O9-BHL-246

FOREIGN POLICIES IN A WORLD OF CHANGE

for Gertrude and Betty

FOREIGN POLICIES

IN A WORLD OF CHANGE

Editors   JOSEPH E. BLACK

Miami University, Oxford, Ohio

KENNETH W. THOMPSON

The Rockefeller Foundation

HARPER & ROW, Publishers

New York, Evanston, and London

ST. PHILIP'S COLLEGE
Not to be taken from the Library
without permission

909.82
B627f

Foreign Policy in a World of Change

Copyright © 1963 by Harper & Row, Publishers, Incorporated

Printed in the United States of America

All rights in this book are reserved.
No part of the book may be used or reproduced
in any manner whatsoever without written permission
except in the case of brief quotations
embodied in critical articles and reviews.
For information address Harper & Row, Publishers, Incorporated,
49 East 33rd Street, New York 16, New York.

B-R

Library of Congress catalog card number: 63–10706

PREFACE

The responsible policy makers in each nation, and the citizenry at large, regard the world from a particular vantage point: that of a separate independent nation with its own geographical location, its unique security and defense problems, and the wide-ranging interests and values it is trying to secure. It is little wonder, then, that most studies of foreign policy are nation-oriented, seen through the eyes of an author who is attached to the goals and aspirations of a particular nation. The observer, like the foreign-policy maker, however, has to come to terms with the fact that as his nation has interests that must be secured, other nations have their own set of foreign policy priorities. Foreign policy in action must be viewed as a process of competition, co-operation, and compromise as the nations are buffeted about the stormy seas of world politics. Within this same framework one may also discern some of the common objectives that bind nations together within the world community.

This book attempts to bring into focus the stubborn truth that, while the foreign policy of each nation has certain unique characteristics, at the same time there is a high degree of inter-relatedness of policies and objectives. The many countries represented in this study also provide a good basis for making comparisons in the foreign policy field.

This study of foreign policies is centered around the concept of "a world of change." The editors and authors of this volume have been acutely aware of the rapidity of change as they have attempted to keep the various contributions current during the preparation of this book. The rapid sweep of events makes mockery of yesterday's headlines. During 1961 and 1962 a dominant movement of international politics was the building of a greater Europe which would include a stronger and broader community encompassing Great Britain and other nations. Now, in the spring of 1963, the bright hopes of a few months ago appear to have been

13622

crushed by General DeGaulle's view of the world and his perception of the role that France should play.

But this is only one act of a larger drama; who can foretell what will happen in the next scene when the repercussions of the recent decisions have become clear or when some of the present leaders of Europe have been replaced by new decision makers? Other changes have followed one another such as revolution in Iraq, the changing orientation of India toward China, the continuing Sino-Soviet split, and even the fall of the Diefenbaker Government in Canada. All are evidence that history does not stand still. Only within the theoretical framework that takes into account a world of change and of competing national interests can we comprehend the larger movements of our time.

A study of this scope could not have been brought to completion without the help of many dedicated individuals. To all who participated in this project, we would like to express our gratitude. It has been a special pleasure to work with the authors of the various chapters in this book. Their patience and forbearance as special problems have arisen is greatly appreciated. We would also like to express our gratitude to the translators of the various chapters. The following professors in the language departments at Miami University have been especially helpful: Dr. Stanford Luce, for his translation of "The Foreign Policy of Switzerland"; Dr. Glenn Barr, for his translation of "The Foreign Policy of Argentina"; Dr. Raymond Maloney, for his translation of "The Foreign Policy of Mexico"; and Dr. Charles Bangert, for his translation of "The Foreign Policy of Germany."

We would also like to thank Professors Dan N. Jacobs and Hans Baerwald for their assistance and comments on the chapters that fell within their special fields of interest. Likewise, we would like to express our gratitude to The Honorable Boris N. Krylov who made the arrangements for the writing of the chapter on the U.S.S.R.

A very special debt of gratitude is owed to the secretaries who helped with the vast amount of correspondence and typing which was required for the completion of this volume. Our special thanks go to Virginia Myers, Ellen Shera, Catherine L. Tolles, Janet Weaver, and Mary White.

For his special interest in this project and for his counsel and advice throughout the preparation of this book, we are especially indebted to Rollin Posey, College Editor of Harper and Row. Initially he suggested this volume to the editors and has given the encouragement necessary to see it through to its completion.

Dr. D. A. Graber, the Harper and Row editor for this volume, brought remarkable skill and forbearance to the task. A foreign policy expert in her own right, her counsel, advice, and persistence have made this a better book than it otherwise would have been.

During the process of translation, rewriting, and revision, two outstanding young scholars at Miami University were especially helpful: Everett Chard and Maynard Grierson. They have demonstrated qualities that augur well for meaningful careers in the years ahead.

Finally, our thanks go to our families who have had to share us with "that *big* book on foreign policy."

Joseph E. Black
Kenneth W. Thompson

New York City
April 15, 1963

vi

CONTENTS

MAPS

Joseph E. Black graduated from Utah State University in 1947 and took his M.A. and Ph.D. degrees at Northwestern University. In 1950 he joined the faculty at Miami University, Oxford, Ohio. He was made Professor and Chairman of the Department of Government at Miami in 1958. Starting in the summer of 1961, he will be on leave from Miami University for two years serving as Professor of Political Science at University College, Ibadan, Nigeria. He will also lecture at Makerere College in Kampala, Uganda, and at the Royal College at Nairobi, Kenya. He is the author of the study, *Chapter Review and Revision, 1955.*

Kenneth W. Thompson is a well-known authority on international politics and American foreign policy. He received his A.B. degree from Augustana College and took his Ph.D. degree at the University of Chicago. He taught at Northwestern University and the University of Chicago before joining the staff of the Rockefeller Foundation in 1955. He is currently Vice-President of the Rockefeller Foundation. Mr. Thompson has written widely on international affairs. His major published works include the following: *Christian Ethics and the Dilemmas of Foreign Policy,* 1959; *Political Realism and the Crisis of World Politics,* 1960; and *American Diplomacy and Emergent Patterns,* 1962. He is co-author of: *Principles and Problems of International Politics,* 1951; *Man and Society,* 1953; *Conflict and Cooperation Among Nations,* 1960.

ABOUT THE CHAPTER

This chapter serves as an introduction to the study of the foreign policies of various nations throughout the world. The authors call attention to the world environment within which nations pursue their policies and to some of the major characteristics of modern world politics. They stress the "revolutionary" nature of the modern world and the impact of changed conditions on foreign policies.

The various approaches to the study of foreign policy are examined briefly, including the current trends in the field. The authors note the merits of the analytical approach and the need to pay heed to a multiplicity of factors when social and political problems are unraveled. Comprehension of the foreign policies of nations requires awareness of the complexities of interests and forces which influence the behavior of states. The chapter surveys some of the factors which must be examined by those who are attempting an analytical study of foreign policy

ABOUT THE AUTHORS

JOSEPH E. BLACK graduated from Utah State University in 1947 and took his M.A. and Ph.D. degrees at Northwestern University. In 1950 he joined the faculty at Miami University, Oxford, Ohio. He was made Professor and Chairman of the Department of Government at Miami in 1958. Starting in the summer of 1963, he will be on leave from Miami University for two years serving as Professor of Political Science at University College, Ibadan, Nigeria. He will also lecture at Makerere College in Kampala, Uganda, and at the Royal College at Nairobi, Kenya. He is the author of the study, *Charter Review and Revision*, 1955.

KENNETH W. THOMPSON is a well-known authority on international politics and American foreign policy. He received his A.B. degree from Augustana College and took his Ph.D. degree at the University of Chicago. He taught at Northwestern University and the University of Chicago before joining the staff of the Rockefeller Foundation in 1953. He is currently Vice-President of the Rockefeller Foundation. Mr. Thompson has written widely on international affairs. His major published works include the following: *Christian Ethics and the Dilemmas of Foreign Policy*, 1959; *Political Realism and the Crisis of World Politics*, 1960; and *American Diplomacy and Emergent Patterns*, 1962. He is co-author of: *Principles and Problems of International Politics*, 1951; *Man and Society*, 1953; *Conflict and Cooperation among Nations*, 1960.

ABOUT THE CHAPTER

This chapter serves as an introduction to the study of the foreign policies of various nations throughout the world. The authors call attention to the world environment within which nations pursue their policies and to some of the major characteristics of modern world politics. They stress the "revolutionary nature" of the modern world and the impact of changed conditions on foreign policies.

The various approaches to the study of foreign policy are examined briefly, including the current trends in the field. The authors note the merits of the analytical approach and the need to pay heed to a multiplicity of factors when social and political problems are considered. Comprehension of the foreign policies of nations requires awareness of the complexities of interests and forces which influence the behavior of states. The chapter surveys some of the factors which must be examined by those who are attempting an analytical study of foreign policy.

FOREIGN POLICIES IN A WORLD OF CHANGE

JOSEPH E. BLACK

Miami University, Oxford, Ohio

KENNETH W. THOMPSON

The Rockefeller Foundation

THE ANALYSIS OF FOREIGN POLICY

Nations pursue their policies within the context of an existing world environment. It is of course obvious that policies designed to serve a pattern of interests in one period under one set of circumstances can be largely irrelevant in another period.

In analyzing foreign policies, the prudent observer must give careful attention to the primary interests of nations as seen by those who are making decisions, and relate them to the great movements by which nations are buffeted about as they strive to reach their goals. This means that specific attention must be given to a broad range of subjective and objective factors which limit choices. Likewise, the student of foreign policy must be aware of the available courses of action.

In any absolute sense this task is impossible; it is difficult enough to understand the major characteristics of an era, let alone perceive the full range of alternatives which confront decision-makers. The difficulty of the task, however, does not excuse him from being cognizant of a multitude of complexities which are operative and which condition the decision-makers' policy choices.

The Greek historian, Thucydides, writing at the outset of the Peloponnesian War, was convinced that far-reaching events unfolding in his day were without precedent. Indeed, to Thucydides, "this was the greatest movement yet known in history, not only of the Hellenes, but for a large part of the Barbarian World—I almost said of Mankind."[1] Likewise, we believe today that the breath-taking events of recent decades are without parallel in history. The attempt to gain perspective by studying the past gives scant comfort. For it is obvious that

[1] Thucydides, *The Peloponnesian War*, New York: Random House, 1951, p. 3.

ST. PHILIP'S COLLEGE
Not to be taken from the Library
without permission

unlike the "great movements" of other periods, the cataclysmic events of our own time have largely re-written the terms for man's continued existence upon the earth.

The rapidity of change taken together with the sheer dimensions of unfolding events is now commonly referred to as "the revolutionary age." With Telstar communications facilities, space capsules circling the globe, and nations racing to reach the moon it is little wonder that man is dazed by the sweep of events. And the "sonic booms" or great shocks and disturbances which follow in the wake of the rapidly moving events of our time provide some of the conditions which must of necessity influence the foreign policies of nations.

Today some hundred and twenty nations face the task of living together upon the planet, earth. Many of the interests these nations seek are widely shared throughout the community; some are limited and parochial and can only be gained at the expense of other nations. The full range of these interests, and the policies being pursued to achieve them must be viewed in the perspective of the fundamental forces of a revolutionary era.

TWENTIETH CENTURY WORLD-WIDE REVOLUTIONS

Any one of the major revolutions of our time would have a significant impact upon international relations. Taken as an aggregate these revolutions have drastically altered the international environment; the relative simplicity of an earlier era will not be restored.

The technological revolution

The revolution in weapons and warfare casts the darkest shadow across the land. With the knowledge that one thermonuclear bomb can carry more destructive power than all the explosives detonated in all previous wars, responsible leaders have coined the phrase "world balance of terror." Some scientists who have given very careful attention to the impact of new weapons and the accelerated pace of development in weapons systems insist that whether we reach the year 2,000 or even 1975 with civilization intact is open to serious doubt. Nuclear weapons testing and the dangers involved in a continuing arms race heighten anxiety for all responsible leaders. Even the spokesmen of small nations make it clear that this matter concerns all nations; survival of the weak as well as the strong hangs in the balance.

Of course, the revolution in weapons and warfare is merely a part of the broader technological revolution. Modern weapons systems are obvious derivatives of the systematic application of scientific knowledge, technical skill, integrated production methods and the allocation of the necessary resources to the achievement of a particular goal: that of controlling and utilizing in a highly concentrated form, fantastic quantities of energy. As chemical and biological warfare systems are developed, it is apparent that they too come from the great strides of science and man's knowledge of the universe.

The systematic search for new techniques, basic and applied research supported on a massive scale, and the orientation of society to rapid change is a characteristic of modern life; it sets this period in history apart from all others. Modern research projects and facilities, including research in the nuclear field, by the new nations can be partially understood as status symbols. But they are more than that. They are indicative of the world-wide search for knowledge and disclose the breadth and depth of the assault being made in an attempt to control man's environment.

On the one hand, we are horrified at the prospects of a global holocaust; on the other, we are heartened by developments in agriculture, medicine and other fields. In any event, it is clear that the age of science conditions both the values of man and his expectations. Indeed, we see on every hand the specter of a child-like belief in ultimate progress: given the proper allocation of resources towards a specific goal there need be no reason for failure. With man grasping for this noble dream, it is ironic that a great "if" stands in the way; "if" the world is not first destroyed by other successes achieved as a result of the technological revolution!

New power alignments throughout the world

Polarization of political power Another major change which provides a part of the framework for the consideration of foreign policy problems is a revolution in the world distribution of power. On the one hand, following World War II, we have witnessed the rise of the two Super-Powers, the United States and the Soviet Union, who vastly exceed all other states in industrial capacity and military power. On the other hand, we have seen the collapse in a few brief years of the old imperial structures which for centuries gave a modicum of order and coherence to the world. While the international system today is not exclusively bipolar in nature, it would be erroneous to underestimate the extent to which affairs of the world are shaped and influenced by the two great centers of power. De Tocqueville foresaw the future more clearly than his contemporaries when he wrote in 1834 of the United States and Russia that even though "their starting point is different, and their courses are not the same—yet each of them seems to be marked out by the will of heaven to sway the destinies of half a globe."[2] Khrushchev gave twentieth century expression to this general view when he declared that

to be more precise about international tension, it is obvious that everything in the end revolves around the rela-

tionship between two countries—the U.S.S.R. and the U.S.A. To illustrate this figuratively, one can say that just as you would have to tear the leaves from a cabbage gradually, one by one, to discover the heart, so if you were to remove one by one all the various undecided or disputed questions among countries then the heart of the matter would turn out to be the contradictions between our two countries, the U.S.A. and the U.S.S.R.[3]

Of course this is oversimplified. The world is in flux and appears to be moving toward more complex forms and not into a rigid East-West mold. The European movement is bringing a form of unity to one of the most important of the high-energy areas of the world. Some Europeans speak fondly of a third great center of power conceived as a "third force" on a par with the United States or the Soviet Union. China with her teeming "millions of blue ants" and a smaller number of engineers and managers, is striving to effect a gigantic program of change. While there are formidable roadblocks to the transformation of China into a major technological complex using high-energy converters, or even maintaining the status quo, she seems destined to play a major role in world politics. Beyond this, who would deny the importance of the great political changes in other parts of Asia, in Africa and in Latin America? It is clear that the old order is passing while a new one is being born.

Emergence of new nations The break-up of the colonial world and the emergence of a large number of new nations are directly related to the political revolution. This great change is still in progress and before the end of the present decade some fifty new nations will have been added to the world community in the post-World War II period. This great increase in the number of actors in international

[2] Alexis de Tocqueville, *Democracy in America,* New York: Oxford University Press, 1947, p. 242.

[3] *Pravda,* May 10, 1957.

affairs has already had far-reaching consequences.

The new nations generally are badly underdeveloped, yet they have plans and ambitions to participate in the way of life of the most advanced nations. They are using their new found status in the world community to pursue their political and economic objectives. Many of them are trying to reweave the intricate fabric of tribal loyalties into a new pattern of nationalism.

The impact of the new nations has had a profound effect upon the United Nations and certain regional arrangements. We hear increasingly of "historic interests" of states that had not existed as separate entities until three years ago and which, to a large extent, are said to have "unnatural boundaries" decided upon by the imperial Powers. We may regret that the new nations were not born into a more seasoned world community.

A symbol of our age is the newest Head of State making his appearance at the United Nations. Full of hopes and plans he presents a stirring speech on the role which his nation will play in world affairs; he also discusses in the general debate the range of problems confronting the world. Whether the impact of the new nation will be as great as the leader envisages or whether it will be able to achieve the goals of a cherished "five year plan" is open to question. But there is no denying the fact that the "new nations" have arrived and are to be reckoned with.

Examples of integration and co-operation
Concurrent with the movement toward fragmentation of areas, "Balkanization" of portions of Africa, and the creation of extremely small states, there is the counter-movement towards integration and co-operation. The ties which hold nations and even regions together are frequently more obscure than the surface picture of dependent territories clamoring for independence—and then achieving that "happy state." Great universal or regional organizations and international conferences are often in the spotlight of world news; but in addition to these there are economic and political ties which help to integrate and give form to the community of nations.

Undoubtedly the most spectacular, and from the standpoint of international relations, the most significant of the moves towards unification and co-operation is taking place in Europe. The Coal and Steel Community, the Common Market, Euratom, and other functional bodies are drawing together separate national communities into a wider regional grouping. The results of this unification are already having a profound effect on nations who have traditionally relied heavily on European markets. The COMECON nations of the Communist world no less than nations in the West are jarred by the effect the new Europe can have on the flow of trade.

There is no need here to catalogue the worldwide movement towards new organizations to achieve common goals. Interdependence has grown along with movements which are divisive and which bring greater instability. While some observers still speak wishfully of federal integration as the only desirable end, other arrangements may prove more compatible with a whole range of values nations have and consequently more in keeping with the realities of our time.

The population explosion

The "population explosion" will have an enormous impact in the coming years both from the standpoint of overall international relations and independent foreign policies. It is clear that the dramatic increase in world population will be as fateful and have an effect as profound as the unleashing of the atom. The change in population has already worked a far-reaching effect on living standards, values, "the way of life" and expectations in many different nations. At one extreme, it means starvation for thousands of people; for others it means growing urbanization and the loss of open spaces. The United States is already feeling the effects of a larger population and the changing way of life following in the wake of the increase. Schools that are overcrowded or on "double shift," the traffic jams on the highways, city slums and sprawling urban areas, chronic unemployment and the entry of thousands of new workers into the labor force each month, the absolute necessity of increasing the rate of economic growth if full employment is to be achieved, are all resounding evidences of the impact of population growth.

The stability of population in past centuries was largely due to the uneasy balance between high birth rates and high death rates. Now mankind confronts a world-wide picture of rapidly declining death rates, with birth rates, with few exceptions, remaining high. The population of the world, which stood at three billion in 1962, is expected to rise to at least six billion by the end of this century.

For many nations the great rise in population will make it difficult, if not impossible, to achieve a genuine increase in the standard of living. Already we read of economic "five-year-plans" being fulfilled, but with fewer calories per capita at the end of the "successful plan." Eugene Black, former President of the International Bank, points to

the plight of the developing countries whose efforts to raise the living standards of their people to tolerable levels are largely vitiated because they direct much of their increasing resources simply to feeding, clothing, housing and training these extra persons.[4]

It is ironic that in the midst of a period of concern with weapons of mass annihilation, the world is also confronted with the specter of a world that is so overpopulated that many of the values and goals which nations and people hold are in danger. Who can doubt that the question of "population policy" will receive increased attention in the future?[5]

[4] Eugene Black, "Population Growth and Economic Development," *The Virginia Quarterly Review*, Summer 1961, p. 329.
[5] See below, p. 18.

These great changes and others related to them—for change begets change—provide the backdrop for the dramatic crises of our time. The concrete problems, which must be dealt with from day to day, are largely related to these and other changes. It may be that the great mass of mankind can ignore them. Weighted down by daily frustrations and problems, it frequently searches for a "devil" responsible for threatening "a way of life." Responsible officials, however, cannot afford this luxury. They have the task of trying to find a way through troubled waters while at the same time persuading reluctant publics to accept some of the hard facts of international life.

A new style of policy-making

In traditional international relations, in a world largely dominated or influenced by Europe, only two distinctions were normally made between states: those that were Great Powers and those that were Small Powers. Great Powers had general interests and the strength to protect their interests in every sphere; Small Powers had only limited interests to match their limited power. Areas which did not belong to the Great or Small Powers were classified as dependencies of one type or another or as "empty spaces."

Discarded precedents　In a less hurried era, the leaders of the Great Powers could meet in private and agree upon spheres of influence or upon the disposition of territories under dispute. There was no great "spotlight of publicity." The leaders did not have to contend with an aroused public opinion at home or worry about the impact their decisions would have on the leaders of some small "uncommitted nations."

As late as 1884–85, with the mad "scramble for Africa" at its height, Germany and France invited Great Britain to the Berlin Conference on Africa. At the Conference, Portugal's claim to portions of the Congo was denied and it was decided that the region of the Congo, an area as large as Western Europe, would become the personal domain of King Leopold of Belgium. Britain's claim to the Niger region was validated and other general territorial agreements were made. No real attention was given by the participants to the question of the logic of the boundaries in light of tribal distribution in Africa; indeed, the question of the wishes of the inhabitants and their loyalties would not have been an acceptable topic for discussion.

Policy-making in the United Nations Contrast this with recent United Nations sessions devoted to the problems of Africa. After debates in open session—but with simultaneous private negotiations taking place—and in front of the news media of the world, resolutions are passed "finding" that certain situations exist, "noting" past resolutions, and "calling" upon colonial nations to grant a greater degree of self-government to a region or to provide certain services for it. For example, in the summer of 1962, with the Congo conflict continuing, a special session of the General Assembly convened to deal with the problem of independence for the Trust Territory, Ruanda-Urundi. After extensive bargaining, a resolution was passed declaring the independence of two new African states, to be known as Rwanda and Burundi. The Assembly sent a special Commission to Africa to help with the multitude of problems confronting the new states. This same session of the Assembly also discussed the situation in Southern Rhodesia and demanded that changes be made in the Constitution of that "self-governing" territory.

Of course, once nations have achieved their independence and taken their place in the world community, there are still stubborn factors which tend to limit the freedom of action of the new state. Even though the older classification of states as great or small is inadequate, it is still obvious, to use Orwell's phrase, that "some are more equal than others." Even though the "imperial" Power has relinquished political controls, there are still economic ties, problems of access to markets, problems of the exploitation and development of natural resources, the need for capital, and the necessity of retaining the services of experts and technicians.

Many new African states, as in French-speaking West Africa, have found that in spite of their new freedom there are still "ties that bind." A recognition of these ties and the mutuality of interests is one of the small steps towards maturity. The complexities of international economics may be disconcerting to new states, but they cannot be ignored. As one astute African leader observed, after listening to a long discussion on Africans trading with Africans and cutting ties with Europe, "Quite right, but how much cotton can you eat?"

Intangible power factors Even though many of the new nations will continue to depend heavily on assistance by the colonial Powers of the past, it is obvious that they still play a larger role in world affairs than might be assumed from any elemental calculation of various power factors. This has also been true in the past: certain nations, because of special attributes or a certain vigor, have played roles all out of proportion to what might be expected. In the case of the new states there are several interrelated factors which help to account for their influence. In the first place, the rise of the new diplomacy and the role of international organizations, together with possibilities for bloc-action, have given the smallest nation a forum and a degree of worldwide attention unthinkable in past periods. As the new nations move towards a clear majority position within the United Nations their influence will be enhanced, not diminished. The relative decline of the Security Council and the ever-broadening role of the General Assembly also enhance the position of small nations.

In the second place, in a bipolar world, the great competition for the loyalty and support of these nations has exaggerated their importance. The courting they have received from other Powers, the support for their resolutions, the economic aid which has been given, can best be understood in terms of power politics. This is not to deny that there has been astute leadership in some of these nations and that some types of aid have been given for other than purely political considerations.

Thirdly, even without the Cold War, many of the smaller nations are located at strategic junctures. Thus Israel and her policies influence the entire Middle East and the positions taken by many of the Major Powers. This tiny nation, counting about two million inhabitants, provides the "mix" which gives "temper" to the entire Arab world. Likewise, the new nations of Southeast Asia are destined to play an extremely important role because of their location, their food surplus, and the Cold War.

Finally, because of the technological revolution, the smaller nations, both actually and potentially, play an increasingly important role. Because of the vast strides in communications even a Small Power like Egypt can beam its voice throughout the entire Middle East and also cover a good portion of Africa. This influence of some smaller nations will undoubtedly become greater as they obtain modern weapons which might be used either to draw the greater Powers into the vortex of the conflict, or, at the least, to threaten the stability of a region.

APPROACHES TO THE STUDY OF FOREIGN POLICY

Historical, legalistic, and descriptive methods

There are many ways in which the foreign policies of nations around the world can be discussed. Diplomatic history has been the traditional approach. The hallmark of the great diplomatic historians has been their insistence on reconstructing the diplomacy of a particular period with accuracy, precision and due attention to the major events. They have not been especially interested in formulating general laws, constructing conceptual schemes or elaborating theories of international behavior. Tra-

ditionally, diplomatic historians have been reluctant to deal with contemporary events or to make policy recommendations for the future. There have been exceptions, of course, from Thucydides to the present day.

The legalistic approach to the study of foreign policy has had widespread influence in recent times. At its best, this approach can lead to a more comprehensive understanding of the world community, of the actual role legal norms play in international relations, and of the problems confronting those who would create a more stable world order. Too frequently, however, those identified with this approach have isolated the legal factor from the political and social framework. Frequently they recommend a "world of law and order" with no evident comprehension of the political, economic and social foundation required for such an order.

This same general approach has been applied to the study of the external relations of states and to internal governmental problems. Attention is focused almost completely on constitutional provisions, laws, treaties and regulations, and on the formal bodies which are established to make or execute policy. Recommended improvements normally take the form of a carefully prescribed re-allocation of authority to existing bodies, or a plan for the creation of new institutions to which particular tasks are assigned.

Obviously, there is a proper place for this approach. Its great weakness has been that it has either underrated or condemned the role of politics, power and interest in foreign policy considerations. Beyond this, extremely complicated problems have been made to appear easily manageable and rather "mechanical" solutions have been prescribed for them.

Another general approach to the study of foreign policy can be classified as "descriptive." A large number of textbooks and treatises on foreign policy fall within this general category. Obviously each author or scholar selects what is to be described, whether it be historical materials, current events or institutions, using his judgment on the weighing of various factors. Within this approach one will find some studies which are rigorous and make some attempt to formulate theories and establish a conceptual framework. Frequently, however, there is little discipline; some attention is given to many items, without full attention to any.

The ideological approach

The ideological approach to the study of foreign policy, has the widest appeal. It is represented in this book by at least one of the chapters. General ideologies which are associated with particular economic, social and political systems or with particular religious beliefs or value systems are applied to the complicated world of international relations and to the foreign policies of nations. Thus, foreign policies are frequently counterpoised as democratic versus aristocratic or authoritarian; peace-loving as opposed to imperialistic or war-loving; free enterprise versus socialistic or communistic; enlightened versus the selfish or unenlightened!

The virtues of simplicity　　All nations, to some extent, use ideological justifications for their policies. One reason is that "action" policies are frequently so complicated that they cannot be described accurately in simple phrases. A more important reason is that all nations, for internal consumption and internationally for ideological warfare, tend to identify their foreign policies in sweeping ideological terms. Thus we speak of the foreign policies of the "free nations" versus the foreign policies of the "captive nations." Of course, this means that all virtue is claimed for the policy goals of a particular nation or group of nations while just the reverse is true of the enemy. This approach is extremely useful because the ideological identification can be understood by the most uninformed citizen without much thought.

In the United States, many individuals have identified foreign policy problems and "power politics" with aristocratic regimes; they have also assumed that democracy was a substitute for the difficult dilemmas of international politics. Some "enlightenment" philosophers assumed that once all nations had democratic governments, wars and international conflicts would cease. Individuals who follow an ideological approach obviously ignore the multiplicity of factors which influence foreign policy; instead, they escape into a dream world where comfort is assured, or at the very least, where the demons are clearly identified.

The influence of ideology on policy　　No one would deny that ideologies do influence the policies of states, though there is much disagreement about the extent of this influence. Frequently ideologies are directly related to value patterns and to both the expectations of men and the general conception of the proper means for achieving desired goals. It is also true that ideologies are used as justifications for policies and that they can be molded to fit the demands of successful political action. Operating within particular ideological systems, one's perception of his own foreign policy and that of other nations is obviously distorted.

Contrast, for example, how Portugal views her years of rule in Angola with the views taken by the new African states. Portugal insists that Angola is a part of her territory, not a colony; she stresses "equality," opportunity, the rights of all individuals regardless of color, and the progress that has taken place. The ringing speeches in the United Nations, by contrast, tell of years of "colonialism," "domination," "modern slavery," and finally of terror and butchery.

Nations frequently find it useful to equate their policies with goodness itself, or with the will of God or some divine plan. When Wilson went to the Peace Conference at Versailles he went not only as a statesman, but also as a missionary from the new world to help bring the truth to those who had strayed from the path. Thus, Lloyd George wrote that part of each Big Four session was taken up with Wilson's views on how European nations should learn to be "moral" like the United States. One day, for example, Wilson raised the following question:

Why has Jesus Christ so far not succeeded in inducing the world to follow his teachings in these matters? It is because he taught the idea without devising any practical means of attaining it. That is the reason why I am proposing a practical scheme to carry out His aims.[6]

Other Americans have been more modest than this, but it is not infrequent that "His plans" for mankind are identified with those of the United States.

Over the years scholars have debated the influence of ideology on the foreign policy of the Soviet Union. Viewpoints cover the spectrum from those who insist that her foreign policy is not influenced by ideology to those who find in ideology both a general framework of objectives and specific guidelines which dictate day to day policy decisions.

There is little doubt that Marxism-Leninism, as re-interpreted through the years, does play a significant role in giving decision-makers in the Kremlin a general viewpoint of the international scene and some operational concepts. It should be stressed, however, that Marxist-Leninist principles do not provide the answers to either persistent long-range problems of policy and strategy or to the daily crises which must be met. Indeed, in many specific cases, ideology has been re-interpreted to fit the requirements of power and policy. Of course, a re-interpretation of ideology does not mean its abandonment. Rather, it recognizes its crucial role and the fact that, whatever the changes in policy, they must appear to be in conformity with "eternal Marxist principles."

The requirement that all policy decisions and all movements throughout the world must be reconciled with ideology also means that, in addition to re-interpreting ideology, there are many occasions when objective facts and truth must be equally flexible and brought into line

with the "eternal principles." Thus there is a certain fairyland like quality to much that is written by Soviet authors. Fact and fiction melt into specific and general statements that are proved to be true by giving them a general "ideological blessing."

Soviet scholars of foreign policy make a clear distinction between the policies of the socialist and capitalist states. When discussing the foreign policy of socialist states, such concepts as "national interest," "competing interests," and "balance of power policies" are completely ignored. Indeed, these scholars insist that socialist states are entirely new and simply do not have the same operational framework as other states. Thus, the establishment of the Soviet system "announced to the peoples that a completely new, hitherto unknown type of state had come into being, and with it a new kind of foreign policy."[7] This new state would not have the same goals and policies as other states but would be based squarely on the struggle for peace!

The analytical method

The ideological approach to the study of foreign policy precludes the careful evaluation of a multiplicity of factors which must be taken into account by responsible policy-makers whether they come from the socialist or capitalistic world. In sharpest contrast to the general orientation of the ideologists stands the "analytical" approach. This approach differs from the others not only in the method of viewing problems, but also in its general orientation to the field of international politics.

The pattern of interests   Those who follow the analytical approach take for granted that nations have a pattern of interests and obligations which provide the general framework for foreign policy formulation and execution. It is

---

[6] David L. George, *The Truth About the Peace Treaties,* London: Victor Gollancz Ltd., 1938, Vol. I, p. 54.

[7] See below, p. 223.

clear that all interests of a state are not of equal value. Within the pattern of interests are some which must be defended or advanced at all costs; others are of a secondary nature and may be modified or even abandoned under certain circumstances; still others are peripheral and not considered central to the well-being of the nation. There are also identifiable interests which cannot be advanced because they are clearly beyond the power of the nation.

Within the pattern of interests, there are contradictions: the achievement of some interests makes it impossible to achieve others. For example, within its pattern of interests a nation may well want to be secure from attack. This may require maintaining a large deterrent force. Another interest may be to utilize the resources of the state for peaceful purposes and thus not have to channel a large portion of state revenues into defense expenditures. Obviously, both of these interests cannot be satisfied simultaneously.

Nor does the pattern of interests exist in a vacuum; it is directly related to groups and classes within the nation and their competition for the achievement of specific goals. One segment of a society may well want a high tariff erected to protect a particular industry or labor group; at the same time another interest wants tariffs lowered or abolished. A study of the interest patterns of a particular state may well start with the vital needs of national security; but it will soon lead into the intricate fabric of a society and the competing claims that various interest groups have.

One of the primary tasks of those responsible for the foreign policy of the nation is to ascertain what the hierarchy of interests is and to relate them to those of other nations within the world community. As nations attempt to secure their interests, there are obviously disputes and the need for compromise and adjustment. There is also the task of developing a community of interests. Indeed, there are many interests already shared by a number of nations which are of a higher priority than some of the particular "national interests." What hopes there are, for example, for effective arms control lie within this area of mutual interests.

Appraising competing interests   Thus, a person using the analytical approach will start from the concept of competing interests. As he views the problems of Britain's entry into the Common Market arrangement, for instance, he must take into account the cluster of British interests, including her ties to the Commonwealth, her reliance on food imports from other countries, her world-wide trading interests, her special ties with the Atlantic nations and her special ties to Europe. Likewise, the positions of other European nations become intelligible only as the patterns of interests are evaluated.

A second factor to be taken into consideration in the analytical approach is the power of nations to achieve their interests. While it is easy to be aware of this factor, it is extremely difficult to evaluate the power of a nation. There are a multitude of elements to be taken into consideration; and, because these elements blend differently for each nation, it is impossible to calculate with any degree of certainty the exact power it has.[8]

A third factor that must be taken into account is the process through which policies are adopted and implemented. Both formal and informal groups which influence the decision-making process must be evaluated. In virtually all states there are recognizable allocations of power between various functional groups within the government. Usually there are ministries, special advisers and planning groups which have particular responsibilities in the field of foreign policy planning.

But the formal and easily identifiable foreign policy agencies are frequently not the vital initiating agencies; the actual decision-making process is often obscure and extremely difficult to comprehend. In addition to individuals within the regular governmental structure, there are centers of power within the society who have their spokesmen and their methods of influencing policy. Obviously there are different interest groups and different pressures applied in each policy area. This makes it im-

[8] See below, pp. 15–20.

possible to work out a complete formula on the "foreign policy process" that has validity for any wide range of policy decisions.

Of course, the method of policy-formulation differs widely from nation to nation. The relatively open access to the policy-making process which is part and parcel of democratic systems is lacking in certain authoritarian systems. Nevertheless, various competing influences are at work in all states, even though they may be limited and obscure.

The analytical approach also emphasizes that the foreign policy process takes place within a complex international environment. The tensions of a particular period, the patterns of co-operation, and the policies of the Major Powers are among the many factors which condition the international environment. Thus, nations are affirmatively attempting to achieve their particular interests at the same time they are reacting and are propelled along by the sweep of events.

Comparative studies

The *comparative* study of foreign policies has received relatively little attention apart from the established study of comparative government. Consequently, the prevailing approach in comparative government is likely to be applied to the study of foreign policy. In the past, the study of comparative government has been primarily descriptive rather than analytical. At present, however, there is a great deal of ferment and re-examination of methodology in this field and there is no doubt that the trend is towards a more systematic and scientific approach. Scholars of comparative government are giving greater attention to conceptual schemes, to the testing of hypotheses and to gathering significant data.[9]

Another major change in the field is relevant to foreign policy analysis. While a few years ago the study of comparative government frequently meant dealing with four or five major European Powers, the present trend is to include a large number of different political systems, including some that are relatively new to the international scene.

There is also a definite departure from the traditional Aristotelian scheme of classifying governments according to whether rule is by "the one, the few, or the many." The newer classifications take into account a multitude of factors: the structure of the society and the patterns of legitimacy which prevail; the distribution of authority within the state; the functions of various existing institutions; the relationship between economic, social and political factors; the process of change within the state, and the factors which both hasten and retard change; the decision-making process within the government; and ideology and belief patterns.[10]

On the one hand, greater attention is being given to the comparison of institutions in different states and to classifications and models which show identifiable similarities between processes and systems. On the other hand, useful case studies in depth are giving us a greater comprehension of unique institutions of individual states and the clear influence of particular historical, geographic, and other considerations which influence a state and its policies. In turn, these case studies furnish the raw material for more intensive and extensive comparative analyses.

[9] Roy C. Macridis and Bernard E. Brown, *Comparative Politics: Notes and Readings*, Homewood, Ill.: Dorsey Press, 1961, pp. 3–11.

[10] For a useful theoretical framework "Models of Political Change in Africa" see David Apter, *The Political Kingdom in Uganda*, Princeton, N.J.: Princeton University Press, 1961, pp. 20–27. For other classifications and identifications of different systems see: Max F. Millikan and Donald L. M. Blackmer, *The Emerging Nations: Their Growth and United States Policy*, Boston: Little, Brown & Co., 1961; Gabriel A. Almond and James S. Coleman, *The Politics of Developing Areas*, Princeton, N.J.: Princeton University Press, 1960; Samuel Beer, *Patterns of Government*, New York: Random House, 1958; and Roy C. Macridis and Bernard E. Brown, *op. cit.*

On the "scientific" study of politics

On the whole, the new approach towards the study of governments and governmental processes is to be welcomed. With a more systematic technique, the willingness to utilize methods employed successfully by sister disciplines and the knowledge now available on data gathering and processing, real progress should be made in our understanding of society, government, and even interstate relations.

The major trend noted above should be viewed within the context of the scientific age in which we live and other major trends in the social sciences. The social scientist is attempting to develop the tools and techniques which will better equip him to investigate and evaluate particular aspects of man's behavior. He is also aware of the fact that the scientific method —developing hypotheses, investigation and data-gathering, classification of materials and then evaluation before coming to conclusions— is less likely to yield error than any other. At the same time, another force is operative; the social scientist is constantly being pressed to "be scientific" and to put his "science" to use. Consequently, the social scientist is busy predicting future consumer preferences, advising advertising firms on how to increase the sale of certain products and calculating who will win the next election.

The attempt to create a "science of politics" and to predict political behavior and policy patterns does raise a series of fundamental issues. Certain limitations should be kept in mind. The intricate behavior patterns, the number and types of conditioning agents, and alternative courses of action open to individuals and groups, are indicative of the complexity of the material with which the social scientist works. He must also keep in mind that history does not really repeat itself and that there is no adequate "laboratory" for testing. Man lives at a certain time and the forces which act and react upon him are constantly in a state of flux. The more complex the environment, the greater the number of factors to be taken into account. When one considers complicated organizations, such as the state and its government, then these complex factors are multiplied many times.

Faced with extremely stubborn and complicated situations, the researcher is frequently tempted to "cut the situation down to size." For example he might: (1) examine facets of behavior that are amenable to scientific inquiry, even though the studies are not crucial or even relevant in terms of any ordering of priorities and problems; (2) simplify or abstract from the complex situation certain facets that can be examined—and possibly even develop an intricate conceptual scheme as a substitute for coming to terms with the knotty realities which surround the problem; (3) create a simplified model that has no practical relationship to any institution or group—but which allows analysis, projections, and comparisons with other models; (4) develop a laboratory situation which is not only removed from reality but from the environment where real choices are made; (5) create a "model organization" or simulate the behavior of men or groups—again removed from the arena where there are real priorities and where men are ultimately responsible for decisions on matters of the highest priority.

In other words, with an extremely complicated world, the social scientist is frequently tempted to know too much that can be "properly verified" while comprehending too little about the contingency of behavior patterns and the harsh obstacles confronting those who must make decisions. There is some validity in the charge frequently made that social scientists ignore the great problems and major dilemmas confronting society and escape into research that is "narrow gauge"—and sometimes hardly relevant.

The scientific approach, with rigorous and systematic research, the gathering of significant data, and the use of models and imaginative concepts is clearly gaining ground. There is obviously a need for greater clarity—to distinguish between value statements, definitional statements and factual statements; there is also a need for greater accuracy, both in the methods used in research and in its presentation. Regularities and uniformities in behavior should be identified, and generalizations should be verified whenever possible. But more sophisticated concepts and theories, and the greater use of quantification and empirical research do not mean that historical perspective, an appreciation of the role of geography and a number of factors of contingency should be ignored. Instead, the new approaches should ultimately lead to a greater willingness to consider all relevant factors in the foreign policy equation, even though they might not be amenable to scientific analysis.

THE PURPOSES AND APPROACHES OF THIS STUDY

This book was planned as a contribution in the fields of comparative foreign policies and international relations. Those responsible for its preparation envisaged a study that would be analytical as opposed to contributions which are primarily ideological in orientation. While each author was given the greatest degree of independence in preparing his contribution, the general orientation of the study was made clear: a multiplicity of factors which might be classed as determinants in influencing the policy of his particular nation were to be given attention. A suggested outline enumerating determinant factors was sent to each author. As expected, the various contributors dealt with the suggested topics in different ways. Following is a brief discussion of the reasons for selecting certain determinants as a framework for each chapter.

The influence of history

It is clear that the foreign policy of every nation is to some extent a product of its own his-

tory. The approach of a nation and its people to foreign policy problems is conditioned by expectations, values and beliefs. The patterns of values and beliefs which emerge over a period of time are largely adjustments to the environment and the limits it imposes. While those who direct the affairs of the nation have some control over history and have some choice between various alternatives, one is still impressed by "how little the course of events is determined by deliberately planned purpose."[11] As Dr. Cancino notes in his chapter on Mexico: "Circumstances give each nation its own historical configuration and mark it with its own individuality."[12]

A number of authors who have contributed to this work have stressed the role of history in determining the boundaries of states and a legacy which furnishes the guidelines for foreign policy at the present time. "France," Mr. J. B. Duroselle asserts, "is much more a 'product of history' than a 'geographic entity.' "[13] And Mr. Saul Rose, in writing about Great Britain, points out that "It is not until a country has become a political entity as well as a geographical area that one can begin to talk about its foreign policy."[14]

The influence of geography

The influence of geography and other relatively fixed factors cannot be denied. As Dr. Eayrs points out: "Pacts may be broken, treaties unilaterally denounced; but geography holds its victims fast."[15]

Geography must be viewed in various differing lights: the extent of territory; the general configuration of the territory; the type of soils, climatic conditions and rainfall; waterways and

---

[11] Harold Nicolson, *The Congress of Vienna*, New York: Harcourt Brace, 1946, p. 2.
[12] See below, p. 643.
[13] See below, p. 58.
[14] See below, p. 25.
[15] See below, p. 675.

geographical barriers; and the location of the nation with respect to other Powers.

The actual problems a nation confronts as well as the perception its people have of the rest of the world have a specific geographic base. Thus, it is ironic that the very isolated geographic position of the United States has been the primary reason why her citizens, until very recent times have virtually ignored the influence of geography on foreign policy.

One might also note that the Russians, whatever the form of government, have been conditioned by the geographic fact that there is an "invasion route to Moscow." President Kennedy is clearly aware that any basic arrangement with the Russians must take their Western vulnerability into account. He pointed out in a major address, "we recognize the Soviet Union's historic concern about their security in Central and Eastern Europe, after a series of ravaging invasions—and we believe arrangements can be worked out which will help meet these concerns."[16]

On the other hand, no one should overstress the immutable quality of geography. It, too, must be seen in relation to changes in technology, power patterns and political arrangements. Thus, the position of Canada was greatly altered by two factors: weapons developments and the bipolarization of world power. "Geography, which so recently conferred invulnerability upon Canada," Dr. Eayrs points out, "now placed it in the forefront of atomic attack."[17] Such changes do not indicate that geography as an element has decreased in importance; they merely suggest that the particular influence of the particular element has been altered.

Natural resources

As a part of the broad geographic base of a nation, we must also keep in mind the natural

[16] *New York Times*, July 26, 1961.
[17] See below, p. 675.

resources of the nation; they include land available for food production, and its mineral, metal and water resources. The policy patterns of some nations can be understood in terms of their food requirements and the fact that they rely heavily on the importation of food. Other nations have a food surplus and are primarily concerned with access to markets.

Modern technology, changes in weapons and warfare, and the amazing developments in communications systems are based squarely on the utilization of high-energy resources. Thus, access to high-energy sources such as coal fields, and oil reserves is an obvious requisite for any nation which expects to compete in the modern industrial world. Mere access to such resources obviously does not guarantee a nation that it will become an industrial state or that it will be able to make use of these resources. Without them, however, a nation is quite clearly doomed to continue as a low-energy society.

Industrial development

The industrial development of a nation becomes one of the key indices of the role that it will play in modern international affairs. The great industrial centers of the world are still limited to a relatively few areas: the United States and Canada, Western Europe, the Soviet Union and, to a lesser degree, Japan. It is interesting to note the close correlation between the nations which have had a paramount influence in international affairs in recent years and these clusters of power.

The complexities and demands of a highly industrial society partially dictate the priorities of the industrial nations and the policies that will be followed. The expectations and priorities of the citizens and the plans and programs of those in authority are directly tied to a continuance of the system and to a constant improvement in industrial techniques. Whether the system is capitalistic like that in the United States, or a state-directed economic system like that in the Soviet Union, there are common problems which are inherent in a highly complex industrial society.

To the underdeveloped nations it frequently appears that the nations which are highly industrialized have solved their problems and that they should now be able to divert massive quantities of capital to the less fortunate nations. While there is some surplus that can be devoted to the development of these areas, the truth is that industrialization has created numerous complicated internal problems. Competition arises from internal groups including, for example, exponents of improved social services and exponents of heightened individual consumption. How ironic that the United States, with the highest per capita standard of living in the world and the greatest industrial complex ever developed is plagued with unemployment, underemployment, a shortage of schools, inadequate housing and the growth of depressed areas! Similarly the Soviet Union, which has succeeded in putting two men into the same orbit, has not solved many of the basic problems in the consumer production field. China and other nations have been annoyed that the Soviet Union has not been willing to share more freely the relative abundance which she enjoys. But the Soviet Union has found that her own priorities and programs, including the maintenance and expansion of her industrial system, limit the export of capital and technicians.

Many nations in the world are classed as "underdeveloped"; they are largely agricultural and pre-industrial. Virtually all of these nations have plans for duplicating the industrial societies which exist. Frequently their plans appear to be more pipedreams than blueprints and the most formidable obstacles stand in the way of their fulfillment. The leaders in China planned a "great leap forward" which would carry China into the category of the highly industrialized nations. But even the will of the decision-makers, the support of masses of people, a great blueprint and the force of the entire political apparatus were not enough. Many of the nations who have just achieved independence are finding the industrial path

rugged for them. Experts suggest that some of them will not make the grade and will continue as agrarian societies, tied to the great industrial centers which already exist.[18]

Military capacity

The *military capacity* of a nation has frequently determined whether or not it would continue to exist as a political entity. Of course this factor, too, must be understood in terms of the wider distribution of world power and the various alliances which bind nations together. Some of the European nations, for example, have decided that independent military establishments would carry little weight in the modern world; they have had little choice but to become a part of the NATO arrangement.

Other nations, such as Mexico, have discovered that military force was quite irrelevant for achieving their objectives. Still others have found that even though their power is practically nil on the world scene that, within a particular region, the maintenance of a relatively powerful military establishment was absolutely essential. Israel, for example, has continued her precarious existence because she had the power to maintain herself within a very hostile environment.

What constitutes an adequate military stance in the modern world? A short time ago many strategists in the West talked almost exclusively of deterrent capability and of a defense system tied entirely to nuclear weapons. It is not without irony, then, that some of the major recent treatises on modern warfare deal with guerrilla tactics and the methods of achieving rather limited objectives. It has become increasingly clear that even though the Major Powers will continue to stockpile nuclear weapons and that even though a major war is deferred, military

[18] For example, see Fred Cottrell, *Energy and Society; The Relation Between Energy, Social Change, and Economic Development*, New York: McGraw-Hill, 1955.

conflicts will continue, and some of the more traditional tactics and weapons will be used.

Population factors

When evaluating the population of a nation one must give attention to both quantitative and qualitative aspects. Quantitatively one must consider the total number of people, the age configuration within the population, distribution according to sex, the rate of population increase or the rate of decrease and the distribution of the population within the nation. Qualitatively, such factors as educational level, skilled versus unskilled, and health factors are frequently taken into consideration.

Traditionally it was assumed that the greater the population of a nation, the greater its power. Examples of the relationship of population to power are not difficult to find. It is clear that neither the United States nor the Soviet Union would have reached their positions in the world without large populations. To take a reverse case, Canada with a territory of over 3,000,000 square miles has a population of some 18,000,000 people. Obviously with this skimpy population she is kept from the categories of the Major Powers despite her great expanse and material wealth.

A nation's population must be evaluated in relation to its other attributes. The question must be faced of how a large population should be used, how it will be fed and what its contribution to the achievement of shared values should be. Consequently, while some states are trying to increase their populations, others have an overpopulation problem. Many nations are finding that a rapidly increasing population hampers the state and makes it virtually impossible to achieve some of its goals.

Recently, several nations have adopted policies to limit the rate of increase of their population. China's population policy is of particular interest. In 1958, after China had officially abandoned her great experiment in birth control, Mao announced at the Party Congress that "our fast expanding population is an objective fact and is our asset."[19] Chou En-lai and others echoed this view by praising "the great flesh-and-blood force of our population, by which we can, or soon can, do anything within the realm of human possibility." What turned out to be "possible" was the continued rapid increase in population. Consequently, it was no surprise to find in 1962 that China had evidently reversed her policy again and that a new program of "family planning" had been instituted.

There are other qualitative factors which should be given attention even though they are extremely difficult to evaluate. What is the influence of the *value structure* of a society and what are the *dominant groups* which influence the choices that are made? What is the role of *ideology* in providing goals and in helping a nation to achieve them? What are the elements which make up the *national character* which tends to give a different quality to the population of each state? How would the *morale* of the people be evaluated and what quality of support will be given to governmental decisions? The illusiveness of these factors makes them difficult to deal with; but they cannot be ignored.

Government

Finally, one is led to a consideration of the qualities of government, leadership and diplomacy. In the final analysis those who have the authority to exercise the power of the state will have to make decisions on the priorities of interests to be achieved and determine the policies for securing them. Some of the elements considered above provide the muscles and sinews of power; the leadership of the society must provide the brains and determine how the strength will be used.

[19] For discussion see, *The Economist*, Aug. 25, 1962, p. 705.

It would be difficult to overstress the importance of the quality of government in determining the role a state can be expected to play in international relations. Governments have the task of bringing into balance the power and resources available to the state and the goals which it hopes to achieve within a given period of time.

In evaluating the quality of government, the student of foreign policy must give attention to a number of factors: the support of the population and the willingness of the government to take into account the major aspirations of the populace; the organization of the government and the processes by which decisions are made; the quality of individuals brought into the government service and their dedication to the broader goals of the society; the balancing of forces within the society and the effect of this balance on the operation of the government.

Those who would understand the foreign policy of a nation must also give some attention to the foreign policy formulation process, including some evaluation of both the formal institutions and the informal arrangements which are used in determining the courses of action on matters of the highest priority. No one would deny the difficulty of analyzing the decision-making process within even the most open democratic society. The difficulty is obviously compounded several times over within the modern totalitarian state. It is because of the dearth of good hard information and because of the closed avenues to ordinary investigation that scholars turn in despair to "Kremlinology," the study of the inner workings of the Soviet system through the evaluation of every tidbit of information available.

Leadership

Obviously, the quality of government cannot be separated from the quality of leadership existing at a particular time. There is frequently a tendency to talk about states and governments as though they were real living entities. But Charles Burton Marshall reminds us:

The terms *state* and *government* convey ideas of hugeness, majesty, and impersonality. These overtones should not mislead us. The state— and this is true also of its agents, government—remains, in Plato's phrase, man written large. It is only man. It is not superman. It is man written large, not limitless. The individual is multiplied in the frame of the state. The individual's limitations are not transcended. The institutions of political life do not add to the dimensions of the human mind. They have no insights denied to individuals. They produce no wisdom beyond the compass of man's mind. The intelligence operating in the lines of decision and execution is but human intelligence. It has the inherent attributes of contingency, fallibility, and subjectivity. Service to the state does not bring to the minds of the servants any additional endowments for perceiving the future. For all its majesty, the situation of the state is still the human situation.[20]

The role that a state plays at a particular time, and the foreign policies that will be followed, are dependent upon the qualities of those who are in the positions to make decisions. Their decisions will frequently be based squarely on information provided by those who are in subordinate positions within the government. The decision to place I.R.B.M.'s in Cuba was made by individuals—not by "the Kremlin." Likewise, the reaction of the United States to this move had to be determined by leaders, not by some generalized agency. Leaders have to decide the allocation of resources and select

[20] Charles Burton Marshall, *The Limits of Foreign Policy*, New York: Henry Holt and Company, 1954, pp. 14–15.

the particular goals which they hope to achieve. In all fields of action the most fateful policy decisions are made by men, not by an abstract state or organization.

At times there are leaders who play such an important role that one tends to think of the leader and the state as a combined entity. Thus one spoke of Hitler's Germany or Mussolini's Italy. At the present time, there are many cases where the role of a nation is tied closely to that of particular individuals. Little wonder, then, when one frequently hears the queries: "What will happen to India after Nehru? Or France after De Gaulle? Or Egypt after Nasser?"

Diplomacy

A factor intimately related to those just discussed is that of diplomacy. Whether or not a nation achieves its particular objectives is frequently determined by the quality of its diplomatic service. Be they the normal day-to-day relations between states or attempts to deal with crisis situations, diplomacy continues to be the channel for furthering co-operative efforts and adjusting existing differences. The United Nations and other international organizations have not diminished the necessity for diplomatic intercourse; rather, the real point is that additional dimensions have been added to the diplomatic process.

The qualities of individuals also must be considered, along with the institutional arrangements for diplomacy. History abounds with incidents when nations have achieved particular objectives through wise diplomacy, even when some of the more obvious elements of power were lacking. Likewise, there are many cases when otherwise powerful nations have failed to play the role expected of them because of weakness in the diplomatic field.

Both the goals and the processes of diplomacy are frequently misunderstood. This fact is especially lamentable in democratic nations where the support of the people is required for

the sustained operation of the government. Many individuals assume that there is something basically wrong with traditional diplomatic procedures. They ask for less secrecy and more democratic procedures in reaching decisions. Some insist that diplomacy should be a "one shot" affair. A certain nation should be given "one more chance" or "one final effort should be made."

But even with improved methods of communication and the establishment of new international agencies, the principles of successful diplomacy have not changed. There is still the requirement of rather continuous contact between the major nations; there is frequently a need for secrecy, at least during actual negotiations; patience continues to be a fundamental feature of diplomacy; and the individuals involved in the negotiations must have confidence in each other.

The test of diplomacy is not whether it is dramatic, whether it is open to the public view, or whether a particular ideology prevails. The test is whether or not there is an effective accommodation of harmonious as well as conflicting interests.

It is no exaggeration to say that the solutions of the problems of the utmost urgency to the world lie within the realm of successful diplomacy. The international control of arms and agreements on limiting tests of nuclear weapons, the arrangements for international inspection, and the delimitation of the number of nations which will be allowed to acquire nuclear weapons, all continue on the agenda of the diplomatists. The solution of a whole range of problems, from the entry of Britain into the Common Market to the future arrangements in the Congo, lie in the province of diplomacy. Even if a more mature world order emerges, diplomacy will be the tool for achieving the new arrangements. There will be no end to the processes of adjusting conflicting interests and obviating misunderstandings.

It was suggested that each of our authors give attention to the process of policy formulation within his state and the process of policy execution. Finally, it was proposed that within limitations of space, attention should be given to some of the major current foreign policy problems.

THE AUTHORS AND THEIR CONTRIBUTIONS

Chapter patterns

The various contributions in this study are not all cut to the same pattern. A variety of reasons are responsible for the lack of uniformity. In the first place, each author, while working within the analytical framework, was asked to use his own judgment in weighing the different factors which influence policy. Secondly, there is limited agreement among social scientists on the merits of the analytical as opposed to other approaches which might be taken. Some authors employed these other approaches in whole or in part. Thirdly, all of the authors were not equally free to subject the policy-making process and other factors to careful scrutiny. Fourthly, it is clear that the proposed suggestions did not fit each of the nations equally well. With the great variety of nations included, there are enough unique circumstances that uniformity proved to be unattainable. Fifthly, the problem of communication itself proved to be difficult. Undoubtedly, there were some misunderstandings on exactly what was expected of the various authors. Finally, the problem of the length of the contributions turned out to be a real stumbling block. Each contributing author had to make difficult choices on the material to be included within the space available.

Choice of authors

The editors of this volume planned that each of the contributions would be written by a leading scholar from the nations included. This plan has been followed with two exceptions where it proved impossible to find native authors who could meet the publication schedule.[21] We were determined in every case that the contributions were to be written by scholars of high ability and broad experience.

The chief value of calling on authors from the nations represented is that the contributions are written by individuals who are intimately acquainted with the foreign policy goals and the foreign policy processes which are followed. It also means that the authors have brought to their task a comprehension of leadership groups who determine policy choices and an understanding of background values and attitudes which are sometimes missed by the foreign scholar.

Of course, the other side of the ledger indicates some special problems which arise with this approach. Some authors may take a very defensive position about their nations and in a sense become special pleaders. There is always the chance, in a symposium of this type, that the author will sense that value judgments are being made about the "worth" of the various nations. This attitude can lead one to "protest too much" and to become an advocate of particular foreign policies. There is an additional problem when the author holds some responsible government position and consequently feels that he cannot be entirely candid about certain policies or governmental processes. As Hans Morgenthau once observed,

One would not expect the pronouncements of any contemporary statesman to tell us what his government is really up to in foreign policy. The degree of distortion, to be sure, differs from statesman to statesman and from nation to nation. It is extreme in totalitarian nations where the conceal-

---

[21] The chapter on China was written by Professor Robert Scalapino of the University of California (Berkeley); the chapter on Nigeria was written by Professor James Coleman of the University of California (Los Angeles).

ment of the true nature of the policies pursued—domestic and foreign—is one of the foundation stones of the very authority of government. It is bound to be great also in democratic nations which play a continuous active part in the affairs of the world; for that role requires continuous competition for the support of opinion at home and abroad, a support which derives not from the rational understanding of actual policies but rather from the emotional commitment to policies desired and expected."[22]

The editors, in making their decision to use national authors, well understood that the price of objectivity might have to be paid for other advantages which could be expected. However, they were also aware that the "outside expert" is not without bias and that the problems of objectivity cannot be assured regardless of the status of the author. In the final analysis, it is the quality and perception of the author that count.

On balance the editors are gratified with the results of this endeavor. Many of the authors have felt entirely free to carefully evaluate the policies of their nations while at the same time bringing a level of understanding and perception that is commendable. Other contributions, while not written in the same objective fashion, do present extremely valuable information which is not usually available to the student.

[22] In introduction to D. A. Graber, *Crisis Diplomacy: A History of U.S. Intervention Policies and Practices,* Washington: Public Affairs Press, 1959, p. v.

They are also revealing in reflecting the power of ideologies in particular countries.

Choice of nations

Ideally this study should have included all of the nations in the world community. Practically, of course, this was impossible and some selection process had to be used. The general objective was to present case studies which would be of the greatest utility to scholars, students, governmental officials and others interested in international affairs. In general, the editors used the following categories in determining which states to include:

1. All of the nations which would qualify as Major Powers;

2. Adequate representation of nations from all of the regions of the world;

3. Adequate representation from the "new" nations as well as from those with a longer history in the world community;

4. The inclusion of states, which, because of particular experiences, have played a special role in world affairs. Switzerland, for example, was included for this reason.

Some nations originally selected could not be included because satisfactory arrangements could not be made with authors or because the pressure of other duties prevented the completion of manuscripts. It is hoped that additional states can be included in subsequent editions.

Others may wish to undertake further study and analysis in this important sphere of comparative foreign policy. If so, a major purpose of the present volume will have been served.

PART ONE

WESTERN EUROPE

ABOUT THE AUTHOR

SAUL ROSE is a Fellow of St. Antony's College, Oxford. He began his studies at New College, Oxford, and received his undergraduate degree before the outbreak of World War II. During the war, he served as an officer in the Intelligence Corps in both the Indian and Malayan Campaign areas. Upon resuming his studies at the end of the war he became a student at Nuffield College. He was appointed Lecturer in International Relations at the University of Aberdeen where he taught for three years. He finished his work for his Doctor of Philosophy during this time and shortly thereafter became International Secretary of the British Labour Party. In 1955 he was elected to St. Antony's College. His publications include: *Socialism in Southern Asia,* 1959 and *Britain and South-East Asia,* 1962. He is editor of *Politics in Southern Asia,* 1962.

ABOUT THE CHAPTER

In this essay Mr. Rose skillfully brings together the factors which contribute to the overall foreign policy goals and policies of Great Britain. He shows how certain formative factors, such as "nation, power and position," along with traditional goals, influence the path that Great Britain has followed in the past and how they will condition her actions in the future.

The author traces the major highlights in Britain's foreign policy, noting that Britain had two traditional objectives in order to achieve security: The first of these was to deny to a potential enemy the control of the area from which invasion might be launched, the second was to forestall on the continent any concentration of power which might threaten to overwhelm Britain.

Mr. Rose is well aware of the main currents and shifts in world politics in recent years and of the major decisions which confront Britain today. Especially interesting are the discussions of the emerging European Community and the tentative decision to "join Europe."

The chapter as a whole is characterized by deep insight into the fundamental factors underlying the behavior of states, particularly how they have influenced the actions of Britain throughout the years.

THE FOREIGN POLICY OF BRITAIN

SAUL ROSE
Oxford University

FORMATIVE FACTORS

Geography

Among the influences which shape the foreign policy of a country, geography appears as one of the most important and constant. Indeed, it has been asserted that "the geographical position of a nation is the chief factor in determining its foreign policy, and indeed the chief reason why it must have a foreign policy at all." Applied to Britain, this observation calls to mind the group of islands, in area nearly the size of the state of Oregon, located off the shore of the European continent from which they are separated at the nearest point by a bare 20 miles of open water. Geography seems to fix the natural frontiers of the country, rendering them immune from the ephemeral

changes of boundaries in Europe; yet this impression is far from reality. From the time of the Roman Empire to that of the Hanoverians, those who held sway over the British Isles also had a connection with the Continent. And the frontiers of the United Kingdom underwent a major alteration as recently as forty years ago by the establishment of the Irish Free State.

There are, therefore, factors in foreign policy which must be considered along with, if not before, geography. It is not until a country has become a political entity as well as a geographical area that one can begin to talk about its foreign policy. Even then, its foreign policy may hardly be worth consideration until and unless the country has attained sufficient power to make its influence perceptible. Here, then, are two additional factors: political entity and power. But what constitutes the power of a country? Referring to the standard analyses of the elements of national power, we find a list something like this: natural resources, industrial capacity, military preparedness, population, national character, morale, diplomacy and finally—geography.

Nation, power and position are the three

basic elements for an assessment of foreign policy. Of these, it is the last which tends to come first to mind, partly because it contributes to forming the other two. Position is usually counted, and rightly so, among the components of a nation's strength—as in the conception of the Heartland, or in the appreciation of the Atlantic and Pacific oceans in American foreign policy. Position also contributes to shape the very idea of the nation. In the case of the United Kingdom, where natural frontiers are, with few exceptions, so clearly marked, that influence has been particularly strong.

England may plausibly claim to be one of the oldest nation-states. The precise moment of this development cannot be pin-pointed; but Shakespeare expresses a national pride and patriotism which was current in the first Elizabethan age. A familiar example is John of Gaunt's paean in *Richard II:*

> This royal throne of kings, this scepter'd isle,
> This earth of majesty, this seat of Mars,
> This other Eden, demi-paradise,
> This fortress built by Nature for herself
> Against infection and the hand of war,
> This happy breed of men, this little world.
> This precious stone set in the silver sea,
> Which serves it in the office of a wall
> Or as a moat defensive to a house,
> Against the envy of less happier lands.
> This blessed plot, this earth, this realm, this England.

These lines are often quoted for their poetry and patriotism; but they also show how strongly the conception of the nation was determined by geography—the "island fortress" theme recurs. From the sixteenth to the nineteenth century this was the dominant theme in British foreign policy. During that period England became the United Kingdom, and developed from a mercantile society to the leading industrial country of the world. But all the time the sea was there to protect it as a moat defensive to a house, setting it apart from the European continent. From the defeat of the Spanish Armada to the Napoleonic Wars and then from the Battle of Trafalgar until the Battle of Britain, the country was free from any serious threat of invasion and was spared the experience of foreign occupation which befell most of the continental states.

An insular position bred an insular outlook. On the occasion of some very rough weather a British newspaper carried the headline "Channel storm—Continent isolated." A good many Englishmen would have to think twice before they saw anything odd in this announcement. English people often talk of going to Europe for their holidays. This attitude, of being in Europe but not of it, had a very real basis for a very long time; and it sank deeply into the British way of thinking about foreign policy. Although it was the reflection of a geographical situation, it acquired a reality of its own; and one of the questions confronting British foreign policy today is whether that attitude is not lingering on as an after-effect when the situation which gave rise to it has fundamentally altered.

Naval power

For geographical situations, too, can alter, and do alter, through the development of communications. The Channel was a moat only because of the difficulty of crossing it. It was harder to transport an invading force across the Channel than across the Rhine or a land frontier. It could be made more difficult still by naval defense, and practically impossible if the defenders had naval superiority. The achievement and maintenance of naval superiority over any hostile force that might be mustered became, at an early stage, a cardinal point of British policy. This policy came to be defined as the maintenance of a two-power standard and was embodied in the Naval Defence Act of 1889. The aim was "that our fleet should be **equal to the** combination of the two next strongest navies in Europe."

Naval superiority was dependent on Britain's economic resources. The problem of reconciling naval requirements with the means of sustaining them is recurrent in British history. The greatest constitutional crisis that England experienced was associated with the demand for payment of "ship-money." Although the country's resources increased with the wealth and size of the population, at any given time they were limited, and at no time would England have been capable of facing the world alone. In order to achieve security, British policy had to adopt two intermediate objectives. The first was to deny to a potential enemy the control of the area from which invasion might be launched. This meant that the Low Countries and the Channel ports should not be allowed to fall into hostile hands. Even as late as 1914 it was the German invasion of Belgium which decided the wavering British Cabinet in favor of war.

Relations with Europe

The second objective was to forestall such a concentration of power as might threaten to overwhelm Britain. This aim is usually expressed as seeking to avert the hegemony of any one Power over the European continent, such as was attempted by Napoleon's France and Hitler's Germany. In practical terms, this meant an addiction to the balance of power. If any one Power or group of Powers appeared to be aiming at hegemony, it was Britain's role to throw her weight into the other scale. There were exceptions to this general rule, through special circumstances or even miscalculation, but this was the norm, dating back to Henry VIII whose motto *"Cui adhaereo praeest"* applied to international as well as matrimonial affairs.

To be able to work this kind of balance of power—the special feature of which is that Britain holds the balance—it was necessary that Britain should be able to shift her weight from one scale to the other as the balance fluctuated. Hence the doctrine of the "free hand": as Lord Salisbury put it, "to keep absolutely clear of engagements and to leave the country free to take any action which it might think fit in the event of war."

Trade

The refusal of England to commit herself to Europe contrasted with heavy commitments undertaken in other parts of the world. This is paradoxical but logical, accepting that it was a consistent aim of England, like every other nation, to augment her wealth and strength. Wealth was to be obtained from trade. Trade of an island nation was necessarily carried in ships. Merchant ships could be used in an emergency as naval vessels—whether to face the Spanish Armada or to evacuate Dunkirk. Warships could be used to protect the British Isles and also to protect British trade. The development of overseas trade and of naval power went hand in hand.

At first the quest for trade was undertaken for enrichment and for reinsurance because trade with the Continent was liable to be cut by a hostile Power. Later, as the industrial revolution gathered momentum and the population of Britain doubled and redoubled, it became a question of survival for a large part of the population. England became dependent on foreign countries for more than half of her food supply. She was also dependent on overseas sources for the raw materials necessary for the manufactures with which that food was purchased. For the British navy, the protection of Britain's trade routes became a duty next in priority to the defense of the British Isles, and not very clearly distinguishable from it. To the doctrine of the free hand was added the principle of the freedom of the seas—at least for British shipping.

THE WESTERN EUROPEAN SETTING

Building an Empire

In the search for trade, more was acquired than goods. The trade routes required staging posts. Bases were needed to protect shipping. Trading centers were established, and also demanded protection. The areas from which commodities were obtained had to be secured. Red patches spread over the map of the world. The flag followed trade; then trade followed the flag. Free trade meant not only freedom of the seas for carrying cargoes but also freedom of access to markets. That access was to be obtained preferably by persuasion and inducement, but if necessary by force. In the nineteenth century China provided a notable example of a country "forced to be free" in this way.

Towards the end of the nineteenth century Britain was faced with a dual challenge: the challenge to the ideology of free trade of which she was the foremost exponent, and the challenge to her industrial and trading supremacy. The raising of tariff barriers constricted British markets, and emphasized the desirability of being able to exercise political control over territories overseas. At the same time, the realization that Britain was being overtaken began to percolate. The U.S.A. and Germany were outdistancing the U.K. in population. By the end of the century the U.S.A. was producing more coal than the U.K.; and Germany as well as the U.S.A. was producing more steel.

The advantages for industrial countries in exercising political control over "underdeveloped areas" as markets and sources of raw materials were generally appreciated. If Britain did not acquire a territory, another country would. Part of the impetus of the "scramble for Africa" came from the desire to forestall a competitor. Colonies, instead of "millstones round our necks," became precious stones in the Imperial crown. The ideology of imperialism gained acceptance concurrently with the recognition of its advantages. "Take up the

White Man's burden" was a call to follow in a well-trodden path. The British had shouldered it with enthusiasm, and empire-builders set out with Bible and bayonet across darkest Africa. As with trade, so with empire: the chain was linked by sea power.

It would be wrong to say that the motive was profit, although the profit-motive was undoubtedly there. But there was also a genuine altruism and a sense of obligation towards "kindred" in the dominions beyond the seas. For all these reasons, just as the defense of the British Isles became linked with the security of trade routes, so the security of trade routes was linked with the protection of the Empire. That was the next priority for the British navy.

TRADITIONAL GOALS

By the end of the nineteenth century, therefore, the experience of centuries had inculcated certain cardinal principles of British policy. These were:

1. the prevention of any one country obtaining the hegemony of Europe, which involved
2. the maintenance of the balance of power by exercising a free hand;
3. the denial of invasion ports i.e. the Low Countries, to a potential enemy;
4. naval superiority, defined as a two-power standard for,
   (a) the protection of the British Isles
   (b) the safeguarding of trade routes
   (c) the security of the Empire.

The myth of isolation

There is a common misconception which should be discarded. The doctrine of the free hand, implying non-commitment, is equated with the policy of isolation, sometimes called "splendid." Although this was indeed the position in which Britain found herself at the end of the nineteenth century, it was the result of circumstances rather than choice, and the epithet "splendid" was merely an attempt to make the best of a bad job—as was shown soon afterwards by the conclusion of the Anglo-Japanese alliance in 1902 and the Anglo-French entente in 1904.

It was true that in the nineteenth century a policy of isolation or non-alignment prevailed for most of the time. This was due in part to the reluctance of British statesmen to enter into engagements to deal with hypothetical situations in the future and to assume obligations on behalf of their successors. For example, Lord Salisbury, as Prime Minister in 1887, declared:

> No English Government can give an absolute guarantee for military and naval cooperation in a future conflict, simply because it is not certain whether Parliament will fulfil those promises.[1]

Potential allies on the Continent also had this consideration in mind, and regarded England as an unreliable partner. Bismarck remarked upon

> the absolute impossibility of confidential intercourse in consequence of the indiscretions of English statesmen in their communications to Parliament, and the absence of security in alliances for which the Crown is not answerable in England, but only the fleeting Cabinets of the day.[2]

These were obstacles to engagement but not to involvement; and although British foreign policy had phases of greater or lesser activity in regard to continental affairs, it was never indifferent. The policy of isolation was not one

of holding aloof but "to avoid needless and entangling engagements." The phrase might be Jefferson's; it is actually Gladstone's. It meant a free hand—with the implication that the hand could be applied as required by the cardinal principles of British policy.

Three principles of policy

This outlook was summed up by Eyre Crowe, then a relatively junior official in the Foreign Office, in his memorandum of January 1st, 1907 to which reference is unavoidable in any study of British foreign policy. In that document, the determining factors were stated:

> The general character of England's foreign policy is determined by the immutable conditions of her geographical situation on the ocean flank of Europe as an island State with vast overseas colonies and dependencies, whose existence and survival as an independent community are inseparably bound up with the possession of preponderant sea power.

From this observation three principles were deduced. The first was that, since it would be

> but natural that the power of a State supreme at sea should inspire universal jealousy and fear and be very exposed to the danger of being overthrown by a general combination of the world,

the policy of Britain had to be directed so as

> to harmonize with the general desires and ideals common to all mankind,

and more particularly to be

> closely indentified with the primary and vital interests of a majority, or as many as possible, of the other nations.

---

[1] Cited in R. W. Seton-Watson, *Britain in Europe*, Cambridge: 1945, p. 563.
[2] Cited in R. W. Seton-Watson, *Britain and the Dictators*, Cambridge: 1938, p. 22.

What were those primary and vital interests? Eyre Crowe contended that:

England, more than any other non-insular Power, has a direct and positive interest in the maintenance of the independence of nations, and therefore must be the natural enemy of any country threatening the independence of others, and the natural protector of the weaker communities.

The second interest of nations, according to Eyre Crowe, was

the right of free intercourse and trade in the world's market.

Therefore England should champion freedom of commerce. In doing so:

She undoubtedly strengthens her hold on the interested friendship of other nations, at least to the extent of making them feel less apprehensive of naval supremacy in the hands of a free trade England than they would in the face of a predominant protectionist Power.

The third principle of British policy was the maintenance of the balance of power:

It has become almost an historical truism to identify England's secular policy with the maintenance of this balance by throwing her weight now in this scale and now in that, but ever on the side opposed to the political dictatorship of the strongest single State or group at a given time.[3]

[3] "Memorandum by Sir Eyre Crowe on the Present State of British Relations with France and Germany, January 1, 1907," *British Documents on the Origins of the War 1898–1914*, ed. by G. P. Gooch and H. Temperley. London: His Majesty's Stationery Office, 1928, Vol. III, pp. 402–20.

This analysis has been cited, not because it is correct, but because it was authoritative and accurate about the way in which foreign policy was approached at that time. The third principle—the maintenance of the balance of power—is put clearly and cogently; but the reasoning of the first and second principles is patently faulty. Granted that all countries wish to maintain their national independence, it does not follow that they wish to maintain the national independence of others. "Do as you would be done by" is a maxim which has yet to gain universal acceptance in international relations. Certainly at the beginning of the twentieth century it was far from being a recognized rule. After the First World War it was embodied in the Covenant of the League of Nations and called "collective security"; but even then performance fell far short of promise. In 1907, when the wave of British imperialism had not yet spent itself, the description of England as "the natural enemy of any country threatening the independence of others" showed a characteristic blind spot.

As for championing the freedom of commerce, this was a policy which commanded diminishing support as protectionism spread. It may have been true at one time that every country, if it could not itself hold naval supremacy, would prefer Britain to have it rather than any other nation. But by 1907 the German Navy Laws had made it clear that there was one country that did not accept the preliminary hypothesis.

The first and second principles stated by Eyre Crowe amount to the contention that what is good for Britain is good for the world, but phrased in the more acceptable fashion that what is good for the world is good for Britain. The tendency to hold this belief is discernible in the foreign policy of most countries. In the previous century it had been asserted that "the cause of America is the cause of humanity." In some cases it may even be true. In regard to Britain at the opening of the twentieth century it probably was; but the real basis of the principles enunciated by Eyre Crowe was not so much that community of interest as the factors outlined earlier which made the balance of power, the free hand, naval supremacy and freedom of commerce established features of British foreign policy.

Eyre Crowe's analysis, however, not only represented a typical view of the time, but by its general acceptance helped to maintain a stereotyped approach to foreign policy. He spoke of "immutable conditions," and so it was natural to suppose that the policies attuned to them should also be unchanging. In fact conditions changed, but policies continued as if nothing had altered.

Continuity of policy

Continuity of British foreign policy has been an observed fact and at the same time a bone of contention. But if foreign policy is determined by "immutable conditions" there would seem to be little point in arguing about it: argument suggests that there is a choice between alternative lines of policy. During the nineteenth century, there was argument in plenty, and yet there was continuity. How is this paradox to be explained? There are two possible answers.

One is that continuity does not mean "no change" but rather "no abrupt change," and consequently there could be modifications of policy while preserving continuity. In the nineteenth century, however, argument about foreign policy was not generally of this kind—at least between the major political parties. The general election of 1880 was one of the rare occasions on which foreign policy was a major issue in an election. Gladstone, challenging Disraeli's Government, enunciated in his Midlothian campaign the six principles on which British policy should be based:

To foster the strength of the Empire;

To preserve to the nations the blessings of peace;

To cultivate to the utmost the Concert of Europe;

To avoid needless and entangling engagements;

To acknowledge the rights of all nations;

To be inspired by love of freedom.

But these generalities were common ground. Disraeli, who summed up his own policy with the phrase *"Imperium et Libertas,"* could hardly take exception.

It was not about the principles of foreign policy that the argument was conducted, but about their application. This provides the clue to the paradox of the combination of continuity and contention in foreign policy. Thus in the great debate on the Eastern Question, Disraeli gave priority to the maintenance of the balance of power. His principal object was "to keep the Russians out of Turkey, not to create an ideal existence for the Turkish Christians."[4] Gladstone, on the other hand, put freedom before the balance of power, not only on grounds of principle but also in Britain's longer term interests:

> You talk to me of the established tradition and policy in regard to Turkey. I appeal to an established tradition older, wider, nobler far—a tradition not which disregards British interests, but which teaches you to seek the promotion of these interests in obeying the dictates of honour and justice . . . It is the populations of those countries that will ultimately possess them— that will ultimately determine their abiding condition. It is to this fact, this law, that we should look.[5]

WORLD WAR I to WORLD WAR II

The Impact of World War I

At the beginning of this century, therefore, the framework of British foreign policy appeared fixed and set, permitting differences in applying

[4] W. F. Monypenny and G. E. Buckle, *Life of Benjamin Disraeli*, vol. II, London: 1929, p. 983.

[5] J. Morley, *Life of Gladstone*, vol. II, London: 1908, pp. 130–1.

its principles but little if any alteration of the principles themselves. Britain's involvement in the First World War came about in consequence of a challenge to the principle that the integrity of the Low Countries must be maintained, and in consequence of Britain's refusal to countenance a hegemony on the Continent. Her alignment in the Dual and then the Triple Entente was in accordance with the principle of throwing her weight into the lighter scale.

The weight that was required to redress the balance was greater than ever before. The size of the British armies sent to fight in foreign fields was unprecedented, and so were the casualties. The effect of this experience was a deep desire to avoid a repetition. "Never again" was the cry which commanded universal assent. It was accompanied by an eagerness to withdraw from the Continent where so much British blood had been spilt. There was a movement back to isolation in Britain as well as in America.

Moreover, when the war ended, the balance of power had shifted. It was France, not Germany, which had the preponderance on the Continent. The most striking feature of British postwar policy was the promptitude with which Britain removed her weight from the French scale, thereby lending confirmation to the French view of *"Perfide Albion."* When the U.S.A. failed to ratify the treaty guaranteeing the French borders, that let Britain out too. But it need not have done. What blocked a British guarantee was the doctrine of the balance of power and the free hand. The balance had now tilted in favor of France: Britain could not both be allied to France and hold the balance.

Co-operation for peace

The League of Nations Anyway, balance of power politics were in disrepute. The keynote of the new world order was to be co-operation, not rivalry. To this end, British policy advocated and contributed to the construction of a League of Nations which would bring security

to each and all. This concept of collective security was in line with British policy during the previous century of getting the affairs of Europe into trim by means of the Concert of Europe, that is, the concerted action of the European Great Powers. The League of Nations was to be a world-wide Concert. In its Assembly it was to provide a meeting ground for all the countries of the world while its Council would give a special position and function to the Great Powers.

But the League turned out to be much less wide than had been hoped. The absence of the United States was not compensated by the presence of Japan. Taking into account the alteration in relative strength of the Great Powers in the past decade, the League seemed likely to bring increased responsibility rather than added security. That apprehension was increasingly felt, especially on the Right wing, while on the Left it was used as an argument for reinforcing the League system. From both points of view, particular commitments were to be avoided. The traditionalists objected on traditional grounds; while the advocates of collective security were opposed to any regional pacts which might seem to detract from the general assurances embodied in the League Covenant. Either way, Britain was to revert to a free hand.

Middle East mandates Yet, Britain showed a willingness to undertake certain commitments. As part of the peace settlement, Britain became the mandatory Power controlling Palestine, Trans-Jordan and Iraq. Added to the position which she already held in Egypt and the bases in Aden and Cyprus, this represented a very considerable involvement in the Middle East.

Originally, Britain's interest in this area had been primarily one of securing trade routes with the East and preventing any other Power, usually Russia, from being in a position to sever them. In accordance with the experience that "a large Empire is the best reason for a larger Empire," once Britain had obtained a position, she found herself obliged to defend it and, in defending it, to extend it. To this double motive was added, at the beginning of the twentieth century, a further consideration of growing importance. Oil was discovered in Persia in 1908 and elsewhere in the Middle East in the following years. With the adoption of oil-burning engines for warships, the control of oil supplies from the Middle East became a major element in Britain's strategy. The revenue from British investments in that area was also a matter of no small account. For Britain, therefore, the Middle East came to mean trade routes and pipe lines and the bases to protect them. While assuming these far-flung commitments, Britain maintained her opposition to a European engagement without anybody apparently noticing the contradiction.

The Locarno agreements This state of affairs could not last. Britain's interest in Europe could be reconciled with such an attitude of detachment only if the guarantee of security through the League of Nations were made effective; and that would have involved a much more extensive obligation. The dilemma was resolved—temporarily—by the Locarno agreements of 1925. They obtained for the British Foreign Secretary, Austen Chamberlain, the order of Knight of the Garter—and rightly so, for they represented almost the optimum expression of two of the cardinal points of British policy: the security of Belgium and the maintenance of the balance of power. Belgium's security was assured by the collective guarantee of the German-Belgian frontier and by an arbitration convention. The balance of power, and Britain's position as the holder of it, was secured by giving the guarantee of the Franco-German frontier to both countries alike. Britain was thus in a position to throw her weight against the country which might attempt to upset the balance. The only drawback was that she was not merely able to do so, she was committed to do so. Her hand was no longer completely free; but the British Government of the day was the only judge of whether there was a flagrant breach requiring immediate action.

The Locarno guarantee was a sign of the changing times. It came after two attempts at building security—the Draft Treaty of Mutual Assistance of 1923 and the Geneva Protocol of 1924—had failed. Austen Chamberlain stated the British objection to the Protocol by adapting a phrase from Bismarck:

> A form of guarantee which is so general that we undertake exactly the same obligations in defence shall I say of the Polish Corridor (for which no British Government ever will or ever can risk the bones of a British grenadier) as we extend to those international arrangements or conditions on which, as our history shows, our national existence depends, is a guarantee so wide and general that it carries no conviction whatever and gives no sense of security to those who are concerned in our action.[6]

A guarantee limited to the Versailles settlement in the West carried more conviction and therefore brought a sense of security—which turned out to be illusory. At the time, however, French anxieties were calmed by the British engagement, and British hesitation was overcome by limiting the commitment to the minimum that would bring reassurance. It was for effecting the compromise between French requirements and British reluctance that Austen Chamberlain earned his Garter.

The Washington Conference The commitment to Europe was a new departure in British foreign policy, but as yet it was minimal. As if in compensation, Britain's engagement in Asia was reduced. The Anglo-Japanese alliance was terminated and replaced by the Four-Power Treaty negotiated at the Washington Conference in 1921. Obligations under this Treaty were very much less than under the Alliance. However, the motive for the change was less the desire to reduce commitments than the

[6] Sir Charles Petrie, *The Life and Letters of the Rt. Hon. Austen Chamberlain*, vol. II, London: Cassell, 1940, p. 259.

willingness to meet the wishes of the Dominions and the U.S.A. regarding the Alliance.

America's new status as a World Power brought about the other major departure from established policy—the abandonment of naval superiority. At the Washington Conference, Britain agreed to naval parity in capital ships with the U.S.A. There was not much option. If Britain had refused, the U.S.A. would obviously win any competition. It was better therefore to bow to the inevitable. The days of Britain's naval supremacy were over; Britannia no longer ruled the waves. It was a consolation that the Power which now shared naval predominance happened to be one with which a conflict was highly unlikely. A decade earlier, Britain had refused to accept a similar claim from Germany. Now the danger of German naval competition had been eliminated. Britain had seen to that at the end of the war by requiring the surrender of the German fleet and the imposition of limits on naval building. The German fleet, scuttled at Scapa Flow, presented no danger at the bottom of the sea.

The only other challenger, apart from America, was Japan; and there was no need for Britain to concede parity in that instance. On the contrary, as long as Britain and America were in agreement, they could force Japan to accept a lower ratio, since they could obviously outbuild Japan if she refused. So the 5–5–3 ratio was arrived at. It is noteworthy that Britain, although accepting a one-power standard in relation to the U.S.A., still maintained a two-power standard in relation to other countries. But a two-power standard in general did not mean much. The important question was how much naval strength could be brought to bear in any given area.

It had to be recognized that under the Five-Power Treaty Japan secured naval supremacy in the China Sea because America had to provide a two-ocean navy and British naval needs spanned the seven seas. If Britain and America were united, their naval strength was more than a match for Japan; but if they were not, Japan could face either of them with equanimity. This was the key to the situation in the Far East in the 1930's. Japan could absorb Man-

churia with impunity because if Britain, in the throes of her economic crisis, were to contemplate intervention at all, it could only be in conjunction with the U.S.A.; and America, despite the resounding declarations of Secretary Stimson, was not prepared to act.

These changes were of a different kind from those which had occurred in the previous century. They were not differences about the application of certain principles but departures from them. The relative power of Britain in the world had declined with the emergence of new Great Powers, and her involvement in Europe had increased with the improvement of communications. These two developments were to transform the position of Britain. The story of British foreign policy in this century is one of gradual and painful adjustment to their consequences.

Air power

It is extraordinary that, after centuries had inculcated the importance of naval supremacy, no corresponding conclusions were drawn about air power. In part this was a result of the ten-year rule—the rule, adopted in 1919 and not abandoned until 1932, that the Service Departments should frame their estimates on the assumption that the British Empire would not be engaged in any great war during the next ten years. The rule itself reflected the mood of the 1920's with its revulsion from war and its belief that disarmament would help to create a peaceful climate. Yet this did not prevent Britain from attempting to salvage as much as possible of her naval position. That was largely a matter of holding on to the strength she had; the creation of an air force would involve expansion, which was quite another matter.

There was also a defeatism and pessimism, which Baldwin later adduced as an excuse, but which he himself helped to spread with his notorious observation in November 1932:

I think it is well also for the man in the street to realise that there is no power on earth that can protect him from being bombed. Whatever people may tell him, the bomber will always get through . . . When the next war comes, and European civilisation is wiped out, as it will be . . .[7]

At all events, the result was that by 1933 Britain was estimated to rank only fifth or sixth in air power, after Russia, France, America, Italy and probably Japan. In 1934 Churchill declared that Britain was only the fifth air power, if that, with strength only half that of France while Germany was arming fast. Baldwin gave assurance that, if efforts for a disarmament agreement failed, the Government would "see to it that in air strength and air power this country shall no longer be in a position inferior to any country within striking distance of its shores."[8] This was the equivalent of a one-power standard in relation to Europe, given the range of aircraft at that time.

As the challenge from Nazi Germany grew, Baldwin added another principle to that of air parity on July 30th, 1934: "When you think of the defence of England you no longer think of the chalk cliffs of Dover, you think of the Rhine. That is where our frontier lies."[9] This was an extension of the traditional doctrine of denying the Low Countries to a potential enemy for invasion bases. The range of aircraft required Britain's forward defenses to be advanced. Baldwin declared the frontier was the Rhine, which was already too close. Yet in 1936 Britain accepted the remilitarization of the Rhineland with only a verbal protest.

Churchill was the most powerful critic of the Government at that time. In a speech to the Conservative Committee on Foreign Affairs in March 1936, he expounded the principles of policy which he regarded as valid under the circumstances:

For four hundred years the policy of England has been to oppose the strongest, most aggressive, most dominating Power on the Continent, and particularly to prevent the Low Countries falling into the hands of such a Power . . . we always took the harder course, joined with the less strong Powers, made a combination among them, and thus defeated and frustrated the continental military tyrant whoever he was, whatever nation he led. . . . I know of nothing which has occurred to alter or weaken the justice, wisdom, valour and prudence upon which our ancestors acted. . . . My three main propositions are: first, that we must oppose the would-be dominator or potential aggressor. Secondly, that Germany under its present Nazi regime and with its prodigious armaments, so swiftly developing, fills unmistakably that part. Thirdly, that the League of Nations rallies many countries, and unites our own people here at home in the most effective way to control the would-be aggressor. . . . For myself, I am for the armed League of all Nations, or as many as you can get, against the potential aggressor, with England and France as the core of it. Let us neglect nothing in our power to establish the great international framework. If that should prove to be beyond our strength, or if it breaks down through the weakness or wrong-doing of others, then at least let us make sure that England and France, the two surviving free great countries of Europe, can together ride out any storm . . .[10]

Citing this speech in the first volume of his memoirs of the Second World War Churchill observed in 1948:

[7] G. M. Young, *Stanley Baldwin,* London: Rupert Hart-Davis, 1952, p. 174.

[8] W. S. Churchill, *Second World War,* vol. I, London: Cassell, 1948, p. 89.

[9] House of Commons, *Debates,* July 30th, 1934, vol. 292, col. 2339.

[10] Winston Churchill, *The Second World War: The Gathering Storm,* New York: Houghton Mifflin Company, 1948, pp. 207–211.

If we add the United States to Britain and France; if we change the name of the potential aggressor; if we substitute the United Nations Organisation for the League of Nations, the Atlantic Ocean for the English Channel, and the world for Europe, the argument is not necessarily without its application today.[11]

What stands out from Churchill's analysis is the recognition of Germany as the potential aggressor and the assertion that the League of Nations was the most effective way of controlling it. Failing that, the essential foundation was the combination of England and France. This was a point of view which the French had held about the League of Nations from the outset. They had always regarded the League primarily as a means of French security against Germany; but it was not the point of view which had been prevalent in Britain. There, the principle of collective security seemed to involve turning a blind eye to the quarters from which danger threatened. There was some wishful thinking—that if the dangers were not seen they were not real; but the object was to avoid discrimination which might be construed as provocation. So the idea of non-discrimination between victors and vanquished, which made sense for the peace settlement, became twisted into non-discrimination between potential aggressor and intended victim, which made nonsense of collective security.

The policy of appeasement

The difficulty was complicated by the Italian adventure in Ethiopia. This attempt by Mussolini to re-create the *Imperium Romanum* confronted Britain and France with a dilemma. On the one hand, they could scarcely maintain their protestations of upholding the principle

of collective security and at the same time do nothing about Italy's flagrant aggression. On the other hand, Germany represented a greater danger than Italy. It was to counter the growing German threat that the three Powers—Britain, France and Italy—had in April 1935 established the so-called "Stresa front." But that front had promptly been undermined by the Anglo-German Naval Agreement concluded, as the French did not fail to note, on the anniversary of the Battle of Waterloo. It could be argued that the intention of this agreement was both realistic and conciliatory. There was no way to stop Germany from naval re-armament. If she were voluntarily to limit herself to a 35 per cent ratio with Britain, that would be better than no restriction at all and might remove a grievance. If the policy of appeasement can be sustained, the Anglo-German Naval Agreement stands with it. But it could not be reconciled with the maintenance of the Versailles settlement: it was a breach of international obligations, and also of the Stresa front.

Ethiopia Italy's attack on Ethiopia was so long in preparation and so open in its coming that it was impossible to avoid recognition of it as a defiance of the Covenant. The British Foreign Secretary, Sir Samuel Hoare, made one of the strongest declarations in support of the League Covenant in an attempt to deter the Italian aggression. But once the attack had been launched, the British attitude reflected the dilemma that was presented. Having recognized a breach of the Covenant, sanctions had to be applied. But it was made clear that sanctions would stop short of war, and so Mussolini was given a veto on the sanctions that would really have hurt. At the same time the Hoare-Laval plan was worked out with a view to appeasing Mussolini's appetite at the expense of Ethiopia with some compensation in the shape of a "corridor for camels." Mussolini had misbehaved and so had to be checked; but the punishment was lenient and was to be sugared with the offer of some satisfaction. The hope was that he could be both deterred and enticed from his evil ways. The enticement, however, was too much for British pub-

[11] *Ibid.*

lic opinion to stomach; and the outcry which followed upon the disclosure of the Hoare-Laval plan was such that the Prime Minister, Mr. Baldwin, found it expedient to jettison his Foreign Secretary.

Rhineland remilitarization Italy's imperialism, and the consequent collapse of the Stresa front, was one of the reasons for the failure of Britain and France to respond to Hitler's remilitarization of the Rhineland in 1936. This challenge to the Locarno agreements came at a time when one of the guarantors was applying sanctions against the other. To stop Mussolini from marching into Ethiopia had proved beyond the combined, though half-hearted, efforts of the League of Nations. It would take more than that to stop Hitler marching into his own backyard. The possibility of the use of force to prevent it was one which the British Government shied away from, although Hitler later admitted that, if force had been used, "we would have had to withdraw with our tails between our legs."

The remilitarization of the Rhineland did have one important effect on British policy. Britain re-affirmed the Locarno guarantee to France and Belgium against any unprovoked aggression, and initiated military staff conversations. This was the first step down from the fence upon which Britain had hitherto been sitting. No longer was it possible to pretend that one could not and should not recognize in advance the potential aggressor. The need to take precautions was accepted. The League of Nations had failed to stop Italy. There might be argument as to whose was the responsibility, but it was difficult to deny the fact. The last resort was the combination of Britain and France indicated by Churchill, to which the military staff conversations now pointed. But the British Government had not abandoned all hope of drawing Italy back into the fold of the Stresa front. It was for this reason that Neville Chamberlain described the policy of sanctions in June 1936 as "the very midsummer of madness" and for the same reason that Britain concluded with the Italian government, in 1937, the "Gentleman's Agreement" which Musso-

lini construed as envisaging the victory of Franco in Spain. It was on this issue of relations with Italy that Eden parted company with Chamberlain in February 1938. He had come to the conclusion that it was futile to continue the appeasement of Mussolini in the hope of breaking the Axis, whereas Chamberlain was prepared to go on pursuing the will o' the wisp of Italian friendship.

The Munich Agreement The *anschluss* with Austria added to the growing alarm, but it was one of the points of the Versailles settlement about which consciences had been uneasy: after all, was not Austria a German state?

The crisis over Czechoslovakia tested the appeasement policy to the utmost. It was clear that Britain and France would have to fight if Hitler marched into Czechoslovakia, and that would mean a general war. As Hitler was apparently determined to acquire the Sudetenland it was necessary, if war was to be avoided, that the Czechs should concede. It was fantastic to prepare for war "because of a quarrel in a far-away country between people of whom we know nothing." Hence the Munich agreement—which was an agreement between four Powers to exact concessions from a fifth. In return there was supposed to have been a guarantee of the remainder of Czechoslovakia. This guarantee was never made specific although the Secretary of State for the Dominions declared that the Government felt under a "moral obligation" to treat it as being in force. But when Hitler marched into Prague in March 1939, the Prime Minister took the view that the declaration of independence by Slovakia had "put an end by internal disruption to the State whose frontier we had proposed to guarantee. . . . H.M.G. cannot accordingly hold themselves any longer bound by this obligation."[12] This attitude could not be maintained. The reaction of public opinion was too strong. The policy of appeasement was not abandoned but supplemented by a policy of firmness.

---

[12] House of Commons, *Debates*, March 15, 1939, vol. 345, col. 437.

The turning point—Poland

The new policy took the unexpected form of a guarantee extended to Poland at the end of March 1939. This was an altogether novel engagement. Fourteen years earlier one Chamberlain had said that no British Government could ever risk the bones of a British grenadier for the Polish Corridor. Now another Chamberlain gave an unequivocal guarantee to Poland. It was even left to Poland to decide whether or not Britain would be involved in war. This was one thing that Lord Salisbury had said no British Government could do, yet according to the guarantee

in the event of any action which clearly threatened Polish independence, and which the Polish Government accordingly considered it vital to resist with national forces, H.M.G. would feel themselves bound at once to lend the Polish Government all support in their power.[13]

At one blow two of the cardinal principles of British foreign policy—the doctrine of the free hand and limitation of commitments in Europe —had been knocked away.

There remained, however, the principle of the balance of power, which in this situation could only mean the mustering of all available strength to counter the threat of German hegemony over the Continent of Europe. It was apparent even to Chamberlain by this time that the Rome-Berlin Axis could not be broken. With America wedded to isolation, the only other possible source of a considerable accretion of strength lay beyond Poland in the Soviet Union. The situation seemed to require the conclusion of a triple alliance between Britain, France and Russia against the Axis, and negotiations were begun with that object.

[13] Royal Institute of International Affairs, *Documents on International Affairs, 1939–46*, vol. I, p. 126.

But they were pursued halfheartedly, partly because Russian military strength was discounted after Stalin's purge of the high command, partly because the attitude of the British Government, particularly the Prime Minister, to Russia was one of distrust, and partly because of the objections encountered from Poland and Rumania who believed, with reason, that if they once allowed Russian troops into their territory they would not get them out again. Britain had, by her guarantee to Poland and then to Greece and Rumania, played her bargaining card with Russia. Britain had nothing more to offer unless she were prepared to enter into arrangements for military co-operation and also countenance precautionary measures by the Soviet Union in the Baltic states. It was on these two points that the negotiations dragged.

When Hitler intervened with a higher bid offering half of Poland, most of the Baltic states and Bessarabia, and at the same time a postponement of Russia's involvement in the war, Stalin accepted the new offer. So Britain went to war over the Polish Corridor, with fatal consequences for more than one British grenadier.

The British-French Union plan

The resistance in the East was shorter than anticipated. With the collapse of the Eastern front, Britain was faced with the more familiar problem of defense in the West. The new and relatively unknown factor was the effect of air power. The development of the air weapon made it desirable to keep enemy air bases as far from the Home Islands as possible. This accentuated the importance of the alliance with France. To the Churchillian argument for alignment with France to maintain the balance of power was added the need to avoid the establishment of aircraft bases within striking range.

The test came in 1940 at the time of the fall of France, when the British Government was moved to make its famous offer of union with France:

At this most fateful moment in the history of the modern world the Governments of the U.K. and the French Republic make this declaration of indissoluble union and unyielding resolution in their common defence of justice and freedom against subjection to a system which reduces mankind to a life of robots and slaves.

The two Governments declare that France and Great Britain shall no longer be two nations, but one Franco-British Union. The constitution of the Union will provide for joint organs of defence, foreign, financial and economic policies. Every citizen of France will enjoy immediately citizenship of Great Britain; every British subject will become a citizen of France.

Both countries will share responsibility for the repair of the devastation of war, wherever it occurs in their territories, and the resources of both shall be equally, and as one, applied to that purpose.

During the war there shall be a single War Cabinet, and all the forces of Britain and France, whether on land, sea, or in the air, will be placed under its direction. It will govern from wherever it best can. The two Parliaments will be formally associated. The nations of the British Empire are already forming new armies. France will keep her available forces in the field, on the sea, and in the air. The union appeals to the United States to fortify the economic resources of the Allies, and to bring her powerful material aid to the common cause.

The Union will concentrate its whole energy against the power of the enemy, no matter where the battle may be. And thus we shall conquer.[14]

[14] W. S. Churchill, *The Second World War: Their Finest Hour* (volume II), London: Cassell, 1949, pp. 183–4.

This declaration is commonly regarded as a freakish aberration of British policy. In fact it was intended much more as an encouragement to the French than as a policy for the future. Even so, it was not out of line with the direction in which British policy had been moving. If Britain's frontier was really on the Rhine and this was the only way to save France, the declaration would have been sound policy. But neither of those hypotheses was correct. Nothing could save France; and it transpired that Britain's frontier was still the Channel. For, although the British Isles were attacked and heavily damaged, they were not invaded. The Channel, combined with naval superiority and air defense, was still a barrier to occupation. That this was so was recognized even when the declaration was made: "indissoluble union" was not taken as far as the transfer to France of the remaining British fighter squadrons. It was not thought—by the British Government —that they could affect the fate of France, whereas they might well decide the issue of the Battle of Britain. And so it turned out.

The impact of World War II

The Second World War had effects similar to those of the first but with greater scale and intensity. Just as in 1918 Britain was obliged to recognize America's ascendancy, so in 1945 she was obliged to accept third place to America and Russia. The relative decline in Britain's world status continued, as greater Powers emerged. Technical development, which had been accelerated by the demands of war, increased Britain's vulnerability and proximity to the Continent. The detonation of A-bombs at Hiroshima and Nagasaki emphasized that the world had become a much more dangerous place than ever before. While the dangers grew, Britain's strength was at a low ebb. The war had drained her economic resources, so that she was a client of the U.S.A. In wartime the special relationship and close collaboration between Britain and America were welcome. But the abrupt cessation of Lend-Lease gave notice that America did not intend it to continue into peace. The main pillar of British support was knocked away.

Yet there were items on the other side of the ledger. There were the imponderables of morale and prestige—the fact that Britain had fought on and emerged triumphant. There was also the fact that, although Britain ranked only third among the Powers, it was a good third, considerably superior to any fourth Power. France was given that position, for example in the occupation of Germany; but it was known to be an act of courtesy, inspired very largely by Britain. Churchill argued that "It was important to re-create a strong France; for the prospect of having no strong country on the map between England and Russia was not attractive." The fifth of the Big Five—permanent members of the United Nations Security Council—was China, and in 1945 that country was too weak and internally divided to be able to exercise much influence. Britain therefore still ranked as one of the Big Three and also had a particular connection with the U.S.A.— besides a common language—which was not altogether severed.

Moreover, the efficacy of the Commonwealth link had been tested and had endured the strain, at least among the self-governing members. Since the Imperial Conference of 1926, if not before, each Dominion had been in control of its own external relations. They were not obliged to declare war when Britain did; but at no time did Britain "stand alone"— the Commonwealth was in it together. From these circumstances arose the pattern of relations which dominated British thinking about foreign policy in the immediate postwar years.

POSTWAR POLICIES

Every country tends to view the world from its own standpoint. The common British view of international relations after the Second

World War discerned four concentric circles, with Britain at the center. First there was the circle of the United Nations which was to be world-wide; then there was the circle of the Commonwealth, that indeterminate association with intangible bonds which had, nevertheless, withstood the strains of war; thirdly, there was the grouping of Europe, of which Britain after all was part; and fourthly there was the Atlantic association, the relationship with the U.S.A. which had attained a special degree of intimacy during the war and was to be tended and fostered.

The United Nations

In the first phase, the main emphasis was placed on working through the United Nations and making the United Nations work. The reason for this shift of emphasis was twofold. One aspect was the recognition of the increased and increasing vulnerability of Britain. A similar situation had given rise after the First World War to the adoption of the League of Nations idea. But at that time collective security was a theoretical concept, based on the argument that war anywhere was liable to involve countries everywhere. "All for one and one for all" was an acceptable maxim so long as it was not put to the test. In the 1930's, as war loomed closer, the more familiar "each for himself" became increasingly attractive. At the time of the crisis over Czechoslovakia the British Prime Minister declared:

However much we may sympathise with a small nation confronted by a big and powerful neighbour we cannot, in all circumstances undertake to involve the whole British Empire in a war simply on her account. If we have to fight, it must be on larger issues than that.[15]

[15] *The Times*, September 27, 1938.

Such an attitude it was now fashionable to condemn as mistaken, if not immoral, and the intention was not to repeat that error. Therefore, in the immediate postwar period the British Foreign Secretary, Mr. Bevin declared:

> What is necessary and what we intend to do is to make the Security Council the place where the questions of policy are resolved . . . This is the major function of the Security Council and we, for our part, intend to do all we can to make it the very centre of the world's international affairs.[16]

The search for security was one motive for Britain's emphasis on the United Nations. The other side of the coin was the belief that the organization offered a fruitful field for the exercise of British influence by virtue of her leadership in Western Europe and as the center of the British Commonwealth and Empire. The notion that Britain also held a special place in American regard may have been an illusion, but it was fondly cherished; and there were hopes of establishing particularly close co-operation with the Soviet Union.

Balancing East and West

Anglo-Soviet relations   The Treaty of Alliance with the U.S.S.R. concluded in 1942 was regarded by the incoming Labour Government as a symbol of a new departure in Anglo-Soviet relations on which they were exceptionally fitted to embark. Admittedly, in domestic politics before the war, relations between the Labour and Communist parties had ranged from coolness to extreme hostility. If this was an example of Left talking to Left, the outlook was not very bright. In international affairs it was hoped that things would be

different—that the Soviet Union would recognize in a Labour Britain a well-disposed and sympathetic collaborator, and that a Labour Britain, for her part, being politically democratic and economically socialist (at least by intention), would be well-placed to act as a bridge or, if need be, a buffer between American democracy and Soviet socialism.

Britain would therefore be able in the United Nations organization to chart a "third way" between East and West. At the same time —and this was a notion very easily confused with the "third way"—Britain as leader of Western Europe and of the Commonwealth could also represent a "third force." This idea was particularly attractive to many who saw with alarm the developing cleavage between East and West, and wished to soften their direct confrontation. From that point of view a multiple balance of power comprising a "third force" was preferable to a simple balance between two blocs, since the latter afforded very little scope for maneuver. For Britain it had obvious advantages if it could be put into practice, since it would restore to her the position of holding the balance which she had enjoyed for so long in the past.

Unfortunately, this notion was based on a fundamental misconception. The Soviet Union, far from regarding Britain as a mediator between herself and America, chose Britain as the main target of attack. In Soviet eyes, what distinguished Labour Britain from capitalist America was a distinction without a difference. Britain was subjected to greater pressure both as the weaker link in the capitalist chain and because of her commitments on the Soviet periphery. The Soviet leaders saw in the British Labour Party not potential comrades and sympathizers, but deviationists and deceivers of the proletariat. Labour Britain was regarded as a rival, not a collaborator. The idea of a "third way" was an anathema. It would simply mislead the workers into believing that there was an alternative to the stark choice between communism and capitalism. Consequently, the more that Labour Britain tried to provide a *via media*, the less it was qualified to mediate.

Soviet pressure and Britain's postwar eco-

---

[16] House of Commons, *Debates,* August 23, 1945, vol. 413, col. 942.

nomic weakness combined to restrict Britain's influence abroad. Mr. Bevin, replying to criticism, pointed out: "I have not had one ton of spare coal to ship to Western Europe to help in rehabilitation. I have had nothing with which to negotiate."[17] Commitments had to be cut. The notification to America in February 1947 of the intention to withdraw from Greece marked the end of this phase. The beginning of the next was the Marshall Plan in June 1947. In this offer Britain saw an economic rescue at the eleventh hour, and Bevin grasped it with both hands. The initiative came from America, but it was the British response which led on to the Organization for European Economic Cooperation. This represented not only a rescue operation but also a shift in Britain's foreign policy.

The Cold War   With the refusal of the Soviet Union to participate in the Marshall Plan, it was no longer possible to maintain the pretense, already rendered transparent by the Soviet abuse of the veto, that the United Nations was the center of world affairs. As a member of the Government put it, the British objective altered at this time from "one world" to "one free world." In other words, Britain had to resign herself to the acceptance of the East-West division of the globe. Moreover, the direction of her alternative policy was towards Europe. This new move was given impetus by the consolidation of the Soviet bloc. After the *coup d'état* in Czechoslovakia the Iron Curtain was rung down over Eastern Europe.

Military engagements followed economic cooperation. The Treaty of Alliance with the Soviet Union had become a dead letter. The Dunkirk Treaty with France made belated amends for the sorry record of the inter-war period. The Brussels Treaty concluded with France and the Benelux countries in 1948 was ostensibly directed against a revival of German aggression, but clearly was a defensive measure against Soviet encroachment. It represented another step in the new British policy, a commitment to the defense of Western Europe.

Atlantic Alliance and European Union

Western organization was proceeding in two directions at once. On the one hand there was the organization of Europe represented by the O.E.E.C., the Brussels Treaty, and then, in 1949, the Council of Europe. These were all in the direction of European consolidation, the first economic, the second military and the third political. The other path to Western consolidation culminated in the Atlantic Alliance in 1949. N.A.T.O. came into being as a response to Soviet pressure in Europe, demonstrated particularly by the Berlin blockade. It incorporated the Brussels Pact and transcended it: for Britain the supreme importance of N.A.T.O. lay in America's participation. European Union and Atlantic Alliance were growing side by side. Britain could only play a distinctive role in both on an inter-governmental footing, not by joining a European federation.

Another objection to Britain's absorption in Europe was provided by the Commonwealth. Since the war, that association had been transformed by the accession of most of the Asian territories to independence and acceptance by all—except Burma—of continued Commonwealth membership. Whether this development was attributed to the enlightened policy of the Labour Government or to the inability of a weakened Britain to hold on to those territories, the result was to give the Commonwealth a new lease on life.

In 1950, therefore, British policy had achieved what was to be the summit of its postwar influence, acting as a link between Western Europe, the Atlantic Alliance and the new Commonwealth. It was further enhanced by the launching of the Colombo Plan to provide assistance to the underdeveloped countries of South and Southeast Asia; and it was strikingly demonstrated by the visit of the Prime Min-

[17] House of Commons, *Debates,* June 19, 1947, vol. 438, col. 2354.

ister to Washington at a critical point of the Korean war in order to dispel any idea of using atomic weapons. This, however, was the limit. The strains imposed by the Korean war began to tell, and in the next phase Britain was compelled to recognize that the role of the indispensable link was no longer within her capacity.

Federalism versus functionalism   Several of the continental countries wished to push ahead with unification of Europe by means of federation, and were not content to have their progress dictated by the speed with which Britain could be persuaded to accompany them. From this arose the great debate between federalism and functionalism. The federalists in the six countries of France, Germany, Italy and Belgium, the Netherlands and Luxembourg, wished to create supra-national authorities as steps on the road towards a united Europe. The British response was to argue for a functional approach through inter-governmental co-operation. This conflict of views had already been manifested at the time of the creation of the Council of Europe in which the Assembly was the focus for the federalists whereas Britain put the emphasis on the Council of Ministers. In 1950 the dispute was brought to a head by the presentation of the Schuman plan for the creation of a Coal and Steel Community on supra-national lines. This posed the question to Britain in the most direct and difficult form: whether she was or was not prepared to accept participation in a supra-national community and so commit herself to integration with Europe.

The answer given by the Labour Government was in the negative. Various reasons were provided: that Britain was not in the habit of accepting a principle without knowing what it would mean in practice; that a Socialist Government was reluctant to surrender to a supra-national authority the economic controls necessary for Socialist planning; that the political orientation of the governments of the Six with whom Britain would be joining was not attractive to the Left. Overriding all these reasons was the conception of the semi-detachment of

Britain from the Continent and the equivalent, if not preponderant, interest in the Commonwealth and across the Atlantic. Dalton, one of the leaders of the Labour Party and a senior member of the Government expressed a very prevalent, if not a very Socialist, sentiment when he said at the Labour Party Conference in 1948:

> It is no good denying that we are very much closer, in all respects except distance, to Australia and New Zealand than we are to Western Europe. Australia and New Zealand are populated by our kinsmen. They live under Labour Government, they are democracies, they speak our language, they have high standards of life and have the same political ideals as we have. . . .[18]

The question was posed again in 1951, this time under the threat of the Korean war and the possibility that what had happened in a divided Korea might be repeated in a divided Germany. This danger gave rise to demands for a German contribution to Western defense. In view of the resistance to this idea, a compromise solution was devised in the Pleven Plan for a German contribution integrated in a European Defense Community under supra-national control. Britain's response, nevertheless, was unchanged: every encouragement to the Six countries to go ahead with E.D.C., but without Britain.

With the failure of the French Parliament to ratify the E.D.C. in 1954, scepticism about this supra-national institution seemed to have been justified; but the breakdown only emphasized that the defense of Western Europe was not a matter from which Britain could be semi-detached. The gap left by the collapse of E.D.C. had to be filled, and it was the British Foreign Secretary who took prompt action to fill it. As the result of his tour of the European capitals, a Western European Union was cre-

[18] Labour Party, *47th Annual Conference Report*, 1948, p. 178.

ated to take the place of the defunct E.D.C. at the price of an unprecedented British commitment to the Continent: the undertaking by Britain to maintain on the Continent of Europe four divisions and her Tactical Air Force.

The Commonwealth

While the necessities of Britain's position in the West were pushing her towards an increasing involvement in Europe, her ties with the Commonwealth were being loosened. The new Commonwealth was linked by the acceptance of the Crown as the symbol of its free association, by the bonds of the past, and by practical co-operation on a basis of certain generally accepted ideals and principles. No longer could it be said that it was a family of nations in the sense of being derived from a common stock. Nor could the head of this heterogeneous family any longer undertake the responsibility for the defense of all its members. During the second world war Canada and the U.S.A. had entered into a defense agreement which still continued, and it was clear that Canada's strategic outlook was primarily that of the American hemisphere. In 1951, as the peace treaty with Japan became imminent, Australia and New Zealand also entered into a direct defense arrangement with the U.S.A. in the form of the ANZUS Pact, from which Britain was excluded. In one way this was a welcome development, for it relieved the strain upon Britain. Yet it had to be recognized that the consequence would inevitably be an increased orientation of these two countries towards Washington rather than London.

Policy problems in Asia   One of the points of difference which had developed between Britain and America in relation to the Far East concerned the recognition of the Peking Government of China. Britain was among the first countries to extend recognition early in 1950. Essentially, the British argument was based upon the realities of the situation. Just

as during the Second World War Britain had differed from the American view that China was a Great Power which must be included in the Big Five, so in 1950 Britain recognized that the China of Chiang Kai-shek was past and that it would be necessary to come to terms with the People's Republic. This appreciation no doubt reflected a desire to salvage what could be saved of British economic interests in China. But, over and above this consideration, the Commonwealth again entered into the picture. It appeared that the Asian members of the Commonwealth would quickly recognize the Peking Government whereas there would be considerable hesitation and reluctance on the part of the "old Dominions." One of Britain's motives, therefore, was to avoid a sharply conflicting alignment of "white" and "colored" members of the Commonwealth on this issue. The achievement of a multi-racial Commonwealth was very recent and not yet firmly established. To foster and secure it was to become one of the new elements of British policy.

There was also the problem of the defense of the Commonwealth in Asia. Admittedly, in regard to India, Pakistan and Ceylon, it was no longer a British responsibility. But it was still a matter for concern, and Britain retained responsibility for the defense of Malaya and Borneo. In line with the policy which had proved effective in Europe—the policy of containment—it was desirable in the British view to draw a line in Asia also which should not be transgressed. For that it would be necessary to have, in Asia as in Europe, the support of the United States. Of this there was no sign until the deterioration of the war in Indochina provoked an American reaction.

The proposal for the creation of what was to become SEATO only became a real possibility when it was espoused by Mr. Dulles. Even then the intention was to create an organization which would be able to render assistance to the French in Indochina. The British response to this was ambivalent. On the one hand, the idea of a Southeast Asia defense organization in which Britain, as well as America, would participate was welcome. On the other hand it was futile, in the British view, to attempt to commit this organization to the cause of the maintenance of French rule in Indochina. The British held that the best that could be hoped for in that struggle was partition. Eden records in his memoirs: "My chief concern was for Malaya. I wanted to ensure an effective barrier as far to the North of that country as possible."[19] There was, therefore a difference of opinion between Britain and America about the function of the new grouping. From the British viewpoint, its purpose would be to guarantee a settlement, if such a settlement could be reached with the Communists over Indochina. Consequently, it should come after, not before, negotiations.

In this argument the British policy prevailed, not so much perhaps on the merits of the case as because the train of events was moving inexorably in that direction. The worsening of the French position in Indochina demanded a settlement on the basis of saving whatever was possible. In the negotiations for this object, Britain was in a strong position to act as mediator. This was the role after which there was constant hankering because of past history. Although there was no question of separation from the United States or an independent policy, yet this opportunity to exercise the skills of traditional diplomacy in a traditional way was one which was most agreeable to Eden. He likened his objective at the Geneva Conference in 1954 to that of achieving a kind of Locarno, a treaty of guarantee. In this he was successful and, like Austen Chamberlain thirty years before, returned to receive the Garter.

The challenge in the Middle East

Negotiations for a settlement in Indochina showed British diplomacy in the guise of moderation and mediation, with due recognition of

the decline in Britain's power and influence and the consequent limitations upon her policy. It is all the more curious to contrast it with the British attitude in the next phase in the Middle East. Eden himself has recorded that he was not convinced when Dulles compared the situation in Indochina with the Japanese invasion of Manchuria in 1931 and Hitler's re-occupation of the Rhineland. Yet he was very soon afterwards to take the view that he "was not so sure about Nasser." Why the challenge in the Middle East should have produced so much stronger a reaction than the situation in Indochina is no doubt partly a matter for psychological analysis; but it was also due to a traditional British interest and a direct British involvement.

Priorities of interests   The Middle East had, in the twentieth century, acquired growing importance in British eyes, not merely as "the life-line of Empire" but also as a source of oil supplies. During the Second World War, there had been an outspoken argument between the Prime Minister and his Chiefs of Staff about the relative priorities of Singapore and the Middle East. The Chiefs of Staff clung to the established view that Singapore was second only in importance to the defense of the Home Islands, but were firmly detached from this by Churchill who insisted that the Middle East came before Singapore. This change of priorities reflected an alteration in relative importance, but also Britain's limitations. It was an estimate not confined to Churchill and the Conservatives. Bevin had reacted in traditional fashion to the Soviet claim to trusteeship of Tripolitania in 1945. Personifying British interests, he is said to have protested: "You can't cut me in half." Attlee has recorded that, when he became Prime Minister,

> Europe came first. In the order of priority in world strategy that was Number One. From our point of view the Middle East was Number Two, although from the American point of view, and probably also that of Australia and New Zealand, the Far East

---

[19] Sir A. Eden, *Full Circle,* London: Cassell, 1960, p. 87.

was. But for us the Middle East was the critical area after Europe. It still is in many ways.[20]

This attitude was reflected in the ambivalent policy towards Palestine and in the willingness of a section of the Labour Government to resort to force in the Persian oil dispute in 1951.

In accordance with the policy of drawing a line and holding it, Britain aimed to consolidate the "northern tier" from Turkey to Pakistan. It was therefore a matter of some congratulation when in 1955 the Baghdad Pact was successfully concluded comprising Turkey, Iraq, Iran and Pakistan along with Britain in a defense agreement. Thus, although this phase of British policy was marked by some recession from the peak which it had reached in 1950, it too could count some successes. The exclusion of Britain from the ANZUS Pact had been made good by the creation of SEATO, and to it had now been added the Baghdad Pact. Britain was substituting for her own individual engagements collective treaty obligations for the same objects. The potential enemy in each case was the Communist bloc—Russia, China or both together. It was no doubt particularly irritating when one of the countries to be protected by this system of defense agreements turned and bit its protector.

The Suez Canal   The full story of Britain's reaction to Nasser's nationalization of the Suez Canal Company has not yet been told. From the British point of view what was at stake was first, freedom of communications via the Suez Canal; second, oil supplies from the Middle East; third, the holding in the Suez Canal Company; and fourth, British prestige—Egypt could not be allowed to dispose of British property with impunity. The fiction of interposition between Israeli and Egyptian forces is apparent even in Eden's account.

The resort to force in this instance suggested that a vital British interest was at stake, a be-

[20] F. Williams, *A Prime Minister Remembers*, London: Heinemann, 1961, p. 175.

lief which was in part due to the influence of a cliché of British policy—that the Mediterranean and the Middle East were "the life-line of Empire." The Mediterranean and the Suez Canal had been closed during the Second World War yet Britain had survived. Nasser remains in possession of the Suez Canal Company yet Britain still survives. It seems reasonable to argue that, if the international organization is unable to take action to uphold international law, individual countries are entitled to do so. But the resort to war in such a case must surely depend on what is a truly vital interest, as the Suez Canal Company obviously was not. All that Britain succeeded in doing was to unite the United Nations against her, to call forth threats of the use of nuclear weapons by Russia, to demonstrate to the world and to herself that she could not mount an effective military action in the Middle East, and to enhance the prestige of Nasser for having not only nationalized the Canal Company but also defied the combination of Britain, France and Israel.

No doubt the Suez action can be regarded as an aberration. But it is important to recognize that the decision had its roots in traditional thinking about the interests of Britain and the methods of sustaining them. Whereas at the Geneva Conference the British Foreign Secretary appeared to be the one who had come to terms with the contemporary situation, two years later, as Prime Minister, he appeared to be harking back to bygone days.

One of the effects of the Suez policy was to set up an extreme tension within the Commonwealth. It had long been recognized that the independent members of the Commonwealth were free to pursue their own foreign policies. To questions about what the Commonwealth was, it became common form to reply that it was an association of nations not necessarily in agreement on policy, but at least agreeing to differ. The Suez affair created a much more serious situation. There could be no agreement to differ. The majority of the Commonwealth were positively opposed to British policy and the new Asian members were extremely hostile. This had been anticipated by the Prime Minister. He says in his memoirs that, as it was known that there would be differences of view among the members of the Commonwealth, consultation would have meant delay in taking action: "Once palavers began, no effective action would be possible." Britain, therefore, went into the Suez operation without Commonwealth consultation. This in itself was a remarkable departure from established lines of British policy.

However, the Suez operation was called off before matters had come to an actual breach between Britain and most of the Commonwealth. The Commonwealth survived, though sorely shaken.

Self-government for dependent territories

There was no change in the general policy, which the Conservatives pursued almost as zealously as Labour, of leading the various dependent territories towards self-government and full Commonwealth membership. New graduates to this status came in quick succession: Malaya and Ghana in 1957, Nigeria in 1960, Sierra Leone and Tanganyika in 1961, and others treading on their heels. With the completion of the process in Asia except for Singapore, Borneo and Hong Kong, attention was focused on Africa. There, the problem of the multi-racial Commonwealth, which had existed since 1947, came to a head.

Rejection of racial discrimination   Warning had been given in 1953 by the controversy over the development of the Federation of Rhodesia and Nyasaland. One of the main motives for the Federation had been to block the spread of the *apartheid* policy northward from South Africa; but the Federation itself seemed not altogether immune from the contagion. How could countries of different racial composition be equal members of the Commonwealth without accepting the principle of nondiscrimination? Mr. Macmillan, who succeeded Sir Anthony Eden as Prime Minister,

recognized the trend in Africa by his "wind of change" speech in 1960. In the following year the decision of the Union of South Africa to become a republic afforded the occasion for a review of her position in the Commonwealth. The policy of *apartheid* was challenged, and not only by the "colored" members. Britain was faced with the necessity for choice between one of the old Dominions and the new multi-racial Commonwealth. The decision went in favor of the latter.

This meant not only the departure of South Africa, but also the introduction of a new principle into the Commonwealth itself. Hitherto it had been said that the Commonwealth was unbreakable because it was so flexible. The rejection of racial discrimination introduced an element of inflexibility. Since the failure of Joseph Chamberlain's efforts at the beginning of the twentieth century, Britain had become reconciled to the idea that the direction of Commonwealth development was centrifugal. The elimination of South Africa in 1961 appeared, paradoxically, a step in the opposite direction, towards greater cohesion.

The gradualist approach   While accepting the aim of decolonization and a quickening of the process, Britain retained a gradualist approach, as was seen in the Congo crisis. United Nations action at first had full support from Britain; but an attitude of reserve developed as the U.N. organization in the Congo came to grips with the Katanga regime. In the voting on the Security Council resolution of November 24th, 1961, which condemned secessionism and authorized U.N. action against Tshombe's foreign mercenaries, Britain—along with France—abstained.

Business interests and "public relations" activity, presenting the image of Katanga as an oasis of security in the chaos of the Congo, had some part in influencing opinion; but there was little need for persuasion that the Congo had reached independence without adequate preparation. The desirability of economic and technical aid given by the former imperial Power to its erstwhile colonies had been impressed upon the British public, and probably had some relevance to the Katanga situation. The drawbacks to imposing federation upon an unwilling people were only too apparent in Central Africa. On what grounds should self-determination be denied to Katanga? These were some of the considerations which led to a distinct cooling of British enthusiasm for the U.N. Congo operation.

In the background lurked a more general uneasiness about the changing character of the U.N. itself. Universality of membership, which Britain had consistently espoused, meant a continuing influx of new states and a growing emphasis on anti-colonialism, accentuated still more by the enhanced role of the General Assembly. Britain tended to resent any questioning about her intention to emancipate her colonies or about her judgment of the time and preparation needed. This was aggravated by the "salt-water fallacy" which exempted the Soviet empire from similar treatment. The contrast between the U.N. reaction to Suez on the one hand and to Hungary on the other did not pass unnoticed. There seemed to be developing a "double standard" of treatment: one for the democracies and another for the Communist countries.

The loosening of Commonwealth ties

The U.N. reaction to the Indian seizure of Goa provoked the Foreign Secretary in December 1961 to a disquisition on Britain's "appalling dilemma," because a large section of the organization condoned the use of force. The main purpose of the U.N. was to maintain peace and security, but a large number of the new members gave priority to the acceleration of decolonization even if it meant using force. However, having drawn up the balance sheet between pessimism and hope, the Foreign Secretary came down decidedly in favor of hope. Still, the fact that he was able to speak of a crisis of confidence in the U.N. indicated the

degree of Britain's disenchantment since the immediate postwar years.

India's Goan adventure had repercussions on the Commonwealth as well as on the U.N. The British Foreign Secretary's censure came oddly from a Government which had launched the Suez operation, but the reaction of other members ranged from condemnation to condonation. Apparently, racial discrimination was now inadmissible, but the use of force for purposes other than self-defense was not ruled out; nor was the maintenance of democracy a necessary qualification, as Pakistan and Ghana showed. The character of the Commonwealth seemed not merely flexible but fluid, and this had a bearing on Britain's relations with Europe.

One of the main arguments against Britain joining a federal Europe had been that the Commonwealth tie would thereby be broken or loosened. Those who favored integration with Europe replied that, whereas the British connection with Europe was unalterable because of the facts of geography and inevitable because of the growth of a united Europe, the Commonwealth was, if not a declining, a disintegrating body; so that, looking to the future, the advantages of joining Europe would progressively outweigh those of clinging to the Commonwealth. The condition of the Commonwealth remains difficult to diagnose, but the situation of Europe has been clarified.

Contrary to the British belief that the Continentals were more prone to words than deeds, European integration, after several setbacks, has become more and more of a reality—from the Council of Europe through the Coal and Steel Community to Western European Union and EURATOM, and since 1957 the European Economic Community or Common Market. These developments have placed Britain in another quandary. Her first reaction to the Rome Treaty which established the Common Market was to set up a counter-grouping in the European Free Trade Area. But the potentialities of E.F.T.A. were recognized to be far inferior to those of the Common Market. For economic motives there is strong pressure for Britain to join with the

Six. There are also those who hold that Britain should cease trying to pretend that she is a World Power. On the other hand, in addition to the objections from British farmers, there are the obligations of Britain towards the Commonwealth countries, and now towards E.F.T.A. There is also a reluctance to acknowledge that Britain is merely one of a number of European countries. Consequently, the position of being both in Europe and in the Commonwealth, which was for Britain a decade ago a source of peculiar satisfaction and influence, has now become an embarrassment and a dilemma. At the end of July 1961, the Government took the plunge and announced that it had decided to make formal application for negotiations with a view to joining the European Economic Community "if satisfactory arrangements can be made to meet the special needs of the U.K., of the Commonwealth and of the E.F.T.A." A motion to this effect was carried in the House of Commons a few days later by 308 to 5. It was significant that the Opposition put down an amendment with a more negative nuance which was rejected by 318 to 201. During the subsequent negotiations, the Opposition held their hand; but increasingly opinion has tended to crystallize for or against "joining Europe."

The H-bomb

Another challenge to the role of Britain in the world is presented by the ultimate weapon. The transformation of Britain's position can be illustrated by two simple comparisons. In 1831 Palmerston was able to say, "No country on the face of the globe is likely to suffer less than England from war." Eighty years later it was not possible to adopt so jaunty an attitude; but it was still possible to contemplate war for prestige. Thus Lloyd George said in his famous Mansion House speech in 1911:

> Britain should at all hazards maintain her place and prestige among the Great Powers . . . if a situation were to be forced upon us in which peace could only be preserved by the surrender of the great and beneficent position that Britain has won by centuries of heroism and achievement . . . then I say emphatically that peace at such a price would be a humiliation intolerable for a great country like ours to endure.[21]

Fifty years later it is generally recognized that war would mean the destruction of Britain along with most of the world.

When the wartime co-operation with America in the development of atomic weapons was brought to an abrupt halt by the Mac-Mahon Act in 1946, the Labour Government, almost as a matter of course, decided to make a British atom bomb. This decision came to fruition in 1952. At that stage, therefore, Britain was one of the Big Three, not only in terms of the general pattern of international relations but also by virtue of her possession of the A-bomb. It was the Conservative Government in 1952 which decided to make the H-bomb. Five years later Britain was still one of the Big Three through the possession of the ultimate deterrent.

There has been much heart-searching: can Britain afford an independent nuclear deterrent? Is it necessary or desirable that Britain should devote resources, which could be well employed in other directions, for equipment in weapons which are already being built by her ally? The U.S.A. already has enough H-bombs. Enough is enough, and more than enough is too much. What purpose does a British H-bomb serve? These questions have been asked with increasing frequency.

They have not yet deflected British policy. The answer given by the British Government is twofold: that conceivably Britain might need the deterrent for her own purposes, and that the possession of the H-bomb gives Britain a

[21] M. Thomson, *David Lloyd George*, London: Hutchinson, 1948, p. 204.

special position in world affairs. This insistence upon retention of an independent British deterrent, while advocating, as all British Governments have done since the war, the closest possible association with the U.S.A., reflects to some extent a lack of confidence in the Atlantic alliance. If closer co-operation could be obtained from America, the arguments for the independent deterrent would be weakened. Failing that, there is a hankering after the leadership of Europe by virtue of the possession of the H-bomb. This line of thought is a reversion to the old Third Force idea, with or without the neutralist implications. At the same time, there is much concern about the spread of nuclear weapons and the "nth power problem," as well as the danger of "escalation" from tactical weapons to the big bang. The solution to these problems ultimately depends upon achieving a measure of effectively controlled disarmament. Meanwhile, majority opinion and governmental policy favor keeping the deterrent, though not necessarily an independent one. There is, however, a minority view which regards the use or threat of the H-bomb as morally insupportable. Another section of opinion considers Britain to be so vulnerable that the prime object of British policy must be to contract out. This is very largely a reaction to a world situation which seems to have got completely out of hand.

METHODS OF FOREIGN POLICY FORMULATION

How does the British Government arrive at decisions on this or any other question of foreign policy? The short answer is: by the same methods as it reaches decisions on political questions generally. There is interaction of Government and Parliament and of political parties, pressure groups and public opinion. Each of them influences the others in varying degrees and some conclusion usually emerges. In regard to foreign policy, however, there are limiting factors which are not present in the determination of domestic policy. The most obvious of these is the simple fact that external affairs are not under the Government's control. The Government can decide to nationalize or denationalize an industry, but it cannot decide to conclude a treaty unless the other party is willing. Consequently, it is not feasible for the Government to commit itself in advance to any particular line of policy except in broad terms. Pressures are generated from time to time in favor of particular policies—for example, unilateral nuclear disarmament or adhesion to the Rome Treaty—but party manifestos tend to be less specific, usually preferring principles to programs. Principles afford room for maneuver, allowing policy to be suited to the exigencies of the particular situation.

The influence of political parties

Another consequence is that foreign policy rarely becomes a major issue in an election campaign. Gladstone's Midlothian campaign has been mentioned; to it might be added the "Khaki" elections of 1900 and 1918, the "Zinoviev letter" in 1924, and the election of 1951 in which the Anglo-Persian oil dispute figured prominently; but these are exceptions. Foreign policy declarations, because they tend to be general in character, do not often provoke conflict between parties. More frequently controversy about foreign policy takes place within the parties in the process of arriving at the party standpoint. These intra-party disputes may well be more heated and acrimonious than the arguments between the parties, as the political system provides a strong incentive to woo the "floating vote" in the middle. The "floating voter" may take fright at an extremist policy. Therefore, party statements often represent a compromise between a pragmatic appreciation of what will please the electorate and doctrinal concessions to appease the party militants.

Party controversy is also muffled by continuity, although that is still a matter for contention as it was in the nineteenth century. It has two aspects, practical and theoretical. In practice, some continuity is inevitable unless there were to be a revolution. Even then, experience of the twentieth century does not suggest that a revolution necessarily changes foreign policy. There are objective factors, which do not change perceptibly from one Government to another, such as the country's position and strength and also the international engagements which it has undertaken and cannot unilaterally repudiate.

Party differences

In theory, however, continuity of foreign policy is not a generally accepted notion. There are those who advocate the subordination of party differences and the presentation of a united front to the outside world. Others maintain that there are differences between the parties in regard to foreign relations and that it would be wrong to blur or bury them. Until fairly recently, the Conservative Party was preeminently the party of Empire, while the Labour Party was anti-Imperialist. Since the development of the new Commonwealth, the gap between parties on this subject has narrowed considerably. Between the wars, the Labour Party was the protagonist of collective security while the Conservatives were more inclined to traditional policies. Since the Second World War there has been no major cleavage of this kind, although the Labour Party was slower and more reluctant to accept the breach with Russia than were the Conservatives. While differences of this sort do exist, yet in the field of foreign policy there is much common ground between the major parties. This is partly due to the recognition of Britain's limitations and restricted scope for maneuver, and also to ways of thought about foreign policy which have been handed down from the past.

The role of public opinion

The influence of public opinion on foreign policy is undoubtedly real but difficult to assess. In ordinary times it is confined to the few who are interested in or knowledgeable about the particular questions at issue. This kind of informed public opinion makes its influence felt through organizations such as the Royal Institute of International Affairs, through the universities and the press, and through pressure groups or lobbies which have a concern in the matter. Britain's entry into the Common Market, for example, is a question which has received much attention both in academic circles and from organizations such as the National Farmers' Union, the Federation of British Industries and the Trades Union Congress.

The opinion of other countries has its impact on British opinion: the views of Britain's associates in E.F.T.A. or the pronouncements of Commonwealth Prime Ministers have some effect. The Government, Parliament and the parties are responsive to the views and interests of the consumers—who are also the voters. Occasionally, a groundswell of mass opinion appears to be set in motion on a question of foreign policy. It rejected the Hoare-Laval plan for Ethiopia. It moved away from the policy of appeasement after Hitler's march into Prague. It brought down the Chamberlain Government after the fall of France and made itself felt again at the time of Suez.

The administrative organization

In speaking of the Government, it is necessary to distinguish between the political and administrative elements, the Cabinet and the departments responsible for the conduct of external relations. The departments concerned are the Foreign Office and the Commonwealth

Relations Office. They, too, constitute a factor making for continuity of foreign policy. Officials will tend to proceed along established lines, unless a new direction is given from the top. This tendency is strengthened by having both departments staffed from bottom to top by career officials. This also applies, with few exceptions, to the appointments held abroad. One or two of the most important embassies may from time to time be allocated to a political nominee for special reasons: for example, Lord Halifax relinquished his position of Foreign Secretary to become Ambassador to the United States during the Second World War.

Ordinarily, the Foreign and Commonwealth services are staffed by professional civil servants appointed on merit after a stiff examination. The Foreign Service is no longer as it was described by John Bright in the nineteenth century, "a gigantic system of out-door relief for the aristocracy of Great Britain." Recruitment is now on a much wider social base. The result is a body of officials who are highly regarded for their competence. It has sometimes been suggested that they might in fact control the minister who is ostensibly in charge of them, since they have the advantage of long experience and technical expertise. Before the Labour Government took office in 1945, fears of this kind had been expressed; but Ernest Bevin was apparently very successful both in directing the Foreign Office and winning the loyalty and affection of its staff. It is perhaps significant that two recent phases of British foreign policy which encountered strong criticism—the appeasement policy of Neville Chamberlain and the Suez policy of Sir Anthony Eden—were times when the Foreign Office was by-passed and the Prime Minister, with an inner group of the Cabinet, took direct control.

The trend is undoubtedly towards enhancement of the role of the Prime Minister in foreign affairs. This is partly due to the increase of summit meetings, partly to the general elevation of the Prime Minister's position resulting from the development of propaganda media, particularly television, and partly to the growing importance of foreign relations which can no longer be treated as an adjunct to domestic politics.

Although the Prime Minister is something more than *primus inter pares* in the formulation of foreign policy, the principle of collective Cabinet responsibility is maintained. The relations within the Cabinet vary according to its composition as well as the attendant circumstances. The decisions reached engage the Government as a whole. In making up their collective mind about policy in a new situation, the Cabinet will take established policy as their point of departure, keeping in view Britain's obligations to other countries and assessing the importance of the British interests involved. Reactions at home have to be considered together with effects abroad. If an unpopular course has to be followed in preference to an attractive policy which might spell disaster, it is the Government's task to give the lead away from the primrose path. Its survival may depend on its ability to educate the public in favor of the straight and narrow. Conversely, public opinion may at times overtake and run ahead of the Government. The critical periods have been those in which a major readjustment of attitude was required by a fundamental change in circumstances.

Britain is currently passing through such a phase. The interplay of forces in the democratic process can be observed; but the outcome is still obscure. The readjustment of attitude required in the nuclear age has undermined traditional patterns of thought about foreign policy. The improvement of communications has transformed Britain's position. The changes in the Commonwealth and in Europe have presented problems of determining British relations with both. The growth of the super-Powers has left the British Isles with their population of 50 million further and further behind. All these developments have presented Britain with the necessity for choice. Is Britain to accept that she can henceforward only be a European country, much like any other? Or is she to maintain that, although the days of the *Pax Britannica* are far in the past and she cannot hope for a place among the super-Powers, she can still, by her exertions and her example, play a special role in world affairs? The idea of Britain providing the link between Europe, the Commonwealth and the Atlantic alliance has faded into a dream. The immediate question is whether Britain can reach the much less ambitious target of reconciling the requirements of the Commonwealth and Europe. The decision in favor of joining Europe has been taken in principle, although it remains to be seen whether and how far the conditions for Britain's adherence will be met.

BIBLIOGRAPHY

Author's Suggestions

Sir Anthony Eden. *Full Circle*. London: 1960.

J. D. B. Miller. *The Commonwealth in the World*. London: 1958.

Royal Institute of International Affairs. *Political and Strategic Interests of the United Kingdom*. London: 1939.

Royal Institute of International Affairs. *Britain in Western Europe*. London: 1956.

Royal Institute of International Affairs. *British Interests in the Mediterranean and Middle East*. London: 1958.

Robert W. Seton-Watson. *Britain and the Dictators*. Cambridge: 1938.

Lord Strang. *Britain in World Affairs*. London: 1961.

C. M. Woodhouse. *British Foreign Policy since the Second World War*. London: 1961; New York: 1962.

ABOUT THE AUTHOR

JEAN-BAPTISTE DUROSELLE is one of the most widely known authorities on contemporary French political developments. His articles have been published in many leading journals and his comments on Europe are frequently quoted.

Mr. Duroselle was born in France in 1917. He holds the following degrees: Licencié en Histoire, Agrégé d'Histoire et de Géographie, and Docteur des Lettres. He has held the following academic positions: Professeur au Lycée de Chartres, Assistant d'Histoire contemporaine à la Faculté des Lettres de Paris, Professor, Lycée Hoch, Professor l'Université de la Sarre, and Professor Université de Lille. Since 1958 he has been Professor at the Fondation nationale des Sciences politiques and Director of the Centre d'études des relations internationales. His publications include: *Les débuts du catholicisme social en France,* 1951; *Histoire diplomatique de 1919 à nos jours,* 1953, and *De Wilson à Roosevelt,* 1960.

ABOUT THE CHAPTER

France, according to Mr. Duroselle, is more a "product of history" than a "geographic entity." In this chapter he discusses geography but clearly demonstrates the accuracy of the view of a "France molded by history."

The author asserts that national interest does not exist in the abstract; different groups have different views on the interests of the nation. The government must decide "the objectives it proposes to reach in foreign policy and the risks it is willing to take in order to attain those objectives." Within this framework the author gives attention both to traditional French interests and policies and to De Gaulle's concept of the national interest and the risks he is willing to take to protect it.

The author discusses a number of specific and general problems confronting France today. The problems of military security and European unification are given special consideration. Algeria gained her independence while this volume was in preparation. The successful negotiations which brought this "nightmare" to a close were a clear victory for De Gaulle's Algerian policy and provided the capstone for his successful policy of decolonization. It is clear from this chapter how closely the policies of France have been tied during the past few years to De Gaulle and his views of France's destiny.

2

THE FOREIGN POLICY OF FRANCE

J. B. DUROSELLE

*Fondation nationale des
Sciences politiques, Paris*

THE ROLE OF GEOGRAPHY AND HISTORY

Geographic determinism

Location and topography Metropolitan France, including the island of Corsica, covers 212,300 square miles. It occupies a singular location in the western part of Europe and, along with Spain, has both an Atlantic and a Mediterranean coastline. It has the shape of a hexagon and is situated in the most temperate zone of the northern hemisphere: the 45° latitude cuts across its southern part, a little north of Bordeaux and a little south of Grenoble. The temperate character of its climate is accentuated by the passage, on the western shore, of a warm sea current, the "North Atlantic Current," a Gulf Stream offshoot.

On this relatively small surface (620 miles from Strasbourg to Brest; 620 miles from Lille to Marseille), French territory offers an extreme variety: two great "basins" formed by hills and low plateaus, the "Parisian basin" in the north and the "Aquitanian basin" in the southwest; two great tertiary chains, the Alps· in the east—elongated by the Jura Mountains— and the Pyrenees in the south; several "massifs," crystalline and primary, of which the most important is the "Massif Central," with satellites on two sides; the Armorican Massif in the west, the Vosges and the Ardennes in the northeast, and, finally, narrow drainage plains, the most important of which are those of the Rhine in the Alsace region and those of the Rhône.

Historical influences That this soil has its "own personality" ("France is a person," Michelet used to say), does not result, however, from its geography. The British Isles and Italy are in well-defined geographic zones on the whole. Germany, quite to the contrary, does not have clear boundaries. France partakes of both these situations simultaneously. The sea, the Alps, the Pyrenees, on five sides of the hexagon, can be considered quasi "natural" boundaries—although in detail, the frontier does not follow the line of the mountain ridges faithfully. But the sixth side, the northeastern, is a product of history, not of geography. The frontier artificially cuts through the farthest reaches of the great plains of northern Europe, then through the high hills of the Meuse and the Moselle. In the endless history of the wars of France, from the Gallic epoch to 1940, the most important always took place in this area of the northeast. It is here that France is "vulnerable." It is here that her frontiers have been in doubt and have given rise to international problems for the longest period.

This brief description leads us, then, to a picture of a France which is much more a "product of history" than a "geographic entity." With the exception of the northeastern frontier, this territory has generally constituted a unit for at least twenty centuries, if not politically, at least in its nomenclature. Moreover, this geographic area has often even belonged to the same sovereign. France is, then, a very old country; for longer than any other, she has been a "person." But that results, let us repeat, from history, and not from geographic determinism.

The quest for "natural frontiers"

If geography does not explain the "personality" of France, is it the basis of a fixed aim of French foreign policy? According to some, from the very beginning this aim was the reestablishment of the "natural frontiers": the Atlantic, the Pyrenees, the Mediterranean, the Alps, and the Rhine. Leaving the sea frontiers aside, the Pyrenees—a quasi-insuperable wall in its center—were definitively considered the frontier in 1659—with an extension of France on their southern slope in the east. The Alps, much easier to cross, did not become an integral frontier until 1860 with the annexation

of Savoy and the county of Nice. There remains the problem, once again predominant, of the northeastern side of the hexagon.

Historical factors   Now, on this point, one should again note that geographic determinism did not play a part. The evidence, given, notably by Gaston Zeller, establishes that the Old Regime, prior to 1789, never made an effort to reach the "natural" frontiers.[1] The idea of "natural frontiers" is recent. It comes, purely and simply, from the French Revolution. Undoubtedly, the intervention of the revolutionaries—Brissot and Danton—rests on a long intellectual tradition. But for the first time it was introduced in deed. "The French Republic," wrote Brissot, "should have no limit except the Rhine."[2] But it was Danton, above all, who formulated the doctrine in a speech at the National Convention on January 31, 1793:

> I say it is in vain that people wish to create a fear of giving too great an expanse to the Republic. Its limits are denoted by nature. We will reach them on all four corners of the horizon: in the direction of the Rhine, the direction of the Ocean, the direction of the Alps. There the limits of our Republic should end, and no human power can keep us from reaching them.[3]

But this doctrine had only limited success. From the time of the French Revolution, it was in opposition with two other doctrines: that of "revolutionary expansion," consisting of a desire to propagate the republican ideal everywhere and to surround France with "Sister Republics"—today we should say with

[1] See, principally, "Histoire d'une idée fausse," *Revue de Synthèse*, 1936, and "La Monarchie d'Ancien régime," *Revue d'Histoire moderne*, 1933.
[2] Cited by Georges Lefebvre, *La Révolution française, Peuples et Civilisations*, XIII, Paris: Alcan, p. 153.
[3] See Louis Barthou, *Danton*, 1932.

satellites; and that of the "frontiers of 1792," which are, with very slight differences, the present frontiers of France.

In 1796–1797, there was a "great debate" on this subject in the heart of the *Directoire*. The Alsatian, Reubell, upheld the natural frontiers. La Revelliere-Lepaux was a mystic of revolutionary expansion. The sage Carnot believed Europe would never tolerate, in the long run, anything but the modest frontiers of 1792. In particular, the English would never accept leaving the French permanently installed in Antwerp. The debate was resolved by the victories and ambitions of a young general, Napoleon Bonaparte, who imposed on the directors the solution of revolutionary expansion. It was only in February 1814, that Napoleon I, vanquished and in retreat, withdrew to the solution of the "natural frontiers." But it was too late. The allies, who were invading France, would have no more of it.

From 1815 to 1848, the monarchy considered itself satisfied with the frontiers preserved—approximately those of 1792. But republican opposition demanded the revision of the treaties of 1815 and the "natural frontiers." However, on assuming power in 1848, the republicans confided the direction of foreign policy to Lamartine. For him, the preservation of peace was infinitely more precious than the acquisition of "natural frontiers." Napoleon III alone was to have inclinations in this direction. It was he who obtained the annexation of Savoy and Nice to France in 1860. In 1866, facing the expansion of Prussia, he tried in vain to obtain from Bismarck "compensations" in the Rhineland or, if that failed, in Luxembourg, or even Belgium. The defeat of 1871 was to ruin, except for certain laggards, the doctrine of "natural frontiers."

Undoubtedly, Clemenceau was subscribing to it on September 15, 1919, when he said in the Chamber of Deputies that "the drive toward the Rhine was the tradition of our ancestors." But he immediately added:

It is not our fault if, today, when I want to go to the Rhine, I encounter German countries between the Rhine and myself, and if I am obliged to take them into account."[4]

Validity of the concept Furthermore, the doctrine of the "natural frontier" is nothing but a "myth." In an extremity, mountains can determine frontiers, although there were mountain states which possessed both slopes: Navarre in the Pyrenees, Piedmont-Savoy in the Alps, and, today, Switzerland and Austria, for example. But in what way does a river constitute a "natural frontier?" "They are ties instead of being obstacles," writes Saint-Marc Girardin in 1863. "It is a curious thing," he adds:

I have never seen a nation which, by virtue of the system of natural frontiers, dreamed of reducing its possessions and its borders. It is always in order to expand its empire that each nation studies the geography of its natural borders."

And he adds in regard to the Rhine:

If the inhabitants of the Rhenish provinces do not want to be French, if our ideas, if our laws, if our administration displeases them, it is useless for you to say that the Rhine is our natural frontier; nature will cede to man's will, for that is the destiny of our century: that the will of the people is stronger than all the fortresses, than all the mountains, than all the rivers, than all the lines of demarcation, natural in name.[5]

Jean Gottmann attributes to the "grand designs" of the 17th century the idea, unknown till that time, that there is a link between poli-

---

[4] *Journal Officiel, Débats parlementaires*, September 15, 1919.

[5] See the article on "Frontières naturelles" in the *Dictionnaire général de la Politique* by Maurice Block, I, Paris: Lorenz, 1863, pp. 1089–91.

tics and geography.[6] Being a myth like, for example, the "Manifest Destiny" in the history of the United States, the doctrine of "natural frontiers" in no way results from geographic determinism.

European versus overseas outlook

However, there is a domain in which geographic determinism has played a role, during the period in which France has been a modern state, that is, since the 16th century. One of the characteristics of France is that she has almost exactly the same length of continental and sea frontiers. As a result of that, there has always been a vacillation between two fundamental choices: a European policy and an overseas policy. While England could always give priority to overseas, and Germany or Austria always to the continent, France was wooed by both appeals. By that fact, she was less favored than England on the seas—hence the loss of Newfoundland in 1713, of India and of Canada in 1763; and less favored than Germany on the continent. It was always sufficient for England to arouse a powerful adversary against France in Europe to keep her from sending sufficient reinforcements overseas. Germany, meanwhile, benefited from the fact that the French forces, often dispersed throughout the colonies and involved in African campaigns, were unable to prepare adequately for scientific modern war.

One can trace the path of this fundamental vacillation throughout French history. The opposition between Louis XIV and his minister Colbert is a good example of it. Colbert was a man with an overseas viewpoint. He wanted to enrich France by great maritime commerce, for this was the way to augment "the power and the grandeur of His Majesty and to lower

those of his enemies and enviers."[7] The war he accepted and even desired was one which was to break the maritime superiority of Holland. Costly continental conquests of little profit he did not desire, but he did want colonies, the source of riches, and a powerful battle fleet. Louis XIV, on the contrary, was little concerned about colonies and about being a merchant king. He had "grand designs" on the continent, directed toward the Spanish Netherlands. For him, war was above all a conquest of fortresses. After Colbert's death (1683) and the maritime defeat of La Hougue (1692), the king was disinterested in the navy and permitted naval supremacy—and consequently colonial supremacy—to pass to England forever.

This does not mean that France had definitively given up overseas interests. From time to time, she again launched herself on a great colonial policy. She succeeded, with Choiseul and Vergennes, after 1763, in reconstituting a strong navy which explains, in part, the victorious outcome of the War of Independence of the United States. But the Revolution and the Empire brought continental politics back to the foreground.

Under the Third Republic, from 1880 on, a whole group of politicians: Jules Ferry, Eugène Etienne, and Gabriel Hanotaux, launched France on the path of great colonial conquests. They preferred to tone down the loss of Alsace and Lorraine, then the great problem, and to maintain good relations with Germany in order to be able to be active overseas. Their adversaries, the "continentals," such as George Clemenceau, violently attacked the colonial policy which, Clemenceau said, made the error of diverting attention from the "blue line of the Vosges."

After the Second World War, the desire to preserve the former overseas "empire" in one form or another, was in direct contradiction with European politics. Europe was definitely no longer oriented toward conquest, but toward "integration." Is it possible to simultane-

---

[6] Jean Gottmann, *La Politique des Etats et leur géographie*, Paris: Colin, 1952, p. 24.

[7] Cited by Ernest Lavisse, *Histoire de France*, VII, Paris: Hachette, 1911, p. 234.

ously exhaust one's forces in Indochina, in Algeria, and at the same time maintain a powerful army on the European continent? The answer is: "No." Consequently, some said, let us abandon all thought of European integration, and particularly of a European army, in order to devote our efforts to the creation of a solid "French Union." Let us abandon, said the others, all thought of maintaining ties overseas since our supreme contribution should be the creation of Europe. In fact, until 1958, and even later, France pursued these two "grand designs" simultaneously; in both cases she was the victim of this basic vacillation.

Let us not think that she will be able to choose permanently between the continent and overseas in the future. The vacillation will persist, for it is determined by geography. It is in a revolution in the traditional concepts of the "continentals" and the "maritimes" that the evolution will take place. But there will always be "continentals" and "maritimes."

THE FRENCH NATIONAL CHARACTER

If purely geographic determinism exists only within certain limits, is it possible to speak of a determinism of men? Can one refer to a French "national character" which has made its mark on the country's foreign policy? Here again, one must proceed with extreme caution. Undoubtedly, the French take pleasure in discovering, in the descriptions Caesar or Strabo give of the Gallic character, certain traits in which they recognize themselves: open, hospitable toward strangers, but vain and quarrelsome; variable and unstable in their sentiments, fond of new things, high-spirited, but quick to be discouraged, and, lastly, very undisciplined.[8] The individualism of which the modern

Frenchman boasts, he rediscovers among his Gallic ancestors.

But, since Gallic times, there have been many contributions of new blood: Romans, Visigoths, Burgundians, Franks, to mention only the principal ones. One would seek in vain to define a French "ethnic." It is rather the subsequent cultural traditions which succeeded in forming a "national character." Salvador de Madariaga compares the "fair play" of the British, "el honor" of the Spanish, and the "Droit" of the French.[9] André Siegfried, in subtle analyses composed of observation and intuition, often attempted to define the "French character." "The Frenchman is first of all an individual; that is simultaneously his grandeur and his weakness."[10]

Countless authors have tried to reveal this national character. But it is so elusive that nothing objective can be said with certitude. Nonetheless, certain facts emerge from the penumbra. The French have a high opinion of their civilization, and an acute sense of right and devotion to what they consider logical. In their colonies, they have therefore been "assimilators" more than the British. Undisciplined and imaginative, they entertain, less than the British or the Germans, the idea of adapting the means to the end, and this has often led them to launch themselves on badly calculated adventures, ending sometimes in disasters. Individualists, they often tend to minimize and to misjudge the interests of other peoples, and to take refuge in xenophobia when they consider themselves misunderstood.[11] Individualists once again, their internal discords sometimes expose them, disunited and weakened, to danger. *Petits bourgeois,* austere and distrustful, they often did not understand the necessity of participating in the great revolutionary movements which transformed international society, such as the industrial revolution and decolonization.

[8] See *Histoire de Jules César,* II, Paris: 1866, pp. 31–32. The author of these books is Napoleon III.

[9] *Anglais, Français, Espagnols,* Paris: 1930, p. 272.

[10] *Tableau des partis en France,* Paris: Grasset, 1930, p. 28. See also his short book, *L'âme des peuples,* Paris: 1950, p. 222.

[11] See the very characteristic book of Edmond Nagelen, *Grandeur et solitude de la France,* Paris, 1956.

However, since one can also find many examples in their history of suppleness and empiricism, a spirit of practicality, generosity in regard to foreigners—the Poles, for example—"sacred unions" in the face of the enemy, and an audaciously revolutionary and progressive spirit, we refuse to believe there is an element of determinism in the Frenchman sufficient to have influenced the country's foreign policy lastingly and systematically.

MAJOR FOREIGN POLICY PROBLEMS OF THE PAST

Hence, French foreign policy, when one examines its principal manifestations, is the product of three basic factors: the aims of the governments, which have varied according to their leaders' ideologies, and even their characters; the external circumstances against which these governments intended to react; and the means at the disposal of the state for action abroad. While it would be useless to summarize this eminently complex history in a few lines, it is nevertheless essential to show what have been, successively, the "major problems" which French foreign policy tried to resolve.

From the Hundred Years' War to Napoleon Bonaparte

When the Hundred Years' War ended and the English were driven out, the unity of the realm was once again restored under Louis XI. Thereafter, the initiative of the kings led France to try to implant itself in Italy. From 1492 to 1519, that was the major concern of French policy; this is the phase of the "Italian wars" which lasted until 1555.

In 1519, however, the hazards of history created a danger which appeared mortal.

Young king Charles of Spain with possessions in Italy, inherited Franche-Comté and the Netherlands from his grandmother, Marie de Bourgogne, and the states of Austria from his grandfather, Maximilian of Hapsburg. Moreover, he was elected Emperor of the Holy Roman Empire. In the north, the east, the southeast, and the south, France was thus encircled by the empire of Charles the Fifth. The breaking of this suffocating menace was to be the major aim of France until 1714. The division of the empire of Charles the Fifth between the Hapsburgs of Austria and the Hapsburgs of Spain, the loss of the Protestant Netherlands by the Spanish—all this was not sufficient for French security. The struggle against the Hapsburgs was the dominant one during two centuries. Conducted with feeble means while France was torn apart by the religious wars in the 16th century, the struggle was intensified in the 17th century. Richelieu and Mazarin succeeded in supporting the parceling out of the empire in Germany, meanwhile cutting the reins of Spanish power. Louis XIV took the initiative and tried to impose his hegemony. The conquest of Alsace, of Franche-Comté, of a solid barrier of strongholds in the north was worth less in his eyes than the final result: the accession of the Bourbon dynasty to the throne of Spain after a terrible war which put an end, moreover, to the desires for domination of France.

Then, for one century, came the phase of the "English wars." From 1689 to 1815, eight wars were fought between France and England. This was the struggle for domination on the sea and in the colonies, a struggle which England won in the end.

But the end of the "English wars" coincided with a phenomenon of quite different dimensions. The French Revolution and its product, Napoleon's Empire, tried, as Louis XIV had done, and with more success for a time, to establish the hegemony of France in Europe. France, from 1792 to 1815, faced a succession of eight coalitions, in which England always took part. It was only when all the great European powers united against her that her desire for hegemony was broken forever.

From the Congress of Vienna to the Cold War

From 1815 to 1870, French foreign policy was more modest. Undoubtedly, the dream of every Frenchman was to demolish "the shameful treaties of 1815." But the Bourbons and Louis-Philippe of Orleans, like the leaders of the Second Republic, enamored by peace, had no desire to take uncertain initiatives, and trust to better times, or to a revolution of the peoples. Napoleon III, on the contrary, a strange and contradictory personage, used the new force of the "nationality principle" to break the treaties of 1815. The misfortune, for him, was that he thereby favored the beginnings of the unification of Germany, without wanting it to be brought to its close. Therein lies the origin of the disastrous war of 1870.

The period of the "German wars" then began. The idea that Germany was the hereditary enemy appeared only toward 1866.[12] Three times between 1870 and 1945, German troops invaded French territory. The loss of Alsace and of Lorraine confirmed the defeat of 1871. The victory of 1918 permitted the recovery of the "lost provinces." Hitler re-annexed them by virtue of his victory of 1940. But France was part of the coalition which crushed him, although she played only a minor role. The provinces, twice lost, rejoined the nation.

Although this phase, from 1870 to 1945, also saw the creation of the colonial empire, the major problem, the one around which all French policy revolved, was uninterruptedly that of relations with Germany. To recover Alsace and Lorraine, to assure the lasting security of France: such were the main preoccupations. The idea of breaking Germany definitively was, again, held by General de Gaulle in 1945–1946, and by M. Georges Bi-

[12] Hans Otto Sieburg, *Frankreich und Deutschland in der Geschichtschreibung, 1848–1871,* "Habilitation" thesis, presented at the University of Saarbrücken, 1957.

dault up to 1948. It was the appearance of a new international system, with all the power of the U.S.S.R. in Europe, and not French hesitancy to dismember Germany, which gradually put an end to the idea that the Franco-German conflict was the essential problem.

Out of all this, hardly any continuous line emerges, unless it is that very general one of European equilibrium. France tried to prevent other Powers—Hapsburg, England, Germany —from acquiring hegemony in Europe. She tried to acquire it twice herself, with Louis XIV and Napoleon I. In the end, it was the establishment of Soviet hegemony in Europe and—to provide a counterweight—the entry on the scene of the United States, which put an end to the secular policy of a "balance of power" within a European framework. Too, the new problems facing French foreign policy since 1945 are only very indirectly connected with the long traditions of the past. It is on an analysis of the new situation, of the new problems, and of the efforts, often hesitant and disjointed, of France to adapt herself, that we wish to concentrate above all.

THE MAKING AND EXECUTION OF FRENCH FOREIGN POLICY

The role of public opinion

France being a democracy, its foreign policy is evolved according to the same general processes as in the other democracies: public opinion plays a role through the intermediary of the people's representatives and also through more direct processes. Every deputy, knowing he will be subject to re-election, must take into account the demands of his electors. These, in France as everywhere in the world, are much more interested in internal policy, of which many aspects concern them directly, than in foreign policy. The candidates' electoral programs make very few allusions to international relations.

Nevertheless, there are two aspects in which foreign policy has had such repercussions on the lives of citizens that they are infinitely sensitive thereto. One aspect concerns the portion of taxes to be devoted to action abroad or to its preparation. This includes outlays for national defense, aid to foreign countries and aid to colonies which have won their independence. The other aspect relates to the duration of military service and, eventually, the recall of reservists.

To give an example, when Hitler reoccupied the demilitarized zone of the Rhineland in March 1936, the vital interest of France—as we now know—was to prevent him from doing so. The dispatch of French troops into the Rhineland was a definite possibility. But the military men consulted declared that, in this case, general mobilization would be necessary for the certainty of its success. General elections were scheduled for the following month of May. Mobilization would have rendered the parties represented in the government unpopular. The Council of Ministers failed to act, and Hitler was able to quietly complete an operation which, by permitting him to erect a powerful line of fortifications along the frontiers of France, ruined the entire policy of French alliances and exposed the country to invasion.

During their histories, all democracies have experienced this choice between a necessary unpopularity and a popularity which is ruinous and, one might say, demagogic. But within this general democratic framework, there are features which are peculiar to France. It is these we must analyze. To do so successfully, we must draw a very clear distinction between the juridical framework and the political realities.

Constitutional provisions—theory versus reality

The theory   Juridically, the Third, Fourth, and Fifth Republics display astonishing similarities in the making of foreign policy; in all three cases, the direction of foreign policy was divided between the President of the Republic, the Council of Ministers, and Parliament.

The constitution of October 4, 1958, while considerably increasing the powers of the President of the Republic—by the right of dissolution (Art. 12), by the right to submit to referendum certain bills, including the ratification of certain treaties (Art. 11), by the right to assume full powers "when the institutions of the Republic, the independence of the nation, the integrity of its territory, or the execution of its international engagements are in grave and immediate danger (Art. 16),"—seemingly does not give him much more extensive privileges in foreign policy than under the preceding regimes. He "is the chief of the armies (Art. 15)," and foreign ambassadors are accredited to him (Art. 14). But the "government," directed by the "Prime Minister," "determines and conducts the policy of the Nation," "disposes . . . of the armed force (Art. 20)." The Prime Minister "is responsible for the National Defense (Art. 21)." Lastly, the Parliament, composed of two equal assemblies, the National Assembly and the Senate, conserves very extensive powers. With certain limitations, the government is responsible to it. As for treaties, the provisions are approximately the same as in the Constitution of 1875: "The President of the Republic negotiates and ratifies treaties (Art. 52)."

> Treaties of peace, treaties of commerce, treaties of agreement relating to international organization, those engaging the finances of the state, those modifying provisions of a legislative nature, those relative to the status of persons, those which permit the secession, exchange, or addition of territory, cannot be ratified or approved except by virtue of a law (Art. 53).

Lastly, "The declaration of war is authorized by the Parliament (Art. 35)."

Practice before 1914   However, in reality, the juridical texts do not mean much. A quick look at their evolution will convince us of this. Under the Third Republic, before 1914, the President of the Republic, who had permitted the majority of his powers to fall into disuse, retained considerable influence in the field of foreign policy, and for a simple reason: at that time, diplomacy consisted largely in secret agreements. Thus the existence of the Franco-Russian military alliance of 1892 was disclosed only in 1897, and its text remained unknown to the public. So that the secret would be kept, only the President of the Republic, the Minister of Foreign Affairs, and the President of the Council knew it. The other ministers were not informed. They therefore left to these three persons the task of formulating foreign policy, but for exceptional cases.

From the Versailles Treaty to the Fifth Republic The advent of open diplomacy, the long debate over the ratification of the Treaty of Versailles, the crises of the twenties and the thirties, followed by the Second World War, gave an entirely changed aspect to the structure of the foreign policy of the expiring Third Republic and the Fourth Republic. Instead of a small group consisting of the President of the Republic, the President of the Council, and the Minister of Foreign Affairs, it is the whole cabinet which now makes the important decisions, and is subject to increasing control by Parliament. The real importance of the President of the Republic, who is not responsible to Parliament, has thus decreased, as has the importance of the Minister of Foreign Affairs. He is no longer considered a special personage guarding secrets to which others do not have access and is no longer in a position to arbitrate among his colleagues. In the cabinet, the Minister of Finance and Economic Affairs—who participates more and more in foreign policy because of the increasing importance of economic and financial problems abroad and the growing need for appropriations—and the Minister of National Defense, have much more effective authority than he. True, this has sometimes been balanced by the foreign minister's greater continuity in office. For instance, Aristide Briand directed foreign affairs from January 1921 to January 1922, then from April 1925 to January 1932; M. Georges Bidault from September 1944 to July 1948, then from January 1953 to June 1954; M. Robert Schuman from July 1948 to December 1952. The latter barely consulted the other ministers before launching the famous "Schuman Plan" of 1950. But in general, as head of a ministry with a feeble budget, the Minister of Foreign Affairs has played a continuously decreasing role.

The growing practice of international conferences between prime ministers further contributed to this decline so that the effective direction of foreign policy, belonging collectively to the cabinet, passed more and more into the hands of the President of the Council. Often—this was the case with M. Mendès-France—the President of the Council kept the portfolio of foreign affairs for himself. As for foreign policy debates in Parliament, they took on another dimension and an importance unknown prior to 1914. It is sufficient to recall the debate over the ratification of the Atlantic Pact from July 22 to 29, 1949, or, again, the famous rejection of the European Defense Community on August 30, 1954.

The de Gaulle era The Fifth Republic, whatever the constitutional texts may be, is completely detached from this evolution. As everyone knows, all important decisions, all long-range plans, stem from the President of the Republic, General de Gaulle, and from him alone. All observers have noted the preference he gives to foreign affairs in relation to internal affairs: "it involves the subordination of domestic politics to the primacy of international affairs."[13] "With some of the perennial conflicts of French Society at least temporarily submerged, de Gaulle, when it comes to foreign policy issues," has been called "a truly national spokesman."[14]

[13] Stanley Hoffmann, "De Gaulle's Memoirs: The Hero as History," *World Politics,* October 1960, p. 145.
[14] Roy C. Macridis, "De Gaulle's Foreign Policy and the Fifth Republic," *The Yale Review,* Winter 1961, p. 172.

Against this authority, which stems from an extremely broad interpretation of the constitution, no serious criticisms are directed. The prime ministers, Michel Debré first and Georges Pompidou later, were devoted to the President of the Republic and never sought to supplant his policy with another, although the Constitution would permit this. The Minister of Foreign Affairs, Maurice Couve de Murville, is a specialist in finance who began his diplomatic career in 1945. While enjoying the prestige of an excellent technician, he does not have the authority which is bestowed on an elected minister by universal suffrage.

Criticism is not mainly against the de facto pre-eminence of de Gaulle. It concerns, above all, his excessive attention to foreign policy which, say the Socialists, makes him neglect urgent social problems. Critics say that the Quai d'Orsay has become purely and simply an executive organ which is kept ignorant of decisions being prepared at the Elysée, decisions which it usually cannot modify. Members of the foreign office have less importance than they have ever had in the elaboration of foreign policy and, discreetly, complain about it. Moreover, at the Elysée, the General Secretary and the Director of the Cabinet usually are career diplomats who have facilities available which enable them to dispense with the Quai d'Orsay if not for the execution, at least for the formulation of policy.

This, then, is the fundamental difference between the Fifth and the Fourth Republic. The extreme instability, the extreme weakness of the executive power, gave the stable and efficacious Civil Service an important, sometimes even decisive, role. Knowing that the current cabinet would have only an ephemeral existence, high officials could practically stifle decisions which did not please them. Or, they could impose their policy on governments which were very weak. This was the case, for example, of French policy in the Saar, which was the work of an energetic and bold ambassador, Gilbert Grandval, much more than it was the work of the cabinet. Or, in an extremity, civil servants could make important decisions themselves. The deposition of the Sultan of Morocco in 1953 took place practically without initiative by the political leaders who did nothing but ratify it.

Today, with a stable government, totally dominated by the exceptional personality of a President of the Republic who expects to govern by himself, the high officials are reduced to executing policy. While, in principle, this is their proper function, they had become accustomed to doing much more.

The Ministry of Foreign Affairs

Aside from the specialized attachés (commercial, military, cultural, etc.) who often correspond directly with their respective ministers, French foreign policy is carried out by the Ministry of Foreign Affairs. This ancient institution, laden with traditions and archives, is located next to the Palais Bourbon on the Quai d'Orsay, and receives its popular name from its location.

Internal organization   The principal lines of organization of the Ministry are as follows: There is a Minister, assisted by a "ministerial cabinet" composed of individuals selected by him to aid him in his everyday work, and in particular, to "filter" people seeking access to him. Since May, 1961, there has been a return to a practice common under the Fourth Republic, that of associating a Secretary of State with the Minister. These two individuals are subject to dismissal under the same conditions as other ministers. Under them is the true head of the Quai d'Orsay, the Secretary General. This office was rendered illustrious by personalities such as Jules Cambon, Maurice Paléologue, Philippe Berthelot, Alexis Léger, François Charles-Roux, to cite examples from the Third Republic. Now it seems to have lost some part of the importance which it had in the epoch of ministerial instability.

Under the Secretary General, the principal divisions are more functional and less geographic than in the United States. There are five general divisions of unequal importance: the General Division of Political Affairs, the General Division of Economic and Financial Affairs, the General Division of Cultural and Technical Affairs, the Division of Administrative and Public Affairs (consular problems), and the Division of Personnel and General Administration. Within the General Divisions, the offices are usually distributed by geographic area.

The personnel directly dependent on the Quai d'Orsay (excluding French professors abroad, of whom several thousand come directly under the General Directorate of Cultural and Technical Affairs) comprise 3,300 individuals: 1,200 in Paris and 2,100 abroad. Diplomats, properly speaking, total a little over 1,000. The others are agents fulfilling auxiliary roles.

Training for the diplomatic service   Normal access to a diplomatic career in France has been, since 1945, through selection in the difficult competition of the National School of Administration. To enter the school, one must either already have certain diplomas and pass an examination known as the "students' competition," or one must have been in government service for five years and pass the examination known as the "officials' competition." Sixty students are admitted to the National School of Administration each year, and of this number, less than ten are admitted to the "Foreign Affairs Section," from which, after three years of study and apprenticeship, the students enter the Quai d'Orsay as "third secretaries." The competition of the National School of Administration gives primary importance to general culture; next come public law, political economy, history, geography, and foreign languages. It is only after entering the National School of Administration that specialized studies begin.

The very difficulty of the examination has given the "Career" a strong *esprit de corps*. Those admitted without undergoing the examination (a certain percent of the higher posts) must assimilate themselves to this corps or be kept apart and oriented toward the less interesting posts.

Co-ordination with other ministries

In our times, foreign policy has taken on so many complex aspects, has expanded itself into so many spheres, that the problem of *co-ordination* assumes enormous importance. Several ministries have interlocking responsibilities: the Ministry of the Armed Forces, the Ministry of Finance and Economic Affairs. Dependent on the latter are two important divisions: "the Division of Exterior Finance," (monetary problems, balance of payments, the movement of capital, credits, the control of exchanges) and the "Division of Exterior Economic Relations," to which the commercial attachés and counsellors are subordinate. This division has close ties with the "General Division of Economic and Financial Affairs" of the Quai d'Orsay, and commercial negotiations are conducted jointly by these two bodies. In 1948, an "Inter-ministerial Committee for Questions of European Economic Co-operation" was created. Since 1958 it has been charged with the co-ordination of French policy in regard to the European Common Market. It is responsible to the Prime Minister.

For cultural affairs and technical assistance, the General Division corresponding to the Quai d'Orsay works in close liaison with the "General Division of Co-operation with the Community and Foreign Countries" of the Ministry of National Education. An "Inter-ministerial Committee for Cultural and Technical Co-ordination" exists, but its role is very limited.

At the highest echelon, co-ordination between National Defense and Foreign Affairs is assured by the "Committee for National Defense," which has some similarities with the "National Security Council" in the United States. Presided over by the President of the Republic assisted by the Prime Minister, it is composed of the ministers of the Armed Forces, Foreign Affairs, Finance and Economic Affairs. Its secretary is the Chief of the General Staff. It meets about once a month.

Pressure groups

What forces bear on the formulation of decisions? General de Gaulle, more than any leader of the Fourth Republic, is inclined to resist the pressures of various groups and even to choose a path unpopular at the moment. This is a result of his constitutional role, but also of his temperament. He defined the true statesman as one who

> chooses his end and holds his line without allowing himself to be stopped by his followers and without waiting for any formula or combination to come to lighten the responsibility which is his obligation and his honor."[15]

This means that unlike the Fourth Republic, in which pressure groups were sometimes capable of provoking the fall of cabinets, General de Gaulle is little accessible to their influence. Whether it is a question of economic pressure groups (for example, the National Center of the French Patronate, or the Committee of Metallurgists), the trade unions (for example, the pressure exerted by the National Union of Students of France to put an end to the Algerian War), the churches or political parties, General de Gaulle pays little attention to their demands. We have little knowledge about the influence of pressure groups on the foreign policy of the Third and Fourth Republics. Pierre Gerbet has shown how the influence of the metallurgists was exerted—with only limited success, because of the personality of the minister, Robert Schuman—when the European Steel and Coal Community, to which they were originally opposed, was instituted.

The current President is able to resist "special interests," because he feels he is supported

15 *Le Monde*, June 2, 1961.

by general opinion. His trips in the departments of France, the study of opinion polls, and lastly, the referendums, show him whether he has sufficient support. In January 1961, he evidently intended to resign if he did not have the support of at least 50 percent of the registered voters. We know that the number of *yes* votes greatly exceeded this percentage, and that 75 percent of the voters at the polls, and 56 percent of the registered voters supported the President's policy.

The very possibility of a referendum greatly reduces the influence of Parliament. The majority of the members, for example, were hostile to the program of atomic armament which the government submitted to Parliament. The threat of dissolving the National Assembly, however, also contributed to Parliament's approval of this program. Members of Parliament complain of this reduced status. But these complaints do not seem to have much effect on public opinion. Nevertheless, a coalition of all the parties, except for the Gaullists, against the election of the President by universal suffrage, substantially decreased de Gaulle's majority on October 28, 1962. At the polls, 61.7 percent of the voters favored de Gaulle's proposal. This represents 46.44 percent of the registered voters. In spite of this decline in support, the President felt strong enough to continue in office.

THE NATIONAL INTEREST OF FRANCE

Difficulties of objective definition

One cannot objectively evaluate the national interest of any nation. Certain groups within a country have specific interests, sometimes contradictory, and nothing proves that the sum total of these interests is the national interest. The question should be presented in another way. In a democratic regime, there is a government which has better precise information on the internal and external situation at its disposal than the public. It is to this government that the task of defining the national interest belongs. It must decide the *objectives* it proposes to reach in foreign policy and the risks it is willing to take in order to attain these objectives. In other words, it is the government which directs the international strategy of the country. To succeed, it must have the *means.* It is by deciding on the *objective,* and analyzing constantly the relations of objective to risk and objective to means, that it determines the policy to follow.

The democratic process permits the elected representatives of the country to control this strategy, that is, to approve, reject, or modify it. This can result in a change of government if the latter has adopted a strategy the majority of representatives disapprove. It can also result in an appeal to the country to settle the quarrel between the executive and Parliament. Lastly, general elections periodically give an idea of the evolution of public opinion.

Consequently, to define the national interest of France at a given moment, is to define the subjective idea those responsible for foreign policy have formed of the stakes, the risks, and the means. Of course, one comes closer to an objective definition if, over a long period, the majority of the governments envisage these various problems in a similar way. The fact that in the United States, foreign policy has been almost bi-partisan and continuous since 1947–1948, shows that so far as that country is concerned, one can approach an objective definition. The case of France is obviously different for various reasons which must first be analyzed.

National aims   In the hierarchy of the aims pursued by every state, one can, we believe, distinguish three spheres, mutually irreducible, even though tightly linked in practice. The effort of a state is directed toward the increase of power, the increase of wealth, and the realization of certain ideals desired more or less clearly by public opinion. Doubtless, all this calls for commentaries and nuances which we cannot supply here. For example, an act which

would increase power may not be feasible because it is contrary to an accepted ideal: specifically, the French could not annex the Saar after the Second World War, not because this was technically impossible, but because public opinion, at least in Europe, rejected the idea of dominating foreigners against their will. The same idea has been progressively extended to the extra-European world. Public opinion is more and more hostile to the conservation of colonial dominions, even where it requires only a limited use of force.

Similarly, if wealth was very closely linked to power under the Old Regime—for the richer a government was, the more soldiers it could hire and the more fortresses it could maintain —the relationship between wealth and power has become much more complex. Goering put this in elementary terms in saying that Nazi Germany preferred cannons to butter. The choice of the portion of national revenue to be devoted to armaments is therefore closely linked to the idea one has formed of the national interest.

Lastly, although nearly all citizens, in the long run, profit by the increase of national wealth, the distribution of this increase can be carried out in a number of ways. The idea of increasing the national wealth may, in some states, appear secondary, the essential being to increase, or even to preserve, the wealth of certain social groups.

Changing concepts of power

If we go back to these three terms—power, wealth and ideals—we can note some important phenomena in 20th century France. The idea of power, linked until about 1815 to that of conquests in Europe—then conquests overseas—or again, to that of "revenge" for the reconquest of Alsace and Lorraine, assumed, from 1919 on, a purely defensive look. The key word of Clemenceau in 1919 after an exhausting war was "security." This is the same idea of security—vis-à-vis Germany—which explains the projects for dismembering that country expressed by General de Gaulle in 1945.

France on the defensive   It is the idea of security vis-à-vis the U.S.S.R. which has dominated French policy since 1947. Like all peoples, the French want to be independent, and with all the more keenness for their having recently, from 1940 to 1944, experienced dependence. The idea of power has evolved then in the last hundred and fifty years from an active and offensive position toward a passive and defensive position. This is, moreover, the usual case for every country which feels satisfied with its territorial limits. The abandonment of the great ambitions for expansion of the natural frontiers, led France to be a typically satisfied country.

But this defensive attitude has another aspect. It consists in wanting to keep what one has. It evokes a conservative attitude. It is interesting to compare the policies of Vichy, the Generals de Gaulle and Giraud, and Admiral Darlan, in regard to the colonial possessions of France during the war. They were absolutely identical. Darlan, meeting Hitler in Berchtesgaden on the 11th and 12th of May, 1941, obtained the promise that France would keep its empire except for Morocco and Tunisia, but with compensations at the expense of the British Empire. The first Churchill-de Gaulle agreement of June 25th, 1940, mentions that "the aim of Great Britain is the complete restoration of French colonial and metropolitan territory." The agreements of October and November 1942, known as "Murphy-Giraud" and "Darlan-Clark" contain exactly the same clause.

The value of colonies   When France, exhausted but on the side of the victors, elaborated the principal lines of its policy in 1944–45, the conservation of the empire, under another name, and with improvements, appeared as one of the basic points. It seemed to many that, territory being a fundamental element of power, France would not again become a Great Power except by keeping its vast posses-

sions. That this underestimated the forces rising in the world, that this rested on a false evaluation of the factors of power in a world in the middle of a technical revolution, was discounted. The national interest of France, once her security was assured, was to conserve territory.

Fifteen years were necessary, many miscalculations, two colonial wars and even the disaster of Dien Bien Phu in 1954 for public opinion—in an ever-growing proportion—and the leaders to discover that colonial territory, far from increasing power in the era in which we live, diminishes it, and that the colonies, sources of strength in 1900, have become, following events outside of France, brakes and not accelerators of power. The humiliation of the defeat of 1940 and the Nazi occupation exacerbated this conservatory tendency. It was psychologically easier for the Britons, unconquered, and important participants in the victory, to make an about-face than it was for the French. Emerging from shadows and suffering, the French automatically made their aspirations coincide with a "back to normalcy" concept. And "normal" meant the conservation of the empire.

Changing concepts of wealth

In terms of wealth to be increased, the situation is radically different. France was ruined by the occupation and by allied bombardments. But the "back to normalcy" would have meant, in the economic field, a return to the mediocre situation of 1938. The record year for French production had been 1929, before the crisis. That was a too distant memory. If the tendency was toward conservation in the sphere of power, in that of wealth, it was clearly toward radical reforms.

By a curious coincidence, the year 1940 marked an important turning point in the demographic history of France. From a country with a low birthrate, sometimes lower than the mortality rate, France had fairly abruptly again become a country with a rising birth-rate. The effects were not felt until after the return of the prisoners. But since 1946, and in a continuous fashion, France has demographically become a dynamic country, clearly surpassing in birthrate Great Britain, Germany, and even Italy.

This phenomenon coincided with a revolution in economic concepts. A new generation of "Saint-Simonians," for whom economic growth, industrialization and modernization were the supreme values, little by little took over the levers of authority. Everything contributed to this: the mental effort of those who may be called "the generation of the thirties;" the concepts of certain technocrats of the Vichy regime; the nationalization of certain big industries (coal, electricity, gas, the Renault factories) which replaced timorous family enterprises in the first ranks of production by a new milieu of engineers and technicians, more avid for progress than for peaceful income, and so on. Undoubtedly there was strong resistance. The electoral success of the Poujadists in 1956 was the last battle of the rear guard of partisans of the small traditional enterprise, surviving only through tariff protection and state aid.

At the moment we are writing, the "Saint Simonians" have won the battle. In terms of foreign policy, this has led to a revolution without precedent. The "exporter" spirit, the spirit of "competition with the foreigner," has replaced the "protectionist" spirit. The slogan of the "conquest of world markets" has overpowered that of "the protection of national labor." The Fourth Republic in its relatively powerless condition, allowed all this expansion to take place on the foundations of disorder, inflation, and American aid. The financial reform of December 1958 by the Fifth Republic and the devaluation of the franc—continuously overvalued until then—are placing the country on healthy foundations: firm currency, balanced budget, lowering of tariff barriers, and growth of the authority of the "Planning Commission."

This intellectual revolution of the producers has had, in foreign policy, incalculable consequences. It alone made possible the Common Market and created a chance for the future political integration of Western Europe. It alone allowed the re-establishment of a certain equality in Franco-American relations. It alone allowed, above all, the rethinking of the problem of power in new terms, no longer connected to territory, but to technical and industrial progress.

Novel applications of traditional ideals

In the face of these two facts, the French *ideal,* inherited from the Revolution, has changed little in its principles. The transformation was in their application. The Revolutionaries did not fail to apply their great principles of liberty, equality and fraternity to foreign problems. The right of the peoples to self-determination has become one of the foundations of the French concept of nationalities.

True, the first use made of this was quite deceptive. When the National Convention, in November 1792, proclaimed that it was going to bring "fraternity and aid to all peoples desirous of recovering their liberty," it gave itself a right of intervention which did not take long to be used as justification for all conquests. It nevertheless subsisted, after 1815, as a constant: that of the favor accorded by the liberal elements of public opinion in France to the principle of national self-determination. The support of oppressed Poland was one of the great aspirations of the liberals. Napoleon III greatly favored the application of this principle to Italy, Germany, and Rumania, and proclaimed it for Poland. The loss of Alsace and of Lorraine were analyzed by Renan, by Fustel de Coulanges, in relation to the desire of the populations to remain French. After the First World War, France resolutely supported the Wilsonian method of plebiscites—inaugurated under the Revolution and taken up again by Napoleon III.

But almost no one—not even Wilson—envisaged the application of this principle to colonies. The idea—widely approved recently in France—appears to be that for certain "uncivilized" peoples, access to civilization is more important than independence. Jurists justified the conquest of African territories by saying that they were *res nullius*—territories belonging to no one. The French concept of the "white man's burden" has this difference from the Anglo-Saxon concept that, convinced of the excellence of their civilization, the French wanted to induce the natives to profit from it. Therefore assimilation has always been a characteristic feature of French colonization.

After the Second World War, it was toward more perfect assimilation, that French policy was first oriented. The Conference of Brazzaville was in no way directed toward the independence of the colonies, but toward the elevation of the natives to the status of French citizens. Universal suffrage was established for both men and women in the major part of these territories. For Algeria, the two extreme choices offered by General de Gaulle were secession—independence without ties to France —and "Frenchification" which would have made Algerian Moslems "full-fledged Frenchmen," with France making a vast effort to increase their standard of living.

After prolonged efforts, the ideal of the "civilizer" and "assimilator" was gradually abandoned in favor of another, much older ideal, which, until then, had been applied only to Europeans and Americans. This was the ideal of the right of self-determination, which implies independence. The Fourth Republic granted it—forced by events—to Indochina, Morocco, and Tunisia. The Fifth spontaneously offered it to Black Africa. Finally, the Evian Agreements of March 1962 gave Algeria the right of self-determination. Algerians used this right to proclaim their independence.

The national interest after 1945

On these general foundations, what have been the concepts of the national interest in the last

fifteen years? Here again it is necessary to emphasize the contrast between the hesitations of the Fourth Republic and the line, which is progressively becoming clear, of General de Gaulle returned to power. Since 1945, three distinct conceptions of the national interest can be distinguished in a study of the programs of the various cabinets.

The "policy of grandeur"   The first was that of General de Gaulle in 1944–1946, continued by Georges Bidault. This is the "policy of grandeur," but a policy of grandeur founded on tradition. Basically it contained three points. The first of these was to dismember Western Germany to assure the security of France. This was Marshal Foch's idea—re-adopted and improved—when he urged the separation of the Rhineland from Germany. The sole concrete result, up to 1955, was the separation of the Saar, economically united to France. Alliances with Russia and England—as in 1914—were to complete this security. A second objective was to conserve the colonial empire, with reforms, certainly, but in its integrity. Lastly, France was to stay out of the growing quarrel between East and West. The presence of Communists in the government until May, 1947, justified this neutral policy. M. Bidault, furthermore, entertained the ambition—a vain ambition, as events have shown —that France could be the *mediator* between the two evolving blocs.

European integration   When the Soviet attitude hardened in 1947, the solidarity of France with the West became evident. The concern for security in respect to the U.S.S.R. dominated all preoccupations. The idea of dismembering Germany disappeared with the London agreements of June 1948. The Berlin blockade redoubled anxieties.

From then on, French policy adopted a line which it was to hold until June 1954: that of European integration. For the concept of the "grandeur" of France, cruelly belied by events, why not substitute that of European grandeur? In unifying Europe, one would form a new Great Power, capable, one day, of assuring its own security and dispensing with the aid, simultaneously indispensable and a little humiliating, furnished by the United States. While waiting, it was necessary to solidify the American alliance. This was accomplished when the Atlantic Pact was signed April 4, 1949. But the idea of unifying Europe appeared to many—particularly to the Ministers of Foreign Affairs of the period, Bidault and Schuman—to be the principal aim. It was Bidault who inaugurated this policy in July 1948. Schuman continued it.

British opposition rendered the first project, that of the Council of Europe, illusory, because the English refused to grant it supra-national powers. We then enter the narrower path of the Little Europe of Six, but with real supranational powers. This led to a success, the "European Coal and Steel Community," a derivative of the Schuman Plan of May 9, 1950, and to a failure, the "European Defense Community," a derivative of the Pleven Plan of October 1950. On the colonial scene, the policy of "conservation" of the preceding years was continued, with more and more difficulties.

Concentration on economic expansion The third kind of policy was that of M. Mendès-France, from June 1954 to February 1955. M. Mendès-France, who voluntarily kept himself "in reserve," came to power because of strong pressure of public opinion, which wanted an honorable end to the war in Indochina. M. Mendès-France formulated his program in June 1953:

I have already said that the fundamental cause of the ills which are overburdening the country is the multiplicity and the weight of the tasks it proposes to assume simultaneously: reconstruction, modernization and equipment, development of countries overseas, amelioration of the standard of living and social reforms, exportation, the war in Indochina, a great and powerful army in Europe, etc. Now events have confirmed what reflection would have permitted forseeing: one cannot do everything simultaneously. To govern is to choose, however difficult the choices may be.[16]

The "policy of choice" of M. Mendès-France was clearly in the direction of a choice for economic expansion. Peace in Indochina—and therefore the abandonment of a former colony—was the first condition for this. Little interested in European integration, the President of the Council allowed the E.D.C. to collapse. He inaugurated a liberal policy in Tunisia. He stayed in power too short a time for his plan of expansion to be elaborated. But this brief interval left a profound mark on the country. The feeble governments which succeeded him had to continue in the path of his choice. It is true that they resumed the line of European integration. A young and brilliant Secretary of State for Foreign Affairs, Maurice Faure, contributed greatly to "European relaunching" with the signing of treaties creating the Common Market and Euratom. But at the same time, a "choice" was made in abandoning the Saar (1955), in giving independence to Morocco and Tunisia (1955–1956), in preparing independence of Black Africa by the *Loi-Cadre* of June 23, 1956.

De Gaulle's concept of national interest

When General de Gaulle came to power in June 1958, the Algerian War, begun under Mendès-France November 1, 1954, had become one of the major preoccupations of the French. The impression that the government was going to solicit the "good offices" of foreign countries to put an end to it, provoked the coup d'état of Algeria, launched by the colons and the army. The total discredit into which the Fourth Republic had fallen explains why the metropolis did not rise to defend the regime, the more so because it had in reserve a

[16] *Année politique,* 1953, pp. 490–1.

man of prestige, General de Gaulle. The decisive moment was that in which the leader of the Socialist Party, Guy Mollet, convinced of the General's democratic sentiments, granted him the support of a large part of the Left.

The arrival in power of such a personality, and, moreover, as we have seen, of a personality passionately attracted to foreign affairs, necessarily involved a profound change in the concept of the French national interest. We shall return, later, in studying some of the present problems, to certain of General de Gaulle's concepts. Let us content ourselves here with indicating some of the basic elements of his policy.

Novel ideas in traditional garb   One must begin by eliminating the totally wrong meaning certain authors, particularly Americans, give to the expression General de Gaulle loves to use: the "grandeur" of France. To numerous commentators, this would mean a return to the past form of grandeur. In their understanding, de Gaulle is a Bismarck, a Clemenceau. He is the most traditionalist, the most backward of statesmen, "the old man." He is launching himself in the most artificial of efforts, the most futile, for what difference does it make whether France is *grande*. He continues to think in terms of force and excessive nationalism. As Stanley Hoffmann puts it so well:

> Some criticisms of "grandeur" are based on a misunderstanding of the General. His *mystique* is not a quest for anachronism, a vain nostalgia for past greatness, a fruitless drive for restoration. This misconception pervades Edgar Furniss' recent study[17] which misses the psychological meaning of de Gaulle's appeals: when he talks to the French about their greatness then and now, it is in order to get them to adapt to, and to act in, the world as it is, not in order to keep

them in a museum of past glories. It is flattery for reform.[18]

In my opinion, which is widely shared, de Gaulle is the complete opposite of the traditionalist. He is the most adaptable of statesmen. The idea of conforming to what he calls "the force of things" dominates his basic concepts. He is, for example, the one who made the mass of Frenchmen understand that power no longer lies in territory, but in economic expansion; that decolonization is an unavoidable phenomenon of our time, and that this phenomenon is not a misfortune for France, but an excellent opportunity. Among his basic ideas, that of the necessity for a collective effort rather than an individual one to aid underdeveloped countries and the idea that the Atlantic Alliance has responsibilities not only in Europe but in the entire world, have been largely accepted, after much resistance, by his partners.

What gives de Gaulle a traditionalist look is his style. He likes majestic traditions. His style is that of Talleyrand or Chateaubriand, and he even employs obsolete words. He is fond of the pomp of parades and ceremonies. He speaks of the U.S.S.R. as "Russia," and, in connection with Eastern Germany, mentions "Prussia" and "Saxony." But does that signify that he is turned toward the past in his ideas?

The grandeur of great enterprises   What does this notion of the "grandeur" which he wants to restore in France mean? His patriotic passion is not a simple sentiment.

> The positive side of my mind convinces me that France is not truly herself except in the first rank; that only vast enterprises are capable of compensating for the ferments of dispersion which its people bear in themselves; that our country, as it is, among others, must, under penalty of

---

[17] *France: Troubled Ally*, New York, Harper, 1960.

[18] "De Gaulle's Memoirs," *World Politics*, October 1960, pp. 150–51.

mortal danger, aim high and bear it-self upright. In short, in my opinion, France can only be France in grandeur.[19]

In the idea that "great enterprises" are necessary to eliminate internal contradictions which exist so easily in this country lies the basic originality of his thought. The whole problem is to know what these "great enterprises" are.

These "great enterprises" are not conquest nor adventure. They vary with the epoch. During war, "The concrete historical content of grandeur can be described by three terms: independence, status, self-respect."[20] In 1945–1946, it was the re-establishment, the reform of the empire. In 1958, it was necessary to take in hand all the potentials, all the dynamism of the country, and intensify them in remaking the state and in solving the bitter problem of the Algerian war. But, once this was done or in the process of being done, the great tasks are on a world-scale and adapted to a certain pride the French have in the universal character of their civilization. As Roy Macridis notes:

The realization of his plan is consistent with his most profound convictions about the role and mission of France in this age of empires. For France remains for de Gaulle as for every French intellectual and statesman the land of balance and moderation, of courage and freedom; the land where man has a mind of his own, with a respect for differences and deference for quality . . . It is not, of course, accidental that the ideal of France is equated with the reality of French Power. Only a strong France can maintain freedom and dignity at home and cultivate it abroad . . . It is part and parcel of Gaullism and it is shared widely by many political leaders and intellectuals.[21]

The "vast enterprises" which General de Gaulle proposes to France are discussed in his speeches and press conferences. Within the general framework of the defense of liberty and peace, three important ideas seem to dominate: that of a definitive reconciliation with Germany, for so long an enemy with, as a more distant perspective, the creation of a "vast confederation of Europe." This confederation would be open to the countries of Eastern Europe when they detach themselves, in the distant future, from the Communist sphere of influence. Then there is the hope of collective world effort, on behalf of the underdeveloped countries in which France has already played so great a role, but which should be organized and made permanent. Within this framework, France would weave special ties with those of its former territories which desire it, and, particularly, with a sovereign Algeria—ties of defense, but above all, economic and cultural ties. Lastly, there is the vision of a vast expansion of the French economy within the framework of the "plan." The terms of General de Gaulle's press conference on May 8, 1961, are particularly clear in this respect:

the condition dominating the entire future of France is that its children unite in a great national task . . . What task? What ambition? Those which are imposed on us by both the character of the times and of the world in which we exist, the necessities of the life of our people, the profound impulse which is already forcing its way through and which the falling into order of a numerous youth will multiply—the development of France![22]

---

[19] *L'Appel*, p. 1.
[20] Stanley Hoffmann, "De Gaulle's Memoirs," *World Politics*, October 1960, p. 145.

[21] "De Gaulle's Foreign Policy and the Fifth Republic," *The Yale Review*, Winter 1961, pp. 185–86.
[22] *Le Monde*, May 10, 1961.

Nuclear weapons   In my opinion, it would be a completely wrong interpretation to put the building of a "striking force" of nuclear arms, within the framework of these "vast enterprises." True, when the first French A-bomb exploded, General de Gaulle congratulated the makers with a "Hurrah!" But for him, the aim is not strength. The A-bomb is not only a means of assuring the security of the country—a thesis which is known to be the subject of discussion by many experts—but above all a means of making France "respected." It is obviously not a question here of the moral respect which could result from the prestige of French culture, but of that sort of respect which is obtained in the international world by following Theodore Roosevelt's precept: "Speak softly and carry a big stick." It is, quite precisely, the path followed by Great Britain. There are, undoubtedly, many good minds in France and abroad which assert that France would be more "respected" if she took the initiative of renouncing such a weapon. But such is not the point of view of General de Gaulle. A large part of public opinion accepts his views on this subject.

Public support of foreign policy   For, ultimately, it is in the positive action of the government that General de Gaulle seems to find the means for developing what is essential: the support, the backing of public opinion. Whatever may be the ultimate fate of the "vast enterprises"—which his subtle adaptability can, moreover, lead him to reconsider or modify— they can only succeed if they are widely supported by the French people. De Gaulle believes that the French people need vast enterprises, on a national, European, African, and world scale. His originality lies in having made them rest on radically new foundations, in strict contradiction with various solidly anchored traditions. For the distrust of Germany and the "conservation" of colonies, he has, in fact, substituted Franco-German collaboration and absolute decolonization.

We have spoken above of the intrinsic conflict between the "maritimes" and the "continentals" which geography imposes on the French. De Gaulle is among those who want both a grand overseas policy and a grand European policy. In this sense he is in Theophile Delcassé's league. But the latter practiced an anti-German continental policy and a policy of colonial expansion overseas at the beginning of the century. General de Gaulle has adapted himself to the conditions of the second half of the century. If, like Delcassé, he seeks the grandeur of the country, if he by no means renounces a "global" policy, this is done on entirely new principles.

I do not hesitate to say that this new concept of the national interest seems to have, at the present time, broad support among the mass of the French people. The idea of "vast enterprises," simultaneously peaceful, generous and grandiose, is particularly agreeable to a people which still feels the effects of "national humiliation." Constantly criticized on the details of the government's policy, details which he calls "trivia" and which hardly interest him, the General thus has the concerted support which he feels is the necessary condition for grand policy.

Lastly, the Gaullist conception of the national interest is opposed to that of the "imperialists." The "imperialists" would like to conserve at least what remains of the empire. They would like "for the populations who have been carried away by the exaltation of liberty to continue to be treated in the terms of an empire." De Gaulle's ideas also are opposed to those of the partisans of "Little France," who are sometimes referred to as "Cartierists" (from the name of the journalist Raymond Cartier, who is quite far from sharing all these ideas). These latter want decolonization, as de Gaulle does, but because "these territories cost us a great deal more than they bring us," they consequently refuse to use the resources of France for aid to underdeveloped countries. "Those," de Gaulle says, "I do not believe to be in agreement with the idea France conceives of herself nor with the idea the world conceives of France."

De Gaulle's ideas differ from those of the Communists, because the "mission of France," as de Gaulle understands it, is founded on the

Western kind of civilization France contributed to making, while the Communists would like to create a new civilization founded on Marxist-Leninist principles. Nor does de Gaulle agree with the "mystics of Europe" who would like to sacrifice French patriotism for a patriotism of a united Europe, because de Gaulle considers that the vital reality in the present world is that of the existing nations.

MAJOR PROBLEMS OF PRESENT FRENCH FOREIGN POLICY

From these "vast perspectives" we must now descend to the more concrete problems facing French foreign policy. Less grandiose, they have the advantage, however, of being current and sometimes burning.

Military security

Above all, it is the *security* of the country which involves the most delicate choices. The French have a horror of war and know that their territory will be ravaged if war takes place even in a conventional form. How can they escape this horror? "Neutralism" resulting in a neutrality of the Swiss type and consequently in a denunciation of the Atlantic Pact is a propaganda weapon of the Communists and, to a lesser degree, the ideal of some intellectuals. Its unreality is too flagrant in the perspective of the cold war for it to have the slightest chance of being adopted. It is within the framework of the Atlantic Pact that the basic problems present themselves.

Joint Western defenses   There, the choice can be clearly drawn between two principal tendencies. One, which is proverbially proclaimed by the United States and supported by the majority of its allies, notably Great Britain

and Western Germany, consists in seeking the maximum integration of the forces at the heart of SHAPE in such a way as to increase concrete solidarity among the allies. Since the presidency of John F. Kennedy, it has another aspect, which is that of increasing the conventional forces in such a way as to open solutions other than that of a nuclear riposte, which would lead to collective suicide. In this system, a division of responsibilities would be adopted. The United States, and, secondarily, Great Britain, would be the sole retainers of the weapon of thermonuclear reprisal. The other allies would contribute to defense by purely conventional divisions.

De Gaulle's views   The other conception is that of General de Gaulle and is quite far from being shared by all responsible French military men. It consists of several points: (1) the Atlantic Pact has a global responsibility, not just a European. On this point, the thesis of General de Gaulle seems, for the time being at least, to have won out since Mr. Dean Rusk lengthily expounded the problem of Cuba to the Atlantic Council meeting in Oslo in May 1961. (2) At the heart of the Atlantic Pact, the basic decisions should be taken not by the United States alone, but by a directorate of three Powers "of global vocation": the United States, Great Britain and France. By his memorandum of September 1958, General de Gaulle requested the formation of the directorate, which would have had the effect of giving France a part in the decisions concerning the use of American thermonuclear weapons— which the United States does not want at any price. This idea also provokes bitter criticism from Germany and Italy who do not recognize France's right to this pre-eminent place in the alliance, and from the British, who would prefer to play the role of brilliant seconds alone. (3) The thermonuclear threat to United States territory itself is making the Americans' resolution to defend Europe at any price more and more improbable. The Europeans, and particularly France, must consequently create their own force of thermonuclear dissuasion. (4) The national defense presumes the sacrifice of citizens to the nation. They will sacrifice themselves less willingly to supra-national entities (the defunct "European army") or even simply integrated bodies. Thence General de Gaulle's evident tendency to oppose the integration of forces at the heart of SHAPE. It is known that he excluded the French air force from it, and, for times of war, the French Mediterranean fleet. He has also refused to allow the installation of American launching sites on French territory.

Of these four points, the third and the fourth raise the most serious problems. The first has apparently been accepted and it appears that President Kennedy has convinced President de Gaulle that the second is absolutely impracticable.

Is the refusal to integrate (point 4) the expression of a certain "neutralism" on the part of General de Gaulle, or rather a certain "patriotic egoism?" Or else, is it only a question of means of pressure for trying to obtain point 2? In this case, the means have been inefficient and clumsy, because they have severely irritated the Americans and other allies of France. But perhaps General de Gaulle would agree to abandon this and to "reintegrate" if he obtained more satisfaction on point 3.

Nuclear weapons for France Objections made to the creation of the French striking force are of various sorts. The British, it appears, dread seeing France gain access to the privileged position they themselves acquired by creating a little stockpile of bombs. The American arguments are more positive: In the first place, the number of people possessing these instruments must not be multiplied, as that would increase the insane risk of a fatal accident. The French effort encourages other countries, and notably China, to follow suit. (One can, however, ask what force in the world could keep the Chinese from aiming at this goal with all their strength, whether France produces bombs or not).

Secondly, if France pursues its experiments, conclusion of an agreement on stopping nuclear experiments becomes more difficult. (It is true that in Paris, President Kennedy, discour-

aged by the Soviet demand for veto rights on the control, seemed sceptical about the possibility of reaching such an agreement). By refusing to take part in the Geneva Conference in 1962, France has raised a supplementary dissatisfaction in the United States. On the other hand, the new nuclear experiments by the Soviet Union and the United States have reduced the French refusal of a moratorium to a problem of insignificant size.

Thirdly, because of the weakness of its means, France risks exhausting its forces in manufacturing for itself an obsolete and inefficient weapon. The Algerian War having prevented it over a long period of time from furnishing NATO with the conventional divisions it promised, if it chooses to provide itself with an atomic weapon in addition, it will no longer have the means for constituting the conventional divisions. American leaders, strongly influenced by Henry Kissinger, Paul Nitze, and Arnold Wolfers, consider that these conventional divisions are a vital necessity.

There is a great deal of speculation as to whether the "little deterrent" France could have in a few years can really play a dissuasive role. If, as General Gallois says, the risk is proportional to the stake, the conquest of France representing a small stake, the risk of destruction France could inflict on its adversaries would be sufficient to end all desire for conquest on their part. Others, however, consider the "big" deterrent the only effective deterrent. France, being incapable of creating this, must then either envisage a "Europeanization" of the manufacture of the bomb (but this poses almost insoluble problems of decision, and Germany has promised not to manufacture nuclear armaments)—or else to rely entirely on American protection, or, an intermediary solution, to do as the British, that is, to consider a national nuclear armament as a small complement to the formidable force of a big ally in defending Europe under any condition.

One wonders then, as we have noted above, whether the creation of the French striking force does not have much more of a political than a strategic role: to elicit a certain "respect" because one possesses a terrible weapon. Also it should convince the American leaders that in order to free a part of the French budget and permit France to create conventional divisions, they would be wiser to decide to give France, if not bombs, at least the very expensive rockets to carry them. Another alternative would be to give France facilities to build atomic submarines with Polaris missiles.

For a while it appeared that some people in the American executive branch of government were not far from a solution of this kind, but President Kennedy himself, in 1962, took a negative position. The American Congress has remained very hostile to the arrangement suggested above and has given no indication that it would be willing to revise the Mac-Mahon law. It is true that General de Gaulle's perspectives always take the long view. Who can say what the situation will be in 1970? For the moment, between the solution of conventional integration and the Gaullist solution, it is evidently the second which has been chosen. There is no sign either to foreshadow the slightest deviation in the attitude of the French president.

European unification

A second basic problem is that of European unification. It can be formulated thus: are there possibilities that in a few years a certain number of Western European countries will accept the constitution of a supra-national government to manage common affairs? Is it in the interest of France to take this path?

Creation of the Common Market   At the time General de Gaulle assumed power in 1958, existing institutions appeared to be doubly menaced. On the one hand there was the new chief of the French government, great adversary of the European Defense Community in his time, little in favor of "technocrats" like Jean Monnet, seconded, moreover, by M. Michel Debré who had always favored the idea

of European integration. Would he not put an end forever to the first effective realization of European unification, the Common Market? On the other hand, the British, very hostile to the Common Market, appeared resolved to "drown" it in a greater "zone of free trade" which, as they presented it, would have placed them at the conflux of two privileged zones, that of imperial preference and that of Europe. Now, the weak cabinets of the Fourth Republic appeared resigned to ceding to British pressure. The profound difference between the Common Market then being born and the zone of free trade is that the zone of free trade limited itself to being a customs union whereas the Common Market envisaged the progressive integration of the economies: mobility of capital and labor, co-ordination of banking systems, salaries, social security, and the like.

Through an unexpected reverse of the situation, perhaps due to the influence of Chancellor Adenauer, General de Gaulle gave evidence from the summer of 1958 on that he intended not only to pursue the creation of the Common Market, but even to accelerate it and above all to defend it from that engulfing which the zone of free trade would have constituted. Strongly supported by Germany and Italy, France won a decisive diplomatic victory. In 1959, the British resigned themselves to abandoning the project of the free trade zone. They tactically created the zone of the "Outer Seven," then "Eight" oriented their propaganda, particularly in the United States, toward the idea that dividing Europe into two blocs was a disaster. Certain German circles—particularly the Minister of the Economy, Dr. Ludwig Erhard—and the Netherlands, more tempted by the commercial aspects of the problem than by integration, supported this thesis. The Republican government in the United States hesitated; but the subsequent Democratic administration clearly aligned itself in favor of the Common Market, to such a degree that President Kennedy, it seemed, exerted strong pressure on Mr. Macmillan for the United Kingdom to join the Common Market. The Prime Minister applied for membership in the Common Market in July 1961.

The problem of economic unification has not been solved, however substantial the progress has been in the integration of economies in the heart of the Common Market. Delicate points remain. One of these points, agriculture, where French pressure results in the maintenance of fairly high tariff barriers, was resolved between the Six in January 1962, after hard but fruitful negotiations. But the British, accustomed to inexpensive food, did not want such tariffs. The question arose whether Great Britain, followed by certain other countries, would agree to join the Common Market, with its substantial amount of integration or whether the process of integration would be slowed down by Britain's entrance. In other words, the question was one of knowing which would win out, economic integration or a simple customs union. The French were disposed not to admit England in the Economic Community without her accepting all that was achieved by the Six. But other members—notably, the Benelux Countries—preferred to have England in the Community, even at the expense of some integrating achievements. If Chancellor Adenauer and General de Gaulle remain at the heads of their respective countries for several years longer, one can estimate that economic integration will triumph, even if it must be delayed, or even exclude British adherence.

Prospects for political integration   On this hypothesis, is progress toward political integration possible? General de Gaulle, undoubtedly impressed by what the "grandeur" of a Europe would be in which France would play the primary role, has not stopped developing his position. He started from what was called "the Europe of fatherlands," to which he prefers giving the name "Europe of States" in which the distinction between nations would remain absolute. But, on the one hand, he requested of his partners—in vain, following Dutch opposition—the creation of a permanent secretariat of the "European Economic Community"; on the other hand, he spoke of the necessity for establishing a "Confederation" and even recognized a "grand and solemn European referendum" which has, until now,

evoked no enthusiasm abroad except in Italy. What he wants is *political* co-operation, not the kind of *technocratic integration* represented by the High Authority of the "European Coal and Steel Community" which does not enjoy his favor.

The last hypothesis: if, when the General leaves the government, economic integration is almost achieved, all the bases will have been established for political integration. In fact, integrated economies presume more than an interchangeability of currencies. The necessity for a common monetary policy implies in effect the creation of a common political organ.

Rapprochement with Eastern Europe   But the originality of the Gaullist position lies in that the General clearly indicated that he believes in a distant, but inevitable relaxation of tensions between the East and West of Europe. When the Soviets sent Gagarin into space, he congratulated Moscow for this great "European" achievement. That is the reason for which, doubtless, he alone among all the Westerners has declared that France considers the Oder-Neisse frontier between Germany and Poland definitive. For him, then, a united Europe will one day stretch toward the East:

> Without a doubt, the Communist regime, applied in Russia for forty-two years, which is opposed in all its ideology to the free world, will lose its virulence under the profound drive of the people toward what man wishes for by nature: a better life and liberty . . . Without a doubt, Soviet Russia, although having helped communism to install itself in China, will realize that nothing can make her be other than Russia, a white nation of Europe, conquering a part of Asia and, in sum, very well endowed with land, mines, factories, and riches, facing the yellow multitude which is China, countless and miserable, indestructible and ambitious, building by trials a power one cannot measure and looking around her at the spaces over

which she will have to spread one day.[23]

Decolonization

The third great problem facing the France of today, as well as all the Western Powers, is decolonization. It involves preventing the newly independent countries from swinging into the Communist camp; of weaving solid ties with them to keep them in the Western camp and to acquaint them with its values. How has France, which so recently was a great colonial Power, solved its colonial problems? For the moment, let us leave aside the most tragic of them, the Algerian affair, and try to give an account of the decolonization undertaken by France.

The early stages   During the first phase, from 1945 to 1958, what could be called "decolonization against the grain" took place. Syria and Lebanon in 1945, Vietnam (North and South), Cambodia and Laos in 1954, Morocco in 1955, Tunisia in 1956—received their independence after successful pressures brought on the governments of the Fourth Republic.

Then came "spontaneous decolonization." It consisted of first offering to various overseas territories the possibility of immediate independence outside the Community if they cast a negative vote in the referendum of September 28, 1958. Only Guinea took advantage of this, and the French government accentuated, doubtless by an error of calculation, the character of rupture invested in the "no" of the Guineans.

But very quickly, membership in a community which kept certain privileges for France, such as, in particular, the conduct of foreign affairs, appeared unsatisfactory to a number of the new "states." Without hesitation, General de Gaulle, preferring good relations to the maintenance of formal ties, offered the members of the Community independence pure and simple, allowing each the conduct of foreign affairs and candidacy for admission to the United Nations. All chose this direction. The same thing took place, through another process, for the two former mandates of Togoland and the Cameroons. Outside of Guinea, this then made fourteen newly independent states (if one does not take into account the temporary federation of Mali formed by Senegal and Sudan).

At present, of the former French colonies, all that remain under French sovereignty are small, scattered territories: (1) the four overseas departments: Guiana; Martinique and Guadeloupe in the West Indies; the island of Réunion in the Indian Ocean. These are territories which chose assimilation: (2) the French coast of Somaliland, with Djibouti, at the entrance to the Red Sea; (3) The Comores Islands near Madagascar; (4) in the Pacific Ocean, the big island of New Caledonia, and French Polynesia (several hundreds of little Pacific islands); (5) the little islands of Saint-Pierre and Miquelon near Newfoundland. The "five cities of India" went back *de facto* to the Indian Republic.

Some of these territories may soon request independence. But the scantiness of their populations or their dispersion, renders independence fairly precarious. The "general councils" (the local assemblies) of the West Indies pronounced themselves as being quasi-unanimous in favor of maintaining the status of French departments, as opposed to the idea of belonging to the Caribbean Federation. The only real political problem is that of Djibouti. Will this territory join big Somaliland, Moslem and strongly influenced by Nasser's Egypt? Or will it join Ethiopia for which it has been the natural market for more than fifty years, thanks to the French railroad line from Djibouti to Addis Ababa? There lies a difficult choice.

French-speaking Black Africa   The problem of the new states of Black Africa is evidently much more important. All are fundamentally

[23] November 10, 1959, *Année Politique*, 1959, p. 633.

French-speaking. Madagascar alone seems capable one day of developing Hova sufficiently to make a native scientific language out of it. This has a basic importance for the policy of French cultural expansion. At the U.N., French —one of the two official languages—has seen its side abruptly increase with the entrance of 14 new French-speaking states.

But their political relations with France are of varied and complex characters. Only the four states of former French Equatorial Africa (Gabon, Congo-Brazzaville, the Central African Republic and Chad), Senegal, Mauritania and Madagascar now belong to the "Community," which has become a sort of Commonwealth where nations are "co-operating" with France by bilateral contracts. But six other countries have moved toward signing agreements of co-operation with France: the four states of the "Council of Understanding" (Conseil de l'Entente)—the Ivory Coast, Dahomey, Upper Volta, Niger—as well as Togoland and the Cameroons. The latter, while not entirely a black country, takes part in the union which was concluded among the other 11 states linked to France. These (11 African states and Madagascar) formed the "Afro-Malgache Union" (Union africaine et Malgache) which is commonly called the "Brazzaville group," a pro-Western and even pro-French group whose most developed points appear to be Senegal, the Ivory Coast, Gabon, and Madagascar.

But, along with the Brazzaville group, another group has been formed, cool or even frankly hostile toward ties with the former metropolis. It is called the "Casablanca group," because Morocco took the initiative of calling a conference of the malcontents. Morocco was embittered by the Algerian war and above all by the independence of Mauritania, which it hoped to annex. Morocco also opposed the retention of French sovereignty over the ex-Algerian Sahara, half of whose territory it also claimed. Guinea and Mali also are members of this group, as is Ghana. A union of Guinea, Ghana, and Mali has theoretically been proclaimed. One of the countries of the "Brazzaville group," Upper Volta, sometimes appears to be attracted by the other group. In any case,

Upper Volta has eliminated its tariffs in regard to Ghana and has maintained them toward other members of the Council of Understanding (Conseil de l'Entente).

These are only the beginnings of a complex process whose future path it is difficult to foresee. It is certain, for example, that the countries of the "Brazzaville group" on the whole approved French atomic tests in the Sahara, while those of the "Casablanca group" protested with indignation and with some exaggeration, and see in these explosions, actually harmless, both a mortal danger for Africans and a symbol of French colonialism. It is probable that the independence of Algeria will make France's position firmer, without eliminating all disagreements.

Aid to the former colonies   In the various agreements of co-operation with France, there are military clauses. France sometimes keeps bases and sends military instructors and officers who assist the small national armies, and participate at times in the struggle with rebels against the central government. For example, France gives support in the Cameroons against the insurgents of the "Union of the Cameroon peoples," who are more or less under Communist direction. In addition, France has occasionally promised its military support to its former colonies.

It seems to me that this policy is not without danger. There is in all the newly independent countries a profound desire for "non-engagement." Rather than seeking ties of alliance, is it not preferable to systematically encourage the tendencies of the new states toward a "positive neutralism?" This ideology—for Africans and many Asiatics—seems to be the best barrier against the Communist ideology. Basically, the Communists are much more hostile than the Westerners toward neutralism; they favor only a false neutralism which would be in reality a weapon of war against the West. The pro-neutralist policy of France in Laos and Cambodia, for example, seems much more healthy for the future than past American efforts to create in Laos an artificial regime, pro-Western, but a generator of oppositions which ultimately favored the Communist Pathet-Lao.

It is on the cultural plane, as already noted, and the economic plane that French efforts should be intensified. France's aid to underdeveloped countries which depended on its sovereignty not long ago is considerable. It represents, compared to United States aid, a distinctly higher percentage of the gross national product (1.7% for France—0.5% for the U.S.A.). This is one of the "vast enterprises" to which General de Gaulle summons the French people: continuing this aid, intensifying it, organizing it, making it stable, while waiting to extend it, collectively, to other underdeveloped regions of the world such as India and Latin America, for example. One of the aspects of the French effort consists, moreover, in inducing its European partners to make a collective contribution to the aid of African countries. The latter are keenly interested in this effort, and participate in the relevant negotiations which take place in Brussels, headquarters of the Common Market. It is there, actually on the basis of equality of rights, that there is a true possibility of realizing the concept, mythical until now, of "Eurafrica."

Algeria

The Algerian problem impeded and delayed all these efforts. It poisoned them because it allowed the idea to develop that France was still "colonialist." But after a cease-fire agreement was reached on March 18, 1962, at the end of long negotiations at Evian, the situation became much simpler.

De Gaulle's proposals   In offering the Algerians self-determination on September 16, 1959, General de Gaulle presented them with a choice between three hypotheses: "joining France"—for which the French of Algeria and a part of the army officers have fought desperately; "Secession"—complete separation from France with a "regrouping" of the French

of Algeria and the pro-French Moslems, resulting perhaps in a division of the Palestinian sort, or the return of the Algerian French to France; and "Association." He clearly specified that the intermediary solution did not signify a half-independence, but implied the total "external and internal sovereignty" of Algeria which would freely associate itself with France through various treaties and would benefit from the latter's massive economic and technical aid. His preference more and more ostensibly went to the third solution. Lastly, he would have liked a truce to precede any negotiation with the nationalist leaders of the "Provisional Government of the Republic of Algeria" (GPRA), but he permitted the beginning of negotiations before the truce. The fact that a part of the army supported the "activists" grouped in the rebel "Secret Army Organization"—OAS, who completely reject Secession and Association—made it necessary to proceed slowly.

Nationalist objections   What were the reasons for the Algerian Nationalists' hesitation to accept these offers? Briefly, the principal divergences stemmed from the fact that: (1) the GPRA wanted to be considered the *sole* representative body of Algerians which, the French felt, did not correspond to reality. (2) The GPRA wanted auto-determination to be applied to Algeria *including* the two departments of the Sahara (Oasis and Saoura). France, in 1957, had artificially detached the Sahara from Algeria. But, from 1898 to 1900, when the Sahara was occupied, it had been equally artificially attached, for reasons of administrative convenience, to Algeria in the north and to French West Africa in the south. This means that in the south, the Sahara is now divided between Mauritania, Mali, Niger and Chad. France, which is interested in the Sahara for economic reasons—the important production of oil and natural gas undertaken in 1954—might abandon its sovereignty in return for an agreement for rights of economic exploitation with the immediate neighbors of the Sahara. But it must be pointed out that Morocco claims the western half of the former

Algerian Sahara. (3) The GPRA appeared little disposed to allow a solution, as was done in Cyprus, in which, in an Algerian republic, the 12 percent of French Europeans would constitute an organized community. They wanted to accept the French only as plain Algerian citizens, or as resident and non-privileged foreigners. The experience of Tunisia and Morocco showed that this would meet with opposition from the French army. (4) The GPRA appeared little disposed toward allowing France to keep her big naval base of Mers-el-Kébir near Oran, but finally, they gave in and agreed to a lease of the base to France for 15 years.

Moreover, the GPRA was certainly divided. Those of its members who followed M. Bourguiba's suggestions accepted the idea of association which also appealed to Tunisia. Those who followed Chinese and Russian advice, wanted a complete break with France with no association of any sort. This tendency was formally denounced by the GPRA. But there were increasing rumors that the military leaders of the FLN did not believe in any "co-operation" with France and preferred a collectivist revolution with the elimination of French influence rather than any French aid, however important that aid could be.

The consequences of disagreement As a result, the Algerian War, painful but not very deadly, at least for the French, lasted seven years. France could not be beaten in it, but neither could the guerrillas be totally crushed. The hope of those who desired the continuation of the war was the "internationalization" of the conflict, that is, a strong pressure exerted on France by the U.S.S.R., or even the United States, obliging it to give in. It is clear that the United States could only be induced to exert such pressure—which risked destroying the Atlantic Alliance—if a massive intervention of Communists, probably Chinese airplanes, had made the Algerian problem an element of the East-West conflict. It is equally clear that the U.S.S.R. and China would have an interest in forcing the hand of the United States.

Conversely, all Africans who feel a large measure of solidarity with the West, like M. Bourguiba or the "Brazzaville group," had a major interest in promoting the negotiations. M. Bourguiba threw all his weight in this direction. Prior to the solution of the Algerian conflict, France was handicapped in all its policies. The policy of security was weakened since the major part of its army was immobilized by a counter-guerrilla war. Its European policy suffered, for its partners did not want to be taken for supporters of colonialism. And its policy of decolonization and agreement with the African countries was hampered because the African countries necessarily felt a solidarity with the Algerians who were fighting for their liberty. Likewise, its policy in the United Nations was made more difficult.

Unfortunately, the Evian cease-fire did not put an end to bloodshed in Algeria. A new revolt had started, a revolt of the "Europeans"—more than one million, including a big majority of poor people—against the Evian decisions. The O.A.S. group of rebel officers commanded by former General Salan, supported by a big majority of the "French of Algeria" started a new guerrilla warfare, which was as bloody and cruel as the earlier fighting, but probably less legitimate. To defend the myth of "French Algeria," they tried to sabotage the armistice by provoking clashes between Moslems and Europeans. They hoped, vainly, that the Army would follow them. The Army did not follow, and this was General de Gaulle's greatest achievement. But while they had no chance at all to win, they were able to create such resentment among the Moslems that co-operation between France and Independent Algeria and between Moslems and Europeans in Algeria became much more difficult.

Fundamental problems The real issue is this: does decolonization in a country with an exceptionally high percentage of settlers imply the departure and exile of those settlers? Or is there a formula which will permit at least a number of them to stay and be integrated in the new state? This problem, which often has led to bloodshed, tears and sufferings, also faces the British in Southern Rhodesia. Colonization implied equality—and some racism—in one direction. When the former subjects become sovereign, will they be rational enough not to create inequality and practice racism in the opposite direction? Economically speaking, will it be possible for the new state to integrate a minority with a higher standard of living than the citizens of the majority? Certainly, it would be economically irrational to get rid of people who are essential for the economic expansion of the new state. Actually, roughly 800,000 French settlers have left Algeria for France and only 200,000 remain. While this creates difficult problems for French internal policy, it is also an economic stimulus. Decolonization is the goal, admitted by the majority of the French of France. But reaching it is far from simple.

Disagreements with the United Nations

Arraigned every year in the United Nations, and often by countries which are little qualified to give lessons in civilization, it is normal for France to feel little solidarity with this organization. The majority of French public opinion is indifferent or hostile to the U.N. General de Gaulle speaks ironically of the "Nations called united." We know that as an adversary of United Nations' intervention in the Congo, convinced of its ineffectiveness, he refused for France to contribute financially.

The wisdom of this position has been questioned. It seems good and salutary to Frenchmen to look reality in the face and, instead of slogans and illusions, to recognize publicly that the U.N. is little capable of maintaining peace and order. In this sphere, "wishful thinking" is more harmful than useful.

But the circumstances in which France expressed the little esteem it had for the U.N. were inopportune. These sentiments were expressed at the moment of the entrance of the French-speaking African states, of whom a great number are ready to support France in numerous cases. Instead of "sulking at" the United Nations, would it not be wiser to "play the game" there—while knowing well that this game does not touch the essence of things? After all, the United Nations has at least the advantage of being the place in which new and weak states can express their opinions and feel themselves the equals of the old and powerful nations. It is the place in which freshly appointed diplomats form and train themselves. It would have been preferable to silence the scepticism and resentment.

This is all the more true because, in the most ambitious of the enterprises of General de Gaulle—collective aid to underdeveloped countries—the United Nations can be essential in making the aid of the rich to the poor lose that aspect of inequality, paternalistic and disagreeable, which it always keeps when aid is unilateral.

If the "grandeur" the present French government is seeking is not the return to the past, but the desire to turn itself toward the future and to make France continue to play a profoundly civilizing role, French policy must avoid being supercilious. Only then can a strong and democratic government which indisputably has the support of public opinion, exert in the world an influence worthy of the proud and generous country whose destiny it has taken in hand.

BIBLIOGRAPHY

Editor's Suggestions

Aron, Raymond and Lerner, Daniel. *France— Steadfast and Changing: The Fourth and Fifth Republic.* Cambridge: Harvard U. Press, 1960.

de Gaulle, Charles, *War Memoirs.* Vol. I, *The Call to Honor,* New York: The Viking Press, 1955; vol. II, *Unity.* New York: Simon & Schuster, 1959; vol. III, *Salvation.* New York: Simon & Schuster, 1960.

Duroselle, J. B. *La Politique étrangère et ses fondements.* Paris: Armand Colin, 1954.

Duroselle, J. B. "French Diplomacy in the Post-World War Period," in Kertesz, Stephen D., and Fitzsimons, M. A., *Diplomacy in a*

Changing World. South Bend, Ind.: U. of Notre Dame Press, 1959.

Furniss, Edgar, Jr. *France: Troubled Ally.* New York: Harper & Brothers, 1960.

Howard, J. E. *Parliament and Foreign Policy in France.* London: Cresset Press, 1948.

Luëthy, Herbert. *France Against Herself.* New York: Frederick A. Praeger, Inc., 1955.

McKay, Donald C. *United States and France.* Cambridge: Harvard U. Press, 1951.

Macridis, Roy C. and Brown, Bernard E. *The De Gaulle Republic: Quest for Unity.* Homewood, Ill.: The Dorsey Press, 1960.

ABOUT THE AUTHOR

SVEN HENNINGSEN was born in 1910. After completing his undergraduate studies at the University of Copenhagen, he continued his
work at the University of Gothenburg where he received his Ph.D.
degree in 1944. Dr. Henningsen currently holds the position of Professor of Contemporary History and Political Science at the University
of Copenhagen. He has also been a visiting professor at the University
of Minnesota and at Makerere College in Uganda. He has written the
following books: *The Polish Corridor and Danzig,* 1936; *The Far East
and the Great Powers,* 1941; *Studies in Economic Liberalism,* 1944;
International Politics, 1946; and *The North Atlantic Treaty,* 1954.

ABOUT THE CHAPTER

The geographic position of Denmark was responsible both for her
growth to the position of a Major Power and then for her decline in
both size and influence. Professor Henningsen carefully evaluates these
geographic factors and then turns to an historical survey of the foreign
policy of Denmark. The author notes that "historical analysis leads to
the conclusion that a small state's power potential, and its ability to
defend vital national interests with its own forces, have rapidly deteriorated and for all practical purposes disappeared."

The largest portion of this essay is devoted to a careful analysis of
the vital national interests of Denmark and how the major problems
of world politics impinge on them. Attention is given both to specific
territorial problems and to broader interests. Within this general framework the author discusses major world problems and the attitude Denmark has taken towards them.

Professor Henningsen notes at the conclusion of his essay that the
currents of world politics since World War II have caused Denmark
to abandon traditional policies of neutrality and side with the West.
He also notes the rapid changes in Europe which call for a continuing
examination of Denmark's goals and policies.

3

THE FOREIGN POLICY OF DENMARK

S V E N   H E N N I N G S E N

University of Copenhagen

THE GEOGRAPHICAL SETTING

Location

From a geographical point of view, Denmark is a connecting link between continental Europe and Scandinavia. The Jutland peninsula rests on the top of the European continent. The Danish Straits—the Belts and the Sound—are links between the Baltic in the south and Kattegat and Skagerrak in the east and north, leading to the west coast of Sweden and southern Norway, but also to Great Britain and the ancient and modern great harbor-cities of Western Europe. Western Jutland is washed by the North Sea. But the lack of natural harbors on this coast was for many centuries one of the reasons why Denmark's interests were primarily directed towards the Baltic area and Scandinavia. The Sound and the Belts thus connected Denmark with the outer world. Through them the seafaring nations of Western Europe reached the Baltic. Likewise, the peoples inhabiting the Baltic's shores had to pass through the Sound and the Belts in order to get out to the oceans. This gave Denmark from an economic as well as a military point of view a key role to play.

The double position of being directly connected with the European mainland, as well as being the doorkeeper of one of Europe's crossroads has, through the centuries, created some of Denmark's most important foreign policy problems. The political, economic and cultural interests and influences, generated by this geographical position, have constantly affected and formed the life of the Danish people. It has been its task not only to adapt these foreign impulses to its own needs and traditions, but also in many instances to be the intermediary between Europe and the rest of Scandinavia. Motivated by either strategic, political or economic considerations, Denmark tried for centuries not only to gain firm control of the Baltic and its shores, but also to dominate Scandinavia.

In evaluating the importance of geographical position on Denmark's foreign policies, it is also significant that the country is placed in one of the corners of Europe. It has been living on the outskirts more or less remote from the main arteries of European politics. That may have saved it from many dangers. But it also excluded it from valuable influences and explains certain isolationist attitudes towards European problems.

The Sound and the Belts were, until the age of railways and airplanes, Denmark's most important means of transportation and communication with the outer world. They also were the connecting links in a country consisting of many islands. Geography has thus been one of the most important factors in creating the Danish state.

Geographical conditions also were instrumental in another respect in establishing the contours of the Danish state. In the south, a big area of woodlands created a natural barrier between the Danes and the Germans. East of the Sound, similar great forests, running through the middle of Sweden, also constituted a rather impenetrable border line between the Danes and the Swedes. The present Swedish provinces of Skåne, Halland and Blekinge thus became Danish, tied to the Danish islands by the passable highroad—the Sound. The disappearance of these geographical borders created foreign policy problems of decisive importance.

Political implications

These basic geographic factors have been a fruitful challenge in the life of the Danish people. They have also been an element of frustration and a cause of Denmark's diminishing size and influence. They help to explain why Danish kings for a long period ruled not only most of Scandinavia and for a short period England, but also parts of northern Germany. This powerful position was gradually lost. When the rivalry between the Danish and Swedish kings over the mastery of Scandinavia weakened

both countries, new European Great Powers—England and Holland, Prussia and Russia—became interested in the Baltic area for economic as well as military reasons. As these new factors in European politics made themselves more and more felt, the relative power of Denmark was further reduced. But the Sound and the Belts retained their influence; they now became an area of interest and conflict between these states and important in their relations with Denmark.

Even under changed conditions of communications and power relations between the states of Europe, the Northern Straits have retained an importance not only in European but, in the age of the Super-Powers, also in international politics. Although the changes in military technology have diminished and certainly changed the strategic problems connected with the Baltic area, the Belts and the Sound are still important in the strategical thinking and planning of the states involved. Any Power who either wants to penetrate into the Baltic or break through to the North Sea and the Atlantic must, in one way or another, win control over the Danish waters.

Being an island kingdom, Denmark became a seafaring state. Seaborne trade with other nations has always been a vital interest and its political and military protection constant problems of foreign policy. Until the beginning of the nineteenth century, Denmark was a strong naval Power. The rule of Danish kings stretched to the Faroe islands, Iceland, and Greenland in the North Atlantic; they had possessions in the West Indies, on the coasts of Africa and in India. This powerful position has gradually been lost. Denmark is today, apart from a small minority of Germans in North Schleswig, a nationally homogeneous nation. Of former possessions, she only retains the Faroe islands and Greenland, which have become integrated parts of the kingdom.

The second decisive geographical factor, constantly influencing Danish foreign policy, has been the land frontier with Germany. The border area, protected by neither mountains nor rivers, has been an easily passable gateway. Since the many islands are unprotected by nature and since Denmark is very small, the country is, from a strategic point of view, vulnerable and difficult to defend, particularly against modern weapons. When nationalism in the nineteenth century became the most important single element in relations between Denmark and Germany, two wars resulted. The German occupation of Denmark during the Second World War illustrates the significance of Danish territory in a great modern war, as well as the importance for Denmark itself of the land frontier with Germany. Since the Second World War, the ramifications of this factor have changed with the presence of great Soviet forces in Eastern Germany. But fundamentally, it is a new version of an old problem.

Through the centuries, geography has thus played a major part in creating Denmark's foreign policies. Two issues stand out clearly: relations with Scandinavia and Germany. The character and content of these issues and their relative importance have changed in the course of history. Other questions—as for example relations with Great Britain and Russia—have been important, particularly in modern times. But the Nordic and German problems have through the ages remained key foreign policy issues.

THE HISTORICAL DEVELOPMENT OF DANISH FOREIGN POLICY

Early history

Since about 800 A.D., when the contours of the Danish kingdom began to crystallize, political actions and reactions towards neighbors, i.e. a foreign policy, are discernible. This foreign policy was vigorous and expansionist in the Middle Ages. But, following the development of the European Great Power structure, an autonomous Danish foreign policy gradually disappeared. It became more and more conditioned by the interests of the European Great Powers, in particular Great Britain. From the beginning of the eighteenth century on Russia, which became the dominating Power in Northern Europe, influenced Danish policy. Later in the same century, Prussia increased its influence when it extended its power into the Baltic area.

Denmark remained neutral while the Great Powers fought on the Continent, in North America and India and, after 1793, the coalition wars against revolutionary France. Danish trade and shipping flourished. In 1807, however, Napoleon and Alexander I concluded the agreement on the Continental System and secretly decided that Denmark, if necessary, should be forced to observe it. Acting on rumors about this, the British government sent an expeditionary force to Denmark. Copenhagen was bombarded and forced to capitulate; the Danish fleet was destroyed.

After that humiliation, Denmark concluded an alliance with Napoleon and was belligerent until 1814. The consequences were catastrophic. Danish overseas trade was destroyed, finances were ruined and, in 1814, Denmark had to surrender Norway to Sweden.

From the 1830's on, German National-Liberals demanded the unification of the duchies of Schleswig and Holstein and their admission into the German confederation, while the Danish National-Liberals favored a fusion of Denmark proper with Danish Schleswig, excluding the German Holstein. Both movements were deeply nationalistic, but simultaneously claimed "historical rights," disregarding actual nationality lines in the duchies.

The first decades of the 19th century saw the dying-out of centuries-old enmity between Swedes and Danes. Liberals in both countries supported the Scandinavian movement instead, and its more ardent adherents hoped for a political unification of the Nordic countries.

The Danes expected from the Scandinavian movement help against Germany, while the Swedes desired to find support for their latent conflict with Russia over Finland. Considering traditionally close Danish-Russian relations, this dichotomy in aims shows the inner weakness of the Scandinavian movement. The negotiations about a Danish-Swedish alliance ended unsuccessfully in 1863, when the dispute over Schleswig led to war between Denmark and Prussia-Austria. The numerically smaller and badly equipped Danish army had to fight the war alone and was decisively defeated. In the peace of Vienna of 1864, Schleswig and Holstein were ceded to Austria and Prussia. Although the loss of the Danish part of Schleswig was never accepted as final, a growing majority of the Danish people after 1864 rejected the idea of regaining it or protecting Denmark's independence through alliances.

The twentieth century

The successive governments after 1864 followed a policy of strict neutrality, conditioned by the balance of power structure of European politics. Germany's overwhelming and growing power, Britain's declining interest in the Baltic area, and the German-Russian animosity after the turn of the century gradually forced Danish politicians, after 1900, to consider whether an alliance with Germany would be the best guarantee for Danish security. This idea remained untried. However, influential Danish politicians and diplomats, on the eve of the Great War, were convinced that in case of a European war Denmark could not under any circumstances permit itself to be among Germany's enemies.

This "realist" approach to neutrality carried Denmark through the First World War without becoming involved. The Versailles Treaty of 1919 made the return of the Danish-minded part of Schleswig possible and solved the one outstanding problem of Danish foreign policy.

Denmark thought that the establishment of the League of Nations and the Covenant's promise of a general reduction of armaments was the solution to the country's security problem. In 1922 a defense law was passed, radi-cally reducing Danish military strength. The dichotomy between reliance on the League and a continuing neutralist attitude was neither faced nor solved.

The weakening of the League system in the 1930's and Hitler-Germany's growing power and aggressiveness led to open neutrality towards the League and the problem of European and international solidarity, and endeavors to extract guarantees from Germany. When Great Britain refused to promise help, the Danish government in 1937 indicated, without success, its willingness to conclude a non-aggression treaty with Germany. Such a treaty was concluded in 1939 when Hitler proposed it and the Danish government did not feel that it was in a position to reject the German offer.

In World War II, Denmark tried again to stay neutral, but the interests of the Great Powers brought Scandinavia into the orbit of war. After the Soviet attack on Finland, the Germans attacked Denmark and Norway on April 9, 1940. Confronted with overwhelming force, the Danish Government decided to capitulate. The attack on Denmark was a secondary, but necessary part of the German plan to occupy Norway in order to prevent a British-French occupation and to give Germany greater operational freedom in the U-boat warfare in the Atlantic.

During the first period of the occupation, a government functioned on the theory of a neutral, but occupied Denmark. Gradually, the connections with the free world were interrupted, and, after successive conflicts with the Germans, the Danish government stopped to function in August 1943.

For the rest of the war, an official Danish foreign policy did not exist. Fragments of a policy were created by diplomats in the United States and Great Britain and by the "Liberation Council," directing the underground war. The purpose of this "policy of resistance" was to create as close connections as possible with the enemies of the Axis and prepare the moment when a Danish government could function again. This happened on May 5th, 1945. A new phase in Danish foreign policy began, which will be described below.

PROBLEMS OF NATIONAL POWER

Problems of national power—defined as a state's capability to defend avowed national interests—have several aspects. National power may be analyzed in connection with specific interests, for example economic aims; it can also be discussed under different circumstances, such as peace or conflict and war. The national interests of Denmark in times of peace will be discussed later on. The following analysis deals with only one vital aspect of the problem: Denmark's ability to protect its integrity and independence.

The diplomatic weapons of small countries

The surveys of geography and history have shown the importance of the Belts and the Sound and the vulnerability of Danish territory in case of war. We have also seen how the power of Denmark declined through the centuries. Consequently, it had to liquidate all aspirations of expansion in its area of interest. Confronted with Great Power ambitions, it was likewise unable to defend its integrity, although in the end, it preserved its independence. Since the 18th century, the major problem has been Germany's, Great Britain's and Russia's changing interest in the area. Each of these Powers either tried to prevent other Powers from controlling the Sound and the Belts and using Danish territory as a base for aggressive policies or attempted to use it themselves for the same purpose.

In trying to cope with these dangers against its integrity and independence, Denmark has shared the fate of other small states. The dependency on Great Power policies can clearly be observed from the 18th century on. As manpower and industry from the 19th century onwards became essential for military strength, it became impossible for Denmark to solve its defense and security problems effectively.

While defense policies and appropriations were constant issues in Danish politics from the 1870's on, the discussions reveal an "idealist" approach, confronted with a "realist" interpretation of national interests, rather than providing rational and adequate answers to strategic problems. Under the circumstances, a Danish military posture could only have two purposes: to defend the territory against accidental violations and, in case of direct attack, to react to the degree which political considerations and the morale of the people as a future independent nation demanded.

In her study of the power of smaller states,[1] Annette Fox reached the conclusion, that their chances of resisting Great Power pressures in times of crises and war depend to a large degree on their diplomacy's ability to play the interests of several Powers against each other. Danish experiences illuminate this concept. The British surprise attack in 1807, the war with the German Powers in 1863–64, World War I and the preceding period, and the German surprise attack in 1940 may be taken as examples of situations of the type, discussed by Annette Fox.

The first and fourth example were *coups,* leaving Denmark no possibilities of playing a diplomatic game. The second example, the war of 1863–64, showed, that Great Britain and Russia were not sufficiently interested to intervene effectively. In the decades before 1914 and during World War I, Denmark succeeded in staying out of conflicts between the Great Powers and war by adapting neutrality to changing situations. In 1807, 1864, and 1940, one Power was capable of applying overwhelming military force. The other Powers were either unprepared, not sufficiently interested in the Danish area, or engaged in other situations of greater importance to them.

In the period from the 1860's to 1918,

[1] Annette Baker Fox, *The Power of Small States,* Chicago: University of Chicago Press, 1959.

Denmark's security problem was dominated by German power. Great Britain did not any longer have a sufficiently strong interest in the Baltic or wanted Germany to balance Russia, and Russia was either more interested in other areas of the world or weakened vis-à-vis Germany. The conclusion must be, that Denmark in the three situations, where its integrity and independence were at stake, was dominated by one Power and of secondary importance to the other states. An attack would not present serious geographical obstacles and military resistance would be of minor importance, not raising serious risks.

The morale of the people

The occupation period from 1940 to 1945 raised, however, new aspects in regard to Danish ability to survive. While military resistance lasted only a few hours, the people's ability to resist the occupying Power's ideological attacks and the fundamentally civilian active resistance, which developed with increasing force and efficiency after 1943, showed that this kind of defense is vital and possible for a small nation. Resistance experiences from other European countries also emphasize this point of view.

The morale of a people is thus important as expressed in its ability to sabotage the intentions of an occupying Power. In this context it is also significant to emphasize the importance of national homogeneity. In Denmark, the national minority group turned out to be disloyal. The unreliability of political movements which had loyalties beyond the national state, was also obvious. This last phenomenon is directly related to another small nation problem in terms of national power: the economic-social stability, expressed in the democratic structure of society, and the loyalty of the overwhelming majority towards this ideal.

This was not only important for purposes of limiting collaboration with the occupation forces to small and insignificant groups; it was also important in regard to the ideals of significant groups within the active resistance movement. Although critical of the attitude of the older political parties, they professed democratic ideals and were at the end of the war willing to co-operate with the prewar political parties and form a coalition government with them.

This short analysis of Danish problems under foreign occupation indicates that, under certain conditions, the small state's power elements are important in solving problems of national interest and survival. But its power elements differ radically from those applied by the Great Powers.

Historical analysis leads to the conclusion that a small state's power potential, and its ability to defend vital national interests with its own forces, have rapidly deteriorated and for all practical purposes disappeared. This was to a great extent true in a world of traditional balance of power relations among several great states. So far, most discussions have reached the conclusion, that it is even more true in a world of bi-polar policies, based on nuclear capacity.

THE FOREIGN POLICY PROCESS

The Minister of Foreign Affairs

The responsibility for conducting foreign policy rests with the Minister of Foreign Affairs, who is a member of the Cabinet. Since 1849, when parliamentary rule began in Denmark, the members of this body have generally been active politicians, most often members of Parliament. For a long period, this was not always true of the Foreign Minister. He was often chosen from among diplomats or the nobility. The reasons for this were many. The party leaders felt that, among their active members, they did not have a candidate who had the desirable knowledge about foreign policy problems. Active politicians rarely had sufficient proficiency in foreign languages, a consideration which became decisive for choosing a diplomat or non-politician. The expenses and social obligations connected with the post may, in earlier times, have played a certain role. Neither did the parties in general encourage members to choose foreign policy as a career.

After 1864, foreign policy issues ceased to play a major part in Danish politics, while problems of domestic policies took on an overwhelming importance. While it is in general true that expertise and influence in domestic issues may lead to the highest posts in politics, foreign policy oriented politicians generally stop short of the premiership. That was particularly true in Denmark during the long period when neutrality was the accepted line of foreign policy, and it was considered a virtue for the country, not to have an active foreign policy.

This attitude has to some extent changed since 1949 when Denmark joined NATO. Although foreign policy is still more or less *terra incognita* for the majority of the members of Parliament, some have devoted more interest to it. The post of Foreign Minister has, since 1949 been filled with a politician of influence and this has given the post increased importance.

While the Foreign Minister has the political responsibility for the conduct of foreign policy and the administration of the Ministry of Foreign Affairs, major decisions are taken, or at least approved, by the Cabinet as a whole, and the Prime Minister has in this, as in all other questions, a decisive influence.

The role of Parliament

The influence of Parliament on foreign affairs has by and large followed the same pattern as in most Western European countries. Parliament has to ratify treaties and pass appropriations, covering the financial obligations originating from them. It also passes the budget of the Ministry of Foreign Affairs. None the less, before the First World War, members in general did not interest themselves to any great extent in foreign affairs. General debates on foreign policy problems were rare and did not betray any great interest or deeper knowledge about the issues.

The Minister of Foreign Affairs and his staff were furthermore very reluctant to give Parliament information about foreign policy issues. The problem, related to foreign policy, which did have a major place in Danish politics and consequently in the interest of Parliament, was defense. After 1870, the political parties disagreed about the type of defense to be chosen and, consequently, the costs. Indirectly connected with this issue was the neutrality policy and the content which the parties gave to it.

The demand for greater popular control of the conduct of foreign policy led in 1923 to legislation establishing a parliamentary committee for foreign affairs (*det udenrigspolitiske nævn*). The task of the committee was to control the conduct of foreign policy by asking questions and receiving information from the Minister of Foreign Affairs and other members of the Cabinet about policy issues and decisions. The sessions of this committee are secret, enabling the ministers to give information which could not be revealed in open meetings or be reported in the press.

Compared with, for example, the appropriations committee, the role of the foreign affairs committee seems, until 1945, to have been rather passive. The committee also had and still has the structural weakness that it does not have a secretariat to furnish the members with relevant information and provide a means for pertinent questions to the ministers and their officials.

After the war, the problem of relations between the authority of international organizations and the constitutional regulations about sovereignty have led to new legislation. The 1953 constitution contains provisions which are important in regard to Danish participation in international organizations with supranational authority. If the government signs a treaty, by which part of the national sovereignty is surrendered, Parliament must accept this by a ⅚th majority vote. If the law does not receive the necessary number of votes, but only the majority which is required for ordinary laws, the government may hold a plebiscite. Then, if a majority of the voters, representing at least 30 percent of those entitled to vote, cast their votes against the law, it is rejected.

The Folketing has the general control over foreign policy enjoyed by parliamentary governments. Parliament may furthermore appoint investigation committees. That happened for example in 1945, when a committee was appointed to investigate events leading to the German occupation in 1940 and the policies of the governments during the occupation period.

Danish participation in international organizations since 1945 has also led to greater parliamentary activity in foreign affairs. The delegations to, for example, the U.N. General Assembly and the Council of Europe are composed of party members who are, in most instances, members of Parliament. The lines to be followed by such delegations are formulated in general instructions, but the delegations have some freedom of action. In general, the debates in Parliament on questions of foreign policy have increased substantially since 1945.

The Foreign Office

The administration and execution of foreign policy is carried out through the Foreign Office, which is organized along traditional lines. The service is unified in the sense that officials alternately serve at home and in foreign posts. The positions as ambassadors or ministers are generally occupied by career diplomats. Since 1945 a few non-career people have been appointed to top positions, but they have then, as a consequence of their appointment, entered the service.

Traditionally, the Foreign Office personnel was recruited from applicants having a university law degree. Special training and entrance examinations are not required. A growing number of economists have, however, since the 1920's entered the service and reached top positions. The Foreign Office posts, particularly the important positions, were for a long period occupied by members of the nobility. This tradition continued longer in the Foreign Office than in other branches of the administration, but has now by and large disappeared. Since 1945 the number of Foreign Office personnel has greatly increased.

The inner organization of the Foreign Office has, however, by and large remained unchanged. While the growing importance of, for example, economic problems has led to the establishment within the administration of a policy analysis and planning organization for economics, this is not the case in regard to foreign policy. An organization like the Foreign Policy Planning Staff in the U.S. State Department does not exist in the Danish Foreign Office.

The director of the Foreign Office is a permanent official who has the administrative responsibility. His influence on policy decisions is important because Foreign ministers rely to a great extent on the advice of the departmental director. In so far as the interests of other ministries are involved, or their advice has importance for foreign policy decisions, their participation in the decision-making process takes place either through discussions among the ministers concerned or the officials. A formal system does not exist. Available information indicates that the liaison between the departments in some instances has been insufficient.

Pressure groups

While the decisions on major issues of foreign policy by and large reflect public opinion, as expressed by the political parties, newspapers, party associations and organizations, which can be labelled pressure groups, it is difficult to reach conclusions regarding the interplay between decision-makers and these groups in the policy-forming process. The debates in Parliament, on foreign policy problems generally move along very broad lines and the same is true about editorials in the newspapers.

Organizations representing economic interests clearly have an important influence on negotiations about trade agreements and economic problems in general. Representatives of such organizations directly participate in negotiations with the representatives of the opposite country or countries. Their influence has also been clear during negotiations about Danish participation in the Free Trade area, and lately the Common Market.

The picture is less clear, when it comes to more general questions about NATO, the United Nations or problems raised by general international events. On such issues public opinion media often limit themselves to purely reporting or expressing "moral" rather than "realistic" opinions. This reflects partly a certain lack of interest in foreign policy issues, stemming from a long period of neutrality, and partly the feeling in a small country of being powerless and therefore without influence.

THE NATIONAL INTEREST

An analysis of the national interest of Denmark and the attitudes which groups and parties take on this question, should start with a broad formulation of the concept of national interest. Denmark desires (1) to preserve the integrity and independence of the country, (2) to acquire and maintain the highest possible living standard, (3) to uphold democratic institutions and (4) to create a peaceful and harmonious world. Although it is difficult to find "the national interest" expressed as a concept, a formulation like this would probably be ac-

cepted by an overwhelming majority of the Danish people. Disagreements will however appear, when it comes to giving these broad aims a specific content, formulating them into policies and executing them. Of course, Denmark's problem is not unique. People of most countries agree on the broad outlines of their national interest, but differ about the means which are best-suited to protect and further it.

Territorial problems

Schleswig Relevant to the first aim is the desire of the majority of the Danish people to uphold the territorial *status quo*. Denmark does not have any *irredenta*. A Danish minority lives in South Schleswig. Immediately after the Second World War, increasing numbers of that group professed pro-Danish sentiments and expressed a desire to use the right of national self-determination. The pro-Danish activities of this group were energetic and found support from the Danish conservative and liberal parties. While a majority in Parliament was willing to support Danish cultural activity, it rejected a policy demanding the return of the province to Denmark. Gradually, this movement and its support from Denmark have lost strength. West Germany's membership in NATO and the prospective Danish membership in the European Economic Union may be said to have settled this problem. It is probably also true that the small German minority living in North Schleswig has given up the hope of a frontier-rectification, which was a latent demand in the inter-war years and a threat to Danish integrity during the occupation.

The Faroe Islands and Greenland While the people of the Faroes in the North Atlantic now and then have expressed dissatisfaction about particular problems relating to their association with the Danes, the majority have clearly expressed their desire to continue their status as part of the Danish Kingdom. Political activity is a relatively new phenomenon in the other part of Denmark in the North Atlantic: Greenland. The postwar situation in this great island has raised new and great problems of economic and political development. But the Greenland people have not expressed any desire for loosening the ties with Denmark. It is, however, obvious that, as Greenland is modernized and westernized, integration of the developing and more and more politically conscious people of Greenland raises great and challenging problems.

The geographical position of Greenland and the Faroes points to another aspect of the problem of maintaining integrity and independence: the ability to protect these parts of Denmark. During the German occupation of Denmark proper in 1940, the communications with Greenland, the Faroes and Iceland—the former Danish possession, which became independent in 1918 with the King as the common head of state—was cut off. Subsequently, British forces occupied the Faroes and Iceland —which in 1944 abrogated the Union with Denmark—while American forces occupied bases in Greenland. These events show, that these parts of Denmark are endangered in a war, in which they might be occupied by the enemies of the great sea Powers. This idea contributed after 1945 to revising Danish approaches to the integrity and security problem.

The experiences during World War II led to a widespread acceptance of the point of view that traditional neutrality no longer protected integrity and independence. As these problems became acute in 1948–49 the Hedtoft government, as will be shown later, decided to conclude an alliance with other Western nations. Elections since then prove that a majority accepts this policy in principle. In discussing concepts of national interest, it is also relevant to point out, firstly, that a policy of alliance for many Danes has very pragmatic overtones; it is accepted as the lesser of evils. Secondly, a neutralist point of view is still maintained by a minority which would prefer that Denmark returned to neutrality.

Economic interests

The desire to maintain and develop the highest possible living standard has important consequences for Danish foreign policy goals. The relatively high Danish living standard depends on an extensive foreign trade. Denmark does not possess the raw materials, which are necessary for modern industry. In order to industrialize, heavy machinery, as well as raw materials and fuel, must be imported since Denmark has neither coal nor oil deposits, nor iron or other metal resources which can be profitably mined. It is furthermore necessary to import a long list of consumer goods, including food products and textiles.

For a long period, the main part of the required foreign exchange was earned by exporting agricultural products. The high production level of agriculture was, however, maintained only by importing feedstuffs. The dependency on agricultural exports, which this economic structure created, has to some extent changed since the end of the Second World War, when industrialization has taken big steps forward. Industry is not only in many areas supplying the home market, but also building up growing exports. But this new development has not changed the fundamental fact that, in order to maintain and develop a high living standard, Denmark must export.

Since 1945 the British market, although still very substantial, has declined in importance, while trade with the United States and the new Asian and African countries has increased and the German market has regained its former significance. These strong trade interests, which make the creation of great- and free-trade areas a vital aim of Danish foreign policy and economically link Denmark with the powerful states of the West, would, from the late 1940's onward, have made it extremely difficult for Denmark to follow a policy of neutrality.

Political and social values

The economic interests, which make a Danish orientation towards the Western states natural, are furthermore supported by a broad harmony in regard to political and social values. Danish developments for more than 100 years have not only lead to political democracy, but also to social democracy. Social democracy involves a wide adjustment of class differences and, since the 1930's, the creation of a modern welfare state. These democratic gains in many and important areas of the nation's life, influence the average Dane's attitude towards the international scene and foreign policy.

The defense of independence and the search for security are linked to the desire to preserve political and economic democracy and a democratic "way of life." While prudence and a desire to preserve peace may lead to a sympathetic appraisal and acceptance of the concept of co-existence with the Communist world, the Danes' fundamental rejection of non-democratic methods and ideals places Denmark solidly in the Western group of nations.

The impact of democratic values on foreign policy discussions goes, however, further than that. It is for example illustrated by the emphasis, which politicians of various parties and newspapers of different political coloring put on the democratic character of NATO. This is based on the belief that an alliance of democratic states can, by its very nature, only be defensive and promote international stability and peace. The need for a moral justification by emphasizing the democratic character of a policy is a recurrent motive in foreign policy discussions.

Since Denmark does not have colonies or an immediate colonial past, this democratic value system also influences the average Danes' attitude towards colonialism, which is considered a policy of the past. The sooner its remnants are abolished, the better.

When a people lose the feeling of having a mission or a responsibility in the world, the foreign policy horizon becomes limited. The desire to acquire material benefits and a secure and comfortable living standard becomes not only a satisfaction but an ideal. Undoubtedly, the historian can find such traits in the development of Denmark since 1864. The "welfare state" has, on the other hand, in the minds of a large part of the Danish people become part of the country's mission. It shows the world that such results are possible in a small, poorly endowed but democratic state, which stays out of international rivalries.

International goals

The rejection of "bigness," because it makes a state aggressive and power-conscious, is combined with adoration of the small and "idyllic." Danish literature and poetry are full of this theme. This reflects the small nation's reactions against a world dominated by unrestrained power. While membership in NATO, therefore, to a certain extent is a controversial political issue in Denmark, membership in the U.N. is not, although the blind optimism of the 1920's towards the League of Nations has been superseded by a more realistic evaluation of the U.N.'s possibilities and achievements.

But the desire for a mission or participation in a missionary task on a world scale is nevertheless also present in a small nation. This is for example illustrated by the interest in aid and help to the developing countries. The Dane, feeling a responsibility in world affairs, will with pride mention that his country proportionally contributes most to technical aid through the U.N. This concern for the developing countries has naturally also an element of economic self-interest: the desire to develop trade and economic relations with those countries.

The counterpart to the desire to promote a peaceful world, is the criticism of Western friends and allies, if—according to Danish opinions—they pursue policies and aims which are not furthering such a world. Although differences of opinion between "Leftist" and "Rightist" groups are easily detected in opinion clashes, it is interesting to observe, that the defense is often weaker than the attack. The point of view for example, that colonialism is anti-democratic capitalism, defended and cloaked in the mantle of anti-communism, is often aired in liberal papers. "Progressive" revolutions and regimes in underdeveloped countries have a wide margin of sympathy and only open and undisguised attacks on democracy and democratic ideals lead to critical evaluations of such regimes.

While press discussions of such problems may show differences of opinion, the anti-democratic policies in the Communist world have been unanimously criticized and condemned. The same is the case with open Soviet intervention in Eastern Europe or Chinese aggressive acts in Asia. The Soviet Union's resumption of atomic tests in 1961 likewise released strong criticism and protests.

These general observations will serve as a background for the following description and analysis of problems since 1945.

POLICIES AND ATTITUDES TOWARDS MAJOR PROBLEMS SINCE 1945

The United Nations

Through the victory of the United Nations and the German capitulation on May 5th, 1945, Denmark's independence was restored. The liberation was carried out by British troops, which soon evacuated the country. The Soviet occupation of the island of Bornholm was also brought to an end in 1946, after the Danish government had assumed responsibility for the future defense of the island without foreign assistance.

During the occupation, many groups were of the opinion that the traditional policy of neutrality had lead to the disaster of April 9th, 1940. In 1944, the council of the resistance movement expressed the point of view that in the postwar world Danish security ought not to be based on an isolated and undefended neutrality, but on co-operation with the United Nations. When negotiations about the first postliberation government began between the council of the resistance movement and the leaders of the political parties, this broad concept was accepted. After the liberation, it was approved by Parliament and a unanimous public opinion.

It was also a widespread opinion, that stability in the postwar world and security for all the nations would only be possible through continued co-operation between the Great Powers in the new world organization. The smaller nations, including Denmark, were not able to carry out an isolated defense.

Danish view of U.N.'s purpose   After liberation, Denmark was invited to the San Francisco conference and became one of the founding members of the United Nations. Acceptance of obligations of a military as well as non-military character, which this membership involved, became thus the basis for the foreign policy of liberated Denmark. The postwar Parliament also decided to postpone its decision on new defense laws, until the U.N. Security Council was ready to negotiate an agreement about Danish military contributions to U.N. forces.

The concept of the United Nations as the center of a universal security system, based on collective obligations, can still be said to be an ideal, which enjoys general acceptance among the Danish people. Although the growing conflict between the Great Powers and the Cold War shattered the confidence in the U.N. security system, the faith in the ideal as the ultimate and best solution is strong in Denmark.

While NATO is now accepted as the military guarantee for Danish independence which, through its very existence, promotes peace, the U.N. is simultaneously considered an important supplementary organization for solving international questions. The Danish attitude is, therefore, that the U.N. ought to be strengthened and as many important international projects as possible be carried out through U.N. organs. This line has been taken in numerous cases as, for example, during the initial discussions about the Marshall plan and discussions about NATO aid to underdeveloped countries.

Collective military action   Danish attitudes and policies in regard to the U.N. as a security system were extensively debated during the U.N. action in Korea after June 25th, 1950. When the war broke out, public opinion, apart from the Communists, agreed that this was a test for the U.N. as a security organization, and the decision to intervene in Korea was generally approved.

Discussions about a Danish contribution to the action betrayed, however, strong divergences of opinion. While some groups and papers advocated sending a military force to Korea, the government's decision was that Denmark ought to limit its support of the U.N. action to a non-military contribution. When in 1951 the U.N. asked for troops, the reaction was, that an eventual Danish contingent ought to be on a voluntary basis or part of a Scandinavian force. The armistice negotiations brought an end to this discussion, which had revealed the conflict between advocates of a more narrow national interest and the principles of collective security.

When the "Uniting for Peace" resolution was placed before the U.N., the government voted for it. The resolution was considered necessary to overcome the abuses of the veto right and strengthen the U.N.

The question of placing troops at the disposal of the U.N. again arose during the Suez crisis in 1956, and Parliament agreed to send a force to Egypt. Since March 1957, when the U.N. took over the surveillance of the Israeli-Egyptian frontier, a Danish force has been included.

While accepting NATO as the protection against a military attack, it has simultaneously

been a strong Danish belief, that the U.N. has an important role to play as a mediator and meeting place for the representatives of all nations. Consequently, there has been strong Danish support for admitting all states as members. This desire to make the U.N. a universal organization has had an important influence on Danish attitudes regarding the representation of China.

After the defeat of the Kuomintang in the Chinese civil war and the proclamation of the Chinese People's Republic, Denmark recognized the new Peking government and also advocated its recognition in the U.N. as representing China. When China intervened in the Korean war, some Danish papers were of the opinion that China, as an aggressor, was not eligible to enter the world organization. But after hostilities ended, the attitude of the Danish delegation gradually shifted from voting against to voting for considering the admission of Communist China. The Danish press has almost unanimously supported the view that Peking ought to represent China in the U.N. and emphasized that this did not imply a position for or against Chinese communism, but simply the recognition of the government in power.

Great Power conflicts   Denmark believes that in conflicts between the Great Powers, the U.N. has an important function to perform by bringing the opponents together and, with the other members as mediating participants, producing a peaceful solution. In this connection it has often been argued by Danes that the smaller and in particular the Scandinavian states have an important role to play. On the other hand, there are those who emphasize that Denmark should not follow too active a line in Great Power rivalries. In conflicts between a strong and a weak nation, the Danish point of view has been, that it is the U.N.'s duty to protect the weaker. The inner conflict between these concepts of the U.N. has never been clearly resolved in Danish debates.

Denmark has strongly supported the proposals for disarmament made in the U.N. and the demand for controlled disarmament. It has also taken great interest in the work of the Economic and Social Council and has actively contributed to technical assistance to underdeveloped countries.

Danish participation in settling colonial questions in the U.N. has been very active. Since Denmark is not a colonial Power, this may seem rather paradoxical. But the general Danish attitude has been that colonialism is now obsolete and that, for the sake of world peace, colonial areas ought to obtain their freedom as soon as possible. Danish representatives have tried to mediate in U.N. bodies between extreme points of view on these questions and have made an effort to prevent excessive pressure on colonial Powers.

In view of Denmark's exposed geographical position and the widespread opinion, that a war between the Great Powers would in the nuclear age lead to total destruction of their country, Danish debates and policies in the U.N. have supported the demand for peaceful solution of conflicts and long-term efforts to produce a more stable and peaceful world through the United Nations. Thus, the United Nations, even after 1949, has had an important place in Danish foreign policy and debates. However, the demand, that the U.N.'s first function is to prevent war has raised many contradictory questions, which remain unanswered. This is true partly because they are by their very nature unsolvable, but also because of the dichotomy between the ideals of the smaller states and their lack of strength and sometimes willingness to carry their ideals out.

Membership in NATO has on several occasions raised the question to what extent loyalty towards allies should dictate voting in the U.N. Although Denmark in general in the U.N. has voted with Great Britain and the United States, it has on several issues followed a line different from the one taken by its great allies. Moreover, it is a recurrent theme in Danish discussions that Denmark ought to follow an independent course in the U.N. and not let its voting be determined exclusively by NATO solidarity.

NATO

Hopes for non-involvement fade The first postwar governments believed that security problems would be solved within the framework of the United Nations. This view was supported by an overwhelming majority of public opinion. The proposals which had been made during the war in the Western World for an alliance between the Atlantic nations were rejected, if they were at all discussed by the Danish public. The Danish foreign minister stated in Parliament that Denmark wanted to be an intermediary between East and West, that the government did not consider entering into alliances with any of the Great Powers, and neither did it want a Nordic bloc. It was at that time known that the Soviet Government was opposed to closer Scandinavian co-operation.

As the postwar conflicts between the wartime allies emerged and demonstrated the weakness of the U.N. as a security organization, scepticism towards the U.N. as a guarantee for security began to appear. But government and Parliament as well as public opinion in general were still unwilling to re-appraise the security problems.

European events in the first part of 1948 became decisive for Danish attitudes towards security and defense. The gradual Communist takeover of control in Eastern Europe had been accepted as an inevitable development. But Czechoslovakia was considered as the democratic bridge between East and West. The Communist coup in Prague on February 24th, Stalin's demand on February 27th to Finland for an alliance, rumors of a *coup* in Denmark during Easter, the signing of the Western European defense alliance in Brussels on March 13th, and the first step leading to the Berlin blockade had a shock effect on Danish public opinion.

A growing number of people realized that

the postwar world was taking a quite different course from what had been hoped for and expected. The realization, that the former allies had become rivals and the fear of Soviet plans in Northern and Western Europe, forced politicians as well as the public to reconsider the problems of security.

Reluctantly, growing numbers of the Danish people came to the conclusion that, considering Denmark's exposed position in a border area between the conflicting East-West interests, the U.N. offered only a slight guarantee against aggressive plans on the part of the new powerful neighbor across the Baltic. The only answer was a defense alliance with like-minded states. The plans for an Atlantic alliance, which began to materialize during the summer of 1948, did not, however, appeal to the majority of Danes in this phase of re-orientation. The old suspicion against being entangled in Great Power politics was still alive.

Attempts to create a Nordic alliance This situation gave new life to old dreams and hopes for a Nordic alliance. The reaction in the rest of Scandinavia, and in particular in Norway, to Soviet expansion had created the same desire as in Denmark for a more stable and reliable guarantee for independence and freedom than the U.N. Statements from the foreign ministers of Norway and Sweden indicated, however, that there were fundamental divergences of opinion between them as to the line to be followed in regard to East-West conflicts.

While the official Swedish attitude expressed a desire to continue the policy of neutrality towards the Great Powers, the Norwegian foreign minister, in a speech in April, said that a situation might appear, which would force Norway to choose a different road from Denmark's and Sweden's. Mr. Lange also said that the military and security problems with which the Scandinavian countries were confronted, were not identical and might create difficulties for them in choosing the same solution.

This Norwegian-Swedish exchange clearly indicated the possibility of a schism in Scandi-

navia. In order to forestall such a development, the Swedish Erlander government obtained from Parliament authorization to initiate negotiations with Norway and Denmark about Scandinavian defense co-operation.

Discussions about the Swedish proposal in May 1948 showed from the beginning the fundamental difference of approach between Sweden and Norway. While the Swedes considered a Scandinavian alliance as the instrument by which Denmark and Norway could be kept outside a Western alliance, the Norwegians wanted it to be the vehicle by which Scandinavia could be brought into an alignment with the rest of the Western democratic nations, if that solution turned out to be the best.

The Danish Prime Minister, Hans Hedtoft, tried to mediate between the Swedish and the Norwegian points of view. In September it was decided to investigate the possibilities of Scandinavian defense co-operation on the basis of the Swedish plan.

A committee presented its report in January 1949. The main points were (1) that a united Scandinavian defense posture would increase the three countries' capacity to defend themselves, and (2) that it was not inevitable that the Scandinavian region would be drawn into a war between the Great Powers. But the report also emphasized, that if Scandinavia became involved in such a war, it could not for any length of time defend itself without help from the outside. (3) A substantial re-armament of Norway and Denmark was necessary while Sweden preserved its present level of armament.

In the meantime the Danish and Norwegian foreign ministers and the U.S. Secretary of State, George Marshall, met during the U.N. General Assembly in Paris in October 1948. The Scandinavian ministers explained the Nordic negotiations. It also seems that Mr. Lange raised the question about American deliveries of arms to a Scandinavian defense alliance.

A Washington statement soon poured cold water on such hopes. It declared, that the United States did not intend to give one-sided military guarantees and that states, which did not join the planned collective security system, would be of secondary importance to the U.S. During the fall, American diplomats tried to convince the Scandinavian states that it would be in their own best interest to enter the planned Atlantic alliance. This obviously had a certain effect in Norway.

At a meeting in January 1949, in Karlstad, the Swedish and Danish delegations submitted draft proposals for a defensive alliance. An important point during the Karlstad discussions was how Denmark and Norway could be effectively re-armed. The economic burdens involved seemed to be overwhelming, necessitating outside aid or at least deliveries at favorable prices. The Norwegians were inclined to take the American statements seriously. The Swedes maintained that a new situation would be created, if the Scandinavian alliance were concluded. This might induce the Americans to change their attitude. The U.S., however, soon made its position clear. Thereafter the Scandinavian alliance negotiations broke down on the question of relations with a North Atlantic alliance.

The Danish government tried to the last to find a Scandinavian solution and approached the Swedish government regarding a Swedish-Danish alliance. When this was rejected by Sweden, the Danes followed the example of Norway and signed the North Atlantic treaty.

Reluctant membership in NATO Membership in NATO meant that Denmark definitely gave up its traditional policy of neutrality and accepted the security which could be obtained in an alliance with the great Western Powers. In Parliament this policy has since 1949 been supported by a majority, consisting of the Social Democratic, the Conservative and the Liberal parties, while the Communist Party and, since 1960, the new Socialist People's Party, have been in constant opposition. The Left Liberals, who originally opposed Danish membership and the commitments gradually undertaken by Denmark, have recently changed their position. This parliamentary situation has corresponded to a pro-NATO at-

titude among the electorate, although criticism or rejection of certain NATO policies has over the years been discernible.

The Danish people are fully aware of their exposed position on the Northern front of the Cold War. In general, they accept the necessity for and desirability of close co-operation with the other Western nations. It is on the other hand felt, that this geographical position dictates a cautious attitude towards the Soviet Union and requires NATO policies that are clearly defensive and which cannot be seriously interpreted as provocative. This attitude is among many Danes combined with a certain scepticism towards the reliability of any alliance. Consciously or unconsciously the memories of 1864 are still alive.

Traditionally anti-militarist and pacifist attitudes on the part of segments of the electorate have also manifested themselves through a certain reluctance in accepting expanded defense budgets and the extension of military service, demanded by the NATO defense planning. It has often been argued that increased defense efforts might threaten economic stability and the living standard of the people and thus lead to a threat to political and social stability.

Consequently there has been a strong emphasis in Denmark on NATO as a peace-preserving organization. The deterrent effect of NATO has been put in the foreground and the containment policy has been accepted, while statements about policies going beyond that, as for example "rolling back Soviet power" or "massive retaliation," have been met with scepticism or outright rejection.

These major aspects of public debates and opinions on NATO have dictated the policies of the governments since 1949. They explain the reluctant negative attitudes taken by Danish governments towards certain proposals in the NATO Council. They express the dilemmas of a small state in an exposed position; the conflict between the desire for greater security and the fear of being overwhelmed by the power and interests of greater nations, and also the fear of being dragged into conflicts which are outside the country's direct sphere of interests. In a world of violent conflicts and growing interdependency, the small state is caught between the necessity of belonging to greater combinations, the fear of losing political identity and the desire for freedom of independent decision.

Membership in NATO made possible the solution of an immediate postwar problem: the continuation of American bases on Greenland in peacetime. After the liberation in 1945 Parliament ratified the Greenland treaty, concluded in 1941 with the United States by the Danish minister in Washington, while Denmark was occupied. After the end of the war it was expected that the American lease of bases would come to an end. However, as the Cold War developed, it became clear that Washington did not feel that the stipulation in the 1941 treaty, extending the American rights until threats against the American continent had passed, had lost its importance. After the North Atlantic treaty had come into force, Danish-American negotiations were renewed. In May 1951 a treaty was concluded which arranged for combined Danish-American defense of Greenland and conceded the right to the U.S.A. to have bases on the island in peacetime.

It was not anticipated in Denmark, nor for that matter anywhere else, that NATO would gradually develop the integrated structural organization which has been established since 1949. The development of a traditional alliance with an international organization with wide ramifications and the admission of new members have, over the years, led to differing attitudes within the Danish government and to lively debates in Parliament and among the public.

Controversial NATO programs The first major debate occurred in September 1950 when, at its meeting in New York, the NATO council decided to establish an "integrated" European force with an American commander. "The NATO parties" in Parliament authorized the government to accept the New York proposals, while the opposition maintained that this step was leading Denmark dangerously

beyond the obligations undertaken in 1949. When the final agreement was ratified by Parliament in 1951, the majority made certain reservations regarding SACEUR's authority in peacetime and emphasized that, as far as Denmark was concerned, it reserved its right to decide on peace and war.

Under the command of SHAPE, the Northern Command, covering the Danish-Norwegian military area, with headquarters in Norway, was created. While the establishment of SHAPE and the selection of General Eisenhower as its commander received Danish approval, the simultaneous demand for the re-armament of Western Germany was met with serious doubts in Denmark, where historical experiences of German military power and recent memories of occupation during World War II created a strong emotional barrier against accepting a new German army. These anxieties were not substantially alleviated when the Minister of Defense in the beginning of 1951 declared in Parliament that a German contribution to NATO defenses would simplify the defense of Jutland. The possibility of solving the German re-armament problem through the creation of EDC was accepted as a good solution and postponed the moment when Denmark had to define its position on this question.

The Danish fear of extending the responsibilities of NATO and—it was felt—thereby the dangers of war, clearly came to the fore in 1951, when the membership of Greece and Turkey came up. Norway as well as Denmark, at the Ottawa meeting, opposed the resolution inviting the two countries to join NATO. As it turned out, the Scandinavians stood alone in their opposition. When Norway changed its attitude, the Danish government asked the foreign policy committee of Parliament to authorize a Danish acceptance. In arguing this change of position, the foreign minister pointed to the fact that Denmark could use its veto. But he deemed this to be a serious step for Denmark to take alone in an organization of democratic states.

The Lisbon resolutions establishing the permanent council and the post of a secretary general met with Danish approval. But the simultaneous demands for a substantial increase in the Danish defense budget and an increase of the military service to 18 months, recommended by the "Wise Men," occasioned serious debates in and out of Parliament. The main argument of the opposition was that an increase would endanger Denmark's economic stability. In the end, Parliament reduced the defense expenses suggested by the Lisbon decisions.

About the same time proposals for stationing NATO air forces on Danish territory were discussed. Military experts believed that this would increase the efficiency of Danish defenses. Although the liberal-conservative government apparently took a positive attitude towards SHAPE's arguments, it soon became obvious that public opinion was against the idea. It was argued that stationing of NATO forces on Danish territory would appear as a provocation against the Soviet Union and would therefore be objectionable from a political point of view.

The vigilance with which even the "Atlantic parties" scrutinized decisions of NATO, which might eventually expand its responsibilities, was demonstrated in connection with the Council's resolution in December 1952, expressing moral support for France's war in Indochina. Not only the traditional opposition parties against NATO, but also the Social Democrats severely criticized foreign minister Kraft for having supported the resolution. Apart from domestic political reasons the criticism expressed a moral rejection of colonial wars and the fear, that this would be the first step, leading NATO into deeper involvement in colonial wars.

From 1953 onwards, the NATO problem, which has been in the forefront of Danish debates, has been Western Germany's admittance into NATO, its re-armament, and the implications of this step for Denmark. The Hedtoft government accepted the London-Paris decisions in 1954. In Parliament the "Atlantic" parties and the Single Tax party carried through the ratification, while the Left Liberals and the Communists opposed it and demanded a plebiscite. The foreign minister explained, however, that a Danish veto would not keep Western Germany out of NATO, but lead to the isolation of Denmark and its withdrawal from NATO. He emphasized the increased protection of the Danish southern border, which would be the result of German land and naval forces.

Although military logic dictated Danish acceptance of a re-armed Western Germany, a prolonged discussion in the Danish public nevertheless betrayed a strong emotional reaction. It reached a climax in 1961 with the establishment of a unified Danish-German command, with a Danish commander and a German deputy. The agreement, which was ratified by Parliament in December 1961, also said, that the unified command would only function in case of war and during NATO exercises. The Danish attitude has been negative or reluctant about arming NATO with nuclear weapons, and the Danish government has rejected proposals for supplying the Danish army with nuclear warheads.

In the non-military sphere, the Danish government has supported the tendencies to strengthen political consultations within the NATO Council. Denmark shares the desire of the smaller member-nations to be informed in advance about the policies and actions of the Great Powers and have a chance to discuss them. A Danish NATO organization actively participates in the wider field of political, economic and cultural co-operation between NATO members. Although sections of public opinion support the idea of closer co-operation with NATO and an ultimate Atlantic Union, other groups and the political parties believe that economic or European cultural co-operation ought to take place through existing organizations. The proposals aiming at an Atlantic Union have been met with a certain scepticism by public opinion. The Danish attitude is, that although such a development is desirable, there is a long distance to go and the tempo ought to be slow. Considering the obstacles to Atlantic Union, there seems little danger that the Danish public will be forced to make an early decision in the matter.

Nordic co-operation

Co-operation with the Nordic countries is an important element of Danish foreign policy. It is based on a strong desire among the Danish people to preserve and strengthen the ties with the Scandinavian sister nations.

Based on bonds of language, religion, identical development of law, in part common origin and common historical experiences, the Scandinavian movement has developed since the start of the nineteenth century. After centuries of conflict and war, the Scandinavian people gradually developed a feeling of solidarity and a desire for understanding and co-operation. The wish to express these somewhat vague feelings in practical policies and concrete actions seems over the decades to have been strongest in Denmark. It was, to a great extent, shared by the Swedes, but met with less interest in Norway and until recently in Finland and Iceland. One explanation of this situation may be, that the demand for independence and consolidation dominated these peoples' attitudes towards their neighbors.

Successes and failures   The Scandinavian movement, which began in the Middle Ages as a movement for political union, changed tactics after 1870 and became more "practical." Seeking a broader basis and finding support from organizations such as the new labor movement, the folk high schools and the democratic political parties, the adherents of the Scandinavian movement worked out plans for Nordic co-operation in economic, social, legislative and, above all, cultural matters. A practical result of these efforts was the Scandinavian monetary union after 1872, which functioned until World War I broke out. This phase of Nordic co-operation culminated during World War I with intimate and extensive co-operation and consultation on the government level. In 1919 the Norden Association was formed, which established branches in all

the Nordic countries. Since then *Foreningen Norden,* with a growing membership in all the Nordic countries, has been the center of propaganda for the Scandinavian idea and the organizer of numerous activities in wide fields of Scandinavian common life.

In the 1920's Nordic co-operation on the political level declined; but the threatening development of European politics in the 1930's gave new impetus to desires for political co-operation. On Danish initiative, the regular meetings between the foreign ministers of the Nordic countries were resumed in 1932, and the governments tried to co-ordinate their endeavors to return to a policy of strict neutrality in regard to Great Power conflicts. The growth of Nazism and Fascism increased the feeling of Nordic solidarity and led not only to greater interest in co-operation in internal Scandinavian matters but also, although unsupported by the governments, to new, but fruitless discussions about Scandinavian defense arrangements.

The occupation in 1940 of Norway and Denmark and Finland's military co-operation with Germany brought Nordic co-operation on the governmental level to a temporary standstill. But it deepened, particularly in Denmark and Sweden, the feeling of Nordic interdependency and a desire for expanding Nordic co-operation after the war. This is the background of the extensive Nordic initiatives after 1945.

Reviewing the results of Nordic co-operation in the postwar world, it must be admitted that on the great political-economic issues, Scandinavian co-operation has failed. As described in an earlier section, the negotiations for a defense alliance in 1948–49, strongly supported by the Danish people and government, were unsuccessful.

The negotiations after 1948 about a Scandinavian Customs Union and a Common Market were likewise unsuccessful. A Scandinavian Customs Union had been discussed as early as the 1880's. After 1945, the interest in a Nordic Customs Union and Common Market gained momentum. In particular, the idea won support in Denmark. In 1948 the governments appointed a committee for economic co-operation to work out proposals for a Customs Union. Although the Committee in its report in 1954 reached the conclusion, that a Scandinavian Customs Union was feasible and in the long run would benefit all countries concerned and stimulate economic progress, the proposals nevertheless met opposition, in particular from Norway. When discussions in the Nordic Council and on a governmental level made little progress, the plans for a European Common Market and for a European Free Trade area forged ahead of the Nordic discussions. The Nordic governments gradually became convinced that the idea of a Scandinavian Common Market must recede into the background.

These failures seem to indicate that there have been and are limits to the scope of Scandinavian co-operation. Those limitations are the results of basic differences of interests and national approaches. It seems clear that since 1945 purely Scandinavian answers to the wider European and world issues are too narrow. Twenty million people and the Scandinavian resources are an insufficient basis for solving decisive military and economic problems. Within problems limited to Scandinavia itself, co-operation has however been extensive and growing. These endeavors have since 1952 been centered in the Nordic Council, whose establishment took place largely under the inspiration of the Danish Prime Minister Hans Hedtoft.

The Nordic council "*Nordisk Råd*" is an advisory and recommendatory body, and consists of members of the Nordic parliaments, chosen by these, and representatives of the governments. The establishment of such a council was already discussed on Danish initiative in the 1930's. The idea was strengthened by the creation in 1949 of the Council of Europe and its formation in 1952 meant a coordination of

already existing Scandinavian co-operation through ministerial conferences, government departments and permanent bodies. But above all, the legislative assemblies are now drawn into the work on a much greater scale than ever before, and consequently Scandinavian co-operation has come to occupy a central position at government level.[2]

Although the results of the work of the Council, which meets annually, have not met the expectations which it raised in 1952, it has nevertheless taken many important initiatives, leading to extended and important Nordic co-operation in cultural, legal and administrative matters as well as in questions regarding social security, health services, transportation and communication and minor economic problems. The first decade of the Nordic Council's existence was crowned in March 1962 with the signing in Helsingfors, Finland, of the Convention on Nordic co-operation.

In international politics the Nordic countries are also co-ordinating their policies. In the United Nations, the Nordic representatives co-operate intimately and the meetings of the General Assembly are preceded by meetings of the Nordic foreign ministers, where a "Nordic" line of policy is discussed and determined. When a Nordic country is represented on U.N. bodies and agencies, it generally speaks for all of Scandinavia. Nordic countries also co-operate in other international organizations and thus continue the traditions from the 1920's and '30's.

A general review of the Nordic movement at the beginning of the 1960's leads to the conclusion that it has created a unique fellow feeling among five states (Denmark, Sweden, Norway, Iceland, Finland) and peoples and made serious conflict—not mentioning war—between them unthinkable. It has also led to important co-operation between them, gradually making the Nordic countries one area in many cultural and social fields. But it is also characteristic of developments in Scandinavia, that in the same epoch the demand for na-

[2] Franz Wendt, *The Nordic Council and Cooperation in Scandinavia,* 1959.

tional independence and the preservation and growth of national characteristics has increased, leading to the dissolution of political unions between them. Confronted with the European tendency towards integration and creation of supranational institutions, an immediate problem for the Nordic states and peoples has been created. The question is whether this tendency towards integration will lead to new developments in Scandinavian policies towards regional integration or create new ties with the rest of Europe, which inevitably will diminish the importance of Scandinavian solidarity and co-operation, even in cultural and social fields.

European integration and economic co-operation

The Danish approaches to the postwar policies of European co-operation and integration have generally had two motivations: a positive economic one and a negative political-cultural one. Although wartime devastations were limited, Denmark shared postwar Europe's need for economic reconstruction. Denmark is to a high degree dependent on a large volume of foreign trade and was therefore after 1945 greatly interested in endeavors to increase international trade by abolishing the restrictions which, in the immediate postwar years, hampered the free flow of goods. Secretary of State George Marshall's Harvard speech in 1948 was therefore greeted with satisfaction. Denmark received about 300 million dollars from the U.S.A., mostly in aid, and participated in O.E.E.C. in abolishing quantitative restrictions on trade. It was however from a Danish point of view a weakness of the O.E.E.C. that agricultural protection was by and large untouched.

A set of inter-governmental rules of conduct was gradually established within O.E.E.C. But being a traditional organization on a governmental level, it did not raise problems of surrendering sovereignty or accepting political

obligations. These questions, however, arose in debates about the Council of Europe, of which Denmark became a member at its foundation in 1949.

Lack of interest in European unification
Danish interests in the postwar European movement had been slight. Danish representatives participated in the conferences of the movement, but when it came to decide the constitution of the Council, the Danish government joined the opposition against a federal solution.

There are many explanations for this Danish attitude. The prewar European movement had left little, if any impact on Danish political concepts. Neither had the growth of the idea of European solidarity during the war influenced discussions about postwar problems in occupied Denmark. The Danish government did not go into exile to London where, during the war years, the future of Europe was discussed formally and informally between a group of men, who became leaders in European politics after 1945. This stimulus to the European movement by and large left Denmark untouched.

But the Danish negative attitude or lack of interest in a European movement in the more narrow sense of the word has deeper explanations. Fundamentally belonging to Northern Europe, Continental political ideas have only a minor impact on Denmark. Although the German problem has had an overwhelming influence on modern Danish foreign policy, the problems of the rest of the Continent have only had a secondary importance from a political point of view. The Scandinavian endeavors in the 1930's to co-operate with the smaller Continental states—the Netherlands, Belgium and Luxembourg—became a temporary and unimportant episode.

Denmark's economic connections with the Continent have first of all been with Germany. Culturally, the influence from the Continent has primarily been German and French, while the impact of cultural life in the rest of the Continental countries has been sporadic and of less importance. If we look at religion, the barrier between Catholicism and Protestantism runs across Northern Germany.

The cultural-social life in Denmark since the middle of the last century—for example the Folk high schools, a broad democratization of schools and general education, emancipation of women, and the Danish welfare system—have developed along lines which the Danes feel, are characteristic of a Danish-Nordic society and somewhat at variance with trends on the Continent. It is feared, that the Danish-Nordic characteristics would be endangered by closer and more intimate political ties with Continental Europe. Confronted with this scepticism towards, or lack of knowledge of, Continental European trends and ideas is the very strong "Nordic" orientation of not only politics, but also social-cultural life in modern Denmark.

Another element in public opinion formation in Denmark in modern times has been the pro-British attitude of the Danish people. This has not only been underpinned by strong economic bonds and the traditional fear of Germany, but also by a broad sympathy and admiration for British parliamentary institutions and British political ideas and behavior. Although clashes between economic interests have occurred since the 1930's and in particular since 1945, this has not changed the Danes' instinctive sympathy for Great Britain and a desire to follow a British line in foreign policies.

All these motivations in regard to the European movement may be summed up in the concept of "defense of sovereignty." The fear of losing control of Danish affairs by joining organizations with supranational organs and losing identity and independence in a close integration with the Continent, explains the Danish attitude towards supranationality.

When the constitution of the Council of Europe was worked out in 1948–49, the Danish representatives joined forces with the rest of Scandinavia and Great Britain to keep the organization politically as loose as possible. In subsequent discussions between "federalists" and "functionalists," the Danish attitude was decidedly for the functionalist approach, although it did not solve the dichotomy between this approach and the gradual sterility of the work of the Council.

Since Denmark did not join the Coal and Steel Community or the European Defense Community, public opinion and the policy-makers were not directly forced to make up their minds about integration and supranational powers. These questions became burning only with the establishment of the European Economic Community after 1957, because it had a direct bearing on primary Danish economic interests.

OEEC, EFTA and the Common Market
The importance of foreign trade to the Danish economy is obvious from the fact, that one-third of the gross national product is exported. In 1960, roughly 30 percent of this went to countries within the EEC, 26 percent to Great Britain, 16 percent to other members of EFTA and 28 percent to the so-called Third Countries. In view of this structure of Danish foreign trade, the Danish government strongly supported the endeavors within OEEC from 1956 to 1958 to reach an agreement between the European Economic Community and the rest of the OEEC countries to establish an extensive European Free Trade Area. When these negotiations broke down in the fall of 1958, the government followed Great Britain and, together with the rest of the Scandinavian countries, joined the EFTA—The European Free Trade Area. The main motivation from the Danish point of view was that EFTA would be a temporary organization, leading to negotiations with EEC about a broad European solution of the market problems, but without the political implications of the Rome Treaty.

Soon, however, it became obvious that EFTA did not lead to this goal. As the tariff decisions of EEC began to be felt, the prospects for Danish exports, first of all to the important German market, became serious. When Great Britain therefore in July 1961 announced its intention to seek admission to EEC, the Danish government and Folketing decided to follow the same course. But they made Danish membership in EEC dependent on a successful result of the British negotiations with the EEC. As long as the question of British membership remains undecided, this important aspect of Denmark's future will remain in suspense, while Danish agricultural exports to EEC, in particular to Germany, are meeting increasingly serious obstacles. In Danish public debates there is a growing understanding that Denmark cannot stay outside the dynamic and important European integration movement. The economic aspects of this policy are accepted, but hesitations regarding the wider political-cultural perspectives of EEC are still strong and are likely to remain so in the foreseeable future.

The foreign policies of Denmark have since 1945 been subject to the revolutionary changes which have occurred within the international society of states. The result has been a gradual modification in the structure of Danish aims and attitudes. This process is still continuing.

So far, it has meant abandoning neutrality and following a policy of alliance in NATO, while at the same time giving close attention to the neighbor in the Baltic: the Soviet Union. It has also meant that relations with some states, for example the Scandinavian states and Great Britain, for a long time based on intimate mutual interests, have undergone certain changes. Other states—the new nations of Asia and Africa, but first of all the United States—have acquired new and greater importance. Of equal significance, from a Danish perspective, have been the new aspects of relations with Germany, not only through common membership in NATO, but also as an eventual intimate partner in the European Community. This, in the 1960's, is developing into the major problem of Danish foreign policy. From the Danish people this process is demanding a re-examination and re-evaluation, not only of aims but also of interests and values. It lends an importance to foreign policy issues, unknown for several generations.

BIBLIOGRAPHY

Author's Suggestions

Fink, Troels. *Spillet om dansk Neutralitet, 1905–1909.* København: Munksgaard, 1959.

Fink, Troels. *Ustabil Balance. Dansk udenrigs- og forsvarspolitik, 1894–1905.* 1961.

Haagerup, Niels J. *De forenede Nationer og Danmarks Sikkerhed.* 1956.

Hæstrup, Jørgen. *Kontakt med England, 1940–43.* 1954.

Henningsen, Sven. *Den nordatlantiske Pagt.* 1954.

Den parlamentariske Kommissions Betænning I og Beretninger. Vols. II–XII. København: 1945–1958.

Reske Nielsen, Erik og Kragh, Erik. *Atlantpagten og Danmark.* København: Munksgaard, 1957.

Schultz Danmarkshistorie. Vols. I–VI. Edited by Aage Friis, Axel Linved, and M. Mackeprang. 1941–43.

Sørensen, Max og Haagerup, Niels J. *Denmark and the United Nations.* New York: Manhattan Publishing Co., 1956.

DENMARK

Wendt, Frantz. *The Nordic Council and Co-operation in Scandinavia.* 1959.

Editor's Suggestions

Danstrup, John. *A History of Denmark.* København: Wind, 1949.

Friis, Henning Kristian. *Scandinavia Between East and West.* Ithaca: Cornell U. Press, 1950.

Lauwerys, Joseph Albert. *Scandinavian Democracy: Development of Democratic Institutions in Denmark, Norway, and Sweden.* New York: American-Scandinavian Foundation, 1959.

Ravnholt, Henning. *The Danish Cooperative Movement.* København: Det Danske Selskob, 1950.

ABOUT THE AUTHOR

Karl Dietrich Bracher is a professor of Political Science and Contemporary History at the University of Bonn in Germany. He completed his Ph.D. degree at the University of Tübingen in 1948 and then engaged in post-doctoral studies for one year at Harvard University. He began his teaching career as a lecturer on Political Science and Political History at the Free University in Berlin and in 1958 was made a full professor. At present, he also holds the position of Director for the Seminar of Political Science in Bonn. Notable among his published works are: Die Auflösung der Weimarer Republik, 1955 (3rd ed. 1960); Staat und Politik (ed. with Ernst Fraenkel, 1957); Die nationalsozialistische Machtergreifung, 1960; Über das Verhältnis von Politik und Geschichte, 1961.

ABOUT THE CHAPTER

A divided Germany in a divided world provides the basic theme for this chapter on the foreign policy of Western Germany. Dr. Bracher deals only briefly with the period prior to the end of World War II. The bulk of this chapter analyzes the policies of the ruler and of the Federal Republic of Germany in trying to come to grips with the problem of a divided Germany and of Berlin which lies a considerable distance within the Eastern zone. The author gives careful attention to the many conferences and policy pronouncements of the Major Powers and to the ups and downs of Adenauer's policies over the years.

A very valuable part of this chapter is the critique of the official policy of Germany and the questions raised regarding possible alternatives which were largely ignored by the Adenauer government. Mr. Bracher carefully relates the policies of the government to the internal politics of the Federal Republic and beyond that to the politics of dealing with the Powers in the Western alliance. The chapter ends with some observations on the New Europe and the problems which confront Germany as the Adenauer era comes to an end.

ABOUT THE AUTHOR

KARL DIETRICH BRACHER is a professor of Political Science and Contemporary History at the University of Bonn in Germany. He completed his Ph.D. degree at the University of Tübingen in 1948 and then engaged in post-doctoral studies for one year at Harvard University. He began his teaching career as a lecturer on Political Science and Political History at the Free University in Berlin and in 1958 was made a full professor. At present he also holds the position of Director for the Seminar of Political Science at Bonn. Notable among his published works are: *Die Auflösung der Weimarer Republik*, 1955 (3rd ed, 1960); *Staat und Politik* (ed. with Ernst Fraenkel), 1957; *Die nationalsozialistische Machtergreifung*, 1960; *Über das Verhältnis von Politik und Geschichte*, 1961.

ABOUT THE CHAPTER

A divided Germany in a divided world provides the basic theme for this chapter on the foreign policy of Western Germany. Dr. Bracher deals only briefly with the period prior to the end of World War II.

The bulk of this chapter analyzes the policies of the allies and of the Federal Republic of Germany in trying to come to grips with the problem of a divided Germany and of Berlin which lies a considerable distance within the Eastern zone. The author gives careful attention to the many conferences and policy pronouncements of the Major Powers and to the ups and downs of Adenauer's policies over the years.

A very valuable part of this chapter is the critique of the official policy of Germany and the questions raised regarding possible alternatives which were largely ignored by the Adenauer government. Mr. Bracher carefully relates the policies of the government to the internal politics of the Federal Republic and beyond that to the politics of dealing with the Powers in the Western alliance. The chapter ends with some observations on the New Europe and the problems which confront Germany as the Adenauer era comes to an end.

4

THE FOREIGN POLICY OF
THE FEDERAL REPUBLIC OF GERMANY

KARL DIETRICH BRACHER

Bonn University

Enough time has passed since the collapse of the National Socialist regime to subject the foreign policy of the Federal Republic of Germany to a fruitful critical examination. As the much glorified Adenauer government approaches its close, the problems posed by Germany's restoration have come to the fore clearer than ever before. Our discussion will concentrate on the manifold aspects of the "German question" as it emerged from the attitudes and actions of German and non-German Powers. It will not suffice to provide a mere historical description of the various stages of development from 1945 through 1962. The examination must be concerned with the hypotheses, the structure, the means and the conditions which have determined and produced this development.

It should be noted at the outset that Germany's foreign policy is limited in two ways. Externally, the occupation of Germany and the international policies of the participating Great Powers have placed narrow limits upon the new German foreign policy. Internally, the attempt to establish and secure a democratic order in Germany for a second time since the failure of the Weimar Republic has imposed very definite conditions on foreign policy formulation and execution.

It logically follows from this that our frame of reference for examining Germany's foreign policy must be this two-fold point of view. We will first consider the situation existing in 1945, including the legacy of the National Socialist regime. This will be followed by an examination of the formation and growth of the Federal Republic and the "German Democratic Republic." After that, we will discuss in detail the further development of the Federal Republic, its political alignments and questions of the "Cold War" up to the crisis of 1956. Finally, we will turn to a critical resumé of the foreign policy of Adenauer, with proper attention being given to both internal and international factors which have been of crucial importance. Such factors include the rising political and economic importance of the Federal Republic and the renewed activity of Soviet Russia's foreign policy since the start of the Berlin crisis in 1958.

THE HISTORICAL AND GEOGRAPHICAL SETTING

The 1945 catastrophe meant a profound, and apparently total, rupture in the historical and political existence of Germany. For the affected population, as well as the critical observer, the situation appeared to be the "Zero Hour," which, if it had not really put an end to German history and statehood, had at least marked what Alfred Weber calls the "farewell from history up to this time."

Dominant factors before World War I

But, of course, the Germany of 1945 was still tied to her past. It soon became apparent that no matter what directions German policy might take, it could not be separated from the specific conditions of German history and the policies of the past century. The legacy of the past, which led to the political unification of Germany and, finally, to the totalitarian experiment of National Socialist imperialism, essentially determined the new beginnings of German policy. These basic conditions were of a varied nature: historical-geographical, political-ideological, and economic-social.

The central location in the heart of Europe and the special position of leadership in the empire of the Middle Ages, after the disintegration of the Reich into loosely connected territorial states, kept Germany from developing into a unified, centralized state, like the other Western Powers. Unlike France, the German states in the eighteenth century had developed a moderate form of enlightened ab-

solutism which seemed to make possible an organic transition to a modern state without revolutionary upheaval. The original enthusiasm for the principles of the French Revolution gave way to a reaction because of the effect of the Terror, the aggressive expansion of the Revolution, and the rise of Napoleon. This forced national interests to the fore in the wars of liberation; restoration dominated again over revolutionary reform efforts.

As a long-range development, the result was an alienation and separation of German political thinking from the West European development, especially after the collapse of the liberal revolution of 1848. The strong liberal movement yielded increasingly to the primacy of the foreign-policy-oriented ideals of "freedom and unity" over the domestic-oriented ideals of "freedom and constitution." This meant the subjugation of the main stream of constitutional-democratic reform to the reactionary forces of the royal courts, of the military and of the bureaucracy.

Bismarck and Prussia, chief pillars and symbols of this reaction of the old regime, forced the formation of the longed-for German national state, the Second Reich, in a revolution from the top. At the same time, with this movement for unity, they could absorb the bourgeois liberal emancipation movement into the structure of a pseudo-constitutional, semi-absolute, feudal, military and bureaucratic state.

In internal politics, this led to tensions and structural mistakes which were only superficially covered up by the splendor of the first years of the Empire. Not only was the development of a functioning parliamentary system and responsible parties hindered, but the military-bureaucratic authoritarian state also blocked the co-operation of the growing masses of workers and their social-democratic organizations and labor unions. The rapidly growing population of a society changed by the industrial revolution was not integrated into the political process. Instead, the tendency grew to neutralize the social forces by deviating the pressure of interests to external affairs.

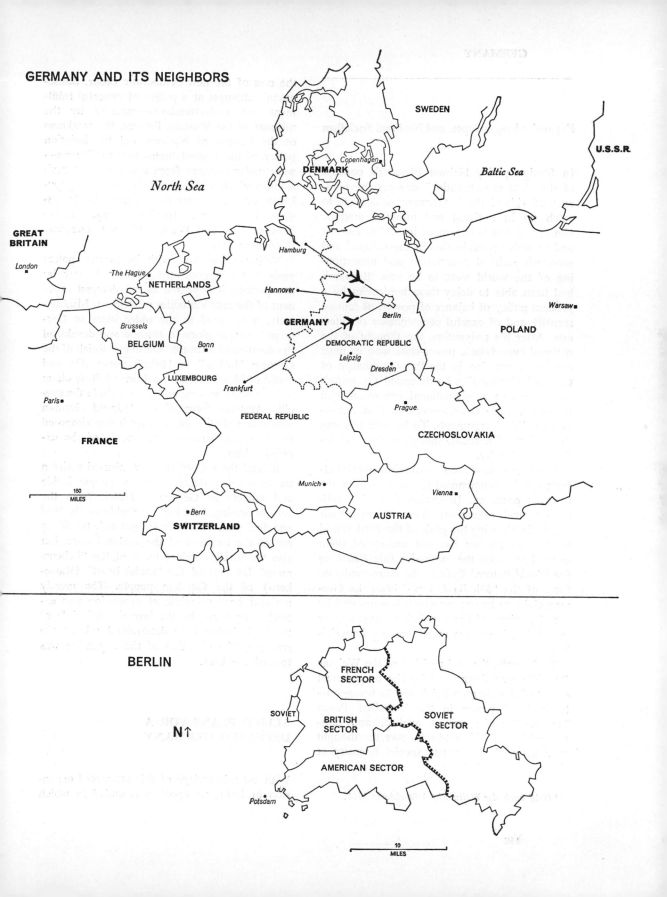

GERMANY AND ITS NEIGHBORS

SWEDEN

U.S.S.R.

DENMARK

Copenhagen

North Sea

Baltic Sea

GREAT
BRITAIN

London

The Hague

Hamburg

NETHERLANDS

Hannover

Warsaw

Brussels

GERMANY

Berlin

POLAND

BELGIUM

Bonn

DEMOCRATIC REPUBLIC

Leipzig

LUXEMBOURG

Dresden

Paris

Frankfurt

FEDERAL REPUBLIC

Prague

FRANCE

CZECHOSLOVAKIA

150
MILES

Munich

Vienna

AUSTRIA

Bern

SWITZERLAND

BERLIN

FRENCH
SECTOR

SOVIET

N↑

BRITISH
SECTOR

SOVIET
SECTOR

AMERICAN SECTOR

Potsdam

10
MILES

Expansionism, collapse, and National Socialism

In foreign policy Helmut Plessner's concept of the "late comer nation" denotes the tendency of wide circles in Germany to demand to catch up in national and imperial matters. German claims to hegemony in Middle-Europe and to active participation in the colonial and economic-political penetration and apportioning of the world were to be met. Bismarck had been able to delay these tendencies by a prudent policy of balance of power, of mutual security and of careful compromises of interests. After his resignation, the thought of the national-imperialistic power-state won its most extreme expression in the Pan-Germanism of the "All Germans" who defended Germany's pretensions to ethnic-national expansion with historical, cultural and—even at that time—racial-political arguments. To be sure this was the policy of a small, though active and influential minority.

More important are the colonial-imperial efforts which accompanied the expansion of the German economy. In conjunction with military-political arguments, these reached their climax in planning the goals of the First World War. Fritz Fischer has just uncovered them in his book with the expressive title *Reaching for World Power*.[1] Even in the more moderate form of the "Middle Europe" idea, the German claim to hegemony which is supported by broad sections of the population, must appear to neighboring states as threatening imperialism.

To be sure, the real position of the Weimar Republic was determined by the unequivocal defeat of the German Reich and its severe curtailment of power in the Versailles Peace Treaty. But the protest against, and non-recognition of, this set-back, gave the thought of a national power-state special intensity at

[1] *Griff nach der Weltmacht.* Düsseldorf: 1961.

the cost of the new democratic order. Stresemann's attempts at a policy of peaceful fulfilment and understanding—impaired by the mistrust of the Western Powers, the weakness of the League of Nations and the isolation policy of the United States toward Europe—were under pressure from a nationalistic revisionism which seized broad circles of the population, especially after the onset of the depression. The Weimar foreign policy, shifting between East and West, could not overcome these dynamics.

National Socialism with its foreign policy goals had two contrasting facets. In day by day politics, it appeared as the sharpest exponent of the anti-Versailles movement. Ideologically, it returned to the older ideas of Germany's unique place in Europe and developed the doctrine of a future "Germanic Reich of the German Nation." In Hitler's personality and world of ideas, this national-imperialistic claim to hegemony was expanded to include the specific Austrian form of the "Grand German idea"; in a significant manner it superimposed the Prussian-German components of the expansion idea.

Behind the veil of cleverly misused revision tactics—which deceived many people inside and outside of Germany—Hitler, from the very beginning, held imperturbably to his fixed and final goal. This included not only the filling out of the territory of the national state, but also the forcible enlargement of the "Lebensraum" far beyond the "racial heart" (Rassekern) of the German people. The merely national state principle of expansion was extended, or burst, by the imperial principle of the biological-racially determined rule of the stronger. The direction of the expansion was toward the East.

ALLIED PLANS FOR A DEFEATED GERMANY

With the miscarriage of this attempted expansion in 1945, an epoch was ended in which

German foreign policy had interpreted its central position and its difficult ethnic-national problems as an invitation to hegemonial claims. Under Hitler, the "solution" to this problem developed into a terror and annihilation policy toward all peoples that were biologically or politically not in favor. To be sure, the problems which had led to such results had not disappeared entirely with the 1945 capitulation. On the contrary, they fundamentally determined the very policies with which the occupying Powers attempted to liquidate National Socialism and to put an end to its hypotheses.

The legacy of the Hitler era

There now began a new epoch in the sad history of the "German question" in which there was no success in completely removing the legacy of past decades. Germany all too suddenly became a focal point in a new constellation of international politics—an East-West struggle in whose causes the "Third Reich" had played such an important part by the destruction of the European balance of power and by Hitler's policy of ruthless expansion. In the future East-West struggle—in its origin as well as its various later stages—the status of the German problem formed one of the central subjects and tests of international politics. There could not be a withdrawal from history and politics as some had hoped.

The previous history of Allied policy toward Germany sowed the seeds of the future German problem. Just as the German catastrophe did not start with the defeat and splitting of Germany in 1945, but really began with the Germans' surrender to Hitler's policies in 1933, so the problem of Germany as a basic element in the future East-West conflict is essentially an outgrowth of that destruction of the European system of balance of power.

By starting the war, Hitler had pushed the democratic Western Powers into an alliance with the totalitarian Soviet Union. But the military end of the war in Europe was darkened by differences of opinion among the victorious Powers. The change of the war alliance into an enduring peaceful arrangement had to reckon with the new problems which resulted from the structural change of international politics, especially from the enormous increase in power of the United States and the Soviet Union.

In the face of the Russian participation in the war, American foreign policy had shown itself quite yielding toward Soviet claims for hegemony in Eastern Europe. The Russian claim to Eastern Poland, established in the secret agreements in the Hitler-Stalin pact of 1939, had already been broadly confirmed in Teheran. This meant, although the details remained unsettled, that the grave basic decision had been made in principle to compensate Poland for her losses in the east by shifting the western boundary at the expense of East Germany.

The conference in Yalta was not able to clarify the fronts and mark out the stages of the future policy on Germany. The question of Germany's eastern boundary, in particular, was reserved for a future peace treaty. But the mass flight of the German population from the territories east of the Oder-Neisse boundary and their administration by Polish authorities under the Russian occupation pointed in advance to a de facto decision. Likewise, the various plans for the division of what was left of Germany, which were discussed by the Russians as well as English and Americans, were left completely unsettled. They were referred for further discussion to special commissions of the Great Powers.

Occupation policies

The pressure of events and urgencies which arose from the military occupation of conquered Germany proved to be stronger and more decisive. Instead of a definite plan for the future, only the boundaries of the occupation zones were fixed in an agreement in November 1944. North Germany fell to the British, South Germany to the Americans and Middle Germany to the Russians. After the inclusion of France and the enlargement of the Three Power Commission to one of Four Powers, parts of the British and American zones were united to form a French occupation zone in southwestern and western Germany. However, the Yalta conference retained the economic unity of Germany instead of a definite plan of division, in consideration of the Russian demands for reparations. The political future of the country remained obscure.

This situation was not changed by the first postwar conferences. At the Potsdam meeting in July 1945, only a few basic principles of the policy for Germany had become recognizable. These had already been fixed in the declaration of capitulation and in the first agreements of the allied military commanders in May and June 1945. According to these regulations, the four allies were to exercise full administrative powers in Germany through their supreme military commanders. Control would be at three different levels: first, within the four zones; second, in the four sectors of Berlin—the city was placed under Four Power occupation and administration—and finally, jointly over all questions affecting Germany as a whole. A Four Power control commission had to agree unanimously in its decisions.

The whole problem of Germany was reflected in the complicated structure of the occupation policy. Only under the conditions of a positive continuation of the war alliance in peacetime could this complicated framework really function, combining as it did the division and unity of Germany at the same time. These conditions were an illusion even though the United States, England, and the Soviet Union expressly agreed in Potsdam to act jointly on Germany as far as possible.

The final agreement on Germany states: 1. that the transferring to Russia of a part of East Prussia and Koenigsberg would also be supported by the three Great Powers "at the approaching peace settlement"; 2. that the remaining German eastern territories, east of the Oder-Neisse line, would be placed under Polish administration until the final determination of Poland's western boundary.

That was a provisional settlement which, because of its obscurity, was open to the most varied interpretations by both East and West. To this day, it burdens not only the policy of the Great Powers, but also the initiation and direction of a German foreign policy toward Eastern Europe. While the Russians and Poles stood firm in their interpretation of the final character of the boundary settlement, and this interpretation was confirmed formally in 1950 by the Communistic regime of the East German "Democratic Republic," the West has emphasized the provisional nature of the arrangement.

Two factors should be noted, however: First, the full acceptance of the expulsion and resettlement of the German population of these territories, which the Western Powers recognized in the Potsdam agreement, contained in itself a de facto acceptance of the Oder-Neisse boundaries. The juristic proviso that a final settlement should be made by a peace treaty remained a contradictory theorem. Secondly, the chance in the near future of a global peace conference which would bring this legal question to a political solution had retreated far away because of the development of international politics.

Taken as a whole the situation of conquered and prostrate Germany presented a dilemma that was like a vicious circle. The ad-hoc limitation of the spheres of influence and power of the Great Powers hampered a secure and lasting settlement concerning the size and status of the future Germany. The increasing tensions between the allies quickly led to a paralyzing of the All-German Control Council and the de facto separation of the Western zones from the Soviet occupation zone. The result of this development—the rise of two German state structures under the guardianship of rival Great Powers—made the state form and sovereignty of Germany dependent on the course of the Cold War.

The more closely the international lines were drawn, the quicker German politics freed itself from the fetters that bound it and the more evident became the provisional nature of the postwar regulations and the need for their reform. That meant a complicated combination of factors and problems which has remained ominously at the basis of the German problem.

The establishment of the Federal Republic of Germany containing almost three-fourths of the German population was undertaken with the idea that it would have an increasingly effective role in decision-making. This corresponded to the ideal of a free democratic policy for a state and led to an alliance on which the Western Powers, in contrast to the Soviet policy, were determined in spite of all limitations. However, the Federal Republic—created to cope with Germany's problems in light of the division—had been founded from the very beginning on the claim that it was to look after German interests as the deputy for All-Germany. The consequence was that it was burdened with the whole weight of the problems of international tensions, boundaries, and re-unification.

This situation, paradoxical and extremely contradictory, did not at first receive due recognition. The full dimensions of these problems and the perils they present for international politics have only become apparent with the passing years.

THE BREAKUP OF THE WARTIME ALLIANCE

The basic goals of Allied policy toward Germany after the capitulation of the Hitler regime included the following: the annihilation of National Socialism and the punishment of the guilty, the complete disarmament and demilitarization of Germany, the curtailment and control of her economic potential, and the supervision and democratization of her public life. But the extensive differences between the Western Powers and the Soviet Union made a uniform policy for achieving these goals impossible.

Yielding to Soviet demands

While Stalin's totalitarian regime was able to concentrate all of its power on the consolidation and extension of the position of power it had won in the war, the Western democracies, in conformity with their nature, had to consider the currents of public opinion, and the changing conditions of internal policies in peacetime. Strong pro-Russian feelings resulting from the wartime alliance, particularly in the United States, the activity of Communist parties in the West—their loyalty extended more to the foreign policy of the Soviet Union than to that of their own country—and above all, war-weariness induced the Western Powers to favor return to a peacetime economy and rapid disarmament. The possession of the atom bomb seemed to the United States to be a sufficient and adequate guarantee of the military and political balance of power. In reality, the West yielded to the Soviets, alternately affected by illusions and fear. By the settlement of the eastern boundary question and, even more, in the matter of the right of national self-determination, essentials of the program of the Atlantic Charter and the "Crusade for Democracy" were sacrificed to the Russian interests.

It was understandable and perhaps unavoidable that consideration be given to the demands for revision and security by Germany's eastern neighbors. However, one must question a policy which accepted the new excesses of a nationalism which, in Hitler fashion, attempted to secure its survival by the mass expulsion of all linguistic-ethnic foreigners. The moral and international legal aspects of Hitler's "total solution" to the nationality problem in Middle and East Europe cannot be examined here. The fact remains, however, that the terrible example of the National Socialist re-settlement and annihilation policy rebounded on the Germans themselves.

The political aspect of those events was to be of great importance in the future. For example, Poland was forced into a close community of interests with the Soviet Union, partially because the latter had made possible, and sanctioned the "cleaning up of the boundary and nationality problems."

To be sure, the role of Germany in the future was given scant attention between 1945 and 1948. Thoughts of national prestige and traditional power politics also determined the new order of the postwar world, contrary to the hopes and expectations of the Roosevelt era. The ideal of "one world" soon clashed on the boundaries of realistic international politics, even after the eager and hopeful founding of a supranational organization in the form of the United Nations. Although this body, thanks to the participation of all Great Powers, promised to be a more effective force than the former League of Nations, still there had already appeared the first conflicts between East and West at the end of 1945 and the beginning of 1946.

Churchill, with the frankness of a private citizen, expressed this growing conflict in a speech which he gave on March 5, 1946, in the presence of President Truman in Fulton, Missouri. From Stettin to Trieste

> an iron curtain has fallen clear across the continent. Behind this line lie all the capitals of Central and Eastern Europe. That is not the liberated Europe for which we fought. It is also not Europe that bears the features of a lasting peace."[2]

In the arguments about Iran and Turkey and later those about Greece, the sharp fronts of the Cold War became clearly evident.

[2] *New York Times*, March 6, 1946, p. 4.

The Truman Doctrine ends Western complaisance

With the proclamation of the Truman Doctrine in March 1947 the turning point was clear for everyone to see. It lay in the resolution of the United States not to withdraw from international politics as it had done after 1918. It also meant a halt to the disarmament policy of the United States and a call to halt the advance of the Soviet Union, not only with diplomatic protests but also with economic and military-political action. The new policy of containment had begun.

This change had decisive results for the allied policy toward Germany. With the breakup of a unified policy by the Four Power Control Council, both internal and external differences became sharper. The apparent peace of 1945 gave way to deep conflicts of opinion about the political, social, economic and intellectual-cultural treatment of Germany. To the American proposals for the demilitarization of Germany presented by Secretary of State Byrnes in the summer of 1946, Molotov replied with the unconditional demand that the period of occupation must be extended to at least 40 years and the "policy of democratization" be carried through consistently in the West, after the model of the Soviet occupation policy. With this plan in mind, Molotov inconsistently called for the re-establishment of German unity (with the final exclusion of the eastern territories), but rejected as premature Byrnes' suggested preparation of a peace treaty.

The immediate result of this conflict was the union of the American and English zones into the "Bizone."[3] Instead of continued industrial dismantling, the thought gained ground that a constructive economic and occupation pol-

[3] In keeping with their original hesitancy and even negative attitude, the French were not ready to form a Trizone until 1948.

icy would contribute to the support of the newly formed Länder governments and serve as a necessary answer to the failure of a unified East-West policy on Germany. To supplement this new policy, the West gradually stopped the dismantling of German industry and rejected Russian demands for reparations from the Western zones.

The new goal of Western policies was the reconstruction and recovery of Western and Central Europe, an area shattered by the war and torn by crises. As the core area, Germany had to be included, disregarding all feelings of antipathy or sympathy. To be sure, the western zones of Germany were under secure control by the occupation forces. A revival of National Socialism was no more a threat than the danger of a seizure of power by the Communists. This danger was less in Germany than elsewhere in Western Europe where the Communist parties had increased their strength during the war and up to 1947.

However, misery and poverty in Western Europe contained definite dangers which were not effectively attacked until the historic establishment of the Marshall Plan in June of 1947. Its fundamental and basic thought was that American help would not be dissipated by piecemeal aid to individual countries but that it would treat Europe as a whole and also include West Germany. As one of the most effective economic operations of more recent history, the Marshall Plan created a new constructive element of international policy. It did this because it was undertaken by the thoroughly well-understood self-interest of the United States and at the same time had laid the basis for a realistically launched policy of European union.

The fact that the original scope of this new undertaking was limited and took on an anti-Soviet accent was a direct result of the opposition of the Soviet Union. Under Russian pressure, Finland and Czechoslovakia had to forego participation in the plan. In this way the Marshall Plan became an economic-political complement to the policy of political containment.

This was the background for the formation of the Federal Republic of Germany (*Bundesrepublik Deutschland*). Oriented toward the West, founded on the de facto division of Germany, it still assumed the claim to represent all of Germany. Thus, it remained confronted with basic problems of past German politics —the position between East and West and the national question. This new Germany was to be a part of the Western alliance. But the transition from an occupation policy to that of ally, with all of its consequences for the revival of a German foreign policy, had its roots in the circumstances of the birth of the Federal Republic.

THE ESTABLISHMENT OF THE FEDERAL REPUBLIC

The political, economic and human effects of complete defeat, the huge stream of expellees, demilitarization, and the denazification of millions had made Germany a vacuum in the years 1945–48. Unlike 1918, the country seemed to be much more exposed to the dynamics of revolutionary developments. However, the rigorous policy of the occupation stood in the way. Large portions of the population—shocked and made miserable by the physical and ideological strains of the "total war"—remained in political apathy expressed by the phrase "*ohne mich*"—without me. Even after the founding of new parties and Länder governments, this apathy could be overcome only slowly. And it had a rebirth after Germany was drawn again into world politics.

Gradual emergence of self-government

The original aimlessness and lack of co-ordination in the Western allies' German policy— complicated as it was by changes in leadership in Washington and London as well as internal problems in France and the willfulness of de Gaulle—gave way in 1946 to a new organization of self-government. It had become clear that the desired democratization or re-education remained mere theory or negative repression as long as it was not oriented toward a government of its own and was unable to fulfill itself in political action and responsibility.

The gradual emergence of self-government in the West was fundamentally different from the measures followed in the Soviet zone of occupation. There all instruments were used to bring about a Communistic unified state. The German Social Democratic Party (SPD) and the German Communist Party (KPD) were forced into one Soviet-controlled "Socialist United Party" (SED).

The actual developments in self-government were far in advance of the slow planning and decision-making of the Control Council. Indeed, the Control Council actually inhibited self-government. The constitutional unity of the many fragments—the four zones, divided Berlin, East Prussia annexed by the Russians, the eastern areas under Polish administration, and the Saar area—was robbed of any reality by the complete legislative power of the allies, their growing political differences and the resulting failure of the Control Council. The Berlin Blockade brought this growing split to world attention and hastened its political institutionalization and stabilization.

Even more quickly than at the zonal level, the Allied Kommandantura of Berlin—the Control Council in miniature—proved how little it could fulfill its task as administrative head of Berlin. The Western Powers never had enough assurance of access to their Berlin sectors. Finally the Soviet Union attempted to break this Western bastion of strength in the middle of her sphere of influence and to demonstrate her superiority by blockading the land access to Berlin.

The political importance of this test of strength lies in the fact that, for the first time, the new American course in the East-West struggle was tested at the point of conflict and was successfully carried on to the end by the use of a great air lift. No less important was the attitude of the West Berliners who re-affirmed their former votes. While they gave this test of power its political meaning, at the same time their decision established an incentive and direction for developing West German politics. It also created a consciousness that there should be a desire to direct her own foreign policy, thus dispelling postwar apathy.

But even with the successful conclusion of the Berlin conflict, the Western Powers were not able to improve the uncertain and poorly functioning occupation agreements with the Soviet Union. Divided Berlin in its island position remained as difficult a problem as ever. The Russians continued to paralyze the joint government.

The formation of two separated German states in the East and West immediately gave the total conflict a new sharpness. For this meant not only the actual collapse of the Four Powers policy—the only bond of political unity—but also the removal into a vague future of the functioning of Berlin as a potential capital of a postwar Germany. It was clear that Berlin could be protected permanently only by an immediate and constantly dependable working agreement of the Great Powers. Yet it was just such an agreement that was endangered by the end of the Four Power occupation policy and the founding of separated states. The West could evade and delay the consequences of this dilemma for ten years by a limited co-operation in Berlin, by ignoring the actual division of Germany and by meticulous adherence to the Four Power statute for the city.

Perpetuating the status quo

The establishment of the Federal Republic and its Soviet satellite imitation, the German Democratic Republic, clearly brought problems for the future. The Germans who wished to have a sovereign state again, as well as the protection of the Western allies, carry a heavy responsibility for this. They chose economic and political resurgence without sufficiently considering the instability of the status quo and the difficulty of combining a policy of consolidation with one of revision.

The new start of a foreign policy in the Federal Republic is continuously determined by this dilemma. The Western policy was tied in all details so extensively to a status quo solution (or apparent solution) of the German problem that it seems neither honest nor realistic to minimize the weight of this decision, as do many current proposals for a solution of the German question. Of course this does not remove the chief responsibility from Germany, since she has made her voice heard and since she has a major effect on Western policy, on international policy concerning Germany, and even on the policy of the Soviet Union.

In retrospect, there has been much noteworthy criticism of the policy which led so quickly to the formation of a German state in 1949. Such criticism cannot be dismissed simply as the opinions of neutralist or pro-Soviet groups and partisans. Shrewd observers of the international scene, such as Paul Sethe, the German political writer, have pointed out repeatedly that there were not sufficiently serious attempts to test the Soviet proposals for a unified German government. Successful negotiations would not have been easy. Certainly there would have been difficulties, perhaps ending in impracticable negotiations concerning the international status of the German state, its limitations, and its place in Europe.

The whole problem of the traditional East-West position of what Gerald Freund calls the "Germany between two worlds" might again have been revived. The reminiscence of a "Rapallo policy" or of the "Stalin-Hitler pact" would again have been a cause for fear. But it is also disadvantageous for the Western position and its credibility if the initiative for such proposals is left to the Soviet Union. The Molotov proposals in June of 1947 and those of Stalin in 1952 would probably not have led to an All-German unification which would have encouraged constitutional development and freedom. Territorial questions such as that of the Eastern boundary also would have been a problem.

But the early demands of the Soviet Union should not have led to an abandonment of all attempts to negotiate for the future status of Germany. Could not such an abandonment be considered a sign of purely defensive thinking on the part of the West? Our criticism does not plead for agreement to the Russian demands, toward which America had to be most cautious because of the world political situation in 1947–48 and again in 1952. It is directed at a policy of giving up on negotiations while still asking the Soviets to give proof of apparent readiness to make concessions.

After the disappointments of the appeasement era of 1945–46, the American decision to accept the consequences of the containment policy—which included Germany—is clearly understandable and perhaps unavoidable. The Americans considered the Soviet policy as a strategy of attrition, against which only a clarification and demarcation of the fronts could help—even though it meant the certain bitter result of division. Moreover, one must not forget that, from the point of view of a constructive policy for Europe and Germany, the Soviet Union on its part had refused to have anything to do with a solution when it declined to accept the Western invitation to enter the Marshall Plan.

BASIC PROBLEMS OF THE FEDERAL REPUBLIC

Three basic factors have greatly influenced the foreign policy orientation of the West German government. (1) The Federal Republic of Germany owed its origin to the trial of strength between the United States and the Soviet Union; its position in this alignment of fronts was therefore predetermined. (2) At the same time, its claim to represent the continuity of an All-German state included with it the protection of the All-German interests. It meant its commitment to demands for the reunion of both parts of Germany, the self-determination of the entire German people, and the freely and con-stitutionally-based order and sovereignty of a future All-German state. However (3) real policy was directed towards a consolidation of the balance of power, as demanded by the role of the Federal Republic of Germany as a central pillar in the Western policies of containment. After the breakup of a Four Power solution, the task of controlling West Germany and fitting it into the Western scheme of things became the job of the Western European alliance.

Adenauer sets a policy course

The election in 1949 of Konrad Adenauer, chief of the CDU, to be the first Federal Chancellor, had been a very close one; Adenauer's own vote was said to be the deciding one. But with the exception of the weak KPD, all parties were, in principle, committed to a Western view. The "Europe Organizations" favored by Germany followed the plan which called for a Council of Europe, oriented toward the West, at the expense of the original idea of an All-European Organization. The Bonn Constitution of 1949 had expressly provided for the limitation of German sovereignty in favor of supranational organizations. The future pattern for a Western security system was thus unmistakable. The question was only what form this co-operation should take and how it should be combined with the desires for a united Germany.

The course of the Adenauer government was not without internal contradictions, when the firm Western policy collided with the All-German goal, and with the policy of continuity which was so firmly claimed by the government's jurists. Unlike Austria at the end of the occupation regime, the possibility of a neutrality solution seemed excluded by the actual split from which the new German state arose. However, the Social Democratic opposition under the leadership of Kurt Schumacher was in accord with strong popular movements when it admonished Adenauer to caution in his

Western policy. It warned him not to jeopardize a future peace treaty for All-Germany by irrevocable "Vorleistungen"—actions or accomplishments made too soon. Even though the area for freedom of decision was limited and the personal passions of the leaders led to exaggerations of the main conflict, still the problems and finally the dilemma of the later German foreign policy undeniably had their beginnings here. The Adenauer government did not thoroughly think through the ambivalence of its motives and interests. Indeed, it often enough damned the alternative suggestions of the opposition as "Communist-inspired."

It seems that the logical consequence of this policy would have been to abandon positively every thought of revision and to examine the real strength of the Federal Republic's claims to represent All-Germany, and to agree to a settlement of the Eastern boundaries and a normalizing of the relations with the Eastern neighbors on the basis of the status quo.

This conclusion was not drawn, mainly because of the duty to represent the oppressed population of East Germany as well as the expellees. There still remained the basic contradiction which the formal construction of the "Hallstein Doctrine"—the negation of the two-states theory—and the continuing Four Power responsibility later tried unsuccessfully to conceal. Above all this policy hurt Berlin whose inclusion in the Federal Republic failed because of makeshift arrangements which proved to be ineffective. The outcome of this policy also hurt the population of the East German Republic which had to pay for its contradictory position by a sharpening of the Communist regime and finally by a complete separation from the West.

And so the course was set, the basic decisions apparently pre-arranged. It remained to be seen what possibilities the activity of the political leadership and the various groupings of the Federal Republic would open up for the easing, or at least partial solution, of the German problem in the advancing course of the East-West conflict. To make the most of these was, to be sure, possible only within the framework of the limitations placed on the constitutional order and policies of the Federal Republic by the new Three Power occupation statute of September 21, 1949, and the Petersberg agreement of November 22, 1949. Under these, the Federal Republic no longer kept free from an alliance with the blocs. Along with the controlling powers over economic and military matters, the Western states claimed control over the direction of foreign policy and the alignment with the West.

The West German government followed this course in full harmony with the will of a parliamentary majority. But a strong opposition rallied to the views of the SPD and its leader Kurt Schumacher. The latter had drawn the conclusion from the sad experience of Social Democracy in the Weimar Republic that the stability of a future democracy in Germany was closely linked with a high regard for national political needs.

Western European unity

Adenauer, the Rhenish politician, sought to tie the CDU to co-operation with the Christian-Catholic sister parties which were in power in other European states. This policy of a community of the "Christian democracies" of Western Europe, with their integration policy, could further the equality of rights for the Federal Republic. The great successes and progress of the policy were undeniable: the reception into the Council of Europe and the solution of the Ruhr control problem by the creation of the Montan Union in 1950 gave Western Europe and the Federal Republic a splendid chance for rapid stabilization and co-operation.

Because of the victory of communism in China, Russia seemed to have shifted its interest to Asia. The negative effects of the integration policy on the problems of division and Berlin were scarcely discernible; the fears seemed exaggerated. Likewise, the way to a German-French partnership had become

visible. This would be the basis for a solution to the German problem in the West. In addition to this, the West German government itself, by March 1950, had developed a proposal for a re-unification of Germany through free elections. The Western Powers had also agreed to this proposal.

With the coming of the Korean war and with the founding of the North Atlantic Treaty Organization, the demand for European integration was quickly tied to that of German re-armament. Here was a warning example of the dangers which threatened Germany and Europe as long as the disarmament and control policy had not yet changed into a positive German policy. For in the meantime, the Soviet-occupied German Democratic Republic had already set up armed police troops, even before they had dared to carry out sham elections for their own parliament (*Volkskammer*). These troops, under the protection of the vastly superior Soviet armed forces, were thoroughly capable of an action similar to the one in North Korea. While the West had extensively disarmed after the end of the war, the Soviet Union had kept its military strength. Also, the situation regarding strategic weapons had definitely changed. The American monopoly of the atom bomb had been broken since the fall of 1949 and the Chinese manpower potential had fallen to the Communist bloc.

Western re-armament

This dangerous shifting of strength was the background for the American decision to re-arm. Necessarily, the re-armament policy spread to Europe and caused the rapid shifting of emphasis from economic reconstruction to military security. It seemed impossible to exclude from this new security area the new, scarcely consolidated Federal Republic in the heart of Europe. To be sure, this made the unsolved German problem even more acute. Adenauer had very early declared his readiness for a military contribution from the Federal Republic. This did not mean a "militaristic" change in this declared civilian but it was thoroughly in accordance with his unreserved Western alignment.

Certainly, the desire to hasten through the military contribution the consolidation of the Federal Republic and its alignment with the West, intensified even more the ambivalence of the West German state's founding, its dilemma between being a state in its own right and the whole assumption of re-unification. The bitter clash of opinions regarding re-armament also touched the moral foundations of the Federal Republic which were anchored in the clear renunciation of the military tendencies and excesses of the German past.

Were there not three dangers involved? In the eyes of the Germans themselves, would not re-armament render unbelievable the avowal of an honest and peaceful new start, and would it not disastrously disturb the democratic growth by such a rapid shift? In addition would not the quick readiness for this change add new fuel to the mistrust in the West and make questionable the earnestness of the avowals for a united Germany? And finally—especially in the East—would not the fear of a new German threat gain bases and arguments, which, in view of the unsettled boundary question, would not be felt as mere propaganda in the Cold War? Behind these could be the double results: the isolation of Germany and the general disinclination of all Powers to really push for re-unification. The West would be opposed because an active policy for re-unification would bring into question the sure integration of the Federal Republic with the West. The East would be opposed because the Western orientation of a newly strengthened and united Germany would appear intolerable.

This was a dilemma which both sides tried to take into consideration in their own way: the West by a plan of integrating the West German forces into a European Defense Community; the Soviet Union by the much discussed projection of the Stalin note of March 1952 for a settlement of the German problem. Both occurred at a time when the occupying Powers

had conceded to the Federal Republic the establishment of its own foreign office after a transitional period. The Federal Republic, whose chancellor had reserved this office for himself, was thereby challenged to develop and test the controversial conception and interests of a German foreign policy on a crucial constellation of states.

To be sure, the government had to reckon with the various groups and media which argued over the means and goals of this foreign policy. The democratic formation of opinion, enlargement of sovereignty, and change of manner of the incessant East-West conflict were the factors of this argument; stabilization, security, integration and German division were the main themes. The problems were as diverse as they were difficult. A profound conflict of interests, virulent and powerful, lay in the background of all the policies—German, European and Western.

SETTING THE COURSE OF GERMAN FOREIGN POLICY

The allied postwar policy had started with the assumption that Germany would have to be kept under control for a long time and be deprived of any real military potential. That policy was based on the conviction that Germany would be able to carry on a pernicious policy if she could play the East against the West. From the historical point of view, this was true at most only for the Second World War; certainly it was not true for the First World War. But the possibility of a revival of the overrated "Rapallo policy" remained a bogy for the West.

Repercussions of East-West tensions

After the final breakup of the Four Power regime in 1948–49, the problem of Germany had two main aspects in which international and domestic German problems were closely intertwined. Germany's refitting into the European system of states and the new beginning of a German policy that could maneuver, were closely linked with the split into two German states, which, on the basis of external power circumstances, began to exist and to develop each in its unique way, under completely different conditions.

In these two fundamental facts there existed, at least in the eyes of the foreign states concerned, a partial solution to the German problem. The co-ordination of the Federal Republic with the West and the German Democratic Republic with the East, seemed to solve two problems at once: it would guarantee in Central Europe a clear demarcation of the military and political spheres of the two blocs and it would prevent the much feared see-saw policy of a newly arisen Germany.

The only question was how this presumed "solution" could be reliably guaranteed and how it could also be firmly established with the consent of the German population and at the same time be brought into harmony with the avowed goal of re-unification. This was not an insoluble problem for the Soviet Union after she had given up hope of drawing all of Germany into her sphere of influence. With a persistent continuation of the occupation policy and with a tightening of the "people's democratic" Communistic course, the German Democratic Republic quickly developed into an unconditionally obedient satellite. Agitation for independence remained ineffectual or was smothered more consistently than in any other satellite state. This was the case on June 17, 1953.

The situation was clearly different in the Federal Republic. Free parties and interest groups, a freely elected parliament, a democratic-legal constitutional order left wide opportunity for the formation of public opinion and decision-making. There were practically no advocates for an alignment with the East, if one disregarded the small Communist party —later forbidden—and a few insignificant groups, mostly directed from the East. But the

growing sympathy for the Western policy and way of life did not mean that serious questions could not be asked. Did not the tie with the West destroy the chance of furthering the re-unification of Germany through neutralization? In the long run, would it be possible to settle the German problem if Germany was tied to the West?

The rapid pace of European integration and the progress of the Western defense system were the important reasons why such considerations and such questions received scant attention. Public opinion overwhelmingly supported the Western orientation of the Federal Republic. This policy met three vital needs: It accelerated the recovery process of West Germany and promised a rapid transition from the occupation regime to political equality; it opened up the view to new supranational principles of value which had largely been ignored in Germany during the Hitler period; it contained for Germany's neighbors a system of guarantees against a new policy of German hegemony.

There were no differences of opinion about these goals, and especially about the need to have Germany become a part of a broader association of states. The only difference was that the Social Democrats advocated as wide an area as possible for European unity—one that would include the Anglo-Saxon and Scandinavian countries and one that would be flexible in regard to the problem of the division of Germany. The Council of Europe in Strasbourg could be considered a suitable starting point for such a union.

Opposed to this, the Adenauer government —in accord with the concrete progress of the integration policy—held to the "little Europe" solution of a Community of the Six. Naturally, there would be a close association with the Anglo-Saxon Powers and a later extension of the community. But the earlier idea of a "third" European force continued to have an effect. Of course the growing sharpness of the East-West conflict and the drawing of a re-armed Germany into the defense system of the West helped to set the tone for the discussion of German foreign policy.

The question of remilitarization

A revived Germany that would be able to help strengthen the Western military potential and at the same time contribute to her own defense would obviously arouse suspicions throughout Europe. Of course, such a revival of power would also bring a strong reaction from the Soviet Union. The United States made every attempt to allay the fears which were expressed in both England and France. The new German military might would not be a danger because it would be completely integrated with the new European Defense Community and thereby placed under permanent control. Naturally, this arrangement depended on the consent of the partners. This consent was withheld, and the plan was finally defeated by France.

The debate over both goals and the method of achieving them continued in Germany. Adenauer insisted that a military contribution to the West would give the quality of complete statehood to the Federal Republic and would benefit his policy for the security and equalizing of Germany within the framework of the Western community. Of course, this stand for a remilitarized Germany meant a revolutionary shift in both policy and fundamental political opinions. Many politicians, not excluding Adenauer, had spoken in the recent past about the need for a German renunciation of military power as provided in the new constitution.

With good reason one might fear that the headlong change from demilitarization to remilitarization might again endanger the tender plant of democracy, disturb her inner and outer growth, nurture old and new painful memories of the Allied postwar policy in this matter. Moreover, it would make the entire German problem infinitely more complicated. The Social Democrats wished to have the German contribution to the defense limited to economic and political aid, at least until the creation of a supranational European author-

ity. There was no real criticism of the principle of European defense and integration, but there were objections to the speed of the German change in orientation.

The great debate over German unification, unity with the West and re-armament did not become simpler as the years dragged on. The Government, by its victory in the campaign of 1953, gained the necessary majority to change the constitution regarding military power. With the defeat of the proposed Defense Community, NATO was adopted as an alternative. But this new arrangement did not solve the basic question of the German problem and was only able to guarantee the status quo.

With the NATO plan adopted, the question of the new German army came to the fore. What would be the status and character of an army that was "half national" and "half integrated" into a supranational force? Certainly this new army would operate within the framework of NATO and within the bounds of the United States' position of hegemony. However, its mere existence would operate to strengthen the "restoring" tendencies in state and society. It clearly offered Soviet propaganda a welcome opportunity to defame the demand for re-unification when this demand was sought by way of a "policy of strength." This also raised grave questions for Germany's neighbors who had been victims of the National Socialist regime. Finally, the continuity of the German Reich in the Federal Republic proved to be a two-edged sword: Germany would be recognized as one of the major Western states, but the problem of breaking with the Hitler years would be very difficult.

ALTERNATIVE SOLUTIONS FOR MAJOR POLICY PROBLEMS

During the first half of the 1950's, following the Korean war, German foreign policy had to adjust to the return to the status quo in a divided world. In the search for possibilities of action and alternatives in a solidified situation, special attention was called for in four problem areas: improving German-Soviet relations, the conditions for relaxing tensions, reviewing military-political power relationships in view of the new atomic equilibrium, and finally, the unfolding of the American policy toward Germany after the transition to the Eisenhower-Dulles era.

Re-unification

The problem of re-unification remained at the center of the German problem. Both the East and the West insisted that, when re-unification took place, it would take place on its terms. According to democratic concepts, the Federal Republic had the stronger, more legitimate position. It was not only the much larger state with three quarters of the German population, but it could, since its policy and government were based on free elections, represent from the very beginning the demand for free All-German elections as the legal and politically legitimate way to a democratic united Germany.

This was an advantage in principle which seriously handicapped Soviet policy toward Germany in the field of international relations and, especially, in the question of the recognition of the German Democratic Republic. At the same time there also remained in the non-Communist world—with all understanding for the legitimacy of the German demands—such a vivid memory of National Socialist Germany that the re-unification thesis of a government representing the continuity of German statehood could not exactly expect complete support.

The result was the unspoken insight, that the Federal Republic must adapt itself to the new situation of the status quo, to the policy of containment; that the security of its existence took precedence over an unsure policy of re-unification. In viewing the situation Adenauer had drawn the following conclusions: The way

to re-unification by way of a Western alliance and the strengthening of the West German position could mean nothing but the primacy of West Germany's freedom and security over the national unity and the freeing of the East German population. How little this decision was allowed to become known, how few were aware of it, was proved by the frightened alarm and indignation of the German public —even within the government camp—whenever the consequences of that course of action were bluntly made clear.

Soviet proposals for a peace treaty

In the meantime, there had been much discussion about alternatives to the policy of the Government. They lay on two different planes that were closely connected: the one was the adjustment of interests and relaxing of tensions between the Great Powers; the other was the development and shaping of a new German-Soviet relationship.

The slogan "co-existence" began to show its influence; it affected the German problem just as it did the new states of Asia and Africa. Even before the death of Stalin and the presidential change in Washington, there seemed to open up a new era of East-West politics with the easing of tensions and disarmament conferences. There appeared with the Stalin note in the spring of 1952 the thought of a partial solution—as in the case of the Austrian question. To be sure, the timing of the Soviet initiative would expose it to the suspicion from the very beginning that it did not deal with a constructive solution but was merely a diversionary action, even if on a grand scale.

On March 10, 1952, the Soviet Union presented new proposals for a peace treaty with Germany. While Moscow, in 1950, had still pushed the formation of a central government on the basis of equality with representatives of the Federal Republic and the German Democratic Republic, now Stalin placed the chief emphasis on the withdrawal of the armed forces and an "alliance-free" re-united Germany. The breaking up of alliances and an exclusion and neutralization seemed more important to the Russians than a "Communistic solution." This change of attitude, so difficult to grasp in all its details, was now to occupy the internal battle of opinion and it continues to do so even to the present day.

It is true that the Soviet proposition belonged within the world political frame of a disarmament campaign which—after the failure of the Korean policy—attempted to attack the newly strengthened Western position in its alliance system. Germany represented the most important and probably *still* the weakest spot. Also, the Soviet Union, which could imagine itself secure in its bloc system, might expect profound repercussions on the attitudes of France and England as the result of such a neutralization of Central Europe. The return to the unsettled alignments of the prewar era, to the French-Russian security alliance might cause a new orientation of the Federal Republic with the American withdrawal from Europe. This would also have its effects on the inner political-power relationships in Germany.

Such considerations make it probable that the possibility existed here for the first and perhaps only time to test seriously the Soviet and Soviet-German claims and protestations for unification. The proposal for free All-German elections for a national assembly on the basis of the election law of the Weimar Republic with which the East German Minister President Otto Grotewohl amplified the Soviet note on March 14, 1952, seemed to offer an astonishingly real starting point, even though the demand for the exclusion from the election of "undemocratic and unpeaceful organizations" might give the Soviet policy various possibilities for intervention.

The surprising thing was that with this proposal Moscow accepted tacitly not only the West German development but also her rearmament. Certainly the national armed forces which it allowed a neutralized Germany would not outweigh or counter-balance the security guarantees of a Western alliance for the Federal Republic. But it is an open question whether, in spite of all these doubts, a delay in the West German reconstruction and alliance policies would not have been justified—while negotiations were going on. The risks and losses which were connected with a serious test of the Soviet proposals were obvious. However, to give careful consideration to any possible discussion about re-unification, about the Eastern boundary line, or the proposals for a peace treaty was the more important since Germany was still occupied. The question of the withdrawal of the occupying powers could not become acute until a satisfactory arrangement for the future of Germany had been achieved.

The Western response

The Soviet proposal was not really considered seriously. The Federal government, instead of asserting some initiative, showed relief at the caution of the West. The great worry of the Government seemed to be that nothing should delay West Germany's climb to sovereignty, the acceptance of the Federal Republic as a full partner in Europe, the strengthening of NATO and European defenses, and, finally, the insistence that nothing should slow the economic progress and material satisfaction of the population of West Germany. Of course this policy made it easy for Moscow to keep disturbing the world and especially German public opinion with calls for "peace movements" and the necessity of a neutral Germany.

Re-unification discussions, had they come to pass, would have presented the Soviet Union with no less difficult problems in regard to the Soviet zone and its satellite regime. But instead of comprehending this fact, the German policy held immovably to its juristic and institutionally anchored positions. A re-unification strategy, to be successful, would have demanded on the part of Germany positive strength, initiative, and the use of political means to gain the desired goal. That was the insoluble contradiction which had characterized the Eisenhower-Dulles era with its vacillation between the theory of the roll-back liberation policy and the practice of a mere status quo and reaction policy while, at the same time, without any checking or questioning, it abandoned to Moscow both initiative and maneuverability.

Here lies the real heart of the problem which was too lightly disposed of by the German government with its allusions to the "utopian" or "nationalist drift" of neutralist groups. It was not simply a matter of groups with their "heads in the clouds," Communist directed or not, but it was a matter of realistically feeling out the interests and weaknesses of the adversary. This must be the central task of every successful foreign policy.

There was no German contribution to the policy formation of the Western Powers, who promptly answered the Soviet proposals on March 25, 1952 with a repetition of the demand which the Eastern bloc had already rejected—that a UN commission should check beforehand the granting of political freedom in all of Germany. To be sure, that would finally lead to the inclusion of all of Germany in the West; no Soviet answer could be expected if the Federal Republic itself had nothing else to say regarding the question of re-unification. The German abstention, which has been repeated many times since, was felt by the other partners in the Western alliance to be "proper reliability." In the long run, it probably proved to be a hindrance which, in reality, narrowed the West's field of action. However, the motives of the other nations were understandable enough. The immediate need for consolidation and security seemed to be greater than the demands for disarmament and re-unification. The specter of Soviet rule, which was very evident in Berlin, added to the demands for security and unity in the West. All of this tended to give the policy of the Federal Republic legitimacy and inevitability, and even seemed to give it the stamp of necessity.

The fact that there was no deep split in the Federal Republic over this policy was due to the loyal, democratic character of the opposition. At the same time, as a result of a certain letup in the East-West conflict, the tempo of the Western policy toward Germany became more organic and at the same time the economic upswing of Europe was of great benefit to Germany. It even placed her into a preferred position. The death of Stalin gave new impetus to speculation about a lessening of international tension. Instead of a European Defense Community, the more elastic NATO solution emerged, with its defensive character which corresponded more to the military and strategic situation.

CONSOLIDATION OF THE SEPARATION

The hopes to break through the vicious circle of defense and threat moved on two levels. Either a global change of the entire world political situation could untangle the complications of the German problem; or, in a more limited area, a new formulation of German-Soviet relations might offer a new starting point for a partial relaxation and removal of tensions. On these two levels lay the main themes of foreign policy discussion which characterized the middle period of the Adenauer era from 1953 to 1958.

Freezing the status quo

The point of departure for both Soviet Russia and the Federal Republic was that the present area of influence and a guarantee of the present power position was the prerequisite for all discussions. This meant that, as in the case of the artificial separation compromise in Korea and Indochina, the German problem remained suspended while propagandistic, psychological and juristic arguments dominated the field. There were even such grotesque plans for a solution as the offer of the Soviet Union to join NATO and thus paralyze the much feared in-

GERMANY

clusion of the Federal Republic. This offer was made at the Foreign Minister's Conference which brought the four Great Powers together in Berlin in January and February, 1954.

If Berlin was at the same time both a symbol of the problem and of hope, then it also showed that the Germans' expectations and fears that the Four Powers could come up with an agreement at Germany's expense were not correct. The problem of Germany was much too closely linked with the bloc system which divided the world. The first step toward a policy of re-unification by way of free elections now implied for the Soviets the abandonment of a major cornerstone of their rule in the entire Eastern bloc. A substantial counter-concession, such as the release of West Germany from the military front, appeared just as intolerable to the West.

With this in mind, the Federal Republic energetically entered the field. It aided and supported the American view which held that a Germany re-united through free elections should be given the opportunity to decide on its own future status. Naturally, in the eyes of the Soviet Union, this was hardly a real concession. There could be no doubt which way a free All-German government would decide.

And so the Berlin conference ended without results. Progress on the German question was of interest to Moscow only if it set limits to the integration and re-armament of the Federal Republic, or even better, if it led to a complete detachment of Germany from the West. On the other side, the Western Powers showed no readiness to risk their newly fortified base in Western Europe under the changed circumstances of the atomic equilibrium.

With the formation of the Western European Union in place of the wrecked Defense Community, and the replacement of the occupation regime by a treaty with Germany—the Paris treaties of October, 1954—the Five Power alliance of the 1948 Brussels Pact, designed to control Germany, was now formally changed into an alliance with Germany. Germany was also formally taken into NATO. With greater participation in European affairs by the Atlantic Powers, French fears were reduced. Paris,

showing the rapid improvement in German-French relations, had given self-determination to the Saar population and released the Saar. It was a magnanimous gesture which set an example for re-unification, even though the conditions were not comparable and the whole matter had taken place without any action on the part of the West German government itself.

Bonn and Moscow restore diplomatic relations

With the continued insistence on the part of the West that re-unification could only take place on Western terms, the Soviet Union assumed a new type of initiative. It was clear from the violent uprising of June, 1953, that a United Germany decision in favor of the Soviet Union could not be expected. The aim of the new initiative was to institutionalize the reality of the two German states both juristically and diplomatically. This new policy reached its height and partial success with Adenauer's visit to Moscow and the resumption of diplomatic relations between Bonn and Moscow in September, 1955. Opinions differed and still differ on whether this change meant another chance toward progress on the German question. To be sure, the Federal government this time had not refused the Soviet request. The question was only whether its acquiescence now and in such a form was very beneficial to the Western and especially to German interests.

The opening of diplomatic relations between Moscow and Bonn should be placed in its proper context. There had been a revival of disarmament and security projects which were presented by East and West in the Geneva summit conferences in July, 1955. The relaxed, even optimistic atmosphere of these discussions resulted from the elasticity with which the Western Powers operated with regard to the German question.

Anthony Eden, following the Berlin Conference of 1954, had launched a plan to combine disarmament and security policies with the holding of free All-German elections. This became known as the "expanded Eden Plan." To be sure, it soon was evident how difficult his prerequisite, the creation of a "military diluted zone," could be, combined with the fact that the Western Powers believed that they had to hold fast to the West European defense system.

One is struck again with the contradictions which had characterized the German problem for a decade. Obviously, the Soviet Union had attempted to solve this problem only on the basis of the recognition of the status quo—even before it had developed its own version, opposed to the Eden Plan—and then had it extended and improved by Poland in the form of the Rapacki Plan. The ratification of the Paris treaties, which incorporated the Federal Republic as a fully equal partner in the Western system and consequently ended the occupation statute, became the occasion for action.

The Soviet Union answered with the lifting of the state of war with Germany and with the demand for normal relations between Bonn and Moscow. Adenauer found himself in a difficult situation. He could not ignore the Soviet advances if he wanted to maintain the position that Germany was independent and able to act as an independent power. But, at the same time, he saw himself faced with the disagreeable position that, with the Soviet recognition of the Federal Republic, there was the simultaneous recognition of the German Democratic Republic. Even when the goal of the German line of negotiations was to make the re-unification problem the central point of the discussions, this other side of the "normalization" had to be considered.

"Normalizing" relations

Another question was: Would not the Soviet Union, as an occupation Power, be released from its responsibility toward a united Germany if, in the future, it faced the West German state only in the relationship of sovereign state to sovereign state? It was not mere

chance that, at the very moment that Adenauer was in Moscow, the East German Minister President Grotewohl was on hand for the settlement of the two-state solution. Then only the Berlin question would remain as the last item and it would be exposed to the full pressure of the de facto events.

A real "normalizing" of relations would have had to be inextricably connected with the conclusion of a peace treaty. Here was the necessary initiative with which the Federal Republic and the West should have approached the Russian request and should have forced it into the frame of the German question. There was a double chance of success. Had not the Soviet Union itself again and again stressed the necessity of a peace treaty and used it for its All-German and world political propaganda? And was not the solving of the unsettled Berlin problem, temporarily shelved in 1949, a test case on which the seriousness of the Soviet desire for relaxing of tensions and "normalizing" might be checked?

Two widely effective arguments of future Soviet propaganda—the demands for a treaty and the Berlin situation—could thus have been used to rally world public opinion to the Western side. The Federal government missed this, for it evidently had not been sufficiently prepared for its Moscow trip. The temporary shifting of Adenauer's position for an improvement of German-Soviet relations gained rather a negative importance for the development of the German question. How questionable a "normalizing" might be, if it renounced a solution of the most important problems, was shown in the assertions of both parties. Adenauer insisted that, in entering into diplomatic relations, there was no recognition of territorial limits prior to a peace treaty nor a renunciation of the Federal Republic's claim for representing all of Germany. The Soviet Union declared that the Federal Republic formed one part of Germany; the German Democratic Republic formed the other part. Bonn's answer was the affirmation of the famous Hallstein-Doctrine; it threatened all the states recognizing the East German regime with the breach of diplomatic relations.

Initially, this policy had the logic of political strength and economic advantage on its side. However, it was again a policy of a purely negative nature, the opposite of an attempt at a solution. It blocked relations with Germany's eastern neighbors; it hindered entering the U.N. The Federal Republic now had relations with Moscow, the patron Power of the German Democratic Republic. The Soviet Union also had control of still another lever: the unresolved tension between the legal declarations and the de facto situation of a divided Berlin in the middle of the Russian dominated German Democratic Republic—a "part-state" which had been declared sovereign.

The reasons for the resulting dilemma lay in the American as well as the West German concept and policy. Since the birth and rise of the Federal Republic were inextricably linked to American policy and necessarily dependent upon it, the clear preference which Eisenhower and Dulles showed to Adenauer's government would necessarily discourage or even refute all internal criticism of the inflexible course of the Bonn government. He would discourage all attempts to develop German initiative, or to make a German contribution to the question of relaxing tension, of security, and of the German question as a whole.

INTERNAL POLITICS AND ADENAUER'S FOREIGN POLICY

The internal political scene of the Federal Republic, during the second half of the '50's, was characterized by the transcending position which Adenauer had won at the head of the "chancellor's democracy." For the first time, a German democracy had a government with a party which had an absolute majority in the legislative body. To be sure, the Social Democratic opposition could claim gains for its position and it could function as a controllable opposition.

But in the meantime nearly all of the smaller parties had been drawn into the wake of the politically and economically successful government party. They had fallen victims to the two-party tendency, the five percent clause of the election law, or had been decimated by Adenauer's divisionary tactics. The reasons were chiefly political: next to the effect of the "economic miracle," it was the continuation of the traditional distinction between "bourgeois" and "socialist" camps which largely determined political consciousness and elections without taking into consideration the social regrouping and leveling—a better term might be assimilation—of West German society.

The result was an immobility in both internal and foreign policy. Undeniably, the constant reference to the advantages and guarantees of the Western alliance, which Adenauer monopolized for his policy and proclaimed as the only policy that would solve the German problem, played an important role. But even more important were his successful tactics toward other organizations and interest groups. Adenauer granted representatives of these groups direct access to the Chancellor's office. He thus succeeded to pass over his own ministers as well as his party and parliament, thereby making his position secure from attack. The catchword "pressure group state" was not unsuitable. The hazards which were connected with this method of governing were apparent, not only for the continued development of the young German democracy but also for its foreign policy.

Adenauer's original strength—contrary to the praises of his admirers and contrary to the complaints of the opposition—lay in the area of domestic politics. The experienced chief-mayor ruled the state. The basic decision to follow the West had been conclusive. The achievement of this statesman for the consolidation of the Federal Republic lies in the art with which he has been able to render harmless the contradictory pluralism of political and social interests, and mold them into the channel of his successful course.

But his basic tactic also has a clearly negative aspect. It made it impossible for Adenauer to use his position of strength to pursue a policy which would have steered a course through the basic contradictions of the Federal Republic in the re-unification, Oder-Neisse, and Berlin policies. It cannot be a surprise that refugee organizations, former nationalists and National Socialists, vested interests of the most varied shades were not ready to contribute to finding a solution to the awful dilemma which confronted the Government in its foreign policy. Foreign criticism of these "revisionist groups" is understandable; but it does not always strike at the essential points. For instance, it seems more important that the concern for groups and movements which Adenauer believed he needed to strengthen and maintain his domestic political position, blocked every foreign policy initiative of the Federal Republic. This relieved the Western allies of the need to give additional attention to the German problem during a period when they were involved with the Suez and East Asian crises.

The shadow of Hitlerism

The much demanded "conquering of the past," which was expensively and successfully carried on in the domestic fields of education and the democratic strengthening of the Federal Republic, did not have a full counterpart in the field of foreign policy. The heavy burden of the past which the Federal Republic bore as the declared successor of the Hitler regime was lightened only toward the West, but not toward the East. Indeed, the Adenauer government had never made quite clear the fundamental difference between the questions of the Oder-Neisse line and re-unification. Such a separation of issues could have been a starting point for German-Polish relations which might have been fruitful at the time of the Polish "thaw" in 1956. It is also clear that there are moral implications of the intransigent policy of the Federal Republic. The Germans beyond the Elbe, though bearing the burden of Hitler's heritage, were given scarcely more consideration than the expellees who had participated

fully in the security and prosperity of the Federal Republic.

All of those who raised serious questions regarding the Eastern boundary were denounced as "renunciation politicians." Meanwhile, the refugees were assimilated and they no longer constituted an important force that had to be accommodated. Even the BHE, the party of the refugees, melted away. But the place of the party was taken by an increasing number of large mass meetings of refugee organizations. At these meetings, responsible ministers conjured up the rosy picture of a return to the East German homeland. To be sure, they did this with the renunciation of the use of any force, and with the promise of an All-European settlement. But were not matters farther away than ever? The claim of the Sudeten Germans was extremely doubtful. In their case, it was practically an appeal to the Greater Germany revision policy of Hitler. Such an appeal could not count on any kind of support from Bonn's allies and would obviously arouse mistrust.

It is difficult to estimate the damage to the Federal Republic which the fear of such an Eastern policy caused, even though it never was undertaken. Not only in the eyes of its Eastern neighbors, but also in the eyes of its Western partners, the Federal Republic of Germany remained a state devoted to revisionism which had not entirely rejected the legacy of the Hitler regime or dared to disown it. It was especially disastrous that thus the re-unification question was likewise moved into the area of "revisionism" even though it belonged on another level. For re-unification was not just a territorial problem. It was a problem of seventeen million people who were being denied the right of self-determination and the free choice of their own government and way of life.

This linking of two unlike problems and subjects proved to be calamitous in two respects. (1) It removed from the Oder-Neisse question the final value which it might still have possessed had it been used at the right time as an object of negotiation by the West. (2) It isolated the position of the West in Berlin, which, now excluded from the German question, was forced to a solution of its own. This also threatened to put an end to the function of Berlin as a potential capital of All-Germany and as the actual show-window and rallying point for the oppressed population of the German Democratic Republic.

THE TWO STATE THEORY

While the world's attention was held by the great international crises of 1956 in Eastern Europe and the Near East, the German problem remained in the state which had been determined by the decisions of 1955. However, realities such as the position of Berlin in the middle of the East-German Republic, the disentanglement of interzonal trade, and relations with the Soviet Union continually forced the Federal government to modify its political position of ignoring the two-state situation. While it observed with mistrust all movements for "softening" its legal position, the policy of Adenauer was still faced with the contradiction which encumbered the genesis, the growth and the pretensions of the Federal Republic.

The status of the *Bundeswehr*

Concretely, it was the debate of 1956–57 on the change-over in armaments which claimed attention. With an active CSU politician, F. J. Strauss, in charge of the Ministry of Defense, the debate turned to the equipping of the new *Bundeswehr* with tactical atomic weapons. This followed the introduction of compulsory military service in July, 1956, and the very slow buildup of the army. It was not until April of 1957 that the first West German volunteer soldiers were called up. The German Democratic Republic had already completed the transformation of the barrack-housed *Volkspolizei* into a "national people's army" a

year earlier with much less furor. The forcible methods of the totalitarian state guaranteed the recruiting of a sufficient number of "volunteers."

Adenauer's repeated demands for the equal status of the *Bundeswehr* with allied armies did not improve the situation, partially because the relation to atomic armament was not clear. The slogans of West German revisionism, revenge, and militarism began a "triumphant march" through the Eastern bloc—and did not leave the rest of the world untouched. With the warning signals for restoration in the Federal Republic, and with support from soldier groups, refugees and veterans, was it not possible that nationalism with anti-Communist direction would attempt to drag the allies to some misadventure? Was there not a hidden danger in the combination of re-armament and demand for revision if every compromise with the East was excluded?

The effect of such fears was all the greater when Adenauer opposed with great firmness all plans to effect a neutralization or formation of demilitarized zones free of atomic weapons. Such an approach to the German problem contained considerable risks in the very period of changeover to atomic weapons. However, the complete rejection by the Germans, even before comprehensive investigation and discussion —as was demanded in England—was no less risky than the blind alley into which the Western policy for Germany had entered.

Soviet tactics

The Soviet Union now took the position that re-unification was an internal German matter between the Federal Republic and the German Democratic Republic. This view was rejected by the Adenauer government because it would have reduced Bonn to the level of the totalitarian satellite regime that clearly existed contrary to the will of its inhabitants and existed only because of the presence and protection of the Soviet Union. Moreover, this view seemed to conjure up a danger which Adenauer feared above all else—the uniting of the Great Powers to relax tensions without considering Germany and, consequently, at her expense.

In the course of the Soviet campaign for lessening tensions, Paris and London actually seemed inclined to give up the priority of the stalled German question and deal with the questions of European security, disarmament, and the lessening of tensions in the East-West conflict. The Soviet Union approached them cleverly, and even made it appear that Washington would accept a global settlement by the Big Two before solving the German and European questions. The West clearly went on the defensive since it neither could nor wanted to make a rapid change of course.

In this situation the "German Democratic Republic" itself became a weapon, in grand style, for the first time in Soviet policy. Toward the end of December, 1956, Ulbricht began openly to launch a plan of "co-operation between both German states" with the goal of an All-German confederation. There could be no doubt that the main purpose of such a project was the general recognition and legitimization of the German Democratic Republic and subsequently the "democratization" of West Germany according to Communist ideas.

To be sure, this plan did not have the slightest chance in Germany itself or in the West. Ulbricht's proclamation was only too transparent since in his projected solution the superior "people's democratic order," the "progressive forces," and the Communistic system of society would win the upper hand. As essential conditions for a confederation, Ulbricht and Grotewohl always listed the demilitarization, the "defascisting," and the socialization of West Germany and, finally, the equal ranking of the two states.

It was clear that Moscow wanted to separate the Berlin question from its connection with the Four-Power responsibility and to make it a starting point for a general settlement put forth unilaterally by the Communists. This general approach has been followed since 1958.

These changes temporarily put Adenauer in a difficult position which, for a short time, amounted almost to a state of isolation. Without any change in his own policy, he seemed to have changed from the model boy of the West to the "mischief-maker" in world affairs. His domestic opposition likewise severely condemned the doubly questionable waiting policy which limited itself to re-armament and repetition of the old claims that, without a re-unified Germany, there could not be an integrated free Europe and therefore no security for the free world. Now for the first time, and then again at the height of the Berlin crisis, Adenauer's course showed its main weakness: the inability to adapt itself to changed conditions. With shocking suddenness it became evident how fragile the Federal Republic's position of strength was.

German responses

In the meantime, however, Adenauer succeeded in overcoming the threatening isolation of the Federal Republic. By concessions towards France, French opposition was decreased and the plans for Europe moved ahead. Euratom and the Common Market were the crystallization points of these efforts and both the Federal Republic and West Berlin were formally included in these organizations.

On the other hand, strong domestic opposition to atomic arms for the *Bundeswehr* continued. When the Federal Government, in its answer to the Soviet protest notes, referred to its right to make its own decisions as a sovereign state, it was formally right. But did this not confirm again the Soviet view of Germany and the two state theory?

Contrary to expectations at home and abroad, Adenauer had almost entirely given up taking advantage of the new relationship with Moscow. The Federal Government limited its efforts to the repatriation of condemned prisoners of war from Russia; it hesitated regarding the desires for trade and cultural relations. Adenauer did not seem to plan for extending his foreign policy to include the Eastern bloc, not even Poland which was of special importance because of the burdens of the past and the plans for relaxing tensions.

Poland had been forced to recognize the German Democratic Republic much earlier, and the Bonn-Moscow relations could serve as a precedent. Disregarding the legal problems, the political and moral aspects of a German-Polish reconciliation possessed a weight which was thoroughly in keeping with the risk of a resumption of diplomatic relations. The most careful attention should have been given by Bonn to the task of aiding Poland's efforts to gain greater independence from the Soviet Union.

During this period, Adenauer held firm to his policy regarding unification and the Oder-Neisse line. But a number of voices were raised demanding that a change be made. In London, Foreign Minister von Brentano declared that one would "some day have to choose between reunion with 17,000,000 Germans in the Soviet Zone and the insistence upon territories behind the Oder-Neisse line." To be sure, there was an immediate denial from Bonn. In the Bundestag, Carlo Schmid, speaking for the opposition, insisted: "The taboos of the Oder-Neisse line must be broken, otherwise it will one day become master over us. It will bewitch us."

Leaders of other nations also voiced their view on this question. De Gaulle openly expressed himself for the recognition of the Oder-Neisse line. When the Soviet Union renewed its guarantee of the Polish western boundary in November, 1956, China and Yugoslavia made corresponding declarations. Poland's Gomulka expressly wished "on the basis of the recognition of the mutual relationships and in the interest of easing tensions in Europe to normalize relations with the Federal Republic."

On the other hand, Bonn insisted on this sequence: All-German Government, peace treaty, boundary settlement. With the coming elections, it even emphasized a strengthening of the policy of "Right to the Homeland." All suggestions for German-Polish talks were pushed aside. When finally Yugoslavia recognized East Germany, Bonn answered with the breach of diplomatic relations in October 1957.

Faced with this complete immobility, the opposition continued to point out other alternatives. According to the SPD, the separation of Germany was a fruit of the East-West conflict; therefore Germany's policy should be directed against the forming of blocs and the armament race and should also declare its interest in regional security pacts, in compromises with the needs for security of the Soviet Union and Germany's neighbors, and, finally, in the simultaneous withdrawal of the Federal Republic and the German Democratic Republic from the military blocs. The SPD believed that, in view of the interests involved, the Soviet Union would be more inclined to participate in constructive German discussions and settlements if she were offered the dissolution of the hostile military alliances and the creation of an all European security system guaranteed by both Washington and Moscow. This would make a questionable neutralizing of Central Europe unnecessary. Above all, this would finally give the West the initiative again.

Adenauer made it abundantly clear that these suggestions were entirely unacceptable. His election victory in September of 1957 had the slogan: "No Experiments." It showed that the demand for security in the German population was stronger than the need for new attempts at solving the problem of Germany. This position was taken although the record of Adenauer's foreign policy showed severe crises and defeats, a falling-off of international interest in the problem of Germany and, correspondingly, anger and disillusionment in Germany itself. But as sharp as the foreign policy discussion had been, domestic and economic policies were again the deciding factors in the elections. No wonder that the interest of the Germans in re-unification became more and more subject to doubt.

THE BERLIN CRISIS CONTINUES

By 1958 there were two major problems which again started the discussion about the question of Germany and pushed it once more into the center of international affairs. (1) The attractive power of a free and flourishing Federal Republic made the continuing flight of refugees from East to West Germany assume such proportions that it was bound to weaken the position of the German Democratic Republic, not only psychologically but also materially, thus shattering its claim to statehood. Daily there were hundreds, and at times over a thousand refugees, who gave the lie to the German Democratic Republic's propaganda. The unyielding appeal to the principle of self-determination, which the refugees demonstrated by their "votes with their feet" stood in sharp contrast to the compulsory elections of the East German regime.

(2) The special position of Berlin brought together all of the problems as though they were under a magnifying glass. Berlin not only represented the remnant of the legal claim of Four-Power responsibility for Germany, it also played its role politically as an orientation point and meeting place of the divided people, and it was an asylum for the refugees.

Soviet arguments for ending occupation

The next moves of the Soviet Union were aimed at these two critical points which threatened Soviet policy for Germany and the very existence of the German Democratic Republic. In this context, the Soviet Union and its propaganda could count on some advantages: Why should not the uncomfortable Hallstein Doctrine be exchanged for a sound and lasting consolidation of the status quo which rearmament and a decade of efforts had not changed? Moreover, were not the bases of the Western rights in Berlin quite disputed and capable of modification? Could not the German Democratic Republic claim complete control of its own boundaries, when the Federal Republic claimed full sovereignty and for all practical purposes recognized the reality of the German Democratic Republic through economic relations and control proceedings? In the

final analysis, was it not an internal German matter after all?

Russian policy, which raised these questions, could not fail to have an effect. At the same time, it became evident that after a decade of armament competition and the firming up of the fronts, the position of the West had not become stronger; indeed it had clearly grown weaker.

In Berlin, the Soviet Union could force negotiations under more dangerous conditions than in 1949, 1952 or 1955–56. The cleverly veiled demands of Khrushchev were not aimed at a maximum all-out settlement but were limited to a "normalizing" of Berlin, to be secured by a peace treaty with Germany. This two-Germany treaty would have established the recognition of the Federal Republic and the German Democratic Republic on equal terms and would have brought the occupation to an end by elevating West Berlin to a "demilitarized free city."

For German policy, this new move was a question of life itself. A policy of simply carrying on with the monotonous assurance of the Federal Republic that there was no occasion for a review of German foreign policy would no longer satisfy anyone. For the Soviet initiative set a time limit of six months. At the end of that period, Russia threatened to transfer control of the access routes to Berlin to the German Democratic Republic, and, if necessary, arrange for a peace treaty with her. This new attack on the German question was not as unexpected as it appeared to some. It was related to two factors: the development of the Berlin problem itself and the immediate events preceding the crisis.

The postwar history of Berlin

Many legal and political factors have formed the postwar history of Berlin to an even greater extent than they have the birth and development of the Federal Republic. One can distinguish three different levels: the international agreements between the four Great Powers, the unfolding of the occupation law and occupation policy, and finally, the effects of the German policy and the consolidation of the Berlin policy since the end of the 1940's. The complexity of the Berlin problem and the vulnerability of "Berlin policy," whether it is conducted from the Western, German or Soviet side, stem from the inextricable entanglement of the conditions—so varied in their origins and directions.

In contrast to the original division of Germany into four separate zones, Berlin as a unit was expressly placed under an inter-allied governmental board (*Kommandantura*). Therefore, from the very beginning, it was not a part of the Soviet zone. It followed from this that all four Powers were to have access to Berlin. But not until the Berlin blockade were agreements made which expressly prohibited limitation of communication with the city. Essentially, the Soviet Union observed these agreements until the Berlin note of 1958.

The Western Powers, in their replies to the Soviet Union, insisted that even if she gave up her rights in Berlin that it would not affect the Western positions. The Western Powers had insisted on continuing the *Kommandantura,* even though Russia had withdrawn in 1948, and on their right to exercise its powers. They admitted however, that for the period of Soviet obstruction "it would be possible to execute their decisions only in the Western sectors." Here lies the central problem of all discussions about the legal status of Berlin—the original form was not given up, but only suspended, through the fault of the Soviet Union. It continued legally in the rump-*Kommandantura,* even though it could not carry out its acts completely.

This state of affairs was also taken into account in the arrangements of 1952 and 1954 under which the occupation regime was ended for the Federal Republic by the Western Powers, and for the German Democratic Republic by the Soviet Union. Not only the Western Powers, but also the Soviet Union, expressly reserved their obligations under the Four Power agreement. Even a unilateral transfer of rights to the German Democratic Republic—as the Soviet Union has threatened since 1958—cannot change this.

This refers particularly to the four Powers' rights of presence and the rights of access connected with them. According to this interpretation, based on international law, the German Democratic Republic can never replace the Soviet Union without the consent of the four Powers because the Soviet Union can surrender only its own powers but not the All-Berlin occupation rights of the four Powers. And she cannot make the sovereignty of the German Democratic Republic complete by a unilateral peace treaty.

Because of its special status within the four zones, Berlin had become a territory by itself, but attached directly to Germany as a whole. The ousting of the constitutional parliament and local authorities from East Berlin in 1948 meant the suspension of an All-Berlin administration, but it did not mean its renunciation. As a result, the seats for the representatives from East Berlin have been held for them, even to the present time. The splitting of the city had come about by *coup d'état* and obstruction; but by no means had it been legalized by such actions; neither could it be made legitimate by the founding of two German states.

The Soviet Union, however, with certain reservations, had not hesitated to permit the inclusion of East Berlin into the German Democratic Republic; indeed, it has become the seat of its government. It is debatable whether the inclusion of West Berlin in the Federal Republic could have been an effective countermove. As a matter of fact, Berlin helped create the constitution and accepted it. But the Western Powers believed that full voting rights should not be granted to the representatives of West Berlin in the Bundestag and the Bundesrat. Therefore Berlin only sent delegates from her house of representatives.

Western policies

In view of this complicated status, the Soviet demand for a "free city" solution for Berlin was able to influence world opinion—poorly informed as it was—because it appeared to end this suspended condition and at the same time take into account Berlin's special position. That this drive was a clumsily plotted fraud was obvious to the careful observer. It would hand over the access ways to the German Democratic Republic, while applying only to West Berlin. The Western Powers were asked to unilaterally give up their existing as well as suspended rights. In addition, the plan sanctioned the inclusion of East Berlin into the German Democratic Republic, contrary to the status of the city.

One could ask whether a prompt reaction to the earlier Soviet and Soviet-zone attacks against the status of Berlin, with a threat to include West Berlin in the Federal Republic, might have made a more favorable starting point for Berlin discussions. From the very beginnings of the Federal Republic there was a strong difference of opinion between the Germans and the Western allies on this very point. Now, after getting accustomed to the special status of West Berlin, the free city and internationalizing plans were discussed only in their unilateral limitation to West Berlin. On the other hand, a firm plan for Berlin's integration into the Federal Republic—after the model of East Berlin—was never discussed. In this connection, the responsibility of the Western Powers should not be underestimated. The initiative was not wrested from the Soviet Union although, in the meantime, West Berlin had been integrated into the legal and economic system of the Federal Republic and the federal laws were automatically binding.

The question remains why the West, apparently unprepared, entered upon the crisis, which was by no means unexpected, and why the foreign policy of West Germany was incapable of developing a real stand against the critical positions of the Soviet Union on Germany and Berlin. How was it possible that in spite of a much stronger Western position, legally, morally and politically, that with certainty could count on a favorable vote of the entire German population, the West, three years after the Soviet ultimatum, still stood

with its back to the wall and had to talk about unilateral concessions?

THE DILEMMA OF GERMAN FOREIGN POLICY

The Western Powers attempted to meet the Soviet position with diplomatic means. They requested Moscow to discuss the German problem as a whole within the framework of the security problem. The Soviet Union answered promptly with the proposal to discuss these questions, including that of a peace treaty, at a summit conference. It remained firm, however, on its position that re-unification could no longer be the object of such discussions, but only a treaty with German governments. Russia included a draft which was clearly in the spirit of Ulbricht's confederation and neutralization propaganda.

With that, the West was forced even more into the defensive. The appeal to the fifty-two enemy states of the Hitler regime to sign a peace treaty with Germany and thus solve the disagreeable questions of Germany and Berlin could be sure of its effect. There was much to be said in favor of taking the Soviet Union at its word and confronting it with such a great conference on Germany. This was also advocated by the governing mayor of West Berlin, Willy Brandt.

A policy of inaction

But again there was a lack of willingness of the Federal government to maneuver. It extended its established criticism of the Soviet draft for a peace treaty to even criticizing the proposal for a conference. Just as consciously as it held to the claim to represent the All-German state tradition, just as little was it prepared to assume the consequences of All-German peace treaty negotiations if they were linked with a grand conference of all war enemies. Again, this was a case of taking the defensive position rather than the initiative. This turned out to be easy, because the Soviet Union did not, in the final analysis, insist on its six months time limit. The waiting of the West could continue while the failures of the conferences and negotiations from Geneva in 1959 to Paris in May 1960, seemed to make the West's readiness to negotiate look amazingly absurd.

Adenauer (and de Gaulle, this time) insisted that one must not negotiate under pressure. He seemed to ignore the possibility that sometime in the future he might have to negotiate under essentially more unfavorable conditions. For Russia still had considerable room for maneuvering and creating *faites accomplis* which could only be met in a military way and not be parried politically. On August 13, 1961, the Berlin wall was started, thus sealing the greatly increased stream of refugees off from West Berlin. With the erection of the wall, an essential political function of Berlin was throttled. No suitable or sufficient reaction was possible. One was pushed into negotiations under the double pressure of accomplished and accepted facts. Once again, the West had suffered losses without securing any equivalent compensation.

Adenauer, after a dismayed moment of helplessness, began to take into account the dilemma into which the many years of waiting had suddenly thrown him. If it is correct that his conversations with President Kennedy in November 1961 no longer excluded isolated Berlin negotiations before re-unification negotiations, then this makes the German tactics since 1955, and especially those since 1959, appear in a questionable light.

Western proposals

The Soviet draft of a peace treaty was doubtless unacceptable as a whole. On the other hand, the Western peace plan, as it was presented to the Geneva conference of foreign ministers in May and June of 1959, was a very concrete plan, in specific stages, for a solution of the Berlin problem by a re-unification of the city through free elections.

This was to be followed by the formation of an All-German committee with twenty-five representatives of the Federal Republic and ten from the German Democratic Republic. By three-fourths majority, they would prepare an election law and hold a referendum. The All-German assembly elected in this manner would then draft a constitution and form a government. This government would sign the peace treaty and have freedom in deciding foreign policy matters. But this "negotiation package" did not touch the center of the peace treaty arrangement which interested the Soviet Union: the boundaries, the status and the form of the future Germany.

The "Germany Plan" offered by the SPD, made public early in 1959, seemed to offer more starting points: with military disarmament it demanded the creation of a central European zone of relaxed tensions which should include Poland, Czechoslovakia and Hungary, along with Germany. It also called for the withdrawal of all foreign troops. This would offer the prerequisites for free elections for an All-German assembly.

The internal criticism of the "Germany Plan" was severe. Indeed it was of such excessive severity that it was suspected of being Communist-inspired. It was quickly passed over by the stream of events. But even this adds to the burden of the Federal government for its rejecting on principle all attempts at compromise. It also adds to the burden of the opposition because its plan was not really clear and realistic.

Today a final judgment is not yet possible. The new Federal government hurried immediately to emphasize the unchanging position of German foreign policy. Adenauer sacrificed Foreign Minister von Brentano, who had done nothing but serve his foreign policy faithfully and persistently. Over the years it is clear that Adenauer has tried to free the Federal Republic from the mortgage of the Third Reich and from its notoriety in defaulting on international agreements. This has been proved through complete and continued identification with the Western alliance.

At the same time, this policy has failed to make a contribution of its own to further development and to relieve the tension of East-West relations. It has also failed to adapt the republic's Western-oriented policy to the changed conditions of the second half of the '50's and the '60's. Both favorable evaluations and unfavorable criticisms of the Adenauer era must be based on a careful weighing of the basic problems and both the positive and negative aspects of the policies put forward to meet them.

Continuing problems

In recent months, the problems of the German position in the final phase of the Adenauer era lie in its relation to the Kennedy plans for exploring and negotiating over the Berlin situation; and the attitude toward the European plans which de Gaulle has developed in connection with the expansion of the Common Market. Both instances appear to be symptomatic of the structural and tactical handicaps of German foreign policy even though they belong within the larger and broader framework of European policy and the East-West conflict.

With regard to the Berlin question, the Federal government finds itself faced with the softening of its basic position because of American plans for compromise which it notes with both reluctance and opposition. The new Foreign Minister, Schroeder, seems to be willing to subordinate the dogmatic line of the Adenauer–Brentano course, with which the names of Hallstein and Grewe are connected, to a more flexible alliance policy which would take the changed situation more readily into account.

Differences of opinion between West Germany and the United States are to be understood as the consequences of this process of change and should not be overrated. Most recent information leaves no doubt that the vast majority of the population as well as the active political forces of West Germany, especially at the present time, adhere more firmly than ever to the Western alliance. This holds true of the opposition, through the voices of Willy Brandt and Fritz Erler, even more clearly than the government which is burdened by the long-standing, historically hardened concept of the Germany of the Adenauer era. There also remain the problems of atomic armament which are closely linked with the controversy about an adequate strategy for the West in a continuing period of atomic equilibrium. The hardening of Western policy exhibited in the Cuban crisis of 1962 may suggest future trends of policy.

On the other hand, the intransigence of de Gaulle's alliance and European policies raises considerable problems which could disturb this process in two respects. With regard to the Berlin and German question, it will strengthen the persevering forces in Bonn. With regard to the Western alliance and European policy, it means a withdrawal into an attitude of sovereignty in terms of small areas. It may even mean a strengthening of nationalism.

While it is clear that Germany does have an interest in the expansion of the Common Market, it is just as clear that she is unwilling to jeopardize the great postwar achievement: Franco-German co-operation. In addition, there is the danger of weakening the political effects of integration in the Common Market if Great Britain and Scandinavia, and eventually the neutral countries, are included. This, of course, is equally true of de Gaulle's plan for a lesser Europe as a "political union" of sovereign states. If the process of political integration is blocked by this, then, in the eyes of West German politicians—as well as in the interest of the Western alliance—an expansion of the Common Market and particularly an inclusion of the most important ally, Great Britain, is most desirable.

Of course, it is not desirable at the risk of a conflict with France. It is at this point, after the end of the war in Algeria and upon reactivation of French European policy, that the second great problem for German foreign policy comes to the fore. Of course, this is above all a problem of French domestic policy after de Gaulle has left the scene. However, the future on this point is truly obscure.

Certainly the chief interests of Germany are clear and unequivocal: orientation toward the West and Europe in particular, re-unification of Germany, liberal democracy, security and freedom. But the internal contradictions of these postulates have not diminished. They are now confronted with the greatest foreign political crisis since the renewal of German statehood. Not only the actual existence, but also the much admired inner stability of the Federal Republic will depend on whether or not it can maintain its place in the community of free peoples and make it clear that it is prepared to make sacrifices for the sake of Berlin and her oppressed fellow citizens. In the final analysis, it also means overcoming the continuing remnants of the Third Reich. This means a reversal in the revisionist and nationalistic thinking with regard to the question of the Eastern boundaries and, to some extent, even a changed approach to the policy of re-unification.

The Bundestag, as well as the public, are showing a growing readiness to approach the German question no longer primarily in terms of restoration of the national state, lost in 1945. Two pre-conditions, though, seem indispensable for any solution of the German question. Firstly, there must be a fully effective guarantee for Berlin to live according to the will of its population, including Willy Brandt's "Three Essentials"—free access, viability, and military presence of the West. Secondly, there must be a liberalizing of human conditions in Germany, at least equal to conditions in neighboring Poland, allowing free interchange of Germans in East and West. This may also lead to a more constructive Eastern policy on the part of the Federal Republic, and thus further a process of relaxation in Europe.

By the unhappy chain of circumstances, Germany has again moved from under the guilt of the Hitler regime into the center of world politics. She can only exist as a dependable democracy if this time, and very different from 1933, she holds firmly that justice and human rights, internal freedom and international co-operation take precedence to national greatness.

BIBLIOGRAPHY

Editor's Suggestions

Almond, Gabriel A. (ed). *The Struggle for Democracy in Germany*. Chapel Hill: University of North Carolina Press, 1949.

Bracher, Karl Dietrich. *Die Auflösung der Weimarer Republik*. 1955.

Bracher, Karl Dietrich. *Über das Verhältnis von Politik und Geschichte*. 1961.

Deutsch, Karl W. and Lewis J. Edinger. *Germany Rejoins the Powers: A Study of Mass Opinion, Interest Groups, and Elites in Contemporary German Foreign Policy*. Stanford: Stanford University Press, 1959.

Edinger, Lewis J. "Continuity and Change: Some Data on the Social Background of German Decision Makers," *Western Political Quarterly*, vol. 14, no. 1 (March, 1961), pp. 17–36.

Edinger, Lewis J. "Electoral Politics and Voting Behavior in Western Germany," *World Politics,* vol. xiii, no. 3 (April, 1961), pp. 417–84.

Freund, Gerald. *Germany Between Two Worlds.* New York: Harcourt, Brace and World, 1961.

Grosser, Alfred. *Die Bonner Demokratie.* Düsseldorf: Karl Rauch, 1960.

Haas, Ernst B. *The Uniting of Europe.* Stanford: Stanford University Press, 1958.

Robson, C. B. (ed). *Berlin: Pivot of German Destiny.* Chapel Hill: University of North Carolina Press, 1960.

Wallich, Henry C. *Mainsprings of the German Revival.* New Haven: Yale University Press, 1955.

Wiskemann, Elisabeth. *Germany's Eastern Neighbors.* New York: Oxford University Press, 1956.

ABOUT THE AUTHOR

JACQUES FREYMOND is presently Director of the Graduate Institute of International Studies, Geneva. He began his academic life with studies at the University of Lausanne, Munich and the Sorbonne. In 1943 he was appointed to the faculty of the University of Lausanne and has held the posts of Professor of Contemporary History, Professor of Diplomatic History, and Professor of History at the Graduate Institute of International Studies. He is now the Director of this institution. He is a corresponding member of the Academy of Political Science. Dr. Freymond has been a Rockefeller Fellow and has studied at Yale and Columbia Universities.

His published works include the following: *Le conflit sarrois,* 1959; *The Saar Conflict,* 1960 (English and German translations); "Die atlantische Welt," in *Propyläen-Weltgeschichte,* 1961; *Introduction à la Première Internationale Recueil de Documents,* 1962; "European Views on Arms Control," in *Arms Control: Issues for the Public,* 1961.

ABOUT THE CHAPTER

Switzerland provides the classic example of the small state which, over the years, has played a role in world affairs out of proportion to her power as it is normally calculated. This chapter deals with the goals and policies of Switzerland and, in addition, throws the spotlight on some of the major problems of international politics. The author raises the question of the future of small states in the world of giants and the trend towards European unification. His conclusions regarding the continuance of the small among the mighty show deep insights into the trends of our times and the processes of international politics.

The chapter deals at length with the unique record of Switzerland as a neutral nation. Both the history of neutrality and the reasons for the relative success of this policy are analyzed. The conduct of foreign policy and governmental arrangements for formulating and executing policy are also discussed.

The chapter presents a most valuable analysis of the problems of national survival and the difficulties of exerting an influence on the Great Powers. Mr. Freymond concludes that nations like Switzerland "must establish durable conditions at home and conduct foreign relations with all necessary prudence, in order to attenuate the repercussions of clashes among the Powers, if possible."

5

THE FOREIGN POLICY OF SWITZERLAND

JACQUES FREYMOND

Graduate Institute of International Studies, Geneva

Switzerland, at first glance, appears a living paradox to the present day observer. In this second half of the 20th century, the world is in a state of upheaval, caught in the throes of a dangerous political and social crisis. A conflict of ideals, which transcends national frontiers, pervades the rivalry of Powers, penetrating into our very lives. To be frank, the world is already engaged in war, a war of a strange character, at times open in certain parts of the world and "couverte," to use Richelieu's expression, in every other. And yet Switzerland, at an epoch when most nations seem to shrink from isolation and endeavor by uniting forces to protect their independence, remains stubbornly apart, clinging to a neutrality which is apparently outdated.

What is the explanation? Is Switzerland blind? This is highly unlikely. Most Swiss, on the contrary, are only too alive to the dangers threatening the world as a whole and especially their own country. Appraisals of the general situation by the press or in conversations have generally been pessimistic right from the end of the last war. While eager to believe that East and West could co-operate, Switzerland clearly perceived the obstacles lining the road to peace. Nor had it any illusion as to the possibility of once more being able to stand aside in the event of another open conflict.

THE HERITAGE OF THE PAST

The precarious nature of Swiss union

This reserved attitude of the Swiss has deep roots and can be accounted for by both history and geography. The building up of the Confederation was a long and painful process. The small communities composing it only gradually grouped themselves around the original nucleus formed on the axis of the Gothard, which, in the Middle Ages, was the route linking up the cities of Italy, Southern Germany, the Rhine and Flanders. The growth of this system of collective security, by the inclusion of communities as different as the cities of Zurich, Berne, or Basle, on the one hand, and the cantons of Central Switzerland or the Grey Leagues of the Grisons, on the other, raised many problems and resulted in more than one crisis.

Diverse backgrounds and interests However conscious they might be of their united front in face of the ambitious scheming of neighboring princes, this alone did not suffice to reconcile the Cantons' conflicting interests. Zurich and Schwytz, for example, allowed themselves to become embroiled in a rivalry that endangered the alliance; Berne, in the heart of the Swiss tableland, was more interested in the possibilities offered by the decline in power of Burgundy than in the undertakings of its confederates in Northern Italy.

In addition to differences of opinion about the Confederation's foreign policy, there was internal political and social strain between the rural cantons and the city cantons. From the 16th century on, there also was religious strife. The very existence of Switzerland was indeed in peril on several occasions and its internal balance was constantly upset. At the time of the French Revolution and the Empire Wars, Switzerland was invaded; between the 15th century and the beginning of the 18th, and again in the middle of the 19th century, it was shaken by several civil wars. Although these experiences have now faded into the past, they have nonetheless left their mark.

The Swiss have learned not to underestimate the difficulty of the problem inherent in the coexistence of communities with different languages and faiths. They know that in these delicate matters, where reactions are governed by emotions, at any time a misguided move may suddenly compromise agreements reached by mutual concession. Every nation's history conceals quarrels ready to flare up again, owing to a change in the attitude which at a given moment had enabled their peaceful solution.

The need for continuous adjustments Switzerland, where the recognition of particularism has been made one of the conditions of the liberties enjoyed by its citizens, is in an even more dangerous position than many other countries. Technical developments and the resulting modification of economic and social structures and of the geographical distribution of the population, require constant adjustments of the sometimes subtle formulas which have enabled the contradictory demands of democracy and federalism to be reconciled.

This prosperous nation is in actual fact a little fragile, not so much on account of its size as of its peculiar features. The will to live united which welds it together must be constantly stimulated and educated anew, as the great cultures to which Switzerland simultaneously belongs vie with one another internally and have a powerful attraction, particularly for young people. This explains the slowness and prudence in important decisions of international policy of a people whose history has taught them that their existence is dependent on the maintenance of balance by means of mutual concessions and remedies administered in homeopathic doses.

Prosperity engenders caution

Prosperity also leads to a certain reserve in foreign policy. A people satisfied with its lot is naturally chary of the risks implied in any change. These are all the greater in that Switzerland's prosperity does not spring from the riches of its soil or subsoil, but almost exclusively from hard work, a constant effort to adapt production to internal economic conditions and a tireless struggle to wedge an entry into world markets.

Everyone who has studied Swiss economy has been struck by the contrast between the poverty of natural resources and the high standard of living. "It should be borne in mind," wrote Wilhelm Roepke three years ago, "that if Swiss prosperity is almost a miracle, it is at all events a miracle which it was by no means easy to bring about and which holds out no guarantee of permanence."[1]

[1] See "La position internationale de l'économie suisse" in the *Revue économique et sociale,* Lausanne, September 1959.

The relinquishment of sovereignty implied in some of the changes contemplated in Europe would result in the responsibility for decisions being placed in the hands of large states. These would necessarily occupy a dominating position; the consideration of the interests of a microcosmic community such as Switzerland would play only a secondary role. Smallness can be a strength if the economic policy adopted by a state takes this factor into consideration. But how could statesmen who have never been confronted by the type of problem which the Swiss encounter daily, be expected to realize the unusual degree of caution and delicacy demanded by this smallness? Engrossed as they are in large designs, how could they divert the necessary attention? It is no wonder, therefore, that the Swiss are scarcely tempted to entrust others with the direction of their economic policy. Their country is too fragile to take the risk of certain experiments from which large states can more easily recover.

The history of Swiss neutrality

Origins Switzerland's reserve is furthermore explained by the particular nature of its neutrality. This was not imposed on the Swiss Cantons by outside pressure. It was born of opposing interests and religious conflict within the early Confederation. The danger of a split, which was sufficiently apparent at the end of the 15th century for Nicholas de Flue, the famous Swiss hermit, to recommend abstention from foreign wars, became even more evident at the beginning of the 16th century. A religious crisis grafted itself on the political and social and foreign policy disputes setting the towns and country at variance with one another. Hence, any siding with one of the parties engaged in the religious wars then tearing Europe asunder, would have engendered a schism in the Confederation which would have brought its downfall. No political engagement that might involve Switzerland in a conflict

could be entered into if the Alliance was to be preserved.

This policy of neutrality was defined and consolidated in the following centuries, in line with the degree to which it proved to be practicable, effective and valuable, not only to the Swiss but to the other European states. Its success was proportionate to the determination shown by the Confederates to assure respect for it by taking the necessary steps for the military defense of Swiss frontiers. But the policy of neutrality is also linked with the development of the policy of European balance of power. Switzerland, in order to preserve its independence vis-à-vis the Great Powers, had to wend its way among them—"keep the balance equal," to quote from the instructions to a British Ambassador.

From the Congress of Vienna to World War II On the strength of this tradition and the unfortunate experiences during the French Revolution and the Empire Wars, the Cantons' delegates to the Vienna Congress requested not only recognition of Switzerland as an independent state, governed by its own constitution, but also of its neutrality. In the same spirit, the Powers agreed that this "neutrality and inviolability of Switzerland and its independence of all foreign influence were in the true interests of the policy of Europe as a whole."

New proofs of the value of this policy were furnished to the Swiss subsequently, in the course of the 19th and 20th centuries. But this did not prevent them from joining in the experiment of collective security at the end of the First World War and from attempting to reconcile the principle of permanent neutrality with membership in the League of Nations. A distinction was made between participation in economic and financial sanctions, which Switzerland agreed to apply, and military sanctions, from which it was exempted.

But this distinction failed to stand the test of reality. The glaring defeat of the League of Nations led the Swiss Government to revert to so-called "complete" neutrality. In the light of events between 1938 and 1945, the Swiss concluded that neutrality continued to be justified. Rightly or wrongly, the fact that their country had not been caught up in the war and that it had survived the terrible disaster which had devastated Europe, was taken to prove that neutrality was still an effective means of assuring national independence.

Since 1945 It is not surprising, therefore, that in 1945 the Swiss Government felt in no hurry to submit its candidature to the United Nations Organization. The matter was naturally one for careful consideration. The hopes held out by the Preamble to the United Nations Charter duly impressed public opinion; nor was the public deaf to the call of duty. But, to those called upon to examine the problem at the time, a neutral status appeared incompatible with membership in the United Nations Organization. The protection that the United Nations Organization would be in a position to offer small nations, moreover, inspired little confidence. The whole mechanism of sanctions risked paralysis in the event the Great Powers opposed each other during a crisis and used the right to veto. The United Nations would only be able to act when the five Great Powers were in agreement, i.e. in the face of minor crises. In a major crisis the veto would tie their hands.

It was therefore decided to adopt a reserved attitude. Prudence was the order of the day for this small country after what had just happened, in the face of an unknown postwar world, dominated by a coalition whose fundamental differences of opinion had visibly undermined it even before the end of the war. This prudence was all the more essential because Switzerland's neutrality was not simply a policy which certain of its governments had adopted for a time, but ranked as a constitutional principle. Applied for three hundred and fifty years, purposely qualified as "permanent," it had become an integral part of the international status of the Confederation. Its relinquishment would imply a complete break with the past, whose consequences both on internal equilibrium and on external relations were not to be underrated. The Government

considered that public opinion, whose influence is decisive, was not yet ripe for such a change.

In the meantime, it is true, the situation has changed. There is a different attitude and neutrality has ceased to be so sharply criticized. Some member states of the United Nations Organization have even adopted a certain neutrality as such. The Korean war, for instance, revealed very divergent positions, ranging from great reserve to whole-hearted support. In admitting Austria, the United Nations even went so far as to recognize that neutrality is not incompatible with membership therein.

This decision, which aroused keen interest in Switzerland, did not, however, incite the Government to depart from its reserve. The possibility of the adherence of a neutral state was merely a matter of opportunity, because the main Powers concerned had considered it advisable to admit that some of the Articles of the Charter would never be applied or at least were unlikely to be. But there still remains a contradiction in terms which, in a period of emergency, might put a neutral state in an awkward position.

THE FUTURE OF SMALL STATES

To what extent is there still justification for the existence of small states, like Switzerland? Are such states compatible with the transformation in methods of production and economic structures, the changes in the swing of power between continents, endeavors to achieve continental integration, the expansion of international organizations? Can small states be kept alive? Is it even in the interest of the members of these small political communities to do so? Does not particularism inevitably lead to recession and eclipse in the long run? That it does, is a widespread conviction. Americans and Europeans are in favor of integration. Heads of new states are battling for the establishment of large economic and political coalitions.

Likelihood of survival

And yet it would not seem that the small state is necessarily doomed to disappear. There is after all no basic difference between the situation of the world of today and that of Europe in past centuries. The small state of Switzerland has succeeded in existing under a system of European balance. It has survived periods of inter-state rivalry and of irreconcilable ideological conflicts in the 16th century and at the time of the French Revolution.

Today we are living under a system of world balance. The situation is perilous. The end of this critical period is by no means in sight. On the contrary, with the development of China it would seem that the tension will be drawn even tighter. The struggles between the Powers, however, assume various shapes and their profiles are shadowy. The uniting of forces is apt to vary with events and with the different views of individuals stepping into the scene. What is Germany's future to be? What do we know of the relations between China and the Soviet Union? Between India and China? What direction is the Middle-East going to take? And Africa? How are the Latin-American states going to solve their economic and social problems? We have nothing which allows us to affirm that the Great Powers will succeed in establishing the empires or continental coalitions they envisage. On the contrary, in each of the groups or blocs, centrifugal forces can be observed. It is evident that bipolarity is merely a convenient figure of rhetoric.

A further characteristic of contemporary developments, apart from this tendency towards concentricity, is the birth of new states. The membership of the international organizations increases year after year and particularism offers food for nationalism, which is visibly and bitterly asserting itself in the Middle East and Africa.

Finally, scientific and technical progress is not only to the advantage of large states; small nations can also benefit thereby. On the military plane, modern atomic weapons can furnish new means of offense, rather than defense, to small states. On the economic plane, small states can share in and benefit from economic progress, to the extent that they have available brainpower and qualified workers. It is Man that counts, with his intelligence and working capacity, not only equipment. This has been demonstrated recently by several states, Israel in particular, which has succeeded in developing despite the hostility of its neighbors and an unfavorable geographical position. The victory is threefold: technical, economic, and political. And if one stops to think that several of the newborn states of Black Africa have turned towards Israel in order to benefit by its experience, it is obvious that it enjoys a certain degree of influence.

It cannot therefore be declared that history has doomed the small state, that it will necessarily be the victim of an irreversible movement. The immutable laws of history have so often been quoted in the course of the last hundred years by founders of empires which today have ceased to exist, or by theorists whose followers have succeeded for reasons which had nothing to do with the lines forecast, that it is advisable to be a little wary in this respect.

But even if the small state is not condemned, there must be the will for it to live. More than any other, it is founded on the will to live together. Its citizens express this will in various ways, by taking part in public life and in the defense of their country. This is especially true of Switzerland.

The need for military preparedness

Training a citizen army   The military efforts of Switzerland are characteristic, and it is worth while to examine their scope and their limits. Financially, they represent approximately 40 percent of the state's annual budget. But heavy as the financial cost may be, it only partly reveals the great sacrifice accepted to protect Switzerland's independence and neutrality. Its army, a militia, based on compulsory service for all citizens, is commanded by only a small number of regular officers and noncommissioned officers. The officers, then, are for the main part militia officers and noncommissioned officers who "instruct while receiving instruction," and thus carry a fairly heavy load alongside their daily work. Approximately sixteen months in-service instruction is required to become a lieutenant and two years to become a captain. To this must be added annual training periods of three to four weeks, and administrative duties throughout the year. The latter are sometimes quite considerable since a militia officer, responsible for instructing his men, has to prepare himself, draw up programs of work and, if he commands a company, keep the register of his unit up-to-date.

These obligations may at first sight appear lighter than those of soldiers in other countries, who have to undergo eighteen to twenty months training. True, the four months training of Swiss recruits is short as compared with the long periods of mobilization imposed on young people in many countries. It is also a fact that the splitting up of periods of service to gain promotion makes it easier to reconcile civilian life and military training. But the obligation to serve and the binding engagements it implies extend over a longer span of life; and the responsibilities of the officers in conjunction with the administration and instruction of the troops, are of a more permanent and hence much more exacting nature.

Our purpose is not to compare the merits of different types of armies or the duties incumbent on each, but to appraise an effort. The splitting up of periods of service, to which we have already referred, would not be possible without the organization of a system of speedy mobilization. The restricted geographic area in which this system is applied makes it possible to avoid long periods of service to protect the frontiers. Under it half a million men can be called up within something like 24 hours. They are all in possession of their own uniform and weapons and the mechanism of mobilization itself is always held ready to operate by men who, for the most part, carry military responsibilities in addition to their duties as civilians.

The deterrent value of small armies The characteristic of this army is its close integration into the nation. Switzerland, which has been spared from foreign war for over a hundred and fifty years and has refrained since the beginning of the 16th century from taking any part in Big-Power politics, has preserved a military tradition, strange as this may seem. It has observed from experience that a neutral status can only be durable if a neutral state is prepared to assure its respect and, consequently, to pay the price. The information on the plans laid by the Germans during the Second World War confirms that it was decided to relinquish an attack on Switzerland simply because the value of the Swiss objective was out of proportion to what the German Army would have to pay for it. The existence of a Swiss Army, which they knew was ready to fight and win the necessary time to destroy the communications required by the German Army, meant that too many Divisions would have to be put into action. In these circumstances, the game was no longer worth the candle.

It goes nonetheless without saying that the Swiss Government has only very modest means of combat to assure independence and neutrality. Its troops are well-equipped with light weapons, but lack heavy arms. They would, however, have the advantage of fighting on familiar ground, of being able to take advantage of the country's natural defenses, which have been constantly strengthened in the course of time, and of being able to rely on depots already installed.

It is not for us to assess the exact value of Switzerland's contribution to a stable political and military situation in Europe. No one can tell, moreover, how an army which has not faced fire for years would react, nor how a nation which, unlike its neighbors, has not experienced war would behave. What should, nevertheless be emphasized is the fact that the great military effort which has been made, testifies to the will to exist as a nation.

The psychological value of small armies

Such testimony is as necessary for Swiss nationals as for their neighbors. However limited the means of a small state are as compared to those of Powers with nuclear and thermonuclear weapons, the will to contribute personally, even in the slightest way, to the protection of national territory rather than leave it to others, is an important political fact. A small country makes it less tempting for a potential adversary to start a military adventure if it puts an obstacle in the way which will have to be destroyed by conventional weapons. Resort to atomic weapons, which would break down local resistance, would modify the nature of the operation and broaden the conflict. The greatest danger for a small country is that of being speedily overrun by a Great Power, thus establishing a *fait accompli,* which the other Powers would be inclined to accept, for fear of being exposed to an atomic conflict, for an objective which, in itself, is of no great importance.

What is most important therefore is for Switzerland to organize its defense in such a manner as to be able to hold out as long as possible, in order to endow its resistance with a symbolic value which would compel all concerned to take sides. This obstinacy, moreover, which may have been looked on as absurd, seems more legitimate at the present time, when the fear of atomic war and the development of local conflicts or subversive operations have demonstrated the permanent value of conventional weapons.

The fact that the will to exist as a nation, as demonstrated by a permanent military effort, likewise strengthens the resistance of public opinion, should not be overlooked either. The public opinion of every nation must always be in a position to resist the ever more frequent attempts at moral pressure and blackmail, aimed at dominating a whole population by

mere threats and reaping the harvest of victory without battle. Whatever its size, an army, provided one is determined to use it, remains an indispensable instrument for effective diplomatic action.

It is by doing their utmost first to guarantee their own existence that small states can claim to render service to their neighbors and other countries. "The Allied Powers," states a report to the Vienna Congress by the Committee on Swiss Affairs, dated January 16, 1815,

have promised to recognize and to have recognized in the period of general pacification, the perpetual neutrality of the Helvetic side, and to restore to it the lands which were taken from it . . . but only to consider these promises as binding insofar as Switzerland, in compensation for the advantages which would be reserved for it, would offer Europe through its own Cantonal institutions as well as the nature of its own federative system, a sufficient guarantee of the ability of the new Confederation to maintain the neutrality of its territory.[2]

This condition, which does not appear in the Final Act, deserves to be mentioned here, for it clearly shows what the Powers are entitled to expect from a small state.

Limits of external political effectiveness

This agreed, the limits set to the influence of a small nation on international policy must immediately be stressed. A small state must know how to be contented with its lot and relinquish any aspiration to play a role. The ambitions of its statesmen must be modest. Nothing is more dangerous than to try to meddle in Big-Power

[2] *Le Congrès de Vienne et les traités de 1815,* I, Paris: Amyot, 1864, p. 619.

politics without the means to do so and to use the tactics of the Great Powers to extend one's sway. The history of international relations is amply marked by disasters suffered by sovereigns or governments which let themselves be tempted to play a game beyond their skill and became unwitting pawns in the politics of Great Powers. Great historical missions, as the Swiss historian Jakob Burckhardt wrote, are reserved for great states. One of the essential qualities of the small state is modesty.

This modesty will also help small states to understand that their influence can be only limited in the international organizations, and that the halo of prestige they may win by becoming the satellite of a Big Power or by bartering their vote, is ephemeral and illusory. The only thing which can sometimes compensate for the relative weakness of a state and enable it to render real service, is the caliber of its representatives. But to be useful, it is not indispensable to be a member of an international organization. On various occasions it has even been demonstrated that certain services could only be rendered by states which were free, as outsiders.

Slender means demand great firmness in the matters of principle and in the conduct of foreign policy. Nothing is more dangerous for a small state, I believe, than expediency, which the large states will inevitably take advantage of sooner or later. Experience has shown the Swiss in this respect that the policy of neutrality cannot be dissociated from the status of neutrality. Hence, certain rules in the conduct of their foreign relations must be scrupulously observed, because one of the factors of their security lies in the "reliability" of their policy. This can enable foreign nations to appraise the Confederation's future conduct accurately in the light of its attitude in the past.

The nature of Swiss neutrality

Neutrality versus neutralism   It is probably this which distinguishes the policy of neutrality practiced by Switzerland from the "neutral-ism" adopted by other states. In reality, the latter simply means refusal, at least for the time being, to take sides with either of the two blocs. The state which adopts this attitude does not consider itself bound by the same formula towards other nations. On the contrary, it considers itself free to act as it pleases on the international scene, to form alliances, join a coalition, intervene by dint of propaganda or of political and even military means. The limits it assigns to its freedom of action correspond to its immediate interests, and not necessarily to the duties of neutral states as progressively defined by international law.

True, the duties of a state which, like Switzerland, practices a policy of neutrality are limited. The Head of the Swiss Political Department briefly summarized them in a lecture on the Confederation's foreign policy:

> A state which comes under a permanent status of neutrality can never launch a war, nor can it take part in a war which breaks out between other countries. In all wars, therefore, it must observe strict neutrality. But it is under the obligation to defend its territory against any aggression, with all the means at its disposal. Its neutrality must be armed. Finally, in time of peace, it is pledged to refrain from taking any engagement whatsoever which might draw it into war.[3]

From the Swiss viewpoint, it is precisely this obligation to refrain from any engagement which might draw it into war that demands a somewhat reserved attitude on the part of a state laying claim to the right of "permanent neutrality."[4]

[3] Lecture by Mr. Max Petitpierre at the *Istituto per gli studi di politica internazionale*, at Milan, on November 9, 1957.

[4] "*The state which desires to preserve its neutrality in a future conflict will therefore refrain from entering into international engagements or taking internal measures which might hamper or even forbid the execution of the legal obligations involved in the right of neutrality.*" Paul Guggenheim, *Traité de Droit in-*

The right to express political opinions Swiss neutrality, however, is of a strictly political and military character. It does not extend— and here again it differs from "neutralism"— to the ideological conflict raging in the world of today. The policy of neutrality practiced by the state, does not imply neutrality as regards personal or collective opinion. Neutrality of public opinion is incompatible with the existence of a democratic state. The Swiss people realize that nothing could be more dangerous for them than the acceptance of a so-called ideological or moral neutrality, for they have often been submitted to contradictory pressures or propagandas in the course of history. They have had to face the threat of National-Socialist Germany, and were able to witness at close hand the dramatic struggle of Austria between 1934 and 1938. The Swiss citizen is entirely free to have his preferences and to express them. The neutral position of the state is not binding on him in this respect. The most that can be required of him is to moderate his words.

Moreover those in charge of affairs have never hesitated to state their opinion. They rightly considered that they were entitled, and even had the duty, to do so. It was during one of the most acute postwar crises, in the autumn of 1956, that Federal Counselor Max Petitpierre clearly defined the distinction between neutrality and "neutralism." Without hesitation, as was his custom, the Head of the Political Department expressed a sound judgment of the Suez and Budapest crises.

These events [in Hungary] mark a turning point in the ideological conflict which has opposed the communist and noncommunist world for nearly forty years. They confirm what was already demonstrated by the risings in Berlin on June 17, 1953, and in Poznan on June 28, 1956, and the events in Poland in September of this year: the weakness of a political and economic doctrine which claims to be the one and only true doctrine and aspires to universality. The Hungarian insurrection proves that, for countries which have experienced democracy, even faulty democracy, which have been free and independent, communism is an unnatural form of government, unable to hold its promises whether political or economic, incapable of subsisting as such, but surviving by means of compulsion due to the presence and intervention of foreign military forces. . . . The events in Hungary show that justice cannot be brought about by unjust means, that peace cannot be established by violence, that man's nature cannot be improved by reducing him to slavery.[5]

In this same speech, after referring to some of the measures taken by the Federal Government during the crisis,[6] Mr. Petitpierre declared:

Recent events and the modest role they have given us the opportunity to play, seem to me to show that there is still a place in the world of today for neutrality such as Switzerland's. This neutrality is not moral, does not denote indifference. It has nothing to do with "neutralism," is not an endeavor to escape from responsibilities, in no ways implies abdication as regards the judgment passed on events, does not seek to evade action when action can be useful to the cause of peace. There are many ways

---

ternational, I, Geneva: 1954, p. 501. In a Note, the author adds *"Certain principles governing the policy of neutrality are only valid under the policy of neutrality of a state which is permanently neutral."*

[5] Reply of December 5, 1956, to the demands for explanations made by the Parliamentary Committees for Foreign Affairs.

[6] Agreement to represent French interests in Egypt, Syria, Jordan and Israel, British interests in Egypt and Syria, Iraq's interests in France; transport of United Nations troops in Egypt; dispatch of relief to Hungary.

of serving peace. Our geographical position, our history have taught us that the Swiss policy of neutrality is one which has stood the test for over three centuries and has weathered all the storms which have swept over Europe.[7]

Thus, the Head of the Political Department, while proclaiming in words and in deeds that Switzerland practiced a policy of active neutrality, did not hesitate to emphasize the contradictions in communism and to condemn its methods, thereby openly expressing his opinion of a regime adopted by one of the Great Powers.

THE CONDUCT OF FOREIGN POLICY

The role of the Federal Council

The Federal Council

> watches over the interests of the Confederation abroad, paying particular notice to its international relations, and has general charge of foreign affairs. . . . It ensures the external security of Switzerland and the maintenance of its independence and neutrality.[8]

This body—a College of Magistrates whose decisions may be made by majority vote—is responsible for directing the foreign policy of Switzerland. Because of the importance of external relations, the Federal Department handling foreign affairs had often been linked with the Presidency of the Confederation. But since the Presidency changes each year, a Federal Counselor has now been placed at the Head of the Political Department on a perma-

nent basis, in the light of the disadvantages inherent in the break in continuity resulting from annual rotation.

This decision was however coupled with a measure which illustrates the extent to which the Federal Council was anxious to avoid any form of personal policy: the Head of the Political Department is assisted by a delegation of three members (all of them drawn from the Federal Council) in studying the most important questions. Thus he has relatively limited freedom of action. The collegial system, which is characteristic of Swiss political institutions, compels him to keep in close touch with his colleagues and to refrain from taking initiatives which would not be approved by the other members of the Government. The Government is composed of men who not only belong to different parties but come from different parts of the country. This means that any decision involves reconciling positions which are influenced by varying traditions or viewpoints. It explains the slow and prudent gait of the Federal Government, but also its firmness when agreement has been reached on what is imperative.

The role of the Federal Assembly

The decisions of the Federal Council are, of course, subject to review and approval by the Federal Assembly, whose authority extends to "alliances and treaties with foreign States," and "measures to insure external safety and the preservation of the independence and neutrality of Switzerland; the declaration of war and the conclusion of peace."[9]

The Government, while reserving its freedom of action in the conduct of diplomacy, keeps in close touch with Parliament, not only through the Committees for Foreign Affairs of the two Houses, which are regularly informed of developments, but through the personal contacts which it is so easy to maintain in a small country. Important decisions, except in

---

[7] Reply of December 5, 1956 to the demands for explanations made by the Parliamentary Committees for Foreign Affairs.

[8] Federal Constitution, Art. 102, paras. 8 and 9.

[9] Federal Constitution, Art. 85, paras. 5 and 6.

emergency situations, which seldom arise, gradually come to a head, as the result of private or unofficial soundings and exchanges of views, which are more or less extensive according to the personality of the Head of the Political Department.

This sounding of opinion moreover often goes beyond the Parliament, involving people who are not engaged in politics. For instance, in 1945, the Head of the Federal Political Department submitted the problem raised by the possible entry of Switzerland into the United Nations Organization to an extra-parliamentary Committee. Similarly, Switzerland's relations with countries working for the economic and political integration of Europe, and questions like technical assistance to countries in process of development, have been submitted on various occasions to *ad hoc* committees, including members and non-members of Parliament.

The establishment of these contacts is evidence of the constant and earnest desire of the Swiss authorities to base their decisions on the *consensus* which is indispensable in conducting the foreign affairs of a Federal State. They are obliged to do so, moreover, because basic decisions affecting a provision of the Constitution have to be submitted to a referendum. The Swiss people had to decide whether Switzerland should or should not join the League of Nations. It would also have to be consulted in the event of adherence to the United Nations Organization or of a decision affecting Switzerland's neutrality.

The Political Department and diplomatic personnel

The conduct of Switzerland's international relations lies in the hands of the Political Department, which directs and co-ordinates the activities of the Diplomatic and Consular Service. This task is steadily becoming heavier owing to the enlargement of the diplomatic field, the spread of international organizations, and international gatherings and conferences and the increasingly marked interpenetration of technical and political matters. A small state experiences growing difficulty in establishing and maintaining contacts with other states, keeping itself informed, and following developments in such a way as to insure the defense of its interests and those of its citizens. As a result of the expansion of international relations and the countless obligations arising from the effort to improve the standard of living in the world, the financial burden is becoming so crushing that a choice has to be made which daily becomes more perplexing.

There is also the problem of personnel. How are enough competent diplomats to be found? How can they be trained to handle delicate questions in a variety of specialized spheres? The Political Department has considered several solutions. It has gradually swelled the ranks of its diplomats by adding experts in economic, military or cultural questions. This has been effected with a prudence and moderation adapted to Switzerland's resources, and to the extent that it has been obviously necessary. Efforts have been made also to improve the recruitment and training of higher officials for the Diplomatic Service, in order to enable them to solve some of the technical problems which increasingly enter into day-to-day work. For certain important issues, resort has been had to the services of well-known men prepared to place themselves at their country's disposal during some negotiation or international conference. In the conduct of its international relations, just as in many other spheres, the Swiss Government is fortunately able to draw on a civic capital built up in the course of a long tradition.

The Commerce Division

The mounting importance of economic diplomacy has, however, called for special measures. Whatever the value of the services rendered by business representatives in the negotiation of commercial agreements, and however much it might be anxious to avoid distending the administrative machinery, the Federal Government could not indefinitely entrust its representation to men over whom it had only limited influence. It required an instrument which would be pliable in its hands, if it wanted to preserve its role of arbitrator.

Therefore the Commerce Division was established during the First World War. This Division is not placed directly under the Head of the Political Department. It is under the Department of Public Economy and is responsible for Switzerland's economic relations with foreign countries and for defending the interests of Swiss economy and conducting economic negotiations. Economic affairs are integrated into the framework of the Confederation's foreign policy by liaison officers who deal with the Political and Finance Departments. In the main embassies, commercial attachés, or diplomats who are experts in economics handle economic affairs.

The role of the Commerce Division has grown with the years. It was especially important during the Second World War, when it had the duty of promoting exports and assuring the necessary imports for the country's subsistence. To it fell the delicate negotiations to prevent economic suffocation, despite the blockade enforced by the belligerent states against a country imprisoned in a Europe controlled by National Socialist Germany and its Italian ally. Furthermore, it was charged with the supervision of imports and exports made necessary by the particular circumstances in which Switzerland found itself. In order to obtain authorization to import from any of the belligerents, it had to be in a position to guarantee that the goods would be used in accordance with the agreement concluded, while at the same time avoiding outside intervention in the internal affairs of the Confederation.

The Commerce Division was only partly freed from this task by the close of hostilities, because of the Cold War and the restrictions this implied in trade between the West and the East. Switzerland, by reason of its neutrality, cannot join in embargoes laid on a group of countries. It has to keep up a "normal flow of trade" with every country, while refraining from taking advantage of the restrictions imposed by one or other of the opposite groups. The Commerce Division has to watch over this. At the same time, it takes a heavy share of responsibility in the increasingly complicated negotiations required by the transformation of the world's political map, the development of international trade and international competition, and, finally, the attempts at economic integration on the regional level.

The conduct of cultural relations

Switzerland's cultural relations with foreign countries also raise several delicate problems. Under federal tradition, these are a matter for the Cantons. There is no Federal Department of Public Education. Although circumstances have led the Federal Government to support the humanities, art, and scientific research, and to induce the Houses of Parliament to consent to Switzerland's participation in international organizations such as UNESCO and CERN, up till now the Federal Government has nonetheless avoided binding itself by cultural agreements whose application might cause difficulties with the Cantons. The reply of the Federal Council to the circular letter of UNESCO dated October, 2nd, 1953, defines this policy: "Switzerland," it states,

has already repeatedly been invited to conclude cultural agreements with foreign countries, not only of recent years, but a long time before the Second World War. The Federal Council has always refrained from acting on these proposals. No doubt such agreements could offer certain advantages and correspond to a desire for understanding and cooperation. It, however, is inclined to prefer the simpler and more practical means of individual arrangements between the competent bodies which are quicker to take effect and less rigid than official overall agreements, stipulating the execution of general long-term programs laid down in advance. This moreover also corresponds to a necessity inherent in the nature of things.[10]

Switzerland's situation and its Federal structure along with the fact that it belongs to several different cultures, seemed to it to require this reserve. This presented and still presents disadvantages, whose consequences should not be underestimated. The exchanges of persons on the basis of private cultural agreements are inadequate to maintain normal contacts between the Confederation and the European countries or those of other continents, in an age when cultural relations have become one of the important elements in international relations and one of the instruments of foreign policy. A small country like Switzerland, which in addition is neutral, is in danger of being isolated. It runs the risk of seeing itself barred from the current of exchanges which is developing among the other countries.

It also finds itself defenseless against a cultural invasion which is increasingly assuming the appearance of propaganda. This danger was obvious enough during the rise of the Hitlerian wave to lead the Federal Council to entrust a body with the twofold mission of "preserving the cultural patrimony of Switzerland" and "developing an understanding of the spiritual and cultural patrimony of Switzerland abroad." This body, the *Pro Helvetia Foundation,* is a public agency and its income is supplied from the Federal budget. It is nevertheless autonomous in the sense that its members, who are appointed by the Federal

Council, have complete freedom of decision within the terms of their mission.[11]

The role of this body in national and in foreign relations has continued to grow. It was particularly useful when there was a question of standing up to National-Socialist propaganda. And it has gained importance in the course of the last few years by reason of the broadening of the diplomatic field. But, however large its role, it need scarcely be said that it does not cover all the cultural relations of a country which long tradition has accustomed to rely primarily on the initiatives of private individuals and groups.

NATIONAL INTERESTS

Their impression of success, the high standard of living and the realization of their limited means all combine to unite the Swiss in a common aim: to survive. Since they cannot exert any influence over the Big Powers, nor turn the tide of history, they can do nothing better than hold to the celebrated maxim of Jakob Burckhardt concerning the mission of the small state. To that end, they must establish durable conditions at home and conduct foreign relations with all necessary prudence, in order to attenuate the repercussions of clashes among the Powers, if possible.

Preservation of the Federal Union

What are the conditions of survival? The Swiss would say that they first lie in the reconciliation of federalism and democracy. There is unanimous agreement that the twenty-two Cantons which make up the Confederation must be maintained. It is, however, realized that they cannot all be placed on an equal

[10] "Rapport sur les accords culturels," Oct. 6, 1954. Published by the Program Commission of the UNESCO General Conference. See also Karl Doka, *Les relations culturelles sur le plan international,* Neuchâtel: 1959, p. 316.

[11] In connection with the activities of the *Fondation Pro Helvetia,* see Karl Doka, *op. cit.,* pp. 263–76.

footing. The relative influence of each must be borne in mind. Also, adjustment must be made to necessary changes in economic and social structure.

History has shown the Swiss that they must know how to be contented with a compromise, in order to preserve a balance between these political bodies, which develop at an uneven rate. Any solution which is too categorical produces, if not a breach, such an acute strain that the whole Confederation is weakened. But it is not in the interests of any of these Cantons, large or small, to break their federal bonds. The only other alternative would be to join up with one of the neighboring countries and this would mean more loss than gain. However strong the cultural links uniting the various parts of Switzerland with Germany, France or Italy, they are not sufficiently powerful to outweigh the consciousness of Swiss national interests.

Hence, the desire to insure the existence of the Confederation prevents those holding the majority from taking advantage of their strength to carry the day. Otherwise, as a permanent minority, there would be no interest for the French and Italian Swiss in remaining Swiss. The federal bond is consequently strengthened by encouraging each Canton to preserve and cultivate its original character. Strange as it may seem, the resistance of the Ticino against the cultural attraction of Italy or a thrust of irredentism, increases in proportion to the degree to which the Confederation helps it to resist the Germanization resulting from the *Drang nach Süden* and affirm its Italian character. National interests demand the maintenance of particularisms. Diversity is the condition of unity and consequently of permanence.

Neutrality and Western orientation

Survival, moreover, is only possible in a world which accepts diversity. Survival has been assured solely by a system of balance which prevented any Power from dominating the European Continent. The Swiss way of life would not survive the victory of a totalitarian imperialism. It is linked with a specific conception—the same as that of most Western states—of the organization of a political association as well as with a particular form of international relations. Switzerland's future is determined by the fact that it belongs to Europe and the West, geographically and historically, that it is associated in their fate and would experience the repercussions of their eventual fall in power just as it has benefited from their rise. Cultural, political and economic reasons all preclude the Swiss microcosm from withdrawing into an ivory tower. Its paltry resources, the poverty of its soil, which compel its inhabitants to work hard, also oblige them to seek elsewhere what is lacking. "Swiss prosperity," observes Wilhelm Roepke, "is a daily effort, and a big effort. Not only do the Swiss have to work hard to assure it, but they have to seize hold of all the advantages that a veritable world economy can offer."[12] National interests therefore, demand an international orientation.

From this springs the contradiction we pointed out earlier, of which the Swiss are perfectly aware. They realize that their present prosperity is largely due to not having been caught in the numerous wars that have torn Europe asunder and wrecked its territory. This is no doubt partly because their country did not happen to be in the direct line of great invasions, but also because it has deliberately refrained from taking sides and has practiced a policy of neutrality. The first reason for this neutrality was to preserve internal unity. It is in protecting themselves from Europe that the Swiss have at the same time benefited from its remarkable development.

But can they hold to this neutrality at a time when the whole of Europe is threatened and the West and its civilization are in peril? Are they not in danger of losing everything because they have failed to enlist in a decisive

12 "La position internationale de l'économie suisse," in the *Revue économique et sociale*," *op. cit.*, p. 100.

battle sufficiently early in the day? What would have become of the Swiss Confederation in a Hitlerian Europe? More than one Swiss has asked himself this question, and is asking it again at a juncture where two conceptions of political life are engaged in a deadly conflict all over the world. How is the international orientation demanded by national interests to be pursued in the circumstances?

THE CHOICE OF A FOREIGN POLICY

Should neutrality be abandoned?

It is consequently not surprising that Switzerland's policy of neutrality and even its neutral status, should have given rise to many debates in recent years.

The case against neutrality   Some have pointed out that armed neutrality involves a financial burden out of proportion to the revenue of a small country, which is not in a position to purchase the whole series of indispensable weapons. The disadvantages of its policy in remaining outside the United Nations Organization and standing aloof from attempts at regional grouping have also been noted. It thereby risks being progressively pushed aside from the channels of intellectual exchanges which are increasingly a part of alliances or regional groups of a political nature. It is also in danger of being unable to procure the necessary equipment for its technical and industrial development. This would not be the case if it were to agree to the political conditions of co-operation with other states.

It has also been stressed that Switzerland's absence weakens, though perhaps only slightly, the international position of Europe, sorely pressed on every frontier and only able to maintain its influence by massing all its inhabitants. The protagonists of these arguments conclude that neutrality ought to be cast aside

because it compromises Switzerland's chances for the future. Europe will save itself without us or against us. Besides, Swiss neutrality reduces the chances of Europe for the future.

The case for neutrality   There is a host of objections to this, however. A referendum would be required for neutrality to be relinquished. The public mind is little prepared for such a decision, which would encounter strong opposition, on the one hand from those who do not want to choose either camp and, on the other hand, from those who would reject the camp suggested. The country, firmly united today, would be divided by a quarrel which would weaken it.

Moreover, which camp should be chosen? The overwhelming majority of Swiss would not dream of opting for the so-called "socialist" camp. It is rather towards Europe that they turn. But which Europe? The Europe of the Six, the only one whose aims imply political adherence? And in that event what would be the consequences?

Switzerland's adherence would imply accepting a Europe governed by a Franco-German Directory and by a definite tradition of centralization. There is a basic difference between the federalist tradition of Switzerland and the political philosophy of European militants. The opponents of adherence observe that the federative structure of Switzerland would be progressively transformed in consequence; particularism would gradually disappear. In the end, Switzerland would be swallowed up in an aggregate which would only be European in name because the large centralized nations would have maintained their predominance.

Has the Europe now being organized acquired any degree of political stability? Can a small state which weds its cause be certain that the decision of governments of the large states would not be modified by a reversal in the quotient of power? The internal situations of France, Germany, and Italy preclude replying to this query with the necessary guarantees.

Furthermore, doubt has been expressed about the value of the military protection the

Europe of the Six—which, owing to the EDC failure, is not a military alliance—is in a position to offer. There is actually a "European" organism, the Western European Union, in which Great Britain is associated. But this merely plays a role within the Atlantic Alliance. Switzerland could assure its relative security only by adhering to NATO. Even then, this would add to its responsibilities owing to its acceptance of the risks assumed by the others.

The pros and cons of economic integration

Naturally, the most extensive and heated debates center around the advantages and disadvantages offered by certain formulas of economic integration. In this brief survey all their ins and outs cannot be explained. Those in favor of Switzerland entering into the European Economic Community emphasize the importance of economic exchanges between Switzerland and the states composing the Europe of the Six. They in particular stress the steady rate of increase in recent years of Swiss imports from and exports to those countries. In 1958, Swiss foreign trade statistics showed that 58.8 percent of imports and 39.2 percent of exports were attributable to the European Economic Community.

Others, however, point out that the share of non-European countries in Swiss foreign trade should not be underestimated. Between 1899 and 1955, exports had risen from 27 percent to 47 percent and stood at 44.2 percent in 1958. Consequently, while Switzerland's participation in the Common Market would offer real advantages and its absence entails serious disadvantages, it is nevertheless unable to take the risk of letting itself be hemmed in by a European economic system which applies a protectionist policy. It would not even be in the interests of Europe, which ultimately benefits from the prosperity of its members, to limit exchanges with the non-European countries. It would be a "first-class calamity" for Switzerland, stated one of the men who had

considerable responsibility in the negotiations relating to European integration, "if tariffs were to be increased." "High customs tariffs," he added,

> are the luxury of Big Powers. Look at the United States! The small country, whose markets are abroad and which lives on its exports, must, on the contrary, keep its cost of production—and hence its customs duties—as low as possible in order to remain in competition.[13]

Opposition to joining the European Economic Community has still other motives. It is the hierarchical conception of inter-state relations inspiring a policy of state control in a distribution of tasks among the countries concerned in proportion to the relative importance of each, which frightens the Swiss. This would force Swiss undertakings to readjust their business, and to content themselves with their apportioned share in the assignment of markets.

Foreign policy, however, is not solely guided by the advantages or disadvantages it implies for the country in question. If a small state wishes to be accepted and respected, it must indeed justify its existence towards others by the service rendered. We must therefore ask ourselves what the group of states which constitute the European Economic Community would gain by Switzerland's adherence. Our contribution would certainly be modest, and would primarily be of moral value. It might be of relative political importance insofar as the participation of another small state could act as added counterbalance, within the Community, to the influence of the large states.

[13] Lecture in Geneva by Olivier Long, Minister, delegate of the Federal Council for Negotiations of Commercial Treaties, on November 11, 1957. It should also be borne in mind, as stated by the "Society for the Development of Swiss Economy," that Switzerland has the highest per capita export figure for industrial products in the world, and that its international exchange of goods and services represents over a third of its national income.

Any illusions on this score should, however, be avoided. Since the large states would inevitably hold the majority of seats, there would be little chance of Switzerland's imposing its federalist conception or influencing the foreign policy of a European community. Nor would Switzerland's adherence offer more than is now offered either on the economic or the military plane.

This brief examination of the conditions ruling the conduct of foreign policy and of the choice that is open to the Swiss once more illustrates the limited freedom of action allowed to a small state. The only consolation it can enjoy, probably lies in the fact that the large states do not have a very much wider margin of action.

Leadership in humanitarian ventures

The Swiss, while remaining attached to a policy of neutrality which has not been found to their disadvantage hitherto, endeavor to compensate its negative effects. They are sensitive to everything going on in neighboring countries. They are afraid of intellectual and moral isolation, whose far-reaching consequences would be as serious for the actual existence of the Confederation as the effects of an economic blockade. This fear has given them an increasingly clear and realistic consciousness of their solid ties with the other European nations and the world at large. The whole population has always spontaneously reacted in this spirit.

The fact that they are not strong enough to prevent conflicts between the Great Powers, has led the Swiss to show their desire of taking part in world life and helping other peoples in the only way which seemed to be fitting: they have endeavored to rise above the contradiction between neutrality and internationalism which disturbed them by conceiving a humanitarian mission. The establishment of the International Committee of the Red Cross is probably one of the best known illustrations

but not the only one. The feeling that they should do something for other peoples as their share, found many different outlets during the last war; for example the dispatch of relief supplies, or the welcoming of children from various countries into the humblest families. After the war the *Don Suisse à l'Europe* and the *Aide suisse à l'étranger* appeared good means of showing their desire to help rebuild the world and re-establish friendly co-operation among the nations.

Critical minds may have regarded these gestures as a way of salving the conscience of a people which could not see the victims of the war without a feeling of guilt. That is a rather harsh interpretation. On the contrary, the whole population, including its poorest members, reacted so spontaneously that it would seem to argue disinterested motives. As to a guilty conscience, this should not be exaggerated. What states entered into the war deliberately? In 1945, when the Swiss looked back objectively over the years that had just passed, they certainly had no reason to blame their Government, but every cause to praise it for the skill with which it had steered through the rocks.

Participation in international organizations

This humanitarian mission is, however, only one aspect, the popular angle, of Switzerland's contribution to international co-operation. Since lasting peace and the development of the international community are in their interests, and since they realize neutrality is only a means of defending their independence, the Swiss must try, so far as possible, to have a part in international organizations. It is not surprising then that Switzerland has joined some of these: the International Court of Justice, UNESCO, the International Refugee Organization, the World Health Organization, the International Labor Organization, the International Civil Aviation Organization, the International Union for Telecommunications, the International Postal Union, UNICEF and, finally, OEEC.

In joining the OEEC the Federal Council attached a Declaration defining the conditions and the limits laid down by the Swiss Government in regard to its country's co-operation. It is interesting to quote this:

1. It goes without saying that Switzerland will not enter into any engagement which would be incompatible with its traditional status of neutrality.
2. The Resolutions of the Conference affecting Swiss economy can only become binding on the Confederation by its own agreement.
3. Switzerland reserves its freedom to maintain the commercial agreements concluded with European States not taking part in the work of the Conference and to enter into new ones.[14]

In stating this, the Federal Government not only emphasizes Switzerland's neutrality, but also its sovereignty, with the intention of recording its opposition to international organizations of a supranational type. It also reserves worldwide trade agreements, which are indispensable for a country whose pattern of foreign trade, low tariffs and particular postwar circumstances, place it, from some angles, in a special position. But these considerations in no way modify the very clear purpose manifested by the partnership of Switzerland in international bodies.

The foreign policy of the Swiss Confederation cannot really be condensed into a single formula, *neutrality,* but rather into two: *neutrality and international co-operation.* Definite and realistic expressions of fellowship are indeed considered as the true means of reconciling a small nation's need for security with its interest in promoting an international community. The Federal Council and the Minister for Foreign Affairs have repeated this again and again. For example, the message addressed by the Federal Council to the Federal Assembly on August 20, 1948, in connection with the adherence of Switzerland to the OEEC, states:

> Our country, situated in the heart of Europe, cannot isolate itself economically, nor can it disinterest itself from events occurring on its borderline. It must, within its modest possibilities, take part in the efforts being made to reconstruct the Continent and by this reconstruction install a climate of mutual understanding, stability and peace. Our neutral status forbids us to join open or disguised political alliances, but it does not prevent us from being associated in the economic recovery of Europe. On the contrary, the solidarity which is the natural complement of this neutrality requires it.

As has been rightly observed,

> Switzerland seems destined by its geographical position and prepared by its past to fulfil the international duties which are increasingly attached to the actual idea of neutrality and strip this of the character of a selfish privilege that generally appears to vilify it in the eyes of belligerents.[15]

The Head of the Political Department again emphasized Switzerland's conception of its mission when there was a question of sending a Swiss Delegation to the Commission of Neutral States which were to control the Korean Armistice. He declared that the work to be carried out by the Commission was for precise and limited purposes of a pacific and humanitarian nature. There was no objection to it so far as Switzerland's policy of neutrality was concerned. On the contrary, Switzerland's action in these two Commissions, undertaken at the

---

[14] "Message of the Federal Council on Switzerland's participation in the OEEC," *Feuille Fédérale, 1948,* II, p. 1136.

[15] *Ibid.,* p. 1113 ss.

request and in the common interests of both belligerents, served the cause of peace and was therefore in accordance with the policy of neutrality as the Swiss had always conceived and defined it.

The Swiss press used an argument of the same type to explain and justify the very discreet role of intermediary played by Swiss diplomacy during the ultimate phase in the organization of the Conference between the French Government and Algerian representatives at Evian.

Aid to underdeveloped countries

Switzerland's growing share in assistance to countries in process of development is another sphere in which this intention of international co-operation is shown. To be frank, public opinion was a little slow in waking up to this. Being accustomed to restrict its vista to European horizons, it had difficulty in grasping the startling revolution implied in the perception by these underprivileged populations of their inadequate living conditions. It was only realized by degrees that these problems would not be solved by charity but politics. Any country which stands aside from the fight to combat underdevelopment, which becomes a struggle for development, is in danger of being swept away by the revolutionary crisis shaking the world. Or it will be put out of competition by rivals in West or East, or by a more permanent deviation of the channels of trade. With the broadening of the sphere of Soviet influence, Western economic influence is shrinking. As this coincides with increased productivity in the West, it is inclined to sharpen competition within the confines of a world which is shrivelling rapidly.

From this angle, it is certainly in the interests of Switzerland to co-operate economically with the underdeveloped countries. This has now become apparent to public opinion, which is supporting a series of private ventures to lend different forms of assistance to the new states.

The Federal Council affirmed this in its message of May 5, 1961, in which it declared:

Assistance to countries in process of development is a way of working for peace. It is commanded by the fellowship which should unite all people and prompt their relations. Without a doubt, they are becoming increasingly interdependent, they are all exposed to the same risks and perils, and one way of avoiding these is by a joint endeavor to place scientific and technical progress at the service of humanity as a whole. Border lines are no longer barriers today, inside which a people can withdraw into itself. For the first time in history perhaps, the fate of peoples and mankind is identical, which implies collective responsibility in building up the world of tomorrow. By helping the countries in process of development we are also preparing our own future.[16]

This declaration was made by the Federal Council as an introduction to a proposal demanding a new financial effort from the Houses of Parliament with a view to expanding multilateral and bilateral assistance. The response with which it met is proof that the greater part of the nation has grasped the political significance of such action.

Relations with European unification movements

Switzerland, we have stated, belongs to Europe. The Swiss realize the duties incumbent on them as members of a common civilization with a common destiny, and they are ready to co-operate in straightening out Europe and enhancing its prestige.

[16] "Message of the Federal Council to the General Assembly Concerning Switzerland's Co-operation with Developing Countries," *Feuille Fédérale*, May 5, 1961, No. 8107.

But they and the promoters of the Europe of the Six vary in their idea of European co-operation. The Swiss are fully aware that adherence to the European Economic Community as it stands today and as it desires to shape itself, would be the downfall of Switzerland. It would abolish the political conceptions on which it has built up an existence throughout the centuries, conceptions whose value is not confined to the small state that proudly claims them. The proof that their sacrifice has simply allowed certain large European states to resume a historic mission—with more extensive means (those of a United Europe)—which does not necessarily correspond to the ideas of the Swiss for their Continent, would singularly detract from the satisfaction of acquiring citizenship in a unitarian Europe. They would find themselves being led by France and Germany, with no right to complain because they themselves would have helped to destroy the political bodies which contributed to the enrichment and prestige of European civilization and which preserved a balance of power within that Continent.

Their refusal to join the European Economic Community is not, therefore, based solely on the classical argument of neutrality, but to a far larger extent on the desire to bring about a simpler, more elastic and broader conception of economic co-operation. This, indeed, was what led Switzerland to enter the European Free Trade Association, whose promoters, as realists, desired to go forward step by step, without any unnecessary bustling of the partners, whose adherence would be all the more effective because it was a matter of free choice.

Switzerland was able to adhere to the EFTA because this did not infer any political engagement contrary to a neutral status. Moreover, its rules are sufficiently flexible to enable the Association to reconcile regional and world programs on the economic and political levels. It was also a duty to adhere, as proof of the intention to assist in strengthening inter-European bonds and building up a huge market of 300 million inhabitants.

It was not the aim of the European Free Trade Association to divide Europe still further but rather to regroup the countries which, for various reasons, had been unable to join forces with the Common Market countries, thus running the risk, if they remained isolated, of finding themselves in an unfavorable position. The peremptory conditions laid down by France and its associates, left no option: a restrained but determined stand had to be made. This is very well expressed in the message of the Federal Council of February 5, 1960:

> The establishment of a free-trade area of this type might revive the desire of the states belonging to the Common Market to avoid a split in Europe and give new impetus to those who have labored to this end. The reason is that the conditions resulting from the first measures of commercial policy taken by the Common Market would no longer be solely to the detriment of the states not belonging thereto. The advantages and disadvantages would be more evenly distributed among the different members of the OEEC.
>
> A free-trade area should be conceived in such a way as to constitute a sound basis for establishing a bridge with the Common Market. It should be used to proceed with the elimination of obstacles to trade, as far as possible at the speed laid down in the Rome Treaty. Any steps which could lead to commercial strife should be avoided. All the members of such an area must constantly aim at restoring the unity of the OEEC and re-establishing the principle of equal treatment therein.[17]

The decision of the United Kingdom Government in the summer of 1961 to request admittance to the European Economic Community has, of course, placed Switzerland in a new situation, in the same way as the other members of the EFTA. But the problem it

[17] Message of the Federal Council to the Federal Assembly on Switzerland's participation in the EFTA, p. 25.

raises, however difficult, is not insoluble. If the United Kingdom does join the Common Market, not only its structure, but its policy will be modified. This adherence will inevitably involve a change in the balance of power within the Community, as well as certain changes of methods. It also implies a broadening of the economic sphere of the EEC, which will help to conciliate regional interests and the world interests of Europe.

These circumstances have led the Federal Government to reconsider its position and to contemplate the possibility—in agreement with the states which are members of the EFTA and especially Austria and Sweden—not of adherence, which would be incompatible with its neutral status, but of association. It made official approaches to the EEC at the end of 1961 in this vein.

At the moment of writing, no one knows how the negotiations will work out. The outcome will depend both on developments as regards relations between the United Kingdom and the Common Market and on whatever changes there may be on either side of the Atlantic.

But this request for association can be interpreted as further evidence of Switzerland's intention to take part—in line with the conditions of neutrality—in any attempt to strengthen international co-operation.

In the course of a more or less long evolution, moreover, it is not impossible that Switzerland may end up by accepting supranational organizations, in the same way as other states. But these would have to correspond to a need and to respect European differences. This does not appear unlikely if one observes the contradictory efforts, so characteristic of our era, of forces directed towards the constitution of large groups and forces which, by contrast, promote the formation of small autonomous communities and work for the disintegration of the big blocs.

The Europe for which the Swiss yearn cannot be a small Europe which has shrunk into itself, hedged in by customs and political barriers. A large federalist Europe, where political bodies balance and sway one another, a Europe which exerts worldwide influence, is what they so ardently desire.

BIBLIOGRAPHY

Author's Suggestions

Bonjour, Edgar. *Swiss Neutrality, its History and Meaning.* London: Allen & Unwin, 1946.

Bonjour, E., Offer, H. S., and Potter, G. R. *A Short History of Switzerland.* Oxford: Clarendon Press, 1955.

Lasserre, David. *Etapes du fédéralisme, l'expérience suisse.* Lausanne: Rencontre, 1954.

Rappard, W. E. *The Government of Switzerland.* New York: D. Van Nostrand, 1936.

Lloyd, William Bross. *Waging Peace, the Swiss Experience.* Washington, D.C.: Public Affairs Press, 1958.

Codding, George Arthur. *The Federal Government of Switzerland.* London: Allen & Unwin, 1961.

Siegfried, André. *Switzerland: A Democratic Way of Life.* New York: Duell, Sloan and Pearce, 1950. (English edition of *La Suisse: démocratie témoin.*)

ABOUT THE AUTHOR

MARIO TOSCANO has combined two careers in a lifetime. His academic achievements start with an LL.B. from Milan University in 1930 and a Ph.D. in Political Science in 1931 from Pravia University. He was Assistant Professor of Diplomatic History, first at Milan University and then at Cagliari University until 1939 when he became full Professor. Since 1952 he has served as Professor of Diplomatic History at the University of Rome.

Concurrent with these achievements have been Dr. Toscano's increasing contributions as a public servant. He has been Historical Advisor to the Ministry of Foreign Affairs since 1946 and is the President of the Commission for publication of Italian diplomatic documents. He has been Chief of the Research Department of the Ministry of Foreign Affairs since 1947 and has represented Italy as a delegate to the last ten United Nations General Assemblies with ambassadorial rank.

His numerous publications include the following: *Guerra diplomatica in Estremo Oriente*, 1950; *Le origini diplomatiche del patto d'acciaio*, 2nd ed., 1956; *Una mancata intesa italo-sovietica nel 1940–41*, 1954; *Fonti documentarie e memorialistiche per la storia diplomatica della seconda guerra mondiale*, 1954; *Lezioni di storia dei trattati e politica internazionale*, 1959; and *Appunti sulla questione dell'Alto Adige*, 1961.

ABOUT THE CHAPTER

As a background for discussing current foreign policy problems, Dr. Toscano gives careful attention to the fixed factors which mold the life of the nation and the historical elements and traditional goals which have guided the foreign policy of Italy. The sections which deal with Italy's political make-up and the forces which influence foreign policy decisions are particularly valuable. Careful attention is also paid to the formal and informal institutions which give direction to the foreign policy of Italy.

In discussing the national interest of Italy, Dr. Toscano notes that her fundamental concern is the same as that of other nations: "insuring the survival of the country's own way of life in an ideologically and militarily divided world." He analyzes the movement towards European integration and the reasons why Italy has been one of the strongest supporters of this movement.

The chapter concludes with a survey of Italy's relations with the major nations and regions of the world. Dr. Toscano also discusses the Atlantic Alliance and Italy's role in the United Nations. The chapter reveals keen insight into the role of Italy in the modern world.

6

THE FOREIGN POLICY OF ITALY

MARIO TOSCANO

University of Rome

FIXED FACTORS INFLUENCING POLICY

The geographic setting

Of the several geographical factors influencing Italian foreign policy, the most important is the exceptionally long land and sea frontier. The Italian state consists of a long peninsula, solidly anchored to the European continent at the Alpine arc, which extends into the Mediterranean for a distance of 706 miles, and of a complex of islands, the largest of which are Sardinia and Sicily. Excluding the islands, the land frontier is 1,155 miles in length, the sea frontier, 2,232 miles; including the islands, the sea frontier is 4,624 miles long. Thus, the combined land and sea frontiers of the modern Italian state total 5,780 miles.

Each frontier, land and sea, involves a different set of security requirements and has had a distinct influence on the conduct of Italian foreign policy. Italy's geographical make-up has also influenced the contacts her population has had with the external world, the ethnic composition of the Italian people and the development of the national culture and traditions. The very variety of problems posed by this peculiar geographic situation, along with a markedly inferior material strength as compared with the other Great European Powers,[1] has caused continental and maritime considerations to alternate as the basic criterion determining the decisions and actions of the Rome government.

The geographic factor, as noted initially, also has influenced the ethnic composition of the nation, the development of the national culture and political traditions, the economy, and the national temperament. The northern part

---

[1] With the sole exception of Germany, all Great Powers in Europe became unified nation-states during the late medieval period, i.e., several centuries before the Italian national unification of 1861.

of the country is projected toward the Continent, the southern and insular part toward the Mediterranean, while the central section of the Peninsula represents, in most respects, an area subject to both Continental and maritime influences. Thanks to the frequent invasions of the Peninsula from north of the Alps, and to far easier peaceful and cultural contacts with the European continent, the North-Italian of today is very similar, even in physical characteristics, to the Frenchman, Swiss and German. In the south, on the other hand, the traces of Greek, Arabic, Norman, Spanish and other Mediterranean influences are quite visible. They have been decisive there in creating the mental outlook, social customs and traditions, physical structure and coloring of the population. In the central zone, these two influences have merged. They have produced a composite type, the connective tissue of which was provided by the original Etruscan imprint.

The demographic variety of the Italian people, is still too great to permit speaking of a single ethnic and cultural type. A century of national independence is too short a period to insure an effective amalgamation, despite the fact that participation in two World Wars and the evolution of the economy and the transportation and communications system have brought about significant advances in this direction. Consequently, the political conceptions of the Italian clearly reflect his point of origin and the ethnic characteristics peculiar to the individual region. The North-Italian, for example, is much more sensitive to continental European problems than the southerner who shows more concern for Mediterranean problems.

Human and material resources and economic development The peculiar geographic structure of the country—along with the effects of a long succession of foreign rule in the various parts of the Peninsula and on the islands—has also been at the root of Italy's uneven economic development. The northern regions are highly developed, even though poor in natural resources, aside from methane gas in the Po River valley and the hydroelectric wealth brought by the rivers flowing from the southern side of the Alpine watershed. The economic development of the north must be attributed not only to the greater facility of trade and communication with the Continent, but also to the cooler climate and the attitudes and interests of the ethnic groups of the area. The southern regions are predominantly agricultural, despite the scarcity of water, the difficulty of exploiting a miserly soil, and the presence, though in limited quantities, of certain raw materials such as iron, coal, petroleum and sulphur. The industrial organization of the north has permitted this part of the country to play a determining role in the choice and pursuit of national foreign policy objectives, even when the country's foreign policy was focused primarily on Mediterranean objectives.

The topographic and soil features of the Italian territory, with its very high percentage (6.7%) of rocky land and about 5,790 square miles of non-productive terrain[2] have given the Italian demographic problem a strong influence on foreign policy. The birthrate (17.9 per thousand) is not the highest in Europe today. Still, it is considerable in an absolute sense. When the high proportion of mountainous, rocky, and otherwise uncultivable land is considered, it becomes almost explosive. Consequently, the current average of 421.7 inhabitants per square mile (227.1 in 1871, 387.9 in 1951) is not comparable with that of the other European states with birthrates almost as high, or higher, than the Italian. The population of the Kingdom of Italy in 1861 was 22,014,000 (26,128,000 within the area enclosed by today's confines); in December, 1960, the figure had risen to 51,152,000. This is the fundamental explanation of the chronic unemployment (about 1,500,000) and underemployment (about 5,000,000) and the constantly heavy emigration to other European countries and overseas.

The movement of Italians abroad was not

---

[2] In addition to the Alpine chain, the entire Peninsula is obliquely crossed by the Appenines. The big islands of Sardinia, Sicily and Elba also are largely mountainous.

and is not so much a manifestation of political expansion. Rather, it is a manifestation of the poor Italian's need to find work. Although the industrialization of the country may create jobs for all citizens in the not-too-distant future, the actual realization of this hope is probably far in the future. Hence, the problem of emigration plays a considerable role in the formulation and execution of Italian foreign policy—and it will continue to do so, in all likelihood, for at least another decade.

On the one hand, the settlement of millions of Italian emigrants in other countries has forged strong and fecund bonds between Italy and the host countries. On the other hand, these settlements have often constituted points of attraction for the Rome government. Frequently, the intention was to open new outlets for national emigration by acquiring not only areas selected for receiving Italy's excess population, but also those toward which the flow of emigrants had already begun independently, with neither encouragement nor direction by the government in Rome. Today, the population pressure and consequent unemployment problems are less acute. Nevertheless, the Italian government still is assiduous in promoting the free flow of labor from one country to another, especially within the European and Atlantic communities. This policy has often been misunderstood in those countries which are almost entirely unfamiliar with the desperate search for employment, the fear of losing a job and the personal drama implicit in losing it when there is little hope of finding another.

Historic factors

The historical vicissitudes of the Peninsula have also created a whole series of traditions which have had and still have a far-from-negligible influence on Italian foreign policy. Throughout the centuries, there have been many Italian states and each of them, from time to time, has tried in different ways to resolve the problems created by Italy's geography. Though

these problems are gradually disappearing with the changes in the economic structure of the country and those wrought by time itself, the historical precedents still represent basic points of reference in the formulation of Italian foreign policy. This is especially true when the formulators succumb to the temptation to take the easier path of imitating the past, rather than the obviously wiser, although more difficult and laborious one, of devising new solutions to fit the times.

For two reasons, historical traditions assume in Italy an intensity unknown elsewhere. The first is the objective circumstance that the grandeur of the Roman Empire is unique and has few points of comparison with the historical experiences of other countries. The second reason concerns a peculiarly Italian mental trait: the penchant for rhetoric. In language, it usually manifests itself in a compulsion to add either an essentially irrelevant elegance of expression or an excessive schematism to the oral description of all objective phenomena, even the most mundane and uncomplicated. If the tendency stopped at this point, it might cause more amusement than concern. Unfortunately, a certain distortion of objective reality is involved. For the Italian, in all sincerity, actually sees the reality in terms of a language image. Where the language is used in the way just described, the inescapable consequence is that reality is viewed highly subjectively. Thus, the rhetorical bent of the Italian mind is an ever-present stimulus to the cultivation of traditions and myths which then acquire the force of a concrete reality in the Italian outlook. As subsequent illustration will show, myths have had and continue to have a highly important place in Italian foreign policy.

During the Classical age, the Italian Peninsula gave birth to a unitary state. In turn, this state generated the Roman Empire, the only empire in the whole of human history that successfully united East and West—as they were then understood and conceived—into a single dominion. To the magnetic attraction of the grandeur of Rome one must add the fact that the Roman tradition constituted, for Italian rulers after 1861, the sole precedent of a unitary state comprising the entire Peninsula. This circumstance explains certain objectives of Italian foreign policy after the unification, just as it explains their attractiveness to many levels of public opinion.

After the unity created by classical Rome disappeared, there was not only a succession of foreign invasions and foreign dominations, but separate states were constructed. Some of these gave birth to particularistic political traditions. Typical, in this respect, were Venice, Piedmont, Tuscany and Naples. The policies of each of these states put the accent on particular requirements. In so doing, they became the fixed reference points of separate traditions. In an Italian environment, this could not fail to influence greatly the selection of the country's foreign policy objectives. These traditions were not and are not solely positive. At times, they were negative and even disastrous to the effective pursuit of their original objectives. On the other hand, the long succession of foreign dominations, the frequent shifts from the glory of the power of Rome to the humiliation of foreign oppression and the fact that for many centuries the consecration of the European empires (German, Spanish, French) always occurred in Italy, permitted the Italians to witness much, to hear much and to undergo many experiences. Thus was bred a profound psychological scepticism which strongly influenced the outlook on international problems.

At this point it is relevant to recall that Italy is and has been the scene of another unique experience in the history of the world: the experience of being the seat of the Catholic Church. Though the Pontifical State has ceased to be territorially important, it has nonetheless preserved a high spiritual value. In the past, the Papal State was a hindrance to unification of the Peninsula. But it was more than that. The presence of the headquarters of the Papacy has given Italians a keen sense of the universal. Undoubtedly this bent stems from the experience of the Roman Empire and, in one form or another, it has kept the idea of a supranational organization alive. Perhaps this explains the present-day fact that the Italians are in the forefront of the movement for European unity and sponsoring supranational conceptions in the international organizations to which they belong.

TRADITIONAL GOALS OF FOREIGN POLICY

Unification of Italian territories

During the first decade of national unity under the House of Savoy foreign policy was dedicated to bringing all Italians into the Kingdom. When the creation of the new state was proclaimed in Turin in March, 1861, two vital areas were still outside the realm: Rome and its hinterland, constituting the Pontifical State; and Venetia, Trento and Trieste, which were still under the Austro-Hungarian Empire of the Habsburgs. The conquest of these territories was the principal objective of the Savoyard monarchy and its parliamentary government. Besides a desire to liberate all foreign-dominated Italians and to unite them to the mother country, it was necessary to guarantee the military security of a state that had appeared almost as if by a political miracle. This state, furthermore, was under attack from abroad and at home, to say nothing of its own organic weaknesses. At the same time, the royal government was under pressure from the south to seek an outlet for Italian emigration and to expand the country through participation in the colonial rivalry of the European Powers, a rivalry then in full swing.

The Veneto and Rome were both brought into the Kingdom during the first decade of unity, but the cost was high. The Austro-Prussian War of 1866 enabled the government to conclude an alliance with Berlin and, consequently, to wrench Venice and the Veneto from Austria-Hungary just after the Battle of Sadowa. Unfortunately, this conquest was more a diplomatic success and the result of the military victory of Italy's Prussian ally than the consequence of the contribution made by Italian armed forces.

The Franco-Prussian War of 1870–71 brought the opportunity to resolve the Roman question. Napoleon III had been one of the most ardent defenders of the Papacy and the French garrison in Rome represented an insuperable physical barrier to the repeated attempts of Italian patriots to bring down the temporal power of the Papacy and make Rome a part of the new nation-state. The French capitulation at Sedan in September, 1870, eliminated this barrier. On the 20th of the same month, the royal troops of the Savoy monarchy occupied the Capitoline city which was immediately proclaimed the capital of the Italian state. By this time, most of the work of national liberation was complete. What remained to be done concerned peripheral provinces. But Rome, too, had cost much, not in the form of human and financial sacrifice, but in the form of open Papal hostility toward the new regime, an antagonism that was not formally buried until the signature of the Lateran Accords of 1929.

Imperialism

Africa　After 1870 the demands for the attainment of territorial objectives other than *Italia irredenta* became firmer. They went hand in hand with the rebirth of the myth of Rome —the sheerly mystical notion that, by virtue of historical precedent, modern Italy had an imperial role to play in the international scramble for colonies, markets and prestige. The clamor for territorial expansion into Albania, Tunisia and Egypt and Italian participation in the race to subject and colonize Black Africa became more insistent. Irredentism, security, increasing the national power and territorial expansion, from that time forward, were the criteria determining the direction of Italian foreign policy.

Italy's African ventures had two outstanding characteristics: they were all geared to the Mediterranean problem and they aimed at insuring both the country's military security and the possibility of emigration. The Italian colonial possessions, though belonging to a notoriously poor country, were not sought for economic exploitation, but rather as military bases or potential recipients of excess population. Consequently, unlike other European colonial Powers, Italy gave its overseas territories much more than it received in return. The Mediterranean-African stimulus was then very strong, reaching its climax during the decade from 1887 to 1896.

The ill-starred battle of Adua on March 1, 1896, in which an Italian force was annihilated by the Ethiopians, did not register at home as a simple episode in the construction of an Italian empire in Africa. The Aduan disaster befalling Italian troops in far-off Ethiopia represented a tremendous blow to the *amour propre* of the Italian military and the shriller advocates of imperial expansion. However, the pause was of short duration. The expansionists soon recovered their dominant influence in the formulation of Italian foreign policy. This time, the objective lay in the heart of the Mediterranean, the only remnant of the Ottoman Empire in North Africa still free from the domination of the competing European colonial Powers: Libya. After intensive diplomatic preparation, featuring agreements with Germany (1891), France (1900–1902), Great Britain (1902), Austria-Hungary (1902) and Russia (1909), the conquest of the Libyan coast and most of the hinterland was effected during the conflict with Turkey (1911–12).

The Libyan undertaking proved so popular that it even surprised the Italian Prime Minister who had promoted the venture. Only the Socialists resisted the euphoria imperialism had aroused. Acquisition of what was called Italy's "fourth shore" satisfied the long-standing desire for expansion in the name of finding new and—most important of all—nearby outlets for Italian overseas emigration. By the time of the Libyan war, emigration had reached almost the million mark annually. Overseas expansion was a keen satisfaction to those who dreamed of Italian hegemony among the Mediterranean Powers.

The Balkans During this period, a new factor in Italian foreign policy made its appearance alongside the traditional irredentist motif. It originated in the desire to affirm fully the interests of a country undergoing full demographic and economic development. The Balkans and the problems of that area now became of vital Italian concern. Albania was the point of key interest. Italian interest in Balkan problems, relentlessly pursued, permitted the Rome government to obtain full recognition of Italy's interest in the Balkans. Italy made secret agreements with Russia and Austria-Hungary, the two Powers which had thus far refused to accept the Italians as legitimate rivals in that delicate sector of the European diplomatic chessboard.

Participation in World War I

The outbreak of the First World War found Italy militarily weakened by her recent conquest of Libya. Nevertheless, the nationalists pressed for Italian intervention in the conflict. The declaration of neutrality at the outset of the War, in accordance with the letter and spirit of the Triple Alliance treaty, laid the country open to the propaganda of the belligerent Powers. Notwithstanding the fact that nationalists represented a minority party, they won the contest for public opinion, thanks to the mustering of popular forces against the Parliament and strong support from the Crown. This dangerous precedent was to facilitate fascism's rise to power.

Italy's participation in the First World War proved much more onerous than anticipated. Six hundred thousand Italians lost their lives and the material costs exceeded the calculations of the most sober proponents of Italian intervention. The effort prostrated the country economically and laid the groundwork for a searing social crisis. At War's end, Italy obtained Trento, Trieste, the Alto Adige, Fiume, Zara, Rhodes, the territory beyond the Juba River, but not part of Dalmatia, nor a protectorate over Albania, nor Smyrna and part of Asia Minor, nor colonial mandates; nor was there even agreement with France regarding the colonial rectifications contemplated in the Pact of London.

Even so, these acquisitions, along with the disappearance of the Habsburg monarchy and Italy's presence among the ranks of the victorious Powers, might have provided considerable satisfaction. But the Italian public, like that of the other European belligerents, was dangerously dissatisfied with the conditions attending the serious economic crisis following in the wake of the War. The nationalists, with little real effort, managed to persuade the population that the victory had been "betrayed," because the peace treaties did not endorse all the provisions stipulated in earlier agreements which had set forth the conditions of Italy's entry into the War.

The attrition attending the war effort had proved so great that the foundations of the state itself were shaken. The disorders promoted by the parties of the Left provoked an even stronger reaction among the Fascists and nationalists. This reaction found its sinews in the support of Italian industrialists, the military and part of the bourgeoisie. The *dénouement* was almost predictable months before Mussolini actually became Prime Minister on October 28, 1922, with the consent, if not the tacit blessing, of the Crown.

Mussolini's policies

In its initial phase, the foreign policy of the dictator was relatively mild. Doubtless it contained within itself the germs of the dramatic developments that were to follow, but the fact was that *il Duce* had not yet made his definitive choice of objectives.

It was the advent of Hitler in Berlin that stimulated a dynamism in Fascist foreign policy. With the Four-Power Pact, the Venice meeting, participation in the Stresa front and agreement to help guarantee Austrian independence, Mussolini initially seemed to be adopting a reasonable attitude. But the Abyssinian undertaking, ill-prepared with the Laval agreements of 1935, constituted the point of departure for a catastrophic evolution in Italian foreign policy. Clearly, the conquest of Ethiopia was, in a very real sense, a continuation of earlier colonialist aspirations. At the same time, it was equally clear that, on the psychological level, the whole adventure was an expression of the myth of Imperial Rome. But whatever the precise nature of the motivation, the venture itself demonstrated no respect for the reality of the postwar epoch. Mussolini underestimated the reaction of the British public—a reaction which, to some extent, surprised even British statesmen—and overestimated the degree of French support. The final—and unhoped-for—military and diplomatic success blinded him and removed his last inhibitions.

The Spanish Civil War exalted the ideological aspect of the position of the Head of the Fascist Government—drove a further wedge between him and the democracies and threw him into the eager embrace of Adolf Hitler. His trip to Berlin in 1937 impressed him greatly and he was to remain a prisoner of this impression for the rest of his career. In November, 1938, when he began his campaign of territorial claims on France for Nice, Corsica, Tunisia and Djibouti, Mussolini deluded himself that his diplomatic victory would be no less facile than Hitler's clamorous successes. He did not realize that he was on the point of becoming the German dictator's puppet, with no hope of regaining his freedom of action.

As an immediate consequence of the increased necessity of German support, the Italian dictator, on January 1, 1939, decided to accept Hitler's offer of an alliance. Later, this evolved into a Tripartite Agreement with Japan. The impression that a political agreement with the democracies was out of the question, along with the German assurances regarding Poland, paved the way for the signing of the Pact of Steel of May 22, 1939, just after the Italian occupation of Albania. The Danzig crisis caused Mussolini to hesitate. Among other

things, he understood now that the possibility of controlling Hitler's actions through consultation, which Mussolini had envisaged in the Pact, was nothing more than an illusion. Berlin had played him for its own ends. Therefore Italy decided in favor of non-belligerence. This decision was in harmony with the frame of mind of the Italian public and with the fact of Italian military weakness, but it definitely contradicted all the theories of imperialism and ideological struggle at the foundation of the regime's propaganda.

When France fell, Mussolini became convinced that the outcome of the war had been decided. Without hesitation, he declared war on France and Great Britain. During the brief period in which the victory of the Axis Powers seemed assured, the Fascist government announced its Mediterranean and Balkan objectives: Malta, Tunisia, Corsica, Nice, part of Morocco and Egypt, Croatia, Greece. The hard military reality soon drove itself into Italian consciousness. The public clearly perceived that the War would find its *dénouement* in an Anglo-American-Soviet victory. A *coup d'état* on July 25, 1943 brought down Mussolini. While it was principally a consequence of the military defeat, it was also the fruit of the illusion that Italy still had a chance to insert herself into the Anglo-American game and thereby earn her return ticket to "respectability" in accordance with the decisions of the Quebec Conference.

The Armistice of September 8, 1943, arrived earlier than Mussolini's successors had anticipated and the Germans immediately exploited the disorientation of the Badoglio government. The consequence was the division of Italy. In the south, the government of Victor Emmanuel III acted as a co-belligerent with the Allies; in the north, Mussolini's puppet regime was under the control of the Germans. It was a tragic and painful period, but it was also one that saw the Partisan "resistance" and the Italian Liberation Corps write heroic pages in the nation's history. But the Peace of Paris turned out to be much more severe for them than the Italians had feared: only the Brenner frontier remained intact. France obtained Briga and

Tenda, Yugoslavia was given Istria and Zara. A special regime was provided for Trieste but was never implemented; Rhodes and all the colonies: Tripoli, Cyrenaica, Somalia, Eritrea, to say nothing of Ethiopia, were lost. The fleet was dismembered, all fortifications were dismantled, and reparations to Greece, Yugoslavia, Albania, and the Soviet Union were stipulated. The imperial dream had come to an end. The country had to be reconstructed. Aerial bombardment and the long, fierce struggle of the Allies to roll back the Germans had reduced the Peninsula to a vast shambles. Even the structure of the state itself was seriously undermined.

TRENDS IN POWER RELATIONSHIPS

Political parties

The condemnation of the Fascist policy which had led the country to defeat in World War II formally manifested itself in the abolition of the Fascist Party (one of the provisions of the peace treaty) and the fall of the monarchy, which was also held responsible for Mussolini's advent to power. The Republic was proclaimed after a referendum on June 2, 1946 registered a 54 percent majority in favor of republican government. The referendum indicated, at the outset of the new republican era, that the defeated forces still retained much influence.

Actually, the disappearance of the monarchy gave rise to an absolutely new balance of domestic political forces. It meant the elimination of an institution which until then had held its ground honorably against the other Crown existing in Italy and Rome: the Holy See. This fact has had a peculiar consequence: among the non-Marxist parties at war's end, the Catholic party (the Christian Democracy), able to count on the support of the Vatican and its parochial network, was in a position to play a principal role. Hence, the Catholics of the

Christian Democracy constitute one of the dominant political forces in the Italian Republic. All Italian governments since 1945 have been headed by a Christian Democrat. In foreign policy the Christian Democracy is strongly pro-Atlantic and European. Its voting strength rests in all social and economic classes, but the predominant element is bourgeois.

The Christian Democrats' strongest competitor for power is the Italian Communist Party, the biggest in Europe outside the Soviet Union. From winning 19 percent of the votes in 1946 (4,356,686), it went on to garner 22.7 percent in 1958 (6,700,812). During the military occupation period, its work was not challenged by the U.S. representatives. In some cases, it even received help. Its electoral support is derived chiefly from workers, but it also includes many intellectuals, artists, clerks, government employees and most of the Partisan survivors of the War of Liberation. It dominates the General Confederation of Labor, the largest and most powerful Italian labor union association. In foreign policy, the P.C.I. is anti-Atlantic and anti-European, never divorcing itself from the foreign policy positions of the Soviet Union. The strength of the Italian Communist Party has grown, too, as a consequence of the fact that most of its political activity is supported by parallel action of the Italian Socialist Party.

In the 1946 elections, the Italian Socialist Party won a higher percentage of votes (20 percent) than did the P.C.I., but in 1947 the secession of the democratic wing headed by Saragat caused a bloodletting of the P.S.I. from which it has still not fully recovered. In the elections of 1958 the P.S.I. carried 14.2 percent of the votes (4,198,522). Its members are mostly workers, clerks, employees of the national, provincial and municipal administrations, and petty bourgeoisie. In foreign policy, the Socialist Party is substantially neutralist, though it has frequently wedded Soviet attitudes. In 1962, the Socialist party decided to back a coalition government of Christian Democrats, Social Democrats, and Republicans. This position, which may continue for a lengthy period, has strained its relationship with the Communist Party.

The right wing of the Italian political party lineup is numerically weak. The neo-Fascists (Italian Social Movement, or M.S.I.) won only 4.7 percent of the votes (1,410,770) cast in the general elections of 1958, while the Monarchists earned 4.8 percent (1,432,515). Despite the slight edge over the M.S.I., the Monarchists have declined steadily in electoral power ever since. Both parties gather their votes from among those whose political vision is still governed by a nostalgia for the Mussolini regime and the monarchy. In foreign policy, they are both pro-Atlantic and European, but the latter position carries an appreciably nationalistic tinge.

During the entire Cold War period, ever since the inauguration of the Marshall Plan, all the Italian cabinets, with very short-lived exceptions, have been constructed on majorities in which certain small anti-Communist parties had a decisive influence.[3] The importance of these smaller parties far exceeds their numerical strength. It derives from the fact that they are considered the only truly democratic parties outside of the Christian Democracy. At least two of them seem indispensable in the formation of a working parliamentary majority in coalition with the D.C. They are also important because of their historical traditions and the quality of their electoral support. Though divided on domestic policy, particularly on the question of how to deal with the Socialist Party, the minor political parties have substantially the same views on foreign policy: all are pro-Atlantic and European.

The President

The fragility of the parliamentary majority on which a truly democratic Italian government can depend (i.e., one excluding the monarchist-

Fascist right, with its 9.5 percent of the Chamber, and the Socialists-Communists, with their 36.9 percent) increases the influence of the other political forces in the development of Italian foreign policy. Of prime importance in this respect is the President of the Republic. Since Italy is a parliamentary republic, the powers of the Italian President are theoretically limited. Actually, the Head of the State has always had a particularly important influence in the molding of foreign policy. Though of extremely differing temperaments, all three presidents of the Republic since the institutional referendum of 1946 have participated actively in the formation of Italian foreign policy, more or less discreetly. Consequently, under existing circumstances and so long as no single party has a majority in the Chamber of Deputies, the Chief of State must be considered one of the formative influences in Italian foreign policy, notwithstanding the parliamentary nature of the government.

Labor and business

The influence of the labor unions is also appreciable. The General Confederation of Labor, as noted above, usually operates in favor of the policies of the Soviet Union, especially with regard to anti-colonialism, disarmament, atomic weapons, the Atlantic Alliance and Europeanism. A general strike over differences regarding the government's foreign policy is always a possibility. The easiest form of labor union opposition to Italian foreign policy is labor agitation timed with international events and pushed to the point where it can actually paralyze government action. Fortunately from the government's point of view, Italian labor is not entirely in the hands of the C.G.I.L. Both the Social Democracy and the Christian Democracy have their labor organizations—the U.I.L. and the C.I.S.L., respectively. These labor associations obviously do not hold anti-Atlantic and anti-European positions. But their desire to increase their membership frequently

[3] The Italian Social Democratic Party gathered 4.6 percent of the votes (1,352,029) in the 1958 elections; the Republican Party 1.4 percent (405,072 votes); and the Liberal Party 3.5 percent (1,046,132 votes).

induces them to take the lead in staging strikes for better wages. These strikes often coincide with extremely delicate international crises. Hence, they, too, must be considered as forces, however indirectly they operate, in the development and execution of Italian foreign policy.

The *Confindustria,* an association of prominent Italian industrialists, certainly holds pro-Atlantic and pro-European views. But its political influence is far from commensurate with its enormous economic power. The explanation is that, unlike other pressure groups, the *Confindustria* makes its financial contribution to the parties of its choice without requiring that the money be earmarked to promote the election of a specific candidate within the party or parties receiving the financial aid. Consequently, the party secretaries are the only persons with a decisive voice in determining electoral preferences. There has always been talk, too, of the financing of Marxist parties by individual industrialists. If true, this represents a practice with precedents in the period of the Partisan war against the Germans and the Salò Republic. On the other hand, the unceasing drive to find foreign outlets for their products leads the industrialists, at times, to favor economic agreements with Communist countries and states whose foreign policy is not pro-Western. This pressure to open up new markets for Italian exports has a strong influence on the formation of Italian foreign policy. The fact that the *Confindustria* is the principal source of that pressure more than justifies placing the organization in the category of forces considered here.

A power unto itself, with no counterpart in the other democratic countries, is the National Entity for Hydrocarbides (*Ente Nazionale Idrocarburi,* or E.N.I.). It is actually a semigovernmental institution whose president is chosen by the Italian government. Nonetheless, the economic power of this formidable industrial complex is so great that it can, and occasionally does, operate without reference to cabinet policy. In fact, the foreign policy of the Italian government is sometimes heavily influenced, if not actually determined, by the activities of E.N.I. abroad. Since the organization is chiefly concerned with petroleum, it operates mostly in the countries of North Africa and the Middle East, as well as in some of the Iron Curtain countries. E.N.I. thus has its own unique attitude towards the Moslem world and trade with the Communist countries.

The public and private oil companies of some of the major countries of the Atlantic Alliance underestimated E.N.I.'s strength and, at one time, assumed a hostile attitude toward E.N.I. interests. Much tension was created. The upshot of the situation was that E.N.I. policies found new support. For the first time—and with particular vigor—E.N.I. introduced the element of "oil diplomacy" into Italian foreign policy. A late arrival in the oil competition, E.N.I. has brought revolutionary conceptions to the struggle. In certain respects, these have been conducive to modifications in the traditional policies of the other exploiting companies, and in the policies of the governments of countries with petroleum deposits in their sub-soil. Among the factors determining Italian foreign policy, therefore, E.N.I. has a unique and important position.

The press

The "fourth power," the Italian press, must be considered in terms of the various categories of newspapers. Almost all large-circulation dailies which are not allied with any particular political party are proponents of Atlantic and European policies, though with varying degrees of conviction. With the advent of universal suffrage in Italy, however, their influence has diminished. The bourgeoisie which, in Italy, makes up the majority of readers, no longer dominates the political scene. In any case, it would seem that the influence of the big independent newspapers on the Italian middle classes is not decisive. Although several of the most important and largest newspapers are pro-Liberal, the Liberal Party itself received only 3.5 percent of the votes in the general elections of 1958. Today, the role of the Italian press is, indeed, far from the one it played in 1915, for example, when the *Corriere della Sera* actually had a decisive influence in determining Italian intervention in the First World War.

The influence of the individual political parties' daily newspapers is as inconsequential as their circulations. The sole exception is the Communist daily, *L'Unità,* which propagates the ideas of the P.C.I. and strongly influences the masses of workers and peasants. Since the art of propaganda is much more efficiently cultivated in the anti-Western camp, it must be recognized that *L'Unità* represents one of the most effective instruments of opposition to the Atlantic and European policies of the Rome government.

The periodical press, on the whole, mirrors the various tendencies of the Italian political spectrum, but its influence is restricted to relatively narrow circles. In fact, it is the expression, far more than the creator, of ideas in foreign policy.

The internal balance of forces

Within this framework of forces participating in the formation of Italian foreign policy, one must keep in mind certain general characteristics of their relations with each other. In the first place, one must note the instability of the balance of power between the various component elements. The political majority held by the democratic governments of the postwar period has always been small. All too frequently, it has been difficult to predict just how long any given majority might be maintained. The various governments have had to keep this in mind—and the problem remains unsolved. Consequently, formulators of Italian foreign policy tend to seek positions that avoid tests of strength that are not absolutely necessary.

Secondly, it must be pointed out that, in a world in which there are only two great pro-

tagonists, the U.S. and the U.S.S.R., Italy has a weaker structure than other Western Powers. Consequently, she cannot yet have any decisive influence on collective Western decisions. Therefore, foreign concepts and outlooks greatly influence the country's foreign policy.

Finally, even among the national democratic forces, polyvalent and sometimes contradictory pressures are operative. The general requirements of belonging to the Western community sometimes conflict with the particular requirements of Italy as a country with a relatively short history as a unified national state.

INSTITUTIONS FOR FORMULATING AND ADMINISTERING FOREIGN POLICY

The organs formally charged with the formulation of Italian foreign policy are the Ministry of Foreign Affairs, the Head of the Government, and the Cabinet.

The Ministry of Foreign Affairs

The Ministry of Foreign Affairs, directed by the Foreign Minister, is headed by two Under-Secretaries of State and a top career official, the Secretary General. The latter is assisted by five Directors General—Political Affairs, Economic Affairs, Personnel and Internal Administration, Cultural Relations with Europe, Emigration—and by the Chiefs of the various Services—Co-ordination, Press, Diplomatic Litigation, Studies, Private Affairs.

The technique used by the Foreign Minister in fulfilling his functions varies according to his individual temperament and is not subject to any fixed rules. Only two officials, the Secretary General and the Director General of Political Affairs, always participate in the deliberations of the Minister. The Under-Secretaries of State and the other officials of the Foreign

Office have never played a consistently influential role in policy-making. In certain periods, this role has been extremely important; even the collegial meetings of the top officials have frequently determined policy. But, in both instances, the degree of influence depends primarily on the temperament of the head of the Foreign Office administration.

The Secretary General   In practice, Secretary Generals, although their office is considered a permanent one, have changed along with Foreign Ministers. Aside from the fact that, even in pre-Fascist times, the changes in Secretaries General occurred much more frequently than is commonly supposed, it is important to recognize the historical evolution of the situation and the gradual appearance of new assumptions regarding the importance of the post. Until the outbreak of the First World War, foreign policy was the monopoly of a restricted group of persons: the Sovereign, the Foreign Minister, the diplomats and the military. The Secretary General insured the "continuity" of foreign policy, which, at times, involved secret agreements. In fact, it meant the continuity of the King's influence.

After the First World War, the appearance of so-called "open diplomacy" caused parliaments and parliamentary governments to assume a dominant role in the creation of national foreign policy. The "continuity" of foreign policy, especially after the disappearance of the Crown, is no longer insured by a Secretary General with permanent tenure, but by the continuity, or lack of it, in the ideas of the governing majority. The office of the Secretary General, though still useful and important, has consequently acquired different characteristics. A relationship of trust between the Minister and the Secretary General has become increasingly necessary.

The place of the Secretary General and his functions are further conditioned by the position of the Chief of Cabinet of the Foreign Minister. This role, too, is partially determined by the temperament of the Minister and the personality of the Chief of Cabinet. Some Foreign Ministers have extensively used the help of the Chief of Cabinet and permitted him to exercise an influence which, in fact, restricted that of the Secretary General. Conversely, other ministers have vigorously circumscribed the activities of their own Chiefs of Cabinet.

Subdivisions   The present structure of the Foreign Ministry of the Italian Republic does not vary greatly from that of the prewar period. It has always been based on a subdivision of functions by "subject matter" rather than "territories." This system, unlike that of other countries, corresponds better to Italian interests and to the individualistic temperament of the Italians. The American and British system of "desks," where all questions pertaining to any given country or single geographic area are handled, might well present greater difficulties in Italy, than the system now used by the Italian Foreign Office. It would be difficult to coordinate the activities of the individual desks. Furthermore, within each of them, the officials concerned with economic, cultural or emigration matters would be relegated to a position of inferiority with respect to their colleagues handling political problems. In turn, this would create a dangerous competition among officials to be assigned to work on political matters. Finally—and the observation is far from a loose generalization—the whole concept of teamwork encounters a spontaneous, often unexpressed, antagonism in the Italian temperament.

With the present system, the selection of young and dynamic Directors General for cultural relations abroad and for emigration helps balance a situation in which the greater prestige is attached to the Political Affairs and Economic Affairs Directorates. The system has a peculiar validity in a country like Italy, whose two principal "natural resources" are precisely her cultural and human patrimonies. Perhaps there is no parallel situation to be found elsewhere, since the other Powers with equally important cultural heritages have fewer human resources, but are much stronger in the military, political and economic fields.

While the Economic Affairs office—except for expansion—is substantially what it was before the War, the Political Affairs office, in its present form, is the consequence of many experiences of the post-1939 period. At the outbreak of World War II, there were three general offices pertaining to political affairs. "Ordinary" political matters were handled by the general office for Europe, the Near and Middle East and the Mediterranean, and by the general office for Transoceanic Affairs. "Extraordinary" political affairs were the competence of the office of General Affairs. Moreover, the post of Secretary General was left unfilled to permit the Chief of Cabinet of the Minister to exert his influence more freely.

After the War, all these functions were concentrated in a single general office of Political Affairs. Only later, when Italy became actively involved in the international community, was a second general office for "multilateral" affairs created. This innovation, however, did not always produce the happiest results. In 1955 the system of a single general office of Political Affairs was therefore re-adopted. The major disadvantage of the current set-up is that it makes it difficult for a single Director General to supervise all political matters, the more so because he is required to accompany the Foreign Minister on his official visits abroad.

With the exception of the office of Cultural Relations Abroad, which has special subdivisions—Schools, Cultural Institutes, Cultural Agreements, Scholarships, International Organizations, etc.—all four of the other general offices are organized on an area basis. Other subject matter areas are assigned to the "Services"—United Nations, NATO, Disarmament, Council of Europe, etc.—under the administrative control and direction of the Director General of Political Affairs. These services are in addition to those already mentioned and to the protocol or "Ceremonial" office. The latter contains two functional divisions: "Ceremonial of the State," which handles protocol matters for the President of the Republic and the Prime Minister; and the "Ceremonial of Foreign Affairs," which looks after specific protocol matters in diplomatic relations. Both of these services have their offices at the Ministry of Foreign Affairs.

On the technical level, co-ordination of the activities of all these general offices and services is the task of the Secretary General, who acts through a Co-ordinating Service. In addition, the Secretary General is the direct superior of the Studies Service and of the Press Service. As in the other ministries of the Italian Republic, there is a Council of Administration, presided over by the Minister or, in his stead, by an Under-Secretary of State. It handles various details of personnel and financial administration.

Personnel The officials of the Foreign Ministry are subdivided into various categories. The three principal ones are the career diplomatic-consular, the commercial and the category dealing with emigration matters. Of the three, the first is by far the most important. For both those going to the embassies and those assigned to the consular service, it is the only channel through which a diplomatic career is possible. There are two other categories, both of modest significance: the press attachés and the technical Commissioners for the East. The non-executive categories are the Chancellories, the local clerks and the wage-earning maintenance force.

War and postwar developments produced a real crisis in the Italian diplomatic career service. At first, the political purge eliminated almost all of the ambassadors and Nazi-collaborators who had given their loyalty to the Republic of Salò created by Mussolini in 1943. Subsequent revisions, however, permitted some of the purged diplomats to return to service, though they are few in number and hold unimportant posts. Political appointees were admitted into the career service by the anti-Fascist governments immediately after the war, but they, too, constitute a small minority of the service. In 1962, only three embassies—Washington, Paris, and Vienna—were headed by diplomats who owed their appointments to their backgrounds of active political opposition to fascism. From 1948 to 1952, young aspirants to the diplomatic-consular service, all of whom must meet difficult competition, were very numerous. Thereafter, however, their numbers fell sharply (today most of them come from the southern regions of the Peninsula), so that it has become a problem to replenish the ranks with qualified people.

Italian diplomats are technically well-trained and many of them have exceptionally high professional capacities. Their approach to international problems, of course, is colored by past traditions, with all their merits and defects. But many have grasped the essence of the evolution of diplomacy in the atomic age and have fully adapted themselves to it. *Esprit de corps* has remained high, but the solidarity of the monarchical epoch is dwindling. Certainly the tendency to find and use outside political support has appreciably increased in recent years. This fact has created internal divisions within the career service. On the whole, however, the Italian diplomatic-consular career service is by no means inferior to that of the major Western states. While Italian diplomats have recently intensified their contacts with the politicians of the Peninsula, one gets the impression that the Foreign Ministry is losing its influence in the country, both in an absolute sense and in the very creation of national foreign policy. If the tendency develops much further, a very difficult situation may arise.

The Prime Minister

The role of the Prime Minister in developing Italian foreign policy has generally been considerable. Aside from the fact that in certain periods De Gasperi, Fanfani, and Pella have combined the two offices of President of the Council of Ministers and Foreign Minister, all the principal decisions of the postwar epoch have been reached through consultation between the Prime Minister and the Foreign Minister. Adherence to the Marshall Plan and the Atlantic Alliance, European policy, the solution of the Trieste question, the position assumed during the Suez crisis are but a few of the salient occasions. They involved, in fact,

initiatives undertaken by the Prime Minister or the implementation of a policy in which the Prime Minister's role was certainly not inferior to that of his Foreign Minister.

This co-operation is not based on fixed rules, although it is formally justified by the fact that the Prime Minister is the head of the parliamentary majority and that the foreign policy of a parliamentary government can be no other than the one approved by the majority. Cooperation may take various forms, running all the way from the Prime Minister's personal participation in high-level foreign policy meetings to simple individual consultation with the Foreign Minister. There is a special office for liaison between the Foreign Minister and the Prime Minister, headed by a career diplomat with the title of Diplomatic Adviser to the President of the Council. A similar office also operates to serve the President of the Republic. The liaison office sends the Prime Minister all the more important telegrams and secret reports from abroad, as well as the summaries prepared at the Ministry on various important questions. All shifts of diplomatic personnel, prior to being submitted for the approval of the Council of Ministers, are discussed and agreed upon in consultations between the Foreign Minister, the Prime Minister and the President of the Republic.

The Council of Ministers, Parliament, and the President

The supreme organ deciding the foreign policy of the Italian government is the Council of Ministers. Both the Foreign Minister and the Prime Minister, who presides over the Council, report foreign policy matters to it. Normally, discussion follows oral reports with almost all the Ministers participating. It is their function to approve certain conclusions, which are then announced in an official communiqué expressing the will of the Cabinet. This procedure, too, is a direct consequence of the Italian constitutional regime.

Finally, both branches of Parliament—Chamber of Deputies and Senate—are required to approve international treaties and the budgets of the Foreign Ministry, as well as to discuss fully all principal foreign policy problems. Italian parliamentarians and ministers take a keen interest in these debates, which, for a complex of circumstances familiar throughout the Western world, have fundamental repercussions on domestic policy.

Enough has been said above about the role which, for all practical purposes, the President has assumed in the making of Italian foreign policy. Any further delineation is therefore unnecessary.

THE NATIONAL INTEREST

Widely-shared goals

Survival and peace   The fundamental concern of Italian policy is the same as that of the majority of the Western Powers: insuring the survival of the country's own way of life in an ideologically and militarily divided world. This necessity is particularly appreciated today, but it has been at the basis of the policy of all Italian governments since the First World War. *Primum vivere* constitutes the principal heritage left by the forebears of modern Italy, who so unstintingly contributed to the creation of the entire patrimony of Western civilization.

Closely related to this supreme interest is the parallel one of safeguarding the peace. Notwithstanding certain apparent contradictions in the past, this is a requirement that accords with the Italians' conception of foreign policy. After the painful experience of the last conflict and America's loss of her monopoly in the field of nuclear weapons, the pursuit of peace seems to be widely appreciated. Everyone clearly understands that a total atomic war would be catastrophic. But the conviction that avoiding it requires Italian membership in the Atlantic Alliance is no longer prevalent to the same degree it was in 1949 when the coalition government headed by De Gasperi made its choice in favor of joining NATO. The significant alteration in the military situation and the atomic stalemate have reinvigorated the neutralist campaign. Although maintenance of peace is considered a fundamental Italian interest by everyone, this view is not accompanied by a clear notion of the dangers to peace implicit in the "competitive" ideological and economic methods now seriously threatening the survival of the Western way of life. But this is a position which is not too dissimilar from that existing in other Western European countries.

European political unity   The two national interests just mentioned are nothing specifically Italian: they derive from the fact that Italy belongs to the free world. Consequently, they are held in common with the other states belonging to that community. On the other hand, interest in the construction of European political unity is typically Italian. The reasons are several. In the first place, Italian historical traditions favor such unity. Italians today recall that military and economic weakness made national unification extremely difficult one hundred years ago. They remember, too, that the same weakness hampered Italy's entry into the ranks of Europe's first-class Powers. In the second place, this consciousness of traditional weakness, amply demonstrated by Italian military experience in World War II, made Italians realize that in a world dominated by a conflict between the American and Russian super-Powers, the old national states of Europe would necessarily lose status as prime influences in international politics. If they were to have any substantial influence at all, it could only be acquired through collective action, through a politically united Europe. Thirdly, the very temperament of the Italians inclines them to understand and support the idea of European unity. They are probably more sensitive to the need of such unity than any other nation of the old Continent. In no other European state is the creation of European unity so genuinely popular and nowhere is the aspiration more compatible with a vital interest of the nation. In a certain sense, the traditional myth of classical Rome has been replaced, in part at least, by the new "myth" of a united Europe, one to which the Italian of the post-World War II epoch tenaciously clings.

Special interests

Territorial claims   The peace treaty of 1947 greatly reduced the territory of the Italian state. Some of these amputations were expected. Others, such as the loss of Pola, Zara and Fiume, truly Italian cities, were deeply resented, while still others (Briga and Tenda, the so-called Zone B of the projected Free Territory of Trieste) seemed highly unjustifiable. Despite this, Italy has no genuine interest in advancing territorial claims, though she is keenly committed to the defense of her own territorial integrity.

It is precisely for this reason that the Alto Adige question is so important in current Italian foreign policy. Eventual loss of this territory would not only be unacceptable to the Italian public, but it would most certainly provoke a crisis capable of reversing the present orientation of Italian foreign policy. The opposition parties would have a field day in pointing to the rebirth of pan-Germanism (which the Kremlin has long been using as a whipping-boy) as the principal explanation of such a development—nor would they be very far from the disagreeable truth. In fact, while it is true that the majority of the inhabitants of the Alto Adige are German-speaking, it is also true that they enjoy exceptionally liberal treatment at the hands of the Italian government. Moreover, out of 240,000 German-speaking individuals, 210,000 wanted—and received—Italian citizenship after 1948. At that time, they did not object, as they now do, to the Italian interpretation of the De Gasperi-Gruber Agreement that the accord envisaged

the creation of a single Trentino-Alto Adige Region.

Interests in the Mediterranean area   while the prewar goals of territorial expansion in the Mediterranean have entirely disappeared from Italian foreign policy, the geographic factor has obviously remained unchanged: the Peninsula still stands in the middle of the Mediterranean. This fact, continues to keep alive a special Italian interest in the political fate of the inland sea which the Italians still regard as *Mare Nostrum*. It is a polyvalent interest involving several diplomatic stances and actions: favoring a reduced role in the area for the other Great Powers, while encouraging the rise of new independent states; participating in the political and economic construction of these nations; maintaining particularly friendly relations with their governments, thereby insuring peaceful outlets for the Italian economy. In other words, it is an up-to-date version of an old interest.

This circumstance explains the fact that Italy favored the rise of the state of Israel no less than that of the Arabic countries and Cyprus. It explains the Italian attitude during the Suez crisis and the policy pursued in the Middle East and toward such Mediterranean countries as Greece, Turkey, and Yugoslavia. Furthermore, it explains why, at times, the policies of Italy in this part of the world and those of her allies diverge, rather than converge. Sometimes, the Mediterranean interest of Italian foreign policy has assumed a most singular form: the myth that Italy is especially qualified to mediate disputes arising in the Middle East and the Mediterranean area. Here again, the rhetorical penchant obscures an unflattering reality: Italy's incapacity, for material reasons, to act as an arbiter or mediator. Other Powers, aware of this fact, have failed to encourage Rome to try the role. Nonetheless, the aspiration is a strong one and is worth noting.

Emigration   Another continuing Italian interest is keeping open the outlets for the flow of emigrants abroad. If the Italian economy continues to flourish at its present remarkable rate, this requirement, for the first time in the history of united Italy, may be eliminated in another 15 years. In any case, it is less vital now than in the past. There have been many particularly important emigration agreements in the postwar period, some of which—such as those with Canada and Australia—have opened up new emigration possibilities of considerable proportions. And, as noted earlier, emigration policies explain certain positions assumed by the Italian government within the Common Market and the Atlantic Alliance. They are involved in the relations between Italy and the countries of Latin America and even in relations with the United States. Nor are emigration policies of negligible importance in relations with Egypt, Tunisia, Libya, Morocco, Ethiopia, Somalia and South Africa.

Certainly the existence of numerous Italian settlements in Europe (Switzerland, Germany, Belgium, France, Great Britain), as well as in the above-mentioned countries, affects Italian foreign policy. While that policy is not planned in detail, the attention of Italian policy makers is directed from time to time toward Latin America, the Mediterranean and Africa, as well as toward the construction of European unity, precisely because the colonies of Italian emigrants in those areas have created a special interest in their fortunes. Developing trade possibilities to the maximum would probably entail serious and detailed planning as well as the creation of additional instruments. But, whether this were done or not, interest in Italian emigrant settlements abroad, with their promise of increased foreign trade, would remain a constant and characteristic aspect of Italian foreign policy.

Thus the postwar period has witnessed, on the one side, the affirmation of an Italian "Western" interest, common to all the countries belonging to the free world community, and, on the other, an up-dating under new conditions, of traditional interests. The myth of Rome has been replaced by two new dreams: a united Europe and an Italy in the garb of the recognized mediator in Mediterranean and Middle Eastern politics.

FOREIGN POLICY TODAY

Revision of peace treaty clauses

As mentioned before, the Italians unanimously condemned the provisions of the 1947 Paris peace treaty as excessively onerous. The disillusionment and bitterness were profound, indeed. The main criticism was that the treaty had ignored the Quebec Declaration of August, 1943, that the Italian contribution to the Allied war on Germany would determine the degree to which the armistice conditions would be modified in Italy's favor. Consequently, when the Italian peace treaty went into effect Italian foreign policy concentrated on three primary goals. These were: 1) revision, through negotiations with the ex-enemy states, of the peace treaty clauses and the solution of pending problems such as the disposition of the former colonies and creation of the Free Territory of Trieste; 2) normalization of relations with all ex-enemy states, particularly with those on Italy's frontiers; 3) Italian entry, on a footing of equality, into international life and organizations.

Reparations   Pursuance of the first objective produced appreciable, if uneven, results. The United States and Great Britain immediately declined the share of the Italian fleet assigned them by the peace treaty, but required its demolition. France partially followed suit; Greece and the Soviet Union, however, made no concessions at all in this regard. As for reparations, Italy could do nothing more than persuade Greece, Yugoslavia, Albania and the Soviet Union to permit paying them in the form of periodic shipments of Italian products. Shipments to Russia were subsequently stopped. With France, the Italian government came to an agreement providing for a limited revision of the Franco-Italian frontier. Since the agreement failed to obtain the approval of the French parliament, it never went into effect.

Colonies   Initially, Palazzo Chigi, the Italian Foreign Office, dedicated its chief effort to the problem of the colonies. In this effort, it was backed by almost all the political parties, including those that later assumed a strongly anti-colonialist position. This phenomenon is quite understandable if one remembers that Italian colonial policy was vigorously supported by even the humbler classes of Italian society. After World War II, the main obstacle to Italy's retention of her prewar colonial empire was Great Britain, the Power in occupation of those territories.

As it developed, Libya became an independent state and Eritrea was annexed by Ethiopia. For ten years Somalia remained under Italian administration as a U.N. mandate. Then it, too, became independent. Through no fault of her own, Italy thus found herself stripped of colonial possessions. This circumstance was to cause a serious weakening of the French colonial positions in North Africa, a fact which Paris had long understood very well. The Rome government, after a period of bitterness and resentment, made use of its new freedom of action by lining up, to the extent possible, in favor of the aspirations of the Arab and African populations. This drew a distinction in this respect between Italy and the Franco-British allies. It was a result anticipated by few persons at the time.

Trieste   To understand the full significance of the Trieste question in the eyes of the Italian public, it must be thought of as having a primarily symbolic value. The Italian public, no less than the Rome government itself, fully expected unequivocal Western support of the Italian claim to the area. The promise of such support, solemnly made by France, the United Kingdom, and the United States on the eve of the general elections of 1948, had, in fact, come to symbolize for the Italians proof that their country had once more become a full-fledged member of the Western community.

Despite pressure from Washington, Paris and London on Belgrade to accept a direct compromise with Rome, matters remained at a standstill. They were aggravated by the tension in Trieste deriving from the prolongation of foreign military occupation. After Tito's defection from the Cominform, it was obvious that the West would never go beyond a certain limit in exerting pressure on the Yugoslavs, even while hoping for a fair solution of the Trieste question.

It was only then that the Rome government tried to begin direct negotiations with Yugoslavia. The first exchanges of views proved completely fruitless. Following the 1953 general elections a new government took power in Rome. Certain semi-official stories of the *Jugopress* regarding a possible imminent Yugoslav annexation of part of Trieste induced Pella, the new Prime Minister and Foreign Minister, to stop procrastinating. Washington and London were asked for permission to replace the Anglo-American troops occupying Zone A of Trieste with Italian forces, thus putting the Italians on a footing of parity in any negotiations with Belgrade. Yugoslavia was already administering and occupying Zone B, whereas Italy had only the Tripartite Declaration of March 20, 1948, with which to back her negotiating position. Given Anglo-American reticence to implement their promise, this was hardly enough to permit Italy to lead from strength in dealing with the Yugoslavs.

It was under these circumstances that Washington and London issued the declaration of October 8, 1953, which provided for the transfer of Allied powers in Zone A to Italy. Tito publicly threatened armed intervention if Italian troops entered Trieste. The Anglo-Americans hesitated, but, after a long, laborious and bitter exchange of views between all countries concerned, Italy obtained almost all of Zone A and Yugoslavia practically all of Zone B.

Faced with the Anglo-American decision of October 8, 1953, and Tito's violent reaction to it, the Italian public began to appreciate the advantages entailed in Italian occupation of

Zone A, even though it was less than Italians had hoped. Popular fascination with the very name of the city of Trieste assured the Italian government full public support at the negotiations. In reaching a solution, the three top Italian political figures involved, President Luigi Einaudi, Prime Minister Scelba and Foreign Minister Martino, were enthusiastically united in their conviction that the settlement proposed and subsequently concluded was the best possible under the circumstances. Removal of the Trieste thorn signalled, finally, the beginning of an improvement in Italo-Yugoslav relations. This made possible Yugoslav Foreign Minister Popovic's visit to Rome in 1960 and Italian Foreign Minister Segni's return call to Belgrade in 1961, followed in 1962 by Vice President Rancovic's trip to Italy. Today the prospects for true friendship between Italy and Yugoslavia are excellent.

Military restrictions   Article 46 of the peace treaty provided that its military clauses would remain in force until the Allied Powers and Italy agreed on modifying them or until Italy became a member of the United Nations by virtue of an agreement between the Security Council and Italy. Thus it was that Italy's request for admission to the U.N. in 1947 and the subsequent developments in the question fall within the framework of the revisionist campaign so tenaciously carried forward by the Rome government. In effect, a Soviet veto kept Italy from being admitted separately from Bulgaria, Hungary, Finland and Rumania, whose peace treaties also provided for their ultimate entry into the U.N. Admission was finally granted in December, 1955.

The long years of painfully embarrassing waiting, created considerable resentment and disillusionment. By the time Italy finally entered the U.N., the Italian motivation in wanting admission was no longer based on the original drive to secure revision of the peace treaty, but on considerations of prestige and the urgently-felt necessity of full participation in the activities of the organization.

The division of the world into two opposed blocs eliminated all hopes of revising the peace treaty in agreement with the Soviet Union even though the Soviet Union had permitted Rumania, Bulgaria and Hungary to escape implementation of the military clauses of the peace treaties involving them. Therefore, Count Sforza approached the problem from a new angle. He wrote French Foreign Minister Schuman a letter in which he asked Paris, Washington and London to "change formally and substantively Italy's international position by announcing the moral extinction of the treaty of peace." Examined favorably in the Anglo-Franco-American meeting in Washington on September 10–14, 1951, this request led to the Tripartite Declaration of September 26, 1951, which favored a limited revision to abolish discriminations concerning Italian sovereignty. In effect, this meant revising clauses dealing with Italy's obligations to its own citizens and with military affairs. With regard to the revision procedure, it was agreed that the three Western Powers would send their Declaration to all signatories of the Italian peace treaty and that the Rome government would send individual notes to each of the signatories. The Soviet Union, Poland and Czechoslovakia, however, opposed this procedure, while Yugoslavia adopted a wait-and-see attitude. Hence, the revision of the peace treaty occurred only in a limited form.

Normal relations with former enemies

The United States   The second objective of Italian foreign policy immediately following the signature of the peace treaty aimed at the normalization of relations with the ex-enemy states. Within this framework, priority was given to re-establishing normal relations with the United States. This objective, of course, was motivated—and inevitably so—by selfish and material considerations because the U.S. was the richest and militarily strongest Power. Nonetheless, a keen and spontaneous sentiment of friendship and ideological understanding was also involved. The presence in America of millions of Italian emigrants was a strong bond, to say nothing of a sense of common ideals. The present-day heirs of the great supernational constructions of Imperial Rome and the Catholic Church, could fully appreciate the generous impulses at work behind the foreign policy of the United States. A decisive development in this Italo-American *rapprochement* occurred during Prime Minister De Gasperi's first trip to the United States in January, 1947. It was then that the basis of a community of outlook and solidarity was laid down, a solidarity that was to develop markedly in subsequent years. One index of this progression was physically manifested in the difference in the formal greeting Washington extended De Gasperi when he made his second visit to America. In 1947, the only U.S. official waiting at the airport to greet the Head of the Italian Government was the Chief of the Italian desk at the State Department, the future Ambassador James Dunn; on September 24, 1951, De Gasperi found President Truman and his entire Cabinet lined up to welcome him to Washington on his second American visit. Ever since that time it has been a tradition that the various Italian Prime Ministers make at least one visit to the States (Scelba, Fanfani, Segni, Pella), almost as a gesture of consecrating the friendship between the two countries. The U.S. visit in 1957 of President Giovanni Gronchi was the first trip abroad of an Italian Chief of State in the postwar epoch.

France Along with the development of Italo-American friendship, the Italian government turned its attention to establishing the most intimate possible relations with France. Faced with the higher necessity of common solidarity in the job of reconstructing Europe, Italy and France quickly forgot most of the frictions troubling their postwar relations.[4]

The *rapprochement* with France was facilitated by the understanding attitude of the various French governments. The French supported the Italian position on colonial matters, the Trieste question and revision of the Italian peace treaty. French understanding, however, never reached the point at which Paris could appreciate the full significance—and complete sincerity—of an unprecedented Italian policy decision. For the first time since becoming a unified national state, Italy was genuinely pre-prepared to accept French primacy in the Latin world and to loyally play the role of a "brilliant second." Italian overtures in this sense met with no positive reaction in Paris. The audacious idea of an Italo-French customs union, which had even been reduced to a concrete and detailed agreement in 1948, was opposed by certain French economic circles and never got past the French parliament. Unfortunate as was this French failure to grasp the opportunity to participate in a truly historic and constructive undertaking, Franco-Italian relations continued to improve.

Today, the relations between the two countries are at an unprecedentedly cordial level and the fact represents one of the fixed reference points of current Italian foreign policy. From the Italian government's point of view, the only currently conceivable possibility of an appreciable divergence of French and Italian policies concerns the European unification problem. As for the construction of a United Europe, certainly the Italians, given their deep-seated belief in its desirability and urgency and their conception of European unity as a community of equals, could neither countenance any action designed to slow down the process, nor accept a possible French claim to the political domination of the Continental European political community. Thus far, however,

---

[4] The French had failed to keep the promise made by General de Gaulle in August, 1944, that France would be content with Italy's definitive renunciation of her rights in Tunisia and Fezzan. As for the rest, de Gaulle had promised that France would guarantee metropoli-

tan Italian territory and the restitution of the country's former colonies. The Paris government subsequently demanded Briga, Tenda, Mont Cenis and, for a certain period, even evinced annexationist aspirations with regard to the Val d'Aosta. It was the Paris government, too, that originated the formula of the Free Territory of Trieste and supported the return to the Alto Adige of the German-speaking inhabitants who had opted for Hitler Germany in 1939 and moved into the territory of the Third Reich.

neither problem has given rise to serious differences between Rome and Paris. However, the recent Franco-German entente and French opposition to Britain's entry into the Common Market could lead to disagreements.

England   Italian overtures to London encountered greater hurdles. After World War I, Anglo-Italian harmony was achieved almost immediately, while relations with France remained tense for several years. After the Second World War, however, tension between London and Rome persisted and the issues between the two governments were settled to the complete satisfaction of neither. London could not quickly forget the peril to England represented by Mussolini's Mediterranean policies, any more than the bitterness caused by finding in the enemy camp a country traditionally considered a friend. If there had not been a certain urgency about coming to a decision regarding colonial matters, as well as Italian membership in the Western European Union and the Atlantic Alliance, this delicate stage of psychological transition would probably have proved less difficult. Unfortunately, the reality was quite different. Sforza's trips to London in 1947 and 1949 helped improve the situation but only temporarily. A lasting improvement in Anglo-Italian relations depended on Italy's active participation in the Atlantic Alliance, the Council of Europe, the W.E.U. and, most of all, on the final settlement of the colonial and Trieste issues.

For several years, London placed the principal obstacles in the way of the construction of European organizations like the E.D.C., the Coal and Steel Community, the Common Market and Euratom. But with the ratification of the Treaties of Rome, establishing the 6-Power Europe, Anglo-Italian relations entered a genuinely friendly phase, formally expressed by President Gronchi's visit to London in 1959 and Queen Elizabeth's trip to Italy in 1961. As matters stand today, the Italians respect and understand Britain's international position and Anglo-Italian friendship is deemed one of the principal bases of Italian foreign policy. For this reason, Italy, possibly more than any other Power, favors Britain's membership in the Common Market.

Greece, Albania, and Austria   The normalization of relations with Greece met with no particular difficulties. On November 5, 1948, Sforza and Tsaldaris signed an agreement marking the resumption of friendly relations between Rome and Athens. Thereafter, it was Italy who proved the strongest advocate of Greek membership in NATO. With Albania, good relations proved particularly difficult. Although diplomatic relations were resumed in May, 1949, Italo-Albanian contacts have never gone beyond the level of "correctness." The Tirana government's entry into the Soviet Union's Iron Curtain system has prevented genuinely friendly relations between Albania and Italy. Only recently has the tension between Moscow and Tirana brought a less polemical tone to the Hoxha government's attitude toward its neighbor across the Adriatic.

It appeared initially that the De Gasperi–Gruber Agreement had removed the Alto Adige question as a possible thorn in Austro-Italian relations. Gruber himself made his first visit to Rome in November 1948. Three developments, however, changed the complexion of the situation. With considerable liberality, Italy agreed to accept once more as Italian citizens those German-speaking inhabitants of the border region who had voted in 1939 for residence and citizenship in the Third Reich; Austria acquired neutral status through the State Treaty of Vienna; West Germany began to assume a political and material importance that re-established the German factor as a force that could not be ignored in Western calculations. The net effect of the new situation was to bring the Alto Adige question once more to the fore, with all the bitterness it involves on both sides of the Brenner. The present status of the Austro-Italian controversy seems to promise an even more serious aggravation of the tension between Rome and Vienna.

The Iron Curtain countries   Italy's membership in the defensive system of the West kept the Rome government from developing friendly relations with the Soviet Union. On the economic level, these relations are normal enough. But the country's political relations with the Kremlin are even more difficult than those of the other NATO countries, precisely because Moscow has always refused to countenance any changes in the Italian peace treaty. In an attempt to find some point of agreement, President Gronchi traveled to Moscow in January, 1960, but, the trip failed in its purposes. The presence in Italy of the strongest Communist party west of the Iron Curtain and the pressure of certain Italian industrial groups desirous of increasing trade with the Soviets undoubtedly represent two significant elements in the development of relations between the two countries. It is true that the sporadic periods of relaxation in East-West tensions have usually improved Italo-Soviet relations. But so long as the present majority of democratic parties in the Italian Parliament is retained, it is highly improbable that a truly cordial diplomatic bond will be established.

With all the other Iron Curtain countries, Italy's relations are cool, but correct. Czechoslovakia can do nothing to improve her standing in the eyes of the Rome government until she calls a halt to the incessant barrage of radio propaganda aimed at the Peninsula. Relations with Poland are probably the most cordial—or least cool—that Italy maintains with the Soviet satellites, thanks in no small part to the tenacious Catholicism of that country's population. As for the Peiping regime, Italy has not yet extended formal recognition, though Rome is painfully aware of the negative consequences—chiefly at the economic level—of this position.

West Germany   The presence at the helm of the West German government of a strong Catholic in the person of Chancellor Adenauer has enormously facilitated the rebuilding of friendly relations between Rome and Bonn. The cordiality has developed to the point where the Italian government is now one of the major advocates of giving West Germany full citizenship in the economic and military

system of Europe and the Western world. The personal meetings between Adenauer and the various heads of the Italian government have become a genuine tradition. Nonetheless, one must recognize that the Austro-Italian controversy over the Alto Adige has already cast some shadows over Italo-German relations. It has stimulated in the Italian public a growing fear of a resurgence of pan-Germanism. Any predictions regarding future relations between Bonn and Rome are quite risky. Both governments are keenly conscious of their common interest in continuing the political and diplomatic collaboration that has hitherto brought advantages to both sides. But the fact remains that the governments themselves are not the only controlling factor in foreign policy in the era of open diplomacy.

Latin America   Latin America was the area toward which postwar Italian policy was first directed. Latin America gave Italy political and economic support in the form of emigration and commercial agreements and openly and unanimously supported Italy on her colonial problems and admission to the United Nations. Even when the horizons of Italian foreign policy began expanding to their present proportions, Latin America continued to occupy an important segment of the arc. The fact is not at all surprising, considering that there are in that part of the world large and industrious communities of Italian emigrants and descendants of Italian emigrants. Nor was it puzzling in the least that President Gronchi's two visits to Latin America (1959 and 1961), and those of his South American opposite numbers to Italy, occasioned significant political and popular manifestations. As matters stand today, the Rome government is convinced it has a unique contribution to make in resolving the present crisis in the relations between the Western community and these countries.

Mediterranean countries   Postwar Italian foreign policy has gradually concentrated its attention on the Mediterranean and the Middle East. Consequently, particularly good relations with newly independent countries (Morocco, Libya, Tunisia, Lebanon, Algeria) and those with longer histories as sovereign states (Turkey, Egypt, Yemen, Iraq, Jordan and Iran) have been established. Two elements explain this situation: the particular Italian interests described earlier in this chapter and the very real Italian sympathy for and understanding of the aspirations and needs of these countries. In this regard, Italy is simultaneously the heir of prewar foreign policy attitudes toward this area and, as a "proletarian" Power, the proponent of a radical revision of the balance of power in that part of the world. As has been pointed out above, this aspect of Italian foreign policy is the one least identified with the policy of some of Italy's Atlantic allies.

Relations with Israel stand in a special category. The Italian government lent considerable effective support to the Jews' successful struggle to carve an independent state for themselves. But there is no denying a certain ambivalence of sentiment behind the Rome government's action. Obviously, limits were imposed by the long-standing prior commitment to maintain friendly relations with the Arab countries, limits of which the Israeli, no less than the Arabs, are quite aware. The problem is shared by other Western European countries. But it is a particularly thorny one for Italian governments who argue an especially favorable status for Italy *vis-à-vis* the Moslem world.

Africa and the Far East   Italy's policy toward the African countries resembles its Mediterranean and Middle Eastern policy, with the chief difference lying in the fact that the Rome government's policy in black Africa has thus far been less intense and less organized. Aside from the traditional interest in Somaliland and Ethiopia, Italian initiative—mostly the consequence of spontaneous activity by economic interests in the Peninsula—has been directed toward finding new markets. In this respect, more than modest successes have been achieved in Kenya, the Sudan, Nigeria and elsewhere. What has happened is that Italy's remarkable industrial development opened up

new and promising horizons to Italian diplomatic action. Italian policy in the Far East and Oceania (Japan excepted) is far more active than it was in the prewar period. But it still is of secondary importance compared to the attention Rome pays to other areas of the world.

Atlantic Alliance   The American invitation of the summer of 1947 to the Italian government to share in Marshall Plan aid was the point of departure for Italian participation in Western collective organizations. The American offer—promptly accepted—caused a violent domestic debate. It is no exaggeration to say that the general election campaign of 1948 was fought out on the primary issue of whether it was in the Italian interest to accept that aid. The electoral victory of the Christian Democracy and its allies was, in fact, a clear public approval of the political choice the De Gasperi cabinet had made earlier.

Italian participation in the O.E.E.C., was only the first step toward re-acquiring full and equal status as a member of the Western community. A little later, the American State Department, asked by the French to sponsor the creation of a military alliance, declared that the United States could envisage defending Europe only if it demonstrated that it was capable of unifying its own military forces. From this requirement derived the Brussels Pact (March 17, 1948), establishing the Western European Union of France, Great Britain, Belgium, Holland and Luxembourg. Europe had the initial impression that Washington intended to require Italian participation. But the American attitude expressed itself as a desire, not a demand, for Italian membership. Thus, the problem of Italy's eventual signature of the Brussels Pact arose and became very acute immediately after the parliamentary elections of April 18, 1948.

The parties of the Left were obviously opposed to the Brussels Pact. They accused the United States of preparing aggression against the Soviet Union and urged a neutralist policy. The parties of the Right viewed Italian membership in the Western European Union as something to be traded for a return of Italy's former colonies and the cancellation of the military clauses of the peace treaty. Caught between these two pressures, the De Gasperi government hesitated. Not even the five member states of the Western European Union wanted immediate Italian participation. Britain was still suspicious of Italian objectives and worried about the eventual disposition of the former Italian colonial empire; the others considered themselves too weak to extend their military commitments to a country unable to make a significant contribution of armed power. For the moment, Italian entry into the W.E.U. was ruled out. When negotiations for the erection of the Atlantic Alliance got under way, however, the picture changed drastically.

The French government, anxious that the line of European defense be established as far south as possible, and now without major grudges against Italy, insisted that Rome be included in the first list of countries invited to enter the projected alliance. At a certain point, France even refused to approve an invitation to Norway unless Rome were also approached. For its part, the Italian government, formerly hesitant about the advisability of joining the Brussels Pact organization, immediately took a position in favor of joining the Atlantic Alliance. Great Britain, Canada and the Benelux countries were still uncertain about Italian membership. But they made it quite clear that if Washington explicitly and firmly favored Italian entry, they would withdraw their objections. This forced the United States to assume full responsibility in the matter and, at the last moment, the necessary declaration was made.

Italian membership in the Atlantic Alliance has been the main pillar of Italian foreign policy ever since April, 1949. Rome's participation has been active and it has never taken the initiative in creating obstacles to the smooth functioning of the Alliance. Naturally, it has tried, on various occasions, to develop and utilize those parts of the Alliance treaty that lend themselves to a more effective defense of specific Italian interests.

With regard to military matters, Rome always favored the integration of the Allied armed forces and accepted bases on Italian territory, including those for the launching of intermediate-range ballistic missiles. Ever since the NATO meeting of Ottawa in 1951, Italy has insisted on the principle of "consultation." However, the Italian interpretation of this principle has, at times, given rise to some perplexity when there were no suggestions for solving the problems on which consultation was to occur, and no willingness to increase Italian obligations. Naturally, the Italian Foreign Office reacted vigorously against the idea of creating a Three-Power political "directory" inside the Alliance and still heads the opposition to de Gaulle's formula.

Actually, Italian persistence in advocating more "consultation" between the NATO allies and the no less tenacious opposition to the establishment of a Three-Power directory within the Alliance represent the surface aspect of a much more fundamental policy objective. Italy, just as most of the other allies of the American and Soviet colossi, has still not made the psychological transition from the pre-World War II power constellation, in which at least half a dozen states ranked as true first-class Powers, to the post-1945 pattern of power relationships in which only Washington and Moscow can justifiably be considered the molders of international political development. In other words, Italy has not yet learned the art of exploiting her present status in such a way as to heavily influence the policies of the United States, an art the British, for example, have learned quite well.

When one recalls the crucial influence on French policy enjoyed by Czechoslovakia as a member of the French-sponsored Little Entente during the post-World War I period, it is obvious that Italians need not rule out the possibility of influencing American policy in the way Britain has done since 1945. Whether or not this role can ever be developed by Italian policy-makers depends on future events, of course. But there is no doubt that Italy's insistence on consultation and her opposition to the de Gaulle formula reflect a first faint perception that her present status need not mean the loss of all effective voice in the determination of free world policy. One final consideration in connection with Italy's NATO role: its continuance and intensity depend on the maintenance of the present democratic majority in the Rome parliament.

European unity   Italy, in the postwar period, has been and still is the strongest advocate of European unity. She was a founding member of the Council of Europe in 1949; she became a member of the European Coal and Steel Community in 1951. In 1952, she used her entire influence in bringing the negotiations for the creation of the European Defense Community to a positive conclusion. When the French parliament refused to ratify the E.D.C. treaty, it was Italy who in 1955 advanced the idea of re-launching the European unity process in the form of a customs union, which culminated in the Rome Treaties of 1957 and the creation of the European Common Market. Within the Six-Power community, Italy always takes the lead in stimulating further development of the E.C.M.

The United Nations   During the past several years Italy has gradually acquired membership in all the international organizations of the United Nations. Nor is it an accident that the first organization joined was the U.N.E.S.C.O. and that an Italian has served as its Director General. Enough has already been said about Italy's entry into the U.N. itself; suffice it to recall here that, within a very short space of time, Italy was elected to the Security Council, the Economic and Social Council, the Trusteeship Council and to the Vice Presidency of the General Assembly. While Italy holds no decisive position in the United Nations Organization, she is certainly to be ranked with the medium-sized countries enjoying great freedom of action: the Latin American, North African and Middle Eastern countries. In participating in the conference on surprise attacks in 1958, and in the negotiations on disarmament in Geneva in 1961 and 1962, Italy's contribution of ideas to the solution of the most serious problems within the competence of the U.N. was appreciable. At the same time, she has long demonstrated that she favors aid to the underdeveloped countries.

In conclusion, it is relevant to point out that Italian foreign policy, during the years since the end of the Second World War, has been a very active one. On the whole, it has been quite successful in achieving for a country desperately weakened by military defeat a positive and vigorous role in international politics. Conceding this record of accomplishment, however, does not obscure the fact that Italian influence in international relations is limited by the country's relative material strength and potential. In relation to the principal protagonists on the world scene, Italy's influence is far from decisive. This, in turn, is not always appreciated by Italian public opinion, especially with regard to the bigger international issues concerning Italy only indirectly. Nonetheless, in certain specific areas and in Six-Power Europe especially, Italian influence is commensurate with, and sometimes greater than, the country's material power.

BIBLIOGRAPHY

Author's Suggestions

Albrecht-Carrie, Rene. *Italy from Napoleon to Mussolini.* New York: Columbia University Press, 1950.

Ciano, Galeazzo. *L'Europa verso la catastrofe (1936–1943).* Milan: Mondadori, 1948.

Currey, Muriel. *Italian Foreign Policy, 1918–1932*. London: Nicholson and Watson, 1932.

Italian Society for International Organization. *Italy and the United Nations: Report of a Study Group Set Up by the Society*. New York: Manhattan, 1959.

Kogan, Norman. *Italy and the Allies*. Cambridge: Harvard University Press, 1956.

Toscano, Mario. *Appunti sui negoziati por la participazione dell' Italia al Patto Atlantico*. Milan: Giuffré, 1961.

Toscano, Mario. *Appunti sulla questione dell 'Alto Adige*. Rome: Ricerche, 1961.

Toscano, Mario. *La ripresa delle relazioni diplomatiche fra l'Italia e la Francia e la liquidazione della questione Tunisina nel corso della seconda guerra mondiale*. Milan: Giuffré, 1962.

Toscano, Mario. *La ripresa delle relazioni diplomatiche fra l'Italia e l'Unione Sovietica nel corso della seconda guerra mondiale*. Rome: Commità Internazionale, 1962.

ABOUT THE AUTHORS

NUÑO AGUIRRE DE CÁRCER was educated in Spain, France and London. He has been associated as a professor with the University of Madrid and the Madrid Foreign Service School where he was Professor of Foreign Policy. He has been active in the Foreign Service of Spain serving in London, Tangier, Karachi, Tunis, Tripoli and the United States. He was Head of the Near East and Middle East Division of the Spanish Foreign Ministry from 1960–62 and is presently Minister in Charge of Cultural Relations in the Spanish Embassy in Washington, D.C. The following are among his published works: *España y la triple alianza*, 1946; *Las Tribunales Mixtos y la evolución político-internacional en Egipto*, 1949; *La ruta del Jordan*, 1955; *La novela del Canal*, 1957.

GONZALO FERNÁNDEZ DE LA MORA Y MON began his academic career as Professor at the Diplomatic School in Madrid; he has also been Professor at the Madrid School of International Civil Servants. He entered the Spanish Foreign Service in 1948 and since that time has held numerous positions both in Spain and on the international scene. He has represented Spain in several international conferences; has been Head of the Division of International Cultural Organizations, Ministry of Foreign Affairs; Vice-Secretary General of the European Center of Documentation and Information and is presently Counselor of the Spanish Embassy in Athens. He has written extensively, including: "La repercusión de la revolución de 1849 en la bibliografía europea contemporánea," Revista *Arbor*, 1949; "Las aporías de Nuremberg," Revista *Arbor*, 1951; *La quiebra de la razón de Estado*, 1956; *Maeztu y la teoría de la Revolución*, 1956.

ABOUT THE CHAPTER

This chapter first considers the role of geography as it has conditioned the relations of Spain with Europe, Africa and the Americas. This is followed by a careful examination of the historical background of modern Spain. We are reminded of the fact that Spain was once a Major World Power and that attitudes and ideals have been developed over the years which persist to the present time. In the historical survey, the authors include a presentation of the role of Spain during World War II as a neutral nation and then examine the diplomatic consequences for the nation at the end of the war.

The major policy areas are discussed, as they have developed over the years. These include Spain's policy towards Portugal, Hispano-America, the European and Atlantic areas and finally Africa. The chapter concludes with a survey of major current foreign policy problems.

7

THE FOREIGN POLICY OF SPAIN

NUÑO AGUIRRE DE CÁRCER
Embassy of Spain, Washington

GONZALO FERNÁNDEZ DE LA MORA
Ministry of Foreign Affairs, Madrid

BACKGROUND FACTORS

Location and size

The geographical position of Spain at the extreme southwest of the European continent conditions the country's role in Europe, Africa and America, the three sectors which have been the main field of her external activities. Spain is not separated from the European continent, but her communications with it are hampered by the difficulty of crossing the Pyrenees. Various authorities have even described her as an American country since the Spanish-speaking nations of the New World are a projection across the Atlantic of the Spanish way of life. It has also been justly observed that, from the geographical point of view, Spain can be considered an African Power. The narrow Straits of Gibraltar were undoubtedly an isthmus in the geological past; Spain has been present in the northwest of the continent since before the arrival of the Arabs. Likewise, the typically Spanish Canary Archipelago, whose origin is lost in legends of Atlantis and the Hesperides, naturally belongs to the African coast zone.

Turning from continents to seas, Spain is both a Mediterranean and Atlantic country, with the advantage—not enjoyed by France, for example—of commanding the gateway between the two. As a Mediterranean Power—preponderant during various periods—her ships have sailed from the Spanish Levant to its eastern end. There is no need to stress the central position in the western Mediterranean of the Balearic Islands, long coveted by England, the nation whose power more than that of any other, has always been based on command of the seas. The western Mediterranean basin has been the natural setting for contacts between Spain and North Africa. The maintenance of peace in this area has been a constant of Spanish foreign policy.

As an Atlantic Power, with the Cantabrian Sea, or Bay of Biscay, to the north, and to the west the North Atlantic, major political axis of the Western Powers, Spain must inevitably be concerned with all matters affecting security and peace in this important region, quite apart from the well-known special interests that link her with the countries along the shores of the southern Atlantic.

The surface area of Spain is 189,500 square miles, which compares favorably with that of other European countries, and is second only to that of France. The size of Spain, combined with her geographical position referred to above, is highly important from the standpoint of international politics. The full value of both factors is brought out in questions of political and military alliance, for they signify the possibility of counting on a vast territory with favorable climatic conditions for making war. They permit the dispersal in the interior of both attacking and defending units, and last, but not least, they make it difficult for any hypothetical, victorious enemy to occupy the country.

Resources

Population   The Spanish population, thirty million inhabitants in the Peninsula and adjacent islands, is the twelfth highest among the world's independent states. But the population density of 57 inhabitants per square kilometer is less than that of the majority of the European nations. The paucity of natural resources of a large part of the country makes any increase impossible in certain regions; in others, such as the Cantabrian and Spanish Levant coast zones, the density reaches the normal degree for level and industrialized European countries (from 100 to 250 inhabitants per square kilometer). In addition, mention should be made of the steep rise in the population, especially noticeable

at the lower levels of the demographic pyramid.

Natural resources   Spain is fundamentally an agricultural country; in an emergency, she could be self-sufficient in agricultural products. However, she is making progress in industrialization. This is having a major impact on the modernization of agriculture and, at the same time, is broadening the total base of the economy.

Spain does fall short in some of the basic sources of power. For example, petroleum has to be imported. There are deposits of two minerals of military importance: wolfram and uranium.

Military resources   The military factor is especially important for the power of the nation if it becomes involved in war. The Spanish human element is impressive: tough and resistant to fatigue or strenuous climatic conditions, frugal in food and other needs, capable of quick on the spot improvisation, and endowed with exceptional valor.

The equipment of the armed forces is being modernized. The Agreement on Aid for Mutual Defense between Spain and the United States has provided funds for this program. The agreement signed in 1953 is valid for ten years with an option for extension for two additional five year periods.

From the strategic point of view, Spain offers a great central redoubt, defended to the north by the Pyrenees, and open to the south and west. The maritime coast is very extensive, and includes natural ports of exceptional importance. The island territories (the Balearics and Canaries) occupy a position of tremendous military value in the western Mediterranean and the Atlantic routes.

These considerations lead us to classify Spain as a medium Power, but one which is increasing its influence by ties of a more spiritual nature with the nations of the American continent which speak her language. Among the special conditions which increase her influence, we must cite the international cohesion of the Spanish people, Spain's recent experience of internal conflict, and a world conflagration which she managed to avoid, and finally, a military tradition which found the best possible school on African territory.

THE FORMULATION AND IMPLEMENTATION OF FOREIGN POLICY

The National Defense Junta named General Franco as Head of the Government of the Spanish State on September 29, 1936. According to the decree, he "assumed all the powers of the new state."

On the first of October, 1936, a law created, among other main organs of the central administration of state, the Technical Board, the General Secretariat of State and the Secretariat of External Relations, run by a diplomatic official. This duplicated the pattern followed during a brief period of the dictatorship of Primo de Rivera.

Early in 1938 provision was made for the organization of the central administration of state into ministerial departments. Among them was the Ministry of Foreign Affairs. The same law formally provided for linking the President of the Government with the Headship of State, noting that according to the decision of the National Defense Junta, the Head of State has full powers.

It is clear, therefore, that the final decision in the most important questions affecting Spanish foreign policy have to be taken by the Head of State, advised by the Foreign Minister who is charged with implementing such policies in accordance with the principles laid down. The Minister regularly informs his Government colleagues about foreign affairs at the meeting of the Council of Ministers, which is presided over by the Head of State.

Some of the constitutional laws do refer to the instances when the Council of the Kingdom and the Spanish Cortes (Parliament) must be heard on foreign policy. For example, the law provides that "The Head of State will hear the Council of the Kingdom without fail on the following matters: the declaration of war or agreement of peace." The Cortes advises on the ratification of treaties. Provision is made for the submission of important questions of foreign policy to a public referendum if the Head of State thinks it is advisable, or if the interests of the public should demand it.

Advisory organs on matters concerning foreign policy include: the recently created Foreign Affairs Advisory Council; the Cultural Relations Board; the Institutes of Hispanic and Hispano-Arabic Culture in the realm of cultural policy; the General Staff and the National Defense Committee on matters which affect the external security of the nation; the CIPAI on international air policy; plus a series of inter-ministerial committees for matters which demand consultations among various departments.

FOREIGN POLICY IN THE HISTORY OF SPAIN

Spain as a Great Power, 1500–1800

Territorial expansion   The reign of the Catholic sovereigns, Ferdinand and Isabella, comprises not only the crucial moment for the formation of the Spanish nation, with its unity of faith, of race, of religion, of political leadership, but also brought the possibility of expansion. Expansion could take place towards America, thanks to the discovery, towards North Africa as the corollary of the reconquest, towards the Mediterranean and Italy—the natural direction of the House of Aragon—and towards Europe through matrimonial links.

The providential coincidence of dates (1492) between the end of the reconquest of Spain—the taking of Granada—and the discovery of America, meant that the vital and warlike

201

spirit gathered for the first enterprise was immediately available for the second, which brought about Spain's greatest contribution to world history. The political genius of Ferdinand the Catholic—living model for the treaties of Machiavelli—and the Mediterranean tradition of the Crown of Aragon, meant that this area and the Italian peninsula would be the theater of operations. France, recently arrived at political cohesion, was destined to be the natural adversary.

But, as well as arms, another element came to establish the supremacy of Spain. This was matrimonial policy. The children of the Catholic sovereigns married as follows: Isabella married the heir of Portugal; Catherine became the wife of Henry VIII; Juana wed Philip the Handsome, head of the House of Burgundy. These marriages determined the territorial expansion of Spain's European dominions under Charles. Combined with the discovery, conquest, and colonization of the New World, they made Spain the foremost World Power.

The balance of power　　G. Schwarzenberger tells us that one of the rules of the "international oligarchy" was that its members should watch each other carefully to prevent any one of them becoming so strong as to menace the existence of the oligarchy itself and bring about world hegemony. France obeyed this basic norm by making herself the center of resistance against world domination by a single Power, although, to do something so much beyond her strength, she had to ally herself with the devil —at that time the Turk, historic enemy of Christianity. Thus was destroyed the vague but genuine feeling for a *"Communitas Christiana,"* and naked power politics was born. Two concepts of power were thenceforth fighting: the Spanish, imbued with medieval ideas on the unity of Christianity, and the modern, represented first by France, and then by England, the Netherlands and a little later, Sweden.

In the period beginning with the first Spanish Bourbon, Philip V, Spain, saddened by the wily appropriation of Gibraltar by the British, could still qualify as a Great Power, but *"minor inter pares."* This was notably true thanks to the survival of the empire of the Indies. to the possession of an important fleet—which received the coup de grâce at Trafalgar—and to the policy of "Family Pacts." These Family Pacts, though they always operated at the expense of the poor relations—Spain—did at least give us a place in the European political combinations, but often only as a silent partner and still more often as the one who foots the bill.

Reaction against this situation led to the idea of neutrality in conflicts which did not directly affect us, an idea which came to dominate our policy from the beginning of the 19th century onwards.

Major contributions　　Despite this evident step backwards, Spain's balance, from the point of view of civilization and culture, is not essentially negative. The tremendous worldwide mission which Spain undertook achieved the Christianizing and Hispanizing of a continent. It preserved Catholicism on a wide European front: in Belgium, half of Holland, the Rhineland and Bavaria, and even, indirectly, in Ireland. It kept the Turks—the "enemy" in those centuries—within bounds without anachronistic crusades or underhand deals à la Francis I. And this does not include the scope of her cultural manifestations in literature, painting, architecture and sculpture, which continue to arouse the admiration of every cultured individual.

Retreat in the nineteenth century

The transition from the eighteenth to the nineteenth century, marked in European politics by the French Revolution and the Napoleonic Empire, coincided with the decline of Spain as a World Power. This fact, plus the absence of any political institutions of prestige, were the excuses used to relegate Spain to an insignificant role at the Congress of Vienna.

The "European Political Concert" which emerged from Vienna was based on the dogma of internal order and monarchical authority.

Because of the internal vicissitudes in Spain during the first quarter of the century, the Major Powers of the new European system not only watched us carefully, but eventually they interfered, even militarily, in our affairs.

The shock to the nation produced by the break-up of our Empire, through the independence of the new American republics, finally reversed the roles traditionally attributed to the Crown, the Councils, the civil bodies and the military. The military now began to seek a field of action in internal politics as a substitute for overseas opportunities.

Apart from a few sporadic episodes—Santo Domingo, Mexico, Cochin-China, the Papal States and the Moroccan War of 1859–60—Spain made no sorties into the international arena. Instead, she devoted herself to civil wars, overthrowing the monarchy, hasty and ephemeral experiments with other regimes, and finally a search for a saving formula which would bring internal peace to the country. It was believed this was found with the restoration of the monarchy in 1875.

From the Restoration (1875) to the Republic (1931)

Canovas del Castillo, Prime Minister and political instigator of the restoration of Alfonso XII to the Spanish throne, was confronted with a number of problems in the international field: the recognition and international status of the new regime; the problem of easing tension with the United States which had arisen over insurrections and uprisings in Cuba; and the attempt to secure agreements on Spanish rights in Morocco. The latter led to an international conference on the Morocco problem in Madrid in 1880. There were also negotiations with England and Germany on the Philippine Sulu Archipelago.

War with the United States The final Cuban uprising began in February, 1895, an uprising which had received the approval of the United States. Spain again found herself plunged into isolation, with only the slightest encouragement and friendly words from some of the European Powers. There is not space here to go into the origins of the war between Spain and the United States. American historians have explained, little by little, the real character of American intervention in the matter. It was the first occasion on which the republic made its foreign policy manifest on a world scale. It is clear that the unfortunate situation in Cuba was mercilessly exploited in order to put at the disposal of the new non-European Super Power, the remains of the Spanish dominions: Puerto Rico, the Philippines and the Pacific. The Count of Romanones, a politician of liberal and impartial ideas, summarized the situation in which Spain was caught thus: "our country was so deprived of allies and international support, that she had to succumb to the weight of this international isolation, an isolation in which she lived not only by counsel of her politicians but also because of the force of opinion."

Surrounded by countries who falsely appealed to principles of international morality, Spain succumbed in the face of a single-minded policy of power. And so ended her work of centuries in the new continent.

The problem of Morocco During this same period, no problem was more persistent and more difficult to deal with than that of Morocco. Indeed, the Morocco affair has had a major impact on an important sector of Spain's international political activity right up until the present time. For both historical and geographical reasons, Spain could have been expected to play a major role in the development of North Africa. However, over the years, Spain's holdings were gradually reduced until almost nothing was left.

The first Spanish-French negotiations ended in November 1902. The resulting agreement granted Spain the dominating influence over an area which stretched from the mouth of the River Sebu in the Atlantic to that of the Muluya in the Mediterranean, including the city of Fez and its province in the south. However, because of a cabinet crisis in Spain, this agreement was stillborn. All of Spain's chances vanished of extending her influence over an important area in North Morocco, instead of the narrow and uncultivated coastal border.

In 1904 the British and French reached an agreement involving their colonial interests in both Egypt and Morocco. Even though the Spanish Government was not consulted, the articles of the agreement "took into special consideration the interests that [Spain] derives from her geographical position and from her territorial possessions in the Moroccan coast of the Mediterranean." The French Government was to come to "an agreement with the Spanish Government" over this area.

The new Spanish-French conversations led to a treaty in October of 1904, but the area left to Spanish influence was greatly reduced from that which had been mentioned in the stillborn agreement of 1902. For example, Fez and the zone between the River Sebu and the 35th parallel, with the city of Uazan, as well as the northern province of Taza, were omitted. This clearly unfavorable position, compared with France, was to remain the goal of successive Paris governments whenever Moroccan affairs were discussed. In spite of tremendous limitations, the 1904 treaty admitted that Spain did have a vital interest in Morocco and in the western part of the Mediterranean.

In 1907 the British and Spanish governments exchanged official notes dealing with this question. These recognized "the importance of Spain's insular positions in these areas" and the common interests of Spain and Great Britain. The notes concluded that "both Governments have come, therefore, to an agreement for the purpose of not only maintaining a 'status quo'" in the region, but also "and which concerns us most of all . . . guaranteeing our communications . . . in the Mediterranean and Atlantic."

During this same period, and under the pressure of Germany, which had hoped to obtain a holding in the Morocco region, the British and the French came to an understanding with Berlin in November 1911, through which recognition was given to France's protectorate over the whole Moroccan empire, infringing upon the rights of Spain guaranteed in the treaty of 1904. Consequently, a new Spanish-French treaty was drawn up in 1912 by which the territory remaining under Spanish protection was reduced to about 20,000 square miles, a tenth of that which was kept by France. The 1912 treaty has been the juridical base upon which the Spanish presence in Morocco has relied for 44 years.

Neutrality in World War I   The new Head of the Government, Dato, proclaimed Spanish neutrality the day after the outbreak of hostilities in the First World War. In spite of a few dissenting voices, that Spain should favor Germany, it is certain that this neutrality corresponded to the desire of the majority of the nation, and also to a tradition more than a century old. This same policy was pursued during the Second World War. In effect, ever since the Napoleonic wars, Spain has refrained from taking part in any of the major European conflicts, not because of convictions, but because no interests of Spain would be served by becoming involved. Unconsciously, this attitude had its most deeply embedded roots in the Spanish tradition of "just war" which was elaborated by our classical international lawyers of the sixteenth century. Consequently, not even tempting offers of the Kaiser—Gibraltar, Tangier, and freedom of action in Portugal— made to Dato by the German ambassador, could change Spain's attitude.

Spanish neutrality actually proved beneficial to the Allies in that it saved France from maintaining forces along the Pyrenean border. At the end of the war, Romanones, the Head of the Government, was in Paris but of course could not participate in the peace treaty negotiations. However, in interviews with Clemenceau and Wilson, he made it clear that Spain was interested in the development of events and desired to be consulted on all matters which affected her interests.

Activities in the League of Nations   Spain was active in the League of Nations, including the Council, from the very beginning. After serving as a semi-permanent member for several successive periods, the Spanish Government applied for admission as a permanent member in 1926, taking advantage of the entrance of Germany into the League. The application of Spain, which coincided with similiar petitions from Brazil, Poland and China, encountered stiff opposition from France and England. This opposition, which coincided with claims concerning the Tangier question, led General Rivera to abruptly withdraw Spain from the League. Her absence was short-lived, however, and she participated in the organization again in 1928. Spain's participation in the League of Nations was at once both idealistic and impartial; she was active in attempts to reform and improve the organization.

Return of dictatorship   The difficulties that were encountered in the total occupation and pacification of the small zone allotted to Spain in Morocco, and especially the ease with which the Riffians obtained armaments, completely undermined the constitutional government which had ruled Spain since 1876. This undermining resulted in the re-establishment of the dictatorship under General Primo de Rivera. The General made it clear that he was "looking for a prompt, worthwhile and sensible solution to the problem of Morocco." He was to reap his greatest successes in the international field when he finally obtained peace, thanks to new military tactics and open collaboration with France. This brought about the surrender of Abd-el-Krim in 1925.

Foreign policy during the Second Republic, 1931–36

The Republic boasted from the very beginning of wanting to incorporate Geneva's postulates in the constitutional texts and converting them into a polestar for her foreign policy. Therefore, article 6 of the 1931 Constitution stated the very words of the Briand-Kellog Pact as follows: "Spain renounces war as an instru-ment of national policy." Article 7 added: "The Spanish state will respect the universal norms of international law, incorporating them into the positive law of the country." Finally, article 77 specified the conduct to be followed by the President of the Republic in the event of international conflict.

Within the professed neutrality in which Spain wished to maintain herself in the struggle for power between the Great Powers, Spain's ideological bent favored the French and English democracies. One of the greatest exponents of Spanish Diplomacy in 1931 synthesized the general lines of the new foreign policy as follows:

1. Spain would try to introduce the directive ideas of her great jurist theologians of the sixteenth century in a modern surrounding, especially the ideas of Fr. Francisco de Vitoria.

2. She would try to enliven the society of nations with a sincere spirit of international co-operation.

3. Spain would not abandon because of this the two ambitions she has the right to have: the restoration of Gibraltar (although this was apparently forgotten during the republic); and an agreement with the two Americas to guarantee respect for her language and culture in the New World;

4. Spain would always try to live in the most close and cordial relationship with Portugal.

5. As regards tactics, Spain would follow a policy of collaboration in Geneva with the smaller democratic nations (the Scandinavian countries, Switzerland, Holland, Belgium and Czechoslovakia) and close contact with France and Great Britain, without, because of this, opposing any other Great Power. She would follow with special interest the work of the

nations of her own tongue and culture in the Nations' Parliament.

In the League of Nations, Spain's points of view were outstanding in the discussions on the eternal question of disarmament; in the project of international organization of air transport (preceding the ICAO); and in the defense of the *international* character of members of the League of Nations Secretariat. Spain was at the time a Permanent Member of the Council.

For the first time since the Bolshevik revolution, an agreement was reached in 1933 between Spain and the U.S.S.R., by which they mutually recognized and decided the interchange of diplomatic representatives. The changes of ministries in Madrid and the desire to reduce the number of components of the future Soviet diplomatic mission, delayed the putting into practice of this agreement. It was again postponed when the Marxist separatist revolution broke out in October 1934, until after the beginning of the National Movement in July, 1936. This did not prevent the Second Republic from supporting and backing the entrance of Soviet Russia in the League of Nations, at the same time as that of Mexico, where it was represented by a notoriously Marxist ambassador, Alvarez del Vayo.

The National Movement, 1936–39

The Spanish state, born on July 18, 1936, was so occupied with the internal struggle for life or death that initially it played a passive role in foreign affairs. Although a few states were to grant recognition during the early stages of the conflict, only two important European Powers were included: Italy and Germany. National Spain did not choose them; at this stage she was playing rather a feminine and expectant role in world affairs. The states which recognized Spain took the initiative. The United States, and many other countries, waited until the civil war had ended in victory for the Na-

tional Movement before they extended recognition. Once begun, however, recognitions came in quick order. By the end of spring, 1939, fifty-three nations had recognized the new government and had sent representatives.

The new state was not presented to the world by France and England, for example, because these states did not want to support the new Spain, and preferred to keep their ambassadors in Madrid. They rendered their material and moral support to the Republican government. The diplomatic possibilities were clearly outlined. The Government of Burgos was faced with an elemental dilemma; either to take refuge in international isolation as had been the custom in contemporary Spain, or establish contact with the important Powers who were willing to do so. She chose the second alternative.

In the three years between 1936 and 1939, the Great Powers were divided into two groups: the majority supported Madrid, either from inertia or sympathy, and a minority recognized the Government of Burgos. The preferences of national Spain, given the limitations mentioned above, were significant: at the difficult time of the uprising, she opted for the political, economic and military collaboration of Italy before that of Germany. And when the moment came for the first pact or agreements in March of 1939, on the eve of victory, she turned first to Portugal, then signed the anti-Comintern agreements, and lastly, drew up a pact of little importance with Germany.

In all of these instruments it was clearly shown that Spain did not intend to commit her destiny to any country in case of war. The idea of neutrality was always in the foreground. There is no need to underline the importance of this action if one takes into consideration the fact that Spain was involved in a civil war, and that Germany and Italy were already involved in expansionist plans and were inclined towards close military alliances which were to come into play with the outbreak of World War II. During these first three years, Spain was willing to accept offers of friendship. But she was clearly unwilling to become involved in any military mortgages for the future.

The Second World War, 1939–45

Hours after the war broke out in Europe, a decree was issued in Madrid establishing "strict neutrality" of the Spanish people. This was communicated to the Great Powers on September 4th, 1939. It was not a surprise. But when in June, 1940, the German army hoisted its flag on the international bridge at Hendaye, any keen-sighted observer would have considered it very doubtful that the Germans would respect Spanish territory, which was the only way through to Gibraltar which formed the gateway to the Mediterranean and North Africa. What at the time looked superlatively improbable, was achieved owing to a very clever policy of some rhetorical, but very few real, concessions.

Relations with the Axis　　Ramon Serrano Suñer was Foreign Minister during the difficult period from December 18th, 1940, to September 2nd, 1942. The initial outstanding fact was Spain's refusal to sign the tripartite German-Italian-Japanese Pact of September 27th, 1940, which was not attenuated by the interviews that took place in Hendaye between Franco and Hitler on October 23, 1940, and in Bordighera with Mussolini on February 11, 1941. Franco always responded by postponing his answers to the German-Italian entreaties.

The German attack on the U.S.S.R. on the morning of June 22nd, 1941, introduced a new factor. The following day, the Blue Division was sent to the Eastern front. All the combatants, including Spanish army officers, were volunteers. The new situation was juridically confirmed by the Decree of December 18th, 1941, which read: "Spain maintains, as in the first stages of the war, her neutrality." This was a new concept introduced in international law, which corresponds to what the 1936 Spanish-Italian Agreement named, somewhat ingeniously "benevolent neutrality."

Spain was obliged at times, although she never went as far as Sweden did in permitting the passage of German troops, to yield to the wind. Thanks to this, she was not dragged into the conflict. Her conduct did not fit into the stereotyped patterns of strict neutrality, but it had the incredible and fabulous virtue of keeping Spain out of the war. And it provided for the protection of the Sephardic Jewish minorities in the Balkans, the salvation of thousands of central European refugees who found either refuge or transit facilities in Spain, and the exchange of prisoners of war. What was more decisive, it left the Mediterranean open, allowed the use of the Rock of Gibraltar, and made the allied landing in North Africa possible.

Relations with the allies　　While the Axis tried to attract Spain, the allies did all that was in their power to keep her apart from the war and reduce as much as possible her trade with and concessions to Italy and Germany, however small. This policy constituted at times a serious obstacle for the development of Spain's economy and was on the point of becoming self-destructive. The British intervention in our sea trade and the oil seizure in January, 1944, would have made Spain surrender to the absolute conqueror in the continent. Fortunately, the Spanish-Anglo-American agreement of April, 1944, re-established the oil supply and solved the acute crisis in favor of Spain's neutrality.

In this respect, Eden, in the House of Commons declared: "In the days of utmost crisis in the war, when we were alone, the attitude of the Spanish Government was extremely helpful to us, particularly at the time of our landing in Africa." In the famous words of Sir Winston Churchill: "When Sir Samuel Hoare went to Madrid four years ago, measures were taken to have his aeroplane ready at the airport, as it seemed almost certain that Spain would follow Italy's example and would join the victorious Germany in the War against Great Britain. If Spain had surrendered to the flattery and pressure of the Germans at so critical a time, our burden would have been very much heavier." The Spanish made a reality of what

Churchill considered an impossibility. In the two tense and difficult three-year periods between 1939 and 1945, Spain's foreign policy can be described with one word which was to acquire considerable proportions: neutrality.

The consequences of the war, 1945–55

Diplomatic ostracism   However, the victorious allies in the Second World War condemned Spain when the solemn hour of dictating peace came. The solicited and progressively imposed penalty took the form of international ostracism without precedents. Alberto Martin Artajo was made Foreign Minister on July 18th, 1945, in order to meet this period of unpleasant consequences. On August 2nd, 1945, the Declaration of Potsdam was made public whereby England, the United States and the U.S.S.R. "felt obliged to specify that, for their part, they will not back any application that the present Spanish Government may file to become a member of the United Nations." The Spanish Government's protest on August 5th was completely disregarded.

In France, the activity of exiled persons and terrorists flared up again, and armed bands crossed the Pyrenean frontier and, although they were rapidly dispersed, penetrated into Spanish territory. A systematic press campaign tried to create a hostile atmosphere for Spain throughout the entire world. The culminating moment was when the "Spanish case" was dealt with by request of Panama, in the United Nations Organization on February 9th, 1946. Before a month had passed, findings against the Spanish regime were made public, in the wake of a tripartite conference held in London. The United States published a "White Book" about Spain, based on documents drawn from the German and Italian files, which thoroughly deserved the opportunity for reply in a similar publication by the Spanish Government. It was then that a brutal and unusual event took place: on March 1st, 1946, France took the one-sided decision to close the Pyrenean frontier.

The attacks continued. It seemed as if the United Nations had nothing else to worry about. During the second week of March, 1946, the U.N. discussed Spain and appointed an investigating committee. Spain was accused of threatening world peace because atomic arms were being manufactured in Ocaña. On December, 4th, 1946, the Spanish Government rejected this fantastic announcement. But the foreign chancellories appeared not to listen to any argument on the matter. On December 12th, 1946, the United Nations approved the withdrawal of top diplomatic personnel accredited in Madrid and the non-admission of Spanish delegates to international organizations. One by one, the ambassadors were withdrawn.

Apart from His Holiness the Pope's nuncio, only the Portuguese ambassador, faithful to the Iberian Alliance, and the Minister of Switzerland, loyal to the serene Helvetic tradition, remained in their places. An impressive popular demonstration took place in the streets of Madrid, congregating in the Plaza de Oriente in a protest against this foreign intervention. It was December 9th, 1946; the Spanish people were tasting the beginning of one of the most bitter moments of Spain's existence and one of the most uncomfortable international events in her history.

Efforts to break the diplomatic blockade
Only by dint of patience and pluck could this international blockade be gradually broken down. Official agents, consuls, ministers and Ambassadors did not once relax in the prudent and uninterrupted task of preaching the truth about Spain. It was a rather unrewarding task, but not long in being felt. The United Nations sessions and the recount of votes concerning the case of Spain indicated the gradual recuperation of our prestige. The six votes in favor in 1946 were increased to 16 in 1947.

However, a fresh blow nearly defeated Spanish resistance. The European Allies, entrusted by the United States with the distribution of Marshall Plan funds, eliminated

Spain from receiving any benefits. This provoked a resolution in the U.S. House of Representatives to include Spain in the distribution; but President Truman vetoed the plan, and not a penny of the Marshall aid reached Spain.

Adverse weather conditions made the economic situation ever worse. The threat of starvation could only be conjured away thanks to the Spanish-Argentinian Trading Covenant of October 30th, 1946, and to the Franco-Perón Protocol of April 19th, 1948, whereby the fraternal Argentine republic supplied Spain, on credit, with all the grain she needed. As in the year 1936, our friends were self-elected. Argentina, the Dominican Republic, Peru, Ecuador, Costa Rica, El Salvador, Paraguay all renewed diplomatic relations with Madrid and assumed the defense of the mother country in the Assembly of the United Nations.

The blockade is lifted   The impossibility to suppress Spain was beginning to make her enemies yield a little. On February 9th, 1948, France re-opened the Pyrenean frontier. The Spanish Government made only one condition: that the gesture should be exclusively on France's initiative. In the 1949 voting, 26 hands were raised in the United Nations in favor of Spain.

On January 19th, 1950, the American Secretary of State, Acheson, presented a plan for the renewal of diplomatic relations with Spain. On August 25th, the American House and Senate approved a loan of $62,500,000 which was to help staunch the economic wounds which, at the end of 1949, forced part of the Bank of Spain's gold reserves to be pledged after Argentina unilaterally decided to stop sending over grain on credit.

The United Nations revoked the resolution of December 12th, 1946, to withdraw ambassadors and ministers. Thirty-eight states voted in favor and there were 12 abstentions. By October 4th, 1950, there were 24 chiefs of mission in Madrid: 14 ambassadors and 10 ministers. The diplomatic blockade had ended. In the course of 1951, the ambassadors of the United States, France, England, Belgium, Holland and Italy presented their credentials. The

United States appointed a military and an economic commission, which were transferred to Spain in order to prepare the meticulous reports that were to be the basis for the new policy that Admiral Sherman initiated in his visit to Franco on July 16th, 1951. Spain's international perspectives had been radically transformed.

PRINCIPAL ELEMENTS OF PRESENT POLICIES

Peninsular policy

Portugal and Spain have spent centuries virtually turning their backs on one another. In fact, this lasted until the national uprising created to a certain extent a community of doctrine and of interests, and a basis of mutual respect on which a firm alliance could be built. A legion of Portuguese volunteers joined the Spanish National Army shortly after the civil conflict began. In 1937 the Lisbon Government sent a special representative to General Franco, and the following year, he presented his credentials as ambassador.

On March 17, 1939, the first international treaty was signed in Lisbon; this marked the first appearance of National Spain as a signatory state. This treaty, with an additional protocol signed a year later, provided for broad mutual obligations. The two nations agreed to honor their respective frontiers and territories and "to commit no act of aggression against the other party." They also agreed they would aid no aggressor or possible aggressor against the other party. Finally, they promised "to *concert* their efforts towards safeguarding, as far as possible, mutual interests." As a means of securing these interests, a number of state visits between Franco and Salazar, as well as between other leading officials, have taken place.

Peninsular solidarity has also been reaffirmed in a number of other ways. The two nations have supported each other in the United Nations, in matters arising from NATO policy, in the case of aggression against Goa and in the "Santa Maria" incident, among others. As the Spanish Foreign Minister, Sr. Castiella expressed it: these "two peoples who have parallel historical destinies" and who wish "to guard and exalt the personality of each" have bound themselves "in a greater alliance to defend themselves against any attack on their independence and common spiritual heritage."

Hispano-American policy

The other immutable trend of our foreign policy, though it has taken different shapes during the last century and a half, has clearly been the one that draws Spain to look with fraternal affection upon the nations either across the Atlantic or on the fringes of Asia which bear the seal of our culture, our language and our common faith. If we examine history with the correct perspective, we see how the emancipation of Hispano-America, virtually complete by 1824, led to a period of tension between the mother-country and the former overseas territories. This tension disappeared only towards the second half of the 19th century, when treaties of recognition and friendship began to be drawn up with the new republics.

However, it was not until after the crisis of 1898, when the last traces of our imperial past disappeared, that a genuine policy of Hispanic friendship began to mature. The dictator Primo de Rivera was a chief mover of this drawing-together, which was symbolized by the Ibero-American Fair at Seville in 1929.

With the creation in 1945 of the Institute of Hispanic Culture (which found a precedent in the Council of Hispanity, born in 1941), began a systematic policy of strengthening the links of Hispanity. Throughout the continent, Cultural Institutes associated with that in Madrid are being established. Moreover, treaties are being signed to cover friendship, culture, mi-

gration and social security, as well as commerce and payments. And finally, treaties of double nationality with a number of countries (Chile, Peru, Paraguay, Guatemala and Nicaragua) raise this Hispanic fraternity to the ultimate limits in law and legislative expression.

A formal body for achieving mutual goals has not been created. Nevertheless, we see how this Hispanic community of nations has, with rare exceptions, voted as a bloc on resolutions of common interest. To a large extent, Spain owes her postwar rehabilitation in international circles to the effective diplomatic action of the Hispano-American republics in international organizations.

It is useful to point out that Spanish policy towards Hispano-America need not necessarily find an obstacle in the policy of the United States towards the countries of the new continent. Rather, we may say that it complements it in a variety of ways. To this end, it is interesting to record that in a toast at an official banquet in Madrid on the 16th of December, 1961, the American Secretary of State, Dean Rusk, favored collaboration between Spain and the United States to further their respective interests in the countries south of the Rio Grande.

European and Atlantic policy

France, England and Germany Although we have no territorial problems with our neighbors, there have been nonetheless repeated moments of tension with France because of the aid and freedom of movement she allowed on her territory to exile groups defeated in the civil war. At the end of the Second Great War, they found more than mere tolerant benevolence in France for their schemes against the legally established government of Spain which, moreover, had been formally and publicly recognized by the great democracies in the spring of 1939. It is, therefore, contrary to all principles that six years later the authorities of the neighboring country should permit themselves to doubt what they themselves had recognized officially only a few years before.

However, the passage of time, the internal changes in French policy, and events of a European and North African nature have served to bring Spain and France together, erasing little by little the traces of the difficult moments they have had to pass through.

The improvement of relations with England is also noteworthy, culminating in the visit of the Foreign Secretary, Lord Home and the Home Secretary Mr. R. A. Butler, to Spain. There always remains however, as a shadow on these Hispano-British relations, the still unresolved problem of Gibraltar, which one day will have to be faced with realism and a sense of history.

Relations with Germany have also tended towards a progressive drawing together, which may perhaps provoke suspicions in some foreign offices.

The United States The effective aid lent by Spain to the British colonies in North America at the time of their emancipation is little known. This fact, combined with the imperishable memory of Castilian colonization in the southern and western territories of the United States—today literally dotted with Spanish place-names—provides a solid base for Spanish-United States collaboration.

Unfortunately, the Cuban question came between the countries. The revelation of the so-called "Ostend Manifesto" in 1854 brought clearly to light the hitherto more or less hidden American desire to appropriate the island. At the end of the century, when their attempt to buy it failed, the United States took advantage of the explosion of the "Maine" to unleash a war of aggression which ended in a Spanish defeat. This serious event, which had such profound repercussions on Spain's life in the twentieth century, took nearly fifty years for its effects to be overcome.

The rise of the United States to the political leadership of the Western World, and the transformation of the old Pan-American isolationism of Monroe into a disinterested, but practically worldwide interventionism, has placed American-Spanish relations on a level which has little in common with that of '98.

The recent co-operation in the area of security and economic affairs has contributed to the improved relations between Spain and the United States. Following the Second World War, the Great European Powers who were on the side of the victors undertook a tacit "diplomatic blockade" against Spain. The military responsibilities of the Pentagon, however, allowed the United States to consider the advantages of an alliance with objectivity.

Starting with the visit of Admiral Sherman, prolonged negotiations over a two-year period finally resulted in the American-Spanish pacts of September 1953. These pacts dealt with both mutual defense and economic aid. The military agreement was extremely difficult to negotiate because the United States wanted a simple concession of Spanish territory for the installation of United States military bases. However, the Spanish view that the bases should be zones "for joint use under the Spanish flag and command" finally prevailed.

The agreement on aid for mutual defense provided for the purchase of war material in accordance with the act of Congress. The Economic Aid Agreement supported a series of measures aimed at stabilization of the currency, a balanced budget, and the development of Spain's foreign commerce.

These agreements have been put into effect. Military bases were built at Rota, Moron, Sanjurjo and Torrejon in close co-operation with the Spanish defensive system. These bases have become a part of the strategic dispositions of the West. The organizations which have administered the programs in connection with these agreements have worked without the slightest incident throughout the eight years of the implementation of these programs.

During this same period, a number of distinguished Americans, including President Eisenhower and Secretary of State Dean Rusk have visited Spain. Consultations between American officials and the leaders of Spain, have helped to develop friendly relations between these two nations.

The existence of a direct alliance between Spain and the United States has made possible the incorporation of our country into the defense of the West against the Communist menace. This has been accomplished without prejudice to Spain's total freedom of movement with regard to the rest of the world.

African policy

Since prehistoric times, the Straits of Gibraltar have served not as a moat, but rather as the natural passage for the migration of peoples and commercial and cultural interchange. Until the 15th century, it was Islam which made its presence felt in the Peninsula; but from then onwards, it was the Iberian peoples who assumed a civilizing function in North Africa. The diplomatic action of Spain in the North Africa zone has been especially active in the last quarter of a century. Its general theme is Hispano-Arab friendship; its two concrete themes are the question of Tangier and the fate of the Protectorate of North Morocco.

Common Hispano-Arab interests Hispano-Arab concord depended on two conditions which were not fulfilled until the second third of the 20th century; namely, relaxation of Hispano-Moroccan tension and the independence of the North African and Middle Eastern nations. The end of the colonial regimes along the Mediterranean coast and the Arab aspiration to international status coincided with the "diplomatic blockade" of Spain, a nation which had no economic interests to defend in the Islamic area, and which had more historic claims than any other European nation to the sympathy of the Arabs.

Since the end of the Second World War, Spanish diplomatic action has always supported the new Islamic states. This has included joint action in international assemblies. In the United Nations debates on the Spanish case—especially in the critical voting of the 16th of May, 1949 and the 4th of November 1950—the Arab

delegates came out solidly and without a single exception in favor of the revocation of the diplomatic ostracism of Spain. This situation was repeated in the rest of the International Organizations, beginning with UNESCO. In the 1956 UNESCO Assembly in New Delhi, the Spanish delegate was elected almost unanimously to the Executive Council, with the support of the Afro-Asian group.

To further Hispano-Arab Co-operation and understanding, the Institute of Hispano-Arabic Culture was created on the 11th of August 1954. This Institute has done important work promoting intellectual exchanges and founding a series of centers of Hispanic culture in the main Moslem capitals.

When the crisis of the traditional regimes in the Middle East reached its critical point in 1958 (the consolidation of Nasser, the revolution in Baghdad, and the Anglo-American landings in Jordan and Lebanon), Franco was the only European Head of State who, in his declaration of the 27th of July 1958, reaffirmed the principle of self-determination and friendship for the Islamic peoples. Censuring the errors committed by the former ruling countries, Franco called for an intelligent approach towards the new Arab states by the Great Powers. Not long afterwards, a good part of the world was to follow his line, so controversial in its day, which reveals once more the far-sighted nature of Spanish foreign policy towards the Islamic world.

Spain, therefore, is not only the sole Mediterranean country against which the Arab peoples harbor no resentment; it is also, by reason of its geographical situation and the historical claim which link it to Islam, the nation best suited to bring together the divergent viewpoints of the West and the Arab East.

Now let us examine the concrete themes around which Spanish diplomatic action in North Africa has turned.

Tangier During the First World War the strategic Tangier enclave fell under the influence of the Allies. At the instance of France and England, the Sultan expelled the subjects and diplomatic representatives of the Central

Powers. The International Statute of Tangier of 1923, modified in 1928, was no doubt incapable of guaranteeing the neutrality of the city and its surroundings in the Second World War. This led Spain to the occupation of Tangier by the Jalifa's troops on July 14th, 1940. The Spanish communiqué of that date was to the point: "In order to guarantee the neutrality of the zone of Tangier, the Spanish Government has decided to assume provisionally the services of vigilance, police and security." The work thus done in Tangier during the period of Spanish administration cannot be denied. Thanks to it, the people of Tangier escaped the hazards of the conflict.

As a result of the Allied victory, which occurred in a period of general hostility to the Spanish regime, a conference on Tangier met in Paris in 1945. France, England, the United States and the U.S.S.R. attended this conference; Spain was excluded. Spain protested against the very holding of the conference and the agreement, which ignored Spain's rights, reached by the Great Powers. Her protests were not heeded.

The administration of Tangier under the new agreement was unsatisfactory. Street incidents occurred in 1952; they were violently suppressed by the French-Belgian police. Spain then requested the rescinding of the 1945 agreement and the return to the previous statutory regime, with modifications. Through negotiations, a new agreement was reached in 1952. It included a protocol modifying the Franco-British agreement and an accord on new international jurisdiction and regulations pertaining to general and special police. Spain's position in the new administration was vastly strengthened over what it had been after 1945. The complex structure of the new international administration, which included Spanish participants, lost its reason for existence with the proclamation of the independent Kingdom of Morocco in 1956.

Morocco The regime of the Spanish protectorate in North Morocco was regulated by the Hispano-French convention of November 1912. A complementary agreement of July 1925 delimited the frontiers of the French and Spanish zones. However, from 1945 on, and with only minor exceptions, France acted in a unilateral manner in the entire region.

A typical superiority complex led France to the extreme of dethroning unilaterally the Sultan, Mohammed V, and installing the aged Ben Arafa. This decision, adopted without consulting Spain, was extremely badly received by Moroccan opinion and created an atmosphere of tension and unbearable instability. In the northern zone entrusted to Spain, on the contrary, the nominal authority of Mohammed V was maintained through the person of the Jalifa, as was his religious authority. In the mosques the prayers continued to be made in the name of the Sultan.

Ben Arafa had to abandon Rabat finally, and on October 30, 1955 he renounced his rights. Meanwhile, a Council of Regency was formed to assume his powers. Eventually, on the 5th of November, France was forced to the humiliating course of re-establishing Mohammed V on the throne. With French prestige and authority thus lost, the protectorate now lacked all meaning. On the 2nd of March 1956, the Declaration and Protocol were signed in Paris by which France recognized as defunct the Treaty of Fez of the 30th of March 1912, and accepted the independence of Morocco within interdependence with France.

To the Spanish representative in Rabat, who went to greet the Sultan on his return from exile, Mohammed V expressed his gratitude for Spain's noble support during his banishment, conduct which "neither his sons nor the sons of his sons would ever be able to forget."

On April 4, 1956, Mohammed V, who assumed the title of King of Morocco, arrived in Madrid. After three days of conversations, he signed the protocol by which Spain recognized as invalid the Convention of 1912; the independence of Morocco was proclaimed.

Jurisdiction over the northern zone was progressively transferred to the Rabat Government. On April 1, 1958, Spain agreed to hand over the southern zone of the Spanish protectorate (Tarfaya), to the north of the Province of Rio de Oro. This completed the independence of the entire territory of the Kingdom of Morocco, without any bloodshed on the part of Spain.

On the 26th of November 1957, armed bands, apparently uncontrolled by the Rabat Government and calling themselves the "Army of Liberation," attacked the zone of Ifni by surprise, forcing the reduced Spanish garrison to retire to the coast where it resisted heroically until the arrival of reinforcements restored normality and inflicted a severe chastisement on the aggressors. Spanish troops reacted with the same speed and success against the attempts of terrorists to disturb order in the Province of Rio de Oro. Today life in these African territories is entirely normal, and the scanty nomad tribes which populate them have once more renewed their loyalty to the legitimate authorities.

The Mediterranean and African regions
Hispano-Arab friendship remains therefore as one of the constant factors of Spain's foreign policy. It is reflected in the similarity of viewpoints, or at least, the broad understanding by Spain shown at the United Nations when matters of special interest to the Arab countries are involved. As a concrete example we may cite Spain's support for the Arab line respecting the Arab refugees in Palestine.

In the Mediterranean sphere, Spanish policy defends the preservation of peace, which can be disturbed only by the presence of political or naval forces proceeding from one or other of the two great centers of Communist power in the world. In this respect, Spanish aims coincide, naturally, with those of the Mediterranean members of N.A.T.O., as well as the deep, though sometimes unexpressed, interests of the Arab nations which line the North African coast from Tangier to Port Said.

With regard to the rest of the African continent, Spain is extending its relations with the newly-independent countries. She already has fully active embassies in Senegal as well as Mauritania, Nigeria, Cameroon and Ethiopia. Only financial or administrative considerations have thus far delayed her plans for diplomatic representation in all the new African nations.

MAJOR CURRENT PROBLEMS

Spain and the United Nations

Admission At the San Francisco Conference certain enemies of Spain had tried to close her way into the United Nations under the pretext that the new Spanish state may have received aid from the countries which fought against the United Nations. A similar resolution was approved at the tripartite Conference of Potsdam. The Polish petition that the mere existence of the Spanish regime should be declared a threat to international peace and security was not approved by the Security Council. However, it was followed by the report of a five-member Subcommittee which classified the activities of the regime as a "potential" danger for international peace, an epithet which has no standing in international juridical language.

On the 12th of December, 1946, the General Assembly recommended the exclusion of Spain from the international organization, as well as the immediate withdrawal of the ambassadors accredited to Madrid. Only four years were to pass before the same United Nations, conscious of the injustice, incongruity and uselessness of the measures recommended, revoked them, on the 4th of November, 1950. Nonetheless, Spain did not present her candidature as a member of the United Nations because of the veto wielded by the U.S.S.R. in the Security Council in these and other matters. Only when the two World Powers arrived at a "package deal" did Spain request her entry on the 22nd of September 1955. She was admitted on the 14th of December of the same year, together with fifteen other countries.

In view of these events, which show clearly that within a year of its foundation the U.N. had ceased to be the ideal envisaged by its creators, it is hardly surprising that the attitude of both the Spanish people and Government was one of annoyance, or at least profound indifference, towards an international organization which could so easily be turned into a toy of naked power politics, or the object of the undertakings or commitments of the two Super Powers.

Organizational and procedural reforms   Despite all this, and from the moment she was admitted as a member, Spain acted in absolute fidelity to the ruling principles of the organization, casting her vote in accordance with the merits of the case in hand. Her general line of conduct has been to support the fundamental interests of the West, to defend the basic interests of the country, and to stay by the side of her faithful friends, without lending herself to maneuvers or seeking the applause of the majority.

Spain believes that plans for the reform of the Charter should be studied by a general "ad hoc" conference, rather than limiting things to minor partial reforms whose only object is to get out of this or that difficulty. With regard to the General Secretariat, for example, it is necessary to uphold the correct interpretation of the Charter, of the Security Council resolutions and the General Assembly. There should be no excesses or abuses of power which might convert this permanent element of the organization into a police instrument on a world scale with unforeseen political and financial consequences. One cannot give a blank check in such a grave matter, nor simply demand afterwards endorsement by every nation. It is necessary to restore the balance of power in the bosom of the organization, and ensure the most perfect geographic distribution, which should not only take into account absolute figures of area or population.

Although Russian attempts either to destroy or reduce the General Secretariat to their service must be opposed, we do not find the very principle of the existence of a veto absolutely inacceptable, though its use should naturally be subject to strict limitations. In the defense of the fundamental interests of the Free World and the high principles of the Western community, the great Western Powers should not systematically deny themselves the use of the veto to which they have a right, according to the Charter, corresponding to their special obligations with regard to the preserving of peace and international security. The use of the veto solely by the U.S.S.R. leads to their being led astray by majorities who are politically thoughtless and very often ideologically tendentious.

Faced with the upset of the political balance formerly existing in the United Nations, caused by the mass entry of the newly independent countries of Asia and Africa, one should consider a policy which would place greater emphasis on joint action by regional zones. This attitude of giving a bigger role to the regional groups would reduce the number of problems finally reaching the United Nations Security Council and General Assembly, because these problems would have been already aired among the members of groups such as the Organization of American States, the Arab League, or the British Commonwealth. This new policy would be reflected in the distribution of posts corresponding to the respective zones in the councils and main organizations, as well as in the higher echelons of the international organization.

But above even that, above all, such cohesion should be reflected in the joint formulation of policies to deal with the great problems of world politics. Spain, which to a greater or lesser extent, has interests in different regional zones (Europe and the North Atlantic, Ibero-America, the Mediterranean and the Arab World as well as Africa) will, for her part, continue to act within the framework of the different regional zones mentioned, convinced that the strengthening of such groups must work in favor of a more stable balance in the bosom of the international society.

Disarmament

Spain, which already paid great attention to the problem of disarmament under the aegis of the League of Nations, has also followed the subject with the interest it deserves in the disarmament discussions within the United Nations, expressing her views on the matter on many occasions. The Spanish position may be summed-up in the following essential points.

Although today the weight of the agonizing decision of peace or war falls basically on the Great Powers, the need for security is not, nevertheless, their exclusive concern. The other nations, above all the medium-sized Powers, such as Spain, always have an important role to play in judging the action, intentions, and projects of those Great Powers on such a vital matter, demanding that they modify their conduct according to the needs of the common and universal good.

Obstacles and ways to surmount them
Given the difficulty of reaching a total agreement on general and complete disarmament, the negotiators must seek workable partial agreements through reciprocal concessions, always in a climate of confidence and mutual understanding.

On the other hand, effective disarmament is not possible without efficient international control, previously established. Inspection, freely accepted by all and made by an international body, does not imply desire for domination or interference with sovereignty. It therefore gives no adequate grounds for rejecting it, once the agreement comes to the point of devising methods of applying it.

Spain, therefore, is not opposed to the adoption of measures of disarmament which are accepted jointly by the great military Powers, always granted that, with a climate of reciprocal confidence re-established, these disarmament measures will definitely be of universal application, simultaneous and effective. For this, it is essential to have an efficient system of control accepted, a system previously arranged and put into effect within the framework of the United Nations, simultaneously with the development of these measures of progressive disarmament.

However, disarmament measures which would alter considerably the present balance of military forces would not be acceptable. For example, the disappearance of means of transporting and launching nuclear weapons, together with the disappearance of bases in foreign countries—in the first phase foreseen by the Soviet resolution on disarmament—would give a tempting opportunity to a Great Power to take advantage of this imbalance, no matter how temporary, to launch an attack.

Nuclear weapons   With regard to nuclear arms tests, Spain approves of their suspension, so long as this is subject to some system of control accepted by all the states concerned, and is not a mere moratorium which could be broken abruptly by one of the Great Powers after secret preparations for these very tests.

Likewise, the production of atomic material for military purposes would have to stop. The entire future production of such materials would have to be devoted to peaceful ends—once an effective control exists over both the stoppage of production and the destruction or neutralization for military ends of the present "stocks."

With regard to the adoption of disarmament measures or agreements not to use certain weapons in a unilateral manner, Spain feels that her defense and security, closely linked with the defense and security of the Free World, must be previously guaranteed by solemn agreements universally accepted, within the framework of the United Nations. Without these guarantees, she cannot renounce the measures she judges necessary for her own security in favor of mere declarations of pacifist principles which, in many cases, do no more than prepare a power vacuum in certain areas which someone ends by filling.

Anti-colonialism

The mass entry of African and Asian countries recently arrived at independence has profoundly altered the geographic composition of the United Nations, thus upsetting a balance of forces which, up to then, we must admit, was really favorable to the West. The trend of voting has altered with this; for the surprisingly disproportionate increase in the number of new members who remain in the neutralist or "non-committed" camp, makes it already very difficult for the Western Powers to achieve sufficiently large majorities in the voting on matters which they consider of the utmost importance to their national interests.

Small Power political maneuvers   These "uncontrollable" majorities reappear, however, with the greatest of ease when the matter suggested by a Great Western Power is by its very nature and contents able to attract them. What happens then is that the states of the "third world" promptly seize the question from the Great Western Power who proposed it, and, taking over the role of patrons, they present the matter—with the modifications necessary to meet their own interests—in such a way as to reap the credit for having raised and pressed ahead with it.

Such a thing has happened, for example, with the United States proposal "Africa: Program of the United Nations for Independence and Development," put forward by President Eisenhower himself during the Fifteenth General Assembly in 1960. It reached the debating stage as a proposal submitted by Ethiopia and 23 other African countries, with some decisive modifications of a political nature.

Two objectives are achieved with this procedure: it neutralizes or mutes all the tremendous efforts made by the Western Powers to raise the standard of living and generally improve the lot of the "third world" countries. At the same time, it introduces into subjects which deserve general approval strange elements, political in type and ephemeral in character.

This precise method was employed with the "General Declaration of Independence for Colonial Territories." Announced by Khrushchev in the general debate of the Fifteenth Assembly of the United Nations, it nevertheless reached the final stage of voting as a proposal headed and elaborated by the great nations among the "neutralists."

Readiness for independence   It is useful to make these points to show the need to follow criteria of one's own on the major aspects of anti-colonialism, based on objective facts about the workability of independence for the countries under consideration, without feeling any uneasiness about being in the minority in various United Nations votes on these matters. An independent decision should be taken at the risk of having this attitude misinterpreted and exploited with evil intent by pro-Communist propaganda.

Spain is fully aware of the direction in which the "winds of history" are blowing, but believes that this evolution towards independence must necessarily take into account a series of factors. Some of these are of a political nature, such as the capacity of the independent peoples for self-government. Others relate to education in general, for a minimum level of culture is indispensable, at least in those who are going to be the ruling "elite." Still other factors are economic, and concern the economic viability of the territories which aspire to independence, even with aid that will not fail to come from one camp or the other. Only with these premises, and with a requisite transitional stage to avoid the abrupt cutting of all previous links, can independence be granted in a manner that will avoid the renewal of chaotic situations like that which occurred in the Congo in the wake of nationhood.

Another interesting aspect to bear in mind is the illogicality for the Great Western Powers to support a policy of declarations limited to certain geographic areas or a single continent, such as the African, for example. It is a somewhat brazen procedure to focus attention on one geographic zone while keeping a free hand in the rest of the world. We believe that the decolonization resolutions, in so far as they receive overwhelming majorities, and above all, the support of the Great Powers on both sides, should be applied simultaneously, in the same manner, in all the geographic zones of the world. There should not be intervention of power politics or reciprocal understandings about zones of influence to preserve the exclusive interests of the Great Powers of the world, to the evident and almost exclusive prejudice of the lesser Powers.

Nor do we agree with the fixing of strict and immutable stages for a process of decolonization which necessarily has to take into account that series of political, educational and economic factors to which we have already referred. To achieve independence, it is necessary to prove, right up to "D-Day" that it is merited; it is not sufficient to go to sleep and wait for the much-desired date, previously fixed.

Relations with former colonizers   Finally, we see that the anti-colonial doctrine focuses less and less attention on the right of free determination of the self-ruling peoples, who apparently are to be guided by "remote control" in one direction only. Any desire shown by these peoples for integration or close association with the former ruling Power is promptly damned by the exponents of anti-colonialism. It is difficult not to realize that, in this way, there is a clear attempt to malign and deny all the work of "colonization"—in the true sense of the word—done by the European Powers, for the exclusive benefit of the non-European colossi.

Though insisting firmly that the interpretations put upon the "anti-colonial" items of the United Nations Charter are abusive, Spain has continued to give proof, spontaneously and generously, of her desire to keep the international organization informed of anything that may happen in her different territories, whether metropolitan, island or African provinces. And on this score, she has received the gratitude of the international forum. Moreover, in a speech at Fernando Po, on October 20, 1962, the Minister of the Presidency, Carro Blanco, stated for the first time that "if the majority wished to modify their status, Spain will not create any obstacle toward reaching an agreement with the [Equatorial] provinces regarding their future."

Nor is there anything in Spain's conduct— the faithful continuation of a tradition uninterrupted since the days of the great geographical discoveries—which might give the slightest

pretext for accusations of racial discrimination towards peoples who form part of our national community, even though they possess racial characteristics distinct from those of the peninsula. The renewed evidence offered publicly in the United Nations by the twenty peoples of our stock is the best proof of this wide and generous Christian concept of the intrinsic equality of the human race. This concept constitutes one of the claims to glory, not even denied in recent or present times, of the Spanish way of life.

Membership in regional organizations

The arrival at the Foreign Ministry of Fernando M. Castiella, a professor of international law, trained in the great European universities and former ambassador to the Holy See, implies the beginning of a process, gradual but irreversible, of drawing closer to Europe. This after all, is the natural scene for Spain's political international affairs. Throughout history, her mission though universal, never ceased to be European. We have already discussed what this trend has meant in bilateral relations between Spain and the main European countries. Now we shall see this same tendency reflected in the attitude to the international organizations within the European field.

European orientation   The advance has been extremely important, with Spain's entry in July 1959 into the European Organization for Economic Co-operation marked out as the vital moment. Spain has taken a full part in the work of this organization, even after its transformation into a new organization, the Organization for Economic Co-operation and Development, which includes the United States and Canada as well as 18 European countries. Spain has belonged to the OECD as a founder member since December 1961.

Although they are organizations of worldwide scope, we would like to draw attention to Spain's participation in the work of the International Monetary Fund and in the International Reconstruction and Development Bank since May 1959; in the International Finance Corporation since March, 1960, and in the International Development Association since 1961.

As far as purely European organizations are concerned, Spain, as a signatory of the European Cultural Convention, takes an active part in the cultural and youth work of the Council of Europe, now centered in the Cultural Co-ordination Council as well as in other activities of a technical nature of the Strasbourg organization. Spain also participates in the European Center of Nuclear Research, in the Brussels Customs Convention, in the European Space Research Organization, in European organizations dealing with maritime affairs, transport, etc. She also took part in the Strasbourg and London preparatory meetings of the European Organization on Ways of Launching Space Vehicles.

Spain has watched closely the evolution of the two great European economic groups, the "6" and the "7," without deciding on joining either of them. This reflects the number of interests which link Spain to each of them. Consequently, she waits for the solution of these conflicting interests, which seems in sight.

The petition of Great Britain, followed shortly by that of Denmark and Ireland, to begin negotiations with the Common Market makes probable, among many other things, the disappearance before long of the European Free Trade Association.

In the early days of 1962, and after interminable discussions, the common agricultural policy of the "6" was approved, and with that, the transition to the second stage of the Common Market. It was at this juncture and after careful consideration, that Spain took the plunge in drawing closer to Europe by requesting on February 9th, the opening of negotiations with a view to possible links with the European Economic Community.

The Common Market   The document setting forth this petition is perfectly explicit; it does not limit itself to vague and general diplomatic terms as employed by other petitioners, but reveals clearly throughout its text not only the reason for such a request, but also the desire that this association could lead gradually to full integration.

Historic considerations are enumerated in this letter: "Spain's European vocation, repeatedly confirmed . . . finds a new occasion to manifest itself at this moment."—Geographic reasons are: "the territorial continuity of Spain with the Community and the advantage that her geographic position might bring . . ."; general economic reasons indicate that "the Spanish Government is deeply concerned with the task of accelerating the economic development of the country . . . and seeks in the link requested, a stimulus to achieve that objective . . . towards which the success of the Spanish stabilization plan has been an encouraging precedent." Commercial reasons designate: "The agricultural exports to the countries of the Community, a fundamental element in Spain's external commerce, the maintenance and increase of which are of maximum importance." Finally considerations of an international nature are that: "The bonds which unite Spain with the American nations could be a positive contribution to the solving of the problems arising between these nations and the Community." For all these reasons, "the Spanish Government request an association [with the European Economic Community] likely to arrive in time at full integration."

A month after its presentation, in the first meeting of the Council of Ministers of the European Economic Community, the Spanish petition was examined. On the 7th of March, official receipt was acknowledged, with the promise to study it carefully. It was impossible to fix a date for the start of the preliminary consultations because of pending negotiations between Great Britain and the EEC. The official organs of the Community explained that the result of such negotiations might determine the attitude later adopted by other countries who had presented similar petitions.

A socialist attempt to obstruct the Spanish case through speeches in the European Parliament session of the 29th of March met no success. When the Political Commission of the Council of Europe studied the matter, it recommended the establishment of some form of economic agreement with Spain. Such was the situation in 1962, and the likelihood was that progress, no matter how slow, would have to be made along this road which Spain is taking towards the United Europe which is now being created.

The Atlantic Community   Spain shows the same attitude with regard to the various projects for establishing an Atlantic Community.

Her special position with respect to the American nations with the same culture, the treaty links with the United States since the 1953 agreements, her status as a member of the OECD—the economic platform uniting the countries on both sides of the North Atlantic—all these reasons make her a potential member of the somewhat vague idea of an Atlantic Community which may yet one day take concrete form. In this, the nation which discovered the New Continent believes that the brother countries of Ibero-America should by right also take their place.

BIBLIOGRAPHY

Author's suggestions

Almagro, Melchor Fernandez. *Historia política de la España contemporánea*. 2 vols. Madrid: Editorial Pegaso, 1956.

Brenan, Gerald. *The Spanish Labyrinth*. Cambridge: Cambridge University Press, 1950.

Doussinague, José María. *España tenía razón* (*1939–45*). 2nd ed. Madrid: Espasa Calpe, 1950.

Hayes, Carlton J. H. *Wartime Mission in Spain* (*1942–45*). Madrid: EEPESA, 1947.

Madariaga, Salvador de. *Spain: A Modern History*. New York: Praeger, 1958.

Pattee, Richard. *This is Spain*. Milwaukee: Bruce, 1951.

Peers, E. Allison. *The Spanish Tragedy* (*1930–36*). 3rd ed. New York: Oxford University Press, 1936.

Thomas, Hugh. *The Spanish Civil War*. New York: Harper, 1961.

Whitaker, Arthur P. *Spain and Defense of the West*. New York: Harper, 1961.

PART TWO

EASTERN EUROPE

ABOUT THE AUTHORS

VLADIMIR MIKHAILOVICH KHVOSTOV was born in June, 1905. Since 1936—with several interruptions—he has been a professor at Moscow University. He was an officer in the Soviet Army during World War II and from 1946–57 he was Chief of the Archive of the Ministry of Foreign Affairs. Since 1959 he has been the Director of the Institute of History of the Academy of Sciences of the U.S.S.R. He is a specialist in the history of international relations and foreign policy. He is currently the Deputy-Chairman of the Commission of the Ministry of Foreign Affairs for the publication of diplomatic documents. Mr. Khvostov has twice been awarded state prizes for his scholarly works and has served on several occasions with the Soviet Delegation to the United Nations. Along with several textbooks he is the author of the following Russian works: *The History of Diplomacy (1871–1917)*; *The Last Years of the Foreign Policy of Bismarck;* and *Forty Years of the Struggle for Peace.*

LEONID NIKOLAEVICH KUTAKOV completed his studies at the Moscow Institute of History, Philosophy and Literature with a specialty in History in 1941. His career was interrupted at this time while he served his country during World War II. From 1946–1951 he was Director of a section of the Archive of the Ministry of Foreign Affairs of the U.S.S.R. Since 1947 he has conducted scientific-instructional activities. He has twice been Deputy Director of the Institute of International Relations and has held the Chair of General History at Moscow University. From 1958 to 1960, his academic activities were again temporarily halted while he served in diplomatic work. Since 1961 he has been Deputy Director of the Institute of History of the Academy of Sciences of the U.S.S.R. and Professor of the Institute of International Relations. He has the scholarly rank of Doctor of Historical Sciences and the title of Professor. His published works, in Russian, include the following: *History of Japanese-English Relations on the Eve of the Second World War; A New History of International Relations (1917–1945)*; and *The Portsmouth Peace Treaty (1905–1945).*

ABOUT THE CHAPTER

This chapter is clearly ideological in orientation and presents the "correct" Soviet point of view. According to the authors, Soviet Russia's foreign policy is determined by the fact that she is a socialist state, not by a multiple set of determinants. As a socialist state, the Soviet Union follows a policy of peace; she is entirely virtuous; international tensions arise because of the capitalistic states. "Thus," according to the authors, "the peace-loving nature of the foreign policy of the Soviet state, like that of any socialist state, is not tactics, not a temporary, transient thing, but a permanent, indispensable characteristic of foreign policy, one determined by the existence of a socialist system."

This chapter surveys the major problems confronting the world and presents the official point of view regarding both the nature of the problems and the methods for dealing with them. It is interesting to note the omission of a number of vital issues which confront the Soviet Union: There is no mention of the conflict with China or any of the satellite states; de-Stalinization and its repercussions are also ignored. Likewise there is no mention of the agricultural difficulties or of any problem which conditions the policy of the state. Everything is explained in light of the socialist system.

8

THE FOREIGN POLICY OF THE UNION OF SOVIET SOCIALIST REPUBLICS

V. M. KHVOSTOV

U.S.S.R. Academy of Sciences

L. N. KUTAKOV

The Institute of International Relations, Moscow

BASIC PRINCIPLES

Desire for peace

The day after the victory of the armed uprising in Petrograd, on November 8 (October 26, old calendar), 1917, V. I. Lenin, founder of the Soviet state, drew up drafts of the first decrees of the Soviet Government. One of these was the Decree on Peace. The Decree was adopted by the Second All-Russian Congress of Soviets that evening.

The government of workers and peasants created by the revolution of October 24–25 and supported by the Soviets of Workers', Soldiers' and Peasants' Deputies, proposes to all the belligerent nations and their governments that negotiations should start at once concerning a just and democratic peace,
the Decree stated.

This appeal, heard round the world at the height of a sanguinary world war, announced to the peoples that a completely new, hitherto unknown type of state had come into being, and with it a new kind of foreign policy. The Decree on Peace proclaimed the new and important principles of the foreign policy of the Soviet state. The struggle for peace was the first of these principles.

One of the basic principles of Soviet foreign policy is recognition of the sovereign right of every nation, large or small, to decide its own destiny. That principle, too, was set forth in the Decree on Peace.

Breaking with the traditions of bourgeois diplomacy, the Decree on Peace was an appeal to the peoples, as well as to governments. "We must help the peoples to intervene in questions of war and peace,"[1] said Lenin in presenting his draft of the Decree to the Congress of Soviets. And the peoples did intervene. Recent history is a picture of their growing struggle against the threat of war.

The profound historic idea lies in the fact that the first act of the Soviet state's foreign policy was dedicated to the struggle for peace. The Decree on Peace marked the beginning of the grand epic of the struggle of the socialist state against the forces of aggression and war.

The peace-loving nature of the foreign policy of the Soviet state, like that of any other socialist state, is not tactics, not a temporary, transient thing, but a permanent, indispensable characteristic of foreign policy, one determined by the existence of a socialist system.

To build socialism in a single country and, what is more, in a country as backward as Russia was up until 1917, the people had to concentrate exclusively on developing their economy and culture. They had to create a powerful industry, build factories, mines and mills, set up entire new industries, primarily a heavy industry, and basically to reconstruct and develop agriculture. War would only interfere with all that, and it did interfere with the building of socialism every time the Soviet state was forced to wage it, in 1918–1920 and in 1941–1945. It is perfectly obvious that without those two wars unleashed against us by the imperialists, the Soviet Union would have been able to improve to a far greater degree the well-being of its people and would have advanced much farther along the road to communism.

That the Soviet state and the Soviet people desire peace can hardly be denied, as the facts show. But perhaps there are factors in the Soviet Union which, running counter to the aims of building communism and raising living standards, create a personal interest in war? The answer is "NO." Such factors would be alien to the Soviet way of life.

In the Soviet socialist society there are no classes or groups of the population that derive profits from war orders or the arms drive. With the disappearance of the capitalist class, there disappears the profit incentive to wage war.

It is often claimed in the West that the Soviet state must wage war in order to implant socialism in other countries by force. But that is not true either. From the Marxist viewpoint—and that is the viewpoint by which the government of the U.S.S.R. is always guided—a revolution arises only as a result of far-reaching historical processes: the growth in the country of the class struggle, which is determined by the action of objective laws of social development. In his writings, Lenin gives a detailed analysis of when and under what conditions a revolutionary situation arises. He does not for a moment allow that a revolution can be made "to order."

In the early months of the Soviet system Lenin wrote, in a controversy with "Left-wing Communists"[2] that they

> believed the interests of an international revolution require that it must be *pushed* and that only war, but not peace, represents pushing of that kind. . . . Such a "theory" would be completely at variance with Marxism, which has always denied the "pushing" of a revolution, which develops to the degree that the acuteness of the class contradictions giving rise to revolution mature.[3]

The Soviet people, it goes without saying, are in full sympathy with progressive movements in other countries. But to sympathize, to give the Communist parties moral and ide-

---

[1] V. I. Lenin, *Works*, 5th ed. (Russian), vol. 26, p. 218.

[2] "Left-wing Communists" is what an anti-Party grouping within the Party headed by Bukharin called itself. This grouping was against the conclusion of peace with Germany, denied the possibility of peaceful co-existence, and supported the "pushing" of revolutions in other countries. It formed a bloc with Trotsky. It did not find support in the ranks of the Party and its views were condemned by the Seventh Party Congress in 1918.

[3] Lenin, *op. cit.*, vol. 27, p. 49.

ological support in their fight against capitalism, has nothing in common with attempts to make a revolution abroad "to order" by interfering in the affairs of another country. Communists are fully aware that it is impossible to make a revolution, even in one's own country, to say nothing of abroad, with the help of plots or upon orders.

Thus we see that war is not in the interests of the Soviet Union, that it is detrimental to those interests.

Co-existence with capitalist countries

Making the preservation of peace their goal, the Communist Party of the Soviet Union and the Government of the U.S.S.R. proceed from a recognition not only of the desirability but also the possibility of peaceful co-existence between the two opposing social systems. In 1917 capitalism ceased to be the only and predominant social system in the world. The October Socialist revolution ushered in an era of the co-existence of the two opposing social systems that has continued up to the present time.

For almost thirty years, a single socialist country existed alone within a capitalist encirclement. This specific condition of the co-existence of the two systems continued until the end of World War II, when a number of countries in Europe and Asia dropped out of the capitalist system, and the socialist system assumed a world character.

The co-existence of the two social systems is an objective fact. The question is: can that co-existence be peaceful? The division of the world into two opposing social systems back in 1917 imperatively posed the question of the relations between them.

Immediately after it came into being, the first socialist country advocated the establishment of peaceful relations with the capitalist countries. Since then, the Leninist principle of peaceful co-existence of the two social systems has unfailingly been the basic line of the for-

eign policy of the Communist Party and the Soviet Government.

However, in proposing the conclusion of a just, democratic peace, without annexations or indemnities, the Soviet Republic from the very beginning met with extreme hostility on the part of all the bourgeois countries. True, Germany, Austria, Hungary, Bulgaria and Turkey declared they were prepared to conclude peace without annexations or indemnities. But their agreement soon proved to be merely a screen behind which they had decided to dismember and plunder the territory of the former Russian empire. During negotiations between the Soviet delegation and the delegations of Germany and her allies at Brest-Litovsk in December 1917, the German representatives declared that Poland, Lithuania, a large part of Latvia, and part of Estonia, that is, regions occupied by Germany, must be detached from Russia.

What was the reaction of the Entente, the military bloc headed by Britain and France, which the United States joined in April 1917? Russia's former allies, who throughout World War I enjoyed the support of the Russian army, which came to their aid when the going was hardest, did not bother to reply to the Soviet Government's appeal to conclude a just peace, although the appeal was repeated several times. Nor did they reply to the proposal of the Soviet Government that economic ties should be developed.

Early in 1918 the Soviet Government had worked out a comprehensive plan for the development of economic relations with the United States. The plan was transmitted to the American government by Colonel Robins, head of the American Red Cross mission. It provided for the export from Russia of 3,000 million rubles worth of raw materials in 1918 alone and the purchase of goods to that amount in the U.S.; it gave Americans permission to exploit coal and other mine and marine riches, and to build railways, electric stations, canals, seaports, etc.

The Entente replied to the peaceable proposals of the Soviet Government with armed intervention aimed at restoring capitalism in Russia and dismembering the country. The aggressors' first objectives were the Caucasus, Central Asia and the Ukraine, which, if they were detached from Russia, would not be able to resist an Entente onslaught.

On December 23, 1917, the Entente leaders signed an agreement on the division of Russia into "spheres of action." After that they landed troops at Murmansk, Archangel, Vladivostok, Odessa, Baku and a number of other places. They also undertook the organization of internal counter-revolution in Russia.

The United States played an active part in the intervention by landing troops in the Russian Far East and in Northern Russia. The American troops conducted military operations against our country. Those facts were long remembered by the Russian people. They could not, naturally, but influence the attitude of the Soviet people toward the U.S. and the other Western Powers in the years that followed.

For three years the interventionists oppressed Russia, waged war against her, incited civil war, and inflicted losses amounting to 39,000 million gold rubles. Such was the answer given by the Entente Powers and the United States to the appeal of the Soviet Government to conclude peace. The initiative in the military trial of strength between the young socialist state and the capitalist world came from the Western Powers. They were beaten, however, in the battles that followed!

But to return to the question posed above. Is peaceful co-existence between the two opposing social systems possible? The answer, in the light of the experience of the first years of the Soviet Union, is: yes, it is fully possible. The facts prove that this is so. Indeed, after it had overcome its enemies, the Soviet state was able to ensure itself peace from 1921 to 1941, that is, for all of twenty years.

The basic principles and goals of the foreign policy of the socialist state took shape during the first few years of Soviet power. These principles are: recognition of the possibility and necessity of peaceful co-existence between countries with different social systems, strict observance of the standards of international law, respect for national sovereignty, recognition of the equality of all nations, large or small, refusal to interfere in the affairs of other countries. All these principles can be combined under a single word—Peace.

ECONOMIC CO-OPERATION WITH CAPITALIST COUNTRIES

After Soviet Russia had won peace for itself by routing the interventionists, the aim of Soviet foreign policy became to preserve it for as long as possible.

In the years of peace the Soviet people built up a heavy industry of their own, carried through the collectivization of agriculture, and built a socialist society. From the ruined, famine-stricken country Russia had been, following the imperialist and civil wars and the foreign intervention, it developed during the years of peace into a great industrial, socialist Power. If the Soviet people had not managed to ensure the preservation of peace during twenty years, all those achievements would, of course, have been impossible.

The government of the Soviet Republic strove to make peace with the capitalist countries as stable as possible. To that end it sought broad agreements with them that would settle the main controversial issues.

Trade agreements with Western countries

On March 16, 1921, a trade agreement was signed with Britain. That was followed during 1921–1922 by trade agreements with Austria, Germany, Italy, Czechoslovakia and other countries. The All-Russian Central Executive Committee, the highest organ of power in Soviet Russia, likewise proposed restoration of trade relations to the United States. The U.S. government rejected the proposal, however, declaring restoration of trade would be possible only if "basic changes," meaning, of course,

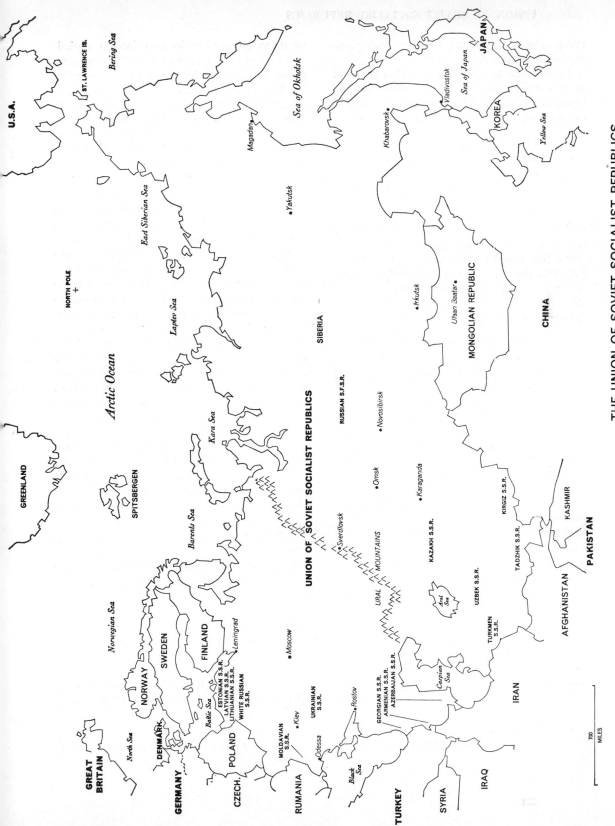

THE UNION OF SOVIET SOCIALIST REPUBLICS

restoration of the capitalist system, took place in Soviet Russia.

In its desire to achieve a general adjustment of relations with capitalist countries, the government of Soviet Russia proposed a speedy convocation of an international conference

> to examine the demands made by other powers on the Russian government and the demands made by the Russian government on other powers and to draw up a final peace treaty.[4]

At Genoa, the Soviet Government attempted to reach a broad agreement with the capitalist world that might serve as the foundation for a long and durable peace and mutually advantageous economic co-operation. It proclaimed the principle of the peaceful co-existence of the socialist and capitalist countries:

> While adhering to the principles of communism, the Russian delegation recognizes that in the present historical period, which makes possible the parallel existence of the old system and the new socialist system that has arisen, economic co-operation between countries representing these two systems of property is imperatively necessary for general economic restoration.[5]

The Soviet Government likewise proposed a universal reduction in armaments. It is regrettable that this proposal did not get the support of the other Powers. Nonetheless, it had genuine historical significance inasmuch as it marked the beginning of the efforts for disarmament which the Soviet Government is still carrying on today.

Thus, the Soviet program at Genoa proclaimed economic co-operation, disarmament, and peace. To achieve those goals, the Soviet Government was willing to make big concessions to the capitalists. It agreed to recognize the prewar foreign debts of the Tsarist government, to give concessions to foreign capitalists, and to relinquish its legal claims to compensation for losses inflicted on the country by the Entente intervention. In return, the Soviet Government asked for a loan to be used to restore the economy of Soviet Russia, which had been ruined by two wars, the world war and the civil war, and, secondly, juridical recognition of the Soviet Government.

Representatives of the Entente rejected that program of peaceful co-existence and economic co-operation. All the same, the Soviet Government was able by that time to break the economic blockade organized by the West.

At the Genoa conference a Soviet-German agreement was concluded—the Rapallo treaty named after the Genoa suburb of Rapallo where it was signed. The treaty put an end to reciprocal financial claims of the two countries. It established further that "diplomatic and consular relations between Germany and the Russian Federation are immediately to be resumed."[6] Steps to develop Russo-German economic relations were also examined. Since then the expression "spirit of Rapallo" has been commonly used to signify a policy of peace, an independent political course for each partner, and relations based on equality and mutual advantage. It was on those terms that the Soviet Government endeavored to establish peaceful co-existence with every capitalist country. It proved impossible at the Genoa conference to reach similar treaties with the other capitalist countries. They continued their attempts to organize intervention, economic pressure and boycott, to create diplomatic isolation, and to employ ultimatums and threats of force.

Agreements with Eastern countries

From the earliest days of its existence the Soviet Government worked to establish friendly

---

[4] *Izvestia,* Oct. 29, 1921.
[5] *Foreign Policy of the U.S.S.R.,* Col. Doc. vol. II, p. 290.

[6] *Foreign Policy of the U.S.S.R.,* Col. Doc. vol. II, p. 297.

and equal relations with economically under-developed countries that were dependent on the West. Especially great efforts were made to establish such relations with its neighbors. From the very beginning the Soviet state based its relations with all peoples on the principles of recognition of the right of each nation to self-determination, the equality of all peoples, strict noninterference in the internal affairs of other nations, and unconditional rejection of all forms of national oppression. Those principles were embodied, in 1921, in treaties which Soviet Russia concluded with Iran, Afghanistan and Turkey.

The Soviet Government gave up all claims, without compensation, to loans which Tsarism had granted to Iran, as well as all concessions, privileges and financial undertakings by Tsarist Russia that had been aimed at enslaving Iran. The treaties with Afghanistan and Turkey were permeated with the same deep respect for the freedom and independence of the peoples. They were the first equitable treaties those countries had ever concluded with a great European Power. The same is true of the treaty which the U.S.S.R. concluded with China three years later.

Russia's struggle for recognition of the full equality of its peoples, the granting of independence to Finland, and recognition of the independence of Poland, all made the Soviet Government a powerful bulwark of the national liberation movement that was rapidly developing among the oppressed peoples. This movement was inspired by the experience of the Russian revolution and the victory over intervention.

The peoples of the East highly appreciated the aid given them by the Soviet Government. Their feelings were reflected in the many statements made by leaders of the national liberation movement of the twenties. Kemal Ataturk, founder of the Turkish Republic, wrote the Soviet Government in 1920: "It gives me the greatest pleasure to tell you of the admiration in which the Turkish people hold the Russian people."[7]

[7] *Izvestia,* Dec. 5, 1920.

The very fact of the existence of the Soviet state as a powerful, anti-imperialist force helped the peoples of the East to ensure their independence. In laying the foundations of friendship between the peoples of the U.S.S.R. and the countries of the East, Soviet foreign policy laid one of the cornerstones of universal peace and security.

Recognition and disarmament

The growth of the economic and military might of the Soviet Union, its invariable love of peace, the interest of certain capitalist circles in economic ties with the Soviet Union, and the friendly attitude of the working class abroad towards the first socialist state, all led to the growth of the international influence of the U.S.S.R. As a result, a considerable number of capitalist countries had to give up their policy of not recognizing the U.S.S.R. and established diplomatic relations with it.

In 1924 the Soviet Union was recognized *de jure* by Britain, France, Italy and a number of other countries, and in 1925 by Japan. Since Germany had done that earlier, the U.S.S.R. was by then recognized by all the Great Powers except the U.S. For another ten years the U.S. government persisted in not recognizing the first socialist state. Only in 1933 did it give up that policy thanks to the astuteness of President Franklin D. Roosevelt. President Roosevelt realized that the U.S.S.R. was growing in stature and strength, irrespective of whether the United States recognized it or not.

In the second half of the 'twenties and the early 'thirties, the Soviet Government continued to work for disarmament. In 1927 it submitted before the preparatory commission for a disarmament conference a draft plan for universal and complete disarmament. The proposal made a tremendous impression on the world democratic public.

It was rejected by the capitalist countries, after which the Soviet Government submitted for the commission, in 1928, a plan for partial disarmament. This, too was turned down. The Soviet Government, however, continued to uphold the idea of disarmament in the preparatory commission and at the disarmament conference itself, which opened in 1932, and held sessions until 1934 without achieving any results.

THE FIGHT AGAINST THE THREAT OF FASCIST AGGRESSION

The establishment of a Fascist dictatorship in Germany greatly complicated the international situation. At approximately the same time, the influence of the extreme militarists grew stronger in Japan where things were, to all intents and purposes, close to fascism.

The Fascists launched a furious campaign of propaganda against the Soviet Union and communism and openly called for war against the U.S.S.R. Fascist aggression grew greater and greater with each passing year. War was being fought in China, Ethiopia, and Spain and was gradually spreading, threatening to develop into another world war.

Collective security

The Soviet Government tried to save its own country and all mankind from the calamity of war and help those peoples that had become victims of aggression to uphold their independence. Guided by those aims, it energetically supported the idea of creating a system of collective security. At the foundation of Soviet projects for the organization of collective security lay the idea that all the countries of a geographical region should join together to repulse any aggression.

In 1934 the Soviet Union and France presented the draft of a treaty dealing with the collective insurance of security in Europe, known as the Eastern Pact. Treaty members were to be the U.S.S.R., France, and all the countries of Central and Eastern Europe. The failure of that project, due to the joint efforts of Britain and Hitler Germany, was a great misfortune. After it became clear that the project for the unification of a broad circle of European countries to fight against aggression had failed, the Soviet Government in 1935 concluded treaties of mutual assistance with France and Czechoslovakia. If the terms of those treaties had been applied, a sufficiently strong barrier to Hitlerite aggression would have been created.

Action through the League of Nations

In 1934 the Soviet Union joined the League of Nations.

In the League of Nations the Soviet Government boldly and consistently supported the countries that had fallen victim to Fascist aggression, among them China, Ethiopia and Spain. Although Fascist aggression did damage to their interests as well, the Western Powers refused to take effective measures against it. They adopted a policy of "non-intervention," which actually was the same as conniving at aggression. In March 1938, after the Hitlerites seized Austria, the Soviet Union proposed immediate discussion, within the League of Nations or outside it, of the joint measures needed to prevent new acts of aggression.

Although this proposal did not gain the support of the Western Powers, the Soviet Government took new steps towards acting together with Britain, France and the U.S. against the aggressor. It publicly emphasized time and again that it would fulfil all the obligations stemming from the Soviet-Czechoslovak treaty on mutual aid. Under the treaty, the Soviet Union was to give Czechoslovakia military assistance in case of aggression, if France would do the same.

In this connection the Soviet Government proposed calling a conference of representatives of the armed forces of the U.S.S.R., France, and Czechoslovakia to determine in detail the forms and nature of co-operation among the three countries. President Beneš of Czechoslovakia was informed by the Soviet side that the U.S.S.R. was prepared to go to the aid of Czechoslovakia alone, that is, even if France should not go to her aid, providing, of course, that Czechoslovakia asked the U.S.S.R. for help and herself resisted the aggressor. A request for aid never came from Beneš, however. He preferred to capitulate rather than to put up resistance to German aggression.

The Munich settlement

The ruling circles of Britain and France rejected the Soviet proposal on aid to Czechoslovakia. Instead of helping her they agreed, at a conference in Munich at the end of September 1938, to dismember the country and hand over a number of important border regions to Germany.

The Munich-men, supporters of the "policy of non-intervention," had very definite aims in view when they made a deal with Hitlerite Germany. They counted on placating the Hitlerites and persuading them not to infringe on the interests of Britain and France. At the same time, this would demonstrate the isolation of the Soviet Union and in that way direct Fascist aggression to the East, against the U.S.S.R.

Here the governments of the Western Powers hoped to kill two birds with one stone: Germany would weaken and perhaps even destroy the Soviet Union and together with it the socialist system, while the Soviet Union, which would be sure to put up stubborn resistance, would weaken Germany as a dangerous competitor. The British government headed by Chamberlain was the inspirer of that pro-Fascist and anti-Soviet Munich policy.

Nor should the regrettable fact be forgotten that many influential representatives of U.S. ruling circles sympathized with the Munich

policy. Secretary of State Hull was no exception as he himself says in his memoirs.

Roosevelt tried to paralyze an Anglo-German rapprochement. He made anti-Fascist declarations. A Congressional majority, however, successfully prevented the President from going farther than verbal statements and taking more effective measures against the Fascist aggressors.

Soon after the Munich conference the Soviet Union proved to be in a very difficult position. On December 6, 1938, came a Franco-German agreement. An Anglo-German declaration signed on September 30, 1938, immediately after the Munich conference, destroyed the hope that Britain would take part in military actions to curb German aggression. To all intents and purposes both the Anglo-German and the Franco-German declarations represented treaties of non-aggression.

After Munich the Soviet Union found itself isolated. Britain and France were obviously evading any counteraction to Hitler's aggression. They sought agreement with the Hitlerites and tried to set them on the U.S.S.R. For the sake of a compact with them, they were ready to give Germany entire countries or else a significant share of the territory of those countries. The idea behind the policy of the Western Powers was to have the Fascists unleash a war against the land of socialism as soon as possible and to avoid a war within the capitalist world.

Hitler violated the agreement reached at Munich, which provided for preservation of the remnants of a Czechoslovak state. The Hitlerites invaded Czechoslovakia on March 15, 1939, and occupied the whole of it, completely destroying Czechoslovak independence. It was obvious that the Hitlerites had no intention of considering their partners in the Munich conference, adhering to the pledges made to Britain and France or, even more, co-ordinating their actions with them. It was clear that the Western Powers had failed to achieve a solid compact with German fascism.

Nor was that all. The consequences of Munich and Franco's victory over the Spanish Republic early in 1939 weakened the British and French position. Among democratic circles in the West the Munich policy was often regarded as treachery. Demands that the aggressor be repulsed grew louder and louder. It was in such a situation that the governments of Britain and France proposed to the Soviet Government that negotiations start on collaboration in a fight against German aggression.

Anglo-French-Russian negotiations

What was the attitude of the Government of the U.S.S.R. to that proposal? The U.S.S.R. agreed to the Anglo-French proposal concerning negotiations. It did not want to miss a single chance of organizing resistance to the aggressor. If it had been possible to create an anti-Hitlerite coalition of the three Great Powers in 1939, it is highly probable that Hitler Germany could have been prevented from violating the peace. It is hardly likely that the Hitlerites would have dared to embark on new acts of aggression in the face of such a powerful coalition.

However, the entire course of the Anglo-French-Soviet talks showed that the Western Powers had not given up their efforts to direct Hitler's aggression against the U.S.S.R. What they wanted was to secure guarantees of support on the part of the U.S.S.R. in case Germany went to war against the West. But they did not want to give the Soviet Union similar guarantees. That became especially clear during the negotiations carried on by the military missions of Britain, France and the U.S.S.R. in Moscow in August 1939.

From the top secret instructions, now made public, which the British military mission was given in London before leaving for Moscow, it is clear that the British government did not want to reach an agreement with the U.S.S.R. on ways of jointly repulsing the Hitlerite aggressors and that it had decided not to conclude such an agreement. The British government, the instructions said, did not wish to assume any definite commitments.

Nor could the Soviet Government ignore newspaper reports of talks between Britain and Germany concerning a big British loan for Hitler Germany. We now know from the documents of Dirksen, the German Ambassador in London, that those reports had foundation. Simultaneously with the three-Power negotiations in Moscow, highly secret Anglo-German separate talks were taking place in London. The British government proposed to the Hitlerites "far-reaching plans for Anglo-German cooperation aimed at opening up new world markets and exploiting the existing markets" and their division on a world-wide scale. Among the territories to be divided, the British side had named China and the Soviet Union,[8] although at that moment the British government was negotiating with the latter on a joint struggle against Fascist aggression!

If a general understanding was reached between Britain and Germany, the British promised to let the Hitlerites take Poland, in violation of all the guarantees Britain had recently given Poland. "Sir Horace Wilson, who was close to Prime Minister Chamberlain," reported von Dirksen, the German Ambassador in London,

> has definitely told Wohltat [the German representative-author] that conclusion of a non-aggression pact would give Britain the opportunity to free herself of the obligations to Poland.[9]

As for the talks with the U.S.S.R., the British promised to break them off.[10]

From all this it is quite obvious that both the guarantees to Poland and the talks with the Soviet Government were small change which the British government was prepared to sacrifice for the sake of an agreement with German fascism. The British government did not want an agreement with the U.S.S.R. All it wanted

---

[8] *Eve of World War II. Documents and Materials,* volume II, Dirksen's Archives, Moscow, 1948, p. 217. (In Russian.)

[9] *Ibid.,* p. 133.

[10] *Ibid.,* p. 219.

was negotiations over an agreement that might make Hitler more compliant to Britain.

The non-aggression treaty with Germany

To sum up, what was the Soviet Union's international position in 1939? On the western borders of the U.S.S.R., war threatened to break out at any moment. By marching through Poland and the Baltic states the German army could be at the borders of the U.S.S.R. within a few days; at that time the borders ran close to Leningrad and Minsk. At the Far Eastern borders of the U.S.S.R., war was actually in progress. In 1938 the Japanese militarists had invaded Soviet territory in the region of Lake Khasan, not far from Vladivostok. They were driven from Soviet territory by the Red Army.

In May 1939 came new trouble-making by Japanese imperialism, this time directed against the Mongolian People's Republic. Japanese troops had invaded the territory of the republic in the region of the river Khalkhin-Gol. Since 1936 the Soviet Union had had a mutual assistance treaty with the Mongolian People's Republic. Always true to its commitments, the Soviet Union sent troops to help the republic. In the summer of 1939, at the height of the Anglo-French-Soviet talks and the German-Polish conflict, the Red Army was engaged in heavy fighting against considerable forces of the Japanese army in the Far East, in the Khalkhin-Gol River district.

The Soviet Union was thus faced with the prospect of simultaneously waging war on two fronts, in Europe and in the Far East, surrounded by a completely hostile capitalist encirclement and lacking allies. The Soviet Government had to do everything possible to save its people from such a danger. In this complicated situation the Government of the U.S.S.R. received a German proposal to conclude a non-aggression treaty.

After the Munich deal, after the Western Powers had let the Fascists smash the Spanish Republic, after negotiations with Britain and France had reached a deadlock owing to their unwillingness to collaborate with the U.S.S.R., after information was received of the secret negotiations between Germany and Britain and, finally, after the Japanese attack in the Khalkhin-Gol region, the Soviet Government, having tried absolutely everything in its efforts to guarantee the security of the U.S.S.R. and to consolidate universal peace in co-operation with the Western Powers, became convinced that this was utterly impossible. The Soviet Government, therefore, decided to accept the German proposal, which, for a time, would save the U.S.S.R. from the threat of fighting a war on two fronts simultaneously without allies and give the country time to strengthen its defenses. The Soviet Government agreed to conclude a treaty with Germany only after it was clear that Britain and France did not wish to join the U.S.S.R. in repulsing Hitlerite aggression.

On September 1, 1939, Germany attacked Poland. After that Britain and France entered the war. War was already raging in Asia and Africa, and now it had flared up in the heart of Europe.

It was perfectly obvious that Germany was preparing to attack the Soviet Union. Under those circumstances the Soviet Government took a number of measures which, the future showed, helped to a certain degree to repel Hitlerite aggression. The Soviet Union sent its troops into the Western Ukraine and Western Byelorussia, which Poland had at one time seized, and thus prevented Germany from capturing the whole of Polish territory. At that time Churchill stated, for instance, that the liberation of Western Byelorussia and the Western Ukraine by Soviet troops was "absolutely necessary for the security of Russia in the face of the fascist threat."

Soviet foreign policy was faced with similar tasks in the Baltic area. For their part, the peoples of the Baltic countries did not want to live under a Fascist yoke. Salvation lay only in returning to the bosom of the Soviet state from which Latvia, Estonia and Lithuania had been forcibly torn by the Entente imperialists in 1919 with the help of German troops. Forcibly and contrary to the will of the peoples! That this is true can be seen from the results of the elections to the Constituent Assembly in November 1917, when in Latvia, for example, the Bolsheviks received 72 percent of the votes.

Now the peoples of the three Baltic republics overthrew their pro-Fascist governments and demanded re-union with the U.S.S.R., which took place in 1940. Bessarabia, which had also been forcibly taken away from Soviet Russia in 1918, rejoined the Soviet Union at the same time.

Meanwhile the Hitlerites, after pausing for a short time following their seizure of Poland, started in the spring of 1940 to overrun one country after another.

The Soviet Government endeavored in every way to prevent the spread of war and aggression to new areas. It succeeded in doing so in relation to Sweden. In April 1940, the Soviet Government indicated to the Hitler government that it was interested in Sweden's neutrality not being violated. The Hitlerites were forced to heed the warning.

After that the Soviet Government endeavored to hinder Hitler's invasion of the Balkans. It pointed out to the Hitlerites that the occupation of Bulgaria and other Balkan countries and the appearance of German troops in Finland would be regarded by the Soviet Union as a threat to its security. The negotiations between the U.S.S.R. and Germany in 1940, no matter what form they took, had as their actual purpose prevention of the seizure of the Balkans by Hitler Germany and at the same time elucidation of the plans and intentions of the Hitlerites.

But the Soviet Union did not succeed in saving the Balkan countries from being captured by Hitlerite Germany. This time the Hitlerites did not heed the Soviet warnings, as they had done in the case of Sweden. In the summer of 1940 they decided to begin war against the U.S.S.R.

After seizing almost all the capitalist countries on the European continent, Hitlerite Germany came into possession of vast material resources. Furthermore, the large number of easy successes had turned the heads of Hitler and his associates. They imagined that they would be able to overcome the U.S.S.R. in the same way they had conquered the countries of Western Europe.

THE GREAT PATRIOTIC WAR AGAINST THE FASCIST INVADERS

At the time it attacked the Soviet Union, Hitlerite Germany had subjugated almost the entire continent of Europe. The countries whose resources Germany had at her disposal produced, in 1940, about 45,000,000 tons of steel and 400,000,000 tons of coal—so great were Hitler's means when he attacked the Soviet Union. In 1940 the Soviet Union produced 18,300,000 tons of steel and 165,900,000 tons of coal.

In estimating the correlation of the economic and military might of the Hitlerite coalition and the Soviet Union, we cannot limit ourselves to a comparison of naked figures showing the volume of output and the number of divisions or aircraft. With its planned economy, the socialist system creates the conditions for an incomparably more productive utilization of all material resources than is possible under capitalism.

Initial reverses

After France's capitulation, military operations on land in the West ceased. Hence, the Hitlerites were able to concentrate against the Soviet Union the main mass of the armed forces of Germany and her satellites, totalling more than 190 divisions having the latest equipment and powerful tank forces—3,500 tanks and more than 50,000 guns and trench mortars. The major share of the German air force—more than 60 percent—acted in coordination with these ground troops. In all of history there is no instance of such a colossal mass of men and material ever having been concentrated to carry out a strategic task.

The nonaggression treaty with Germany enabled the Soviet Union to gain some time to increase the country's defensive capacity. Much was accomplished, but the Soviet Union did not manage to complete its preparations for defense by the summer of 1941.

The suddenness of the German attack, due in great measure to Stalin's miscalculations of the time of the expected invasion, enabled the Hitlerites to achieve important successes. The Soviet armies were forced to retreat and German troops occupied an extensive territory. But the Hitlerites were unable to smash the resistance of the U.S.S.R. The giant death-dealing machine of the Hitlerite armed forces, which had swept the armies of the West European countries out of its path, misfired for the first time on the plains of Russia. The land of socialism withstood the impact of that machine, although two of the imperialist Great Powers of the West had been unable to do so. With their victories at Moscow, Stalingrad (now Volgograd) and in the Kursk bulge the Soviet armed forces inscribed wonderful pages in the history of warfare.

The contribution of the Western Allies

The Anglo-Soviet-American coalition formed after the U.S.S.R. entered the war is an example of close collaboration among countries with different social systems. The creation of the anti-Hitlerite coalition and its practical activity show how correct is the idea by which Soviet foreign policy is constantly guided— that such co-operation is possible if both sides want it. The formation of the anti-Hitlerite coalition implemented the idea of a joint rebuff to the aggressor for which the Soviet Government had worked during the prewar years.

Immediately after the German attack, the governments of Britain and the United States declared they would help the Soviet Union in the war. On July 12, 1941, an agreement between the Soviet and British governments on joint action in the war against Germany was signed. Later, on May 26, 1942, the U.S.S.R. and Britain signed an agreement on alliance in the war against Hitler Germany and her accomplices in Europe and on co-operation and mutual aid after the war.

The United States did not conclude a treaty of alliance with the U.S.S.R. The two countries limited themselves to an agreement on the principles to be followed in giving mutual assistance in waging war against the aggressor, an agreement devoted in the main to regulating the procedure for furnishing American military supplies. Although in content the Soviet-American agreement was far narrower than the Soviet-British treaty of alliance, it was also evidence of close co-operation between the U.S.S.R. and its allies. It confirmed the possibility of co-operation between countries with different social systems.

The Soviet people waged the war against nazism to uphold their independence and freedom and also to deliver the peoples of Europe from Hitlerite domination. The Soviet Union did not carry on the war against Hitlerism alone. Many freedom-loving peoples fought side by side with it. The United States and Britain also fought against Hitlerite Germany. But it was the Soviet Union that made the decisive contribution to victory over Hitlerism. None other than Churchill confirmed that. "The Red Army," he wrote in February 1945, "celebrates its twenty-seventh anniversary amid triumphs which have won the unstinted applause of their allies and have sealed the doom of German militarism."[11]

It was the operations on the Soviet-German front that decided the outcome of World War II. This was the main front of the war. Its decisive significance is confirmed by the fact that, throughout the war, Hitlerite Germany's

[11] Correspondence between the Chairman of the Council of Ministers of the U.S.S.R. and the Presidents of the U.S.A. and the Prime Ministers of Great Britain during the Great Patriotic War of 1941–1945, vol. I, p. 305.

main ground and air forces were concentrated against the Soviet Union.

In 1942 about 80 percent of Germany's land forces—178 divisions and 8 brigades out of 232 divisions and 12 brigades—and 4 out of 6 air fleets, as well as the forces of Germany's allies, faced the Soviet Army.

Even in summer 1944, when the "Second Front" finally emerged, there were 228 enemy divisions and 13 brigades at the Soviet-German front, whereas the Germans had 60 divisions in the West. By the time the second front was finally opened in France in 1944 after endless delays, Germany had actually already been smashed in the East by the Soviet forces.

Attempts have been made to belittle the Soviet Union's part in the defeat of fascism in World War II, and to minimize the Soviet people's sacrifices to deliver mankind from the Fascist fiends. The main argument usually advanced is that the Soviet Union would not have been able to defeat the Hitlerites without the U.S. lend-lease shipments of armaments and various other supplies. The fact is, however, that all the manufactured articles shipped by the Allies throughout the war amounted to only four per cent of the Soviet industrial output. Of course, the shipments helped the Soviet Union to fight the war, but they were incapable of influencing the outcome decisively.

The second front in Europe

Inasmuch as the Soviet Union had taken on itself the main burden of the war of liberation against fascism, victory over Germany and the end of the tremendous bloodshed could have been hastened above all by lightening the Soviet people's burden. The most effective way would have been for the United States and Britain to open the second front in France at the earliest possible date. If that had been done in time, the contribution by the two Western Powers to the liberation of mankind from fascism would indeed have been great. Unfortunately, that was not the case.

In violation of the official and unconditional obligations which the American and British governments had undertaken towards the Soviet Union, they did not open the second front even in 1943. In an Aide-Mémoire dated June 10, 1942, the British Government said:

> . . . we are concentrating our maximum effort on the organization and preparation of a large-scale invasion of the Continent of Europe by British and American forces in 1943.[12]

This commitment was confirmed by the United States in a joint message from the U.S. President and the British Prime Minister to the Chairman of the Council of People's Commissars of the U.S.S.R. on January 26, 1943. In this letter, a definite obligation was undertaken to land large forces in France in August or September of 1943. This was a clear and official commitment, binding both juridically and morally on the governments of the United States and Great Britain, but they did not carry it out. The flouting by the Allies of their commitments meant protraction of the war, frustrating the Soviet Government's efforts for a speedy victory and the establishment of peace.

The Soviet people were fighting for their very existence and were being bled white on all the fronts stretching from the Arctic Ocean to the Black Sea. The enemy had approached close to Moscow, the heart of our country; besieged Leningrad was starving. It is not surprising that the Soviet people and the Soviet Army regarded the repeated delays in opening the second front as a move by the American and British governments to save their own forces and at the same time to weaken their ally, the U.S.S.R., to a great degree, so that the Soviet people should suffer the maximum losses and become dependent on the United States and Britain after the war. Such a goal had been publicly confirmed by Harry Truman when still a Senator. "If we see," said Truman, "that Germany is winning, we ought to help

[12] *Ibid.*, vol. I, p. 385, note 23.

Russia, and if Russia is winning, we ought to help Germany, that way let them kill as many as possible."[13] Analogous statements were made by some members of the ruling circles of Britain. It goes without saying that the constant delays in opening the second front, plus statements like the above, cut the Soviet people to the quick.

The opening of the second front was dragged out until a time when the defeat of Hitler Germany was already assured even without it, thanks to the victories of the Soviet Army. In 1944 the American and British ruling circles were not concerned with alleviating the position of the Soviet Union—which by now had ceased to be in need of such an alleviation—but with occupying as large a part of Europe as possible and bringing it under their influence before the inevitable collapse of the Hitlerites. The delays of the American and British governments in opening the second front in France cost the Soviet people enormous losses.

The defeat of Germany and Japan

After liberating its native land the Soviet Army continued to push forward. In the second half of 1944 and the beginning of 1945, it drove the Fascist invaders from Rumania, Bulgaria, Poland, Czechoslovakia, Hungary, Austria and the northern part of Norway. Its successes preordained the liberation of the whole of Europe from the occupying forces.

As soon as the countries liberated by the Soviet forces ceased to be in the zone of direct military operations, the Soviet command transferred the entire civil administration to the local national authorities. This was done in conformity with the Soviet Union's foreign policy principle of noninterference in the domestic affairs of other countries. In this way the Soviet Union created important requisites for a lasting peace.

[13] *New York Times,* June 24, 1941.

With the defeat of Hitlerite Germany, and of Japan three months later, the aggressors who had violated peace throughout the world were smashed. World War II ended under conditions in which all the victorious Great Powers were allies. All this created, it would have seemed, the possibility of a really lasting peace.

That was precisely what the Soviet Union desired. Its aims in the war had been to "free the peoples of Europe from Fascist oppression" and help them "to regain their freedom and independence . . . by giving them the full right to choose the state system they desired." At the same time, the Soviet Union wanted "to see a situation in Europe that would completely exclude the possibility of further aggression by Germany" and would guarantee lasting economic, political and cultural co-operation among the peoples of Europe on the basis of mutual trust and mutual assistance." The Soviet Union desired to achieve these aims jointly with its allies—Britain, the United States and France. It regarded collaboration of this kind as the best means of consolidating peace in Europe and the world.

These aims were made public on the occasion of the 26th anniversary of the October Revolution. Thanks to the efforts of the Soviet Government, these aims were reflected in the joint decisions the three leading Powers of the anti-Hitlerite coalition—the U.S.S.R., the United States and Great Britain—took during the war. The Moscow conference of the three Foreign Ministers in October 1943 established that the three governments were unanimous about continuing in the postwar period the close collaboration which had taken shape during the war.

A declaration of four countries (including China) was adopted about universal security, outlining joint actions in the organization and maintenance of peace and security after the war. This declaration recognized the necessity of establishing an international organization for the maintenance of peace and security, later founded as the United Nations. The declaration pointed to the need for co-operation with a view to general agreement on disarmament. Declarations on Italy and Austria were also adopted. They outlined joint co-ordinated policy with regard to these countries.

At their conference in Teheran, November 28–December 1, 1943, the Big Three confirmed the resolve of the United States, Britain and the U.S.S.R. to "work together in war and in the peace that will follow."[14]

At a conference of the Big Three, held in Yalta, in the Crimea, in February 1945, when the defeat of Hitlerite Germany was already near, problems relating to the establishment of a lasting peace after the war were discussed. The representatives of the three Powers agreed on a common policy concerning the unconditional surrender of Nazi Germany. The "inflexible purpose" of the Allies was declared to be "to destroy German militarism and nazism and to ensure that Germany will never again be able to disturb the peace of the world."[15] It was decided to disarm and disband all German armed forces, to break up for all time the German General Staff, to eliminate or control all German industry that could be used for military production, to bring all war criminals to just and swift punishment, and to wipe out the Nazi party, the Nazi laws, organizations and institutions. It was agreed that Germany should pay reparations in view of the tremendous damage she had inflicted on other countries.

Agreement was reached on major questions concerning the United Nations, namely, the principle of unanimity of the voting of the five permanent members of the Security Council— the Soviet Union, the United States, Great Britain, France and China—was established. At the Yalta Conference it was agreed that two or three months after Germany's surrender the Soviet Union would enter the war against Japan. Agreement was reached that the Russian territory of Southern Sakhalin, which had been seized by the Japanese, would be returned to the Soviet Union, and that the Kuril Islands,

which also had belonged to Russia since ancient times, would be turned over to the Soviet Union.

After Hitler Germany attacked the Soviet Union, the Japanese militarists also prepared to attack it. But they decided to wait for further successes by the German Fascists. It was only the turn in hostilities on the Soviet-German front in favor of the U.S.S.R. that held the Japanese rulers back from aggression against the Soviet Union. Throughout the war, however, the Japanese kept their best ground forces, the Kwangtung Army, in Manchuria, thus threatening the Soviet Union's security in the Far East and thereby helping Germany.

In the course of the Soviet-German war, the Japanese militarists provoked incidents on the Soviet-Manchurian border, violated the freedom of navigation in Far Eastern waters, and wrung various concessions from the Soviet Union. From these facts alone it is clear that Japan pursued a most unfriendly policy towards the Soviet Union in gross violation of the Soviet-Japanese Treaty of Neutrality of April 13, 1941, Article I of which bound the two sides to "maintain peaceful and friendly relations."[16] Furthermore, Japan was at war with the Soviet Union's allies. In view of all that, the Soviet Government denounced the Soviet-Japanese Treaty of Neutrality in full accordance with the denunciation procedure stipulated in the treaty. The Soviet Union carried out to the letter the commitments it had undertaken towards its allies at the Yalta Conference. On August 9, 1945, it declared war on Japan.

Until the Soviet Union's entry into the war, the United States had borne the brunt of the military operations against Japan, which were waged chiefly at sea and around naval bases. Japan retained large ground forces both on the islands and on the mainland of Asia. In connection with that, the Anglo-American command had planned to carry out large-scale operations against Japan in the second half of 1945 and in 1946. Churchill assumed that the

[14] *Foreign Relations of the United States. The Conferences at Cairo and Teheran,* Washington: 1961, p. 640.

[15] *Foreign Relations of the United States. The Conferences of Malta and Yalta,* Washington: 1945, p. 970.

[16] *Foreign Policy of the U.S.S.R.,* Coll. Document, vol. IV, p. 550.

war against Japan might end only in 1947. The United States and British governments were therefore extremely desirous of the Soviet Union's aid in the war against Japan. That is admitted by President Truman in his memoirs[17] and by other American and British statesmen.

By a swift and powerful blow the Soviet forces smashed the Kwangtung Army in Manchuria. This made further resistance by Japan hopeless and predetermined her surrender. In the light of the above, the two atom bombs which the United States dropped on Japan did not, in substance, change anything. Japanese militarism had already been crushed by that time.

The Soviet Union's wartime collaboration with the Western countries and the joint Allied decisions should have ensured universal peace and security if, of course, the decisions were carried out to the letter by all their signatories.

THE STRUGGLE FOR PEACE IMMEDIATELY AFTER WORLD WAR II

The Soviet Union has had to conduct its fight for peace since the close of World War II under conditions radically different from those prevailing on the eve of the war. The most aggressive imperialist Powers—Germany, Italy and Japan—had suffered defeat. The Soviet Union's influence, on the other hand, had soared, not only because of the tremendous military and political power which had enabled it to crush Hitlerite Germany, but also because the nations justly saw it now as their deliverer from the horrors of Fascist slavery, as the savior of their freedom and of world civilization. On liberating the peoples of Europe, the Soviet Union gave them every opportunity to decide their own fate and so acted in a spirit of genuine internationalism.

---

[17] H. S. Truman. *Memoirs*, vol. I, Garden City: Doubleday, 1955, p. 411.

The end of the war was accompanied by another break, the second since 1917, in the capitalist system and capitalism's loss of quite a number of countries. People's democratic government was established in those countries, and they embarked upon the road of socialist construction.

Western propaganda tries to depict those events as the result of "interference from Moscow." But that is not the case. The countries of central and southeast Europe, China, and several other Asian countries have been the scene of events which have radically changed the face of a large part of our planet, as well as the destinies of vast human masses. Such profound changes in the life of peoples do not take place accidentally and cannot be instigated at will or through intrigues of any other countries. The breaking away of many countries from the capitalist system derives from the operation of the inner laws of capitalism and has resulted in a general crisis of the capitalist system. In the first stage of that crisis, during World War I, Russia broke away from the capitalist system.

As a result of World War II and the new upheavals which beset the capitalist system, it lost a number of countries in central and southeast Europe. The democratic forces headed by the Communists came out during the war as fighters against the Fascist invaders, and that heightened the political organization and prestige of those forces, especially of the Communist parties. A powerful anti-Fascist movement swept all the countries of central and southeast Europe.

Even before the war, the Communists were very influential in a number of the countries that have since left the capitalist system—Bulgaria, Czechoslovakia, etc. Most of the local bourgeoisie and land-owners of those countries were hopelessly compromised by their acts of national treason and collaboration with fascism. The ruling classes could not go on governing in the old way. Thus the breaking away of Poland, Czechoslovakia, Hungary, Rumania, Bulgaria, Yugoslavia and Albania from the capitalist system was deep-rooted in their inner development.

The role of the Soviet Union lay in helping the People's Democracies' chances of independent development. By defeating the Hitlerite coalition, the U.S.S.R. helped to liberate central and southeast Europe from Fascist slavery. At the same time, it helped those countries reconstruct and develop their national economies. What is more, the U.S.S.R. supported their fight against foreign imperialism's attempts at intervention, undertaken with the aim of restoring the old and reactionary way of life. Without that support, the democratic forces of those countries might have come up against a situation similar to that which Greece encountered in December 1944 as a result of the military operations of the British troops. The Soviet Union's support gave the peoples of the countries that broke away from the capitalist system the opportunity to freely determine their own destinies.

In 1949 capitalism suffered a particularly grave defeat. Its domination in China came to an end. After half a century of revolutionary struggle, the most numerous nation in the world threw off the yoke of imperialism and reaction.

Aid to People's Democracies

One of the foremost tasks of Soviet foreign policy since the war has been the extension of all-round help to the People's Democracies. All in all, since the end of the war, the U.S.S.R. has given the socialist countries long-term credits totalling approximately 8,580,000,000 U.S. dollars. Soviet trade with the People's Democracies, which is conducted on the basis of long-term trade agreements, has expanded considerably. The U.S.S.R. has given the People's Democracies substantial aid in restoring and developing their economies by building large enterprises in those countries and supplying them with industrial plants, etc. Scientific, technical and cultural co-operation has grown. The Council of Mutual Economic Assistance, established in 1949, is promoting the organization of economic co-operation among the socialist countries.

Of the same vast scale has been the Soviet Union's help to the People's Democracies in defending their national independence. The Soviet government concluded treaties of friendship, mutual assistance and postwar co-operation with Czechoslovakia and Poland. In 1948, agreements on friendship, co-operation and reciprocal aid were signed with Hungary, Rumania and Bulgaria. All those agreements set the goal of repelling any attempt at a renewal of aggression by Germany or any other power aligned with it for purposes of aggression. Like the Soviet Union's treaties of 1942 and 1944 with Great Britain and France, they aimed at repelling new German aggression.

In 1950 the U.S.S.R. and Chinese People's Republic concluded a Treaty On Friendship, Alliance and Mutual Assistance. The Soviet Union and People's China are linked by relations of the most sincere fraternal friendship and co-operation. Their treaty provides that both Powers shall take all steps to prevent a new aggression and the violation of the peace on the part of Japan or any other state directly or indirectly allied with Japan in acts of aggression. In the event of an attack against either of the contracting parties by Japan or its allies, the other side shall help in every way it can. When Chiang Kai-shek, with U.S. help, engaged in provocative operations in Taiwan waters in 1958, the Soviet Government expressed its full support of China. In July, 1962, N. S. Khrushchov warned: "The one who dares to invade the Chinese People's Republic will meet a shattering rebuff from the great Chinese people, the peoples of the U.S.S.R. and of the whole socialist camp. Let nobody entertain any doubt on that score."

International relations of an entirely new kind have evolved between the states of the socialist camp since the war. That hitherto unknown type of relations rests upon complete equality between the states, large or small, upon non-interference in one another's internal affairs, upon respect for independence, territorial integrity and sovereignty. But while these new relations are based on strict observance of the above principles, they do not stop there. The new socialist relations between the states also presuppose warm fraternal friendship and the most generous mutual assistance and co-operation in the economic, technical and cultural spheres, joint defense against enemies, and a struggle for peace. With the victory of the people's democratic system in a number of European and Asian countries, socialism transcended the boundaries of a single country and became a world system.

At the moment when the war ended, all the Great Powers of the anti-Hitlerite coalition were allies. Peace would have been lastingly assured if it had been possible to preserve co-operation of the victor countries and to prevent the reappearance of militarism and reactionary governments in the vanquished countries, and so guarantee that their development would follow democratic lines. The compacts concluded by the U.S.S.R., the U.S.A. and Britain in Yalta at the end of the war were designed to prolong the co-operation between those countries so as to reach a peaceful settlement on democratic foundations in both Europe and Asia.

Those compacts were supplemented in July and August 1945 by the Potsdam agreement of the three Powers on Germany and the Potsdam Declaration of the U.S.A., Britain and China on Japan, with which the Soviet Union aligned itself after joining the war in the Far East. Those highly important acts are known to have envisaged the democratization and demilitarization of both Germany and Japan.

Agreement was also reached at the Potsdam Conference concerning Poland's western frontier along the Oder–West Neisse line, and on a number of other questions. The idea was for the Polish frontier to be conclusively established at a future peace conference. These territories were placed under the administration of the Polish state. Proceeding from the fact that the question of the Polish frontiers was conclusively decided, the Control Council on Germany, comprising the commanders-in-chief of the Soviet, American, British and French occupation armies, adopted a decision on, and carried out the resettlement of over three

million Germans from those areas to German territory. The Polish government, in turn, populated those old Polish lands with Polish settlers. The resettlement of millions of people proved that the governments of the four Great Powers and Poland itself considered the decision final and not subject to change.

In the states of the West powerful forces hostile to the policy of co-operation with a socialist Power and indifferent to the establishment of a lasting peace, were at work. In the richest country of the West, the United States, there were plenty of influential people determined to ensure for the United States a dominant world role. That has in fact been accomplished everywhere, excepting the U.S.S.R. and the other countries that have taken the road of socialist development. This circumstance, in our opinion, explains the postwar U.S. propaganda campaign of hatred against the U.S.S.R.

But soon after the war and increasingly as the postwar years passed, the difference between the two courses in world policy, corresponding to the division of political forces on the world arena, has become manifest. The vital difference in Soviet and Western policy has, perhaps, expressed itself most vividly in the following and obvious fact. During the war against Nazi Germany, Japan and their allies, the armed forces of the U.S.S.R., U.S.A., and Britain were stationed on the territories of quite a number of states in Europe and Asia. The Soviet Union demonstrated its peacefulness and respect for the sovereignty of other states by deed, and evacuated its troops without delay from the alien territories—from Norway, from the Danish island of Bornholm, from Yugoslavia, Czechoslovakia, Bulgaria, China and Iran. The Soviet forces were withdrawn from the territory of the latter in May 1946. They stayed on only in Germany, Austria, and North Korea, whose occupation by the victorious countries was stipulated in the joint wartime agreements. They also stayed in Poland, Hungary and Rumania on the basis of the same agreements, to protect the communications of the occupation forces stationed in Germany and Austria. The Soviet Union withdrew its forces from Korea as early as 1948. The Soviet Union also gave up its two bases: Port Arthur, on Chinese territory, and Porkkala-Udd in Finland, while the Western Powers increased their armed forces and bases abroad.

Disarmament

New tasks of the utmost importance arose in the sphere of disarmament after the war. The atom bombing of two Japanese peace-abiding cities during the last days of the war, an act unjustified from any military standpoint, gave humanity a visual demonstration of the terrible destructive power of that new weapon of mass annihilation which hits the civilian inhabitants of the large cities most severely. The Soviet Union took the lead in the fight for the prohibition of nuclear and other types of mass destruction weapons, and also for marked reductions in the size of armed forces and conventional arms.

As early as 1946, the Soviet government advanced the idea of the immediate prohibition and eradication of atomic weapons. It was there that it saw its chief task, dictated by the interests and future of humanity. On June 19, 1946 the Soviet Government submitted to the Atomic Energy Commission of the U.N. Security Council a proposal on the conclusion of an international convention banning the production and use of weapons utilizing fissionable materials and providing for the destruction, under international control, of all stockpiles.

Its June 11, 1947 draft plan presented an even more comprehensive proposal for a system of disarmament control. It provided for the creation of an international control commission within the framework of the Security Council. This commission was to be invested with broad powers essential to the implementation of the convention banning atomic weapons and essential to the exercise of international control over the use of atomic energy. That control commission would operate on the basis of its own procedural rules, which would provide for the adoption of decisions by a majority vote, rather than by the principle of unanim-

ity. The suggestion was for control and inspection to begin as soon as the convention banning atomic weapons went into effect. It was to be control of the ban on atomic weapons, and not control over the economy and domestic life of individual countries, as provided for in the Baruch plan.

In submitting these proposals, the Soviet Government proceeded from the conviction that control should be instituted only if an unequivocal agreement banning atomic weapons existed. According to the Soviet proposal, the control commission could investigate the activity of undertakings engaged in the extraction of atomic raw materials and production of fissionable materials and atomic power. It could also check up on their reports. It could institute special investigations, once suspicion arose that the convention was being violated. The signatories to such a convention promised not to prevent such investigations.

Later the Soviet Government added to these proposals, pointing out that inspections should not be only periodical but function on "a permanent basis." The Soviet Government suggested that both conventions, on the prohibition of atomic weapons and on control, should go into effect simultaneously.

Almost simultaneously with its proposals on the prohibition of atomic weapons, the Soviet Government also came out for the general reduction of armaments. In 1948, it suggested that the five Great Powers begin to reduce their armed forces and conventional arms, as a first step, by one-third in one year.

In 1947 and 1948, the Western Powers revealed a tendency to fight shy of any measures concerned with the regulation and curtailment of armaments, under the pretext that such measures could only be implemented in an atmosphere of international confidence, after the conclusion of a German peace treaty. Even after it had the atom, and then the hydrogen bomb, the Soviet government continued to work with the same zeal for the prohibition of mass-destruction weapons and reduction of conventional arms. After the atomic weapon tests in the U.S.S.R., the Soviet government, in calling for the conclusion of a peace pact between the five Powers at the fourth session of the U.N. General Assembly repeated its proposal for a ban on atomic weapons.

At the fifth session of the Assembly in 1950, the Soviet Government came before that body with a Draft Declaration on removing the threat of another war and consolidating the peace and security of the nations. The Draft proposed that a ban be adopted on atomic weapons and strict international control be established over its implementation. The Draft Declaration also repeated the previous proposals for the conclusion of a five-Power peace pact and for a one-third cut in the size of the armed forces in one year.

All its proposals were rejected by the Western Powers. Instead of disarmament measures, the Western ruling circles tried to put through control over armaments and the collection of information about existing armaments and armed forces. The U.S.A. and its allies persisted in their evasion of an agreement to ban atomic weapons.

The Soviet Union proved its desire for disarmament not only by its proposals, but also by its deeds. After the end of the war, the Soviet Government put through the demobilization of 33 recruiting age groups and reduced the size of its army to dimensions not exceeding the prewar 1939 level.

In 1947 the U.S.S.R. submitted a proposal to the U.N. on measures against war propaganda and got the General Assembly to adopt a resolution condemning such propaganda. Subsequently, on March 12, 1951, the U.S.S.R. Supreme Soviet adopted a law On Defense of Peace. War propaganda was declared a grave offense.

During the most serious complications that arose in the international arena, the Soviet Union submitted proposals offering a basis for the peaceful settlement of those controversial issues. That was the case with regard to the war in Korea, for instance. In 1951, proposals were submitted by the Soviet side, with the concurrence of the Chinese People's Republic and Korean People's Democratic Republic, which laid a foundation for the subsequent truce talks.

The German question

In the opinion of the Soviet Government, one of the chief guarantees of a stable peace should be a demilitarized and democratized Germany as envisaged at Potsdam. In keeping with the spirit and letter of the Potsdam Agreement, the Soviet Government has undeviatingly pursued a course aimed at the speediest possible conclusion of a German peace treaty and formation of an all-German government.

The Soviet proposals towards the speediest possible reunion of Germany as one peaceful democratic state were not accepted by the United States, Britain and France; they chose quite another course. The merger of first the British and American occupation zones in December 1946, and formation of "Bizonia," and then the alignment of the French zone with it and opposition of all three Western zones to the Soviet zone, the separate monetary reform in the three Western zones (1948), which deepened economic dissidence of Germany and publication of an occupation statute in April 1949, were the steps that led to the splitting of Germany.

A Federal German Republic with its capital in Bonn was set up in September 1949 by the three Western Powers. The Soviet Government vehemently denounced the formation of a separate state in western Germany, characterizing it as the "culmination of the policy of dismembering Germany pursued by the government of the United States, Great Britain and France."

After the formation of the separate West German state, the democratic organizations of the eastern part of Germany, where demilitarization and democratic changes had been implemented, took steps of their own. The German Democratic Republic with its center in Berlin was proclaimed in October 1949. This new state undertook the task of struggling for national unity, peace and democracy.

Inasmuch as the rebirth of militarism in

West Germany represents a very grave threat to peace in Europe, the fight against the re-militarization of West Germany has become an important element of the Soviet Union's work for peace. Anxious to achieve a solution of the German problem, the Soviet Government on March 10, 1952 requested the governments of the United States, Britain and France to again take up the question of a German peace treaty, and submitted the draft of the basic principles of such a treaty. Simultaneously, the Soviet Government requested them to discuss the conditions conducive to the speediest possible formation of an all-German government capable of expressing the will of the German people. But the governments of the United States, Britain, and France again refused to consider that Soviet draft. Neither did they advance any proposals of their own.

On April 9, 1952, the Soviet Government stated that it considered it essential for the governments of the U.S.S.R., U.S.A., Britain, and France to get down without delay to a discussion of the question of free all-German elections. No sooner was that proposal submitted by the Soviet side, than the Western Powers made haste to go back on any genuine preparations for free elections.

Peace with Japan

In the matter of a peace settlement with Japan, the U.S.S.R. has always favored the return to that American-occupied country of its status of a fully independent state. U.S. activities in Japan evidently were designed to turn Japan into a U.S. military base and drag out the occupation of Japan by the American army. The Soviet Government demanded the conclusion of a just peace treaty with Japan and withdrawal of the occupation forces.

But these proposals were not accepted by the U.S.A. and its allies, who joined hands in drafting a peace treaty which violates the international agreements on Japan adopted at the conferences in Cairo, Yalta and Potsdam, as well as the principles of the policy charted by the allies in their Far Eastern Commission. While their draft treaty says that Japan must surrender its rights to the territories it previously seized by aggression—Taiwan, the Pescadores, Southern Sakhalin, and the Kuril Islands—it fails to say that those territories must be returned to China and the U.S.S.R. as stipulated in the agreements adopted at Cairo, Yalta and Potsdam.

At the San Francisco conference of September 1951, the Soviet Government submitted a number of amendments and additions with the aim of improving that draft treaty. But the United States and its allies rejected the proposals of the U.S.S.R. and the other Powers. As a result, the Soviet Government refused to sign the treaty. On the day when the peace treaty was signed, the American government also concluded a so-called "security pact" with Japan which gave the United States the right to retain its armed forces on Japanese territory.

SOVIET EFFORTS TO LESSEN INTERNATIONAL TENSION AND STRENGTHEN PEACE, 1953–1962

Great Power conferences

In the postwar period, the Soviet Government consistently strove for the peaceful settlement of international issues.

Supporting the initiative of the Chinese People's Republic and the Korean People's Democratic Republic and backed by the irrepressible yearning of the peoples for peace, the Soviet Union facilitated the signing of a truce in Korea in 1953.

At a Big Four Foreign Ministers' Conference in Berlin in early 1954, the German problem was discussed. The Western Powers wanted to have all-German elections held in a foreign-occupied Germany on conditions stipulated by the occupying Powers. The U.S.S.R. maintained that all-German elections, to be free, indeed, must be prepared by the Germans themselves. There must be a provisional all-German Government which includes representatives of the parliaments of both parts of Germany; further occupation troops must first be withdrawn.

Though no understanding was reached over Germany, the Soviet Union was able to get the three Western Powers' consent to a new Foreign Ministers' conference, at which the Chinese People's Republic would be represented, to discuss the conclusion of a final peace in Korea and the termination of war in Indochina.

The Foreign Ministers of the U.S.S.R., the Chinese People's Republic, the Korean People's Democratic Republic, the U.S., Britain, France, and other countries met in Geneva in April 1954. The delegation of the Korean People's Democratic Republic proposed that Korea be reunified by holding, under the supervision of a Commission consisting of representatives from both North and South Korea free elections to an all-Korean National Assembly which would, accordingly, form one single Government for all of Korea. The withdrawal of all foreign troops from Korea was also stipulated. The U.S.S.R. fully supported this proposal declaring that it was prepared to guarantee with the other states Korea's peaceful development. Unfortunately for peace and the prosperity of these areas, these constructive proposals were not accepted. Korea is still divided. Soviet troops had been withdrawn from North Korea in 1948; meanwhile foreign troops are still stationed in South Korea.

The Soviet Government vigorously facilitated the attainment of a cease-fire agreement in Indochina. Under this agreement hostilities were terminated in Vietnam, Cambodia and Laos. The agreement forbade the entry into the Indochinese states of troops or arms and also the establishment of military bases in their territories. As co-chairmen of the conference, the Soviet and British foreign ministers were authorized to examine the fulfilment of the agreement. The U.S.S.R. addressed itself

repeatedly to Britain and the other parties to the Geneva agreement, insisting upon fulfilment of the agreements and protesting against their many violations by the U.S., such as the import of arms into South Vietnam, the sending of military personnel there, etc.

The Soviet Government's next major move to reduce international tensions was to facilitate the conclusion of the Austrian State Treaty which, for ten years after the war, had been impeded by the U.S. and its NATO partners. Austria was still occupied by Soviet, U.S., British, and French troops. In 1955 the Soviet Government invited the leaders of the Austrian Government to Moscow. In the talks between the Soviet and Austrian government delegations, preparations for the conclusions of the Austrian State Treaty were completed. On May 15, 1955, the representatives of the Four Powers and Austria signed in Vienna the State Treaty on the restoration of an independent and democratic Austria. Austria pledged to adhere constantly to a policy of neutrality, and the Big Four—the U.S.S.R., the U.S., Britain, and France—promised to respect Austria's neutrality. Europe had now one more country which was not a member of any military bloc —a real contribution to maintaining peace.

Friendly relations with Western countries

The establishment of firm and friendly relations between the world's two biggest Powers, the U.S.S.R. and the U.S., would greatly enhance the prospects for peace. To this end, the U.S.S.R. proposed in 1956 that a treaty of friendship and co-operation be concluded between it and the U.S. However, the Soviet initiative failed to meet with due understanding and support from the ruling quarters of the U.S.

Desirous of ensuring the peaceful coexistence of states with different social systems, the Soviet Government also strove consistently to improve relations with Britain and France. The U.S.S.R. shares many common interests with the peoples of these countries, especially the common concern to prevent war in Europe.

The U.S.S.R. established diplomatic relations with the Federal Republic of Germany and with Japan. Steps were taken to improve relations with the Scandinavian states. Soviet commercial and cultural ties grew. A definite relaxation of international tensions was achieved. This was not to the liking of the monopolists in several Western countries and they took steps to spike an international relaxation of tension.

The first blow was dealt at Egypt. The aggressors were Britain, France, and Israel. The Soviet Government's emphatic warning compelled them to cease hostilities against Egypt.

Almost simultaneously with the anti-Egyptian aggression, imperialist forces launched an offensive against the socialist camp. In Hungary, a Fascist insurrection to restore the old regime was engineered with the help of foreign agents. Its victory would have signified the appearance of a hotbed of war on the banks of the Danube. At the request of the legitimate Hungarian Government, the Soviet Union helped Hungary to quell the insurrection.

The Soviet Government continued to pay great heed to questions of European security. In the period under review, militarism in West Germany came to represent a new threat to European security. These designs, initiated by U.S. and West German revanchists, began to assume quite tangible form after 1950. Since the Soviet people had lost millions of human lives in the war against Hitler Germany, it could not but view West Germany's armament as a threat to itself and European peace.

Collective security in Europe

At the 1954 Berlin conference, the Soviet Union had proposed a draft treaty for an All-European system of collective security, believing that the U.S. could also subscribe to this treaty. After all, only a system of collective security, in which all the states would pull to-

gether to preserve peace, can guarantee real peace.

In August 1954, the French National Assembly rejected the West German armament plan known as the "European Defense Community." This reopened the door for Big Four discussions of German reunification and, in particular, the holding of free all-German elections, the withdrawal of occupation forces from Germany and the convocation of an all-European conference to institute a system of collective security in Europe. It was in these conditions that in October 1954 the Soviet Government informed the three Western Powers of its desire to have these questions discussed. These facts debunk Western propaganda allegations that the Soviet Union objected to free all-German elections. Actually it was the U.S. and the West Germans who obstructed the holding of such elections.

Despite EDC's failure, West Germany was remilitarized, and incorporated in NATO. In response, the U.S.S.R. and the People's Democracies, against whom this undertaking was directed, were compelled to take due precautions. In the spring of 1955, the representatives of eight states, including the U.S.S.R. and seven European People's Democracies signed in Warsaw a Treaty of Friendship, Co-operation and Mutual Assistance. All the signatories mutually pledged that in the event of an armed attack in Europe on any of the parties to the treaty, they would at once help it with every means at their disposal, including the use of armed force.

All the provisions of the Warsaw Treaty are in strict conformity with the U.N. Charter. The Warsaw Treaty is open to other states, regardless of their social systems. Thus, in contrast to the aggressive blocs, this purely defensive alliance of peace-loving states is by no means a closed grouping of the type of the North Atlantic bloc, whose true character was exposed by its members themselves when they refused to admit the U.S.S.R. to membership in it. One of the articles of the Warsaw Treaty declares that it will be invalidated should a system of collective security be established in Europe. The Government of the Chinese People's Republic declared its solidarity with the decisions of the Warsaw Conference and its support for the Warsaw Treaty.

When the Paris Agreements went into force, a new situation came into being in Germany. The Federal Republic of Germany went still further along the road of militarization and mounting reaction. This all put well nigh insuperable obstacles in the way of German reunification.

The working people of the German Democratic Republic, which is quickly advancing along the socialist road, cannot agree to a mechanical merger with such a militaristic and reactionary state as the Federal Republic of Germany. Furthermore, the West German Government has agreed to its country's occupation till 2005. The conclusion of a peace treaty and the settlement of the West Berlin problem, coupled with the institution of a confederation between the two German states, would supply a trustworthy and painless solution for the German people's national problem.

The Soviet Government has pointed out that the Big Four have no right to decide this question without the German people. From the Soviet point of view, as N. S. Khrushchov has said in the German Democratic Republic's People's Chamber,

it is the duty of the four powers to help the German people in every way to decide their national problems by themselves on a peaceful democratic basis through direct negotiations between the two German states.[18]

The Soviet Government supported the East German Government's proposal for a German confederation.

In accord with the basic principles of its foreign policy, the Soviet Government has repeatedly proposed to the Western Powers to start a co-ordinated stage-by-stage withdrawal of troops from Germany.

The program of Adenauer and his Western patrons provides for the gobbling up of the German Democratic Republic, the abolition of all the gains of the working people of East Germany, the conversion of East Germany into the domain of the Junkers and monopolists of the Rhine and Ruhr and the use of all of Germany as the principal military base of NATO directed against the U.S.S.R. and the other socialist states. The U.S.S.R. cannot support this program and it categorically spurns it. A joint statement issued by the U.S.S.R. and East German governments in January 1957 pointed out that "any attempts to use violence to solve the German question and any attempts to undermine the people's democratic system in the G.D.R. by hostile actions will be cut short."[19]

On January 10, 1959, the Soviet Union again put before the states and the world public the draft of a German peace treaty which fully accords both with the German people's national interests and with the security interests of all the other European nations.

The Soviet draft repeats the principles set out by the Soviet Union from 1952 to 1954, however, taking into consideration the circumstance that owing to the policy of the Western Powers, Germany's division has become a hard fact. Hence the immediate unification of the two states is unreal. The Soviet draft consequently provides for the possibility of concluding a peace treaty with the two German states or with an all-German confederation. It entitles Germany to have its own national armed forces necessary to ensure its defenses. At the same time, it forbids Germany to possess nuclear weapons, rockets, and guided missiles, and to join any military grouping directed against any country that had been in a state of war with Hitler Germany.

The conclusion of the peace treaty would terminate revanchist propaganda for the return of what they call the "alienated territories." The peace treaty would also solve the problem of West Berlin, which has become a

---

[18] N. S. Khrushchov, "For a Lasting Peace and Peaceful Coexistence," Moscow: 1958, pp. 149–150.

[19] *Pravda*, Jan. 8, 1957. Joint statement of the governments of the U.S.S.R. and G.D.R.

bridgehead for subversion against the G.D.R. and the other socialist countries.

In several of N. S. Khrushchov's speeches and in notes and statements of the Soviet Government, the concrete conditions on which West Berlin could become a free, demilitarized city, are formulated. These conditions are: the abolition in West Berlin of the remnants of the occupation regime and the conversion of West Berlin into an independent political unit with its own constitution based on democratic principles. The free city's communication with the outer world would be guaranteed to ensure the free passage of people and goods to and from West Berlin. In 1961 the German Democratic Republic, exercising its sovereign rights in order to protect its security, placed the border with West Berlin under strict control.

On January 16, 1963, N. S. Khrushchov declared: "The socialist countries are ready to give the free city the fullest guarantees of non-interference in her affairs, and free choice of the social system which the people of West Berlin would prefer. The U.N. would guarantee this. As promised, the G.D.R., the U.S.S.R., and their socialist allies will even agree for the international forces under the U.N. flag to remain in West Berlin for a certain period of time." The conclusion of a peace treaty and a normalization in West Berlin would enable one of the thorniest issues to be solved at the earliest date and would greatly contribute to stronger peace in Europe. However, the Western Powers bristled up at these proposals of the Soviet Government.

The struggle against colonialism

In the years since the end of the war, the crisis of imperialism's colonial system has become intense in the extreme. In Asia and Africa a great number of countries broke away from the colonial yoke and formed independent national states. However, the newly independent nations are forced to defend their independence not only from the old colonialists such as Britain, France and Portugal, but also against the allies of these colonialists. In this struggle against the colonialists, the peoples of these countries have the U.S.S.R.'s powerful support.

The U.S.S.R. is helping the Afro-Asian states in their effort to achieve full economic independence. It grants credits, delivers equipment and builds industrial establishments for them. The U.S.S.R. does not attach any strings to its assistance that would infringe upon the independence of the states whom it is helping. Soviet assistance to the Eastern countries is not confined to the economic sphere alone. The U.S.S.R. is also giving them vigorous political support in their struggle for independence.

After the termination of Anglo-Franco-Israeli aggression against Egypt, the Soviet Government called on the three Western Powers on February 11, 1957, to adopt a joint commitment to solve peacefully all issues related to the Near and Middle East, to keep out of the internal affairs of the countries of this area, to refrain from involving them in Great Power military blocs, to abstain from arms deliveries to these countries, to withdraw foreign troops, and to facilitate the economic development of the Near and Middle East countries, without attaching any political, military or other conditions, that would be incompatible with the dignity and sovereignty of these countries. The U.S., Britain, and France showed no readiness to accept these proposals. Then on April 19, 1957, the U.S.S.R. Government suggested as an initial move towards an amelioration and normalization of the climate in the Near and Middle East, that the Big Four condemn the use of force as a means for solving the outstanding issues related to this area. Again the Western governments failed to support this Soviet proposal.

In the summer of 1958, the Soviet Government likewise categorically objected to U.S. and British intervention against Lebanon and Jordan and insisted that they terminate armed intervention.

The Soviet Government took active measures to support the liberation movement of the African peoples as well as their struggle for independence. It consistently championed the rights and independence of the African nations.

N. S. Khrushchov, in September–October 1960, at the U.N. General Assembly's 15th session, made a proposal to abolish colonialism. The General Assembly, despite the resistance of the colonial Powers, approved unanimously. As was pointed out earlier, the Soviet Government made a tremendous effort to discontinue the war in Indochina in 1954. Later on it systematically advocated the establishment of a democratic and neutralist Laos. However, in 1961, the Phoumi Nosavan faction revolted against the legitimate government of Prince Souvanna Phouma.

At the 1961 Geneva Conference, the Soviet Government invariably supported the idea of a conciliation between the hostile Laotian groupings and of a coalition cabinet capable of guaranteeing peace and neutrality in Laos. The Soviet position facilitated the establishment of a coalition government headed by Souvanna Phouma.

The Soviet Government helped the Cuban people when they were subjected to economic, political, and military pressure by their powerful neighbor. The U.S. had severed diplomatic relations with Cuba and had declared an economic blockade of the island. In April 1961, counter-revolutionary bands had invaded Cuba.

In the fall of 1962, Cuba was threatened with new aggression. To prevent it, Cuba asked the U.S.S.R. to place middle-range ballistic missiles on the island. The missiles were brought to Cuba exclusively to prevent aggression against it. N. S. Khrushchov declared: "In the age of intercontinental and global missiles, Cuba, this small and distant island, 50 km wide in some places, is of no strategic significance to the defense of the U.S.S.R."

The naval blockade of Cuba, and the placing of U.S. and allied armed forces on a war footing to invade Cuba, gave rise to a menace of a nuclear world war. Therefore, on October 27, 1962, the Soviet Government announced its readiness to remove from Cuba the equipment which the U.S. called "offensive," if the U.S. undertook not to invade Cuba and to keep its allies from doing so, too. President Kennedy agreed. The U.S.S.R. removed its missiles and bombers from Cuba. Prime Minister Nehru of India aptly praised the role of the U.S.S.R. and Mr. Khrushchov in this international crisis: "Your wise statesmanship helped to avert the direct danger." The U.S. lifted the naval blockade of Cuba and rescinded the other military measures. Mutual concessions have ended the dangerous tension.

The struggle to ease tensions

At the U.N. General Assembly's 12th session in the autumn of 1957, the Soviet Government proposed the adoption of a Declaration on the Peaceful Coexistence of states. The idea of peaceful coexistence is winning increasingly wider recognition, and was supported by most of the participants at the session.

On December 21, 1957, the U.S.S.R. Supreme Soviet made several concrete proposals with the aim of reducing international tension. In particular the Supreme Soviet expressed its profound conviction in the expediency of personal contacts between leading statesmen to discuss burning international issues.

On the basis of this decision, on January 8, 1958, the Soviet Government circulated among all U.N. members its proposals for a lessening of international tension, in which it emphasized the need for ending the testing of, and prohibiting, nuclear weapons, of forbidding war propaganda and of concluding a non-aggression pact between the NATO and Warsaw Treaty countries. To ameliorate the climate in Europe, the Soviet Government suggested adopting Poland's proposal for an atom-free zone in Central Europe, concluding a non-aggression pact between the NATO and Warsaw countries, and reducing the strength of foreign troops in Germany and other European states.

The Soviet Government suggested discussing at a summit meeting measures to reduce international tensions. Though these proposals were supported by the broad world public they did not meet with understanding from the Western countries.

The Soviet Union came out with a new idea in 1958 which was in harmony with the vital interests of all the peoples of the world. The Supreme Soviet decided on the unilateral cessation of A- and H-weapon tests by the Soviet Union. The Supreme Soviet voiced the hope that the Soviet Government's example would find support among the Western Powers. However, this call went unheeded.

In the spring and summer of 1958 the U.S. carried out more than 50 test explosions of nuclear weapons. The British conducted explosions at the same time. This compelled the Soviet Government to resume nuclear weapon testing. However, though it resumed testing, the Soviet Government still adhered to the view that testing should be completely prohibited. It declared its preparedness to cease testing at once should the U.S. and Britain agree to conclude the appropriate treaty.

Attaching particular significance to the promotion of good relations with the U.S., and in order to reduce international tensions and develop personal contacts, N. S. Khrushchev visited the U.S. in the autumn of 1959. This visit was a great mission for peace. In the course of negotiations with President Eisenhower, an understanding was reached to arrange a Big-Four heads-of-Government meeting in May 1960. However, the incursion into Soviet air space of American spy planes, especially the widely and sadly notorious U-2, produced an extremely negative impression upon the Soviet people. President Eisenhower made it clear that the sending of military aircraft and violation of Soviet sovereignty constituted the national policy of the U.S. administration which it planned to continue. These actions on the part of the U.S. Government resulted in the breakdown of that summit meeting to which the world public had so eagerly been looking forward.

An objective assessment of all these facts will show that the Soviet Union continued in these years, as hitherto, to take the initiative in the effort to abolish the "Cold War," and vigorously strove for the promotion of peaceful co-operation.

THE DISARMAMENT PROBLEM

Partial disarmament

A new stage in disarmament negotiations began when it fully dawned upon the West that the Soviet Union had put an end to the U.S. nuclear monopoly.

On April 24, 1952, the U.S. put before the newly created U.N. Disarmament Commission a six-point document which spoke in general terms of the need for reducing armed forces and armaments and of the withdrawal from use of all means which could be employed for mass destruction. The elaboration of a control system was demanded as a preliminary.

In May 1952, the Western Powers suggested concrete armed forces limits—of from 1,000,-000 to 1,500,000 each for the U.S.S.R., the U.S.A., and China, and of from 700,000 to 800,000 each for Britain and France. On June 11, 1954, Britain and France presented a memorandum which qualified, to some degree, the stage of disarmament at which they were prepared to abandon nuclear weapons. The measures they suggested could have served as a basis for disarmament and the Soviet Government duly appreciated this. In its draft of a resolution at the Ninth U.N. General Assembly session of September 30, 1954 and still more in its proposals of May 10, 1955, it went forward to meet halfway the Western viewpoint as expressed in the Anglo-French memorandum.

Before, the U.S.S.R. had proposed reducing armed forces by a definite fraction, namely one-third. Now it accepted the proposal to cut them to an established figure, as the Western Powers suggested. This meant less of a reduction than the Soviet Union would want. But, to achieve the earliest attainment of a disarmament agreement, it met the West halfway. The Soviet Union also agreed to put off the prohibition and withdrawal of nuclear weapons till conventional armaments would have been cut to three-quarters of the agreed reduction program.

But the U.S.S.R. proposed definite time terms for each stage of disarmament. This was something the Western draft did not have. The Soviet Union also contributed several proposals to consolidate the area of international confidence. This included in particular the abolition of military bases in other countries and the withdrawal, except for strictly limited contingents, of foreign troops from both parts of Germany. Of particularly great importance were the Soviet Government's new, far-reaching proposals on the organization of control and the scheme for setting up ground control posts at big ports, railway hubs, motorroads and airfields.

However, in August 1955, the Western Powers led by the U.S. went back on their own proposals. Instead of a discussion of earlier proposals, Mr. Stassen, the U.S. delegate in the Disarmament Sub-committee, demanded the advance acceptance of Eisenhower's aerial photography proposal made at the Geneva summit meeting of 1955. On September 6, 1955 Stassen, naturally acting in conformity with the State Department's directives, announced that all previous proposals of the Western Powers would be put off, pending a "study" of the methods of inspection and control.

In actual fact, the Western Powers had in general abandoned every serious disarmament undertaking. At the Geneva Big-Four summit meeting, British Prime Minister Anthony Eden suggested establishing a zone of arms limitation and inspection in Europe. The Soviet Government at once supported this useful proposal. But as soon as the U.S.S.R. agreed with the British proposal, the Western Powers, including Britain itself, abandoned it.

In 1956–58 the Western representatives in the Sub-committee already declared quite candidly that their governments were reluctant to abandon nuclear weapons as they believed them "essential for their security." In conformity with Dulles' directives, Stassen stated in the Sub-committee that the U.S. "will not

agree to the full abolition of its nuclear weapons." An analogous statement was made also by the British representative.

A no less disheartening impression was produced by the abdication by the three Powers of their own proposals as concerned armed forces ceilings. Very soon they were demanding in the Sub-committee that the U.S.S.R. agree to incomparably higher ceilings—2,500,000 men each for the U.S.S.R., the U.S. and China, and of 750,000 men each for Britain and France. This proposal actually spelled the U.S.A.'s refusal to make any cut in the strength of its troops, as they were in the vicinity of 2,500,-000 at the time. Still, in striving to achieve a disarmament agreement, the U.S.S.R. consented to this proposal as well, provided however, that later on there would certainly be a much bigger reduction.

However, this overture was also declined. More than that. Barely had the U.S.S.R. agreed to the 2,500,000 ceiling, then the Western representatives began to hedge their willingness to agree to such high ceilings with sundry additional stipulations and reservations. They made all headway in disarmament dependent on the preliminary settlement of other political issues. It was plain that the complication of the thorny disarmament problem with the preliminary solution of other still thornier issues, could not be viewed otherwise than as a desire to impede disarmament.

Very indicative from this point of view is the further lot of the question of reducing conventional armaments and armed forces. Since the Western representatives claimed that they could not give up A- and H-weapons because the U.S.S.R. possessed an advantage in conventional armed forces and armaments, the Soviet Government suggested coming to terms at first on the reduction of conventional armaments and armed forces, without having this question linked up with a nuclear weapons ban. The question of nuclear disarmament would be settled later. However, the Western Powers found it impossible to start disarming even in the sphere of conventional armaments. More than that. In 1956 and 1957, both in the London Sub-committee and later in the U.N. Disarmament Committee, Western delegates in general announced as unthinkable every radical disarmament solution. Now they insisted upon the necessity of having the matter confined to "partial undertakings."

Reluctant to let slip a single chance of attaining a disarmament agreement, the Soviet Government, in its turn, put forward a project for partial undertakings. It met the U.S. halfway, agreeing to the establishment of a zone for aerial photography in Europe and in Eastern Asia. Appropriate international control over the observance of all these rulings was envisaged. These proposals were also declined.

Rocketry development and the launching of the first intercontinental ballistic missile in the Soviet Union radically changed the strategic situation. The U.S.A. a great distance away had been relatively invulnerable before. But with the appearance on the scene of the intercontinental missile, this advantage of the U.S. became irrevocably a thing of the past.

Its rocketry achievements and the unprecedented consolidation of its strategic positions did not detract the U.S.S.R. from the vigor it invested in the effort for disarmament. It took several new unilateral actions to reduce armaments.

Complete disarmament

On September 18, 1959, at the U.N. General Assembly's Fourteenth session, N. S. Khrushchov proposed general and complete disarmament.

This opened a new chapter in the history of disarmament. The idea of general and complete disarmament removes the main obstacles that have lain in the way of limiting armaments and armed forces or of banning different individual types of weapons. In the case of partial measures, the states would still have the potentialities for launching an attack. While the danger of attack exists, and there is consequently the need for defenses, we still have military secrets. The organization of defenses

and the military industry cannot be revealed without impairing national security.

The history of the disarmament talks plainly shows that control was always made one of the main obstacles to the attainment of agreement. And this is not at all the question of whether control is necessary. "We," N. S. Khrushchov told the Fourteenth General Assembly session, "have always been and will always be for strict international control over the fulfilment of a disarmament agreement when it is achieved."

The history of disarmament negotiations discloses difficulties of still another nature, which also doomed talks to failure. While the idea was to disarm only partially, so that after the fulfilment of the disarmament agreement there would remain one or another type of arms, and consequently the possibility of conducting war, the question was: how will disarmament measures affect the international balance of forces?

But in the case of complete and general disarmament, there is absolutely "no possibility of creating any military advantages for one or another state or group of states,"[20] as N. S. Khrushchov noted at the Fourteenth General Assembly session. The proposal for general and complete disarmament differs from all other disarmament proposals in that its realization totally precludes all possibility of unequal armament conditions.

The Soviet Government put forward a four-year three-stage program. During the first stage, the strength of the armed forces of the U.S.S.R., the U.S. and People's China was to be reduced under due control to 1,700,000 men each and of Britain and France to 650,-000 men each. Arms were to be reduced accordingly. The second stage provided for the complete abolition of armed forces still at the disposal of states. All military bases in other territories were likewise to be abolished. The third stage envisaged the destruction of all types of nuclear and rocket weapons, military aircraft, and so forth. Research for purposes of

[20] N. S. Khrushchov, *World Without Arms, World Without Wars,* vol. 2, Moscow: 1962, p. 159.

war or the manufacture of arms and military materiél would be prohibited, war ministries and general staffs, as well as all military and paramilitary establishments and organizations would be abolished, all kinds of recruitment and military training would cease, there would be no military service in whatever form and no allocations would be made for military purposes. An international control agency was suggested, with the volume of control and inspection to be defined according to the respective stage of disarmament.

When putting forward its program for general and complete disarmament at the Fourteenth U.N. Assembly session, the Soviet Government declared that, should the Western Powers be loath to agree to it, the Soviet Government was prepared as hitherto to reach an understanding on appropriate partial disarmament undertakings and the consolidation of security.

Prime among these, in the Soviet Government's opinion, are: 1) the establishment of a zone of control and inspection coupled with the reduction of foreign troops, in the territories of the respective countries of Western Europe; 2) the establishment of an atom-free zone in Central Europe; 3) the evacuation of all foreign troops from the territories of the European states and the abolition of military bases in the territories of other countries; 4) the conclusion of a non-aggression pact between the Warsaw and NATO treaty states, and 5) an agreement on method to forestall a surprise attack. At the same time, the Soviet Government declared that it stood as hitherto for the termination of nuclear weapons testing once and for all.

The idea of general and complete disarmament that N. S. Khrushchov proposed was unanimously approved by the U.N. General Assembly. Unfortunately, however, the corresponding resolution that the General Assembly adopted has still not been realized. In 1960, throughout the entire proceedings of the so-called 10-Nation Committee, the Western delegates evaded discussion of the program of general and complete disarmament. The Western delegates insisted that the Committee instead discuss projects for certain separate undertakings pertaining to control. However they did not propose control over disarmament for the foreseeable future, but over available armaments.

The Soviet Government put before the General Assembly's Fifteenth session the draft of "The Basic Provisions of a Treaty on General and Complete Disarmament." This plan is a revised edition of previous Soviet proposals, which takes into consideration sensible suggestions voiced in the meantime by other governments or the public of different countries. It largely meets several Western wishes.

Measures for effective international control over every stage of disarmament are given in greater detail. In accordance with the French proposal, the Soviet draft envisages already during the first stage, the destruction and the prohibition of manufacture of available means of nuclear weapon delivery including aircraft, missiles of both strategic and operational and tactical designation, etc. Accordingly, the very first stage provides for the abolition of all foreign military bases in other countries. These measures would actually banish in a most reliable way the danger of a surprise attack.

With account taken of the remarks made by the U.S. and other Western representatives, the first stage provides for the prohibition of the orbiting or placing in outer space of vehicles capable of carrying weapons of mass destruction. Rockets should be launched only for peaceful purposes and under international control, including the inspection of launching sites. The first stage envisages on-the-spot control of the destruction of all means of weapon delivery and over the abolition of military bases in other countries. The withdrawal from these countries of foreign troops to their own national boundaries is likewise provided. Also envisaged is the establishment of control at airfields and ports so as to guarantee that they will not be used for military purposes. The control agency must have free and unhindered access to all establishments manufacturing the means of nuclear weapon delivery. Permanent control teams may be instituted. Rocket devices, etc are to be inspected.

Effective control is to be instituted also over undertakings slated for the second and third stages. The control system remains in force after the completion of the entire program of total disarmament. But should this be thought inadequate, Soviet representatives are prepared, as they have declared, to discuss any other plan provided it means control over disarmament.

The Western Powers also submitted proposals at the General Assembly's Fifteenth session. Chief among these were the plan of the U.S., the United Kingdom, and Italy, and the United Kingdom's own separate project. The three-Power plan proclaims general and complete disarmament as its "ultimate aim," but gives no concrete program of how and when this is to be achieved.

The three-Power plan, though it names disarmament undertakings, supplies no plan to put them into force. They thus are merely a vague "ultimate aim." Many prime and absolutely essential measures, as, for instance, the abolition of military bases in other countries, are again omitted. Such "omissions" can only be judged as an attempt on the part of the Western Powers to obtain unilateral advantages.

In summing up, one should say that the gist of the difference between the Soviet and Western proposals is that while the Soviet plan is aimed at the earliest abolition on a strictly defined date of every type of weapon including rocket and nuclear weapons, the Western plan seeks to retain these weapons. It is from this difference in the approach to disarmament that the difference derives in the approach to control. The U.S.S.R. is for stringent international *control over the abolition of weapons*. The West meanwhile is *for control over retained armaments*. This control serves war in the same way as weapons do. It gathers information about the enemy or, in other words, discharges the functions of an espionage service.

The role of control will change fundamentally if complete disarmament is effected simultaneously with the introduction of control. When no arms are left, no one will expect control to be used to spot targets for a nuclear missile blow. Control over armaments cannot be substituted for disarmament. "If our disarmament proposals are accepted," N. S. Khrushchov, the head of the Soviet Government, has declared, "we are prepared to accept any Western proposal on international control." These words hold out the broadest possibilities for reaching agreement and they demonstrate with the utmost clarity that it is by no means the Soviet attitude which obstructs the attainment of a disarmament agreement.

When the Fifteenth General Assembly session resumed its work in March 1961, the Soviet Union called for the continuation and completion of disarmament discussions, so that this same session might reach agreement about a co-ordinated basis for negotiating a treaty on general and complete disarmament. However, this was followed by the expressed desire of the new American Kennedy Administration to put off disarmament discussions for the time being, because of its being unprepared to conduct such negotiations. The Soviet Government complied. Instead of disarmament discussions at the second half of the General Assembly's Fifteenth session, there would be Soviet-American talks on disarmament in June–July 1961.

This bilateral exchange of views yielded definite positive results. Despite difficulties of no mean magnitude and different views on many major aspects of disarmament, the two sides succeeded in evolving a joint statement on agreed principles for disarmament negotiation. However, the basic difference was not overcome. This was: Should the matter be one of disarmament and control over disarmament —which is what the Soviet Government is pressing for—or should it be control over armament—which is the cornerstone of the Western position?

Before Soviet-American talks started, the Geneva conference on nuclear weapons test stoppage resumed work in March, 1961. Previous negotiations, initiated in late 1958, showed that from the projected treaty on the stoppage of tests, the West desired to exclude a definite category of tests, namely underground explosions. In plain words the West wanted to retain possibilities for perfecting nuclear weapons.

They directly stated that after the moratorium —which they wanted to make too brief—expired, they would automatically acquire the right to resume underground explosions. It was expected in the U.S.S.R. that the new U.S. administration would put forward a constructive feasible program. However, its proposals of March 21, 1961, yielded little new. This was a grave disappointment for the U.S.S.R.

While conducting negotiations with the U.S.S.R., the Western Powers endeavored to exacerbate the international situation, by utilizing Soviet intentions of signing a German peace treaty in 1961 as a pretext for stepping up the arms race, building up armed forces, and trying to exert pressure on the countries of the socialist camp. Threats to start a nuclear war against the U.S.S.R. in response to the conclusion of a peace treaty with East Germany were made in the Western press and in speeches delivered by responsible personalities. In the summer of 1961, President Kennedy announced a "new course" envisaging a marked increase in the U.S. military budget—up to 56,000 million dollars—a speeded-up nuclear missile program, the multiplication of the armed forces, etc. The arms race was whipped up also in certain other Western countries, especially West Germany.

The Soviet Union could not but react to intensified preparations for a war against it, and was compelled to temporarily suspend the Soviet armed forces cut slated for 1961 and to increase budgetary allocations for defense needs. It was no longer possible to overlook the nuclear tests conducted by France. Since France is a member of NATO, it is quite obvious that the advantages stemming from the French tests could easily be used for the needs of the entire North Atlantic bloc. This put the U.S.S.R. at an absolute disadvantage. And realizing that war might be started against it, the U.S.S.R. was compelled to resume nuclear weapon testing.

While regarding general and complete disarmament as the principal means of securing a lasting peace, the Soviet Government, at the same time, does not rule out the possibility of agreeing to several measures that would tend to reduce international tensions and strengthen the area of international confidence, thereby facilitating the realization of general and complete disarmament.

With these aims in mind, the Soviet Government proposed to the Sixteenth U.N. General Assembly session a whole series of undertakings providing for the pegging of national military budgets at the January 1, 1961 level, the adoption of declarations repudiating the use of nuclear weapons, the prohibition of war propaganda, the conclusion of a nonaggression pact between the NATO and Warsaw Treaty states, the evacuation of foreign troops from other countries, the taking of steps to prevent the further spread of nuclear weapons, the establishment of denuclearized zones, and the taking of definite control measures to diminish the danger of surprise attack.

While not considering these proposals exhaustive, the Soviet Government declared that it was prepared to give attentive study to any constructive considerations that might be voiced on the score and to exchange views on these questions in any form suggested.

An 18-nation Disarmament Committee, which the U.N. constituted from representatives of the Western Powers, the socialist states, and the neutralist countries, started work in Geneva in March 1962. For the first time, a disarmament organ had an agreed basis for its work—the joint Soviet-American principles for a disarmament agreement. The participation of the delegates of the eight neutralist states in Committee proceedings was unquestionably a positive sign.

Displaying a businesslike and constructive approach to disarmament, the Soviet Government at once put before the Committee a detailed draft treaty for general and complete disarmament over four years under strict international control. In its proposals, the Soviet Government always pointed out that the disarmament problem could be solved if confidence among the countries was strengthened. Solution of such an urgent problem as, for example, the conclusion of a German peace treaty would give a new stimulus to a disarmament agreement. Thus N. S. Khrushchov, in his speech on January 16, 1963, pointed out that: "Disarmament is possible only if the international situation is cleared, that is to say if confidence among countries is strengthened, when conditions are created which are not favorable to armaments expenditure and to the increase of armed forces." The Soviet Union also submitted the simple and very effective proposal of terminating nuclear weapon tests under reciprocal control, effected with the help of national means of detection—since the experience accumulated in past years has shown that any nuclear weapon tests, whether conducted underground, in the atmosphere or underwater, are easily recorded simultaneously in several countries. As to the underground tests, the U.S.S.R. suggests to continue negotiations to work out the system of control and to stop the tests for the period of negotiations.

However, the U.S. and Britain declined the offer. They also refused to accept India's proposal for a nuclear test moratorium while the Committee was discussing a test stoppage. The Soviet Government, on the contrary, said it was prepared to agree to this proposal. The eight neutralist states evolved their own compromise plan for the solution of the question of the nuclear test stoppage. The Soviet Union welcomed this initiative, too. The Soviet Government agreed to accept the neutralist states' plan as a basis for reaching an understanding on the termination of all nuclear tests. However, these proposals were also rejected by the U.S. and Britain. As the facts showed, the U.S. meanwhile was completing preparations for a new series of atmospheric nuclear weapon tests, which it started in late April, 1962. Notwithstanding, the Soviet Government continues to strive for an effective agreement.

THE TASKS OF THE FOREIGN POLICY OF THE U.S.S.R.

At its 22nd Congress in October 1961, the Communist Party put before the Soviet people the stupendous task of laying the material and technical foundations for a Communist society. The program envisages a tremendous rise in the people's material standards and the advancement of science and culture. Naturally, all these aims can be achieved only in conditions of peace. It is quite plain that a country that puts itself such vast tasks in the economic and cultural fields and in the advancement of material standards, cannot be seeking war.

The Soviet people and their government are striving to make peace and the security of all nations a constant norm of international relations. Today, when a tremendous technical revolution has taken place in the military sphere and the use of modern nuclear missile weapons spells death to hundreds of millions of people, war cannot and must not be used as a means to solve controversial issues.

In its foreign policy the Soviet Government has always guided itself by the Leninist principle of peaceful coexistence and it continues to do so. Proceeding from this principle, the CPSU Program sets before the Soviet Government the task of securing conditions of peace for the building of a Communist society in the U.S.S.R. and the development of world socialist systems and, together with all peace-loving peoples, of saving mankind from a destructive world war.

The main problem of our time is the problem of war and peace. It has become the problem of life and death for hundreds of millions of men and women. That is why the main task is to prevent a thermo-nuclear war. By uniting the efforts of the powerful socialist camp, the peace-loving non-socialist states, the international working class, and all the forces defending the cause of peace, it is possible to prevent world war. To do away with war, to establish eternal peace on the earth is the historic mission of communism.

The Soviet Government believes that war cannot and must not be used as a means for solving international disputes. Peaceful coexistence or disastrous wars—no other alternative is given by history.

Peaceful coexistence means: repudiation of war as a means for solving controversial issues among states, the solutions to be achieved through negotiations; equality, mutual understanding and trust among nations, who take into consideration each other's interests; noninterference in internal affairs; recognition for all nations of their rights to solve all the problems of their respective countries independently; high respect for sovereignty and territorial integrity of all countries; development of economic and cultural co-operation on the basis of complete equality and mutual benefit. The Soviet Union has consistently upheld and will uphold the policy of peaceful coexistence of states having different social systems.

BIBLIOGRAPHY

Editors' Suggestions

Aspaturian, Vernon V. "Soviet Foreign Policy," in Macridis, Roy C., ed., *Foreign Policy in World Politics*. Englewood Cliffs, N.J.: Prentice-Hall, 1962.

Beloff, Max. *The Foreign Policy of Soviet Russia, 1929–41*. New York: Royal Institute of International Affairs, 1947.

Brzeninski, Zbigniew K. *The Soviet Bloc*. Cambridge: Harvard University Press, 1960.

Fischer, L. *The Soviets in World Affairs*. 2 vols. Princeton: Princeton University Press, 1951.

Garthoff, Raymond L. *Soviet Strategy in the Nuclear Age*. New York: Praeger, 1958.

Jacobs, Dan N., ed. *The New Communist Manifesto and other Documents*, 2nd ed. New York: Harper and Row, 1962.

Kennan, George. *Soviet Foreign Policy Under Lenin and Stalin*. Boston: Little, Brown and Co., 1961.

Mosely, Philip E. *The Kremlin and World Politics*. New York: Vintage Books, 1960.

Rubinstein, Alvin Z., ed. *The Foreign Policy of the Soviet Union*. New York: Random House, 1960.

Authors' Suggestions

An authentic and correct exposition of the foreign policy of the U.S.S.R. is contained in the speeches and statements of N. S. Khrushchov. Representative compilations are:

Conquest Without War, An Analytical Anthology of the Speeches, Interviews, and Remarks of N. S. Khrushchov. XI. New York: 1960.

For Victory in Peaceful Competition with Capitalism. New York: Dutton, 1960.

N. S. Khrushchov in America. Full Text of the Speeches Made by N. S. Khrushchov on His Tour of the U.S., September 15–27, 1959. New York: 1960.

Other source materials are:

Correspondence Between the Chairman of the Council of Ministers of the U.S.S.R. and the President of the U.S.A. and the Prime Minister of Great Britain During the Great Patriotic War of 1941–1945. New York: 1958.

Falsifiers of History. Moscow: 1951.

The Truth About Western Policy on the German Question. Moscow: 1959.

ABOUT THE AUTHOR

DYURA NINCIC studied at Belgrade University and the London School of Economics, receiving his LL.D. in 1954 from Belgrade University. He was an active participant in the National Liberation Movement in World War II and joined the Yugoslav Foreign Office in 1946. He has served with the Permanent Mission of Yugoslavia to the United Nations as Counsellor and Deputy Permanent Representative and as Alternate Representative to the Security Council and the Disarmament Commission. He represented Yugoslavia in all sixteen sessions of the U.N. General Assembly. Since 1959 he has been Director of the International Organizations Department in the Secretariat of the State for Foreign Affairs with the rank of Minister Plenipotentiary.

His articles and studies on international relations and international law include the following: *The U.N. Charter and the Problem of Domestic Jurisdiction*, 1954; *The Question of Self-Defense in International Law*, 1955; *The Problem of Collective Measures*, 1956; *The Question of a United Nations Force*, 1960; *The Evolution of the United Nations*, 1961; *The Disarmament Problem and the Struggle for Peace under Contemporary International Conditions*, 1961.

ABOUT THE CHAPTER

"In the final analysis, foreign policy is a result of the complex interplay between the goals a nation seeks to achieve in the international sphere and the general context within which these goals are to be attained." In this chapter Dr. Nincic depicts the major goals of Yugoslavia and the world-wide struggle for power which stands in the way of their attainment.

The author gives the highest priority to Yugoslavia's desire to be independent from foreign influence and especially from the two Major Power blocs. Attention is directed to the difficulties Yugoslavia has had in maintaining a position of non-alignment and in resisting the pressures from both the East and the West. Ironically, while this book was in preparation, the pendulum in Yugoslav-Russian relations was swinging again towards closer ties between these two nations. The author revised the chapter, accordingly.

The last part of the chapter is devoted to an exposition of the major foreign policy principles followed by Yugoslavia. Attention is given to both general problems confronting the world community and to particular problems, such as Yugoslavia's relations with her immediate neighbors.

9

THE FOREIGN POLICY OF YUGOSLAVIA

DYURA NINCIC

Ministry of Foreign Affairs, Belgrade

The elements that shape a country's policy are many and varied, and they are subject to change. While the conduct of a country's foreign affairs naturally reflects its internal political and social structure, and its historical background and geographical environment, foreign affairs are also fashioned by the broader international setting within which the country has to operate. In the final analysis, foreign policy is a result of the complex interplay between the goals a nation seeks to achieve in the international sphere and the general context within which these goals are to be attained. It is essential, therefore, if a country's policy is to be properly understood and correctly assessed, to grasp and evaluate these various factors in their dynamics and interaction. This is what we shall seek to do here with regard to the foreign policy of Yugoslavia, a foreign policy whose understanding will be interesting and useful in piecing together the overall picture of present-day world affairs.

THE BACKGROUND

Geography and natural resources

The general background of Yugoslavia's foreign policy is somewhat complex, both in its "constant" and its "variable" elements. In terms of geography, Yugoslavia belongs to the Balkan, the Central European and also the Mediterranean area. This explains the various influences, cultural, political and religious to which the population has been exposed at various stages of its history. With the exception of the fertile Pannonian Lowland in the Northeast, Yugoslavia is largely a mountainous country, where the people have had to wage a constant struggle for their very existence. Probably, this helps explain—without any facile resort to "geographical determinism"—some of the sturdy features which are generally recognized to form part of the "national character." The country's natural resources are abundant. She has one of the richest deposits of high-quality bauxite, the largest copper mine in Europe, the greatest unexploited reserves of hydro-energy on that continent, after Norway, as well as large deposits of coal and lignite.

The road to nationhood

Prewar Yugoslavia was, nonetheless, a backward agrarian country, with one of the lowest literacy and one of the highest infant mortality rates in Europe. That, of course, is explained by the vicissitudes that marked the history of the peoples of what was later to become Yugoslavia. Yugoslavia as a state did not come into being until 1918. Prior to that, the nations that were to become part of the Kingdom of the Serbs, Croats and Slovenes, as it was originally called, had travelled different paths. Serbia, once a powerful medieval empire, had been conquered by the Turks. It only regained its independence in the nineteenth century after two major uprisings and full-scale wars, as well as a series of diplomatic battles, against its Ottoman rulers.

At almost the same time, the newly independent state had to resist various forms of pressure on the part of its powerful neighbor, the Austro-Hungarian monarchy, a pressure which reached its climax in the notorious 1914 ultimatum, which touched off World War I. Montenegro had also been an independent kingdom and had had to pay a high price for its freedom. Croatia and Slovenia had been part of the Dual Monarchy and had been compelled, through the centuries, to wage a constant struggle to preserve their national identity and to become masters of their own fate. Macedonia had remained under Turkish rule until the Balkan Wars of 1912 and had then been incorporated into Serbia, while Bosnia and Herzegovina, formerly Turkish provinces, had been annexed by Austria-Hungary in 1908.

Despite the obstacles which history and power politics had placed between them, all these branches of the South Slav family had much in common. Situated astride Europe's traditional invasion routes, surrounded by powerful and usually greedy neighbors, they have, over the centuries, had to wage a grim and unremitting struggle for their independence, indeed, for their very survival, a struggle the twin weapons of which were arms and diplomacy. In this struggle, they developed a growing unity, arising not only from racial, cultural and many other affinities, but also from a yearning for freedom they all shared and a sense of common destiny. These strivings were expressed, in prose and in verse, by the best minds among the South Slavs, and particularly by liberal thinkers of the nineteenth century.

From World War I to World War II

Their dreams were brought to fulfillment in 1918, though not quite in the way that had been hoped. The new Yugoslav state was a result of the struggle of the different South Slav nationalities and of the victories of the Serbian army. It was also part of the system of Versailles, which the triumph of the Allies had brought to Europe. The internal structure of the new multi-national state was rigidly centralized, with all power in the hands of the Serbian ruling circles. These circles had to quell vigorous revolutionary movements of the working class in the aftermath of the war and in the days of the October Revolution. The centralized system was aggravated by a monarchist form of government, and was as oppressive as it was generally inefficient and corrupt. It aroused the mounting resistance of the other nationalities, and placed an increasing strain on the entire fabric of the new state, notwithstanding temporary accommodations between the bourgeoisie of these nationalities and the Serbian ruling circles. Economically, Yugoslavia was a backward agrarian country. An overwhelming part of its natural resources were owned and exploited by foreign businesses, which wielded substantial political influence, too. These factors, of course, largely conditioned Yugoslavia's prewar foreign policy.

In the early days, Yugoslavia, which had partly been a product, and had become one of the mainstays of the Versailles system and of the pattern of alliances which France had established in support thereof, closely aligned her policies to those of France, both with regard to the former enemy states and to the Soviet Union. She did not even recognize the Soviet Union diplomatically until shortly before World War II. Her own major concern was to stave off the revisionist pressure to which she was exposed on the part of at least three of her neighbors—Italy, Hungary and Bulgaria. The latter were not slow in seeking to make use, for their own purposes, of the growing and perfectly legitimate dissatisfaction of some of the oppressed nationalities and they found allies in the more reactionary sections of the bourgeoisie of these nationalities. As the system of collective security which France had endeavored to establish in Europe began to disintegrate under the impact of the mounting Fascist offensive and the sapping influence of appeasement policies, the Belgrade ruling circles switched their allegiance to the Axis Powers in their quest for support against the growing democratic and national movements within the country. In so doing, they displayed an increasing readiness to surrender portions of their nation's independence. This culminated in the Yugoslav government's adhesion to the Three Power Pact on March 25, 1941.

The Government that had accomplished what the overwhelming majority of the population viewed as a flagrant act of treason, was overthrown two days later. This, too, was in a way a climax—the climax of the twin struggle the people had been waging for democracy and independence. On April 6, 1941, Yugoslavia was attacked on practically all her borders by Germany and her satellites. Rent from within by the dissensions that had accumulated during almost a quarter of a century of national, political and social oppression, betrayed by the powerful fifth-column elements that had worked their way into some of the key positions in the governmental and military structure of the country, Yugoslavia was able to put up little more than a token resistance to the onslaught of Hitler's divisions. The Army surrendered and the King and the government fled the country.

It was then, and then only, that the real fight began. The struggle of the Partisans which started in the early days of July 1941, less than three months after the collapse of the prewar Yugoslav state, and continued until V-E Day, tied down considerable parts of the Axis forces, succeeded in liberating large parts of Yugoslav territory and, by November 1943, laid down the foundations of the new Yugoslav state right in the midst of Hitler's European fortress. This war for national liberation was led by the Communist party, which had been driven underground and bitterly persecuted by the old regime, but which was alone capable of launching an all-out struggle against the invaders and their lackeys. This struggle finally resulted in the complete liberation of Yugoslav soil from the Fascist forces.

Internal changes during World War II

One of the basic features of Yugoslavia's victorious liberation struggle—and one that goes a long way towards explaining the success of that struggle—was the fact that it was a revolutionary struggle as well as a struggle against the various forms of oppression that had plagued prewar Yugoslavia and that had finally helped bring about her downfall. It was a struggle both against the Fascist invaders and against a return of the old order which had, in a very real sense, paved the way for the invasion. The process of liberation was at the same time a process of change in the political, in the social and in the economic field. The Yugoslavia that had emerged from the throes of World War II was a very different country from the one that had collapsed only four years before.

Internally, the transformation was a twofold one. On the one hand, Yugoslavia had changed from a rigidly centralized state to a federation, with a full measure of self-government for, and complete equality of, the different nationalities. An answer to the national question, which had been one of the country's basic weaknesses, had thus been found and the continued existence of Yugoslavia as a state ensured. This was one of the major results of the liberation struggle, which had, in fact, had a double aspect: it had been a fight for the liberation of the country as a whole from the Fascist invaders and for the liberation of each individual nation from the national oppression to which it had been subjected under the prewar regime.

At the same time, the liberation struggle had brought about a radical change in the basic structure of political power. As the liberated territory expanded, the local authorities which had become subservient to, or had been imposed by, the occupation forces and their quislings, had naturally been removed. They had been replaced by new officials which had emerged from the liberation struggle and embodied the strivings of the people as expressed through that struggle. By the end of 1943, a Provisional Parliament known as the Anti-Fascist Council of National Liberation met and established a new form of government in place of the Government in Exile. The latter not only symbolized the past and all its implications, but, as we shall see in a moment, had actually thwarted the liberation struggle through its representatives inside the country.

In other words, a new form of government was established throughout the liberated territory which, by the end of the War, coincided with the national territory as a whole. In some cases it even covered areas which were not included within Yugoslavia's new boundaries. Thus, the liberation of the country also meant the completion of a sweeping political revolution which divested the former ruling classes of their power. Henceforth, power was placed in the hands of the social strata that had borne the brunt of the war of liberation and had carried out the revolution.

Yugoslav socialism   A revolution, accomplished under these conditions, was bound to have far-reaching social and economic implications. The shift in the relationship of social forces had necessarily led to a change in the pattern of property ownership. The measures of nationalization, taken after the War, had been a natural sequel to the liberation struggle. The property that was taken over was, in the main, the property of those who had sided with the enemy in that struggle. Moreover the country had to be rebuilt and the tremendous damages wrought by the War had to be repaired. Vast common efforts were required to do this, as well as the pooling of what little resources remained. This, too, precluded any return to the curious "free" enterprise system that had prevailed before the war. There was, however, a deeper reason why the country embarked upon a course that was to lead to socialism. Socialism was, in fact, the only way for it to emerge from its previous state of backwardness and to lay solid foundations for independent progress. The generation that had led the liberation struggle believed strongly that the future belonged to socialism, as a more advanced and more equitable social order.

The foundations for Yugoslavia's further evolution were thus laid, an evolution from which her distinctive pattern of socialism gradually emerged. In the early postwar years, the reconstruction of the war-ravaged country was the most pressing need and the essential material prerequisites for the advance towards socialism had to be created. The economic life of the country was therefore, of necessity, subjected to a centralized system of controls. This was the period known as "administrative socialism."

As soon, however, as the basic aims were more or less achieved, as the nation's economy began expanding and the forces of production gained momentum, this system of controls was increasingly becoming a brake upon, rather than an incentive to, further economic and social progress. It also was fraught with bureaucratic tendencies which were naturally inimical to the growth of genuinely democratic institutions. When that stage was reached, in the early nineteen-fifties, a transformation of the basic forms of political and social organization firmly grounded on the social ownership of the means of production, set in. This transformation is still in progress.

The general line of advance was that of growing self-government at all levels of economic and political organization. The process began with the introduction of workers' management in industry (i.e. the control and operation of the industries by the workers themselves) and was soon followed by various forms of what was to become known as *social management* (i.e. the management of various social institutions, services, etc. by the citizens concerned). It was accompanied by a growing measure of political or territorial self-government which grew into a system of *communes,* where we find the essential elements of direct democracy in the social, political and economic spheres and where the individual and the common interests blend to an increasing degree.[1] This, obviously, was a bold and largely unchartered course to take and one beset by many difficulties. The fact that it has proved successful is, we feel, the best evidence that it corresponds both to the particular needs of our country and to the overall requirements of socialist advance in the mid-twentieth century.

The political and social transformation of the country also modified the mainsprings of its foreign policy. Thus, socialism and independence—both of which were a fruit of the liberation struggle—became closely linked in the minds of the people and in the practical policies of the country. An essential prerequisite

[1] This process developed alongside, and on the basis, of the growth of the forces of production arising from the rapid industrialization of the country. This rapid process of industrialization has, of course, changed the face of the country and, in particular, modified the structure of the population. While, out of a prewar population of around fourteen millions, more than 70 percent were engaged in agriculture, the percentage of those employed in industry has now risen to over 50 percent. At the same time, industrial output has risen four and a half times, as compared to that of the last prewar year—1939.

for both was *peace,* as a nation that had lost more than one tenth of its population in the War, was fully in a position to realize.

THE STRUGGLE FOR INDEPENDENCE FROM FOREIGN INFLUENCE

The political and diplomatic struggle for independence had actually started during the War as part of the national liberation movement. It was not so much a struggle for renewed independence which the peoples of Yugoslavia had enjoyed in the past and had lost in the war and which was, at best, a rather dubious and precarious one, but for the country's future independence, which they were determined to make far more effective and enduring. It was, from the outset, a struggle for the recognition of Yugoslavia's rightful place—a place she had long won in the field of battle within the United Nations, as the war-time coalition came to be known. It was also a struggle for the acknowledgment of Yugoslavia's right to independent development in the postwar world. Nor was it an easy struggle. The opposition encountered was not easily overcome. The goals which the Yugoslav Liberation Movement had set itself, while fully in keeping with the declared policies of the Allies, especially as expressed in such documents as the Atlantic Charter, did not quite fit into some of the actual schemes they were devising for the postwar period.

East and West seek dominance

The main pressure, at first, came from the West. For a long time during the War, the Western Allies had supported the Royal Yugoslav Government in London and the Mihailovic forces within the country. This was done primarily because these forces were an anti-Communist element, required for the building of the postwar order which the Western Allies visualized, as a means of extending their own sphere of influence at the expense of that of the Soviet Union. It was only when it became glaringly obvious that the rightist forces in Yugoslavia were not only wholly ineffective from the military point of view in the fight against the Axis, but that their political value had itself become seriously impaired through their increasingly overt collusion with the Axis, that the Western Allies decided to extend a somewhat grudging recognition and a measure of support to the Partisans. There was also some evidence of displeasure on the part of the Soviet Government at what they apparently felt, was an excessive proclivity towards independence among the leaders of the Yugoslav Liberation Movement.

The pressure to which Yugoslavia's independence was exposed did not cease with the end of the fighting—it merely assumed new forms. Basically, it was part of an attempt to keep Yugoslavia within one or the other of the two spheres of influence into which Europe was about to be split and which were subsequently to grow into hostile military and political groupings. There were even attempts to carve Yugoslavia herself up on a fifty-fifty basis between the two spheres. Indicative in this regard was a colorful episode which Winston Churchill relates in his World War II Memoirs:

> The moment was apt for business, so I said: "Let's us settle about our affairs in the Balkans. Your armies are in Rumania and Bulgaria. We have interests, missions and agents there. Don't let us get at cross-purposes in small ways. So far as Britain and Russia are concerned, how would it do for you to have ninety percent predominance in Rumania, for us to have ninety percent of the way in Greece and go fifty-fifty about Yugoslavia." While this was being translated, I wrote on a halfsheet of paper:
>
> Rumania:
> Russia 90%
> The others 10%
> Greece:
> Great Britain 90%
> (In accord with USA)
> Russia 10%
> Yugoslavia 50%–50%
> Hungary 50%–50%
> Bulgaria:
> Russia 75%
> The others 25%

> I pushed this across to Stalin, who had by then heard the translation. There was a slight pause. Then he took his blue pencil and made a large tick upon it. It was all settled in no more time than it takes to set down.[2]

This shows the mood in which the problems of postwar settlements were approached then.

Unsatisfactory peace treaties

The pressure, however, continued as the struggle for mastery in Europe between the two camps became more severe. The West was by now inclined to regard Yugoslavia, with the Communist party in power, as part of the Soviet orbit and acted accordingly. This was particularly obvious when the time came to sign peace treaties with some of Yugoslavia's neighbors who had been Hitler's allies. For Yugoslavia this was a moment of great importance, because it provided an opportunity for her to complete the liberation struggle, by freeing those of her nationals who had remained outside her borders as a result of the territorial settlements that followed World War I. In Italy, in particular, there had been a large Slovene and Croat minority which had been subjected to a particularly severe form of oppression under the Fascist regime. These minorities had

[2] Josip Broz Tito, "On Certain Current International Questions," *Foreign Affairs*, October 1957, pp. 68–76.

joined the liberation movement in large numbers. The movement had, in turn, inscribed the freedom of these Yugoslavs on its banners.

When the time came, at the Paris Peace Conference of 1946, to rectify previous injustices, the Western Allies strenuously endeavored to keep those changes of the Italian-Yugoslav border which could not be avoided, as limited as possible. Thus, they tried to prevent Yugoslavia's borders from moving further West, with scant heed for ethnical considerations or for the respective roles played in World War II by the two countries concerned. The consideration that seems to have weighed most heavily with the Western Powers was to halt any advance of what was deemed to be the Soviet sphere of influence, particularly towards the Mediterranean region. Yugoslavia was then considered—how wrongly was soon to become apparent—a vanguard of Soviet penetration.

The Soviet Union, on the other hand, generally supported Yugoslavia's claims, although not always with the degree of enthusiasm which the Yugoslavs felt they had the right to expect. As they were later to learn, Yugoslav national interests constituted for the Soviet Government of that time only one element in the complex power struggle they were engaged in with their war-time Allies, an element upon which greater or lesser insistence was placed in relation to the overall state of the game. In these circumstances, Yugoslavia had to accept a compromise whereby a substantial number of Slovenes remained under Italy. A Free Territory of Trieste was established, but never actually came into being, so that the Trieste question remained for several years a bone of contention between Yugoslavia and Italy, and a means of Western pressure upon Yugoslavia.

Early postwar relations with the power blocs

Relations between Yugoslavia and the Western Powers began improving when the latter realized: a) that Yugoslavia's independence could not be curbed through the various forms of pressure which they had at different times sought to bring to bear upon her, and, b) that Yugoslavia's independence was genuine and that Yugoslavia was not, and never had been, subservient to the U.S.S.R. or to any other country for that matter. Naturally enough, after the crisis with the Eastern European countries had occurred in 1948, Yugoslavia's relations with the West entered a new and, broadly speaking, more favorable stage.

There was, however, the danger which at times became quite apparent, that some Western Powers might seek to use Yugoslavia's very considerable difficulties with the Soviet Union, to renew their pressure to bring her within the Western field and even into a certain state of dependence upon the West and to induce her to alter her economic and social system. This, of course, was merely a revival of old ambitions under a new guise and under changed conditions. When this pressure proved no more successful than previous attempts along similar lines had been, relations with the Western Powers and with the United States and the United Kingdom, developed fairly smoothly, despite certain ups and downs. The "downs" were usually caused by tactless and fruitless attempts on the part of certain circles in the West to interfere with, or at least influence, various aspects of Yugoslavia's foreign or domestic policies.

Difficulties with the Soviet Union   The story of Yugoslavia's struggle to resist pressure from Stalin and his acolytes, is fairly widely known by now. While the vicissitudes which Yugoslavia's relations with the Soviet Union and some of the other countries of the Soviet camp went through at the time are familiar to most students of international relations, the underlying causes are still not always fully grasped. Yugoslavia's difficulties with the Stalinist regime did not begin in 1948, when the official break came. The break was actually merely the culmination of a lengthy process which had started during the War—and, in a sense, even earlier—in the relations between the Yugoslav Communist party and the Soviet-dominated Comintern. The war-time friction stemmed from causes whose full significance was only later revealed.

Under Stalin, Soviet policies had generally speaking been those of a Great Power with its own specific interests to which other considerations—including the liberation of the different countries—were subordinated. In this particular case, they were to be subordinated to the needs of the Soviet Government's accommodation with its war-time Allies,[3] on the one hand, and to the requirements of extending the Soviet Union's sphere of influence at the expense of those self-same Allies, on the other. The Yugoslav Liberation Movement and the Communist party which led it, were determined to pursue Yugoslavia's own national aims. They felt that these aims were fully in harmony with the broader interests of both the immediate anti-Fascist struggle and the long-range interests of the growth of socialism in the world. But these aims did not necessarily coincide—and could, in fact, hardly be expected to coincide—either with Stalin's tactical aims or with his hegemonistic ambitions. Frictions thus soon developed, although their full significance was not realized at the time or for many years later.

In the immediate postwar years, in the deep after-glow of the victory over the common enemy in which the Soviet Union had played so prominent a part, and to which the Yugoslav Liberation Movement had made its contribution, the difficulties were dimmed by the feeling of common elation, and what were felt to be the common goals of socialism, as well as by the support the Soviet Union had given Yugoslavia in her efforts to withstand pressure from the West. The sources of friction, as was soon to become apparent, not only remained but tended to increase. The basic point at issue was the same: Yugoslavia's determination to assert her right to her own line of advance towards socialism, which was once again a form of her struggle both for socialism and for independence.

[3] Josip Broz Tito, Report to the Congress of the Socialist Alliance of the Working People of Yugoslavia, April 18, 1960.

The trouble broke out in 1948, when Stalin and Molotov addressed, on behalf of the Communist party of the Soviet Union, a number of letters to the leaders of the Communist party of Yugoslavia. These letters brought forth a number of charges the burden of which was that the Yugoslav Communists had strayed from the true path of Marxism-Leninism (as interpreted by Stalin!) and had shown hostility to the Soviet Union. The Yugoslav leaders refuted these charges and insisted upon their right to independence and equality in relation to the other Socialist countries and Communist parties.

Then came the famous (or infamous) meeting of the Cominform in Bucharest, where the Yugoslav Communist party was tried and condemned *in absentia*. This marked the beginning of a violent campaign of political, ideological, economic and even military pressure, against Yugoslavia. While resisting this pressure—and this demanded considerable determination and no small sacrifice on the part of the people— Yugoslavia affirmed certain basic views, certain fundamental tenets of her political philosophy, concerning relations between Socialist states and within the international labor movement in general. The Stalinist view was based on the concept of the leading role of the Soviet Union within the Socialist camp. Since the latter was equated with socialism as a system, the interests of the Soviet Union became both identical and coextensive with those of socialism, and transcended those of the other Socialist countries and of the working-class movement as a whole. This was the Stalinist understanding of "proletarian internationalism," which was but a very thin disguise for Soviet Great Power hegemony.

In resisting this hegemony, the Yugoslavs had of necessity to combat the ideological guise under which it was presented. Yugoslavia thus denied the concept of a "leading nation" within socialism and insisted instead on full equality— political, economic and ideological—among Socialist countries. The Yugoslavs also rejected any uniform pattern or blueprint, either for the working class movement or for the construction of socialism. They demanded instead for each country the right to build socialism through a creative rather than dogmatic application of Marxism and in accordance with its specific needs and conditions. In the Yugoslav view, a rigid pattern or a centralized leadership for the international working class movement would only stultify the general advance towards socialism for which the times called. In other words, a country's independence, a nation's right to self-determination, necessarily meant its right to elect its own form of government, and to choose its particular line of progress towards socialism.

MAJOR POLICY PRINCIPLES

Non-alignment

Thus Yugoslavia has had to wage a determined struggle to keep clear of the spheres of influence into which Europe had been split and to fight shy of the political, military and ideological alignments—both East and West—into which they had subsequently grown. She soon came to realize that an essential precondition of her independence in general and of her independent advance towards socialism in particular, was to remain outside groupings which, by their very nature, would have tended to bring her into line with the general political and ideological outlook associated with that particular grouping. That is why she displayed no inclination, even at the time when she was under the most severe pressure from the East, to join the Western alliance, just as she never construed the improvement of her relations with the Eastern European countries as implying an intention to enter the Warsaw Pact.

Dangers of the policy of alignments   Nor is it merely a question of keeping aloof from "en-

tangling alliances." Yugoslavia's opposition to the policy of military and political alignments is of a more fundamental nature. The policy of alignments, in the Yugoslav view, is both a source and a result of the difficulties, of the tensions and perils, through which the world has been passing during the last decade and a half. They are fraught with the danger of war, at a time when it is more or less generally recognized that a nuclear war would spell suicide for mankind. They increase artificial divisions at a time when the forces of history are leading towards growing world unity. The state of tension they maintain, and the hegemonistic tendencies that are apt to develop within their fold, hamper the growth of progressive trends in the world.

The ideological overtones which the military and political power groupings were soon to acquire only made things worse. By the very fact that it injected ideological elements into the international arena, the policy of blocs made outstanding problems more difficult of solution and existing differences more profound. The blocs tended to turn into closed economic systems, which not only warped the normal growth of the world economy, but also added to the prevailing political divisions.

Thus, to the Yugoslavs—and their views on the matter were solidly rooted both in their own experience and in their analysis of world currents and trends—the blocs and all they stand for, are not merely an evil to shun, but a danger to be fought. That is why Yugoslavia never accepted the label of "neutralism" with regard to her foreign policy. While she might be neutral in the struggle *between* military alignments, she was anything but neutral in the struggle *against* the policy of alignments. Nor was she neutral when it was a question of supporting the trends which she considered consistent with the needs of our times and which, objectively, work against the entire structure of international relations of which the alignments are a part. The Yugoslavs have never, of course, thought it possible that the alignments could be done away with overnight. They could only be done away with gradually to the extent that the cause and conditions that had brought them into being were removed.

Newly-independent countries favor non-alignment   There was a time, not so many years ago, when the countries that did not owe allegiance to either of the blocs were almost looked upon as freaks of international life, as countries which had not "yet made up their minds" where to go, when non-alignment was viewed as "sitting on the fence" and neutralism described as "immoral." It was the time when blocs were regarded as a normal and immutable fact of international life. This, of course, led to the prevailing mood that "those who are not for us are against us."

Those who attended the sessions of the UN General Assembly in those days will recall the picture of a House rigidly divided along bloc lines, with automatic majorities and minorities operating with unerring precision and with a few "neutrals" either seeking refuge in abstention or endeavoring to narrow the gap between the blocs through compromise proposals. It was apparently overlooked at the time that the two camps into which the world appeared to be irremediably split, covered only one third of mankind—the most vocal, highly developed and powerfully armed third, it is true, but only a third nonetheless. The remaining two-thirds were still, to a very large extent, under various forms of colonial domination and shockingly underdeveloped, but they were on the move. As their movement gained momentum and the shackles which had held them in bondage began falling apart, their role on the international scene started to grow and grow at an accelerated pace. Not only was the membership of the UN vastly increased, but its entire structure became radically modified.

The newly independent countries of Asia and Africa began acting together on a number of issues, first on the colonial issues which were their immediate concern, and then also with regard to other international problems, including those which had hitherto been considered as coming within the exclusive scope of East-West relations. These countries, with a few rare exceptions, showed no inclination to join the existing power alignments, with whose aims and purposes they could not sympathize and towards which they adopted an attitude rather similar to that which Yugoslavia had already taken.

Non-alignment becomes a positive policy
Yugoslavia very soon established close working relations with most of these countries, with which she obviously shared a common approach to the basic problems of international relations. A growing measure of co-operation was established both in the UN and on a bilateral basis. President Tito's visits to Asia and Africa helped to make these links even closer, in particular with such countries as India, Indonesia, the United Arab Republic, Morocco, Ghana and others. This general trend led to their concerted action at the fifteenth session of the UN General Assembly, where they tabled a number of important resolutions. Among them was a resolution calling for immediate contact between the President of the United States and the Premier of the Soviet Union for the purpose of easing world tensions, as well as a draft resolution setting forth some of the basic principles along the lines of which future disarmament efforts could develop. A further and important step in that direction was the Conference of the Heads of States and Governments of the Non-aligned Countries, which assembled in Belgrade on September 1, 1961, where the fundamental tenets of non-alignment were restated and the approach of the non-aligned countries to some of the major international problems defined.

The policy of non-alignment thus became considerably more than mere opposition to the system of blocs and all they stood for. Nor did the proponents of this policy rest content with seeking to steer an illusory middle course between the opposing positions of these blocs. Rather, they sought to work out a positive approach to the basic issues confronting the world and to point to a way toward their solution. These transformations of the policy of non-alignment were a result both of the growing strength of the non-aligned countries and of their concerted action. When we speak of the "strength" of the non-committed countries, we are, of course, not thinking in terms of military might or economic power, because these countries possess neither. And when we refer to their "concerted action" what we have in mind is not any trend towards the establishment of a "third bloc," since such a trend would be self-defeating and constitute a denial of the very principles of non-alignment. What we are thinking of is the obvious fact that the number of non-aligned countries is increasing and that non-alignment, as a policy, is spreading, and, most important perhaps, that this policy corresponds more and more clearly to the needs and possibilities of the present-day world.

Co-existence and peace

"Co-existence," as a Yugoslav representative put it at one of the sessions of the UN General Assembly, "merely means to bring our thinking and our policies into line with the technological and scientific progress in the world as it is to-day. It is as simple—and as complicated—as that." Co-existence is simply based on a recognition of the fact that the present-day world consists of countries with different economic and social systems, and at varying levels of development, that these countries have their differences and that these differences, in this nuclear age of ours, can be solved only by peaceful means if the world is to be spared general destruction. Co-existence then, in the Yugoslav view at least, is not one of the possible policies among which the world is at leisure to choose, it is *the only* policy. As President Tito expressed it in his speech at the fifteenth session of the General Assembly of the United Nations, it is the only alternative "to an almost constant cold war, to moving on the brink of war, and finally to real war which would mean complete destruction."

Co-existence is, moreover, the Yugoslavs are convinced, a realistic and fully attainable goal.

Marx once said that mankind sets itself those tasks only which it is in a position to solve. We are convinced that peace, through co-existence is, in our day, a feasible proposition for two basic reasons. On the one hand, the very destructiveness of modern weapons would appear, in any rational terms, to rule war out as "a continuation of politics by other means"—to use Clausewitz's now grimly obsolescent dictum. On the other hand, the forces working for peace—and among these the non-aligned countries have an important place—are constantly gaining in strength and are increasingly capable of preventing countries, who would be prepared to do so, from unleashing a nuclear catastrophe. Peace and co-existence demand a constant struggle—a struggle which, however, offers growing prospects of success.

The requirements of active co-existence
Co-existence, as the Yugoslavs understand it, is not a passive state of merely living side by side, of eking out a kind of existence together. Co-existence, in the interdependent world of ours, implies co-operation. That is why we, in Yugoslavia, speak of active and not merely of "peaceful" co-existence.

Furthermore, when we speak of co-existence, what we have in mind is not merely co-existing blocs, but *co-existence among states* both with similar and with dissimilar social and political systems. Co-existence between the existing political and military blocs, while it is obviously better than open conflict between them, is a highly precarious state of affairs and one which, moreover, implies the continuance of the alignments themselves. In fact, the blocs have, in a sense, been co-existing all along and it can hardly be claimed that his has been a very felicitous condition of affairs. Co-existence, as we see it, should lead to the gradual disappearance of the blocs. Therefore, co-existence between the blocs can at best only be the starting point of a process in the course of which they are to "wither away," and co-existence will extend to all states, regardless of their social and political structure. Differences in forms of government or political and economic systems are unavoidable at the present stage of history, but should not be a source of international conflict or an obstacle to co-operation among states.

Co-existence, as the Yugoslavs understand it, does not, moreover, in any way imply a freezing of the social and international status quo. Far from stultifying either progress or change, co-existence is, in the present-day world, alone able to create genuinely propitious conditions for both progress and change and for socialism in particular. A creative application of Marxist theory to existing world conditions, has led Yugoslavia to the conclusion that socialism is a process which embraces the entire world, makes its way through all the pores of society, and evolves various forms according to the specific conditions of the different countries. It is therefore up to individual countries, or rather to the social forces in these countries to solve the problems of socialism and social progress in general, by their own means and in accordance with their own lights. The struggle for socialism thus has to be fought within each country and not on the international level, between countries or groups of countries. If this view is accepted—and the alternative is fraught with extremely dangerous possibilities in terms of "revolutionary wars" for the purpose of "spreading socialism"—then it becomes perfectly clear that it is under conditions of co-existence and of a more stable peace, that the natural trends of social development can most easily make headway. This point is succinctly put by Edvard *Kardelj* in a recent book entitled "Socialism and War":

> Naturally, the policy of co-existence is not and must not be a policy of defending the status quo either in international relations, and still less in international social relations. It simply means renouncing war as a means for settling international contradictions, and relying, at the same time, on the results of internal social development, which will, as a final result, change international relations as well. . . . For us, the struggle for peace and for peaceful co-existence is, above all a

component part of the struggle for Socialism.[4]

Now, it is obvious that co-existence as a pattern of international relations and of co-operation among states must rest on certain clearly defined principles. These principles are embodied in a number of international documents ranging from the Atlantic Charter, to the *Panch-sheel,* the principles of Bandung and the more recent Belgrade Declaration. These principles offer a standard of international conduct which all states should observe in their relations, if they are to live and work together. These principles have been set forth in various ways, but they actually boil down to three basic rules which President Tito mentioned in his address to the fifteenth UN General Assembly.

"The first of the fundamental principles of co-existence, as we understand it," he said,

> is that differences of social systems must not be a reason for armed conflict or an impediment to peaceful co-operation among states. Controversial issues should be settled by peaceful means, and force and war should be eliminated from the practice of international relations. The third basic principle is respect for the obligation of non-interference in the internal affairs of other nations and states and the right of every nation to organize its own life.[5]

Such, then, in broad outline, is the policy of co-existence, both peaceful and active, which the Yugoslavs firmly believe is the only possible policy under existing world conditions if the survival of mankind is to be assured. We shall now try to show how Yugoslavia has sought to apply this policy in practice.

[4] Edvard Kardelj, *Socialism and War*, Belgrade, 1960, partially reprinted in Dan N. Jacobs, editor, *The New Communist Manifesto and Related Documents*, 2nd ed., Evanston, Ill.: Row, Peterson and Co., 1962, pp. 183–212.

[5] Josip Broz Tito, Speech at the Fifteenth Session of the General Assembly of the United Nations, September 22, 1960.

CURRENT FOREIGN POLICIES—
THE PRACTICE OF CO-EXISTENCE

We shall examine Yugoslavia's relations with her immediate neighbors, with the Major Powers and with her associates in the struggle for co-existence. We shall also discuss some of the international issues upon the settlement of which peace and co-existence depend.

Yugoslavia's relations with her neighbors, both capitalist and Socialist, provide a vivid example of how she has endeavored, albeit with varying degrees of success, to translate her idea of co-existence into practical terms.

Relations with neighboring countries

Italy   The manner in which relations between Yugoslavia and Italy have evolved is of particular interest in this regard. Here are two countries which practically everything seemed to divide. There was a bitter aftertaste of centuries of strife marked by strenuous resistance to Italy's desire to take large parts of Yugoslavia and to Fascist aggression and occupation. Their political and social systems and foreign policies differed, Italy being a member of NATO and Yugoslavia pursuing a course of non-alignment. The dispute over Trieste, moreover, had been one of the major hotbeds of crisis in postwar Europe. And yet, relations between the two countries are now friendly and even close. Their trade is lively and their frontier probably one of the most open in the world. Visits among leading statesmen are a frequent occurrence, and cultural exchanges take place on a considerable scale. In a word, it may safely be claimed that relations between Yugoslavia and Italy provide today a striking example of active co-existence and good-neighborliness in practice. How was this brought about? Through the fact that the two countries, once the Trieste question had been settled by mutual understanding, resolutely turned their back upon an unpleasant past. Without in any way overlooking their dissimilarities, they sought gradually to extend the area of agreement which was solidly grounded in their mutual interests.

Greece, Austria, and Albania   Not dissimilar has been the story of Yugoslavia's relations with Greece. The two countries had been friends and allies in two world wars, but, in the early postwar years, there had been serious difficulties between them. Here, too, vast differences of political and social systems and of general outlook were involved. Despite these differences, relations between Greece and Yugoslavia have become generally friendly and co-operative. With Austria, too, relations which had been burdened by many a painful memory of things past, have been developing satisfactorily. As regards Yugoslavia's neighbors, which belong or had belonged to the Socialist camp, they have followed the general pattern of the evolution of our country's relations with that camp. An exception to this has been the case of Albania. Ever since 1948, Albania has pursued a course of consistent hostility towards Yugoslavia and has engaged in constant vilification campaigns and subversive activities against our country and its government. Notwithstanding this attitude of the Albanian Government, Yugoslavia has for her part, unswervingly supported the independence and territorial integrity of her small neighbor, which she considers to be vital to the peace of the area.

Relations with Major Powers

Of Yugoslavia's relations with the Major Powers and the alignments they have created, fairly extensive mention has already been made. These relations have, despite their ups and downs, been developing upon a basis of co-existence towards which Yugoslavia has consistently been striving. Both camps, apparently, accepted Yugoslavia's independent course in world affairs and her own advance towards socialism. Her attitudes are still sometimes, it is true, misunderstood and misconstrued. But this is, as often as not, part of the high price that still has to be paid for a genuinely independent policy. Relations with the West have, in spite of this, been developing to the mutual advantage of both sides and in keeping with the requirements of co-existence. Yugoslavia has received valuable economic assistance from some of the Western Powers, especially the United States.

As regards the Soviet Union, the changes that have been taking place in Soviet policy since the close of the Stalinist epoch, have made it possible to develop generally satisfactory relations and a similarity of views on some important issues has emerged. The same holds true of relations with most of the other countries of the Socialist camp, despite intermittent revivals of various "ideological" charges, which are sometimes permitted to affect inter-state relations. In this latter regard, the attitude of the Chinese leaders has been particularly virulent. This is fairly easily explained by their general attitude to international affairs and to the problems of socialism.

Relations with non-aligned countries

We have already described Yugoslavia's relations with the non-aligned countries of Asia and Africa—her allies in the fight for peace and co-existence. These relations are, we submit, a vivid illustration of active co-existence in the true sense of the word. Differences between Yugoslavia and these countries, and among these countries themselves, are vast, in terms of geography, of historical and cultural background, and, in many cases, of social and political structure. Yet, the bonds that have gradually brought them together—and that keep them together—have proved stronger than these differences. These bonds, as we have tried to show, have been forged by a common

approach to the problem of peace. These states have, in a sense, found themselves on the same side of the "barricade"—not of the military or of the ideological barricade, but of the barricade of peace and co-existence.

Yugoslavia's early steps towards co-operation with these countries, both in the United Nations, and in the general field of international relations, often aroused suspicion. They were even derided by those whose sole terms of reference are provided by the existing alignments and their policies. What could Tito be doing in Asia and Africa, but seek to undermine the East or the West, as the case might be? Even when the Belgrade Conference of the non-aligned countries met in September 1961, serious doubts were expressed, on the one hand, as to whether "such different" countries would be able to find a common language; on the other hand, the conference as a whole was judged solely in terms of the benefit it would yield to the two opposing sides in the acute international crisis prevailing at the time. The Conference, which climaxed a long period of growth of the policy of non-alignment, provided an answer to both these lines of thinking. It did find a common language on all the main questions of peace and co-existence and it did not lend its support to either of the sides in the crisis. Rather, it addressed itself to the origins of the crisis in order to seek its elimination.

Korea and Suez

To complete our outline of Yugoslavia's policy of co-existence in practice, perhaps a few words should be said at this stage about her attitude on some of the major problems around which the possibility of co-existence primarily revolves. Yugoslavia has played an active part both in the efforts to quell conflicts and to do away with their underlying causes. In the first category, the case of Korea might perhaps be mentioned. From the very day the Korean war broke out, Yugoslavia, although

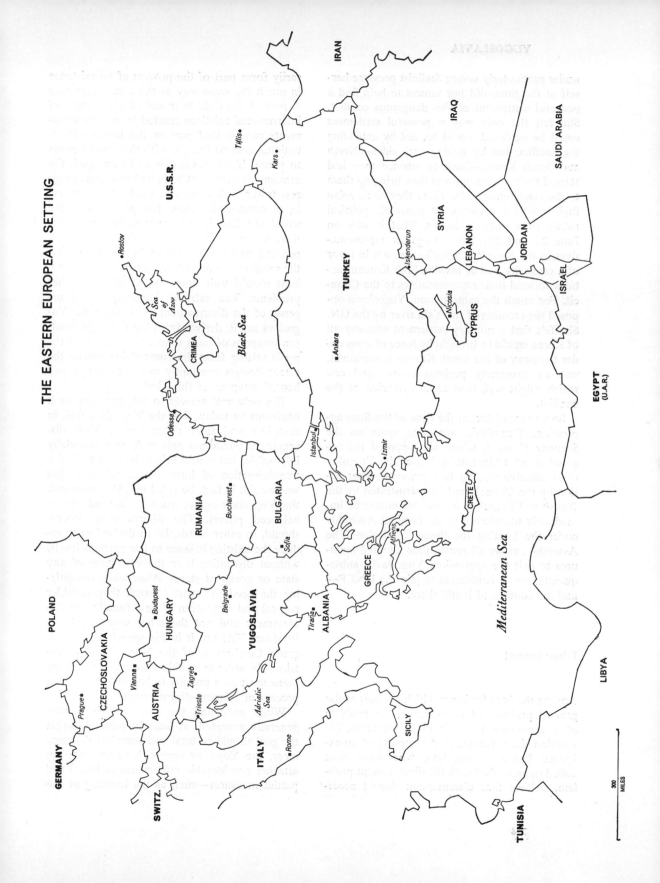

THE EASTERN EUROPEAN SETTING

under particularly severe Stalinist pressure herself at the time, did her utmost to help find a peaceful settlement of this dangerous conflict. She felt the only way a peaceful settlement could be achieved would be, not by extending the conflict, but by getting both sides—North and South Korea—back to whence they had started their operations and then bringing them to the conference table. There they could solve their political disputes by peaceful, political rather than military means. That is why on June 25 and 27, 1950, Yugoslav representatives in the Security Council came out in favor of a cease-fire and of inviting both Korean factions to send their representatives to the Council. For much the same reason, Yugoslavia opposed the crossing of the Yalu river by the UN. She felt that a military settlement whereby all of Korea would be brought by force of arms under the sway of the South Korean government, was an extremely perilous course and one which might well lead to an extension of the conflict.

Some years later, at the time of the Suez aggression, Yugoslavia was once again on the Security Council, where she opposed the aggression most vigorously. It was the Yugoslav representative who in fact proposed, after action by the Council had been frustrated by the British and French vote, that the matter be immediately transferred to the General Assembly under the Uniting for Peace Resolution. The Assembly, as we all recall, then adopted measures to halt the aggression. Yugoslavia, subsequently, sent a contingent to join the UNEF—and the contingent is still there.

Disarmament

Among the broader issues which are part of the general problem of co-existence, the problem of *disarmament* certainly ranks foremost. We mention disarmament in the context of co-existence because Yugoslavs, who have been called upon to deal with the disarmament problem, believe that disarmament should necessarily form part of the process of co-existence in much the same way as the armaments race is part of the Cold War and of the pattern of international relations created by it. The armaments race is thus part of the broader international context fraught with the gravest perils to peace. If this context is to be changed, the armaments race must be halted and some progress towards disarmament made; the converse is, of course, also true. The problems of the world are thus interdependent. However, this does not mean that they should be made dependent upon one another in the sense that the solution of one problem or one set of problems should wait upon the solution of other problems. The extreme importance and urgency of the disarmament problem, as the Yugoslavs see it, derives from the nature of modern weapons of mass destruction and from the perils arising from the competition among the Great Powers constantly to build "bigger and better" weapons of this kind.

The only real answer to this problem, as it confronts us today, lies, the Yugoslavs feel, in complete and total disarmament. Such disarmament would not only make war materially impossible, but would bring about so radical a transformation of international relations that war would, in fact, be ruled out. Disarmament, the Yugoslavs agree, must be carried out in balanced phases. The disarmament process should, in other words, be so devised as to reduce the existing balance to less perilous levels, without disrupting it to the advantage of any state or group of states. Also, while recognizing the need for strict control, they consider control and inspection to be a function of disarmament and not the other way round. As President Tito put it in his speech at the Belgrade Conference of the Non-aligned Countries: "In order to be able to control something, there must be a process to be controlled, i.e. a process of genuine disarmament."

While endorsing the idea—which is now generally accepted, at least in principle—that the goal should be total and complete disarmament, the Yugoslav approach to the problem attaches considerable importance to initial and partial measures—such as the banning of nuclear tests,[6]—which are likely to lead to other and more far-reaching measures in the field of disarmament, to start the ball rolling, as it were. Yugoslavia has endeavored, to the best of her abilities, to help towards progress in this vital field. Not only have the Yugoslav representatives, time and time again, emphasized the importance of the problem and the imperative necessity of doing something about it, but they have made a number of proposals, especially in the General Assembly of the United Nations, on the disarmament problem in general and on certain of its major aspects. These proposals include a resolution calling for initial and partial disarmament measures, submitted in the UN Disarmament Commission in 1956 and a draft setting forth certain basic directives for progress towards disarmament, which Yugoslavia and eleven other non-aligned countries placed before the General Assembly at its twelfth regular session.

Yugoslavia has come to believe that the non-aligned countries have an extremely important contribution to make to a solution of the disarmament problem, particularly in view of the complete deadlock reached by the Great Powers and their military alliances in their negotiations on this problem. This deadlock is itself hardly a matter of surprise, because the negotiations that led up to it were generally conducted in a Cold War context, amidst mounting tensions and towering armaments. The negotiations thus tended to blend with this context rather than seek to modify it through some measures of progress in disarmament. If the deadlock is to be broken, a new approach to the problem has become essential. Such a new approach can obviously come most easily from those countries whose attitude on disarmament is not burdened with bloc considerations or interests. Such countries are particularly well placed to view the problem in the light of the actual requirements of progress towards a solution. It is for this reason that Yugoslavia has

been insisting that the non-aligned countries should be included in the disarmament talks, if these talks are to make any headway. The role the non-committed countries have been playing in the Geneva Disarmament Committee would seem to prove that she was right in her insistence.

The problem of Germany

As one of the major victims of German aggression in World War II, Yugoslavia has been much concerned that the German question has become a source of recurring tension among the two blocs. She has the greatest misgivings about the efforts to re-arm West Germany and to revive German militarism which has, in the past, brought such untold sorrow to so many European countries. She has also deplored the tendency to ignore the existence of East Germany which is, whether one likes it or not, one of the facts of postwar international life. She also feels, and has said so all along, that a solution should be sought, not by building positions of strength on both sides of the dividing line, but through negotiations and by bringing the two Germanys together.

Colonialism

One of the major features of Yugoslav foreign policy, and one closely linked to her general attitude on the problems of peace and co-existence, is her steadfast opposition to colonialism. This opposition stems from a number of obvious reasons. For one thing, we consider colonialism to be a denial of the right of self-determination and of equality among nations, of that very same right for which Yugoslavia has herself had to wage such a harsh struggle and which has always constituted one of the basic elements of her political philosophy. Colonialism has, besides, long been doomed by history, as any perceptive study of historical trends will reveal and as the occurrences of the

---

[6] Yugoslavia has, for her part, strongly and steadfastly opposed such tests, from any quarter, under any pretext and in any environment.

last decade have so clearly confirmed. Last, but by no means least, colonialism, as recent events have only too abundantly shown, poses a constant threat to the peace of the world. On the one hand, the colonial Powers' attempts—invariably futile in the long run—to resist liberation movements by force of arms, lead to serious conflagrations, which are always liable to spread. On the other hand, colonialism frequently tends to become involved in the Cold War, or rather the Cold War naturally tends to spread to colonial areas in fermentation and tends to draw them into the East-West conflict. This adds fuel to the conflict and exacerbates the colonial issues themselves. Considering colonialism to be a cancerous growth which needs removing with the utmost determination and dispatch, Yugoslavia has taken a consistent part in the struggle against its various manifestations.[7]

The problems—and they undoubtedly rank among the most serious problems of our time —arising from this closing chapter of colonialism's harrowing history, come under three main headings, some of which are now mainly of historical interest, while others still retain a very definite current significance. There has, in the first place, been the immediate threat to international peace and security arising from the attempts of the colonial Powers to quell the struggle of the dependent peoples for their freedom by force of arms, as happened in Indonesia, Tunisia, Morocco, Algeria and now in Angola.

All these matters came up before the Security Council or the General Assembly of the United Nations and proved that the colonial issue is but one aspect of the general problem of peace. In all these cases, the Yugoslav representatives joined with what was gradually to become the anti-colonial majority, in urging

the United Nations to take the measures enjoined by the Charter to remove the danger to peace created by the stubborn colonialist attempts to stem the tide of history. The UN did, in fact, in many cases help these peoples gain their freedom, contributing thereby towards diminishing the dangers to world peace.

Then there was the question of ensuring application of the Charter provisions on Trust and Non-Self-Governing Territories to make the UN into an effective instrument for assisting the emancipation of dependent peoples. These provisions—explainable in terms of the actual conditions in which the UN came into being—were, in a sense, an exception to the application of the right of self-determination solemnly proclaimed in the Charter as a legal, rather than a solely political or moral right. The Charter also provided means for gradually reducing the scope of the exception and finally, doing away with it entirely. In the case of the territories under trusteeship, the exception itself was fairly limited. The degree of UN supervision over the territories themselves was quite substantial, and what was required, therefore, was to make the best possible use of these means.

As regards the Non-Self-Governing Territories, the situation was very much different. The area covered was immense and the means at United Nations' disposal were extremely slender—these were the colonies in the traditional sense, where the writ of the colonial masters ran unchallenged. The "wind of change" very soon began sweeping these vast expanses under alien rule, and the membership of the United Nations also began changing as part of the same general process. In turn, there was a growing demand for a more effective UN role in the Non-Self-Governing Territories, which, of course, required a broad interpretation of the relevant Charter provisions. All this was part of the general struggle of the anti-colonial forces which, with the influx of new members into the UN, became a powerful anti-colonial majority. In this struggle, Yugoslavia played, from the very outset, a very active role, as witnessed by the various proposals she initi-

---

[7] It is true that colonialism is disintegrating at an accelerating pace and that the area it covers has shrunk substantially. The remaining ramparts, however, are being held with ferocious tenacity. Its dying spasms still pose a threat to the peace—witness Angola, Rhodesia and, in a somewhat different sense, South Africa.

ated, usually in conjunction with the Asian and African countries most directly affected by these issues.

As a result of the general disintegration of the colonial system in the accepted sense of the word, the struggle has been shifting to the various forms of what has become known as neo-colonialism—the attempts to deprive the newly acquired independence of the former colonies of any real substance by maintaining them in a state of actual dependence, political, economical or both. Yugoslavia considers that this is a particularly dangerous aspect of the broader colonial problem as it confronts us today. This explains her active part in the Congo crisis, where she requested, among other things, an urgent meeting of the Security Council to deal with the situation created by the overthrow of the Lumumba government. That explains her opposition to foreign bases—particularly on the territories of states which are unwilling to have them.

It, also, explains our country's steadfast hostility to all forms of economic domination, particularly in the newly independent countries, whether in the form of political "strings" to various forms of economic assistance or of attempts to maintain key positions in the economic life of politically independent but economically weak countries, or of various types of economic pressure and discrimination. Genuine and enduring political independence requires stable economic foundations. In the absence of economic equality, political equality is bound to remain precarious. Yugoslavia has, herself, suffered too long from these various attempts at economic domination, not to realize their perils and their far-reaching implications.

The demand for economic development

An essential part both of the struggle for the general emancipation of the dependent countries and the efforts towards a more stable peace and a betterment of international rela-tions in the broadest sense, is the problem of economic development of the underdeveloped countries and areas—one of the major problems of our time. Its importance is manifold, both economic and political. Economically speaking, a healthy world economy obviously and urgently requires that the yawning gap between the developed and underdeveloped countries should be successfully overcome. Politically, as we have seen, economic backwardness is not only a result of, but also an invitation to, political domination, with all that the latter implies, not least of all in terms of the Cold War struggle. The need of assisting the underdeveloped countries in making up for the time they have lost, through no fault of their own, is now generally recognized. What is not always fully grasped, at least in practice, is the scope of the aid which is now required and the form in which it should be extended. The aid is still inadequate in scope and is not always motivated by economic considerations such as a desire to promote the development of the underdeveloped countries. Rather, it is still frequently prompted by political aims and by the overall strategy of the Cold War.

If this danger is to be obviated, if the aid is to achieve its essential purpose, not only should it be increased very substantially, but it should, wherever possible, be channeled through the United Nations. That is why Yugoslavia has fought, for many years, for the establishment of a United Nations Fund for Economic Development (SUNFED), as well as for other forms of aid through the United Nations, such as technical assistance, UNICEF aid, and the like. She has, for her part, endeavored to contribute to UN projects of this kind, to the extent of her capacities. Yugoslavia's natural preference for multilateral UN assistance does not, of course, imply the rejection of bilateral aid, provided it is devoid of political strings. In fact, she has herself been both at the receiving end of such aid and at the giving end, particularly in the case of the less developed African countries.

The same general considerations have led Yugoslavia to oppose the various obstacles which are raised, both for political and for economic motives, to the flow of international trade and the exchange of commodities and which often have a directly adverse bearing on the problems of the less developed countries. A word should perhaps be said in this connection about Yugoslavia's views on the integration processes which have been involving the more highly industrialized countries and, more particularly, the European Economic Community or Common Market. While recognizing economic integration to be a natural and generally healthy outcome of the present stage in the growth of the forces of production, Yugoslavia, like many other countries, objects to the discriminatory effects of the closed economic groupings upon other countries, especially upon the less developed ones. She also objects to their tendency to merge with political and military alignments, whereby they become a divisive, rather than a genuinely integrating factor, speaking in global terms.

The United Nations

All this naturally brings us to the question of Yugoslavia's attitude to the United Nations. Her non-aligned status, her opposition to bloc divisions, her support of the principles of co-existence, all these naturally incline Yugoslavia to take a favorable view of a universal, democratic and peace-preserving organization, such as the United Nations. Yugoslavia's general understanding of the basic processes at work today is that they are making for an increasing degree of unity of the international community, despite all the artificial barriers and divisions. The momentous technological and economic advance underlying these processes, naturally result in a growing number of problems which can successfully be dealt with on a broad and permanently multilateral basis. This trend, which the program of the League of Communists of Yugoslavia describes as the "trend towards closer co-operation among peoples and towards the unification of the world," has called into existence a world organization, both broader in scope and more closely knit than previous ones.

At the same time, the other aspect of the same basic trend—the progress towards independence and equality of nations, required the new organization to build upon foundations of sovereign equality of states and the right of peoples to self-determination. Another, far less desirable consequence of the technological revolution of our time, the emergence of nuclear and thermonuclear weapons of mass destruction, underscores the need for excluding war as a means of settling differences and for seeking settlements by peaceful means only— as the Charter prescribes in perfectly clear terms. The principles upon which the United Nations is built, are thus an expression of the needs of our time; they are also a consecration and an application in the field of international relations, of some of the major values which form part of the democratic and progressive heritage of mankind.

On the other hand, the actual machinery devised at San Francisco to carry these principles and purposes into effect, reflected the actual conditions under which the United Nations came into being. The United Nations was, thus, in a sense, or was at least intended to be, a continuation of the war-time coalition. This explains the privileged status granted the leading Powers of the coalition, the absence of universality, the emphasis placed upon enforcement measures for the maintenance, or rather the re-establishment of international peace and security, and several other features of the organization's structure. Such then in the Yugoslav view are the main influences that brought the United Nations into being and determined its basic features.

In practice the United Nations has proved to be an "irreplaceable instrument of peace" as one official Yugoslav statement put it. It has, in particular, been an instrument of co-existence. The principles of the Charter are those of co-existence and the United Nations has, in a very real sense, been breeding co-existence, even at a time when the international climate was anything but favorable. The United Nations has, in practice, revealed a number of substantial weaknesses. These were not due to any failing of the basic premises upon which the organization stood, but rather to the uncongenial environment within which they were applied. The Cold War could not but affect the United Nations. The Great Powers and their alignment usually either tended to ignore and circumvent the organization, or to use it as a tool for policies which had very little in common with the purposes set forth in the Charter such as Cold War and, in some cases, even "hot" war policies. This, of course, tended to deflect the United Nations from what should have been its course, to impair its usefulness and, generally, to weaken it.

The main purpose of Yugoslavia's far from inconsiderable activities in the United Nations, was to resist pernicious effects of the Cold War on the United Nations and help to make it an increasingly effective instrument of co-existence. This purpose was stated in President Tito's address to the Belgrade Conference of Non-aligned Countries. "As regards the political strengthening of the UN," he said that it was, above all,

essential to wage a determined struggle against all the tendencies which circumvent and weaken the Organization and distort its role. It is, at the same time, necessary to influence, through and with the aid of the UN, the course of international relations towards peace and peaceful co-existence. That means, concretely speaking, not only that the basic international questions should be dealt with in the UN, but that they should be dealt with in such a way as would enhance the role and the standing of the Organization itself and contribute to the positive development of relations in the world.[8]

This is the general line that Yugoslav delegations at successive sessions of the various UN

bodies have tried to follow in, what I think, a fairly consistent manner. In seeking to strengthen the organization—and it has been the very strong Yugoslav view that no effort should be spared to achieve this—the purpose has not, of course, been to make it into a super-state or a "world government." Rather, the purpose has been to ensure its universality by expanding its membership, and by refusing to close one's eyes to the realities of the Chinese situation. Another goal is to safeguard its unity by eliminating the divisive effect of Cold War influences. It is also important to increase its effectiveness, not so much as an enforcement agency based on the concept of eliminating war through military action, but rather as a genuine peace-preserving and peace-making organization, called upon to tackle the problem in all its multiple aspects, economic, social, as well as political. The UN should become more democratic, too, by increasing the role of the smaller nations, particularly in the General Assembly. Yugoslavia has never opposed a broad interpretation of the organization's powers, provided they were exercised in conformity with the principles and purposes of the Charter. While the Charter has, on the whole, proved to be a flexible and adjustable instrument, certain changes of a structural nature may be called for to enable the UN to keep abreast of a swiftly moving world. The expansion of the membership of certain bodies like the Security Council or the Economic and Social Council are, in fact, considerably overdue.

HOW YUGOSLAVIA'S FOREIGN POLICY IS MADE

A few words should perhaps be said, before concluding, about the processes which lead to the formation of Yugoslavia's foreign policy and about the machinery used to put it into effect. These processes and this machinery reflect the country's Socialist and Democratic

[8] Josip Broz Tito, Speech delivered at the Belgrade Conference of Heads of States and Governments of the Non-aligned Countries, September, 1961.

evolution, as well as the development of its foreign policy.

Foreign policy issues and world affairs in general are matters of lively interest to the broadest masses of the population and are discussed in their political organizations and in their representative bodies, with the Federal House of the National Assembly and its Foreign Affairs Committee at their apex. The responsibility for the conduct of foreign policy rests with the Federal Executive Council, a branch of which is the State Secretariat for Foreign Affairs. This Secretariat and the foreign services in general are staffed by men and women who are part of the national liberation movement and the postwar struggle for the construction of socialism.

Yugoslavia has today diplomatic missions in most of the countries of the world and is represented at the meetings of the various United Nations bodies and of the other international organizations. Yugoslavia is a member of all the specialized agencies and of a large number of governmental and non-governmental organizations. An active part in developing Yugoslavia's foreign contacts, in the broader sense, is carried out by the Socialist Alliance and the Trade Unions which co-operate closely with the different progressive parties and national liberation movements throughout the world.

Conclusion

Such, in Yugoslav eyes, are the broad outlines of Yugoslavia's foreign policy. We have sought to indicate the various factors that have helped shape it and make it what it is today. We have dwelt, with what some may possibly feel to be excessive length, on certain elements, such as the theoretical considerations underlying our country's foreign policy. We have done so because these elements are of considerable importance in understanding our policy.

Yugoslav foreign policy does, we feel, in many ways and for reasons that have been suggested here, reflect the broader complexities of the present state of international relations. If, in describing the basic aspects of our country's foreign policy, we have contributed in some small measure, to a better understanding of the overall world picture, this chapter will have amply served its purpose.

BIBLIOGRAPHY

Author's Suggestions

International Affairs, a fortnightly government publication (also published in English), sets forth the official views of the Government of Yugoslavia on current problems.

Kardelj, Edvard. "Socialism and War" (Excerpts from a Series of Articles Published in Belgrade, August, 1960), in Jacobs, Dan N., ed., *The New Communist Manifesto and Related Documents.* 2d ed. Evanston, Ill.: Row, Peterson and Company, 1962, pp. 183–212.

Popović, Koča. See statements in the general debate at the 10th, 11th, 12th, 13th, 14th and 16th sessions of the General Assembly of the United Nations.

Tito, Josip Broz. "On Certain Current International Questions," *Foreign Affairs,* Vol. 35, No. 1 (Oct. 1957), pp. 68–76.

Tito, Josip Broz. Speech at the Fifteenth Session of the General Assembly of the United Nations. *Official Records of the General Assembly, Fifteenth Session (Part 1), Plenary*

Meetings, 1960, Doc. A/PA.864–907, pp. 51–58.

Yugoslavia's Way, Program of the League of the Yugoslav Communists. New York: All Nations Press, 1958.

Editor's Suggestions

Bass, Robert, and Marbury, Elizabeth, eds. *The Soviet-Yugoslav Controversy, 1948–1958:* *A Documentary Record.* New York: Prospect Books, 1959.

Dedijer, Vladimir. *Tito.* New York: Simon and Schuster, 1953.

Djilas, Milovan. *Conversations with Stalin.* New York: Harcourt, Brace and World, Inc., 1962.

MacLean, Fitzroy. *The Heretic: The Life and Times of Josip Broz Tito.* New York: Harper, 1958.

PART THREE

THE MIDDLE EAST
AND NORTH AFRICA

ABOUT THE AUTHOR

Diplomat, scholar and writer, NURI EREN, has served for twenty-four years in every phase of Turkey's foreign relations—as economic expert and negotiator, as public relations counselor and chief, as diplomatic representative in various capitals and with various international organizations such as the Council of Europe, the North Atlantic Treaty Organization and the United Nations. He has received commendations for his singular achievements from Presidents Bayar and Inonu and Prime Ministers Saydam and Menderes.

He left the Foreign Service at the peak of his career in May 1960 as Minister Plenipotentiary and Deputy Permanent Representative to the United Nations. In 1961 and 1962, Mr. Eren was at Princeton University as Senior Research Associate in International Relations. He is currently engaged in writing and research at the United Nations in New York.

ABOUT THE CHAPTER

Using the historical method, Mr. Eren traces the Turkish struggle for independence from foreign intervention during the post-World War I period. Careful attention is given to the various international agreements through which the independent status of Turkey was secured. The author stresses the necessity of recognizing the fact that a nation can be and is only what her environment and inheritance have made her. He reminds the reader how new Turkey is as a nation in the modern sense.

Mr. Eren then turns to the World War II period and to the reasons for the non-involvement of Turkey in that conflict. He discusses the world during the post-World War II period and the reasons for Turkey's alignment with the Western bloc. To Turkey, membership in NATO provides the security she had long sought against the Soviet Union. Beyond this, it means a community of interests and that Turkey's orientation toward the West has achieved its goal.

The chapter concludes with a survey of Turkey's main foreign policy problems, an examination of the foreign policy formulation process, a note on the diplomatic corps and a brief discussion of economic, social and geographical factors which must be understood if one is to comprehend the continuity of Turkey's foreign policy.

10

THE FOREIGN POLICY OF TURKEY

NURI EREN

Princeton University

Republican Turkey has such a completely new identity that the world views her as an altogether new creation with only incidental connections with the Ottoman Empire. Indeed, in every phase of her national life she presents a radically different picture from that of the Ottomans. But, even so, a nation's identity, like an individual's, bears inevitably the stamp of environment and inheritance. The present international posture of Turkey rests rooted in her Ottoman past.

THE INFLUENCE OF GEOGRAPHY AND HISTORY

First, if not always foremost, she bears instincts absorbed from her environment. In her period of expansion, geography was her great ally, but it turned into her greatest peril in a period of contraction. Her intercontinental position offered a natural springboard to her foes for expansion in every direction: for Russia to the south, Britain and France to the north, and Austria to the east. All four imperialist Powers, in their rival zeal to outgrow each other, converged on Istanbul, the ancient capital city of Constantinople.

Turkey and the Great Powers

In the 19th century, Turkey was the prime target of European diplomacy. Karl Marx, who erred so gravely in his socio-political prognostications, cast a discerning light on Turkey's compelling geo-political nature. In an article in the *New York Tribune* of August 12, 1853, he wrote,

Constantinople (Istanbul) is the golden bridge between the East and the West, and Western Civilization cannot, like the sun, go round the world without passing that bridge; and it cannot pass it without a struggle with Russia.

Truly, Constantinople had been the object of Russian ambitions for more than a thousand years when Grand Duke Sviatasloff in 789 A.D. had declared "the Greek Empire in Europe, together with Bohemia and Hungary, ought to undergo the rule of Russia," and rushed to bring it about. But the attempt was frustrated in Silesia and the Grand Duchy of Moscovy had to wait another thousand years before a Russian could lay claim again to the "eternal city of the East." Significantly, this messianic urge, long embedded in the Russian soul, was expressed, not by a ruler or a military commander but a man of letters. Dostoevski, in a newspaper article in 1877, wrote:

> the Golden Horn and Constantinople —all this will be ours . . . the time has come . . . this is the natural solution . . . it must be ours, not only because it is a famous port, because of the Straits, as the center of the universe, the navel of the earth; not from the standpoint of the long-conceived necessity for a tremendous giant like Russia to emerge from his locked room, in which has already grown up to the ceiling, into the open spaces where he may breathe the free air of the seas and oceans . . . Our task is immeasurably deeper. We Russians are really indispensable and inevitable both to all Eastern Christianity and to the whole future of Orthodoxy on earth, in order to achieve its unity . . . Therein lies our final conflict with Europe and ultimate union with her but only upon new, mighty and fruitful foundations . . .[1]

Beginning with the Russian attack on Azov in 1663 and ending with the First World War Turkey fought thirteen wars with Russia. The in-between periods were never peaceful but red hot with the tensions of Cold War. Muscovite

[1] See Fëdor Mikhailovich Dostoevski, *Journal d'un écrivain,* 3 vols., 1927.

"Moskof" became synonymous with "enemy" in the Turkish language. Mindful of Dostoevski's warning that the path to the domination of Europe lay through Turkey, the Turkish people acquired a strong consciousness of their focal position in the struggle for intercontinental supremacy.

Secondly, they learned that a country could never count on constant friends but must operate on the basis of constant interests. In 1878, Britain's hasty appetite for Cyprus, in return for her support in the Congress of Berlin, taught them the lesson. The ally of today could turn into the mortal enemy of tomorrow. Self-preservation was the constant by which they had to steer their besieged ship of state.

Thirdly, military defeats forced them to the conviction that in the face of a changing Europe, Ottoman institutions and culture could no longer generate the means of survival. The disenchantment with the traditional past started in the 18th century when the proud Ottoman army began to discard its traditions and adopt Europe's new weapons and methods of war. Continued insufficiency against the West spread the discontent to the form of government. After a while, with agonizing deliberation, disenchantment with the whole Ottoman outlook reduced Turkish self-esteem to the lowest denominator. In the nineteenth century national poets sang:

> Christian lands I visited,
> palaces I saw,
> Moslem lands I visited,
> ruins I saw.

By the twentieth century foreign policy goals were determined by the urge of integration with Western civilization.

Renunciation of the Empire

Finally, the strongest instinct that the Republican Turks developed from their Ottoman past was the irrevocable renunciation of the Empire with all its non-Turkish territories. They aspired, instead, to the creation of a compact, ethno-culturally homogeneous nation-state within the confines of Asia Minor and Eastern Thrace.

The nation arrived at this conviction grudgingly, forced by the inexorable march of events towards national self-determination. The defection of the Greeks in 1829 heralded the first stage of the Empire's dissolution. But the idea of Imperial destiny was not easily given up. The Ottomans sought to counter national secessionist movements by the creation of an Ottoman nationality—a federation of different races and religions. It was a hopeless, senseless, uphill effort from the very beginning.

The rising tide of nationalism was compounded by their growing cultural inferiority and the corroding pressures of the rival Imperial Powers. By 1914, they had settled for a Moslem Empire when the unexpected defection of the Arabs left them naked against the world. A Turkey of the Turks became a matter of deep, almost religious, conviction. Ever since, this has been the most faithfully, fanatically held principle of Turkish foreign conduct.

THE LESSONS OF WORLD WAR I

The desire to stay neutral

Turkey was dragged into the First World War under the compulsion of the first three of these cardinal considerations that dominated her instincts in international affairs. She realized she was the most coveted prize in the intercontinental struggle as a land bridge between the three continents. She sought to neutralize herself by seeking guarantees against aggression from all major contestants. When war became imminent Cemal Pasha, one of the ruling triumvirate in the Ottoman Government, traveled to Paris for a Turco-French agreement. But with their eye on the opportunities that the

dismemberment of the Ottoman Empire offered, the French refused him.

Enver Pasha, the second and more powerful member of the triumvirate, on August 9, 1914, approached Russia. Turkish neutrality, at that critical moment, would guard the Russian flank. But Russia's immediate military advantage floundered on the rocks of her historic ambitions for Constantinople. The Turks, turned down by the Allies, their instincts with respect to Russian designs strengthened, their suspicions of Western imperialism confirmed, thrust themselves into the eager and conniving arms of the Germans. Germany, at least, offered an alternative against the principal enemy, "the Muscovite."

The progress of the war confirmed the validity of the Ottoman instincts regarding Turkey's world position. The Allies entered into various arrangements for the partition of the Ottoman Empire. In diplomatic exchanges between March 4, 1915, and April 10, 1915, Britain and France awarded to Russia her traditional claim to Istanbul and the Turkish Straits. The London Agreement of April 26, 1915, the Sykes-Picot Agreement of April–October 1916, and the Saint Jean de Maurienne Agreement of April–August 1917 completed the dismemberment of the Ottomans.

The Turks fought, not for the Empire, but for their own independence. In effect, by October 1918, when they signed the Armistice of Modros, they were confined to the Turkish heartland. But the Allies, disregarding their obligation to retain the positions they occupied when the Armistice was signed, proceeded to occupy the country. Relieved by the Bolshevik Revolution of their commitments to Russia, and disregarding their pledges to each other, they hastened to grab as much of the Turkish territory as they could.

The British moved into Istanbul, the French into the Adana region, and the Italians into Antalya. Large segments of Eastern and Northern Turkey were marked for carving into Armenia and Kurdistan. On May 15, 1919, the Greeks occupied Izmir and its hinterland, proving that the Turks would be deprived even of their homeland.

National resistance to dismemberment

This threat revived national resistance. "Defense of Rights Associations" organized themselves across the country to fight enslavement, becoming the embryo from which the Turkish National Republic, led by Mustafa Kemal Ataturk, developed. On September 4, 1919, convening as a national congress in Sivas, the resistance movement drafted a document proclaiming its aims. On January 28, 1920, the newly elected Ottoman Legislature in Istanbul endorsed it. This was called the National Pact and became the Magna Carta of Nationalist Turkey's policy. It is quoted below because of its great importance. It has provided the terms of reference for every Turkish international move ever since. It continues to embody present day national consensus on Turkish foreign policy:

> The Members of the Ottoman Chamber of Deputies recognize and affirm that the independence of the State and the future of the Nation can be assured by complete respect for the following principles, which represent the maximum of sacrifice which can be undertaken in order to achieve a just and lasting peace, and that the continued existence of a stable Ottoman Sultanate and society is impossible outside of the said principles:
>
> ART. 1. Inasmuch as it is necessary that the destinies of the portions of the Turkish Empire which are populated exclusively by an Arab majority, and which on the conclusion of the armistice of the 30th October 1918 were in the occupation of enemy forces, should be determined in accordance with the votes which shall be freely given by the inhabitants, the whole of those parts whether within or outside the said armistice line which are inhabited by an Ottoman Moslem majority, united in religion, in race and in aim, imbued with sentiments of mutual respect for each other and of sacrifice, and wholly respectful of each other's racial and social rights and surrounding conditions, form a whole which does not admit of division for any reason in truth or in ordinance.
>
> ART. 2. We accept that, in the case of the three (Kurdish) Sandjaks which united themselves by a general vote to the mother country when they first were free, recourse should again be had, if necessary, to a free popular vote.
>
> ART. 3. The determination of the juridical status of Western Thrace also, which has been made dependent on the Turkish peace, must be effected in accordance with the votes which shall be given by the inhabitants in complete freedom.
>
> ART. 4. The security of the city of Constantinople, which is the seat of the Caliphate of Islam, the capital of the Sultanate, and the headquarters of the Ottoman Government, and of the Sea of Marmora must be protected from every danger. Provided this principle is maintained, whatever decision may be arrived at jointly by us and all other Governments concerned, regarding the opening of the Bosphorus to the commerce and traffic of the world, is valid.
>
> ART. 5. The rights of minorities as defined in the treaties concluded between the Entente Powers and their enemies and certain of their associates shall be confirmed and assured by us —in reliance on the belief that the Moslem minorities in neighbouring countries also will have the benefit of the same rights.
>
> ART. 6. It is a fundamental condition of our life and continued existence that we, like every country,

should enjoy complete independence and liberty in the matter of assuring the means of our development, in order that our national and economic development should be rendered possible and that it should be possible to conduct affairs in the form of a more up-to-date regular administration.

For this reason we are opposed to restrictions inimical to our development in political, judicial, financial, and other matters.

The conditions of settlement of our proved debts shall likewise not be contrary to these principles.[2]

The Pact remains as valid as the day it was proclaimed, in spite of the changes that have overtaken the world. It remains valid not only because it reflects the aspirations of the Turkish people but because it is based on currently accepted political principles: (a) self-determination for the Turkish people within a homogeneous Turkish state; (b) renunciation of empire and rule over foreign populations; (c) freedom from foreign intervention within national boundaries through the establishment of unconditional sovereignty; and (d) dedication to domestic development within the irrevocably limited national boundaries.

POSTWAR DIPLOMACY

When the Pact was proclaimed, the more populous sections of the country were under occupation. The Nationalists in Ankara were a handful of insurgents without a single ally. Their only strength derived from the will of the people. Determination for survival and genius in the combined use of diplomacy and force achieved the almost impossible.

[2] J. C. Hurewitz, *Diplomacy in the Near and Middle East*, vol. II, Princeton, N.J.: Van Nostrand, 1956, p. 74.

What Karl Marx had observed in the *New York Tribune* on April 19, 1853, came to pass:

From the battle of Navarino to the present Eastern crisis, the action of the Western Powers has either been annihilated by squabbles among themselves or that action has been in the direct interest of Russia alone . . . [the] Turkish Government has, in every instance been obliged to throw itself upon the mercy of Russia and to seek protection from that power which openly avows its firm intention to drive the Turk across the Bosphorus, and plant the cross of St. Andrew upon the minarets of the Aya-Sofyeh. . . .

Relations with Russia

Cornered by the Western Allies, Mustafa Kemal Ataturk perceived the opportunity offered by the Revolutionary Government of Russia and set out to exploit it. The first contact was established in May, 1920. But there was protracted negotiation before agreement was reached.

The Russian negotiators revealed that Russia's historic instincts remained in spite of the change in the regime. They pressed for keeping Turkey's south-eastern gates within their hold. They insisted on dividing eastern Turkish territory between an independent Armenia, Kurdistan, and Georgia. Obviously, they desired a Turkey free from Western domination, but under the Russian thumb. The Turks also realized that a new element had crept into the Russian calculations. In addition to the strategic advantages of a Turkish Alliance, Moscow searched to exploit Turkey's traditional prestige, as the leading Islamic Power, for spearheading revolutions in Asia and Africa.

These terms were not only contrary to the National Pact but extremely dangerous to Turkey. Under such conditions, an alliance promised unlimited expansion for Russia. Turkey's and—in a world of independent nation states —Russia's interests precluded any expansion. Confined within their own boundaries, the two countries were natural allies. Engaged in expansion they would become natural antagonists.

Seeking a permanent basis for her international relations Ataturk's Turkey desired Russian co-operation as a permanent means for the preservation of the status quo between the two. At the same time, a bona fide Turco-Russian Alliance would secure both of them from exploitation by third parties of their great strategic advantages against each other. The agreement was signed when Turkey felt that these conditions were fulfilled. Significantly, the Russians acquiesced after the Turkish armies reconquered the Eastern provinces and the Greeks suffered their first major defeat at İnönü, in January 1921.

The Treaty of Friendship and Brotherhood signed on March 16, 1921, skyrocketed Nationalist Turkey's posture to international importance. But its significance is more abiding, for it continues to reflect the basic principles of Turkey's attitude towards her Northern neighbor: (1) It accepts the Turco-Soviet border as permanent. Articles VI and VII abrogate all previous treaties, contracts and obligations and provide for a completely new beginning. (2) Article VIII renounces subversive propaganda by the parties against each other, and provides the basis of co-operation between the two national governments, irrespective of ideological considerations.

(3) The preamble of the Pact declares, "in the common struggle undertaken against imperialism, foreseeing that the difficulties arising from the one would render worse the position of the other . . ." and thereby acknowledges the equal danger of a power conflict to both. It forbids engagements with third parties against each other. (4) Both the preamble and Article IV refer to "the principle of the liberty of nations, and the right of each nation to determine its own fate." Russia embraces self-determination for the peoples in the area and renounces imperialist aims.

The Lausanne Agreement

The Turco-French Agreement of October 21, 1921, is the second international document reflecting basically a Nationalist approach to foreign policy. No doubt, the immediate interests of the Nationalists dictated a rapprochement with France, which provided for the evacuation of the French occupied southern provinces. Securing their southern borderline the Nationalists could concentrate their limited forces against the Greeks on the western front.

But the agreement had a double significance. It realized Turkey's desire to relieve herself from exclusive dependence on Russia, and it also expressed an urge to build a similar relationship with the West. On the other hand, it proved to the West Turkey's unshakable determination to abide by the conditions of the National Pact. For instance, Turkish negotiators, even though hard pressed by a war on two fronts, would not forego their rights to Alexandretta (Iskenderun).

By September 1922, the Turkish mainland had been cleared of the Greek invader; the Nationalist Government had received international recognition. Total Ottoman defeat by the Allies had been converted into a victory for the New Turkey. By the most skillful combination of military force with diplomacy, Turkey had regained her ability to stand up for her rights. The stage was set for the emergence of the New Turkey as defined by the National Pact. The Lausanne Treaty sealed this acceptance. Ambassador Joseph C. Grew, the United States representative at the Conference admitted that it "was probably the greatest diplomatic victory in history."[3]

The Turks, although victorious in arms, were facing the most powerful coalition in the

[3] Joseph Clark Grew, *Turbulent Era*, vol. I, Boston: Houghton Mifflin Co., 1952, p. 569.

world, and they were alone. The Allies were not always united but still in the major issues they acted together. Their co-operation could extend as far as to join in an ultimatum against the Turks. On February 3, 1923, the third month of the Conference, they presented their proposals to the Turkish delegation and pressed them to accept within twenty-four hours. Lord Curzon, the British representative, prepared to leave the next day. He waited an extra hour at the station for Ismet Inönü, the Turkish delegate to give in—but he waited in vain. The Turks refused any conditions contrary to the National Pact.

The burden of the negotiations at Lausanne rested principally on three major issues: the capitulations; the control of the Turkish Straits; and territorial rights.

The capitulations   The capitulations were the immediate cause of rupture in the first stage of the negotiations. Article 6 of the National Pact declared: "It is a fundamental condition of our life and continued existence that we, like every country, should enjoy complete independence and liberty . . ." This was a reference to the capitulatory system that limited Turkish sovereignty within Turkey, and which even the late Ottomans had found extremely obnoxious. Through the nineteenth century Ottoman diplomacy had steadfastly struggled for the abolition of the system but with no avail. Though abrogated during the war, the capitulations were re-instated by the Allies right after the Armistice.

The capitulatory system had its origin in the practices of the Middle Ages when foreign merchants were excused from the jurisdiction of the local authorities. Turkish emperors, after their establishment in Istanbul, had confirmed the international usage and granted extraterritorial rights to foreign traders in the Ottoman Domain. In the 19th century, the West, stepping into the vacuum created by Ottoman stagnation, had stretched its economic and political power and had extended the capitulatory privileges. As a result, the Ottomans had lost jurisdiction over their international trade and also over many of their

subjects who bought papers of citizenship from Western Powers. Ottoman independence had become a travesty. The New Turkey could not possibly accept this limitation of her sovereignty.

On the other hand, the Western Powers were equally adamant. For France, Britain, and Italy, the issue transcended their relations with Turkey. They all enjoyed capitulatory rights around Africa and Asia. An adverse decision in Turkey would affect their privileges elsewhere. Thus from the first day of the Conference, November 22, 1922, to the last, July 24, 1923, the capitulatory system remained the major point of contention between the two parties.

The Conference came to a successful end only after the Western Powers realized that the outdated privilege had to give way before a universally accepted right. Article 28 gave Turkey her full sovereign rights within her national territory: "Each of the High Contracting Parties hereby accepts, in so far as it is concerned, the complete abolition of the capitulations in every respect . . ." Yet, to this day, Turkey remains extremely sensitive to any kind of political, cultural or economic foreign privilege or concession.

Territorial questions   The territorial settlement did not provide an equally full satisfaction. When the Conference ended, Turkey's northern borders were drawn to her satisfaction. The French agreement, with the special dispensation on Alexandretta (Iskenderun), provided a temporary acceptance of her southern borderline. At the other end, her European frontiers with Greece and Bulgaria were subject to protracted discussion. But these were finally resolved to her satisfaction. By foregoing her claims on Turkish-populated Western Thrace, Republican Turkey planted the seeds of her future rapprochement with Greece at Lausanne.

But the question of her border with Iraq remained unsolved. Britain, in control in Iraq, would not forego the oil in Mosul. The Conference delegated the problem to Turkey and Britain for bilateral negotiation. They failed to agree and the dispute was referred to the League of Nations which awarded the territory to Iraq. Turkey accepted the verdict. In 1939, after the return of Iskenderun, the goals of the National Pact were attained. Today Turks consider the national domain as final, and have no claims on any of their neighbors.

The Turkish Straits   The status of the Turkish Straits was the third but by no means the least important issue before the conference. One of the major campaigns of the war had been fought over the area and the British had suffered their one, irredeemed disaster of the war at Gallipoli.

Through the nineteenth century, the Straits had been the principal object of Russian, as well as Western diplomacy. Black Sea traffic flowed into the Mediterranean through them. After Russia's descent into the Balkans and the Caucasus, the Straits acquired global importance. As Karl Marx had said, Constantinople was the Golden Bridge to intercontinental power. "Let Russia get possession of Constantinople and her strength is increased nearly half, and she becomes superior to all the rest of the world." On the other hand,

> vital interests render Great Britain the earnest and unyielding opponent of the Russian project of annexation and aggrandizement. England cannot afford to allow Russia to become the possessor of the Dardanelles and the Bosphorus. Both commercially and politically such an event would be a deep if not a deadly blow to British Power.[4]

In the course of the 19th century, Russia came twice literally within an inch of the physical possession of the Straits. In both instances she was obstructed from the final realization of her goal by Britain and her Western Allies. In mid-century, Britain and France actually fought her over the issue.

[4] *New York Tribune,* August 12, 1853.

Denied territorial satisfaction, Moscow turned to diplomatic means of control. She pressed the Ottomans to consider them an inner waterway for the Black Sea countries, open to their ships but closed to others. She sought bilateral agreements that bound the Ottomans to the joint defense of the area with Russia. Britain, on the other hand, insisted that the waterway was international. Passage through the Straits had to be unrestricted both in time of war and peace. Dominating the Mediterranean by sea power, she sought to stretch her naval supremacy into the Black Sea as a counterweight to Russian pressure on land.

The Ottomans wavered between the two pressures. From 1774, when the Sultan relinquished his absolute control of the passage, to the Montreux Convention in 1936, the Turks had to accept ten different regimes governing the area. The Nationalists came to Lausanne with the desire of ending this pendulum-like role of the Straits in the power conflict.

They accepted, in fact, they welcomed, an international agreement acknowledging the importance of the Straits to the commerce and the peace of the world. Such an agreement would provide a collective guarantee for the inviolability of the area and immunize Turkey against pressures from the north, as well as the south. The area would cease to be an object of rivalry.

With Article IV of the National Pact they called for the opening of the Straits to the commerce and traffic of the world by an international agreement. They proposed to regulate the passage of warships in a manner that would eliminate the potential use of the area for offensive action in either direction. They also sought full responsibility for implementing this agreement as the sole and undisputed owners of the waterway.

At Lausanne, the negotiations, as expected, proved very difficult. Britain had attained her historic goal. She aimed to keep it by limiting Turkey's sovereignty, and placing the area under international jurisdiction. Only Soviet Russia sided with Turkey's efforts to obtain recognition of her unlimited rights of ownership. But the joint Anglo-French and

Italian point of view prevailed and Turkey had to accept restrictions on her sovereign rights. The area was demilitarized and an international commission was entrusted with the supervision of navigation. In one important respect, however, Turkey was satisfied. The passage of warships, both in time of peace and war was restricted, confirming Turkish desire to eliminate passage for warlike purposes.

This failure in the attainment of basic national goals was remedied on July 20, 1936, when the Montreux Convention abrogated the Lausanne agreement and granted to Turkey full sovereign rights over the Straits. All restrictions with respect to militarization were lifted. The International Commission was dismissed.

AN INDEPENDENT TURKEY

Ismet Inönü, the Turkish victor at Lausanne, described the Treaty as the creator of a homogeneous, fully independent Turkey. Truly, the Turks, with the abolition of the capitulations, achieved not only territorial but also political, juridical and economic freedom. All through the 19th century, Turkey had sought to become an equal member of the European comity of nations. The Treaty of Paris, following the Crimean War, had attained for her this ambition, but only in name. Now, with her sovereignty regained in full, there would be no question. But even so, Mustafa Kemal Ataturk never allowed Nationalist Turks to delude themselves. Lausanne was the direct result of their military successes. To retain their independent status in the councils of the world, they needed sustained effort.

Internal development and Westernization
Indeed, the first decade following Lausanne was a period of intense exertion for the development of Turkey's new stance. Two cardinal principles of her new attitude were in obvious operation. She directed all her energies to domestic reconstruction, ever conscious

that ultimately her security rested on her own strength. It was the period in which her instinct for modernization was most active. Daily life was reorganized on a secular basis. Women were liberated from dogmatic confinement; the alphabet was Latinized; the dress was modernized. Social and cultural alignment with the West was the principal driving motive.

Renewed friendship with Russia

Strangely, this was the period of her political alienation from the West. As she struggled to attain a Western mode of life, she was also exerting herself for the preservation of an independent stand between Major Powers. She found herself closer to Russia than ever before. The temptations of complete commitment to the Soviets were greatest in the face of Soviet sympathy as against Western diffidence.

When she transferred her capital from Istanbul to Ankara, France, Britain and Italy protested, exhibiting the old tendency to dictate even in matters of domestic concern. Daily annoyances persisted. The French objected to conforming their missionary schools in Turkey to Turkish academic regulations. Mussolini publicly requested economic concessions and inferred that she lay within Italy's Lebensraum. The Mosul dispute with Britain dragged on. Suspicions of British involvement in the revolt of the Eastern provinces, next to the disputed Iraqi border, were confirmed.

On the other hand, Russia continued to give full diplomatic support. The Turco-Russian Treaty of Neutrality and Mutual Non-Aggression was signed the day following the decision of the League of Nations to award Mosul to Iraq. In 1927 a commercial treaty doubled trade between the two countries. In 1928 Litvinov proposed and effected Turkey's participation in the Preparatory Disarmament Talks. This was Republican Turkey's first appearance in an international gathering. In 1929, the Assistant Soviet Commissar for Foreign Affairs, Karahan, visited Ankara and the Turco-Russian Non-Aggression Pact was re-affirmed.

The Turco-Russian Treaty of Neutrality and Mutual Non-Aggression of 1925 deserves to be fully quoted for it shows how cautious Ankara remained against full commitment even at a moment of diplomatic isolation from the rest of the world. The treaty is of interest not only because it constituted the basis of Turco-Russian relations for twenty years but because, in spite of its denunciation, it still contains Republican Turkey's basic attitude towards Russia: live and let live, in diplomatic parlance, renunciation of aggressive intent and action against each other. The Treaty reads:

> Art. 1. In the case of military action being taken against either Contracting Party by one or more other Powers, the other Contracting Party undertakes to maintain neutrality as towards the first Contracting Party.
>
> *Note:* The expression "military action" shall not be held to include military manoeuvres, since they do not cause any prejudice to the other Party.
>
> Art. 2. Each Contracting Party undertakes to abstain from any aggression against the other; it likewise undertakes not to participate in any alliance or agreement of a political character with one or more other Powers directed against the other Contracting Party, or in any alliance or agreement with one or more other Powers directed against the military or naval security of the other Contracting Party. Furthermore, each of the two Contracting Parties undertakes not to participate in any hostile act by one or more other Powers directed against the other Contracting Party.
>
> Art. 3. The present Treaty shall come into force as soon as it is ratified and shall remain in force for three years. After that period the Treaty shall be regarded as extended auto-

matically for a period of one year, unless one of the Contracting Parties notifies its desire to terminate the Treaty six months before its expiration.

> *Protocol* I. It is in any case understood that each Contracting Party retains full freedom of action as regards its relations of all kinds with other Powers outside the limits of the undertakings the conditions of which are laid down in the present Treaty.
>
> *Protocol* II. The two Contracting Parties agree that the expression "of a political character" as used in Article 2 of the Treaty of today's date should include all such financial or economic agreements between Powers as are directed against the other Contracting Party.
>
> *Protocol* III. The two Contracting Parties also undertake to enter into negotiations to determine the methods of settling disputes which may arise between them and which it may not be possible to settle through the ordinary diplomatic channels.[5]

Restoration of Western friendships

This period is noteworthy for the development of Republican Turkey's relations with the world. For instance, British adamancy in Mosul failed to divest Ataturk from his zeal to re-establish the traditional friendship with the West, an inheritance from the liberal Ottomans of the 19th century. On June 5, 1926—within six months of the League's decision—he recognized the secession of Mosul to Iraq, opening the way to the resumption of cordial relations. The Turco-British rapprochement was reinforced by the Turco-French Treaty of May 30, 1926. In 1927, Ankara exchanged

[5] Hurewitz, *op. cit.,* vol. II, p. 142.

ambassadors with Washington. On May 30, 1928, Ataturk signed a Treaty of Friendship and Non-Aggression with Italy.

Within five years of her founding, the Republic established co-operation with the West. Both the Italian and the French treaties conformed to the pattern of the Turco-Soviet Pact. They renounced participation in diplomatic and military activities against each other and pledged neutrality in case of an attack by a third party on one of them. All these pacts, including the Turco-Soviet Agreement, reflected Republican Turkey's determination to keep herself free from any entanglements in the power conflict between major nations. Her desire to renounce war in the solution of international disputes was expressed in these pacts by the pledge to submit differences to arbitration.

Ties with small neighbors

Within the same space of time Turkey consolidated her relations with her immediate neighbors and smaller nations. On the West she signed friendship agreements with Yugoslavia in 1925, with Hungary in 1927 and with Bulgaria in 1929. On the East, in 1926, she signed a treaty of benevolent neutrality with Persia, and in 1928 a treaty of friendship with Afghanistan. All of these agreements attempted to resolve outstanding disputes, if any, between the parties and establish the basis of friendly co-operation, confirming Turkey's peaceful intentions and her satisfaction with the status quo.

October 30, 1930, the date of the signature of the Greco-Turkish Treaty of Neutrality, Conciliation, and Arbitration, inaugurated a new era in Turkish diplomacy. Truly, the Treaty terminated the century-old feud between the two nations. In spite of occasional ups and downs, it has continued to serve as a valuable frame for Turco-Greek co-operation. But its transcending importance resides in marking the beginning of Turkish activist

diplomacy. The immunization of the Balkans and the Middle East from Major Power politics became Turkey's principal goal in the next nine years. With Greece solidly on their side, Ataturk and Inönü embarked on the creation of a Balkan Union to protect the area against the swelling ambitions of Italy and the rising might of Germany.

Balkan Union and Saadabad Pact

Initiated by Greece and Turkey, the First Balkan Conference met in 1930 with all the six Balkan Powers attending. During the next three years, Turkey exerted great diplomatic effort and skill to congeal the relationship into a binding, political agreement. Beginning with Greece in September, 1933, and following it up with Rumania in October and Yugoslavia in November of the same year, she negotiated a series of friendship and non-aggression treaties which formed the core of the Balkan Pact signed in 1934. In spite of all Turkish remonstrances, Bulgaria, which had territorial claims on Greece and Rumania, and Albania, under Italian pressure, remained out, thereby jeopardizing the Pact's effectiveness.

The Pact is an important landmark in the philosophy and practice of Republican Turkey's foreign policy. By obligating herself to the joint defense of her Balkan neighbors' frontiers, Turkey was departing from a neutral stand of non-involvement. However, her entry into the League of Nations in 1932 had already implicated her in collective defense. The Balkan Pact, aiming to preserve the status quo, merely sought to keep the area from involvement in the power conflict that had begun knocking at the Albanian door.

In the meantime, Turkish attempts to close the ranks of her neighbors against strife within and threats from beyond the area extended to her Eastern neighbors. As in the Balkans, she proceeded by strengthening her relations with each neighbor separately. In this area, border disputes with Persia had been a chronic headache. Coupled with Iran's dispute with Iraq, over the control of Shatt-ul-Arab, they had inhibited joint action. However, in November of 1933, a settlement with Iran opened the way to a larger agreement.

The Italian adventure in Ethiopia provided the final incentive. On July 8, 1937, the Foreign Ministers of Iran, Iraq, Afghanistan and Turkey signed the Saadabad Pact, which committed them to respect each other's territorial integrity. Like the signatories of the Balkan Entente, they pledged themselves not to participate in any aggression against each other. But, unlike the Balkan agreement, they did not undertake a mutual guarantee of their joint frontiers. The Pact remained free of any military commitments. Both Afghanistan and Persia bordered the Soviets; and Turkish diplomacy continued to remain sensitive against assuming responsibilities that could bring her into conflict with the Soviet Union.

In spite of Turkey's friendly relations with Egypt and her renewed assurances of good faith towards the Arab world, the pact was received with mixed feelings by Arab Nationalists. A segment of Arab opinion feared that Turkey was seeking re-entry into the Arab World. This reaction to the Saadabad Pact is significant from the point of view of subsequent events and Arab reaction to the Baghdad Pact.

TURKEY AND "THE GATHERING STORM"

The year 1935 is another landmark in the evolution of Republican Turkey's basic foreign policy principles. The Italian aggression in Ethiopia, almost involving Britain in a war with Italy, destroyed Turkish confidence in the ability of Major Powers to preserve peace among themselves. As a result, she was forced to re-appraise her policy of non-involvement in Major Power conflicts and accept involvement within a general international frame. She was not only a participant but a prime mover in the sanctions against Italy. As her immediate response in Korea seventeen years later proved, reliance on collective defense had become one of the principal pillars of her foreign posture.

The Montreux Convention

The Ethiopian struggle, coupled with German re-armament and revisionism, revealed to the Turks the extreme precariousness of the status quo in Europe. The impunity with which Italy and Germany broke their international engagements bared the nakedness of the Turkish position in the Straits. The Turks could no longer count, as they had hoped to when demilitarization was imposed upon them in Lausanne, on the balance among the Great Powers to keep them safe from aggression. As a result, the natural desire to assume full control over the most strategic segment of national soil became an urgent necessity for national security.

In April 1936, Turkey presented a formal request to the League of Nations for revision of the Treaty. This request was supported by the Soviet Union which had desisted from signing the Lausanne Convention. In the exposed state of the Straits, an Italy in naval domination of the Mediterranean and supported by Germany was a grave threat to both Ankara and Moscow.

Furthermore, this was another opportunity for the Soviets to try for their traditional objective which, even at their most anti-imperialist period, had remained awake. On April 23, 1919, *Izvestia* had declared,

> Now the Turkish Revolution is returning the Dardanelles to the toiling masses and through them to the world proletariat which also includes the Russian. Thus what Russian imperialism failed to realize will, now, fall as a ripe plum to the Russian masses.

The outcome of the negotiations kept the Straits out of the Soviet grasp and left Moscow displeased. As in Lausanne, Russia sought to close the waterway to the non–Black Sea Powers and restrict its international character to the Black Sea nations. But the Convention, even though limiting the access of the non–Black Sea Powers, refused to accept the Russian principle. The Soviets this time adhered to the Convention, but not with willingness.

The Montreux Convention, signed on July 20, 1936, permitted Turkey to assume military control of the Straits. The international commission was abolished. The Convention simply laid down detailed regulations for the passage of warships. In the long run these have proved beneficial. Without impairing Turkish rights of ownership they established an international regime which barred one-sided pressure on Ankara. From Turkey's point of view, the goals of the National Pact were achieved and her security requirements fulfilled.

Alignment with the West

1937 marked the final step in Turkey's gradual and enforced departure from a policy of non-involvement with a Major Power. Originally, she had aimed at a neutral status between major contestants and signed non-aggression pacts with the Soviet Union, France, Italy and all her neighbors. Later, she had sought to create a Neutral Power bloc in the Middle East and the Balkans. When the Japanese adventure in Manchuria and the Italian invasion of Ethiopia proved that war was still conceivable, she had accepted involvement through collective security. But collective action by the League had failed against Italy. What chance would it have against a re-armed Germany?

In 1937 Turkish statesmen saw a Europe divided into two. The Axis Powers were arming rapidly for a quick take-over of Europe. The weak-willed democracies were wallowing in a half-hearted effort to cover their weakness. Turkey's northern neighbor wavered in impotence between the two camps.

Over 60 percent of Turkey's trade was with the Axis. The teeming industrial populations of Italy and Germany had become the hungry customers of Turkish agricultural products. Berlin had pressed her advantage with easy trading terms and generous credits which Turkey needed badly for her industrialization. Strangely, however, the economic benefits offered by Germany had an adverse effect, alerting Turkish instincts against a German alignment. Ankara hastened to strengthen the precarious balance of Europe by offering to join in a defensive alliance with Britain.

Cool, calculated interest dictated the choice. Turkey believed that her accommodation with the West was definitive. It had been won hard, but it would be mutually respected. Also, the Western Powers had their global responsibilities for and benefits from their empires. Turkey did not offer any additional gains. By contrast, both Germany and Italy expected to enrich their meager natural resources from the East. Moreover, the Allied potentials were limitless. They would be reinforced by American participation, which Turkish leaders viewed as inevitable. The Axis had little chance against these odds. Finally, avoidance of inimical entanglement with Russia remained one of her prime instincts. She felt that the Western Alliance would guard her best against such an eventuality. Under the Nazi threat of expansion, the West loomed as the Soviet's natural ally.

The final Turkish commitment with Britain and France was effected in May 1939. Negotiations that had been dragging on for months assumed urgency when Italy, by invading Albania, initiated her thrust into the Balkans. Thereupon M. Vladimir Potemkin, Soviet Vice-Commissar of Foreign Affairs, hastened to Ankara to urge the Turkish Government into a Franco-British Alliance. The Turks, in their turn, irked by the mutual reluctance of the Soviets and Western Democracies to forge a common front, proposed a Turco-Soviet Mutual Assistance Pact which they hoped would serve as the link bringing Moscow in line with Paris and London.

These exchanges resulted in the joint Turco-British Declaration of May 12, 1939, that committed Turkey publicly to the Peace Front of the Western democracies. A similar declaration with France followed on June 23, 1939. The Turkish Foreign Minister was invited to Moscow and the Turkish Government was expecting to conclude a similar agreement with the Soviet Union in the course of the summer when the war exploded.

In spite of the surprise and disappointment of the Nazi-Soviet Pact, Turkey proceeded with her schedule. In September, the Turkish Foreign Minister went to Moscow for the conclusion of the Turco-Soviet Alliance of Mutual Assistance, completing the link in the chain of Turkey's defense arrangements with the Western Democracies. Since the twenties, Republican Turkey had come to accept Russia as a "status quo" nation, opposed to any violent disturbance of the existing international boundaries. When the Russians now demanded the joint defense of the Straits, contrary to the conditions of the Montreux Convention, the bottom fell out of Turkey's carefully fostered attitude towards the Soviets. Plainly, this was reversion to the traditional Tsarist policy of control of Turkey. It left a permanent scar against Russia in the Turkish national conscience.

On October 19, 1939, two days after the Foreign Minister's return from Moscow, Turkey signed the Tripartite Alliance with Britain and France. The important articles of this document are quoted below in full. They are of utmost importance because they served as the basis of Turkey's stand in the War.

Article 1: In the event of Turkey being involved in hostilities with a European power in consequence of aggression by that power against Turkey, France and the United Kingdom will co-operate effectively with Turkey and will lend her all aid and assistance in their power.

Article 2: In the event of an act of aggression by a European power lead-ing to war in the Mediterranean area in which France and the United Kingdom are involved, Turkey will collaborate effectively with France and the United Kingdom and will lend them all aid and assistance in her power. In the event of an act of aggression by a European power leading to war in the Mediterranean area in which Turkey is involved, France and the United Kingdom will collaborate effectively with Turkey and will lend her all aid and assistance in their power.

Protocol II appended to the Treaty: The obligations undertaken by virtue of the above mentioned Treaty cannot compel that country to take action having as its effect, or involving as its consequence, entry into armed conflict with the Soviet Union.[6]

WORLD WAR II

As the war clouds on the Western front gathered for their inevitable spread around the world, Turkey had two definite commitments. First, the Balkan Entente obligated her to come to the assistance if a signatory was attacked by another Balkan Power. Second, under the Tripartite Treaty with France and Britain, she was committed to intervene if any of her allies became involved in hostilities in the Mediterranean.

Only one of the commitments, the Anglo-French, became operative in the course of the conflict. This was on June 11, 1940, when Italy declared war on the Allies. But Turkey abstained, and in the latter years of the war this abstention became a major point in contesting her true attachment to the Allied cause. Now that the historical perspective has

[6] Hurewitz, *op. cit.,* vol. II, p. 226.

emerged more clearly, Turkey's decision to withhold commitment is accepted not only as diplomatically valid, but as having been beneficial to the Allied cause.

Reasons for non-belligerency

Turkey excused her conduct on the basis of Protocol II quoted above. She argued that Turkey's intervention would extend the war to the Balkans and the Middle East, involving her in war with the Soviet Union. However, the considerations that determined her conduct were more than juridical.

Since the Axis was pressing for a decision on the Western front, Turkish leaders believed that their country's intervention would have no effect on the outcome. On the contrary, it would extend the conflict to the Middle East and the Balkans where Allied commitments were widespread. Turkish invervention would mean peripheral efforts for Britain and France.

The Treaty had obligated the Allies to modernize the military establishment of Turkey. But this obligation had not been fulfilled. In the face of the progress of the campaign on the Western front, Turkey's inability to fight a modern war was apparent, and she would be a liability instead of an asset. By conserving her resources from ineffective use, Turkey would be of greater help to the Allied cause in the future. Moreover, Turkey's inaction did not mean her defection from the alliance. She was determined to remain true to its letter and spirit.

The British Ambassador to Ankara, Sir Hugh Knatchbull-Hugessen, in his memoirs entitled *A Diplomat in War and Peace* remarks:

To plunge thus handicapped into the melee at a moment when one of their allies was down and out and the other in deadly danger might have earned for Turkey imperishable memories of heroic self-sacrifice but it would have done very little good. Indeed by becoming a liability to their already

strained ally they might have done incalculable harm.[7]

From the opposite end of the picture Franz von Papen, the German Ambassador in Turkey, in his *Memoirs* raises the same point: "It seemed a lot to ask Turkey to expect her to enter the war at the time of France's debacle and the disaster of the British Expeditionary Forces at Dunkirk."[8]

In effect, the exigencies of the Turkish position were officially recognized by the British Government itself on June 11, 1939. In a statement in the House of Lords, Lord Halifax declared, "His Majesty's Government fully appreciated the circumstances which had led to this decision of the Turkish Government, who throughout have kept in close contact with His Majesty's Government."[9]

Nevertheless, psychologically the decision had been very hard on both the government and the nation. Their instinct for strict adherence to contractual agreements was so strong that in spite of all the practical exigencies and the legal justification of the situation they were not altogether happy.

On July 12, 1940, defying the Italian threat knocking on her door and the awakened appetite of the Soviets, the Turkish Prime Minister, Refik Saydam, announced to the Grand National Assembly Turkey's continued loyalty to the Western Alliance. In spite of the French capitulation and British isolation, "Turkey would remain faithful to her commitments to England." During the whole course of the War adherence to the West was a cardinal concern of Turkish policy. Sir Hugh Knatchbull-Hugessen's testimony with respect to this issue is of interest:

that Turkey's natural political orientation was towards Great Britain and the Anglo-Turkish Alliance was in Turkish eyes, a permanent feature in her international life and not pri-

---

[7] London: John Murray, 1949, p. 166.
[8] London: Andre Deutsch, 1952, p. 461.
[9] Knatchbull-Hugessen, *op. cit.*, p. 167.

marily, as with us, an element in the international grouping necessitated by the immediate German menace.[10]

Turkey was never obligated to fulfill her second commitment which called for assistance under the Balkan Entente. The Italian attack on Greece on October 28, 1940, absolved her of any responsibility. The treaty between the Entente members guaranteed their borders only against each other. But by warning Bulgaria that any intervention would bring Turkey into the conflict, she helped secure Greece's back door and enabled her to withdraw much needed troops and equipment from the Bulgarian borders to the Italian front.

In February of 1940, at a meeting of the Balkan Pact Powers, Ankara had sought once again to solidify the Entente against Major Power intervention. She had proposed to extend their mutual obligations to cover each other against outside attack. But she had failed again. The Entente simply re-affirmed its neutrality. The progress of the hostilities wore out even this flimsy bond. Rumania openly embraced the Nazi cause. Yugoslavia gave in to Nazi pressure. Bulgaria, encouraged in her revisionist aims, asked them in. By April 1941, the Germans had reached the Turco-Greek borders without fighting.

In this first phase of the war, Turkey confronted the Axis with all her international arrangements disrupted. The Balkan Entente was smashed by German occupation of the Balkans. The Axis ruled over the Mediterranian. France had capitulated and the Tripartite Alliance had lost its effectiveness. Britain was laboring for her own survival. Moscow's reversion to the traditional policy of the Tsars had turned the U.S.S.R. into a deadly antagonist.

The Turkish Government learned that in negotiations for a treaty for joint action between Germany, Italy, Japan and the Soviets, in November 1940, the Soviet Government had introduced her Turkish ambitions to the international mart. As the price of her co-operation,

she had demanded the establishment of a base for land and naval forces of the U.S.S.R. within range of the Bosphorus and Dardanelles and the recognition of the area south of Batum and Baku in the direction of the Persian Gulf as the center of the aspirations of the Soviet Union.

In the second phase of the war, during the final Axis bid for world dominion that brought the Germans to Stalingrad and to the gates of Egypt, Turkey's principal concern was to pursue "peace with honor," without altering her fundamental pro-Western outlook. As early as April 1941 when Italy was pressing for a German push into Egypt through the East, Hitler had told Ciano that "One must exclude the possibility of pushing through Turkey by force. Apart from the resistance of the Turks which would be considerable, the distances would render perilously risky any military action. . . ."[11]

As the British ambassador to Ankara expressed it, "There was never any doubt where the President's sympathies lay. The problem before him was how far he could go to express them without involving his country in disaster."[12]

Pressures from the Axis

In July, 1941, the Germans pressed for the passage of troops and arms from the Balkans to Syria and Iraq. In compensation, they offered parts of Greek Thrace and some of the Aegean Islands. The Turkish refusal was categorical. The Germans had to contend with a Treaty of Non-Aggression and Friendship, which allowed the Turks to guard their commitments to Britain. On July 24th, in a statement to the House of Commons, the Foreign Secretary, Anthony Eden, acknowledged Britain's tacit consent to the Turco-German pact.

[10] *Ibid.,* p. 145.

[11] Altemur Kilic, *Turkey and the World,* Washington, D.C.: Public Affairs Press, 1959, p. 86.
[12] Knatchbull-Hugessen, *op. cit.,* p. 193.

Since the Mutual Aid Pact we signed with Turkey in October, 1939, our relations have continued to be on a very special footing. Turkey is our friend and ally. As we were fully informed of the course of the negotiations between the Turkish and German Governments the agreement comes to us as no surprise at all.[13]

The mounting score of German successes in Russia and Africa resulted in mounting pressure on Turkey. Japan was urging Hitler for a quick thrust into the Persian Gulf and India for a dramatic union of the two partners in the Indian Ocean. On the other hand, Italy was anxious to insert her fleet into the Black Sea where she hoped it could be effective in harassing the Russian rear in the Crimea. Finally, the German High Command had become increasingly restive at Allied shipments into Russia through Iraq and Iran.

But Turkey resisted every effort to draw her away from her non-belligerent attitude. She would not commit herself to assist Germany in any way. In reporting to his government on the Turkish scene on January 5, 1942, the German Ambassador, Von Papen, wrote:

Turkey reiterates and repeats her unchanged desire to keep out of hostilities and to refuse to let herself be drawn into the struggle for any interests which do not directly concern her. . . . any attempt to force the Turks to pronounce themselves definitely would cause Turkey to adhere to the enemy.[14]

During these years the incessant threats and profuse complaints from the German side were compensated by generous expressions of gratification from the Allies. In a New Year's message in 1941 Churchill cabled, "In these times of distress we are encouraged by

loyal friends." On January 19, 1942, Joseph Stalin instructed his ambassador in Ankara to express the Soviet Government's gratitude to Turkey for its conduct in the war which he specified as reward-worthy.

The country backed this attitude by keeping herself fully mobilized with almost a million men under arms; vulnerable Thrace lived under a state of emergency, strategic spots in the country were screened off. In the meantime, in co-operation with the Allied Middle East Command, Turkey proceeded to re-equip and modernize her army. The nation lived on the alert, not knowing what to expect from day to day, dreading, on the one hand, a German invasion and fearing, on the other, the ultimate aims of the Soviet Union. Since these aims had been pressed on the Turkish Foreign Minister in Moscow in 1939, and followed up with Hitler in 1940, they would certainly be reasserted as soon as the thrust-back of the German invasion began.

Pressures from the Allies

Winston Churchill's visit to Adana, where he met President Ismet Inönü, opened the third phase of the war for Turkey. During this period, the Allies replaced Germany in pressuring her to involve herself in the conflict. Psychologically, this was the most difficult phase of the war for the Turks. Beyond their diplomatic commitment to the West they desired an early Allied victory, but found themselves physically inhibited. The *Luftwaffe* controlled the skies in the Aegean. The *Wehrmacht* in the Balkans was intact. The Turkish Army could not match remotely their crushing armor. Across the flat plains of Thrace the Germans could cross to Istanbul and Gallipoli overnight.

Turkey's strength against Germany lay, as did Russia's, in the long, treacherous distances of the heartland of the country. In an offensive campaign, Turkey would be a liability. The kind of vengeful destruction that the *Luftwaffe* rained on Belgrade and Rotterdam would de-

[13] Kilic, *op. cit.,* p. 90.
[14] Von Papen, *op. cit.,* p. 480.

stroy the few metropolitan centers like Istanbul, Izmir and Ankara that the nation possessed —centers that were more than urban conglomerations. There the spirit of modern Turkey subsisted. There the few industrial establishments she was able to develop in thirty years existed as the base of her new economy.

Furthermore, both the United States and the Soviet Union were determined to mount the final assault on the western front and not through the Balkans. All the Turkish sacrifice would be for a diversionary cause. In the final analysis it could turn fatal for Turkey and vitally detrimental to the Allies.

The Turkish leaders realized that the establishment of a new order in Europe in full partnership with the Soviet Union, which the Anglo-Americans projected, did not conform with the aroused appetites of the Russians. In an exhausted impoverished Europe, the Soviets would prevail. Neither England nor the United States could stop their expansion. Turkey would not be liberated, but German captivity would be succeeded by Russian invasion. If Turkey participated in the war, she must do so with the certainty that her territory would keep free from invasion and her defensive capacity remain intact for coping with the uncertainties of the postwar era.

In 1943 Turkey agreed in principle to intervene in the war. The British undertook to clear the Aegean and drive the Germans back from the islands surrounding Turkey. In the meantime, they promised to increase deliveries in heavy arms and planes. But none of these conditions were fulfilled when the Teheran Conference met and decided to bring Turkey into the war. The attempt to clean the Aegean had ended with a defeat proving the Turkish contention about German strength in the area.

When Ismet Inönü was invited to Cairo to receive the tripartite Teheran decision, Roosevelt had to admit that naturally the Turks "would not like to be caught with their pants down" and if he were in their position he would keep insisting that they would be properly armed before they undertook to act. Nevertheless, Ismet Inönü scaled the re-armament program down to the minimum neces-

sary for the containment of a joint German-Bulgarian attack.

But the British failed to produce even this limited amount. As a result, Turkey did not physically participate in the conflict. In August 1944 she severed relations with the Axis Powers. In February 1945, at the request of Great Britain and the United States, she declared war against Germany and Japan.

Turkey's role in the war

Turkey's role in the war has been variously appraised. After 1943, the Soviets accused her of aiding the German cause. For the historical record, the conclusions of the man most immediately responsible for the Turkish attitude towards the Allies in those critical years deserves mention. Sir Hugh Knatchbull-Hugessen, in *Diplomat in War and Peace* states:

> If I were asked for my personal opinion as to whether the non-participation of Turkey in actual hostilities on our side had been a benefit or reverse I should answer, with very little hesitation, that things were better as they were . . . for Turkey to go to war in 1940, when Italy joined the Axis, or in 1941 when Germany attacked Greece was recognized as inadvisable. Possibly the risks of disaster decreased as the war progressed and certainly the Allied position improved, but even in 1943 and especially at Adana at the beginning of that year it was recognized that Turkey could be expected to risk her whole existence by coming in. In 1944 too it was felt that there was justification in a great part at least of the Turkish argument of unpreparedness. . . . There would be at any time an element of gamble in Turkish belligerency. On the other hand, by making her general sentiments plain

and by opposing throughout the war a block of resistance to German penetration into Iraq, and Syria, Turkey rendered a service of the first importance. There were moments when in reliance on this "protective pad" we were able to move forces into North Africa which would otherwise have to be held inactive elsewhere to contain a possible German diversion. In this way Turkey played a valuable part while avoiding anything which might have increased our liabilities. This view found expression also in the Soviet Press, which though prone to attack Turkey for her inaction, agreed that Turkish neutrality had played a positive part in favour of the Allies earlier in the war by reason of the fact that it barred to Hitler's armies the road to Egypt and Persia.

One thing was never in doubt, namely Turkey's intense desire for an Allied victory and her recognition of the fact that her prosperity if not her existence depended on the close friendship of the Allies. . . ."[15]

It seems, almost, a miracle that Turkey, in one of the most critical areas in the conflict, could have escaped belligerency, even though all belligerents, at the point of a bayonet, strove to push her into the fray. Turkey owes this miracle first, to the wisdom and courage of her leaders who were able to keep their nerve under the most arduous pressures and to see beyond the immediate exigencies of the day. Secondly, she owes it to the policies and spirit inherited from the Ataturkist Revolution: a determination to remain immovable against any temptations beyond her borders; confidence to accept sacrifice for self-defense; ability to make this determination credible to friend and foe alike. Finally, in neither the first nor the second phase of the war was she in the direct path of the ultimate outcome. Her greatest mo-

ment of peril developed late in 1940 when Hitler toyed with the idea of appeasing Russia in an all-out effort to finish up the British Empire. Then Ankara would have been on the path of prime German objectives and nothing could have saved her.

As soon as the German objective shifted to Russia, her status became peripheral. From the German point of view, she was no longer worthy of a major campaign. Churchill's desire to force the issue by an assault through the Balkans again placed Turkey in a focal position. As soon as that policy was abandoned, she assumed peripheral status. She could thus exercise her will and could prevail against pressures from the major contestants.

THE POSTWAR WORLD

Pressure from Russia

The end of the War found the Republic under continuing tension. Looking back, she felt herself in greater isolation than at any time since 1923. After Lausanne, she had had the friendship of the new Soviet state and her territorial integrity was secure. Now, the Soviets had repudiated their friendship and declared their claims. For the first time since 789 A.D. Grand Duke Sviatasfaff's ambition to control Byzantium, Hungary and Bohemia seemed within their grasp.

True, Turkey was allied to the Western democracies but the worth of the alliance appeared questionable. Under the leadership of the United States, the democracies were engulfed in comatose co-operation with the Soviet Union. They were intent on preventing such a secondary matter as a piece of "Turkish real estate" to distract them from their great ally.

In effect, the Russians, with their usual foresight and intuition in propaganda matters concerning the Anglo-Saxon world, had initiated their campaign against Turkey after Stalingrad.

[15] *Op. cit.,* pp. 203–204.

By exploiting the natural envy of the victims of the disaster for those who had escaped it, they presented the Turkish people as chiselling their way through the conflict. As a result, at the end of the war they had isolated Ankara psychologically from her Allies and prepared themselves to pounce on her.

On March 19, 1945, they informed the Turkish Government that the traditional Turco-Soviet Treaty of Neutrality and Non-Aggression of 1925 no longer conformed to the new situation. In June they spelled out their conditions for a new treaty. These conditions were the same as those they had proposed to Hitler. They demanded the control of the Turkish Straits. They asked for bases in the area. At the same time, they pressed for the change of the eastern border. With a view of opening the heartland of Anatolia to a drive from the north they demanded Kars and Ardahan—the natural mountain barrier between the two countries.

Obviously, these were not simple requests for updating the contractual agreements between the two countries. The Soviets were aiming at the subjugation of Turkey. They intended to break her principal points of resistance both on the east and the west.

Force was given to these claims by the attempt to establish an independent Kurdestan and by the initiation of the Communist campaign in Greece. The frontal diplomatic attack was re-inforced by an attempt to envelop Turkey in a military pincer. Tactically, the move was perfect, and it could not have been better timed.

The Turkish Straits had been discussed in Potsdam, and both the United States and Britain had agreed to the revision of the Montreux Convention. In fact, on November 2, 1945, the United States had taken the initial step in that direction. In a note to the Turkish Government, it had revealed a dangerous surprise by proposing free passage for Russian warships at all times. On November 21st, the British had indicated that they were agreeable to the American proposals. Turkey, on her part, was ready for a revision. But she pressed for an international conference and not a convention of Black Sea Powers such as the Soviets desired.

When Turkey refused to capitulate, the Soviets increased their military pressure on Greece and enhanced their efforts to disintegrate Iran and Iraq through the Kurds. Their open drive to the Indian Ocean and Africa caused the Allies to re-evaluate their Russian policy and precipitated the United States into action. In January 1946, President Harry S. Truman declared:

> Russia intends an invasion of Turkey and the seizure of the Black Sea to the Mediterranean. . . . Unless she is faced with an iron fist another war is in the making . . . to allow Russia to set up bases in the Dardanelles . . . would in the natural course of events result in Greece and the whole Near and the Middle East fully under Soviet control.[16]

In March 1947, a joint session of Congress was called and the President asked and obtained aid for Greece and Turkey. This revolutionary departure in American policy, also inaugurated a new era in Republican Turkey's basic foreign posture. She dropped a cardinal tenet of her foreign policy: the principle of non-alignment against the Soviets. She had given it primacy in all her deals with other Powers and guarded it meticulously through the vicissitudes of the war. But Russian aggressiveness rendered alignment with third parties imperative. Henceforth, the development and extension of this alignment would be her main concern.

Turkey in the Western alliance

When the Republic was founded, Turkey accepted modernization as a cardinal principle of her new existence. This process, initiated as a means of securing herself against a modernized world, had developed into an ideological com-

[16] Kilic, *op. cit.*, p. 128.

mitment. Ataturk struggled to extend the political ties with the West to cultural bonds. Right after the war, under Ismet Inönü's leadership, Turkey terminated the one-party dictatorship and moved into a multi-party parliamentarianism, gaining thereby ideological association with the Western community.

These domestic moves towards Western alignment were reinforced by diplomatic moves to tighten Turkish bonds with Western Europe and the United States. Even though the United States had declared herself committed to Turkish independence, and the Tripartite Alliance with the French and the British had been officially revalidated, Turkey's sense of security was never completely restored. She remembered the wartime aspirations for creating a new order in Europe with the Soviets and the consequent Anglo-American coolness towards her territorial integrity, which, luckily the Soviets themselves had dispelled by their greed. She realized the necessity to set herself on guard against any possible future collusion between a wiser Russia and an overzealous West. Her one great nightmare was exclusion from any Western combinations, political, economic or even cultural.

Economic and military assistance   Thus, the Turks became the most ardent proponents of European integration which was sparked by Russian aggressiveness. But curiously, in almost every instance, they had to fight to join. First, they were left out of the European Council. In a year they pushed their way in. In July 1948, they were invited to the Organization of European Economic Co-operation without much ado, since this was an extension of the Truman Doctrine of military and economic aid, from Turkey and Greece, to the whole of Europe. Under this program Turkey has continued to receive aid from the United States without any interruption. What Dean Acheson said with respect to the necessity of American support on March 20, 1947, still applies:

Turkish economy is no longer able to carry the full load required for its national defense and at the same time proceed with that economic development which is necessary to keep the country in a sound position.[17]

By 1962 American aid had totalled 3.7 billion dollars of which 2.1 billion was military and 1.6 billion economic. This has enabled Turkey to modernize her army and to keep twenty divisions under arms for immediate use by the North Atlantic Treaty Command. At the same time, she has doubled her gross national income and built some of the social and industrial infrastructure necessary for further and self-sustained growth.

Turkey never liked the idea of economic aid detached from political considerations. Her outlook ran against the neutralist concepts. In 1948, Foreign Minister, Necmettin Sadak defined her attitude towards aid programs as follows: "Turkey, already more than an ally of the United States, is looking forward to a crystallization of this relationship in an Alliance." To the Turks the aims and goals of Soviet imperialism were clear. Only full political, military and economic integration could counter them. Europe had succumbed to Hitlerism because she had failed to integrate political, economic and strategic defenses. Economic co-operation coupled with political and ideological neutralism furthered only the cause of the aggressor.

Efforts to enter NATO   From 1948 onwards, Turkey's principal diplomatic efforts were directed towards the realization of this full commitment with the West. The rape of Czechoslovakia and the pressure on Berlin had forced the Western democracies to the consolidation of their joint defense against the Soviets. On April 4, 1948, they signed the North Atlantic Treaty Organization. Turkey, recalling that she had been the first to stand against Soviet aggression, expected to become a member of the new association. Deprived of her aid, the Germans had failed in the Mediterranean; with her help the Soviets could now outflank

---

[17] United States, Department of State, *Bulletin*, vol. XVI, Supplement, May 4, 1947.

Western European defenses and reach the shores of the Atlantic as fast as their ships could carry them.

But she met opposition from every quarter. First, France and Britain balked. They still had an influential position in the southern Mediterranean, and feared to dilute it with the intrusion of the North Atlantic Treaty Organization. They proposed a separate Middle Eastern Alliance with links to NATO. The smaller Benelux and Scandinavian countries, none wiser from their experience with Hitler, feared that the exposed positions of Greece and Turkey would increase their chances of conflict with the Soviets. Moreover, they calculated that two more partners would divide American aid into two more slices. The United States, on her part, still stunned by the revolutionary changes that had overtaken her international relations and laboring for a psychological adjustment to these involvements, advanced the lame excuse that this was a regional pact confined to the Atlantic states. This certainly was an illogical assertion in view of Italian and Algerian accession to the pact.

The exclusion of Greece and Turkey from the NATO Alliance had encouraged the Soviets. They recognized that under the existing arrangement the two countries were expendable military outposts. They redoubled their efforts to exploit the gap. The stick had not worked, they tried the carrot. A friendly ambassador, Anton Lavrischev, was dispatched to Ankara. Radio Moscow and the Russian press changed their angry tone to a friendly chatter.

Nevertheless, Turkey was never deceived. On the contrary, President Inönü proposed to the United States a bilateral alliance. Secretary of State George Marshall refused it on the grounds of its inacceptability to American traditional instincts against entangling alliances.

Turkey persisted against the illogic of the situation. As an alternative, she called for United States adherence to the Tripartite Treaty of Mutual Assistance of 1939 between Turkey, France and England. This was considered politically infeasible. Ankara came up with another suggestion: an Eastern Mediterranean Alliance, including Britain, France and the United States.

Turkish insistence, on the one hand, and NATO refusal, on the other, went on for two years until the Korean War substantiated the Turkish argument that "geographical areas not under contractual agreement permit free play to international greed and open the way to aggression. . . ." Even so, there were another two years of wrangling before Greece and Turkey were admitted as fullfledged members of the North Atlantic Treaty Organization.

Membership in the North Atlantic Treaty provided Turkey with the security she had been seeking against the Soviet Union since the war. However, from the people's point of view, it carried a deeper significance. NATO, to the Turkish public, was more than a military alliance. It was a community—the Western Community. Turkey's adherence to that community proved that her orientation towards the West had attained its goal.

Turkey and the United Nations

Turkish efforts after her admission to NATO offer insight into another part of her international outlook. Although NATO provided the only available effective guarantee against aggression, Ankara continued actively to seek strengthening collective security both in the United Nations and through regional agreements. The underlying belief behind these efforts was expressed by Prime Minister Adnan Menderes in July 1950, when he explained the Turkish Government's decision to aid the Security Council against aggression in Southern Korea:

> If the United Nations were to fail to take action against an aggression in no matter what part of the world, this would pave the way to further aggressions and would constitute a sort of premium for them. Our Government is convinced that the strong-

est guarantee for the safeguarding of peace, is to recognize it as an indivisible whole. . . .[18]

In July, 1950, Turkey was among the first to rush with military assistance to Korea, in the same manner that she had favored sanctions against Italy in the Ethiopian War and joined the Nyon Patrol in the Spanish War. She believed that in an awkwardly balanced world of intercontinental missiles and supersonic jets, a spark in Patagonia could set off a prairie fire in the Mediterranean. Peace was indivisible and had to be sought and guaranteed globally. In the fifties Turkish policy followed exactly the pattern of the thirties: support of the international organization's peace-keeping powers, but reliance on collective defense commitments with the West, these to be reinforced with defensive arrangements with immediate neighbors.

CENTO

After the war, the Turkish Government engaged in the laborious process of recreating her prewar arrangements in the Balkans, as well as the Middle East. In 1946 Nuri Said of Iraq was invited to Ankara. Through the course of the war, Turkey had continued her friendship with her southern neighbor in the spirit of the Saadabad Pact. She had also supported Iran in the evacuation of Azerbaijan by the Soviets, and had pressed for the independence of Syria, Lebanon and Jordan. She was very sensitive to the boiling cauldron in the Middle East. Conflict among the Arab States or between the Arabs and Zionists could invite Soviet incursion and place Turkey between two fires.

She sought to cultivate the co-operation of Egypt. But the emergence of Israel had alienated the Arab World from the West. British reluctance in confirming Egyptian independence solidified Arab adversity into active animosity. In October 1951, Egypt refused a joint Middle Eastern Command with Turkey, France, Britain and the United States. Exchanges with other Arab States revealed that the Arab World did not feel menaced by the Soviets. On the contrary, they were eager for Soviet co-operation for spiting the detested West. A defense in depth, as Turkey visualized it, aligning the Arab World with the West and immunizing it against the exploitation of regional differences in the international power struggle of communism proved impossible. Turkish diplomacy reverted to the principles of linear defense on the basis of the Saadabad Pact.

Among the Arab nations, Iraq already had the tradition of an alliance with Turkey. Moreover, she was suffering from Soviet pressure. The Kurdish portion of her population was under a barrage of subversion from the North. Mahmut Barzani, a tribal leader recruited by the Soviets, was agitating for an independent Kurdistan to encompass large tracts of Iraqi territory. Iran's position vis-à-vis the Soviet Union was still more perilous. Pakistan viewed Soviet attempts to penetrate Afghanistan with increasing anxiety and desired to reinforce her security.

In May 1951, Secretary of State John Foster Dulles visited Ankara and baptized the Northern Tier Concept of a Middle Eastern Alliance. The chain of agreements that led to the Central Treaty Organization was inaugurated by the Turkish-Pakistan Treaty of Friendship of July 1951. But it took another four years, and Soviet co-operation with Nasser, to crystallize the effort into a regional pact.

Iraq held back. Arab opinion was adverse to the West and Baghdad abstained from breaking the joint Arab front until Nasser's bid to capture the Arab World with Soviet backing imperiled the Iraqui regime. In February 1955 Baghdad signed the agreement with Turkey for co-operation in national defense. The ice was broken. Britain was the first adherent in April, 1955. She was followed by Pakistan, in September, and by Iran in November.

---

[18] *News from Turkey*. New York: Turkish Information Office, July, 1952.

The original Turco-Iraqui Agreement of 1955 has now developed into a skeleton regional alliance. It is organized more or less on the same basis as the North Atlantic Treaty Organization. It has a Permanent Council, composed of the Foreign Ministers of the signatories, meeting at least once a year. It has set up a Secretariat in Baghdad which, after Iraq's defection in 1958, moved to Ankara. It differs from the NATO Alliance in not providing for integration of the armed forces nor a joint command. Neither does it offer automatic help in case of aggression.

The United States, which fathered the pact, has abstained from joining it as a full-fledged member. It participates in the work of the military and economic committees and provides funds and arms. The American Secretary of State attends the meetings of the Permanent Council. The United States has withheld her full membership for fear of antagonizing Nasser and Nehru. Turkish policy has sought America's full adherence, believing that her absence could, at a moment of weakness, be utilized in bringing Iran into the Soviet orbit as long as she remains uncovered by any Western guarantee.

Balkan diplomacy

While the process of forging a regional alliance with her south-eastern neighbors continued, Turkish diplomacy was also busy with Balkan neighbors. During the war, Turkey had tried to alleviate the Greek ordeal by large shipments of food. In the postwar years, subjected to the same Soviet pressure, the two countries were drawn closer. The Truman Doctrine of joint aid had further strengthened their friendship. They waged the same diplomatic battle to get into NATO. In 1950 they enjoyed a complete identity of purpose. When Stalin attempted to satellize Yugoslavia, they rushed to win Tito to their side.

Diplomatic exchanges led to staff talks which, by August 1954, eventuated in the Balkan Defense Pact, and went far beyond the original Balkan Entente of the thirties. They agreed that armed aggression against one would be considered aggression against all; and they undertook to render immediate assistance to the attacked. In NATO pattern, they established a permanent council. The general staffs were directed to work jointly.

The Balkan and Baghdad Pacts completed Turkey's diplomatic arrangements in meeting the dangers of the postwar period. From the isolation of 1945, she had attained as complete a defensive arrangement as was available to her. In the NATO councils, as the contributor of the largest European contingent, and as the king-pin of the land defenses of the eastern Mediterranean, she has continued to hold an important position in spite of political and economic difficulties. Within the Central Treaty Organization, as the strongest and most advanced Middle Eastern partner, her counsel, naturally, carries great weight.

The defection of Iraq has strengthened CENTO. Slowly but steadily, it is increasing mutual help among its three regional partners. Only the Balkan Pact has failed to meet its promises. Tito's slip into pro-Soviet neutralism, compounded by the Turco-Greek dispute over Cyprus, has pushed it into the attic where it is gathering dust without being officially discarded.

The Cyprus accord

Since the Turco-Greek reconciliation in 1930, Cyprus introduced the first real discordance between the two countries and nearly broke the genuine friendship between the two peoples, which had grown almost into a tradition. The dispute was not in the main a Turkish creation. True, eighty percent of the Island's population called themselves Greek but this statistical fact concealed issues equally relevant to the principle of self-determination. Twenty percent of the people on the Island were Turks and for centuries they had lived an independent life from the Greeks. In fact, on the basis of the old Ottoman system, each community had enjoyed civil autonomy, running its own schools, its own courts, its own municipality within each city. Self-determination which rested on the principle of the individual's right to self-rule under the traditional way of life of the islanders had to apply to Turk and Greek alike.

At the same time, geography operated against the Greek majority. The Island, hundreds of miles away from Greece belonged to the Turkish mainland. The question arose whether eighty thousand Greeks within the geographic complex of twenty-eight million Turks were entitled to assert a right of self-rule. International recognition of such a principle could create a precedent leading to all kinds of irrational claims around the world. For instance, it could provide a basis for a cluster of Cubans occupying an island or a key on the coast line of Florida to claim union with Cuba. On the basis of such considerations the international community could not give satisfaction to Greek aspirations. The dispute continued year after year to embitter the relations between Greece, Turkey and Britain, crippling Western co-operation in a most crucial area of the world.

As the traditional allies of the Greeks, the British were embittered because this attempt aimed to deprive them of their last stronghold in the region—a stronghold that had served Greece well in the war, providing the Allies a base for their liberating operations against the Germans—a stronghold that could serve the same purpose against the Soviets. Greek pressure for annexation also trespassed on vital Turkish interests. Cyprus commanded the southern approaches to the Turkish heartland. During the war—any war—the island provided Turkey's only access to the West. For Greece she was only a matter of sentiment, for Turkey she could be life or death.

The Greeks were exasperated because "their Turkish friends" deprived them of a "legitimate heritage." The Turks were mad because "their Greek friends" invaded their threshold. Greece tossed the dispute into the arena of international debate in 1954 when Prime Minister Marshal Papagos requested United Nations' intervention. From then on it became subject of an increasingly bitter debate among Greece, Turkey, and Britain. It aroused intense national sentiment in all three countries and stretched their relations to a breaking point. But in spite of extreme domestic pressures, official determination for agreement persisted.

After protracted discussion and negotiation and repeated failures, the three governments finally agreed to create an independent Cyprus. The Treaty of London of 1959 provided each party satisfaction of minimum but rational claims. For Greece and Turkey, Cyprus was the severest test of their friendship. They emerged from the ordeal convinced that no matter how bitter their squabbles, when the chips were down, the sense of their common destiny was strong enough to pull them together.

Yugoslavia sided with Greece in Cyprus, and relations between Ankara and Belgrade cooled. Also, Turkey's active conviction of the indivisibility of peace contradicted Tito's pro-Soviet neutralism, stretching their differences. Nevertheless, increases in mutual trade, reinforced by the belief that their destinies were linked against potential Soviet expansionism, helped to keep their diplomatic relations correct.

CURRENT POLICIES AND OUTLOOK

The Balkans   In the Balkans, Bulgaria and Romania are within the Soviet orbit. They have no independent policy. But, Turkey has exchanged diplomatic representatives with them, and tries to cultivate good neighborliness within the limits of their allowances from Moscow. The prewar idea of a Balkan Union embracing all the six Balkan states is no longer feasible.

Iraq   Ankara's relations with Iraq have been normalized. The downfall of the Hashemite monarchy in June 1958 could have resulted in a very dangerous international situation for Turkey, as well as Iran. But General Kassem has succeeded in keeping Iraq free from communism and out of the Soviet camp. The pulls of *Realpolitik* make for a close co-operation between the two countries. Iraq cannot afford to forget that her northern Kurdish section is within only a few hundred miles from the Soviet border. Ever since her independence, relations with Turkey have been subject to this strategic reality. Unless she is totally engulfed by communism, change of government will not affect this basic policy, and increasing co-operation with Turkey will be inevitable.

Syria   Among Turkey's neighbors, Syria is unique. Since the establishment of the Turkish Republic, Syria has emerged as the only neighbor with territorial claims on Ankara. True, in 1945 the Soviets demanded Kars and Ardahan, but their claims never went beyond diplomatic juggling. In any event, the claims were officially withdrawn in 1953. On the other hand, Syria is constantly seized with the fever of Iskenderun (Alexandretta) Irredentism. Politicians use it to distract attention from their domestic failures. The Soviets fan it to ferment discord against Turkey. During the short-lived United Arab Republic, Nasser exploited it for generating Syrian loyalty for himself.

The trouble stems from the Franco-Turkish agreement of October 20, 1921, when the French forced Turkey to concede Iskenderun to their rule as a result of which the area remained the only piece of Turkish soil outside Turkish jurisdiction after Lausanne. Nevertheless, the Franco-Turkish Treaty had recognized its Turkish character. Article VII stipulated a special regime apart from the Syrian Mandate: "The Turkish inhabitants of this district shall enjoy every facility for their cultural development. The Turkish language shall have official recognition."

In the memorandum attached to the treaty, the right of the inhabitants "to adopt a special flag containing the Turkish flag" was recognized. In 1939, on the basis of these stipulations, the region was returned to Turkey, with

90 percent of the population opting for reunion with the mother country. Since the Turkish character of the area is indisputable, Turkey expects that when Syria settles down to the serious and more rewarding business of domestic development, the Irredentist fever will subside and Turco-Syrian relations will assume their natural and cordial course. For among the Arab states, economically and culturally, Syria is the closest to Turkey.

An overall appraisal

Turkey has lived through much better days—centuries of great might and wealth. But her bonafide acceptance among the comity of nations was never as widespread as today. In fact, her foreign relations constitute the one undisputed aspect of her national life today. There is a wide and deep consensus of satisfaction in the nation about their foreign stance. Even the violent upheaval of May 1960 failed to produce any discordant note regarding foreign relations. The present freely-elected administration has vouched for the continuation of the same policy, in spirit and letter. This widespread domestic satisfaction is paralleled by similar widespread approval internationally.

In the Atlantic community she is accepted as a staunch ally, dependable and determined. In the Balkans, both Greece and Yugoslavia recognize her friendship. Left to themselves, Bulgaria and Rumania would return easily to the cordial relationship of the prewar period. Her Middle Eastern partners appreciate her efforts in their behalf in the NATO councils. The Arab bloc begrudges her the recognition of Israel and her influence with the West, but is free of any basic animosity. With proper informational effort and better spokesmen in the Arab World Turkey could constitute a successful example of modernization for her Muslim neighbors.

The neutralist Afro-Asian world disapproves of her Western alignment, but is increasingly impressed by her sincere dedication to collective security and national freedom for the small countries. Even the Soviets appear to be convinced of the correctness of her attitude and seek to make amends for their past offenses.

In the life of a nation, thirty years cannot amount to more than a wink. Yet Republican Turkey has been able to forge a universally recognized tradition of constancy and credibility in her foreign relations. Various factors in her national inheritance and her present national makeup have been instrumental in this achievement.

(1) The Republic defined her international aims before she was born. They reflected the national will and remained constant—free from the changing opportunities and perils of the international arena. They expressed Turkey's permanent image of herself in the modern world.

(2) The image was based on a realistic estimation of her national status in the existing order of the world. Free from the inhibitions of an imperial past, the image focused on a limited national future. Global geographic importance was kept in balance with the nation's actual limitations in industrial and human resources. It confirmed the realities of the international situation. It was inspired by a genuine desire for liquidating ancient feuds and establishing a friendly new order.

(3) Also, it harmonized with the spirit of the times. It was based on the principle of self-determination for others, as well as for herself. It proposed negotiation and arbitration as the solution of international differences. It advanced international co-operation, not only as a means of national defense, but as the road to economic, social and cultural development.

(4) The nation had an inherited instinct for international affairs. Backed by well established and nationally accepted procedures for the execution and administration of policy, she was able to pursue constant goals, in spite of the changing tides of war and peace. She knew how to be resilient in form in order to remain firm in substance.

Nevertheless, the nation cannot afford to rest on her laurels. The path in the future will be steeper. The nuclear weapons have shifted the weight of the bi-polar conflict from physical imperialism to a competition between communism and democracy. Henceforth, Turkey's natural geopolitical advantage at the meeting point of three continents and the confluence of three seas will weigh less and less. Her present hard-earned place among the comity of nations will depend on her ability to increase her tempo in pulling herself up socially, culturally and economically, to the level of the Western democracies.

Economic problems

The pains of growth have ruffled Turkey's stable surface. An initial crack-up in economic inertia that produced a period of affluence has been succeeded by the strictest austerity since the Republic. Rising aspirations have outstripped production. Record increases in population, averaging an annual growth of three percent, are pressing hard on natural resources. No longer are new minerals, or new products sufficient to advance the country's low standards. For the first time, the farmer must raise more per ploughed acre, and the worker must produce more per man labor or grow poorer. Even improved techniques and mechanization in agriculture, better seeds and new crops, are only a fraction of the solution.

Compared to one out of ten in the United States, seven in Turkey still live on the land and produce less than half of the national product—and these nine million souls, out of a working population of fifteen million, are idle half of the year. Only new urban industrial centers can utilize their wasted energies. Only by improving the quality of their work and their minds can these under-employed, unskilled rustics rise to the requirements of industrial effort. In short, Turkey needs rapid industrialization along with intensified effort to educate her people in new skills. Both of these require large outlays of capital which is in exceedingly short supply.

For the last ten years, Turkish exports have paid for only three-fourths of her imports. The balance of payments has been continuously in the red, averaging an annual deficit of 125 million dollars. In addition, she has incurred 1.3 billion dollars of foreign debt, which she has contracted to pay off in installments averaging over 100 million dollars annually. Under these circumstances, even to subsist at the present level, with a three percent increase in population, presents a grave problem. But to subsist and, also, to grow, with the inescapable standards of a twentieth-century existence, requires continuous aid.

This she has obtained from her Western allies with the United States as the principal supplier. In contrast to other countries, such as India, economic dependence on the West has not constituted a domestic problem. For Turkey's commitment to the West reaches far deeper than the expediency of a counterforce against Russian pressure. Since the Ataturk Revolution, Westernization has been the national orientation. "Attainment of progressive Western mode of life" topped the program of every political party in the elections of 1961.

At the same time, Turkey's tie with the democracies, in the words of the Republican People's Program "was an undetachable element of her foreign policy." All other parties, including the Justice Party, the Nation Party, and the New Turkey Party, agreed.

FOREIGN POLICY FORMULATION

Political consensus about foreign policy is of paramount importance. For Turkey is a Republic, based on parliamentary democracy. The constitution of 1961 has instituted a bicameral system, dividing legislative power between the Senate and the lower chamber. The Prime Minister and his Cabinet wield the executive power, formulating and complementing policy. But since they derive their power from the legislature which can vote them out, in the final analysis, national policy rests in the lap of the

Parliament, which, in turn, speaks with the voice of the political parties.

The parties themselves, determine their ultimate programs and policies at their national conventions. These gatherings are attended by local party representatives from all around the country. They bring to the convention the ideas and aspirations of the common people in their localities. The party platform takes shape within the frame of these ideas and aspirations. The platform of the winning party becomes national policy.

President, Cabinet, and Ministry of Foreign Affairs

The President is only the nominal head of the executive branch. The actual exercise of power is vested in the Cabinet. But, by tradition, the President in Turkey has exerted considerable initiative in the foreign policy process. At critical moments of decision affecting the country's foreign stance, he has used his constitutional prerogative of presiding over the Council of Ministers. Undoubtedly the tradition will continue.

In matters of lesser importance, the Prime Minister and the Council of Ministers act on their own. Routine matters are the sole responsibility of the Minister of Foreign Affairs. In the determination of a line of action, the ministry receives recommendations from its representatives abroad. These recommendations are sifted within the ministry. When a decision is reached, depending on its scope, the Minister decides himself or discusses it with the Prime Minister and, if necessary, with the President.

If the issue does not involve national policy, and does not necessitate legislative deliberation, decisions are made without further ado. Otherwise, the case comes before the Council of Ministers. If legislative action is necessary, such as the ratification of a treaty, then the Foreign Affairs Committee of the Parliament enters into the operation. So far this Committee's role in the foreign policy process has remained passive. But if alternatives develop, it can become as important as the Foreign Affairs Committee of the United States Senate.

In short, national policy rests on the inspiration and consent of the common people who voice their ideas through the political parties. These exercise their power in the parliamentary process. However, the day-to-day follow-up of policy lies within the responsibility of the Ministry of Foreign Affairs, with the ultimate control of implementation resting in the Council of Ministers and, by tradition, in the President.

The Diplomatic Corps

The Foreign Minister who heads the Ministry of Foreign Affairs is a political appointee. But the ministry is a civil service organization, composed of career officers who provide for a steady continuity of action and decision free from the vagaries of politics.

For this reason, Turkey has had no incompetent ambassadors and is not likely to have any. She is represented by a professional corps of diplomats with a long tradition of an established service behind them, their professional proficiency nurtured by the age-old national acumen in international affairs. Higher education and fluency in English and French are the first two prerequisites in a very rigid, selective test. After acceptance, the career officer must serve two years of apprenticeship in Ankara before he is appointed abroad. Each foreign assignment is limited to four years, alternating with two years at the ministry. The diplomat must have approximately twenty years of experience before he becomes eligible for an ambassadorial post.

As a consequence of this apprenticeship, Turkish representatives have won a world-wide reputation for their all-around knowledgeability and steady diplomatic correctness. They never make any mistakes. Neither are they often touched by a stroke of brilliance. Like many of the older countries, Turkish bureauc-

racy has failed to understand the new dimensions in the foreign policy process and lagged in retooling itself for the requirements of our age.

In the nineteenth century, the Ottoman Empire was blessed by a profusion of great ambassadors. Posted at the cross-streams of world focus, they were able to sense the determining currents of their times and to guide the Turkish ship through its dangerous eddies, unharmed. Their leadership, as much as the rivalry of Western imperialists, kept the Empire afloat.

The inbreeding of diplomatic bureaucracy has deprived the Republic of the benefits of this great tradition. The candle has burned at both ends. On the one hand, at the crucial spots of international influence, the nation's voice has been muted. On the other hand, the country's leaders have lacked the illuminating guidance that great emissaries should impose upon political leadership, which is engrossed in domestic affairs.

Although the world has remained constantly impressed with the constructiveness of Turkish policy, the Turks themselves have continued incensed by the belief that their full impact on the comity of nations was not being exerted. The spectacle of Greek, Iranian, and Lebanese emissaries carrying their voices much further than Turkish spokesmen, has aroused the public's ire. Truly, the implementation of policy has lacked the personal imagination and initiative that is Turkey's due as an experienced and mature nation. National sensitiveness on this issue has been well grounded, since the country did not lack the talent necessary for brighter representation.

In professional gatherings in the world, brilliant Turkish scholars, writers, industrialists, and bankers have proved their shrewdness and sophistication. Only the vested interests of bureaucracy have limited the utilization of these talents in diplomatic tasks in the international organizations, such as the United Nations and NATO, where the nature of the work requires instincts and abilities other than the habits and attitudes of chancellery-diplomacy to which career officers are limited.

This same traditional attitude has, also, inhibited the understanding of the new dimensions in international affairs. The foreign service has, for too long, remained unorganized, untooled against the incursion of economics, of public opinion, and of military strategy, into the process of international diplomacy. For instance, although relations with Greece, with the Arab World, and with Soviet Russia constitute the sensitive points of the country's foreign posture, the service has no Arabists, Greek or Russian experts. There are few, if any, career officers who claim proficiency in these languages. They were never given an opportunity and personal initiative and effort would not have been rewarded.

Turkish diplomacy is still conducted on the basis of 19th century concepts by generalists: those who have gained great proficiency and skill in the general rules of diplomacy, but lack the depth of knowledge that the present interdependence between domestic and foreign affairs requires in dealing with a foreign country. Luckily these short range deficiencies have been redeemed by the foresight and perspicacity of the country's statesmen, writers and parliamentarians.

The new leadership

Editorialists such as Nadir Nadi, Falih Rifki Atay, Huseyin Cahit Yalcin, and Ahmet Emin Yalman, have kept Turkey appraised of the rhythm of world currents. Parliamentarians such as Kasim Gulek, Nihat Erim, Cihat Baban, Turhan Feyzioglu, Bulent Ecevit, Suat H. Urgublu, and Fahrettin K. Gokay have been a source of policy inspiration and guidance. Statesmen like President Ismet Inönü, Prime Minister Refik Saydam, and Foreign Minister Necmettin Sadak have bridged the gap with their own good judgment and discernment.

Recently, inspired by public criticism, encouraged by the younger crop of foreign service officers, and supported by the political leadership, the foreign service establishment

has undertaken changes in its structure and mentality that will remedy the deficiencies of an otherwise efficient and conscientious organization. The Ministry has set up a general-directorate for cultural affairs, a directorate of information, and a department of economics and finance, taking into its fold economists and financial experts. The missions to the United Nations and the North Atlantic Treaty Organizations have been reinforced by scholars, economists, and soldiers. Ambassadorial posts have been opened to talents in the national arena, other than career bureaucrats.

Other elements of strength

Consistency in national aims, backed by a national consensus, and implemented by a proficient organization of professional diplomats have helped to place Turkey among the more influential Middle Powers. Other human factors contribute to enhance Turkey's position. The Turks are a martial race. Their ability to put up a dogged fight under the worst conditions has been proved once again in Korea. In spite of great economic stress, the nation has continued to sustain a heavy military burden without fuss and flurry. She keeps twenty divisions under arms; service without pay remains an obligatory national duty.

In addition, the Republic enjoys the blessing of a homogeneous population, in direct contrast to the Ottoman Empire that embraced more varied races and creeds than the tower of Babylon. According to the census of October 1960, the Republic totalled 27,809,831 souls. Turkish citizens had more than doubled since 1927 (13,636,265). Of these, 98 percent are Muslims. Some two hundred thousand Christians are concentrated in Istanbul. There are also some 40,000 Turkish Jews. Scattered about the Eastern provinces are a million and a half people that speak Kurdish, and some call themselves Kurds.

In Turkey, racial mixtures have had a longer past than anywhere else; it is hard to ascertain the truth of the ethnic Kurdish contention. But, the Kurdish speaking people in Turkey have remained immune to Soviet blandishments in favor of Kurdish nationalism. Neither during the opportunities of the war, nor under the divisive influences of party politics, has their loyalty to Turkey been breached.

The articulate élite of this group has always found complete satisfactions for its aspirations within the Turkish setup. They have suffered no discriminations; neither have they felt a chip on their shoulder. All professions and public offices, including the Army, have been open to them without any distinction. If the aroused economic aspirations of the common people in this area are not frustrated in favor of other sectors in the country, the common cultural and religious background will no doubt gradually obliterate the linguistic difference.

This advantage of homogeneity is compounded by the national consensus for the existing form of government. Politics remains within the frame of normal party conflicts, revolving around economic, social and personal differences, free from the deep, volcanic convulsions in the structure of the state and society. The military coup of May 1960 was undertaken to perpetuate the Republic and the Revolutionary reforms of Ataturk. The easy transfer of power from a military to a representative government in October 1961 has reinforced the strength of the consensus for the Republic.

Finally, with her 300,000 square miles, Turkey is the largest country in Europe outside of Russia. A peninsula, that is bordered by three seas—the Mediterranean, the Aegean and the Black Sea—provides easy access to sea-borne allies. This topographic advantage is further strengthened by the shape of the land, a central plateau surrounded on the north, west and south by ranges of mountains that rise higher, and ruggedly wilder, as they reach the internationally sensitive spots on the Russian and Iranian borders, a natural phenomenon that adds to her defensive capacity.

Moreover, even the intercontinental position that increases her peril in times of international conflict, contributes to her stance in times of international peace. Much of the commerce of the world flows through the Straits. Most of the flights between Asia and Europe cross her skies. Also, she is a bridge between the Muslim World of the Middle East and the Christian World of the West. She is the intermediary between the industrial West and the developed East, serving as the example for a partnership in which the East and West join in complete harmony and trust.

But all these elements of strength: geographic accessibility, demographic homogeneity, the structural stability of her social and political setup, the consistency of her foreign policy, and the steady statesmanship in the pursuit of her aims, will no longer suffice to preserve her present posture as an influential Middle Power in a world of atomic explosion and stratospheric flight. For the conquest of the atom and the stars is only a symbol of the accelerated tempo and of the deepening fathom of change. Turkey will hold her place among her partners in the West, and set the pace for her neighbors, by speeding her own tempo of change and closing her cultural and economic gap. Of this the nation seems to be keenly aware.

BIBLIOGRAPHY

Author's Suggestions

Beloff, Max. *The Foreign Policy of Soviet Russia*. New York: Oxford University Press, 1947.

Craig, Gordon A. and Gilbert, Felix, eds. *The Diplomats: 1919–1939*. Princeton: Princeton University Press, 1953.

Grew, Joseph C. *Turbulent Era*. Boston: Houghton Mifflin, 1952.

Hoskins, Halford L. *The Middle East*. New York: Macmillan, 1954.

Kilic, Altemur. *Turkey and the World*. Washington, D.C.: Public Affairs Press, 1959.

Knatchbull-Hugessen, Sir Hugh. *Diplomat in Peace and War*. London: John Murray, 1949.

Lausanne Conference. *Records of Proceedings and Draft Terms of Peace*. London: H. M. Stationery Office, 1923.

Lenczowski, George. *The Middle East in World Affairs*. Ithaca: Cornell University Press, 1952.

Von Papen, Franz. *Memoirs*. London: Andre Deutsch, 1952.

The Problem of the Turkish Straits. Washington: U.S. Government Printing Office, 1947.

ABOUT THE AUTHOR

BOUTROS BOUTROS-GHALI has travelled widely throughout the world in the capacity of student, lecturer and teacher. He was educated in Egypt and in France where he received his Doctorate in international law. He has lectured on international relations at universities in America, India, Poland, Yugoslavia, Holland, France, Jordan and other countries. He has held a professorship at the Academy of International Law at the Hague. At present he is professor at Cairo University, and a member of the Board of Trustees of the Egyptian Society of International Law and the Egyptian Society of Political Science.

Mr. Boutros-Ghali is the author of several books and essays in Arabic, French and English on subjects in the fields of international law and international organization. He is the editor of *Al Ahram Iktisadi*. Among his forthcoming publications is a study of international military alliances.

ABOUT THE CHAPTER

Professor Boutros-Ghali starts his chapter with an examination of some of the basic factors which influence the foreign policy of Egypt. He notes in particular the necessity of harnessing the Nile and the moral problem which has confronted Egypt's rulers in deciding how the wealth of the country should be used.

The chapter is organized into five major sections: The relationship of Egypt towards Africa, Islam, Europe, Arabism and neutralism. The author notes that Egypt is a part of Africa and underlines the fact that, in addition to her direct interest in the waters of the Nile, there is a broader interest in the African community and its development. Of the major concepts around which Egypt's foreign policy revolves it is made clear that neutralism plays a very important role. The author mentions the strong pull of non-alignment for many of the new nations of the world and shows that neutralism actually works with Arabism as an organizing force.

Professor Boutros-Ghali is aware of the difficulties which must be faced by Egypt. He notes in particular the underdevelopment of the country and the opposition of other nations and power groups. He concludes that the geopolitical position of the U.A.R. does not allow the country to adopt a policy of isolationism and that it imposes on her a "dynamic foreign policy which compels her to squarely meet new challenges which arise."

11

THE FOREIGN POLICY OF EGYPT

(United Arab Republic)

BOUTROS BOUTROS-GHALI

Cairo University

BACKGROUND FACTORS

The challenge of the Nile

From Cheops to Mohammed Ali, from Mohammed Ali to Gamal Abdel Nasser, Egyptian foreign policy has been dominated by two challenges: the first has been the physical task of mastering the waters of the Nile; the second has been the moral task of deciding how the Egyptian rulers should use the wealth resulting from the cultivation of the Nile Valley. To master the Nile waters was a challenge which demanded centuries of back-bending toil in draining the jungle marshes and reclaiming the land which lay along the river, and then centuries of weary labor to carry the river water to the greedy desert.

Today, in the atomic age, the first challenge still remains: Egypt must conquer new territories, must reclaim the deserts and drain the swamps to nourish her increasing population. The never ending toil of bringing water to the fields remains the burden of the Egyptian peasant. Without his struggle to make the most lasting and economic use of the waters, Egypt would be a still narrower land, and famine would be her fate.

The second challenge also remains unchanged. How shall the rulers of Egypt make the best use of Egyptian wealth? In few countries are the differences and inequality in the distribution of wealth more glaring; in few countries is the distribution of authority between the ruling minority and the subject majority more uneven. The sway of the ruling minority, over the wills and actions of the Egyptian peasantry, regardless of its composition, has been absolute. How are the rulers of Egypt to dispose of its wealth? Will they use it for the betterment of the lot of the peasantry who made them the masters of that wealth? Or will they dissipate it in military adventures and in the pursuit of dreams of power and influence?

Another factor in foreign policy has been the physical isolation of the habitable land, confined as it is to a narrow strip on either side of the Nile. To the west and east of the valley lie forbidding deserts, impassable barriers to any army. To the south, the region beyond the first cataract is inhospitable, with no arable land; the second and third cataracts offer serious obstacles to navigation. To the north, along the Mediterranean coast, the delta is a land of swamps with no natural harbors other than Alexandria and Damiette at the two extremes of the area. Surrounded by sea and desert, the country is, in effect, a long oasis. Neither the Turks, who reached the Suez Canal in 1915, nor the Germans, stopped at El Alamein in 1942, nor the Israelis in 1956, quite succeeded in breaking through Egypt's desert defenses.

However, the generalization that Egypt is secure against aggression from outside is relative. There have been periods both in ancient and in modern history when forces have broken through the barriers of desert and sea. Moreover, the rapid development of weaponry has made geographical isolation an insecure defense. Nevertheless, this physical isolation has left a deep and happy sense of security even down to the present time. It has given rise to a popular feeling that Egypt has a unique and exceptional destiny because divine providence has set her apart—distinctly apart—from her neighbors.

Population

A fourth influence which must be considered is Egypt's extraordinary concentration of population. Only one-thirtieth of the modern state of Egypt is habitable; more than 95 percent is barren desert. The density of population is more than 1300 to the square mile; small villages lie close together creating a pattern of "semi-urbanism," a pattern of close contacts, which facilitates supervision and control of the people. Internal rule is consequently a rela-

tively simple problem for any ordinary government, thus opening the opportunity of adopting an active foreign policy.

Some writers have noted two other factors: (1) Egyptians show an apathy toward government and politics, partly as a result of the exclusion of the masses from political participation, partly as a result of history.

> For over twenty-five centuries Egypt was never ruled by Egyptians. The seat of Government might be in Persepolis, Rome, Constantinople, Damascus, Baghdad, or it might be in Alexandria or Cairo. But the rulers, the army and the higher ranks of the bureaucracy were almost without exception foreigners.[1]

This may explain why the formulation of foreign policy, even today, is strictly the prerogative and sole responsibility of the Chief Executive. The extent to which the Executive is guided by the counsel of his principal associates, including the Minister of Foreign Affairs, is a matter of his personal choice, made in the light of the interests of the state. (2) Due to the unbroken unity of the country throughout six or seven millenniums and due to the absence of a local autonomous aristocracy, the people of Egypt show a marked homogeneity.[2]

Culture

Geographically and culturally, Egypt is not simply one country, but four: an African country, a Mediterranean country, an Islamic country since the 6th century A.D., and an Arab country. This quadruple identification, and her unique geographical situation at the crossroads of three continents, are factors that have in-

[1] C. Issawi, *Egypt at Mid-Century,* London: Oxford University Press, 1954, p. 5.
[2] *Ibid.,* pp. 1–3.

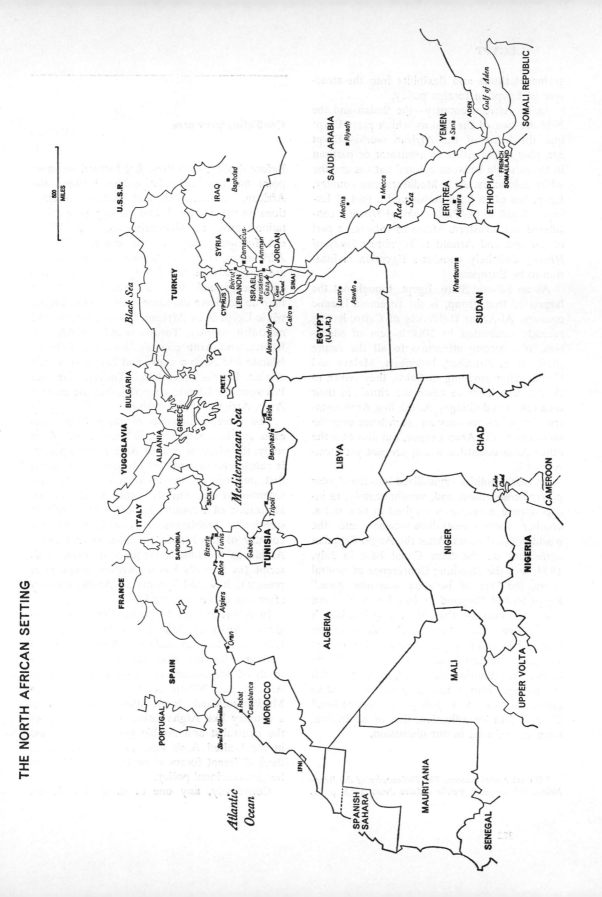

THE NORTH AFRICAN SETTING

grained latitude and flexibility into the structure of Egyptian foreign policy.

As an African country—the Sudan and the Nile are two of the factors which press Egypt into the heart of the African world—Egypt can play a role either as arbitrator or partisan in the struggle between colored natives and the white colonizers. As a Mediterranean country, Egypt has often been considered a part of Europe. Hegel, in his *Philosophy of History,* considered northwestern Africa as forming a part of Europe, and Arnold J. Toynbee's *Study of History* definitely considers Egyptian civilization to be European.

As an Islamic State, Egypt, though not the largest of that group, is the foremost Islamic country. Al-Azhar University of Cairo, having recently celebrated its 1000th year of education, is a strong attraction to all the future sheiks from Zanzibar, Indonesia, Malaya and China. After studying in Cairo, they return to their native lands to teach the rituals in their own towns and villages. As the first Arab country, Egypt has not only an ascendance over the members of the Arab League, but also over the other Arab countries which are not yet members of it.

As world politics crystallized into the bipolar power arrangement and, simultaneously, as independence movements resulted in new states, another force—neutralism—came onto the world political scene. After the Anglo-Egyptian agreement on the Suez Canal base in July, 1954, and the Bandung Conference of neutral states, the "era of isolation was now gone." Egypt looked "beyond its frontiers to find out where the currents that affect it spring, how it should live with others . . .[3] This transition from a bilateral foreign policy with Great Britain and a regional policy with some Middle Eastern neighboring countries, coincided with the change from a foreign policy oriented to Great Britain to a policy of "neutralism." Thus, a fifth identification, that of neutralism, must be included in our discussion.

[3] Gamal Abdel Nasser, *The Philosophy of the Revolution,* Washington: Public Affairs Press, 1955, p. 53.

Conflicting pressures

Before dealing with these five factors, we must point out the inter-relationships between the African, Islamic, Arab, and neutralist orientations on the one hand, and the opposing orientations towards a Mediterranean, or pro-Western foreign policy on the other. Although Africanism, Islamism, Arabism, and neutralism are obviously related through their anti-Western background, they are not identical and they do not have the same limits. For example, while Egypt is an African, Islamic, Arabic and neutralist country, Tunisia is only an African, Islamic and Arab country. Jordan is only an Islamic and Arab country and Lebanon is only Arabic. On the other hand, Turkey, Iran and Pakistan are Islamic countries, but are neither Arab, African, nor neutralist.

The inter-relationship of these four processes can be analyzed in different ways: Arab unity, the ultimate goal of Arab foreign policy, is considered in terms of Muslim policy as the first step toward the creation of the Muslim Commonwealth. On the other hand, the Islamization of a country has often been the first step for its Arabization. If Somalia, an African country of the Muslim religion, should adopt Arabic as the official language or even Arab script (as Somalia has no written language at present), it would become an Arabic country after one or two generations.

In relations with Lebanon, Egyptian policy gives priority to Arab policy because of the Lebanese Christian majority. When Egypt was dealing with the non-Muslim Chief of the south of the Sudan, emphasis was placed on African and Nilotic solidarity. Emphasis on Muslim solidarity is essential in dealings with a country like Afghanistan. A combination of the neutralist and Arabic policies culminated in the United Arab Republic in 1958. Thus, these different forces allow Egypt flexibility in her international policy.

Conversely, any one of these four forces

could conflict with another one and give rise to an open struggle, such as Islam versus Arabism, or a simple competition, such as "Africa First" versus "Arab Unity First." It will always be problematical which of these forces should be given priority in the formulation and execution of foreign policy.

We propose now to deal successively with the attitude of Egypt towards Africa, Islam, Europe, Arabism and neutralism. While this approach may at first appear somewhat artificial, due to the close relationship between several of these forces, I believe that such an examination will offer the reader the clearest understanding of the development of Egyptian foreign policy.

EGYPT AND AFRICA

The relation between Egypt and Africa for several thousands of years has been summarized by Burghardt Dubois:

In Ethiopia the sunrise of human culture took place, spreading down into the Nile Valley. . . .

Beyond Ethiopia, in Central and South Africa, lay the gold of Ophir and the rich trade of Punt on which the prosperity of Egypt largely depended.

Egypt brought slaves from Black Africa as she did from Europe and Asia. But she also brought citizens and leaders from Black Africa.

When Egypt conquered Asia, she used black soldiers to a wide extent. When Asia overwhelmed Egypt, Egypt sought refuge in Ethiopia as a child returns to its mother, and Ethiopia then for centuries dominated Egypt and successfully invaded Asia.[4]

[4] Burghardt Dubois, *The World and Africa*, New York: 1947, p. 117.

This poetic, but controversial interpretation of history has at least the merit of showing the emotional and psychological links which bind Egypt to Africa and the Sudan.

Ancient history

In ancient Egypt, the African policy was one of conquest and integration. This received priority over the Asiatic policy which was secondary and dealt with defensive measures until the Hyksos, coming from Asia, conquered the country. Just as today, Egypt felt that the Nile Valley should be unified.

During the Middle Kingdom, the frontier lay at the second cataract, but Egyptian interests extended further to the south. Indeed, Egypt maintained a resident colony and a fortified trading post at Kerma, a town south of the third cataract and a transshipping point for vessels and caravans. This trading post known as "The Walls of Amen-em-het the Justified" was placed in charge of a high Egyptian official who, as commercial agent enjoyed a "status like that of Clive or Hastings in India or like that of an American Indian agent."

When the Hyksos invaded Egypt, the Sudan and Ethiopia became a refuge, both physically and culturally, for the Egyptians. Noble Egyptian families migrated to the Sudan and Ethiopia and intermarried; one such family formed the eighteenth Dynasty which rescued Egypt. From that time, larger parts of the Sudan and Ethiopia were incorporated into Egypt—"and we may properly speak of an African empire."

Among the officials of the Pharaoh was the "King's Son of Kush" or Viceroy of Ethiopia. Queen Hat-Shepsut sent a commercial expedition by sea to the land of Punt (Somalia) and Arabia Felix (Yemen). In the succeeding centuries the African Empire crumbled. Around 720 B.C. came the first successful invasion from the south. From a capital at the fourth cataract, Napata Pi-ankhi, an Ethiopian, invaded Egypt and founded the twenty-third Dynasty.

Almost 1400 troubled years passed until Egypt fell to the Arab Caliphate and then reformed its relations with the different Sudanese kingdoms and tribes through a series of treaties. Islamization and Arabization spread to the Sudan from Egypt until the two countries were united by one religion, one language and intermarriage.

Start of the modern age, 1820–1898

In modern times, the political reunion of the Nile Valley was first accomplished by Mohammed Ali's sons Ismail Pasha and Ibrahim Pasha, who in 1820 retraced the steps of their Pharaonic ancestors. Their goal was to explore the Upper Nile and to exploit gold mines, which proved to be non-existent. They were able to bring all Sudanese provinces under Egyptian control by October of 1822. Finally, the conquest of Kassala in 1840 marked the complete success of Egypt's African foreign policy.

In 1841 when Mohammed Ali agreed to evacuate Syria and Crete, the Ottoman Sultan formally recognized the Pasha government of the "provinces of Nubia, Kordofan, and Sennar with all their dependencies," that is to say with all their adjoining regions outside the limits of Egypt.

Mohammed Ali's grandson, the Khedive Ismail, adopted an African policy coupled with a pro-Western policy. In fact, any new expansion towards Asia and Syria would have created a conflict with the Ottoman Empire and Great Britain. As Palmerston had said, Egypt "should stay in its African shell." The Khedive based his African policy upon geographical discovery, scientific research, anti-slavery and the ambitious scheme of opening Africa to modern civilization. Furthermore, the unification of the Nile basin from the Mediterranean sea to the source of the Nile became imperative as Egypt introduced the system of perennial irrigation. Herodotus' observation that Egypt is a gift of the Nile remained true as long as Egypt could secure and protect the sources of the river.

Khedive Ismail annexed all of the African coast of the Red Sea, the coast of Somaliland, the coast of the Indian Ocean as far as Ras-Hafoun and Kismayou on the Aden Gulf. The southern boundaries were placed at the great lakes of Uganda, Ounyouro and at the Equator. Although some of the Egyptian pro-consuls were unpopular, Egyptian administrators gave the African peoples equal rights with Egyptians. The draft electoral law of June 5, 1879 allotted sixteen seats in the Egyptian Council to the representatives of the Sudanese people. The Democratic Constitution of March, 1882, assigned them 17 out of 125 seats in the Chamber of Deputies. However, the elections could not be completed because of the British intervention in Egypt which occurred that same year.

In 1881, a certain Mohammed Ahmed proclaimed himself to be the Mahdi of the Sudan. His mission, he explained in his various proclamations, was to first win the Sudan, and then march on Egypt. A number of other crises, such as the Oraby revolution in Egypt, the bombardment of Alexandria, and the defeat of the Egyptian army at Tel-el-jebur, prevented Egyptian soldiers from quashing the Mahdi succession.

Then in January of 1884, Lord Cromer forced the Egyptian Government to withdraw all troops to Wadi Halfa and to abandon the southern part of the Nile Valley. According to the British point of view,

> the whole edifice of territorial aggrandisement in Africa, which Ismail Pasha and his predecessors had in an evil moment planned for their country, toppled to the ground. It was built on no sure foundation. The power gained by semi-civilized skill over the wild tribes of the Sudan had been grossly misused.[5]

[5] Earl of Cromer, *Modern Egypt*, New York: Macmillan Co., 1911, vol. I, p. 353.

Of course the Egyptian Prime Minister, Sherif Pasha, objected strongly to the abandonment of the Sudan. He pointed out that

from the point of view of civilization, however well founded may be the criticisms directed against the Egyptian Administration in the Sudan, it is nevertheless true, that it is owing to the efforts of Egypt that the regions as far as the lakes, form at the present time a part of the known world. It is equally due to Egypt that European houses of commerce have been able to establish themselves in the Sudan, that the scientific exploring expeditions have been undertaken, and the Christian missions have been able to settle there.[6]

British influence in Egypt and the Sudan

In 1898, a joint Egyptian-British expeditionary force, commanded by Lord Kitchener, reconquered the Sudan. Egypt contributed four-fifths of the troops and two-thirds of the campaign expenditures. She was unable however, because of British predominance, to fully re-establish her authority and was obliged to sign a convention on January 19, 1899, which formally established the Anglo-Egyptian Sudan. A few years later, Britain took over almost complete control of the administration and the condominium became practically a British colony.

Two other events even more drastically limited Egyptian influence in the Sudan: On December 18, 1914 a British protectorate over Egypt was proclaimed. The decision to terminate the protectorate on February 29, 1922 and to recognize Egypt as "an independent

sovereign state" did not affect the status of the Sudan. A continuation of the agreement of 1899 was one of the reservations limiting Egypt's new "freedom." Secondly, in November 1924, the murder in Cairo of the English Governor General of the Sudan and the Commander-in-Chief of the Egyptian army stationed there, resulted in forcing the immediate evacuation of all Egyptian troops and most Egyptian officials from the Sudan.

During the next decade, Egypt obtained the following concessions in the Sudan: (1) The Anglo-Egyptian Nile Waters Agreement of 1929 which stipulated that "no irrigation or power works or measures are to be constructed or taken on the Nile River and its branches . . . so far as all these are in the Sudan or in countries under British administration" without the agreement of the Egyptian Government. (2) The Anglo-Egyptian Treaty of August 26, 1936, which abrogated the drastic measures taken by the British in 1924. Egyptian troops were to be re-admitted and the British Governor-General, in making new appointments to posts for which qualified Sudanese were not available, was to select "suitable candidates of British and Egyptian nationality." Egyptian immigration into the Sudan was not to be restricted.

After World War II, at the Peace Conference of Paris in 1946, Egypt presented claims for all of Eritrea and the Red Sea port of Massawa, but without result. But the Sudan question came close to being solved in the agreement between Bevin and Sidky in March of 1946. The agreement called for the "recognition of the unity between the Sudan and Egypt under the common crown of Egypt," and further provided that the Sudanese would have the right to determine their own future. The contradiction between these two items brought about the collapse of the agreement. Egypt stressed the fact that the Sudan was to be a part of Egypt and that the Sudanese could only choose the form of their association with Egypt. Great Britain insisted that the agreement meant the right of self-determination for the Sudan. Unable to reach a compromise, Prime Minister Sidky Pasha resigned.

[6] Egyptian Royal Ministry for Foreign Affairs, *The Sudan Question Based on British Documents,* Cairo: Misr Press, 1952, p. 23.

Sidky's successor, Nokrachi Pasha, broke off negotiations with the British, announcing to Parliament his decision to appeal to the United Nations. The Security Council considered the Egyptian demand in August and September 1947, but was unable to solve the matter. The British further strained Anglo-Egyptian relations by making administrative and constitutional changes in the Sudan without Egypt's consent. Finally, on October 15, 1951, the Egyptian Parliament adopted decrees denouncing the treaty of 1936 and the agreements of 1899. Farouk was proclaimed King of Egypt and the Sudan.

Independence for Egypt and the Sudan

The change in government due to the military revolution of 1952, led to a new approach in Egypt's African policy. The policy of previous Egyptian governments was reversed (1) by separating the demand for the withdrawal of British troops from Egypt from the Sudan question; (2) by offering priority to the Sudan question and reserving the question of the Suez Canal base for further negotiations; (3) by accepting the thesis that the Sudan should not be made subject to the Egyptian Crown without its consent.

The Anglo-Egyptian Treaty of February 1953 regarding the future of the Sudan was clearly a victory for Egypt. It proved to the Sudanese public that the British were attempting to retard their attainment of self-determination. The elections which followed in the summer of 1953 resulted in a victory for the National Unionist Party which favored union with Egypt. However, the pro-Egyptian policy of the National Unionist Party gradually changed after the party assumed power. The Sudanese Parliament, in December 1955, unanimously adopted a resolution declaring that the Sudan should become an independent sovereign republic; it called upon both the British and the Egyptians to recognize this new status.

On the first of January 1956, the system under which the Sudan had been administered since 1899 came to an end and the Sudan emerged as an independent state. A few days later, the Sudan was elected unanimously as the ninth member of the Arab League, thus transferring Egypto-Sudanese relations from the African sphere to the Arab sphere.

Egypt's hope was that a successful Arab policy would gradually establish Egyptian leadership throughout the Arab world; this would automatically involve the integration of the Sudan into the new Arab state. The military coup of November 1958 in Khartoum interrupted Egyptian efforts to bring about the unity of the Nile valley. However, the U.A.R. was the first state to recognize the new Sudanese regime. The conclusion of the Nile Waters Agreement between the two countries in November, 1959, proved that the Government of Egypt had opted for a functional and non-political approach in an effort to promote the unity of the Nile valley after the approach to this goal through popular support had failed.

The philosophy of Africanism

Egyptian policy towards Africa, however, is neither limited to Nile unity nor to the "Arab approach"; it is a broader and larger policy which proposes to bypass the Nile valley and to transcend Arabism through Africanism. President Gamal Abdel Nasser in his work *Philosophy of the Revolution* expresses this policy as follows:

> . . . we cannot, in any way, stand aside, even if we wish to, away from the sanguinary and dreadful struggle now raging in the heart of Africa between five million whites and two hundred million Africans. . . . The people of Africa will continue to look up to us, who guard the northern gate of the continent and who are its connecting link with the world outside.

We cannot, under any condition, re-linquish our responsibility in helping, in every way possible, in diffusing light and civilization into the farthest parts of that virgin jungle. . . .[7]

Favorable factors   While neutralist in the Cold War, Egypt is committed in the African struggle. This policy of commitment is based on the following facts: (1) The struggle for Africa is indivisible, from Algeria—an Arab African country—to Kenya or South Africa—two non-Arab African countries. So long as the whole of Africa is not liberated, Egypt (U.A.R.) will feel itself threatened.

This deep sense of African solidarity is not confined to Egypt but is shared by other African countries. Dr. Kwame Nkrumah, for example, writes on the last page of his autobiography: "Our task is not done and our own safety is not assured until the last vestiges of colonialism have been swept from Africa."[8] This view was also affirmed by President Sekou Touré when he declared: "We are conscious that, so long as the whole of Africa is not liberated, Guinea will feel itself threatened."[9] African nationalism not only shares with Arab nationalism the spirit of anti-colonialism, but also the awareness of the artificiality of boundaries drawn by the colonial Powers and the determination to transcend them through new unions and regroupings.

(2) Arabic-speaking Islam enjoys a splendid opportunity for cultural and political expansion in Africa. In fact, the Islamic religion can be considered as the African religion *par excellence,* Christianity being discredited in the eyes of many Africans and identified as a "white man's religion." There exists, of course, an indigenous oriental Christianity in Egypt and Ethiopia, which does not suffer from this onus.

How can one explain the success of both the Islamic religion and the Arabic language in spite of Christian missionary work and in spite of the impact of Western civilization through the channel of the various European colonial administrations?

In the first place, Western Christian civilization is relatively new in Africa, while Islam made its appearance there more than a thousand years ago. The Islamic world was a curtain which separated Europe from Africa and gave Islam a monopoly which led to the conversion of a large part of the African population.

In the second place, the doctrine of Islam is simple; its promises are direct and unconditional. The convert is not burdened with a system of doctrines which he must learn; all that is required is a confession of faith which can be pronounced in less than a minute. Finally, the difference in culture and manner of life between the African negro and Muslim communities were not so great as to make it impossible for the two to live together in fellowship. Islam adopted African forms to such a degree that it almost became an indigenous religion.

The Arabic language has been another instrument of cultural penetration. Religious books written in Arabic find a wide circulation. Moreover, the example of Arab literature has encouraged and taught Muslim Africans to write their own vernacular languages in Arabic characters. Arabic has the distinction of being the first to raise African languages such as Swahili, Hausa, Kanuri, Tul and Mandingo to the level of literary form.

Africanism shares with Arabism its devotion to neutralism. Even if we must agree with Hamilton Fish Armstrong, that "the best description of . . . neutrality is the one given of women in the old song: you never see two alike in any one place; you never see one alike twice," it is still true that African neutralism is *very* much like Arab neutralism. When Africans talk of doing things "in the African way" they mean neither the Western way nor the Eastern way but the neutralist way. When Dr. Nkrumah said that Africa "is not an extension either of Europe or of any other conti-

---

[7] P. 70.

[8] Kwame Nkrumah, *Autobiography,* Paris: Presence Africaine, 1960, p. 291.

[9] Sekou Touré, *La Guinée et l'Emancipation Africaine,* Paris: Presence Africaine, 1950, pp. 75–83.

nent . . . thus we wish to develop our own community at the same time as an African personality," he expressed the very deep meaning of Egyptian and Arab neutralism.

Methods In her reach for Africa, Egypt, and later the U.A.R., have used different channels: support to nationalist leaders who have fled or have been thrown out of Africa's former or remaining colonies; active participation in the different Pan African conferences, creation of the Casablanca organization,[10] bilateral treaties of economic and cultural assistance, scholarships for African students, organized missionary activity, Al Azhar, Egyptian professors teaching in different African countries, and many others.

From the foregoing analysis it is clear that Africanism does not compete with Arabism; on the contrary, Africanism reinforces Arabism. It must not be forgotten that sixty-six percent of the Arab community and seventy-two percent of the Arab lands are in Africa. Thus Africanism is a defense in depth for Arabism, a source of solidarity, and a new opportunity for the Arab world situated as it is between Europe and Black Africa. It is destined to bring white and black races together in a harmony of mutual interests.

EGYPT AND ISLAM

From the time of the conversion of the mass of the Egyptian population to Islam in the

---

[10] The Casablanca organization created in January, 1961 associates: the Algerian Republic, the Republic of Guinea, the Kingdom of Morocco, the Republic of Ghana, the Republic of Mali, and the United Arab Republic. Co-operation among the member states of the African Charter of Casablanca is effected through the following organs: an African Political Committee, an African Economic Committee, an African Cultural Committee, a joint African High Command, and a liaison office. These different committees meet in Cairo, Bamako, Rabat, Conakry, and Accra. A number of resolutions have been adopted and are at the point of being implemented.

ninth century, that religion has played an important part in the formulation of Egyptian foreign policy. In the early militant days, Islamization of Egypt cut the country off from Christian northern Mediterranean lands with which it had been in close contact for several centuries. At the same time, it joined the Mediterranean and the Indian oceans by filling the thousand-year old gap formed by the Roman-Persian frontier. The pendulum once more swung back to Asia.

Muslim leadership—the Caliphate

For about two centuries, Egypt was governed by the Arab Caliphate from Medina, Damascus and Baghdad. Then in 969 the Fatimites conquered the country from the West, founded Cairo, and inaugurated one of the most brilliant periods in the history of Muslim Egypt. The government of Egypt was wrested from the last of the Fatimites by Salah El-Din El-Ayyuby, who saved Egypt from the Crusaders in 1163.

The Ayyubid dynasty was supplanted by the Mamelukes, who maintained their rule after the Turkish conquest of 1516. The Mamelukes of Egypt ruled as deputies of a branch of the Abbasid line who were maintained as pensioners in Cairo with the sole function of investing successive Mameluke Sultans with lawful authority. When the Ottoman Sultan Selim I conquered Egypt, he carried the puppet Caliph al-Mutawakil with him to Constantinople but allowed him to return to Cairo where he died in 1543. With him the shadowy Abbasid Caliphate of Egypt may be said to have ended, opening again the problem of the legitimate Caliphate, the oldest problem Islam has had to face.

The first known diplomatic document which applies the term Caliph to the Ottoman Sultan and recognizes his religious authority over Muslims outside of Turkey is the Russian-Turkish treaty of Kuchuk Kay Marji, signed in 1774. From this time on, the Caliphate ceased to be merely titular and became an active factor in international relations.

This revival of the Caliphate institution was due to the reaction of Islamic society to Western imperialism. The subjection of Muslim populations to non-Muslim Powers created a new sense of Muslim solidarity. Abdul Hamid II (1842–1918), as the ruler of the only Muslim country still independent, was in a favorable position to exploit the institution of the Caliphate for his own ends.

This approach was enthusiastically received in Egypt and throughout the Muslim world. The periodical *Al Urwah al Wuthqua* published by Gamal al-Afghani and Muhammad Abdu stirred Muslim consciousness as perhaps no other paper had done before. In its pages the idea of pan-Islamism was given form with special emphasis on the role which Egypt could play. The occupation of Egypt had profoundly moved the Islamic world.

The faithful look upon Egypt as part of the Holy Lands. It has a place in their hearts which no other country can occupy. It is the gateway to Mecca and Medina and any disturbance in it is bound to produce an effect on all Muslim lands.[11]

Why this surge of feeling? Lord Cromer in his book, *Modern Egypt,* has pointed to one cause:

The Egyptian . . . holds fast to the faith of Islam, that noble monotheism belief which takes to a great extent the place of patriotism in Eastern countries, and which serves as a common bond of union to all Moslems from Delhi to Fez, from Stamboul to Zanzibar, as they turn to pray towards the cradle of their creed.[12]

The pro-Muslim policy was doomed to failure. On November 23, 1914, the Sultan Caliph Mohammed Rashad proclaimed the Holy War (*Jihad*). All Muslims were called to take up arms and fight side by side with the Muslims of the Ottoman Empire. The call went unheeded. Lingering on after the war, the institution of the Caliphate was abolished in 1924 by the Turks, who were more interested in saving a Turkish national home than in retaining their leadership over the Muslim world. Again the Islamic world was without a head.

Attempts to restore Muslim unity

Egypt's initial reaction was one of surprise and consternation. Three major groups made their influence felt: (1) the supporters of the deposed Caliph, (2) the Muslim activists, and (3) the Egyptian nationalists. The supporters of the deposed Caliph were a group of Egyptian ulema of Al-Azhar; they published a proclamation to the Islamic world declaring that the action of the Turkish Government could not invalidate the allegiance which the Muslim world had given to the former Caliph.[13]

The Muslim activists, under the leadership of the religious authorities, saw a favorable opportunity for recovering their position of primacy in the Islamic world, a position they had held from the fall of Baghdad down to the Ottoman conquest. They were encouraged secretly by King Fouad, who saw in the Caliphate a new opportunity to strengthen his throne against parliamentarism and Wafdism.

The Wafdist, on the other hand, were inclined to seek salvation by standing on their own feet and developing a national life for Egypt along Western lines, rather than falling back upon the Islamic past.[14] Furthermore, they were opposed to any change in the political

---

[11] J. M. Ahmed, *The Intellectual Origins of Egyptian Nationalism,* London: Oxford University Press, 1960, p. 28.
[12] *Op. cit.* vol. II, pp. 132–3.

[13] See Declaration of Mohammed Hassanein, former rector of Al-Azhar in *Al-Ahram,* March 6, 1924.
[14] See *Al Sissa,* Feb. 2, Feb. 26, Feb. 28, 1926.

organization of the country which might strengthen the position of the King. Saad Pasha Zaglul, then the Prime Minister, declared that the Egyptian Government intended to maintain the strictest neutrality in regard to the Caliphate question.

In spite of the Government's official negative attitude, an Islamic Congress met in Cairo in May 1926. No important resolutions were passed and no decisions regarding the Caliphate question were made. In June and July of the same year, King Abdul el-Azis Ibn Saud convened the "Congress of the Islamic World" at Mecca. It was to give attention to the affairs of the Hejaz and the Holy Cities. An official delegation from Egypt attended this Congress.

A proposal was drawn up for the holding of an annual congress at Mecca for the discussion of Islamic affairs; there would also be a permanent committee of the congress. Neither the committee, nor the congress were ever called into existence. The main reason for their failure was the reluctance of Ibn Saud, who had not obtained the advantages for which he had hoped from holding the first congress, and the negative attitude of Muslim governments toward committing themselves to membership in a permanent organization.

Islamic congresses since 1930

Five years later, Haj Amin El-Husayni, Mufti of Jerusalem, called an Islamic Congress to meet in Jerusalem "for the purpose of investigating the actual situation of Islam and measures to be taken in defence of its interests." The congress was to deal with (a) Muslim co-operation; (b) the diffusion of Islamic culture, (c) defense of the Muslim Holy places, including Jerusalem; (d) preservation of the tradition of Islam, (e) establishment of a Muslim university in Jerusalem.

As in 1924, Egyptians were divided on the question of actively participating in the congress. The Muslim activists were strongly opposed to the establishment of a university which

could compete with Al-Azhar. Moreover, they were worried by the fact that initiative and leadership had passed from Cairo to the Muslims of Palestine and India. A second group declared the congress to be reactionary and contrary to the evolution toward national states. A third group saw the congress as an opportunity for Egypt to take over the leadership of the Muslim world.

Although the Egyptian Government was not officially represented, there were delegates from a number of Muslim associations and political parties. The congress adopted a recommendation for the establishment of a Muslim university at Jerusalem and one for the incorporation of the congress into a permanent institution. A general assembly was to be held every two years in Jerusalem with an executive council and a bureau.

The Executive Council was very active during the first year of its existence. The Bureau was formed with an Iranian as Secretary. Protests were dispatched to the League of Nations; manifestos and appeals were issued to the Muslim world. In the spring of 1934 when the war broke out between Saudi Arabia and Yemen, the Executive Council appointed a peace delegation to arbitrate the dispute. This delegation participated in the negotiations which led to the treaty signed at El-Taif in May of 1934. The congress however, showed no further sign of activity and never met again.

Twenty years later, in 1954, Zafrullah Khan, the Pakistani Foreign Minister, suggested that an Islamic Congress should be held in Jerusalem to discuss the problem of the Holy places there. The initiative was taken by Egypt. In agreement with Saudi Arabia and Pakistan, Egypt suggested a revival of the Islamic Congress to be held annually at Mecca during the period of the pilgrimage.

This idea had been eloquently developed by President Abdel Nasser in *Philosophy of the Revolution*. In the concluding pages of the book, President Nasser analyzed the "circles" in which the Egyptians must revolve if they are to play their destined part in the world. He found three circles: the Arabic, the African and the Islamic. According to President Nasser:

. . . the third circle goes beyond continents and oceans; I referred to this as the circle of our brethren in faith who turn to us, whatever part of the world they are in, towards the same kiblah in Mecca, and whose pious lips whisper reverently the same prayers. My faith in the positive efficacy which can be the outcome of further strengthening the Islamic bonds with all other Moslems became deeper when I went to the Saudi Kingdom with the Egyptian mission who went there to offer condolences on the occasion of the death of its late king. As I stood in front of the Kaaba and felt my sentiments going forth into every part of the world to which Islam had been extended, I found myself exclaiming, "our idea of the pilgrimage should change." Going to the Kaaba should never be a passport to heaven, after a lengthy life. Neither should it be a simple effort to buy indulgences after an eventful life. The pilgrimage should be a great political power. The press of the world should resort to and follow its news; not as a series of rituals . . . but as a regular political congress wherein the leaders of Moslem states . . . draw up in this universal Islamic Parliament the main lines of policy for their countries and their co-operation together until they meet again.[15]

Recent developments

In 1954 King Ibn Saud, Prime Minister Nasser and Prime Minister Mohammed Ali of Pakistan met at Mecca during their pilgrimage and announced throughout the Muslim world their intention to create a Muslim Congress. Anwar

[15] *Op. cit.,* p. 72.

el-Sadat, a member of the Egyptian Revolutionary Council was appointed Secretary General of the Congress. In September 1954, the Secretary General issued the draft Charter of the proposed Congress.

The aim of the Congress is to spread Islamic culture free of all inhibitions, and to co-ordinate the economic policies of all Muslim nations. In pursuit of these purposes, the Congress is to co-operate with the Arab League, with Muslim organizations in all parts of the world, with international groupings holding similar principles, such as the Asian-African bloc, and with the United Nations. An Executive Council, a General Assembly and a Secretariat were to be established.

A few observations should be made, in spite of the fact that this new organization has never really come into being. This Muslim organization and the rules of procedure have been projected entirely along Western patterns. It was to be an organization both of governments and individuals; the differentiation between "Arab circle" and "Muslim circle" was maintained; nothing was said about the Caliphate which was the original reason for calling the first Muslim Congress. In the projected organization, the Caliphate was replaced by an elected President or a Supreme Council. The Congress never met again, however, and it appears that the whole project was reduced to a cultural institution whose operational center was located in Cairo.

Why did Islam fail to be an important factor in the foreign policy of the Government of Cairo, even though President Nasser gives attention to Islam as the "third circle?" It would appear that the answer lies in the development of a "fourth circle" which had not clearly emerged when President Nasser wrote his book. This fourth circle is the "neutralist circle." Neutralism has proved to be more powerful in foreign policy than a common religion. The common neutrality shared by the U.A.R. with India in Asia, Yugoslavia in Europe, and Cuba in America, has proved a much closer political bond than a common religion shared with such predominantly Moslem countries as Pakistan, Turkey, or Nigeria.

EGYPT AND EUROPE

Methods of analysis

Relations between Egypt and Europe may be analyzed from several different approaches. They may be studied as a part of the historical incompatibility between spirituality and materialism, between nomad and sedentary, between Turan and Iran, between intuition and logic, between mechanical precision and "wide dreams." One is reminded of the view voiced by Rudyard Kipling: "Oh, East is East, and West is West, and never the twain shall meet . . ." When pro-European Egyptian rulers, politicians or scholars seek to reject this truth, they simply deny that Egypt belongs to the East. Thus Khedive Ismail claimed that: "Egypt is a part of Europe now" and more than half a century later, Taha Hussein wrote:

> We Egyptians must not assume the existence of intellectual differences, weak or strong, between the Europeans and ourselves or infer that the East mentioned by Kipling in his famous verse . . . applies to us or to our country.[16]

Again, relations between Egypt and Europe may be approached from the point of view of the reaction of Islamic society to Western civilization. This reaction has produced two groups of thinkers and politicians. The fanatics, who in their contact with a different civilization have developed a fear and a distrust of innovations, react by falling back on their own traditions, especially those which are opposed to Western civilization—the Muslim Brother-

hood is an example. The progressives have opted for imitation, assimilation and collaboration—the Wafdist attitude. Of course, there are middle of the road reactions, but these two extremes have tended to prevail, not only in Egypt but throughout the Muslim world.

Relations between Egypt and Europe also may be analyzed from the angle of the Ottoman question. "In that shifting intractable and interwoven tangle of conflicting interests, rival peoples and antagonistic faiths that is veiled under the easy name of the 'Eastern Question,' " Egypt has played a vital role as a potential rival of the "sick man," as a ground for Anglo-French rivalry until the *entente cordiale,* as a forerunner of Western penetration in Africa, and as a market for European investments.

Western intervention in Egypt

French influence Although there have never been long periods when contact between Egypt and Europe was completely interrupted, Napoleon Bonaparte's occupation of the country can be taken as the beginning of a new relationship between Egypt and the West. Egyptian reaction to French occupation was one of resentment, hate and distrust; Napoleon and his army were Christians and infidels. The resistance aroused by Napoleon's occupation awakened what we call Egyptian nationalism. Nevertheless, French occupation made possible the process of Westernization by breaking the power of the Mamelukes, and by opening up new fields of learning for some Egyptians.

In spite of the success of Egyptian collaboration with the West in domestic policy—a success largely due to the fact that foreigners were servants and not the masters of the state—the treatment of Mohammed Ali by the European Powers increased Egyptian distrust of Europe. The importation of Western experts and Western techniques were not the only transformation which took place. In the field of political thought the transformation of "Muslim

---

[16] Taha Hussein, *The Future of Culture in Egypt,* Washington, 1924, p. 9.

nationalism" to an "Egyptian nationalism" was an important element for a rapprochement between Egypt and Europe.

The successors of Mohammed Ali (Abbas and Said), did not leave a profound mark on the relations between Egypt and Europe. However, Khedive Ismail (1863–1879) brought Europe to Egypt and transformed Egypt into a Western colony. As Mohammed Ali had foreseen, the existence of the Suez Canal proved incompatible with Egyptian independence. Khedive Ismail's indebtedness became the excuse rather than the reason for the intensification of foreign interference. His deposition in 1879 marked the triumph of European intervention in Egypt.

British influence   The fall of the anti-Western regime opened the door to the military occupation of the country by Great Britain; this occupation lasted seventy-two years. The history of these years of occupation is the history of Great Britain and other European attempts, first to incorporate Egypt and the Arab territories into their colonial empires or spheres of influence, and, when this had failed, to bind the newly independent countries into the Western network of alliances. These attempts at direct, and later indirect, domination were sometimes peacefully adjusted; sometimes they were stubbornly resisted.

Adjustments took place under the influence of the moderate nationalism represented by the Europeanized constitutional liberalism of the Pashas; they were also furthered by the attitude of a group of political thinkers who believed in the necessity of a rapprochement with the West. As Lutfi Al Sayed wrote in *Al Jaridah* (Sept. 14, 1922): "The dominant civilization of today is European, and the only possible foundation for our progress in Egypt is the transmission of the principles of that civilization." At another time he noted: "In Egypt we are the pupils of Europe in everything at the moment. There is no good purpose served in hiding this. . . ."

The first legal expression of this attitude was the 1936 treaty. This treaty made Egypt an ally of Great Britain and recognized Great Britain's "vital interests" in the Suez Canal. British forces were to be moved from Cairo and Alexandria to the canal zone. The treaty succeeded in obtaining for Britain all of the military advantages of a protectorate while softening Egyptian suspicion with *de jure* recognition of her complete independence. For the first time, the British position was regularized by a formal alliance.

Another example of the rapprochement between Egypt and the West was the Bevin-Sidky draft treaty. At this time, partisans of the pro-Western policy suggested the transformation of the Arab League into a Mediterranean League with participation of such countries as Greece, Turkey, Italy and Spain. Such a suggestion had already been made in October of 1945 by the former Secretary of the Arab League, Abdel Rahman Azzam. The association of the Arab League with the Atlantic Pact by means of a new Middle East Defense Organization was another proposed Mediterranean policy. As will be developed later, the Anglo-Egyptian agreement of October 1954 was a new compromise between Egypt and the West, but it was a compromise without results.

Resistance to Western imperialism

Active resistance to British imperialism and Western influence was largely due to the extreme nationalism represented by the small middle class, the university students, the Egyptian-born officers of the army, and the ulemas of Al-Azhar. Sayed Kotb, for example insisted in his book, *Social Justice in Islam,* that "the gulf which history had dug between Europe and the Islamic world remained still unbridged. Dislike of Islam thus became a fundamental part of European thinking. . . ." The Arabi Regime, the Wafd Revolution of 1919, the policy of the Muslim Brotherhood, the denunciation of the 1936 treaty, and the military revolution of July 1952 were all different expressions of this attitude.

The triple aggression of October 1956 by Israel, Great Britain and France, destroyed any real prospect of an Egypt-Western rapprochement. This Western plot aroused again a deep distrust and exasperation towards the Western world.

At the beginning of 1960, relations with Great Britain were partly restored and British observers began to look with optimism to the future position of the West particularly of Great Britain, in the region. There were sound reasons for optimism. Today the principal importance of Egypt and the Arab world lies not in its position on the map, but in the minerals which their lands contain: their geology and not their geography has become decisive. However, a continuing surplus of oil production in the world is transforming the oil market from a seller's to a buyer's market. There is, therefore, a trend towards a calmer and more rational calculation of mutual interest between Western Europe and the Arab world. Furthermore, risk of war has been greatly diminished since the arrival of the nuclear stalemate.

Conflicting interests with the West

This cautious optimism, however, is subject to many reservations: (1) Any new pro-Western foreign policy implies a compromise with Israel which is, in effect, a Mediterranean and Western country in the heart of the Arab world. (2) The West is still the natural ally of the archaic regimes of the Hashemites, the Saudis, and other dynasties which are delaying access of the Arab world to the political ideas and social standards of the 20th century. (3) It is in the interest of the West, and of Great Britain in particular, to maintain an unequal distribution of oil among the different Arab states and within each of the oil producing countries themselves. As a simple example, the Sheikdom of Kuwait, a former British protectorate, supplies fifty percent of the oil consumed in Britain and, at the same time, is the largest single investor on the London Stock Exchange!

(4) In the expression of its four non-Western policies—the African, the Arabic, the Muslim and the neutralist—Egypt may hope to enjoy a role of leadership. On the contrary, in any pro-Western policy, Egypt has always played the role of a vassal state—Ottoman suzerainty until 1914 and British suzerainty until 1954. At the very best, it will never reach a situation more favorable than that of the weaker partner. (5) During the period when a pro-Western policy was advocated by a sophisticated elite, Western Europe in general, and Great Britain in particular, was leading the world. Today, in the era of mass influence and in a divided world, any pro-Western policy seems out of date. Furthermore, the African, Muslim, Arab and neutralist policies are based essentially on opposition to the pro-Western policy. Ever since the Napoleonic intervention the West has been largely blamed for all of the evils now prevalent in the Arab world.

EGYPT AND ARABISM

Attempts to create Arab unity

The historical past   Efforts to unify what is now the Arab world can be traced back several thousands of years. Tutmosis III (1450 B.C.) of Egypt was the first Pharaoh to introduce a formal and consistent policy of military alliances with the various Asian kingdoms in the Middle East. Gaza in Palestine was the administrative center and served as the control station of the great road through Palestine to Syria.

This first Middle Eastern arrangement lasted less than a hundred years. Its dissolution followed the invasion of Syria by the Hittites from the north and the Khabui people from the eastern desert. However, a Middle East empire was created by Ramses II and his successors. The crowning achievement was the Egyptian-Hittite alliance (1280 B.C.) between Ramses II and Hattusibis III.

The Egyptian-Asiatic alliance crumbled away in succeeding centuries under the growing weakness and decadence of the Pharaohs, coupled with the invasions by Libyans and other sea-faring Mediterranean peoples. For many hundreds of years, Egypt was a dependent part of Middle East empires even though there were a few feeble attempts to restore Egypt's independence.

The glory was over and the land of the Nile had become a dependency of other Powers: the Assyrians, Babylonians, Persians and Macedonians. When Egypt once more became independent under Ibn Tulun, she repeated a classic pattern—the annexation of Syria. With Mohammed Ali as master of Egypt and his son, Ibrahim Pasha the governor of Syria (1833) the pattern of Thutmosis, Ramses, and Ibn Tulum was repeated.

For a time it looked as if Ottoman rule might be overthrown. Arab national consciousness was nonexistent, however, and there was no political or ethnic system on which a commonwealth could be built. Furthermore, Mohammed Ali and his son were outsiders (Albanians) and therefore lacked the appeal which an indigenous Arab leader might have had. Finally, British pressures were exerted against any dismemberment of the Ottoman Empire.

Between two World Wars   After the outbreak of World War I, a radical change took place in British policy towards the Arab world. Britain abandoned her policy of maintaining the integrity of the Ottoman Empire and replaced it with a plan to build an Arab Empire. She exploited Arab nationalism, which Mohammed Ali had neglected, in order to integrate and reinforce an Empire which could inherit the triple function of the defunct one: to serve as a friendly guardian of the British route to India, to act as a buffer against Russian expansion, and to restrain potential Egyptian expansionism in the Nile valley.

However, the British project was doomed to failure because of territorial, dynastic and personal rivalries which divided the numerous Arab groups, and because of French and Zionist intervention. As a result, instead of achieving unity and independence, the Arabs saw their lands divided and their freedom restricted. The postwar peace settlement legalized the Balkanization of the Arab world.

What was the policy of Egypt towards the Fertile Crescent and the Arabian Peninsula during the four years which intervened between the armistice of 1918 and the final imposition of the postwar settlement in 1922? It was a policy of aloofness and even more of opposition between the Egyptian movement and the Hashemite movements towards independence. Egyptians were fighting the British and the Arabs of the Fertile Crescent. The Arabian Peninsula allied itself with the British. The two movements found themselves working at cross-purposes. The separation between Arabs in Asia and Arabs in Africa was total.

Between the two World Wars, the only legal expression of a rapprochement was the conclusion of the Treaty of Friendship and Perpetual Peace signed in 1936 between Ibn Saud and Egypt. Four years after the independence of Iraq in 1937, Egypt changed its consulate at Baghdad to a legation. However, the same diplomat had to represent Egypt at Teheran, Baghdad and Djeddah. He resided in Teheran, the capital of a non-Arabic country. During this same period, Egypt failed to participate in the different Middle-Eastern pacts and alliances such as the Tripartite Treaty of Arab Brotherhood.

The Palestine problem put an end to Egyptian isolationism. The participation of Egypt in the Palestine Conference in London in 1939 was the first formal international recognition of the existence of Arab solidarity.

During World War II, after the capitulation of the Vichy government in Syria and Lebanon, the United Kingdom again pursued its objectives of unification—the plan of 1915—and a new Arab-Asiatic empire under the leadership of the Hashemite dynasty. The first Arab steps were taken by Nuri-al-Said, Prime Minister of Iraq. He proposed a union among the Arab-Asian countries *exclusive* of the countries of the Arabian Peninsula and Egypt.

The project failed again, partially because of the opposition of Egypt, who feared the resurrection of a new Hittite or Ottoman Empire which might threaten her position of pre-eminence. Two other factors weighted the scale in favor of the Egyptian position: Ibn Saud was unwilling to accept any unification under the rival Hashemite clan, and Syria and Lebanon feared that their newly-won independence would be jeopardized by submergence in a larger federation.

The Egyptian plan

At this point the initiative was taken by Egypt, which once again felt ready to play the role of unifier of the Arab world. Why did Britain accept the Egyptian pre-eminence? Why did she not build up an Arab Empire in spite of the Egyptian opposition, according to her original plan? Three explanations can be offered.

(1) For many reasons, it was inevitable that Egypt would be the leading partner. She was the wealthiest, the most populous, the most advanced technically, and generally the most powerful of the Arab states. Geographically and culturally, Egypt occupied the position of a bridge between Western Europe and the Arab world.

(2) There was a possibility of channeling "Egyptian expansionism" into the Asiatic area, by involving Egypt in the Arab-Asiatic puzzle so that Britain might gain the opportunity and the time to detach the Sudan from Egypt and to reorganize her African Empire. The Palestine question had diverted Egypt's attention from important developments which had occurred in the Sudan.

(3) An Arab federation of all the countries of the Middle East still remained a first step which could give birth later to the Greater Syria Plan. The expulsion or withdrawal of Egypt would be a second step in this plan.

On September 25, 1944, after nearly two years of consultations, an Arab conference, presided over by Nahas Pasha, Prime Minister of Egypt, and attended by delegates from Iraq, Jordan (then Transjordan), Lebanon, Saudi Arabia, Syria and Yemen, met in Alexandria. While there was clearly support for the idea of Arab unity, there was also a good deal of suspicion and hesitancy about its practical application.

Suspicion was aroused because the project had the blessing of Great Britain; there was jealousy because of Egypt's assumption of leadership; Lebanon with her Christian majority was reluctant to commit herself to any scheme of Arab unity; Ibn Saud suspected the motives of what appeared to be a British inspired *Wafdist-Hashemite* combination; the Imam Yehia was afraid of losing his superb isolationism; and the Hashemite and the Egyptian programs still remained in complete disagreement. However, the persuasion of the British resulted in agreement on the principle of a loose association. The conference drew up the Protocol of Alexandria which formulated the aims and a proposed constitution of an Arab League. Six months later, the Pact of the Arab League, based on this protocol, was signed at Cairo.

The Arab League

The pact provided for a Council which was to convene twice a year, as well as in extraordinary session, upon the request of two member states. It provided for permanent committees dealing with economic affairs, communication, cultural activities, legal affairs, social affairs, and health affairs. It also provided for a permanent Secretariat-General.

Briefly, the purpose of the Arab League is to protect and safeguard the integrity and independence of its members and to insure broad co-operation in economic, social and cultural affairs. An annex to the pact proclaims that Palestine will be independent and not subordinate to any other state; this provides for the potential membership of that country. Another annex provides for the participation of non-independent Arab countries in the work of the League and pledges the League to work for their independence. The first annex was to counter any attempt to integrate Palestine into a Greater Syria Plan; the second annex was to open the door to Egyptian influence in the North African countries—Libya, Tunisia, Algeria, Morocco.

It is unnecessary to examine in detail the machinery of the League; it is important to note two fundamental characteristics of the organization. The first is the obvious Egyptian influence in the League. The Secretary-General of the League has always been an Egyptian; Cairo is the headquarters of the organization. More than fifty percent of the officials of the Secretariat are Egyptian and Egypt contributes about forty percent of the budget.

During the first decade of the League, the internal balance of power was clearly in favor of Egypt; for all important matters, Egypt enjoyed an assured majority in the Council. She has had the support of Saudi Arabia, Lebanon, and, to a certain extent, Yemen and Syria. The key to the Egyptian majority lay in Syria. If Syria had broken with her pro-Egyptian policy within the League, Lebanon would have been compelled to consider seriously whether her independence would not have been better served in the Greater Syria group—Iraq, Jordan and Syria.

After the fusion of Syria and Egypt, the balance of power inside the League was still in favor of this "new member state." However, the admission of Libya, Sudan, Tunisia and Morocco, along with the various disputes which have arisen, have lost to the Government of Cairo the majority she had formerly enjoyed within different organs of the League. Despite this "new look," however, there is no reason why the League should not continue to play the role of arbitrator and conciliator, which it has played for more than sixteen years.

The second characteristic of the League is the basic compromise on which the League was built: the compromise between the Nuri-al-Said scheme—the Greater Syria Plan—and the Egyptian-Saudi program—the maintenance of the status quo. This compromise can be seen in the text of the Arab Pact. Article 8 stipulates that each member state of the League will respect the system of government established in the other member states and will abstain from any action calculated to change established systems of government; this article confirmed and legalized the Balkanization of the Arab world. Article 9, on the contrary, is a concession to the Nuri-al-Said scheme: "States of the Arab League which desire to establish closer co-operation and stronger bonds than those provided in the present pact, may conclude among themselves whatever agreements they wish for this purpose." This article offered an opportunity for the initiation of the Greater Syria Plan. No real reconciliation was achieved between the Hashemite and Egyptian-Saudi policies.

The Greater Syria plan

The opposition of these two tendencies was even more pronounced during the Palestine campaign. Jordan, supported by Iraq, favored the annexation of Palestine in order to make possible the Greater Syria plan; Egypt and Saudi-Arabia desired an independent Palestine under the presidency of the Grand Mufti of Jerusalem, so as to preserve the *status quo*. The Egyptian program failed. Israeli troops broke the second truce, attacked in the Negeb on December 22, 1948, and forced the Egyptian army to retreat. The Council of the Arab League was informed by the Political Committee of the annexation of East Palestine to the Hashemite Kingdom of Jordan. This brought to an end the first stage of the struggle between Hashemite and Egyptian-Saudi policy.

Strengthened by their victory, the supporters of the Greater Syria plan became more active and resumed the next stage of their program: union between Iraq and Syria. Egypt countered by inducing the League to adopt the "Treaty of Joint Defense and Economic Co-operation" in June, 1950, designed "to consolidate the relations between the States of the Arab League . . . corresponding with the desire of their peoples. . . ."

The new treaty provided for pacific settlement of disputes, and for an automatic collective security system, including the use of armed force to repel aggression, in conformity with Article 51 of the United Nations Charter. The treaty also provided for the establishment of a Joint Council, composed of the foreign and defense ministers of the participating states, and for a Permanent Military Commission representing the general staffs of the armies of the member states. It was also stipulated that the contracting states would not conclude any international agreements which might be contrary to the provisions of the treaty, nor act in a way which might be contrary to its aims.

The treaty came into force on August 23, 1952. But in spite of several meetings of the Defense Council, there has been no real implementation of the treaty. This is the result of the old feud between the Saudi-Egyptian and Hashemite blocs and because of the lack of arms and necessary equipment for the new Pan-Arab army.

Iraq joins Western defense pacts

In 1954 the Western Powers urged Iraq to become a party to the Agreement of Friendly Co-operation between Pakistan and Turkey. Her participation was strongly opposed by Egypt which needed, above all, the maintenance of Arab solidarity in bargaining for the British evacuation of the Suez Canal base. The Political Committee issued a communiqué worded as follows: "Every member [of the League], declared that its government has not been invited to adhere to this Pact and had never thought of joining it. . . ."

After the conclusion of the Anglo-Egyptian Agreement of October 19, 1954, Iraq felt that the necessity for an Arab united front had diminished and announced its intention to conclude a military alliance with Turkey. Despite mounting Egyptian pressure inside and outside the League, including sponsorship in Cairo of an emergency meeting of the premiers and foreign ministers of the Arab League, Iraq

signed the Alliance insisting that this was necessary for the defense of its "northern tier," Baghdad being the only Arab capital situated nearer to the Soviet border than to Tel-Aviv. The existence of such a treaty seemed to offer the only available opportunity for the receipt of arms and equipment.

The Egyptian-Saudi position was strongly opposed. It was alleged that the action of Iraq had destroyed Arab solidarity in international politics by placing her own interests before those of Arab solidarity. In a certain manner Iraq had become "the ally of the ally of Israel." The price of any understanding with Turkey should have been much higher, such as the breaking of economic relations between Turkey and Israel and a settlement of the question of the Sanjak of Alexandretta which had been annexed by Turkey from the Arab world.

The Baghdad Pact, as the Turco-Iraqi treaty became known, was concerned with "the maintenance of peace and security in the Middle East region in accordance with the United Nations Charter and the Treaty of Joint Defense between the Arab League States." The pact provided for mutual co-operation in the field of security and defense for a period of five years. It was stipulated that the pact should be open to accession by any member of the Arab League, or by any state actively concerned with the security of this region, which was fully recognized by both of the contracting parties. This last stipulation was designed explicitly to exclude Israel from the pact and to re-affirm the fact that the treaty was compatible with the principles of the Arab League.

The treaty provided finally for the creation of a permanent council at the ministerial level, as soon as four Powers should become parties to the pact. This provision was put into effect when Britain and Pakistan acceded to the pact. The council of the pact convened in Baghdad in November of 1955 under the chairmanship of Prime Minister Nuri-al-Said. It was attended by the premiers of Iran, Pakistan and Turkey, the foreign minister of Britain and observers from the United States.

Yet this important diplomatic meeting was eclipsed by a more important and spectacular event which took place two months earlier: On September 27, Prime Minister Nasser announced that he had concluded an agreement with Czechoslovakia for the purchase of Czech heavy weapons. The main argument of Nuri-al-Said—the need to obtain arms and equipment through the channel of the Baghdad Pact—was thus destroyed.

At this point the initiative was taken again by Egypt, which attempted to conclude a tripartite treaty with Saudi Arabia and Syria to counter the Baghdad Pact. Egypt failed in this but was able to conclude bilateral treaties with each of these two states.

The anti-Baghdad bloc

On January 16, 1956, the new Egyptian Constitution was proclaimed. For the first time in Egypt's modern history, the Constitution of the state announced that Egypt was "an Arab state" and that the Egyptian people were "a part of the Arab nation" transferring the "Egyptian-Arab policy" from foreign to domestic policy.

On April 21, 1956, the new anti-Baghdad bloc was enlarged by the adhesion of the Yemen to a tripartite treaty concluded between Egypt, Saudi Arabia and the Yemen, for five years. Egyptian diplomacy was working to obtain the adhesion of Jordan, and thus to isolate Iraq, when Israel and then France and Britain invaded Sinai and Port Said in November 1956. These various defense treaties were not effective during this aggression. However, Egyptian jet planes found refuge in Saudi Arabia and Syria, pipe lines were blown up, and petrol was cut off from Britain and France.

When the aggressors withdrew from Egypt in conformity with the United Nations resolutions, Egypt again took up its program of Arab unity. The "Treaty of Arab Solidarity" was concluded in January 1957 among Saudi Arabia, Egypt, Jordan, and Syria for a period of ten years. During this period, Jordan was supposed to receive the financial support previously given by Great Britain, the annual shares being two and a half million pounds for Syria and five million pounds each for Egypt and Saudi Arabia. The Jordan revolution of April 1957 put an end to this treaty and redressed the balance of power in the Arab world between the "pro-Westerners" and the "neutralists."

In September 1957, during the Turkish-Syrian crisis, the Egyptian-Syrian Mutual Defense Pact of October, 1955, was first invoked and basic elements of the Egyptian armed forces were moved to Syria. In the same month, Syria and Egypt established a Joint Committee charged with making recommendations for the unification of the economies of the two states. In March there was an agreement on cultural unity. All of these agreements were successive milestones designed to lead to final political unity.

Partial Arab unity

Formation of the U.A.R. Finally, on November 19, 1957, a Syrian-Egyptian parliamentary session held in Damascus unanimously approved a motion urging negotiations for the creation of a federal union of the two countries. Events moved rapidly and the merger of Syria and Egypt was announced in Cairo on the first of February. The proclamation announced that

the participants declare their total agreement in the necessity of uniting Egypt and Syria into one state to be named "The United Arab Republic." In deciding on the unity of both peoples, the participants declare that their unity aims at the unification of all the Arab peoples and affirm that the door is open for participation to any Arab state desirous of joining them in a union or federation. . . .

The formation of the U.A.R. and the election of Gamal Abdel Nasser as its first president were the object of two plebiscites in February, 1958. The Constitution was promulgated in March. Article I of the constitution stated that the new union was democratic, and that its people were a part of the Arab nation. It was clear that this was thought of as a first step toward the creation of total Arab unity.

Five weeks after the founding of the U.A.R., the announcement was made by President Nasser and the Crown Prince of Yemen of the formation of a confederation between the U.A.R. and the Yemen. This was another step toward the unification of the Arab world.

The Hashemite reaction to the formation of the U.A.R. was the federation of Iraq and Jordan in the Arab Union; this crumbled a few months later with the Baghdad revolution of July, 1958. At this stage, Arab nationalism was triumphing over political fragmentation. The classic feud between the Egyptian approach to unity and the Hashemite plan was abruptly ended. A majority of the people in Jordan and Lebanon were ready to merge with the U.A.R. or adopt a close association with the new republic; public opinion throughout the Arab world was ready to accept U.A.R. leadership.

Israeli opposition   However, this new opportunity was doomed to failure because of Israeli threats and Western intervention. Israeli troops were ready to march to the west bank of the Jordan in the event of Jordan's fusion with Iraq or the U.A.R.; American troops made a landing south of Beirut and British paratroops were flown into Jordan.

In spite of all the signs of unity, political co-ordination between Baghdad and Cairo was still lacking. Neither the Egyptian-Syrian army, nor the Iraqi army could afford a clash with the British troops in Amman, the American troops in Beirut or the Israeli troops in Palestine; nor could they risk a new coalition between Western imperialism and World Zionism, as in November 1956.

When American and British troops were withdrawn, the chance of Arab unification under U.A.R. leadership was ended. Furthermore, a quarrel occurred between General

Quasim, a partisan of the status quo, and Colonel Aref, a partisan of a close association with the U.A.R. Later, this quarrel revealed the existence of much deeper differences between Arabism and communism, with the weak Government of Quasim trying to hold the balance between the two opposing Powers.

In March, 1959, a group of pro-U.A.R. officers revolted in Mosul, giving a new opportunity for Arab unification. However, the revolt failed and the classic relationship between Baghdad and Cairo re-asserted itself, blessed by Western and Soviet diplomacy, fulfilling their desire to perpetuate, even though for different aims, disunity in the Asiatic part of the Arab world.

Syria secedes   At the end of September 1961, a secessionist movement in Damascus put an end to the union between Egypt and Syria. On October 4th the President of the United Arab Republic officially recognized the secession reserving, however, formal recognition of the secessionist government. The new Syrian republic was duly admitted to the United Nations, as well as to the Arab League, the organization which assumed an active role in adjusting the controversial issues between Cairo and Damascus. Some months later, on December 23, 1961, the United Arab Republic terminated the union of the United Arab States established in 1958 between the U.A.R. and the government of Yemen. The union was considered to be incompatible with the new socialist orientation of the U.A.R.

In spite of the failure of these two efforts at union, Egyptian policy towards the Arab world continues on a steadfast course: *First,* through the instrumentality of the Arab League, which emerged unscathed, if not indeed reinforced by the ordeal imposed on the Arab world by the break-up of these two limited unions. *Second,* through a direct appeal to the Arab people. Not only does Egypt continue to call itself the United Arab Republic but she continues to make an appeal to the ideals common to all Arab states, and still has the goal of a federation of all Arab states. *Finally,* Egypt offers to the disinherited Arab masses the attraction of a socialist policy. While such a policy displeases and creates anxiety among the monied minorities, it reaches across frontiers and channels an irresistible current which is carrying forward men, tribes, and groups of states towards the formation of a nation.

EGYPT AND NEUTRALISM

Historical origins

Egyptian neutralism is not a new policy and is not, as has often been stated, the result of the Cold War. It is not merely a demand for complete withdrawal from all associations which involve partisanship in major conflicts of interest between East and West. Egyptian neutralism in particular, and Arab neutralism in general, goes back to the intervention of European imperialism in the Middle East and Africa at the end of the last century. It finds its psychological and popular basis in xenophobia. Its roots in Egypt reach back into a century or more of foreign exploitation and domination. Furthermore, the exploitation of xenophobia by certain elements of the ruling class has resulted in diverting attention from internal unrest and in postponing internal reform.

The effects of British imperialism   Internal tensions were channeled against a safe target, British imperialism, and later, Western and Zionist imperialism. Some historical examples will make it clear that the roots of Egyptian neutralism are found in the attitude of Egypt toward international situations prior to the Cold War. The Constantinople Convention of 1888 provided that "The Suez Maritime Canal shall always be free and open in time of war as in time of peace, to every vessel of commerce or of war, without distinction of flag." One should also note that Egypt failed to participate actively in World War I and was neutralist

during World War II. It is thus clear that neutralism had already been adopted by Egypt and the Arab world in 1940. The Rashid Ali *coup* against the Taha Hashimi government in Iraq was an isolated material expression of alignment. The Holy war (*Gihad*) which Rashid Ali declared against Britain in 1941 was not echoed elsewhere in the Arab World.

This deep indifference, coupled with xenophobia, which is the popular infrastructure of Egyptian neutralism, was not understood by Western scholars. Owen Tweedy, for example, in *Political and Economic Survey of the Middle East,* observed that when the German Afrika Corps with its Italian allies under General Rommel captured Tobruk, and it was not clear that Egypt could be defended, "the Egyptian public stood remarkably steady . . . and despite all the past efforts of Axis propaganda in Egypt, there was no single case of sabotage of vital military communications across the Delta to Alamein . . ." This was true but the writer fails to appreciate another aspect of the attitude: The Egyptian population stood remarkably indifferent to the difficult position of the allied armies fighting for Western democracy.

It was the ruling class, or at least King Farouk and his advisers, who in their own interest adopted what was practically a policy of positive neutralism. In order to ensure the maintenance of the dynasty, it was necessary first to avoid provoking British hostility by undue opposition to British goals and secondly to avoid identification with British interests in the eyes of the Axis Powers, who might at any time supplant Great Britain in Egypt. Furthermore, the Arab countries declared war on the Axis Powers only at the last moment in order to be invited to the San Francisco Conference. Egypt's declaration of war did not prove entirely bloodless: it cost the life of Ahmed Maher, the prime minister who was assassinated by a fanatic defender of Egyptian neutrality.

The effects of the Palestine war   The Palestine question also influenced the development of Arab neutralism. This development passed through three successive phases: before, during and after the Palestine war. Before the Palestine war, the Arab League, which the British Government had expected to act as a tool for political and economic integration, became nothing more than an Arab alliance against Zionism. Anti-Zionist defense became the only activity of the League; economic rehabilitation, social co-operation, and regional integration were relegated to places of secondary importance.

For example, during the first ten sessions of the Council of the Arab League, 74 resolutions were adopted concerning the Palestine problem and only six concerning economic co-operation and five concerning social co-operation. In other words, the institution created for the rapprochement between the Arabs and the United Kingdom became, because of the Zionist movement, an institution which widened the gap between the Arabs and the West.

The Arab defeat in the Palestine war created a crisis of confidence between the Arabs and the rest of the world which had deliberately espoused the Zionist cause. It also created a crisis of confidence between the Arabs and the United Nations which had decided in favor of partition and had imposed the first armistice of June, 1948, which had led to the defeat of the Arabs. It finally led to a crisis of confidence between the Arabs and Britain, the supposedly trustworthy ally, which in less than a generation betrayed the Arabs for a second time.

Soviet-Arab relations   On the other hand, there was practically no direct relationship between the Soviet Union and the Arabs. Communist groups throughout the whole Middle East were weak and divided. When they were called on to adjust their line in keeping with the Soviet support for a Jewish state in Palestine, they lost all power and popular appeal. In the face of such a revolutionary situation dominated by humiliation, frustration and anger, no dialogue with the West or the East was possible. The neutralist attitude imposed itself.

After the Palestine war came another blow. The "state" of Israel was admitted to the United Nations with the support of the Soviet Union and the Western bloc, even though those two blocs had reached a deadlock on the admission of more than twenty other states.

The Palestine war also left as a legacy to the Arab Middle East strategic and political problems which were in conflict with Western policy in the region. Until 1948 the Arab world and the Western world had a common interest in defending the area against any foreign invasion. The only Powers likely to invade or to threaten Egypt and the Arab world were Major Powers whose hostile action would be part of a general war against Great Britain.

With the creation of the state of Israel the situation changed completely. On the one hand, Israel was a state created by the West, which desired to include it among the other Middle East states in a general organization for the defense of the region. On the other hand, Israel was a Power whose expansionism and hostility the Arabs feared and whose annihilation they desired. While the West urged Egypt to dovetail its military establishment into a general plan for defense against Soviet Russia, Egypt viewed her problems of defense as being primarily directed towards the possibility of a local war with Israel. The Cold War with Israel loomed larger than the East-West Cold War in which the Arab world could only be a satellite.

The pro-Zionist policy of the two blocs and the creation of the Zionist state were terrible blows to their respective relations with the Arab world. However, because of the weakness of the different Communist groups, resulting from the Soviet absence from the Middle East, the Soviet attitude was considered rather as an unfriendly gesture taken by a foreign state, than the betrayal of an ally. Furthermore, the official Communist party line for the Middle East was to favor Arab nationalism and to counter Zionism, officially described as a *petit bourgeois* capitalist ideology and an instrument of British imperialism.

On the other hand, because of the presence of the British troops in the Arab Middle East, and because of the different political, cultural, and economic ties which link the Western world to the Arab world, the pro-Zionist policy of the West was considered as a real betrayal. The difference between an unfriendly gesture and a betrayal may well explain the new attitude of Egypt towards the Cold War during the next decade.

Neutralism becomes official policy

At this stage of the situation three important trends of opinion appeared in the Egyptian press, and public opinion circles. A first trend called for the neutrality of Egypt according to the rules of international law. A leading article published in the Wafdist newspaper *Al-Misri* expressed this view:

We ought to declare the neutrality of the Suez Canal as well as that of Egypt . . . If the British finally leave Egypt and the various States guarantee the country's neutrality, we shall be, like Switzerland, sheltered from the spectre of the war which threatens the world with ruin.

A second view advocated the conclusion of a non-aggression pact with the U.S.S.R. And a third opinion expressed the fear that Egypt might become involved in a third World War in which she had no interest because both blocs are tyrants and colonizers.

These three main currents of opinion, combined together, gave birth to the first official manifestations of Egyptian neutralism towards the Cold War. Egypt, a member of the Security Council, abstained from voting in favor of the United States' resolution requesting the United Nations to intervene in Korea. Nothing could better illustrate Egyptian neutralism than the explanation given in the Security Council on June 30, 1950. Referring to the fact that he had not been able to participate in the voting on the resolution three days earlier because instructions had not arrived from Cairo, the Egyptian representative declared:

I am now in a position to state, on behalf of my Government, that Egypt would have abstained from voting on the resolution adopted by the Security Council . . . had the representative of Egypt been able to participate in the voting. This attitude is dictated by the following two reasons: first, the conflict under consideration is in fact but a new phase in the series of divergences which threaten world peace and security; secondly, there have been several cases of aggression against peoples and violations of the sovereignty and unity of the territories of states, members of the United Nations. Such aggressions and violations have been submitted to the United Nations, which did not take any action to put an end to them as it has done now in the case of Korea.[17]

This manifestation of neutralism was without doubt an expression of public opinion not only in Egypt, but in the different Arab countries. This is demonstrated by the fact that the pro-Western politician, Nuri-al-Said of Iraq, was forced to come out for neutralism at the thirteenth session of the Arab League in late 1950 and early 1951. A resolution adopted by the Council of the Arab League was the first of the Arab League's contributions to neutralism which three years later was to have such an appeal throughout the whole Afro-Asian world.[18]

Arab governments at this period were almost without exception very much dependent on public opinion in their foreign policies. They were doubly dependent because they did not wish to yield to public opinion in domestic policy which would involve social reforms and political changes; this meant they needed a popular neutralist foreign policy as a safety-valve.

[17] United Nations, Security Council, *Official Records*, 5th year, No. 17, 475th meeting.
[18] See text of Resolution in *Egypt and the United Nations,* New York: Manhattan Publishing Company 1957, p. 128.

Decline of pro-Western attitude

Even among the Pashas and the large owners of property, support for the West was not very strong. They believed that the community of interests with the West was not strong enough to warrant Egyptian support and the establishment of close relations. They knew, of course, that they might lose their privileges without the support of the West; they also knew that they would lose them more rapidly if they were to advocate the unpopular idea of closer association with the West. A neutralist attitude was the only attitude possible.

Even if the majority of the politically active elements of Egypt did not follow the neutralist attitude, there were fewer and fewer political leaders like Ismail Sidky Pasha, former Prime Minister of Egypt, who advocated an open alignment with the Western bloc. Furthermore, the neutralist and even pro-Soviet sentiment which existed found expression in various political and large anti-imperialist fronts which, if not Communist, were at least animated by their ideology.

With the end of martial law and the return of the Wafd, most Communists were released from concentration camps and the Leftist front was tolerated. Student and mass demonstrations were encouraged. Ahmed Hussein, a former Fascist, created the Socialist party; its foreign political orientation was neutralism. His weekly periodical *Al-Ishtirakia* preached friendship with Russia, recognition of Red China, and cancellation of all treaties with the West.

This anti-imperialist campaign culminated in the abrogation of the 1936 Treaty on October 8, 1951, and the burning of Cairo on January 26, 1952. In Iraq the anti-Western Istiqlal party demanded neutrality between the two blocs and praised the decision of Egypt not to support the West in the Korean war. In Syria, after the downfall of the Husni El-Zaim regime, the Islamic Socialist Front engaged in a concentrated pro-neutralist and anti-Western campaign. The peace movement had considerable success and a large number of prominent personalities signed the Stockholm Appeal.

The military revolution in Egypt in July 1952 offered promises and opportunities to the West to engage in a new dialogue with Egypt. British diplomacy did not miss this opportunity and on October 19, 1954, Egypt and the United Kingdom reached an agreement on the Suez Canal base. Commenting on this agreement, United States Secretary of State John Foster Dulles declared in a statement to the press: "This agreement eliminates a problem which has affected not only the relations between the United Kingdom and Egypt but also those of the Western nations as a whole with the Arab States."[19] In the House of Commons, Anthony Eden stressed the importance of the agreement, saying that it was essential to win the good-will and friendship of Egypt so as to assure stability in the Middle East.

These statements made it clear that the Anglo-Egyptian agreement was considered by the West as the first step for a general organization of the Middle East. However, the same treaty was considered by the Egyptians as "our final liberation from imperialism," although it would have been indelicate to suggest that Egypt had no intention of observing the spirit of this agreement which was, in fact, incompatible with Egyptian neutrality. The circulation of leaflets denouncing the Suez agreement by Leftist groups and the Muslim Brotherhood was another confirmation of the strength of neutralism in Egypt.

Western diplomacy tired of waiting for further results, utilized other channels, and began to encourage bilateral treaties outside of the framework of the neutralist Arab League. Britain veered back to the policy of supporting pro-Western Iraq against pro-neutralist Egypt for the leadership of the Arab world. Despite mounting Egyptian pressure, inside and out-

[19] U.S. Department of State, *Bulletin,* vol. XXI, No. 789 (Aug. 9, 1954), p. 198.

side of the League, Iraq entered the Western bloc through the Baghdad Pact.[20] This was a serious blow to the neutralist policy of Egypt.

Neutralism broadens its ranks

However, at this point Egyptian neutralism was rescued and strengthened by the following events: (1) The conclusion of an Indo-Egyptian treaty of friendship on April 6, 1955, transformed Egyptian neutralism from a national policy to an Afro-Asian ideology. The Egyptian Ambassador to India gave expression to this widening of Egyptian neutralism when he said: "It is a great honour for both countries to face the world with a common stand at all international gatherings."[21]

A short time later in a joint statement issued by the prime ministers of India and Egypt the following was included:

The Prime Ministers would like to reiterate their conviction of the urgent necessity of furthering the cause of world peace and of reducing tensions that exist in various parts of the world. For this purpose it is their conviction that involvement in military pacts or alignments with great Powers does not serve the cause of peace and, indeed, often has the opposite effect.[22]

(2) The Bandung Conference of April, 1955 enabled Egyptian public opinion to see neutralism as a part of the general Afro-Asian movement to contract out of the Cold War. (3) In September, 1955, Egypt concluded an agreement with Czechoslovakia for supplying heavy weapons, including tanks, jets and submarines, in exchange for Egyptian cotton and rice. Before this agreement Egypt and other Arab states had relied on the West for their supplies of arms and ammunition.

(4) The Brioni Conference on July 20, 1956, advanced Egyptian neutralism from an Afro-Asian movement to a world-wide movement. The participation of Yugoslavia, a European country, meant that neutralism was adopted not only by countries which refused alignment with Western imperialism, but by a country which had refused alignment with Soviet imperialism.

These events, in strengthening Egyptian neutralism, gave new aims to it. Before 1954, neutralism was used as a tool to obtain the evacuation of British troops. After 1955, neutralism became a new means for improving Arab solidarity. Neutrality and unity versus alignment and disunity became the new motto of Egyptian foreign policy.

The Anglo-French invasion and its aftermath

Egyptian diplomacy and propaganda were moving along this line when the United States Government, followed by the British Government and the World Bank, withdrew its provisional offer of a loan for the High Dam. On July 26, 1956, President Nasser announced the nationalization of the Suez Canal Company. This act of nationalization, viewed from the angle of neutralism, gave new impetus to this policy, just as the Czechoslovakia arms deal had done the year before. It was an assertion both of Egypt's independence and of her neutrality. Egypt's action was viewed with approval throughout the Arab world.

It was also clear that there was great hostility to the foreign policy goals of the Western Powers. The British, French and Israeli aggression against Sinai and Port Said brought this anti-Western feeling to a point of exasperation. The association of the West with World Zionism clearly proved to the most pro-Western Arab politicians that collaboration with the West was disastrous.

Even the Iraqi rulers, who had hoped to se-

---

[20] *Ibid.*, p. 49.
[21] Text of document issued by the Lok Sabha Secretariat, New Delhi, October, 1958, p. 119.
[22] *Ibid.*, p. 185.

cure the fall of President Nasser by "playing a waiting game," resented the British aggression which ruined their own policy. It destroyed the chance they hoped for: that of exercising leadership over the Arab world. In consequence, Iraq took the lead, supported by Pakistan, in proposing the exclusion of Britain from the Baghdad Pact. Saudi Arabia and Syria broke off diplomatic relations with France and Britain. Jordan denounced the Anglo-Jordanian treaty. In addition to this, pipelines were blown up and riots and strikes broke out in several of the Persian Gulf Sheikdoms.

Because of the anti-Western and the pro-Russian propaganda, the last minute American intervention in favor of the Arab cause went unobserved. Public opinion, except in certain ruling circles, identified the United States with the Anglo-French invasion. On the other hand, the Russian threat to attack London with missiles and the Russian promise to send volunteers to fight in Egypt created a widespread belief among Arabs that the Soviet Union had saved them from Western imperialism. In the eyes of the Arab world, a resounding victory had been won against the Western bloc. For the first time in history international public opinion had forced the abandonment of an attack by two Great Powers. The policy of neutralism had been successful.

After the aggressors had withdrawn in conformity with the United Nations decision, Egypt again took up its program based on neutrality and the unification of the Arab world. The Eisenhower Doctrine, the visit of Ibn Saud to the United States, and the Jordan revolution of April 1957 all were new attempts of the West to weaken the Egyptian-Arab neutralist camp.

The see-saw continued, with the collapse of the Eisenhower Doctrine and the merging of Egypt and Syria. Almost all Arabs viewed the Eisenhower Doctrine not as a proposal for insurance against communism but as an American campaign against neutralism. On the other hand, the union of Egypt and Syria was seen as a victory of the neutralist policy. In fact, support by Egypt and Syria for Arab neutralism was among the main factors contributing

to the creation of the United Arab Republic.

The Iraqi revolution of July, 1958, was another victory for neutralism. However, the classic feud between Baghdad and Cairo was to rise again and to make it impossible to really join Arabism and neutralism. Two major centers of power continued to exist in the Arab world.

The nature of Egyptian neutralism

The foregoing analysis of Egyptian and then Arab neutralism leads to certain conclusions: Egyptian neutralism expresses the very deep feelings of the Egyptians because it corresponds to the geographical position of Egypt and the Arab world, placed as they are between two enemy blocs; because it conforms to the Muslim political ideology; and because it has improved Arab solidarity. Egyptian neutralism is a part of the general Afro-Asian neutralist policy; the solidarity of the have-not countries of the world corresponds to the present stage of economic development of Egypt, which is clearly among the poor nations of the world.

Egyptian neutralism, in contrast to European, Indian or Indonesian neutralism, has always been very harshly criticized. Among the explanations for this attitude are the fact that Egypt is not backed by any real power; it lacks a doctrine to explain neutralism; neutralism is incompatible with the Arab policy working for the extinction of Israel as a political entity; and, finally, Egypt's very aggressiveness.[23]

[23] Barbara Ward in her book, *Five Ideas that Changed the World*, London: Hamish Hamilton, 1959, p. 136, gives an example of Western subjectivity when she writes: *There are, in fact, two kinds of neutrality. It is difficult to define which kind deserves the adjective positive or indeed what the adjective is supposed to mean. But the distinction is clear. There is a neutrality, a non-alignment between military blocs which seem by all means to lessen the conflicts between them, to suggest solutions, to mediate difficulties. . . . I believe the Swedes have made a consistent effort to*

The real explanation seems to be that Egyptian neutralism, and more recently, Arab neutralism, is still very deeply involved with Arab nationalism. Arab unity has not yet been achieved in the Middle East; thus, neutralism is a tool for achieving unity, rather than a tool for achieving conciliation outside the Arab world. It is a partial and subjective neutralism rather than an objective neutralism; it will remain so until Arab states pass from the confederation to the federal stage.

GENERAL CONCLUSIONS

In this chapter we have dealt first with the attitude of Egypt towards Africa. This attitude continues to be of vital importance for both political and economic reasons. Then we considered Islam, which for more than a millennium has been a basic element in the policy of Egypt. It was challenged successfully at the beginning of the last century by the Western European Powers. The struggle of these forces —Islam versus Westernization—gave birth first to nationalism and later, as a second step, to Arab federalism. Then the opposition of Western imperialism and World Zionism to Arabism gave birth to a new policy with much wider scope: neutralism.

In our age, following the re-emergence of independent African countries, new opportunities are offered to Islam and Arabism in Africa. The U.A.R. policy towards Africa has become again its most important policy.

However, outside of Africa, Islam has lost much of its importance in the field of foreign policy. No longer does it appear that the real

use their non-alignment for this purpose. . . . But there is another non-alignment which regards neutrality as a sort of see-saw in which, by playing one bloc off against another, now swinging down with Communist support, now soaring up with Western backing, local plans, plots and objectives can be secured. Yet, what kind of security is to be found on a see-saw . . . ?

struggle is between Islam on the one hand and the camps of the East and the West on the other. Neutralism has emerged as a new ideology and has proved to be more important in the field of foreign relations, than a common religion. Obviously, neutralism is incompatible with any pro-Western Mediterranean policy which attempts to form a bloc of the Arab states; likewise it is incompatible with any particular designs that the Soviet Union might have on the Middle East. Arabism, on the other hand, has suffered some setbacks with the break-up of the union between Egypt and Syria and with the re-emergence of the conflict between Baghdad and Cairo.

Finally, in evaluating the foreign policy of Egypt, due account must be given to the difficulties which constantly confront it. The underdevelopment of the country, the insufficiency of capital, and the lack of modern techniques and technicians have placed many obstacles in the path of exploiting diplomatic successes. The foreign policy of the U.A.R. has found it difficult to reach the second step, the *institutional* stage in international relations. The infra-structure of the country does not yet match the dynamism of its foreign policy.

There is the opposition of centrifugal forces working against the U.A.R. within the African world, the Muslim commonwealth and the Arabic nations. Such forces are based on archaic systems exploited both by Western and Soviet imperialism. A negative aspect of the neutralist policy must also be noted. While it offers to the U.A.R. the possibility of an independent policy, it forecloses any support from the West or the East for Arab unity or African solidarity, such as the help that was forthcoming in the case of Indian unity, Western European integration, and Warsaw group solidarity. On the contrary, any scheme proposed by the U.A.R. will be opposed from without by Zionism and probably by Western and Eastern Powers.

Thus, some scholars have asked whether Egypt reaps any advantage from adopting the African, Arabic, Muslim and neutralist policies at the same time. They wonder whether Egypt can achieve a sort of *Pax Egyptica* with the country secure as the center of four overlapping spheres of influence: the Arab World, Africa, Islam, and the neutralist bloc. Should the U.A.R. not accept more modest ambitions? Will she not be compelled to renounce any attempted role of leadership in Africa or in the Arab world and to apply her energies to the more humble task of developing the country as a modern welfare state?

The foregoing analysis shows that the unique geopolitical position of the U.A.R. does not allow the country to adopt any such policy of isolationism. It imposes on her a dynamic foreign policy which compels her to squarely meet a new challenge: how to discharge today the obligations of her unique geopolitical and historical position with the power and means at her disposal.

BIBLIOGRAPHY

Author's Suggestions

Ahmed, Jammal Mohammed. *The Intellectual Origins of Egyptian Nationalism.* London: Oxford University Press, 1960.

Carnegie Endowment for International Peace. *Egypt and the United Nations.* New York: Manhattan Publishing Company, 1957.

Issawi, Charles. *Egypt at Mid-Century.* London: Oxford University Press, 1954.

Nasser, Gamal Abdel. *The Philosophy of the Revolution.* Washington, D.C.: Public Affairs Press, 1955.

Royal Institute of International Affairs, Information Department. *The Middle East: A Political and Economic Survey.* London: 1950.

Wilson, John. *The Burden of Egypt: An Interpretation of Ancient Egyptian Culture.* Chicago: University of Chicago Press, 1951.

ABOUT THE AUTHOR

His excellency, HABIB BOURGUIBA, JR., was born and educated in France and graduated from Law School (Paris, Grenoble), in 1953. He took an active part in the National Liberation Movement, especially during 1951–1954. His career has been closely tied to building the Diplomatic Service of his country. He participated in the establishment of the Department of Foreign Affairs for Tunisia and has held a number of important diplomatic posts. In 1959 he represented Tunisia on the Security Council Subcommittee for Laos; he was a member of the Tunisian delegation to the United Nations in 1960. Mr. Bourguiba has served as Ambassador to Italy and to France. At the present time he holds the concurrent posts of Ambassador to the United States, Canada and Mexico.

ABOUT THE CHAPTER

This chapter is a vigorous presentation of the goals, aspirations and limitations of a new nation which gained her independence only in 1956. Ambassador Bourguiba gives attention to the geographical setting of Tunisia and to the historical background which influences the values and aspirations of the nation.

The idealism of this young nation is clearly seen in the exploration of the objectives and goals of Tunisia as outlined by her leaders. This idealism, however, has not prevented her leaders from being very much aware of the world of power politics and of the long-range nature of many of the problems which must be solved. The chapter was written during the final phases of the struggle of Algeria for independence and clearly reflects the sentiment of the nations of the Maghreb as they attempt to deal with the problems of the present and plan for the future.

Ambassador Bourguiba includes a survey of present foreign policy goals as well as some of the problems which will make it difficult to achieve them.

12

THE FOREIGN POLICY OF TUNISIA

HABIB BOURGUIBA, JR.

Ambassador of Tunisia, Washington, D.C.

After a short fight and long negotiations, Tunisia emerged to independence on March 20, 1956. The last months of the negotiations were spent by the Tunisian leaders in trying to overcome the reluctance of the French to give Tunisia the two fundamental attributes of sovereignty: a national army and diplomatic representation.

Tunisia never meant her national army to be an instrument of foreign policy. She is too small and too weak a country to nourish such an ambition. Besides, she has nothing to fear from her immediate African neighbors, at present or in the near future. They are very much linked to her by sentiment or interest. They are kept busy by their own problems and they know that, should they attack us, they would have to face a quick condemnation by world public opinion and effective action from the United Nations. On the other hand, the greatest armed forces we could afford would still be far from strong enough to crush any attack by any European country. Therefore, the tiny army we are keeping has been used exclusively for police service inside the national territory.

When we finally gained independence, we were confronted, among other problems, with the challenge to establish a diplomatic service starting from nothing, to have it work properly and carry on a coherent foreign policy in accordance with our potentialities and needs.

PERMANENT FACTORS

To begin with, let us examine the fixed factors we had to take into consideration when formulating our foreign policy, those factors which have influenced it and will continue to influence it in the future.

The geographical setting

Tunisia enjoys a very typical "crossroad location." She lies at the intersection of three "worlds": the African world to which she is linked by the Sahara desert; the Arab world of which she constitutes a portion of the "west" wing; the European world to which she is connected by the Mediterranean Sea. Such a location enriches the Tunisian personality; being at the same time African, Arab and, to a certain extent, European, Tunisia cannot be considered as being typically African, or Arabic, or European. She is rather a synthesis, a combination. As far as foreign policy is concerned, she finds it necessary to conciliate different sets of specific imperatives.

Tunisia is certainly not as African as, let us say, Ghana, because her inhabitants are mostly fair-skinned and belong to a Mediterranean civilization which has not much to do with the ones which flourished south of the Sahara. This does not prevent Tunisia from being in complete solidarity with the African continent, since, like most of the African countries, she experienced a colonial or semi-colonial regime. The factor of African solidarity is geographical and political, and possibly economic.

On the other hand, Tunisia is certainly not as Arab as, let us say, Saudi Arabia, because throughout her history, she was exposed to some European influences which do not belong to the background of the Arab peninsula. This difference does not, however, prevent Tunisians from being an important part of the Arab-Moslem world, sharing with the other Arab countries their language, religion, their past history and present political aspirations.

A comparable thing can be said about the European aspect of Tunisia. Our country is not a part of Europe, geographically speaking as Switzerland, or from the sociological point of view as the United States or New Zealand. But it is a fact that the Roman and the French occupations of Tunisia as well as the proximity to Italy left very strong influences on the way of life of our country and on its economy.

It is significant that the first part of Africa to be known to the Europeans is Tunisia. In ancient times it was called Afrika (which became Ifrikia in Arabic), a name which was to designate the whole continent later on. This illustrates in a striking way the fact that Tunisia

has always been a sort of a bridge, a link between Europe and Africa. Tunisia is neither exclusively a part of the African, the Arab or the European areas, but partakes of the heritage of all three. She is, unquestionably, a typically Mediterranean country. As such, she has something in common with Syria, Lebanon and Spain, with Italy, Greece and Egypt. Tunisia separates—or unites—the oriental and the occidental basins of the Mediterranean Sea, a privileged position which could not be claimed by any exclusively Arab or African country.

All the characteristics evident in Tunisia apply to Algeria and Morocco as well. They, too, are Arab, Mediterranean and African countries. They, too, might be considered as a bridge between southern Europe and Africa, south of the Sahara. They share with Tunisia one and the same historical past, including a common French occupation, and an Arab-Moslem background. Geography also unites them in one and the same ensemble. This is why the permanent factor which is most immediately felt by the people and the leaders of Tunisia is their belonging to the "Maghreb." Maghreb means "west" in Arabic, North Africa being the western part of the Arab world.

General principles of policy

It goes without saying that Tunisian foreign policy reflects all the preoccupation resulting from the geographical setting of the country and the historical setting of the people. But like most of the newly emerged inexperienced nations, and unlike most of the sophisticated old Powers, Tunisia naïvely believes that a minimum of morality should govern international relations. She acts accordingly at the risk of sometimes jeopardizing her immediate interests.

First of all, we believe that any international policy should not in any way jeopardize freedom, justice, and dignity of individuals on one side or the other. We believe that the "law of the jungle" must be eliminated from international relations. A policy of hegemony, such as practiced until World War II, can only lead to tragic adventures like the Fascist and Nazi adventure in Italy and Germany and the militarist adventure in Japan. Unfortunately, after the war, a certain form of international gangsterism was still practiced. Colonial wars in Vietnam and Algeria, aggression against the Suez Canal by France, the United Kingdom and Israel, and intervention in Hungary by the U.S.S.R. are examples of ventures which are incompatible with such values as the respect for human dignity. As long as certain Powers will continue to act in this way, international peace will be threatened; and if peace is constantly threatened, nothing valuable can be achieved by men in this, our world, let alone the risk of blowing it up once and for all.

This is why Tunisia considers that her first duty is to co-operate in maintaining peace everywhere in the world and support all forms of peaceful co-operation between all nations. Since she believes that the United Nations Organization is one of the best means to promote such co-operation, she favors a powerful United Nations Organization and backs its action everywhere.

As a former colonized nation, Tunisia stands for the principle of complete and total decolonization for all peoples. We back all nations still colonized—be they from Africa or any other continent. Opposition to colonialism is a question of human dignity which goes far beyond geography or race. Co-operation is certainly a better relationship than domination. No nation is entitled to rule another nation.

Another principle of our foreign policy, linked to the first two, is self-determination. We believe that liberty should be given to all peoples to freely choose their destiny. However, this liberty must be limited in order to prevent any fractioning, hence weakening, of former colonized nations. Thus Indonesia was weakened when it became separated from West Irian, as was nearly the case of Algeria and the Sahara. This principle of self-determination, extended to the limits of the former colonial administration, is one of the most important principles of our foreign policy. Should every nation comply with it, we would save a great deal of trouble in Africa, in Europe and elsewhere.

Another aspect of our foreign policy is non-alignment. We believe that the best way for the developing countries to work for peace and eliminate the Cold War is to abstain from being integrated militarily or politically into either of the two blocs which are challenging each other in pursuing our support. We do not say we are neutral, because complete neutrality is impossible. But we try to approve of this or that bloc in so far as it acts in accordance with highly acclaimed moral principles on one particular issue. Similarly, we might side with the other bloc on another issue. If it happens that one of the two blocs is, during a certain period, more often on the side of justice, we shall be more often on its side, without systematically supporting it on any issue. That is what we understand by non-alignment.

Last but not least, while standing for the rights of the individual, for peace and international co-operation, for decolonization and self-determination, for non-alignment, we try to keep the respect of all nations by the only weapons we have at hand: moderation, seriousness, good-will, good sense and loyalty to high principles, whatever the immediate consequence might be. These pragmatic efforts to avoid any excess, any extremism are essential to every young nation.

We are an African state but we do not feel like adopting a systematic "Africanism" directed toward the outside. We are an Arab country but we resent a certain kind of "Pan-Arabism" solely based on sentiment. We are geographically and philosophically close to Europe but we do not feel like adopting any of its political theories. We asked for self-determination for the Algerian people from France, our former adversary, but also for that of the Mauritanian people from Morocco, our closest friend. We share with the West certain values and high principles, but we condemned it on Suez. And if we condemned the East in Hungary, it is not out of a permanent policy, but rather because, in this particular case, the East denied any right of self-determination to the Hungarian people.

Always firm on principles, we seek a greater flexibility by reasonable concessions in the methods of carrying on our foreign policy in order to contribute constructively to peace and justice throughout the world.

NON-PERMANENT FACTORS

Political elements

Let us consider now the non-permanent factors of our foreign policy, those which existed when we gained our independence in March 1956, but the effects of which are likely to fade away in the more or less foreseeable future.

French troops in Tunisia While recognizing our full independence and sovereignty, France maintained a large number of troops on our national territory. These troops remained in Tunisia solely according to the right of force. They were stationed all over the country and behaved with the Tunisian population and authorities as if Tunisia had never become independent. There were nearly one hundred thousand troops while the Tunisian armed forces were practically non-existent. This was an ever-present threat to our national security, the more so because some French politicians were publicly saying that Tunisia should be reconquered, while local French officers were taking bold initiatives without the knowledge of their central government. There have been various developments since then, but until 1958 and again in 1961 and 1962, the troop situation was the most important element taken into consideration by the Tunisian government when formulating its foreign policy. One must add that Tunisia has always had the entire support of many democratic and liberal French statesmen, together with the overwhelming majority of French public opinion. This also was weighed in our decisions and policies.

The Algerian war The situation in Tunisia is linked to that in Algeria. Never was it more closely linked to it than in the early months of our independence. A war had been raging for one and a half years between the Algerian Nationalists and the French Army in Algeria. More than one hundred thousand Algerian refugees had by then poured into Tunisia across the Algerian borders. What is more important, about ten thousand Algerian freedom-fighters—far more men and much better armed than our national army—were stationed in Tunisia and, curiously enough, sometimes in the same town or village as the French soldiers. This explosive situation was aggravated progressively by the policy pursued by France in Algeria and its reaction on the Algerians who were pressing us to get into war with France in order to help them obtain their independence. The Algerian leaders, whether in Cairo or after they settled in Tunisia, were encouraged in this policy by the Egyptian government.

Friction with Egypt This brings us to another factor which had some weight around 1956. Since the negotiations for our internal autonomy and the cease-fire of 1954, the Egyptian Government had criticized us publicly, charging the Tunisian leaders with treason towards our Algerian brothers and the entire Arab world. Somehow, the Egyptian Government felt responsible for the welfare of the Tunisian people, as indeed of all the Arab people, without taking into consideration the fact that the Tunisian leaders, who had fought twenty-five years for the well-being of their people, were the best judges in the matter.

The public criticism by the Egyptians did not stop, even after we gained full independence without useless losses and after the Algerians admitted that a peaceful, independent Tunisia would better serve their cause than a fighting but non-sovereign state. As a matter of fact, Egypt was sheltering an important Tunisian extremist leader, Salah Ben Youssef, sentenced to death in absentia by a Tunisian tribunal for plotting against national peace and sovereignty. Therefore relations between Tunis and Cairo were in a state of permanent crisis. Egyptian radio broadcasts and propaganda and open encouragement of subversive action against Tunisian leaders, particularly against President Bourguiba, made matters worse. The difficulties with Egypt and the passivity of the other member-states of the Arab League had a profound impact on the young Tunisian nation which had longed for generations to orient itself towards the holy places where Islam and the Arab nation were born.

Relations with the Eastern and Western blocs

In 1956 most African countries were still under foreign domination. They had neither political power nor an international audience. Contacts and communications, if any, between the leaders and the masses of Africa were still very difficult. The most optimistic observers did not expect so soon the tremendous changes which were to bring political independence to most of the African nations in less than five years. Nobody foresaw in such a near future the importance of Africa in international affairs and particularly in the United Nations, and the emergence as a group of the young underdeveloped and poor nations of the world. Nobody realized that this group would have to be reckoned with whenever one considered the relationship between East and West.

What was the relationship of Tunisia with the West and the East in 1956? Tunisia won her independence thanks to the unflagging struggle she had been fighting against colonialism during many decades. But she was helped by the action of French liberals and the sympathy of French public opinion. Furthermore, once Tunisia became independent, she enjoyed the sympathy of the French Government and indeed of all the Western nations, particularly the United States.

Generally speaking, the relations were very good between Tunisia and the Western bloc as a whole. The Tunisian leaders were convinced that should some difficulty arise between Tunisia and France about the decolonialization process in Tunisia, the United States would be best-suited to help both parties solve their difference. The Tunisians thought that only a

powerful friend of France could prevail upon her to abide by her own pledges and the necessities of true decolonization. Only such a friend could handle the problem without hurting the good relations which existed between Tunisia and France and which both, and particularly Tunisia, needed badly.

On the other hand, the Tunisian leaders thought that Russia would not be very eager to intervene in any difference between Tunisia and France as Russia was then reluctant to support overtly the Algerian freedom fighters. The reason is that North Africa was considered in terms of world politics as a *"chasse-gardée* [sphere of exclusive influence]" for France. Russia believed that the weakening of French influence in North Africa would lead to American influence in the area, which would be worse, from the Russian point of view. Since they could not weaken the French influence for their own profit, they preferred to abstain from any initiative favorable to the interests of the peoples of North Africa, Tunisia in particular.

Add to the picture that the Tunisian Government and the people did not know much about the Russians, whom they considered a mysterious people living in a vast, remote country. By contrast, they had seen a lot of American and British soldiers during World War II. The travels made by Tunisians before independence to gain support and assistance made the Americans and the British seem familiar and somehow reliable people to the Tunisian officials.

These are the political elements the Tunisian leaders took into consideration once they had assumed responsibility for Tunisian foreign policy. Let us consider now what men and institutions influenced this policy.

The men and the institutions

The struggle for independence in Tunisia was led by the Neo Destour Party since its creation in 1934. Its founder, Habib Bourguiba, proved to be a dedicated, wise, clever and admired leader throughout the struggle. He was called by the Tunisian people "The Supreme Combatant" because of the statesmanship, loyalty and tenacity he displayed during the political or armed fighting as well as during the negotiations with France. Although he was not always unanimously followed, he was the only policy maker of the Neo Destour during the pre-independence period. Once independence was achieved, he became Prime Minister and when monarchy was abolished, he was elected as the first President of the Republic of Tunisia.

Constitutional provisions In theory, the Tunisian regime is a Presidential Republic having certain similarities with the United States system. One must bear in mind that in foreign policy, as in any other field, we are still in the experimental stage. Therefore it would not be quite correct to compare our institutions to those of a well-advanced nation. We adopted a formula which will be amended and changed little by little. The ultimate stage will be a full-fledged democracy adapted to our national characteristics and the aspirations of our people. A dynamic perspective is shaping up our institutions and the relationship between one institution to another, particularly as regards foreign policy.

Right after our independence, when the National Constituent Assembly was still drafting our constitution, Premier Habib Bourguiba (monarchy was not yet abolished) took the initiative of presenting the budget to the Assembly. He made a precedent in order to give to the first representatives ever elected by the people of Tunisia the sense of their responsibility and power. Later, certain articles of the constitution provided an embryo institutional procedure, as far as foreign policy is concerned. Articles 30, 43 and 49 read as follows:

Article 30: Permanent Committees will be elected from among the Deputies. They will remain in session constantly, even during the recess of the National Assembly.

Article 43: The President of the Republic shall draw up the general policy of the country and control its execution. He shall keep the National Assembly informed of the development of this policy. The President of the Republic shall choose the members of his Government, who shall be responsible to him. The President of the Republic may address the National Assembly in person or by message.

Article 49: The President of the Republic ratifies treaties, declares war and makes peace, with the agreement of the National Assembly.

We do not yet have a specialized committee for foreign affairs. The political committee takes care of them.

On the whole, there is a beginning of cooperation between the legislative and executive branches. During the formative period, President Bourguiba has not missed any occasion to address himself to the National Assembly or directly to the people to inform them and seek their support after they have considered the issue. Thus he is but continuing the methods of seeking popular participation and support, methods he used to apply during the struggle against colonialism. Presently, he enjoys such great prestige among the people and the members of the Government, because his ideas have so often proved accurate and convincing, that his decisions are always executed entirely and faithfully.

The result is that, owing to his legendary past, and to the powers granted him by the laws and by the people, President Bourguiba happens to be, roughly speaking, the only policy-maker in the Tunisian Government, although he may follow the advice given to him in Government sittings or party meetings. That is why, to fully understand the foreign policy practiced by Tunisia since its independence, one should try to discern what Bourguiba has been thinking since 1956, what his ideas were before independence and how they are likely to evolve.

Bourguiba's ideas   The very creation of the Neo Destour, which was the result of a split from the Destour Party in 1934, is a good example of one of the greatest qualities of Bourguiba: realism. The Destour had been formed by elements belonging to the upper class who did not have any contact with the people. They were learned, cultured persons who considered politics as a social and part-time activity designed to give them added prestige and authority in society. They were very jealous of the Tunisian cultural and social heritage and demanded too much from France while doing too little to have it granted. Bourguiba and the Neo Destour decided to reach and mobilize the masses, to do more and ask for less, at least at the beginning. He carried politics out of the social clubs and academic discussions of the well-to-do people to the masses who knew best the miseries of the Tunisian nation and were more eager to fight for their dignity and prosperity.

This realism was to guide him all the way throughout his political career. Sometimes it forced him to oppose intense but wrong sentimentality at home or abroad. On each of these occasions his prestige allowed him to impose his realism on a reluctant people against their sentiments. His reward was that a grateful people strengthened their confidence in him every time because his views were confirmed by facts. And he is likely to be followed indefinitely as long as facts confirm his predictions.

Another major quality of Bourguiba is his passionate love for the liberty of the individual and his inherent dislike for any kind of political doctrine based on oppression and domination. This was evident in the early 40's when he was released by the Axis Powers from a French jail and was given an enthusiastic reception by the Fascist authorities in Rome. They used every means to rally his support, at a time when most of the Tunisian people were sympathetic to the Axis Powers for having chased the French out of Tunisia. For, as the saying goes: "the enemy of my enemy is a friend to me." Nevertheless, Bourguiba resisted and sent to

Habib Thameur, one of his collaborators in Tunis, a message which later became famous urging the Neo Destour to work hand in hand with the Allies.

After World War II, this choice made by Bourguiba was emphasized and confirmed again and again in public statements endorsing the Western ideology with its principles of freedom and dignity of the individual. He expressed the greatest admiration for the French democrats and liberals, for the ideas of Woodrow Wilson after World War I, and those defended by Franklin D. Roosevelt during World War II, which led Roosevelt to promise to the Sultan during the war that Morocco would become independent. Nor did Bourguiba ever miss an opportunity to express his personal views on the ideology of the Eastern bloc and its methods.

He does not believe that the speeding of economic progress should be achieved by depriving the people of their fundamental liberties. He stated again and again that what gives the human being his superiority over other creatures, is that he puts "dignity before bread." The Tunisian people revolted against France, not because of the economic exploitation of the country and the people, but rather because she humiliated them in their individual dignity and national pride. Once national pride is restored through the recovery of sovereignty, the first thing to proclaim and keep from deterioration is the dignity of the citizen.

President Bourguiba does not think that the government should sacrifice the welfare of the living in order to build a better world for those who are not yet born. The government should take, in his view, equal care of the present generation and of the generations to come. Finally, he does not think that communism, which has already split into three different approaches in the U.S.S.R., Yugoslavia and China, is the only way for young nations to conquer underdevelopment.

President Bourguiba also believed very deeply in the friendship and the necessity of co-operation with France. His generosity and absence of bitterness toward a nation which had persecuted him for years is very well known. This attitude is the more remarkable because, for some time, it was not shared by the Tunisian people and the other leaders of the Neo Destour. It has always been condemned by the other Arab nations and their leaders who considered Bourguiba as too soft a nationalist. And last but not least, it has been often discouraged by French leaders when they were under the pressure of internal political necessities.

These are some of President Bourguiba's personal views on some problems, regardless of any political consideration. We shall see to what extent they inspired him in his dealings with France, the Arab and African countries, the East and the West. We shall wonder if he had to reconsider them under certain circumstances.

THE OBJECTIVES OF OUR FOREIGN POLICY

Now that we have seen what permanent and non-permanent factors have influenced Tunisian foreign policy from the start, let us examine what objectives the Tunisian leaders chose to give to their policy when they first assumed the responsibilities of government.

First, let us say that, unlike other countries, Tunisia has no traditional policy for many problems. As we shall see later, she is still far from having completed an adequate network of diplomatic representation throughout the world. Although inexperienced in formulating her policy, she has had to cope with the tremendous changes which are sweeping the whole of the African continent and staggering the traditional United Nations membership. Besides, she has not been on the international scene long enough to judge the accuracy of specific policies on the basis of their results.

Therefore, we can only examine here the past and present intentions of the Tunisian leaders. We shall then review some of the most important questions pertaining to regional or international issues, on which Tunisia adopted a clear-cut position. Then, perhaps we can try and find out what Tunisia did achieve, and what lessons she is learning from her past and present experience.

Independence and economic development
The most important objectives of our foreign policy are summarized in the first three operative paragraphs of the Preamble of our Constitution which read as follows:

> We, the Representatives of the Tunisian people . . .
> Proclaim, that these people, who have liberated themselves from foreign domination, thanks to their solidarity and to their struggle against tyranny, exploitation and retrogression, are determined:
> . . . on strengthening national unity and upholding human principles, accepted among peoples who safeguard human dignity, justice and freedom and who work for peace and progress and for free co-operation between nations,
> . . . on remaining true to the teachings of Islam, to the ideal of a Union of the Great Maghreb, to their membership in the Arab family, to their co-operation with the African peoples in building a better future and to all peoples struggling for justice and freedom . . .

This means that one of our immediate objectives was to make France realize the consequences of her recognizing our independence. We had to take over every sort of authority within the country and outside. We had to exercise all police and defense responsibilities. French colonial occupation had to be ended so that we might control every parcel of our national territory. This may seem to go without saying. Unfortunately it did not appear so obvious and logical to France and we are still fighting for it.

The second objective was and still is the struggle against underdevelopment in all its implications. One of the nationalist leaders' slogan was "dignity before bread." This was before we won independence. Once independence was achieved, even though not quite completely, people began to think that bread is rather important too. They expected that their own leaders would bring them a prosperity which the colonial rulers had failed to bring. As a matter of fact, the leaders tried to meet these aspirations. They considered that independence is not an end in itself but a means to achieve freedom and dignity for the individual and prosperity for all.

They knew they could count on the enthusiasm of the people and the resources of the country. But they also knew that nothing could be achieved without a great amount of foreign assistance in capital and technicians. So the whole problem was to devise a proper foreign policy which would attract foreign assistance without jeopardizing the sovereignty and security of the country.

Co-operation for peace To be "true to the ideal of the Union of the Great Maghreb" could be interpreted as paving the way for unity by helping the Algerians win their independence and by co-operating with Morocco. The "belonging to the Arab family" and the "co-operation with African peoples" are general objectives, without specific implications. But they are clear enough to show the general direction Tunis is committed to follow in light of the changes which are occurring in the Middle East, and the revolution which is staggering the African continent.

In 1956, the Tunisian leaders also had the great ambition to make Tunisia a model among the young nations. It was hoped that she would set an example through the progressive methods she has been using to gain independence, build a modern state and conquer underdevelopment, while keeping good relations with every Eastern and Western nation, including France, the former colonizer of Tunisia. We were determined to do all we could to have this method—which we call "Bourguibaism"—

succeed so that it could be profitably used by others.

But our main objective in the international field has always been to help promote peace, understanding and co-operation between all the nations of the world. This is as vital for small Tunisia as for the U.S.A. or the U.S.S.R. And we do believe that Tunisia or any other small country can do as much for international peace as either of the two leaders of the world.

Whether it be over Berlin or disarmament, over Red China or Cuba, over the Congo or the United Nations, any difference which arises between the two blocs is based on distrust in the first place. And this is where small, uncommitted nations can play a great part in having the two parties take into consideration the wishes of the majority of the nations of the world. For none but these weak, disarmed nations can fully express the sincere and deep anxiety of mankind while the two Super-Powers are consciously and methodically preparing for a third world war which, they know, is likely to be the last deed of men on earth.

Limitations

These are the main objectives of our foreign policy. Before we see how these general principles have been translated into a day to day policy applied to particular cases, let us examine what were and still are the limitations to our endeavors.

The limitations spring from the fact that Tunisia is a young, small and underdeveloped country. To properly carry on a policy, a country needs able men working within a well-organized administration, and a wide representation throughout the world. Unfortunately, we faced and are still facing difficulties in these three domains.

When Tunisia became independent, it had comparatively many able and experienced men to take over some of the responsibilities previously shouldered by the French civil servants. Our needs being smaller than those of similar countries, we thought that it would make our problems easier to solve. This was not the case. From the moment they had a Tunisian boss and a few Tunisian colleagues, a great number of French civil servants quit their jobs, while in other countries they stayed because their bosses and most of their colleagues remained French. That made our task more difficult, even though our needs were less demanding. Having to face the sudden departure of French civil servants in all our departments, we had difficulties finding able people to work in a brand new department, created over-night, where all the civil servants had to be Tunisian. It is one thing to create a foreign service when it becomes a historic necessity and to develop it little by little, taking generations to form an elite to run it. It is quite another thing to try and create such a service over-night in a world where foreign politics are dominating the life of the nation, and where other countries have developed a formidable, complex machine to take care of their relations with the rest of the world.

People who have not lived through such an experience can hardly imagine the difficult administrative problems the young nations are facing, which in turn hinder their efficiency in formulating and properly carrying on their foreign policy. Tunisia was not among the lucky countries whose independence had been decided long ahead by the colonial Power and whose diplomats were training in that Power's embassies until they were able to fly on their own. It will take us many years to have a perfect instrument. Until then, our objectives are more difficult to define and to attain.

Another limitation comes from the fact that we cannot afford to be as fully represented as we would wish. Six years after independence, we had diplomatic representation in only a very small number of countries. And in those countries our staff was very small. For instance, we had only two ambassadors in the whole Western Hemisphere. One was accredited to the United States and Mexico, the other to the United Nations and Canada. Apart from Mexico, we had no accredited representative nor even an office in the whole Latin-American continent. And the whole United States was supposed to be covered by a staff of five officers in Washington, D.C.!

We are about to open new embassies in Africa, south of the Sahara, but in 1962, we were represented only in Accra, Leopoldville, and Dakar. Not until 1960 did we open an embassy in Moscow. And we had no diplomatic mission in the whole Asian continent in 1962! Financial difficulties were keeping us from any diplomatic contact with the overwhelming majority of the Afro-Asian countries with which we have so much in common.

PRESENT FOREIGN POLICIES

Now that we have discussed the factors which are influencing our foreign policy, its objectives and limitations, let us examine the stand Tunisia took on some of the most important issues she had to consider since she became independent.

France

During the first years of our independence our foreign policy was, of course, dominated by our relations with France. Our attitude towards France was defined long before we won independence, during the very struggle that led to it. In the darkest hours of colonialism, we always realized that, should we become independent, we would have to share many things with France in the political, economic and cultural fields. Therefore we never wanted to jeopardize the future good relationship between our two countries. We tried to progress step by step, asking only for reasonable changes. Unfortunately, the French attitude compelled us to abandon negotiations and use violence.

Reforms before independence Before independence, any true reform attempted by a Resident General was stopped by the French settlers in Tunis and the North African lobby in Paris. This was the case for the policies advocated by Mr. Armand Guillon in the mid-thirties and Mr. Louis Perillier in the early fifties. During the latter's proconsulate, the Neo Destour Party even agreed to participate in the government. This was of no help. The nationalist movement tried then to mobilize international public opinion, but France would not abide by the wishes of the majority at the United Nations. She did not even recognize that organization's right to discuss the matter. Then the Bey of Tunis endorsed the nationalist thesis and asked for reforms which would lead Tunisia to autonomy. But France, after having rejected the request of the true representatives of the people and that of world public opinion, ignored the plea of the legal ruler of Tunisia. There was no other solution than armed struggle against France which the national movement decided to embark upon and undertook with success.

Such a struggle is common to all nationalist movements. What distinguishes the leaders of Tunisia is that they became the champions of a progressive decolonialization which would save many human lives and promote a stable young nation with the agreement and support of the former colonial Power. Although the leaders remained firm on principles, their attitude was not always understood in Tunisia and abroad.

As soon as Tunisian autonomy was recognized by the French Government, in July 1954, Bourguiba, speaking of Mendès-France's offer said:

These proposals are a substantial and decisive step toward the restoration of the complete sovereignty of Tunisia. Independence remains the ideal of the Tunisian people, but the progress towards this ideal will no longer be achieved through a struggle between the Tunisian people and France. It will be achieved through

amendments and adjustments between the French and the Tunisian Governments in mutual confidence and renewed friendship.[1]

Full independence was to be granted to Tunisia on March 20, 1956.

Major difficulties in Franco-Tunisian affairs Throughout the long struggle for independence, Habib Bourguiba had been, as Félix Garras, a French writer and journalist, wrote:

a loyal adversary. He never gave up believing in France, the friendship of which he pursued unflaggingly. His achievements are evidence that between colonialism and an impossible holy war, there is room for a modern policy of free co-operation, a word he shouted as a challenge at a time when revolt and despair were supreme.[2]

Co-operation was what Tunisia offered to France. In order to make it possible, the Government guaranteed the total and complete security of the French population in Tunisia. Economic and cultural ties were kept or even strengthened. We even accepted the provision that the French army should remain in Tunisia for a certain time.

There were two main problems in our relations with France: the complete decolonization of Tunisia, and the Algerian war; these two questions were linked together. First the Algerian war: On November 1, 1954, the Algerian nationalists started a liberation war against France. The Tunisians had then already stopped fighting against the French. They were engaged in a series of negotiations in order to gain full independence. During the negotiations, 15,000 French troops were placed along the Tunisian side of the Tunisian-

---

[1] Quoted in Félix Garras, *Bourguiba et la Naissance d'une Nation,* Paris: Juilliard, 1956, p. 255.

[2] *Ibid.,* p. 281.

Algerian border to prevent any infiltration of the freedom fighters and their arms from Tunisia to Algeria. Although the Algerians were far from having their full strength and organization, these French troops were not able to stop such border crossings.

When Tunisia became independent, she did not have more than 3,000 men to watch the border, a force which was not even enough to deal with whatever smuggling might occur. So it was materially impossible to keep Tunisia strictly neutral in the Algerian war. We believe it was also morally impossible and politically undesirable.

The Tunisians and the Algerians are one and the same people. They share the same language, religion and civilization; they suffered from the same colonial domination. Many Algerians have lived for generations in the Tunisian area along the border. The Tunisians could not humanly forbid the Algerian fighters to use their soil for transit. It would have meant treachery to their own people and denial of their own struggle. No government would have even thought of doing so, the more so because the French were occupying large areas of Tunisia and using them for strategic purposes in their military action against the Algerians.

Politically, it would have been a mistake not to help the Algerians: they would have sought help from other countries much more inclined to extremes and much less friendly to France and the West than Tunisia. This would have jeopardized the future of a united Maghreb linked to France, a combination long desired by the Tunisians and often mentioned by President Bourguiba in public.

France never completely accepted our point of view. She understood our difficulties, she appreciated the efforts we were making to maintain peace for the French troops, and security for the French citizens, but she still was unhappy about what she called "our interference in her internal affairs." President Bourguiba said in a public speech in August 1957:

> Therefore none should feel privileged to trouble peace and tranquillity in our Republic . . . Because of the desperate, ferocious war they have to wage against the very adversary which was ruling Tunisia—French colonialism—our Algerian brothers should understand that Tunisia, an independent nation, has the right and the duty to express to them her solidarity. But she cannot admit that they consider her territory as an operational zone, or a base for launching attacks against the French forces.[3]

On the other hand, not one French citizen living in Tunisia has ever been hurt by an Algerian or a Tunisian. As a matter of fact, even after the incident of Sakiet which we shall consider in a moment, the Tunisian people and Algerian freedom fighters in Tunisia remained quiet, thus abiding by the request President Bourguiba directed to them on February 8, 1958:

> I ask you to keep calm, to assure the security of the territory, and not to forget that we all are responsible for the lives and properties of the French people living in our country. Our dispute is with France and the French Army, not with the French citizens who live here. And this applies to other foreigners.[4]

The ideas expressed by Bourguiba were put into facts as soon as we became independent. We did our best to keep the country out of the war. We believe France could not reasonably ask for more. But there were some political leaders in Paris and some French officers in Tunisia and Algeria who did not forgive us our attitude towards the Algerian freedom fighters and who were even thinking of the reconquest of Tunisia. This led to a great many incidents along the Algerian border. French troops, crossing the border, began to organize daily

[3] See Tunisian daily papers of August 14, 1957.
[4] *Ibid.*, February 9, 1958.

raids in Tunisia which resulted in human losses and property damages.

Sometimes these attacks were even made by French troops stationed in Tunisia. This was the case in July 1956 at Thelepte, in southwest Tunisia. After having attacked the Algerian freedom fighters stationed nearby, the French troops ferociously repressed the Tunisian population in the whole area. For them, Tunisians and Algerians were alike, so much so, indeed, that on February 8, 1958, a Tunisian village, Sakiet Sidi Youssef, was bombed by French planes on a market day, killing one hundred Tunisian civilians, among whom 80 per cent were old people, women and children.

These are some of the problems which Tunisia had to face in connection with the Franco-Algerian war. We Tunisians have been caught in a very awkward situation, as President Bourguiba said "between the French, our friends, and the Algerians, our brothers." We could not possibly do more than keep Tunisia at peace and appeal to both parties, as did President Bourguiba in July 1956 when he said:

I appeal to the Algerians and the French to respect the autonomy and the sovereignty of Tunisia. Until the problem of the French troops in Tunisia is solved, the Tunisian Government will firmly work to keep in Tunisia an atmosphere of peace and security.[5]

And yet, France was not satisfied. She took exception to our position in the Algerian affair and cut out, in May 1957, the economic assistance ($45,700,000 yearly) she was prepared to give to an independent Tunisia for willingness to keep in common with France a customs union and a currency parity. She grew also more and more reluctant to sell us the very small quantity of arms we needed for our police and growing army, and finally re-

[5] Secretary of State for Information, "La bataille de l'evacuation," March 1, 1959, p. 14.

fused altogether to deliver them. At the same time, she put heavy and effective pressure on Belgium to refuse to sell us anything, and Italy to deny its own promise to sell us arms. And when we asked the United States and the United Kingdom, France made clear and public her position: nobody should interfere between her and Tunisia. This position constituted an infringement on our national sovereignty, which leads us to my second point.

Complete decolonization

Since the first day of our independence, France tried by every means to keep an exclusive bilateral relationship with Tunisia, which she continued to consider as a kind of protectorate. She did not want any nation, even an ally, to give us economic assistance, to deliver arms to us, to support us politically. When we asked for an international contingent to blockade the Tunisian-Algerian border and thus do away with all our common problems, she publicly refused because she considered this an interference in her affairs.

It is of interest to recall the protocol signed in March 1956 between Tunisia and France:

The two Governments recognize that the peaceful harmonious development of Franco-Tunisian relations accords with the necessities of the modern world. They notice with satisfaction that this evolution allows the accession to full sovereignty without any suffering for the people or disturbance for the State. They assert their conviction that, by basing their relations on full mutual respect of their sovereignties and the independence and equality of both States, France and Tunisia are strengthening the solidarity which unites them for the benefit of both.

After the inaugural address by the President of the French Government and the answer of His Highness, the Bey, reasserting their common will to promote their relations in the same spirit of peace and friendship, the two Governments opened negotiations in Paris in February 1957.

Consequently:

France solemnly recognizes the independence of Tunisia and agrees

A) That the treaty concluded between France and Tunisia on May 12, 1881 cannot regulate Franco-Tunisian relations;

B) That those dispositions of the June 3, 1955 Conventions[6] which would be in contradiction with the new status of Tunisia as an independent and sovereign State, will be amended or abrogated.

Likewise France accepts:

C) The exercise by Tunisia of her responsibilities in matters of Foreign Affairs, Security and Defense as well as the constitution of a Tunisian National Army.

With respect to their sovereignties, France and Tunisia agree to define or complete the modalities of a freely achieved interdependence between the two countries, by organizing their co-operation in the fields where their interests are common, particularly defense and foreign relations.

The agreements between France and Tunisia will establish the modalities of the assistance France will grant to Tunisia in the creation of the Tunisian National Army.

The negotiations will resume on April 16, 1956, in order to conclude, as soon as possible and according to the principles stated herein, the agreements necessary to their application.

As one can see, this was a clear and definite recognition of Tunisia as an independent sov-

ereign state. No treaty of any kind was binding Tunisia to France. Free negotiations were to open on an equal basis, to try and work out plans for co-operation. It may be fastidious to go back to this document more than five years after we gained our independence. The fact is that, unbelievable though it may appear, France is not yet willing to accept the consequences of our independence. Many signs have made it clear that she was and still is thinking of Tunisia in terms of colonizer and colonized, or at least with a paternalistic approach.

Why French troops remained in Tunisia

From the start, the French Government publicly stated that the continuing occupation of Tunisia by the French army was considered as a condition for granting independence to Tunisia. They gave three reasons for this theory, but no legal justification. The reasons were as follows: (1) The French army should stay in Tunisia in order to cover Algeria, strategically. One may easily guess what the Tunisians thought of this reason, considering that the conquest of Tunisia in 1881 was likewise undertaken to "cover Algeria." (2) The French army should stay in Tunisia to protect French citizens living there. This made one wonder which authority was in charge in Tunisia, not to mention the fact that no Frenchman, indeed no foreigner, has ever needed any special kind of protection. (3) The French army should stay in Tunisia until the two Parties (France and Tunisia) had agreed that the Tunisian army was capable of defending the Tunisian territory. Thus France would be the only judge of whether the Tunisian army was fit for its mission while, at the very same time, France refused to help us to build it.

One can easily imagine that, under these conditions, no negotiation and no co-operation were possible between France and Tunisia. The only way left to us was political and diplomatic pressure. The only prospect for the relationship between the two countries was gradual deterioration.

For more than two years, the French forces occupied Tunisia, controlling the borders, ar-

---

[6] By the Conventions of June 1955, France had granted internal autonomy to Tunisia.

resting Tunisian citizens and foreign diplomats, jeopardizing peace and defying Tunisian local and national authorities. One might also mention the daily incidents the French army stationed in Tunisia or Algeria was provoking on the Tunisian territory, incidents which caused continuous losses in Tunisian property and human lives.

This lasted until the incident of Sakiet in February 1958. Then the pressure of world public opinion and the good offices of the United States and the United Kingdom caused France, after an internal revolution and the ascendancy of General de Gaulle, to evacuate most, but not all, of the Tunisian territory. This was in June, 1958. Then, as always, France had given up too late. Our rights were recognized only after the Sakiet-Sidi-Youssef incident, added to many others, had destroyed confidence and made co-operation doubtful.

Economic grievances This co-operation was to receive more severe blows from France in the economic field. As mentioned earlier, for political reasons France cut her economic assistance to Tunisia in May 1957, although it had been a consideration in return for certain privileges we were giving France in the economic field: we belonged to the Franc Zone, leaving to France the control of our share in foreign currency and aligning our currency with the French franc. This meant that France was actually controlling our foreign exchange. She could also impose upon us any devaluation of her own currency, such devaluation being decided according to her exclusive interest and internal policy. Besides, we belonged to the same customs area as France, being thus compelled to apply the French customs policy, regardless of the fact that our interests might be contradictory. As a matter of fact, they are clashing in most cases. Despite our political independence, France kept the economic relationship unchanged. She opposed our efforts and did not even try to placate us.

In 1957 the French Government decided to devaluate the franc, the fifth manipulation affecting the franc since 1945. This time the main reason was political, connected with the war in Algeria. Tunisia was merely "informed" of this measure, which had a profound impact on her economy. French officials said at that time that Tunisia considered the advantages and disadvantages of the operation and decided to follow France's lead. The truth is that we were put before a *fait accompli*. We had not been consulted, we had no other currency than the franc, we lacked the technicians and the means necessary for an autonomous conduct of our economic and financial affairs. These reasons made us follow a measure disastrous for our economy and dangerous for our political sovereignty; but the lesson was not lost. We created a national bank and issued a currency of our own, the dinar, which was worth one thousand French francs.

Two months after we issued the dinar, France once again devaluated the franc without consulting us. This started an economic crisis between France and Tunisia which, like the political crisis following the bombing of Sakiet, was to pull Tunisia a little further away from France. Tunisia refused to follow a devaluation which was determined only by the French internal situation. The attitude of France, and the failure to reach an agreement with her on common economic problems she had ignored for so long, led the Tunisian Government to retire from the Customs Union dominated by France. This withdrawal became effective in August 1959. From then on, we fixed our customs duties and organized our foreign exchange on the sole basis of our interest and according to our own economic structures.

Here again, France did her best to keep us in a dependent position, accepting under pressure and often too late, measures which could have been the basis of true co-operation. But the worst was still to come. After the bombing of Sakiet, President Bourguiba said in an interview:

I do not know if co-operation [between Tunisia and France] is still possible. Of all the countries Tunisia could co-operate with, France is the one with which it would be the most natural. I shall continue to hope for such co-operation. But for the present, I am no longer confident.[7]

The occupation of Bizerte After Bizerte, little room was left even for hope. When the French evacuated most of the territory in June 1958, it was decided that negotiations should start right after the evacuation was completed to settle the problem of Bizerte. But France never wanted to enter into negotiations. She stayed in Bizerte by virtue of her military strength. Once more, it was evident that the French were thinking in different terms than the Tunisians. When they said we were a protectorate, we actually were a directly administered colony little different from Algeria or Senegal, for instance. Between 1954 and 1956, what they called "internal autonomy" was a kind of protectorate and what they called full independence was similar to a grant of internal autonomy. They never wanted to give up. President Bourguiba said in this respect, on July 17, 1961, on the eve of the Bizerte drama:

> I have repeated over and over again that, as far as France is concerned, the recognition of independence does not bring the struggle for independence to an end. Other powers repress the nationalist movement for some time; but as soon as they have granted independence, they accept all its consequences and thus put an end to the conflict. But France, the country of Descartes, disregards this elementary logic.[8]

Indeed, France disregarded this simple fact so much that, more than six years after our independence, the colonial occupation was still in effect in Bizerte—a naval base with complete extra-territorial status—and along our southern border.

The Tunisian Government never missed an opportunity to ask for negotiations. The French position can be summarized as follows: Peace is threatened and there is danger of war in the world. Tunisia feels solidarity with the Free World and is devoted to the principles of liberty, but nevertheless there are no agreements in existence which tie her down to the West. In these conditions, France cannot feel secure. In order to be prepared for a war which might break out any time, her defense and her security make it necessary for her to stay in Bizerte. Moreover, France has commitments towards the Free World. Staying in Bizerte safeguards the West of which Tunisia herself is a staunch friend.

Thus France was basing her claim to stay in our country by force of arms on the fact that we support the West, to which she belongs. She was forgetting that the reason why we felt respect and solidarity with the West was precisely because it claimed to be founded on the respect and dignity of peoples, on their independence and liberty. And it is worth noting that the NATO Powers, consulted one by one, have made it clear that with the latest developments in armaments and strategy conceptions and with the proximity of bases in southern France and Italy, Bizerte was not essential either to France or to NATO.

By the end of June 1961, the military authorities at Bizerte seemed to want not only to overlook our will but to aggravate the situation by extending the airstrips outside the limits of the base. President Bourguiba sent a message to President de Gaulle by special messenger, thus showing the importance he gave to the matter. He wrote in this message:

> . . . I wish to state again that as far as we are concerned, we want to act so that what is today a matter of dispute will be in the future the starting point of a free and fruitful co-operation between our two countries.
>
> Mr. President, you have yourself stressed enough how "intolerable it

[7] Interview published by the Tunisian Secretary of State for Information.

[8] Speech before the National Assembly. See Tunisian daily papers of July 18, 1961.

is for a state to have its destiny decided by the action and decision of another state, however friendly it might be," to easily understand our feelings and our decision.

He ended the message by saying:

The man who has also given the best of himself to restore the independence of his country and who wishes, on his part, to dedicate his last efforts to the recovery of his homeland, to its progress and prosperity, adjures you to save our two countries from new and useless trials.[9]

But all that was in vain. President de Gaulle did not even answer that message. While the Tunisian population was manifesting its feelings in the streets of Bizerte, the French sent paratroopers to reinforce the base, ignoring a solemn statement by the Tunisian Government forbidding the overflight of our national territory.

Armed conflict and its aftermath At 5:30 P.M. on July 19, 1961, Tunisian troops fired the first warning shots at a French aircraft flying over our territory. The shots did not harm anyone, since France had seen to it that we did not have adequate anti-aircraft armament. As everyone knows, the reaction was very quick. In three days, the French troops occupied the whole area, destroying the city of Bizerte and killing more than two thousand persons, mostly civilians.

Tunisia asked the Security Council to meet on July 21st. The Security Council voted a resolution urging a cease-fire and withdrawal of all the French troops to the positions of July 19th. The French Government declared publicly its refusal to comply with the Security Council resolution. Then President Bourguiba invited the U.N. Secretary General, Mr. Ham-

marskjöld, to come to Tunis and visit Bizerte, which he did. But France refused to co-operate with him, and charged him with complicity with Tunisia.

The second meeting of the Security Council could not reach any decision, mainly because of the support given to France by the Western member states. A special meeting of the General Assembly was then held—France did not attend this meeting—during which a resolution was voted (by 66–0, with 30 abstentions) which noted "with regret" that France did not abide by the decision of the Security Council, recognized that France was violating Tunisian sovereignty and asked both parties to enter into negotiations in order to reach an agreement on the evacuation of French troops from Tunisia. But this did not bring any change in the attitude of France who continued to defy the highest moral principles as well as the public opinion of the whole world. Several weeks later, France agreed finally to withdraw her troops within the limits of the base and to evacuate whatever territory she had occupied after July 19, 1961. But her troops are still in the base.

In December 1961 in Rome, and January 1962 in Paris, we made two further attempts to solve the Bizerte problem through negotiations. These efforts remained fruitless until a few months later, when France began to evacuate the southernmost part of the base. Then in July 1962 during a new meeting in Paris, the French Government gave the impression that it really wished the Bizerte problem to be solved. Consequently, the two countries resumed their diplomatic relations and negotiations. Only the future will tell what will come out of these last developments.

A consequence of the Bizerte crisis among others was that the French Government, for political reasons, detained the French teachers who were under contract with the Tunisian Government for several weeks. This delayed the start of the academic year, due to the large place the French language is occupying in our schools and colleges. We saw no reason to mix culture with politics and to deal with the cultural relations the same way we dealt with the

[9] Message of July 6, 1961. See *Jeune Afrique*, No. 40, July 17th, 1961.

political or economic relations. But this is not the French point of view. The result is that we may feel compelled to change our educational policy in the future so as to keep us from any dependence on France in this respect. Thus the last possibility of co-operation between our two countries may be wrecked by the anachronistic neo-colonial policy France has been practicing in Tunisia since our independence was proclaimed.

I have discussed our relations with France at length because they are by far the most essential for us. They condition our very existence as a free and independent nation. They are influencing our relations with the other countries of the Maghreb and the Arab world. The policy France has been pursuing in Tunisia will also have a great impact on the African countries, and on the attitude of these countries and particularly Tunisia towards the East and the West.

I have tried to show how our relations with France have been steadily deteriorating throughout the years mainly because of the war in Algeria and the French policy in Tunisia. Now that Algeria has gained independence and France's policy seems to change in Tunisia, things might change. But now, the choice might not be that of Tunisia alone. It might be that of the whole, integrated Maghreb.

Maghreb

This brings us to my second point: the policy of Tunisia towards her sister nations of the Maghreb.

I have already said that geography, history, religion and solidarity against the same colonialism are factors of unity for the nations of the Maghreb. This unity is more and more considered an economic necessity at a time when even the well-advanced European nations are integrating into a large economic ensemble which is already trying to have at least part of Africa under its economic control.

Algerian independence   The first step towards unity was, of course, the emerging of Algeria as an independent state. In this matter, both Tunisia and Morocco helped the Algerians a great deal. The Algerian Provisional Government and more than twenty thousand Algerian freedom fighters were stationed in Tunisia which was also sheltering nearly 150,000 Algerian refugees. Tunisia missed no chance to support the Algerian cause through the usual diplomatic channels, at the United Nations and by other means.

In October 1956, the King of Morocco, Mohammed V, flew to Tunis for a conference with President Bourguiba and the Algerian leaders to make a common offer to France as regards Algeria and the whole Maghreb. This conference could not take place because the French authorities in Algeria highjacked the Moroccan plane which was taking the Algerian leaders from Rabat to Tunis, as guests of Mohammed V, and arrested them.

Sixteen months later, in April 1958, a conference took place in Tangier between leaders of the three major political parties: the New-Destour (Tunisia), the Algerian National Liberation Front (Algeria) and the Istiqlal (Morocco). In their final resolution, they recommended the formation of an Algerian Government in exile which was to be known as G.P.R.A. Among other decisions, they also recommended the eventual establishment of a North African Federation.

As one may suppose, the decisions taken in Tangier could not be carried out until and unless Algeria was independent. Nevertheless, they showed the spirit in which the leaders of the Maghreb were foreseeing their common future. A treaty of friendship, co-operation and mutual assistance signed between Tunisia and Libya in February 1957 and a similar one signed between Tunisia and Morocco in March of the same year were further evidence of this spirit.

But Algerian independence remained Tunisia's first preoccupation. In a speech he made before the Congress of the Neo Destour at Sousse in 1959, President Bourguiba urged France to practice decolonization by putting an end to the war in Algeria. On another occasion, President Bourguiba went so far as to offer France to stay in Bizerte with his consent, should she consider to bring the Algerian war to an end. When he paid a state visit to France in February 1961, an important part of his conversation with President de Gaulle was about Algeria.

It was in conformance with our general policy to urge the settlement of peace anywhere in the world. But, naturally, to us, the Algerian war was a matter of gravest concern. It threatened our country more than once as shown by the bombing of Sakiet in February 1958, innumerable border incidents, and French aggression on Bizerte in July 1961. We endured this tragedy side by side with our Algerian brothers who were always supported by the unsparing efforts of President Bourguiba. From the war was born a spirit of solidarity and bonds of intimate friendship were forged.

The French-Algerian agreements—signed at Evian on April 19, 1962—and the emergence of Algeria to independence represent the outcome of a policy of wisdom forever preached by President Bourguiba. It was obvious that the French army would never succeed in subduing a whole people united in the same struggle. It was equally obvious that the Army of National Liberation could not, militarily and without external assistance, break down the highly trained, potentially superior French troops. Wisdom was to acknowledge these facts.

Besides legally terminating the conflict, the cease-fire agreements and the independence of Algeria also constitute the prelude to close co-operation between the French and the Algerians. The first manifestations of this co-operation were the combined efforts of both the French and the Algerians to crush the fanatic extremists of the OAS and negotiate solutions to the problems facing an independent Algeria.

Today, Tunisia is the first to rejoice over the independence of Algeria; indeed, peace at our borders means for the people of Tunisia the end of a tragedy, the disappearance of a permanent threat and, we hope, the beginning of

an era of stability in which we can devote the best of our efforts and resources to the task of renovation which Tunisia has assigned to herself. We were longing intensely for this decolonization era. It will mean, above all, an era of co-operation between France and the three North African countries.

Obstacles to unity　　This co-operation will be beneficial to all concerned but mostly to France whose interests will be guaranteed and, beyond France, to the Free World which is mortally torn between the principles it proclaims and the policies applied by some of its members, policies forcing other members to a passive attitude which has been interpreted by the victims involved as a sign of complicity. This contradiction was bound to serve the purposes of the enemies of the Free World, and they used it as a ready-made freely furnished argument.

Now that Algeria is independent, the problem of building a "Great Maghreb" (Tunisia, Algeria, Morocco and, we feel, Libya and Mauritania) is getting closer to its solution. This does not mean it is going to be solved in a few months or even in a few years. It would be more realistic to think that its solution will need another generation.

Young North Africans who have not yet reached their teens will grow up with the idea of unity. To them, it will not be psychologically difficult to relinquish some of the attributes of one entity's independence for the sake of a larger entity: namely a North African ensemble, the Maghreb.

There is, at the present time, a problem between Mauritania and Morocco. Mauritania, a former French colony, has been granted independence by France although her territory was claimed by Morocco as an integral part of Moroccan national territory. All the Arab countries supported Morocco in her claim, all but Tunisia which recognized the Islamic Republic of Mauritania. This brought a crisis between Morocco and Tunisia. Our position is that, since the Mauritanians are not willing to be a part of Morocco, then by virtue of the right to self-determination, they should form their own state. Our policy has never been "to support our brother right or wrong" but to support justice even against our brother if need be. Furthermore, we understand the Maghreb to be a group of peoples who are willing to build their union out of free choice. Mauritania, an Arab Moslem country, should be able to decide her own destiny and her integration into the Maghreb.

In fact, the Mauritania incident did not have a lasting impact on Tunisian-Moroccan relations because we have so much in common and we stand to gain so much by getting even closer to one another. We cannot afford tension between us. We also feel that all the problems involving demarcation of frontiers and related to the North-African Sahara will be settled in a spirit of friendship and co-operation and in the light of the "Maghrebian Idea."

Arab world

Similar dreams are linking the Tunisian people to the other Arab nations. Language, religion, a brilliant past, these are what ties Tunisia to the Arabic Middle East. Before independence, our nationalist leaders made of Arabism a weapon against the assimilating forces of colonialism. The very persons who struggled against fanaticism and introduced reforms in the Islamic traditions of independent Tunisia, had been encouraging any form of conservatism while fighting against the French influence. Thus they were the first to bring Tunisia closer to her Arab-Moslem heritage.

When the Tunisians stopped fighting against the French and started negotiating, their attitude was resented by most of the Arab countries. These countries condemned our moderation. They could not understand our attitude towards France, let alone our so-called treason against our Algerian brothers. They went on criticizing us even when we definitely gained our full independence and even when the Algerian leaders moved to Tunis, thus approving of our way in helping them.

When we entered the Arab League in October 1958, we found that the League was not able to solve the difference we then had with the U.A.R. Consequently, apart from rare occasions, we abstained for some time from attending its meetings. This is by no means a denial of our belonging to the Arab world. As a matter of fact, most of our problems are solved by now, due to changing attitudes within the League. But we are still adhering to the three conditions for efficient work stated by President Bourguiba in October 1958, when we first entered the League: (1) Between brothers, as in any other circumstances, no co-operation is fruitful without the respect of personal dignity and mutual interest. (2) No Arab leader can better judge the situation of an Arab state than the very leaders of that state. And (3) interference in the internal affairs of another state should be avoided.

In spite of all that may happen, we cannot forget the assistance the Arab nations gave us during our struggle against colonialism. We cannot forget their support during one of our most painful hours: the Bizerte crisis which was an occasion for us to see who, among all the nations, were indeed our friends when we were in need. Therefore, although we believe more strongly in the Maghreb than in a huge Arab state that would stretch from Morocco to Iraq, we are determined to work, whenever we are given a fair chance, for the strengthening of Arab solidarity and co-operation.

Africa

Until recently, if one wanted to go from Tunis to Accra, the quickest way was first to go northward to Paris or London, and then southward to Accra. There was no direct service between these two cities, or between many other places on the whole African continent. This gives an idea of the barriers which existed between African countries which opened only towards Europe. Hence, the first problem to be solved by any new African country is to grow familiar with the other countries, and know their people and understand their problems. There is a real need for true friendship and solidarity.

Tunisia is trying to satisfy this need in three ways: (1) Through our embassies in Africa, although, as I said earlier, our representation in Africa is still very insufficient. Pending the creation of new posts, we are multiplying our visiting missions which visit whole areas from time to time, thus keeping permanent contacts. (2) Through the many meetings, seminars and conferences, some of which we sponsored and organized. Among these we may cite "The Conference of the African Independent States," "The All-African People's Conference" which gathers representatives of political parties, trade unions, women's and youth organizations from all the African countries, independent or not; and trade union, youth and women's congresses. (3) Last, but not least, this need is satisfied through the different delegations to the United Nations where among the Afro-Asian delegations an African group is emerging as a distinctive entity.

The more we know the other African countries, the more we are convinced of the similarities of our problems and the necessity to harmonize our policies inside Africa and outside. That is why we do not approve of the creation of some groups—such as the Casablanca group, Monrovia group, Brazzaville group—which, while claiming to have similar views, contend that they are different from those of the rest of the continent. We aim at a larger universality. We think that Africa is bound to achieve it when all the African nations are emancipated and when they find out that in other parts of the world and particularly in Europe, peoples with much greater differences than ours are trying to unite to be stronger in the economic field and thereby become stronger in the political field.

Africa is still searching for the proper solution to its many problems. There is much to do to help the struggling peoples achieve their full independence; build prosperous states; create regional federations; harmonize economic policies; and stand politically united

against any European neo-colonialism or any tendency of the two blocs to introduce the Cold War in Africa.

We hope to convert our African brothers to our views by the example of a successful policy inside and outside the country. This may seem presumptuous, but one must keep in mind that, although she is less than ten years of age, independent Tunisia seems a very old lady among the young African "debutantes" which came into existence in 1960, 1961 and 1962. As a matter of fact, she happens to have sponsored their "debuts" in the United Nations.

We are trying to give them the example of a peaceful, stable nation where the government and the people work in harmony to build a modern state. Our stability and harmony inside the country allow us to turn to the international field and to play a part out of proportion with our size and power. Because of our international prestige, we were of great help to the Algerians and the Congolese at the U.N. and elsewhere. And it is not without significance that the first African to be elected to the Presidency of the General Assembly of the U.N. is Mr. Mongi Slim, a Tunisian. This brings me to our policy in the U.N.

The United Nations

Much has been said and written about the United Nations Organization, about its weakness and strength, its achievements and failures. I shall not repeat that. I shall only express wonder why many nations, including Great Powers, are not paying any attention to the very valuable lessons history has been teaching us since the collapse of the League of Nations led humanity to the most tragic adventure of all times. Nor shall I comment on the high political and moral principles which led to the creation of the U.N. and which have never been more badly needed by individuals and nations than in this our time.

To all the good reasons which made such an

organization as the U.N. desirable after the Second World War, we should add a major one: the struggle many peoples have been fighting against colonialism, and the consequent emergence to nationhood of a large number of young, underdeveloped countries which more than doubled the number of U.N. member states. It is to the U.N. that all peoples have been turning when fighting for independence. It is from the U.N. and its specialized agencies that all young nations are most willing to ask technical and economic assistance because there are no strings attached to it.

The future of the United Nations is most promising when it deals with the problems of the weak nations of the world because what it will undertake will not be questioned by the Great Powers. Everybody agrees that history is irreversible and that all nations should be politically emancipated. The shrinkage of our world is also making more and more urgent an active solidarity among nations, comparable to the solidarity among the citizens of a particular state. In promoting these two goals, no Power and no regional organization can replace the United Nations in the long run. Besides, while the U.N. is useful to all nations, it is most needed by the small and the weak, those who cannot take care of their own problems. It is better for them to accept an imperfect decision, than no decision at all.

That is why we have dedicated all our efforts on the international scene to strengthening the U.N. Our aim is to keep it working, whatever might happen. Because the more people are accustomed to it, the more they will need it, and the more powerful it will grow, for the benefit of all. This is the reason why we have always adopted moderate positions, with a better chance of acceptance, rather than extreme positions which would meet no wide approval but which would have given us the satisfaction to completely express our views.

Our concern for the United Nations' efficiency, among other things, led us to oppose the proposition of replacing the late Mr. Dag Hammarskjold with three secretaries with veto power (one Russian, one American and one neutral). We believe that the world political situation is such that whatever pleases the United States has no chance to be accepted by the U.S.S.R.; and that whatever is presented by the U.S.S.R. is rejected by the U.S.A. Consequently, part of the solutions proposed to a three-man Secretariat would be blocked by the East, and the other part by the West. The United Nations Organization would collapse out of helplessness—and so would our dreams, and any chance to see wisdom prevail among nations.

We have come to a crucial point: East-West relations. The most immediate duty of the United Nations is to solve the problems presented to the world by the aggressive competition known as Cold War, with all its implications, political and military. In the United Nations and outside the organization, great responsibility lies with the leaders of the two blocs. But the responsibility is not only theirs. We, the small nations, also have our share, since we face the same dangers. That entitles us to express our views and to judge the leaders of the two blocs on their policies, since these policies can bring to the whole world peace and prosperity or war and destruction. This brings me to our position vis-à-vis the East and the West.

East and West

From the start, independent Tunisia has not made any mystery about her belonging to the Western bloc. There were two main reasons for this: (1) The leaders of Tunisia sincerely believe in the high principles of liberty and justice defended by the Western nations. Most of these leaders have a background of French culture. All of them remember the role played by Wilson in the creation of the League of Nations and that of Franklin D. Roosevelt and Winston Churchill in the drafting of the Atlantic Charter. (2) It did not take us long to find out that France was not ready to give us real independence. She was militarily occupying the country and controlling a great number of services. The best support we could hope for to help us with France was a loyal friend of hers —a Western Power—which would be at the same time a friend of ours.

Indeed, facts were soon to justify this policy brilliantly. As soon as France stopped her economic assistance, the United States offered us aid which was of great help. Besides, a few months after we gained our independence, the United States, leader of the West, seemed to reconsider her policy towards her European Allies in questions involving the African nations.

Breaking up the solidarity she used to manifest towards her allies and friends at the United Nations, the United States deliberately supported some just causes, at the risk of being in conflict with her European partners. The results of this attitude were the inscription on the U.N. Agenda of the Algerian question and the condemnation of France, Great Britain and Israel's aggression against Egypt. We were the more pleased by this attitude because we were in turn siding with the West on almost every important issue, such as the Hungarian drama, not without being criticized by many a nation.

During that period, as soon as President Eisenhower had formulated his political doctrine for North Africa and the Middle East, President Bourguiba gave it his full adhesion. We were completely, unequivocally associated with the West for better or for worse. But in the very speech by which he supported the Eisenhower doctrine, President Bourguiba, speaking of the new orientation of United States policy, said in January 1957:

We hope that the U.S. will keep this orientation and confirm it without reservation, particularly as regards the Algerian question which is about to come before the United Nations. If the United States, during this debate, sides with justice and helps find a solution based on the right of the Algerian people to sovereignty and independence, while taking into consideration

her friendship and alliance with France, together with France's prestige; if the United States could reach such a solution through conviction and friendly pressure, directly or through the United Nations, then there would be no more reason for one nation on earth to pay any attention to communism. On the contrary, all the peoples would turn to the nations that are respectful of liberty and human dignity.[10]

Thus our position was very clear; we were with the West. But we expected the West to solve in one way or another the deepest contradiction of its history: The West, and particularly the United States, had a great appeal for the Afro-Asian countries owing to the high principles on which she had built her society. But at the same time, some members of the West, particularly the Europeans, were pursuing in Africa and elsewhere a colonial policy which was in complete contradiction with these very high principles.

Consequently the United States, a friend of all the European colonial Powers, could not help the African peoples in their fight for independence while the U.S.S.R. missed no occasion to express her support of these peoples and to claim for them the right to emancipation and self-determination.

For good reasons, this consideration had and still has for the Africans much more importance than any U.S. economic assistance. In our particular case, the good done by the United States in moral and economic support was outweighed by the harm France was doing in Tunisia and Algeria, without the United States being able to alter the situation.

President Bourguiba made several statements on this. I have mentioned the difficulties we once had in buying arms from France or any of its Western allies, particularly Belgium, Italy, Great Britain and the United States.

---

[10] Speech published by the Tunisian Secretary of State for Information.

Bourguiba said on that occasion (November 1958):

> The problem does not concern France alone, but rather the whole Free World. If it does not offer the means for this country to assure its future, to safeguard the dignity of its regime, and to realize the conditions of prosperity, we shall no longer be interested in solidarity and co-operation with it.[11]

Ultimately, the U.S.A. and Great Britain sold us a small amount of arms which kept us from turning to other countries, less friendly to France.

The situation was even worse in Algeria where France was using U.S. made armaments (given her through NATO channels) and U.S. financial help against the Algerian freedom fighters while the United States was giving steady support to France in the United Nations.

In consequence, Tunisia was little by little abandoning her clear-cut pro-Western attitude. A very close analysis of our policy was made by President Bourguiba in April 1960 when he said:

> The free world, in fact, attracts us in so far as it stands for liberty, respect and dignity. Since it professes to believe in these principles, we appeal for our liberty and rights. But what are we to think when these principles are belied by this so-called free world? What conclusions can we draw when we see the colonial spirit lingering on, when we see superior strength being used to impose upon weaker countries, or when we witness wars of reconquest, racial discrimination, military occupation imposed by force of arms, or atomic explosions in a land which belongs to us? France cannot continue to explode atomic bombs

and then consider herself morally absolved by verbal appeasement or by the pretext that she has taken all necessary precautions.

Consequently if the free world gives moral support to France's attitude, we shall in no way feel bound to it. It is rather the reverse which will take place. We warn France and her allies. We shall turn away from the free world the moment that it proves that its fine principles are a mask for quibbling and deceit. It will no longer be able to turn to advantage the respect for liberty, if it is proved that it is only prepared to defend the liberty of certain European peoples against the threat of communism and that it cares very little about the liberty of those peoples who live outside Europe and who are not members of the Atlantic Pact.

Such discrimination can only signify that humanity is treated differently according to its geographical area, its color and creed; that man has no inherent rights; that liberty, independence and dignity remain the privilege of certain white people living in specific countries, whereas other peoples exist in order to be dominated and, even though their independence and sovereignty are recognized, they are expected to be dragged against their will into coalitions and conflicts which are of no interest to them.[12]

This was more than one year before the Bizerte crisis. During the military fighting in Bizerte, in the Security Council meetings, during the General Assembly special session, during the mission Mr. Dag Hammarskjold undertook in Tunisia, France stayed firm, ignoring the United Nations decisions, insulting its Secretary General and humiliating the Tunisian

---

[11] See Tunisian daily papers, November 14, 1958.

[12] "The Impotence of the U.N.," speech before the National Assembly, April 7, 1960, p. 9.

people. The United States was not able to support de Gaulle against the Russians in Berlin and, at the same time, support the Tunisians against de Gaulle in Bizerte. It was evident that the contradiction of the Western position was not yet solved.

This led us to proclaim our complete noncommitment which President Bourguiba expressed during the Belgrade Conference:

The third and most important characteristic is that the states represented at this conference are completely free from any commitments towards the two blocs and are consequently able to decide for themselves without any preoccupation other than that of preserving peace and international security, or of contributing to peaceful and fruitful co-operation between peoples.[13]

Now let us not forget that among the "uncommitted" nations which were represented at Belgrade there were many differences, many nuances. We have been considering ourselves as "non-aligned" for a long time. We do not think that the label "uncommitted" or "non-aligned" is sufficient to define our policy. Facts only matter; those of our foreign policy will be determined in great part by the future attitude of the West towards the problems of decolonization and the economic development of the newly emerged nations of the world.

[13] Published by the Tunisian government, September, 1961.

BIBLIOGRAPHY

Author's Suggestions

Bourguiba, Habib. *La Tunisie et la France.* Paris: Julliard, 1954.

Garras, Félix. *Bourguiba et la naissance d'un nation.* Paris: Julliard, 1956.

Hahn, Lorna. *North Africa: Nationalism to Nationhood.* Washington: Public Affairs Press, 1960. (Introduction by President John F. Kennedy.)

André Raymond. *La Tunisie.* Presses Universitaires de France, 1961.

PART FOUR

AFRICA
SOUTH OF THE SAHARA

ABOUT THE AUTHOR

JAMES S. COLEMAN is numbered among that select group of American scholars who have made major contributions to our understanding of underdeveloped areas in general, and the new African states in particular. He received his A.B. degree from Brigham Young University and his M.A. and Ph.D. degrees from Harvard. He has received awards for study and research from the Rockefeller Foundation and Carnegie Corporation. In 1959 he received the Woodrow Wilson Foundation Award from the American Political Science Association for his major book on Nigeria.

Throughout his academic career Mr. Coleman has been associated with the University of California at Los Angeles. He is currently a professor of political science at that institution and is also director of the African Studies Center.

His publications include: "Togoland," *International Conciliation*, 1956; and *Nigeria: Background to Nationalism*, 1958. He is co-author of *Politics of the Developing Areas*, 1960. He is co-editor of the forthcoming book, *African Political Parties*.

ABOUT THE CHAPTER

Observers of Nigerian development have frequently commented on the relative restraint and moderation of this new nation. But in many ways her policies and behavior are similar to those of the other new African states. Mr. Coleman sets himself the dual task of examining the distinctive "factors and forces in the Nigerian situation which help to explain her unique pattern of development" and that of identifying and analyzing "the more generic elements in the African situation that shape and determine not only the foreign policy of Nigeria, but of other African states as well."

The author first examines a number of major factors which affect Nigeria's role in world affairs. The geographical setting, the demographic pattern of the nation, the historical background and some economic factors are all considered. The author then turns to an analysis of the political organization of the nation and to the processes of decision-making. As the framework for analyzing the content of Nigeria's foreign policy, the author gives special attention to her relationship to the Commonwealth, to the United Nations, to the Western and Eastern blocs, and to the other African states.

13

THE FOREIGN POLICY OF NIGERIA

JAMES S. COLEMAN
University of California, Los Angeles

The foreign policy of the Federation of Nigeria is in certain respects atypical, in others fairly representative, of the role assumed by the array of new African states which have joined the world community since 1960. On many African and international issues, its policy has been surprisingly modest and restrained. This is a quite remarkable position, considering the fact that it is not only Africa's first, and the world's thirteenth, most populous state, but also that several Nigerian leaders pioneered in the African nationalist awakening.

Its record of comparative "moderation" stands out in sharp contrast to the far more dramatic and militant assertiveness of certain smaller African states such as Ghana and Guinea. It is a record that has brought considerable satisfaction to those in the Western world who had looked forward with the hope that, on entering the world stage, the Nigerian giant would become a major stabilizing force on the African continent. But it is a record that has brought no little disappointment to those Nigerian patriots who had hoped that their country would assume a more "dynamic" role of leadership in African and world affairs, a role they believed it was destined by size and population to play.

However evaluated, the fact is that much of Nigeria's external record since independence in October, 1960, reflects that pattern of peaceful change, accommodation and compromise that has characterized Nigerian political evolution since the end of the Second World War. One of our major purposes in this chapter is to examine those distinctive factors and forces in the Nigerian situation which help to explain this unique pattern of development.

There are other aspects of independent Nigeria's external record which reflect more general factors and forces that underlie, condition, or affect, the foreign policies of most of Africa's new states. On several occasions since Nigerian independence, the federal government has taken a firm stand on such issues as neutralism, racialism, residual colonialism, and other affronts to African dignity and independence. These are issues that deeply concern the leaders of all of Africa's new states. In confronting such issues, Nigeria's capacity for positive action was dramatized by the fact that it was the only African state to sever diplomatic relations with France over nuclear testing in the Sahara.

Its determination to demonstrate complete independence in foreign relations has been repeatedly manifested in its voting record in the United Nations on certain Cold War issues. Indeed, since becoming independent on October 1, 1960, its record reveals a shift from an initial position of cautious restraint to a more assertive one on these and other issues. In large measure, this is a reflection of its response to general continent-wide pressures and trends dominant in the post-colonial African scene. Thus, our second major purpose here is to identify and to analyze the more generic elements in the African situation that shape and determine not only the foreign policy of Nigeria, but the foreign policies of other African states as well.

MAJOR FACTORS AFFECTING NIGERIA'S ROLE IN WORLD AFFAIRS

Governing elites of most new states enjoy considerable autonomy and freedom of action in their conduct of foreign relations. There are many explanations for this fact, such as the absence of institutionalized restraints upon their exercise of authority, the undeveloped or inchoate character of public opinion, the unintegrated character of the societies they govern, and the lack of a clear conception of the various factors which, in their totality, constitute the "national interest."

Their freedom of choice of alternatives, however, is not absolute; like all governing elites, they are ultimately constrained by those basic factors that everywhere define the limits of the possible. Thus, at the outset, we must be concerned with how Nigeria's foreign policy is affected by such basic factors as Nigerian geography, the character of the Nigerian population, as well as the relevant aspects of Nigeria's history, early as well as recent, her economy, and her political system.

The geographical setting

The historic isolation of the peoples of Nigeria from the mainstream of world affairs is largely the consequence of geographical features that made human intercourse virtually impossible. Bounded on the south by a dense coastal swamp forest, and on the north by the southern reaches of the Sahara, communication and relationships with the external world were infrequent or nonexistent. The only significant exceptions to this isolation were the late medieval and early modern links via the trans-Saharan trade routes with the Maghreb, Tripolitania and Egypt.

The principal legacy of these early connections with the outside world was the spread of Islamic culture to the whole of the Western Sudan, including, in particular, northern Nigeria. This cultural diffusion of Islam into sub-Saharan Africa provides a basis for the close relationships between Nigeria and the predominantly Muslim states of North Africa and the Middle East.

Like most of the international boundaries of former colonial areas, those of Nigeria were arbitrarily laid down during the scramble for Africa. None are "natural" boundaries in the sense of being demarcated by striking physical features or a defense rationale, or of separating distinctive cultural groups. Indeed, two of Nigeria's major cultural groups—the Yoruba of the Western Region and the Hausa of the Northern Region—were bifurcated by the colonial mapmakers.

A significant portion of the southern part of the Republic of Dahomey, Nigeria's western neighbor, is inhabited by Yoruba-speaking peoples; and an even larger area of the Republic of Niger, the northern neighbor, is inhabited by Hausa-speaking peoples. Neither of these potential irredenta, however, have yet threatened to become issues affecting Nigeria's foreign relations. In part this is due to the fact that throughout most of West Africa the impact of

French and English cultural influences and languages upon at least the politically relevant elite groups has been far more pervasive and decisive in differentiating neighboring French- and English-speaking territories as wholes than have pre-colonial cultural or tribal bonds that may transcend or fragment those regions.

The anti-traditionalist, anti-tribal orientation of modernizing elites has further strengthened the tendency towards the sharpening of territorial individuality and the weakening of trans-territorial tribal or cultural bonds. In most of post-colonial Africa, territorial nationalism commands far greater respectability than those tribal or sub-territorial nationalisms which might threaten the integrity of the new states. Thus, unless deliberately activated and manipulated by political leaders, it is unlikely that a Pan-Yoruba or a Pan-Hausa nationalism will emerge as a source of tension between Nigeria and the Republics of Dahomey and Niger.

Nigeria is divided roughly into four physical regions. Ranging south to north, there is the swamp forest on its South Atlantic coastline; then the tropical rain forest and oil-palm bush; followed by the open woodland and grass savannah; and, finally, the semi-desert of the far north. The variations in climate, rainfall, vegetation, soil fertility and food crops produced by this natural differentiation have resulted not only in complementary economies supportive of internal Nigerian unity, but also in the development of a variety of agricultural exports, thus reducing the vulnerability of the Nigerian economy as a whole.

A final geographical feature that should be noted is the fact that Nigeria stands as a giant surrounded by four new states that are sparsely populated and economically and militarily weak, and, therefore, constitute no threat to her. This has contributed to an official Nigerian posture of magnanimity and benevolent restraint towards its small neighbors—a position that only freedom from insecurity permits. It also has allowed Nigerian leaders to concentrate the attention and energies of their people mainly upon the massive internal problems with which they are confronted.

This happy situation might well be only a function of the foreign policy of moderation of the Federal leadership since independence. Given a more militant "Pan-Africanist" leadership, a policy of intimidation and aggrandizement might be pursued. For the immediate post-colonial period, however, the absence of a threatening neighbor, among other things, has served to minimize Nigerian preoccupation with foreign relations.

The demographic pattern

Cultural factors There are several characteristics of Nigeria's population that have had and will continue to have very significant consequences for Nigeria's foreign relations. One is the fact that the people of Nigeria represent Africa's ethnic and cultural heterogeneity in its richest and most diversified form. Situated at the linguistic, cultural, and religious crossroads of tropical Africa, Nigeria is in many ways a microcosm of the middle two-thirds of the continent.

It is the key juncture of the major language families of the sub-continent; its traditional societal base comprises indigenous societies ranging in scale from the smallest autonomous village "tribe" to the largest kingoms and empires of pre-colonial Africa. Within its borders one finds, on a more massive scale than elsewhere, the confrontation of the principal proselytizing Christian sects, institutionalized Islam, and traditional African religions.

Among the many consequences of this great diversity of indigenous cultural patterns and traditions are two that are particularly in point. One is that Nigerian unity—indeed, the survival of Nigeria as a sovereign entity—is threatened by the lack of national integration. Nigeria is plagued by strong local parochialisms, sectional and tribal separatism, and other fissiparous tendencies characteristic of most of the new states of Africa. The other, more constructive, consequence is that the very fact that such diversity exists has contributed no

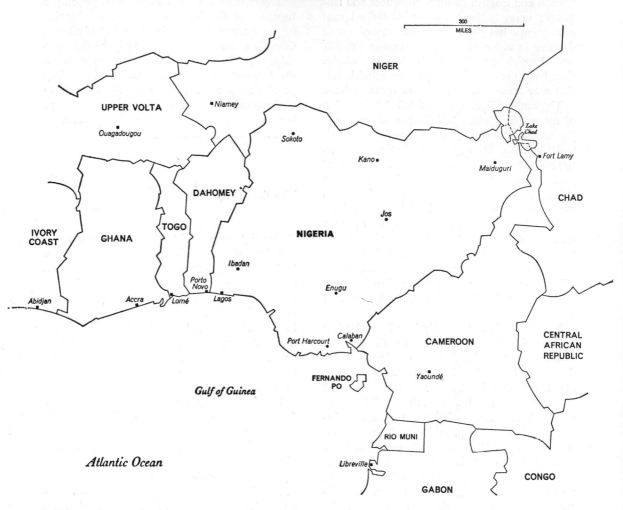

WEST AFRICA

little to a spirit of ethnic and religious tolerance among Nigerian political leaders, as well as to a pragmatic and eclectic orientation towards foreign systems as models for Nigerian development.

The religious composition of Nigeria's population provides the basis for external links that are relevant factors in Nigerian foreign policy. There are more than two million Nigerian Christians, concentrated in the Eastern and Western Regions and the "Middle Belt" of the Northern Region. The political power of the Catholics in the Eastern Region of Nigeria has

been demonstrated on several occasions. The Anglican community is quite sizeable and embraces a significant element of the southern educated elite.

Of even greater political significance, both domestically and externally, is the fact that nearly one-half of Nigeria's population is Muslim. This provides the basis for efforts that have been made since independence to establish or to strengthen spiritual and fraternal links between Nigeria and the Muslim states of North Africa and the Middle East. Moreover, there is also a very large number of Nigerian

Muslims each year travelling en route to or from Mecca on pilgrimage. This has dictated the development of very close diplomatic relationships between Nigeria and the Republic of the Sudan and Saudi Arabia.

Composition and distribution   The size and the geographical distribution of Nigeria's ethnic groups have profoundly affected the development of Nigeria's political system and pattern of politics. The latter, in turn, has a very direct bearing upon the character of Nigeria's foreign policy. Although there are around 250 separate language groups (inaccurately referred to as "tribes") in Nigeria, three of these (the Hausa in the Northern Region, the Yoruba in the Western Region and the Ibo in the Eastern Region), each numbering more than five million, comprise more than half of Nigeria's total population.

Thus, each of Nigeria's three regions has a sizeable cultural core area of comparatively high ethnic homogeneity, and a peripheral area composed of several ethnic minorities. Each core area has provided a fairly secure political base for one of the three major Nigerian political parties: the Northern People's Congress (NPC) in the north, the Action Group (AG) in the west, and the National Convention of Nigerian Citizens (NCNC) in the east. This political-cultural pattern, strengthened by certain facets of British policy during the colonial period, is the primary explanation for Nigeria's federal system of government in which the three regions have a wide measure of autonomy.

It is the density of Nigeria's population—an estimated 45 million in 1962—that sets it apart from most of the rest of Africa, Ruanda, Burundi and the Nile Delta region in Egypt excepted. Although there are parts of Nigeria that are sparsely populated, the eastern region of Nigeria is among the most densely populated rural areas in the world. Given the pressure upon the land, the lack of employment opportunities, and a rapidly expanding educational system, a substantial number of persons inhabiting areas of high population density have migrated for seasonal or permanent employment to other areas of Nigeria and West Africa over the past fifty years. Such labor mobility within Nigeria has furthered the development of a Nigerian consciousness and unity among the persons concerned.

Those who have migrated for work beyond the borders of Nigeria, however, pose a special foreign policy problem between Nigeria and the labor-receiving countries. Spain has recruited a large number of Nigerian laborers for plantations on the island of Fernando Po. In the English-speaking western province of the Republic of Cameroun there are more than 50,000 rather unwelcome Nigerians (mainly Ibo) from the Eastern Region engaged in petty trade—which they tend to monopolize—and in skilled clerical and other jobs. In Ghana a sizeable number of eastern Nigerians work in service industries, and northern Nigerians (Hausa) are engaged in petty trade. The conditions of employment and the treatment of these various categories of Nigerian citizens working abroad have already been the basis of some concern and diplomatic exchanges between the government of Nigeria and the countries concerned.

Another unique demographic feature in Nigeria is that it has the smallest proportion of aliens or non-Africans to its total population of all new states of tropical Africa. This is the result, in part, of climate and health conditions prevalent in Nigeria during the active period of European settlement in Africa; and, in part, of an early British policy of protecting indigenous land tenure, forbidding the establishment of European plantations, and maintaining a firm control over immigration. Thus, Nigeria has had no experience with the "white settler." With few exceptions, the only Europeans who came to Nigeria were transient traders, administrative employees of firms, technicians, missionaries, or government administrators. None of these persons regarded Nigeria as their country of permanent residence or retirement.

This has meant that relationships between independent Nigeria and European countries, and particularly the United Kingdom, are not complicated by either the rancor, or the need for elaborate protective devices which the "settler factor" elsewhere produced. In fact, the only significant "alien" element in the Nigerian population that could become an issue in Nigeria's foreign relations is the relatively small Lebanese community which plays such an influential role in the commercial life of Nigeria. Next to the "Big Firms," the Lebanese are the main target of resentment of the expanding class of Nigerian entrepreneurs, if for no other reason than that they are the most visible evidence of continued alien control of the economy.

The historical legacy

Among the myriad events and aspects of the history of Nigeria's peoples, there are several that have a special significance for the external relations of the new state. We have already noted the important historical links established as a result of the spread of Islam between northern Nigeria and the Muslim world and early trans-Saharan trade.

Another historical encounter was that between Nigeria—the "Slave Coast" of West Africa—and the slave-receiving countries of the New World. For more than 400 years the West coast of Africa, particularly that part of the coastal regions now included within the boundaries of independent Nigeria, was the principal reservoir of slaves for the New World. In addition to the devastating impact of the slave trade upon African societies, two other consequences should be noted. One specific legacy is the presence in several countries (e.g., Brazil, the West Indies, and Sierra Leone) of groups of persons of African descent among whom there are surviving cultural links with Nigeria. A more general legacy is the suspicion and hostility which have colored, and will continue to affect, relationships at both the interpersonal and international levels between Africa and the Western world.

The slave trade, like colonialism, was a historical experience they suffered which helps to provide some plausible explanation why Africa is so backward and underdeveloped. It also provides a rationale for Africans to make a special claim upon the external world for assistance to help them modernize rapidly and catch up with the rest of mankind.

The most determinative period of Nigerian history was the sixty year span of formal rule by Britain. The entity of Nigeria was solely a British creation and the concept of a Nigerian nation is a legacy of the British presence. The imposition of a common government, lingua franca, and currency system, as well as the establishment of internal peace and the maintenance of law and order, provided a framework in which a Nigerian consciousness among the politically relevant strata of the population could develop. These constitute, of course, the legacy of any colonial system. What, among several things, was a distinctively British contribution was the concept of local government and regionalism— the dispersion rather than the concentration of power. Nigeria was the showpiece of indirect rule, where the "natural" units were the building blocks of the larger society. As a result, Nigeria today not only has a federal form of government, but Africa's most pluralistic political system.

Another important historical aspect of the British connection is that it was terminated progressively, by negotiated stages, and without acrimony or deep scars affecting post-colonial Anglo-Nigerian relations. This example of peaceful transfer of power is explained partly by Nigeria's size and complexity, partly by Nigerian and British statesmanship, and partly by Nigeria's peculiar regional power structure and federal system of government.

None of the three constituent regions of the federation was prepared to secede and destroy Nigeria as Africa's greatest Power, yet none could single-handedly either dominate the whole federation or force any other region to do its will; each "national" party was based upon a regional power center and required an alliance with at least one of the others if it wished to participate in the national government. The result was negotiation and compromise among Nigerian regional leaders regarding both the tempo of movement towards independence and the character of the political system of independent Nigeria.

Throughout the whole process of decolonization the British government in London and in Nigeria more or less used its "good offices" to facilitate the intra-Nigerian compromises that were reached. The end result was a graceful British departure with Commonwealth commitments strong and Anglo-Nigerian relations remarkably friendly.

Another significant historical fact of the colonial period is that close fraternal ties developed among members of the older generation of educated nationalists from the several territories of former British West Africa—Nigeria, the then Gold Coast, Sierra Leone and the Gambia. Although these ties were never as intimate or as continuous as those among the educated political elite of French-speaking Africa, they were nevertheless quite close and meaningful. An important segment of the top political and intellectual leaders of these countries is on a first-name basis, having shared experiences abroad as students in British or American universities, or having participated jointly in agitational and political action movements.

The two associations which both reflected and furthered this close association were the short-lived National Congress of British West Africa, formed immediately after World War I, and the much more durable West African Students Union (WASU) in London. Although the emergence of sovereign states has tended to formalize relationships, the memory and the continued existence of these more informal channels of contact can serve to ameliorate interstate tensions and to further Pan-Africanism.

The economic base

With a per capita income of about $84, Nigeria ranks among the poorest of the world's underdeveloped countries. Its economic growth potential, however, is regarded as very high. It is endowed with relatively fertile land, adequate for its population. The latter is sufficiently dense to be a positive factor in development. It has substantial coal and petroleum deposits, and a great hydroelectric potential in its river system. It has demonstrated a capacity to attract substantial foreign investment. Assessments of its economic potential are strengthened by the fact that, over the past decade, it has maintained an impressive rate of growth, averaging around four percent.

Unlike Ghana, the per capita income of which is nearly double, Nigeria is not dangerously dependent upon one export; rather its exports include several major commodities, including palm oil products (25%), cocoa (20%), groundnuts (20%), cotton (6%), rubber (6%), and a variety of other tropical products. The really critical factors in the development of its economy are not resources, but capital and trained manpower. For both of these Nigeria, like most new African states, is heavily dependent upon the external world.

Capital and manpower needs The magnitude of Nigeria's dependence upon external capital is revealed in the fact that forty percent of the funds for the Nigerian Federal Development Plan of 1955–1962 had to be secured from abroad. Even more illuminating are the plans for financing the six-year (1962–1968) $1,892,800,000 "National Plan." It is hoped that $949.2 million (50%) will be obtained from external grants and loans and $560 million (30%) from external private investment, and that the balance of 20% will be raised locally.

Given this awesome gap between its capital needs and domestic capacities and the fact that each year there is a much greater balance of payments deficit due to vastly increased imports, the Nigerian government has placed very heavy emphasis upon expanding both external private investment and exports. These twin imperatives—the critical need for new sources of capital and new markets for Nigerian exports—are crucial determinants of Nigerian foreign economic policy.

The second major requisite for Nigeria's rapid economic growth is high-level manpower. Here again Nigeria confronts an alarming deficiency not readily overcome. According to Professor Frederick Harbison "Nigeria has not now, nor will she have in the next few years, the capacity to generate the high-level manpower necessary to make rapid economic growth possible." By his 1960 calculations, Nigeria's ten-year minimum requirement for high-level manpower to meet its development goals would be around 85,000 persons. Of this number Nigeria now possesses only about 30,000, and the shortage in the present output of Nigerian graduates from institutions of higher education in Nigeria and abroad is around 5,000 per year. The implications are clear: there must be not only a massive expansion in post-secondary education in Nigeria (which the new development plan envisages), but also continued heavy dependence upon foreign (expatriate) high-level manpower at least until 1970.

As support for education in the annual budgets of the federal and regional governments is already extremely high, and grossly disproportionate to other expenditures, the financing of the expansion of higher education must be obtained largely from external sources. Moreover, if development is to take place on the scale envisaged, high-level manpower recruited from abroad must be doubled by 1965, and the number reduced only as trained Nigerian replacements become available. Thus, Nigeria confronts the striking paradox of most of post-colonial Africa, namely, heightened dependence upon the external world during the first decade of independence. The psychological and political consequences of this fact constitute a crucial element in the foreign relations of all of Africa's new states.

Foreign trade   Nowhere is the preponderant economic role of a colonial Power more visible than in the foreign trade pattern of its dependent territory. As the table on page 388 shows, during the colonial period the United Kingdom was far and away Nigeria's best customer and its dominant supplier. Yet the table also reveals other relevant facts regarding Nigeria's external economic relationships. It shows that, although still preponderant, the role of the United Kingdom is markedly declining; that trade with the six West European countries constituting the European Economic Community (E.E.C.) and with the United States and Japan is very important to Nigeria; and that trade with other African countries, with countries of the Commonwealth other than the United Kingdom, and with the Communist bloc, has been and remains insignificant. Although the trade pattern has changed in certain key respects since 1946, and current efforts to expand exports will undoubtedly lead to greater diversification, it is doubtful that there will be any dramatic change in the present basic pattern until Nigerian industries are developed on a wider scale, or unless there is a revolutionary change in Nigerian political leadership.

Nigeria's foreign trade pattern is directly related to two key foreign policy issues: Nigeria's relationship to the E.E.C. and intra-African economic integration. The issue of association with the E.E.C. is of central importance in view of the fact that Nigeria is the most important supplier of tropical produce to the countries of the E.E.C., and that more than 80 percent of Nigeria's export trade will be affected.

If Nigeria declines to become an associated member of the E.E.C., she would not only lose the preferences now given to some of her products by the United Kingdom, her best customer, but as a member of the E.E.C., Britain would be obliged to apply E.E.C. tariffs to Nigerian products and also to admit duty-free similar products from the French-speaking "associated" states of Africa, Nigeria's chief competitors. If, on the other hand, Nigeria becomes an associated state, not only would her products be guaranteed continued free entry into the United Kingdom market, and current E.E.C. tariff discriminations in favor of Nigeria's African competitors removed, but she would as well be eligible on equal terms for E.E.C. development grants. There can be little question that, in the short run, the potential economic benefits to Nigeria of E.E.C. associated status outweigh the economic disadvantages.

Despite these demonstrable economic benefits, however, there is strong opposition in Nigeria, on political, psychological—and also economic—grounds, to becoming an associated member in the E.E.C. The arguments against association are many: (1) that granting E.E.C. industrial products free entry into Africa will delay, if not prevent, the industrialization of Nigeria; (2) that the maintenance of vertical economic links with Europe prevents the development of closer economic, and ultimately political, unity among African states; (3) that such status is nothing more than a postcolonial continuation of a master-servant relationship wherein African countries supply raw materials for European industries, thereby widening rather than narrowing the gap between highly industrialized Europe and non-industrialized Africa; and (4) that the maintenance of such an unbalanced economic relationship with one of the two sides in the Cold War makes a mockery of Nigeria's declared policy of nonalignment.

These and other arguments have been advanced; some are informed, others are not. For example, associated countries, as distinguished from full member countries, are free to protect their nascent industries. Also, would not the present division between non-associated and associated territories be removed and West African regional economic integration enhanced, if the former joined the E.E.C.? On the other hand, there can be little question that, in the long run, associated status would prolong Nigeria's economic dependency, unless the short-term benefits of that status are deliberately used to industrialize and diversify the Nigerian economy.

It is the overriding desire for full independence—for the total consummation of the freedom sovereign statehood was supposed to bring—that will undoubtedly prevail. As the Prime Minister stated in October 1962:

As an African country, we consider that the Common Market is essentially a European affair and has political overtones which cannot appeal to Africans. We are, therefore, naturally distrustful of any institutions which may cause our future industrial goods to be discriminated against either outside or within the Continent, and which operate in a way to keep Africans perpetually as primary producers. This sense of dependence is itself an unstable basis for relations between the former metropolitan countries and the newly independent countries. We are also anxious to expand our trade outside traditional markets, for so long as the trade and industry of Africa are conducted with only one area of the world, so long will a feeling of dependency persist. In other words, having secured political independence, we are determined to see that this is also expressed in economic terms.[1]

An African Common Market   The idea of an "African Common Market" has become a shibboleth in the public statements of leaders in Nigeria and other English-speaking West African countries not associated with the E.E.C. The popularity of this notion has many possible explanations: the obeisance all African leaders feel stimulated or compelled to give to the goal of African unity; the strong nationalist impulse to reject continued economic dependence upon, or an unbalanced "neo-colonialist" relationship with, Western Europe, and to find an "African" solution to the problem; and sheer lack of knowledge either of what a "common market" is or of the cold realities of the economies of West African states.

The fact is that the economies of Nigeria and its West African neighbors are not complementary; indeed, for most commodities they

[1] Sir Abubakar Tafawa Balewa, "Nigeria Looks Ahead," *Foreign Affairs* (October, 1962), p. 136.

387

are competitive. As a consequence, intra-African trade is relatively insignificant. Ghana, for example, is Nigeria's largest African trading partner (see table, below). Yet in 1961, Nigerian trade with Ghana amounted to no more than one-half of one percent of the total foreign trade of Nigeria, and trade with all African countries combined was less than one percent. This pattern will probably continue for the foreseeable future, unless radical changes are forced by the political imperatives of Pan-Africanism.

PATTERNS OF NIGERIAN FOREIGN TRADE

COUNTRIES	IMPORTS				EXPORTS			
	1939	1946	1958	1961	1939	1946	1958	1961
Commonwealth	62.0	75.9	50.2	45.0	62.6	81.3	57.2	46.4
United Kingdom	54.8	65.5	44.3	38.8	60.8	75.6	56.4	44.8
Canada	00.5	00.7	00.1	00.8	00.1	04.1	00.0	00.3
India	06.4	09.7	03.7	03.2	00.0	00.0	00.2	00.4
Hong Kong	00.3	00.0	01.9	01.9	00.0	00.0	00.0	00.2
Ghana	00.0	00.0	00.2	00.3	01.7	01.6	00.6	00.7
European Community	19.0	7.3	19.2	22.0	24.6	2.95	32.1	34.8
Germany	07.7	00.0	07.5	07.5	10.9	00.0	08.9	07.8
Netherlands & possessions	07.2	05.0	06.3	06.3	06.1	02.9	13.7	12.8
Italy	01.8	01.4	02.4	03.6	00.4	00.0	06.3	04.8
Belgium & Luxemburg	01.2	00.9	01.3	01.6	00.9	00.05	01.6	03.0
France & possessions	01.1	0.0	01.7	03.0	06.3	00.0	01.6	06.4
Japan	03.2	0.0	11.8	13.8	00.0	00.0	00.8	02.0
U.S.A.	07.2	09.7	05.9	05.4	10.0	10.6	06.1	11.2
Eastern Europe	00.5	00.4	01.9	02.1	00.2	00.0	.31	00.4
Czechoslovakia	00.5	00.4	01.2	01.2	00.2	00.0	00.3	00.4
Eastern Germany	00.0	00.0	00.7	00.9	00.0	00.0	00.01	00.0
Others	08.06	06.7	11.0	11.64	02.6	05.15	03.49	05.2
Norway	03.4	00.4	03.7	02.7	00.4	00.4	00.4	00.1
Iceland	00.0	00.0	00.8	01.2	00.0	00.0	00.0	00.0
Denmark	00.0	00.0	00.3	00.5	00.0	00.0	01.0	00.7
Eire	00.0	00.0	00.1	00.2	00.0	00.0	00.0	00.2
South Africa	00.06	00.0	00.5	00.04	00.2	00.0	00.1	00.01
All others	04.6	06.3	05.6	07.0	02.0	04.75	01.99	04.19

The political framework

There are at least three aspects of the Nigerian political system that are significant for an appreciation of independent Nigeria's foreign policy: (1) the fact that it is a federal system with a fairly wide sphere of autonomy for the three constituent regions; (2) the fact that it is a competitive system with rival national parties competing in periodic elections, an official parliamentary opposition, and a free press; and (3) the fact that the federal government has been and remains a coalition of elements representing rather widely differing political orientations.

The federal system   The Nigerian federal system is not one that was selected arbitrarily in the last stages of colonialism as the most appropriate political framework for an independent Nigeria; rather, it is the end product of several decades of evolution. The principal considerations in that evolutionary process have been Nigeria's distinctive three-core area ethnic pattern previously described; the "regionalized" colonial administrative system first established in 1900 (between the Northern and Southern Provinces) and further divided into a three-region pattern in 1939 (when the Southern Provinces were divided into the Eastern and Western Regions); the progressive devolution of authority to Nigerianized regional governments via a series of constitutions (Orders in Council and their amendments) of 1947, 1951, 1954, 1957, and 1959; the different patterns and rates of economic, educational and political development of the three regions during the colonial period; and, after more than a decade of political struggle and compromise among regionally-based elites and parties, the final striking of a balance between the forces of regional separatism and those of unitary centralism.

The main center of political gravity between 1952 and 1959 was in the regions. Since 1959, however, it has progressively shifted to the federal government, a fact dramatized by the dismissal of the Western Regional government in the spring of 1962 and the appointment of a Federal Administrator by the federal Prime Minister. The reasons for the shift are numerous and include the following: the decision of two of the three major party leaders (Awolowo in the west and Azikiwe in the east) to move in 1959 from the regional to the federal political arena; the emergence of Sir Abubakar Tafawa Balewa, federal Prime Minister, as a national leader in his own right; the entrance of a new generation of more nationally-minded activists into politics; the coming into force upon independence of certain powers and functions granted by the constitution to the federal government; the assertion of federal supremacy and leadership in the formulation of a national development plan; and the growing importance of foreign relations, constitutionally a distinctly federal responsibility.

Federal control over foreign policy   The supremacy and exclusive competence of the federal government in the field of foreign affairs, however, is something that had to be asserted and established. It has not been easy; and the principle is still not scrupulously and universally respected. The process of consolidating federal supremacy has involved the progressive curtailment and suppression of a pre-independence pattern of what was tantamount to regional foreign relations.

Such a pattern emerged during the period of regional ascendancy from 1952 to 1959. The governments of each of the three regions were endowed with a sphere of autonomy, formalized by the grant of full self-government in 1957 to the Eastern and Western Regions (1959 in the Northern Region) in those matters within regional competence under the Constitution.

It was during this period that the three main party leaders—Sir Ahmadu Bello, leader of the NPC in the Northern Region, Dr. Nnamdi Azikiwe, leader of the NCNC in the Eastern Region, and Chief Obafemi Awolowo, leader of the AG in the Western Region—held the premiership in the regions whose governments their party controlled. It was also a period of regional competition in awarding scholarships abroad, in recruiting expatriate personnel, and in carrying on public relations activity directed at expanding trade with and attracting investment to their respective regions.

For these purposes a facility was needed in London. In due course, each of the three regions appointed a Regional Commissioner to the United Kingdom whose office increasingly resembled a regional embassy in the imperial capital. This was supplemented by a steady stream of official missions sent abroad, composed of parliamentarians, ministers and premiers in varying combinations and numbers, who visited Western countries to stimulate trade and investment, to extend goodwill or to learn how foreign ways might be instructive for the development of Nigeria.

Throughout this period of intense regional activity abroad, the function of conducting the foreign relations of Nigeria as a whole was the responsibility of the British Governor-General of the Federation, the representative of the Queen. As Nigeria was still a dependency, however, it was the United Kingdom government that in fact handled such matters. Control over foreign relations and defense were the last functions to be handed over to the federal government of Prime Minister Balewa on Independence Day, October 1, 1960. Only on that day could Nigerian federal leadership, possessed of full sovereignty, commence to engage in formal relationships with foreign governments and give expression to a Nigerian foreign policy.

The historical fact that Nigeria approached final independence via an intermediate stage of regional self-government largely explains the special post-colonial problem of curtailing regional intrusions, and establishing federal supremacy in the conduct of foreign relations. Yet several factors continue to exist in the Nigerian situation that make a complete resolution of this problem unlikely in the foreseeable future. One is that, by *convention*, constituent units (i.e., states, provinces or regions)

of federal systems within the Commonwealth are permitted to appoint an Agent General in London, without diplomatic status, to cater for trade and students. Accordingly, at independence, Nigeria's regional Commissioners in London became regional Agents General, and the federal Commissioner became the Nigerian High Commissioner, the Commonwealth equivalent of ambassador. Although this change made the latter solely responsible for official Nigerian relations with the United Kingdom government, the Agents General of the regions continued to handle many of the functions previously handled by the regional Commissioners, including investment promotion, student affairs, and recruitment of expatriate staff.

Another factor is the provision in the Nigerian constitution giving the regional governments a nullifying power over the implementation of certain treaties. According to Section 69, any law enacted by the federal Parliament for the purpose of implementing any international treaty, convention or agreement concerning matters not falling within the exclusive or concurrent powers of the federal government, "shall not come into operation in a Region unless the Governor of that Region has consented to its having effect."

Still another factor is the provision in the Nigerian constitution endowing both federal and regional governments with concurrent jurisdiction over "industrial development." It was under this authority that regional governments conducted their extensive activities abroad prior to independence, and it is the retention of this provision in Nigeria's Independence Constitution which accounts for a continuation of the earlier pattern.

Thus, in August 1961, nearly one year after independence, the western regional government opened a "Western Nigeria Information and Industrial Development Office" in New York City. The federal government ordered that this office be closed, but it has not moved to discourage or to stop what has become a regular feature of Nigeria's relations with the external world, namely, frequent missions of goodwill and investment-seeking abroad by regional premiers and regional ministerial delegations.

These missions are undoubtedly valuable when they achieve their stated purpose, namely, when they secure investment capital for Nigerian development. They also perform an educative function for the visiting Nigerians and for their hosts. But they can be expensive; and, for the host countries, they are frequently confusing, particularly when several apparently competitive delegations from different regional governments, as well as from the federal government, visit the same country within a short period of time seeking similar ends.

Regional views on foreign affairs   It is when official members of the regional delegations, particularly those holding high office in their regional governments, go beyond the promotion of investment capital, and make unco-ordinated and unauthorized statements on foreign affairs, that such visits confuse the external image of Nigerian foreign policy. This is especially true in the case of statements made by regional premiers, who, on their visits, are frequently received by the head of state and/or the foreign minister of the host country.

Cases in point include public statements made in August, 1961, by Dr. Michael Okpara (eastern regional Premier) that Nigeria's membership in the E.E.C. would be a "step in the right direction," at a time the federal government remained uncommitted and generally negative regarding associated status. Again, in New Delhi, he stated that a Third Power bloc of Afro-Asian nations "was the only hope of the world," at about the same time the federal Prime Minister declined the invitation to attend the Belgrade Conference of non-aligned states on the grounds that Nigeria was opposed to blocs. An added element of confusion in the case of Dr. Okpara is the fact that he was at the time, and continues to be, National President of the N.C.N.C., one of the two parties comprising the federal coalition government.

It was in the course of an official tour of Middle Eastern states by the premier of the Northern Region, Sir Ahmadu Bello, that the greatest controversy was created regarding the propriety of a regional premier making statements on foreign policy. In the course of his tour, he held conversations with several heads of state and government (King Saud, President Ayub Khan, the Shah of Persia, the prime ministers of Lebanon and the Sudan, and President Nasser) with whom he discussed the desirability of convening a conference of heads of Muslim states to discuss Muslim unity. His remarks at news conferences and his other public statements made abroad were widely reported in the Nigerian press.

He was alleged to have urged the heads of state he met to join in the formation of a "Commonwealth of Muslim States," to have promised Jordan he would "exercise his influence in international circles to support Jordanian questions and that of the refugees," and to have stated at a Cairo press conference that "Israelis are out for domination," and that the Prime Minister of Nigeria was his "first lieutenant." He qualified his remarks by observing that he could only speak for the north, that "Nigeria is not a Muslim country," and that the federal government was a coalition, and, therefore, in the case of the Israelis, who had "got a footing in the East and in the West" prior to independence, it could not "expel them overnight." The press in southern Nigeria sharply attacked the premier for encroaching on the powers of the federal government; but the Prime Minister defended Sir Ahmadu who, he said, had "every right to call for closer co-operation between Muslim leaders."

Parliament and the party system

Although the federal form of government has made it more difficult to project a single Nigerian voice in world affairs, it is this very same structural feature that largely accounts for Nigeria's democratic multi-party system. At the *federal* level, Nigeria is unquestionably the most free and open polity in all of newly independent Africa. The political process and trends within each of the three regions controlled by one of the three major "national" parties, are, however, more akin to the one-party-dominant pattern prevailing in other new African states.

At the *regional* level, one finds at work the same, apparently inexorable, trend towards the consolidation and strengthening of one-party control as evidenced in the gradual diminution of the electoral strength and political significance of opposition elements. In effect, therefore, the party system of the Federation of Nigeria is made up of essentially three competing one-party sub-systems, none of which has been, or is likely to be, able to control the whole. One of the great imponderables of Nigeria's future is how this rather unique situation of structured multi-partyism will be affected by the prospective creation of a fourth "Midwest" Region (to be carved out of the present Western Region) or by the deep factional split that occurred within the Action Group which resulted in the federal government assuming temporary control of the Western Region in the spring of 1962.

The foreign policy of independent Nigeria has been formulated and expressed, as well as criticized and debated, within the framework of Nigeria's federal parliamentary system. It is a system modeled after that of the United Kingdom, wherein the Government of the day possesses policy initiative and assured majority support in the parliament on all money bills, treaties, and other measures it requires to implement policy.

During the life of the present Parliament, elected on December 12, 1959 for a five-year term, Nigeria's foreign policy has been the subject of wide-ranging debate in the federal Parliament on several occasions. Foreign policy issues also figure prominently during the Question Hour. Outside of Parliament the dialogue is carried on by a very active press, representing very different shades of opinion, in which foreign policy questions are analyzed, international developments fairly objectively reported, and the government's position attacked or defended. Nowhere in Africa has there been,

both inside a representative assembly or among the "attentive public," such free and open discussion of policy issues and such frank and unrestrained criticism of official policy.

The first government   The combination of a parliamentary system and of regionally-based parties made a coalition government at the federal level inevitable. The first coalition government of independent Nigeria was established following the federal election of December 12, 1959. In that election, the Northern People's Congress (NPC) won 142 seats, the National Council of Nigerian Citizens (NCNC) and Northern Elements Progressive Union (NEPU) alliance won 89 seats, the Action Group (AG) gained 73 seats, and independents secured the remaining 8. Sir Ahmadu Bello, Leader of the NPC, preferred to continue as premier of the Northern Region.

Accordingly, Sir Abubakar Tafawa Balewa, Deputy Leader of the NPC, was reappointed Prime Minister. He immediately formed a coalition government of ten NPC members, seven NCNC members and 2 independents. Dr. Nnamdi Azikiwe, then President of the NCNC, became President of the federal Senate, an interim appointment pending his moving up after independence to the Governor-Generalship of the Federation, the role he was presumably promised in the NPC–NCNC coalition agreement. Having failed in his efforts to form a coalition with either the NPC or NCNC, Chief Obafemi Awolowo, leader of the Action Group, became official Leader of Opposition in the federal Parliament.

One of the most striking features of Nigeria's federal coalition is that it brings together two very different groups: the aristocratic, conservative, gradualist, pro-British Northern People's Congress and the egalitarian, radical, impatiently nationalist anti-British National Council of Nigerian Citizens. It was this very incongruity, however, that led many outsiders to regard it as the perfect compromise for a peaceful and stable Nigeria. As Wallerstein has noted: "It was led by a 'moderate' Balewa; Azikiwe was out of politics; the 'radical' NCNC and NEPU were tamed by their membership in the coalition; and the opposition was headed by 'responsible Chief Awolowo.' " Above all, it was a coalition that brought the north and the south together.

If there was to be an alliance between a northern and a southern party, why was there not an NPC-Action Group coalition? Certainly on most counts they seemed to be much more compatible. The leaders of the NPC and the Action Group, at the time of the 1959 federal elections, were much closer to each other in their outlook on many major issues, such as the role of traditional elements (emirs and chiefs), the role of the state and of foreign investment in the economy, and, above all, independent Nigeria's foreign policy. In their opposition to Pan-Africanism and in their support for continued close ties with the Western World, the NPC and the AG had almost identical platforms for those elections.

By contrast, the NCNC leaders were supporters of Pan-Africanism and strongly critical of the pro-Westernism of the other two parties. Moreover, for many years the NCNC had provided very considerable support to NEPU, the militant opposition to the NPC in the Northern Region. In the 1959 federal elections, the two parties formed an electoral alliance. Despite all of these considerations, the NPC–NCNC coalition was formed, and Mallam Aminu Kano, NEPU leader and First Vice President of the NCNC, became Chief Whip of the federal government!

The reasons for the NPC–NCNC coalition

Although the full details of how and why the NPC–NCNC coalition was formed are not known, certain considerations should be noted. Despite the apparent compatibility of the NPC and the AG, there were also grounds for mutual distrust, if not outright hostility, between their respective leaders. One of these concerns the character of the Action Group. From the very beginning, it contained within both its leadership and its membership two distinct tendencies—one that was conservative, "moderate" and pro-West, and the other that was rather far Left, perhaps even more militantly radical in its orientation, and inflexibly purist in

its ideological commitment, than its counterpart in either the NCNC or NEPU. Chief Awolowo's rather contradictory position on various issues over the years reflected the fluctuating ascendancy of these two tendencies in his party.

Thus, the generally held image of the Action Group as a "moderate" bourgeois party has been a distorted one. There has been this element—i.e., the "big trader," "transport magnate," "cocoa farmer," traditional ruler, etc. the so-called Akintola faction—in the party. But there has also been a more radical Socialist wing over which Awolowo finally assumed leadership in 1960 when the AG became the opposition at the federal level. The existence of this radical element in the Action Group was not unknown to the leaders of the NPC; indeed, the latter were among the main targets of its criticism.

Another basis for an NPC animus towards the Action Group was the latter's long-standing campaign to carve up the Northern Region into additional states. The purposes of the AG were straightforward and understandable. (1) An undivided Northern Region, with a majority of Nigeria's population, could potentially dominate the federation permanently—not a healthy state of affairs for any federal system. (2) The Action Group, on grounds of principle, supported the creation of new states in the Eastern and Western Regions; it was only reasonable that the north be similarly divided up. (3) The boundary between the Northern and Western Regions should be redrawn so as to reunite the half million Yoruba living over the border in the Northern Region with the main body of Yoruba in the Western Region. This should be done not only because regional boundaries everywhere should respect ethnic groupings, but also because the Yoruba in the Northern Region had a right to self-determination, i.e., liberation from allegedly reactionary northern rule.

Given the profound insecurity most northern leaders have had regarding the potentiality of the backward north being dominated by a more developed south in an independent Nigeria, it is easy to understand their deep resentment of and passionate opposition to the Action Group campaign. To divide the Northern Region would be to deprive the dominant elite of the upper north of the only security they had against southern supremacy. Their fears were greatly heightened by the vigor and effectiveness of the Action Group in winning parliamentary seats in the minority areas of the Northern Region during the federal election campaign of December 1959.

If the NPC had won all 174 Northern Regional seats, the party would have had an absolute majority in the federal Parliament and could have formed an NPC government. The 24 seats won by the Action Group in the Northern Region made it necessary for the north either to form a coalition with one of the two southern parties or to allow an all-southern coalition to rule the federation. The latter would have been intolerable. As the NCNC neither actively campaigned nor won any seats (although its NEPU ally won eight seats) in the Northern Region, it is understandable why the NPC selected the NCNC over the AG as its coalition partner.

The fruits of coalition   The NPC–NCNC coalition has survived three years, and shows no immediate signs of disintegration. There can be little question but that the interaction between the two elements in the coalition has had a significant impact on foreign policy. Nigeria's policy has probably been less "dynamic" than it would have been had the NCNC been solely responsible for policy. By the same token, however, the policy has most likely been far more assertive, Pan-Africanist, and neutralist than it would have been had the NPC had exclusive control. The result of the interaction can be seen in the progressive, but undramatic, shift to a less conservative and less openly pro-West position since independence.

During the first year, Sir Abubakar kept the Ministry of External Affairs and Commonwealth Relations under his personal control, even though it had allegedly been promised to Mr. Jaja Wachuku (NCNC) as part of the original coalition agreement. It was not until August 1961 that Sir Abubakar relinquished the Minis-

try to Mr. Wachuku who, until then, had served as Minister of Economic Development. In the interval, however, Mr. Wachuku had played a very active role as a member of the Nigerian delegation to the United Nations, and, more particularly, as Chairman of the United Nations Conciliation Commission to the Congo.

In addition to this personnel change, there has been a shift since independence on specific issues in a direction that is clearly more in tune with the spirit of African nationalism. Three examples will suffice. One was the reluctant decision of the Prime Minister to accept the resignation of a senior British official, serving as Secretary to the Cabinet, following unrelenting criticism that the continued presence of such a person close to the *arcana* of foreign policy was not only incompatible with sovereign independence, but implied actual subservience to Britain. Another was the decision (mutually arrived at with the United Kingdom government) to abrogate the Anglo-Nigerian Defense Pact which despite the innocuous character of its actual terms had become so stigmatized as "neo-colonialism" that it was an expendable irritant. The third example was the decision of the government, in the summer of 1961, to negotiate formal trade agreements with Communist bloc countries, and to exchange ambassadors with the Soviet Union.

In each of these cases, the Prime Minister was under strong attack not only by the opposition, but by the more nationalistic elements in the NCNC. The nature of this criticism, as well as its implications for the coalition and Nigeria's future will be examined in greater detail in the following discussion of the actual policy positions the Federal Government has taken on specific issues.

THE FOREIGN POLICY OF INDEPENDENT NIGERIA

The major principles of Nigeria's foreign policy were announced by the Prime Minister in a statement made before the Federal House of Representatives on August 20, 1960, several weeks before independence. These were re-affirmed immediately following the independence in his speech before the General Assembly after Nigeria's unanimous acceptance as the 99th member of the United Nations:

First, it is the desire of Nigeria . . . to remain on friendly terms with all nations and to participate actively in the work of the United Nations Organization. Secondly, Nigeria . . . has absolutely no territorial or expansionist intentions. Thirdly, we shall not forget our old friends and we are proud to have been accepted as a member of the Commonwealth, but nevertheless we do not intend to align ourselves as a matter of routine with any of the power blocs. Fourthly, Nigeria hopes to work with other African States for the progress of Africa and to assist in bringing all African territories to a state of responsible independence.[2]

Since independence, Nigeria's policy on specific issues quite faithfully reflects the principle embodied in this succinct and carefully worded statement. The nature of that policy can most conveniently be examined in terms of Nigeria's relationship to the Commonwealth, to the United Nations, to the Western and Eastern bloc, and to other African states.

Nigeria and the Commonwealth

Nigeria's membership in the Commonwealth was never seriously questioned by any political leader or group. All of the major parties favored it during the 1959 election campaign.

The strong views of the Prime Minister regarding the importance of the British and Commonwealth connection were expressed publicly as early as October 1958. At a press conference in London he observed that:

However tempting it may be to adopt a neutralist position in world affairs, I myself very much doubt whether Nigeria will be wise even to contemplate such a course. She will depend to such an extent for her successful development on the goodwill of the people and Governments of Great Britain, of the British Commonwealth and of the Western world, that I don't myself see any future Government of the Federation being in much doubt about the main principles on which to base its foreign policy.[3]

Although in subsequent official statements, made both immediately before and since independence, his pro-West orientation was never quite so explicit, the high value he places upon preserving links with Britain and the Commonwealth has been clearly demonstrated by his stand on particular issues.

The nature of Commonwealth ties Although all of Nigeria's principal leaders enthusiastically supported Nigeria's membership in the Commonwealth, there has been since independence growing agitation for a "purification" of the relationship such membership implies. This agitation, which has not been confined to any particular party, although characteristically it has been most sustained and emphatic on the part of the Opposition, is directed towards Nigeria becoming a republic, towards the extinction of residual links with Britain insofar as these suggest a relationship of unequals, and towards the extinction of racialism and colonialism wherever it may persist within the Commonwealth. Regarding Ni-

[2] *Federal Nigeria*, vol. III, nos. 9/10, Sept./Oct. 1960, p. 9.

[3] *News from Nigeria*, Nigeria Liaison Office. Washington, D.C., Oct., 1958.

geria's becoming a republic, there is no disagreement in principle. The case is clearcut. In the nationalists' view, all self-respecting states must have their own head of state, their own sense of complete identity and sovereignty and their own national symbols for which a foreign monarch is hardly a substitute.

The critical issues do not center upon whether Nigeria should become a republic. Rather, they involve such questions as what type of republic, how much power should go to the head of state and to the head of the government, and above all, who should hold those roles. Seeking answers to these could unsettle the delicate balance and gentlemen's agreement underlying the present coalition.

Nigerian nationalists tend to distinguish sharply between membership in the Commonwealth as a loose, multi-racial, rather innocuous, association of sovereign equals, and the maintenance of special ties with the United Kingdom, the former colonial Power, particularly if such links were conceived or instituted prior to independence. Acceptance of the former and rejection of the latter point up several facets of post-colonial nationalist psychology which it is critically important to appreciate. Namely, there is a strong impulse to make a clean break and establish relationships afresh as a sovereign actor (the "tabula rasa complex"), a compulsive drive to achieve what Touré calls "integral decolonization," and the instinctive suspicion that all special relationships with the former colonial Power are by definition "neo-colonialist" in character.

Continued heavy dependence upon the former colonial Power, whether freely agreed to or not, tends to exacerbate an already profound sense of frustration over the fact that there has been no visible consummation of the great revolution independence was supposed to bring. Thus, while Sir Abubakar and others like him would be inclined to regard continued close ties with the United Kingdom as obviously natural and manifestly beneficial, the more nationalistic Nigerians would regard such relationships not only as compromising Nigeria's declared policy of nonalignment, and therefore making her a hypocrite, but also as

perpetuating a dependency relationship in which Nigeria could not help but be subservient to Britain.

The views of the opposition   The foregoing are the themes that run through the relentless criticism of Sir Abubakar's policy of maintaining close ties with the United Kingdom. The chief critics have been the Action Group, the more nationalistic elements in the NCNC, and particularly the smaller and more militant groups such as the Nigerian Youth Congress and the Dynamic Party. As Chief Awolowo bluntly put it in a speech in London in September 1961:

> Nigeria is a submissive British subaltern or satellite . . . on major issues affecting Nigeria, Africa and the world, Sir Abubakar has never had the courage and initiative to declare the stand of his government until after he has had a chance of personal contact with Mr. Macmillan or one of his lieutenants.[4]

In the same vein, Sir Abubakar has been attacked by his critics for pushing through Parliament the innocuous but very unpopular Anglo-Nigerian Defense Pact (now abrogated), and for concluding the usual state-succession agreement with the United Kingdom wherein Nigeria undertakes all the rights and obligations of Britain under any valid international instrument insofar as they were applicable to Nigeria before the latter's attainment of independence. Awolowo argued that if Nigeria is to be a party to an international agreement "we must do so in our own right as a sovereign state, not as Britain's underling or foster child." The obsessive concern over any possibly undue influence from the United Kingdom even prompted the serious suggestion that the official residence of the United Kingdom High Commissioner to Nigeria should be physically

[4] *The Service* (Lagos), vol. I, no. 52, Sept. 16, 1961, p. 10.

relocated as it was too close to the official residence of the Nigerian Prime Minister.

Nigeria and the United Nations

One of the principles of Nigerian foreign policy which Sir Abubakar's government has most strongly emphasized is Nigeria's firm commitment to the United Nations Organization. Nigerian support has been repeatedly affirmed—not at all perfunctorily, but with great sincerity and emphasis. Several reasons have been given. One is the belief, frequently encountered among the leaders of uncommitted nations, that the world organization provides a forum in which they can play a constructive mediating role. As the Prime Minister put it:

What we now want is to reduce the differences between nations and to bring the world together. The United Nations Organization is the best instrument for this purpose and it is my hope that African countries will be given an effective voice in that Organization. Our presence in the Security Council will, I am sure, have a salutary effect on the Great Powers and will enable us to make our contribution to the cause of world peace.[5]

There is also the belief that the organization offers neutral protection to fragile and defenseless new African states. "The newly independent countries of Africa," Nigerian Ambassador Udochi noted, "have a greater need of the world organization as a means of safeguarding their independence and freedom than the older and better armed nations of the world." Also, in their view the U.N. is the best instrument for keeping the Cold War out of Africa. On these points, there is no disagreement among Nigeria's principal leaders; all strongly support the United Nations.

[5] *West African Pilot* (Lagos), August 9, 1961.

Nigeria's commitment to the United Nations has been demonstrated on many occasions. Among African states, it is by far the heaviest contributor to the United Nations budget; indeed, its representative at the United Nations demanded that "punitive measures" be taken against nonpaying members. Again, immediately after independence, Nigeria sent an army contingent to the Congo to serve in the U.N. operations. This Nigerian contingent was the third largest among the U.N. troops, and by far the largest of any new African state. Nigerian officers and men served with distinction, frequently on some of the most thankless assignments. Nigeria was among the first five African states to subscribe to the U.N. bond issue covering the Congo operation. It was consistently a strong supporter of the late Dag Hammarskjøld, and continued that support to Mr. U. Thant, openly opposing the Soviet "troika" plan when proposed.

Nigeria's representatives at the United Nations, and particularly its colorful and controversial Foreign Minister, Mr. Jaja Wachuku, have been very active and articulate on a variety of world and African issues. Nigeria's influence was significant in the creation of the UN Conciliation Committee for the Congo, of which Mr. Wachuku was chairman. Nigeria took the leadership in the Fifteenth Assembly struggle to defeat Portugal and secure a seat for Africa on both the Security Council and the Economic and Social Council.

Its spokesmen have been very articulate in all discussions of racial discrimination and residual colonialism. It has consistently voted with the more militant anti-colonial groups on all such issues. On Cold War issues involving East-West tensions, Nigeria has pursued quite an independent line. It has voted as frequently with the Soviet group as with the West, or it has abstained.

Despite Nigeria's U.N. voting record of militancy on racial-colonial issues, the Nigerian government was strongly attacked, both inside the Nigerian Parliament and by nationalist elements in Nigeria and other African states, for the resolution introduced by Mr. Wachuku in the Sixteenth (1961) Session of the General Assembly calling for an end to colonialism in all parts of Africa by 1970. In the United Nations itself, Afro-Asian states were so divided on the issue—the more militantly anti-colonial states violently opposing the motion—that the Nigerian representative withdrew the motion in the interest of African unity.

However, the very fact that it was introduced illuminates a rather characteristic "Nigerian" style and orientation to such problems growing out of Nigeria's own peaceful and unhurried evolution towards independence, as well as the sobering experience of the Congo tragedy. In support of his "1970 freedom resolution" Mr. Wachuku stated frankly that the federal government believed in a process of gradual and orderly evolution in Africa because it did not want plans and money earmarked for development to be diverted to military channels: ". . . if we had half the money spent in the Congo operation we would have no trouble implementing the Ashby Report. . . . We don't want the Congo situation to occur in any other part of Africa."

This is an argument with which most Nigerians would agree in private and rational discourse, but they would lament the fact that it has to be said and above all that a Nigerian spokesman says it. This is the agony of a contemporary African who is both a reasonable man and a nationalist. It is summed up in the following characteristic retort of a Nigerian nationalist to a compliment paid his Prime Minister. "Yes, probably he seems good to you Americans. He is what you want. But for us he is too moderate. He needs more fire, more nationalism."

Nigeria and the Cold War

Western orientation All of Nigeria's major political leaders have at one time or another made statements indicating a basic sympathy for or commitment to Western values. Some have been more categorical and explicit in their sentiments than others. We have already noted the strongly pro-Western statement of Sir Abubakar made in London in 1958. An even more eloquent statement was made by Chief Awolowo, leader of the Opposition, in his Presidential Address to the Seventh Annual Congress of the Action Group on September 19, 1960:

> Because I believe that the ideals and aspirations of Nigeria should consist in individual freedom, the rule of law, liberal democracy, and the pursuit of a welfare state, I unhesitatingly declare my sympathy for and association with the Western Bloc in whose fold these ideals and aspirations are firmly upheld and faithfully practiced. . . . I believe in the ends which Communism professes . . . but I seriously doubt the honest pursuit of these ends by Communist leaders, and in any case wholeheartedly abhor the methods by which they try to achieve these admirable ends. . . . What I have preached and still preach is close and unwavering collaboration with Britain and the Western World in the defence and propagation of the ideals of liberty, equality, respect for human dignity . . . for which they stand in contradiction to the Communist Bloc.[6]

It is difficult, of course, to judge how genuine and deep is the pro-West attachment of those leaders who declare themselves so committed. Certainly there are overwhelming domestic and external political pressures in contemporary Africa nudging all leaders and governments towards greater purity in their "non-alignment" position and towards a more diversified dependence upon the external world. How deeply concerned political leaders are regarding their vulnerability to the charge of being pro-West is reflected in the demand made upon the Federal Government in October 1961

[6] *Daily Express* (Lagos), October 4, 1960, p. 5.

by the National Executive Committee of the NCNC that it "pursue its policy of non-alignment with the utmost vigor in order to dispel the impression in certain quarters that Nigeria is pro-West." It is not only fashionable, but a political imperative to be non-aligned in contemporary Africa.

Sir Abubakar's government has followed a policy of independence, stressing Nigeria's desire "to remain on friendly terms with all nations," and, in Sir Abubakar's words, not "to align ourselves as a matter of routine with any of the power blocs." Indeed, he has repeatedly condemned the formation of blocs either within or outside of the United Nations. His opposition to blocs was the main reason he gave for Nigeria not participating in the Belgrade Conference of Non-Aligned Powers in September 1961. He has argued that "when a neutral country joins a neutral bloc it ceases to be neutral. We want to pursue an independent view, which is not the same as neutralism."

Nigeria's record in the United Nations, as already noted, has in fact been remarkably independent. It unquestionably has been more pro-West than that of Guinea or Mali, but it has also been more pro-East than that of the Philippines or Senegal. But this is an unsatisfactory mode of evaluation, and certainly it provides no basis for prediction. The basic motivation of Nigeria's representatives in the United Nations has been to dramatize their independence, to demonstrate their determination not to be guided by prejudices inherited from their historic tie with Britain and the West, and to do precisely what the Prime Minister stated as his government's policy, namely "to judge each problem on its merits and to follow the path of truth wherever it may lead."

Relations with Communist countries Despite Nigeria's declared policy of non-alignment, and notwithstanding the relatively independent position it has taken in the United Nations on Cold War issues, direct relationships between Nigeria and countries of the Eastern bloc have been marked by a coolness and restraint on the part of the Nigerian government that is all the more pointed because of its sharp contrast to the more relaxed and extensive relations she has with Western countries. The evidence the critics of the government cite in support of their charge that Sir Abubakar's policy of non-alignment is hypocritical and dishonest centers mainly upon a continuation after independence of the anti-Communist, anti-Soviet policies of the British colonial administration. These include a ban on Communist publications, prohibition of the employment of Communists in Government agencies, denial of passports to Nigerian Communists and to students desiring to study behind the Iron Curtain, official obstacles and indifference to the development of trade with Communist countries, and evasiveness and obstructionism in connection with repeated overtures by the U.S.S.R. to establish an embassy in Nigeria.

By mid-1961, the government commenced to change its policy on relationships with the Communist world. An agreement was reached with the U.S.S.R. in March of 1961 to exchange ambassadors, and the Soviet embassy was opened in Lagos in late December 1961. In the same month, the Prime Minister announced the repeal of the 1955 ban against the importation of Communist publications, but pointedly added that he would not hesitate to reimpose the ban if his faith that the Nigerian people had the maturity and self-confidence not to be misled by "literature of this sort" was misplaced. In mid-1961, a Nigerian trade delegation visited Eastern Europe, Russia and Communist China and trade agreements were signed with Poland and Czechoslovakia. Nevertheless, Sir Abubakar's government moved cautiously and by the end of the second year of independence, official contacts between Nigeria and the countries of the Sino-Soviet bloc were still rather cool and formal, standing in sharp contrast with contacts with such new states as the Sudan, Ghana and Guinea.

The most likely explanation for Sir Abubakar's disinclination to plunge indiscriminately into formal diplomatic relationships with the Sino-Soviet bloc are not that he was under the influence of Britain or the West, or that he had a consuming fear of communism, but that he was deliberately pursuing a rational, economizing and pragmatic course of gradually establishing Nigeria's relationships with the external world. Moreover, such a cautious and non-compulsive policy was an accurate reflection of the unemotional and self-confident political style of Sir Abubakar himself. Unlike other less secure personalities, he did not feel driven to embrace the Communist bloc at the time of independence as a petulant gesture of defiance of the West in order to prove that his non-alignment policy was bona fide.

Expansion of diplomatic activities   He had a specific predetermined plan for the progressive expansion of Nigeria's formal relations with foreign countries. In the case of foreign representatives in Nigeria, this plan envisaged the formalization of relationships first with countries of the Commonwealth and with those countries which already had consulates or representation in Lagos, and then acceptance of representatives of additional countries on the basis of demonstrated need and the merits of each case.

The plan for Nigerian representation abroad envisaged the opening of embassies according to three lists of countries, in descending order of priority, in which the governing criteria would be availability of qualified Nigerians, finance, and Nigeria's national interest. As the data in the table on page 401 indicate, Sir Abubakar proceeded cautiously; each country has a justification under these criteria. The rationale for representation in London is obvious. Elsewhere, it is also strong; with Ghana and Sierra Leone there are historic links and they are co-members of the Commonwealth; with the United States there is substantial trade, a large number of Nigerian students in American universities, and a high level of developmental assistance; with West Germany there is substantial trade and economic assistance; with Saudi Arabia and the Sudan there are the problems connected with Nigerian pilgrims to Mecca; with the Republic of the Cameroun there are historic ties with West Cameroon, a large number of Nigerians living in the Cameroon and a long common border; with the Congo (Leopoldville) there is the sizeable Nigerian contingent serving with the UN forces; and with Senegal, Ivory Coast, Liberia and Guinea, there is the fact that these are the other key West African states—the former three, leaders in the so-called Monrovia Group to which Nigeria belongs, and Guinea, with Ghana, a leader in the Casablanca Group. In balance, it is fair to say that while the West is overwhelmingly preponderant in both sending and receiving representation, it is a pattern explained by historical reasons and by an objective assessment of Nigeria's national interest in the immediate post-colonial period.

Nigeria and Africa

General policy principles   As Nigeria approached independence, her leaders expressed a self-consciousness of the continental leadership they believed she was destined to assume, as well as a spirit of benevolent restraint and humility. Sir Abubakar appealed to every Nigerian to assist in making Nigeria a strong and united country "so that she might fulfill her destiny as the leader of the African continent," and become the great "stabilizing force in Africa." Yet this spirit of "Manifest Destiny" was usually tempered by the oft-repeated admonition that Nigeria should not misuse her great power.

This latter strand is brought out clearly in an article by Dr. Nnamdi Azikiwe, Governor-General, entitled "Nigeria in World Politics," published just before independence.

> In the arena of world politics, Nigeria should not seek to impose its leadership on Africa or elsewhere and it should not attempt to browbeat the rest of Africa or [force] any nation to bend their knees in acknowledgment of the existence of a colossus that it is. Rather, a free Nigeria should dedicate itself to co-operate with Africa and the rest of the world

CATEGORY	COUNTRIES REPRESENTED IN NIGERIA	COUNTRIES IN WHICH NIGERIA HAS EMBASSY	COMMITMENTS FOR RECIPROCAL EXCHANGE—1962
COMMONWEALTH	Australia	—	—
	Canada	—	Canada
	Ghana	Ghana	—
	India	—	India
	Pakistan	—	Pakistan
	Rhodesia & Nyasaland	—	—
	Sierra Leone	Sierra Leone	—
	United Kingdom	United Kingdom	—
	—	—	Tanganyika
COMMUNIST COUNTRIES	U.S.S.R.	—	—
	—	—	Poland
NON-COMMUNIST COUNTRIES	Belgium	—	—
Western Europe	Germany (*Bonn*)	Germany (*Bonn*)	—
	Ireland	—	—
	Italy	—	Italy
	Netherlands	—	—
	Norway	—	—
	Portugal	—	—
	Spain	—	—
	Sweden	—	—
	Switzerland	—	—
	*United Kingdom	*United Kingdom	—
Western Hemisphere	*Canada	—	*Canada
	United States	United States	—
	—	—	Brazil
Middle East and	Israel	—	—
North Africa	Lebanon	—	—
	Saudi Arabia	Saudi Arabia	—
	Sudan	Sudan	—
	Turkey	—	—
	U.A.R.	—	—
Asia	*India	—	*India
	*Pakistan	—	*Pakistan
	Japan	—	—
Africa	Cameroun	Cameroun	—
Monrovia Group	Chad	—	—
	Dahomey	—	—
	Ethiopia	—	Ethiopia
	Ivory Coast	Ivory Coast	—
	Liberia	Liberia	—
	Niger	—	—
	Senegal	Senegal	—
	—	Congo (*Leopoldville*)	—
	—	—	Tanganyika
Casablanca Group	*Ghana	*Ghana	—
	Guinea	Guinea (*from Liberia*)	Guinea

* Duplicate listing of member of Commonwealth

towards the maintenance of peace everywhere in the world, the revival of the stature of man everywhere in the world, and the extermination of man's inhumanity to man everywhere in the world.[7]

Nigeria's policy on African affairs since independence has reflected this spirit of "good neighborliness" and co-operation.

There are three main aspects of Nigeria's policy regarding her relationships with other African states that warrant mention, namely, nonintervention, functional integration, and nonviolent resolution of Africa's remaining colonial and racial problems.

The rule of nonintervention   Since independence, Nigerian spokesmen have been vehement on many occasions regarding the inviolability of the present international boundaries of Africa's new states. While acknowledging that Africa's international boundaries are artificial and capriciously drawn, Sir Abubakar repeatedly insisted that they must remain "the recognized boundaries until such time as the peoples concerned decide of their own free will to merge into one unit."

Largely under Nigerian leadership, all facets of the general principle of nonintervention were explicated more fully in the five principles[8] agreed to by the 21 Heads of State at the Monrovia Conference in May 1961. Subsequently, in a bilateral Nigerian-Guinean communiqué, issued after talks between Balewa and Touré, this principle was re-affirmed.

Nigerian spokesmen have not been content merely to give lip service to the principle. Her foreign minister, Mr. Jaja Wachuku, has stated bluntly that Nigeria will enforce that principle: ". . . Nigeria considers it her duty to instill confidence in the new African states. They must feel secure. They must be assured that no

new African state is going to bully them. We will not tolerate any form of bullying by one African state of another." While frequently stated in one form or another as a general principle, such remarks are most likely pointed at Ghana, whose spokesmen have from time to time employed threatening language regarding little Togo. This has not, of course, helped Nigerian-Ghanaian relations. In any event, Nigeria has emerged as one of the leading defenders of the territorial status quo in Africa.

Pan-African unity   A second major principle is Nigeria's firm commitment to the achievement of the goal of Pan-African unity through functional co-operation rather than political unification. The Nigerian case has been put very succinctly by Mr. Wachuku:

> . . . while we want Africa to live in peace, we do not want her to continue in pieces. Nigerians believe in the integration of the African continent. . . . Pan-Africanism is no longer merely a theory; it is a fact. But, while all Africans agree on that, our methods of pursuing this goal differ. There are some who want political union now—with themselves on top. We in Nigeria believe in being realistic about Pan-Africanism. . . . We believe that the African states must first come together on the cultural and economic level.[9]

It is this difference in the *theory* of how Pan-African unity can most effectively be achieved that sharply divides the Casablanca Group (Ghana - Guinea - Mali - Morocco - UAR) — the political unificationists—from the Monrovia Group (Nigeria, Liberia, Ethiopia, Somalia, and all French-speaking new states except Guinea and Mali), who are the functionalists.

Among the more important reasons why Nigeria supports the functional approach to African unification are the pragmatic, unemo-

---

[7] *Presence Africaine,* vols. 4/5, nos. 32/33, p. 30.

[8] Sovereign equality, no forceable annexation, right of voluntary integration, noninterference in domestic affairs of another state, no harboring of dissident or subversive persons or groups hostile to a neighboring state.

[9] Jaja Wachuku, "Nigeria's Foreign Policy," in *Africa: The Political Pattern,* Toronto: University of Toronto Press, 1961, p. 71.

tional and nonideological orientations of most members of Sir Abubakar's government. Moreover, Nigerian leaders have had the sobering and instructive experience of wrestling for more than a decade with the problem of how to achieve and maintain the unity of Nigeria. Both the internal policies and practices—doctrinaire socialism and one-party democratic centralism—and the external policies—"positive" East-leaning nonalignment—of Ghana, Guinea and Mali are incompatible with the stated political values and commitments of the present governing elite of Nigeria.

An added consideration is that Nigeria's late entrance into the arena of interstate politics in Africa posed a dilemma: she would either have had to join the already formed Ghana-Guinea-Mali union, which psychologically would probably have been unbearable, or she would have had to join in the formation of a rival political union, which would be self-defeating in terms of the goal of African unity. Moreover, as the African colossus, she would always be in any political union particularly vulnerable to the charge of disproportionate influence or of territorial aggrandizement. The fact is, however, that for several years all of Nigeria's leaders advocated the functional approach to African unity, and the preservation of the sovereign equality of states irrespective of their size.

The majority of Africa's new states have associated themselves with Nigeria in the functional approach to African unity. Nevertheless, there can be little question that despite all the manifest obstacles to its realization, the idea of Pan-African political unity has acquired a mystique of great political relevance. Moreover, in the eyes of the more nationalist elements, and particularly the upcoming generation of younger leaders, the political unificationists (Ghana, Guinea and Mali) are regarded as the carriers of this mystique and the consummators of the unfinished African Revolution. Pan-African political unity, together with the African personality, African socialism and positive non-alignment constitute a constellation of ideals. Their realization will complete the revolution and will finally redeem Africa as a continent and Africans as a race.

Faced with the overpowering magnetism of the Pan-African mystique for the younger nationalist generation—a group upon which present elites must increasingly depend for support —most of Nigeria's major political leaders have responded in one way or another to the challenge it poses. Sir Ahmadu Bello, northern Premier, has remained singularly indifferent to the political attractions of Pan-Africanism; rather he has endeavored to further the ideal of Pan-Islam and a Muslim Commonwealth. He has said that "Islam is mankind's common denominator."

Dr. Nnamdi Azikiwe, Governor-General, one of the venerated fathers of Pan-Africanism, has sought to maintain the popular Africa-wide image of his identification with the objectives of political Pan-Africanism, without compromising Nigeria's official policy of functional integration. His remarkable talent for projecting an image of himself as passionately in favor of a nationalist objective, while at the same time protecting himself from being connected to any specific course of action, is revealed in the following quotation from a widely-publicized public address in London in August 1961 entitled "The Future of Pan-Africanism":

. . . it is my firm belief that an African leviathan must emerge ultimately: it may be in the form of an association of African States or in the form of a concert of African States; but my main point is that so long as the form of government is clearly understood and an efficient machinery for organization and administration is devised, backed by multi-lateral conventions which would enhance the standard of living of Africans, safeguard their existence by collective security and freedom under the law in addition to the fundamental rights, the dream of Pan-Africanism is destined to come true.[10]

[10] Dr. Nnamdi Azikiwe, "The Future of Pan-Africanism," *Presence Africaine,* vol. 12, no. 40, p. 29.

Sir Abubakar recognized the political importance of reckoning with the Pan-African movement by appointing a special Adviser to the Prime Minister on African Affairs and by authorizing the convening of an All-Nigeria Peoples Conference, composed of 300 Nigerians, representing all political parties and all shades of opinion in the country. In his opening remarks the Prime Minister stated that the object of the Conference was to "examine all our problems whether common or varied [involving relations with other African states] and then try to find solutions to them." The conference recommendations covered most of the principal criticisms which had been made on many previous occasions by the Opposition and by dissident elements in the following of the coalition parties. Significantly, the first recommendation was that "Nigeria should accept, in principle, the political union of African States on a continental basis." The calling of such an unconventional conference for the purpose of popular consultation on Pan-African affairs is a measure of the seriousness the Nigerian Government attaches to the generalized discontent regarding Nigeria's position on political Pan-Africanism.

The most astonishing volte-face of any Nigerian leader on the Pan-African issue was performed by Chief Obafemi Awolowo, Leader of the Opposition, who, after a visit to Ghana and an interview with President Nkrumah in June 1961 advocated that Nigeria join the Ghana-Guinea-Mali union. This declaration was particularly electrifying because Awolowo and the Action Group had for years been among the most articulate and forthright proponents of functional integration and the most forceful critics not only of the idea of political Pan-Africanism but of two of its principal advocates, namely, Nkrumah and Nasser.

Although Awolowo subsequently sought to clarify his stand to show that it was consistent with the development of his thinking on the issue, the main point is clear. Awolowo's spectacular shift is partly the result of the greatly increased strength of the more ideological and militant nationalist elements in his own party, and partly a consequence of his realiza-

tion that, rightly or wrongly, the political unificationist states were riding the African "wave of the future," which it would be political folly—particularly for an opposition leader—to resist.

Racialism and colonialism The third strand in Nigeria's official inter-African policy, namely, the advocacy of a progressive and nonviolent—as distinguished from an immediate and revolutionary—resolution of residual racialism and colonialism in Africa, is also under strong attack by more nationalistic Africans inside and outside Nigeria. Here again Nigeria's policy stands in marked contrast to that of the political unificationist states which, as a matter of declared policy, support nationalist and revolutionary leaders and movements from areas still under white European domination. It is this contrast that has provoked the Opposition criticism that Nigeria's policy is "too slow and dull in African affairs" and too lacking in dynamism and revolutionary fervor.

There can be little question that Nigeria's policy regarding racialist and colonial regimes in Africa is remarkably—indeed, unnaturally—conciliatory and gradualist for an African government. Sir Abubakar has explicitly rejected proposals that Nigeria support revolutionary action against such regimes. Thus, when asked during the Bizerte crisis if Nigeria would provide military support to Tunisia, Sir Abubakar observed that Nigeria was militarily weak, but, in any case, he did not think it right for African countries to give military aid to their neighbors. Again, when he was approached for aid in May 1962 by Holden Roberto, Angolan nationalist leader, he stated that Nigeria would help train administrative and medical staff for the "Provisional Government of Angola," but would not train Angolan armed forces or police "because it will mean that we are training you to fight your African brothers in the south." This cautious position is, of course, related to, indeed, it flows from, the Nigerian policy of nonintervention and of opposition to over-hasty decolonization previously discussed. The rationale of this position is best expressed in Sir Abubakar's own words:

The unity of Africa presupposes the independence of all African states. Those that are now independent have a responsibility, therefore, to aid their fellows to freedom. We abhor violence because its memories persist and haunt the country long after independence has been won. Also, Nigeria's position, born of her experience, has been that peaceful and constitutional methods must first be exhausted in the struggle for freedom. In accordance with this belief, we have given, and will continue to give, moral and material support to dependent African states fighting for freedom.[11]

Not only does the Nigerian government refuse to become an operations center for the liberation of Africans in colonial Africa, but

Sir Abubakar has continued to maintain links with the European-dominated regimes concerned. Portugal and the Federation of Rhodesia and Nyasaland have official representation in Lagos. In fact, Nigeria has committed itself to send a High Commissioner to the Federation of Rhodesia and Nyasaland, a white-dominated political system which African nationalist leaders are currently seeking to destroy. Moreover, Sir Abubakar has indicated that he is interested in visiting the Federation, indeed, that he would even consider visiting South Africa. He has emphasized, however, that this did not mean any lessening of Nigeria's strong opposition to the policies of the governments concerned. "We shall," he has declared, "continue to use all the means at our disposal, especially at the United Nations, to ensure that the last vestiges of racialism and colonialism are wiped off the face of Africa."[12]

[11] Balewa, *op. cit.,* p. 138.

[12] *Ibid.*

BIBLIOGRAPHY

Author's suggestions

Azikiwe, Nnamdi. "The Future of Pan-Africanism," *Presence Africaine,* vol. 12, no. 40, 1962, pp. 7–29.

Azikiwe, Nnamdi. "Nigeria in World Politics," *Presence Africaine,* vols. 4/5, nos. 32/33, 1960, pp. 19–30.

Balewa, Sir Abubakar Tafawa. "Nigeria Looks Ahead," *Foreign Affairs,* vol. 41, October, 1962, pp. 131–140.

Coleman, James S. *Nigeria: Background to Na-tionalism.* Berkeley and Los Angeles: University of California Press, 1958.

Cowan, L. Gray. "Nigerian Foreign Policy," in *The Nigerian Political Scene,* Robert O. Tilman and Taylor Cole, eds. Durham, N.C.: Duke University Press, 1962, pp. 115–143.

Sklar, Richard L. *Nigerian Political Parties* Princeton: Princeton University Press, 1963.

Wachuku, Jaja. "Nigeria's Foreign Policy," in Millar MacLure and Douglas Anglin, eds. *Africa: The Political Pattern.* Toronto: University of Toronto Press, 1961, pp. 62–73.

ABOUT THE AUTHOR

J. G. KIANO began his formal education in Makerere College in Uganda and finished with his Ph.D. degree in Political Science at the University of California, Berkeley, in 1956. In the interim he earned a B.A. degree in economics at Antioch College in Ohio and a Masters degree at Stanford University. His career started as a lecturer in Economics and Constitutional Law at The Royal College at Nairobi, but soon turned toward political and governmental service in Kenya.

He has been a member of the Kenya legislature since 1958, Minister of Commerce and Industry, 1960–61, and is presently Mr. Kenyatta's Parliamentary Secretary for Economic Planning. He is the Secretary/Treasurer for the Kenya Branch of the Commonwealth Parliamentary Association, member of the Kenya African National Union, member of the Executive Council of the World Without the Bomb Assembly, Accra, Ghana, and was the founder and the first President of the Ralph Bunche Academy in Nairobi. Mr. Kiano was one of the founder members of the Pan-African Freedom Movement of East and Central Africa. He has also published a number of articles on political and economic matters in East Africa.

ABOUT THE CHAPTER

This chapter is slightly different from the others included in this book. With the increasing voice of the African states in world affairs, it appeared highly desirable to have East Africa represented in this study. Because of the close relationship between Uganda, Kenya, and Tanganyika, it seemed logical to have one article dealing with the East African point of view.

Dr. Kiano first describes the legacy of the slavery period and the period of colonialism. He then considers the attitudes in East Africa which condition the types of policies that will be followed. The author also analyzes the various Pan-African movements. He correctly notes the different paths that are being followed and the rivalry among the different African nations.

The relationship of the new African states to the Commonwealth and the changing nature of this voluntary association are examined. Dr. Kiano defends the position of non-alignment and insists that Africa "cannot be bought" and that it will follow its own independent course of action.

14

THE FOREIGN POLICY OF EAST AFRICAN COUNTRIES

J. G. KIANO
Treasury Office, Nairobi

To every realm shall peace her charms display,
And heavenly freedom spread her golden ray.
                                    Phillis Wheatley[1]

The above-quoted words of Phillis Wheatley, described by her biographer as a "frail mite of a child, dark as chocolate, cute, shy and rather pretty in an exotic African way," express in a nutshell most Africans' aspirations regarding the bold new world of which they now are an integral part. Before analyzing the fundamental assumptions upon which these aspirations are founded, it will be helpful to take a quick look at the historical pattern of relations between Africa and the rest of the world during the last two centuries.

BACKGROUND FACTORS

Trade and religious contacts   Trade relations between Africa and the other continents

[1] 1753–1784, in her poem "Liberty and Peace."

have gone on for centuries. Traders from India, Arabia and other parts of Asia visited, traded with, and sometimes even settled among, coastal Africans throughout the eastern regions. Europeans from the Mediterranean area, ranging from the Asia Minor borders to the Spanish peninsula, not only kept in close touch with North Africans but also ventured farther and farther south along the West African coast, as well as the Red Sea coastline.

Some religious proselyting did accompany the trade contacts, as evidenced by the long history of the Coptic (Christian) Church in Ethiopia as well as the existence of Moslem African groupings along the eastern coast and the area bordering the famous Sahara desert.

But despite these contacts, which were often sporadic and somewhat haphazard, relations between the very largest of the masses of the African people and the outside world were never institutionalized in any permanent systematic form until recent times. Accordingly, these trade contacts and sporadic religious proselyting did not contribute much to the formulation of the African peoples' attitude toward the rest of the world.

Slavery and colonialism

The first major impact which the outside world made upon African life and thought, unfortunately was the deplorably inhumane slave trade. Britons, Spaniards, Americans, Germans, and practically everybody else in Europe and the Western Hemisphere, captured, bought, enslaved or otherwise directly or indirectly victimized African peoples in the western regions of Africa, while the Arabs did likewise in the eastern regions. African kingdoms were annihilated, tribal societies were ruthlessly dissipated, individual Africans were marketed like sheep or cattle. Whatever African civilizations were flourishing or budding during this era were extinguished.

Thus the first major and effective contact between the African peoples and non-Africans could only give birth to an attitude of bitterness and suspicion in African minds toward foreign Powers. The existence of the racial problem in the United States, among other factors, continues to remind the African of this most tragic episode in African history.

This attitude of bitterness might have been mitigated by the historical fact that Western philanthropic organizations and individuals, such as William Wilberforce and his Anti-Slavery Movement and the Abolitionist Movement in the United States symbolized by irrepressible John Brown, played a very large part in inducing their governments to take effective measures to end the slave trade.

But, again most unfortunately, the abolition of the slave trade was succeeded immediately by wholesale colonization, characterized at its initial stage by exploitation and degradation, often reminiscent of the slave trade activities. Military expeditions by European Powers to subordinate reluctant tribes to colonial authorities, as was the case in many parts of Southern Africa; grabbing of Africans' agricultural lands by colonial settlers as was the case in Kenya, the Rhodesias and elsewhere; massacres

such as took place in the Congo under King Leopold II, as well as in Uganda where different foreign religious factions started battle after battle for African converts; and fraudulent treaties which tricked many African rulers into colonial domination while they thought they were seeking friendship or protection from the foreign Powers: these happenings far outweighed the impacts of genuinely philanthropic missions and services rendered at this crucial period, known so aptly in British history books as "The Scramble for Africa" period.

Resistance to colonialism

By the turn of the century, practically all Africa was subject to one foreign Power or another. The bitterness and confusion caused by the slave trade and colonization gradually gave birth to nationalist movements against colonialism. There were those rulers and tribal leaders who still thought of continued military resistance to colonial Powers. There was, for example King Mwanga of the Buganda Kingdom in the territory of Uganda whom the British banished from his Kingdom for leading a military uprising and causing a good number of Christian converts to be burned alive to weaken foreign influences in his territory. There was Chief Waiyaki from the southern part of the Kikuyu region in Kenya. He led his armies against the incoming British agents and was to be banished to the coast; he mysteriously died on the way. There were the Mohammedan leaders who fought against British armies in the Sudan.

Religious-political movements Following the complete establishment of colonial Powers in Africa, resistance to the non-Africans' authority took three forms mainly. The first manifestations were politically-inspired but nevertheless religious movements seeking to establish heavenly conditions, not only in the theological world, but also in this real world of ours. Some of the best known movements of this kind were the Kibangu Movement of the then Belgian Congo which was led by Prophet Kibangu at the beginning of the nineteen-twenties and the Israelite Movement of South Africa which trained soldiers in the tabernacles for a Holy war against South Africa's European authorities.

Participants in these movements thought that religion was not supposed to concern itself only with the next world. Political injustices, economic exploitation and racial victimization, all of which were part and parcel of foreign colonial rule, were as much a concern to religion as they were to politics. Thus, these religious movements became an effective vehicle for spreading to the masses political attitudes regarding Africans' relations with foreign Powers and institutions such as foreign missionaries, industries and other non-African organizations.

Workers' organizations　　The second type of resistance took the form of workers' organizations. While experiencing a lot of difficulties in the attempt to have them established and recognized by governments, workers' organizations did mushroom in Africa in search for justice and fair play for the African masses. Nearly all Africans during this early part of the century were either self-employed peasants in the rural districts or actual laborers in the industrial, commercial and agricultural concerns. Foreign employers viewed them as cheap labor pools to be employed by them whenever necessary.

Until the post World War II period, workers' movements in colonial African territories were barely able to survive due to the very restrictive laws and regulations against workers' organizations. But it is significant that whenever a trade union movement was banned by law or otherwise disbanded, a new one was soon created, often by the same leaders. Thus mass consciousness about injustices suffered by the African people under colonial rule and foreign economic subjugation became intensified as time went on.

Political groups　　Hand in hand with workers' movements, purely political organizations were formed as an additional weapon to struggle against foreign colonial rule. It has often been said that the leaders of such movements did not have the people with them and that they really were a small group of disgruntled elite amidst ignorant masses, disinterested in politics as such. Nothing could be further from the truth. It is quite correct to say that the leaders were, more often than not, the few literate and otherwise acculturated individuals in any given African colonial territory. Nevertheless, these very persons were the ones who commanded most influence among their fellow countrymen. Furthermore, one does not have to be educated to know when one is being maltreated socially and politically.

Colonialism is now defeated in Africa, even though the Portuguese and the white Afrikaaners in the Union of South Africa still blindly refuse to acknowledge the rising African power in the Continent. A combination of workers' movements and nationalist organizations, aided, particularly at the earlier stages of the struggle for independence, by politically inspired religious sects, has ushered in a new era in the history of this vast continent.

What is significant is that the masses have been very much a part of the struggle. Since the days of the slave trade, through the colonization period, to the present day of nationalistic triumph, these masses have resented profoundly the type of relations with foreign Powers that began when John Hawkins in Western Africa and Arab traders in Eastern Africa initiated the slave trade. What is the new type of relationship that the African masses and their leaders now desire to be established following Africa's independence? In this chapter we will examine the approach to foreign relations now being adopted by the territories in Eastern Africa.

Mental attitudes

The region referred to in this chapter as Eastern Africa includes essentially the countries of

Kenya, Uganda, Tanganyika, Zanzibar, the Rhodesias and Nyasaland. What are the mental attitudes in this region that are shaping the decisions regarding foreign policy? The conditions against which Africans in this region have had to struggle in search of political independence and economic fair play remind the leaders very much of the conditions that existed for the working class in Europe during the last century.

The appeal of socialism　　Until the somewhat belated reforms during the last quarter of the century, political power in Europe was in the hands of the wealthy few. Conditions of the workers were far from satisfactory, and safety for human life was almost ignored. The capitalist system of that period in Great Britain and elsewhere in Europe was essentially a system in which the rich entrepreneurs shamelessly exploited the working masses. This situation led Karl Marx, the Fabian group and other thinkers to develop socialist ideas.

In Eastern Africa, labor laws had been designed by colonial authorities to protect the few foreign employers and curb the influences of trade unions. Mr. P. de V. Allen, former Labor Commissioner in Kenya, expressed this view very frankly in 1939 when he said "I am not in favor of trade unions for natives; the time is not ripe for this."[2] A memorandum presented to the Conference of the Southern Rhodesia Trade Union Congress, which was exclusively for white employees in industries, stressed the same viewpoint when it stated: "the duties and responsibilities of modern trade unionism cannot be foisted upon people who are only beginning to emerge from the state of feudalism in which they have lived for some time."

This attitude of the rich white minority, coupled with the racial antagonism between proletariat black masses and white capitalist cliques in the respective territories, has made most African leaders look with favor upon socialist systems. In their foreign policy ap-

proach, therefore, countries that classify themselves as "socialist" tend to be more revered than those that profess to champion capitalism. That does not mean that Eastern African countries favor the East in the Cold War. It simply means that the African is psychologically or emotionally not committed against the Eastern bloc. Instead, he maintains a friendly outlook toward Communist countries and judges their utterances on foreign policy matters on their merit, as situations arise.

Skepticism and racial pride　　There is also a high degree of skepticism toward those who profess humanitarian motivations to justify their foreign policies. This applies to both the East and the West. There is a tendency these days for governments of Major Powers to stress humanitarian aspects of their policies toward Africa and other less developed areas. The trouble is that in Africa feigned humanitarianism has been used a bit too often to justify imperialistic designs. As a result, most Africans take a thoroughly pragmatic approach and seek to find where the interests lie in any particular policy or project. Africans prefer and respect confessed self-interest rather than the feigned cloak of humanitarianism.

Race relations between Africans and the immigrant communities in the continent were worse during the colonial period in East Africa than in West Africa. Consequently, racial issues have been more prominent in the politics of Eastern Africa. In foreign relations, this factor must be taken into account. There is much racial identification, for example, with the American Negroes who have been suffering racial discrimination in their own country. The sufferings of Asians in Asia, as colored people, receive a lot of sympathy. Because India is just on the other side of the Indian Ocean, and because many Indians have suffered racial discrimination together with Africans in the Rhodesias, in Kenya, and elsewhere in Eastern Africa, a sympathetic attitude toward Asian nations has developed in this region. The constant reference to the Afro-Asian group in the United Nations has strengthened this feel-

[2] *Mombasa Enquiry Report,* 1939, Kenya.

ing of comradeship between African and Asian peoples in international matters.

Thus far, we have discussed background factors which have influenced the thinking of the people of Eastern Africa in their approach to foreign relations. Let us now examine specific courses of action.

MAJOR POLICIES

The meaning of an "independent" foreign policy

International relations have in recent years been dominated by the conflict between the Western and Eastern Powers. It is most regrettable that in this conflict smaller nations have been involved directly or indirectly and some of them have taken sides. Pakistan, for example, is squarely in the Western bloc while North Korea and North Vietnam are squarely on the side of the Eastern bloc. In Africa, there is a new form of "Scramble for Spheres of Influence" in the continent, very reminiscent of the scramble for Africa during the latter half of the last century.

Attitude towards Communist Powers   The Western Powers, claiming to be the champions of freedom and democracy, have done much to woo the newly emerging African nations. Knowing of the African aversion to dictatorship, mass arrests, imprisonment without trial in courts of law, and curtailment of individual freedom, the Western Powers have disseminated high-powered propaganda, painting the Communist countries as the citadels of such vile practices. Unfortunately for this kind of propaganda, little success has been achieved. This is because the masses of the Africans who have suffered such practices under colonial Powers have had practically no contacts with Communist Powers. Only a few leaders have had such contacts.

The effect of the propaganda has consequently been the rousing of curiosity among the African masses regarding communism. They ask themselves, who are these people of whom our former colonial masters seem to be so afraid? Are they really as bad as these former imperialistic countries tell us? Are the things for which they blame the Communists not very much like the things they have done to us during the colonial era? Curiosity about Communist countries, not adherence to their doctrine, now characterizes the African masses' approach to the Eastern Powers.

This curiosity becomes all the more intensified when the masses hear that communism is some form of socialism. It was pointed out earlier in this chapter that the concept of socialism strikes a sympathetic note among many Africans due to their dislike of capitalistic practices in African territories during the colonial period. Curiosity regarding communism does not imply acceptance of the doctrine or approval of the policies and intentions of the Eastern bloc; it is only a desire to know more about what is going on behind the Iron Curtain and to maintain friendly relations with those countries as well as the countries of the West.

Attitude towards Western Powers   Curiosity about Eastern countries is not accompanied by an aversion against the Western Powers. People who have lived under Western colonial Powers would ordinarily be expected to be anti-West in their approach to international politics. This is not the case in Africa, particularly the Eastern African Region. In addition to curiosity about communism, there is in many parts of Africa unabashed admiration for the way parliamentary democracy operates in some Western nations, particularly in the United Kingdom, West Germany, and in some of the Commonwealth countries. What is more, arrangements for technical and financial aid have already been concluded with many of these Western countries.

"Independent" versus "neutral"   What does all this mean? It means that the African countries, particularly those on the eastern side of the Continent, absolutely refuse to be tied to

either the Eastern or the Western bloc. Instead they want to vigilantly guard their independence and be friendly with any country of their choice. They refuse to give loyalty to any Power bloc irrespective of any issue that may arise. Their foreign policy is strictly independent. It is more or less the same type of policy advocated by the so-called non-aligned countries.

While this type of policy has been called "the policy of neutralism," the people of Eastern Africa prefer to call it "independent" for several reasons. First, the term "neutral" implies a disinterested attitude to what happens to this world of ours where our neighbors live. We are aware that this is not what neutral countries really stand for. We know that they want peace and freedom and prosperity for every single country or bloc of countries. Nevertheless, to avoid misunderstandings, we do not wish to parade as neutral people in a world full of conflicts and misunderstandings, a world threatened with nuclear warfare. We cannot be neutral to that. We cannot be neutral to the denial of political freedom to our neighbors or fellow men. We cannot ignore the hunger that less fortunate people of this world have had to endure. We realize that the countries classified as neutrals are fully with us in this regard. But instead of calling them "neutrals" we would rather have them called, with us, "the independents."

Ideological orientation

It is well known that within the group known as the neutral or "non-aligned countries," there are some fundamental differences both in approach and in ideological propensities. For instance, Yugoslavia is included in the non-aligned group. Yugoslavia is certainly not in the Eastern bloc headed by the Soviet Union. Yugoslavia is a political fellow-traveler of India, the United Arab Republic and Ghana, among others. Yet, ideologically, Yugoslavia is a Communist country. She has tried her best to be as close as is possible to the Communist goal of economic and political statism.

Relevance of the Indian approach   India, on the other hand, has a mixed economy, in which both the state and private capital play decisive roles in the economic development of the country. Politically, she can be classified as a parliamentary democracy. Though Mr. Nehru is a professed Socialist—perhaps of the Fabian type—the most pronounced aspect of Indian economic and political life is the pragmatic approach rather than the ideological approach.

Leaders in the Eastern African region come quite close to the Indian pattern in their thinking. Pragmatic socialism, and rejection of a doctrinaire approach to decision-making are the most outstanding characteristics. This, of course, is not surprising. The struggle for freedom by India was closely watched by the African people in this region. The name of Mahatma Gandhi became an inspiration to freedom fighters in Eastern Africa. The jail sentences endured by Gandhi and Nehru stressed the meaning of sacrifice for the sake of freedom. The political weapon of non-violence, as taught by India's nationalists is a respected weapon in the movements led by Jomo Kenyatta of Kenya, Julius Nyerere of Tanganyika, Kenneth Kaunda of Northern Rhodesia, Joshua Nkomo of Southern Rhodesia and Dr. Kamuzu Banda of Nyasaland. It is also revered by Prime Minister Milton Obote of Uganda and his opponent Mr. Benedicto Kiwanuka. In foreign policy, therefore, as in domestic politics, India's pattern is quite detectable here.

Integrity and determination   Adopting an independent foreign policy, and carrying on friendly relations with both the Western and the Eastern bloc does not necessarily mean indulging in some form of international political blackmail. This is a very important point. There may be some countries which refuse to be in either the Eastern or the Western bloc, not because of any convictions or principles, but simply to provide situations for playing one bloc against the other to procure the largest amount of aid.

I am reminded of my student days in the United States when an American magazine published a cartoon which summarized this method of international blackmail most vividly. According to the cartoon, the chief of a cannibal tribe in some unnamed territory was faced with a crisis. He and his people had eaten all the neighbors around and famine threatened the tribe's well-being. Aid had to be secured from international sources. After much deliberation, the chief hit on the most practical idea. "We shall send the word around that we are in a state of political instability and ferment. The Communists, in order to make the best of the situation, will send their agents here. The Americans, in order to stop communism spreading among us, will also send their agents to our territory. When agents from both camps are here, we shall eat them up."

This form of neutralism in foreign policy matters, the refusal to favor one camp or the other for the purposes of fleecing both sides, is the kind of international political blackmail that we in Africa do not respect or wish to see practiced. Going to Washington and saying "You'd better give me some money from your foreign aid sources or else I'll rush to Moscow" is not statesmanship. It is selling oneself and one's country. I am proud to say that the Africans' conscience is not for sale. Yes, *Africa is not for sale.*

Adopting a neutral or independent foreign policy must not be a cover-up for having no policy whatsoever. Nor should this label be a cover-up for an essentially pro-Eastern or pro-Western attitude which may be impolitic if candidly acknowledged. It has become fashionable in most nationalist circles in Africa, the Middle East and Asia to profess non-alignment with the two Power blocs. Yet, essentially, some of these nationalists would prefer to be allied with Western Powers or Communist Powers. Other nationalists may not have developed any systematic thinking about the issues concerned due to their preoccupation with the struggle against colonialism as such. To them the issue of foreign policy may not have been much of an issue—just a sporadic question that arises when some form of crisis or heated debate af-

fects domestic politics. We in the Eastern African region do have a policy as the subsequent sections of this chapter indicate.

Pan-Africanism

Since the early nineteen-twenties, the concept of Pan-Africanism has periodically been voiced and given general approval by African leaders. There were the days when Dr. W. E. B. Du Bois, the famous American Negro writer and scholar, organized Pan-African Congresses which were attended by many African leaders as well as foreign citizens of African origin. After the Second World War, men like Jomo Kenyatta, Kwame Nkrumah, Dr. Nnamdi Azikiwe, and the late George Padmore of the West Indies revived the African movement in Great Britain where they were residing at that time. Their activities in co-operation with other leading Africans residing in Europe and Africa made Pan-Africanism a most cherished concept in African politics. Unity among African peoples would, among other things, strengthen the African political forces against European colonialism.

The Accra Conference of 1958 In December, 1958, Pan-Africanism reached its highest peak. An All-African Peoples' Conference was held in Accra. Political parties and factions from all African territories attended that Conference through their duly authorized delegates and observers. It was agreed that the Conference would have a permanent secretariat in Accra. It was also agreed that a standing committee was to be set up to keep Pan-African affairs in the forefront.[3]

During the conference, a number of points received widespread approval. First, the delegates from all over Africa rejected the idea of

[3] Being a member of the steering committee that organized the conference, I was elected to be in the follow-up standing committee.

being tied up with either the Western or the Eastern bloc. Secondly, the delegates pledged themselves to do all in their power to spread freedom throughout the continent and elsewhere in the world where colonialism and political oppression were still active. All forms of racialism throughout the world were rejected. The delegates pledged themselves to find ways and means of influencing those foreign governments that either allowed racialism to operate in their areas or had proved unable to stamp it out completely. In short, African leaders from all over the continent seemed to be in general agreement on these major policy matters affecting emerging African nations and their relations with the outside world. Two other conferences on an all-Africa basis have taken place since then.

The Casablanca and the Monrovia group
During the year 1961, there emerged some differences of approach between two groups of African nations in matters of foreign policy and matters related to translating Pan-Africanism into day-to-day political and economic activities. One group came to be known as the Casablanca group with Ghana and Morocco as the leading lights. The other group is known as the Monrovia group with Nigeria and Liberia as the strongest members. It is difficult to pinpoint the ideological or tactical differences between the two groups. The Monrovia group is alleged by the Casablanca group to be essentially a pro-Western group of African nations with Right-wing politicians holding sway. Another allegation is that Western capitalists are practicing neo-colonialism in the Monrovia member nations with full knowledge and approval of the African leaders there. The Monrovia group, which has been very reluctant to see their brother nations refuse to join with them hand in hand, reply that the Casablanca group is somewhat too Leftist. Though not pro-Communist, they consider the group too tolerant and friendly with the Eastern Powers and too vehement in attacking the West.

The Pan-African Freedom Movement   In this most unfortunate development within the

Pan-African context, where do we in the Eastern African region stand? In September, 1958, leaders from Kenya, Tanganyika, Uganda, Zanzibar, and Nyasaland met in Mwanza, Tanganyika, and formed the Pan-African Freedom Movement of East and Central Africa, better know as PAFMECA.[4]

In February 1962, the PAFMECA Powers met in Addis Ababa, Ethiopia. There they were joined by representatives from both independent states and nationalist movements throughout East, Central and Southern Africa.[5] At the opening of the Conference, taking note of the broader representation, the organization changed its name from PAFMECA to PAFMECSA (Pan-African Movement for East, Central and South Africa). Emphasizing the importance of the southern part of Africa, Mr. Kenneth Kaunda, leader of the United Independence Party of Northern Rhodesia, was elected chairman for 1962.

In addition to passing a number of resolutions dealing with major problems confronting Africa and the rest of the world, the Conferees pledged to work for a federation of East African states as soon as Kenya, Uganda and Zanzibar had achieved independence. The participants also hoped for a gradual broadening of the proposed federation to include other East, Central and South African states. And they called for increased co-operation in the economic, educational and social fields. It was clear to the observers present that unity is growing throughout East, Central and Southern Africa.

---

[4] I represented PAFMECA at the First All-African Peoples' Conference at Accra later that year. There I stood firm for a genuinely independent stand in East-West Cold War politics.

[5] In addition to delegations from Tanganyika, Kenya, Uganda and Zanzibar, there were delegates from governments or national groups from Ethiopia, Somalia, Urundi, Nyasaland, Northern Rhodesia, Southern Rhodesia, Mozambique, Republic of South Africa, South West Africa, Basutoland, Bechuanaland, and Swaziland. Although no delegates from the Congo (Leopoldville) or Angola attended, it was clear that these areas were within the scope of interest of the Conference.

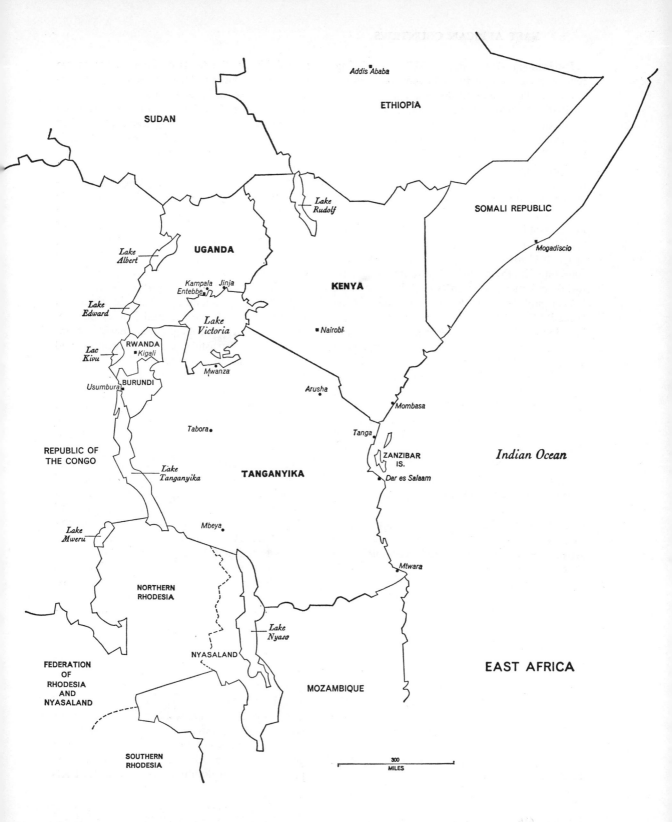

SUDAN

ETHIOPIA

Addis Ababa

SOMALI REPUBLIC

Lake
Rudolf

Mogadiscio

Lake
Albert

UGANDA

Lake
Edward

KENYA

Kampala
Entebbe

Jinja

Lake
Victoria

Nairobi

Lac
Kivu

RWANDA

Kigali

Mwanza

BURUNDI

Usumbura

Arusha

Tabora

Mombasa

REPUBLIC OF
THE CONGO

TANGANYIKA

Lake
Tanganyika

Tanga

ZANZIBAR
IS.

Indian Ocean

Dar es Salaam

Lake
Mweru

Mbeya

Mtwara

NORTHERN
RHODESIA

Lake
Nyasa

FEDERATION
OF
RHODESIA
AND
NYASALAND

NYASALAND

MOZAMBIQUE

EAST AFRICA

SOUTHERN
RHODESIA

300
MILES

By January, 1963, PAFMECSA was being recognized as a vital force in African politics. Peter Mbiyu Koinage, the Secretary-General of PAFMECSA and other leaders of the organization played a major role in the effort to achieve unity for the Congo. A "summit conference" of PAFMECSA leaders was held in Leopoldville in an effort to persuade the British that obstruction of the United Nations' Congo efforts was misguided and should be changed. PAFMECSA leaders, disturbed over the delays in independence for Kenya, also were working for African unity within that territory. Similarly, PAFMECSA may well have the task sometime in the future of arranging a territorial settlement between two of its members: Kenya and Somalia. Many other tasks confront PAFMECSA as it labors toward the goal of bringing Africans to power in all of Central and Southern Africa while at the same time striving for African co-operation and unity.

African leaders in the PAFMECSA region have indicated their serious distress regarding the apparent split which has developed among supporters of Pan-Africanism. Dr. Julius Nyerere, President of the Tanganyika African National Union, has publicly expressed regret and has shown his great desire to reconcile the groups. The Hon. Jomo Kenyatta is also very eager to act as a mediator and heal the split. This means that the Eastern African region is neither in the Casablanca group nor in the Monrovia group. It seeks to champion a United African Front in international matters. It also seeks to make sure that the United African Front is genuinely independent from Western neo-colonialism and Communist infiltration.

Common economic and social interests   In addition to the Pan-African movement which is drawing this region together, one should also note the functional arrangements which are already in operation. For example, when Tanganyika received her independence in 1961, the new East African Services Organization came into existence.[6] This organization has some re-

sponsibility in the fields of finance, commerce and social services in Uganda, Kenya, and Tanganyika. Responsibility for its operations rests with the elected leaders of these states. Even though some political differences are bound to exist between groups and between states, it is clear that common interests can transcend these differences.

Below the surface of current political differences are many common social and economic interests in East Africa. These run the gamut from co-operative programs in the field of health, finance and banking, social services, transportation, and education. The University of East Africa is one of the most impressive international ventures in the field of higher education. It brings together colleges in Kampala, Uganda, Nairobi, Kenya, and Dar es Salaam, Tanganyika. These colleges operate with a common board of trustees, a vice chancellor, and an overall educational directive. They reflect an effort to develop a university program with specialized fields of interest in the several countries. Thus Makerere College in Kampala, Uganda, is the institution most active in the medical and agricultural fields. The Royal College in Nairobi specializes in architecture and engineering. University College of Tanganyika is the location of the law faculty. These several programs are organized in such a way that young men from Kenya, Tanganyika and Uganda may study in whichever university college is strongest in their field of interest.

Similarly, the Central African Airways serve the whole of East Africa. Like the Scandinavian air services, they bind together the separate countries through a single air service.

These co-operative activities in the economic and social field are that part of a larger iceberg which is not visible above the surface. The crises and conflicts that fill the newspapers occur on the surface of the iceberg. The more lasting objective interests that draw East Africans together must be sought below the level of day-by-day clash and debate, in the realm of politics and economics.

These common interests will have even greater importance in the future, given the expansion and development going on in East Af-

---

[6] It was the continuation of the East African Commission established in 1948.

rica. More and more Africans are taking responsibility in public services, education and social services, and in the fields of water-supply, communications, agriculture, and industry. As time goes on, trained Africans will play an even more decisive role in the development of the area. The existence of a fabric of unity at the level of ordinary workaday concerns of the African peoples is one of the more encouraging signs for the future.

Membership in the Commonwealth of Nations

The usual pattern has been that when a former British colony attains self-government, it joins the Commonwealth of Nations. Except in the case of Burma, and the recent expulsion of the Union of South Africa from the Commonwealth, this pattern has been followed by all former parts of the British Empire.

One may now forecast, however, that this pattern is coming to an end. Britain's application to join the European Common Market has brought many persons within the Commonwealth to question the significance of retaining membership in this loose organization of former British colonial territories. It is clear from the discussions at the Commonwealth Conference in London in September of 1962 that grave questions are being raised about the future of the Commonwealth arrangement. The final communiqué of the conference cannot obscure the fact that changes are ahead and that basic decisions will have to be made.

Impending changes   One of the suggestions currently being discussed is creating economic ties between the European Common Market countries and the members of the Commonwealth. Generally speaking, many African countries do not favor such ties if they are to be so formalized as to compromise the independent foreign policy of the associated countries. After all, the European Common Market is part and parcel of the Western bloc. Associating with it means favoring the West against the East, because NATO powers are also members of the European Common Market. Eastern African countries may, as a result, remain in the Commonwealth for a very short period and then leave it to make their own arrangements.

If the Commonwealth does survive the stresses and strains of modern international politics as well as current economic struggles, the member-nations must accept some reorganization of the existing pattern. Most of the non-European nations in the Commonwealth remain there purely for economic and technical aid arrangements which help their economies. They are not there because of the so-called family-type of sentiment toward Britain.

Functional reorganization   There is, therefore, a strong case for reorganizing the Commonwealth from a functional point of view. Economic development programs, mutual exchange of research data and of scholars or technicians, banking facilities and expansion programs, all of these require some form of a clearing-house with a full-time staff. Meetings of the prime ministers need not be held every year in Great Britain with the British Prime Minister as chairman. Rather, chairmanship should rotate and the meetings should be held in the country of the current chairman. This would strengthen the feeling of co-operation among the member nations. It would also make the masses in the countries outside Britain more conscious of membership in the Commonwealth. The Commonwealth Clearing House could be situated in London, but meetings of the ministers must rotate from one country to the other within the Commonwealth. In short, the Commonwealth of Nations must be an effectively organized, functionally coordinated group, able to produce evident results for the betterment of the member-nations, or else it will die.

The Commonwealth is a very significant link between African and Asian countries on the one hand, and Western European-type nations on the other. It is thus a vital part of the international community and should not be allowed to wither away by failing to bring it up-to-date organizationally and administratively. It is all the more important to do this, when one considers the fact that the Commonwealth of Nations is not an ideological camp by any definition. Some member nations are neutralists in the East-West struggle while others are fully in the Western bloc. The Commonwealth maintains significant co-operation between these members without being distracted by the verbal battles and ideological maneuvering all too prevalent in the United Nations.

Financial and technical aid for non-aligned nations

Discussion of Commonwealth problems brings to the forefront the whole issue of financial and technical aid from the more industrialized nations. It is a chilling and humbling fact that no underdeveloped country can hope to achieve rapid development on the basis of revenues collected within its borders. Peoples' incomes are low. Consequently, revenues collected from them either in the form of direct or indirect taxation are inadequate, not only for meeting the necessary recurrent expenditures, but also for development projects which these countries must initiate to accelerate economic growth. The problem then becomes one of deciding what type of aid to accept and how to preserve political independence while relying so extensively on foreign Powers for economic development.

Use of international agencies   The preferred form of aid for underdeveloped countries is, of course, aid through international agencies, particularly the United Nations. By this method the more industrialized nations deposit aid with the international organization which, in turn, distributes the resources in accordance with the needs of the underdeveloped countries and also in accordance with the merits of the development projects for which aid is sought. In this method, economic control of the receiving countries, through the power of the purse, is likely to be negligible.

Contributions to an International Pool for Economic Development, following the graduated taxation method—i.e., the richer nations paying a higher percentage of their national income than the percentage paid by the poorer nations—would greatly facilitate international co-operation for fighting against poverty, disease, and technical backwardness which now plague two-thirds of the world's population.

Bilateral aid   But, unfortunately, foreign aid is an integral part of the rich countries' foreign policy. Such countries wish to give help to the poorer ones for clearly understood political or business ends. *There is no aid without strings attached.* The problem of the underdeveloped countries is to decide which strings are straight business obligations or *quid pro quo* contractual arrangements, and which strings are essentially politically inspired to draw the receiving country closer and closer to the Power bloc involved.

Leaders in Eastern Africa are, generally speaking, of the opinion that the safest way to receive foreign aid and, at the same, preserve political independence as well as some degree of economic integrity, is to amass such aid from a multiplicity of sources so that no one nation or Power bloc has a monopoly. Each form of aid must be examined thoroughly in terms of resultant obligations and technological involvements so that the receiving country does not find itself tied up inescapably to the donating country's economical or technological or political pattern.

MAJOR POLICY GOALS

Revolutionary nationalism has proved triumphant in Africa. Territories previously told by their colonial rulers that it would take them years to attain their independence, are now flying their freedom banners as sovereign states. Whatever explanations, excuses or apologies political analysts or commentators may provide, African masses and their leaders throughout the continent give credit for this victory to their "home-made" revolutionary nationalism.

It is perfectly true to say that in Eastern Africa the policies and patterns of colonialist administration in Uganda differ in details from those in Kenya which, in turn, differ from Tanganyika's. Nevertheless, as these territories are contiguous, and as they have been under the same colonial power, Britain, and further, as they have shared for years some common interterritorial economic and communication services, the characters of their revolutionary nationalist movements have much in common.

Racial equality

The pattern of the past   By having African, European, Asian and Arab communities living side-by-side, racial problems and political conflicts have been very intermingled in this area. Until recently, the very pattern of administration in this region was racially organized—practically all services were categorized as African, Asian, Arab, European or other. This was most pronounced in Kenya and least in Zanzibar. But throughout the whole region, racial separation of the communities was the fundamental administratives pattern. Racial separation leads to racial animosity. In the case of Kenya, it went as far as leading to bloodshed during the Mau Mau rebellion.

Again, until only a few years ago, racial categorization meant racially separate economic and employment compartments. Africans, though they constituted the overwhelming majority of the population throughout the region, nevertheless never attained managerial or executive positions in business, civil services, or industrial enterprises until nationalism began to be triumphant in the late fifties.

As the non-African communities, generally speaking, could educate their offspring far above what African parents could, not enough attention was paid to higher education for African youths since the non-African ones were generally available to man the vacancies arising in governmental and commercial or industrial spheres. This led to widespread resentment against non-Africans by the Africans. Africans felt that their advancement was deliberately held back by the presence of the considerable non-African communities in their midst. This was made all the more pronounced by looking at West Africa where there are relatively fewer non-Africans and consequently a much greater number of highly trained Africans and also Africans in managerial or other executive positions.

The path to the future   I have, of necessity, over-generalized the facts and conditions that have shaped the East African outlook towards non-Africans in political and racial relations. Nevertheless, these facts and conditions have proved to be decisive in the East Africans' approach towards "outsiders." They have led to: (a) racial pride, which is really a defiant answer to the bigotry of some imperialist and racist non-Africans; (b) vigilant devotion to African freedom both as a right and as a shield against exploitation or victimization by non-Africans; (c) a profound desire to liberate all other persons of African origin, wherever they are, from non-African domination in order to ascertain that a black man—as we Africans proudly call ourselves—is and shall always be secure from racial bigotry everywhere in this whole wide world.

Because of these factors, we East African leaders, as I have said above, find the word "neutral" somewhat unsatisfactory as a description of our foreign policy approach. We are positively devoted to freedom, peace and prosperity. Having struggled so hard for our independence, we cannot tolerate enslavement, direct or indirect, economic or political. We have rejected colonialism because it contains within it an element of dictatorship—government without the consent of the governed. To give our loyalty to any given Power bloc would be to subject ourselves to a new form of dictatorship. By so doing, we would become "rubber-stamps" of the leading nation or nations of that Power bloc.

It is fitting to call our foreign policy the Pan-

African Independent Foreign Policy. We are first and foremost burningly desirous to free from racial or political domination every African brother and sister within our continent and in America, Britain and elsewhere where people of African descent abide. Protection of the dignity of our race, which for years and centuries has been trampled on, is therefore a major item in our approach toward non-Africans. Human dignity, particularly for peoples of African descent, comes first in our emotional make-up. As I would quite frankly put it:

> I am superior to no man and no man is superior to me. I claim no racial superiority to any other racial or national community. At the same time I shall fight and struggle to the bitter end to render inoperative any policy or practice smelling of racial bigotry toward my race.

Economic development

The next basic item in our foreign policy has to do with peace and prosperity. To us, these two should always be considered together. In a world where high standards of living have been achieved—in America, Canada, the United Kingdom, Federal Germany and the U.S.S.R., for example—it is only logical for our people to feel that they, too, have a right to live better than ever before. If our standards of living decrease after independence, we will be spawning a revolution within our borders. Without prosperity there can never be lasting peace.

Our approach to foreign policy therefore is very involved with existing and future technical, financial and developmental international programs, bilateral or multilateral. But, being fiercely in love with independence, we carefully scrutinize any financial or other foreign aid program to make certain that our political independence will not be jeopardized or compromised by our participation in such programs.

Neo-colonialism is the villain we are determined to put to the gallows. We realize that financial or other economic exchanges carry with them unavoidable obligations. To say a country will not accept aid unless there are no strings attached is somewhat unrealistic. But there are strings which reduce the receiving country to neo-colonialist status. Such strings are anathema to us. We are prepared to undertake strictly commercial or fiscal or foreign exchange obligations in return for aid or loans received by us. But the moment the giver or givers seek to directly or indirectly control our internal governmental processes and our foreign policy approach, it becomes a case of colonialism in disguise. The aid must be immediately rejected and the giver publicly denounced.

We have great faith in the United Nations. We would like to see international aid channeled through the U.N. But we realize that national interests of the member nations are not identical. Therefore one cannot rule out the role of bilateral or even multilateral programs of aid outside the United Nations. But such aid must be genuinely free from political maneuvers.

Our foreign policy approach also takes into account the East-West struggle and its effects on Africa. We are a pragmatic people, not a doctrinaire lot. We know with absolute certainty that there is no economic, political or ideological panacea or formula that can cure all ills in all countries in this world. We therefore are not impressed with the argument that the East-West struggle is a struggle for men's minds or, in short, an essentially ideological battle.

American-type capitalism has so drastically changed that Adam Smith or even the 19th century capitalist economists could hardly recognize it now. The same applies to Khrushchev's socialism. Neither Karl Marx, nor even Lenin, ever foresaw the politically-inspired economic arrangements and diversities now existing side by side within the Communist orbit. The East-West struggle, in our view, is first and foremost a struggle for survival and for power. We consider this a most tragic approach to international politics.

Our view is the same view that Jeremy Bentham once expressed. "Nations are associates and not rivals in the grand social enterprise" of maintaining peace, prosperity, and true justice for every human being. By taking this line of approach, we know we can make a positive contribution toward ending the Cold War. As the American magazine, *Monthly Review,* put it "Cold War cannot continue in its present form. Things must get better or worse eventually. They cannot keep on oscillating from better to worse. We want to help them get better."[7]

Democratic government

This down-to-earth pragmatism, nevertheless, operates within a specific context of principles, which may appear homespun but, nevertheless, guides us in evaluating any foreign nation's political system and aspirations. For example, we ask ourselves to what extent are the lawmakers and lawgivers responsible to, and really influenced by, the people they govern through periodic elections? Elections in the Communist countries, for example, seem to us to bring practically no changes at all in terms of political personalities or government policy. Peoples' democracies, as they prefer to call themselves, are therefore socialistic oligarchies. We do not want to live under any form of dictatorship, oligarchy or autocracy feigned or apparent. Therefore, we have made up our minds that, while maintaining friendly relations with all these countries, we shall not risk being within their orbit. Unless elections mean the exercise of peoples' will and power to approve, reject, modify, or even completely dismember governmental institutional arrangements, they are not genuine elections. We passionately uphold the right to cast a meaningful vote!

The right to cast a meaningful vote goes hand in hand with the freedom of expression

[7] May 1953, p. 6.

and association. We realize that all freedoms have their limitations. But we believe that such limitations should not be imposed in order to entrench permanently one person or one party in power. This belief is based on our intolerance towards any dictatorial features in a political system.

Another issue with which we concern ourselves very much, is the problem of utilization of natural and human resources for the benefit of the greatest number of people. Exploitation of the masses, either by a foreign clique or an indigenous one may appear to raise the total national product of a country. But it does not necessarily mean an increase in the peoples' standard of living. Like most leaders in underdeveloped areas, we incline toward pragmatic and democratic socialism in our economic thinking. Accordingly, our foreign policy approach favors any move that will bring about the abolition of exploitative capitalism while, at the same time, safeguarding the masses from dictatorial socialism.

DANGER POINTS

The South African question

Two other matters must be mentioned here to complete the picture of our foreign policy considerations. They are the South African question and foreign military bases. The Union of South Africa merits special mention in this analysis of our foreign policy because it is in the African continent and yet, as an independent republic, has a political system which seeks to keep the African rigorously oppressed by the white minority residing there. We are a non-violent people. We hate war, bloodshed, and violent clashes. Yet one wonders what non-violent channels are now left by South Africa to change the apartheid system which all Africans throughout the continent cannot tolerate much longer. When the matter of African oppression in South Africa is raised in the United Nations, South Africa complains that this is a domestic issue. But surely oppression and violation of human rights cannot be allowed to go on under the cloak of "domestic affairs." If any country is jeopardizing world peace, that country is South Africa.

All African nations are determined to liberate their brothers in the Union of South Africa; if South Africa refuses to heed the instructions of the United Nations, then other methods of destroying apartheid will have to be found. Economic sanctions may not prove effective, because South Africa is not too dependent on other African countries for trade or investment. That is why I consider the situation as a danger to world peace. If non-violent methods fail we, nevertheless, shall not give up our determination to liberate our brothers in South Africa.

South Africa is part and parcel of the Western bloc. So is Portugal. Yet these two countries are the Africans' most disliked enemies because of the way they treat black people. Little wonder, therefore, that the Western bloc is not too popular with many of our people. Few Africans have traveled outside the continent. Few have seen the American democracy in operation or the high standard of living enjoyed by Americans. Few have witnessed the liberty enjoyed by Canadians or New Zealanders or Frenchmen. Most African contacts with members of the Western bloc are through their knowledge of affairs in South Africa or through the colonial ties which, thank God, are now rapidly disappearing. Much work to help Africa develop rapidly must be carried out by Western countries before the African attitude toward them will improve. At the same time, the battle for African rights in South Africa must be wholeheartedly joined by all freedom-loving nations as a positive contribution toward total liberation of all peoples, wherever they may be.

Foreign military bases

The second point involved with foreign policy matters is connected with the military aspect of the East-West struggle. Despite calls for peace in the United Nations and on public platforms, military and other defense arrangements are constantly being made by members of the two blocs and their associates. One of the most controversial of such arrangements is the establishment of military bases at home and abroad. In East Africa, attempts have been made by Great Britain to establish a naval base at Mombasa and a military base at Kahawa near Nairobi. Americans have shown considerable interest in utilizing the Island of Zanzibar for their world-wide defense arrangements.

Nationalists throughout East Africa are uncompromisingly opposed to this. Having rejected being part and parcel of the Western bloc, we cannot indirectly take sides in the East-West struggle by allowing any members of these two blocs to have military establishments in our territories. A country that allows such establishments for either bloc may deny being in the bloc; but the fact of the matter is that its foreign policy is not in the neutralist category.

It is true that all independent nations have their own land, sea and air forces. That is a national necessity for the maintenance of order and peaceful administration. But this must not be confused with foreign military bases whose essential purpose is to defend the East against the West or vice versa. East Africa is in a very strategic position vis-à-vis the East-West struggle. As such, the temptation for the Western Powers to establish bases is understandable. But, just as we are not going to allow such bases for the Western Powers, we shall also say "No" to Eastern Powers. We desire to reconcile, not to aid, one bloc against the other.

Africa is on the rise. With so many African territories becoming independent and joining the United Nations, we Africans are quite aware that the line we adhere to in international relations will decisively affect world politics. It is a great responsibility for us and we shall measure up to it.

BIBLIOGRAPHY

Editor's Suggestions

"Africa and International Organization," special issue of *International Organization*. Spring 1962, Vol. XVI, No. 2.

"East African Call for Government," *African Special Report*. March, 1962 (Vol. 7, No. 9), p. 2.

Kiano, Gikonyo. "The Pan-African Freedom Movement of East and Central Africa," *Africa Today*. Sept. 1959 (Vol. 6, No. 4), p. 11–14.

Legum, Colin. *Pan Africanism: A Short Political Guide*. New York: Praeger, 1962.

"Pan African Conference," *African Digest*. Nov.–Dec. 1958 (Vol. 6, No. 3), pp. 90–91.

ABOUT THE AUTHOR

COLIN DE BERRI WEBB, after completing his B.A. degree at the University of Witwatersrand in 1951, took a first in the History Honours School of that University in 1952 with a thesis on the background of the Jameson Raid. Two years later he secured the Higher Education Diploma of the University of Pretoria and in 1955 went to Clare College, Cambridge, where he read for the History Tripos. After completing his degree at Cambridge, Mr. Webb was appointed to the staff of the University of Natal where he was made a Senior Lecturer in History and Political Science in 1961.

Mr. Webb's research interests have carried him into the fields of South African history and political studies. He has contributed articles to the *Chamber's Encyclopaedia* and to various learned journals. At present he is conducting a major research project, supported by the South African National Council for Social Research. The project aims at the production of the first complete history of Natal.

In his research into South African foreign policy and Natal history, Mr. Webb has been working under the Head of the Department of History and Political Science at the University of Natal, Professor Edgar Harry Brookes, M.A., D. Litt. (S. Africa), Hon. LL.D. (Cape Town). For many years Mr. Brookes was a member of the South African Senate. He also was a foundation member of the South African Institute of Race Relations. Mr. Brookes is the author of numerous works on racial questions and political problems in South Africa, including *South Africa in a Changing World* (1954), and *The City of God and the Politics of Crisis* (1960).

ABOUT THE CHAPTER

The Union of South Africa has chosen to swim against some of the major currents of the postwar era. This chapter gives special attention to some of these currents and to the reasons for South Africa's decisions.

While most of the chapters in this book give first consideration to geography as a policy determinant, Mr. de Webb correctly gives first priority to the racial question and to the white supremacy policy of the government of South Africa. Indeed, the racial question permeates a large part of the discussion even when the issue is one of Commonwealth relations or the role of the United Nations in world affairs. The author clearly indicates his views of the course his nation is taking and the economic and political consequences which must be faced.

The chapter concludes with an analysis of the problems of conducting foreign policy in a nation torn with racial strife. The views expressed are obviously a dissent from the official policies of the government. Indeed, Mr. de Webb finds it a tragic paradox that the leaders of South Africa in the name of Western civilization are following policies "which have set it apart from the West."

15

THE FOREIGN POLICY OF
THE UNION OF SOUTH AFRICA

COLIN DE B. WEBB

University of Natal *

In a speech in London in 1943, the South African Prime Minister, General Smuts, directed attention to the new world that was taking shape as a result of the war then being fought. "We have moved into a strange world. . . ." he said.

The old Europe which we have known . . . has gone. The map is being rolled up and a new map is unrolling before us. We shall have to do a great deal of fundamental thinking and scrapping of old points of view, before we find our way through the new continent which now opens up before us.[1]

In 1943 it was impossible to know how strange that new world would be. Even for

Smuts, with his feet in Africa, the focus in international relations was still upon Europe. It was there that the significant changes in the political kaleidoscope were anticipated; elsewhere, the blocks of color, particularly those representing Europe's empires, appeared to be fixed and unchanging. The new map which Smuts saw unrolling was still a map with Europe at its center, but redrawn and extended to show the two great flanking Powers whose influence Europe would henceforward have to accept. And the rethinking and scrapping of old points of view which he recommended was a prescription for coping with the problems which that new world would produce. "You will therefore have these three Great Powers:" he said,

Russia the Colossus of Europe, Great Britain with her feet in all continents but crippled materially here in Europe, and the United States of America with enormous assets, with wealth and resources and potentialities of power beyond measure. The question

---

* With the advice and co-operation of The Hon. E. H. Brookes, M.A., D.Litt. (S.A.), Hon. LL.D. (C.T.).

[1] N. Mansergh, *Documents and Speeches on British Commonwealth Affairs 1931–1952*, Vol. 1, London: Royal Institute of International Affairs, O.U.P., 1953, pp. 568–69.

is how you are going to deal with that world situation.[2]

The analysis was of course correct, but only so far as it went. For South Africa and her old associates, many of the most important issues of foreign policy in the postwar world were to be those raised, not by the new Europe, but by the new world that was to shape itself beyond.

THE POSTWAR MILIEU

South Africa has certainly not escaped the consequences of the developments that have occurred in that North Atlantic–European world of which Smuts was thinking. The rise of the Russian Colossus, the intensification of the ideological struggle, the vast developments in science and technology which have brought the peoples of the earth together into one small neighborhood—all these have made their impact. Isolationism as a policy has been no more desirable for South Africa with practically no international responsibilities than for the giants who face one another in the Cold War. For all alike, great and small, the postwar world has been a world of no escape, and the governments that have directed South African foreign policy have known this.

Under Nationalist Party rule since 1948, as under United Party rule before, South Africa has sought its "circle of friends," and its governments have indicated their willingness to shoulder the burdens that friendship may demand.[3] Yet the country's international position has steadily worsened. The circle of friends has dwindled and the circle of critics and opponents has grown. Isolation has come where isolation was never wanted. Even in the Common-wealth—that intimate "family circle" in whose international company South Africa took its place in independence in 1910—the South African government had by 1961 ceased to feel itself at home. With the constitutional change from a monarchy to a republic, the old ties with the Commonwealth were at last broken.

The circumstances that have produced this drift to isolation must be considered more fully later. The fundamental consideration, however, is the one which was missing when Smuts directed the attention of his London audience to the new world which was already forming in 1943. The pressures on South Africa have come not so much from a reshaped Atlantic-European world, as from the reshaping of the map elsewhere. The Balkanization of Asia and Africa, the anxiety of the governments of South Africa's old associates to retain the good-will and the confidence of the new non-White nations, intensified public opposition to racial discrimination all over the world—these are the things that have separated South Africa from the circle of friends that its governments have desired to cultivate. For the political attitudes of those who govern South Africa remain, on the question of race, the attitudes of the prewar era. A dominant White minority, whether it supports the apartheid policies of the Nationalist Party or the alternative White Leadership policies of the United Party, seeks to preserve a quasi-colonial system when colonialism has been execrated by the rest of the world.[4]

Future historians may well judge that, for South Africa, the decisive theater of war in the great holocaust of 1939–45 was not Europe but the Far East. For it was there, with the Japanese attack on Southeast Asia, that the first of the deathblows was struck at that world of European political ascendancy in which the South African system had had its appropriate place. Increasingly in the mid-twentieth century, the apostles of racial apartheid have found

---

[2] *Ibid.,* p. 570.

[3] See, for example, *South African Senate Debates* (Official Report), speeches by Dr. D. F. Malan, April 8, 1949, coll. 1435–6; and Mr. J. G. Strijdom, June 17, 1955, col. 4392.

[4] See L. Marquard, *South Africa's Colonial Policy,* Johannesburg: South African Institute of Race Relations, 1957.

the "apartheid" of international isolation approaching their frontiers.

THE DETERMINANTS OF POLICY

White supremacy

It is thus upon the Whites of South Africa that attention must to a large extent focus, for foreign policy, in the case of South Africa, is a reflection of the national interest as conceived by this minority group, some three million strong, whose members have preserved themselves as the "colonial masters." The other elements of the population, the eleven million Africans, one and a half million Coloreds, and half million Asians are, to all intents and purposes, without the constitutional means to make their political influence felt.[5]

It is in a White parliament, elected almost exclusively by White voters, that the legislation is made by which the affairs of this complex multi-racial society are governed; and it is from the party majorities in that White legislature that the cabinets are formed which direct South Africa's foreign relations. Although only one fifth of the population, the Whites are for all practical purposes "the nation" and think of themselves as such. Speaking in the debate on South Africa's entry into the war in 1939 the Prime Minister, General Hertzog, referred to the difficulties facing South Africa "with its small population of two million people."[6] He was using the terms which most South Africans use. Beyond the White nation, there are no South Africans; there are only "backward peoples" and "problem groups," to whom the Whites stand in the relation of trustee within their own land.

Whites as "Africans" In this, the Whites of South Africa are probably unique. The most numerous group of their kind in Africa, they have also struck deepest root. From their point of view, there is not only a valuable material heritage at stake, but a rich spiritual heritage. For they have gone further than any other "European" group on the Black continent in acquiring that identity which comes to a people with a history and culture of its own.

They are not, as were so many of the Whites of the Belgian Congo, out on a tour as the agents of business or the administrators of government; nor are they, like so many of the Whites of Central and East Africa, settlers of the first or second generation, maintaining ties with the land of their origin; they are not even, like the *colons* of Algeria, able to look across a narrow moat to the citadel of their erstwhile compatriots. They are "Africans," but of a unique kind, isolated both by time and distance from the lands of their origin. They are not an island people like New Zealanders and Australians, secure behind the frontiers which nature has provided, but a continental people, conscious of this fact and conscious also that there are no frontiers except artificial ones behind which to shelter from the alien millions with whom they share a fatherland.[7] Should South Africa bow to the pressures that are upon her from the outside world, it will be more than a system of privilege that will crumble, more than deep-rooted prejudices that will suffer; a nation will lose its identity.

The reasons for apartheid It is this situation that is the basic determinant of all policy, foreign as well as domestic. As for the new state of Israel, so for White South Africa, national survival in an alien milieu is the ever-present issue and takes precedence over every

---

[5] Figures based on preliminary results of 1960 census, *Annual Register of World Events*, 1960, p. 93. The Colored population of the Cape Province possesses a qualified franchise which permits the election of four White representatives to the House of Assembly.

[6] *South African House of Assembly Debates* (Official Report), September 4, 1939, coll. 17–23.

[7] See J. D. B. Miller, *The Commonwealth in the World*, London: Duckworth, 1958, pp. 189–90.

other consideration. What has kept the Nationalist Party in power since 1948 has, to a large extent, been its apartheid program. White supremacy is to be ensured by the perpetuation of racial and cultural differences under a rigidly applied system of separate development for the different ethnic groups. Where non-Whites have shared facilities with the Whites, they are to be deprived of these rights, and provided, in separate areas, with facilities of their own "suited" to their cultural traditions.[8]

The United Party, which was in office until 1948, and which vies with the Nationalist Party for governing power, is more flexible in its approach to the racial question, less doctrinaire in the remedies which it prescribes; its spokesmen prefer the euphemism of "White leadership" where Nationalists talk of "White supremacy." Nevertheless, it is true for the United Party as for the Nationalist Party, that the ultimate object of policy is to secure "the White man's claim to the land which he occupies."[9] For the foreseeable future, therefore, provided the White man is able to maintain the power which he holds, South Africa's foreign policies are likely to be decided, as they have been in the past, by a "nation" which is only one-fifth of the population, but which is determined to preserve its supremacy.

Boer versus Briton

Against this first great theme of Black-White relations there must, however, be set a second theme, more stridently proclaimed at times, and hardly less important as a determinant of the country's external relations—the theme of Boer and Briton. As it is now modified in the

[8] See G. M. Carter, *The Politics of Inequality*. London: Thames and Hudson, 1958, *passim*.

[9] *Ibid., passim*. See also *Race Relations Journal*, Vol. XXVII No. 4, Oct.–Dec. 1960 (South African Institute of Race Relations, Johannesburg) pp. 139–52, Symposium on Racial Policies of South Africa's Main Political Parties.

twentieth century, it is the theme of Afrikaner nationalism against a broader, more comprehensive White South Africanism. The "Europeans" of South Africa, who form "the nation" when they face outward towards the Black continent, are two nations when they look inward upon themselves, and tend to conceive the national interest in different terms, according to where their loyalties are involved.

Historical factors   Whereas the first theme, that of Black-White relations is, even in its simplest terms, the product of a complex of geographical and historical influences—of the fact that a White nation has taken root on a Black continent—the second is much more directly the product of history. It springs from the fact that, in the nineteenth century, after the acquisition of the Cape by Great Britain, the original Dutch colonists found their identity and their way of life threatened by a new influx of settlers of alien stock and alien language, and by a colonial Power whose ways were not theirs. Eventually, even when they had sought their liberty from that Power in the isolation of the interior, it overwhelmed them.

Afrikaner nationalism in the twentieth century has been an attempt to undo these facts of history. There is a desire to reassert in a form cleansed of alien British influence that cultural identity which was already shaping itself amongst the Boers of the nineteenth century and to restore, in something like its pristine form, the political independence which was lost when the Boer republics fell to the might of Imperial Britain in the first years of the present century. In its very exclusiveness, however, Afrikaner nationalism has divided the White nation. For there has been no place in it for the English-speaking section, or for those among the Afrikaners who have desired to forgive and forget in order to build a new future in co-operation with their old enemies.

Moderating influences   It was from Botha and Smuts, two of the Boer generals who had fought most bitterly against Britain, that there came after the Anglo-Boer War, the strongest appeals for the spirit that has opposed the nationalism of militant Afrikanerdom. "The Boer has fought for independence; the Englishman for his Empire," Smuts declared; "all have fought for what they consider highest . . . Now the highest is Union . . . not of top dog and under dog, but of brothers."[10] Although support for this policy has come principally from the numerically weaker English-speaking section of the population, amongst whom there was little reason not to forgive and forget, and good reason to fear the beating of the nationalist drum, there have nevertheless been many Afrikaners who, through the years, have remained loyal to it, believing like Smuts that "two such peoples as the Dutch and English must either unite or continue the attempt to exterminate each other."[11]

Diversity of economic interests Other factors have also contributed towards the difference in outlook between the two White groups. Support for Afrikaner nationalism comes very largely from the White artisan class, and from the farmers of the *platteland* districts of the Western Cape Province, the Transvaal and the Orange Free State. The forces that oppose it, on the other hand, draw their strength from the professional classes, from the business, financial and industrial elements in the large towns, and from the predominantly English-speaking rural districts of Natal and the Cape Eastern Province. With their eyes on the London money market, on international trade routes, and on the bonds of culture and tradition that form the fabric of the Commonwealth, the outlook of these opponents of Afrikaner nationalism has tended to be a wider one than that of the White worker, concerned principally to protect himself against the competition of Black labor, or the *platteland* farmer, concerned principally to pass on an undisturbed patrimony to his heirs. They have seen the national interest to depend, not simply on saving White civilization from the Black deluge, but

[10] J. C. Smuts, *Jan Christian Smuts,* Cape Town: Cassel, 1952, p. 111.
[11] *Loc. cit.*

upon saving South Africa from isolation in a hostile world.

Lines of policy

Against this background—with the lines of policy being determined by a nation at once united and divided—South Africa's external relations have shaped themselves. During the fifty years of the country's existence as a self-governing state, external threats to the survival of the White nation have been anticipated from four *possible* quarters: from direct acts of aggression by new "imperialist" Powers; from unfavorable political developments in neighboring territories resulting in the isolation of South Africa on the African continent; from unsatisfactory economic relations depressing the South African economy and so stimulating unrest amongst the non-Whites; and finally, and more particularly in the period since 1945, from the insidious operations of revolutionary international communism. On these four issues, consequently, there has been broad agreement within the White nation. Whether the political parties have been in occupation of the government or the opposition benches, they have seen the national interest in generally similar terms: South Africa must be re-insured against wanton aggression by maintaining membership of collective arrangements such as the United Nations; her political influence must be extended in Africa to prevent developments occurring that will endanger the survival of the White race; the conditions for an expanding economy must be promoted; and finally, in the struggle against international communism, the country's security arrangements must be linked with those of the West.

Against this unity of purpose, however, must be set the elements of disunity. For although, so far as these four objectives are concerned, foreign policy has had a bi-partisan character, there has been disagreement over the best means of achieving these ends. Still more bitterly, there has been disagreement over the policies to be pursued in a fifth field affecting the national interest—that of South Africa's relations with the Commonwealth. On these issues, the disunity that exists within the White nation has emerged sharply. Differing in their sympathies, their traditions and their outlook, the two sections of the White population have sought to secure their common interests by different means; in the field of Commonwealth relations, they have seen the national interest in markedly different terms.

From these various threads, and from the different values which successive governing parties have attached to each, the fabric of South Africa's foreign relations has been woven. If it is a fabric with the threads broken in places and running loose in others, the explanation lies in the fact that those who have been responsible for South Africa's external relations have found the warp of the postwar world far less serviceable for their purposes than that with which their predecessors were able to work before 1939. In all its aspects, South African foreign policy since 1945 has become a study in frustration.

THE INSTITUTIONS FOR ADMINISTERING POLICY

Diplomatic and consular services

Yet South African governments have maintained an extensive and vigorous diplomatic service to promote the national interest. The foundations were laid in 1927 when a Department of External Affairs was established under ministerial control, to supervise all consular and diplomatic matters. From these small beginnings, the Union had by 1939 developed the most extensive foreign representation of any of the Dominions.[12] After the war the expansion

of those services was carried still further. New embassies and new legations were established, the Ministry of the Exterior was separated from the office of Prime Minister to which it had previously been an appendage, and the State Information Office, until 1955 under the Minister of the Interior, was transferred to the Department of External Affairs, to act as an additional agency for the promotion of South Africa's cause in the external world. Apart from South African High Commissioners in Britain, Australia, the Central African Federation and Canada, and a permanent representative at United Nations headquarters, the government was by 1960 maintaining embassies in Belgium, France, Italy, the Netherlands, Portugal and the United States, and legations in Argentina, Austria, Brazil, Chile, Finland, Greece, Spain, Sweden, Switzerland and the United Arab Republic.[13] There were hopes for further expansion in the future.

Excluding special attachés, there were twenty-eight senior diplomatic officers representing South Africa in various capacities abroad, and a foreign staff of 330 in the service of the Department.[14] Of this staff, between fifty and sixty have been located in Africa, where South Africa's interests have been further served by the close liaison that has been maintained with the metropolitan governments responsible for the administration of African territories, especially with the British Government through the Commonwealth Office in the period before the establishment of the South African Republic in 1961.[15]

It is, therefore, not primarily for lack of institutional facilities that South Africa's foreign policy has become a study in frustration. The reason lies in the international response which the country's domestic policies have provoked.

[12] See Miller, op. cit., p. 201.

[13] Official Year Book of the Union of South Africa, No. 30, 1960, p. 94.
[14] Statement by Mr. E. H. Louw, Minister of External Affairs, Senate Debates, May 23, 1956, col. 3724.
[15] The Union's Attitude to Africa, Fact Paper 72, May 1959 (South African Information Service, Pretoria), pp. 8–9.

THE COMMONWEALTH

Of the threads now broken the one with the longest history behind it is that of South Africa's relations with the Commonwealth. For a time, in fact, it was the dominant element in the pattern of the country's external relations. For in common with Canada, South Africa was concerned to secure for the Dominions that full sovereignty that would insure control not simply over domestic affairs but also over foreign policy.

By 1934, as a result of the enactment in the British Parliament of the Statute of Westminster and the passage in the South African Parliament of the Status of the Union Act, these things appeared to have been achieved.[16] The bonds of Empire which had dragged South Africa into the First World War and provoked an armed rebellion amongst Afrikaner patriots, had been transformed into the gossamer threads of Commonwealth. Although linked to Britain and to the other Dominions by a common allegiance to the Crown, South Africa faced the rest of the world in sovereign independence, free not only to manage its domestic affairs, but free also to conduct its external relations in terms of the national interest rather than overriding Imperial interest.

Divided public opinion

Despite that, however, the Commonwealth connection has remained the aspect of external relations that has generated the most heat and

opened up the deepest divisions within the White nation. On the one hand, there has been that section of the population, predominantly but not exclusively English-speaking, which has held fast to the vision of Botha and Smuts, believing that the national interest could best be served by preserving for South Africa undisturbed its place amongst the nations with which history had linked its fortunes. In conversation with his Canadian colleague, Sir Robert Borden, Botha once said:

I fought against the British, but I am a firm upholder of the Commonwealth. In South Africa we enjoy all the liberty we could have as an independent nation, and far greater security against external aggression; we have complete powers of self-government; we control the development of the country; and in the affairs of the world we take a place far higher and render a service more notable and useful than we could attain or give as a separate nation.[17]

It is to this view of the national interest that the opponents of Afrikaner nationalism have held fast. Apart from the security to be found in continued co-operation with a group of sister nations who share the same interests and the same traditions, there has been the vision of a South Africa made greater than itself by the enlarged field of action which membership in the Commonwealth makes possible. Even more than Botha, Smuts tried to translate this concept of the national interest into a reality.

The policies of General Smuts

For it was on the stage of the Commonwealth rather than on the cramped space of a South

16 See *House of Assembly Debates,* speeches by Mr. O. Pirow, Minister of Railways and Harbours, March 28, 1934, coll. 1864–9; Mr. L. Blackwell, April 9, 1934, coll. 1879–87; and General J. C. Smuts, Minister of Justice, April 11, 1934, coll. 2072–82.

17 W. K. Hancock, *Survey of British Commonwealth Affairs 1918–36,* Vol. I, London: Royal Institute of International Affairs, O.U.P., 1937, p. 70.

African political platform that Smuts, a true internationalist, felt himself at home and found scope for his talents and statesmanship. During his two periods as Prime Minister, from 1919–24 and from 1939–48, it was a Commonwealth policy that was pursued rather than a specifically national one. Even when out of office or serving as second-in-command to others, the influence which he exerted was towards developing the Commonwealth and cultivating his country's place in that association. South Africa was to be strengthened by strengthening the Commonwealth, her influence extended by extending the influence of that association, her specific interests served by the general interests of the Commonwealth being promoted. What was ultimately desired was a powerful Commonwealth whose contribution to the world and to its several members would be the example of peace and co-operation between nations.

Even in the radically altered circumstances that followed 1945, Smuts retained this view. Speaking in a debate on foreign affairs in the Upper House of the Union Parliament in 1947, he warned that South Africa by itself must inevitably "remain a very small show," and continued:

> I do not like this position of two Super Powers. I think it is necessary for the peace of the world that Britain should recover her position. This immense group of which she is the leader should maintain itself also as a Super Power in the world . . . The way that Great Britain and the whole British group of nations are pulling, and will continue to pull, for peace and good government, for what we call democracy, for human liberty, for human advancement, will probably equal that of any other group in the world. I go so far as to think and to say that I look upon the British group as a safer guarantee of peace in this world than U.N.O. itself.[18]

[18] *Senate Debates,* May 27, 1947, coll. 2337–46.

The views of Nationalist Party leaders

Yet, in the long run, it has not been the vision of Botha and Smuts that has determined South Africa's relations with the Commonwealth. In 1948, the year after his speech in the Senate, the United Party, which Smuts had lead, was displaced from governing power by the victory at the polls of Dr. Malan and his Nationalist Party. It has been this group with its apartheid policies and republican program that has forced the pace of adjustment and change.

For the Nationalist Party the cardinal issue through the years has remained the fact that the "British connection" came originally as something imposed upon a small and helpless people in the hour of its greatest grief.[19] In addition to the issues of sentiment, however, militant Afrikanerdom has conceived the national interest in terms markedly different from its political opponents. In place of the vision of a South Africa made greater than itself by its participation in the affairs of a community of states circling the globe, there has been the vision of consolidation of White solidarity against Black Africa and the rest of the world; of a nation disentangled from foreign commitments and made stronger by the removal of alternative loyalties. "I do not think," said Dr. Malan in the House of Assembly in 1937, "that the monarchy forms any bond in the direction of the preservation or strengthening or unity of the population." On the contrary, he argued, it "accentuates the differences that are in the way of the uniting of our people" because it "conflicts with the ideals and sentiments" of the Afrikaans-speaking section of the population and "strengthens the feelings" of the English-speaking section that "they have a king of their own" and "form part of a nation overseas."[20] Almost a quarter of a cen-

[19] See, for example, *Senate Debates,* speech by Dr. H. F. Verwoerd, April 17, 1961, col. 3150.
[20] *House of Assembly Debates,* January 25, 1937, coll. 578–82.

tury later, his successor in the leadership of the Nationalist Party, Dr. Verwoerd, was to be heard echoing the same arguments.[21]

The policies of the Nationalist Party

Since 1948, South Africa's relations with the Commonwealth have thus been directed by a Party which, for reasons of sentiment as well as political expediency, has had as one of its ultimate objectives the winning of the final victory in the Anglo-Boer War. Yet it is not primarily as a result of "Sinn Feinism" that South Africa's relations with the Commonwealth have been disturbed. With the responsibilities of office upon its shoulders, the attitude of the Nationalist Party towards the British connection changed. There has been little evidence of the aggressive, anti-British policies which might have been expected from a Party whose Federal Council declared in 1941 that "Afrikanerdom is . . . unanimous on the breaking of the British connection," and whose leader called during the war for a separate peace with Germany and the immediate establishment of a republic free from any association with Britain.[22]

Alarmed by the prospect of isolation in a world threatened by international communism and unsure of their support at home, the Nationalist governments that have ruled South Africa since 1948 have been cautious in their handling of the Commonwealth question. For more than a decade, they were prepared to allow the republican victory to remain an ultimate objective of policy rather than an immediate goal. For a time, after the decision had been taken at a Prime Ministers' Conference in 1949 to reframe the structure of the Common-

wealth in order to allow for the continued membership of republics, reconciliation to the British connection appeared to be almost complete.[23] Anxious to secure the final victory in the Anglo-Boer War, yet equally anxious not to lose for South Africa its circle of much-needed friends, the government of Dr. Malan saw in a Commonwealth with accommodation for republics the answer to the problems that were perplexing it in the postwar world. Since then, although affection for the Commonwealth as an association of states has cooled, Dr. Malan's successors have, each in their turn, indicated their desire to maintain the closest relations of friendship with Britain and with the old Dominions of British stock.[24]

The changing racial composition

What has wrecked South Africa's relations with the Commonwealth is not anti-British sentiment, but the changed character of the Commonwealth itself. From a sisterhood of White nations it has become a brotherhood of men dedicated to the principles of multi-racial co-operation. From the point of view of the Nationalist Party, there has ceased to be any prospect of promoting the interests of a nation committed to racialism and White supremacy in such an association. As early as 1955, a leading Nationalist newspaper, *Die Burger*, wrote:

Open-hearted and fruitful exchanges of ideas have already become impossible on many matters. For example, we believe that military and African affairs cannot with advantage be . . . discussed in the presence of India. As

---

[21] See, for example, *House of Assembly Debates*, speeches by Dr. H. F. Verwoerd, January 20, 1960, col. 109, and January 30, 1961, coll. 329–31.

[22] See N. Mansergh, *Survey of British Commonwealth Affairs 1939–52*, London: Royal Institute of International Affairs, O.U.P., 1958, pp. 76–79, 155–60.

[23] See, for example, speeches by Dr. D. F. Malan, *Senate Debates*, May 12, 1949, coll. 5659–60, and *House of Assembly Debates*, May 11, 1949, coll. 5551–65.

[24] See, for example, *Senate Debates*, speeches by Mr. J. G. Strijdom, June 17, 1955, col. 4392; and Dr. H. F. Verwoerd, April 17, 1961, coll. 3161–2.

common ground diminishes in future, so the Commonwealth conference will more and more become a forum for platitudes while the real relations between Commonwealth countries . . . will be maintained through other channels. It is those mutual relations between two or more Commonwealth countries that trust one another in matters of common importance that are advantageous and have meaning. . . . The meaning of South Africa's Commonwealth membership is in our relations with individual . . . members rather than with the whole wide heterogeneous circle.[25]

For a time, Dr. Malan attempted to use South Africa's position within the Commonwealth to prevent its character changing. Repeatedly he warned that the destruction of what elements were left of a homogeneous White Commonwealth would deprive that association of real value so far as South Africa was concerned. He demanded that the old White Dominions should be given a say equal to that of Britain in deciding the developments which were transforming the British colonial empire into a multi-racial association of free and independent states.[26]

His efforts failed, however, and White South Africa has had to accept that, even in so intimate an association as the Commonwealth, it is the lot of the less powerful to have their relations determined for them, and not for them to dictate. Like a South African Canute, Dr. Malan was obliged to see the tide of anti-colonialism advancing despite his behests. His successors have been left with no Commonwealth policy to pursue beyond accepting that,

unless South Africa modifies its racial policies, the basis for co-operation has gone.

The decision to leave the Commonwealth

Partly, at least, it was in recognition of this that the decision was taken to leave the Commonwealth rather than sacrifice any longer certain other objectives of policy. More important to the Nationalist government by 1961 than continued Commonwealth membership, was the desire to satisfy an Afrikaner electorate that had already been kept waiting too long for its republican victory. No less important was the desire to strengthen the nation's defenses against Black nationalism, by securing that solidarity amongst the Whites which, it was believed, would follow, once the republican issue had been removed from the political arena.[27] It may even be, that by 1961 there were members of the government who welcomed the prospect of a break with the Commonwealth, believing that the perils of isolation would compel the political factions within the White nation to close their ranks behind Nationalist leadership.

Accordingly, when in March 1961, South Africa submitted her application for readmission as a Republic, and the delegates attending the Commonwealth Prime Ministers' Conference responded by demanding the modification of the government's racial policies, the decision was taken to withdraw. From the point of view of Dr. Verwoerd and of many of his followers, the hostility that manifested itself against South Africa was proof that the basis for continued co-operation had gone; willingness to leave the Commonwealth was simply *realpolitik* in a South African setting.[28]

For all that, however, the element of frustration remains; South Africa's "Commonwealth"

[25] Quoted in translation in *The Times*, London, January 15, 1955.

[26] Interview with *Die Burger*, Cape Town, February 24, 1951, published in translation in Mansergh, *Speeches and Documents*, Vol. II, pp. 1287–88. See also *Senate Debates*, speeches by Dr. D. F. Malan, June 19, 1951, col. 6584, and September 18, 1953, col. 618.

[27] See, for example, *House of Assembly Debates*, speeches by Dr. H. F. Verwoerd, January 20, 1960, coll. 106–9, and January 30, 1961, coll. 327 & 331.

[28] Dr. H. F. Verwoerd in *Senate Debates*, April 17, 1961, coll. 3161–2.

policies are now reduced to seeking bilateral arrangements with Britain and the old White Dominions with whom once she was so intimately associated. Both before and after March 1961, Dr. Verwoerd expressed his belief that it would be easier to secure co-operation on this basis than on the basis of Commonwealth membership, when Britain "had continually to be in the centre between two interests both of which she sought to serve."[29]

There is little evidence of any success in this direction, however. South Africa's old associates appear to be determined not to lose the trust of the new non-White members, or to devalue Commonwealth membership "by giving to those who are not members all the privileges of those who are."[30] Lacking the strength to impose her own terms, yet adamant in her rejection of the terms of others, South Africa has been left isolated even amongst those who were once her White "sister-nations." In place of Smuts' vision of a South Africa that would be "the brains and imagination of a big Commonwealth," the White nation faces the prospect of becoming "a Robinson Crusoe island."[31]

THE UNITED NATIONS

What saves South Africa from complete isolation is membership in the United Nations. Like other small or middle-sized states, South Africa has looked with hope towards improved collective arrangements on the international level as a means of increasing her own security, extending her influence, and limiting arbitrary action on the part of the Great Powers. It was from South Africa that there came after the First World War a blue-print for a new international order, in the form of Smuts' pamphlet *The League of Nations: A Practical Suggestion.* What South African governments have continued to desire since then is an "organ of the ordinary peaceful life of civilisation," powerful enough to "vindicate violated rights" between states, and ready with the resources "to protect the weakest . . . from destruction" by the strong.[32]

In most respects, consequently, South Africa has been a model member of the great international organizations that have taken shape in the present century. Her governments have kept up their financial contributions with exemplary regularity; they have been prepared to shoulder their military responsibilities; and it has been their policy to stand squarely behind collective action to prevent breaches of the peace and acts of aggression in various parts of the world.

Attacks on South African policies

Yet, in contrast to the position under the League, there has, in the case of the United Nations, been a steady worsening of South Africa's position. As the Charter, with its emphasis on human rights and fundamental freedoms gave warning, that secure world of European ascendancy over which the League presided, has passed away. Since the first United Nations session in 1946, South Africa has had to face annual attacks in the General Assembly, and has had to face them on three fronts: in connection with her treatment of peoples of Indian origin; in connection with South West Africa, a Class "C" League mandate which she has refused to place under

---

[29] *Loc. cit.* See also *House of Assembly Debates,* speech by Dr. Verwoerd, January 30, 1961, col. 329, and January 20, 1960, col. 107.

[30] Statement by the Secretary of State for Commonwealth Relations in the British House of Commons, March 22, 1961. Press Note No. 134, United Kingdom Information Office, Cape Town.

[31] G. B. Shaw, *John Bull's Other Island,* Act I.

[32] See, for example, speech by South African delegate, Mr. C. Te Water, before Assembly of League of Nations, July 2, 1936. Quoted in Mansergh, *Speeches and Documents,* Vol. I, pp. 155–59.

United Nations trusteeship; and in connection with her racial policies.[33]

It is the latter issue that has, in fact, been the overriding concern of South Africa's critics and opponents. Even the South West Africa question, which is fundamentally a legal one, has been fought on the political level in the hope of scoring a victory over the latter-day exponents of an outdated racialism. As in the Commonwealth, so in the United Nations, South Africa has had her relations determined for her by the international response which her White supremacist policies have provoked.

Reasons for continuing membership   Nevertheless, despite the discomforts of the position, it has been the policy of South Africa's governments to cling to United Nations membership. Outside the United Nations, South Africa would be completely isolated. The other international bodies on which representation is maintained are all specialized agencies or technical commissions of one sort or another. They consequently provide no facilities for diplomacy. Nor do they provide the nation with any defense pacts or security arrangements.

Furthermore, whereas the securing of the Republic provided reasons for risking Commonwealth membership, there has been no cause to be served by withdrawal from the United Nations. The attacks upon South Africa would not cease—probably they would increase in virulence—in the event of membership being abandoned. While South Africa retains her place at the United Nations, her governments have the chance of pleading their own cause, of watching over their legal rights under the Charter, of furthering their diplomacy in an international forum, and of seeking shelter for South Africa under the collective security arrangements which the United Nations offers.[34]

Response to the critics   In this situation—unwilling to withdraw from membership yet under almost constant pressure—South Africa has moved increasingly onto the defensive. The United Party government of General Smuts was prepared to discuss the issues raised by South Africa's critics at the United Nations, and was willing to go some way at least towards satisfying the wishes of the majority with regard to South West Africa, by continuing to submit reports, and by abandoning the plans which had been formulated for incorporating the territory as an integral part of the Union.[35]

Since the Nationalist Party assumed power in 1948, however, far less conciliatory policies have been pursued. On the two closely related questions of the treatment of Indians and of race relations in South Africa, there has been an uncompromising insistence on South Africa's rights under Article 2(7) of the Charter, accompanied at most sessions by a rigid refusal to participate in discussions or co-operate in any other way that might suggest even a tacit recognition of the United Nations' jurisdiction in these matters. The conflict has thus become one between an accused, determined to protect her rights under the strict letter of the law, and a growing array of prosecutors equally determined to see the spirit of the law honored.

In the case of the South West Africa issue, there has been even less willingness to co-operate. The annual reports have been stopped; the competence of the United Nations to exercise any supervision over the administration of the territory has been denied; South West Africa has, for most practical purposes, been incorporated as an integral part of South Africa. The advisory opinions of the International Court of Justice have been disregarded, except where they accord with the South African government's own views on the case.[36]

In 1962, it is true, there appeared to be a softening of the South African attitude, when the Government granted permission for the

[33] For brief summaries of the three disputes see *Everyman's United Nations*, 6th ed., New York: U.N. Information Office, 1959, pp. 146–52, 374–9.

[34] See, for example, *House of Assembly Debates*, speech by Dr. D. F. Malan, March 21, 1949, col. 2419. See also speech by Mr. E. H. Louw, Minister of External Affairs at Calvinia, August 17, 1961; report in *Natal Daily News*, Durban, August 18, 1961.

[35] *Everyman's United Nations*, op. cit., pp. 374–75.

[36] R. B. Ballinger, *South-West Africa*, Johannesburg: South African Institute of Race Relations, 1961, *passim*.

territory to be visited by the Chairman and Vice-Chairman of the United Nations' Special Committee on South West Africa. But the permission was granted on the express condition that it did not imply any recognition of United Nations' supervisory authority. The subsequent imbroglio, arising out of the report on South West Africa submitted by the visiting Commission, has resulted in a new hardening of White attitudes towards United Nations interference.[37]

In 1961, the Indian delegate complained that, in its handling of the racial question, the United Nations had, year after year, been met by "a solid wall of intransigence" in South Africa.[38] The same complaint might, with equal cause, have been voiced in connection with the South West Africa question. Instead of cracking the granite walls of apartheid, the United Nations' assault has led to their re-inforcement.

How long can the U.N. be defied?

Racial policies   At the same time, however, there is mounting evidence that the South African government's policies may eventually have boomerang effects, for intransigence is begetting intransigence. "The United Nations must," the Indian delegate argued in 1961, "go on giving expression to world opinion . . ." on the question of South Africa's racial policies, "until . . . the rulers of South Africa . . . recognize that the only thing to do . . . is to remodel society and government in South Africa on the basis of equality for all and freedom from racial discrimination."[39] Thus, tired though the delegates may be of the "hardy South African annual," the debates on the racial question are likely to continue.

While they continue, the South African government is, amongst other things, likely to be faced by aggravated "racial tensions" at home, for there are many amongst the non-Whites who are encouraged by the evidence of sympathy and support at the United Nations to engage in more determined resistance to apartheid.[40] Furthermore, while the debates go on and South Africa's racial problems continue to receive publicity in a world forum, an inflamed international opinion is likely to grow more and more vociferous in its demands for boycotts and official sanctions against South Africa.

South West Africa   In the case of the South West Africa question, the dangers are even greater. The Minister of External Affairs, Mr. Eric Louw, once argued that *de facto* possession is nine-tenths of the law.[41] There are others at the United Nations, however, who are determined to see all ten points of the law respected, and are bent on using the tenth point to prevent *de facto* being converted into *de jure* possession. In 1962, after the visit of the Carpio Commission to South West Africa, a resolution was unanimously adopted in the Special Committee, calling for resolute action by the United Nations to take over the control of the territory.[42]

What has endangered the South African position more than anything else has been the refusal of the South African government to accept the 1950 advisory opinions of the International Court of Justice as a basis for a settlement with the United Nations. Should the Court at any stage give a further advisory opinion to the effect that South Africa has disregarded her international obligations by refusing to act in accordance with the terms of the 1950 judgment, the way will be open for South Africa's opponents at the United Nations to call for collective action, and no question of interference in a domestic matter will be involved.[43]

---

[37] See, for example, *Natal Mercury,* August 7, 1962.
[38] Speech by Mr. C. A. Jha before the General Assembly's Special Political Committee, March 22, 1961, reported in *Natal Daily News,* March 22, 1961.
[39] *Loc. cit.*

[40] Statement by Mr. Louw, Minister of External Affairs, *Senate Debates,* March 5, 1947, col. 1626.
[41] *House of Assembly Debates,* March 19, 1947, col. 1327.
[42] *Natal Mercury,* September 1, 1962.
[43] Ballinger, *op. cit.,* p. 40.

REPUBLIC OF THE CONGO

TANGANYIKA

ANGOLA

NYASALAND

Lake Nyasa

NORTHERN RHODESIA

FEDERATION OF RHODESIA AND NYASALAND

Kariba Lake

MOZAMBIQUE

• *Salisbury*

SOUTHERN RHODESIA

• *Beira*

SOUTH-WEST AFRICA

BECHUANALAND

Indian Ocean

WALVIS BAY

■ *Pretoria*

• *Lourenço Marques*

Johannesburg

SWAZILAND

N↑

Atlantic Ocean

BASUTOLAND

• *Durban*

UNION OF SOUTH AFRICA

300 MILES

SOUTHERN AFRICA

Cape Town

• *Port Elizabeth*

Anti-racialism of Western bloc   South Africa's position is thus far less secure than the adamantine policies of the government may suggest. The danger of United Nations action —possibly in the form of sanctions—has moved perceptibly closer, and South Africa's isolation within the United Nations is now virtually complete. Two things in particular have contributed to this: in the first place, the admission of new members, giving the Afro-Asian states a clear majority; secondly, South Africa's decision to withdraw from the Commonwealth.

It was the hope of Mr. Eric Louw, that the increased number of Black states would at last make the Western bloc value South Africa's vote, and that a more friendly disposition would result.[44] The very reverse has been the

[44] *Senate Debates*, March 5, 1957, col. 1631.

438

case. With the West anxious above all to avoid alienating the emergent states of Africa, delegations which were once prepared to vote against resolutions affecting South Africa, or at least to abstain on such issues, have been giving increased support to moves against South Africa initiated with mounting frequency by the nations of the Afro-Asian bloc.

The Commonwealth decision has had the effect of practically completing the process, for even those old "friends in need," Britain and Australia, are now no longer so readily available to speak in South Africa's cause. In the United Nations more starkly perhaps than anywhere else, South Africa is confronted by the fact that diplomacy based upon the old assumptions about co-operation between states is no longer valid. There are new interests at stake, and new bases for co-operation; and nowhere is there room for racialism.

POLICIES IN AFRICA

The obsolescence of isolationism

Excluded from the Commonwealth and isolated at the United Nations, South Africa faces a situation in which she must depend increasingly upon what can be achieved by routine diplomacy. If political isolation could still be guaranteed to provide some measures of insulation from the affairs of a meddlesome world, there might be many amongst the Whites of South Africa who would be content with the situation. Some, in fact, would be happy to see the last remaining diplomatic threads broken. Withdrawal into isolation would satisfy the same deep-rooted conservative prejudice which led the Boers of the frontier to trek away from British rule at the Cape in the nineteenth century. What produces the frustration of the twentieth century is the knowledge that this is no longer possible; even in isolation, there is no longer any escape.

Leadership of White Africa

The context in which South Africa has felt this most strongly is in its relations with the rest of the African continent. For, since the nineteenth century, frontiers have been marked out which are frontiers of contact, not lines of separation insulating a small and unique community from developments elsewhere. On the political level as well as on the economic level, the future welfare of South Africa is directly dependent on what happens in the rest of Africa. With untoward developments—the spread of alien ideologies, for example, or the triumph of Black nationalism in the territories that are South Africa's immediate neighbors—the White nation faces more than geographical isolation. It stands to lose what should be a natural hinterland for trade and economic expansion. Worse still, it may find itself confronted by a powerful Black irredentism within its own frontiers.

Control over Protectorates   In the forefront of the objectives of foreign policy, there consequently remains the desire to secure good relations, enhanced prestige and extended influence for the Whites of South Africa in the affairs of the continent. The prospects of success are diminishing, however. Already, two of the oldest objectives of policy in Africa have had to be abandoned. One was the acquisition of political control over the Protectorates of Bechuanaland, Basutoland and Swaziland, three Black enclaves which remained as British High Commission territories when the Union was formed in 1910. Economically and geographically they are integrated with South Africa. Their continued existence under independent political control is, therefore, from the point of view of the Whites, an anomaly which unnecessarily complicates South Africa's Native policies and defense arrangements. It is also, from the point of view of Afrikaner nationalism, an affront to national pride. For, while the territories survive as Protectorates, the Union Jack continues to fly over Southern African soil.[45] South African Native policy militated against the transfer that was contemplated at the time of Union, and the Protectorates have now passed beyond the grasp of South Africa by being set along the road that will lead to self-government. By one of the strange ironies of the South African situation, racialism on the domestic level has done more than defeat a cherished objective of external policy; it has left the White nation with the nightmare prospect of Black states evolving towards responsible self-government within the frontiers of South Africa itself.

Alliance with northern settlers   The other objective that has to be abandoned is that of promoting closer political co-operation with the settler communities to the north. What was once envisaged was a broad belt of White territory, running along the "backbone" of Africa, from the Cape in the south to Kenya in the north—in its most desirable form, a political federation of ex-colonial territories under South African leadership. Alternatively, there was hope for an alliance of White supremacist states pursuing "a common Native policy . . ." and "directly flowing from the common Native policy, a common defence policy."[46]

Political developments to the north have gradually killed these ambitions. Where British settler communities exist, they are being directed into accepting some form of partnership with the Blacks whom once they might have hoped to rule. Elsewhere in Britain's African territories, it is the Blacks themselves who are becoming the masters in their own houses. In the Portuguese territories (the only other near neighbors which South Africa has), policy is determined by the theory that the colonial territories are overseas provinces, subject to the same laws as apply in the mother country. Consequently, whatever difficulties Portugal may encounter in her African territories, she is unlikely to accept a White supremacist alliance with apartheid South Africa. For in such an arrangement, the moral defense for her policies would be destroyed.

Co-operation with emergent states

Faced by the prospect of these developments, the government of Dr. Malan's successor, Mr. Strijdom, formulated a new Africa policy in the years after 1955.[47] With the exception of the changed approach to the Commonwealth, it is the most fundamental adjustment that has been made in South African foreign policy since the war. General Smuts and Dr. Malan had both set themselves against colonial emancipation in Africa.[48] With Mr. Strijdom, the fulminations ceased, and they have not been heard again. Acknowledging that South Africa lacks the power and the influence to induce any changes in the colonial policies of the imperial Powers, the fight against emancipation in Africa has been abandoned; instead, the Nationalist government has, since 1955, sought to mark out for South Africa a place of leadership in the affairs of the continent by cultivating friendly relations and close co-operation with the emergent Black states. Mr. Louw, the Minister of

---

45 E. A. Walker, *The British South African Territories,* in *African Affairs,* Royal African Society, Vol. 44 p. 67. See also *Senate Debates,* speeches by Dr. D. F. Malan, May 1, 1950, coll. 1691 ff.; June 19, 1951, coll. 6605 ff.; and September 18, 1953, coll. 623–4.

46 Statement by Mr. O. Pirow, Minister of Defence, reported in *Cape Times,* Cape Town, February 6, 1935. See also E. A. Walker, *A History of South Africa,* London: Longman's, 1940, pp. 668–69; and W. K. Hancock, *Survey of British Commonwealth Affairs, 1918–39,* Vol. II, Part 2, London: Royal Institute of International Affairs, O.U.P., 1942, pp. 1–2.

47 The first announcement of the new policy was a statement by Mr. J. G. Strijdom to the Natal National Party Congress, August 25, 1955. See *The Union's Attitude to Africa,* Fact Paper 72, May 1959, Pretoria: South African Information Service, p. 5.

48 For the attitude of Smuts towards colonial emancipation, see J. C. Smuts, *op. cit.,* pp. 507–8. For the attitude of Dr. Malan, see *Senate Debates,* May 13, 1952 coll. 2635 ff., and September 18, 1953, coll. 620 ff.

External Affairs, explained in 1957 that South Africa must "accept its future role in Africa as a vocation, and must in all respects play its full part as an African power."[49]

Scientific and technical aid By placing South Africa at the service of the rest of Africa, and more particularly by making its specialized scientific and technical knowledge available, the Nationalist government has hoped to demonstrate to the emergent Black states the value of the survival on the continent of a society that has preserved its "White and Western identity." In this way, too, it is believed, South Africa may be able to establish herself as "a permanent link between the Western nations on the one hand, and the populations of Africa South of the Sahara on the other."[50] What is ultimately desired is that the African peoples of the territories to the north should accept that apartheid constitutes "no threat whatsoever" to their own interests, and should combine with White South Africa to protect the continent against external interference.

Although initiated by Mr. Strijdom in 1955, the new Africa policy has been elaborated and most fully developed by Mr. Eric Louw. The type of co-operation and the conditions which are desired were described by him in a major policy statement in 1959, in which he said:

When facing dangers, or possible dangers from outside, I think it is good policy for those who are "inside" to face such dangers together. The Union of South Africa is an African state, as are the emergent states in the North. Let those states recognise that fact, and in so doing accept South Africa's offer of friendship and co-operation in regard to matters of common concern. . . . One can only hope that the time will come when the independent and emergent states of Africa will realise that it is in their interests to co-operate with the Union of South Africa in defence of our common heritage—Africa.[51]

Obstacles to success Yet the investment in the new Africa policy is paying very small dividends, if any at all. For real co-operation and fruitful contact between South Africa and the territories to the north remains impossible while the White nation has its face set against co-operation and contact with its own peoples of color. South Africa, it is true, has an important and useful role to play in bodies such as the Commission for Technical Co-operation South of the Sahara (CCTA) and the Scientific Council for Africa (CSA); but beyond co-operation on that level, nothing has been achieved to strengthen South Africa's relations with the emergent states. Certainly, there has been no justification for the optimism expressed by Mr. Louw in 1957, when he looked forward to "more intensive co-operation" with South Africa's Black neighbors, and spoke of the member-states of bodies such as the CCTA and CSA "getting to know one another . . ." and "more important . . . learning to trust one another."[52] Even the exchange of diplomatic representation with the Black African states has been frustrated because of the mores of a White supremacist society.[53]

The emergent states on their side, have evinced little enthusiasm for a society which plans to entrench a system of tutelage in many respects more rigid than that against which their own liberatory struggles have been directed. Able, as they are, to bid for the favors of the Great Powers, the emergent states of Africa can afford, not only to disregard the over-

---

[49] Address at Graduation Day Ceremony, University of Pretoria, March 1957; reprinted as Fact Paper 33, April 1957, Pretoria: State Information Office, p. 9.

[50] *Ibid.*, p. 9 and *passim.*

[51] Address to Tenth Annual Congress of South African Bureau of Racial Affairs, Durban; reprinted as *The Union and the Emergent States of Africa,* Pretoria: South African Information Service, 1959, p. 15.

[52] Fact Paper 33, p. 8.

[53] *The Union and the Emergent States of Africa, op. cit.,* p. 14.

tures of White South Africa, but to engage in operations designed to sap the foundations of the apartheid fortress. Consequently, while racial supremacy remains the overriding concern of those who govern South Africa, there is little prospect of an effective Africa policy being pursued beyond the White nation looking to its own defenses.

NEW IMPERIALISMS AND COMMUNISM

In the period since the Second World War, external interference in the affairs of the continent has been feared from two principal sources—from India and the Communist East.

Fear of Indian imperialism

Suspicion of Indian ambitions was strongest in the immediate postwar years, when the first adjustments were being made to that new international milieu in which Black states would take their places in independence by the side of the older White ones. India, liberated from the restraints imposed upon her by the British raj might, South Africans believed, become the new imperial Power in the lands bordering the Indian Ocean, and seek an outlet for her teeming millions in the wide spaces of Africa. It was a fear shared by Nationalists and non-Nationalists alike; in fact, some of the strongest warnings came from the United Party opposition benches in the early years after Dr. Malan and his followers had come to power.[54]

Gradually, however, the fear of the "Asiatic horde" has abated. The pacifism of Mr. Nehru and the evidence that India is as firmly opposed

[54] See, for example, *House of Assembly Debates*, speech by Mr. S. Waterson, May 12, 1949, col. 5666, and *Senate Debates*, speech by Mr. Heaton Nicholls, April 8, 1949, coll. 1462–3.

to Russian imperialism as she is to the old imperialism of Western Europe has done much to remove the apprehension that was once felt.

Communist imperialism

The real menace so far as most White South Africans are concerned is not India, but communism. The move of the Russian Colossus to the center of the international stage, and the indications that China is ready at any moment to make its debut from the wings are—apart from the stirrings of the African Giant itself—the two developments of the postwar period that have most alarmed the Whites of South Africa. While sharing the attitudes of other Western peoples towards communism, South Africans also have additional reasons for misgivings. For the doctrines of the new "faith" are fundamentally irreconcilable with the system of political and economic privilege which the Whites desire to preserve. Consequently, these doctrines are likely to have a particularly strong appeal to the politically underprivileged, economically depressed and ill-educated Black millions whom the Whites rule.

Partly because of this, the response of the White nation to the Communist menace has been very different from its response to the Nazi menace in the prewar years. Hitler's imperialism offered no threat to White supremacy. On the contrary, the racial doctrines of Nazism tended to provide theoretical confirmation for the system of discrimination that had established itself in South Africa.

Consequently, what was paramount in the minds of White South Africans in the period before 1939 was not how international relations and foreign policies would affect Black-White relations, but how they would affect the old issue of Boer and Briton. Whereas the upholders of the Commonwealth concept believed that a conflict between Nazi Germany and Britain must involve South Africa too, since the political traditions and interests of the whole "British group" of nations would be affected, there were others who argued that what happened in Europe was no concern of South Africa and that the Union must prove its political maturity by remaining outside another "British war." Some even looked with expectant hope towards the day of deliverance, when the shackles of Empire and Commonwealth would be forcibly broken by the superior might of Germany.[55]

Views of the major parties   No such division exists within the White nation on the question of the Russian menace. Where there have been differences of opinion, they have been over the best means of securing South Africa against possible Red aggression. The United Party government of General Smuts placed its faith in a strengthened Commonwealth able to intervene as a powerful third force and so bring down the scales on the side of the democracies of the West.[56] Dr. Malan and his successors have been anxious for political and military arrangements of a more formal type. Before coming to office in 1948, Dr. Malan declared his party's dedication to the task of rescuing South Africa from "the ever-encroaching and all-destroying Communist cancer." One of his first moves as Prime Minister and Minister of External Affairs, was to bid for the extension of the North Atlantic Pact to include South Africa.[57]

Since then, the new Africa policy has been formulated. One of its principal objects is to make Africa indispensable to the West. In 1958, Nationalist Senators mooted the idea of an African organization "like SEATO in Eastern Asia and NATO in Europe" to contain the spread of communism.[58] Ultimately, the Nationalist Party believes, the Western Powers will have to come to terms with White South Africa, for they will need a reliable ally on the African continent. "In these circumstances [i.e.

with the emergent states of Africa adopting a neutralist position] there is. . . ." said one of the sponsors of the 1958 proposal for an Africa organization,

only one steadfast, certain anchor for the preservation of Western influence on the continent and that is European South Africa. . . . It is only South Africa that is affiliated with the Christian, civilised West European world. . . . Other free states in Africa, like Ghana, Sudan, Abyssinia, Libya may —and I want to emphasize the word *may*—remain allies of the West or remain pro-West, but South Africa can never be anything else but an integrated part of the Christian civilised European bloc. The others *may* still be allies because they have a choice, but we can never break away. That means a South Africa in which the European will remain sovereign. If the European in South Africa should lose his authority, then all the doubts and question marks will arise in South Africa which characterise at present the new, black, independent states as allies of the West. If the Western world wishes to retain its influence in Africa—and the West will have to retain its influence in this strategic continent if it wants to prevent the threat of Communism and the danger from the East —it will have to start mobilising its strength in South Africa, and will have to build on the alliance, whether political, economic or military of European South Africa. . . .[59]

Alliance with anti-Communist nations   The desired alliance has shown no signs of materializing, however. It may be true, that the safest investment for the West is a White supremacist South Africa which, from the very nature of its own predicament, can never be anything but a

[55] See debate on South Africa's entry into the war, *House of Assembly Debates,* September 4, 1939, coll. 17 ff.

[56] *Senate Debates,* May 27, 1947, coll. 2344–6.

[57] *Senate Debates,* April 8, 1949, coll. 1455–6.

[58] *Senate Debates,* July 15, 1958, coll. 34 ff.

[59] *Loc. cit.*

faithful ally. Nevertheless, while the struggle in Africa remains a struggle for men's minds, in which success depends not simply upon securing military allies and strategic bases, but upon laying the ghost of imperialism and persuading the new states that their real interests lie in continued co-operation with the democracies of the West, it is unlikely that the "free world" will embrace with open arms a state which, in the eyes of much of the rest of the continent, has become the symbol of oppression and of colonialism in its most uncompromising form. For the small or middle-sized state, diplomatic strength is directly dependent upon the ability to threaten "unfaithfulness" in favor of another choice of friends. South Africa's problem is that, from the very nature of the situation, it can never make these threats.

Since 1960, the government has been pursuing policies which are an acknowledgment of these realities. It is still assumed that the West will, in the long run, be unable to afford to abandon White South Africa. Certainly, in the event of a "hot war" South Africa's mineral resources and her strategic position on the vitally important sea route between the Atlantic and Indian oceans will, government spokesmen believe, assure the country of allies.[60] But in the Cold War, they accept that she is now isolated.

The emphasis is no longer upon securing support from the West, but upon the White nation mobilizing its own resources to defend itself against indirect Communist aggression in the form of armed insurrection within the country, or a "proxy war" waged against South Africa by puppet African forces from neighboring territories. With the White nation maintained on a "battle-ready footing," with its defense forces equipped for combat under the special local conditions of Africa, and with the civilian population, women as well as men, trained in the use of fire-arms, the government hopes to tide South Africa over the interim period until the pendulum swings and the West

accepts her back into closer military, security and political partnership.[61] The conversion of the White nation into a neo-Spartiate citizen army is, however, the real measure of South Africa's predicament.

ECONOMIC RELATIONS

Efforts to avoid isolation

What complicates the difficulties is the fact that in addition to political isolation—in fact, partly as its consequence—South Africa faces growing economic isolation. The government, on its side, has made, and is continuing to make, vigorous efforts to promote the country's economic interests beyond its frontiers. Through the State Information Office, which operates under the Department of Foreign Affairs, information is widely disseminated; trade representatives are maintained in various parts of the world; special trade missions have been dispatched to the four corners of the globe to explore the possibilities of opening up new markets for South African produce.

Particularly in the period since the fiasco of Sharpeville in 1960 and South Africa's withdrawal from the Commonwealth in 1961, both of which seriously shook international confidence in the country's economic future, the government has by deed as well as word, attempted to demonstrate that industrial peace can be preserved without resort to violence, and that the best guarantee of a stable economy is the continuance of White rule.[62] "Not for

---

[60] See, for example, speech by Dr. T. E. Dönges, Minister of Finance, *House of Assembly Debates,* January 31, 1961, col. 459.

[61] See, for example, *Senate Debates,* speech by Mr. J. J. Fouche, Minister of Defence, June 8, 1961, coll. 4970–2; and Mr. E. H. Louw, Minister of Foreign Affairs, June 7, 1961, col. 4901.

[62] On March 21, 1960, approximately 15,000 to 20,-000 Africans, as part of a wide-spread, non-violent demonstration against the South African Government's Pass Laws, presented themselves at the Police Head-

us," said Dr. Verwoerd in a message to the world on the occasion of the establishment of the Republic,

the sudden upheavals which created the chaos of the Congo, and the struggle of multi-racialism elsewhere, where each group seeks to dominate and lack of confidence in what may happen creates economic uncertainty. . . . Here, the solution is sought by openly retaining the White man's guiding hand, where elsewhere it is the hidden guarantee that the administration and industrial development will not fail.[63]

Economic problems mount

Despite these efforts and these assurances, however, the economic problems have continued to mount, for the political uncertainties of South Africa's international position, as well as the uncertainties on the domestic level, have made it increasingly difficult to maintain the conditions that are necessary for buoyancy in the economy. Loss of Commonwealth membership has cost the country certain assured trading advantages; the calls for boycotts against South African goods, and for concerted international action, possibly in the form of sanctions, have been more and more stridently voiced.

On the African continent, South Africa's natural assets as the leading industrial state have been off-set by her inability to cultivate relations of cordial co-operation with her Black neighbors. The result has been an accumulation of agricultural and other surpluses, for which no adequate markets can be found. What is most disturbing to the White nation, however,

is the fact that South Africa has lost the attractiveness which she once enjoyed as a field for the investment of foreign capital. Racial tension within the country, political pressures from without, and increased international isolation, particularly since the break with the Commonwealth, have combined to undermine international confidence. The further expansion of the economy has come to depend, very largely, on the uncertainties of domestic capital formation.[64]

Political consequences　In this situation, the South African government is faced by what are, perhaps, its most fundamental problems. It is true that the bulk of the support for the Nationalist Party comes from the *platteland* farming districts, which are to a large extent insulated from the shocks that affect the industrial economy. The government is likely, therefore, to be able to weather short-term economic setbacks, without losing votes.

There are other considerations, however, that make the government as anxious as any of the industrial and business interests of the towns to avoid recession. In the first place, should the economy stagnate, it may prove virtually impossible to hold down non-White resentment.[65] It will also prove increasingly difficult to finance the costly defense arrangements on which the survival of the White nation has now come to depend. There is another consideration, however. If South Africa's international position is ever to improve, without the policy of White supremacy being abandoned, the country's rulers must be able to provide the world with tangible evidence of the benefits which the non-Whites are deriving from the system. And, since the Whites are not prepared to share their facilities, the provision of the evidence depends, in the last analysis,

---

quarters of Sharpeville, an African Township, to be arrested for non-compliance with these laws. Violent disorder ensued with the police firing on the Africans. There were 67 fatalities and 186 wounded as a result of this incident.

[63] Reported in *Natal Mercury*, Durban, June 1, 1961.

[64] For a brief analysis of South Africa's dependence upon British capital investment, see H. M. Robertson, *Can Industry Afford to Break the Economic Link?* in *Optima* (Anglo-American Corporation of South Africa, Limited, Johannesburg), September 1960, pp. 134 ff.

[65] See Miller, *op. cit.*, p. 190.

upon the full-scale development of the so-called "Native reserves"—the areas that have been scheduled for African occupation.

Development of Native reserves   Yet the cost of developing these reserves and providing them with the facilities that might at last confound foreign criticism is a staggering one. Investment on a massive scale is necessary over a long period of time. According to the report of the government-appointed Tomlinson Commission, the "Bantu areas" require a twenty-five to thirty-year plan of development, and the provision of £104 million during the first ten-year period.[66] A buoyant and expanding economy is therefore essential.

It is in these facts that the White supremacists, whether they support the Nationalist Party or its alternative, the United Party, face their most fundamental dilemma. Their policies must be made to work and they must be made to work for the material benefit of all sections of the population. Yet White supremacy itself is driving away the foreign capital and crippling the foreign trade upon which success ultimately depends.

FOREIGN POLICY
AND THE MULTI-RACIAL NATION

Views of the Nationalist Party

The South African predicament has done little to shake the confidence of Afrikaner nationalism, however. The government continues to assure its followers of the rightness of its policies and remains convinced that they are the only policies which can succeed. Any relaxation of strong White rule, any modification of the

[66] M. Horrell, *A Survey of Race Relations in South Africa 1955–1956*, Johannesburg: South African Institute of Race Relations, p. 141.

apartheid program, any concessions to the demands being made upon South Africa by its friends and critics abroad would, the government argues, weaken the dykes which are at the moment saving the country from chaos and keeping out the flood-waters of communism. Responsible, efficient, experienced White government must be maintained, even at the cost of contemporary isolation, a temporary decline in living standards, and the temporary conversion of the White nation into an armed camp. The great majority of Afrikaner nationalists would probably remain loyal to the government which they have voted into power even without the persuasion of these arguments and assurances. Antipathy towards racial equality and assimilation is rooted in the deep soil of sentiment and conviction, and it remains unshaken by the winds of change that blow above.

The history which the Afrikaner knows is a history of privation and struggle; the prospect of privation and isolation in the mid-twentieth century is consequently seen simply as another challenge in a long series, to which the present generation must respond with the same fortitude as their forefathers did of old. In these views, the Afrikaner is reinforced by his religious faith—the Calvinism of the South African Dutch Reformed churches, which support apartheid. In Old Testament terms they preach that the White race has been chosen and placed on the southern tip of Africa for a Divine purpose, the fulfilment of which depends upon the European preserving the identity of his race and culture. It is the duty of every Christian, therefore, to combat any extraneous influences which may lead to the undermining of White Christian leadership.

Views such as these are not confined to the pulpit. They are carried into the political arena, where they strongly influence the public mind and the handling of the problems which the country has to face. "We on this side of the House," said a Nationalist Senator in a foreign affairs debate, "earnestly believe that it was the will of the Almighty that we should remain European and that we are the bearers of the Christian civilisation amongst the non-Europeans."[67] These convictions, expressed in 1956, remain the convictions of probably the majority of those who support the government, despite the repercussions that have been felt on the international level. Within the ranks of the Nationalist Party, the waverers are few.

Views of the United Party

However, amongst the opponents of the ruling party, particularly amongst its White opponents, doubts and misgivings are rife. In isolation, they believe, South Africa may be unable to withstand the pressures that are upon her from the outside world. The major opposition group, the United Party (although it stands in a position not far removed from that of the government in its belief that White leadership must be maintained) lacks the conviction and the sure sense of dedication that have equipped the Nationalist Party to pursue radical and even revolutionary policies in the face of mounting opposition at home and abroad.

The approach of the United Party to the political questions of the day is the empirical approach of true conservatism. It concedes the need for adjustment from time to time, but abjures policies which involve a radical disturbance of the *status quo*. In foreign policy, it has agreed with many of the objectives of the Nationalist Party: it has supported the government in resisting United Nations interference in South Africa's domestic affairs; it agrees that South West Africa should not be placed under trusteeship; and it has indicated its approval of the efforts which the government has made from time to time to deal with the problems of Africa and of communism.

Nevertheless, its spokesmen continue to accuse the government of mishandling the actual business of foreign relations. South Africa, they argue, has been needlessly exposed to dangerous isolation by a fanatical devotion to the apartheid ideal and uncompromising rigidity in the handling of external relations. Less intransigence at the United Nations—a willingness at least to talk and submit reports on South West Africa; a less bristly insistence on South Africa's rights under Article 2(7) of the Charter; a less aggressive and provocative statement of South Africa's case—would, United Party leaders claim, have done much to ease South Africa's position.[68] Similarly, a few timely concessions on the domestic level would, without any danger to White leadership, have eased South Africa's relations with those "who were prepared to make common cause with her in the past."[69]

In the opinion of the United Party, the major foreign policy blunder of the government was the decision to press forward at last to the republican victory, regardless of the possible consequences so far as Commonwealth membership was concerned. With much of its support coming from the English-speaking section of the population and from the business and industrial elements in the large towns, the United Party remains convinced that, however uncomfortable South Africa's position in the Commonwealth may have been, membership should nevertheless not have been risked. Within the Commonwealth, South Africa enjoyed advantages, political as well as economic, which are available nowhere else. There is no alternative to the Commonwealth Relations Office as an agency for keeping the South African government supplied with a valuable fund of diplomatic information; nor is there any alternative to the council room of the Commonwealth Prime Ministers' Conference as a venue for the South African government to further its diplomacy and "listen in" to points of view

[67] Speech by Senator G. P. Wessels, *Senate Debates,* May 23, 1956, col. 3762.

[68] See, for example, *House of Assembly Debates,* No-Confidence Debate, January 24, 1961, coll. 44 ff., and *Senate Debates,* speech by Senator J. W. Butler, January 26, 1961, col. 71.

[69] Speech by Sir de Villiers Graaff, Leader of United Party, Pietermaritzburg, June 2, 1961; reprint from United Party Office, Durban. See also *Senate Debates,* May 23, 1961, coll. 4832 ff.

from many different parts of the world. Outside the Commonwealth, South Africa has, the United Party believes, lost the last means that were still left open for maintaining, in some measure, at least, the already dwindling confidence of most of the countries of the Western world.[70]

Views of the Progressive Party

The only other Parliamentary party of any consequence, the Progressive Party, attacks the government's policies on a far more fundamental level. So long as the ticket that secures admission to the political nation remains a White one, South Africa, the leaders of the Progressive Party believe, will be unable to improve its international position. If the country is to recover Commonwealth membership, and escape from the predicament that has developed at the United Nations; if it is to assume its rightful place as the leading African state and combat the spread of communism; if it is to escape economic disaster, the White nation must accept the non-Whites into political partnership, with a franchise determined by educational and property qualifications applicable to all irrespective of race.

In such manner, with "a government which will govern all South Africans on the basis of individual merit instead of colour," the Progressive Party believes South Africa may weather the international storms that lie ahead, without sacrificing the standards and stability that are necessary for the maintenance of the Western pattern of life.[71] The Progressive Party enjoys comparatively small support amongst the Whites, however; and the backing it receives from the non-White population is even thinner.

Views of the non-White population

Amongst the politically articulate sections of the non-White population, the dominant issue remains the domestic struggle. External pressures upon South Africa, likely to create strains and tensions within the White nation have been welcomed, as have measures involving an increase in the country's isolation. Early in 1961, a spokesman of the South African United Front, an overseas organization of exiled leaders from various South African and South West African political bodies, announced the desire of his organization for "the complete isolation of South Africa," as the only peaceful means of bringing about a change of government. There have been calls from the non-Whites for United Nations intervention. In the same quarters, the withdrawal of South Africa from Commonwealth membership under pressure from the Afro-Asian states was greeted as a "resounding victory" for the non-White peoples in their struggle against apartheid.[72]

Principally because the domestic struggle is so all-absorbing, few of the major non-White political organizations have presented a clear formulation of their own approach to the problems of international relations. However, the general position appears to be one of hostility towards the West because of the past association of so many of the members of the Western alliance with colonialism, balanced by a strong suspicion of Russia as the potential imperialist Power of the future.

The indications, therefore, are that in its present mood, articulate non-White political opinion would probably seek a neutralist position in collaboration with the other newly independent states of Africa and Asia. There are

[70] *Senate Debates*, April 17, 1961, speech by Senator G. J. Sutter, Coll. 3205 ff.

[71] Statement by Dr. J. Steytler, Progressive Party Leader, reported in *Natal Daily News*, March 16, 1961.

[72] For a brief statement of South African United Front policies see *Manchester Guardian*, January 16, 1961. For South African non-White reactions to loss of Commonwealth membership, see *Race Relations News*, April 1961.

close bonds between the South African Indian Congress and the Congress movement in India. And the Pan-African Congress, as its name suggests, looks with hope towards schemes such as those formulated by Dr. Nkrumah, for a strong and independent United States of Africa.

Considerable uncertainties remain, however. Organizations such as the banned African National Congress and Pan African Congress, and the South African Indian Congress are far from representative in their membership. Large reservoirs of unformed opinion, particularly amongst the Africans of the rural areas, are only beginning to be tapped and channelled into a political mold. The government itself is conducting an intensive and not wholly unsuccessful campaign to persuade the non-White peoples that salvation lies in acceptance of the apartheid blue-print.

There are other influences that are likely to be felt as well. As South Africa becomes further separated from its old associates, some of the hostility which the non-Whites have felt towards the West may disappear. At the same time, however, in isolation, South Africa will be an open target for Moscow, which is almost certain to make generous offers of support to the non-Whites in their liberatory struggle.

A Cold War battleground

Ultimately, therefore, unless there is a rapid and radical change in the structure of domestic politics, South Africa is almost certain to be faced by the unhappy fate of becoming one of the battlegrounds in the Cold War. The chances of a radical change in policies are slender. As has already been pointed out, support within the White nation for policies such as those advocated by the Progressive Party is thin.

Even if the Nationalist Party were to be shaken from office, therefore, it is unlikely that it would be succeeded by a radical reforming party. The most likely successor is a party or coalition of parties advocating the continuance of "White Leadership" as the United Party now does. Yet a government committed to such a program has little hope of leading South Africa out of the international wilderness. The United Party, dedicated though it was to the Commonwealth connection, now admits that there are certain prices which it is not prepared to pay for re-admission, amongst them the abandonment of the traditional pattern of White leadership.[73] If the recovery of Commonwealth membership is unlikely, so is the recovery of South Africa's international position elsewhere.

Thus the prospect for South Africa is that of remaining the one "apart" in a dangerous world where the fundamental issue is that of saving Western ideals of human liberty and human dignity from the encroachments of totalitarian communism. The tragic paradox of the South African situation is that it is Western civilization which the White nation claims to be defending with the policies that have set it apart from the West.

[73] Speech by Sir de Villiers Graaff, Pietermaritzburg, June 2, 1961.

BIBLIOGRAPHY

Editor's Suggestions

Ballinger, R. B. *South-West Africa*. Johannesburg: South African Institute of Race Relations, 1961.

Brookes, Edgar Harry. *South Africa in a Changing World*. New York: Oxford University Press, 1954.

Brookes, Edgar Harry, and Macauley, J. B. *Civil Liberty in South Africa*. New York: Oxford University Press, 1959.

Carter, Gwendolen Margaret. *The Politics of Inequality: South Africa Since 1948*. New York: Praeger, 1958.

Mansergh, N. *Survey of British Commonwealth Affairs, 1939–1952*. London: Royal Institute of International Affairs, O.U.P., 1958.

Miller, J. D. B. *The Commonwealth in the World*. London: Duckworth, 1958.

Scholtz, G. D. *The Origins and Essence of the Race Pattern in South Africa*. Stellenbosch: SABRA, 1958.

PART FIVE

ASIA

ABOUT THE AUTHOR

ISHTIAQ HUSAIN QURESHI was educated at the University of Delhi and Cambridge University in England. He began his academic career in India at the University of Delhi and advanced there to the rank of Dean of the Faculty of Arts. He is presently the Vice-Chancellor of the University of Karachi.

Dr. Qureshi has served not only in the teaching and educational administrative fields but also as a member of the Pakistani Government. With the establishment of Pakistan he became a member of the Constituent Assembly and in 1949 became active in the administration of the new Government. He held the positions of Deputy Minister, Minister of State, and Minister with cabinet rank during the period 1949–54.

He is a past president of the Pakistan Political Science Association and the Pakistan History Conference. He has also served as Director of the Central Institute of Islamic Research. He was a visiting professor of History at Columbia University from 1955–60.

ABOUT THE CHAPTER

After a survey of the geographical location of Pakistan and the problems inherent in administering a state consisting of two provinces separated by nearly 1,100 miles of foreign territory, the author of this chapter turns to an examination of the historic foreign policies of the nation. He evaluates the power relations within her region and concludes that "Pakistan has cordial relations with only one (Iran)," of her six next-door neighbors, "correct and polite relations with two (China and Burma) and an unfriendly relationship with the rest (Afghanistan, India and the U.S.S.R.)."

Considerable attention is given to the conflict with India. The author notes that the "most vital consideration for any country is security and safeguarding of its freedom." He then shows why Pakistan feels that her security is endangered by the policies of India and why the foreign policy of Pakistan is dominated almost exclusively by a fear of that nation. A careful reading of this chapter throws some light on Pakistans attitude towards the India-China conflict.

The author also considers two other major factors which influence Pakistan's foreign policy: ideology and the necessity for economic development. Of special interest is the discussion of the population factor in Pakistan and the problems of economic advancement in view of the high rate of population growth.

16

THE FOREIGN POLICY OF PAKISTAN

ISHTIAQ HUSAIN QURESHI
University of Karachi

THE GEOGRAPHICAL SETTING

Borders

Pakistan consists of two provinces separated by nearly 1,100 miles of foreign territory.

West Pakistan   West Pakistan, the larger of the two in area, extends roughly between 24° north and 37° north. On its south lies the Arabian Sea and the Rann of Cutch, a desert full of stretches of salt water and sand. On the west it adjoins Iran and Afghanistan, while on the north lies another strip of Afghan territory less than 25 miles wide which separates Pakistan from the Central Asian territories of the U.S.S.R. The north-western frontier of West Pakistan thus runs along the land-locked country of Afghanistan which has an area of a

quarter million square miles and a population of 12 million.

The slopes of Pamir run into the highlands of the north. In this area are situated the picturesque lands of Hunza, Gilgit and Chitral. Of these, Hunza has been made famous by writers who praise its sound methods of agriculture and the good health and longevity of its people. These writings tend to paint Hunza as a Shangrila where prudent habits and natural conditions combine to create an atmosphere of bliss.

Wedged in between these mountainous territories of West Pakistan, the Indian Punjab and the Chinese Empire, lies the disputed territory of Kashmir. The richer and more populated portion of Kashmir is under Indian occupation. The mountainous range of the Afghanistan-Pakistan border is pierced by a number of passes which, since the dawn of history, have provided the routes for peaceful trade between the desert areas of the tableland in the west and the rich Indus Valley in the east. These routes have also been followed by immigrants in search of pasture or a better standard of life. Very often they have been used by invaders who have been attracted by the wealth of the fertile plains of the basins of the Indus and the Ganges.

South of Afghanistan, the western boundary of West Pakistan runs along with that of Iran which has an area of more than half a million square miles and a population of about 20 millions. Iran occupies the greater part of the Great Iranian Plateau which in the east holds portions of Afghanistan as well as of West Pakistan. In places its eastern slopes come up to the Indus. On the east lie the territories of the Indian Union from the Rann of Cutch right up to the Cease-Fire Line in Kashmir. This border is about 800 miles long.

Of the two provinces, West Pakistan, with an area of 310,298 square miles is the larger. It is divided into two unequal parts. Its western and northern areas consist of tableland and mountains which form the eastern ramparts of the Iranian Plateau. In the north the mountains run to lofty heights: Nanga Parbat is 26,-600 feet and Godwin Austin, the popular K2, is 28,250 feet. The other section is the valley of the Indus. The mountains here are mostly barren, though they enclose some green valleys. Of these, Kaghan Valley is famous for its landscape. The richer and the more populated part of this section is the basin of the Indus which holds one of the most elaborate systems of irrigation in the world. The Hindu Kush, which divides Afghanistan into two distinct parts, also serves to separate Central from Southern Asia.

East Pakistan   East Pakistan is bounded on the north by the hilly regions of Jalpaiguri, Darjeeling and parts of (Indian) Assam. In the south lies the Bay of Bengal. In the west it adjoins the Indian provinces of West Bengal and Bihar and in the east the Assam province. The narrow strip of the Chittagong Hill Tracts connects Pakistan with Burma, though the frontier is difficult because of lush jungle growth combined with mountainous terrain.

To the northeast, beyond Burma, is the great Republic of China. It extends from the borders of Hunza all along the northern marches of the sub-continent. The Indo-Chi-

nese frontier beyond Thailand is less than 500 miles from the eastern extremity of East Pakistan. About 1,000 miles from Dacca lie equidistant the cities of Kunming in China and Bangkok in Thailand.

Not far from the Pakistani frontier lies the Burmese territory of Arakan with a substantial majority of Muslims in the population.[1] In Burma as a whole there are many Muslim groups, mostly the descendants of those who migrated from time to time from the sub-continent in pursuit of trade and occasionally for other employment. Towards the southeast of Burma lies a Muslim area stretching as far as the eastern limits of Indonesia. This unsymmetrical conglomeration includes a part of Thailand, Malaya, Indonesia and portions of Borneo and the Philippines.

Topography and climate

A brief look at Pakistan's topography and climate will complete this picture of the geographical setting. West Pakistan presents a varied landscape ranging from the snow-covered peaks of the upper Himalayas to the unbearably hot desert of Sind. The northwest area is dry and continental. It has a Mediterranean type of climate, and is hilly except in the southeast parts. The bulk of the Punjab is plain. Sind is dry, with a small hill tract in the west, the Indus valley in the middle, and a desert tract in the east. Baluchistan is dry and tableland.

East Pakistan is sub-tropical and mostly plateau. It occupies the greater part of the deltas of the Ganges and the Brahmaputra; a good part of it is criss-crossed by the branches of the two rivers. Towards the east, there is hilly country in the Sylhet and Chittagong areas. The entire province is brilliantly green.

West Pakistan is subject to extremes of cli-

---

[1] *Pakistan: Facts and Figures*, Karachi: Department of Advertising, Films and Publications, n.d., pp. 1–3.

mate, except for the coastal strip of Sind. East Pakistan is sub-tropical from March to October, with high temperatures, humidity and heavy rains. For the rest of the year it is cool with scanty rainfall.[2]

HISTORICAL FOREIGN POLICIES

Persian, Greek, Scythian, and Hun invasions

The fabled riches of northern India have been throughout the ages a coveted prize for invaders. In pre-history, more than three thousand years before Christ, there thrived a civilization in the Indus Valley whose remarkable ruins have been excavated at Harappa and Mohenjodaro. There are reasons to believe that this civilization was destroyed by the immigrating Aryans. According to our earliest recorded information, the Indus region was incorporated into the Persian Empire some time between 520 and 515 B.C. If Herodotus is to be believed, the people of this region then paid more than the equivalent of ten million rupees as tribute to Persia, which was "proportionately larger than the rest."[3]

But the great Persian Empire did not last forever. In the Hellenic world, there arose unexpectedly a young man of high ambitions. In 330 B.C. Alexander led a victorious army into Persia; the Empire of Darius fell like a house of cards. Three years later, the young Macedonian was in the plain of Peshawar from where he successfully led his armies beyond the present frontier of West Pakistan. There his war-weary soldiers refused to go any further, and Alexander had no option but to go back along the Indus and through the desert of Makran. This was the first full-scale invasion of India of which history provides details.

[2] *Ibid.*, pp. 3–5.
[3] Herodotus quoted in Pakistan History Board, *A Short History of Indo-Pakistan*, Karachi: Pakistan Historical Society, 1960, p. 44.

However, the impact of Greek civilization did not come to an end with Alexander's departure. Twice the Greeks and semi-Greeks invaded the territories of West Pakistan—once about 200 B.C. under Euthydemos, and again about 162 B.C. under Eucratides—penetrating into Baluchistan, the northwest frontier, the Punjab and Sind.

Next to come through the passes of the Hindu Kush were the Scythians in about 65 B.C. They controlled the Indus Valley and the Punjab, but later surrendered it to the Parthians. Their domination, however, came to an end in the middle of the first century after Christ.

India was momentarily free from foreign invaders till about 500 A.D. By that time the Persian Empire had been overthrown and the Gupta Empire in India was weak. This gave the Huns an opportunity; Toramana quickly established himself in the Punjab and later extended his domain up to Malwa. The Hun power was not liquidated till 528 when Yashodharman, a Malwa military adventurer, annihilated the last Hun ruler.

Muslim domination

Though there had been Muslim settlements on the coast of peninsular India, a Muslim army invaded India for the first time in the reign of al-Walid (705–15), the Umayyad, when the teen-aged Muhammad bin Qasim marched into Sind through Makran. After defeating Raja Dahir at Rawar, he advanced to conquer Aror and Multan. Muslim rule was thus established in Sind.

The next Muslim ruler to invade India was Sabuktigin (977–97). He occupied all the territory in the northwest up to Peshawar. A few years later began the repeated incursions of Mahmud. In 1008 he conquered all the area up to Kangra. In 1014 Jehlum was taken and Thanesar was occupied. The Punjab now became a part of the Ghaznavid Empire. In 1018 Mathura and Kannauj fell; Kalinjar fell next

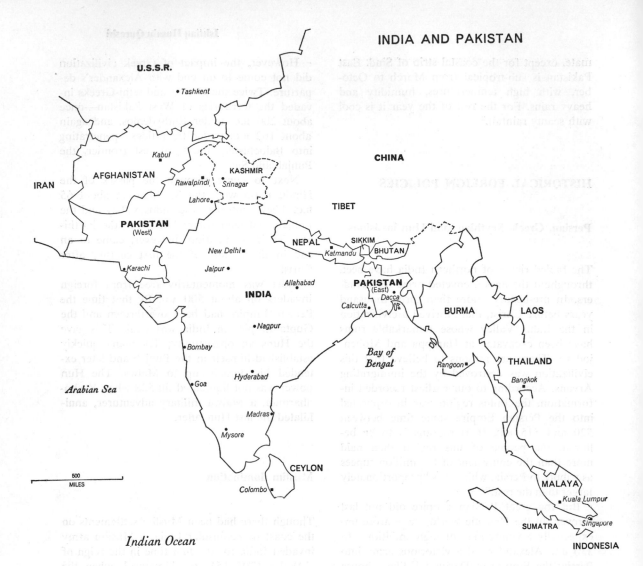

U.S.S.R.

• Tashkent

CHINA

Kabul

AFGHANISTAN

KASHMIR

Rawalpindi Srinagar

IRAN

Lahore

TIBET

PAKISTAN
(West)

NEPAL SIKKIM

New Delhi Katmandu BHUTAN

PAKISTAN
(East)

• Karachi Jaipur Allahabad Dacca

INDIA Calcutta BURMA LAOS

• Nagpur

Arabian Sea • Bombay Rangoon THAILAND

Bay of
Bengal Bangkok

• Goa Hyderabad

Madras Bombay

• Mysore

CEYLON MALAYA

Kuala Lumpur
500
MILES Colombo Singapore

SUMATRA

INDONESIA

Indian Ocean

in 1021. In 1026 came the famous conquest of Somnath. In 1027, for the last time, Mahmud invaded Sind. His successors lost large areas of their empire to the rising power of the Seljuks and were soon threatened to such a degree that they were hardly able to maintain themselves at Lahore.

With the rise to power of the Shansabanis of Ghur the stage was again set for invasion from the northwest. In 1175 Sultan Muizuddin Muhammad bin Sam marched through Baluchistan and conquered Multan and Uchh. He took Peshawar and then in 1189 marched to Lahore, which surrendered without fighting.

Three years later he took the port of Debal in Sind. In 1183 Sialkot was annexed. In 1190 when he was on the point of returning after seizing Bhatinda, news came that Prithwiraj, the Chief of Delhi and Ajmer, was advancing to recapture the fortress. The two large armies met at Tarain, between Karnal and Thanesar. The Sultan was defeated and withdrew to Lahore and then to Ghaznih. He returned in 1192 with more than a hundred thousand soldiers and this time Prithwiraj and his chieftains were completely defeated. Ajmer was also conquered. Delhi followed and then Kol (modern Aligarh). In 1196 Kannauj was captured. Now the frontiers of his domain were pushed up to Monghyer. On his orders Gujarat was taken by Qutbuddin Aibak in about 1196 and Bihar and Bengal by Muhammad bin Bakhtiyar.

Mongol attacks

Then the famous Mongol warrior, Genghis Khan, appeared on the frontiers in 1221. But, through their foresight, the new Muslim dynasty did not come into conflict with him. This proved to be but a short respite and the Muslim empire in the subcontinent was the target of many Mongol invasions. The more famous of these were the invasions of 1292, when the Mongols were defeated by Jalaluddin Khalji, and of 1299, when they invaded Delhi under Qutlugh Khawajah, and Alauddin Khalji managed to repulse them with great difficulty. The Sultans of Delhi throughout the thirteenth century were constantly harassed by the Mongols. There were decades of respite but the danger never completely disappeared. The armies of Delhi did succeed in defending the empire, but the Sultans had to be constantly vigilant. The fourteenth century began in the same way. But with the conversion of the Mongols to Islam, the danger gradually subsided.

Timur's empire   However, when a new conqueror in the person of Timur appeared, the situation again changed. Timur, known to Europe as Tamerlane, is the hero of many legends. He succeeded, by the end of the fourteenth century, in establishing a large empire in Central Asia. In 1398 he sent his grandson into the sub-continent. He took Uchh and Multan. Then came Timur himself. City after city surrendered to him, until Delhi fell and was plundered.

The Sultanate was already in a state of decay when Timur took Delhi. When he left, the entire area fell into a state of anarchy. This produced a power vacuum which was partly filled by the rise of small provincial dynasties.

But the more interesting phenomenon was the establishment and consolidation of an Afghan empire through migration and consolidation. As there was no power to resist the newcomers they just came, settled down and began to rule. Their empire was still seeking stability when it was invaded by Babur, once again from the northwest. In 1526 the fateful Battle of Panipat was fought which established Mogul rule in the sub-continent. The Afghans, united under the able and energetic Sher Shah, turned out Babur's son Humayun. However, after seventeen years, he found his opportunity and re-established his rule in 1555.

Akbar and his descendants   Under Humayun's son, Akbar, began the most glorious period of Muslim rule. For about a century and a half the Mogul empire continued to be the wonder of the world because of its wealth, splendor and culture. During this period there were no foreign invasions, except the loss of Qandahar to the Safawids of Iran. It would, however, be incorrect to assume that the northwest frontier of the empire caused no worry. The rise of the three great empires of the Persians, the Uzbeks and the Moguls brought stability to the sensitive areas now forming Iran, West Pakistan, Afghanistan and the Soviet Republic of Central Asia, but the Moguls had to be vigilant. They assiduously cultivated good relations with Iran, but were not unaware of the ambitions of either of their neighbors. When the Mogul empire weakened, Nadir Shah of Iran invaded it in 1739 and left the dynasty prostrate.

The last of the invaders from the northwest was Ahmad Shah Abdali, a famous general of Nadir Shah. His first attack in 1744 failed. He re-appeared two years later but confined his activities to plundering a part of the Punjab. Again in 1751 he returned and seized the Punjab and Kashmir. Later the Mogul minister, Imadul Mulk, reconquered the Punjab and re-incorporated it into the Empire. This was a challenge to Abdali, who now came post-haste to claim his territory. The weak Mogul Emperor, instead of fighting, preferred giving him Kashmir, Sind and Sirhind. In the process of this visit, Abdali also beat the Marathas near Delhi. When Abdali's back was turned on India, the Marathas started encroaching on the Punjab. A final showdown with them was now inevitable. The last major Hindu-Muslim conflict was also staged on the windy plain of Panipat in 1761. Once again the Marathas were crushed and their power in northern India was broken.

British control

By the middle of the eighteenth century, the great empires of Asia had fallen into decay and were incapable of holding their own against the rising power of Europe. The subcontinent saw the establishment of the British Empire. When the third battle of Panipat had been fought in 1761, the British had already built for themselves the nucleus of an India empire and a powerful army. The destruction of the Maratha power left the British free to expand their influence. By the middle of the next century they became the sole masters of the sub-continent.

The revolt of 1857 having failed, there was little danger to British authority from within for more than three quarters of a century. The rise of Napoleon Bonaparte had, however, led the British to take measures to safeguard their interests by interfering in the affairs of Iran and Afghanistan. The rise of the Russian empire once again emphasized the importance of the northwest frontier, as well as Afghanistan and Central Asia. British policies in these areas were greatly motivated by a suspicion of Russia. The Anglo-Persian convention of 1908 was a successful attempt to stabilize the situation; however, this stability changed soon after the establishment of the Communist government in Russia.

This brief survey shows that the subcontinent has always been sensitive to any developments in Iran or Central Asia because there has been a long tradition of invasions from these areas.

FORCES AND TRENDS IN POWER RELATIONSHIPS

A glance at the map of Asia will show that Liaquat Ali Khan was not exaggerating when he gave the title "Pakistan: The Heart of Asia" to the collection of his speeches delivered in the U.S.A. in 1951. K. M. Pannikar once told Alan Campbell-Johnson that the two parts of the proposed Pakistan would be like two ears of the elephant that was India. He proceeded to remark that the elephant could live without his ears,[4] implying thereby that the ears could not live without the elephant. In reality, the elephant would be exposed to all kinds of dangers if the ears were removed.

The two most sensitive frontiers of the Indo-Pakistan sub-continent lie in the northwest, now the northwest frontier of Pakistan, and in the east, now part of East Pakistan. The former has always been the traditional route for all invasions by land; it now adjoins the powerful U.S.S.R. and a strip of Communist China. The latter has recently gained great significance by the presence of Red China and the Communist pressure in South East Asia. The result is the curious fact that Pakistan bears a major share of responsibility for defending and protecting the Indian mainland.

Neighbors to the north and east

Pakistan's immediate neighbors include some of the most formidable military Powers of the present-day world. The U.S.S.R. and China are both giants before whom Pakistan's military strength pales into insignificance. A war

---

[4] See Alan Campbell-Johnson, *Mission with Mountbatten,* London: Robert Hale, 1951, p. 47.

with either one of them would obviously be a one-sided affair. Pakistan realizes this and cannot contemplate a struggle with them without the fear of disastrous consequences. It was this fear and the traditional fear of inimical developments in Central Asia that led Pakistan into an alliance with the non-Communist nations of the Western world, especially with the United States of America. For in alliance with militarily strong nations lies Pakistan's only hope for survival if its giant neighbors should decide to attack.

Afghanistan is weak economically, politically, and militarily. In itself it is no source of concern to Pakistan. However, since the establishment of Pakistan, it has adopted an unfriendly attitude. It has been following a policy of irredentism regarding the Pushtu-speaking areas of Pakistan. In recent years it has been receiving generous aid from the U.S.S.R. This has helped to make Afghanistan's attitude towards Pakistan even more belligerent. Its troops have repeatedly violated Pakistan's frontier and its propaganda machine attempts to create discontent among the warlike tribes. Since the U.S.S.R. has given open verbal support to Afghan claims, Pakistan is always left wondering how far Afghanistan's efforts are subsidized by the Kremlin.

Iran is a friendly Power, an ally in the Central Treaty Organization (CENTO), with deep-rooted cultural links. Militarily it is not significant in spite of large doses of American aid. Strategically it is important, for if it falls into Soviet hands, the whole problem of the defense of northwest Pakistan would assume graver proportions.

To the east of East Pakistan lies Burma with its internal law-and-order problem and its inherently weak defenses. It is not a party to any defense alliances, but that does not matter much. Its strategic position in Southeast Asia is yet to be appreciated by the Great Powers of the Western bloc. In the immediate future it cannot be a source of worry except indirectly, if Red China pushes south in its expansionist mood and considers it expedient to devour it. In that case, East Pakistan would be fully and dangerously exposed to the Chinese threat.

Relations with India

That leaves India which poses the greatest danger for Pakistan. It is a big neighbor with long common boundaries. It is hostile in its attitude. Its leaders and large sections of its population have not reconciled themselves to the creation and existence of Pakistan. It has made no serious effort to solve its disputes with Pakistan. Its forces occupy a large part of the state of Jammu and Kashmir which is a disputed territory with an overwhelmingly Muslim population. The dispute has been pending for years now before the United Nations. India's record in Junagadh and Hyderabad is not calculated to create confidence in its sense of justice and fair play. In sheer size, it dwarfs Pakistan. In industrial output, it is far advanced. Its military strength is in keeping with its size and resources.

Pakistanis believe that Indian hostility poses a far greater problem to them than Chinese expansion or Soviet threats, neither country having a dispute with Pakistan. Besides, Pakistan is too small to worry them. Unfortunately India has done nothing to reassure Pakistan of her peaceful intentions. Her Western allies have never supported Pakistan against India, even on points such as Kashmir, where the moral strength of Pakistan's stand is not in doubt. Western attitude has also been lukewarm in Pakistan's dispute with Afghanistan. This makes the Pakistanis feel all the more defenseless in spite of security pacts and defense alliances.

In the eyes of Asian countries, India's prestige is high because of her neutrality. India points an accusing finger at Pakistan for bringing the Cold War to India's doorsteps. Many Asian countries are suspicious of Pakistan because of her alliance with the West. For the loss of this prestige, Pakistan has not gained even the support of her Western allies. Thus out of her six next-door neighbors—the U.S.S.R., China, India, Afghanistan, Iran and

Burma—Pakistan has cordial relations with only one (Iran), correct and polite relations with two (China and Burma) and an unfriendly relationship with the rest (Afghanistan, India and the U.S.S.R.). This configuration of power relationships must be understood and appreciated if Pakistan's foreign policy is to be viewed in correct perspective.

FORMULATING FOREIGN POLICY

Before the 1958 revolution

Pakistan was a parliamentary democracy until 1958. Her foreign policy was made by the Cabinet with the explicit or implicit approval of the Parliament. Most of the prime ministers took an active interest in foreign affairs and, in many ways, the Foreign Office received greater attention from the Prime Minister than any other department. One reason for this was the importance and usual urgency of "effective" foreign relations in the early years of independence. In fact, so vital was a correct formulation of policies and so clear the national interests that even the Governor-General, who enjoyed only constitutional powers, took a hand in it. The third Governor-General, Ghulam Muhammad, went to the U.S.A. himself in 1953, prior to the signing of a mutual defense treaty with that country. Before that, it is generally known that the Quaid-i-Azam, Mohammed Ali Jinnah, besides taking a deep interest in foreign relations, was actually the fountainhead of all our policies towards India. These were, of course, times of exceptional stress and strain. But, as a general proposition, it would be true to say that hardly any foreign minister was allowed to build up a foreign policy on his own. On important occasions the Cabinet discussed and approved all decisions and shifts in policy. This was only natural under the system of collective responsibility, and was the norm, though there are good reasons

to believe that on one or two important occasions the decisions of the Cabinet were flouted.

In the final analysis, however, the foreign policy was formulated by the Governor-General, the Prime Minister and the Foreign Minister. Efforts were made to make the decisions legal by securing in some instances, *post facto*, the consent of the Cabinet. There is no evidence to show that the British tradition of consulting the leader of the Opposition concerning major crises was followed. Foreign policy was in Pakistan much more of a party issue than it generally is in Britain or other parliamentary democracies.

Parliamentary approval of the officially-adopted foreign policy was constitutionally essential, but here again the Assembly was seldom taken into confidence on important issues. This is obvious from the fact that foreign policy debates in Parliament were infrequent and, when held, were only of a general nature.

After the 1958 revolution

Since the 1958 revolution, the formulation of foreign policy has been in the hands of the President and his Cabinet. Parliamentary approval is no longer necessary as the Constitution was abrogated. The President is obviously the most important person in the making of policy, but generally the whole Cabinet makes all significant decisions with the Foreign Minister playing a major role.

Foreign policy has come to assume greater significance since 1958, as compared to the earlier period, for three reasons. First, more money is required for the new ambitious development plans. This can only be secured by a better and more effective conduct of foreign affairs. The President has, therefore, been visiting all major aid-giving countries like the United States, Britain, Germany and Japan. In the second place, the revolutionary regime had to vindicate its professed ideals and intentions, and therefore to inform the world of its ability and competence to maintain a stable government and a strong national economy. Finally, breaches in our foreign policy, bequeathed to us by the pre-1958 administration, had to be repaired. To meet these new requirements, therefore, the Foreign Office has been expanded and foreign policy enjoys priority.

Pakistan has recently adopted a new constitution and a national legislature has been restored to the country. It is premature to speculate about the role of this legislature in formulating foreign policy. It seems clear, however, that the new legislature, as well as provincial legislatures, will take a considerable interest in foreign policy. The reorganized political parties will also play an important role.

The role of public opinion

Unfortunately very little work has so far been done on relating foreign policy to public opinion. It is difficult, therefore, to analyze the role of public opinion in the formation of Pakistan's foreign policy. The press here has never been as serious and well-informed a medium of knowledge and opinion as in many advanced countries. Moreover, with some exceptions, the general newspaper reader has not been deeply interested in world affairs. Domestic events, particularly in the economic and political (party) fields, have commanded attention out of proportion to their intrinsic importance.

The exceptions have been Indo-Pakistan relations and the problem posed by the creation of the State of Israel. The former evokes an interest almost bordering on obsession, partly because of historical reasons and partly because of a natural concern for security. The latter has stirred public opinion because of religious bonds with the Arabs and a feeling for the solidarity of the world of Islam. This latter exception demands good relations with the Muslim countries of the world.

Among the instruments of educating the public may be mentioned the Pakistan Institute of International Affairs with its headquarters at Karachi. It has maintained a well-equipped library, has published a journal, arranged lectures, conferences and discussions and published books. It has affiliated institutions located at Lahore and Dacca.

On relations with Afghanistan, India, and the Muslim world, the newspapers and other media of public opinion have been vocal as well as consistent. On the whole, these issues have been kept above party politics. Unanimity of opinion on them has been as natural as the lack of it on other points. On Indo-Pakistan relations, especially Kashmir, and on Israel, official foreign policy has faithfully reflected public opinion. Only on the problem of our relations with the Middle East has the zeal of public opinion sometimes outrun the discretion of the Government, particularly during the Suez crisis. On other topics there has been the usual debate, sometimes well-informed and sometimes ill-informed, sometimes intelligent and moderate, at others obtuse and intemperate.

Foreign policy has rarely been a major issue in the elections held between 1947–1958. It is true that election manifestos of all parties contained certain well-known statements on foreign affairs, but no issue of this kind ever played a decisive role in either the election campaign or its results. Perhaps we do not yet have a public opinion sophisticated enough to take a stand on a foreign policy and make it an important factor in any political debate or conflict. Therefore, the formulation of foreign policy has been in the hands of an exclusively official and political elite.

THE ADMINISTRATION OF FOREIGN POLICY

The Ministry of External Affairs

The administration of foreign policy, as distinct from its formulation, is, as everywhere, in the hands of the permanent staff of the Ministry of External Affairs (formerly known as the Ministry of Foreign Affairs and Commonwealth Relations). The highest civil servant is the Secretary to the Ministry, who corresponds to the British Permanent Under-Secretary of State. He supervises the entire administration of the department, advises the Minister on all points and helps in all deliberations and decisions. Under him are two or more Directors-General (till recently known as Joint Secretaries) who are charged with the general supervision of the work of their subordinates. Then come a large number of Directors or Deputy Secretaries, each in charge of a specific division devoted to a particular branch of administration.

All these senior officers belong to either the Civil Service of Pakistan or the Pakistan Foreign Service, the two most coveted careers for young men of university education. There has been a small research cell in the Foreign Office to supply data and required information to the Minister and the departmental officials. This is the general organization of the Ministry which has remained unchanged almost since its inception in 1947, and there is no apparent reason for looking forward to any change in the future, except, one hopes, for the broadening of the research organization which is totally inadequate for the purpose it is intended to serve.

The diplomatic corps

Outside Pakistan, the administration and application of foreign policy is in the hands of Pakistan's diplomatic envoys, especially those accredited to the Big Powers and the United Nations. They are the people who, by their speeches, negotiations, and day to day work, apply the foreign policy formulated at home and transmitted to them through the Foreign Office.

Like judges who make law in the process of administering it, these diplomats also formulate foreign policy while carrying out the President's or the Cabinet's instructions. The Home Government can only send general instructions. While remaining within the terms of his instructions, the diplomat can still, by carefully phrasing his thoughts or cleverly putting an emphasis, give a new shift to the policy. He has not disobeyed his superiors, but by his own peculiar approach he has done something more than merely broadcasting what he received from the Foreign Office. When he has stayed at a station for a number of years, he has built up an image of his foreign policy in the mind of that country which is as much his own handiwork as that of his superiors. That is how diplomats formulate foreign policy, even on central issues.

At the time of independence, Pakistan did not possess a single foreign service career diplomat, because India, being a British dependency, did not conduct her own foreign relations. A brand new foreign service had thus to be created through stiff competitive examinations. All senior posts were filled either by experienced civil servants or by old politicians as well as one or two university teachers.

This stop-gap arrangement, intended to last until the new foreign service men were experienced enough to take over, was highly unsatisfactory. It denuded the ranks of experienced civil servants who were already in short supply due to low Muslim strength in the old Indian Civil Service. It helped to create a sort of spoils system under which a dishonest or weak government could use highly important diplomatic assignments to reward its followers or silence its critics. It also adversely affected the conduct of foreign relations, for most of the people appointed to responsible positions had neither diplomatic training nor ability. There may be two opinions on the inevitability of this arrangement, but there is no doubt that it must bear a major share of responsibility for the unsatisfactory manner in which foreign policy was handled for many years. With the training of a new foreign service corps, the expertness with which Pakistan's day-to-day foreign relations are conducted should improve steadily from year to year.

THE NATIONAL INTEREST

Pakistan's national interest in relation to its foreign policy may be treated under three headings: security, ideology and economic development.

Security

Obviously the most vital consideration for any country is security and safeguarding its freedom. Pakistan is no exception to this. Before all other aspects, she has always paid heed to the necessity of maintaining her territorial integrity and independence. The fear of Indian aggression is real. The Pakistanis feel that India wants to annul the division of the subcontinent. India's diplomatic missions abroad and even her citizens who visit foreign countries generally work against Pakistan. Her attitude on Kashmir and other Indo-Pakistan disputes is unreasonable and high-handed. She maintains a large army which is mostly concentrated on the Pakistan frontier. She shows open hostility to any effort by Pakistan to strengthen herself. For instance, she showed undisguised hostility to Pakistan's defense alliances with the West. Through her pressure upon the West, the utility of these alliances to Pakistan has been considerably reduced.

The fear of India has always dominated Pakistan's foreign policy. The problem of Pakistan's defense in the eyes of the Pakistanis is mostly the problem of defense against India. The dangers of Communist infiltration or an actual Communist attack have been subordinate factors, because, compared to the Indian threat, they have always looked remote and indirect. The immediate and continuing danger in the peculiar circumstances seems to come from India.

The size and resources of India make this danger more real. She is five times the size of Pakistan in population. Her superiority in resources is obvious. Her economy has a stronger industrial base than Pakistan's. She inherited the most industrialized portions of the subcontinent. Add to this the fact that she has steel and coal in abundance, which are being well-exploited. Moreover, her armed strength is three times Pakistan's.

In comparison, Pakistan is a small country with poor economic resources. The existence of the large Indian territory between the two parts of Pakistan is a further source of weakness. Her economy is weak, and though there is room for development, the prospects of rapid industrialization are meager. She has neither good coal nor steel nor the amount of public or private capital that India can command. For these reasons alone, Pakistan will not be in a position to go to war with India.

India has continuously strengthened her striking power against Pakistan. Simultaneously she has missed no opportunity of branding Pakistan as a stooge of imperialism, oblivious of the fact that India's own policies and threats have thrown Pakistan into the arms of the Western Powers. Proud of her "neutrality" India claims a superior morality, but sees nothing wrong in extracting aid from both the blocs.

The fact seems to be that India has not reconciled herself to the creation of Pakistan. India has not yet mentally accepted the two-nation theory on the basis of which India was divided in 1947.[5] With one set of arguments she captured Junagadh and Hyderabad; with another set, she claims Kashmir. Principles seem to change according to Indian interests.

The history of Indo-Pakistan relations shows that India has made every effort to make it difficult for Pakistan to exist. India first refused and then delayed the dispatch of military assets and financial balances which had fallen to Pakistan's share. India diverted the waters of the Ravi in 1948. She refused to accept Paki-

[5] See K. Sarwar Hasan, *Pakistan and the United Nations*, New York: 1960, pp. 36–37.

stan's decision of not devaluing her currency and suspended all trade. She announced her intention to control and utilize the waters of the three eastern rivers, thus turning West Pakistan into a desert. She defied every United Nations move on Kashmir and refused to hold a free plebiscite to which she is committed by her own statements. The attitude of the Indian press, the statements of Indian politicians and the resolutions of Indian political parties are all equally remote from being reassuring.

In view of all this, Pakistanis feel justified in believing that India wants to see Pakistan remain weak, so that after some time she can, perhaps through a so called "police action," quietly annex her to the Indian Union, thus satisfying elements and their leaders who have for their political goal the re-absorption of Pakistan into the Indian Union.

Ideology

The ideology of Pakistan is based on the principles of Islam. This bare statement makes for two vital factors in her foreign policy. First, it means that Pakistan is religiously, culturally, and emotionally allied to other Muslim countries of the world. Secondly, it means that Pakistan cannot voluntarily accept communism as a way of life. Let us study these two implications more closely.

Affinity with Muslim states Pakistan feels a special affinity with other Muslim states. One of the directive principles of the 1956 Constitution laid down that the "State should endeavour to strengthen the bonds of unity among Muslim countries." Public opinion has always goaded the Government to support the Muslim nations in all their quarrels with other peoples. In 1949 Mr. Liaquat Ali Khan had thrown a feeler to see if it was feasible to hold an Islamic conference of all Arab and non-Arab Muslim states. Nothing came out of it. Similarly, plans for organizing an Inter-Islamic Consultative Body failed to materialize.

On the unofficial level, Chaudhri Khaliquzzaman, then President of the Muslim League, started the Islamistan movement, formed a Muslim Peoples' Organization and, in 1952, held an international conference in Karachi. Another organization, the Mu'tamar-i-Alam-i-Islami (World Muslim Conference) held two conferences in Karachi in 1949 and 1951. Pakistan officially sponsored the International Islamic Economic Conference, which held its first session at Karachi in November 1949. It was attended by 18 Muslim countries. The Conference set up the International Islamic Economic Organization, which held a few more conferences and then disintegrated.

On the diplomatic level, Pakistan and Iran signed a Treaty of Friendship in 1950. Treaties of friendship with Iraq and Syria quickly followed. In 1951, Pakistan signed such treaties with Turkey, Egypt and Saudi Arabia. Similar agreements followed with Yemen in 1952 and Lebanon in 1953. Then came Cultural Agreements with Turkey, Egypt, Syria and Iran. Military goodwill missions were exchanged with Iran, Turkey, Egypt, and Iraq. Heads of states of many Muslim countries have visited Pakistan, and Pakistani leaders have paid return visits. As we shall see later, Pakistan is a member of the Central Treaty Organization which includes Iran and Turkey. With Indonesia and Malaya, Pakistan has friendly relations.

In addition, Pakistan has generally supported all Muslim causes in the United Nations. Pakistani delegates to the world organization have always sided with the Muslim stand on all major issues—Palestine, the Italian colonies in North Africa, Tunisia, Morocco, Algeria, Indonesia, and Egypt.

There is no doubt about the presence of a strong feeling in Pakistan that its people form part of the Muslim world which has common problems; hence they must stand together with other Muslims in matters of common interest. Unfortunately, these Pakistani sentiments have not been reciprocated. One Muslim country after another has demonstrated the lack of common feeling for the problems of the Muslim world. The feeling is growing in Pakistan that this unilateral solicitude for other Muslim countries is hardly fair to herself. If things remain as they are, there is a probability of Pakistan revising her attitude of indiscriminately giving all-out support to every Muslim country.

Opposition to communism   As the philosophy of communism is distasteful to the average Muslim mind, Pakistan seeks to save herself from it. The broad ideals of the Western democracies are based on the Judeo-Christian ethics. The similarity of this foundation with that of Islam makes for an easy entente between Pakistan and the West. They share many values of life and political ideals. Both emphasize the importance of the individual soul and the role of the individual in society. If Christianity is incompatible with communism, so is Islam.

Islam is theistic and individualistic, communism is atheistic and communal. Superficially, both seem to share a dislike of super-accumulation of wealth in the hands of individuals. But in fact, the ideas of the use of wealth and the means and ways of stopping its accumulation differ in the two social systems. Islam will never surrender its unique character by accepting communism, even if the bait is that of rapid economic advance.

Above all, Islam puts its faith in God. Communism rejects God and is essentially a theory of material power, and hence unacceptable to the Muslims. It must be admitted, however, that the faith of the Muslims can be subverted like any other faith. But so long as Islam is the dominant ideology in Pakistan, it has well defined repercussions in the field of foreign affairs. The Islamic nature of Pakistan as a people and as a state has, on the one hand, created a link between it and other Muslim peoples throughout the world, and, on the other, has created an equally natural reluctance to identify itself with Communist countries.

It must be emphasized, however, that Pakistan has no quarrel with the Communist bloc. The primary reason for joining the Western bloc is her fear of Indian aggression. A common mental approach to the West is of sec-

ondary importance only. It is doubtful if Pakistan would have so readily lined up with the West, had there been no Indo-Pakistan difficulties. Here it must be remembered that the Soviet hostile attitude, particularly on Kashmir, came after, *not* before Pakistan's indication of her preference for friendship with the West.

Economic development

Foreign aid   Second only to the integrity of her territories, the greatest single interest of Pakistan lies in rapid economic development. She is an underdeveloped country whose natural resources have yet to be exploited. Her severely limited finance and the low level of her national income are serious curbs on her economic progress. Indigenous capital, public or private, is insufficient. Thus the only alternative is to get foreign aid. So far, foreign economic assistance has played an important role. By the end of 1959 it had reached the figure of 1,541,680,000 U.S. dollars.

Beginning with the Point Four Program of President Truman in 1950, by far the largest amount has come to Pakistan from the U.S.A. Out of the total figure mentioned above, the American share has been no less than $1,118,-000,000. Compared to this, the total receipts from the United Nations and its specialized agencies have been a mere ten million dollars. The Ford Foundation alone has given $15,-020,000 in aid to Pakistan. The total allocation from the Colombo Plan comes to about 150 million dollars.

The defense budget   To safeguard its frontiers, and especially to be prepared for any aggression from the Indian side, Pakistan has been obliged to spend a high percentage of its revenues on defense. In 1959–60 the total expenditure on defense met from revenue was 100,540,000 rupees out of total revenues of 175,840,000 rupees. This is obviously too heavy a burden for Pakistan's economy in the present state of development. If she goes on devoting such a large portion of her income to defending her borders, the speed of her industrialization and of economic progress is bound to be adversely affected.

In fact, however, the gap is certain to widen. For the trend is now towards new and more expensive weapons, which also require superior industrial capacity. The defense budget will go on increasing throughout the foreseeable future. There are, consequently, two ways open to Pakistan. One is to depend on the help of advanced countries, the other is to keep an army in proportion to its resources. The latter is impossible in the present situation. Pakistan has been pursuing the former method since its military pact with the United States of America in 1954. This military aid has now been coming regularly all these years. But that has not caused a decrease in Pakistan's defense budget.

The need for greater economic assistance remains. The second Five Year Plan can only be implemented if sufficient funds in the shape of foreign aid are forthcoming. Pakistan has no option but to accept this aid from any quarter, for the stakes involved in economic development are exceedingly high. Recently Pakistan has entered into an oil pact with the U.S.S.R. This does not denote any significant shift in Pakistan's foreign policy, but it shows the extent of her need.

Population and resources   During the decade from 1951 to 1961, the population of Pakistan rose from 75.86 million to 93.80 million, registering a rise of 17.94 million or 23.66 percent. The density per square mile has gone up from 208 to 257. This population, however, is not evenly spread out, because the mountainous and arid areas are thinly populated. Ten of the 17 districts of East Pakistan have a density of 1000 people per square mile.[6] As the standard of living is low and there are shortages both of food and manufactured goods, it is

[6] *Census of Pakistan, 1961, Provisional Tables of Population, Census Bulletin No. 1.* Issued by Population Census Commissioner, Ministry of Home Affairs, Government of Pakistan, Karachi, Feb. 1961.

necessary to speed up the program of economic development, which must not lag behind the increase in population if it is to be effective. Pakistan is carrying on a vigorous campaign to make family-planning popular among the masses, but the villagers are difficult to reach and the establishment of clinics to make remedies available to the people in villages will take time.

Pakistan has made considerable progress in improving her agriculture as well as industry. She is, however, hampered by the shortage of available water resources. A dispute about water was a contributing factor in the unhappy relations with India. For industrial development, Pakistan has to rely heavily on foreign aid, the bulk of which comes from the U.S.A. This naturally limits Pakistan severely in her foreign policy. In view of the needs of her people, she cannot risk the abandonment of her development projects by annoying her Western allies to an extent that they stop their support of her economic progress.

Thus foreign policy is closely tied up with the urgency of economic development. The population is increasing at an alarming rate and will adversely affect the rate of progress. Economic necessity will not wait. If Pakistan economizes on her defense, she exposes herself to external aggression. If she continues to spend so much on defense, her development program will suffer with a proportionate lowering of the standard of living. Poverty will increase and bring with it social instability and probably political chaos. In that contingency the ideological barriers against communism may not stand the onrush of stark necessity and dire penury.

CURRENT RELATIONS WITH INDIA

Junagadh

As has been mentioned already, Pakistan's foreign policy has been mostly affected by her relations with India. In this field, the most important issue has been Kashmir. But before discussing that problem, it is necessary briefly to look at the Indian annexation of Junagadh and Hyderabad, because it is highly relevant in this context.

Junagadh, with an area of 4,000 square miles and a population of 800,000 acceded to Pakistan on September 12, 1947. India vehemently objected to this on the grounds that the state was geographically contiguous to India and that its population was predominantly Hindu. India insisted that the question of accession should be decided by a plebiscite to be held under the joint supervision of the governments of India and Junagadh. She imposed a severe economic blockade on Junagadh, and her troops surrounded the state. A "Provisional Government" of Junagadh was set up in Bombay, which organized raids into Junagadh territory.

On November 7, 1947, a force of 20,000, calling itself Azad Fauj, and equipped with all the modern weapons of warfare obviously supplied by the Indian Government, marched into Junagadh. The state was occupied by violence and later a plebiscite was held, under conditions dictated by India, by which the people were reported to have voted for accession to India. Pakistan considered this vote farcical and refused to accept the result of this plebiscite held under the shadow of bayonets. She put the case before the Security Council and that is where it lies up to this day.

Hyderabad

Hyderabad, with an area of 82,000 square miles and a population of 20 million, had a majority of Hindus living under a Muslim ruler. The ruler, the Nizam, did not want to accede to any dominion, but desired a special treaty with India aimed at a limited measure of independence. Pending the signing of such a treaty, he entered into a standstill agreement with India. Then India began to exert pressure on Hydera-

bad through Lord Mountbatten, and demanded that it should accede unconditionally. When the Nizam offered to hold a plebiscite to decide the issue, India demanded that the accession should take place prior to such a plebiscite.

Hyderabad was subjected to an economic blockade. Finally on September 11, 1948, Indian troops marched into the state and occupied it. This happened when Hyderabad's complaint against India was still pending before the Security Council. Technically the matter is still *sub judice* in the United Nations.

Kashmir

Indian political and military activities   Kashmir has an area of 84,471 square miles and a population of about 4 millions, 77 percent of whom are Muslims. The affinities between Kashmir and Pakistan are far stronger than those between her and India. Even before the plan of partition was announced in 1947 by the Viceroy, the ruler of Kashmir, a Hindu, had been visited by the President of the Congress Party. A little later the Maharajas of Patiala, Kapurthala and Faridkot called upon him. In August Mr. Gandhi himself went to Srinagar and conferred with the Maharaja. Obviously strong pressure was being put on him to accede to India.

The Maharaja, however, presumably to play for time, entered into a standstill agreement with Pakistan, which placed on Pakistan the same responsibilities as were formerly borne by the British Crown before independence. The Maharaja's intentions were, however, betrayed when, even before the announcement of the details of partition, he started negotiations with two minor princes whose states lay on the Indian side of the border for the building of a road which would debouch into India. But when the Award gave the Muslim majority Tehsils of Gurdaspur and Pathankot to India, there was no longer any need for such an expensive road. Steps were then taken to build a road linking Pathankot with Jammu and a bridge over the river Ravi. Without this road, Kashmir's accession to India was not practicable.

In July, the Maharaja ordered the disarming of his Muslim subjects and of Muslims in his army. In August, militant Hindu and Sikh bands arrived in Jammu. A reign of terror started. The people of Poonch organized a resistance movement and begged the tribes of the North West Frontier for succor. The people did not resort to fighting until the Maharaja's repressive measures became intolerable. In one area alone reported *The London Times* correspondent, 237,000 Muslims were exterminated. On October 22, Pathans from the tribal areas entered Kashmir to help their Muslim brethren. On October 25, the Maharaja fled from Srinagar. The next day, from Jammu, he wrote to Lord Mountbatten asking for help and offering accession to India. On October 27, Mountbatten accepted the accession and on the same day at 9:00 A.M. Indian troops landed in Srinagar.

In Mountbatten's letter of October 27, he had said that "as soon as Law and Order have been restored in Kashmir and her soil cleared of the invaders, the question of the State's accession should be settled by a reference to the people." This undertaking of holding a plebiscite in Kashmir to settle the issue of accession was later repeated by Nehru and all Indian delegates to the United Nations. But afterwards the Indian Government changed its attitude and, taking shelter behind the argument that Pakistan's acceptance of American military aid had introduced a new factor in the situation, evaded the issue of ascertaining the will of the people. It is difficult to understand how the American aid to Pakistan affects the Kashmiris' right of self-determination.

It is of little use to recount every stage of negotiations and arguments before the United Nations.[7] It suffices to say that on every occasion that the United Nations or its Commis-

sions have suggested a way out, India has flatly refused to accept the suggestion or whittled it down. Kashmir is now, according to Indian claims, a part of India, and the question of a settlement does not arise.

Strategic importance   To appreciate the gravity of this issue, the geographical and strategic position of Kashmir must be kept in view. To its north lies Sinkiang and the narrow Wakhan strip of Afghanistan. Beyond these is the Soviet Union. Pakistan lies to Kashmir's west and southwest, India to its southeast. In the east lies Tibet. Kashmir's common border with Pakistan is 902 miles, with India it is only 317 miles. The only two roads linking the state with the outside world lie through Pakistan. It is in Kashmir that three main rivers of West Pakistan—the Indus, the Jhelum and the Chenab—rise. The largest source of Kashmir's revenue was, and probably still is, timber, and it was exported by being floated down the rivers to Pakistan.

From the strategic point of view, Kashmir is vital to Pakistan; for if it is in Indian hands West Pakistan is continuously threatened. Pakistan's land communication with the historic defense line of the Khyber Pass lies within 30 miles of the Kashmir boundary. Culturally, Kashmir is a part of Pakistan. According to the 1941 census, Muslims had a majority of 93 percent in Kashmir province and 61 percent in Jammu province. Gilgit, a very large and strategically significant area, is 100 percent Muslim. Generally speaking, there is hardly any difference between the people of Kashmir and of West Pakistan in habits, customs, dress, food and social structure.

Unless there is a settlement of this explosive issue, there will be no peace between India and Pakistan. Even if at any future time the Government of Pakistan wants to play down the importance of the problem—an extremely remote chance—public opinion will not let it do so. From Pakistan's point of view, there is an apparent contradiction between India's claim that she desires friendly relations with Pakistan and her refusal to settle the Kashmir dispute.

[7] For full details of these three disputes see K. Sarwar Hasan, *op. cit.*, ch. 4.

Water supplies

Cause of disputes   Another Indo-Pakistan dispute of almost equal seriousness has been that of canal waters. The Indus Basin supplies water to 74.8 million acres of West Pakistan and 7.6 million acres in India. Irrigation facilities have yet to be supplied to 44.1 million acres of land in West Pakistan and 5.5 million in India. The Radcliffe Award of 1947, which partitioned the Punjab, placed India in control of the headworks for some of the principal irrigation canals of West Pakistan. For instance, the Madhopur Headworks controlled the irrigation of 661,000 acres of Pakistan and the Firozepur Headworks of 1,041,000 acres of Pakistan.

Starting from April 1, 1948, India was periodically shutting off water supplies to Pakistan. When Pakistan proposed to submit the dispute to the International Court of Justice, India rejected this move. She refused to negotiate unless Pakistan accepted India's sole right to the use of the waters of three rivers—the Ravi, Beas and Sutlej. Obviously, India wanted to deprive Pakistan of its historic share of waters, and for this exploited her occupation of Kashmir and possession of two vital canal headworks.

The Indus Water Treaty   In 1951 the President of the World Bank, Eugene Black, offered the good offices of the Bank for the settlement of this dispute. This offer was based on the proposal of David Lilienthal who had earlier studied the problem on the invitations of the governments of India and Pakistan, and who had reached the conclusion that this was essentially an engineering problem. Mr. Black's offer was accepted by both countries and negotiations started in 1952 between the Bank on the one hand and the two governments on the other. It was not until September 19, 1960, that a treaty was signed finally.

The Indus Waters Treaty[8] allocates the waters of the three eastern rivers—Ravi, Beas and Sutlej—to India, with certain exceptions. The waters of the three western rivers—Indus, Jhelum, and Chenab—are for the use of Pakistan. India has undertaken to let flow, for unrestricted use by Pakistan, all the waters of three rivers. Pakistan will construct, during the transition period of ten years, a system of works to replace the water which has hitherto been met from the eastern rivers with water from the western rivers. India will contribute to the Indus Basin Development Fund a sum of about 174 million dollars in ten equal annual installments.

A permanent Indus Commission has been set up which will be generally responsible for implementing the provisions of the treaty. Where differences cannot be resolved by agreement between Commissioners, the treaty establishes machinery for resort to a neutral expert who is to be a highly qualified engineer. The total cost of the program of construction works will be about 107 million dollars, of which 87 million will be spent on works in Pakistan and 20 million in India. This huge development program will be jointly financed by Pakistan, India, the United States of America, the Federal Republic of Germany, Canada, New Zealand, Australia and Britain.

Public opinion in Pakistan is not satisfied with the arrangements but it is reconciled to them because nothing better could be achieved. As happens in international disputes, the bigger country has received the lion's share.

However, it must be realized that so long as India is in possession of Kashmir, she will always be in a position to interfere with the flow of waters of the three western rivers that have been allotted to Pakistan under the Indus Waters Treaty. Therefore, to say that the treaty has reassured Pakistan would be misleading, unless the other dispute with which the waters problem is closely tied is settled.

[8] For text see Aslam Siddiqi, *Pakistan Seeks Security,* Lahore: 1960, pp. 195–6.

Border problems

Besides these two major disputes between India and Pakistan there have been many others. One that still lingers on is the question of the demarcation of borders and the elimination of border skirmishes. In 1956 Indian armed forces occupied Chhad Bet in the Rann of Cutch, an area which has long been under dispute. The next year, in February, Indian troops were threateningly massed on Pakistan's borders, and the situation became so dangerous that the President and the Prime Minister had to make public protests.

In April 1958, Indian border forces started firing across the Cachar-Sylhet border of East Pakistan. These skirmishes continued to happen at different points until, at the initiative of President Muhammed Ayub Khan, a series of ministerial level conferences were held in 1959 and 1960. As a result of these deliberations workable solutions were found for most of the differences. To avoid future unpleasant incidents, detailed ground rules were framed to be observed by the border security forces of the two countries. The remaining outstanding dispute relates to the Cutch-Sind border, about which the two governments decided to postpone a final decision pending the collection of more data and information.

Goa

Since independence, India had been endeavoring to annex the Portuguese enclaves. Of these, the territory of Goa was the most important. It had been under Portugal for more than 460 years. Out of a population of 650,000 no less than 40 percent are Catholics.[9] They had con-

siderable influence and it was quite likely that in case of an impartial plebiscite, Goa might have opted to remain under Portugal or secure complete independence. India, however, was not willing to solve the problem in a legal manner.

In 1955 the ruling Congress Party launched a movement against the Portuguese. At a seminar held in New Delhi on August 17, 1961, organized by the Indian Council for Africa, Nehru hinted that the use of force could not be ruled out as a means of solving the Goa problem.[10] At the same time, the groundwork for the invasion of Goa by the Indian Army was prepared by the Indian Communist Party which had demanded military action in their Vijaywada session in April, 1961.[11] At last Goa was invaded on December 17, 1961 and within a few days the Indians were in complete control.[12]

Pakistan felt seriously perturbed for various reasons. She had maintained friendly relations with Portugal. There is a small but influential community of Goanese descent in Karachi whose emotions were involved in an invasion of their ancestral land. India had defied world opinion in invading a weaker neighbor.

Pakistan could not but take note of the fact that the allies of Portugal did not come to her help in the hour of her need. Would the world or Pakistan's allies move even a little finger if

---

[9] *The British Survey*, January, 1962, Main Series, N.S., No. 154, London: British Society for Interna-

tional Understanding, pp. 14–20; for the Portuguese point of view see, *The Case of Goa No. 1* issued by the Portuguese Ministry of Foreign Affairs, Lisbon: 1955, and also the text of Salazar's speech to N.A. on January 3, 1962 reproduced by the Portuguese Government under the title *The Invasion and Occupation of Goa by the Indian Union*, Lisbon: 1962; for the Indian case see, Pundlik Guitonde and A.D.Mani, *The Goa Problem*, Indian Council of World Affairs, 1956. Also see Homer A. Jack, *Inside Goa*, New Delhi: Information Service of India publication. For general analysis, see Stephen Barber, "Behind India's Goan Adventure," a leading article in the *Daily Telegraph*, London, Friday, December 15, 1961.

[10] *The Times of India*, August 17, 1961; see also the next day's editorial on Goa.

[11] *The Times of India*, April 11, 1961. See the text of the speech made by Ajoy Kumar Ghosh and his reference to Goa.

[12] *Dawn*, December 20, 1961.

Pakistan happened to be the victim of aggression? The easy victory in Goa resulted in considerable sabre rattling in India. Responsible Congress leaders started talking of dealing with Pakistan in a similar manner.[13] Hostility to Pakistan became an important plank in the Congress Party platform and proved a good vote catcher, quite as much as the triumph in Goa.

RELATIONS WITH THE UNITED STATES OF AMERICA

The story of Pakistan's friendly relations with the United States of America began in 1950 when Mr. Liaquat Ali Khan visited that country. His speeches there left no room for doubt that, ideologically, Pakistan was pro-West. In 1952–53 Pakistan was faced with a food crisis. The U.S.A. offered as a gift 610,000 tons of wheat. This timely and generous gesture helped to remove Pakistan's hesitation in agreeing to further arrangements. The U.S.A. at this time helped Pakistan and Turkey to have closer relations with each other.

Military aid

Finally, in February 1954, President Eisenhower announced the decision to give military aid to Pakistan. This agreement between the U.S. and Pakistan aims at fostering "international peace and security within the framework of the United Nations," at promoting "individual and collective self-defense" in support

of the purposes and principles of the Charter. It re-affirms determination to give full cooperation "to the efforts to provide the United Nations with armed forces as contemplated by the Charter." Under the Mutual Defense Assistance Act of 1949 and the Mutual Security Act of 1951, the equipment, materials or services provided are to be used solely to maintain Pakistan's internal security and for its legitimate self-defense or to permit it to participate in the defense of the area of which it is a part.[14]

The news of the American decision to give Pakistan military aid was bitterly castigated in India. Nehru feared that this aid "might possibly be used against India." To this, Pakistan's reply was that India's acceptance of large scale economic assistance from the U.S.A. had not brought the Cold War nearer to her borders. Pakistan pointed out that American aid to India helped her to divert large sums of money to the armed forces and there is thus no substantial difference between military and economic aid.

The amount of military aid has generally been running at about 80 to 90 million dollars a year. This is not adequate to meet Pakistan's own and regional defense commitments. Therefore, it was rather disconcerting for Pakistan to find that certain American political quarters were critical of this aid. In November 1958, Senator Fulbright said that American military aid to Pakistan was excessive and that it forced India to divert funds from economic development to military purposes. In 1959 Senator Morse was of the opinion that Pakistan was maintaining armies that would be of no use to the U.S.A. in the event of a war with Russia. Senator Albert Gore saw no sense in giving, on the one hand, military assistance to Pakistan and, on the other, economic aid to India with which she buys Canberra Bombers. "We are paying the bill on both sides," he said.

In accepting aid, Pakistan had run many risks. There was deterioration in relations with India. Pakistan incurred the enmity of the Russians and other Communist countries. A num-

[13] *The Times of India,* January 7, 1962. At the 67th session of the Indian National Congress, Nehru's statement on Kashmir and Pakistan and also speeches of Sanjiva Reddy and other Congress leaders' reference to Pakistan in their speeches at subsequent sessions are relevant.

[14] Hasan, *op. cit.,* pp. 60–61.

ber of Arab countries were alienated and the Pakistanis received general abuse by being called "camp followers" and "stooges" of the imperial and colonial Powers. Therefore this criticism in the U.S.A. produced a sharp reaction in Pakistan. So strong was this reaction that President Ayub had to issue a formal statement on June 22, 1959, in which he warned that if Americans "think that they can lead us to confused thinking against the hard facts of life, then we just cannot oblige." If the Middle East goes under, the next direct attack will be on America. The Americans, he concluded, are not "doing any great favor" by giving Pakistan military aid; it is "in their self-interest" to do so.[15]

Regional defense pacts

The Middle East   American interest in the defense problems of Pakistan was also instrumental in bringing her into certain regional pacts. In October 1951 the Western Powers and Turkey had proposed an Allied Middle East Command; this was rejected by Egypt. About a year later, another plan was made for a Middle East Defense Organization. But it had to be abandoned because of British disputes with Egypt and Iran and Arab-Israel hostility. It was then that the U.S.A. thought of bringing Turkey—to which she was already giving aid—and Pakistan together in some sort of association. Consequently the Turko-Pakistan Pact was announced on February 19, 1954, and signed on April 21, 1954.

A mutual co-operation pact between Iraq and Turkey followed in February 1955. This came to be known as the Baghdad Pact. Britain joined the Pact on April 5, 1955. Iran followed suit in November. Pakistan's adherence to the Baghdad Pact had distinct disadvantages. It made Pakistan unpopular with the "non-committed" Afro-Asian countries. It also made her

unpopular with the Arabs who were against lining up with the West. But, most important of all, the U.S.S.R. started vetoing any effective action on Kashmir by the Security Council. Pakistan, however, has shown no vacillation.

In 1958 a revolution took place in Iraq and the new regime withdrew from the Pact the following March. Thereupon it was renamed Central Treaty Organization (CENTO).

South East Asia   The eastern wing of Pakistan, as we have seen, faces South East Asia as the western section faces the Middle East. The geography and the small size of East Pakistan present serious problems in organizing its defense. To have a real deterrent to aggression and to obviate the need of fighting any military action inside East Pakistan, a shield of protection is required. For this reason, Pakistan was persuaded to join the South East Asia Treaty Organization (SEATO). The emergence of China as a Communist Power in 1949 changed the balance of power in Asia. Her neighbors felt alarmed. But any attempt at having a regional alliance was nipped in the bud by the U.S. Secretary of State Dean Acheson, who, on January 12, 1950, declared that, except for the Philippines, South East Asia was not an area vital to the security of the United States.

Then came the Korean explosion, and the House of Representatives Committee on Foreign Relations at once suggested a mutual security pact in the Pacific. Urgency was imparted to this proposal by the war in Indochina and the fall of Dien Bien Phu. In July 1954, the Geneva Agreement removed all doubts, if there were any, as to the dire necessity of collective defense in South East Asia. Therefore, at Manila, on September 6, 1954, the delegates of Australia, France, Britain, New Zealand, Pakistan, the Philippines, Thailand and the U.S.A. met for consultation. A treaty was born.[16] The U.S.A., however, refused to become a member. There was an "understanding" that her adherence to the Pact was directed

---

[15] All quotations from Siddiqi, *op. cit.*, pp. 106–7.

[16] Text in *ibid.*, pp. 191–4.

against Communist aggression only, and that in the event of other aggression she would consult with other signatories. The area covered by the treaty includes both East and West Pakistan and excludes Formosa.

Appraisal What has Pakistan gained from membership in these pacts? If she had sought security, it is obvious that the most serious threat to her existence has not been met. Pakistan has gained in military strength, but her dependence on the United States has increased considerably. She has received substantial aid for economic and other purposes through the instrumentality of these alliances.

On the other hand, these pacts have also created problems and enemies for Pakistan, some of which have been mentioned earlier. For instance, on the Kashmir issue, Pakistan has been disappointed in the attitude adopted by her allies, none of whom has given substantial support to Pakistan. Those in Pakistan who are opposed to the pacts have not failed to compare the Soviet approach to Kashmir with that of the U.S.A. and Britain.

It is true that Pakistan has joined these alliances in her own interest and voluntarily. But she has in the process also taken on risky obligations. She is paid for running these risks. But there are people who point out that India is also being paid without assuming any obligations. And she is getting this aid from both sides without diminishing her international prestige. Many Pakistanis feel that their expectations have not been fulfilled and that their allies have not proved "friends in need."

RELATIONS WITH AFGHANISTAN

Recurrent difficulties

Among Pakistan's neighbors, strategically the most important is Afghanistan. Unfortunately, Pakistan's relations with her have never been

good. After the independence of the sub-continent, Afghanistan was the only country in the United Nations to vote against the admission of Pakistan to that body. A little later, she unilaterally denounced all former treaties regarding the old Indo-Afghan border and staked her claim to the formation of a Pathan State inside the borders of Pakistan. This proposal has of course been unacceptable to Pakistan, in view of Afghanistan's long acceptance of the Durand Line, drawn by the British in consultation with Afghanistan. This has remained the international frontier between the two countries.

The demand for Pushtunistan, an independent state of the Pathans, was made in December 1947. The timing was well-chosen, for at that time the Indian Army was poised for a rapid march in Kashmir towards Pakistan. Since then, there has been a disturbing coincidence of Indo-Pakistan border raids and raids from Afghanistan. Pakistanis believe that India is encouraging Afghanistan. There is considerable evidence for a conclusion of this sort. The All-India Pakhtoon Jirga was organized in Delhi. The Indian broadcasting service has repeatedly made its facilities available to the Afghan Ambassador in India for making anti-Pakistani speeches.[17]

From time to time, Afghanistan has been conducting raids and forays into Pakistani territory. Attacks were made on Pakistan consulates in Kandahar and Jalalabad in 1955. The Pakistan Embassy at Kabul was stoned and damaged.

Some effort at mediation has been occasionally made, but to no avail. Anwar Sadaat of Egypt and Prince Musaid of Arabia tried in 1955 to find a basis of settlement. But Afghan intransigence stood in the way. They had to announce the failure of their mission on account of, to use their words, "a singular lack of spirit of reconciliation and compromise by the party in the wrong."[18]

In this, Afghanistan has been encouraged by

[17] Aslam Siddiqi, *Pakistan Seeks Security*, Lahore: 1960, pp. 26–27. Pakhtun, Pathan and Pakhtunistan are variants of Pushtun and Pushtunistan.
[18] Quoted in *ibid.*, p. 28.

the Soviet Union. In December 1955, Mr. Khrushchev applauded the idea of Pakhtunistan and gave it his support. At the same time, generous Soviet aid to the country was announced. By 1959 this assistance was estimated to have reached the sum of 240 million dollars.[19] The Afghan army is being equipped and trained by Russians. Strategic roads are being constructed. Today Afghanistan is completely dominated by Soviet Russia in the economic, military and commercial fields.

Disputes since 1961

Relations between Pakistan and Afghanistan worsened in 1961. The President of Pakistan revealed at a press conference in London on March 17, 1961 that five to six battalions of Afghan troops were concentrated on the Pakistan border in the Kunar Valley. In the following month, Nikita Khrushchev and the Afghan premier, Daud, who was on a visit in the U.S.S.R., expressed in a joint communiqué complete identity of views on international problems including Afghanistan's claims to Pakistan territory. Simultaneously, the activities of the Afghan agents in Pakistan's territory were intensified. On May 7, therefore, President Ayub was constrained to warn the Kabul Government.[20]

However, these activities did not cease. Three posts in the Bajaur area were attacked by Afghan regulars with mortars and machine guns. The Pakistan Air Force repulsed the Afghans with heavy losses.[21] It was found that the Afghans had used Russian arms.[22] The government of Pakistan lodged a strong protest with the Afghan Government against this aggression. A suggestion by the Government of Pakistan to hold a meeting of the Foreign Secretaries of the two countries to discuss matters of

mutual concern received no response. Afghan incursions continued and, as late as October 4, an Afghan army had to be repulsed from the Bajaur area.

The Pakistan Consulates and Trade Agencies in Afghanistan were harassed and subjected to crippling boycotts. The Afghan Consulates in the tribal territory were being used for carrying on propaganda in the tribal territory. Pakistan asked the Afghan Government to close its Agencies and Consulates in Pakistan.[23] Afghanistan demanded the revision of this decision[24] and, on Pakistan's refusal, severed diplomatic relations on September 6, 1961.

It is interesting to note that the attitude of the Indian Prime Minister and the Indian press alike were openly hostile towards Pakistan. Pakistan had to lodge a protest with India. On September 8, the Soviet official newspaper, *Izvestia* carried a story accusing the CENTO Powers of planning to partition Afghan territory between Pakistan and Iran.

Pakistan kept its borders open for transit trade, but Afghanistan refused entry to goods or vehicles from Pakistan. Afghan goods imported through the port of Karachi remained uncleared. The resulting congestion in the port, railroad sheds and wagons was so severe that the Ministry of Foreign Affairs delivered an *aide-memoire* to some heads of diplomatic missions on the subject. It attracted the immediate attention of the State Department in Washington.

President Kennedy decided to send Livingston T. Merchant as his special emissary on a "good offices" mission to try to bring about a resumption of transit trade between Afghanistan and Pakistan. In spite of all endeavors of Mr. Merchant, he had to declare the failure of his mission. Since then, there has been a stalemate in the relations of the two countries.

---

[19] *Ibid.*, p. 31.
[20] *Dawn*, May 5 and 8, 1961.
[21] *Dawn*, May 22, 1961; May 23, 1961.
[22] *Dawn*, May 24, 1961.

[23] *White Paper*, September 2, 1961, entitled "Closure of Pakistan Consulates in Afghanistan and Afghan Consulates and Trade Agencies in Pakistan," was issued by the Ministry of External Affairs, Government of Pakistan. The text was published in *Dawn*, September 3, 1961.
[24] *Dawn*, August 31, 1961.

The only change has been that Afghanistan permitted American AID goods lying in Pakistan into its territories.[25]

Prospects for the future

This bad blood between two countries with so many cultural ties and other links is very regrettable. At the time of independence, Pakistan was looking forward to having a staunch friend and ally in Afghanistan. These hopes have been betrayed. Recently, in answer to the Afghan-Soviet joint communiqué proposing the implementation of the principle of self-determination to settle the destiny of the Pathan people on the basis of the United Nations Charter, the Pakistan Foreign Minister suggested the holding of a referendum to determine whether the Pathans in Afghanistan wanted to opt for Pakistan or Afghanistan. This may or may not be acceptable to Afghanistan. In the 1947 referendum in the North-West Frontier Province, 99 percent of the votes were cast in favor of Pakistan.

It is worth seriously considering if the two countries can join in some sort of a federal union for mutual benefit. This is the age of large countries and many small areas in newly-liberated Africa are contemplating such moves. Land-locked and comparatively underdeveloped Afghanistan is bound to gain more than Pakistan would from such an arrangement. And, of course, Pakistan's infinitely superior armed strength should be welcomed by the Afghan state with its sensitive frontiers. This solution is at present not generally acceptable in Pakistan, however, because of the general backwardness of Afghanistan. If Afghanistan, with the aid of industrially advanced countries, or through United Nations efforts, develops rapidly within the coming decades, Pakistan's attitude may change considerably.

[25] *Ministry of External Affairs Hand-out* issued by the Press Information Department, dated June 30, 1962.

CONCLUSIONS

Pressures—persistent yet changing

From the North and West The reader will conclude from this brief survey that Pakistan is really pressed by two traditional forces which have remained constant throughout the ages, whatever might have been the nature of the governments in the areas which surround it. The first of these has been the pressure from Central Asia and the northwest. In the beginning, it took the shape of large-scale migrations of peoples in search of more hospitable pastures and lands. This continued until Islam introduced the element of an ideology into a pattern that had existed previously.

It is strange that the element of ideology has entered into the situation again. Today Islam is on the defensive in Pakistan and communism is on the march. Communism is strong by itself and needs no allies if it comes to a showdown. But it is to its advantage, if it can create local conflicts, as it is seeking to do by encouraging the Pushtunistan propaganda of Afghanistan and by supporting the Indian claims in Kashmir.

Friendship between Afghanistan, Pakistan, and India will strengthen the region and weaken the chances of its disruption. Conflict will ultimately create a power vacuum into which the U.S.S.R. or China or both could intrude. The only new element in the situation is that now the pressure does not come from ill-organized tribal groups, as it did at the dawn of history, but from a Super-Power and its great ally which is another Super-Power in the making.

From India The other historical pressure is from within the sub-continent itself. Whenever a strong state has emerged in the Ganges plain, its desire has been to expand towards the ramparts of the mountains in the west and the north. The Mauryas and the British alike did it. Now it is the turn of the Indian Union. The desire in the Indian Union is likely to be strong because of the traditional ideas of Indian unity. Hindu patriots, since the eighteenth century, have succeeded in giving Indian patriotism a mystic and somewhat religious significance by introducing the worship of *Bharat-mata* (Mother India) who has been depicted as a goddess with a trident in her hand.[26]

The territories of Pakistan have always formed part of this picture. It was this association of the idea of the unity of the sub-continent with religion that led Gandhi to compare the division of the British Indian Empire into India and Pakistan to the vivisection of the cow, which is sacred to the Hindus. This involvement of emotions has been the main cause of India's antipathy for Pakistan and has led to unfortunate relations between the two countries. It is this sentiment that has sometimes led India to take the Communist challenge from the north less seriously than her hostility towards Pakistan.[27]

To Pakistan, because of her comparative weakness, this emotional attitude of India is frightening. If problems had been approached rationally, India and Pakistan should have been desirous of establishing the friendliest relations between themselves. Then they could convert the sub-continent into a citadel of strength. It is for this purpose that the President of Pakistan has, during the last three years, been holding out the offer of entering into a defensive alliance with India to establish a policy of joint defense against all outside aggression. India's emotional antipathy has been the main cause of her refusal to look at such an offer.

The Sino-Indian conflict The prospect of massive military aid to India by the Western Powers to help her resist Chinese attacks in the border regions has aroused feelings of dismay and apprehension in Pakistan. The government and people are afraid that India will not use her augmented power against China alone. Pakistan thinks that India is sure to make a bid for absorbing Pakistan and the West might welcome such a move because it might erroneously think that a reunited sub-continent would be stronger and better equipped to fight China.

This fear has so gripped Pakistan that there is a general feeling that the sovereignty and freedom of the country are in peril. President Kennedy and Prime Minister Macmillan have tried to persuade Nehru to hold talks with Pakistan on the problem of Kashmir but the Pakistanis are not hopeful because they see no change of heart in India. They know that the West will support India in her dispute with China, and Pakistan will be isolated. As has been mentioned, Pakistan is more afraid of India than of China against whom it has no outstanding dispute.

Pakistan feels somewhat reassured because of the unwillingness of China to push the dispute to extremes and the prospects of the cessation of hostilities. The willingness of China to demarcate her frontiers with the Pakistani-held territories has tended to diminish the feeling of being on the horns of a dilemma, but there is little comfort for Pakistan either in the attitude of India or that of her Western allies.

Re-union with India Many well-meaning outsiders think that Pakistan should be forced into entering into some kind of re-union with India. Indeed there have been occasions when such pressure has actually come from some of Pakistan's allies. They seem to forget the hard realities which brought Pakistan into existence.

This is not the place to discuss the genesis of Pakistan. It would be sufficient to point out that the British were proud of building up a united India and were reluctant to divide it into two parts. They were forced to accept partition, as indeed was the Indian National Congress, because it became obvious that a forced unity would be a cause of weakness and might result in anarchy.

Pakistan's nationalism is a fact today which cannot be ignored. A population of ninety

[26] This picture ultimately became so popular that innumerable wall calendars displayed it.
[27] *Manchester Guardian*, June 15, 1961.

million cannot be forced into an artificial union without disastrous consequences. The progress that communism has made among the Muslim intellectuals of the present Indian Union because of their frustration should be an eye opener to any advocate of a forced reunion of India and Pakistan. That will be the surest way of losing the Muslim majority areas to communism.

Frustration and insecurity

Because of such statements and attitudes Pakistan is, at present, suffering from a deep sense of frustration which may ultimately prove highly dangerous. She feels isolated. She feels that she has failed in winning any friends who could come to her rescue in the hour of danger. Her allies have never understood her problems; at least she cannot rely on them. Even if the pressure is from communism, she does not feel certain that she will receive necessary support. She has a lurking suspicion that the allies will consult their own convenience rather than her need. The attitude of the United States towards the Russian-supported activities of Afghanistan within Pakistan territory does not inspire her with confidence.

In case of Indian aggression, she can get no help. It will be just another *anschluss,* a re-union, on which no tears will be shed except by the helpless men, women, and children of Pakistan. Pakistan, however, would be willing even to sell her soul to save herself from such an eventuality. This may sound emotional, but it does reflect the mood of her people.

A constructive approach to these problems is not impossible. But little importance is attached to them by Pakistan's allies, because they are dismissed in a cavalier fashion as "merely local conflicts." It is not understood that such conflicts might be veritable powder magazines. The First World War was ignited by "an isolated incident" in "a local conflict." Serious, patient and wise efforts in resolving such conflicts are bound to bear fruit.

A good example is the successful negotiation of the Indus Basin Treaty through the efforts of the World Bank. Pakistan feels that she has not received what she was entitled to get, but she has accepted the solution and one irritant has disappeared from the area. If similar efforts are made by the leading Western Powers, other conflicts also can be resolved. No party may get all it wants, but acceptable compromises might be discovered. If the Pakistanis are given a feeling that their problems are engaging the attention of their friends, the frustration will be reduced considerably.

It is not pleasant for a country to be wedged in between two enormous pressures which are both historical and ideological in their content. No thoughtful Pakistani looks upon the scene with relish. Sometimes the press shows petulance, which is natural but neither dignified nor helpful. With grim determination and enormous sacrifices, Pakistan has built up a defense force which is intrinsically a great achievement. If it comes to the worst, Pakistanis will fight with their backs to the wall. As has been demonstrated so often in history, that may not save them. Their fall, however, will remove a pillar of strength from the region and a good deal will come tumbling down which may not be easy to reconstruct within a foreseeable period.

BIBLIOGRAPHY

Author's suggestions

Callard, Keith B. *Pakistan: A Political Study.* New York: Macmillan, 1960.

Callard, Keith B. *Political Forces in Pakistan, 1947–1959.* Vancouver: Institute of Pacific Relations, 1959.

Choudhury, G. W. and Hasan, Parvez. *Pakistan's External Relations.* Karachi: Pakistan Institute of International Affairs, 1958.

Das Gupta, Jyoti Bhusan. *Indo-Pakistan Relations, 1947–1955.* Amsterdam: Djambatan, 1958.

Hasan, K. Sarwar. *Pakistan and the United Nations.* New York: Manhattan Publishing Co., 1960.

Malik, Hafeez. *Moslem Nationalism and India and Pakistan.* Washington: Public Affairs Press, 1962.

Moon, Penderel. *Divide and Quit.* Berkeley: University of California Press, 1961.

Pakistan History Board. *A Short History of Indo-Pakistan.* Karachi: Pakistan Historical Society, 1960.

Siddiqi, Aslam. *Pakistan Seeks Security.* Lahore: Longmans, Green & Co., 1960.

Symonds, Richard. *The Making of Pakistan.* London: Faber & Faber, 1959.

ABOUT THE AUTHOR

A. Appadorai is Director and Professor of International Relations at the Indian School of International Studies, New Delhi. He was formerly Secretary-General of the Indian Council of World Affairs. In 1948 he was advisor to the Indian Delegation to the United Nations. Dr. Appadorai has travelled extensively and has attended several international conferences. Notable among his published works are: *Dyarchy in Practice; Revision of Democracy* and *The Use of Force in International Relations.*

ABOUT THE CHAPTER

While this book was in preparation, two major events brought India into the limelight of world affairs. One was India's invasion of Goa and the other was the Chinese-Indian border conflict during the fall months of 1962. It is to Mr. Appadorai's credit that, although revisions of his chapter were required to take account of rapidly moving events, the basic framework of his chapter did not have to be altered. The assumptions on which the chapter rests are that "every nation is concerned primarily with securing its national interests . . . that the commitments that a nation enters into . . . are related to its capacity for fulfilling them . . . and that every nation is interested in securing the support of world opinion on its side." Given this orientation it was not difficult for Mr. Appadorai to account for the Indian action in Goa or the mobilization of India when faced with the threat of China.

Of course, attention is given to the unique policies of India which are related to her economic needs and to her desire for a policy of non-alignment with the Major Power blocs. The chapter also contains a rather detailed analysis of India's role in the United Nations and a discussion of India's relations with the major nations of the world.

17

THE FOREIGN POLICY OF INDIA

A. APPADORAI

Indian School of International Studies, New Delhi

India became an independent state on August 15, 1947. The foreign policy of India can, however, be dated from September 2, 1946 when an "Interim Government" was formed and it was understood that India was, in effect, free to follow her own foreign policy. Prior to that date, India's foreign policy was directed by Great Britain to which India was politically subordinate.

THE MAIN ELEMENTS IN INDIA'S FOREIGN POLICY

The essential elements in India's foreign policy are all contained in Jawaharlal Nehru's speech broadcast five days after the Interim or Provisional Government was formed on September 2, 1946. The following extracts from that speech form a good starting point:

We hope to develop close and direct contacts with other nations and to co-operate with them in the furtherance of world peace and freedom.

We propose, as far as possible, to keep away from the power politics of groups, aligned against one another, which have led in the past to world wars and which may again lead to disasters on an even vaster scale. We believe that peace and freedom are indivisible and the denial of freedom anywhere must endanger freedom elsewhere and lead to conflict and war. We are particularly interested in the emancipation of colonial and dependent countries and peoples, and in the recognition in theory and practice of equal opportunities for all races. We repudiate utterly the Nazi doctrine of racialism, wheresoever and in whatever form it may be practiced. We seek no domination over others and we claim no privileged position over other peoples. But we do claim equal and honourable treatment for our people wherever they may go, and we cannot accept any discrimination against them.

The world, in spite of its rivalries and hatreds and inner conflicts, moves inevitably towards closer co-operation and the building up of a world commonwealth. It is for this One World that free India will work, a world in which there is the free co-operation of free peoples, and no class or group exploits another.

In spite of our past history of conflict, we hope that an independent India will have friendly and co-operative relations with England and the countries of the British Commonwealth.

We are of Asia and the peoples of Asia are nearer and closer to us than others. India is so situated that she is the pivot of Western, Southern and South-East Asia. In the past her culture flowed to all these countries and they came to her in many ways. Those contacts are being renewed and the future is bound to see a closer union between India and South-East Asia on the one side and Afghanistan, Iran, and the Arab world on the other. To the furtherance of that close association of free countries we must devote ourselves. India has followed with anxious interest the struggle of the Indonesians for freedom and to them we send our good wishes.[1]

At a press conference held on September 26, 1946, the Prime Minister elaborated these aims which have essentially remained the aims of India's policy ever since: promotion of international peace, co-operation with the United Nations, friendliness with all nations, more particularly with neighboring countries in Asia, membership in the Commonwealth of Nations, freedom of dependent peoples and opposition to racial discrimination.[2]

Neither in the broadcast speech nor at the press conference was there any reference to the promotion of India's national interest as an objective of India's foreign policy. Why was it not mentioned? I believe that it was not mentioned because it was taken for granted. In Nehru's own words:

> Whatever policy we may lay down, the art of conducting the foreign affairs of a country lies in finding out what is most advantageous to the country. We may talk about international goodwill and mean what we say. We may talk about peace and freedom and earnestly mean what we say. But in the ultimate analysis, a government functions for the good of the country it governs and no government dare do anything which in the short or long run is manifestly to the disadvantage of that country.[3]

What is India's national interest? The concept of national interest, in all its elements, is not a static one; its content changes with the varied needs of countries and the changing needs of the same country, and to some extent even with the views of the particular governments in power in that country. There seem to be two elements in India's national interest. One of these, the preservation of national freedom, is common to all countries. The other—to lay firmly the social and economic foundations of her young democracy—has become important to India on account of her recent history. The second element needs some elaboration if it is to be intelligible.

It is true that India has a civilization and

[1] Broadcast from New Delhi, September 7, 1946; text given in Jawaharlal Nehru, *India's Foreign Policy, Selected Speeches,* September 1946–April 1961, The Publications Division, Government of India, 1961, pp. 1–3.

[2] See *The Indian Annual Register,* July–December 1946, Vol. II, Calcutta: pp. 251–58.

[3] Speech in the Constituent Assembly (Legislative), December 4, 1947; *see* Nehru, *India's Foreign Policy, op. cit.,* p. 28.

culture dating from several centuries ago; but her democratic development is quite new. Some historians believe that centuries ago there were republics in India, and have tried to find in the institutions of those republics democratic elements similar to those of modern democracy.[4] It is not necessary here to enter into a debate on this question. Even granting that genuine democratic institutions existed in ancient India, all traces of them had disappeared by the beginning of the nineteenth century; the institutions of social democracy in modern India are of recent origin. The demand for them goes back to 1885 when the Indian National Congress demanded *inter alia* the presence of elected members in the provincial Legislative Councils, the right to discuss the budget and ask questions, and the right to refer to a Standing Committee of the House of Commons issues between the provincial Legislative Councils and the government. An act passed by the British Parliament in 1892 in response to this demand, recognized, though only indirectly and inadequately, the principle of election to both the Council and the local Legislatures. It took India some sixty years, till January 26, 1950, before a full-fledged democracy, with adult suffrage, periodical elections and the essential freedoms such as those of speech and the press, was established.

The point of this very brief recount is that the most important national interest of India today, outside of preserving her national integrity and security, is to see that her infant democracy is established on the firmest social and economic foundations, and to this objective her government and people are firmly committed. In the social structure, where caste is the key institution, the most important liberal development needed is mobility from group to group; in the economic field, the most important development needed is, indeed, development: improving living standards by increased production and equitable distribution. Such economic development will also improve the social structure. The per capita income of India is estimated at $61.00 in 1961, among the lowest in the world. The leadership in India is convinced that if democracy is to survive and develop, especially in the light of the disturbing trend towards totalitarianism in various parts of the world, planned and quick economic development (insuring balanced development of industry and agriculture) is basic. It is equally convinced that such planned development is possible only if there is peace in the world.[5] For securing assistance from developed countries in capital and technical personnel, so essential for developing an underdeveloped country, cannot be thought of if there is any large-scale war. Hence the Indian approach to problems of war and peace, as will be indicated later in this study.

Changes since 1946

The basic elements of India's foreign policy aims as stated above have remained fundamentally the same since 1946, even though the last fifteen years have no doubt been a revolutionary epoch. Developments, such as the emergence of several new nations in Asia and Africa, the increased perfection of weapons of destruction and the attainment of parity by the Soviet Union with the U.S.A. in atomic strength and the emergence of China as a powerful Communist State have served to underline the strength of India's aims. Peace is more urgent, not less; the need for the liquidation of colonialism and racial discrimination, the paramount urgency of being friendly with all nations, and the need to strengthen the United Nations are as valid today as they were in 1946. However, the fuller implications of some of the stated aims, have, with experience, become clearer to Indian statesmen, and minor shifts of

---

[4] See K. P. Jayaswal, *Hindu Polity*, Bangalore: 1955.

[5] See *The Review of Economics and Statistics* (Cambridge, Mass.), Vol. XLIII, No. 2, p. 126; among 106 underdeveloped countries listed, India is the 90th.

emphasis may be noticed by the careful student. For instance, there has been a growing realization that while India should stand unequivocally for the liquidation of colonialism and for a clear international responsibility for the welfare and progress of dependent peoples towards self-government, she must also take note of the complexities presented in some cases, such as the multi-racial plural society of Kenya or the presence of a large number of European settlers among native peoples as in Algeria. "The Government of India realize," said Nehru in the Lok Sabha on May 22, 1956, that *"there are special factors and complexities in the Algerian situation, but they, however, should not be permitted to bar settlements. These call for negotiation and accommodation."*[6]

On the imperative of world peace, India has been as clear as ever; in achieving it, she has perhaps shown greater preparedness to shoulder responsibilities than appeared likely from earlier statements. She has been willing to shoulder the responsibility of being Chairman of the Neutral Nations Repatriation Commission in Korea and of the International Supervisory Commissions in Vietnam, Cambodia and Laos. She has stood ready to send "peace" troops to Korea and to the Gaza Strip, and to send fighting troops, at the call of the United Nations, to the Congo. In other words, there has emerged an active peace policy of reconciliation, supported even by fighting forces, if requested by the United Nations. Enlarging the area of peace, not by forming a bloc but by bringing together like-minded nations in declarations supporting what is known as the Panch Sheel[7] seems to have emerged as a positive way of furthering the attainment of world peace. Finally, there has been a clearer perception of

the close connection between foreign policy and internal developments, in particular of the need to evolve a proper economic policy.

DISTINCTIVE ASPECTS

The student of comparative foreign policy will doubtless be interested to know what, if any, are the distinctive features of India's foreign policy, as related to India's traditions and the particular geographical and historical setting in which she is placed. If there are no distinctive features, what features at any rate, mark out her policy from the policies followed by some other nations both of the East and the West? To this important aspect we now turn.

The foreign policies of all nations are broadly identical in three major respects: every nation is concerned primarily with securing its national interests, and the foreign policy pursued must be attuned to the securing of those interests; secondly, the commitments that a nation enters into in foreign relations are related to its capacity for fulfilling them; and thirdly, every nation is interested in securing the support of world opinion on its side. India falls in line with the rest of the world in these three respects.

The really noteworthy features of India's foreign policy, in a broad sense, are three: her policy of non-alignment; her desire to follow the Indian tradition that the right means must be adopted to achieve a desired end, however much she herself might fall short of the ideal; and her approach to questions of war and peace with what may seem an undue emphasis on negotiation as a means of securing agreement on points of difference.

Non-alignment

In our listing of India's foreign policy aims, we did not include non-alignment, though non-alignment is the keynote of India's foreign pol-

[6] Statement in Lok Sabha, May 22, 1956. *Lok Sabha Debates,* Part II, Vol. V, No. 70, col. 9108. Italics added.

[7] Panch Sheel (Five Principles): Mutual respect for each other's territorial integrity and sovereignty; non-aggression; non-interference in each other's internal affairs; equality and mutual benefit; and peaceful co-existence.

icy. We did not include it among the aims because non-alignment is best considered as a *means* to achieve the basic aims, and not as an *end* in itself.

Non-alignment is best defined as not entering into military alliances with any country, and in particular with any country either of the Western or of the Communist bloc. The United States has military alliances with some fifty countries, and the Soviet Union with some eleven countries. The essential feature of these alliances is that an attack on one member of the alliance system is considered as an attack on all the other members of the system, which would, subject to their respective constitutional processes, go to the rescue of the member attacked. India considers that her joining one bloc or the other would lessen the chances of using what influence she has or would have in the cause of world peace. Let this argument be put in the Prime Minister's own words:

. . . If by any chance we align ourselves definitely with one power group we may perhaps from one point of view do some good but I have not the shadow of a doubt that from a larger point of view, not only of India but of world peace, it will do harm. Because then we lose that tremendous vantage ground that we have of using such influence as we possess—and that influence is going to grow from year to year—in the cause of world peace.

What are we interested in world affairs for? We seek no dominion over any country. We do not wish to interfere in the affairs of any country, domestic or other. Our main stake in world affairs is peace. . . .

The supreme question that one has to face today in the world is how we can avoid a world war. . . . I should like this House and the country to appreciate what a world war means, what it is likely to mean. It just does not matter who wins in the world war because it will mean such utter catas-

trophe that for a generation or more everything that we stand for in the way of progress and advancement of humanity will be put an end to. That is a terrible thing to contemplate and everything should be done to avoid this catastrophe. . . . I feel that India can play a big part, and may be an effective part, in helping in the avoidance of war. Therefore it becomes all the more necessary that India should not be lined up with any group of powers which for various reasons are in a sense full of fear of war and prepare for war.[8]

Self-respect demands, according to Nehru, that India should be free to express her opinion on the merits of each question:

By aligning ourselves with any one Power, you surrender your opinion, give up the policy you would normally pursue because somebody else wants you to pursue another policy. I do not think that it would be a right policy for us to adopt. If we did align ourselves we would only fall between two stools. We will neither be following the policy based on our ideals inherited from our past or the one indicated by our present nor will we be able easily to adapt ourselves to the new policy consequent on such alignment.[9]

Elsewhere, he has added that, keeping self-respect apart, "purely from the point of view of opportunism, if you like, a straightforward honest policy, an independent policy is best."

I think not only in the long run but in the short run, that independence of

[8] Speech in the Constituent Assembly (Legislative) March 8, 1949, *Constituent Assembly of India (Legislative) Debates,* Part II, Con. 14. 9(II). 49/906, pp. 1234-5.

[9] See Jawaharlal Nehru's Speeches, 1949–1953 (Delhi, 1954), pp. 192–3.

opinion and independence of action will count. . . .

We want the help of other countries; we are going to have it and we are going to get it too in a measure—I am not aware of this having been denied to us to any large extent. Even in taking that help, economic or other, or even in getting political help, it is not a wise policy to put all your eggs in one basket. . . . and more especially at the cost of one's self-respect. Because then you are not respected by any party; you may get some petty benefits but ultimately even those may be denied you.[10]

The geographical situation of India also suggests a non-alignment policy for her. A look at the map will show that the two leading Communist Powers are on or near her border, China's international boundary touching hers, and the Soviet Union's being some twenty miles from hers. Military alliances with countries of the Western bloc are ruled out by this factor, as such alliances will be considered unfriendly by the two Communist Powers and the impact of any war between the two blocs will immediately make itself felt on India; an alliance with the Communist countries is ruled out because, by her traditions, India cannot approve of the Communist ideology, a point which is elaborated elsewhere in this paper.

Before we pass on to the traditional basis of non-alignment, three possible misconceptions may perhaps be removed. First, as Nehru was careful to explain in Parliament, non-alignment (not being a party to military alliances) does not involve any lack of close relationships with other countries. "So our policy," said Nehru on March 8, 1949, "will continue to be not only to keep apart from power alignments but trying to make friendly co-operation possible."[11] The large number of agreements entered into by India with several nations since 1947, of a cultural, economic and political (promotion of peace) character will testify to this desire to be friendly with all nations.

Secondly, non-alignment does not mean neutrality. Neutrality, as a policy has little meaning except in times of war. In a sense, it is true that if we take into account the Cold War between the two blocs, India might be said to be neutral in so far as she has decided that she would not join either bloc. But the term neutrality is inapplicable to India's policy because "neutrality" may connote that the country which adopts such a policy has no positive opinions on the issues which divide the blocs and that certainly is not true so far as India is concerned. On the significant world issues, especially so far as they are related to war and peace, India has spoken, clearly and with conviction. To cite a few: She condemned the British and French invasion of the Suez as a "naked aggression" (1956); she condemned, although belatedly, Soviet interference in Hungary (1956); she earlier considered North Korean troops marching into South Korea as "aggression" (1950). Speaking at a Press Conference at the U.N. Correspondents' Association, New York, on October 4, 1960, Nehru brought out this aspect forcefully:

Some people use the word "neutral" in regard to India's policy. I do not like that word at all, having myself been in the past, perhaps even now to some extent, not exactly a negative individual but a positive individual working for positive causes, working with all the vigour and strength that I could command for those causes, and having, if I may say so with all respect, a certain contempt for a neu-

---

[10] From Speech in the Constituent Assembly (Legislative), March 8, 1948, *Constituent Assembly (Legislative) Debates,* Vol. III—No. 2, Con. 14, III. 2.48/904, p. 1768.

[11] Speech in the Constituent Assembly (Legislative) March 8, 1949. *Constituent Assembly of India (Legislative) Debates,* Part II, Con. 14. II. 9(II).49/906, p. 1234.

tral person who has no views at all. . . .[12]

Again, speaking in Lok Sabha on November 22, 1960, he said:

As I have said repeatedly, I do not like the word "neutral" as being applied to India. I do not even like India's policy being referred to as "positive neutrality" as is done in some countries. Without doubt, we are unaligned; we are uncommitted to military blocs; but the important fact is that we are committed to various policies, various urges, various objectives, and various principles; very much so. . . .[13]

Thirdly, non-alignment does not imply that when a war breaks out, India is bound to be neutral; the misconception is so widespread that it is worthwhile to remove this by quoting the Prime Minister on this aspect of non-alignment. Said Nehru in the Constituent Assembly on December 4, 1947:

We have proclaimed during this past year that we will not attach ourselves to any particular group. That has nothing to do with neutrality or anything else or passivity. If there is a big war, there is no particular reason why we should jump into it. Nevertheless, it is a little difficult nowadays in world wars to be neutral. . . . We are not going to join a war if we can help it; and we are going to join the side which is to our interest when the choice comes to it.[14]

The raison d'être of non-alignment has been explained above, as far as possible, in Nehru's own words; it is important to add that the pol-

icy has its basis also in Indian tradition: ". . . all that I have done," said Nehru in Lok Sabha on December 9, 1958 "is to give voice to that policy (non-alignment). I have not originated it. It is a policy inherent in the circumstances in India, *inherent in the past thinking of India, inherent in the whole mental outlook of India, inherent in the conditioning of the Indian mind* during our struggle for freedom and inherent in the circumstances of the case today."[15] The essence of that mental outlook is a spirit of tolerance among the common people in India, who have inherited the tradition from their scriptures and from their history.

It is common knowledge that Hinduism has been essentially catholic; religious beliefs in India have not assumed one uniform shape. There are various shades of difference, ranging from monotheism to polytheism. This clearly indicates that a man's religion is not something to which he is required to conform but something which should fit in with his cultural attainments and his status in life.

A reading of Indian history also suggests that the idea of tolerance was not merely confined to the books but was a reality in the social tradition. Many immigrants and invaders came to India through the centuries. Since these were gradual and protracted infiltrations, these people were assimilated into the society, each group retaining its own characteristics. Asoka's inscriptions on his rockpillars highlighted the prevailing idea of tolerance:

The King, beloved of the gods, honours every form of religious faith, but considers no gift or honour so much as the increase of the substance of religion; whereof this is the root: to reverence one's faith, and never to revile that of others. Whoever acts differently injures his own religion while he wrongs another's. . . .

The rise of communal outlook in the first half of this century ending in the partition of India,

[12] Nehru, *India's Foreign Policy, op. cit.*, p. 85.

[13] *Ibid.*, p. 86.

[14] Speech in the Constituent Assembly (Legislative) December 4, 1947, *Constituent Assembly of India (Legislative) Debates*, Vol. II—No. 5, Con. 14. II. 5.47/904, p. 1260.

[15] *Lok Sabha Debates*, December 9, 1958, Vol XXIII, col. 3961. Italics added.

and the prevalence of untouchability as a custom—notwithstanding the clear injunctions of
the Constitution and the law of the land to the
contrary—warn us that one can never be com-
placent of the strength of the tolerant attitude
in all the people. Nevertheless, basically the
tradition of tolerance is part and parcel of the
thinking and the life of the common people in
India.

The tolerant attitude is one major factor in
understanding the non-alignment policy which
India has followed since 1946; this has been
testified to by the Prime Minister himself.[16] In
the cold-war politics of today, India has studi-
ously avoided taking sides: the pluralistic outlook of the Indian mind has made the Indian
people react instinctively against communism
and its claim to be the sole truth; likewise it has
prevented them from joining the anti-
Communists and regarding communism in as
horrid a way as anti-Communists do. Violence,
the Communist method of realizing the aim of
an egalitarian society, repels them as its basis
is intolerance, though the social content of
communism—the ideal of egalitarianism, sympathy for the under-dog and economic betterment—has some appeal for them. Similarly, the
bitterness and hatred with which communism is
regarded in Western countries is a puzzle to the
Indian people as such an attitude also has its
roots in intolerance and an unwillingness to
learn from other social systems. Yet India,
clearly, shares with the West its values of the
dignity and freedom of the individual, which a
true social democracy alone will help to promote.

Means and ends

A second traditional value which has come
down through the ages is that the means to be
employed to achieve an end are as important as

the end itself and both should be according to
moral law—an idea which has found its best
expression in recent times in Mahatma Gandhi's writings.[17] Many quotations could be cited
from ancient sayings in support of this view,
such as:

"One should not do a good thing by following a bad path."[18]

"Avoid at all times action that is not in accordance with the moral law."

"Success achieved without minding the prohibitions of the moral law brings grief in the
wake of achievement."

"To seek to further the welfare of the State
by enriching it through fraud and falsehood is
like storing water in an unburnt mud pot and
hoping to preserve it."[19]

The equation of right means with right ends
is, in my opinion, in the main Indian tradition;
however, there are texts in ancient books which
take the contrary view and hold that while the
end must be good, the means may not be so. A
well-known political thinker, Kautilya, for instance, in his *Arthasastra*,[20] recommended the
adoption of methods of statecraft according to
circumstances and expressed the view that
what produces unfavorable results is bad policy: a policy is to be judged by the results it
produces. For him diplomacy was an art, not
concerned with ideals but with achieving practical results for the state. For instance, "when
any one of these is on the point of rising against
a weak king," says he,

> the latter should avert the invasion by
> making a treaty of peace, or by taking
> recourse to the battle of intrigue
> (*mantravudha*), or by a treacherous

---

[16] See extract from Nehru's speech cited earlier in this
chapter.

[17] E.g., see D. G. Tendulkar, *Mahatma*, Bombay:
1954; Mahatma Gandhi, *Young India*, 1924–26, Madras: 1927, pp. 364, 435; M. K. Gandhi, *Sarvodaya*,
Ahmedabad: 1954, pp. 6–7.

[18] Manu, *Dharma Shastra*, IV, 199.

[19] *The Second Book of Kural*. A selection from the
old Tamil Code for Princes, Statesmen and Men of Affairs. Translation and Notes by C. Rajagopalachari.
Madras: 1937, pp. 49–50.

[20] See Kautilya, *Arthasastra*, tr. by R. Shamasastry.
Bangalore: 1915, Bk. VII, pp. 327–89.

fight in the battlefield. He may reduce the enemy's men either by conciliation or by giving gifts, and should prevent the treacherous proceedings of his own men either by sowing the seeds of dissension among them or by punishing them.[21]

The existence of this tradition, taken together with the record of events in our history, shows, first, that Indian rulers did not always accept the equation of public and private morality, and second, that social theorists were aware of the difficulty in such equation. Modern political theorists also have failed to meet this difficulty effectively. While an individual is free to go to the limit, even to the extent of facing death in trying to follow a moral principle, a statesman acting on behalf of the state, is likened to the trustee acting on behalf of his ward. In deciding on his action, he has to take into account the interests and the wishes of his people.

In this context, it is sufficient to say that (1) to the extent that the tradition that bad means should not be used to attain a good end has taken roots in India, it should help the furtherance of India's policy of working for peace through peaceful means; (2) that India's leaders have accepted the principle that the right means must be adopted to achieve a good end; and (3) in their view, using violence is essentially a bad means of achieving a good end, such as peace. How far in the implementation of foreign policy, India has kept up to the ideal is a matter for investigation of each specific instance;[22] it is sufficient in this context to note one of the guiding threads of India's foreign policy, as declared by her Prime Minister and as based on India's traditions. "We believe," Nehru told Mr. Bulganin and Mr. Khrushchev at a banquet in New Delhi on November 20, 1955, "not only that the ends to be achieved should be good but also that the means employed should be good, or else new problems arise and the objective itself changes."

[21] *Ibid.*, Bk. XII. Ch. I.
[22] See footnote 97.

Approach to questions of war and peace

There are two parallel ways to peace, one to tackle the roots of conflict (social, economic and political) and the other to attempt to resolve a given conflict without recourse to violence so that there may be a reduction of international tension arising from that conflict, even if the conflict itself may not be resolved.[23]

The ending of colonialism and racialism, the raising of the living standards of people in underdeveloped countries and the promotion of the temper of peace in as wide an area as possible will help to tackle the roots of conflict. The promotion of the temper of peace will be facilitated by disarmament and by the "recognition of each other's sovereignty, independence and integrity, or non-interference in the domestic affairs of each other or of other countries, and by the promotion, both for themselves and for the world, of the approach and conditions of peaceful co-existence"—principles which are all to be found in the United Nations Charter. Wars arise in the minds of men and the promotion of the temper of peace will help to promote a climate of peace.

This, clearly, is a long-term approach and recognized as such not only by India but by other countries. India knows that conflicts, nevertheless, do and will occur as verbal statements are not always kept. Panch Sheel may be broken as she realized most clearly in the case of Hungary in 1956 and that of China's encroachment on Indian territory in 1959–60 and 1962–63. When conflicts have arisen, India's view is that the manner of solution must be peaceful—not one of hatred and revenge, but a friendly one. In the words of the Prime Minister:

[23] Acknowledgment is due to *International Relations*, October 1960 for this paragraph and a few succeeding ones taken from the author's Article "On Understanding India's Foreign Policy," *International Relations* (London), II, October 1960, pp. 69–85.

Whatever the problems, difficult or simple, the manner of approach will make a difference. And you know if you approach them in anger, hatred, in a spirit of violence, then the problems become difficult and indeed much more difficult and much less amenable to solution. So the Indian approach, whether you live up to it or not is a different matter, but the philosophy behind the Indian approach is, as far as possible, a friendly approach: not giving in or accepting what we consider wrong, nevertheless, trying to tone down, first our actions and words, and if possible, our thinking to some extent from cold-war thinking . . . to hold to what we consider right, firmly and without fear and yet not to speak about opponents in terms which would worsen the situation . . . it may be said by many that it is an idealistic way of approaching world problems . . . and yet this is not only an idealistic way but in the circumstances of the world today, I submit, the only practical way, strictly from the practical point of view and that is why the leaders of other countries not accepting perhaps the philosophy of this practically are functioning or coming round to functioning on those lines.[24]

The Indian approach proceeds on the assumption that peace cannot be promoted by creating positions of strength by military alliances. On the contrary, the creation of positions of strength might become a threat to peace—for every party will naturally try to increase its strength *vis-à-vis* its competitors for power, and such an attempt is suicidal in the atomic age. Entering into military alliances and establishing military bases in foreign territory accentuate discord and the possibility of war.

The peaceful approach has to be tried if only because there is no other alternative. Its essential is the determination to avoid force; hence discussion, negotiation, and accommodation are the only way left for the settlement of differences.[25] It is remarkable that the Eisenhower-Khrushchev statement issued after the talks at Camp David during September 25–27, 1959, accepts this position. "The Chairman of the Council of Ministers of the U.S.S.R. and the President of the United States agreed that all outstanding international questions should be settled not by the application of force but by peaceful means through negotiation."[26] On the eve of his tour to the Far East in June 1960, President Eisenhower again emphasized that among most of the world's peoples, there is a genuine consensus of conviction that we can, by negotiation, solve even the most difficult of international problems.

Does such an approach guarantee peace? No, but neither did the traditional power approach guarantee peace. It is India's view, however, that those who approach problems in a peaceful way do not close their door to negotiation, but emphasize it. They are careful more than others to watch for opportunities for negotiation and try to make a success of it; the truces secured in Korea and Indochina are cases in point. It is true that the unwillingness of the parties to the conflicts to use their destructive weapons supported the temper of peace, or perhaps vice-versa, in the instances cited; but that exactly is the utility of the approach in present conditions in the world. The temper of peace is no panacea for the evils of international power politics; but it is supplementary to power.

The essence of this view is that when differences of opinion have arisen between two or more parties, a stable resolution of the conflict depends on a settlement in which none of the parties suffers a significant loss.[27] This is not a

---

[24] Address to the Indian Council of World Affairs, April 5, 1960 (unpublished).

[25] See footnote 97.

[26] See *Keesing's Contemporary Archives,* 1959–60, p. 17082.

[27] This statement excludes stable results achieved by means of war, e.g. war did settle the relation between

distinctly Indian approach; it is integral to true negotiation as such. But the tradition is explicitly mentioned in the Indian epic, the *Mahabharata*. When Sri Krishna was about to negotiate a settlement between the Pandavas and Kurus, he summarized the object of his mission in the following words: "Yes, I will go to King Dhritarashtra, desirous of accomplishing what is consistent with righteousness, what may be beneficial to us and what also is for the good of the Kurus."[28]

This has been the universal tradition, not always consistently followed but, nevertheless, more often followed by negotiators in every country than statesmen are prepared to admit. The willingness to submit a dispute to a third-party judgment, as may be seen in the numerous cases referred to arbitration, can be explained only by the existence in the disputants of that spirit of accommodation and of willingness to see the other man's point of view which is so essential in order to avoid a breakdown. The Indian emphasis on negotiation as a way to peace only highlights a well-known technique and its utility in the atomic age. However, China's aggression on India's soil shows that it is very important for a non-aligned country, especially, to have its defenses in readiness, in case the other party is not prepared to negotiate on just conditions.

executive in Britain. Making foreign policy is essentially the responsibility of the Cabinet as a whole. The Cabinet discusses foreign affairs, usually on the initiative of the Minister for External Affairs who decides what matters should be brought before the Cabinet. Normally, important policy and administrative matters are brought before the Cabinet. The Cabinet acts at the highest level of co-ordination because all important ministries are represented in the Cabinet.[29]

For the more efficient transaction of business and better co-ordination, Cabinet committees have been constituted to deal with various subjects. Since 1957, there has been a Standing Committee on Foreign Affairs in the Cabinet. It has, at present, a strength of six Cabinet ministers, including the foreign minister. This committee acts as a center of co-ordination in the transaction of business which pertains to foreign affairs. It might take decisions on behalf of the Cabinet or make recommendations to it, enabling the Cabinet to take quick decisions. Co-ordination between foreign affairs and domestic affairs is also sought through other Cabinet committees like the Economic Committee.[30]

The Minister for External Affairs heads the Ministry of External Affairs. He is, therefore, the link between the Cabinet and the administration in foreign affairs. The decisions of the

THE MAKING OF FOREIGN POLICY

The role of the Cabinet   India has a parliamentary executive more or less similar to the

---

Britain and the thirteen American colonies more or less on a stable basis.

[28] The *Mahabharata* (translated into English prose) by Pratapachandra Roy, Udyoga Parva (Calcutta, 1920) Vol. III, p. 329. The ancient epic recounts the adventures of the Pandavas and the war against the Kurus. Krishna served as the plenipotentiary of the Pandavas during the final negotiations with their opponents.

[29] The Cabinet system is not based on any formal provision in the Constitution of India. The Constitution recognizes only the Council of Ministers (Art. 74). The functioning of the Cabinet is one of "the major inarticulate premises" of the British Constitution and has been adopted in this country on a similar basis.

The composition and size of the Cabinet are decided by the Prime Minister. There are no fixed rules to guide him in this respect. Generally, the more important members of the Council of Ministers will constitute the Cabinet and all important ministries will be represented in it. The present size of the Cabinet is known to be twelve.

An excellent account of the working of the Indian Cabinet System is given in Asok Chanda, *Indian Administration,* London: 1958, pp. 55–93.

[30] Under the present arrangements, there are ten standing committees and other *ad hoc* committees. For details see, Asok Chanda, *op. cit.,* pp. 89–91.

Cabinet and the Minister are implemented by the Ministry of External Affairs and its field establishments.

This bare statement of the formal position must be supplemented by some indication of the influences that bear on this process. Here, the most important single matter is the personality and the background of Jawaharlal Nehru who has been the Prime Minister and Minister for External Affairs during the last few years, ever since India became independent in 1947.[31]

Nehru's role   In the shaping of foreign policy, the predominant role has been Nehru's. This has been due to various factors relating to his personality: the traditional role he has played in the formulation of the foreign policy of the present-day ruling party—the Indian National Congress—in the pre-independence days; his immense personal popularity among the people of the country which transcends party frontiers and is truly charismatic; his predominant position in his own party; the combination of the leading posts in the government as Prime Minister and Minister for External Affairs; and his long experience in administration which is greater than that of nearly all his colleagues in the government.[32] The absence of strong opposition parties in the country or in Parliament, able to challenge effectively the virtual monopoly of power of the ruling party and form an alternate government, is a further factor of importance in understanding this role. Moreover, all the major parties in the country have accepted in principle the basic concepts of his foreign policy, even if there are occasional differences on details.[33]

This does not mean that there are no controls or checks on his authority. Like any other political leader in a democracy, he has to compromise with a variety of forces like the prevailing trends of public opinion and differences of opinion within his own party or outside. Like any other foreign minister he is also advised by his senior officials in the Ministry or the Ambassadors abroad and has to delegate a large part of his work to his junior ministers or officials in the Ministry. He has also his own personal circle of advisers. For example, it is generally known that he frequently consults Dr. S. Radhakrishnan, the President of India and Shri V. K. Krishna Menon, who was Minister for Defence for many years.[34]

The rank and file   The Secretary-General of the External Affairs Ministry is "the principal official adviser to the Foreign Minister on matters relating to foreign policy and is responsible for the supervision and co-ordination of the whole."[35] Below him is a hierarchy of officials forming a chain of command downwards and of responsibility upwards. The ministry functions on the basis of division and delegation of work. The basic units of administration in the ministry are called "divisions" and are organized on a territorial and functional basis. The advisory and executive functions of the

---

[31] Mr. Nehru assumed charge as Vice President and Member for External Affairs and Commonwealth Relations in the Interim National Government formed in September 1946. With the partition of the sub-continent and the formation of the two independent Dominions of India and Pakistan on August 15, 1947, Nehru became Prime Minister and Minister for External Affairs.

[32] Nehru has been associated with the administration since September 1946. (See footnote 31 above.) There is only one other cabinet Minister in the Government of India, Mr. Jagjivan Ram, with the same length of experience of administration as Minister, though not handling the same portfolio.

[33] The Swathantra Party, formed recently, is perhaps the only important party in India which has expressed open disagreement with these principles. Small right wing Hindu parties like Jan Sangh, Ram Rajya Parishad and Hindu Mahasabha have been demanding a more "militant" policy towards Pakistan and have in very recent times engaged in more open criticism of the foreign policy. The left wing Praja Socialists and Communists, which form the most effective opposition parties in the country, have openly recorded their acceptance of the principles of nonalignment, the former more critically and the latter only after 1956.

[34] On this informal circle of advisers see Vincent Shean, *Nehru: The Years of Power*, New York: 1960, pp. 231–55; Michael Brecher, *Nehru: A Political Biography*, London: 1959, pp. 569–75.

[35] *Report of the Ministry of External Affairs 1960–61*, p. 1.

ministry and its officials enable them to play some direct and indirect role in the making of policy.

The organization and working of the overseas missions and posts are broadly similar to those of other countries, like Britain. Their number has shown a tremendous increase during these past few years, though it is still far from adequate.[36] They act as the field establishments of the ministry, reporting and advising from abroad and implementing the directions from headquarters.

The personnel at the headquarters of the ministry and the overseas missions is organized as two Services—the Indian Foreign Service (A) and Indian Foreign Service (B).[37] The former is comparable to Branch A of the British Foreign Service and forms the higher hierarchy of the Foreign Service; the latter is comparable to Branches B and C of the British Foreign Service and mostly renders junior executive and clerical assistance. After an initial scheme of emergency recruitment in 1947–48, when the service needed sudden expansion, the recruitment to these services has been based on annual competitive examinations conducted by the Union Public Service Commission. The probationers for the higher service are then put

under training, covering a study of such subjects as Indian History, Constitution and Administration; the history of international relations, international law, and international economics; and a foreign language, other than English. Besides the career personnel who form the hard core of the foreign service, there are also in the overseas missions and posts the "specialists" who belong to other services like the Defence Service and the home civil services and are drawn from other ministries and numerous locally recruited persons for clerical and other assistance of a non-confidential nature. Ambassadors and other Heads of Missions are recruited either from the career service or from public life and the liberal professions. They are normally chosen by the Foreign Minister.

Decision-making is a cumulative process involving a number of elements and a complex procedure. It is, of course, difficult to delineate any fixed pattern of the actual process, because much depends on such variable factors as individual personalities and the nature of the situation whose combined effect cannot be precisely gauged. But in any proper assessment of the factors shaping foreign policy, none of these numerous elements can be ignored.

INDIA AND THE UNITED NATIONS

Ever since 1947 when India became independent, she has taken an active part in the work of the United Nations. Testifying to the useful and effective part that she has played, Lord Birdwood, a member of the United Kingdom delegation to the Fourteenth Session of the General Assembly, stated that India was "an effective and balancing influence in world affairs so far as the United Nations' Organization is concerned."[38] India has been active because

---

[36] In September 1946, when the Interim Government was formed, Indian overseas establishments numbered 13. By August 1947, when India became independent, this had grown to 23. At the end of 1960, there were 111 such overseas establishments. These consisted of 54 embassies, 9 High Commissions in Commonwealth Countries, 6 legations, 3 Special Missions, including the permanent delegation at the U.N., 9 Commissions in certain non-self governing territories of Britain, in Africa and elsewhere, 3 Trade Commissions, 3 Trade Agencies and 24 consular establishments. The annual Reports of the Ministry of External Affairs, published by the Ministry itself since 1949, give the lists of such missions for each year.

[37] For details, see the very informative article on, "The Organisation of Consular and Diplomatic Services in India" by H. Dayal, at present Indian Ambassador in Nepal, in *India Quarterly*, XII (1956) pp. 268–82; and the present author's article on "Indian Diplomacy" in *Diplomacy in a Changing World*, edited by Stephen D. Kertesz and M. A. Fitzsimons (University of Notre Dame Press, 1959) pp. 266–300. These articles are, however, a little out of date on details.

[38] Lord Birdwood, "United Nations and Asia," *Journal of the Royal Central Asian Society* (London), XXXXVII, p. 188.

she believes in the purposes and principles of the United Nations. As her Prime Minister once remarked, "in spite of these faults, the United Nations serves an essential purpose and if we did not have it today, undoubtedly countries will have to come together to build up something like it again."[39]

A study of the speeches of the members of the Indian delegation to the General Assembly and the resolutions introduced by them reveals that she has taken greater interest in some of the United Nations activities than in others. Broadly India's interest has been focussed on: 1) the pacific settlement of international disputes and 2) the strengthening of the foundations of peace. The latter objective requires international assistance in the progress of dependent peoples to self-government, the elimination of racial discrimination, the economic development of underdeveloped countries and the fight against malnutrition, disease and illiteracy in underdeveloped countries.

Pacific settlement of international disputes

India has taken the view that the collective security functions of the United Nations as envisaged in Chapter VII of the Charter should not be emphasized because of the Cold War which developed soon after the Charter was signed. For the assumptions under which that chapter was included in the Charter and agreed to by member states when they signed it no longer holds good. This assumption was that there would be continuing unanimity on fundamental world issues among the five permanent members of the Security Council who were given the veto power. The cold war has made it difficult for the permanent members to implement Article 43 of the Charter; the agreements by which armed forces were to be made

available to the Security Council for the maintenance of security were never made. In the circumstances, it is idle to talk of effective enforcement provisions of the Charter.

Therefore, when an attempt was made by the General Assembly in November 1950, through the Uniting for Peace Resolution, to emphasize the collective security functions of the United Nations, India abstained on the resolution. Under that resolution, it will be recalled, the General Assembly assumed power to act "if the Security Council, because of lack of unanimity of the permanent members, fails to exercise its primary responsibility for the maintenance of international peace and security in any case where there appears to be a threat to the peace, breach of the peace or act of aggression." It is not India's view that such a resolution was *ultra vires* of the Charter. The Assembly has been given some responsibility by the Charter for the maintenance of international peace, and, under that provision, it would clearly not be illegal for the Assembly to make recommendations authorized by the Uniting for Peace Resolution. Rather, India felt that the passing of such a resolution was politically unwise because, under the Uniting for Peace Resolution, it is possible for the United Nations to undertake enforcement action even though there is no unanimity among the Big Five; more, it could undertake enforcement action even against one of the Big Five. It is difficult under the Charter to think of a military action sponsored by the United Nations against a permanent member of the Security Council, since each can invoke the veto in the Security Council. The Uniting for Peace Resolution, passed by the Assembly, substantially alters this situation.

Besides, it may be argued that the Charter implies that United Nations military action can be taken only with the unanimous consent of the Big Five and at least two other members of the Security Council. The Charter does not contemplate the possibility of placing any member in the embarrassing situation of having to take sides, in a military action under United Nations auspices, with one of the Big Five against another of the Big Five. Members

[39] From reply to a debate on Foreign Affairs in Lok Sabha, June 12, 1952, *Parliamentary Debates*, Part 2, par. S. 2. 16. II. 1. 52/982, col. 1671.

could reasonably argue that it was on that assumption that they joined the Organization. The gist of this argument is that a division of the United Nations is made possible by the implementation of the resolution which, India felt, was politically unwise.

That India represented the *real* consensus of member states on the subject (though the resolution itself was passed by the requisite majority) may be seen from the fact that the significant provisions of the resolution have been, in effect, a dead letter:

The Uniting for Peace Resolution had given rise to the work of the Collective Measures Committee whose studies concerning the means of effectuating the principle of collective security had been safely filed away, along with papers indicating that States had no intention of following through on the recommendation that they develop military units for possible use under United Nations auspices.[40]

India's abstention on the Uniting for Peace Resolution should not be interpreted as a desire to weaken the Organization. This is evident not only from the pronouncements of her Prime Minister that he would like to see the United Nations grow from strength to strength,[41] but also from the consistent support that India has given to the United Nations when the Organization tried to reduce international tensions by what may be called the diplomacy of reconciliation. In 1956–57, after the outbreak of hostilities in Egypt, the General Assembly authorized the Secretary-General immediately to obtain compliance of the withdrawal of foreign forces. He was requested to submit a plan for a United Nations force to "secure and supervise

the cessation of hostilities" and subsequently he was instructed to take all necessary administrative and executive action to organize this force and dispatch it to Egypt.

It is well-known that the UNEF has been performing a most useful function in keeping the peace. The fact that it is constituted largely of contingents from the smaller and uncommitted nations is of special significance in keeping it out of Cold War politics. The decision to dispatch the UNEF to Egypt was taken *not* under Chapter VII of the Charter (enforcement provisions) but under Chapter VI (pacific settlement of international disputes): the force was organized on the assumption that the contingents and the force "would not have any further tasks than those which were necessary in order to support an operation of reconciliation," and especially they would not be a fighting force. India willingly complied with the request of the U. N. Secretary-General that Indian troops be sent to the Gaza Strip.

Again in 1958, when the U. N. Secretary-General decided to send an Observation Group into Lebanon to insure that there was no infiltration of personnel or supply of arms or other materiel across the Lebanese border to either of the contending parties in the civil war there, and when he asked India to assist, India complied with the request. Speaking to the members of the Indian Council of World Affairs on March 19, 1959, U. N. Secretary-General Hammarskjold paid a tribute to India for her willing co-operation with the United Nations in the following words:

I would like to end these words by repeating our gratitude for the co-operation of the Indian people and the Indian Government first of all and still on a very large scale in the Gaza operation with a very quick response, with a very noble response because the Indian units in the Gaza were of a very very high quality. I can speak from personal experience and I am not flattering you. And also in the second case by the invaluable assistance in the Lebanese affairs through

---

[40] I. L. Claude, Jr., "The United Nations and the Use of Force," *International Conciliation* (New York), March, 1961, No. 532, p. 369.

[41] See Nehru's speech to the United Nations General Assembly on November 10, 1961, as reported in *The Hindu,* November 12, 1961.

the work done by the High Commissioner Dayal. Both those contributions are very valuable contributions to the whole development of the U. N. security and legal system on which it is possible to build the future.

One more instance of the same willingness to co-operate with the U. N. in her diplomacy of reconciliation is India's compliance with the Secretary-General's request to send a unit of Indian forces to the Congo. The U. N. decided to keep the peace in the Congo, asked India to assist and India responded; no question was raised by India of the wisdom of the U. N. decision.

Strengthening the foundations of peace

The government of one people by the government of another, the practice of racial discrimination, the gross underdevelopment of many nations in their economy and the widespread existence of malnutrition, disease and illiteracy, according to India's view, corrode the foundations of peace. It is urgent to supply correctives through international action so that the peace, which the people of the world desire, can be built up on solid foundations. It is not necessary in this context to argue out these fundamentals which have been substantially accepted by most peoples. In accordance with these postulates, India has taken the lead, or supported the lead taken by the delegations of other member states in the United Nations, to work out acceptable ways of achieving the desired goals.

Progress of dependent peoples to self-government   The basic objectives of the trusteeship system are sound: to further international peace and security; to promote the political, economic, social and educational advancement of the inhabitants of the trust territories, and to promote their progressive development to-

wards self-government or independence as may be appropriate to the particular circumstances of each territory; to encourage respect for human rights in the territories; and to ensure equal treatment therein for all members of the United Nations in social, economic, and commercial matters. The Trusteeship Council and the General Assembly have had various opportunities to implement these objectives, in particular when the terms of trusteeship agreements were approved, the annual reports of the administering Powers were considered and the petitions from nationals and associations in the trust territories were heard. The speeches of the members of the Indian delegation indicate the general Indian approach.[42] Indians believe that the United Nations must have the ultimate power to supervise the administration of the trust territories, and the administering Powers should act only as the agents of the United Nations; early steps should be taken to grant complete self-government to the people of the territories; no form of racial discrimination should be practiced in the territories; the terms of the trusteeship agreements and of the Charter should be observed by the administering Powers in a broad and liberal spirit.

When the draft trusteeship agreements were considered at the second part of the first session of the General Assembly in 1946, India submitted various amendments to circumscribe the authority of the administering states in the trust territories. One such amendment provided for the inclusion in all agreements of the following clause:

> The Administering Authority shall administer the Trust Territory on behalf of and solely for the benefit and in the interest of its people, and on the termination of the Trusteeship, all the powers of the Authority shall cease and it shall surrender the Territories to the peoples whose sovereignty and whose right to self-government or in-

[42] See *India and the United Nations,* New York: 1957, p. 78.

dependence shall always be recognized.[43]

Non-self-governing territories The same desire to assist dependent peoples to self-government is revealed in the support which India gave to the achievement of independence of Indonesia (July 30, 1947), the former Italian colonies of Libya, Eritrea and Italian Somaliland (1949–52), Morocco (1951–56) and Tunisia (1952–56) and so on.[44] In drafting or supporting resolutions on these matters, India worked in close co-operation with the Asian-African group, of which she is an active member.

India has also worked on the Committee on Non-Self-Governing territories. The key Article in the Charter relating to these territories is Art. 73 (e) which instructs the administering authority

to transmit regularly to the Secretary-General for information purposes, subject to such limitation as security and constitutional considerations may require, statistical and other information of a technical nature relating to economic, social, and educational conditions in the territories (other than the trust territories) for which they are respectively responsible.[45]

Progress of dependent peoples to self-government was made easier through proposals made by members from non-administering Powers in the Committee, India supporting them and often taking the lead. They suggested that although the administering Powers were under no obligation to submit information about political developments in the territories, they should be encouraged to do so voluntarily in view of Article 73 (b) which emphasizes the po-

litical advancement and the progressive development of free political institutions in the territories. Secondly, the information received by the United Nations was to be analyzed with a view to ascertaining what progress was being made towards self-government in these territories.

Racial discrimination Year after year since 1946, India has raised in the Assembly the question of treatment of people of Indian origin in the Union of South Africa, particularly emphasizing that racial segregation is a violation of fundamental human rights. Race conflict in South Africa, resulting from the policy of *apartheid* of the Government of the Union of South Africa, was also brought to the Assembly's attention in 1952 by thirteen Asian and African States, including India. Though some of them have abstained on the resolutions, practically all the member states of the United Nations broadly support the principles advanced by India[46] and established by scientific research that there is no foundation for the belief in superiority and inferiority on the basis of race.[47] Racial discrimination is not only a flagrant violation of the basic principles of human rights and fundamental freedoms enshrined in the Charter, but, if persisted in, constitutes a threat to international peace.

Economic development of underdeveloped countries It is now widely accepted after Marx that even if economic conditions do not determine historical change, they form a vital factor in that process. For world peace, the vital economic factor is the appalling contrast between the countries in the West or the East with high living standards and those with low standards. There is no reason to think that, science having shown the way, economic inequalities among nations should continue to be as great as they are. For instance, Indonesia has a per capita income of $23.00 and India

[43] *Official Records,* First Session of the General Assembly, Fourth Committee, Pt. II, p. 235, 1946.

[44] See *Everyman's United Nations,* 6th ed., New York: p. 112 ff.

[45] See M. S. Rajan, *United Nations and Domestic Jurisdiction,* Bombay: 1961, Appendix II, p. 482.

[46] *Everyman's United Nations, op. cit.,* pp. 146–52.

[47] See *The Race Question in Modern Science,* London: 1956.

has $61.00;[48] on the other hand, New Zealand has $736 and the U.S.A. has $1291.[49] While the economic progress of the advanced countries must be maintained and even carried further, efforts must also be made by international action to speed up the development of the less developed countries. There is fortunately widespread recognition of the validity of Aristotle's thesis that inequality is the root cause of revolutions—and war is the international expression of revolution. The international community cannot afford to neglect the advancement of the less developed countries if only to be true to, and preserve, itself.

The United Nations has realized the need to do its best for promoting economic and social development. TAA, the work of the International Bank and its newer affiliates, the International Finance Corporation, the International Development Association and the United Nations Special Fund, the World Health Organization and the UNESCO testify to this realization. To take a few examples: Through the help of the International Bank, substantial improvements have been made in the Indian railway system, thermal power projects have been developed, the production of coal and steel has been stepped up and large tracts of land have been reclaimed in Central India. The credit made available by the International Development Association will finance almost one-half of the expenditure planned for the improvement of the national highways under the Third Plan. Likewise, the installation of 800 tube wells to increase irrigation in the Indian state of Uttar Pradesh will be facilitated. Through the assistance of the Special Fund, fifteen projects comprising five training institutes, eight research institutes and two surveys have been developed, the Fund contributing one-third of the cost, and the Government of India two-thirds. The function of the Special

Fund is a most important one in pre-investment activities such as the making of intensive surveys of natural resources, the creation and expansion of industrial research institutes, and the carrying out of enlarged programs for the training of strategically skilled manpower.

While the assistance in all these forms has been valued by India, the fact remains that developmental capital is now secured by her mostly through bilateral negotiations. India is deeply appreciative of the economic aid she has secured from a number of friendly countries for her Five Year Plans. However, Indian public opinion shares the general view of underdeveloped countries that, as and when it is practicable, capital aid is best channelled through the United Nations. This should explain the remark made by Sir Benegal Narsingh Rao in commending an Indian draft resolution linking up the reduction of armaments with the creation of development funds, that

> since astronomical sums were being spent on destructive arms, it was obvious that a very small part of these enormous sums could, if directed to constructive purposes in the underdeveloped areas in the world, serve to wipe out the root-cause of all disorder.[50]

This explains also why India has consistently supported the establishment of SUNFED (Special U. N. Fund for Economic Development), which in principle has been accepted by the General Assembly as the Capital Development Fund.

Fight against malnutrition, disease and illiteracy Space prevents even a summary of India's efforts especially in the Economic and Social Council and the various Intergovernmental Agencies related to the United Nations such as the FAO, WHO, and the UNESCO to

---

[48] Taken from, *Monthly Abstract of Statistics,* New Delhi: Central Statistical Organization, Govt. of India, August, 1961, p. 90.

[49] Except in the case of India, the figures quoted (approximate) are derived from *U. N. Statistical Yearbook,* New York: 1960, p. 459.

[50] *Official Records,* Fifth Session, the General Assembly (1950), First Committee, Political and Security Questions including Regulation of Armaments, Summary Records of Meetings; Vol. I, September 20–December 18, p. 204.

promote international co-operation to fight against malnutrition, disease and illiteracy; nor is it necessary, as there is widespread understanding of and support for such humanitarian work. India is one of the several countries, developed and underdeveloped, which show unabated interest in providing better food, health and education to peoples in underdeveloped countries through the skillful use of international resources, especially through technical assistance and the popularization of new ideas.

Structure of the United Nations

Does the structure of the United Nations need revision because of the significant changes which have taken place in the world since 1945? In particular, the membership of the organization has grown from some 50 in 1945 to well over 100 in the 1960's, including many newly independent states of Asia and Africa; the Soviet Union has achieved atomic parity with the U.S.A., and ideas of the potentialities of international organization have become clearer in the minds of people.

India has taken the view that revision is needed; but changes should be effected with the consent of the permanent members of the Security Council. At least on two occasions the matter came up before the General Assembly, first in 1947–49 when an extensive debate on reforming the voting procedure in the Security Council was held, and second in 1955 when a resolution was introduced, and adopted, to the effect that a Committee consisting of all the members of the United Nations be appointed to consider, in consultation with the Secretary-General, the question of fixing a time and a place and procedures for a review conference.

On the voting procedure in the Security Council, the main issue discussed was how to prevent the abuse of the veto. For instance, could decisions on certain matters be taken by the vote of any seven members of the Security Council? Could the permanent members of the Security Council be asked to exclude certain decisions from their veto power when seven of the Council's eleven members had cast affirmative votes, and so on? India's spokesman told the Interim Committee, to which the matter had been referred, that although he was not a supporter of the veto rule and hoped it would eventually be dispensed with, he did not "regard it as an evil in itself, but rather as the reflection of fundamental differences between the Great Powers" and added, "only if the Great Powers were in accord with each other could international peace be ensured." This has been the view that India has taken also since then: the unanimity of the Big Powers is necessary to ward off threats to peace and security; the ineffectiveness of the United Nations cannot be attributed to the Big Power veto; the symptom should not be mistaken for the disease, and one should not imagine that by verbal changes in the text of the Charter, the ways of states can be changed.

On Charter review, including review of the question referred to above and others such as increase in the membership of the Security Council, a change in the formal amending process and the grant of authority to enable the General Assembly to make decisions instead of recommendations, Krishna Menon told the Assembly in the second debate referred to above:

We think that the Charter can be reviewed only if there is unanimity, and if there is unanimity the main reasons for amending the Charter will disappear. In other words, without unanimity we cannot revise the Charter, and if there is unanimity the reasons for reviewing it will be very small.

In any case, our view is that this is not the appropriate time; there are more pressing problems and without being cynical, one could say that it is not the Charter that is wrong, it is we ourselves . . .[51]

[51] *Official Records,* Tenth Session of the General Assembly (1955), 533rd Plenary Meeting, October 4, 1955, p. 234.

It is remarkable that, in substance, this view is the same as the one expressed by spokesmen for the United States and the Soviet Union.

Several other member states of the United Nations, who are listened to with respect in the Assembly such as Sweden and Canada hold more or less identical views. India has also felt a legal difficulty in pressing for revision without general agreement. Since the Charter is a multilateral treaty and since such treaties cannot be changed without the consent of all the signatories, unanimity is essential.[52]

Finally, reference may be made to the proposal made by the Soviet Union that the office of the Secretary-General should be placed in charge of three persons representing three political groups, Eastern, Western and Neutral. It is possible that such a proposal was made because the late Secretary-General Hammarskjold had been interpreting the nature of his office in a dynamic way. His own conception of his office had, in effect, expanded the political functions of the Secretary-General as distinct from his administrative duties. Whatever the origin of the proposal, India had no hesitation in opposing it.[53] Apart from the obvious defect of the proposal of a partitioned executive, it conflicts with the essentially international character of the office of the Secretary General. Article 100 of the Charter lays down the wholesome principle that in the performance of their duties the Secretary General and the staff shall not seek or receive instructions from any government or from any other authority external to the organization. They shall refrain from any action which might reflect on their position as international officials responsible only to the United Nations. Each member of the United Nations undertakes to respect the exclusively international character of the responsibilities of the Secretary-General and the staff and promises not to seek to influence them in the discharge of their responsibility.

India suggested that it might be useful to have three Deputy Secretaries associated with the Secretary-General "who could bring to bear on his mind the reactions, the thinking, of the various parts of the world."[54] The suggestion is admittedly vague, but perhaps worthy of further investigation.

RELATIONS WITH PAKISTAN, VIETNAM, CHINA, THE U.S.A. AND THE U.S.S.R.

The foregoing pages have attempted to give an outline of India's foreign policy—basic objectives, distinctive aspects and some idea of India's participation in the activities of the United Nations. It is appropriate now to test this general analysis by considering certain key areas of India's foreign relations.

Pakistan

First in importance comes Pakistan which is our neighbor. Relations with her have involved the most complex internal and foreign problems which any state in history has had to face. The story begins with the partition of British India on August 15, 1947 into two independent states, India and Pakistan.[55] It should have been expected that there would be normal friendly relations between India and Pakistan because the partition itself was effected with the consent of the leaders of the two areas. The people of the two states had shared a common history for some centuries; economically the two states were complementary to each other, and politically there was much to be gained by liv-

---

[52] See Lakshmi N. Menon, "India and the Review of the U.N. Charter," *Revision of the United Nations Charter, Symposium,* London: 1956, p. 51.
[53] See *Foreign Affairs Records,* VI, 1960, p. 437.

[54] *Ibid.*
[55] Pakistan reckons August 14, 1947, as the date of her independence.

ing as friendly neighbors. But that was not to be. As a foreign observer has put it, . . . "India and Pakistan have been in a state of undeclared war, with varying degrees of intensity, throughout their brief history as independent states."[56]

I believe that the unfriendliness has been due primarily to two causes: the haste with which partition was effected and the differing interpretations by the two states of the basis of partition. Partition, admittedly necessary, was effected in haste and adequate precautions were not taken to provide for the solution of the social and economic problems which were certain to arise when millions could be expected to be on the move. Hence the mass killings, the problem of recovery of evacuee property, forced conversions, the abduction of women and the like. These problems have now been more or less solved; their solution involved several meetings of representatives at ministerial and secretarial levels, and more than once at the level of prime ministers. It is not necessary here to go into these problems or to discuss how they were solved. Suffice it to say that they added to the psychological tensions between the peoples of the two countries which were primarily due to the problem of Kashmir (discussed below).

If partition had been accomplished with less haste, the recurring disputes about the borders might perhaps have been avoided; in particular the dispute over the demarcation of the boundary on the ground on the basis of what are known as the Radcliffe and Bagge awards.[57] Since these have been solved to mutual satisfaction, there is no need here to discuss them further.[58]

Another dispute, the Canal Waters Dispute, cannot be ascribed to the haste with which partition was implemented. This dispute over the division of the Indus and its tributaries has now happily been settled through the good offices of the World Bank. The settlement shows that, given goodwill and a sense of compromise, the keynote of India's foreign policy, the most vital problems can be solved to mutual advantage.

A second cause for tension between India and Pakistan is more basic. Partition was advocated and accepted by Pakistan leaders on the basis of a two-nation theory, i.e. the Hindus and the Moslems were two nations and, therefore, should have their separate homelands. Indian leaders, while accepting partition sincerely, never approved the two-nation theory. They accepted partition on the basis of some kind of territorial self-determination.[59] "It was perfectly clear," said Nehru,

that it was quite impossible to divide it [India] on the basis of separating religious groups on one side or the other. They overlapped. So it was clearly understood that those communities which became the minority communities on this side or that must have the fullest protection and fullest security of their lives; otherwise, the whole structure which we had built up collapsed.[60]

A division of the Indian sub-continent on the basis of religion would be impossible if it is realized that India has the largest Moslem population in any state excepting Pakistan and Indonesia. The Kashmir question is essentially a consequence of this divergence in the interpretation of partition.

[56] Michael Brecher, *Nehru—A Political Biography*, London: 1950, p. 576.

[57] See Nehru's statement in Rajya Sabha, August 26, 1958, *Parliamentary Debates*, Rajya Sabha, R. S. 10. XXII. 7.58/550, cols. 1048–9.

[58] See Nehru's reply to debate on Foreign Affairs in Lok Sabha, December 9, 1958. *Lok Sabha Debates*, cols. 3958–87. See also Nehru's reply to discussion on an adjournment motion to Lok Sabha on March 12, 1959 for some details of the border problem. *Lok Sabha Debates*, cols. 6031–39.

[59] A third reason should be added for completeness: after the assassination of Liaquat Ali Khan on October 16, 1951, there was a lack of national leadership, which tempted successive governments to hold on to Islam and to the "liberation" of Kashmir for rallying popular support.

[60] Speech in Parliament, March 17, 1950, *Parliamentary Debates*, Par. S.2.III. 3.50/821, p. 1700.

The story of the Kashmir question can be simply told: Under the terms of the Independence of India Act of 1947, the sovereignty of His Majesty over the Indian states lapsed. It was open to them to accede to India or to Pakistan, or, if they so chose, to remain independent. In October of that year, faced with the invasion of the state by armed raiders, the ruler of the state, backed by the leader of the popular organization, requested India to accept the accession of Kashmir to India and to intervene with her armed forces. India accepted the accession and Kashmir became part of Indian territory. Lord Mountbatten's letter of October 27, 1947 accepting Kashmir's accession to India said that "as soon as law and order have been restored in Kashmir and her soil cleared of the invaders, the question of the State's accession should be settled by a reference to the people." Indian troops were sent and they helped to save the valley of Kashmir from falling into the hands of the raiders. As, however, fighting continued and it was clearly known that the raiders were using Pakistani territory as a base of operations and were being assisted directly and indirectly by Pakistan nationals as well as by military and civil Pakistan government personnel, India decided to refer the matter to the Security Council on December 30, 1947. Ever since then, there have been long discussions in the Security Council and outside it, including discussions between the Prime Ministers of the two countries. United Nations Commissions and mediators came to Kashmir and examined the problem. A cease fire was brought about on December 31, 1948 and has been kept, with occasional breaches, since.

The significant international aspects of the issues are the following: Pakistan first denied and later admitted that she had sent her troops to Kashmir (Sir Owen Dixon, the U.N. mediator, said in effect that Pakistan's action was a breach of international law). In the discussions in the Security Council till 1957, several countries including the U.S.A. and Britain took a line unfriendly to India. The grant of military aid to Pakistan by the U.S.A. since 1954 has complicated the problem. India thinks such military aid adds to Pakistan's military strength which she might use against India, notwithstanding the clear assurances by the U.S.A., and accepted by India, that such aid was given only to nations requesting assistance against armed invasion from any country controlled by international communism.[61] India has declared unequivocally that unless Pakistan quits the areas occupied by her in Kashmir, India cannot fulfill her part of the agreement. "There is no settlement of the Kashmir problem if the manner of settling it leads to fresh conflict with Pakistan." Since 1948 when India agreed to a plebiscite, various changes have occurred in the situation. Therefore, India believes that a consideration of the problem on fresh lines is called for—a point recognized by the Swedish diplomat Jarring. In his report, published on May 1, 1957, Jarring said that "the implementation of international agreements, which had not been achieved fairly speedily, may become progressively more difficult because the situation with which they were to cope has tended to change." Since India is committed to a peaceful solution of the problem, she is prepared to agree to a division of Kashmir on the basis of the existing cease fire line. But the deadlock continues.

The question which a student of international affairs must ask is how is it that even if, as is absolutely clear, India, without a single dissenting voice at home, considers her case in Kashmir just, the deadlock continues and part of Kashmir remains under foreign occupation. Has there been something wrong in the diplomatic handling of the question by India during the last fifteen years? One critic has taken the view[62] that it was a mistake on the part of the

---

[61] Pakistan has interpreted the agreement with the U.S.A. differently. Mr. S. A. Baig, the then Foreign Secretary of Pakistan, is on record as having said that "the agreement was a guarantee against aggression 'from any quarter' " and that "there was no reason to believe that the U.S. would put any interpretation on the word 'aggression' other than 'ours'." See debate in Rajya Sabha on March 6, 1959, *Parliamentary Debates*, Rajya Sabha, R.S. 10.XXIV. 21.59/550, col. 2825. See also statement laid on the table of both Houses of Parliament on March 13, 1959.

[62] See Frank Moraes, "Visit to Kashmir: VII—Add-

Government of India to take the Kashmir issue to the Security Council under Articles 34 and 35 of Chapter 6 of the U.N. Charter which is entitled "Pacific Settlement of Disputes" instead of under Chapter 7 which is specifically concerned with "Acts of Aggression." This criticism forgets that clear proof of Pakistan aggression was available only some four months after India referred the matter to the Security Council and after Pakistan committed the act of aggression. But the same critic appears to be on firm ground when he refers to other tactical mistakes of the Government in their diplomatic handling of the question:

India needlessly placed herself at a tactical disadvantage by later adopting the term "plebiscite" which does not occur in the earlier communications. The first document emanating from Delhi after the Maharaja of Kashmir's accession was Lord Mountbatten's letter of October 27, 1947 accepting the accession. "It is my Government's wish," wrote the Governor-General, "that as soon as law and order have been restored in Kashmir and her soil cleared of the invaders the question of the State's accession should be settled *by a reference to the people*.". . . The later intrusion of the term "plebiscite," although conditional, has enabled India's critics to fasten on the plebiscite while forgetting the conditions.

. . . In our anxiety to reach a settlement we have undoubtedly made certain tactical mistakes which our critics have quite naturally attempted to turn to their advantage. We have, for instance, in the protracted process of negotiation allowed ourselves to be persuaded to sidestep certain preliminary hurdles, which action has later quite unjustifiably been interpreted as

acceptance by us of these preliminary points.[63]

While there is something in this criticism, my view is that the trouble has arisen and continued essentially because of the holding on to the two-nation theory by Pakistan and her skillful propaganda. India has rightly stressed her legal rights in Kashmir, but, to counter Pakistani propaganda, she could also have put across the idea that the bid by Pakistan for Kashmir on this basis could have far-reaching reactionary and undemocratic effects. Acceptance of the assumption that religion is the basis of citizenship and nationality would have the consequence that every Moslem in India and every Hindu in Pakistan will be an alien. This is not only undemocratic but is a repudiation of the secular character of the Indian state. The modern mind—especially the democratic and pragmatic British and American—would have understood this argument; and, perhaps, their unfriendly attitude in the earlier years, though primarily due to their cold-war position, could have been changed. This, however, is wisdom after the event, but one can always learn. Looking back, the student cannot but feel that the trouble over Kashmir could have been avoided if only the Kashmir ruler had not vacillated but accepted the advice of Lord Mountbatten[64] to take a quick decision on the question of accession to Pakistan or India "after a reference to the people." Any decision taken by him, after such reference, would have been willingly accepted by India.[65]

---

[63] *Ibid.*

[64] *"He (Mountbatten) said that while urging the Maharaja to make up his mind about accession before the transfer of power, he had all along, from his visit in June onwards, exerted his whole influence to prevent him from acceding to one Dominion or the other without first taking steps to ascertain the will of his people by referendum, plebiscite, election or even, if these methods were impracticable, by representative public meetings."* Alan Campbell-Johnson, *Mission With Mountbatten*, London: 1951, p. 224.

[65] Alan Campbell-Johnson writes: *". . . the Indian Government's policy has been to refrain from inducing Kashmir to accede. Indeed, the States Ministry, under*

---

ing up the Balance Sheet," *The Times of India* (Bombay), April 16, 1957, pp. 6, 11.

Vietnam

As a result of the failure of sixteen months' negotiations between the French Government and Bao Dai, the Supreme Counsellor of State of Ho Chi-minh's Democratic Republic of Vietnam, fighting started in Vietnam in December, 1946. The French granted independence to Vietnam, under the government of Bao Dai, in March, 1949. Thereafter, both Ho Chi-minh and Bao Dai claimed to represent the government of Vietnam.

In this situation, India insisted on guaranteeing the independence of Indochina and insuring peace in the area by means of peaceful negotiation and not by military intervention in or partition of the country. Opposition to partition was precisely the reason why India recognized neither the Democratic Republic of Vietnam (Ho Chi-minh) nor the Republic of Vietnam (Bao Dai).[66]

By the beginning of the year 1953, the Vietminh forces had frequently succeeded in their war against the French, thus engendering in the West a desire to seek assistance from the United States in solving the tangle. Consequently, on March 30, 1953 a Franco-American statement was issued declaring the total defeat of communism in Indochina to be the objective of France. On February 22, 1954 the Indian Prime Minister made an appeal in Parliament for a cease-fire "without any party giving up its own position or whatever it might consider its right." On April 24, Mr. Nehru put

forward a six-point plan for the solution of the problem. These points included promotion of an atmosphere of peace and negotiation and dissipation of an atmosphere of suspicion and threats, cease-fire, France's promise for the independence of Indochina, direct negotiation, complete non-intervention, and keeping the United Nations informed of the progress of a conference called to settle the problem. It may be mentioned here in passing that the six-point plan received the support of Asian nations in general at the Colombo Conference held in April–May 1954. The success of India's proposal was helped by the unwillingness of Great Britain to risk a major war in Vietnam. Mr. Krishna Menon had informal discussions at Geneva with foreign ministers. Ultimately, on July 20, the Geneva Agreement was signed. India served, by unanimous choice, as chairman of the International Armistice and Supervisory Commission with Poland and Canada as other members.

Thus India's efforts succeeded at least in bringing about a halt to fighting in Indochina, although the crisis is not yet finally resolved. The story of Vietnam since the signing of the armistice suggests that freedom from Cold War politics is a prerequisite for any feasible plan for the peaceful settlement of an international dispute.

China

India's relations with the People's Republic of China since 1949 perhaps show at their best application of the principles of her foreign policy as well as their limitations. India was the second non-Communist country to recognize the People's Republic of China on December 30, 1949. From that date to about July 1958, the mutual relations could properly be described as friendly, except for an important disagreement on the question of the "liberation" of Tibet, dealt with below. The establishment of China-India Friendship Associations, the visits of cultural delegations to and from

---

Patel's direction, went out of its way to take no action which could be interpreted as forcing Kashmir's hand and to give assurances that accession to Pakistan would not be taken amiss by India. The Maharaja's chronic indecision must be accounted a big factor in the present crisis." Ibid., p. 223.

[66] The Government of Ho Chi-minh had been recognized by the People's Republic of China and the Soviet Union in January 1950 and that of Bao Dai by the United States and the United Kingdom in February 1950.

China, visits of important personalities—Chou En-lai and Madame Sun Yat-sen to India, Nehru and Dr. Radhakrishnan to China—the conclusion of trade agreements, the visits of sportsmen and artists, participation in industrial and cultural exhibitions, and the visits of technical experts—an Indian team, for instance, to study the working of agrarian cooperatives in China—evidenced growing confidence between the two countries. Thus Chou En-lai was able to declare at Bombay on December 2, 1956 that friendship between India and China was undoubtedly the most important factor in safeguarding world peace. India sponsored People's China's admission to the United Nations and played an important part in making known her views on the possible consequences of the crossing of the 38th Parallel by United Nations troops during United Nations' action in Korea (1950–51). China publicly supported India's claim to Goa[67] and criticized the U.S.-sponsored resolution on Kashmir in the Security Council in January 1957.[68]

The exception to which we referred was on the question of China's relations with Tibet. In October 1950, China's military advance to Lhasa for "liberating" Tibet became known to the world. Believing rightly that China had no *sovereignty*, as distinguished from suzerainty, over Tibet, the Government of India sent a note to China regretting the invasion of Tibet by Chinese troops. A most unfriendly reply to the note was received. After various exchanges, the Government of India finally recognized the *sovereignty* of China over Tibet in 1954. It is correct that India renounced her extra-territorial rights in Tibet which were a legacy from the British period in India which free India, believing in the freedom of all nations, did rightly

to give up. But, one cannot escape the conclusion that there was no need on any ground to recognize the sovereignty of China over Tibet.[69]

Since July 1958, as is now well-known, there have been serious border disputes with China. In Ladakh, along the northwest border, more than 12,000 square miles of Indian territory have been occupied by China. Chinese maps showed large parts of Indian territory as Chinese; when India protested she was told that they were old maps and their revision would be taken up later when the Chinese had leisure to do so. In a letter dated September 8, 1959, Chou En-lai claimed the areas in India which had been included in the Chinese maps as Chinese. Negotiations have taken place between the prime ministers, and teams of officials from both countries have gone into the evidence, historical, traditional, geographical, etc. Though the evidence, as marshalled and published, fully justifies India's stand, China, instead of withdrawing from Indian territory, occupied additional territory in the North East Frontier Agency (N.E.F.A.) in October 1962. This has made the Indian people seriously think of the effectiveness of Panch Sheel as a way of defending national interests. The government has declared that effective steps have been, and will continue to be, taken to prevent any further encroachment on Indian territory, and also to get back the territory occupied by the Chinese.[70] Contrary to earlier intentions, foreign aid will be accepted for this purpose.[71]

---

[67] December 25, 1955 joint statement issued by the Chinese Premier and the Premier of the German Democratic Republic in Peking.

[68] Addressing a Press Conference at Katmandu, Chou En-lai said that the United States had not done a good turn to India on the Kashmir issue and also expressed the view that no useful purpose was served by referring the case to the Security Council. He advised the two parties to peacefully settle this problem through direct negotiations. *The Hindu*, January 30, 1957, p. 5.

[69] For a discussion of the status of Tibet before 1951 see an article by the author in collaboration with R. Vasudev Pillai and Mahendra Kumar, "Bases of India's Title on the North-East Frontier," *International Studies* (Bombay) April, 1960, pp. 361–8. Nehru stated in Parliament on December 6, 1957 that India recognized Chinese *suzerainty* over Tibet. See *Parliamentary Debates* Par. S. 2. VI. 17. 50/836, col. 1267. Again, Nehru clarified that he had used the word *suzerainty*, not *sovereignty*, the earlier day. See *Ibid.*, Par. S.2. VI 8.50/836, col. 1384.

[70] Nehru's statement in Lok Sabha, December 21, 1959, which refers to the use of peaceful means only, has been invalidated by events. See *Lok Sabha Debates*, XXXVII. 27.59, col. 6268.

[71] See Nehru's reply to debate in Rajya Sabha, De-

The U.S.A.

It has been pointed out above that India as a non-aligned country has not taken sides in the Cold War that developed between the U.S.A. and the U.S.S.R. after 1946, that both countries misunderstood her position in the early years, and that, especially from 1956 on, both countries have understood and even appreciated her non-aligned position in world affairs. As India judged every international question independently on its merits, it was inevitable that her views on some questions would differ from those held by the two great countries. This general statement will be clearer when we refer, though only briefly, to India's relations with the U.S.A. and the U.S.S.R.

That there is much in common between India and the U.S.A. is realized by the Government and the people of India. In his speech to the House of Representatives and the Senate in 1949, Nehru pointed to the common ground that exists:

> Like you, we have achieved our freedom through a revolution, though our methods were different from yours. Like you we shall be a republic based on the federal principle, which is an outstanding contribution of the founders of this great Republic. We have placed in the forefront of our Consti-

tution those fundamental human rights to which all men who like liberty, equality and progress aspire—the freedom of the individual, the equality of men and the rule of law. We enter, therefore, the community of free nations with the roots of democracy deeply embedded in our institutions as well as in the thoughts of our people.[72]

It was natural, therefore, that on many questions such as the status of the people of Indian origin in South Africa, the freedom of Indonesia (1949) and of the former Italian colonies and on such international questions as the aggression of North Korea on South Korea (1950), and of Israel, Britain and France in Egypt (1958)—all relating to human rights and the progress of dependent peoples to self-government—there should be substantial agreement between the two countries.

There have been differences on questions relating to Algeria, Morocco, Tunisia, South-West Africa etc. But a study of the records indicates that the differences of view have been more on the procedure of and the timing for attaining the desirable end rather than on the end to be attained. Such differences have sometimes led to criticism in India that the U.S.A. was too cautious and tied up with her allies in the struggle against international communism, and in the U.S.A. that India tended to brush aside difficulties which should be obvious. I am inclined to concur with the view expressed in a recent study that "there is a wide area of fundamental agreement about the inalienable rights of man which most Indians and Americans share with each other."[73]

The main difference in the two nations' attitude to international problems has arisen from the fundamental fact that America believes that containment of communism by creating a position of strength is the only way to

---

cember 9, 1959 for an exposition of earlier views. The following is worth quoting: *"There is one fact which might be remembered when people think so much sometimes of obtaining outside aid. Maybe, they imagine that in my conceit I say that I will not take outside aid. Well, it is not for me to judge myself but I certainly have a little conceit about India's standing on its own legs. Of course I cannot say what in an eventuality we may do; that is a different matter but I do not want this idea to go out to our people that others will preserve our freedom, that others will help us."* *Parliamentary Debates*, **Rajya Sabha**, R.S. 10. XXVII. 18.59/550, cols. **1989–90.**

[72] See Nehru, *India's Foreign Policy, op. cit.,* pp. 590–1.
[73] See Phillips Talbot and S. L. Poplai, *India and America,* New York: 1950, p. 169.

peace. Therefore, she has concluded regional pacts such as the NATO, the SEATO, and the CENTO (the former Baghdad Pact), has acquired bases in the territories of the allies linked through these pacts, and has piled up armaments. But India, as explained, would seek peace through peaceful means and peaceful co-existence; as India's spokesman said at Bandung "One does not seek peace through security, but security through peace." Holding such a view, India developed a conception of collective security which brought about sharp differences between her and the United States both in and outside the U.N. These differences were highlighted in the discussions on the Uniting for Peace Resolution, on termination of military action in Korea, on questions concerning Vietnam and Laos, on the holding of nuclear tests, and on the conclusion of a treaty with Japan. The differences between the two countries on Kashmir, American military aid to Pakistan and on the admission of the People's Republic of China to the United Nations are all projections of the same difference in their fundamental approach to the question of peace and security.

American military assistance to Pakistan was the most important single factor that created a misunderstanding between India and the United States. Indians could not appreciate U.S. global military objectives which apparently dictated a military alliance with a South Asian nation. The manner in which the alliance was consummated did not assuage Indian misgivings. On the other hand, the angry outbursts against the United States served to make many Americans wonder whether India was incredibly naïve about the threat of Communist expansionism from her north. In recent years, however, while neither side has changed its stand, there has taken place a distinct improvement in mutual understanding even on this issue. Informed Americans have come to realize that the military alliance with Pakistan has not served to promote stability in the region and, further, that Indian opposition to the alliance was not prompted by any antagonism to the United States. Chinese actions in Tibet and aggression on India's borders have contributed

to a better understanding by India of the problems involved in protecting her northern borders.

To conclude, the differences that arose between India and the U.S.A. since 1946 are largely explained by the experiences of the two countries in the recent past, by geography, and by the different ideas they have on the means by which their national interests can be secured. These have been alluded to already. It is significant that these differences have not affected the friendly relations of the two countries. Far from that, the substantial economic aid which America has given to India for the development of her Five Year Plans shows that the democratic basis of India's constitution and her efforts for the reduction of international tension have made an appeal to the American mind which should help to consolidate the friendly relations already developed. The United States has supported India's stand in the border conflict with China and has granted valuable assistance, especially by furnishing much-needed military supplies.

The Soviet Union

Two significant facts have shaped India's relations with the Soviet Union since 1947: firstly, the Soviet Union is her neighbor who has a social and political system different from India's; and secondly, India avows a policy of non-alignment and peaceful co-existence. The Soviet Asian republics were invited to send delegates to the unofficial Asian Relations Conference held in New Delhi in 1947 and the invitations were accepted. Several goodwill and cultural delegations have been sent to and received from the Soviet Union. Barter agreements—e.g. in 1949 for the supply of wheat to India and jute and tea to the Soviet Union—and trade agreements have been concluded. Economic and technical assistance has been accepted, though on a smaller scale than from the U.S.A. Statistics published in 1958 revealed that Indo-Soviet trade had increased over fifteenfold since the Agreement of 1954. On February 12, 1960, an Indo-Soviet Cultural and Technical Aid Agreement was signed. It provided for the exchange of scientists, educators, artists, professors and lecturers and for joint research work and the promotion of tourism. Both parties were to encourage the translation of each other's literature, exchange of books and periodicals of a nonpolitical nature, organization of exhibitions and exchange of films, radio and television programs. On several questions, more especially relating to the progress of dependent peoples to self-government and on disarmament, there has been more or less identity of views between the two governments. On the Kashmir issue, the Soviet Union has lent her support to India's stand. Broadly speaking, on how far the United Nations should apply the principle of collective security at the present stage of its development and on the admission of the People's Republic of China to the United Nations, India's views have tallied with those of the Soviet Union.

The question of Hungary (1956) A clash of views between the Indian and Soviet governments has occurred on two questions: When a nationalist rising took place in Hungary in October 1956, the Soviet forces suppressed it. India expressed herself in favor of the Hungarian desire for freedom and against the continuance of the stationing of Soviet forces there. India's condemnation of the Soviet position was, unfortunately, a little belated, and critics in India and abroad were not slow in adversely commenting on India's vote in the United Nations Assembly against a resolution condemning the Soviet Union. The issue is so important that some parts of Prime Minister Nehru's statements on the subject should be cited:

> We are concerned with an attack on freedom anywhere in the world. We are concerned also with strong nations dominating, by armed force, weaker countries. In regard to Hungary, the situation was obscure for some days, and it was only gradually that the story of the tragic events that have taken

place there, became known. From the very beginning, we made it clear that, in our opinion, the people of Hungary should be allowed to determine their future according to their own wishes and that foreign forces should be withdrawn. That has been and is our basic view in regard to Hungary. This has been repeated in the joint statement of the four Prime Ministers (of Indonesia, Burma, Ceylon and India).[74]

> There was a resolution in the United Nations General Assembly in regard to Hungary, sponsored by Pakistan, Cuba, Italy, Peru and Ireland, against which we voted, and as some criticism has been made in regard to our vote on this resolution, I should like to remove any misunderstanding that may have arisen. The resolution was, in our opinion, improperly worded. But the most objectionable part of it demanded that elections should be held in Hungary under the supervision of the United Nations. We took strong exception to this because we felt this was contrary to the Charter and would reduce Hungary to less than a sovereign State. Any acceptance of intervention of this type and foreign supervised elections seemed to us to set a bad precedent which might be utilized in future for intervention in other countries. The resolution was voted paragraph by paragraph. We abstained from voting on all the other parts of the resolution. . . . When the whole resolution including this paragraph was put to the vote, we also voted against it because of that particular paragraph to which we objected strongly.

> This voting on this particular resolution was entirely in consonance with our general policy and instructions. It

[74] *Lok Sabha Debates,* Vol. IX—No. 3, November 16, 1956, cols. 265–7.

seemed to us that this resolution, apart from the basic objections we had to it, would not prove helpful to Hungary at all. We were trying to get the Soviet forces withdrawn from Hungary. What was proposed in the resolution would come in the way of that withdrawal and an attempt thereafter to intervene with armed force would have led to a major conflict. It might well have led to Hungary perishing in the flames of war.

The tragic dramas that have been enacted almost before our eyes, have demonstrated the inherent dangers of a recourse to arms to settle any problem. . . . The recourse to force and the armed intervention in Hungary have not only cost the lives of many brave men and women, but have also checked a progress towards greater freedom which we had welcomed.

. . . .

. . . all these events have powerfully affected the prestige of the Soviet Union in such matters not only in the many countries which are supposed to be uncommitted countries but more in countries and governments which believe in that country, European countries including, if I may say so, the people of the Soviet Union itself.[75]

Resumption of nuclear tests In 1961, when the Soviet Union unilaterally renewed nuclear testing, India condemned it. During his recent visit to the United States, Nehru said in New York on November 5, 1961:

I consider the whole nuclear test business and the hydrogen bomb as evil things. . . . I am dead against any nuclear tests whatever happens. . . . It is obvious that in this particular matter (resumption of nuclear tests by the Soviet Union) the Soviet Union broke

the moratorium, or whatever it is, and therefore they were largely responsible for this new phase.[76]

CRITIQUE

The foreign policy of India has had its critics both within India and abroad. In order to evaluate the policy properly it will be useful to have some idea of these criticisms. They are three: (1) India's policy has not been really non-aligned and independent; it has been, according to some, pro-West, according to others, pro-Soviet; (2) the vital interests of India have not been advanced by the policy which has been followed; and (3) the Indian approach to peace ignores the place of power in politics.

Non-aligned?

Accepting our definition of non-alignment, the criticism that India has not been really non-aligned is meaningless, for you have or have not a military alliance; it is a matter of fact that India has not concluded a military alliance with any country.[77] The criticism itself needs an explanation and this can perhaps be best done by citing some examples.

He [George Meany] "felt stronger than ever that (Nehru) is an agent of the Soviet Union, and I hope to see him and tell him so to his face."[78]

[75] *Ibid.,* November 19, 1956, col. 385.

[76] *New York Times,* international edition, November 6, 1961, p. 1.
[77] The Case of Nepal is *sui generis.* There was an understanding between the governments of Nepal and India that the two governments would consult each other in case of threat to the security of either and devise effective counter-measures. "It was no military alliance." See for details, Nehru's Statement in Rajya Sabha on December 8, 1959, *Rajya Sabha Debates,* cols. 1717–8.
[78] Quoted by Selig S. Harrison, "Nehru's Visit in

. . . with regard to the viewpoint of the Government of India on what it regards as deplorable, the Central People's Government of the People's Republic of China cannot but consider it as having been affected by foreign influences hostile to China in Tibet and hence expresses its deep regret.[79]

"In foreign policy, India is being progressively drawn into the orbit of the Anglo-American bloc."[80]

What the critics really mean is that, though professedly independent, India's foreign policy was in fact pro-Soviet or pro-American. It is interesting to note that India herself sensed this reaction, though she maintained that such criticisms had been made because foreigners could not make out at what we were aiming:

> There was a suspicion in the minds of one group that really we were allied to the other group in secret, though we were trying to hide that fact and the other group thought that we were allied to the first group in secret though we were trying to hide the fact.[81]

It is unnecessary to examine these criticisms here as, from all accounts, India's non-alignment policy which was misunderstood up to 1956 is now clearly understood in the West.[82] With the passage of time both groups have been convinced that India's policy was really independent and indeed that the pursuit of an independent policy by a state like India was advantageous from some points of view.

In June 1956, the then President of the United States, Mr. Eisenhower, at a press conference defended the right of nations to be neutral. He remarked that a decision to keep clear of military alliances could be accepted as natural and even prudent.[83] In the Report of the Central Committee of the Communist Party of the Soviet Union to the 20th Party Congress, the following passages occur:

> The Great Indian Republic has made a big contribution to strengthening peace in Asia and the whole world.
> The tasks confronting the Party in the sphere of foreign policy . . . are:
> To consolidate untiringly the bonds of friendship and co-operation with the Republic of India, Burma, Indonesia . . . to support countries which refuse to be involved in military blocs. . . .[84]

Indian critics of non-alignment strike a somewhat different note: in applying the principle of non-alignment in the case of the U.S.S.R. and China, India has been weak and afraid to take the risk of displeasing them.[85] Thus India's condemnation of Russian action in Hungary in 1956 was so halting and belated that it lost its merit. We were more forthright in condemning British, French and Israeli action in Egypt, and also American and British sanction in West Asia, when troops were landed in Lebanon and Jordan. In the case of Tibet . . . our attitude from the beginning has been in contradiction with

---

Retrospect," *New Republic* (Washington), CXXXV, (December 31, 1956), p. 8.

[79] China's reply (October 30, 1950) to the Indian note on Tibet of October 26, 1950. See Margaret Carlye, *Documents on International Affairs, 1949–50,* London: 1953, pp. 551–2.

[80] *New Times* (Moscow), January 12, 1949, p. 11.

[81] Nehru in the Constituent Assembly (Legislative), December 4, 1947, *Constituent Assembly of India (Legislative) Debates,* con. 14.II.5.47/904, p. 1261.

[82] See Alan de Rusett, "On Understanding Indian Foreign Policy," *International Relations* (London), April, 1959.

[83] Quoted by Hamilton Fish Armstrong in his "Neutrality: Varying Tunes," *Foreign Affairs* (New York), XXXV, October, 1956, p. 57.

[84] Report of the Central Committee of the Communist Party of the Soviet Union to the 20th Party Congress, February 14, 1956, Moscow: 1956, pp. 31 and 47.

[85] See Acharya J. B. Kripalani, "For Principled Neutrality," *Foreign Affairs* (New York), XXXVIII, October, 1959, pp. 46–60.

our avowed principles. It has had the appearance of weakness and opportunism, of purchasing Chinese friendship at the cost of Tibet.[86]

Our survey of India's relations with the U.S.S.R. and China made earlier in this paper would have shown that there is, clearly, substance in this criticism. The only answer to the criticism is the one offered by the critics themselves that "after all India is new to diplomacy, and the world situation is extremely complicated." It is also relevant to note that the critics agree that the principles upon which the Indian policy of non-alignment is based are correct, are generally accepted by the country and are in keeping with the genius of the Indian people.[87]

India's vital interests not advanced

The criticism that India's foreign policy does not advance her vital interests has become somewhat vocal since the news of China's occupation of Indian territory became public in 1959. It may be summarized in the words of Kripalani.

Whatever may have been the failings of the Congress Party government in international affairs, it could always with some justification show that it had added to the prestige and standing of India in the international world. But all this prestige did not advance any vital interests of India or diminish tension on her borders. Our relations with Pakistan are as strained as ever. The Kashmir issue remains internationally confused. In the case of the tiny Portuguese imperial possessions in India, no progress has been made; indeed the

situation has deteriorated. On her northern frontier, India allowed the annihilation of the buffer kingdom of Tibet without a protest; we have recognized the legitimacy of the Chinese claim there. The question of the citizenship of Indian nationals domiciled for decades in Ceylon still hangs fire. There is no improvement of our relations with South Africa.[88]

The facts are not disputed. Naturally the blame is attributed to the policy of the Government, or to its implementation, which has not, in particular, prevented the occupation of one-third of Kashmir, and thousands of square miles of territory by foreign countries. This is all the more so as the Indian people are, to a man, convinced that India's case in Kashmir and in respect of Indian territory taken by China is just without any doubt; the documentation on the subjects is complete.[89]

In the debate in Parliament on China, the Prime Minister confessed that he had not expected there would be aggression on the part of China.[90] It had, however, occurred; what was to be done? He assured Parliament that the government had not neglected the necessary preparations for the defense of India and was confident that under war conditions India would not give in and a united Indian people could throw back the invaders. But war was a terrible thing and should not be lightly resorted to or invited. Negotiation would be tried and he was hopeful that China would realize her folly. Nor was there a mistake, he said, in the policy of non-alignment.

So far as I am concerned and so far as our Government is concerned, our foreign policy is as firm as a rock and it will remain so. The present Govern-

[86] *Ibid.*, p. 58.
[87] *Ibid.*, p. 57.

[88] *Ibid.*, p. 49.
[89] See *White Papers*, published by Ministry of External Affairs, Government of India.
[90] See Nehru's reply to debate in Rajya Sabha on September 10, 1959. See Nehru, *India's Foreign Policy, op. cit.*, p. 348.

ment will hold to non-alignment because it is a matter of principle, not of opportunism or the convenience of the day.[91]

The criticism that the Government has not been able to protect the vital interests of India through its policy is, in reality, bound up with the third criticism to which we have referred, the charge that the Indian approach to peace ignores the place of power in politics, and to this we now turn.

Sanctions

That the Indian approach to peace ignores the critical place of power in politics is pointed out more especially by Western critics who believe in the balance of power as the effective principle in international politics.

This argument has been recently stated admirably by Alan de Rusett: Power held in reserve has been, through history, the central factor in preserving peace. Negotiation and other peaceful means of adjustment of international disputes have always been conditioned by this factor as parties know that, in the last analysis, the relative distribution of power between the parties—including in the estimate of power relations alliances to which the parties are committed or might be committed—will decide the issue. No doubt the balance of power system is not the best way of maintaining peace, a world government being the ideal. But, in the absence of either a balance of power or a world government, the will to negotiate vanishes when all can freely choose between negotiation and the violent achievement of their ends. The courage to trust disappears when the price of miscalculation is total conquest. The Indian approach to peace—the Panch Sheel, the enlargement of the area of peace and emphasis on the role of the United Nations for the

tasks of peace rather than of war—ignores the vital lesson of historical experience.[92]

The Government of India's view, as expressed by its spokesmen, is somewhat as follows: The balance of power, whether it was useful or not to maintain peace in the pre-atomic age, cannot preserve peace in the atomic age. Such precarious peace as it was able to maintain in the seventeenth to nineteenth centuries was due to the prevalence of an intellectual and moral consensus in the European society at that time, and to the existence of some four to six not very unequal Powers with one Power (Britain) who was able, so to say, to keep the balance. These conditions no longer exist with the rise of the Soviet Union and the U.S.A. as Super-Powers, with deep ideological cleavages. Further, the discovery of nuclear weapons, bringing with it what Winston Churchill called "a balance of terror," has made the balance of power entirely outdated. The implications of this, in the context of the theory of the balance of power, have not been adequately realized. The achievement of atomic parity between the Soviet Union and the U.S.A. would help to maintain the balance of power if such parity were an effective deterrent to attack by either. But if it is not an effective deterrent, it may lead to total destruction. In India's view, the possession of nuclear weapons by both the Super-Powers is *not* a clear deterrent. *Prima facie* it would be consoling to think that either party, certain of having to face retaliation if an all-out war is begun by the other, is bound to desist from an attempt which is certain to destroy itself. But a deeper analysis would indicate that a military balance is "a slender reed" to lean upon for two reasons: historically it is an ironical but demonstrable conclusion that nations which have armed themselves to preserve the peace have seldom been able to avoid war if only because reason cannot always control political passions and, even if it does, accidents play a part in events. And, secondly, an atomic stalemate can continue to be a stalemate only

---

[91] *Ibid.*

[92] See Rusett, *op. cit.*

so long as the two Powers who possess the destructive weapons, continue always to be equal in their power. Such an assumption can be valid only if technology is stabilized. But we know for certain that this is far from being the case where weapons development is concerned.

In these circumstances, India would subscribe to the view expressed by the President of the Bandung Conference, Dr. Ali Sastroamidjojo[93] "We know too well from the lessons of history that power politics, with an uneasy balance of power in its wake, cannot guarantee peace but will lead sooner or later to war," which, with the hydrogen bomb may, in Einstein's view, lead to the *annihilation of any life on earth*.[94]

Hence the Indian approach to peace, which is to explore more fully than was perhaps necessary in an earlier age, the potentialities of negotiation and other means of peaceful settlement of conflict and to promote the active peaceful co-operation between states and agreements on non-aggression and mutual respect. If it be asked "Is your system likely to succeed, can you rely on it?" the answer, in the words of India's spokesman in the United Nations General Assembly, Mr. Krishna Menon, is:

With great respect, we are entitled to ask: have the other systems succeeded? Can anybody turn round to us and say that the doctrine of the balance of power is more likely to help us, or to succeed—that doctrine which is the legacy of Metternich, of Castlereagh and of Talleyrand, which wrecked the principle of universalism and culminated in the war of 1914, and which to this day is making its incursions into international affairs? I am reminded of the statement of a great Frenchman, Rousseau, who said that the

strongest is never strong enough to be always master unless he transfers strength into right and obedience into duty.[95]

This answer is not satisfying: at best it only means that one is not sure if either the balance of power, or the alternative offered by India can deliver the goods. The India-China dispute compels a rethinking of what India can do or suggest to do if a party to a dispute, in spite of the justice of the case of its opponent, is determined to hold on to the fruits of its aggression.

It appears to me that India's foreign policy is on the cross-roads, not in the sense in which some members of the Indian Parliament viewed it—substitution of alignment for non-alignment—but in the more fundamental sense of finding adequate sanctions for a policy based on Panch Sheel. A vicious circle, so to say, develops in the argument: The application of force in a nuclear age to achieve peace, is a contradiction in terms in so far as it may lead to total destruction; it is against the principle of equality of means and ends. A limited war, it is agreed by experts, has the potentiality of developing into a global war. If an aggressor is amenable to reason, negotiation will succeed; if he is not, he gets away with the fruits of his aggression, and therefore the application of force is called for to prevent a result which is undesirable. It seems that the vicious circle may be broken on one difficult assumption only. That assumption is that mankind, groping in the dark for a solution, may accept, in William James' telling phrase, a moral alternative to war, the alternative preached and practiced by Mahatma Gandhi and a number of idealists before him; non-violence, i.e. resisting force by love, and by self-sacrifice. A fearless nation believing in non-violence, prepared for annihilation but unwilling to yield to aggression, can set the example of such a moral alternative.

[93] See text of his speech in *Asian-African Conference*, issued by Information Service of Indonesia, Embassy of Indonesia, New Delhi: 1955, p. 34.

[94] *New York Times*, February 13, 1950.

[95] Krishna Menon's speech in U. N. General Assembly on October 4, 1955. *Official Records*, United Nations General Assembly, tenth session, 533rd plenary meeting, p. 244.

Nehru has, however, for understandable reasons, declared that as a statesman in charge of government he is not prepared to take the risks involved in the adoption of non-violence as a way of resolving international disputes. Nevertheless, as Michael Brecher rightly points out, the non-violent tradition is an integral part of the thinking of Indian leaders and "is inevitably reflected in their attitude to foreign affairs."[96] The Indian approach to war and peace, developed earlier in this paper, emphasizing peaceful means to maintain peace, is a reflection of this attitude. "The most striking example of its influence is Delhi's restraint on the problem of Goa."[97] But the achievements of a partial adoption of non-violence cannot be as satisfying as the achievements of violence in an earlier age or as the achievements of non-violence possible according to its exponents. Indian critics, who say that the Government of India has failed to advance vital national interests by its policy, as well as the government, are certainly aware of the central problem we

[96] Michael Brecher, *India's Foreign Policy: An Interpretation,* Secretariat Paper No. 1, prepared for the Thirteenth Conference of the Institute of Pacific Relations, Institute of Pacific Relations, (N.Y.).

[97] One week after this paper was sent to the editor, Goa was taken by India through what the Government has officially termed police action; fighting with the Portuguese troops lasted not much more than one day and Goa has now become part of India. The Government in a public statement explained that it had taken this action with great pain and only after it was satisfied that Portugal, even after she had been advised by her allies, would not enter into negotiations on the subject, and that they were under great pressure from public opinion at home. The Indian people believe that Goa is physically a part of India. Colonialism is permanent aggression—the United Nations General Assembly has officially refused to consider Goa as part of metropolitan Portugal and had listed it as a non-self-governing territory—and the feeling in India was unanimous that the independence of India would be incomplete so long as Goa remained in the hands of a foreign Power, and could be used by enemies in the event of war. It need only be added that in this particular instance, the dilemma we have posed at the end of this paragraph was solved by the Government by deciding to use force. At the same time the Prime Minister has categorically declared that India's foreign policy with its reliance on peaceful means remains unchanged.

have posed; until a decision is taken to use physical or moral force, either of which has incalculable risks, the results must necessarily be unsatisfying.

An assessment

It seems true, therefore, that in some respects the vital interests of India have not been adequately advanced by our foreign policy and its implementation—a criticism which will apply with equal force to the foreign policies of many aligned nations. It is, however, too one-sided and pessimistic a conclusion that India's foreign policy has no achievements to its credit. Only history can measure the success which has attended the foreign policy of a country during a particular period. Fifteen years are in any case too brief a period for taking stock of a dynamic and revolutionary situation. Further, it is an obvious fact that such success as any country sees in the fulfillment of her aims is due to the co-operation of several like-minded states and to several other factors among which her effort is just one. Viewed against this background, several policies supported by India have gained wide acceptance. There is a growing realization of the urgency of international action in developing underdeveloped countries, economically and socially; there is increasing participation of Asian and African states in international counsels; and world public opinion has almost unanimously accepted the undesirability of colonialism and racialism. Again, India can have legitimate satisfaction that she is now widely trusted in international councils. The invitation to her by the parties concerned to be Chairman of the Neutral Nations Repatriation Commission in Korea and of the International Armistice and Supervisory Commissions in Vietnam, Cambodia and Laos are proof of this. On account of the greater trust she commands, she has been able to contribute a little to whatever reduction of international tensions has been possible. Above all, India has been able to secure considerable international assistance by way of capital aid and technical help for development.

While India's efforts in some directions of her foreign policy are bearing fruit, Korea, Vietnam, Palestine, Formosa and Berlin remind us that there are still many trouble spots in Asia and elsewhere. Chinese aggression on Indian soil has to be repelled. Disarmament and the banning of hydrogen bomb explosions are yet to be agreed upon; there is still much to be done to establish international responsibility for has-

tening the development of dependent peoples to self-government; racialism remains alive, more particularly in Africa; and we are still far away from an assurance of world peace. The mere enumeration of these—and there are many other unsolved problems—only shows that problems of international relations have a way of creating new ones, even in the course of our partially solving an old one, and need continued vigilance and effort for their satisfactory solution.

BIBLIOGRAPHY

Author's Suggestions

Berkes, Ross N. and Bedi, Mohinder S. *The Diplomacy of India: India's Foreign Policy in the United Nations.* Stanford: Stanford University Press, 1958.

India, Lok Sabha, Secretariat. *Foreign Policy of India: Texts of Documents, 1947–1959.* 2nd ed. New Delhi: 1959.

Indian Council of World Affairs. *India and the United Nations: Report of a Study Group Set up by the Indian Council of World Affairs.* New York: Manhattan Publishing Co., 1957.

Karunakaran, K. P. *India in World Affairs, August 1947–January 1950.* Bombay: Oxford University Press, 1952.

Karunakaran, K. P. *India in World Affairs,* *February 1950–December 1953.* Bombay: Oxford University Press, 1958.

Kundra, Jagdish Chandra. *Indian Foreign Policy, 1947–1954: A Study of Relations with the Western Bloc.* Groningen: J. B. Wolters, 1955.

Nehru, Jawaharlal. *India's Foreign Policy: Selected Speeches, September 1946–April 1961.* Delhi: Publications Division, Ministry of Information and Broadcasting, 1961.

Talbot, Phillips and Poplai, S. L. *India and America.* New York: Harper, 1958.

Das Gupta, Jyoti Bhusan. *Indo-Pakistan Relations, 1947–1955.* Amsterdam: Djambatan, 1958.

ABOUT THE AUTHOR

YOSHIHIKO SEKI has spent his life in academic pursuits and his contributions have been numerous in this field. He was graduated from Tokyo University in 1936. He presently holds the position of Lecturer at Tokyo University and Full Professor at Tokyo Metropolitan University. His published works, in Japanese, include *British Socialism* and *Socialist Policy of the British Labour Party*. An article in English on "New Trends in Japanese Socialism" appears in the *Japan Quarterly*, Vol. VII, Number 2.

ABOUT THE CHAPTER

A nation is largely the product of its physical environment, its cultural make-up and its historical development. Mr. Seki considers each of these in turn as he introduces us to the role of Japan in international affairs. He gives careful attention to the unique geographic position of this island nation, to the cultural homogeneity of her people, and to her historical traditions which make her actions in international affairs understandable.

The author then turns to an assessment of Japan's current national power with special attention to the thriving economy of the nation. The nature of Japan's military power and the political stability of the nation are also examined. In his discussion of foreign policy formation the author considers both the formal institutions and the role played by public opinion.

Professor Seki concludes his chapter with an analysis of a number of specific foreign policy problems which confront Japan and gives a brief assessment of the difficult choices which face the nation in the field of national security. He notes the general agreement in Japan on the need to promote the nation's prosperity and security. The real conflict centers around "the methods of guarding the national interest."

18

THE FOREIGN POLICY OF JAPAN

YOSHIHIKO SEKI

Tokyo Metropolitan University

GEOGRAPHICAL AND CULTURAL FACTORS

Location and size

Japan is often compared geographically with England which is located at the opposite side of the Eurasian continent. They are both island kingdoms in the temperate zone having similar climatic conditions. This is, however, just about as far as one can go in pointing out the similarities between the two countries.

Examine the map of the world. You see the Empire of Japan curving along the sea coast of East Asia and stretching down as far south as the Ryukyu Islands. The country's northernmost tip, Hokkaido, reaches to latitude 40. The total distance from the northern tip to the southern tip comes close to the distance be-

tween New England and the State of Florida. As far as the domination of the sea is concerned, the situation of Japan in relation to the Pacific Ocean is therefore a great deal more important than that of England in relation to the Atlantic Ocean. If the East Asian countries should ever start haggling with the countries on the other side of the Pacific over the command of the ocean, Japan could not possibly avoid getting involved in the turmoil.

The term, Far East, was created in Europe. It implies that Japan actually was the country farthest away from Europe which was the center of international politics, at least till the end of the 19th century. This very fact enabled Japan to close her outward doors and thereafter to concentrate mainly on Asia, without becoming entangled in international affairs. Besides being isolated from Europe, Japan is cut off from Asia proper by the Straits of Chosen. These are some hundred miles wide—roughly six times as wide as the Straits of Dover which separate England and the European Continent. Moreover, the Straits of Chosen make up only one sixth of the total distance between Japan and China, the central axis of East Asia.

Prior to the invention of the steam engine, communication between Japan and the Asian continent was attended by many dangers. While national prestige was on the upswing, the governing classes encouraged more vigorous intercourse with Korea and East China. Nevertheless private communication on a people-to-people basis presented far greater difficulty between Japan and Asia proper, than was true between nations of Europe. This lack of opportunity for contact with peoples of different tongues and customs has created a rather intense curiosity towards foreigners and the tendency to have one-sided viewpoints on international problems.

The size of a country is another important factor influencing its international position. Japan consists of four main islands and many smaller adjacent ones. The total area, including the Ryukyu Islands and the Bonin Islands amounts to some 142,641 square miles. This is smaller than the State of California, though a little larger than England or Italy. Besides, Japan's mountains take up the greater part of the land mass, leaving only about 15 percent of the total area available for cultivation.

Though the abundant rapid streams provide rich water resources, there are no other power sources except coal. Mineral resources are poor. Moreover, Japan does not produce cotton, wool, rubber, or sugar. Just imagine, more than 92,000,000 people living in this small, resourceless land. (The population reached the mark of 30,000,000 even one century ago.) It is one of the most densely populated countries of the world. That Japan is small in size, that the four islands are strung together close enough for the inhabitants to commute quite freely and that it is isolated from the continent, all these factors helped brew and strengthen the racial homogeneity of the Japanese people.

A country of limited size is generally vulnerable to foreign aggression. Unlike Russia, Japan cannot possibly lure an enemy into its own territory to deliver a fatal blow. On the contrary, such an attempt would mean the immediate and total crumbling of its power to resist. In the past, Japan always sent her troops out of the country to carry out war. This, naturally, forced her to keep the military forces, both the army and the navy, constantly strong. Undoubtedly, it was a great strain on a resourceless country like Japan to maintain both land and sea forces strong and in tip-top condition for action. Consequently, the well-being of the people was sacrificed to achieve this end. As a result, the people began to think that the standard of living could be raised only by winning an aggressive war.

Religion

The homogeneity of the Japanese people is found not only in race and language, but also in religion. Shintoism has been the official religion of Japan; its essence is spirit worship. In ancient times, natural disasters were considered to be the deeds of *Kami* ("Gods" in English but, more properly, "Superiors"), which the people idolized and worshipped in the hope of evading such disasters. *Kami,* they thought, existed in everything: on the top of a mountain, in houses and animals. A man after his death was thought to become one. All these concepts led to the ritual of ancestor worship. Each family, it was believed, possessed its own *Kami* and so did each clan. The Great Shrine of Ise, which had been dedicated to the *Kami* of the Imperial Clan, namely the Yamato Kingdom, eventually became the highest among the *Kami* and continued, thereafter, to hold sway over the entire people of Japan.

The period from the sixth to the eighth century A.D. saw active communication between Japan and China, thereby bringing into Japan many cultural imports of foreign character. Among these was Buddhism.

From the early stages of its introduction into Japan, Buddhism managed to merge with Shintoism quite successfully. It was taught that the *Kami* of Shintoism were a mere transfiguration of those of Buddhism. Therefore, there was no contradiction at all between the two. Consequently, no one thought it wrong

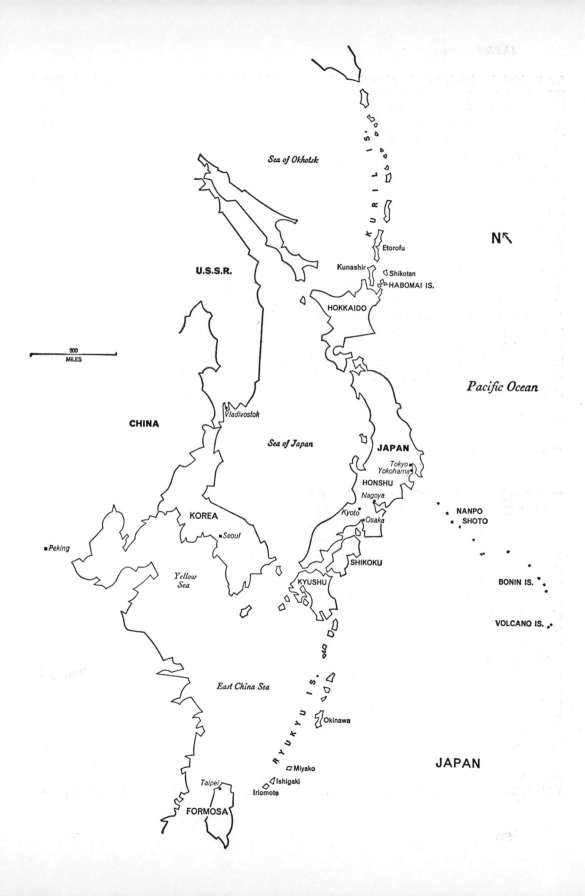

Sea of Okhotsk

KURIL IS.

N

U.S.S.R.

Etorofu

Kunashir

Shikotan

HABOMAI IS.

HOKKAIDO

Pacific Ocean

300
MILES

Vladivostok

CHINA

Sea of Japan

JAPAN

Tokyo

Yokohama

HONSHU

Nagoya

KOREA

Kyoto

NANPO
SHOTO

Osaka

Peking

Seoul

Yellow
Sea

SHIKOKU

BONIN IS.

KYUSHU

VOLCANO IS.

East China Sea

RYUKYU IS.

Okinawa

JAPAN

Miyako

Taipei

Ishigaki

Iriomote

FORMOSA

for Buddhistic rituals to take place in a holy Shintoist shrine. Many a Japanese has belonged to a Buddhist sect, while being a faithful Shintoist. Thus, Buddhism and Shintoism existed side by side without too obvious antagonism or persecution.

Along with Buddhism came another significant import: Confucianism. This is more a code of social ethics than a religion. Its original characteristic, i.e. advocation of the family system based on the concept of filial piety toward parents, gradually was transformed in the feudal age into a code of strict obedience to feudal lords and, in general, all seniors. Furthermore, it strengthened the class distinctions characteristic of feudalism. Thus, there was formed in the country of Japan a people of incomparable cohesion and virtually unparalleled racial, linguistic and religious homogeneity. Japan had developed a culturally unified people centuries before it established a politically modern state.

General outlook

How then have such traditions merged into the political life of the Japanese? First, owing to the hybrid nature of their culture, the Japanese do not regard it to be superior to others. Nor do they have any feeling of religious mission toward foreign countries, comparable to that of the Jew, or the Pan-Slavism of the Russian. Despite political command over its colonies prior to the war, Japan never interfered in the religious or cultural affairs of these countries.

The Japanese never attempted to conquer nature, but rather tried to learn how to adjust themselves to it. Rather than denying and opposing the strong or the superior, they obeyed it and absorbed from it whatever they felt digestible. Thus they learned to utilize foreign civilizations which were superior, by skillfully adapting them to their own tradition. This trend was evident when Japan imported from China Buddhism, Confucianism and various

political systems and also when the Japanese reopened their eyes in the middle of the 19th century toward Western culture. No other nation in the East has ever been under such strong influence of the West nor assimilated so cleverly the impact from abroad.

Secondly, since the nature of Japanese culture is intuitive and contemplative, the Japanese often react emotionally towards political issues. Shintoism denies strongly any rational approach but rather points the way to adjust to nature. Buddhism, too, puts more emphasis on the subjugation of confronting subjects and objects through intuitive thinking, rather than pointing the way to philosophical thinking. In dealing with a political problem, the aesthetic and speculative nature of Japanese culture tends to give more emphasis to the problem of emotional balance than to clarifying the fundamental issues through reasonable thinking. In consequence, public affairs are in many cases resolved in the midst of moody, impulsive excitement.

Thirdly, the general populace of Japan is realistic. To the Japanese, neither Buddhism nor Shintoism is considered to be anything more than a social code. In this respect, they are perhaps the most secular people. But at the same time, the Japanese react very strongly to any kind of humiliation. As Ruth Benedict states in her *The Chrysanthemum and the Sword,* the moral concept of the Japanese is based not on the feeling of guilt but rather on the sense of disgrace. As long as fair profit in life is possible and unless their daily life is somehow disturbed, the Japanese are mostly indifferent to internal politics or foreign relations. Once, however, the country has suffered an affront, they will react to it immediately, and in most cases violently.

Fourthly, the Japanese possess culturally intimate feelings toward China. Formerly the Chinese classics were taught in schools just as the Greek and Latin classics were in the West. The older generations, especially, feel this way. This is probably why they do not have any ill feelings toward Communist China, while they have no friendly feelings toward Russia.

Lastly, probably the most important point is

that in Japan the concept of the personal dignity of each individual does not have as much weight as it does in the West. Certainly, Buddhism taught mercy and the equality of human beings. But it does not distinguish between men and animals. Confucianism was in principle a social moral code, based on the concept of filial piety. But soon it began to pave the way to complete submission to political authority.

The absence of the concept of individual rights has wiped away the possibility of social equality among the people. Human relations have been looked upon vertically rather than horizontally, that is in terms of class or rank differences. This fact alone not only makes it quite hard for a democratic social system to ripen in Japan, but it also makes association with foreign nations on strictly equal terms extremely difficult. In the minds of the Japanese, both an inferiority and superiority complex vis-à-vis foreign countries exist side by side.

HISTORY OF JAPAN'S FOREIGN POLICY

The formation of the modern state

In 1603 the political center of Japan moved northward to Yedo (now Tokyo), where the Tokugawa Shogunate established its administration. For about two centuries thereafter Japan was governed by the Tokugawas, sealed in a feudal system and separated from the rest of the world. This state of affairs lasted until the so-called Meiji Restoration, when some lower class samurai from the western provinces of Japan attempted to tear down the long entrenched feudal regime. On succeeding, they established a modern nation state. Under the influence of classical history scholars, the samurai advocated the return of the reins of government to the Emperor and, at the same time, insisted on the expulsion of foreigners from the country.

In 1854 the Shogunate, pressured by America, Russia, and Great Britain, was compelled to open up the doors of the country to the world. This attitude encountered roaring opposition from those in favor of the Restoration who considered such a policy a national humiliation. By 1867, however, most of the Restorationists, having successfully accomplished their initial purpose, now reversed themselves and began to support the opening of the country more realistically. They recognized the astonishing strength of the foreigners and concluded that it was no longer possible to maintain Japan's independence just by keeping it free from foreign influences.

This was the beginning of their effort to strive for national independence not merely by accepting whatever foreign civilizations could offer, but rather by actively approaching these civilizations and learning from them the latest academic, technological, and industrial knowledge of the West. In the face of the colonial policies of the Western countries, Japan directed an all-out effort toward industrial development and toward re-inforced armaments.

The samurai had no sooner succeeded in establishing a centralized government and unifying the state, than they at once turned to promoting more vigorous assimilation of Western civilization. Of all the foreign countries then in communication with Japan, none had a stronger influence on the political leaders of Japan than Germany, which had just achieved statehood under the leadership of Prussia. Japan learned a great deal from that absolute monarchy, especially in the fields of military affairs, education, and constitutional law.

What the leaders were concerned about was the modernization of the state from *above;* the encouragement of industries by the state, the spread of education, and the establishment of military forces. The tax law was revised so that the farmers mainly paid, in the form of tax, the expenses for education and the military forces. The state itself engaged in the textile, iron, and ship-building industries, which later were turned over to private companies in an attempt to encourage national industries.

These efforts toward building up a nation

state reflected on the diplomacy of Japan. Soon after the Meiji government was established, certain elements believed that a campaign should be undertaken against Korea for the purpose of enhancing the national glory. But the majority were of the opinion that Japan's national strength should be built up before such an attempt was made. Thus, the northern and the southern boundaries were fixed between China and Russia, and Japan began to engage in active diplomatic intercourse and trade with foreign countries. All in all, every effort was made to strengthen national prestige merely to keep pace with the rest of the world.

The most important and first major diplomatic problem requiring settlement by the Meiji government was the revision of the unfair commercial treaties which the Tokugawa Shogunate had previously been forced to conclude with foreign countries. The treaties impaired customs autonomy and granted extraterritorial rights to Western countries. Particularly, the grant of extraterritorial rights was considered a national disgrace and every effort was made by the government to revise the treaties. The negotiations reached a deadlock many times, and sometimes they had to be altogether abandoned. In 1894, however, the government achieved success when it revised the treaty with Great Britain and it did not take very long before the rest of the countries followed suit. Thus, by 1911, customs autonomy was recovered and all of the commercial treaties, long the target of public criticism, were finally revised.

Imperialistic expansion

Just as the stability of the Low Countries was important to the security of Great Britain, Korea meant a great deal to the well-being of Japan. Unlike Japan, Korea, when it was pressed by invaders, divided into two forces: progressive pro-revolutionists and feudalistic anti-revolutionists. The former asked Japan for assistance and the latter turned to China for

help. When minor internal crises broke out, as they did, China did not waste a second to send a great army into Korea to suppress them. Japan, on the other hand, was only concerned that Korea might be controlled by China. On detecting that America was rather in favor of the Japanese position, Japan declared war against China in 1894.

The Sino-Japanese War lasted for a year, ending in 1895. Victory in this war brought Japan Formosa and the Liaotung Peninsula along with reparations. The peace treaty also forced China to acknowledge the independence of Korea. Ultimately, however, Japan had to give up the Liaotung Peninsula under the pressure of Russia, Germany, and France. This so-called Triple Intervention implanted in the mind of the Japanese a sense of deep humiliation. The whole nation criticized the government for its weakness. The leaders were, on the other hand, convinced that under the circumstances, Japan had better accept the humiliation, awaiting some future revenge.

War with Russia   Russia, having opposed Japan's position toward China by the Triple Intervention, dispatched a large army into Manchuria, even after the suppression of the Boxer Rebellion. Furthermore, she attempted to threaten the independence of Korea. In Japan, on the other hand, some leaders were of the opinion that an agreement should be reached in such a way as to put Manchuria and Korea under the control of Russia and Japan, respectively.

But the central government recognized the necessity of balancing powers in order to challenge the strength of Czarist Russia. Japan, therefore, concluded an alliance with Great Britain in January, 1902. If either party became involved in a war—for Japan it was most likely with Russia—the other party would prevent other nations from attacking its ally. Japan was thus protected from becoming isolated in the event of war against Russia. Russia, however, showed no intention of pulling its army out of Manchuria and even began to threaten the peace in Korea.

War was declared against Russia in 1904.

Japan threw everything it had into the game and managed to come through with a victory. But there is no doubt that it was certainly a once-in-a-lifetime trial for the people of Japan. The Treaty of Portsmouth was signed in 1905, and Japan acquired the southern half of Sakhalin, leaseholds to Kwantung province and various Russian railway and mining rights in southern Manchuria. Japan's paramount position was also conceded. The overall outcome of the Portsmouth Treaty, however, did not satisfy the general public of Japan who had overestimated the victory. The government, consequently, was subjected to severe, thundering protests and demonstrations. But it stood steadfastly by its initial policy.

Other military successes   In 1905, Korea became Japan's protectorate and was annexed to the Empire in August, 1910. Thus, Korea which had been, since the earliest part of the Meiji period, one of the most important areas for the security of Japan finally came firmly under the control of the Empire.

When the First World War broke out in 1914, Japan declared war against Germany in consequence of the Anglo-Japanese Alliance and seized Kiaochow Territory—Germany's base in the Far East—Tsingtao and the island colonies of Germany in the Pacific Ocean. While the European countries were preoccupied with the gigantic struggle in Europe, Japan presented China with the so-called Twenty-One Demands. These demands confirmed Japan's newly won position in Shantung Province—which had previously been under the control of Germany—a 90-year extension of the leaseholds to Port Arthur (Lüshun) and Talien (Dairen) and territorial rights in Northern China, Manchuria, and also in Mongolia. Thereafter, by concluding an alliance with Russia, Japan tried to solidify its control over China.

Japan's triumphant victory in the Russo-Japanese War greatly astonished and impressed the Asian peoples. Japan showed the world for the first time that an Asian state could overpower a Western state. Postwar Japan proved its power to be equal to the Western imperial-istic countries; but, at the same time, Japan disappointed the Asian peoples through its China policies which were none the better for the change. There is not much doubt that the wars against Russia and China were indispensable for the stabilization of Korea, and a necessary evil for maintaining Japan's independence.

Japan's victories in these two major wars deprived her people of the virtue of modesty and replaced it with a Big-Power complex. Economically, Japan was beginning to expose its imperialistic character by gradually expanding its territory to secure markets for its growing mass capital. The Southern Manchuria Railway Company, which was established after the Russo-Japanese War, together with the leaseholds to Manchuria, became stepping-stones for Japan's future political and economic advance into Manchuria.

Period of choice

Internal developments   After the First World War, Japan's industrial power made great strides and the country entered a period of economic maturity. Industrial development, however, brought along with it a rise of a new proletariat and, consequently, a socialistic movement. Besides, the democratic ideas of America and Great Britain also were flowing in as a result of Japan's participation in the First World War as one of the allies bearing the slogan "Make the world safe for democracy."

Up to the end of the Russo-Japanese War, Japan, whose leaders and general public were firmly cemented together by the Bushido spirit —that mixture of Shintoist ideas, Confucianism, and Zen—was only striving to join the first-class Powers of the world. But as those leaders left the scene, Japan moved into a period of spiritual vacuum. Public opinion concerning the future course of Japan was divided into two groups: pro-Anglo-Saxon and pro-democratic, and anti-Anglo-Saxon and anti-democratic. The influence of the democratic and socialistic ideas was manifested in the two-party system of national politics which appeared between 1924 and 1932.

In 1928, members of the House of Representatives were elected by general suffrage for the first time. The Meiji Constitution had provided that the Cabinet was to be responsible not to the Diet but to the Emperor. Likewise, the military was directly connected with the Emperor instead of being placed under the control of the Cabinet. Under these circumstances, Japan managed to form, in a short period of time, the broadest possible democratic political system.

The two major political parties then ruling the country were the Seiyukai and the Kenseikai (later Minseito). The former, supported mainly by farmers, was comparatively anti-democratic in character and stood for expansionist foreign policies, while the latter, firmly rooted in cities, stood for comparatively prodemocratic ideas and took up milder policies in line with the idea of international co-operation.

Shidehara diplomacy   Shidehara diplomacy, based on the policies of the Minseito, represented Japan's foreign policy for a longer period. Prior to the formation of party cabinets, Japan had become a permanent member of the Council of the League of Nations and had returned Kiaochow Bay to China. Japan also signed the Nine Power Treaty by which all the signatories agreed to respect the independence, sovereignty, and territorial integrity of China. In the Four Power Treaty, Japan, along with the United States, Great Britain, and France, agreed to respect their respective rights in relation to other insular possessions and insular dominions in the Pacific. At the Washington Conference, Japan conceded its claim and consented to reduce its capital ships.

Shidehara diplomacy kept on pushing forward its basic principle of promoting straightforward, friendly relations with all foreign countries on the ground that any international problem was essentially a question of morality. Japan stopped interfering in China and favored China's nationalistic movement. It with-drew the army from northern Sakhalin and concluded a pact with Soviet Russia in an effort to restore diplomatic relations with that country. It went as far as actively reducing Japan's army and signing the London Disarmament Treaty, notwithstanding the booming opposition of the navy and the elder statesmen as well.

But, this trend did not necessarily reflect the internal political state of affairs. The Seiyukai cabinet (April, 1927–July, 1929) was still representing the expansionist forces. When the Chang Tsolin Incident broke out, it favored those who were responsible for the incident. But the general state of public opinion at the time is revealed in the fact that even the Seiyukai cabinet sent its representatives to the conference on the Anti-War Pact in Paris.

Thus, after the First World War, Japan stood at the crossroads of two courses: to switch to a policy of international co-operation or to stick to conventional expansionism. The prevailing mood of peace and democracy helped, even for a short time, to promote the policy of international co-operation and favoring China's nationalistic movements. But in 1931, Japan made that ill-fated choice of going to war and began walking the path to total destruction.

The downfall of the Empire

The period from 1931 to 1945 witnessed Japan's reckless attempt to expand its territory without, beforehand, settling its internal disorders. Eventually it saw the fatal downfall of the Empire of Japan after the aimless war against America. Japan was aware that China's nationalist movement, growing after the successful revolution, might, by the force of circumstances, threaten Japan's rights and interests in Manchuria. In 1931 the Japanese army attacked Chinese forces in Manchuria. This action was taken independently by the army stationed there, without any order from Tokyo. This Manchurian Incident resulted in the formation of a puppet government, Manchukuo.

From the beginning, the Japanese government was literally dragged into this incident by the militarists and could do no better than withdraw from the League of Nations and from the Washington Treaty. Japan became completely isolated from the Anglo-American Powers and, instead, joined hands with Nazi Germany. After the successful conquest of Manchuria, the militarists furthered their ambition of marching into northern China. Again without consulting the central government in Tokyo, they cooked up an incident and expanded over central and southern China.

When the Second World War broke out in Europe in 1939, Japan decided not to intervene in the struggle. But when France was shattered by the so-called blitzkrieg tactics of Hitler, Japan did not dare waste the chance and immediately invaded French Indochina. The Triple Alliance between Japan, Italy, and Germany followed. Despite the widely extended battle front, Japan's ambition of knocking China out never materialized. If Japan had withdrawn the army from China and concluded a peace treaty with Chiang Kai-shek's nationalist regime, Japan could have secured its territories and have managed to survive thereafter. But the militarists would have never countenanced such action just for the sake of their honor. Thus the worst came. The frantic militarists of Japan went into an absolutely suicidal and hopeless war against America just to suffer, in the end, a complete and decisive defeat.

The militarists take over It would be extremely difficult to give a rational explanation of Japan's foreign policy during that period. Unlike Nazi Germany whose expansionist policy was practiced on the basis of a consistent blueprint by Hitler himself, Japan's expansionism had no unified principle. It is understandable, though not right and proper, that the Japanese militarists reacted rather sensitively to China's threat against Manchuria, which had a considerable weight in the national defense policy of Japan.

But the expansionist policy taken by the military was generated by another motive: an attempt to accomplish domestic reform by way of foreign policies. In other words, young officers, disgusted with the deteriorating party politics and the impoverished conditions of the rural communities, took such radical measures as assassinating politicians and businessmen in an effort to reform Japan into a militaristic, despotic state. Unable to cope with the increasing pressure by the militarists, the upper circles produced a government consisting of senior statesmen who were not connected with any political parties. But that was still far from what the young militarists demanded.

The militarists at first had attempted to generate a feeling of national danger among the people. Then they established Manchukuo. This, they figured, would put pressure on Japan to bring about internal reform. Those who were fed up with the incompetence of party politics welcomed this policy and eagerly supported it. Some liberal party politicians resisted the trend, but to no avail. Every order dispatched by the central government contrary to an expansionist policy was ignored by the troops stationed in China.

The resulting disunity was not by any means peculiar to the relationship between the military and the civilian government. Oddly enough, it also existed between the army and the navy. The latter was always critical of the China policies taken by the former. Even within the army, real power was in the hands of the field officers, who were not necessarily bound together by any unified thought. The result was that Japan's political system became entirely irresponsible.

General characteristics of Japanese policy
On careful observation of the history of Japan, as I have outlined it so far, one notices several vitally important points. First, the Japanese public does not necessarily possess a proper understanding of international issues. That they opposed the retrocession of Liaotung, resulting from the Triple Intervention, and the foreign policies of the government in connection with the Portsmouth Treaty, only proves their overestimation of Japan's power. When the

country was on the way to conquering China after the Manchurian Incident, the people somehow supported the move, though rather passively, and consequently doomed it to failure. The political leaders of the Meiji period fully understood the nature of international political issues. They took measures proportional to Japan's power. Regrettably, this was not the case with the people. An emotional people, lacking rational knowledge, often tends to make serious mistakes in dealing with international problems.

Secondly, Japan's relations with Korea and China seem to have been rather a fatal error. China was an indispensable export market and source of raw materials for Japan. Such being the case, it was unfortunate for Japan that China was carved up and divided among the Big Powers of the world. It was indeed vital to Japan to advance into China and Korea if only to compete with other imperialistic countries and survive. But while doing so, the Meiji government skillfully adopted a policy of befriending distant states and antagonizing neighbors. For instance, at the time of the Sino-Japanese War, Japan secured America's friendship before plunging into war. Before declaring war against Russia, the Japanese were careful enough to conclude an alliance with Great Britain.

After 1931, however, Japan, notwithstanding her own internal disorders, did not bother to assist the Chinese in their nationalistic movement, nor did she strive to secure a *modus vivendi* between Japan and China. On the contrary, Japan attempted to invade China, having America and other Western countries against her, and failed. This was indeed the result of a Big-Power complex, arrogance, and the lack of a proper estimate of Japan's ability.

Japan has a lot to learn from her past experiences. While there is a Japanese saying which goes, "Once bitten, twice shy," it may be even more dangerous to fall so far back into extreme negativism as to withdraw from all external relations by stubbornly overguarding against repeating the same mistake. In the past, Japan overestimated her ability. But are we not, right now, underestimating what we have to do and what we can do?

EVALUATION OF JAPAN'S NATIONAL POWER

The international situation of postwar Japan

When the Japanese, who had always been taught that Japan was invincible (the Divine Land), found themselves completely defeated at the end of the Second World War, the overwhelming majority realized that Japan must not get involved in another war. As a reaction to the defeated imperialistic policy, the people began to withdraw from international politics. The six-year occupation period intensified this reaction. Yet, the realities of world power politics did not permit Japan to remain idle very long. When Japan, the central Power of prewar East Asia, collapsed, creating a vacuum in the balance of power, the United States and the Soviet Union, as the world's Big Two, took over. Japan moved under the influence of the United States, while China and North Korea joined the Soviet bloc.

As mentioned earlier, Japan is located in a strategically important area of the West Pacific. If Japan were a tiny, weak country, it could, to a certain extent, remain aloof from the complications of the Cold War. But Japan is by no means a small country, nor is it economically weak. At least foreigners do not think so. Listen, for example, to an American, George Kennan, who said:

> . . . In a day when large-scale warfare has become a matter of highly complicated and expensive weapons and of central control over great masses of manpower, military strength on a major scale, and particularly strength of an amphibious nature, capable of reaching our homeland and disputing our power within it, can be

produced only in a limited number of parts of the globe.[1]

He goes on further and says that there are only four such points on earth, one of which is Japan. Whether or not this is fact, at least the American people seem to think that Japan will play an important role in the power politics of the Cold War.

Japan is as important to the Soviet Union as it is to the United States. As far back as 1922, the Soviet Communist Party and Comintern already had pointed out the vital importance of the revolution in Japan in their plans to communize Asia. Even after the Second World War, the Soviet Union has kept up its effort to disrupt the peace in Japan and, specifically, to drive the United States armed forces from Japan. In 1950, the Cominform ordered the Communist Party to concentrate on pushing the United States armed forces out of Japan and try to lure the Japanese into the Soviet bloc. Later in 1958, the Soviet Government shifted its policy, this time endeavoring to neutralize Japan first. Accordingly, since that time, the Soviet Union has been proposing and advocating a policy of neutralization for the Japanese Government.[2] It is not necessary to explain that, for the Soviet Union, the neutralization of Japan is the shortest and most direct way to communize it. In any case, the degree of Soviet pressure only proves how important Japan really is to Russia.

The decisive factor in raising Japan's international position so rapidly was the communization of China. If the Chiang Kai-shek Government had continued to control the Chinese Continent, the Cold War in Asia would not have become as critical as it is at present. Consequently, Japan would probably never have been considered so important a country by the United States.

[1] George Kennan, *Realities of American Foreign Policy*, Princeton: Princeton University Press, 1954, pp. 63–64.
[2] For example, the memorandum handed over by Soviet Foreign Minister Gromyko to Japanese Ambassador Kadowaki on December 2, 1958.

The communization of China changed the picture completely. If Japan ever becomes communized, it will be a great help to Communist China in absorbing South East Asia into the Communist bloc. On the other hand, for the Western camp, Japan is the strongest bulwark in defending Asia against the threat of expanding communism. At least this is how both blocs evaluate Japan. Under these circumstances, Japan cannot remain passive in international politics. Japan has no other choice, therefore, but to direct its foreign policy in accordance with its national power.

Therefore, the evaluation of Japan's national power becomes very significant. It is doubtful that the Japanese evaluate their country's national power in the same way as foreigners do. Foreigners seem to overestimate Japanese national power, while the Japanese tend to underestimate it. Let us, then, examine the problem objectively to determine just how strong Japan really is. We shall deal with the problem of economic power and defensive power.

Economic power

When the Second World War was over, every one of the major cities of Japan had been razed nearly to ashes. This meant a fatal collapse of Japan's industry in view of the fact that the major industrial firms were located in the big cities. Immediately after the war, the industrial efficiency of Japan dropped to 13 percent and the income of the people was cut to half of the prewar standard. It is said that 5 to 6 million people or more would have starved to death without prompt assistance from outside sources. The occupation policy of the United States accounts for the fact that most people managed to escape starvation.

Let us leave this immediate postwar period with all of its unpleasantness and contrast it with the present situation in Japan. If we examine the annual rate of economic growth for the 1950–1958 period, we find that Japan achieved 8 percent as compared with Germany's 7 percent and Italy's 5 percent. In 1959, it went up as high as 16 percent. The increase in the average gross national product since the war is 30 percent. Thus, Japan has been enjoying unprecedented economic prosperity. For the last couple of years its international income and expenditures have been in the black.

Naturally, the per capita national income is still far below the international level; it is roughly one eighth of that of the United States. Nevertheless, if this high rate of economic growth keeps up for another ten years, it will not be just a dream for Japan to bring her national income up to a much higher level, even as high as that of the Western countries.

In measuring Japan's national power it should be noted that, along with the economic growth of the country, her industrial structure has been undergoing a process of reorganization around heavy industry. In the development stage of Japan's economy in the late 19th century, the textile industry held the leading position. In the 30's, thanks to the increase in munitions production, heavy industry nosed out other industries. Though a fatal setback was suffered during and after the war, this area of Japan's economy continued to grow. The development of the mechanical industry, especially since 1955, is worth particular notice. The rate of increase in this area has tripled during the past four years. The automobile and consumer durable goods industries have also shown remarkable improvement.

The amazing growth of Japan's national economy has brought about a noticeable increase in Japan's exports. During the 1953–59 period, the world's total exports increased by 36 percent; during the same period, Japan's exports nearly tripled. This could be the result of the fact that Japan has successfully drifted with the tide of the world-wide consumption increase. At the same time we should note that the international competitive power of Japanese industries increased as the result of technical improvement and a drop in production cost.

In the six year period from 1953 to 1959, prices in the Western countries rose by 5 to 15 percent, while no such change took place in Japan. That was because Japan kept the wage cost low and made every effort to improve material-saving techniques and manufacturing processes, despite the fact that Japan had to import most of her industrial raw materials. The rise of the annual average productivity of manufacturing industries during the period, 1953–58, was 7.6 percent, while that of wages was only 5.5 percent. The international comparative cost of heavy industries—iron, nonferrous metals, cement machinery, etc.—is still relatively high, but that of textiles and miscellaneous merchandise is rather low.

So far Japan has developed soundly in terms of the rate of economic growth and the rise of international competitive ability in industry. In this respect, Japan is perhaps the most economically advanced nation in Asia. There is, however, no assurance that this trend will continue in the future. The important factor is whether or not a continuous supply of high quality labor is available. Another factor, perhaps equally important, is that the long ignored overhead capital such as roads, harbors and railway facilities must be accumulated if we are to maintain economic growth at this high level.

Furthermore, the absence of control over excessive competition among large enterprises might very well lead to overproduction. In view of the fact that Japan's economy owes its remarkable growth to the prosperity of overseas markets and that the trading competition is likely to be intensified in the future, it is very doubtful that more production can be expected by raising the costs. Considering the fact that most of Japan's industrial raw materials are imported from abroad, more overseas markets have to be exploited by cutting down manufacturing costs, if the country is to prosper in international economic competition or even survive in it. This is by no means an easy thing to do.

In contemplating the future of Japan's economic power there is no reason for optimism, even though it has so far been lucky enough to remain the strongest economic power in Asia. However, in view of its highly developed industry, coupled with the diligence and high degree of culture possessed by its people, Japan's decision as to which camp it belongs to under the present international state of affairs certainly proves to be decisive for the international balance of power.

Defensive power

Constitutional provisions   Japan, despite the current stability of such objective conditions as population and economic power, as we will see, is politically quite unstable. A major cause of this instability springs from the fact that public opinion on the issue of national defense is fatally split. Article 9 of the new Constitution, enacted after the war, states:

Aspiring sincerely to an international peace based on justice and order, the Japanese people forever renounce war as a sovereign right of the nation and the threat or use of force as a means of settling international disputes.

In order to accomplish the aim of the preceding paragraph, land, sea and air forces, as well as other war potential, will never be maintained. The right of belligerency of the state will not be recognized.

Whether these paragraphs were included voluntarily by the Japanese authorities or whether they were forced upon them by the occupation forces is a subtle question. But regardless of their origin, Japan swore to the world that it would never again possess a military force.

After the Korean war, the occupation forces began to shift their policy towards rearming Japan so that the United States could use Japan as part of her Far East defense plans. Beginning in 1950, overtures were made in this direction by the establishment of a Police Force Reserve functioning on a voluntary basis. The name of this organization was subsequently changed to the Safety Maintenance Forces.

This trend toward the establishment of a Japanese military force was carried one step further in 1954 when the controversial Self-Defense Forces were born. There is no doubt that they are substantially an army.

As the title changed from one to another, so also did the governmental interpretation of the two paragraphs of the Constitution quoted above. At present, the government maintains that the Constitution does not necessarily prohibit Japan from possessing defensive power for the purpose of protecting itself. The Self-Defense Forces Code describes its role as follows:

The Self-Defense Forces assume the responsibility of defending the country against any direct or indirect aggression in order to maintain the security and to protect the independence and peace of the country.

In Japan's prewar military forces, the general control of troops was in the hands of the Chief of the General Staff and the Chief of the Naval Staff, who were both under direct control of the Emperor. The ministers of the Army and the Navy were in charge of military administration and had the right, independent of the Prime Minister, to report to the Emperor. This made it possible for the military to control the nation's defense policy independently of the government.

In order to avoid making the same mistake again, the Self-Defense Forces Code enacted after the Korean war holds firmly to the principle of civilian supremacy. The Prime Minister assumes the entire responsibility for the nation's defense through the Chief of the Defense Agency. This is one of the external departments of the Prime Minister's Office under which is placed the staff board. Legally, therefore, it is impossible for the militarists to meddle directly in national politics.

Strength of the Self-Defense Forces   At present, the Self-Defense Forces consist of three divisions: land, sea and air. As of 1960, these divisions numbered 170,000, 27,667 and

32,225, respectively. All are volunteers and, in the case of regular soldiers, they are required to serve for two to three years. They are free to serve continuously thereafter. Most of the equipment possessed by these units is supplied by the United States Army. In view of the fact that the Self-Defense Forces are designed only to defend the nation and not to assume any aggressive role, these weapons are strictly limited to those of defensive potential. No offensive equipment such as aircraft carriers or bombers are allowed to be included among these weapons. The role of the Naval Defense Force is to protect marine transportation. The fighters of the Air Defense Force guard the nation's sky and the Land Defense Force fortifies the nation against foreign invasion and fifth column activities.

Compared to other Asian countries, the overall strength of the Self-Defense Forces is considerably inferior. Disregarding Communist China's mammoth 2,500,000 man land force, even North Korea and South Korea possess armies of 450,000 and 600,000, respectively. It is clear, therefore that Japan's defense forces are too weak to be practical. They can hardly be considered an army unless backed by United States forces under the provisions of the U.S.–Japan Security Pact.

At present, the main body of the United States Far-Eastern forces is stationed in the Ryukyus. Only air force and naval bases are in Japan. In the event of aggression, the Self-Defense Forces, assisted by the U.S. air force are presumed able to resist the aggressor. But chances are they will not be able to hold out until reinforcements arrive from overseas. If such aggression happens to be a large scale outright invasion we cannot expect the Self-Defense Forces to successfully fulfill their assigned mission.

The Liberal-Democratic Party Government is planning gradually to strengthen the Self-Defense Forces and to modernize their equipment. The problem it faces, however, is that, in addition to the opposition party, which challenges the fundamental raison d'être of the Defense Forces, many other Japanese citizens openly oppose the policy of strengthening the Defense Forces. The Liberal-Democratic Government, as has been pointed out, maintains that the Self-Defense Forces, so long as their activities are confined to national defense, are fully constitutional. The government is, for tactical reasons, opposed to bringing nuclear weapons into Japan and also to sending the Defense Forces abroad, even when this action might be taken in conjunction with the United Nations Police Force.

On the other hand, the Socialist Party, the leading opposition, maintains that the Self-Defense Forces themselves are unconstitutional and should be disbanded. The Democratic Socialist Party, a party which split from the Socialist Party in 1959, agrees, apart from the constitutional issue, to "minimum defensive measures." Among its members there are some, however, who lean towards the position held by the Socialist Party on this particular issue. The Anti-Defense Forces group seeks to reorganize the troops into something resembling Land Development Troops.

Popular views about military needs   What is the consensus of the general public about the Self-Defense Forces? Though various kinds of public opinion polls have been taken, it is quite hard to sum up the opinion of the Japanese people in a few short statements. Some polls taken since 1955 show that about 60 percent of the nation agrees to the existence of the Self-Defense Forces, however less than 50 percent approves of strengthening them. Another poll reveals that when asked: "Should Japan possess nuclear weapons in the future?" more than 65 percent answered "No!" One third of the nation does not approve of the Self-Defense Forces. Under these circumstances the Self-Defense Forces present many problems.

Parallel to this attitude toward the problem of Self-Defense Forces, is the negative tendency of public opinion toward the problem of regional collective security, that is to say the U.S.–Japan Security Pact. Nearly half of the people are critical of the pact and voice a preference for a policy of neutralism. Many public opinion surveys show this trend; however, they do not make clear whether those in favor of neutralism insist on the immediate abrogation of the pact or whether they prefer neutralism as the future course to follow.

Political stability

Japan is the only country in Asia, from the standpoint of its population and its economic strength, that is strong enough to grapple effectively with Red China. However one factor is absent which keeps all these qualities from coming into full play; political stability. Foreign observers never fail to praise Japan's high economic growth but no one ever speaks highly of its political performance. Why is this so?

The new Constitution   The biggest political event in Japan since the end of the Second World War was the adoption of the New Constitution in 1946, under the tutelage of the occupation forces. The new Constitution stripped the Emperor of his imperial power and rendered him merely a symbol of the unity of the people. In contrast, the people, whose rights had been very much restricted under the old Constitution, now were given their fundamental rights: life, liberty and the pursuit of happiness. Under the new Constitution every citizen was fully guaranteed freedom of thought, religion, assembly and organization. The Constitution also provides for the election of the members of both Houses of Parliament by universal suffrage, a parliamentary cabinet system, and the separation of the three powers of government. It may justly be said, therefore, that the Constitution is the most democratic of all existing codified constitutions.

The Diet consists of two houses: the House of Representatives and the House of Councillors. The former has more power and the term of office of representatives is four years. So far, since the end of the war, six general elections for the House of Representatives have been held. Each time more than seven out of ten eligible voters participated. This certainly would give the impression that the Japanese are the most election-minded people in the world.

Party politics   Not only the voting rate but also outward manifestations of party politics seem to indicate that all is well with Japan. For a while after the war, there were two or three conservative parties, one or two social democratic parties and the Communist Party. But in 1955, the two-party system came into being with one conservative party, the Liberal-Democratic Party, and one party of opposition, the Socialist Party. The Communist Party managed to elect only two or three representatives at this time and thus its power became negligible. Ever since, during six consecutive elections, the Liberal-Democrats have won the elections.

Nevertheless, the Socialist Party has gradually been increasing in strength. When the Socialists are united with the Democratic-Socialists, who split from the Socialist Party in 1959, the total number of opposition representatives accounts for more than one-third of the total seats. The Japanese party system resembles the situation in Great Britain where two parties, the Conservatives and the Labour Party, vie with each other for control of the Parliament.

As far as outward appearances are concerned, Japan's politics are based on a perfect parliamentary democracy. But this is only an outward appearance with little bearing on the true facts. It is a frequent experience to find the representatives engaging in fist-fighting within the Diet. The minority often resorts to violence in its attempts to prevent bills from passing, while the majority party pushes through its measures by force of numbers without allowing enough time for thorough discussions and thus slighting minority rights. Furthermore, as demonstrated when the new U.S.–Japan Security Pact was adopted, the Socialist Party mobilizes mass movements outside the House, often causing complete disorder and ugly physical violence.

While the mass violence by the Leftists considerably obstructed the principle of parliamentary politics, political terrorism by Rightists also has upset the nation's political affairs. Intelligent and well-informed citizens are worried that Rightist terrorism, reminiscent of that which solidified the position of military dictatorship thirty years ago, may be returning, though not a single representative has been elected to the Diet from the organized ultra-nationalist party.

Defects in the political system   Considering the fact that neither the Communist Party nor the ultra-nationalist Rightists possess any apparent power, what is the reason for this political instability? First, neither of the parties, Conservative or Socialist, has evolved into a real parliamentary party. Despite the people's sincere outcries and demands that the general elections be freed from the disease of election law violations, many of the candidates are prosecuted for breaches of these laws, very often for buying votes. It is very likely that most of the candidates pour more money into the campaigns than they are legally permitted to use. These practices are more apparent among the Liberal-Democrats, though they exist among Socialists, too. The people cannot be sure, therefore, whether the majority party really represents their opinion.

How then, does the Liberal-Democratic Party manage to win majority support time and again? The answer is simple: the opposition Socialist Party is not supported by the general public, either. The Socialist Party is backed by organized workers—mostly the labor unions belonging to Sohyo, the General Council of Trade Unions of Japan. Even supposing that all of such organized workers did vote for the Socialist Party, they would not account for over one-fifth of the total votes in a general election. Unless they manage to secure the votes of farmers, small and independent manufacturers and unorganized workers, Socialist ascendency to power is a mere dream. Unfortunately, the Party's policies do not appeal to these segments of society.

The present Japanese Socialist Party was organized after the war by several groups which joined together under the banner of socialism. In reality, it was a mixed brigade consisting of three divisions: first, a group on the right in-

fluenced by the Fabian socialism of England; second, the non-Leninistic Marxists (akin to the German Socialist Democratic Party under Kautsky); and third, the Marx-Leninist Leftists who were, however, not in agreement with the Communist Party from a tactical standpoint. Ever since its foundation, the Socialist Party has always drawn a clear line between itself and the Communist Party. Some of the party leaders actually have strong feelings against the Communist Party.

Yet, it is true that the officers and lower level members of the party are rather strongly influenced by Marx-Leninism. In addition, most of the supporting organizations like the Anti-Atomic and Hydrogen Bomb National Congress, the Sino-Japanese Friendship Association or the Anti-Security Pact National Congress include among their members as many Communists as Sohyo members. In fact, they form a united front. Moreover, the Socialist Party is not a genuine parliamentary party like the British Labour Party; this is another reason for the political instability.

In 1960, a minority of the Socialist Party members were so discontented with the party attitudes that they bolted and organized a new party, the Democratic-Socialist Party. It is based on the principles of democratic socialism of the Socialist International and regards the Communist Party as a product of a distorted interpretation of true Socialist ideals. The new party lost about 60 percent of its original representatives in the Diet in the first election after its inception. It is not strong enough to influence the general course of politics.

FORMATION OF FOREIGN POLICY

The role of public opinion

The Japanese have, in the past, been taught to be indifferent to politics or diplomacy. In the main, they have followed this idea closely.

However when they do show interest in these matters, they tend to react to them rather emotionally, as demonstrated by the "up-with-the-country" indignation at the time of the Portsmouth Treaty. Restricted by the old Constitution, based on the theory of the inviolability of the Emperor, the people were never allowed to participate in reasonable discussions on political issues. Thus, in Japan, public opinion on political or diplomatic issues is often expressed by a few so-called opinion leaders, who make no attempt to sound out the general public.

In the current social system, only those who can make use of the mass media are able to join this group. The first newspapers in Japan were published by political groups, especially those of the Opposition. Ever since then, the press has grown as a forum for political opinion. Even the commercial press, which developed out of this party-affiliated press, retained an anti-government flavor, although this was one of the phenomena resulting from the reactionary nature of the government itself. Generally speaking, the outlook of these papers has been, more often than not, critical of the policies of the government.

In Japan, there are several high-level magazines dealing with the nation's political, economic and social issues. The largest of these has a circulation of well over 300,000 copies a month. They play a very important role in forming the opinion of the intellectuals. As is the case with such magazines as *Chuokoron* or *Sekai*, the editors of the high-level magazines have often been solid Marxists. Accordingly, these periodicals tend to go farther to the left than the press.

The contributors to these magazines and papers consist mainly of university professors, writers and professional critics. It is interesting that, as far as international politics is concerned, the public seems to listen more to those who are not scholars of international politics: namely the writers and social critics. This stems from the fact that the writers' sentimentalism, reflected in their political writings, seems to appeal to the emotional character of the Japanese.

Even more basic, however, is the fact that Japan lacks professional scholars of international politics. In prewar days, most of the universities offered courses in international law and diplomatic history, but very seldom in international politics. Besides, the few who took these courses were mostly budding diplomats. As a result, not very many professors or students are presently majoring in international politics. After the Second World War, a considerable number of students went to the United States to study in this field, but there still are not enough. Consequently, not very many books have been written on this subject by Japanese scholars.

As a result, outsiders with no adequate background meddle in the discussions of various international issues. They never attempt to analyze issues objectively but rather engage in *a priori* polemics on the basis of established dogmas, one of which is Marxism. Their arguments generally follow the line: "America is a capitalistic country. Capitalism is inevitably imperialism. Therefore, American policies are all imperialistic, while the Soviet Union is a socialistic country and socialism can do no evil. . . . ," etc. Thus, in their eyes, the Cold War is the confrontation of decaying capitalism and growing socialism. Although this predominantly Marxist attitude is decreasing of late, these magazines were loaded with all sorts of articles based on this viewpoint until the 20th Communist Party Convention of 1956.

Many non-Marxists have also been rather skeptical of the foreign policy of the Japanese government. Possibly no other country in the world experiences such an intense degree of antagonism between the government and the intellectuals. The intellectuals feel that the U.S.–Japan Security Pact, along with the creation of Self-Defense Forces, has increased the possibility for the revival of Japanese imperialism and that the Pact and the Forces have brought Japan considerably closer to another war. Naturally, Communist propaganda directed toward Japan has a great deal to do with this attitude among the intellectuals, but the point is that the intellectual movements are unstable enough to be influenced by such propaganda.

Deliberative organs of foreign policy

The old Constitution required every Minister of State to assist the Emperor and thus fulfill his responsibility. In practice this meant that if the Minister of War opposed the foreign policy of the government and thereby caused a disunity of opinion within the Cabinet, the Cabinet had to resign. Many of the prewar Cabinets were thus destroyed. The old Constitution also provided for the establishment of a Privy Council to examine important national issues and ratify treaties. It also investigated the various diplomatic positions taken by the Cabinet. In addition, there was a provision for a supra-constitutional organ called the *Genro*. Important elder statesmen, for example, ex-Prime Ministers, through the *Genro,* possessed the independent right to participate in the discussions of the nation's foreign policy.

Role of the Diet   Under the new Constitution, the Diet is considered the supreme organ of sovereign rights. The Diet elects the Prime Minister who, with the other ministers of state whom he nominates, forms the Executive Branch of the government. The Minister of Foreign Affairs, thus nominated, drafts the foreign policy on the basis of information supplied by ambassadors abroad and presents it to the weekly Cabinet meeting for discussion. Any necessary contact with foreign countries must go through his office. The Prime Minister generally makes overall decisions on all foreign and domestic issues but, as in Great Britain, he concerns himself with diplomatic problems frequently. After the war, the Minister of Foreign Affairs was given a comparatively important position and his term is generally longer than that of other ministers. The Prime Minister has the right to recall any Minister. Since the war no Prime Minister has taken this action toward his Minister of Foreign Affairs.

The Diet consists of two independent Houses; the House of Representatives and the House of Councillors. Each independently controls the Cabinet through its power over budgets and each discusses treaties and other bills. The Diet asks the Cabinet through the Budget Committee and the Standing Committee for Foreign Affairs about the general principles of its foreign policy. The Diet may reject any of the agreements and treaties proposed by the Cabinet. Every treaty and other important agreements must be approved by a majority vote in the Diet.

Both Houses have equal rights as far as treaties and budgets are concerned. In the event of disagreement between the two Houses, the decisions of the House of Representatives prevail. However, the House of Representatives must repass the legislation by a two-thirds or more majority of members present, after waiting thirty days from the time of the disagreement. The Emperor only attests the instruments of ratification and other diplomatic documents.

The Cabinet and the Minister of Foreign Affairs   In Japan, all diplomatic organs come under the control of the Minister of Foreign Affairs. There are no agencies in the Japanese Government which correspond to the Economic Co-operation Administration in the United States, a diplomatic organ which is independent of the State Department, or the Commission in charge of disarmament under the direct control of the President. Most of the ambassadors are professional diplomats, but occasionally journalists or scholars are appointed from outside the career service.

Though it is true that the Diet is the Nation's supreme legislative organ, decisions by the Cabinet are not likely to be rejected in the Diet because, as in Great Britain, the majority party always forms the Cabinet. On reaching agreement with foreign governments through the diplomatic organs, the Minister of Foreign Affairs first signs the document with the approval of the government party and then he presents it to the Diet. The Liberal-Democratic Party, the current government party in Japan, represents various opinions existing in and out of the party. However, considering the various factions existing within the party, unless the Prime Minister's position in the party is fairly solid, his policies or viewpoints may not prevail without serious challenge.

On the occasion of the Reparation Agreement signed with Indonesia and the Philippines, the influences of intra-party pressure groups were so strong that the original plans drafted by the Ministry of Foreign Affairs had to be frequently altered. In Japan, the divergence of opinion between the government party, namely the Liberal-Democratic Party, and the Socialist Party, on diplomatic issues is so great that preparatory talks of any sort or exchanges of information and ideas have rarely taken place in the past.

PROBLEMS IN THE PRESENT FOREIGN POLICY OF JAPAN

Japan's security

Ever since Japan was admitted into the United Nations in 1956, the Japanese government has repeatedly stressed three basic principles of Japan's diplomacy: the principle of United Nations first, the promotion of closer relations with the free nations and co-operation with the Asian countries. The first principle relates to enhancing the principles of the United Nations in order to promote its activities and strive for accomplishing the mission to which it is dedicated. The second is based on the thesis that the current unstable peace of the world is maintained only through the unity among the free nations and Japan should strive wholeheartedly toward strengthening that unity. The third principle is that Japan should recognize its importance and responsibilities in Asia and help to strengthen unity and stability in this area.

These principles, of course, are not always perfectly compatible. In any case, the most fundamental of all these principles for the government of Japan is to keep in close contact with the free nations, especially the United States. After Japan regained its independence in 1951 in San Francisco, the United States demanded that Japan conclude a U.S.–Japan Security Pact in order that the U.S. might maintain armed forces in Japan for strategic reasons. Realizing its inability to defend itself, Japan accepted this proposal and concluded the pact, thereby casting its lot with the United States.

The intellectuals and labor unions stood steadfastly opposed to the treaty on the ground that a treaty to which the Soviet Union objects, automatically seals Japan's international position. As long as the Security Pact was inseparable from the peace treaty, signing the peace treaty would pull Japan into an anti-Communist military alliance and, in the end, would lead Japan into another war. Thus, a group of pacifists and the left-wingers in the Socialist Party opened an extended campaign against the ratification of the treaties.

Opponents of the peace treaty, in 1956, after the Japan-Russia Joint Declaration on the Restoration of Diplomatic Relations was issued, turned to attack the U.S.–Japan Security Pact, demanding its total abolition. They also pressed the government to shift its policy toward the establishment of a state of neutrality for Japan and the assumption of an "independent" foreign policy. After Gromyko dispatched a communiqué demanding Japan's neutrality, the Communists and their sympathizers shifted radically to neutralism.

Alternative policies   Apart from the camouflaged neutralism of the Communists, the following three counterproposals for the security of Japan have been presented. The first is what we might call the Locarno treaty method in Asia, proposed by the Socialist Party. It would involve multi-national non-aggression pacts among America, Russia, China and Japan. The security of Japan would be guarded by the other three nations.

The second was proposed by Yoshikazu Sakamoto, a scholar of international politics, who holds that Japan should not be armed. Instead, its security should be guaranteed by a United Nations Police Force consisting of armies furnished by neutral nations all over the world. Sakamoto's point of view has been further elaborated upon by Michio Royama, who proposes that Japan should conclude with the Security Council of the U.N. an agreement based on Article 43 of the Charter in order to have the Self-Defense Forces of Japan recognized as official United Nations Forces.

The third proposal deals with armed neutrality. It demands the dissolution of the U.S.–Japan Security Pact and insists that the neutrality of Japan should be maintained by the Self-Defense Forces of Japan. This view seems to find many supporters among the general public but no party has as yet adopted it.

The government, on the other hand, counters these proposals by contending: "Neutralism is a mere fantasy." It has been quite consistent in gradually strengthening the Self-Defense Forces and maintaining Japan's security on the strength of the U.S.–Japan Security Pact.

The new Security Pact   In 1960, the old Security Pact between Japan and the United States was revised and, in the midst of great political confusion, a new version was ratified. The new Security Pact clarified Japan's relationship within the United Nations Charter, emphasized the economic co-operation between Japan and the United States and, further, declared the responsibility of the United States to defend Japan. The period of validity of the pact was set to be ten years. The terms of the treaty changed the disposition of the U.S. armed forces; prior consultation was prescribed in the event of any combat action. In this respect, the provisions of the new version of the U.S.–Japan Security Pact were considerably more favorable to Japan.

The advantages to Japan in the new Security Pact did not, however, change much of the overall picture. Japan refused to send its defense forces abroad under any circumstances due to the limitation of Article IX of the Japanese Constitution. The availability of Japan's forces to the United States was now limited to their use within the territory of Japan. Further-more, Japan declared itself opposed to bringing nuclear weapons into the country.

The U.S.–Japan Security Pact is the only treaty of this kind that Japan has so far concluded with foreign countries. For instance, when the Soviet Union proposed the establishment of an atomic-hydrogen bomb-exempt peace zone around the Pacific Ocean and the Far East area (January, 1959, Address by Khrushchev at the 21st Communist Party Congress), Japan did not react to it, nor did it make any counter-proposal. Japan has been quite indifferent to the possibility of China's having nuclear weapons. Japan is solely depending on the United States at present for its defense.

Diplomatic relations with neighboring countries

With the San Francisco Peace Treaty, Japan terminated the state of war with many of the foreign countries involved in World War II. Nations such as India, Nationalist China and Russia, which were not present at the San Francisco Peace Treaty Conference, were later contacted and steps were taken to resume diplomatic relations. Thus far Japan has entered into diplomatic relations with most of the countries of the world. Still, there are a few nearby countries with whom Japan has not yet been able to resume normal diplomatic relations.

The Soviet Union   First, the Soviet Union, which had boycotted the San Francisco treaty conference, did not come into the picture until Prime Minister Ichiro Hatoyama went to Moscow in 1956 and signed the Joint Declaration on the Restoration of Diplomatic Relations. The Soviet Union was then moving towards "the thaw." The negotiations faltered over and over again on the issue of the islands: Habomai, Shikotan, Kunashiri and Etolof. Japan insisted that these islands do not belong to the Kuriles, while Russia stubbornly insisted that only Habomai and Shikotan could be turned over to Japan. In spite of efforts, the peace treaty was pigeon-holed, but diplomatic relations between the two nations have been restored. Later, the conclusion of the new U.S.–Japan Security Pact in 1960 worried Russia so much that she notified Japan that a Russo-Japanese treaty had to be concluded and all the foreign armed forces had to be evacuated before Russia would consider returning Habomai and Shikotan.

Another serious diplomatic problem between Japan and Russia is the question of fishing rights in the North-West Pacific. Before the war, that area of the Pacific Ocean was one of the important fishing grounds for Japan. After the war, however, Russia proposed, under the pretext of protecting the marine resources, to restrict the catch of salmon and trout. Russia proposed also to restrict the fishing ground for crabs. Year after year, a series of conferences have been held between the two countries to set up mutual restrictions. It is very likely that Russia is trying to stir up public opinion in Japan by repeating these conferences year after year, and Japan has not been able to present any effective countermeasures.

Communist China   Probably no other issue presents more difficulty to the Japanese government than that of restoring diplomatic relations with Communist China. After the San Francisco peace treaty, Japan, as former Prime Minister Shigeru Yoshida had promised, recognized the National government in Formosa, which had not been present at the San Francisco conference. However, after the treaty had been concluded, notes were exchanged between Japan and the Formosa government stipulating that the treaty was only applicable within the area administered by the National government and would not extend to the mainland. The Peking government flatly denies the validity of the agreement. If Japan is to restore diplomatic relations with the Peking government, it has first to stop relations not only with the United States but also Formosa, for neither Peking nor Formosa approves of "two Chinas."

The nation's opinion regarding this issue is unfortunately divided. Peking naturally demands that Peking-Toyko relations be restored

immediately. The Government, on the one hand, is taking a wait-and-see attitude because of relations with the U.S. and the Formosa government, and is calmly watching developments. The Socialist Party, on the other hand, holds that the relations should be restored as soon as possible and that Formosa should be put under the control of the Peking government. The fact that the Japan-China Friendship Association, an organization founded to promote friendly relations between Japan and China, has among its members some Liberal-Democrats, indicates that the restoration of diplomatic relations is desired by many people regardless of differences of party alignment.

It should be noted that many people want to restore diplomatic relations and to promote friendly relations with Peking. In addition to the fact that this would end the state of war between the two nations, a pro-Peking mood exists, motivated by such factors as the traditional cultural relationship between the two nations, a materialistic interest in expectation of trade, and a form of guilty conscience towards China for what Japan did during the war. It is perhaps also true that exaggerated rumors and propaganda regarding recent development in Communist China have aroused awe in the people of Japan. But, over and beyond Japan's relations with the United States, no clear answer has so far been given about what to do about the Formosa government.

Though many desire the restoration of diplomatic relations, no concrete policy has yet evolved on this issue. Some of the intellectuals have advocated a two-China policy. But in view of the complexity of the present international situation, the Government still veers away from this issue.

In this connection, the reaction of the Japanese toward the joint communiqué, issued by the People's Institute for Foreign Relations in Communist China and the delegation of the Japanese Socialist Party to Peking in January 1962, is worth noting. The communiqué reconfirmed the validity of the notorious statement made by the late Secretary Asanuma in which he remarked that American imperialism is the common enemy of the Chinese and the

Japanese and pledged mutual support in combating it.

Almost all of the Japanese newspapers severely attacked the Socialist Party on the grounds that the statement made clear the subjugation of the party to Communist China. The repercussions to the statement indicated that most of the Japanese are not ready to take sides with Communist China in foreign policy matters against the U.S., even if some of them are rather skeptical of the soundness of U.S. policy toward China. In short, it can be said that the Japanese people are ready to recognize the Peking government as the legitimate authority over the mainland but they do not approve of its aggressive foreign policy.

South Korea   Korea presents similar complications. However, unlike the case of China, the Government is willing to patch up relations with South Korea (The Republic of Korea). The Socialist Party holds that as long as Korea remains split, Japan should not limit its ties to South Korea only. But the attitude of the Republic of Korea has prevented the two nations from restoring friendly relations and no change in attitude seems in sight.

At present, Japan associates with the Republic of Korea only through the mission, which was established during the occupation. There are a number of difficult problems between the two nations; among these are the issue of claims of properties of Koreans which were damaged during and before the war and the territorial complications connected with Takeshima Island. In addition, the Rhee Line presents a great deal of trouble to Japan. This line, established in 1952, marks the sovereignty of the Republic of Korea over contiguous territorial waters, for the purpose of conserving marine life in the defined area. Moreover, Syngman Rhee had always been rather stiff-necked and emotional towards Japan, partly due to his internal unification policy. Only after his downfall did Korea begin to show favorable reactions towards Japan.

The existing Republic of Korea government, led by General Pak, is very eager for normal relations with Japan. The Japanese government also shows the same attitude, despite the opposition of the Socialist Party. Official discussions have been held several times between representatives of both governments. Prime Minister Pak himself showed his eagerness by visiting Prime Minister Ikeda on his way to the U.S. But differences of opinion on both sides, concerning the claims on property, are so great that patient and strenuous negotiations will be required before any agreement can be reached. Even Japanese people who do not share the view of the Socialist Party are not so eager to promote the immediate restoration of relations with South Korea under present circumstances. They fear that a generous attitude on the part of Japan might encourage the militarist and dictatorial domestic policy of the Pak government, thus increasing future difficulties.

North Korea   As for North Korea, no formal relations have been established, due primarily to the bitter feeling generated during the Korean war when Japan acted as the military base for the United Nations troops. The Socialist Party, however, maintains its pro-North Korean attitude. Many Koreans living in Japan since prewar days have wanted to go back to North Korea. In 1959, an agreement was reached through the Red Cross to send these Koreans back to North Korea. The Japanese government supported the project purely from a humanitarian standpoint, not for political reasons. There is no doubt that the majority of the Japanese people earnestly wish Korea to be united into a democratic state. Under the circumstances, they feel that at least South Korea should be one, for, geographically speaking, the communization of Korea would be a considerable threat to the well-being and safety of Japan.

However, it is doubtful that South Korea will become a democratic nation in the near future. Japan can hardly expect much from negotiations with Korea until the internal state of affairs there becomes more stabilized. Japan is quite powerless to improve this situation. It is most willing to help facilitate economic recovery in Korea, although it could not possibly recognize such a reckless policy as the Rhee

Line. Of course, the Japanese feel that there is no sense in helping the Koreans if they do not show signs of becoming a democratic nation in the not-too-distant future.

Okinawa and the Bonin Islands   Another issue appealing greatly to the national sentiment of the Japanese is the question of Japanese territorial rights on Okinawa and the Bonin Islands. These islands were put indefinitely under the control of the United States in consequence of the San Francisco peace treaty. In essence, this is not a territorial issue in that the United States government recognized Japan's potential sovereignty over these islands, but wishes to maintain its present administrative rights for military reasons.

The inhabitants of the Bonin Islands are not allowed to go back to the islands, and Okinawa is still administered as a foreign territory notwithstanding the people's wish to be returned to Japanese control. The Communist Party takes full advantage of this situation in its anti-American propaganda, calling it a typical manifestation of American imperialism. Most people recognize the American administration of the islands as a necessary evil. At the same time they cannot remain indifferent to the fact that every Okinawan, no matter how well he is doing economically under the American administration, earnestly wishes to participate in politics as a Japanese, to benefit from a unified economy and to attend Japanese institutions. It is only natural for the Japanese to insist that Okinawa should revert to Japan as soon as possible, even if the American army should be permitted bases on some part of it.

In March 1962, the U.S. government revised its polity toward Okinawa on the basis of various reports presented by the American delegations. The Japanese people welcomed that part of the statement of policy which reconfirmed the American intention of restoring Okinawa to Japan as soon as tension in the Far East is eased, but they were not so happy to find out that existing conditions were not altered very much by the new policy.

Besides expecting expansion of economic aid to Okinawa, they also had hoped for participation by the Tokyo government in the administration of Okinawa in one way or another. This problem is connected not only with the strategic needs of the American Army but also with the delicate problem of Article IX of the Constitution. At any event, the problem of Okinawa remains a latent issue which the Leftists are ready to exploit in order to stir up public opinion concerning political problems. It may safely be said that a single mistake in dealing with this issue could affect the future friendly relations between Japan and the United States.

Relations with the United States

The basic principle of Japan's diplomacy since its re-emergence in 1951 as a free nation has been close contact with the United States. With this basic principle, it has endeavored to bring about its own economic recovery, taking advantage of various forms of economic aid from the United States and leaving its defense mainly in the hands of the U.S. Most of the Japanese people are aware of the generosity with which the American people granted much aid to their former enemy.

Nevertheless, as described in preceding paragraphs, some segments of the people do not have a genuine affection for the U.S. The confusion created by the massive demonstrations staged on the occasion of the ratification of the Japan–U.S. Security Pact in 1960 should not be taken as an indication of the people's ill-feeling against the U.S., but rather as a protest against the Kishi government's disregard of constitutional procedures to push the bill through the Diet. However, it cannot be denied that there have been a lot of people who are critical of American foreign policy, even apart from Socialists who regarded the U.S. as an imperialist country in accordance with Marxist-Leninist dogma and pacifists who wanted to sever all military ties with any foreign country, fearing possible involvement in another international conflict.

Lack of popular understanding There are many reasons for this. But one of the reasons lay—at least till recently—in the misunderstanding of American policy toward Japan. Many American diplomats and civilians have sincerely endeavored to further better understanding between the two countries. So far, it seems, however, that the main American effort toward reaching the Japanese has been conducted with the upper classes of society and conversation with intellectuals has been neglected. This is the reason that U.S. diplomats in Tokyo misjudged Japanese public opinion regarding international problems on which intellectuals have exerted such a great influence. A number of Japanese people have regarded American policy as one of consolidating the vested interests of the upper classes in Japan, to the detriment of the common people.

In this regard, the new outlook of the Kennedy Administration was observed with keen interest by Japanese intellectuals. As the first embodiment of its new policy, the appointment of Professor Reischauer as ambassador at Tokyo was welcomed, because he has long been highly esteemed among Japanese intellectuals as a distinguished scholar of Japanese classics. It is certain that many lectures and round-table discussions with Japanese which he has given and taken part in since his appointment as ambassador have impressed many students and scholars very much.

Many round-table conferences, too, such as those held in Japan since 1961 by ministers, scientists and educators on both sides, stemming from the Ikeda-Kennedy talks in Washington in 1961, have contributed to better understanding of American policy towards Japan. Although some Japanese who had expected immediate benefits from those conferences were disappointed on seeing the move in the U.S. to raise tariffs, thus shutting Japanese goods out of the American market, most Japanese seem to be satisfied with seeing Japan treated by the U.S. as one of the most important countries in the world. Anyhow, it should be acknowledged that many things remain to be done to encourage better understanding between the two countries.

International co-operation and economic diplomacy

Support of the United Nations After a long period of international isolation, following its withdrawal from the League of Nations at the time of the Manchurian Incident, it has been Japan's persistent dream to get into the United Nations. When that dream came true in 1956, the nation not only rejoiced but also held great hopes for the United Nations. Some thought, for instance, that the United Nations would guarantee the security of Japan thereafter. It is indeed ironical from a historical point of view that, while the European countries which formerly supported the League of Nations are now rather skeptical of the role of the United Nations, Japan, which was so responsible for the destruction of the League of Nations, is now somewhat overestimating the power of this organization.

The United Nations is perhaps the only instrument at the moment through which Japan can express its desire for the peace of the world, secure its right to speak and, further, exalt its national prestige. Though Japan has supported, in principle, the policies of the United States on the disarmament issue, it has done a great deal to bring together the policies pursued by the United States and other European countries with those of the Asian and African countries. However, since Japan cannot wholeheartedly subscribe to the neutralism of the Asian and African countries, its position in this regard seems shaky. Japan often boasts of its role of a balancer between the European and the Asian countries and it has sometimes, although not always, been successful in this endeavor.

Aiding underdeveloped countries There is another vital problem for Japan in her relations with other Asian nations: the problem of assisting the economically and technically underdeveloped countries. Japan has already concluded reparations agreements in consequence of the Second World War with such countries as Burma, South Vietnam, the Philippines and Indonesia. The San Francisco peace treaty required of Japan only service reparations to such countries. Japan, however, realized the urgent need for these countries to develop their national economies and accepted a limited amount of product and pecuniary reparations. Moreover, Japan has been assisting them in the construction of dams, harbors and industrial firms, thereby exporting Japan's industrial and technological knowledge. This seems to have proven very advantageous for Japan and it has done a great deal in substantially assisting these countries.

Japan has 5,000,000 yen deposited in the Export-Import Bank of Japan as an Asian Development and Co-operation Fund to be used for all kinds of economic assistance. Furthermore, Japan has actively co-operated in strengthening the World Bank, increasing the capital of the International Monetary Fund (I.M.F.) and also in establishing the Second World Bank.

Japan does not yet positively support the proposal made by the United States in 1961, that one percent of the total national income should be allotted for economic assistance to underdeveloped countries. But if Japan is to prosper along with other Asian nations, its policies have to be directed along these lines. It is often said that Japan is a part of Asia. But regrettably, this is a mere phrase and most people are quite ignorant of the present state of affairs in Asia. Most Japanese seem to respect the West more than Asia. Many problems remain to be settled in this regard.

A good-will tour of some Asian countries recently made by the Crown Prince and Princess as well as that by Prime Minister Ikeda in 1961 were regarded as successful to some extent in stimulating interest in Asian countries among the Japanese. Although Ikeda could not reach full agreement with Prime Minister Nehru about world problems, he promised an increased effort to push economic aid for the development of Thailand. This might encourage better relationships between Japan and other Asian countries.

General economic diplomacy   Finally, let us look at the ever important issue of general economic diplomacy. I have already shown how significant a meaning international trade possesses for Japan's well-being. Under the I.M.F. Agreement, Japan has hitherto been allowed to limit its foreign exchange as a temporary measure to cope with its deficit in international payments.

On the other hand, by resorting to the provisions of Article 35 of GATT (General Agreement on Tariffs and Trade), the Western countries have discriminated against Japan's trade by such measures as restriction on import exchange on many of the imports from Japan. As a result of overestimating Japan's economic power, the United States and some other nations are strongly demanding that Japan liberalize its trade. Japan is heading in that direction, except for certain agricultural and industrial products. At the same time, it is most desirable and indeed indispensable for the future development of world trade that Western countries cease the application of Article 35 of GATT.

The most serious of all the problems connected with Japan's trade concerns the import restrictions against Japan imposed by such countries as the United States, Canada and Australia. In the United States, for example, such Japanese products as textiles, sewing machines, transistor radios and notions are being banned. These are mainly the products of small enterprises.

The Japanese government, while trying to control voluntarily the volume of export in order to avoid trade restrictions, has been appealing to the United States government not to take any legal measures towards banning these Japanese products. If Japan cannot expand its foreign trade in the Free World, it has no alternative but to look toward the countries in the Communist bloc for outlets for its goods. The Free World countries concerned should, therefore, look ahead and find a reasonable, long-term solution to this problem, without being tempted by short-term gains.

Recently, Japanese businessmen have been watching the development of the EEC with keen interest. It is certain that the economic prosperity of Western Europe will provide a promising market for Japanese goods in the long run. But regarding their short term interests, they are afraid that the marketing of Japanese goods might be made more difficult due to the discriminatory policies of the EEC. It is theoretically conceivable to create a counterpart in Asia to vie with the EEC, but practically it is hopeless, at least for the time being. Japanese businessmen are beginning more and more to feel left behind world trends. Some sort of steps should be taken to increase trade among countries of the Pacific area in order for the Japanese economy to survive in the severe competition for world markets.

Policy on nuclear armament

Public pressure groups   Probably no nation is as sensitive to matters of nuclear armament and control as Japan. As the only nation to have suffered the calamities of the atomic bomb during World War II, the Japanese people as a whole, quite naturally, fear involvement in another war, especially atomic war.

After the Second World War, groups of Tokyo housewives voluntarily formed an organization calling for peace and the abolition of atomic weapons. The mass movement, stemming from this humanitarian group, spread all over Japan within a few years and led to the formation of the Congress for the Prohibition of Atomic and Hydrogen Bombs (*Gensuikyo*). In the course of events, Communists gradually infiltrated the organization and began to occupy strategic posts, but the main body has consisted of women's organizations, youth organizations, religious groups and some trade unions.

Activities of the Congress, including its mammoth annual conference attended by many thousands of people, contributed greatly toward intensifying a psychological clamor for peace on the part of the Japanese. But, as the Communists succeeded in permeating the organization, its activities gradually deviated from its original humanitarian purpose and eventually became an instrument through which the Com-

munists were able to stage anti-American campaigns. In September 1961, following the sudden resumption of nuclear testing by the Soviet Union, this organization's policies became completely confused because it could not take a definite stand toward Russia and began to lose much of its earlier prestige.

In reaction to this group, another organization, called the Congress for Peace and for Prohibition of Nuclear Weapons, which had bolted from the *Gensuikyo* a few years earlier in protest to its predominant leftism, intensified its own activities. Not hesitating to blame the Soviet government for the resumption of nuclear testing, this second Congress staged demonstrations in front of the Soviet Embassy in Tokyo and succeeded in gaining a degree of support from the people.

Government policies   Under the pressure of popular sentiment calling for the prohibition of nuclear weapons, the Japanese government also has consistently protested to any country which conducted nuclear tests. In this regard, there is no difference of opinion between the Government and the opposition. The widespread nervousness of the Japanese people and the unity of public opinion with regard to the subject of nuclear testing have caused the Japanese government repeatedly to make clear its stand that it would not allow the American forces to bring atomic weapons into Japan. On this basis also, the Government rejected the proposal that an American submarine visit Japan.

Japanese government policy toward nuclear weapons consistently maintains that not only should an international treaty banning nuclear weapons be concluded with provisions for effective international inspection but also all nuclear testing should be stopped immediately regardless of the conclusion of a treaty between East and West. When the Soviet Union resumed testing in 1961, the Japanese government sent a bitter note of protest. It also transmitted a protest to the American government when the latter declared its intention of resuming atmospheric tests, if the Soviet Union did not agree to international inspection.

There is no doubt concerning the sincerity of the Japanese people in their desire to avoid war or about the consistency with which the Government has protested against all nuclear testing. It remains to be seen, however, how strongly these peace-loving sentiments will be maintained and how well-considered the Government's policy has been. There remains a question as to whether this attitude or policy is merely an emotional reaction or mood rather than a calculated conclusion derived objectively from judgments on international situations.

It is very doubtful that the conclusion would be the same if they considered the possibility that the Soviet Union and its bloc might surpass the Free World in military capacity if the United States refrains from testing while the Soviet bloc does not. It is also not easy to predict the attitude of the Japanese people if they were faced with the even more serious problem of Communist China's acquisition of nuclear weapons. The problem of nuclear weapons remains a problem filled with dilemma, a problem which all nations inevitably must face.

NATIONAL INTERESTS AND POSTWAR DIPLOMACY

As described in the preceding section, there are many more complicated problems that are waiting to be settled, such as the problem of restoring diplomatic relations with Korea and China, territorial problems with the Soviet Union and the problems with Australia in connection with the continental shelf. Japan has been approaching these problems gradually, in line with the growth of its national power and consistently avoiding international complications which might slow down the nation's economic growth. This passive policy on the part of the Government naturally becomes an ideal target for criticism from Socialists and intellectuals. How does one evaluate the contrast-

ing viewpoints of the Government and the Opposition?

All people agree that the nation's policy should be aimed at promoting the nation's prosperity and security. However, the issues in conflict evolve around the methods of guarding the national interest, or rather what policies should be pursued to achieve these desired ends. It is basically, as in the case of any political issue, a question of value judgments and these cannot be dealt with from a scientific point of view alone. Yet, it is not impossible to deal with them reasonably, following definite premises.

Protecting the nation in a bipolar world
First of all, the security of a nation means not only the sanctity of its territory but also the protection of its well-being against any kind of external threat. With regard to the nation's well-being, the majority of the people desire to adhere closely to the provisions of the new Constitution. Because of the psychological traditions of the people, their behavior occasionally gives an impression of being anti-democratic; nevertheless it is generally correct to assume that the Japanese people do wish to live up to the Constitution, preferring to live in a democratic society.

If this assumption is correct, Japan is unlikely to drift consciously towards communism. If this holds true, then Japan is faced with another serious problem in regard to the Communist bloc. As long as the Soviet Union and China retain their ambitions of conquering and communizing the world and demonstrating their military strength, Japan will be forced to re-evaluate its policies and desires to maintain its national integrity and safety without the use of military power.

In this light, the Japanese are left with two choices: armed neutrality or regional collective security arrangements with the free nations. The former is the policy followed by such countries as Sweden and Switzerland. Under certain circumstances, Japan may follow this example. At present, appropriate factors do not exist to make it possible for Japan to follow these nations. These countries have remained neutral for more than a century. Japan, on the other hand, occupied by the United States until the San Francisco treaty was concluded, found itself among the members of the Western alliance. In view of Japan's overall strength and its position in Asia, its withdrawal from the U.S.–Japan Security Pact and neutralization would be a grave matter. From the point of view of international power balances, such a change could very well result in another war.

In addition, it is too great an economic burden for Japan to possess an army strong enough to protect itself independently. Japan would have to increase its national defense budget several times to accomplish this. Furthermore, since democracy has not fully developed in Japan, there is always the danger that a strong army would help the militarists reassert themselves again and thereby threaten the principle of democracy itself.

This leaves Japan only one course: to maintain an army strong enough to cope with small-scale acts of aggression and to rely on the United States in the event of a larger conflict. Meanwhile, Japan can establish itself as a welfare state and a politically consolidated democracy. Japan should not fail to maintain friendly relations with neighboring countries in order to expand its foreign trade. For the sake of national interest, Japan should be friendly with Communist China, but friendly relations with the United States rank first in importance.

The foreign policy of the Socialist Party   In this respect, the Socialist Party's non-armed neutralism is far from realistic. It is true that there are some Communists and disguised Communists among the Socialist Party as well as among the intellectuals. But it is wrong to assume that all of the members of the Socialist Party or those who support neutralism are Marx-Leninists. On the contrary most of them are ideologically against Soviet communism. We might say that their neutralism is at least subjectively genuine. There are also among these groups pacifists who are quite similar to the conscientious objectors in European countries.

It is not difficult to comprehend the positions taken by many Japanese people. The public is accustomed to leaving all diplomatic problems up to a group of politicians and never has learned to face these issues directly. The socialist parties in Japan, unlike those in Europe, have not experienced responsibility for war. In Japan they began to grow to the position of a major party only after the Second World War. They do not, moreover, consider international relations the result of power politics, but rather, like the Socialists and intellectuals in Europe between the two World Wars, they tend to look at all international issues from a utopian viewpoint. They feel that slogans or declarations are enough to secure world peace and that even with dictators, all problems can be settled by negotiations without force. This attitude is reminiscent of the appeasement policy which the Socialists in Europe practiced against Hitler.

To say that the foreign policy of the Socialist Party is nothing more than 19th century isolationism or utopianism, does by no means justify the policy taken by the Government of the Liberal-Democratic Party. The Government should be given credit for the degree of prosperity in Japan, protected by the U.S.–Japan Security Pact. But we must also point out the failure of the Government to enlighten the public on the importance of international issues. In every general election, the Liberal-Democratic Party has always put forward various domestic platforms. But it has avoided announcing its international policies thus failing to gain popular support for them. There is an office in the Ministry of Foreign Affairs responsible for enlightening the public on international issues, but the Government as a whole does not play an active role in any domestic information program.

Policies of the Liberal-Democratic Party
This inattentiveness on the part of the Liberal-Democratic Party government to domestic publicity has a great deal to do with the party's general character. The leaders of the party are mostly bureaucrats who still seem to think that the public need not, or rather should not, worry about politics at all. They

are supported by the public not in terms of their policies but because of personal relations. In addition, the fact that among the party leaders are a number of war criminals, responsible for the Second World War, is enough to cancel out any active propaganda by the Government to win the nation's full support.

So far, the Liberal Democratic government's Asian policies have been following those of the United States. The Americans, afraid of the expansion of communism into the South East Asian countries, have concentrated on supplying these underdeveloped countries with military aid. But such aid is actually not enough to stop communism in Asia. Military aid must be accompanied by economic and ideological programs in order to be effective. In this respect, Japan, being closer to these nations culturally and geographically, has a most important role to play. Japan must acquire enough knowledge and power to be able to give suggestions to the United States in connection with its Asian policies.

The same things can be said in regard to China. As far as trade is concerned, China is not as important as some businessmen in Japan might expect, at least under controlled trade conditions. Yet, it is necessary for a country like Japan, whose national economy is based primarily on foreign trade, to seek markets in China as well as in the Western countries. Apart from the trade issue, it is ill-advised, even dangerous, for Japan to have as a neighbor a country with whom a peace treaty is so long overdue.

Of course, this problem is intertwined with the question of relations with Formosa and, therefore, is even more complicated. Yet it is not actually justifiable to insist that association with the Peking government means disapproval of the Formosan government. On the contrary, Japan can contribute a great deal to world peace by breaking the ice between Washington and Peking. In this regard, criticism by the Opposition of the Government's passive attitude towards the United States–Communist China problem is not wholly unjustified.

Prospects for the future   What Japan can do for the future community of nations is to assume the role of a bridge or barometer between the Afro-Asian countries and Western society, including the United States. Many newly independent nations are likely to lean towards a rather emotional nationalism due to their age-old antipathy for colonialism. They may stand firmly against all foreign countries in an effort to ease their people's discontent resulting from difficulties in domestic economic development. Still, the European countries may insist on their vested interests. This is where Japan could and should play an important part in world relations.

It should, on the one hand, help the underdeveloped nations develop their economy and also assist in their social revolutions toward breaking away from feudalistic social systems. It should, on the other hand, guide them in avoiding the same mistakes that Japan made in the past. The Japanese people, who have in the past successfully managed to adopt and assimilate both the Chinese and the Western civilizations, can help fuse the cultures of the East and the West, thereby becoming a bridge between Asia and Europe.

Foreign policy must, on the one hand, aim at maintaining an idealistic approach and, on the other hand, it must take into consideration the balance of power. The Socialist Party is too unrealistic in its foreign policy, while the Liberal-Democratic Party lacks imaginative programs for the reconstruction of Asia. These two positions must be balanced, if Japan is to become strong enough to exert leadership on the international level and gain the full respect of world opinion.

BIBLIOGRAPHY

Author's Suggestions

Maki, John. *Government and Politics in Japan, The Road to Democracy.* New York: Frederick Praeger, 1962.

Mendel, Douglas. *The Japanese People and Foreign Policy, A Study of Public Opinion in Post-Treaty Japan.* Berkeley: University of California Press, 1961.

Morley, James W. "Japanese Image of the Soviet Union 1952–61," *Pacific Affairs,* Vol. 35, No. 1, Spring, 1962.

Morris, Ivan. "Foreign Policy Issues in Japan's 1958 Elections," *Pacific Affairs,* Vol. 31, No. 2, September, 1958.

Morris, Ivan. "Japanese Foreign Policy and Neutralism," *International Affairs,* Vol. 36, No. 1, January, 1960.

Reischauer, Edwin O. "The Broken Dialogue with Japan," *Foreign Affairs,* Vol. 39, No. 1, October, 1960.

Reischauer, Edwin O. *Japan, Past and Present.* New York: Knopf, 1953.

Reischauer, Edwin O. *The United States and Japan.* (Rev. ed.) New Haven: Harvard University Press, 1957.

Scalapino, Robert A. "The Foreign Policy of Modern Japan," in Macridis, Roy C., Ed. *Foreign Policy in World Politics.* Englewood Cliffs, N.J.: Prentice Hall, 1962.

Scalapino, Robert A. and Masumi, J. *Parties and Politics in Contemporary Japan.* Berkeley: University of California Press, 1962.

ABOUT THE AUTHOR

ROBERT A. SCALAPINO is widely known for his scholarly contributions on Far Eastern affairs. He received his B.A. degree from Santa Barbara College and took his Ph.D. degree at Harvard University. He has taught at Santa Barbara College, Harvard University and the University of California, Berkeley and is currently Professor of Political Science and Chairman of the Department of Political Science at Berkeley.

Mr. Scalapino has served as a consultant to many groups, including the Rockefeller Brothers Fund, the Ford Foundation and the Senate Foreign Relations Committee. He has published numerous articles and books, including the following: *Democracy and the Party Movement in Pre-War Japan,* 1953; *Reflections on American Relations with Japan,* 1953; *The Chinese Anarchist Movement* (with George T. Yu), 1961; *Parties and Politics in Contemporary Japan* (with Junnosuke Masumi), 1962. Mr. Scalapino is the editor of *Asian Survey.*

ABOUT THE CHAPTER

Mr. Scalapino starts his chapter with the assertion that the emergence of China as a Major World Power may well be one of the most significant developments of the later part of the twentieth century. The importance he attaches to the challenge of the new China sets the tone for the discussion. The author examines three major forces which he insists must be taken into account if one is to make sense of developments in China: tradition, nationalism, and Marx-Lenin-Maoism. This is followed by an examination of the foreign policy apparatus with attention being given to emerging institutions of government and to the small group of men who constitute the inner power circle of the Communist Party.

A major portion of the chapter deals with the content of Chinese foreign policy. The Sino-Soviet alliance is discussed with careful consideration to the cleavage within the Communist world. Attention is also given to the whole range of policy problems which confront the leaders of China. Some of these problems are clearly of a territorial nature; others are ideological and are related to the struggle for leadership in the Communist world. The chapter concludes with a brief summary of Chinese foreign policy and the observation of the author that the leaders of this nation can take "considerable satisfaction in her foreign policy achievements after thirteen years in power."

19

THE FOREIGN POLICY OF THE PEOPLE'S REPUBLIC OF CHINA

ROBERT A. SCALAPINO

University of California, Berkeley

In the light of history, the most significant event of the late twentieth century could easily be the emergence of China as a Major Power. We now seem to be witnessing the opening stages of that drama. Although the "People's Republic of China" has been in existence less than fifteen years, it has already had a profound impact everywhere. Chinese influence throughout Asia has immeasurably increased. Chinese missions are operating in Africa and Latin America. Chinese representatives must now be invited to certain international discussions despite the fact that Communist China is not a member of the United Nations. And the Chinese role inside the Communist bloc has become vitally important to the entire world.

Meanwhile, within China, a gigantic upheaval continues, marked by significant achievements and notable failures. There are "big leaps forward" and subsequent retreats; bitter hardships and enticing promises—above all, there is movement and experimentation under some of the most difficult circumstances that any society has ever faced. The future seems to hold more of the same. Continuing mass poverty and rising state power are likely to be linked together. This is an explosive combination. How to connect China with some workable system of international law and order will remain a critical world problem. As we examine Chinese Communist foreign policy, we should keep these central points in mind.

SOURCE SPRINGS OF CHINESE FOREIGN POLICY

In Communist China's foreign policy there are three all-pervasive influences: tradition, nationalism, and Marx-Lenin-Maoism. Their nature, extent, and interrelation must be understood.

Geopolitics and tradition

Area   First, let us set forth a few geopolitical factors that have influenced attitudes and policies in the past and in modern times. As is well known, China is a nation huge in size and in population. It is, indeed, nearly one-half of Asia. This in itself is significant in terms of the way in which power is constructed in the modern world. We live in an age when power is held by continental mass societies such as the United States and the Soviet Union. The time is ripe for Chinese ascendancy.

In the mid-nineteenth century, world power was acquired by a small group of European states that had come to modern nationalism and the industrial revolution early. These states, which had no vast indigenous resources, had the advantage of timing. With that advantage, they developed world empires to supplement their deficiencies. The basic, long-range sources of their power, however, lay extensively outside their own society. Great Britain, France, Belgium, and the Netherlands belonged in this category, as did Japan at a later point.

A century afterward, global power was wielded by two massive societies that were just reaching their full industrial stride. These societies—the United States and the Soviet Union—were true continental Powers containing within their own areas an impressive quantity of raw materials, manpower, and energy. To be sure, Western Europe is now combining its facilities in such a fashion as to represent at least potentially another continental mass society. Will China also join the category of mass societies that attain major power? Certainly she qualifies in terms of sheer magnitude. The difficult question is whether her population-land-raw materials balance is so unfavorable as to be a source of continuous weakness rather than strength.

Population   Today the population of China presumably stands at about 650 million, although this is a subject of debate. Some observers doubt the reliability of the Chinese Communist census of 1953. According to that census, the population of the mainland was 583 million. It has been generally assumed that the population has been growing at a rate in excess of 2 per cent per annum, adding some 12–14 million to the population yearly. Recent hard-

ships may have slowed that growth. No matter what the precise facts, however, it seems safe to say that China has a huge population most of which is now living at marginal levels.

A colossal population represents a problem —and a potential. To draw up a precise balance sheet is difficult. If such a population can be mobilized effectively, much can be accomplished in peace and in war. But in recent years, the Chinese Communists appear to have overestimated what they could do by substituting manpower for machinery, and to have misjudged the industrial-agrarian balance necessary to carry out successful modernization. Moreover, any substantial population increases would negate increases in production. A huge population may also breed certain types of attitudes. No doubt, Chinese confidence and toughness are connected with sheer size. Especially in this age, when *mass* is power, bigness in itself creates a sense of power in the minds of leadership. Perhaps a nation of 650 million can even face the prospects of global atomic war with some confidence of survival. The adventurist attitudes derived from bigness may be in part illusory or dangerous, but they cannot be ignored.

Neighbors   Size also presents China with many neighbors. Few if any countries in the world have common boundaries with as many different peoples as does Communist China. Along her extensive southern borders lie most of the countries of south Asia: Afghanistan, Pakistan, India, Nepal, Sikkim, Bhutan, Burma, Laos, and North Vietnam. To the west and north, China shares a common boundary with Outer Mongolia, North Korea, and with the Soviet Union for thousands of miles. To the east, China looks across a narrow strip of water to states she currently regards as hostile: Japan, Taiwan, and the Philippines. All are affiliated with her deadly enemy, the United States. At present, the most dangerous barbarians (now read "imperialists") come from the east.

It is understandable why the Chinese would choose the name *Chung-kuo,* "Central" or "Middle Kingdom" to identify their country.

CHINA AND ITS NEIGHBORS

SAKHALIN

U.S.S.R.

Khabarovsk

Tomsk

Irkutsk

Harbin *Vladivostok*

Sea of Japan

Tokyo
Yokohama

Ulaan Baatar

JAPAN

Mukden

MONGOLIAN REPUBLIC

Nagoya

Kyoto *Osaka*

Pyongyang

Seoul

Peking **KOREA**

Paotow *Tientsin* *Pusan*

INNER MONGOLIA

Yellow Sea

SINKIANG

Alma Ata

Nanking

Shanghai *East China Sea*

Kashgar

CHINA

Hankow

nagar

KASHMIR

TIBET

Chungking

Taipei

FORMOSA

elhi
New Delhi

NEPAL SIKKIM

Katmandu BHUTAN

Canton

Hong Kong

Pacific Ocean

PAKISTAN
(East)

Kunming

Manila

Calcutta

BURMA

Hanoi

HAINAN

INDIA

LAOS

VIETNAM

PHILIPPINES

Hyderabad

Rangoon

Vientiane

THAILAND

South China Sea

Madras

Bangkok

CAMBODIA

Bay of Bengal

Phnom Penh *Saigon*

CEYLON

NORTH BORNEO

BRUNEI

Colombo

MALAYA

SARAWAK

Kuala Lumpur

CELEBES

Indian Ocean

Singapore

BORNEO

SUMATRA

INDONESIA

500
MILES

To them, China was the hub of the universe, the center of civilization. On its peripheries, where the fertile valleys gave way to arid waste-lands or towering mountains, lived a great variety of barbarians. These barbarians differed in many respects, particularly in the degree of danger they represented to China, but they shared one common trait: they were un-Chinese, and hence, to the Chinese, they were uncivilized. Like the ancient Greeks and the modern French, there has been a conspicuous tendency among the Chinese to divide the world into two categories: Chinese and barbarian. This tendency, moreover, projected itself into modern times. It is one of the reasons why the Chinese were so slow in adjusting to the Western impact, so tenacious in clinging to their traditions. Only at a late date and through a series of harsh revolutions was China wrenched away from the past—and then, not completely.

Ideology Ethnocentrism is still a factor with which to reckon in China. The old strains of cultural superiority and exclusivism are not dead. One still detects the xenophobia, the racism that is a legacy of the Chinese past. It is true that all of this violates Marx-Leninism and is properly denounced by the current leaders. But are not these leaders themselves in an ambivalent position? The old Bolsheviks who control China today are both Communist *and* Chinese. Mao Tse-tung is an excellent example. In some respects, he is a scholar-bureaucrat of the traditional mold. His education and life-experience have been totally within China. In these respects, China is his universe. The two brief trips to Moscow after 1949 scarcely count. Mao writes Chinese poetry, retreats periodically to contemplate long-range policy and to philosophize, and excels in quoting the classics when it serves his purposes. Nor is this unique among the men who rule China today. These men are dedicated Marx-Leninists, and implicit in their philosophy is the world view. But many of them know the world only as it has been strained through Marxian literature. They have had little practical contact with it, except for a few, like Chou En-lai. It was pre-

cisely this type of ignorance that cost nineteenth century China so heavily, when scholar-bureaucrats who knew the world only as it was strained through Confucian literature, totally misjudged their situation and their times.

The present leaders are in power today because they know China. Mao is hailed as the man who "has applied the universal truth of Marx-Leninism to the revolutionary reality of China, and by interpreting the experiences of the Chinese revolution, enriched and developed Marx-Leninism." Clearly, the *Chinese* quotient in Marx-Leninism is rising for the Chinese Communists. The applicability of the Chinese experience for other peoples, moreover, is increasingly stressed in Chinese writings. The Chinese-Marxist way of life is intended to have the same guidance role for the Afro-Asian-Latin American world of today that the old Celestial-Confucian way of life had for the barbarians of yesterday.

Isolationism As China reaches out to the world, however, she also seeks to insulate herself against it in certain respects. Authoritarianism always finds selective isolation an extremely valuable weapon. When a people are under intensive ideological discipline and also under unprecedented pressure to conduct a one-generation industrial revolution, it is important to regulate their contact both with ideas and with people. Promiscuous relations can be dangerous to the central object of such regimes: to create true believers who are completely loyal because they know that their way is vastly superior to the way of others. Thus, on the one hand, Communist China has turned outward to the world with missions, aid, and propaganda, and has also brought a portion of that world to China; but on the other hand, the traffic in both ideas and people has never been more carefully controlled and regulated. The people must be protected against the contamination of liberalism or the liberal, and that portion of China that is "backward" must remain secluded from unfriendly eyes.

Once again, geography and the traditions which it helped to shape have bequeathed a legacy. In the pattern of Chinese history, world involvement and isolation were always interwoven. Despite the thousands of miles of frontier contacts with other peoples, traditional China was precluded by geography from having close or continuous contact with another great civilization. The distances and the natural obstacles separating China from India and the Middle Eastern societies were formidable. Contacts did exist, and some cultural borrowing of importance took place. But the kind of cultural intimacy characteristic of the ancient Mediterranean area was not possible. Undoubtedly, this fact heightened the uniqueness of Chinese culture, and also the sense of that uniqueness, the feelings of cultural superiority.

Isolation, however, was more than a natural phenomenon. It was also a conscious policy. "Keep the barbarians out of Peking!" was a stern injunction of long standing, even in periods when there were scant military means to enforce it. Some barbarians, whom the Chinese wanted to impress, or with whom they had established tributary relations, were invited to the capital where gifts were exchanged and the proper courtesies observed. But dangerous barbarians were kept as far from the centers of authority as possible. The attempt of Chinese officials to confine the Western barbarians to Canton is a classic example of this policy.

In summation, we can say that tradition, as it interacted with the geographic circumstances of China, produced both a set of attitudes and a set of policies governing the relations of China to the larger world. The attitudes were largely those of a people who considered themselves "advanced," capable of setting the cultural tone for their world, a people who might be conquered by crude force but who could never be surpassed in cultural attainments or civilization. In Chinese diplomacy, suavity, patience, brutality, sensitivity, and condescension all played their parts, along with a disinterest in and ignorance of the rest of the world that was with a few exceptions, monumental.

Relations with other Powers　　The central problem of Chinese foreign policy was generally the question of how to handle the barbarians. To this question, Chinese authorities provided a variety of answers. When resources permitted, force was used to pacify unruly elements and extend the bounds of Chinese rule. Periodically, great empires were built, albeit often under the aegis of foreign rulers in Peking. But when China did not wish to use force, or was unable to do so, other means of pacification were tried. Some techniques involved military defense, such as the Great Wall. Others involved the use of the tributary system to tie various small countries to the Central Kingdom. From the Chinese standpoint, this system was an acknowledgment by small states and rulers of the suzerainty of China. To the tributary states, it was not necessarily more than an opportunity for trade combined with some insurance against Chinese interference in their affairs.

It is interesting that in the pre-Western era, Chinese influence was generally greatest in northeast Asia and in the far west, once extending to the gates of Vienna. (Are the Chinese striving to get there again, this time ideologically?) In southern Asia, Indian influence predominated, and the rough cultural boundary line, curiously enough, was that between Vietnam and Cambodia. Once more, that line has some meaning, just as Sino-Indian rivalry is again on the ascendancy.

Confucianism　　Before we examine the other broad components of Chinese Communist foreign policy, we must touch upon one additional element of tradition, namely, Confucianism. Some elements of Confucianism have significance today because they suggest areas of receptivity to Marxism, especially among the Chinese intelligentsia. Confucianism staunchly upheld the concept of the educative state, with its rules being interpreted by a scholar-bureaucracy. The wise—those who had shown their mastery of truth, as evidenced in Confucian principles—should rule. Ideally, moreover, they should rule by example rather than by law. Their conduct should be a guide to the common people. They should serve as tutors to the governed. In theory at least, there were few limitations on the scope of their authority. Music, literature, art—all were a part of basic values and thought, and hence were subject to state control.

Confucianism, however, was no crude philosophy of control through force. Coercion might have to be used, but heavy reliance was placed on persuasion. Indeed, even the concept of introspection was developed. Every person was to look into himself and find *the truth,* and having found it, abide by its dictates. Despite this use of introspection, however, Confucianism was not a philosophy of the individual. It was rather one of the earliest philosophies attuned to the organizational man. Man was never an entity unto himself; he was a part of a larger unit and derived his meaning from that unit. Confucianism saw the smallest and most stable unit in the family, and it sought to use the familial rules as the foundation for state rules. In this sense, it became involved in a dilemma. To which should the priority of loyalty go, family or state? Communism has solved that dilemma, establishing state priorities firmly and without equivocation. But there was no need to change the organizational concept of man that had held sway in China for nearly 2500 years.

Confucianism also contained within its doctrines the right of revolution. One could not revolt against a ruler because, by definition, a ruler was just. But when a ruler ceased to abide by the mandate of heaven, by *the truth* as interpreted by the scholar-bureaucracy, he ceased to be a ruler, and became a tyrant. Anyone could overthrow a tyrant. This doctrine is of particular interest because, as we shall note, the Communists have a parallel doctrine which can be put to excellent use in foreign policy. It is the doctrine of the infallibility of the people. One cannot revolt against the people because, by definition, the people are right. But when some people refuse to abide by the principles of justice and *truth* as interpreted by the Marxist scholar-bureaucracy, they cease to be people and become enemies of the people. Anyone can overthrow the enemies of the people. On this basis, as we shall note, the Chinese Communists have made it a cardinal principle to distinguish between certain foreign governments (which have become enemies) and their

people who, by definition, are peace-loving, democratic, and friendly.

Nationalism

Pre-Communist period Another basic determinant of Chinese foreign policy is nationalism. As we have noted, China has long had a great cultural heritage, and from this has derived a certain unity, as well as a firm belief in the superiority of the Chinese way of life. But this cultural nationalism was not easily translated into political nationalism. China did have her periods of empire, but these empires were usually short-lived, held together essentially by military power and a system of nepotism that ended in struggle and parcellation. Even within China proper, the huge area involved, the entrenched power of provincialism, and the intensive ties of family and clan provided major barriers to the emergence of a truly centralized nation-state. The form, to be sure, was that of a centralized monarchy. But this form could exist only because in fact there was a high degree of local autonomy and an extensive role for private as opposed to public government. The family and clan undertook many functions that were essentially political and governmental. Thus, the loyalties of the people remained divided. In a sense, the family was always at war with the state. Again and again in modern times, the Chinese were described as a sheet of loose sand.

It is not surprising that Chinese patriots— non-Communist and Communist alike—regard the last 150 years as a period of degradation for their country and their people. China was the sick giant of Asia, hopelessly backward and divided, in a world dominated by Western technology and power. Chinese territory was annexed, and spheres of influence were established in many of the remaining areas. The very survival of China as an independent state was long in doubt. Chinese like Sun Yat-sen, in describing their plight, were fond of using such terms as hypo-colony or quasi-colony. Many articulate Chinese considered themselves second-class citizens in their own country.

Communist period   The Chinese Communists effectively utilized the frustrations and bitterness implicit in this situation. Indeed, they came to power primarily because they captured the nationalist movement in the course of a patriotic war. Like the Yugoslav Communists whom they now revile, the Chinese Communists moved from impotence to prominence by employing "united front" tactics against the "Fascist invaders," by appealing to the masses of people to be patriotic and struggle against the Japanese foe. This, together with their promises of "bourgeois" type economic, social, and political reforms constituted the basis of Communist success.

In the chaotic period that followed World War II, the Communists continued to fight vigorously to hold or capture the nationalist banners. Taking advantage of the mass base they had developed during the Anti-Japanese War, they proclaimed themselves the spokesmen for a "New Democracy," for a China totally purged of external control. They sought to pin the label, "running dogs of American imperialism," upon the Kuomintang. And when they triumphed in 1949, they proclaimed that the "New China" would be completely free of Western domination. From the beginning, moreover, they underlined those words with a tough attitude toward the West, particularly the United States.

Since 1949, the Communist authorities have created a giant, monolithic structure that represents the strongest government that China has ever known. The authority of the central government has been extended to the utmost reaches of the country, into every rural hamlet and urban block. This unprecedented control over the Chinese people is not a product solely of coercion, or even organizational efficiency. Rather, the nationalist appeal has been used effectively and with all emotional stops pulled, especially to youth. It was to patriotism that the Communists appealed when they exhorted the Chinese to "volunteer" their services to protect the motherland against American ag-gression during the Korean War. Indeed, the United States has served well as a major target and a valuable rallying-point for Chinese nationalist antipathy throughout the period of Communist rule. The fight against American encirclement, American occupation of Chinese soil (Taiwan), and American militarism has been a constant theme. But patriotism could be directed toward the economic front also. "Eradicate Chinese backwardness" became a war-cry. "The Big Leap Forward" was launched with all the fervor of bayonet-brandishing troops storming the enemy's stronghold.

Symbols and slogans   Whether directed against America or against poverty, Chinese Communist nationalist propaganda is surfeited with military symbolism. In part, this is a legacy of world communism. In many respects, however, it is a legacy of the historical experience of the Chinese Communists themselves. *One must never forget that Mao Tse-tung and his veteran compatriots spent thirty years in the trenches.* They have thought, written, and acted in military terms almost all their lives. It is probably impossible for them to give up this flavor, this tone, this general intellectual framework.

Not unnaturally, the Chinese Communists are proud of the power they have created in slightly over one decade of rule. Boasted Teng Hsiao-p'ing, Secretary-General of the Central Committee of the Party:

The people of all nationalities in China stand united around the Chinese Communist Party, like a giant. In the past, the imperialists mocked the Chinese people by calling them "a heap of sand." Now they can only tremble in the face of the united Chinese people.[1]

Reported Chou En-lai at the same time:

---

[1] Teng Hsiao-p'ing, *The Great Unity of the Chinese People and the Great Unity of the Peoples of the World* (written for *Pravda* in celebration of the 10th anniversary of the People's Republic of China) Peking: 1959, p. 2.

Our motherland has become a big family in which all nationalities are completely equal and give fraternal aid to one another. The country has achieved a unity of unprecedented firmness. Bandits, gangsters, superstitious sects and secret societies as well as prostitutes, beggars, gambling houses and narcotic drugs have all been swept away; there is law and order everywhere.[2]

Although they proclaim proudly the independence and glory of the "New China," the Communist leaders are quick to denounce "bourgeois nationalism" and proclaim their loyalty to "proletarian internationalism." Always, Communist spokesmen have insisted that the Chinese Communist movement is a part of the world Communist movement, a further step along the path that was first illuminated by the "Great October Revolution."[3] In their words, the unity of the Chinese people is the beginning of a continuum that will ultimately lead to the unity of all peoples under the leadership of the great socialist family of peace-loving nations. Teng has stated the CCP position succinctly:

We stand for proletarian internationalism as opposed to all kinds of bourgeois reactionary ideologies of big-nation chauvinism and narrow nationalism. The modern revisionists, as represented by the Yugoslav ruling clique, use bourgeois nationalism to oppose proletarian internationalism,

use the nation as a cover to oppose international solidarity and have fully become an echo of imperialism. The Central Committee of the Chinese Communist Party and Comrade Mao Tse-tung have told the entire Party and people time and again that we must always unite with the proletariat and the peoples of the world and make proletarian internationalism our rule of conduct.[4]

Objectives There is no need to question the sincerity of the Chinese Communist leaders when they utter these words, as they have been doing, indeed, for over forty years. At the same time, there is no reason to ignore deeds in favor of words. And when one reflects upon the foreign policies of the Chinese Communists since 1949, the problems of reconciling nationalism and internationalism, of meshing national interests and international commitments seem no less difficult for a Communist state than for a democratic one. Perhaps, given the nature of Communist requirements, they are more difficult. In any case, for a decade now, Communist China, all speeches to the contrary, has acted very much like any other great rising nation-state. This is now recognized in Asia, and one can be certain, in the Soviet Union as well.

When a new nation with great potential emerges, its pattern of action, within broad limits, can be predicted. First, it will seek to define and defend its boundaries. The definition, of course, will be in its favor to the fullest possible extent, and the defense will be militant. Almost simultaneously, it will seek security in depth, through the creation of some type of buffer-state system. Perhaps, in this atomic-hydrogen age, there is no possibility of security in depth, and the concept of buffer-states has become outmoded. Nonetheless, no major Power has yet indicated such a change by its attitudes and actions. Finally, this new state will gradually strive for hegemony in the general area around it seeking, at the same time,

[2] Chou En-lai, *A Great Decade*, Peking: 1959, p. 13. Recent reports coming from China (1961) indicate that in the wake of serious food shortages, some begging and prostitution have returned. Indeed, certain foreign observers have asserted that there has been a general decline in law and order, measured against the earlier "puritan" days. The extent of this decline, and the question of future trends cannot be gauged accurately at this time. There is no indication, however, that the generalizations given above yet require substantial modification.

[3] Liu Shao-ch'i, *The Victory of Marxism-Leninism in China*, Peking: 1959, p. 1.

[4] Teng, *op cit.*, p. 15.

world recognition and prestige and a portion of the global decision-making power that it considers its due.

Thus far, Communist China has acted in accordance with this pattern of behavior. Ironically, it took Marxism to bring nationalism to its zenith in China. Belatedly, this huge nation has arisen, still weak in many respects, wracked by revolutionary convulsions and bitterness, moving forward in jerky, uneven fashion, possessed, in its elite, of a deep pride, self-confidence, and endurance capacity. As we proceed to explore Chinese policy toward the Communist bloc, the Afro-Asian world, and the United States, the transcendent importance of nationalism will appear again and again.

Chinese Marxism

Under no circumstances, however, should Marx-Lenin-Maoism be slighted. It is clearly a basic determinant of Chinese values, attitudes, and policies today. To add "Maoism" to Marx-Leninism does not mean that all new elements were Mao's personal contribution. Rather, it means that the *Chinese* quotient in Chinese Marxism is substantial and important. The Chinese Communists, incidentally, do not use the term Maoism—yet.

The nature of the real Chinese contributions to Marxist theory and practice is less significant for our purposes than the fact that the Chinese variety of Marxism is vitally important to any understanding of Communist China. The leaders of contemporary China are true believers in the fullest sense. They have been put to all the tests and remained faithful. For them, Marx-Lenin-Maoism is not only a philosophy, it is a way of life, an article of faith, the supreme revelation of truth. And in all of this, they feel themselves confirmed *because it has succeeded*. Perhaps the next generation of Chinese leaders will be different. Perhaps they will be less interested in faith or theory. Perhaps they will really be proletarians, like Khrushchev, instead of intellectuals. But at

present we are dealing with Mao Tse-tung, Liu Shao-ch'i, Teng Hsiao-p'ing, Chou En-lai, and men of similar type.

There is no need to undertake a full analysis of Chinese Marxism here, but certain major points which are of significance in terms of foreign policy should be indicated. The following four points are worthy of brief note, and we phrase them in the terminology of the Maoists:

1. Marx-Leninism must be adapted and adjusted to fit the needs and nature of each society. In this process, each society will be enabled to make its own creative additions to that ideology. Indeed, assert the Maoists, this is what has occurred in the case of China. Out of forty years' experience, Mao Tse-tung has been able to enrich Marxism. And so have the masses. When hundreds of millions of people are on the march, they are bound to discover new truths, because the masses go by the logic of life itself. Hence they instinctively find truth if they are provided with Marxist guidance.

This general point, long ago stressed by Mao in his *On New Democracy*, was recently rephrased by Teng as follows:

Marxism-Leninism always opposes the solution of new problems in life by resorting to ready-made formulas from books. In carrying out socialist construction in a country like ours, with a very large population and backward economy, we cannot possibly avoid a host of extraordinary difficulties and complicated problems. We must depend upon the living experience of mass struggles to overcome these difficulties and solve these problems. The Chinese Communist Party and Comrade Mao Tse-tung consistently maintain that the universal truth of Marxism-Leninism must be integrated with the practice of the Chinese revolution. This means applying and developing Marxism-Leninism through the practical struggles of the Chinese people.[5]

[5] *Ibid.*, pp. 8–9.

At least two meaningful points are to be drawn from this first theme. China has a significant role to play in the development of Marxism as a "living, advancing science." Moreover, the Chinese model of Marxism may offer assistance and hope to other people, especially those of the non-Western world.

2. Mao's great success in the *democratic stage* of the Chinese revolution was his correct handling of the peasant question. He recognized the importance of the peasant, mobilized and led him, thereby creating the mass basis for revolutionary success. Liu Shao-ch'i captured the essence of this theme when he wrote:

China was a big, backward country. Over 80 per cent of her people lived in the rural areas; 70 per cent of this rural population were poor peasants and farm labourers. The peasant question was the central question in our democratic revolution. The rule of reaction in old China was extremely barbarous. The masses of the people had no rights whatsoever. Progressive revolutionaries were subject to mass arrests and execution. In the democratic revolutionary period, the Chinese Communist Party, therefore, went deep into the villages and for 22 years led the armed revolutionary struggle which used the villages to encircle the cities. What the Party adopted was the mass line policy of resolutely relying on the peasants' political consciousness and organized strength, mobilizing the peasants to save themselves . . .[6]

Once again, this theme has obvious implications for the non-Western, non-industrial world. These implications, moreover, involve a

Chinese view of that world and the Chinese relation to it.

3. Perhaps the greatest contribution of Maoism to the theory and practice of Marx-Leninism was its success in uniting the theory of revolutionary stages—first a democratic-bourgeois revolution, then a socialist revolution—and the theory of uninterrupted revolution—a continuous revolutionary flow. In short, the Chinese Communists now claim that Mao—first in practice, then in theory—successfully harmonized the two-stage revolution and permanent revolution theses which earlier provoked such controversy in Communist circles. Again, Liu has put this claim succinctly:

Contrary to left and right opportunism, the correct policy represented by Comrade Mao Tse-tung in guiding the Chinese revolution was: On the one hand, by following the Marxist-Leninist theory of revolutionary development by stages, a clear distinction was made between the revolutionary tasks of the two stages, the democratic and socialist revolutions; on the other hand, by following the Marxist-Leninist theory of uninterrupted revolution, the two revolutions were closely linked together and every means was sought during the stage of democratic revolution to create the conditions for the future realization of socialist revolution, so that the struggles of the socialist revolution could be waged without interruption immediately after the nationwide victory of the democratic revolution.[7]

4. The accomplishment of an uninterrupted revolution is possible only when the proletariat seize the leadership of the revolution *in the course of the democratic revolutionary phase.* This is another major Maoist contribution to Marxism in Chinese eyes. In the democratic phase, it is essential to cast the widest possible net. One must build a worker-peasant coalition,

---

[6] Liu Shao-ch'i, *op. cit.*, pp. 5–6. At a later point in this essay, Liu asserts that neither the "right" opportunists nor the "left" opportunists understood how great was the significance of the peasant question for the Chinese revolutionary cause. *Ibid.*, p. 7.

[7] *Ibid.*, p. 4.

and encompass also the national bourgeois, simultaneously co-operating with them and struggling against them. Only in this fashion can the democratic-bourgeois national-liberation movement have a proper mass base. At the same time, however, unless the proletariat captures the leadership of this movement while it is in process, and is thereby enabled to control its course, the smooth, uninterrupted movement from democratic to socialist revolution will not be possible.

Note the following very significant passages from Liu's recent essay:

The firm grasping of the hegemony in the democratic revolution by the proletariat through the Communist Party is the key to ensuring the thorough victory of the democratic revolution and the successful switch-over from the democratic revolution to the socialist revolution.[8]

As far as the main question of the revolution is concerned, i.e., the question of state power, the founding of the People's Republic of China marked the end of the democratic revolution and the beginning of the Socialist revolution in China. While leading the democratic revolution to victory, the Chinese proletariat firmly established its political control of the state; therefore, there was no longer any need to conduct another struggle for the seizure of state power to ensure the victory of socialism.[9]

This last theme has been stressed because it has a certain significance in terms of Chinese foreign policy. It suggests the underlying ambivalence with which China must approach some of the national liberation movements now sweeping over the Afro-Asian world, despite the paeans of praise sung to these by Chinese spokesmen. We shall return to this point later.

The above themes come out of the practical experience of the Chinese Communist movement. They are a part of the Chinese national emergence. There is no need here to argue the question of originality. The important point is that China has established herself as an entity in the stream of practical Marxism, and through the person of Mao, has claimed credit for making significant contributions to Marxian "science."

Is there a connection between the basic theories which the Chinese Communists have accepted in the course of their forty years' experience on the domestic front, and their attitudes and policies in the field of foreign policy? The answer clearly is "Yes." The proletariat on the international scene are the "fraternal socialist countries." At this point, Mao's famous writings on the possibility of contradictions *within socialism* and *within the working class* appear to have unexpected significance in the light of the Sino-Soviet dispute. There is also a parallel between the Chinese Communists' domestic concept of the "united front" of worker, peasant and bourgeois and their international concept of a union between "National Liberation Movements," "neutral states," and the "peace-loving peoples of the socialist camp." The emerging, non-Western world is like the peasantry and a portion of the national bourgeoisie. This is the world that must be united with, and led by the socialist camp. The national bourgeois element in the Western world, too, must be won, or at least neutralized at the same time as it is fundamentally undermined. Finally, like the compradores, the landlords, and the bureaucratic capitalists— the enemies of the people—there are the governments considered hostile to Communist China, especially "the leader of the imperialist camp, the United States." In general terms, this is the Chinese Communist image of the world, an image derived largely from their indigenous environment and from their faith in the Marxist gospel as "enriched" by their own experiences. Before examining the specific policies pursued by Communist China, however, let us briefly explore the men and institutions responsible for the conduct of Chinese foreign relations.

[8] *Ibid.,* pp. 4–5.
[9] *Ibid.,* p. 9.

THE FOREIGN POLICY APPARATUS [10]

Policy formulation   As is well known, ultimate power in a Communist society is held by a small group of men who constitute the inner circle of the Communist Party. The People's Republic of China is no exception. Final authority in matters of foreign policy, and domestic policy as well, currently rests with leaders such as Mao Tse-tung, Liu Shao-ch'i, Chou En-lai, Chu Teh, Ch'en Yun, Peng Chen, Teng Hsiao-p'ing, and Ch'en Yi. These are the men who have long led the Party and who hold such state offices as they determine. In terms of individual decision-making power, it must be assumed that Mao stands in a class by himself, followed by Liu and Chou, with the latter having a special voice in foreign policy matters. Chou has been the leading diplomat among the top Chinese Communists for many years, even before the Yenan era. Until 1958, he served concurrently as Premier and Foreign Minister. Then, the latter post was given to Ch'en Yi, Marshal of the Red Army and high-ranking Party member. Chou must still be considered the leading spokesman on foreign affairs, however. When an issue of importance is at stake, his voice is inevitably heard.

There can be little doubt as to the group of men who formulate the major guide-lines in Chinese foreign policy; but our knowledge of the decision-making process within top Party echelons is too limited to permit any detailed description of how such guide-lines are determined. We can assume that significant differences of opinion on foreign policy issues do develop on occasion, producing spirited discussion and debate at the Politburo or Standing Committee level. It has often been suggested that, in some form, two broad factions exist, a "moderate" group (symbolized by Chou En-lai) and an "extremist" group (symbolized by Liu Shao-ch'i) and that these factions have meaning both with respect to domestic and foreign policy. Undoubtedly, this formulation is too simple and too rigid. While there may well be differences that can be measured along a moderate-extremist line, it is also likely that given individuals shift positions in accordance with circumstances. On the whole, the Chinese Communist leaders have shown a fairly high degree of flexibility, a willingness to change policies when confronted with failure.

Personnel   When the Communists came to full power in China in 1949, they faced a serious problem in recruiting personnel to run the government at every level. Nowhere was this problem more critical than in the area of foreign affairs. For many years, the Communists had been engaged in guerilla warfare, fought from interior bases. They had been relatively isolated from the world. Most high Party members had been denied adequate formal training; contact with foreigners had been very limited; overseas experience was almost non-existent. The veteran Communists were at home with the peasant perhaps, but not with the world. Indeed, this profound ignorance of the world still casts a long shadow over some of the men at the very top of the Chinese Communist hierarchy.

To staff such agencies as the Ministry of Foreign Affairs with individuals who were both "red" and "expert" was extremely difficult in those early days. Thus, use was made of many individuals who did not have a lengthy Communist background, providing they had the type of training necessary. Indeed, a number of individuals formerly affiliated with the Kuomintang were utilized. At the same time, however, attention was quickly turned toward programs to train professional Communist diplomats and foreign affairs experts. Immediately, various institutes specializing in foreign affairs were established or refurbished. Inten-

[10] I am greatly indebted in this section to the work of Donald W. Klein, "Peking's Evolving Ministry of Foreign Affairs," *The China Quarterly*, No. 4, October–December 1960, pp. 28–39; and H. Arthur Steiner, "Communist China in the World Community," *International Conciliation*, No. 533, May 1961, pp. 389–454.

sive language training centers were opened, and in this field, there is evidence of notable success. Gradually, a professional group of foreign officers of relatively high caliber has been developed.

It must still be difficult to supply individuals of training and experience, as well as loyalty, to meet the rapidly developing needs of Chinese Communist diplomacy. At present, the People's Republic of China has over thirty embassies abroad. It has unofficial or quasi-official contacts with more than eighty nations via an extensive "cultural relations" program. A world-wide "informational" service exists, as extensive as that of other Major Powers. Chinese technical assistance teams are working in Asia and Africa, and aid programs totalling nearly one billion U.S. dollars have been projected or undertaken in the past decade. Finally, the Chinese Communists are already deeply involved in bilateral and multilateral negotiations with many nations, including the United States. From all indications, international diplomacy within the Communist bloc is especially arduous at present.

Party and cultural agencies No one agency is sufficient to handle these multitudinous activities. Clearly, the Party itself is directly involved in matters of bloc relations, since these, in their most important facets, represent inter-party relations. Thus, delegations from the CCP attend the vital Moscow conferences in an effort to hammer out common policies for the Communist Commonwealth. Chou En-lai attends meetings like the 22nd CPSU Congress in his capacity as party leader, not as Premier. Certainly, no area of foreign policy is more vital to the Chinese Communists today than their relations with the CPSU and other Communist Parties. Undoubtedly, Party leaders get vital assistance from professional foreign office personnel, but basically this is an area of Party supremacy. Within the Central Committee apparatus, there is an International Liaison Department which presumably is the official Party agency for dealing with the world Communist movement.

To handle the many unofficial aspects of

Chinese Communist diplomacy, there are a number of organizations having no direct connection with the Ministry of Foreign Affairs. To reach nations with whom China has no official relations, the Communists use the technique of "cultural exchange" and "friendship missions." They also establish contact through attendance at such conferences as those of the Afro-Asian Peoples' Solidarity Conference, or the Stockholm Peace Conference. A large number of "Friendship Associations" attuned to each individual country or area have been created to service some of these aspects of Chinese diplomacy. These Associations operate under the general guidance of two agencies: the Commission for Cultural Relations with Foreign Countries and the Chinese People's Association for Cultural Relations with Foreign Countries. They are normally headed by a prominent individual—the Sino-Soviet Friendship Association, for instance, is headed by Madame Sun. Together with other "mass organizations," they are available for a great variety of functions: when foreign visitors arrive, they provide hospitality; they provide also some of the writers and speakers who convey the Chinese message at home and abroad. When demonstrations or rallies are needed, or petitions must be signed by millions, their leaders serve as organizers. These leaders also attend various international conferences or go abroad on "cultural missions." The Chinese People's Institute of Foreign Affairs plays a similar role, and there are corresponding functions for the All-China Federation of Trade Unions and Youth Front. Much of Chinese diplomacy in the last decade, it should be stressed, has operated via these unofficial or quasi-official organizations. Within the State Council, the general governmental structure, there exists a General Office for Foreign Affairs. It would appear that this Office co-ordinates these varied aspects of Chinese diplomacy.

The Ministry of Foreign Affairs The Ministry of Foreign Affairs handles the more conventional type of foreign relations. In organization, it is similar to the Foreign Ministries of other nations. The divisions within the Ministry are partly area, partly functional. The former include the divisions of USSR and East European Affairs, First (non-Communist) Asian Affairs, Second (Communist) Asian Affairs, West Asian and African Affairs, West European Affairs, and American and Australian Affairs. The functional divisions consist of a General Office, Consular Affairs, Protocol, Treaty and Law, International Affairs, and Information.

Those who have dealt professionally with Communist diplomats and Foreign Office personnel in recent years have considerable respect for their training and ability. It would appear that these qualities rather than long-term Party membership have generally determined appointments at the top-rungs of the foreign service ladder. Perhaps this has been particularly true in terms of the men appointed to Western posts or to negotiation teams with the West. The Chinese are well aware of the high stakes in such situations. To bloc countries, it has been customary to send individuals of the Party functionary type. This could be explained on two grounds: it is in these areas that the Party itself plays the largest role, and in theory at least, a Party functionary would have some advantages in understanding these governments.

The Ministry of Foreign Affairs is not confined to official and formal diplomacy merely because of the existence of other agencies. Undoubtedly, there is duplication in the execution of Chinese foreign policies as there is in most other nations. Chinese embassies operate on a wide front through their various officials: thus the cultural attaché maintains contact with the local Friendship Association if it exists, arranges exchanges, and may be particularly active with student groups. He also supervises some of the Chinese propaganda effort, having liaison with such organizations as the New China News Agency and the Foreign Language Broadcast Division of Radio Peking. The economic section seeks to facilitate trade and, in certain areas, has aid programs to administer. Wherever the Bank of China exists, the embassy undoubtedly maintains a liaison, and

through this, has contacts with various nationals.

The armed forces and the people   Thus far, the Chinese military do not appear to have played any significant *organizational* role in formulating Chinese foreign policy, although military considerations are important, even decisive in connection with many foreign policy problems. It must be remembered again that while the Chinese Communist Party has always kept an iron-control over its military, the top Communists pride themselves upon being quasi-military men, having fought revolutionary battles for thirty years and having formulated a political-cum-military strategy for victory. Thus in the past, the separation between "civilian" and "military" was not easily made in terms of men like Mao. Whether the development of a professional military force equal to the tasks of the nuclear age will gradually force this separation is unclear, but seems likely.

What role do the Chinese people play in the foreign policy of the *People's* Republic of China? A brief but accurate answer to that question would be that the people are "educated" to understand what are "correct" foreign policies, and then caused to participate *en masse* "enthusiastically" on behalf of those policies. Huge demonstrations, protest rallies, parades, and signatory campaigns are held, sometimes involving millions of people. Discussion of foreign policy issues is encouraged at the local commune, factory, or street associational level. The mass organizational approach is applied to foreign as to domestic policy.

However, the individual citizen has no role in formulating the policies he supports, nor can he object to them. The National People's Congress, "the supreme organ of state power" according to the Constitution, is at present a completely powerless body, convened merely to listen to policies as enunciated by Party leaders and approve them "unanimously." In all situations, however, the citizen *must* participate. One foreign observer who witnessed a recent six-hour parade in Peking noted that those weary marchers who sought to drop out were all rebuffed except one ingenious man who grabbed a small child, and indicated that rest room facilities were necessary! The common man has been discovered in Communist China, and henceforth he shall have no rest. Whether eventually, he will share in real authority cannot now be foretold. A look at developments in other Communist states gives little encouragement that the common man will eventually come into his own.

In sum, the diplomacy of Communist China is handled at the summit by a small cadre of men who have run the Communist Party for thirty years, men who have learned to work together despite any policy differences, perhaps because the supremacy of Mao Tse-tung has long been firmly established. They are supported by a growing core of professionally trained career officials who appear to be chosen and advanced on the basis of competence and intellectual ability, assuming always the existence of an absolute loyalty to the state. The people serve to provide the mass base to this elitist structure. Relying upon the cadres, Party officials can bring them into the streets on any occasion, or indoctrinate them on the issues of the day through mass media and compulsory discussion groups.

It is not possible to know how effective this system has been. We cannot be certain as to what the average Chinese thinks today about his government, himself, the world. The evidence suggests that where the Communists move with the tide, i.e. nationalism, they are more successful than when they seek to move against it, i.e. "the Russians are our brothers."

No doubt the process of formulating Chinese foreign policy will become increasingly complex in the years ahead. The problem of policy co-ordination is likely to contribute to the continuing importance of unity among the handful of men who really govern China. Professionals, be they foreign service or military, will take their orders from the men who constitute the inner core of the CCP Politburo. These facts should be kept in mind as we turn to the substantive issues of Chinese foreign policy.

THE CONTENT OF CHINESE COMMUNIST FOREIGN POLICY

Current Chinese Communist foreign policy should be viewed against the background of tradition, nationalism, and Marxian ideology sketched earlier. Before taking up specific issues, let us first present a general synopsis of that policy as interpreted by top Communist leadership. Speaking on the occasion of the 40th anniversary of the founding of the Chinese Communist Party on July 7, 1961, Liu Shao-ch'i summarized China's foreign policy:

Since the founding of the People's Republic of China, the basic policy of our international relations has been to develop relations of friendship, mutual assistance and co-operation with the Soviet Union and the other fraternal socialist countries; to strive for peaceful coexistence with countries of different social systems on the basis of the Five Principles and to oppose the imperialist policies of aggression and war; to support the revolutionary struggles of all oppressed peoples and nations against imperialism and colonialism. This is the general line of our foreign policy.[11]

The Soviet Union, as always, is given a paramount position in Liu's remarks. It is entirely appropriate, therefore, to begin our analysis of contemporary Chinese foreign policy with a study of the complex, intriguing, and rapidly shifting nature of Sino-Soviet relations.

[11] Liu Shao-ch'i, "Speech Delivered at the Meeting in Celebration of the 40th Anniversary of the Founding of the Communist Party of China," *Peking Review*, Nos. 26–27, July 7, 1961, pp. 6–12 (p. 11). The "Five Principles" are explained on p. 575 below.

The Sino-Soviet alliance

It would be difficult to surpass the eulogies that Chinese Communist leaders have bestowed upon the Soviet Union in the years since their rise to power, and in the earlier period as well. Teng Hsiao-p'ing's remarks in 1960 are typical:

> The great Soviet Union is the most faithful friend of the Chinese people. After the founding of the People's Republic of China, the two great socialist countries—the Soviet Union and China—formed a solid and close alliance. The unity of the Soviet Union and China plays an extremely important part in the unity of the peoples of the world. . . . The socialist camp headed by the Soviet Union is the reliable guarantee of world peace and human progress. The People's Republic of China has joined this camp, and shares the same destiny and life-breath of this camp. In the big family of socialism, the national economies of all the socialist countries are surging forward together; the friendship and unity among us are being strengthened and consolidated day by day.[12]

Mao and all other top Chinese Communist leaders have repeatedly acknowledged the Soviet Union as the leader of the Socialist camp, the vanguard of the Socialist revolution, the friend and protector of fraternal socialist nations. They have warmly thanked the Soviet Union for its economic aid and technical assistance. For example, in 1960, various Chinese spokesmen asserted that close Sino-Soviet co-operation in the economic and technical fields had made "a striking contribution" to economic growth in both countries. China's volume of trade with the Soviet Union was listed at 50 per cent of her total volume of trade. The Soviet Union, it was acknowledged, had helped China to build 166 core projects during the first Five Year Plan period, and was scheduled to assist China in the building of an additional 125 projects during the current Plan. In the ten-year period beginning in 1950, more than 10,800 Soviet experts had been sent to China, according to Chou En-lai, and he added:

> Our achievements are inseparably linked with the enormous aid given by the peoples of the fraternal countries. The Chinese people will never forget their love and friendship. We must forever adhere to the Marxist-Leninist principle of combining patriotism with internationalism and continuously consolidate and develop our brotherly co-operation with them.[13]

The Soviet Union has also been credited with major assistance in the development of Chinese science. Said Ch'en Yi:

> In the last ten years, there has been a tremendous development in scientific and cultural co-operation between the two countries. Since the conclusion of the Sino-Soviet agreement on scientific and technical co-operation in October 1954 and the agreement on cultural co-operation of 1956, scientific and cultural co-operation and exchange between the two countries have been expanding in a still more planned way. In 1956, the Soviet Union sent a goodly number of top-notch scientists to help China work out her 12-year programme of scientific development. In 1958, the two countries once again signed a proto-

---

[12] Teng Hsiao-p'ing, *op. cit.*, pp. 15–16.

[13] Chou En-lai, *op. cit.*, p. 37. See also Ch'en Yi, "Sino-Soviet Alliance is the Mighty Bulwark of World Peace," *Sino-Soviet Alliance*, Peking: 1960, pp. 19–21.

col providing for 122 major scientific and technical research projects to be executed by the two countries jointly or by China alone with Soviet aid. Great aid has been given China by the Soviet Union in the study of the peaceful uses of atomic energy. All this has been a great stimulus to scientific and technical research in our country creating the conditions for China to scale the summits of science and culture in not too long a historical period.[14]

The Sino-Soviet alliance has also been given credit for defending world peace and repeatedly "crushing imperialist war schemes." Said Ch'en Yi, "The existence of the powerful Sino-Soviet alliance and socialist camp constitutes the greatest obstacle to the imperialist goal of world domination."[15]

The Sino-Soviet cleavage

Yet in spite of all these words of eulogy and pledges of undying support for socialist unity, no one can doubt any longer that relations between China and the Soviet Union have been marked by increasing tension in recent years, and, at the moment, are in a state of crisis. Perhaps the difficulties can be solved, or reduced, although this is by no means certain. The fact remains that the current cleavage between China and Russia is real, and it is serious. Some aspects of the quarrel are still obscure, but there is now enough hard evidence to indicate its dimensions and its major causes.

Albania and deStalinization   In 1961–1962, Sino-Soviet differences were focused sharply upon two concrete issues: Albania and deStalinization. The rift broke into the open during the 22nd Congress of the Soviet Communist Party, held in Moscow in October 1961. On October 17, as is well known, Khrushchev attacked Albanian Communist leaders in a public address before the Congress. Two days later, Chou En-lai electrified the same audience by charging that to attack a fraternal Party in the face of the enemy "cannot be regarded as a serious Marxist-Leninist attitude." A few days later, he abruptly departed from Congress, not waiting to hear Khrushchev's second spirited assault upon Hoxha and his companions.

In the months that followed, China strengthened her alliance with Albania, and sought to pull other Communist parties to her side, despite the barrage of Soviet attacks upon the Albanians, culminating in a complete severance of Soviet-Albanian relations. During this period also, Albanian leaders shouted defiance of Khrushchev, and in their words, we can read Chinese thoughts. Khrushchev, according to the Albanians, was a revisionist who sought to change the teachings of Marx and Lenin on the reactionary and aggressive character of imperialism, and treated in "opportunistic fashion" such questions as peaceful coexistence and the national liberation struggles. He sought to appease Kennedy and the "treasonous Belgrade clique" while attacking Albania (China), "a stalwart defender of the purity of Marx-Leninism." Anyone who questioned Khrushchev's "opportunistic and erroneous views" was called anti-Marxist, nationalist, and dogmatic by him. Nor could the Albanians accept deStalinization. To them, Khrushchev was criticizing Stalin "in order to impose his revisionist views on the communist and workers' parties of other countries."

The Soviet leaders and their allies answered in kind. Hoxha and his "stooges" were bloody tyrants, guilty of crimes worse than those of the Czars; they were slanderers, disrupting socialist unity; they were dogmatists and false Marx-Leninists. Yet in the face of these charges, Chinese Communist leaders gave Albania maximum support. On January 13, 1962, China and Albania signed five agreements providing for economic, scientific and technical

---

[14] *Ibid.*, p. 21.
[15] Ch'en Yi, *op. cit.*, p. 22.

co-operation. At that time, Premier Chou gave a banquet in honor of the Albanian delegation, and his remarks there were most revealing:

> Dear Albanian comrades: Although China and Albania are separated by many mountains and seas, yet we are closely linked by the great cause of communism. The Chinese people are happy to see that under the correct leadership of the Albanian Workers Party headed by its long-tested leader, Comrade Enver Hoxha, the heroic Albanian people have overcome one obstacle after another on their road of advance by rallying themselves around great goals and working painstakingly, and have won important achievements in the cause of building socialism.[16]

Chou went on to laud the Albanian government for adhering to a foreign policy of peace, resolutely opposing aggression and the imperialist bloc, striving for peaceful coexistence, and promoting the cause of human progress. He called the Albanian Party "a staunch and militant Marxist-Leninist Party," one consistent with the principles of proletarian internationalism, loyal to the decisions of the Moscow agreements, firmly defending "the purity of Marxism-Leninism."

It is difficult to imagine a more sweeping challenge to Nikita Khrushchev and the CPSU. Every charge levelled against Albania by Soviet spokesmen was flatly contradicted by Chou. But while Chou's speech was, in many respects, the most dramatic illustration of the Sino-Soviet cleavage up to that point, it was by no means strikingly new. Albanian students, thrust out of the Soviet Union, had been streaming to Peking. Grain, badly needed by the Chinese, was being diverted to Albania. Chinese technicians were replacing Russians in Tirana and other Albanian cities. And throughout the fall of 1961, many of the themes set

---

[16] Chou's speech was broadcast by Peking *NCNA* on January 13, 1962. A summary is contained in *Peking Review,* No. 3, January 19, 1962, pp. 10–11.

forth boldly by the Albanians and labelled as Khrushchev errors were being stressed in Chinese journals, though without any direct reference to Khrushchev or the Soviet Union.

The issue of deStalinization was also one deeply dividing Chinese and Russian leaders. Prior to his departure from Moscow, Chou had significantly laid a wreath on the tomb of Stalin with the inscription: "To J. V. Stalin, great Marxist-Leninist." This inscription was published in the Chinese press, but not in the Soviet press. In its May Day 1962 celebration, moreover, the portrait of Stalin was prominently displayed along with those of Marx, Engels, and Lenin, notwithstanding the serious crimes and blunders of which Stalin now stood accused in Moscow.

Basic conflicts   What lies behind these dramatic events? The major issues between Communist China and the Soviet Union would appear to be these:

1. *The nature of decision-making inside the Communist bloc.* Success has created new and difficult problems for world communism. For more than a quarter of a century, only one source of final authority existed in the Communist world. In the final analysis, Moscow alone could establish legitimacy, provide sustenance, determine orthodoxy, pass judgment. Today, there are various sources of "supreme authority" in the Communist world. There are a number of Communist states having some degree of independent power and therefore able to sustain decisions made in their own interest. The new term used by some to describe internal power relationships within the bloc is *polycentrism*. Even this term, however, is rejected by many Communists, including those who want to establish in fullest measure the principle of "independence and equality" among bloc members.

It is natural that Communist China, as the most important new member of the bloc, would ultimately lead the struggle against Soviet monolithism. There is reason to believe that the Chinese Communist leaders have long harbored doubts that Russian leaders were correct in their political assessments of the world, particularly the non-Western world. They themselves came to power more in spite of Russian advice than because of it. Certainly now that the Chinese Communists have come to power, they are not prepared to accept unilateral decisions by Soviet leaders affecting Chinese interests.

Intellectually, Khrushchev and other Soviet leaders can accept the necessity for a new approach to decision-making within the international Communist movement. Indeed, it was Khrushchev himself who in 1960 rejected a proposal that the Soviet Union be labelled the leader or head of the Communist world. The Russians sponsored the all-party Moscow conferences of 1957 and 1960, attempts to hammer out a unified position for the Communist movement to which all could subscribe. The new formula for Communist decisions was: *within one party,* "democratic centralism"— discussion, debate and then majority rule, with the minority pledged to accept the decision; *among parties,* consensus and unanimity—the procedure of compromise and adjustment so that the final product can be supported by all participants, as was the case with the Moscow Declaration of 1957 and the Moscow Statement of 1960. Under this formula, each party in theory at least becomes "a free and equal member of the fraternal socialist camp."

To all of this procedure, both Moscow and Peking adhere. But can consensus and unanimity truly be achieved when fundamental differences are developing within the movement? Moreover, given the heritage of Russian authority and the continuing fact of Russian primacy in power and responsibility, can there be equality? All parties signed the Moscow statements, but in fact these statements contained something for everybody. One was free to interpret or emphasize according to taste. In this fashion, it was possible to sign a common statement without reaching a common agreement. Everyone supported such broad principles as "proletarian internationalism" and "Marxism-Leninism," but the central question remained: who determines the substantive content of such principles and the proper tactics/strategy to be employed in realizing them?

The disputes over Albania and deStalinization are related in part to these issues. The Chinese regarded Khrushchev's open attack upon the Albanian leaders as a unilateral action in violation of proper bloc decision-making procedures. According to the Chinese, there had been insufficient private discussion and concession. Thus "proletarian internationalism" had been damaged and the Communist movement embarrassed before the enemy. Khrushchev's analysis of the perfidy of Albanian leaders and of the valiant attempts of the Soviet Union to guide the Albanian Workers' Party back to correct Marx-Leninism has not been accepted by the Chinese. Indeed, the attempt to "guide" Albania they regard as interference in internal Albanian affairs.

Khrushchev's rolling deStalinization campaign has also involved a violation of the true spirit of "proletarian internationalism" in Chinese eyes. This campaign did not encompass the type of prior consultation with fraternal comrades, or consideration for their interests, that should mark bloc relations. DeStalinization is regarded as a self-serving set of unilateral actions by Khrushchev and his followers, actions dangerous if not disastrous for the world Communist movement. In sum, the Chinese Communist leaders have fought against what they regard as "Big-Power chauvinism" on the part of the Soviet Union, a penchant for demanding that bloc members accept decisions made by Soviet leaders and in their interests.

2. *The policies and priorities to be pursued toward the West and toward "National Liberation Movements" in the non-Western world.* Communist China has given ample evidence of being worried lest the Soviet Union, because of fear of global war and the burdens of multiple commitments, follow a policy of appeasement toward the West, one making dangerous concessions that weaken the Communist global position or spoil the opportunities for Communist gain. Chinese arguments suggest a fear of Big Power agreement between the Soviet Union and the United States that would be deleterious to Chinese interests.

Moreover, Chinese Communist leaders have

567

repeatedly sounded an alarm lest any search for accommodation with the West or preoccupation with Soviet internal development lead to the neglect of all-out support for "National Liberation Movements" in the non-Western world. It is through the success of these movements, and their capture by the "proletarian vanguard," that the Chinese see both the success of the world Communist movement and the growth of their own power. At this juncture, China can only compete with an advanced society like the United States indirectly—through a world revolution that saps American strength.

These issues come to focus on such questions as how much emphasis to give "peaceful coexistence" and how to define it; how gravely to view the threat of "imperialism" and "imperialist-sponsored wars"; and how firmly to denounce the actions of Yugoslavia which, in taking up a neutralist position, serves as "traitor" and seeks to split the ranks of the "socialist camp." The lengthy, involved arguments that have taken place over these issues in recent years suggest differences of degree, not kind, perhaps, but these have proven to be significant differences nonetheless.

3. *The policies to be pursued toward "fraternal Socialist allies."* Despite the extensive public praise accorded the Soviet Union by Chinese leaders, there are many indications that the Chinese are deeply unhappy about the limited aid given them and the other "backward" segments of the Communist world. They see the Russians devoting increasing attention to consumer goods for their own people and providing minimal assistance to comradely nations.

Some Chinese appear to argue that it is most "unCommunist" for the Soviet Union to concentrate on the rapid development of its own productivity, and thereby to allow the gap between the USSR and other Communist states to widen. Mr. Khrushchev's answer is that communism is not a group of people sitting around an empty table, all very equal, and very "progressive."

4. *Personality differences and issues related to the internal politics of each society.* It is impossible to know the extent to which personality clashes and involvement in each other's internal politics have exacerbated the Sino-Soviet cleavage. It is not difficult, however, to see how the broad, impersonal cultural gulf which separates the Soviet Union from China and the vital difference in the timing of the Russian and Chinese revolutions might be personified in a fundamental incompatibility between men like Nikita Khrushchev and Mao Tse-tung. Both men are dedicated Marxists— but Marxists who in the course of capturing and holding power, have been schooled to the necessities of pragmatism. Yet there the similarity ends. Mao is a revolutionary intellectual. Khrushchev is an able politician of peasant stock. Mao is a Communist mandarin, quiet, reflective, ruthless if need be, but possessed of a basic dignity and culture. Khrushchev is shrewd, uninhibited, with an earthy quality. He is frequently boisterous in manner and impetuous in action, a man both direct and devious, a gifted exhibitionist, a most uncommon, common man.

Are not such differences as these reflections in a broader sense of the diverse cultures and stages of development characterizing these two massive societies? One senses a disdain among the Chinese intellectuals who lead the revolution today for the qualities of boorishness, ineptitude, and impetuosity that to them mark Russian diplomacy and, on occasion, seem personified in Nikita Khrushchev. Where is the finesse, and where, *above all,* the basic understanding of the world (read "Chinese" world) necessary for Communist success? For example, how could a man be so insensitive to the feelings of others as to suggest a Big Power conference on the Taiwan Straits crisis without Chinese participation? How could he conduct a vigorous deStalinization campaign without consultation or warning? The Chinese pride —and sense of the professional—could not have been unaffected by such brusque and unilateral actions.

The Russians, for their part, find the Chinese Communist leadership immature, romantic, and prone to adventurism. Like old trade-unionists fighting young intellectuals within a labor movement, the Russians pose their practical experience against Chinese theories. Basically, they have developed a hostility to this first generation of Chinese leaders who plunge China into "unrealistic" programs despite urgent Russian advice, and seek to involve the Soviet Union in commitments beyond her wishes or means.

Is it also possible that China and Russia have deliberately or unavoidably meddled in each other's internal politics? Clearly deStalinization is now inextricably connected with the continuing struggle waged by Khrushchev against Molotov and company, the "anti-party" group. But it was this same Molotov who reportedly circulated a letter denouncing Khrushchev's "revisionism" and taking positions similar if not identical to those of Peking. Whether Molotov had contact with the Chinese leadership or not, the identity of views must have strained Sino-Soviet relations. There is no firm evidence of Russian involvement in Chinese politics, but one would like to know more about the purge of Peng Tu-huai. Once again, in Peng's case, or in that of others, could a "coincidence" of views between some Chinese and the Khrushchev group have created additional tension in Sino-Soviet relations? Certainly these possibilities cannot be ruled out. We know that the execution of pro-Khrushchev elements in Albania was one of the reasons for Khrushchev's rage at Hoxha. It is difficult to believe Sino-Soviet differences have not led to some repercussions in the internal politics of these two states, and hence to further complexities.

Underlying causes of conflict   These are the basic issues that have been at stake between China and Russia. What are their underlying causes? Some have already been suggested. Russia and China are two continental-mass societies with a considerable legacy of aloofness from the world, self-sufficiency and ethnocentrism. Today, they are not merely Communist societies—they are homogenized national-Communist states, and indeed, in each, the nationalist quotient is high, higher than it has ever been. Thus each state interprets "correct" Marx-Leninism in the light of its own historic experiences, contemporary situation, and future needs. In each of these respects, there are some fundamental differences between the Soviet Union and Communist China at present. It has been nearly a half-century since the Bolshevik Revolution, and the Soviet Union is now a Major World Power governed by second and third generation Communists. These men inherited the Soviet Union; they did not make it. Both they and their society differ greatly from the era of the first generation. Some of the ardor is gone, and the puritanism. And now, there is vastly more to be defended.

In general terms, Russia is satisfied at present with her boundaries, her buffer state system, her world prestige, and despite numerous problems, her potential for internal development. She is willing, therefore, to put more faith in long-range political and economic competition with the West. Moreover, the Soviet Union has acquired the caution that must inevitably go with global power and global responsibility. For Russia, the dilemma over how to commit her available resources is a serious one. Four priorities vie with each other: swiftly mounting internal pressures from the Russian consumer; the need to attain or hold military parity with the United States; the economic and technical requirements of the Communist bloc; and the aid-diplomacy necessary to compete for the emergent non-aligned world. Like the United States, the Soviet Union cannot afford adventurism.

Communist China, on the other hand, is in the raw, militant opening stage of her revolution. The quotients of puritanism, spartanism, and bitterness are high. The Chinese leaders represent first generation revolutionaries, and they are profoundly dissatisfied with the world as it is. They are not satisfied with their boundaries, their buffer state system, or their world prestige. Internal problems are serious and unresolved. The external challenge, symbolized to the Chinese by the United States, is almost an obsession.

China cannot think realistically in terms of economic or military competition with the United States for the foreseeable future. Hence, the Chinese short cut to security and power lies only in world revolution. They are thus the true Bolsheviks of the 1960's, and in some senses, challenging the Soviet Union for revolutionary leadership in the world.

Future Sino-Soviet relations

For the future, three broad alternatives in Sino-Soviet relations appear to exist. One possibility would be a mending of the present breach. The advantages this would have for the Communist bloc are obvious. China and Russia need, or can use each other, in many ways. The present tension, moreover, greatly complicates the situation for the small Communist parties and states. If it continues, it is likely to produce many splits and further fragmentation within their ranks. But it will be exceedingly difficult to find any fundamental solutions to problems so deeply rooted. Many words have been uttered which cannot be taken back. Violent arguments have occurred. Firm positions have been established. Pride, both individual and national, is at stake. A basic, long-range settlement that would produce Sino-Soviet intimacy seems most unlikely. Only if some of the main actors on the present stage were removed does the prospect of "forgive and forget" seem conceivable, and even then, given the impersonal factors operating, it appears to be a remote likelihood.

A second and opposite alternative would be an open, declared break between China and Russia. Could the situation reach the point where these two nations would attack each other in the same fashion as they now attack Yugoslavia and Albania respectively? Such a possibility cannot be ruled out. We have already indicated, however, why such a dramatic step is likely only under extreme circumstances, or as the culmination of a long series of intolerable provocations. An alliance can stand very severe strain as long as it appears to serve the most fundamental interests of the participants, or when no better alternative is in sight.

A third alternative would be the continuation roughly of the present relationship. This would mean an alliance filled with problems, encompassing differences, even containing a certain atmosphere of "limited warfare," but one sustained because the dangers involved in abandoning it seemed greater than those involved in retaining it. Under present circumstances, this is the most likely prospect: relations between China and Russia that fall short of harmony on the one hand, or rupture on the other. For this alternative to prevail, however, progressive deterioration will have to be arrested. A *modus vivendi* acceptable to both parties will have to be found.

The future thus appears to lie with either the second or third alternatives sketched above. Meantime, China will intensify her efforts to establish close relations with the smaller Communist states and parties, especially those in Asia, Africa, and Latin America. For this new power, hegemony is conceived partly in regional and partly in global terms.

Outer Mongolia, North Korea, North Vietnam

Outer Mongolia   In this context, let us note first Chinese relations with the three small Communist regimes of Asia: Outer Mongolia, North Korea, and North Vietnam. Outer Mongolia, geographically, is in the classic position of a buffer state between Russia and China. This has taken on new meaning, of course, since the advent of the Communists to power in China. For many years, Outer Mongolia, cut off from the outside world, looked only to the Soviet Union under whose aegis the present state was established in 1924. Russia still plays the dominant outside role in the Mongolian People's Republic. Many of the Mongolian elite were educated in the Soviet Union, and both political and economic guidance came solely from Russian sources until recently. Even now, according to Mongolian sources, Soviet aid accounts for more than 75 percent of all external assistance, whereas only about 20 percent comes from Communist China.

Will this condition prevail a decade from now? China is certainly a new force of importance in Mongolia. By the end of 1961, China had granted nearly 50 million dollars to the Outer Mongolian Republic in loans and long-term credit, and helped in the construction of various projects, notably power stations, roads, and irrigation works. Some 10–12,000 Chinese workmen were reportedly in Mongolia at the end of 1961, assisting in construction work. Cultural missions moved between Peking and Ulan Bator. Will a younger generation of Mongols look East instead of West? The Chinese face one serious obstacle: Mongolian nationalism, which appears to be very much alive, has always been aimed primarily against China.

North Korea   North Korea is another state established initially under Russian supervision. When they marched into Korea at the close of World War II, the Soviet forces brought various Koreans with them, including a group of Russianized Koreans who had long lived in the Soviet Union and who immediately became a powerful force in the new government. Kim Il-sŏng, the North Korean leader, was not a Russianized Korean in this sense, although he had been in Siberia after the Japanese drove him out of Manchuria with his guerilla forces in 1941. However, Kim who had been selected by the Russians, was long regarded as a pure Moscow satellite. It now appears that the situation in North Korea was always much more complicated than has been realized.

At first, the North Korean Communists were divided into three major factions—Moscow, Yenan, and indigenous—namely, those elements who came from the Soviet Union and/or were aligned with it; those who came from China and had their primary ties with the Chinese Communists; and those who had been part of the old underground and had their ties primarily within Korea. Through a series of purges and demotions, all three of these factions have been largely eliminated in favor of a Kim faction. Kim appears to be the undisputed leader of North Korea, and the men at the top are men personally loyal to him, many of them from his old Manchurian guerilla unit. Kim, incidentally, is one of the few men in the world to have belonged to the Communist Party of three different countries: China, the Soviet Union, and Korea. At present, the adulation given Kim knows no bounds. This is truly a Stalinist era for North Korea, a fact that undoubtedly complicates relations with the Soviet Union.

Thus North Korea is a state which has had a history of internal complications connected with Sino-Soviet differences. It is also a state toward which the Chinese commitment has steadily risen. The Russians were not popular in North Korea with the general populace, partly as a result of very bad discipline among Russian troops and numerous incidents. The well-disciplined Chinese troops that came into the country in 1950 created a much more favorable impression. As is well-known, the Chinese Communists, only one year after they had come to power, took a major gamble by sending military forces into Korea to save their comrades from disaster. Undoubtedly, this was a gamble taken primarily in the Chinese national interest, not from altruism or any intense internationalist spirit. Communist China wanted no unified, anti-Communist state on its Manchurian border aligned with American and Chinese Nationalist power.

The Chinese gamble succeeded, but the war left North Korea totally devastated. China then proceeded to establish her first foreign aid program in November 1953, extending credit equivalent to approximately one-third of a billion dollars to the North Korean government. This aid was to be used for economic rehabilitation during the period 1954–1957. Further aid in the form of long-term loans was advanced in the fall of 1958. Following the extensive conversations between top Chinese leaders and a Korean delegation headed by Kim Il-sŏng in late November and early December 1958, a joint statement was issued which pledged increasing economic, cultural, scientific and technical co-operation between the two countries and the further development of the friendship of two peoples, a friendship "cemented with blood shed in their struggles against imperialist aggression."[17]

Chinese troops had been withdrawn from Korea in October 1958 just prior to the establishment of this new assistance program. On July 11, 1961, moreover, China and North Korea signed a Treaty of Friendship, Co-operation and Mutual Assistance. Interestingly, this treaty was somewhat more comprehensive than a similar treaty signed at the same time with the Soviet Union. The Sino-Korean treaty provided for mutual defense in case of attack upon one of the parties, mutual consultation "on all important international questions of common interest to the two countries," mutual treatment in accordance with the Bandung Principles, and a continuation of maximum co-operation including "every possible economic and technical aid in the cause of socialist construction of the two countries."

North Vietnam   Toward North Vietnam also, the Chinese can claim a generosity that compares favorably with that of the Soviet Union. One estimate is that Chinese loans and grants through 1965 will total 457.5 million dollars as against a Soviet total of 365 million dollars.[18] The first major Chinese grant to Hanoi was given in July 1955. In 1959, an additional program of assistance from China to North Vietnam was announced which included technical aid and funds for industrial and communications development.

In his report to the 2nd session of the National Assembly in 1961, Premier Pham Van Dong asserted that the successful completion of the Three-Year Plan (1957–1960) was due to the "great and invaluable assistance of the socialist camp."[19] He singled out the Soviet

Union and China for having supplied capital, equipment, technicians and assistance in training cadres. Dong went on to report that new long-term economic and cultural agreements had just been signed with both countries, auguring well for the first Five Year Plan (1961–1965).

Chinese military assistance to North Vietnam, while not on the lavish scale provided North Korea, is nonetheless believed to have been substantial. As the guerilla war in South Vietnam is stepped up by the Communists, Chinese military intentions in this area assume major importance. In December 1961, a Chinese military mission headed by Marshal Yeh Chien-ying visited Hanoi, presumably to counteract the earlier American mission headed by General Taylor, and pledges of American military support to the Diem government. Marshal Yeh declared that the Chinese people could not remain "indifferent" to American "adventurist activities" in South Vietnam.[20] As yet, however, there has been no open military alliance between the Chinese Communists and the North Vietnamese government.

Chinese versus Soviet influence   Now moving toward the middle of their second decade in power, the Communist leaders of China are re-establishing a major role for China in Asia, as the above facts make clear. Already, this has had repercussions within the Communist bloc. The extensive economic, technical, cultural and military assistance given by China to North Korea and North Vietnam in recent years is undoubtedly one reason why both states have taken a position of non-alignment in the current Sino-Soviet dispute. Indeed, both states have, in fact, defied the Soviet Union. They have joined Peking in sending congratulatory messages to the Albanian leaders on recent ceremonial occasions despite the Soviet ostracism of Albania. They have also implied that they will take an independent attitude toward Stalin, and not necessarily hew to the

---

[17] "Sino-Korean Joint Statement," *Peking Review*, No. 42, December 16, 1958, pp. 16–17 (p. 17).

[18] William Kaye, "A Bowl of Rice Divided: The Economy of North Vietnam," *The China Quarterly*, No. 4, p. 92.

[19] "Struggle for Peaceful National Reunification and Development of International Relations," Excerpt from Report of Premier Dong, in *The Problems Facing the Democratic Republic of Viet Nam in 1961*, Hanoi: 1961, pp. 33–59 (p. 52).

[20] "Chinese Military Mission in Viet Nam," *Peking Review*, No. 51, December 22, 1961, pp. 16–17.

Khrushchev line. And in their various statements, they have emphasized many of the same sections of the Moscow statement as the Chinese: the supreme importance of the unity of the *twelve* (Albania thereby included) socialist states; the absolute independence and equality of all members of the Communist Commonwealth; the need for making decisions within the bloc in accordance with the rules of the Moscow agreement; and the importance of keeping a resolute guard against imperialism led by the United States and giving high priority to the national liberation movement.[21]

Outer Mongolia, on the other hand, remains within the Soviet orbit, at least for the present. The leaders of the Mongolian Peoples' Revolutionary Party lined up solidly with Khrushchev in the aftermath of the 22nd CPSU Congress. Mongolian leaders expressed the opinion that Albania was undermining socialist unity, slipping into the bog of nationalism, and being untrue to Marx-Leninism.[22] They also expressed their open disagreement with the position of the Chinese People's Republic on this issue. On deStalinization too, complete loyalty to the Soviet position was exhibited. Indeed, Premier Tsendenbal announced a campaign against the cult of personality that had developed around former Premier Choibalsan who died in 1952. Moscow could not have asked for greater support than this!

The strikingly different positions taken on these issues by Outer Mongolia on the one hand, and North Korea and North Vietnam on the other are some measure of trends in connection with Chinese versus Soviet spheres of influence. It would be wrong, however, to assume that the latter two states were now Chinese satellites. One must always remember that nationalism has not only survived communism, it has flourished under it. Traditionally, the nationalism of all of these peoples—Mongolians, Koreans, and Vietnamese—has been directed primarily against the Chinese. Thus it is probable that a majority of the Korean and Vietnamese Communists hope to establish a position of independence, and in some measure, play the role of buffer states, securing aid from both sides but fully committed to neither. Hence the present emergence of a type of neutralism within the Communist bloc. It must be noted, however, that even this represents a gain for China, a gain symbolizing a new era of Chinese influence in Asia.

Relations with Communist parties of non-Communist states

In her relations with the Communist parties of non-Communist states, China is faced with certain problems and complications. To give such parties financial or political support is to violate principles that China constantly proclaims: peaceful coexistence with states having different social systems and non-interference in their internal affairs. If Chinese direct involvement in the politics of another state could be proven, it would seriously jeopardize certain broader objectives of Chinese diplomacy, especially if a non-aligned nation were involved. China has been extremely cautious, therefore, in rendering direct assistance to Communist parties in most areas where they are not in power. Reportedly, the Chinese have told their foreign comrades: "We did it mainly on our own, and you will have to do it the same way." On the other hand, the Chinese experience is available to all; Chinese propaganda circulates widely throughout the world, and in every form. There are also numerous scholarships and travel grants, and one would presume that an excellent counseling service exists in Peking. In some areas, moreover, the Bank of China is available for loans, and it is virtually impossible to keep track of the uses to which Chinese money is put.

[21] See the report of Kim Il-sŏng to the Central Committee of the Korean Workers' Party on November 27, 1961, as reported by New China News Agency, and The Vietnam Workers' Party Communiqué, issued by Hanoi Radio on December 4, 1961.

[22] See the report of L. Tsend to the Ulan Bator Party Aktiv, November 28, 1961, as reported over Radio Moscow.

Clearly, China has some special advantages in appealing to the Communist movement of the non-Western world, especially in Asia. In addition to the factors noted above, it has the advantages of culture and timing. Chinese traditions are more in accord with many of these societies than those of the Soviet Union. Of at least equal importance, its stage of development is closer to that of the Afro-Asian world; hence its revolutionary procedures may have more applicability. For similar reasons, the Chinese Communist world view is likely to be more appealing to Asian Communists at present than that of the Soviet Union. Chinese dissatisfaction with the status-quo and its militant opposition to the West may well be closer to the attitudes of the Asian Marx-Leninists. The political force that is most radical always picks up a sizeable portion of the protest vote.

Present indications are that Chinese influence is rapidly rising within the Communist parties of Indonesia, Japan, Pakistan, Thailand, and Malaya. Significantly, none of these parties has yet been willing to support the Khrushchev line on Albania or deStalinization. Most of them have exhibited the same general positions as North Korea and North Vietnam. Even in India, where nationalist sentiment is running strongly against China, there is a militant pro-Chinese minority in the Indian Communist Party that made it difficult for that party to take an official stand on the 22nd CPSU Congress.

In all of the Asian Communist Parties—and elsewhere in the Communist movement as well —the Sino-Soviet split increases the likelihood of factionalism and disunity. The strong possibility of "pro-Russian" and "pro-Chinese" factions, or at least, factions taking different positions in line with these two major contestants, is the great danger posed by the Sino-Soviet split to the smaller Communist states and parties. The one possible benefit of the split is the enhanced opportunity which it offers for greater independence from Moscow, and development more in line with indigenous conditions. Both of these tendencies are now apparent in the Asian Communist movement. For the foreseeable future, therefore, bloc

politics will be an important and exciting part of Chinese Communist foreign policy.

The neutralist nations

Let us now turn to another major element of Chinese foreign policy, namely relations with the governments of non-Communist Asia, Africa, and Latin America. These are the "peasant-national bourgeois" countries to be wooed and won, to be organized into a united front that will ultimately come under "proletariat" leadership. In April 1961, a rally was held in Peking to celebrate the sixth anniversary of the Bandung Conference. Liao Cheng-chih, the chairman of the Committee for Afro-Asian Solidarity, made the major address. Summing up Liao's remarks, a *Peking Review* writer sketched the following accomplishments for China in the period 1955–1961:

> Guided by the Ten Principles formulated at the Bandung Conference as well as the Five Principles of Peaceful Coexistence, China during the past six years has made remarkable progress in forging friendly ties with Afro-Asian and Latin American countries. Particularly in the past year or more, it has signed treaties of mutual non-aggression or of friendship with Burma, Nepal, Afghanistan, Guinea, Cambodia, and Indonesia (and earlier with the Yemen). It has settled the boundary question with Burma and concluded a boundary agreement with Nepal. It has reached agreement with Indonesia on the arrangement for implementing the treaty on dual nationality. It has established diplomatic relations with Cuba and a number of newly independent African states. Vice-Premier Chen Yi's successful visit to Indonesia, Prime Minister U Nu's fruitful sojourn in China, and the arrival in Peking of the Ghanaian and Congolese

Ambassadors—these events of recent weeks are new manifestations of China's growing friendship with Afro-Asian nations. Besides, China has exerted efforts which are well known to the world for a settlement of the Sino-Indian boundary question.[23]

While this summary omits some of the problems and contradictions of Chinese policy toward the non-Western world, it does signal the accomplishments and goals of recent years. Since Chinese leaders continuously refer to the "Bandung Spirit" as their guide and hallmark in dealing with peoples living under "different social systems," we should first explore this term briefly.

The Bandung spirit   Twenty-nine Asian and African countries met in Bandung, Indonesia from April 18 to 24, 1955, "to promote goodwill and cooperation among the countries of Asia and Africa, to explore and advance their mutual as well as common interests and to establish and further friendliness and neighbourly relations."[24] The sponsoring nations were Burma, Ceylon, India, Indonesia, and Pakistan. Chou En-lai headed the Chinese delegation, and took a very active role in the Conference. In the main, he set a tone of moderation and conciliation, a position aimed at attaining the widest possible unity and support from the Afro-Asian world.

In his major speech, Chou talked about the common desire of the peoples of Asia and Africa to safeguard world peace, to win and preserve national independence and to promote friendly co-operation among nations. As against these desires, there was the threat of a new colonialism more insidious than the old, the establishment of an increasing number of

military bases in Africa and Asia by outside powers, and the growing threat of war. The United States, of course, was Chou's primary target. Toward all of the Afro-Asian countries, however, he extended the olive branch:

By following the principles of mutual respect for sovereignty and territorial integrity, non-aggression, non-interference in each other's internal affairs, equality and mutual benefit, the peaceful coexistence of countries with different social systems can be realized. When these principles are ensured of implementation, there is no reason why international disputes cannot be settled through negotiation.[25]

These were the famous "Five Principles," and Chou asserted that they had already become the guiding principles in the mutual relations of India, Burma, and China. He noted that China and Indonesia were making good progress in discussing the problem of the Overseas Chinese, that China was prepared to develop friendly relations with the states of Indochina, and that there was no reason "why the relations between China and Thailand, the Philippines and other neighbouring countries cannot be improved on the basis of these five principles." Chou also indicated his interest in normalizing relations with Japan. He further proposed that governments, parliaments and people's organizations of the Asian and African countries make friendly visits to each other's countries, launching a program of "people's diplomacy."

In subsequent sessions of the Conference, Chou stressed the fact that China was not raising issues that might disrupt the unity of the nations assembled. In a small, private session, he assured certain delegates that China was willing to enter into negotiations with the United States "to discuss the question of relaxing tension in the Far East, and especially the question of relaxing tension in the Taiwan

[23] "The Bandung Spirit Grows," *Peking Review,* No. 16, April 21, 1961, p. 12.

[24] Memorandum from Prime Minister Ali Sastroamidjojo of the Republic of Indonesia, to Prime Minister Chou En-lai, dated January 15, 1955, in *China and the Asian-African Conference* (Documents), Peking, 1955, p. 61.

[25] "Main speech by Premier Chou En-lai," *Ibid.,* p. 17.

area." This pledge was reiterated in his final address to the Conference, along with the following observation:

> This Conference has also reflected the fact that our approaches to and our views on many questions are different. We have also discussed in part our differences. However, such different approaches and views did not prevent us from achieving common agreements. We have been able to make achievements in opposing colonialism, safeguarding world peace, and promoting political, economic and cultural cooperation because we peoples of the Asian and African countries share the same fate and the same desires.[26]

Impartial observers agreed that Chou and his delegation scored impressive gains with the Afro-Asian countries at Bandung. The object was to make further inroads against the isolation which the United States and others had attempted to impose upon China. The technique in part was to create an image of China as a moderate nation, willing to discuss all issues with all parties, and anxious to live in peace, abiding by the Five Principles. This formula was in reality the historic Chinese Communist one used in creating a united front at home, that of minimizing differences and long-range objectives in favor of areas of agreement and short-range tasks. Chou has always been one of its most effective expositors on the international scene.

Cultural relations diplomacy　Even before Bandung, Communist China had established a broadly gauged program designed to circumvent her isolation and win support from the world, especially the non-Western world. It was a program aimed both at governments and at people. One of its most important aspects was that of "cultural relations diplo-

macy," to which we have briefly alluded earlier. Already, by 1954, a steady stream of foreigners from every area and every walk of life was coming to Peking on invitation of the Chinese government. Many of them took conducted tours to various areas, with the best accommodations China could offer, special attention designed to inflate the ego, and all expenses paid.

In 1960, for instance, more than 400 delegations from 79 countries visited Communist China, including some 40 from 18 "capitalist countries" of Europe, North America, and Australasia. Over 200 Chinese delegations went to some 48 countries, although the bulk of them went to "fraternal socialist countries." Nevertheless, in that year, China had cultural contacts with a total of 84 countries and areas. These contacts ranged from the purely political to the artistic, and involved representatives of diverse fields: politics, labor unions, business, journalism, education, the arts, and many others.

By 1961, China had concluded cultural agreements with the governments or "people's organizations" of more than 50 countries. Chinese publications were available at cheap prices in many parts of the world and in many languages. From one of the most powerful transmitters now existent, Chinese radio programs were being beamed to Asia, Africa, and other regions in languages ranging from English, Spanish, and French to Swahili and Arabic. Chinese films were also widely circulated. Chinese opera and drama troupes, and Chinese athletes were performing in many areas.

In one week, a 55-member Cuban Ballet Company might perform in Peking, while Chairman Mao received a visiting delegation of African youth, and a 10-member delegation of the All-China Federation of Trade Unions paid a "friendly visit" to Japan. In another week, the dance troupe would be from the Sudan, Chairman Mao would receive a visiting Yemeni Moslem delegation, and a Chinese opera troupe would be performing in Canada. In the earlier period, the emphasis had been largely upon Asia. Now it is at least equally focused upon Africa and Latin America.

[26] "Speech of Premier Chou En-lai at the Closing Session of the Asian-African Conference," *Ibid.*, p. 30.

576

The exchange of state leaders has also been promoted. In 1960–61, the number of top foreign dignitaries visiting New China exceeded any previous period: from Asia, General Ne Win and Prime Minister U Nu of Burma, Prince Sihanouk, Premier of Cambodia, Prime Minister Koirala and King Mahendra of Nepal, President Sukarno of Indonesia, Prince Souvanna Phouma of Laos, and of course, President Ho Chi-minh and Premier Pham Van Dong of North Vietnam, Premier Kim Il-sŏng of North Korea, and Prince Souphanouvong, leader of the Pathet Lao; from Africa, Premier Ferhat Abbas head of the provisional government of Algeria, Premier Sékou Touré of Guinea, and President Nkrumah of Ghana; and from Latin America, Ché Guevara and President Dorticos of Cuba and Vice President Goulart of Brazil. In return, Chou En-lai and Ch'en Yi visited Burma, India, Nepal and Cambodia.

Perhaps massive cultural relations have been nowhere more exemplified than in recent contacts between China and Burma. In the fall of 1960, some 300 Burmese led by Prime Minister U Nu and General Ne Win visited Peking on the occasion of National Day in China. To reciprocate, over 400 Chinese, led by Premier Chou En-lai came to Burma to help celebrate the 13th anniversary of Burmese independence and to exchange the instruments of ratification of the Sino-Burmese Treaty in January 1961. To commemorate this latter occasion, the Chinese government gave 2.4 million meters of printed cloth and 600,000 pieces of porcelain plates to the some 1,200,000 Burmese citizens living along the border. In return, the Burmese government presented the people living on the Chinese side of the border with several thousand tons of rice and salt.

At the conclusion of the Chou visit, the Peking *People's Daily* spoke lyrically thus:

Now the Chinese Government Delegation headed by Premier Chou En-lai has concluded its friendly visit to the land of our *paukphaws* (kinsmen). All the people of our country put a high value on the tremendous achieve-

ments scored by the Chinese Government Delegation on this friendly visit to Burma. The Chinese people boundlessly treasure the friendship between China and Burma. Together with the Burmese people, we will unswervingly safeguard this solidly built, impressive and magnificent edifice of Sino-Burmese friendship and make it ever more majestic year by year and everlasting through the ages! [27]

Is this not reminiscent of traditional Chinese diplomacy in many respects? To be sure, modernity and ideology have interacted to provide various modifications. Today, the tribute system is directed toward the common man not merely the elite. The articles exchanged are utilitarian or in the form of mass entertainment and "enlightenment." They are not ivory, gems, and brides. Moreover, the Chinese are scrupulously careful to establish equality. Chinese leaders return visits, and sometimes initiate them. The Chinese Emperor, however, (if we may so designate Mao for the moment) remains in the Central Kingdom, home of his ancestors except for his two brief visits to Moscow. All visitors come to him, as in ancient times.

Economic relations diplomacy   In her relations with the vast and crucial Afro-Asian-Latin American world, China does not depend upon cultural relations alone. At the same time as the border settlement with Burma, for example, an Agreement on Economic and Technical Co-operation was signed. This agreement provided for a long-term loan of 30 million pounds sterling to Burma without interest, as well as various equipment and technical experts. Such economic and technical assistance has been given to a number of non-Communist countries on a similar basis: Nepal, Guinea, Cuba, Cambodia, and Ghana. Coupled with the aid given to various Communist states, this

[27] *Jen-min Jih-pao* Editorial, "Lasting Friendship Between the Chinese and Burmese Peoples," *Peking Review*, January 13, 1961, p. 11.

represents a substantial outlay, especially when viewed against the serious economic problems confronting China.

Despite the sacrifice involved, China clearly regards this outlay as in both her national interest and that of the Communist bloc (naturally, for China, these are identical interests). Among other things, this program permits the placement of funds and personnel in the three great areas of strategic and political importance to China: Asia, Africa, and Latin America. In trade relations also, China has sought to expand her contacts with the non-Communist world in such a fashion as to combine economic and political advantage. Numerous barter arrangements have been concluded, through both government and private channels. Most Chinese trade is still conducted with the bloc, but non-bloc ties are now significant. China's problem, of course, is the scarcity of foreign exchange, and this is likely to remain serious, especially if food purchases have to continue and China repays loans from Russia on schedule.

In addition to these cultural and economic measures, China has concluded treaties of friendship and non-aggression with such states as Burma, Nepal, Afghanistan, Indonesia, Cambodia, Guinea, and Ghana. These treaties have been based upon the Bandung principles and represent yet another aspect of "peaceful coexistence" diplomacy. Each party accepts the Five Principles and the Ten Principles set forth at Bandung, agrees to settle all disputes by peaceful negotiations, and pledges to develop both economic and cultural relations with the other party.

Successes and failures   Taken together, the Chinese approaches to the "peasant-national bourgeois" states are substantial. Yet Chinese policy toward these states has not been uniformly successful. Indeed, in the five years that followed the Bandung Conference, China slipped badly in her relations with some of the non-aligned states of Asia. The Bandung image of a moderate China gave way in some instances to the image of an arrogant China, militantly nationalist, uncompromising and potentially aggressive. The hope for Asian brotherhood went down before a host of suspicions, fears, and rivalries by the late 1950's. Now it was recognized that power politics would operate in Asia as in the West.

Partly, this was a natural product of an era when new nations were emerging everywhere, with nationalist currents running strong, and when the confrontation of these nations was in some cases occurring for the first time. The rising power of a nation of 650 million people would naturally create apprehensions among the other nations in its vicinity. But China did little to allay those fears in the years immediately after Bandung. Tibet, a serious dispute over the Overseas Chinese question with Indonesia, the Sino-Indian border dispute, unresolved border problems with Burma and Nepal, and a progressively tough policy toward Japan were among the developments that tarnished the Bandung image of China.

Perhaps the Chinese position on some of these issues was not illogical. Perhaps also one should recognize that a country like Communist China, so self-righteous, so nationalist, operating under so much pressure, and with such limited experience in terms of modern international diplomacy, will make mistakes. Certainly some of the actions of China on the international scene between 1957 and 1959 appear to have been mistaken, measured in terms of her own self-interest. And by 1959, a reassessment appears to have been undertaken. After that period, China sought to improve her position and regain, in some measure, the Bandung posture in Asia, while at the same time expanding her contacts and influence in Africa and Latin America.

After some initial toughness which certain Indonesians are not likely to forget, China ultimately showed considerable generosity in reaching a settlement of the Overseas Chinese issue. Relations with Indonesia were climaxed by the signing of cultural and friendship agreements in 1960–61. Border settlements were also reached with Burma and Nepal on reasonable terms, accompanied by the economic-technical assistance and cultural interaction noted earlier. In some facets of policy, China remained "tough," but once again, "Chouism" was the order of the day.

Border disputes with India

During the past decade, China has continuously sought to define and defend boundaries that accord with her own views of her rights, even when this jeopardizes her relations with a significant neighbor like India. For the first time in history, China is insisting that precise boundary lines be drawn along the whole southern border. One must wonder about those Chinese maps that show some Soviet territory in the west and north as actually belonging to China.

Nationalism, in the form of the issues of Tibet and the border question, has produced a major rift between China and India. From the beginning, China was determined that Tibet must be considered an integral part of China, not a border state. In this, the Communists were merely following their Chinese predecessors, with the difference that they had the power to enforce their position. Nevertheless, this was a bitter pill for India to swallow, especially since it was clear that the Tibetans wanted to be independent. Following the incorporation of Tibet into China, the buffer states became Nepal, Sikkim, and Bhutan. A dangerous game is now underway, with Indian influence in these areas at stake. China has made it clear that she will not accede to Indian demands with respect to the border issue. She is willing to fight for the border regions which she claims as belonging to her. And she seeks to isolate India by pursuing a moderate policy toward the other states of this region.

In the past several years, this policy of moderation has paid dividends. Relations have improved with Indonesia, Burma, and Nepal as noted above. In this fashion, China is now shaping her "buffer state" policy. To "peace-loving" states, China promises coexistence, cultural exchange, and aid of various forms. And how does China define "peace-loving"?

To the Communist Chinese, the practical definition of a "peace-loving state" is a state not connected militarily or economically with the Western bloc, particularly the United States. But peace-loving states can, of course, be connected militarily and economically with the Communist bloc. This is because the "socialist camp" is itself peace-loving, and dedicated to opposing the imperialist, militarist bloc headed by the United States.

In this manner, the Chinese leaders seek to develop a global united front encompassing both non-aligned and Communist states. Their policy looks beyond mere "buffer state" relations or even regional hegemony, and seeks to take full account of the mid-twentieth century, interdependent world. And it is here that Marx-Lenin-Maoism is supremely important. China sees herself as a revolutionary model and leader of the whole non-Western world. Thus she is actively dedicated to spurring on the revolutionary movement everywhere.

Relations with "non-peace-loving" states

But what is the Chinese attitude toward the "non-peace-loving" states of Asia or elsewhere, toward those states she believes to be aligned with the United States? The Chinese Communists make a sharp distinction between people and government. The people are, by definition, friends of New China and desirous of cordial relations. They are to be cultivated by every possible means. The government, on the other hand, must be considered a lackey of imperialism, an enemy of its own people, and unrepresentative of their interests. In noting briefly the current relations between Communist China and the governments of India and Japan, we can underline these facts.

India   Initially the Chinese Communists took a soft line with respect to the Nehru government, even after the disputes over Tibet and the border issue broke into the open. Public criticism of Nehru and the Congress Party government was avoided. Chinese leaders contented themselves with statements insisting that China was the party being wronged, that China would do everything possible to settle the dispute in a harmonious fashion, and that Chinese agreements with other Asian states proved how reasonable China could be. However, the Chinese government did not give any ground on the basic issues. Finally, after Prime Minister Nehru charged further Chinese aggression on Indian soil in the fall of 1961, the Chinese press and government moved to the attack.

According to Chinese sources, the Indian Congress Party was worried about its ability to win the 1962 election and thus was whipping up narrow-minded nationalist sentiment as a means of dealing blows against India's "progressive forces." Moreover, charged the Chinese, the anti-Chinese campaign in India was inseparably bound up with increasing American aid to India. India might not be in military alliance with the United States, but it was becoming increasingly dependent upon America economically. Thus, its true neutralism was in question. The Chinese could not deny that to their "surprise and regret," even Ajoy Ghosh, Secretary General of the Indian Communist Party, had criticized Chinese incursions. China's general attitude towards India was well expressed in the following *People's Daily* editorial exerpt from December 7, 1961:

> As to the anti-Chinese campaign, it will eventually boomerang against those who stage it, be they U.S. imperialism, Nehru or anybody else. In the world as a whole, only the imperialist elements, and reactionaries and their followers, who altogether make up only a very small number, take their stand against China; while the workers, peasants, revolutionary intellectuals, and anti-imperialist, anti-colonialist national bourgeoisie and all other people with a sense of justice who form the overwhelming majority of mankind, are not anti-

Chinese but stand for friendship with China.[28]

Japan From the beginning of its existence, the People's Republic of China has taken a dim view of the conservative governments of Japan. On February 14, 1950, China and the Soviet Union signed a thirty year alliance whereby each agreed that if the other were attacked by Japan "or any state allied with her," the other party would immediately render military and other forms of assistance. Subsequently, Chou En-lai offered to "revise" this treaty *if* the United States would withdraw its armed forces from Japan and enable Japan "to gain full independence." Toward the successive Liberal-Democratic governments of Japan, however, the Chinese Communists have shown unrelenting hostility. The following charges are typical of those levelled against Premiers Yoshida, Kishi, and Ikeda:

> In his policy statement [following the establishment of the 2nd Cabinet in June 1958] Nobusuke Kishi borrowed many phrases about democracy and peace. But these cannot in any way camouflage his home and foreign policies which are: to keep tailing after the United States, to continue to create "two Chinas," to maintain stubborn hostility to the Chinese people, to carry out active economic expansion in Southeast Asia, to plot the resurrection of Japanese militarism and to suppress the Japanese people.[29]

Just prior to the May elections in Japan in 1958, Communist China cancelled the China-Japan trade agreement which had been signed on March 5. The reason given was the assault

[28] "The Truth About the Nehru-Instigated Anti-Chinese Campaign in India," *Jen-min Jih-pao* editorial, December 7, 1961, reprinted in English in *Peking Review*, No. 50, December 15, 1961, pp. 11–14 (p. 13).
[29] *Jen-min Jih-pao* editorial of July 7, 1958, "The Chinese People Firmly Oppose Japan's Latent Imperialism," reprinted in English in *Oppose the Revival of Japanese Militarism*, Peking, 1960, p. 31.

upon a Chinese Communist flag at Nagasaki and the fact that Kishi "personally took the lead in repeatedly making slanderous statements against China." If this move was intended to influence the elections, it failed. Japanese sources were quick to charge interference in Japan's internal affairs. The Liberal-Democrats won by their usual margin. Since that time, however, Communist China has taken a relatively tough line toward Japan. It has made abandonment of the military alliance with the United States and the "two Chinas plot" virtual conditions of improved relations. It has insisted upon a neutral Japan, and one having ties with only *one* China, namely the People's Republic. And always the distinction is made between "the peace-loving Japanese people" and the "militarists, Fascists, and reactionaries" who compose the government, "oppressing their people and threatening China."

On October 7, 1961, Mao told a visiting Japanese delegation:

In Japan, except for pro-American monopoly capital and the militarist warlords, the broad masses of the people are our true friends . . . Nobusuke Kishi and Hayato Ikeda of Japan are good friends of U.S. imperialism and the Chiang Kai-shek clique, while the Japanese people and the Chinese people are good friends.

It is U.S. imperialism which has compelled us, the Chinese and Japanese peoples, to unite. The people of both countries have been suffering from U.S. imperialist oppression. We share the same destiny and therefore we are united. We should expand the scope of unity and bring together in unity the people of all Asia, Africa, Latin America and the world as a whole; excluding the imperialists and reactionaries of various countries, they constitute more than 90% of the world's population.[30]

[30] "Chairman Mao Receives Japanese Friends," *Peking Review,* No. 41, October 13, 1961, p. 6.

Mao's remarks constitute a beautiful illustration of the tactic of separating "the people" and "the enemies of the people." They are also an excellent illustration of the use of the Chinese Communist historical experience and tactics on the world stage.

The Chinese Communists have invited a wide range of Japanese representatives to visit New China: literati, trade unionists and socialists, business men, even ex-Generals and conservative politicians, especially those from factions opposed to Kishi or Ikeda. The attempt is obviously to build up cumulative pressures too strong to be resisted by the Japanese government. Their major success thus far has been in establishing an unofficial alliance with the Japanese Socialist Party. This was first developed when Inejiro Asanuma was Secretary-General of the Socialist Party, and branded American imperialism as the common enemy of the Chinese and Japanese people. The alliance has been underlined by the recent Chang-Suzuki Joint Statement of January 13, 1962, made at the conclusion of another visit by a Socialist delegation. In this statement, Suzuki supported all basic Chinese themes including that of a common struggle against U.S. imperialism. In truth, of course, the Japan Socialist Party is by no means as united, nor as dedicated to the Chinese position as such episodes would seem to indicate. But the fact that the American alliance has been largely with the Japanese conservatives, together with the general nature of Japanese politics, have combined to produce this impression.

Once again, trade between Japan and China is increasing, based upon the private barter system under which Japanese companies are screened by Chinese authorities. This too could mean a mounting pressure upon the Japanese government to shift its China policy. Some business groups have always looked longingly at the China market, even though they recognize that prewar conditions cannot prevail. The rising tension between the Soviet Union and China has created new hope, since Japan's industries might be a logical supplier in place of Russia. Up to date, however, the China trade has represented an infinitesimal fraction of total Japanese trade, and there have been sizeable political strings in the form of demands that Japan accord full recognition to the People's Republic as a condition of trade normalization.

General principles   In summary, Chinese policy toward the "peasant-bourgeois" world represents a combination of Chouism and Leninism, with the proportions capable of being altered in accordance with circumstances. Chouism—the Bandung Spirit—is the policy of peaceful coexistence and friendly aid. Leninism is the traditional Bolshevik policy of support by any means of the "progressive forces" of the world. This may mean propaganda, subversion, or even direct intervention. As noted earlier, China has been extremely cautious about employing Leninism openly in most instances, because of the dangers implicit in such a policy. But the paradox symbolized in these two forces—Chouism and Leninism—can never be fully resolved in the foreign policy of Communist China. While this constitutes a weakness, it also constitutes a strength. The threat of Chinese subversion or involvement serves to deter smaller or less mobilized societies from "unfriendly" acts. It encourages their neutralism, even their acquiescence. Fear has always been an important element in preserving the international order.

Chinese foreign policy toward the non-Western world faces another and possibly more serious paradox. As noted repeatedly, the primary objective of China is to neutralize and woo this world, to establish a global united front, thereby combining that "90% of the world's people—the workers, peasants, intellectuals, and national bourgeoisie" against "the enemies of the people—the imperialist camp led by the United States." At the same time, Marx-Lenin-Maoism—also produced out of Chinese experience—has advanced the thesis that the proletariat must capture the leadership of the bourgeois democratic revolution *during its course* if an uninterrupted revolutionary progression to socialism is to take place. This is a radical position directly challenging all non-Communist leadership in the

non-Western world. It is, indeed, more radical than the theories currently being enunciated by Moscow. To the extent that the Chinese diverge from their pragmatic policies of dealing with anyone who will do business with Peking, and actually attempt to adhere to the policies implicit in this doctrine, they are likely to arouse deep suspicion and hostility. This radicalism, combined with the militant nationalism that China has shown under the Communist regime, account for the fact that China, despite her emphasis upon the Bandung Spirit, has a considerable distance to go in allaying the doubts and fears of her neighbors, and many leaders in the non-Western world.

Current relations with Africa and Latin America

With these points in mind, let us look briefly at current Chinese activities in Africa and Latin America, two other important parts of the "emerging" world. As noted earlier, the Chinese have established various unofficial or quasi-official "Friendship Associations" available to entertain foreign guests, produce rallies and demonstrations, sponsor cultural exchanges, make friendship tours, and coordinate all activities. Thus for Africa, there is the Chinese African People's Friendship Association. In addition, China has permanent representation on the Afro-Asian People's Solidarity Council in Cairo. Many contacts with individual Africans have been initiated through this source.

Chinese attention to Africa was first directed toward Egypt, where economic and cultural ties were established early. The Suez crisis gave China the opportunity to pledge its complete support to Egypt. In recent years, major attention has been given to Algeria; leaders of the National Liberation Front have been feted, and this seems to be one of the areas where China has demonstrated more concern for the liberation movement than the Soviet Union. Tunisia also received assurances of support from China at the time of the crisis over Bizerte. North African policy is interrelated to the Middle East. Various friendly contacts have been established with Syria, Iraq, and Yemen in particular.

In West Africa, Communist China appears to have scored its most notable gains, especially with Guinea, Ghana, and Mali. Each of these states, while pledging its neutrality and independence from bloc politics, is dedicated to the Socialist way, and has accepted Chinese economic and technical assistance. Gifts have been proffered. When President Sékou Touré of Guinea visited China in the autumn of 1960, the Chinese government promised and later delivered ten lorries, ten cinema projectors, ten electric generators and more than one hundred cases of drugs. President Nkrumah of Ghana received major attention as a state guest, and the Sino-Ghanaian Friendship Treaty is rightly hailed as a triumph for Chinese united front tactics. With the so-called Brazzaville group of African states, China has been less successful. These states, in the main, have avoided official political or economic relations as yet. With the demise of the Lumumba government in the Congo, moreover, China suffered a set-back there, and once again, according to rumor, the Congo problem produced a policy difference of serious proportions between Russia and China.

In East Africa where independence has come only recently or is still in the offing for most areas, the Chinese have generally proceeded on a more informal basis. Usually, they have selected an individual, advanced funds or equipment to him, gambling upon his success—and loyalty—to advance their cause. Thus in Somali, Kenya, Uganda, and Zanzibar, the Chinese have given funds to individuals for journalistic or political activities. Representatives from these areas, and from Tanganyika, Ethiopia and the Sudan as well, have visited China as state guests or as a part of cultural missions.

The approach to Latin America is similar. Except for Cuba where Communist China has made major aid and trade commitments, and where official relations are fully established, the

Chinese Communists work through individual and group contacts. Friendship Associations are established. Representatives of the trade union movement, youth groups, parliaments, local officials, and literati are brought to China as well as trade delegations. The hope is that these groups will return home to increase the pressure upon their governments for a shift in policy and attitude.

Admission to the United Nations

What kind of positive gains has China scored from this vast and relatively expensive program? The United Nations vote of 1961 seems to indicate that recent gains have been limited. In 1960, when the issue was whether to discuss the entry of Communist China into the UN, the vote was 42 to 34 against discussion, with 22 abstentions. In 1961, discussion of Red China's admission was accepted by almost all UN members, and the issue was whether to give Communist China the seat held by the Nationalist government. It was first decided that this was "an important question" requiring a two-thirds majority. In the final vote that followed, Communist China received 36 votes, 48 votes were cast against her, and 20 nations abstained. In 1962, the corresponding vote was 42 to 56, with 12 abstentions. Most observers interpreted this as a serious defeat for Communist China since it had been expected that she would at least come close to obtaining a majority of the votes.

However, more than one-half of the nations of the General Assembly failed to support Nationalist China, either by voting for Communist China or abstaining. This group, moreover, included most of the important states of the Afro-Asian world. In 1961, when the issue was fully debated, Communist China got the votes of Afghanistan, Burma, Cambodia, Ceylon, Ethiopia, Ghana, Guinea, India, Indonesia, Iraq, Mali, Mongolia, Morocco, Nepal, Pakistan, Sierra Leone, Somalia, Sudan, Syria, United Arab Republic, and Yemen. A number of African states, mainly from the Brazzaville group, abstained. The Afro-Asian states voting against Communist China were Cameroon, Nationalist China, Gabon, Iran, Japan, Jordan, Laos, Liberia, Libya, Malagasy Republic, Malaya, Mauritania, Philippines, Senegal, South Africa, Tanganyika, Thailand, and Turkey.

The future of China in the United Nations is unclear at this point. Decisive in the defeat of Communist China in the 1961 session was the Latin-American vote which, except for Cuba, was solidly against the Communists. Some European states supported the admission of Communist China to the UN, including Great Britain, Denmark, Finland, and Sweden; Austria, Iceland, the Netherlands, Norway, and Portugal abstained. Obviously, many states voting to admit Communist China to the UN did not do so because they approved of the policies and attitudes of the Communist government, but rather because they believed that this government has *de facto* control over its people, is the only government of mainland China, and must be brought into the world organization if many basic problems are to be tackled. Perhaps the issue that kept the vote for admission of Communist China relatively low was the unsettled question of Taiwan. Despite the fact that both the Nationalists and the Communists have denounced any "two Chinas" or "one China—one Taiwan" approach, a very sizeable number of countries favor this as the ultimate solution.

Europe and the United States

Toward Europe, as toward the Afro-Asian world, Chinese policy has been relatively flexible on issues like trade, cultural relations, and related matters. Trade with the West, particularly with Great Britain and West Germany (which does not recognize Communist China) while small is not without significance. As is well known, the Chinese in late 1961 agreed to purchase six commercial jet liners from Great Britain. In the context of Sino-Soviet troubles, this raised the question whether China might seek increased trade with such countries as Great Britain and West Germany (as well as Japan), assuming suitable credit terms could be arranged.

There remains the major problem of relations between Communist China and the United States. As should now be abundantly clear, Communist China regards the United States as her Number One Enemy. Indeed, the indications are that the Chinese Communist leaders feel that war with the United States at some point in the future is entirely possible. Hence their own policy is a rigid one, and they are putting maximum pressure upon the Soviet Union to pursue a similar policy.

The flavor of Chinese policy was well conveyed by Foreign Minister Ch'en Yi in an interview given at Djakarta on April 2, 1961. In response to a question asking for his opinion on Sino-American relations, he made the following comments among others:

> We are willing to improve Sino-American relations, particularly in view of the fact that the traditional friendship between the peoples of China and the United States has had a long history of development. . . . By Sino-American relations is not meant the relations between the peoples of China and the United States. Their relations and friendship have always been good. . . . But the rigid policy of the U.S. Government created a situation in which relations between the two countries cannot be improved. As I see it, the Kennedy administration has basically made no change in the policy towards China as pursued by the Eisenhower administration. Would our American friends give a cool-headed consideration to this, that is, while the United States is using its armed forces, including the powerful Seventh Fleet, to occupy Taiwan, and is supporting the Chiang Kai-shek rebel clique, and if

this situation is not changed, how can the deadlock in Sino-American relations be broken?[31]

China's grievances   From the standpoint of Communist China, the primary problems are these: the United States occupies its territory, Taiwan; advocates a "two Chinas plot" whereby recognition would be extended to both China and Taiwan as two separate *de facto* governments having control over their respective peoples; is prepared to support such a policy by force, with a network of bases that surround China, stretching from Japan to Pakistan; until this plot can be effectuated, seeks to isolate China in every possible manner from normal intercourse with other nations, sowing hatred against China and threatening those nations that might otherwise recognize the People's Republic.

There can be no doubt that the American policy of seeking to contain China by isolation has shaped both the nature and the intensity of the Chinese counterattack. Toward the United States—more specifically toward American leadership and policy—the Chinese Communist leaders exhibit extraordinary bitterness. Chinese traditional pride, Chinese nationalism, and Chinese Marxism combine in answering American policy with all of the venom, all of the toughness, and all of the ingenuity that a China which is still militarily and economically weak, can muster.

Enmity toward the United States is truly a powerful force in Chinese Communist foreign policy today. On occasion, indeed, it seems to dominate that policy. The United States is blamed for almost every evil deed in the world, castigated for its every action. According to official Chinese accounts, the United States is obstructing the formation of a truly neutral government in Laos; constantly violating Chinese territorial waters and airspace, and maintaining a huge military force in the Taiwan Straits to threaten China; driving Japan toward

fascism and militarism; keeping lackeys like Diem in power over the strenuous opposition of their own people; seeking to buy India and many other countries with an "aid" program that in reality benefits the American monopoly capitalists; thwarting the legitimate aspirations of the African people by openly or secretly supporting imperialism; applying Yankee imperialism against the people of Latin America. The charges are endless.

Probably Communist China damages her case in the court of world opinion on the issue of the United States by engaging in excessive exaggeration and distortion. Exaggeration and distortion are not uncommon practices in the political arena. The Russian Communists have made the same charges against America. At present, however, Communist China is not prepared to make the slightest concession to American policies or attitudes, except for the policies and attitudes of a mythical American "people" who supposedly stand in violent opposition to the policies of their government.

Undoubtedly there is an element of fear present in Chinese Communist appraisals of American policies and intentions. The United States does have powerful military forces in the Western Pacific, and her alliance with the Nationalists is a fact. While she has sought to rule out a Nationalist attack upon the mainland, Nationalist leaders continue to reiterate their determination to regain China. Could not an incident develop involving the United States and China in war?

Changes in the status-quo   More important than fear in Chinese Communist psychology, however, is frustration. The Chinese Communists are profoundly dissatisfied with the status-quo as it relates to them, to Asia, and to the world. They intend to change many things, and they see the United States as the chief obstacle to these changes. American power blocks the "liberation" of Taiwan, the "forward progress" of the liberation movements, and the revolutionary process throughout the world. But one should not underestimate either the element of pride and anger in the Chinese Communist attitude toward the United States.

[31] "Vice-Premier Ch'en Yi Answers Questions at Djakarta Airport Press Conference," *Peking Review*, No. 15, April 14, 1961, pp. 5–6 (p. 6).

To ignore China or treat it as a moral leper is unforgivable to men who combine in themselves the legacy of Chinese greatness with the puritanism implicit in any group of first-generation revolutionary zealots.

Communist China professes to great optimism concerning the future. The East wind is prevailing over the West wind. The imperialist camp is weakening and going down to defeat. The socialist camp is scoring one victory after another. If such views are sincerely held, is there any need to make basic compromises with the forces of decadence and defeat? "We can afford to wait—at least on certain issues," various Chinese Communist leaders have said. It seems likely that they would rather wait than compromise on the issues nearest to their hearts. As yet, Communist China has given no indication that she will compromise on the issue of Taiwan, for example. Repeatedly, Communist spokesmen have said that they would not under any condition sit with an independent Taiwan or acknowledge by any action the existence of such a state. The Communists have refused to have diplomatic relations with states recognizing the Nationalists. They have insisted that Taiwan is an internal issue over which China alone has competence. To the Nationalists, the Communists have ceaselessly appealed: "Come home, accept positions under the new government, and serve the nation loyally. Otherwise," they warn, "the United States will ultimately desert you in favor of a Republic of Taiwan, and you will thus be participants in the treacherous act of dismembering your nation."

In truth, Communist China prefers the present American policy to any policy that would involve "Two Chinas" or "One China—One Taiwan." Communist leaders believe that the present American position is too unrealistic to command world support or last indefinitely. But they realize that an independent Taiwan would attract support and they are determined to prevent such a development if possible. In all probability, this is one main reason why the Communists do not attack Quemoy-Matsu. To be sure, such an attack would result in heavy casualties, but the Communists could take

these islands if they wanted to pay the price. However, to hold Quemoy-Matsu would create a *de facto* "Two Chinas" because then all of the mainland and adjacent islands would be Communist-controlled. Nationalist territory would be confined to Taiwan and the Pescadores, many miles away, and a clear separation would have been effected. Probably, the Communists have no interest in seeing this come to pass.

Sino-American relations are likely to remain troubled for the indefinite future. Basic compromises satisfactory to both parties are not easy to discern, and there is no indication that one party will surrender to the other. Will both sides continue a policy of extreme rigidity, and will this ultimately lead to war? Or will time and events produce changes? Already, perhaps, some change is en route. Until a few years ago, Communist China saw the United States as her sole major opponent and problem. Hence she could afford to concentrate upon this obstacle. Now, however, in different ways, India and the Soviet Union constitute problems. On the other side, in the United States there is increasing recognition that Communist China must be involved in world affairs if we are to find a solution or even a *modus vivendi* for any of the pressing problems of our times. In such trends, at least the terrifying simplicity and extremism of recent Sino-American relations is challenged.

A summary of current foreign policy

How does one summarize the foreign policy of Communist China today? We have suggested three main sources of that policy: tradition, nationalism, and Marx-Lenin-Maoism. Tradition and the geopolitical factors that interact with it have influenced various attitudes, techniques and approaches used in contemporary Chinese foreign policy. The New China is not completely new. Nationalism is only now reaching its zenith in modern China, and its influence is upon all that the Chinese state does. If one has to emphasize one determinant over the others, this must be the one. However, one cannot dismiss Marx-Lenin-Maoism which is itself partly—but only partly—the product of Chinese experience and is now being offered to the world.

To date, Chinese Communist foreign policy has been an interesting mixture of success and failure, simplicity and complexity, uniformity and contradiction. Undoubtedly these are factors implicit in the foreign policy of any major society. In broadest terms, China sees the world through Marxian lenses, and she finds her policies in the Maoist adaptations of Marxism. First, there are the proletarian forces, as represented by the "fraternal socialist societies." Toward these countries, China pledges undying loyalty and support. To uphold proletarian internationalism and the unity of the socialist camp is the sacred obligation of every Marx-Leninist. But in fact, China is presently engaged in a serious conflict with the Soviet Union over such basic issues as decision-making for world communism, the meaning of peaceful coexistence, the amount of support to be given national liberation movements, and the degree of militancy that should be exhibited on behalf of communism. In this conflict, moreover, the nationalist quotient seems high on both sides. Clearly modern Communist states have not yet abandoned national interest for international duty, nor been able completely to reconcile the two.

The states of Asia, Africa, and Latin America represent the vast peasantry of the world, with elements of the working class, intellectuals, and national bourgeoisie. To woo and win this major portion of the world is to set the stage for final victory. The object now is to create a united front, an alliance of the uncommitted and the committed, the non-aligned and those aligned with the Communist bloc. To this task, Communist China has harnessed her economic, cultural, and political policies with remarkable energy. Yet, as the results thus far have indicated, it is not an easy task to accomplish. It is helpful, of course, to make the division between the "people" who constitute 90 percent of the world and the

"enemies of the people" who constitute only 10 percent. If the enemies can be isolated and the people won, Maoism will succeed.

But once again, nationalism—and ideology —sometimes gets in the way. When Chinese nationalism reveals itself in arrogant or rigid forms, such "people" as the Indians are not easy to win. In her quest for territorial rights, buffer state protection, and regional-global prestige, Communist China has behaved remarkably like other Major Powers in the course of their rise to eminence. It should not be surprising, therefore, that she has also reaped the same kind of suspicion, resentment, and fear reserved for Major Powers by small neighbors. There is, in addition, the ideological problem posed by Maoism: how to unite with and struggle against the world peasantry-national bourgeoisie simultaneously. Is there not a striking paradox between the Bandung Spirit and the dedication to proletarian capture of the world revolution before its democratic-bourgeois stage has been completed? How are pragmatic policies to be reconciled with radical theories, and will the peasant-bourgeois world remain always oblivious to the problem?

There is finally the landlord-monopoly capitalist world as represented by the United States. To this world, Communist China presents a posture of seemingly implacable hostility. Against America, the Communist leaders have combined the forces of tradition, nationalism, and ideology. The American policy of attempting to contain China by isolation has produced feelings of bitterness and hatred, as has continued American support for the Nationalists on Taiwan. In the long run, the Chinese Communists are confident that they can undermine the American position in Asia, as they are confident of the general demise of the "capitalist" world. In the short run, however, the Communists fear that world support may grow for some "Two Chinas" solution to the Taiwan issue, and they are determined to counteract that trend. Hence they have made relations with the United States and its allies contingent upon a "One China" position.

The future is unpredictable, but it would seem safe to suggest that China will continue to exhibit mixed characteristics. Toward her enemies, she will display qualities of arrogance, rigidity, and confidence, combined with a considerable ignorance about the real world. Toward "peace-loving" peoples, on the other hand, she will display qualities of suavity, flexibility and patience for the time being. China is likely to continue a pragmatic, moderate policy toward those whom she wishes to woo and win without giving up the radical ideology within which this policy is encased. She is also likely to continue a tough policy toward the United States and its allies without precluding forever a policy shift if it seems to serve her national interests. Toward Russia, China faces a major policy dilemma. There are many reasons why China cannot afford and does not want a break with the Soviet Union, but there are other reasons why she cannot capitulate to current Russian views. Hence, this is a dangerous, fluid period in Sino-Soviet relations.

Despite the many problems confronting her, however, Communist China can take considerable satisfaction in her foreign policy achievements after thirteen years in power. She has made her presence felt on every continent of the world. Before another decade has passed, Chinese Communist leaders hope and expect their country to be accepted as one of the Great Powers, even by its opponents.

BIBLIOGRAPHY

Author's Suggestions

Baerwald, Hans and Jacobs, Dan N. *Chinese Communism: Selected Documents.* New York: Harper & Row, 1963.

Barnett, A. Doak. *Communist China and Asia: Challenge to American Policy.* New York: Harper, 1959.

Hudson, G. F., Lowenthal, Richard, and MacFarquhar, Roderick. *The Sino-Soviet Dispute.* New York: Praeger, 1961.

Liu Shao-ch'i, *Internationalism and Nationalism.* 3rd ed. Peking: Foreign Languages Press, 1952.

Mao Tse-tung. *Selected Works.* 4 vols. Peking: 1954–1961.

Peking Review (Weekly). Peking.

Steiner, H. Arthur. "Communist China in the World Community," *International Conciliation,* No. 533, May 1961.

Tang, Peter S. H. *Communist China Today,* Vol. I, *Domestic and Foreign Policies.* 2nd ed. New York: Praeger, 1961.

U.S. Consul, Hong Kong. *Translations of the China Mainland Press.*

Zagoria, Donald S. *The Sino-Soviet Conflict, 1956–61.* Princeton: Princeton University Press, 1962.

PART SIX

THE WESTERN HEMISPHERE

ABOUT THE AUTHOR

J. J. SANTA PINTER is currently Professor of Law at the Catholic University of Puerto Rico. Prior to this appointment he served as Professor of Law of the Political Science Faculty, Salvador University, Buenos Aires. He was founder and first Director of the School of Diplomacy at Salvador University. He has also served as Professor of Law at the Superior School of Gendarmeria, Argentine Army, Buenos Aires.

Mr. Santa Pinter received the degree Doctor of Law from the Pontifical University of Lateran in Rome and the Diploma of Comparative Law from International University, Luxembourg. His studies have taken him to universities in Hungary, Spain, Argentina, Germany and the United States.

Among his numerous articles and books, the following might be mentioned: *System of Anglo-Saxon Law,* 1956; *System of Soviet Law,* 1957; *Theory and Practice of Diplomacy,* 1958; *Reservations to Multilateral Conventions,* 1959; *Humanism and Foreign Policy,* 1959; and *The International Community,* 1959.

ABOUT THE CHAPTER

The close relationship between international law and the foreign policy of Argentina is the central point of this chapter. The author makes it clear that the geographic position of Argentina "directs her policy towards well-delineated areas" and even her contributions in the field of international law can be largely understood in light of particular geographic factors.

Mr. Santa-Pinter gives careful attention to Argentina's contributions to public international law and to the particular international problems which gave rise to the major "doctrines." The reliance of Argentina on international law as a means for dealing with harsh political problems can be understood in light of her geographic position and her power position within the world community.

Similarly, in reviewing current international problems which confront Argentina the point is underscored that whether one is dealing with the Falkland Island controversy, the problems of defense of the South Atlantic, or the development of a free trade zone in the Western Hemisphere, that the location of a nation must be kept in mind to comprehend the priorities of her interests and the policies that will be pursued.

20

THE FOREIGN POLICY OF ARGENTINA

JOSÉ JULIO SANTA PINTER

Catholic University of Puerto Rico

This brief study deals with the general orientation of the foreign policy of Argentina, taking into account the permanent factors which constitute the bases of her national life. These factors include: geography, ethnic composition, and historical tradition. These factors mark the unavoidable point of departure for every Argentine government which comes to power.

We will then consider the formulation and administration of Argentine foreign policy. Attention will also be given to the guiding principles by which foreign policy is combined with international law. The relation between foreign policy and international law has been so close that political problems which gave birth to particular "doctrines" have been resolved—or at least would have been resolved had it not been for unforeseen and foreign factors—in accord with the principles stated in them.

Then follows a brief analysis of the behavior of Argentina in international or diplomatic life, because her behavior has been the object of criticism. Finally, attention will be given to the fundamental features of both the permanent and short-range foreign policy objectives of Argentina.

PERMANENT FACTORS

The influence of geography

The geographic position of the Argentine Republic directs her policy toward well-delineated areas. These might be summed up in the following points: (1) historical consciousness of belonging to the group of American Republics and especially to the community of nations of Iberian origin; (2) traditional orientation towards the peaceful integration of territories considered to be a part of Argentina, such as the islands of the South Atlantic and the Argentine sector of Antarctica; (3) recovery of territories which are presently under foreign domination—the Falkland Islands—and which have never ceased being considered as an integral part of the national territory; (4) a sense of responsibility for the defense of the South

Atlantic which involves Argentina's own national security as well as that of the entire region; (5) finally, as a negative factor, the great distances which separate Argentina from other civilized areas of the earth. This explains, as we shall see, her attitude of abstention in the past from active participation in international politics in distant regions which do not affect Argentina directly. This attitude has changed recently due to the economic factor, as will be shown later in this study.

The geographic factor has also had an important influence on particular Argentine doctrines of foreign policy and international law. Geography influences the characteristics of the people of all of her regions who have added their contributions to the great spiritual reserve of the nation. The same may be said also of the *material wealth* of her regions, which extend from the subtropics to the frozen lands of the south, and which form the basis for economic policy. There is obviously a close relationship between geography and the Argentine views on historical bays, the local origin of the Tejedor Doctrine, her position with respect to territorial waters, as well as her views on other problems of the Western hemisphere.

Ethnic features

A contemporary author, who was formerly the Foreign Minister as well as the permanent delegate of Argentina to the United Nations, once noted:

> Our psychological make-up shows a curious paradoxical duality of inclinations. We Argentines are, on the one hand, jealous of our personal worth and exaggeratedly concerned about maintaining our individual prerogatives. But at the same time there co-exists in us an open generous disposition toward others. These two attributes which coexist with difficulty,

explain the very basis of our international conduct.[1]

Another author stated with deep patriotism, and even with poetic elegance, the true feeling of the Argentine people, when he said:

> This region of America is called upon to influence the course of history by responding to the international yearning which strives to constitute a community of free peoples. Because here the weary immigrants rest from their ocean voyages, and deposit the biological inheritance of all races. From this incomprehensible and contradictory heterogeneity will come the harmonious homogeneity of the future. From the rough stone will come the work of art. From the humble seed the shady plant and the proud flower will develop. Because Argentine land is open to all winds, it is not the sterile land of small localized people who respond to sentiments of regression. In it palpitates the breath of mankind. It is not confined within walls of stone raised toward the sky. It breathes the air of the sea and of the Rio de la Plata.[2]

The real substance of the ethnic basis of Argentine life is derived from a mixture—sometimes spontaneous, other times artificial—of two fundamental factors: the American and the European. The American factor is divided into three parts: the indigenous mixed with creole and gaucho elements; the continental or inter-American; and the North American. The European factor can be divided into two important divisions: The Spanish influence and the general European influence—admiration for what is French, the influence of British

---

[1] Mario Amadeo, *Por una convivencia internacional; Bases para una Communidad Hispánica de Naciones*, Madrid: Cultura Hispánica Edition, 1956, p. 101.

[2] César Díaz Cisneros, *La Liga de las Naciones y la actitud argentina* (con texto del Tratado), Buenos Aires: Imprenta Mercatalia, 1921, pp. 150–51.

Caribbean Sea

SOUTH AMERICA

PANAMA

CANAL
ZONE

TRINIDAD

Caracas

VENEZUELA

BRITISH
GUIANA

FRENCH
GUIANA

SURINAM

Bogotá

COLOMBIA

Belém

Quito

ECUADOR

Manaus

Recife

PERU

BRAZIL

Lima

Brasília

Lake
Titicaca

La Paz

BOLIVIA

Rio de Janeiro

São Paulo

PARAGUAY

Asunción

Pacific Ocean

Atlantic Ocean

CHILE

Córdoba

URUGUAY

Santiago

Buenos Aires

Montevideo

ARGENTINA

800
MILES

FALKLAND ISLANDS

penetration, and adoption of what is Italian, and so on.[3]

It is clear that these elements of biological character should be taken into account as they condition Argentine character and her conduct in the international field. This is true whether we consider her international conduct theoretically, that is to say doctrinairily or practically which means politically.

Historical foundations

The borders of the nation   Although one of the fundamental bases for the location of the borders of the Argentine Republic was the *uti possidetis iuris* of 1810, the year of the revolt against Spain,[4] nevertheless, the country suffered serious dismembering of the territory of the old River Plate Vice Royalty (about 3,000,-000 square kilometers) from which were formed new nations: Bolivia, Paraguay and Uruguay. Later arbitration deprived it of still more territory.[5] All this did not prevent Argentina from demonstrating, first a loyalty toward her sister countries, and, second, a respect for international compromise.

In the same spirit, Argentina signed the boundary treaties with her respective neighboring countries. With Chile treaties were signed in 1881 (Irigoyen-Echeverría), in 1893 (the Quirno Costa-Errázuriz), and in May, 1902. The principle was to fix the boundary "by the highest peaks" of the Andes Mountains (*divortium aquarum*), with the Pacific side for Chile and the Atlantic side for Argentina. This same principle was also followed in the Straits of Magellan. The Treaty or definitive pact of 1925 with Bolivia granted to Bolivia the town of Yacuiba. Treaties were concluded with Paraguay in 1876, 1905, 1907, and 1939. A satisfactory compromise was reached when both parties renounced their maximum claims. Paraguay gave up the Chaco as far as Bermejo, Atajo Island and Misiones, and Argentina relinquished the Chaco as far as Bahía Negra. The problem with Uruguay has been solved by the Treaty of 1916 in agreement with the *thalweg* principle. In 1961 Congress ratified the new treaty with Uruguay which has definitively fixed the frontier line between both countries along the Uruguay river. The boundaries with Brazil had an international character due to the colonial status of both countries. The Treaty of 1828 was signed on the basis of the independence of Uruguay. In 1927 a complementary agreement was signed making the mouth of the River Cuareim in the Uruguay River the limit of Brazilian territory.

Argentina is in a favorable position since no country has any territorial disputes with her. The few pending problems with Chile—(the Beagle Channel and Palena or the zone of the River Encuentro)—and, with Paraguay—the Pilcomayo river which continuously changes its course—have been solved or are on the way to a satisfactory solution.[6]

General orientation of policies   As we shall see in the following pages, the pronouncements and the attitude of the Argentine governments, since the beginning of national life, leave no doubt for the objective observer that Argentine foreign policy is inspired by a desire for peaceful and cordial relations with all peoples. "We have engraved this declaration in our

[3] José Julio Santa Pinter, *Teoría y práctica de la diplomacia,* Buenos Aires: Roque Depalma, 1958, p. 65. See Austin F. MacDonald, *Latin American Politics and Government,* 2nd ed., New York: Thomas Y. Crowell Co., 1954, pp. 24–30.

[4] Díaz Cisneros, mentions the following sources of norms for the formation of the territory of the Argentine Republic: laws dictated by the Spanish Crown during the colonial period; international treaties; bases of independence and finally the *uti possidetis iuris* of 1810 (*Límites de la República Argentina, Fundamentos Histórico-jurídicos,* Buenos Aires: Depalma, 1944, p. 26 ff.

[5] The decisions of President Hayes in 1878, with respect to Paraguay and of President Cleveland in 1895, with respect to Brazil.

[6] The Falkland Islands and the Argentine sector of the Antarctic will be considered later in this chapter.

hearts, say the men of 1816—never to desist fighting for it," said Senator Molinari in his discourse in the Senate on the ratification of the Charter of the United Nations and the Act of Chapultepec, August 19, 1946, "and the time to make manifest to the nations of the world the reasons that have moved us to take this position, we have the honor of making public our intention to live in peace with everybody," and he added what President Yrigoyen affirmed: "with no one against anyone, and with all for the good of all."[7]

The maintenance of "good relations with foreign powers" is a constitutional precept (Art. 86, paragraph 14) and it means precisely that there will be no discrimination whatsoever. In conformity with that principle the Argentine Republic has been developing a general foreign policy of cordiality and co-operation. "Our relations with foreign powers are maintained under the most perfect cordiality, as a necessary consequence of the respectful, economic, and courteous standards which have inspired the foreign policy of the Republic at all times," said President Roque Sáenz Peña.[8]

Argentina's position is a traditionally peaceful one, inspired by the principles of *peace, the good neighbor, non-intervention, peaceful settlement of international disputes, inter-American solidarity, justice, respect for the rights of others, and democracy.*[9]

On these bases we can interpret the declarations of former Chancellor Taboada with respect to the meeting and resolutions of San José, Costa Rica:

We lend our collaboration to every peaceful settlement of the differences that may arise. But that position of peace and the good neighbor cannot

inhibit Argentina from taking the defensive measures which she considers necessary for her tranquillity and that of the other countries of America, if the case for applying such measures arises.[10]

And on another occasion he noted: "At the same time that Argentina adheres profoundly to the principle of non-intervention she believes that nations should observe those obligations with respect to human rights and democracy outlined by the Charter and fortified by the Conference of Santiago."[11] Roque Sáenz Peña himself stated: "Argentine policy has been and will be peaceful, because it is a conservative democracy."

These quotations demonstrate the coincidence of the different points of view followed throughout history by various Argentine governments. We can add the following: "No one can side track us from our natural route," Senator Miguel Cané affirmed in relation to the Drago Doctrine on March 27, 1903,

we shall pay our debts as we have always done, we shall sell our products to whomever pays the best price, we shall buy what is necessary from whomever sells them to us at the cheapest price, we shall link ourselves, with all our intelligence and all our heart to those nations which send us more men to populate our deserts and more capital to develop our wealth. The fact is that this course, gentlemen, is never determined by passion nor is it subject to the whim of fantasy; the permanent interests of the country point out the line to follow without exception.[12]

These principles have been repeated by all the recent Foreign Ministers of Argentina. We

[7] *Discurso pronunciado por el Senador Dr. Diego Luis Molinari,* edition prepared by the Senate, 1946, p. 33.

[8] Roque Sáenz Peña, *Escritos y discursos,* 2 vols., Buenos Aires: Peuser, 1915, II, p. 485.

[9] Provisions from *Charter of Bogotá,* and Resolution XXII of the Third Consultative Meeting of Ministers of Foreign Affairs of the American Republics.

[10] *El Mundo,* August 14, 1960.

[11] *La Razón,* August 19, 1960.

[12] See Luis M. Drago, *La República Argentina y el caso de Venezuela,* Buenos Aires: 1903, pp. 138-9.

quote, for example, former Chancellor Roberto Etchepareborda who insisted that "Argentina's foreign policy will not vary as regards its basic and Christian principles"[13] as well as Chancellor Bonifacio del Carril of the Guido regime who said in an official statement that Argentina's traditional foreign policy, inspired by ideals of peace, freedom, equality and democracy, will be reaffirmed with the greatest possible force by the new Guido government: In other words: "We are with the West because we are the West."[14]

FORMULATION AND EXECUTION OF FOREIGN POLICY

The role of the executive branch

Article 27 of the National Constitution of 1853 decrees that "The Federal Government is obliged to guarantee its relations of peace and commerce with foreign powers by means of treaties which are in conformity with the principles of public law established in this Constitution." The chief-executive is given specific responsibilities. As "supreme head of the Nation" he has charge of the general administration of the country which also includes the formulation of foreign policy; "he names and removes the plenipotentiaries, ministers and the chargés d'affaires with the consent of the Senate"; he "concludes and signs treaties of peace, of commerce, of navigation, of alliances, of boundaries, and of neutrality, concordates and other negotiations required for the maintenance of good relations with foreign powers"; "he receives their ministers and admits their consular officers"; and, finally, he "declares war, with authorization of Congress." All of these powers are performed with the supervision and approbation of the National Congress.

Hipólito Yrigoyen was one of the Argentine presidents who played a most personal role in the conduct of foreign policy. His conception of the basic principles governing the foreign policy of the Argentine Republic were discussed by former Ambassador Gabriel del Mazo at a conference in Montevideo. They might be summarized as follows: (a) autonomy of decision of the American countries, confronted with the First World War; (b) affirmation of international private rights as the world was faced with a new division decided by the victors in the war; (c) affirmation of the individual personality of the Latin-American nations as independent sovereignties. These principles

> aroused faith and confidence. . . . the master key for every policy for an effective community of nations. Such a policy will not be attained by knavery or calculation, but by frankness, based on high purpose and by setting up the moral fortitude of ideals to protect the weakness of countries which are materially weak.[15]

On the basis of these principles we can understand his instructions to his Minister Alvear on the occasion of the adherence of Argentina to the League of Nations in July 1919 and also the instructions to the Argentine delegation in December of 1920, which caused the withdrawal of Argentina from the Assembly of the League.

Within this same framework we might also briefly mention the trip of former President Arturo Frondizi to Europe in 1960. At that time he stated that he hoped to interpret by "person to person diplomacy" the feeling and thought not only of the Argentines but also of all Latin Americans through his dealings with European governments.[16] It is also suitable to mention his trip to Antarctica in March of 1961

---

[13] *Buenos Aires Herald,* March 31, 1962.
[14] *Ibid.,* May 4 and May 5, 1962.

[15] *La Nación,* May 16, 1960.
[16] *La Nación,* June 13, 1960.

for the purpose of "reaffirming Argentine sovereignty" in that area.

The role of the National Congress

Aside from what we have said about the control by the Senate in particular and by Congress in general over the actions of the executive branch in matters of foreign policy, Article 67 of the Constitution enumerates the exclusive powers of the National Congress. These refer to the establishment and security of borders, commerce, foreign debts, treaties with foreign Powers, authorization to the executive to declare war or make peace, the entrance into the country of foreign troops and the departure from the country of national armed forces, and finally, admission into the territory of religious orders other than the ones already in Argentina.

Senator Joaquín V. González analyzed the "diplomatic powers" of Congress on the occasion of the inauguration of the statue of Bernardo O'Higgins and the 108th anniversary of the independence of Chile on September 24, 1918. He noted that the entire Congress, and not just the Senate, takes part in all governmental acts of an international character by mandate of the Constitution. But the Senate has a particular role because it is a consultative council composed of what were originally called "ambassadors of the states or provinces." Thus, the totality of the corporate sovereignty of the component states of the federation is represented in the Senate.

Besides the constitutional precepts, there exist also parliamentary customs derived from these express authorizations. In addition, there are actual constitutional practices which the authorities have always used in conferences or whenever there are private or official meetings in committee or in the halls of Congress. Cooperation is practiced among all these powers because

regardless of how penetrating, or how inspired or how illumined the Presi-

dent feels about the wisdom or the thought of all ages, he cannot claim for himself the omniscience, the complete embodiment of all the powers and sentiments of his country.[17]

We might also note that the participation of the National Congress in matters of foreign policy is stipulated in the regulations of both legislative chambers. For example the Regulations of the Senate of 1862 provided for this body to "examine and pass judgment on every project or matter of constitutional, political and diplomatic character, on treaties and constitutional business." In the same manner, in 1939 the Senate Regulations provided that the Committee on Foreign Affairs would pass judgment on all matters concerning the relations of the Argentine Republic with foreign states. In 1952 and 1955 the Regulations of the Chamber of Deputies of the Nation provided that the Chamber would pass judgment on international treaties, conventions, conferences, and congresses and other matters which concern the maintenance of relations of the nation with foreign states.

Pressure groups

Under this heading we should point out briefly the so-called pressure groups which influence domestic policy and may exercise influence or at times serious pressure on the foreign policy of the government. Among such groups one might point to the political parties, youth and student groups, labor unions, the press, public opinion, the Church, large industry, big business and the armed forces. Also deserving special mention are the opinions of jurists, technicians and persons of political, social and economic importance, and the tradition of the Supreme Court of Justice.

[17] Universidad Nacional de La Plata, *Obras Completas de Joaquín V. González,* Vol. X, Buenos Aires: 1935, p. 468.

Of course, the President decides whether or not he wants to listen to these opinions, and follow their suggestions. However, even though the final decision is his alone to make, it is scarcely probable that the government ever ceases to lend an ear to the above mentioned "pressure groups," because lack of attention could very easily cause serious consequences. It could even jeopardize the stability of the government.

We may mention two special cases of the direct intervention of the Argentine armed forces in foreign policy. The first was after the Punta del Este Conference, in January 1962, the second occurred after the March 18, 1962 general elections. In the first case, the armed forces compelled President Arturo Frondizi to dismiss high ranking officers, including Minister Cárcano in the Foreign Office, as well as to break diplomatic relations with Cuba in spite of the official Argentine position taken in Punta del Este by former Chancellor Cárcano. This was the result of the dangerous "double game policy" of the President *with* Communist Cuba *against* communism. In the second case the armed forces, which are certainly against communism as well as against the return of any kind of Peronism, overthrew President Frondizi because of—once more—his double game policy *with* Peronist elements *against* Peronism. The Provisional President of the Senate, Dr. José María Guido came into office in the absence of a Vice President of the Republic. The vice presidency had been vacant since the early days of the Frondizi regime when Vice President Alejandro Gómez resigned his office after an "official family" dispute.

The Ministry of Foreign Affairs

The organic law concerning ministries decrees that the Ministry of Foreign Affairs handles "the maintenance of relations of the nation with foreign states and entities of international character." The internal organization, although changed frequently by the minister, corresponds more or less to that of other chancellories with a few national variations. The official name of the foreign office is "Ministry of External Relations and Cult (or Worship)." There are two sub-secretaries in the Ministry, one for external affairs and another one for religious—cult—matters, according to constitutional provisions which place religious matters such as admission of new religious orders, the public control of all religious sects and movements, and the like, under "external" affairs.

We should also note the special position of the Argentine Foreign Minister in the Council of National Defense because of his important role for mobilization of the nation and organization for war. He also is the one who carries on the foreign affairs of the nation by delegation of presidential authority to him. He is the one who makes decisions for the defense of the country. The duties of co-ordination of defense activities rest with the External Security Cabinet. This body is made up of the Secretaries of State in the departments of Foreign Affairs, War, Navy and Air. Its meetings are called and presided over by the Minister of Foreign Affairs on his own initiative or at the summons of any of the ministers who make it up, "provided that they do not request the decision of the President."

The Foreign Service

A foreign service is provided for by law. Specific provisions deal with the classification of diplomatic and consular agents, recruitment, the duties and rights of diplomatic agents, the functions of the Classification Board, schedule of transfers, salaries, leaves and disciplinary measures.

The Argentine foreign service is the object of continuous criticism by public opinion as well as by the press. This criticism is due, generally speaking, to the policy of appointment of the members of the foreign service. Appointments are reserved for a special social class as well as for some "politically well-located" people and are considered an easy means of obtaining economic advantages.

GUIDING PRINCIPLES OF INTERNATIONAL LAW

National sovereignty

Sovereignty, in general, and its attributes and practical manifestations, in particular, are the firmest bases of the Argentine position in international relations. This position is not unique because it coincides in its fundamental outlines with the position of other states, especially, the Ibero-American, as well as with the principles of the Charter of Bogotá and the Charter of the United Nations. However, Argentina takes a uniquely firm stand on the preservation of its sovereign rights.[18] Chancellor Ruiz-Guiñazú, on the occasion of the Third Consultative Meeting of Ministers of Foreign Affairs in Rio de Janeiro, in 1942, noted:

The conjunction of national interest and international interest in a single policy is not a paradox. It implies a problem of synthesis. And thus, with foreign policy being determined by sovereignty, which in its own reason for being, is inexorably ruled by the supreme interest of the nation, as a free independent entity in the determination and execution of its own acts.[19]

This firm idea of national sovereignty produced the opinion in various foreign circles

that Argentina had set itself, as McGann states, as a "self-styled champion of America and all mankind."[20] In other words, the Argentines are called "the Yankees of the South," which cannot mean, in our opinion, any offense if one takes into account the virtues of the North American people; on the contrary, it can be interpreted as the position of an independent nation with freedom of action in the international field, co-ordinating nevertheless, its national and international interests. From the point of view of the philosophy of democracy, this position should be the object of praise. If the countries of the Western hemisphere insist on their complete freedom of action, the United States will never be accused by extra-continental countries of a supposed hegemony over her sister American countries.

At this point we might mention the position taken by the Perón regime vis-à-vis the United States. Former President Perón took a strong stand on national "sovereignty" which was not compatible with the policy of so-called "American interference" practiced by the U.S. Ambassador. That anti-American position changed in the very last moment of Perón's regime and, ironically, this change—petroleum concessions to United States business interests—contributed to his overthrow by the *Revolución Libertadora* in 1955.

Some years later, it was charged, that certain international and foreign elements interfered during the last moments of the Frondizi

[18] See J. J. Santa Pinter, "Sovereignty as a Basis of Argentine Foreign Policy," *World Affairs,* Vol. 123, No. 4, Winter 1960, p. 107. This has also been the Argentine position in the Eichmann case.

[19] See Ministerio de Relaciones Exteriores y Culto, *Tercera Reunión de Consulta de Ministros de Relaciones Exteriores de las Repúblicas Americanas,* etc. 1942, p. 10.

[20] Thomas J. McGann, "Argentina at the First Pan-American Conference," *Inter-American Economic Affairs,* I, No. 2, Sept., 1947, p. 53. "Argentina aspires to leadership, at least in the southern part of South America, and it resents the dominant position of the United States." See also Austin F. MacDonald, *Latin American Politics and Government,* 2nd ed., New York: Thomas Y. Crowell Co., 1954, p. 692. In this respect one should not forget the negative United States reaction with reference to such famous Argentine doctrines as the Calvo Doctrine and the Drago Doctrine, so that we are now faced with a vicious circle of actions and reactions between both countries. Jesús de Galíndez agrees with the authors quoted in this note, see *Iberno-América: Su evolución política, socio-económico, cultural e internacional,* New York: Las Americas Publishing Co., 1954, pp. 338, 522.

regime. The American Ambassador in Buenos Aires was said to have played a decisive role in making attempts to save the Frondizi Administration.

The origin of principles such as the principle of sovereignty we are discussing here, may be theoretical or doctrinaire. Or, it may happen that a situation in fact gives rise to the appearance of a doctrine. We shall see how this has occurred in some instances.

Territorial waters   The Civil Code states that "The waters adjacent to the territory of the Republic to the distance of a marine league, measured from the line of the lowest tide" are public properties of the state. But "for the right of policing for the security of the country and the observation of fiscal laws, they extend to the distance of four marine leagues measured in the same manner." The same provision of the Code speaks of "internal waters, bays, inlets, ports and anchorages" and mentions the islands already formed or which may be formed in territorial waters. In this connection one should also note a provision of the Treaty of International Penal Law of Montevideo in 1889 which provided that "territorial waters, for the effects of penal jurisdiction, include those which extend five miles from the coast of the mainland and islands which form part of the territory of each state." This provision was not recognized by Great Britain in her dispute with Uruguay in 1906 when she insisted that the width of the territorial sea, including the River Plate, was just three miles. Argentina signed and ratified this Montevideo agreement.

Admiral Storni of Argentina submitted to the meeting of the International Law Association in Buenos Aires in 1922 a plan according to which territorial waters ought to have *different* measurements.[21] In reality, what Storni proposed was to put this worldwide problem in order, because national criteria are very divergent. It is interesting to note that no agreement on the width of the territorial sea

[21] Segundo R. Storni, *Mer Territoriale*, 1922.

could be reached at the international conferences at Geneva in 1958 and 1960.

Some years ago, an Argentine professor, José León Suárez, claimed that territorial waters should include those that cover the continental shelf, especially with reference to fishing. A similar—if not identical—criterion was upheld in two decrees of the President in 1944 and in 1946. In these decrees the President categorically claimed sovereignty over the Argentine continental shelf. The decree of 1946 also declared that the Argentine continental shelf is under Argentine sovereignty, guaranteeing, however, freedom of navigation. Present day Argentine policy seems to have abandoned this thesis in favor of the traditional three mile limit. It is interesting to note that the earlier decree of 1946, proclaiming sovereignty over the continental shelf, involves among other concepts the unity of the continental shelf and the continent, morphological and geographical unity, and the biological development of the waters which form it. Following U.S. and Mexican precedents, this decree expressly admitted that each country has the right to consider as national territory all extension of the subcontinental ocean and the adjacent continental shelf.

Historical bays   Luis M. Drago, in his dissenting opinion, in the 1910 Arbitration case between the United States and England over the problem of fishing in the North Atlantic, supported the doctrine which later became known as "the doctrine of the historical bays." This doctrine, in general, affirms that bays belong to the territorial waters of the respective states under certain conditions. These are: first, if the corresponding sovereignty has been exerted over them "since time immemorial"; second, if their measurements conform to the established geographical configuration; and third, if they are necessary for national safety and defense. This famous dissent noted:

> So it may be safely asserted that a certain class of bays such as Chesapeake Bay and Delaware Bay in North America and the great estuary of the

River Plate in South America, form a class distinct and apart and undoubtedly belong to the littoral country, whatever may be their depth of penetration and the width of their mouths, when such a country has asserted its sovereignty over them, and particular circumstances such as geographical configuration, immemorial usage and above all, the requirements of self-defense, justify such a position.[22]

A document of the Argentine Navy affirms that the gulfs and bays which Drago called "historical bays" belong to the Argentine Republic, even though the mouth may exceed ten miles, when their use over a prolonged period is required to protect the vital interests of the nation. Independently of the doctrine of the historical bays enunciated by Drago, and applying the rule of the ten-mile limit—adopted by the Conference for the Codification of International Law at The Hague in 1930—the gulf of San José with a four-mile-wide entrance is entirely within Argentine territorial waters, as is the Gulf Nuevo (New Gulf), with a seven-mile-wide entrance. Both of these are on the Valdéz Peninsula.

National and international rivers   The recognition of sovereignty over rivers had its origin in the protracted conflict between Argentina and France; later the dispute also included England. The two European Powers tried to establish their dominion over the region of the River Plate in 1838–40 and 1848–50, respectively. This occurred long after the "English invasions" (1806 and 1807), which had been repulsed heroically by popular action. The victory over the English gave rise to a national holiday, "The Day of the Reconquest," which is celebrated on the 12th of August. It also influenced the May Revolution against Spain in 1810.

The conflict with France and England over the River Plate was resolved and the Arana-Southern Agreement signed in Buenos Aires on November 24, 1849. This agreement recognized that "the navigation of the River Paraná" was "navigation within the Argentine Confederation, and subject only to its laws and regulations, the same as that of the Uruguay River which is controlled by Argentina and Uruguay." The question of international rivers thus was positively decided by dividing rivers into groups, national and international, the first under the sovereignty of the respective states and the second under international control.

A few years later, in 1852, General Urquiza proclaimed free navigation of rivers as "a means of placing the nation in the irrevocable possession of them." Alberdi affirmed in this respect that

free navigation of the affluents of the River Plate is the only means of reducing to practice the freedom of foreign commerce within inland America, by opening all the ports, markets and new means of communication with which that region is endowed.[23]

This same principle was incorporated in the National Constitution of 1853, with the provision that there was free navigation for vessels flying all flags within the interior of the country, subject only to national legislation.

Diplomatic protection

The Tejedor Doctrine   As a result of certain attacks by Indians against some cities of the southern portion of the Province of Buenos Aires in the second half of the last century, the inhabitants of that region, who were of English origin, solicited the help and protection of the English Minister in the capital city. The

[22] *American Journal of International Law*, vol. 4, 1910, pp. 988–1000.

[23] Juan B. Alberdi, *Organización de la Confederación Argentina*, new ed., vol. II, Madrid: 1913, p. 561.

Minister insisted that his Government should give protection to all British subjects wherever they might be.

Chancellor Carlos Tejedor, in his note of January 22, 1872, replied that foreigners who enter a country are subject to the laws and authority of that country, because

> the foreigner, for the protection of his rights as well as for civil and criminal complaints to which he believes himself entitled, has to go, as do the citizens of the country, to the authorities who administer the laws.

He further pointed out that

> if they enter the desert for commercial purposes, they do so at their own risk, since the State cannot give them the protection which its own subjects lack there. . . .

Otherwise,

> the group of foreigners would be a state within another state, a political monstrosity.[24]

This doctrine, which denies diplomatic protection to foreigners resident in the country, coincides with the National Constitution and with the Charter of the Organization of American States.[25]

The Yrigoyen Doctrine   The principle announced with reference to private foreign inhabitants was applied to *juridical entities* by Chancellor Bernardo de Yrigoyen, in 1876, when the manager of the branch of the Bank of London and South America in Rosario,

Province of Santa Fe, was detained by order of the provincial authorities. This event brought a strong protest from the English Minister in Buenos Aires who threatened to send a warship to Rosario. Chancellor Yrigoyen proclaimed:

> The Constitution and the laws of the nation and of Santa Fe offer full recourse before the courts for the complete defense of individual rights and interests. It is only when there has been a denial of justice, when due process of law has been denied or notoriously obstructed by the agents charged to apply it, that a matter which affects foreign interests can come to diplomatic discussion.[26]

He went on to note that such entities as the bank in question "owe their existence exclusively to the law of the country which authorizes them, and consequently, they are neither nationals nor foreigners," and although they have been constituted exclusively by foreign inhabitants, they would lack the right to diplomatic protection because "the capital of stock companies does not have nationality."[27]

This doctrine has been discussed over the years and its position vis-à-vis the "nationality of capital" is debatable even when legislation and court decisions have attributed nationality to capital for certain exemption and jurisdiction purposes. It seems clear, however, that this does not detract in any way from this Argentine doctrine. The Tejedor Doctrine, applied to juridical entities, clearly denies them diplomatic protection.

Responsibility of states

The Calvo Doctrine   The Calvo Doctrine declares that private debts cannot be collected by

---

[24] See text in Ruiz Moreno, *El derecho internacional publico ante la Corte Suprema.*

[25] "The jurisdiction of the States within the limits of their national territory is exercised equally on all inhabitants, be they nationals or foreigners." (Art. 12). See the Argentine Reservation on signing the "Pact of Bogotá."

[26] See text of note in Ruiz Moreno, *El derecho internacional público ante la Corte Suprema,* **pp. 253 ff.**
[27] *Ibid.*

diplomatic or military means for the simple reason that a foreigner cannot demand privileges that the nationals of the country do not have. In other words, the responsibility of the government cannot be greater in the case of foreigners than in that of its own subjects. Carlos Calvo, a prolific writer on international law, maintained that this should be the rule in spite of some precedents in the past and the insistence of European nations that "foreigners deserve more consideration, more respect and greater privileges than those accorded to the nationals of the country where they reside." He took a very strong stand in favor of consistency and in opposition to the European practice of discrimination. He insisted that the European practice was "intrinsically contrary to the law of equality of nations and is very lamentable because of its practical consequences."

Calvo's doctrine has been analyzed and discussed at length in treatises on international law. We agree with the conclusions of one author who insists that it is not possible to separate this doctrine from other passages in the works of Calvo. Calvo criticized the abuses committed by strong nations against the weak, by following in their relations with each other a norm different from the one followed with the weaker nations. Calvo also deplored the practice of granting to foreign residents special privileges which were not available to its own citizens.[28]

The applications of the Calvo Doctrine have been extensive, and it appears to us that its extension is both lawful and suitable to the new states of our era. If we did not apply this rule to the new states we would fall into the same arbitrariness which is so clearly condemned by the Doctrine.

The Drago Doctrine   As Chancellor Yrigoyen transferred the Tejedor Doctrine from physical beings to juridical entities, so we ob-

serve that the Calvo Doctrine, which was concerned with private debts, was applied by Drago to the sphere of public debts. The Drago Doctrine originated in a note sent by Chancellor Drago on December 29, 1902 to Martín García Mérou, the Argentine Minister in Washington. This was during the period of conflict between Venezuela and certain European Powers.[29] This doctrine sustains, in reality, several principles and not just the one which is known generally as the doctrine of prohibition of the compulsory collection of public debts.

Other principles include: First, juridical equality of states:

Among the fundamental principles of international public law which humanity has accepted, one of the most valuable of all specifies that all states, whatever may be the strength that they command, are entities of the law, perfectly equal among themselves and reciprocally deserving, therefore, of the same considerations and respect.[30]

Second, this juridical equality does not exclude a *de facto* difference:

Of course, one notices in this respect, that the capitalist who provides money for a foreign state, always takes into consideration what the resources of the country are in which he is going to operate, and the greater or lesser probability of the contracted agreements being fulfilled without any fault.[31]

And then follows the passage of special interest with respect to this point:

[28] Alwyn F. Freeman: "Recent Aspects of the Calvo Doctrine and the Challenge to International Law," in *American Journal of International Law,* vol. 40, no. 1, (January, 1946), p. 132.

[29] Luis M. Drago, *La República Argentina y el caso de Venezuela,* Buenos Aires: Emprenta y Casa Editora de Coni Hermanos, 1903; text in English in Supplement to the *American Journal of International Law,* vol. 1, 1907, p. 1.

[30] *Ibid.*

[31] *Ibid.*

All governments enjoy different credit according to their degree of civilization and culture and their conduct in business, and these circumstances are measured and weighed before contracting for any undertaking, by making the condition more or less onerous, with an arrangement for precise facts which the bankers have recorded with exactness.[32]

Third and fourth principles are, repudiation of European territorial expansion in America and repudiation of oppression of the people:

Motivated by the events in Venezuela, the one thing that the Argentine Republic sustains, and which it would gladly see accepted by a great nation like the United States, which enjoys such great authority and power, is the principle already accepted that there cannot be further European territorial expansion in America, nor oppression of the peoples of this continent, because an unfortunate financial situation might cause some of them to defer the fulfillment of their agreements.[33]

Fifth and sixth principles concern the unrighteousness of compulsory collection of the public debt and of the occupation of any soil in the Americas by a European Power.

A seventh point relates to dangers:

The creditor knows that he is making contracts with a sovereign entity and that it is an inherent condition of all sovereignty that he cannot undertake nor execute actions against it, since this method of collection would compromise its very existence, and make independence disappear and nullify the action of the respective governments.

. . . the compulsory and immediate collection of debts by means of force, would bring nothing but ruin to the weaker nations and the absorption of their governments and their inherent authority, by the powerful nations of the earth.[34]

The eighth principle deals with the form of liquidation of debts:

The acknowledgment of the debt, the liquidation of its amount, can and should be done by the nation, without any impairment of its original rights as a sovereign entity.[35]

Dangerous precedents are mentioned in a ninth statement which declares that: the Argentine people were greatly alarmed to learn

that the lack of payment of the services of the public debt of Venezuela is given as the major reason for the capture of her fleet, of the bombardment of one of her ports and the establishment of a war blockade on her coasts. If all of these procedures are definitely adopted, they will establish a dangerous precedent for the security and the peace of the nations of this part of America.[36]

The tenth and eleventh principles relate to Argentine policy and American confraternity. They invoke "the sentiments of justice, of loyalty and of honor, which permeate the Argentine people and have inspired their policy for all time," and make a call to "the sentiment of continental confraternity" of the peoples of America.

Viewing these principles from our vantage point in history, it is not difficult to discover the close relationship of these principles and

[32] *Ibid.*
[33] *Ibid.*

[34] *Ibid.*
[35] *Ibid.*
[36] *Ibid.*

those stated in the Charter of Bogotá and their relationship to other concepts accepted by inter-American theory and practice. Although the delegation from the United States to the Peace Conference at The Hague, in 1907, succeeded in having a fundamental modification of this doctrine accepted, the actual acceptance and triumph of this doctrine dates from The Hague Conference. As a final observation we should point out that the application of this doctrine apparently has been extended from the Americas to the new states of other continents as a result of Article 2, paragraph 4, of the United Nations Charter.

ARGENTINA AND INTERNATIONAL ORGANIZATIONS

The League of Nations

Argentina has frequently been criticized for her withdrawal from the Assembly of the League of Nations. It should be noted, in all fairness, that there were some clear principles which dictated her action: the principle that all states should be admitted to the League of Nations—a true universality of membership; the principle of acceptance of the jurisdiction of the International Court of Justice; the principle of acceptance of the election by annual rotation of the members of the Council, and the principle of the limitation of armaments.

From the legal point of view and that of democracy, these principles should be recognized as unobjectionable; but, from a political point of view, they may be questioned. It has always been the Argentine position to start from fundamental principles and later deduce the conclusions that follow from them. The Argentine Government placed so much emphasis on this point that it preferred to proceed in a known manner, that is, it preferred to withdraw from the League because "only vigorous action is capable of shaking a reactionary atti-

tude to the acceptance of those principles." However, the objectors to Argentina's conduct have taken the argument from the field of principles to the minutiae of legal procedure.

Argentina withdrew from the Assembly on instructions from the Argentine President. The instructions to withdraw were inspired by the "democratic spirit which inspires the traditional foreign policy of the Republic and in recognition of the equality of all sovereignties."[37] It was also clear that withdrawal from the Assembly was not to be construed as a withdrawal or even separation from the League itself. This was confirmed in 1933 when Argentina rejoined the major body of the League. Three years later Chancellor Carlos Saavedra Lamas presided over the Assembly.

The United Nations

Just as Argentina was criticized because of her attitude toward the League of Nations, so she has also been the object of censure with reference to her deliberation and careful consideration of the Charter of the United Nations before she ratified it. We should recognize first that each country and its government are empowered, and even obliged by its political makeup (if the country in question is democratic), to analyze and ponder the reasons for and against its position when faced with proposals of a universal character. Secondly, we should note, that blind belief, without reservations, in the League or even in the United Nations, does not appear in the religious or political decalogue of any country. Consequently, Argentina has the right to discuss freely and democratically her adherence to such international organizations. This was the procedure followed with respect to the Charter of the United Nations—which was finally accepted by the National Congress.

[37] Message of the Executive (President Alvear) to Congress, June 6, 1923.

Her attitude towards the United Nations should not be censured by her critics, because Argentina has never abandoned her Western position nor renounced the traditional principles which inspire her foreign policy. The reasons for this can best be explained by the words of Mariano J. Drago when he said: "faithful to her tradition and her present desires, Argentina can be nothing unless she is together with the free world. And this should be the basis of her present and future foreign policy."[38]

The Organization of American States

A sure compass for the orientation of the foreign policy of Argentina is her membership in the American community. "May America be for humanity," Roque Sáenz Peña exclaimed when he finished his speech on the American *Zollverein* during the first international American Conference in Washington, 1889–1890, in which he wished to offer America to men of all the world just as the preamble of the Argentine Constitution of 1853 offered them Argentine land.

"Our country has always proceeded, inspired by a spirit of frank and loyal Americanism," affirmed Chancellor Taboada, because it has a profound sense of Americanism. Further testimony of this is also found in the decree of May 27, 1945 by which Argentina adhered to the Act of Chapultepec, declaring war against Japan and Germany. In his speech of August 24, 1960, during the Seventh Consultative Meeting of the Ministers of Foreign Affairs, Chancellor Taboada affirmed the Argentine position when he condemned international communism because "of our unreserved adhesion to the inter-American system and obligations," and then went on, "we shall struggle to find all adequate means to fortify the inter-American system and continental solidarity, to preserve representative democracy and to guarantee human rights and inter-American peace."[39]

Argentine participation in inter-American activities has been loyal throughout, even when inter-Americanism was called "Pan-Americanism." This is true in spite of certain internal political difficulties in regard to the ratification of some international or inter-American agreements which bring with them certain military commitments. However, these internal difficulties have been exaggerated by some foreigners. Argentina has participated actively in inter-American meetings at all levels and has adhered to the resolutions which have been adopted.

Participation in international conferences

We mention briefly, in order to complete this panorama, that the Argentine Republic has participated in the great majority of congresses or other international meetings to which she has been invited, even though her attitude towards the International Labor Organization on some occasions has been the object of criticism. We should also note that Buenos Aires has been the site of a great number of international meetings.

FOREIGN POLICY OBJECTIVES

General principles

Although the Argentine Republic attempts to maintain good relations with all countries, it places them in two categories: first, there are

[38] Mariano J. Drago, "Nuestra politica exterior," *La Nación*, May 22, 1960, p. 14.

[39] *Séptima Reunión de Consulta de Ministros de Relaciones Exteriores*, San José, Costa Rica, 1960, Document 27.

the sister countries of America, and second, the countries outside of America which include not only those of Europe but also those of other continents, including the "new states."

This arrangement makes sense in commerce and other relationships with all countries as well as with regard to the right to remain neutral in certain periods in history. There are many Argentine writers who take the position that the right of—or perhaps more properly "to"—neutrality is one of the attributes of the highly appreciated sovereignty. In light of this, one can better understand the abstention of the Argentine government from participating in World War II.

Different factors influence her objectives; among them those of an economic nature occupy a pre-eminent place. Roque Peña doubtlessly referred to this in his message to Congress on October 12, 1910:

I participate in the Pan-American concept, as far as it means the indisputable respect for sovereignties, harmony and friendship among the states of the continent, without excluding the reciprocal co-operation, which our economic development requires. It is not suitable for Argentine policy to be either particularly American or exclusively European.[40]

President Frondizi affirmed in his letter to President Kennedy regarding the *Alliance for Progress* that the "magnitude of this undertaking requires not only assistance from all American nations but from the countries of Western Europe as well."

The Antarctic and the islands of the South Atlantic

This topic should be considered under several headings: Argentina's views on the position of

[40] Roque Sáenz Peña, *op. cit.,* p. 42.

these regions; the Argentine foreign policy regarding the Antarctic Continent, and finally, the implications of the Treaties of Rio de Janeiro in 1947 and of the Antarctic in 1959.

Argentina's views   The position of the Argentine Republic is adequately known with reference to the "Argentine sector" of the Antartic as well as with respect to the islands of the South Atlantic. This position is based on the principles of territorial continuation, effective occupation, the popular Argentine feeling towards the Antarctic and the islands, and positive exercise of acts of sovereignty. The position of Argentina has been made abundantly clear, through her literature, statements of national leaders, and a number of proclamations. Although this aspect of the problem is important in the foreign policy of the Republic, it is more domestic than international, since it is a question of territorial integration.

The Antarctic Treaty   Argentina participated actively in the Washington Conference which culminated in the signing of the Antarctic Treaty on December 1, 1959. This action, however, does not imply in any manner that Argentina has renounced her previous position and her territorial claims in the Antarctic. The long and tumultuous discussion of this treaty in Congress before its ratification in 1961 is very eloquent evidence of the strong national sentiments concerning the Antarctic matter.

Although there was some opposition to the treaty among various segments of the Argentine public, Article IV of the treaty apparently contains the necessary guarantees for the position taken by Argentina. In answering certain foreign publicists and statesmen who seem so anxious to internationalize the Antarctic, the following points should be made: they come from countries which were never permanently present in the Antarctic. Consequently, for them it is a question of internationalizing and thereby sharing in an area that belongs to somebody else. Their position would not be so easy for them if the region under discussion were one in which they held a position similar to that of Argentina in the Antarctic, both *de jure* and *de facto*.

The Rio de Janeiro and Washington treaties

On signing the Antarctic Treaty, Secretary Christian Herter declared in the name of the governments of the United States, Argentina and Chile that the Treaty did not affect the obligations these nations had under the Inter-American Treaty of Reciprocal Assistance. We definitely do not share the opinion of an author who asserted that "such statements are easy enough to make but are of no legal consequence."[41] On the contrary, we insist that Article 4 of the Treaty of Rio de Janeiro, which defines the area protected, includes the Argentine and Chilean sectors of the Antarctic. Consequently, Herter's declaration was very well taken. In case of aggression or attack in the area included under the Treaty, the obligations of the nations involved are clearly understood. Consequently, the signing of the Antarctic Treaty in no way undermined the obligations assumed under the Pact of Rio.

The Falkland Islands

The Argentine position with reference to the Falkland Islands (Islas Malvinas) is consecrated as much in instruments of government and declarations of an international character as in abundant juridical, historical, geographic, sociological, demographic, economic, political, and literary and poetic literature of the Argentine people.

Another factor influences the policies of every Argentine government, regardless of political outlook or party affiliation. That factor is the existence of a popular and national sentiment over the years that the Malvinas are Argentine, even though they are under English

occupation, and that they will over a period of time be recovered. Thus, in the case of the Malvinas we are face to face with the problem of territorial *reintegration,* which is distinct from the problem of national *integration* which exists with reference to the islands of the South Atlantic and the Argentine sector of the Antarctic.

For political reasons Argentine governments at times keep silent about the "Malvinas affair." But when the issue is posed, no Argentine government can refrain from making the claim, now of long standing, that these islands belong to Argentina and that they must be recovered.

A recent example of this was the reaction in Argentina to the creation by the British of a new Antarctic colony early in March 1962, at the very moment of the visit of Prince Philip to Argentina. A spokesman for the Argentine Foreign Office stated on that occasion:

> We respect the right of the British to change the different sections of their Foreign Ministry, but this will not change the traditional Argentine stand on her right to the Islas Malvinas, South Georgia, the Sandwich Islands and the Argentine Antarctic.[42]

Participation in the Common Market

Universal interdependence, a new situation in international relations, makes it clear, as President Frondizi pointed out, that "the solution of national problems always has causes and effects which transcend the frontiers of each country and, consequently, it is necessary to face these solutions within the currents and forces which operate in the world environment."[43] In agreement with this presidential view, Argentina has adopted two lines of pol-

[41] Robert D. Hayton, "The Antarctic Settlement of 1959," in *American Journal of International Law,* vol. 54, No. 2 (April 1960), p. 366.

[42] *La Nación,* March 10, 1962.
[43] *Ibid.,* June 13, 1960.

icy: (a) participation whenever possible in the European Common Market, and (b) the creation of a similar common market among the nations of the Americas.

Because of the transformation and amplification of the European Common Market, Argentina, through its embassy in Paris, presented on June 1, 1960, a memorandum requesting her admission to the organization. The document expressed the concern of the Argentine government that a number of the participants of the Common Market were introducing "discrimination with respect to countries equally interested in objectives which are common not only to present members of the organization, but also to the Latin Americans and, therefore, to Argentina." It further noted that Argentina was interested in participating in every collective action tending to assure the most extensive reciprocity possible by means of international co-operation and co-ordination.

Argentina has been quite aware of the contrast between the liberalization of trade in industrial products and the highly restrictive tendency of the rules and regulations applied to interchange of agriculture and livestock products by the majority of industrialized countries. Argentina is trying to find the ideal balance between the exportation of agricultural and livestock products and the importation of manufactured products from the member nations of the Common Market. Such an equilibrium would favor Argentine foreign commerce, as President Frondizi expressed it:

The present position, by itself restrictive and unjust, could be changed into an even more protectionist tendency for the agricultural and livestock sector, especially of the countries of the European Economic Community. The immediate result of such an action would be to stimulate an uneconomic autarchy in the agricultural production of those countries. Such self-sufficiency would prejudice the interests of Latin American exporters who are in a position to produce on an economic and competitive basis.[44]

"That excessive protectionism," President Frondizi points out,

which deprives us of markets for our primary products, may make it impossible for us to acquire in those countries the technical elements which we need for our development and which they have the ability and the necessity of exchanging.[45]

This statement by Frondizi indicates the realistic policy of the Argentine government. Although the situation does not seem to be very promising at the present time, we believe that Argentina's participation in the Common European Market, although *indirect,* could become a reality through the association and direct co-operation of the Latin American Zone of Free Commerce and the European Common Market.

This must be the reason for sending so many special trade missions to Europe in the administrations of President Frondizi and President Guido and others, as well as the establishment in 1961 of a permanent Argentine Embassy accredited to the European Economic Community in Brussels.

The Latin American Zone of Free Commerce

An outstanding role fell to Argentina in the preparations for the negotiations which led to the signing of the Treaty of Montevideo on February 18, 1960. This Treaty established a Zone of Free Commerce and brought into being the Latin-American Association of Free Commerce. Even though we must recognize that this treaty in itself "is not a magic formula

[44] *Ibid.*
[45] *Ibid.*

which will solve all the problems and the structural faults of Latin-American economics," we believe that it will provide markets of adequate dimension, which will stimulate an increase in the investment of capital funds coming from abroad. The flow of foreign capital is made difficult at the present time by the existence of closed markets which greatly restrict the circulation of wealth.

This national effort, joined with similar efforts of other sister countries of the continent, should be taken into account whenever the problem of international economic co-operation is considered. If this is not done, in the words of President Frondizi, "there could be a change in the harmonious structure of the continental bloc, to which Latin America belongs because of historical, spiritual and religious reasons." The dangers implicit in the "Cuban Affair" are the type of situation President Frondizi had in mind. While this matter was being considered at San José, Minister Taboada stated clearly that the "problem waits for an answer here and now," because "Latin America needs to duplicate the experiment which international co-operation made possible in the reconstruction of Europe." In this same spirit the Argentine delegation presented a plan to call a special conference to constitute an Inter-American Organization of Economic Co-operation.

We should also briefly mention the regulations regarding foreign investment in petroleum in Argentina. According to the present law, the rights of private individuals existing as of May 1, 1958 will be respected. Subsequent to that date only new concessions involving a fifty percent participation by the Provinces will be granted. Mineral deposits inside the national territory and the territorial waters (including the islands of the South Atlantic and Argentine Antarctic sector) are exclusive property, absolute and inalienable, of the federal state and belong to the provinces, to the National Territory of Tierra del Fuego, or to the above mentioned islands and to the Argentine Antarctic. The signatories of the Treaty of Montevideo declared in a Protocol of the same date that the treaty did not apply "to the obligations of

buying and selling of petroleum and its derivatives, resulting from agreements made by the signatory countries of the present protocol before the date of the signing of the treaty."

Political defense against communism

Argentina has participated in the Inter-American meetings where all foreign totalitarian doctrines have been condemned. These include a great number of conferences over a twenty year period. Domestically, we can point to a decree in 1956, communicated to the Organization of American States, stating the adherence of Argentina to the Caracas Resolution dealing with "solidarity for the conservation of political integrity of the American states against the intervention of international communism." Other decrees prohibit Communist activities in all the territory of the nation; such prohibitions extend to publications, to all kinds of propaganda and to acts of proselytism. The Foreign Ministry has also requested the reduction of the diplomatic personnel from Communist countries in Buenos Aires to the number equal to those making up the Argentine diplomatic representation in the respective countries.

As a consequence of certain events—discovery of subversive activities which brought about Federal intervention in the Province of Córdoba; a doctrinaire development of the practical knowledge of communist tactics of "revolutionary warfare" and of guerrilla warfare in the institute of higher education of the armed forces—Chancellor Taboada proposed, in the Seventh Meeting of the Foreign Ministers in San José in 1960, that a special conference should be called to prepare an inter-American agreement on the defense of the Western Hemisphere against communism. "The theory and practice of the international Communist movement demonstrate," Taboada pointed out,

> that its objective is the domination or control of the political institutions of

the state, if necessary by the establishment of regimes of a Marxist ideological content whose political dependence on Chinese-Soviet Communism may not be manifest. . . . the international communist movement is aimed at the destruction of the American democratic concept. . . .

One of the conditions for the success of revolutionary warfare is the decline and the disorganization of the state and of society in each national area, brought about by psychological action which facilitates its control without the necessity of resorting to the use of armed force, usually used in war.[46]

Minister Taboada made it clear that Argentina very definitely condemns Soviet intervention in American affairs and that she was disposed to adopt, together with the other governments of the Organization of American States, the necessary means to make this position effective: "we shall act with equal energy with respect to the action of Chinese-Soviet communism in America." Consistent with Taboada's point of view, Argentina signed the Declaration of San José on August 28, 1960.

In January, 1962, the Eighth Consultative Meeting of American Foreign Ministers met at Punta del Este to consider the problem of Communist penetration in the Western Hemisphere. It is still too early—adequate documents are not yet available—to make a satisfactory evaluation of the Argentine position at the Conference. However, the following is clear: the official position of the Argentine government was vociferously attacked publicly and in the press. The public was convinced that former President Frondizi and his government had taken a pro-Communist stand at the Conference. In overthrowing the Frondizi government, the armed forces responded to the opinion that the government had been wrong with

regard to communism on the one hand, and with regard to Peronism on the other. Thereafter, in October and November, 1962, Argentina participated in the U.S. blockade of Cuba.

Defense of the South Atlantic region

This problem of security and strategy, which vitally interests Argentina, has a triple aspect: (a) political defense, as we have just stated; (b) collective military defense within the framework of the principles of security and reciprocal help of the Treaty of Rio de Janeiro; (c) defense of the South Atlantic—parallel to that of the North Atlantic—which, although within the system of Rio de Janeiro, would involve more direct participation and action by nations of the hemisphere.

Argentina's special role   Of the aspects mentioned, the third is the one that requires some additional examination. We believe that for several obvious reasons, a special and decisive role belongs to Argentina in preserving the security of the southern region of the Atlantic. In this connection we might note the guiding principles of the action of the provisional government of General Aramburu in November of 1956 when an Argentine delegation was named to the Conference of the South Atlantic.

This country has ratified the Inter-American Treaty of reciprocal assistance signed at the Conference for the Maintenance of Peace and Security on the Continent, and the Charter of the Organization of American States. All of this indicates the fundamental orientation followed by Argentina in relation to the rest of the American countries.[47] General Aramburu then went on to point out

---

[46] *Séptima Reunión, op. cit.,* Document 10.

[47] *Boletín Oficial,* November 23, 1956.

that the invitation to the sister nations—Brazil, Uruguay and Paraguay—to concur in the resolutions relative to the South Atlantic corresponds to the concept of co-ordinating the duties and interests in this area of common responsibility.

This Conference was held in Buenos Aires with the participation of a delegation from the Inter-American Defense Board headed by its President, General Lemuel G. Shepherd, Jr. of the United States. Its sessions were secret. Eighteen resolutions were approved, showing that there had been a unanimity of ideas beforehand.

> These ideas would reject as inadmissible any regionalist idea, and would refute as unnecessary the signing of other treaties, because those already existing satisfy with complete amplitude the defensive demands of the continent and would put to one side any initiative that might involve the excessive acquisition of armaments, beyond the normal amount and which already form a part of the budget of each country.[48]

At the closing session of the Conference, Provisional President Aramburu emphasized the fact that there is a common will and a clear necessity for nations to co-ordinate their efforts for the good of the continent and civilization.

Co-operation with NATO countries Another part of the story of defense of the South Atlantic is that of the joint maneuvers called "Operation Unitas" carried out by the naval units of the United States, Argentina, Brazil, and Uruguay in 1960. Even though there is no special regional pact for the defense of the South Atlantic, it is interesting to speculate on the arrangements that might be made for the defense of this region and the role which Argentina might hypothetically play in such arrangements. NATO could be brought into the picture through a treaty between Argentina and a state which is both a member of NATO and also has a special interest in the defense of the South Atlantic. That Power could be either European or American. If it were European, it would have to be England, which has interests in the zone because of her occupation of the Falkland Islands.

But such a treaty would be absurd, because it would bring with it the interference in the American Continent of an extra-continental country. ("Extra-American" would be a better term because England is "extra-continental" in Europe and is not really a part of European Continental history.) One reason why such a treaty would be impossible is because of the long-standing dispute between Argentina and England over the Falkland Islands. This dispute presents an insurmountable obstacle for a defense treaty between these two states. In this respect we might note the case of Ireland. In 1949 Mr. MacBride, Minister of Irish Foreign Affairs, in discussing NATO made the following point:

> With the general aim of the proposed pact, Eire is in general agreement. In the matter of military measures, however, they are faced with an insuperable difficulty from the strategic and political point of view, because six of the north-eastern counties of Ireland were occupied by British forces against the will of the overwhelming majority of the people of Ireland.[49]

Consequently, there would be only the American countries, Canada and the United States as members of NATO which could fill the role. And Canada would have to be eliminated, not because of her present military sta-

---

[48] *La Nación*, May 31, 1957.

[49] "*As long as partition should last, any military alliance must be quite out of the question as far as Ireland was concerned*"; Andrew Boyd and William Metson, *Atlantic Pact, Commonwealth and United States*, London: Hutchinson, 1949, p. 68.

tus but because of her negative position in the inter-American system.

Thus, the only country which remains for such a pact is the United States, which has a three-fold interest in the problem: namely, as a member of the Organization of American States, as a member of NATO, and finally because it is undeniable that she has a vital interest in the security of the zone. To this triple aspect is also added her military power.

Creation of new defense alignments   A direct agreement with the United States would be more effective and would bring fewer complications of procedure and of political character, if it was based only on her interests in the zone and her military power, without taking into account her membership in the O.A.S. and in NATO. This is even more true when one disregards the inter-American system, or more expressly, the Rio Treaty. We say this because the interests of the United States in the South Atlantic could outlive the present system of inter-American collective defense.

In both cases, the agreement could be and should be extended to other countries directly interested in the defense of the region, such as Brazil and Uruguay, to which we should doubtlessly add Chile and Paraguay.

Finally, it is clear that in spite of the secret character of the Conference of Buenos Aires in 1957 there is anxiety in official and governmental circles of the Argentine Republic. It is clear that any action for the defense of this region would have to be collective, since in the present stage of weapons and warfare, no country would be able to face a major attack alone.

In considering further a defense arrangement with the United States, a number of points might be made: (1) Any attempt at collective defense of the nations of the area would fall short of effectiveness without the direct intervention of the military power of the United States. (2) Individual local defense, with the help of another Power, could be arranged by means of bilateral treaties. Already Brazil, Chile and Uruguay have such treaties of defense and reciprocal assistance with the United States. These states have set a valuable precedent for Argentina. (3) There could be direct help from the United States which could be accomplished *loco temporeque conveniente,* as a result of the Rio Treaty of 1947, even without a previous bilateral treaty. We note this for two reasons: when the Treaty of Rio starts to function in any given case, nations far-removed in distance from the region may start to mobilize. Even with forces assembled in the region, there is no doubt that the very presence of the military power of the United States would be of vital importance. (4) Another possibility would be the defense of the region vital to the security of the United States, with or without the co-operation of the local countries such as Argentina. Such a situation would clash with the principles of sovereignty, held so dear by the Ibero-American republics. Obviously this would not be a satisfactory solution. It is also clear that the United States, regardless of how powerful she may feel militarily, would still desire regional co-operation, since she is already seriously involved in all regions of the earth—some of these very far away and of doubtful strategic value. One other possibility should be weighed: (5) Defense could be entrusted to the United States, with the concurrence of the other countries directly interested, but with the necessary exclusion of the European countries which still have an interest because of their remaining colonies in the Americas.

Practical considerations   The theoretical and general plan mentioned above might become necessary in circumstances such as the fall of a coastal country on the neighboring continent of Africa to an extra-continental or anti-American influence. This would not necessarily imply an attempt at a naval war. Instead, there would be the possibility of constructing missile bases or preparing radio-controlled weapons to be launched from submarines. Another variant of this threat would be the fall of a country in the Atlantic zone of the American continent to an anti-American influence.

Argentina is not the only country directly interested in the security of the South Atlantic.

Obviously the other states mentioned are also interested. But it is also clear that there is a reverse side to this: Argentina cannot exclude herself nor be excluded from defense planning in this region. This conclusion carries with it the logical sequel for Argentina to enter into an arrangement with her neighbors. This arrangement could take one of the forms mentioned above.

It is clear that some sectors of Argentine public opinion are presently opposed to agreements such as those just discussed. The government should first find a formula for quieting certain fears or misgivings, by showing the benefits which such a plan would bring to the country. We say this because, in a democratic country, harmony should exist between its foreign policy and its national aspirations. Secondly, Argentina should also convince the United States, and the governments of other states, not only of the necessity of such co-operation but also of the reciprocal benefits available. As President Truman noted, "a special responsibility for leadership rests upon the United States in this matter because of the preponderant technical, economic and military resources of this country."

We might note one very acceptable example of co-operation with the United States in this region. Brazil and the United States, by a treaty concluded in 1957, established a radio-controlled arms installation on the island of Fernando de Noronha. This facility is under the command of a Brazilian official and only the Brazilian flag flies over this island. Juan I. Cooke, the former Argentine Foreign Min-ister, gave approval to this type of arrangement when he stated that "the principle of military bases for the defense of the continent is an excellent idea so long as such bases are manned by soldiers of the country in which the bases are located."

Argentina has sufficient resources of a very wide variety to make a co-operative effort attractive to the United States. But any arrangement with the United States would have to guarantee that there would be no lessening of national sovereignty. For her part, Argentina has a strong respect for all sovereignties and for a defense system which will protect them.

Conclusion

This brief presentation has given an overview of the foreign policy of the Argentine Republic. Naturally, there have been some vacillations in the execution of that policy. However it is not difficult to discover general lines which can be regarded as permanent or in any event, periodically returning.

We are convinced that it is impossible, if one wishes to be really impartial, to object to the rectitude of a position, founded on principles as noble as those which we have tried to emphasize throughout this chapter. They are the principles which, hopefully, constitute the basis for the traditional behavior of the Argentine Republic in the field of foreign policy.

BIBLIOGRAPHY

Author's Suggestions

Amadeo, Mario. *Por una convivencia internacional.* Buenos Aires: Editorial de Autores, 1954.

Calvo, Carlos. *Le droit international théorique et pratique précédé d'un exposé historique de progrès de la science du droit des gens.* 5th ed., 5 vols. Paris: Arthur Rousseau, editeur, 1896.

Díaz Cisneros, César. *La Liga de las Naciones y la actitud argentina* (con texto del tratado). Buenos Aires: Imprenta Mercatali, 1921.

Drago, Luis M. *La República Argentina y el caso de Venezuela.* Buenos Aires: Imprenta y Casa Editora de Coni Hermanos, 1903.

Sáenz Peña, Roque. *Escritos y discursos.* 2 vols. Buenos Aires: ed. Peuser, 1915.

Santa Pinter, J. J. *El servicio exterior. Régimen argentino de franquicias aduaneras para diplomáticos.* Buenos Aires: ed. "La Ley," 1959.

Santa Pinter, J. J. *Humanismo y política exterior.* Buenos Aires: ed. "del Atlántico," 1959.

ABOUT THE AUTHOR

NELSON DE SOUSA SAMPAIO was born in the State of Bahia, Brazil in 1914. He graduated from the Law School of Bahia in 1937 and began a diversified career which included activity in the fields of law, education, politics and writing. He maintains an active law practice and has advanced his academic career to the position of Dean of the School of Law at the University of Bahia. Presently he is also professor of International Law in the School of Economics and professor of Political Science in the School of Administration at the University of Bahia. His political career has included the position of deputy of the State of Bahia Legislature for three terms (1947–1959). His published works include the following: *As Idéias-Forcas da Democracia*, 1941; *A Desumanizacão da Política*, 1951; *Ideologia e Ciência Política*, 1953; *O Poder de Reforma Constitucional*, 1954; *A Arte de Ser Livre*, 1957; and *O Diálogo Democrático na Bahia*, 1960.

ABOUT THE CHAPTER

Even though Brazil is the fifth largest nation in area and ranks eighth in the world according to population she is still, according to our author, a "well-known unknown." To help remedy this situation Mr. Sampaio discusses background factors such as geographic expanse, the demographic make-up of the nation, and the cultural and political factors which are basic to an understanding of Brazil.

Brazil's involvement in world affairs can conveniently be divided into three periods: (a) the period of isolationism combined with territorial consolidation; (b) the period of extra-continental initiation lasting from the end of World War I until the end of World War II; (c) the present phase which the author identifies as "apprenticeship for world power" and a greater involvement in world affairs. The outstanding characteristic of this new phase is the "tendency to make foreign policy an instrument of our economic development." Mr. Sampaio deals with some basic economic problems, including the "population explosion" and the very clear demands of the populace for an absolute increase in living standards.

The chapter concludes with an examination of some current directions in Brazil's foreign policy and a brief note on foreign policy formulation and forces that influence foreign policy decisions.

21

THE FOREIGN POLICY OF BRAZIL

NELSON DE SOUSA SAMPAIO
University of Bahia

INTRODUCING BRAZIL

Just as one cannot understand the behavior of an individual without having some contacts with him or some information about his past and present, so it is unwise for a political scientist to separate or overlook certain facts about the people and the country whose external and internal policies he wishes to analyze. Usually the student of international relations begins by getting together a mountain of data about the territory, the demography, ethnic composition, economic conditions, standard of living, cultural situation, and the political structure of the state being studied. Without such elements, any analysis of the international relations of a given nation is made in a vacuum because of lack of knowledge of the factors which shape and determine the direction of these relations.

For the more important countries this in-formation can be taken for granted. This is not the case with Brazil, however, which is still, internationally, a "well-known unknown," in spite of the curiosity that the world has begun to show toward it. We think, therefore, than an introduction to Brazil should begin with a look at the map of the country.

Territorial and demographic conditions

Brazil is a federation with 22 member states, a federal district, and four territories. Altogether Brazil covers an area of 3,286,969 square miles and borders on all South American countries except Ecuador and Chile. Its land boundaries extend 9,766 miles, and it has a coast line totaling 4,602 miles. Since Brazil has its back to the Andes and its face to the ocean, on whose shores are found the major demographic concentrations, the geopoliticians like to speak of the Atlantic destiny of our country. This is further pointed up by the fact that the point in this hemisphere nearest to Africa, the bulge jutting out at the narrowest part of the South Atlantic, is Brazilian territory.

This country of continental proportions is peopled by more than 70 million inhabitants,[1] giving it a density of twenty-one inhabitants per square mile, one of the lowest in the world. The geographic distribution of the population is very irregular, leaving vast areas almost unpopulated, as can be seen in the following table:

The table shows that 69.08% of the Brazilian population is localized in 24.50% of our territory, in the southern and eastern regions. Indeed, the unbalanced geographical distribution of inhabitants is even greater than these figures show, since within each region there are differences in population density. The north, and west and central regions, which represent about two-thirds of our territory (64.11%), contain only 7.19% of the Brazilian

GEOGRAPHIC DISTRIBUTION OF BRAZILIAN POPULATION

Regions[2]	Area (Sq. Kms.)	% of the country	Population	Pop. per Sq. Km.	% Total Population
North	3,573,718	41.98	2,321,461	0.65	3.50
Northeast	969,736	11.39	15,731,916	16.22	23.73
East	1,261,027	14.81	23,107,600	18.32	34.85
South	825,357	9.69	22,693,558	27.51	34.23
West & Central	1,884,006	22.13	2,447,736	1.30	3.69
Brazil	8,513,844	100.00	66,302,271	7.79	100.00

[1] The statistics are for the year 1960 and come from *Anuário Estatístico do Brasil 1960*, I.B.G.E. The results of the 1960 general census have not yet been published. A provisional estimate made by I.B.G.E. (*Instituto Brasileiro de Geografia e Estatística*) places the total population figure at 70,528,625 inhabitants.

[2] The official Institute of Statistics previously cited (I.B.G.E.) divides the country into five regions. The northern region includes the States of Amazonas, Acre, and Pará and the territories of Rondônia, Rio Branco, and Amapá. The northeast covers the States of Maranhão, Piaui, Ceará, Rio Grande do Norte, Paraiba, Pernambuco, and Alagoas. The east is composed of the States of Sergipe, Bahia, Minas Gerais, Espírito Santo, Rio de Janeiro, and Guanabara. The south consists of the States of São Paulo, Paraná, Santa Catarina, and Rio Grande do Sul. The west and central region is made up of the States of Mato Grosso, Goiás, and includes the Federal District (Brasília).

population. The Amazon region, with more than two-fifths of the area of Brazil, has a density of a little more than one-half an inhabitant per square kilometer, (0.65). There are great empty areas, as shown on the population map, and these greatly concern our statesmen from the point of view of national security.

The nationalist feelings, which increased after the Revolution of 1930, brought restrictions which hindered the mass entry of foreigners to populate the country's empty reaches. However, some population experts believe that the problem of peopling these areas should not be taken too seriously, because it will be resolved naturally with the high rate of population increase in Brazil, which follows the dominant tendency in Latin America. As is well known, in Latin America as a whole population shows the greatest rate of growth in the world. Although the Brazilian birth rate has decreased a little (in the census of 1950 it was 43.5 per 1,000), the decrease in the mortality rate has progressed with greater rapidity (19.7 per 1,000 in 1950).[3]

We have, then, an explosive rate of population growth of about 2.4%. According to the provisional estimate of the 1960 census, this rate jumped to 3.05% as the annual medium for the decade of 1950–1960. In concrete terms, this means an annual increase of more than two million people. Should we continue at this rate, it is expected that in 1980 our population will total 100 million, and that we will begin the year 2000 with 150 million inhabitants. Even with this estimate, our population density at the beginning of the next century will still only be approximately that of the United States today. An increase in the number of people, by itself, will not bring about the populating of the less dense regions of Brazil, if the present tendency toward industrial concentration in the Rio-São Paulo area

or in the other large coastal cities continues. Such centers will continue to attract the prolific rural population, thus raising the demographic density of the remote interior very little.

As for the division between the city and the country, in 1950 we had the following distribution: 36.12% urban and 63.78% rural population[4]—percentages that have undoubtedly been modified in favor of the city in the last years because of the growing industrialization.

Cultural situation

As a result of the high birth rate and the rather low average life expectancy—only 43.7 years in the decade from 1940 to 1950—the Brazilian population is predominantly young. The proportion of people under 20 years of age was 52.36% in 1950. This raises the percentage of economically dependent persons and necessitates expenditures for education greater than the public resources available. This phenomenon, together with the economic conditions and the preponderance of rural population, explains why in 1950 more than half of the Brazilians ten years old and up were illiterate (51.65%). At the intermediate and upper levels of education there is a deficiency of scientific and technical instruction. The young people prefer careers of a more humanistic or erudite nature which traditionally have given them the social prestige attached to the title of "doctor." The schools of higher education existed separately until 1920 when they started to group themselves into universities. In 1959 almost one-half of the students enrolled in universities attended the Schools of Law (25.4%) and Phi-

[3] The difference in the rate at which these two indices have gone down can be seen in the following figures: in the period from 1872 to 1950 the birth rate dropped from 46.5 to 43.5 per 1,000, while the death rate was reduced from 30.2 to 19.7 per 1,000.

[4] These figures are from the I.B.G.E., whose concept of urban population is purely administrative and does not follow the international criteria. On the latter basis, the total Brazilian rural population would be higher. According to the *United Nations' Demographic Year Book for 1952*, we had 30.8% urban population and 69.2% rural in 1950.

losophy (20.9%). Students of Engineering represented only 12% and of Medicine 11.6%.

Ethnic conditions

Racial composition   The Brazilian population is one of the most variegated in the world, with the blood of races from four continents running in its veins. The basic components were European, Amerindian, and African, later joined, though on a smaller scale, by Asiatic blood, principally Japanese. The dominant share is, of course, European, principally Latin. Of the latter, the Portuguese who discovered Brazil in 1500 and colonized it, continue to predominate in the number of immigrants. They took the lead in 1903 from the Italians, who had held first place since the intensification of immigration beginning in the 1880's.[5] The Brazilian capacity for assimilating these aliens has been outstanding, justifying the statement of a French sociologist: "Brazil is digesting the immigrant after having swallowed the Indian and the African."[6] Thanks to this, Brazil shows, in spite of the dispersion of its population, great national homogeneity—a country without national minorities. This homogeneous character is strengthened by the fact that the country has only one language, Portuguese, and practically only one religion, Catholicism. In the 1950 census, Catholics represented 93.50% of the population. Protestants were in second place with 3.35%, while some minor sects and persons with no religion made up the rest.

[5] From 1884 to 1958 Brazil received 4,814,952 immigrants. It is estimated that approximately one and one-half million did not remain in the country. Principal national groups represented in the influx of immigrants are shown in the following table. The preponderance of Latin elements is evident:

Italians 1,514,897
Portuguese 1,479,545
Spanish 663,512
Japanese 215,770
Germans 193,339
Other nationalities 747,829

[6] Bastide, Roger, *Brasil—Terra de Contrastes*, São Paulo: Difusão Européia do Livro, 1950, p. 177.

Ethnically, the most salient factor about the Brazilian population is its tendency to become whiter in color of skin. In 1835, according to the writer Afranio Peixoto, the blacks constituted a majority of our inhabitants, with 51.4%, while the whites had 24.4%, and the *mestizos* or half-breeds 18.2%. In this century, after 1920, the whites were no longer in the minority in relation to the colored (black and mulatto) population. The percentages given in the census of 1950 are the following:

White 61.66%
Pardo[7] 26.54%
Black 10.96%
Yellow 0.63%
No color given 0.21%

Various factors explain this growing whitening of the Brazilian population. The slave traffic was abolished by Brazil in 1850, although slavery was abolished only in 1888. Soon after the Africans stopped entering the country in the middle of the last century came the great flow of immigrants, all of them white with the exception of a small contingent of Asiatics, chiefly Japanese, who arrived in this century. Besides, the fertility rate of the black woman is less than that of the white and the half-breed, whereas the mortality rate (infantile as well as adult) is higher among the blacks because of their economic and social conditions, which are lower than for the rest of the population. Interracial marriages also contribute in an appreciable extent to the diluting of the African blood. Such marriages are less frequent between persons with distinctly different skin color, but are common between individuals of nearly the same shade. The poorer the social level the easier it is for the couple to cross the color barrier.

Racial prejudice   It is often said that racial prejudice does not exist in Brazil. The assertion,

[7] The designation *pardo* includes mulattos (crossing of white with black), *mamalucos* (white with Indian), and *cafuzos* (black with Indian). Pure Indians are less than 100,000.

Population density of Brazil according to the 1950 census

Less than one inhabitant per square kilometer

From one to five inhabitants per square kilometer

From five to twenty-five inhabitants per square kilometer

More than twenty-five inhabitants per square kilometer

however, is an idealization not entirely borne out by the facts. Racial prejudice does in fact exist. Our folklore is full of proof of this. Until recently Negroes were barred from diplomatic and consular service as well as from officer rank in the armed forces, especially the Navy and the Air Corps. Among our intellectual elite there existed what some called a general "feeling of racial inferiority," and our statesmen tried to hide from the eyes of other peoples the colored aspects of the nation's population. This racial prejudice was limited only to the blacks. The Indians were defended by the Jesuits from the colonial period on and exalted by the nativistic sentiments of our independence period. Such eminent intellectuals as Euclides da Cunha, Nina Rodrigues, João Ribeiro, Oliveira Viana did not hesitate to deem the Negro blood one of the factors for our backwardness or to regard the half-breed as a cause of degeneracy.

Today these ideas are banished from the midst of our elite, but it would be inaccurate to say that we do not know racial prejudice. To be more precise, we should say that we have a prejudice more of color than of race. While in the United States an individual is either white or Negro, in Brazil we recognize a chromatic scale to classify persons from white to coal black. The placement on this scale does not follow any rigorously objective criteria but depends upon subjective factors also, such as the congeniality or friendliness the person classified displays. Wealth, also, many times helps to "whiten" the individual or improve his chromatic classification. It is customary to use euphemisms such as *"escurinho"* (little dark one), *"roxinho"* (little purple one), etc. and to avoid using the word "Negro" so as not to create touchiness or friction in dealing with colored people. The word "Negro" often is equivalent to scolding, according to the circumstances and the tone with which it is pronounced.

The darker the skin of an individual the more unfavorable is his situation in social competition; he has to make greater efforts to succeed than do his competitors with lighter skin. It is a subtle prejudice, disguised, practiced quietly, whispered. But the proof of its existence is that Public Law Number 1,390 of March 3, 1951, called the Afonso Arinos Law, made it a misdemeanor to practice any acts of discrimination against colored people in public and private schools as well as in government bureaus and commercial and industrial establishments. Even as recently as March of 1961, President Jânio Quadros gave instructions to eliminate whatever vestiges of racial prejudice there might be, no matter how veiled, in the Ministry of Foreign Relations.

It is, therefore, a prejudice that people try to hide, striving to keep its manifestations from the public. When this does not succeed, the "ideology" that Brazil is a "racial democracy" makes people react loudly against the "racists," who become the target of condemnation by the press, the politicians, and public opinion in general. For this reason, the amount of racial prejudice is reduced to as little as can be found in the world today, thus making Brazil an example to other people as being a country where different races live together harmoniously. Racial prejudice does exist, although in an amount so diluted that many people do not notice it, but a racial problem does not exist as we have neither segregation nor race riots.

Political situation

Politically the history of independent Brazil is divided into two periods—the monarchy and the republic. Brazil has the distinction of having been the only monarchical country in this hemisphere, if we except Canada and the short-lived adventures in Mexico of Augustin Iturbide and the Emperor Maximilian, the latter imposed by France. The monarchy lasted from 1822, when independence was declared, until 1889. There was an attempt to follow the English model of cabinet government, during the reign of Pedro II from 1840 until the fall of the monarchy. It went so far as to use the two party names, Liberal and Conservative. But instead of a true parliamentary system, there was only a façade behind which was hidden the power of the Emperor directing an oligarchy of great land owners.

The history of the republic can be divided into five parts. The First Republic, ruled by the Constitution of 1891, endured from 1889 until the Revolution of 1930. The Second Republic had two phases: the provisional government of Getulio Vargas from 1930 until the Constitution of 1934; and the constitutional government of Vargas from 1934 to 1937. The Third Republic began with the coup d'état of 1937 which instituted the dictatorship of Vargas under the name of *Estado Novo* (New State), and ended with his overthrow by the military in 1945. After that came the Fourth Republic, governed by the Constitution of 1946. Then, on September 2, 1961, as a result of a serious politico-military crisis provoked by the unexpected resignation of President Jânio Quadros, the Constitution underwent a profound change. The presidential system, traditional since the fall of the monarchy, was abandoned and a parliamentary government adopted. That date marks the beginning of the Fifth Republic. However, the parliamentary system did not last long. In January, 1963, the presidential system was restored when nationwide elections favored it by a five to one margin.

The Republic transformed Brazil into a federal state. The national parties of the Empire were replaced by state parties, ephemeral and of weak discipline, usually organized on the eve of elections. Until the Revolution of 1930 the Republic altered very little the oligarchical practices of the Monarchy. With the lack of consistent national parties, the presidents of the Republic depended upon the governors, who were the chiefs of the local oligarchies. This so-called "politics of the governors" was dominated by the larger states, especially the richest and most populous states of Minas Gerais and São Paulo. From these two states came all of the civilian presidents of the Republic until the Revolution of 1930, with the single exception of Epitácio Pessoa of Paraiba. The revolution of that year sought to correct the manipulation of elections by the government by establishing the secret vote,

thus permitting greater participation in the political life by the urban middle class that had begun to arise after the great industrial spurt following the First World War. These institutional changes did not have time to produce their expected fruits because they were interrupted by the establishment of the dictatorship of the *Estado Novo* that sought to imitate the Fascist models in ascension in Europe.

After the Second World War representative institutions were restored, proportional representation was adopted, and parties of national scope were founded. The number of these parties grew to thirteen, not counting the Communist Party, which was declared illegal in 1947. With the Fourth Republic the armed forces showed a greater respect for constitutional legality. The political participation of the people, especially the urban middle class, increased. Since then, elections have been the most democratic in the country's history, although the power of money in elections has grown in unprecedented fashion. It is felt also in the politics of patronage, in administrative corruption, and in pressure groups. But, the old days when the government always won the elections are finished. Since 1950 this situation has practically reversed itself, with all government-sponsored candidates for the presidency and for many state governorships being defeated. Inflation is undoubtedly the chief reason for this phenomenon, quickly wearing out the popularity of governments and becoming a great ally of the opposition. This factor and the profound longing for public morality and administrative efficiency explain the great victory of Jânio Quadros in the 1961 presidential election.

These changes, judged in the light of the territorial dimensions and the population of Brazil, make it the most stable of the Latin-American countries. It is also the one in which social changes have taken place with the least violence and bloodshed. But it is a fallacy to speak of Brazilian moderation as an attribute of the "national soul" (*Volksgeist*) in the way that the romantics used to use the expression. Whatever collective, permanent qualities there are do not come from the nature of a people, but rather from historic conditions. In Brazil such conditions made possible a social evolution without major violence and with the maintenance of representative government and civil liberties. The great question for Brazil today is this: To what degree will these institutions be able to resist the impatience of the poor, forgotten masses of our population awakened by the so-called "revolution of aspirations" that beckons them with prospects of a better life? The record of strikes in 1960 showed that the tolerance of the Brazilian people was reaching its limits in the face of the constant increase in the cost of living provoked by the soaring inflation. The electoral triumph of Jânio served as a substitute for revolution. But his sudden resignation from the presidency after seven months in office[8] showed the underlying elements of instability and created new ones: aggravation of the internal dissensions among the military, crisis of leadership, general bewilderment, a new wave of inflation, emotional agitation of the young, and uncertainties about the new experiment with the short-lived parliamentary system of government.

Economic situation

A decisive answer to the question raised above depends upon the rhythm of Brazilian economic expansion. Until now it has been suf-

---

[8] His renunciation, made on August 25, 1961, has not yet been fully explained. The most plausible version is that Jânio, a great political strategist, tried a maneuver to resume office with greatly increased, perhaps dictatorial, powers. But he overestimated his popular support. The people, who had been tolerating the sacrifices of Jânio's regime of austerity, did not clamor for his return to power. Will they do this if their disillusions increase and Jânio acquires a messianic enticement? The future will answer. An attempt of this kind, however, would probably provoke an armed conflict. Thus, because of one of those ironies of history, the man who seemed to be a factor of political stability for five years has become a thorn in the side of Brazilian social unrest.

ficient to create opportunities for the most active elements and those with the greater capacity for leadership and thus deter them from devoting their energies to revolutionary action. Taking the nation as a whole, Brazil is an underdeveloped country, with a per capita annual income of $230 (US) in the years 1952 to 1954. However, its rate of economic growth is one of the most rapid in the western world, and it is already the most industrialized country of Latin America.

But economic progress has been disorganized and has caused great social tensions. The most salient features of this development are, in brief, 1) imbalance between the growth of agriculture and industry; 2) chronic instability of the balance of foreign payments; 3) inflationary pressure; 4) aggravation of the economic differences between social classes; and 5) accentuation of regional differences.

Industry has grown at a more accelerated pace than agriculture. Although we occupy third place among all countries in the amount of arable land, our agricultural methods are still very rudimentary and we have to import wheat.

We now produce almost all consumer goods within our own borders, but we depend upon the foreign market to supply many products, including petroleum, of which our domestic production only comes to about one-third of national consumption. Industrialization has increased the necessity for imports, but our capacity for importing has not grown at a parallel rate, since our exports are made up almost entirely of mineral and agricultural products. These products are subject to the frequent oscillations of the international market, a condition which constantly unbalances our international accounts and causes great instability in our economy.

The chronic inflation, even now on the ascent, adds to the economic distance between property owners and those who live on fixed salaries and incomes. This inflation generates constant salary increase demands and social discontent because of the uncontrollable rise of the prices of goods and services essential to community life.

With industrialization localized in a limited area, as mentioned, its expansion has increased regional differences as far as standards of living and sharing in the national income are concerned. The French professor, Jacques Lambert, gave the title *The Two Brazils*[9] to his excellent work about our country. Actually, it is possible to discern four Brazils. The first is located from Guanabara to the south, including, in addition to the former Federal District, the States of São Paulo, Paraná, Santa Catarina, and Rio Grande do Sul. If Brazil were made up of only this industrialized region, which also includes the most productive agriculture in the nation, it would be classified as a semi-developed country. Southern Brazil is steadily increasing its contribution to the national income. It acts as an economic metropolis for the other areas, which, to a certain extent, have become internal colonies, compulsory consumers of national industrial products. The second Brazil is the northeast. It was the first region colonized by the Portuguese but fell into economic decline during the last century and is now one of the regions of greatest poverty in the world. Eastern Brazil occupies a position halfway between the other two, both from an economic and a geographic point of view. Finally, the fourth Brazil takes in the northern and the west and central regions, which represent the vast frontier awaiting effective economic exploitation.

The task which the Brazilian people face is to link together all of these Brazils, with their vast differences of production methods and economic stages, into one economic system, and then to integrate the whole into one great internal market.

Brazil's international profile

From these data we can deduce some characteristics which give to Brazil an outstanding

position among the nations of the world today. It is the fifth country in territorial size, coming after the U.S.S.R., Canada, Communist China, and the United States of America, although in continuous area it is actually larger than the United States. In the amount of arable land Brazil is in third place, and in population, it is eighth.[10]

In certain aspects Brazil calls forth various superlatives: it is the largest Latin country in territory and population, representing almost half of South America in both respects; it is the largest Catholic country of the globe, also in both categories; it is the most industrialized nation of Latin America, and it is probably the country with the least amount of racial prejudice in the world.

THE THREE STAGES OF BRAZILIAN FOREIGN POLICY

The combination of attributes of Brazil indicates the raw material of a Great Power, which, as a matter of fact, is already in a state of gestation. But Brazil's international age is still very young. When a North American was once told that Brazil was an adolescent on the international scene, he retorted that the adolescent was the United States, a Power that was called when very young to a position of international leadership, without having passed through the long phase of preparation in this domain which other nations have known. On those terms, one must consider Brazil as an international child which is only beginning its biography in the international field.

Today, however, all the nations, young and old, are called to the international scene. The

[9] *Os Dois Brasis,* published by the Centro de Pesquisas Educacionais, Rio, 1959.

[10] Ahead of Brazil in population are the Peoples' Republic of China, with 640 million; India, with 398 million; U.S.S.R., with 200 million; the United States of America, with 175 million; Japan, with 92 million; Indonesia, with 87 million; and Pakistan, with 86 million.

growing and tumultuous political integration on our planet impels even recently formed nations to participate in the international drama. The Cold War drives them in various directions, and the embryo world parliament—the United Nations—has been drawing them since their beginnings into a difficult diplomatic apprenticeship. There have always been internal and external political forces exerting pressures on people in their international policies. But until World War I the nations, at least those of lesser importance, could live relatively isolated behind their boundaries. Today the age of isolation has passed for every country, large or small. Even the nations adhering to permanent neutrality, such as Switzerland and Austria, do not sleep behind that fragile political curtain. Quite to the contrary. They watch the outside world uneasily.

The evolution of Brazilian foreign policy resembles that of the more important nations of this hemisphere, including the United States. In the beginning there was isolation; then the first tentative steps into extra-continental politics; and finally, the present search for direction in world affairs. Brazilian international policy can then be divided into three stages: 1) territorial diplomacy, that of establishing the boundaries, which lasted until 1917; 2) the phase that we could call extra-continental initiation, lasting from 1917 to 1945; 3) the present phase, which opened after the Second World War, and which we can call the apprenticeship to become a World Power.

There is no neat separation among these periods and the interests and preoccupations of one stage have not disappeared with the beginning of the following. For example, in spite of the terminology employed to delineate the three international ages of Brazil, one cannot say that boundary problems have disappeared in our own days; one certainly could not say that they had vanished by 1917.

In a general manner, one may say that as we pass from one stage to another, the international objectives of Brazil become less simple. Its external policy grows more complex and there is more controversy about national objectives. Correspondingly, institutions that formulate this policy also become more diversified. Popular participation increases in proportion to the increased activity of the representative machinery. The variety of pressure groups and forces that mold public opinion grows, likewise.

Territorial diplomacy

The first phase of our diplomacy—which we could also call *geographic diplomacy*—covers almost all of Brazilian history. It embraces the colonial epoch. For Brazil, since independence, has only consolidated the work of territorial expansion of the Portuguese colonizers. Only a little territory has been added. Brazil had reached its present territorial extent almost completely by the middle of the eighteenth century, while the United States did not achieve this result until the last century.

Consequently, when Brazil became independent, it received this great territorial heritage and the politico-juridical principle of *uti possidetis,* which operated to conserve it. And that was the policy which independent Brazil followed. However, if national unity had not served as a foundation, Portuguese America would have broken down into small republics like Spanish America. The monarchy acted as the cement of unity. The crown symbolized national unity and avoided, thanks to the dynastic principle, the struggle for power among the *caudilhos,* or local chieftains. Such a fight would certainly have brought territorial fragmentation. This interpretation is corroborated by the fact that the period in which our unity was most threatened was exactly that of the Regency, between the abdication of Pedro I, in 1831, and the declaration of the majority of Pedro II, in 1840. The declaration was hastened (since the monarch was only fourteen years old) especially to pacify and unite the Brazilians.

Brazil's wars   Brazilian foreign policy has been dominated ever since by these two major concerns:[11] to fix the limits of our territory and to accomplish a balance of power with our neighbors, especially those to the south. This was not done without some armed conflicts. The four wars, the only ones in which Brazil participated on this continent, all had their origins on the southern borders.

In 1825 Argentina helped Uruguay, which had been annexed by Brazil in 1821 under the name of Cisplatina Province, fight for independence. But as the Argentines, in their turn, proclaimed the incorporation of Uruguay to the United Provinces of the River Plate, Brazil entered into war to avoid that outcome. The solution was the independence of Uruguay (1828) as a buffer state between the two rivals. The interests of England, which co-operated diplomatically in the settlement, were also considered.

Our second conflict was in 1851, against the Argentine dictator Manuel Rosas who, besides trying to close navigation in the Parana River, attempted a new annexation of Uruguay. The third fight consisted of an intervention in Uruguay, in 1864, motivated by internal factions and border incidents which constantly frightened the people of Rio Grande do Sul. The Brazilian army deposed President Aguirre,

chief of the party of the "Blancos," hostile to our country, and helped into power the "Colorados," our friends.

Uruguay was once again the seed of discord in the fourth and last conflict, the biggest in South American history. The Brazilian intervention in that country aroused protests and even a proposal of mediation from Paraguay, which alleged that its security was menaced. We had certain boundary problems with Paraguay and an interest in assuring free navigation on the Paraguay River, means of access to the province of Mato Grosso. When the offer of mediation was refused, Paraguay opened hostilities against Brazil. The Paraguayan dictator, Francisco Solano Lopez, wanting to attack Rio Grande do Sul, invaded Argentine territory, and Argentina placed itself on our side. The Uruguayan government did the same, having been raised to power with the support of Brazil.

Since this conflict, which lasted more than five years—from 1864 to 1870—and ended with the defeat of Paraguay, Brazil has resolved all its territorial problems by peaceful means. At the fall of the monarchy in 1889, Brazil had already established its boundaries with Venezuela (1859) and Paraguay (1872). The new-born Republic became very active in South American diplomacy. So involved was Brazil that she refused an invitation to the First Peace Conference in 1899 because, in the words of Foreign Minister Olinto de Magalhães, "our attention is turned toward South America."[12]

The achievement of Rio Branco   It is not surprising, then, that the biggest figure in Brazilian diplomacy is the champion of peaceful solution of boundary problems, José Maria da Silva Paranhos, Baron of Rio Branco, the man who was Minister of Foreign Relations for longer than any other (1902–1912), and served under four presidents. So outstanding was his contribution that a Brazilian historian ob-

[11] During this period Brazil also had to defend its rights as a sovereign nation against some unfriendly interventions from England. The English repression of the slave traffic was one of the causes of friction between the two nations. After the Aberdeen Bill (1845) England extended its policing to Brazilian territorial waters and even to the rivers of Brazil. Later two incidents worsened the relations between the two countries: the sack by private individuals of an English vessel shipwrecked on the southern coast of Brazil in 1861; and the imprisonment, in 1862, of two officers of the British Navy who, in civilian clothes, engaged in disorderly conduct in Rio de Janeiro. The arbitrary demands of the English ambassador, William Dougal Christie, on account of these two incidents led to a misunderstanding, referred to as the "Christie question," which provoked the rupture of diplomatic relations between our country and the United Kingdom. The last disagreement with England occurred in 1895, when England occupied the island of Trindade off the coast of the State of Espírito Santo, claiming dominion over it. They vacated the island the following year through the mediation of Portugal.

[12] Delgado de Carvalho, *História Diplomática do Brasil (Diplomatic History of Brazil)*, S. Paulo: Cia. Editora Nacional, 1959, p. 246.

served that one could divide the foreign policy of the Republic into three periods: before, during, and after Rio Branco.

> After his death in 1912, his influence came to constitute, along with the imperial precedents, the pacific tradition of Itamarati, which is essentially to preserve the territorial and moral patrimony of the nation through the body of laws that shape, even today, all the foreign policy of Brazil.[13]

In fact, the incorporation of more than 200,000 square kilometers into Brazil is due to him. Even before becoming Foreign Minister, he was known as our major authority in questions involving territorial limits and was the lawyer for the Brazilian interests in various famous cases: the dispute with Argentina about the territory improperly called the Missões, which was resolved in 1895 through the arbitration of President Grover Cleveland, and which resulted in the acquisition of 36,000 square kilometers by Brazil; the establishing of territorial limits with French Guiana (1900), through which the region of Amapá came within Brazilian confines.

During Rio Branco's ministry the case of Acre was resolved and the limits were established with British and Dutch Guiana, and with Colombia and Peru.[14] The most important case was that of Acre, a vast, almost uninhabited region north of Bolivia which began to be populated by Brazilians, chiefly from Ceará, about 1877, when the rubber fever was beginning to spread. In 1899 these Brazilian residents rebelled against the Bolivian authorities and even tried to proclaim independence for Acre. Four years later the Treaty of Petropolis (1903) resolved the problem with the inclusion

of Acre in our territory with adjustments at certain points of the border, and indemnification of two million pounds sterling to the Bolivian government, the obligation of Brazil to construct the Madeira-Mamoré railroad and permit Bolivia freedom of fluvial navigation to the ocean. But this addition of 19,412 square miles was not accomplished without arousing suspicions and censure from various South American countries against Brazil, accusing it of an imperialistic thirst for territory. The criticism renewed the protests of the epoch of Brazilian intervention in the affairs of its southern neighbors. Such anti-Brazilian reactions were not lasting, however, and were later dissipated almost completely, thanks to a policy of good-will toward our neighbors.

The truth is that Brazil, its territorial expansion completed, felt satisfied within its large perimeter of 9,766 miles and was primarily interested in preserving the *status quo* on the continent. Its pacific aims had been proclaimed more than once since the Empire, and the Republic had given them solemn consecration in Article 88 of its first Constitution (1891): "The United States of Brazil will in no event commit itself to a war of conquest, directly or indirectly, for itself or in alliance with another nation."[15]

The extra-continental initiation

The First World War took Brazil out of continental confinement and opened the second phase of its diplomatic history, which lasted only the short space between the two world conflicts. During this period the dominant characteristics of our foreign policy can be summarized as three: a) two experiences in extra-continental politics interspersed by return to the old isolationism; b) a continuation of the

[13] Hélio Vianna, *História Diplomática do Brasil* (*Diplomatic History of Brazil*), S. Paulo: Edições Melhoramentos, p. 135.

[14] After this intensive diplomatic activity, there only remained to be resolved small, localized border questions and the boundary line with Bolivia. The latter was settled by the Treaty of 1928. The remaining task was simply the demarcation of the limits.

[15] Similar articles appeared in later Constitutions (Constitution of 1934, Article 4; Constitution of 1946, Article 4), but were excluded from the dictatorial Constitution of 1937.

concern with territorial integrity, although the fears were caused less by the bordering countries, all of them underpopulated, than by European nations with population expansion who might covet our almost empty spaces; c) finally, closely linked to the previous motive, the desire to preserve to the greatest possible extent the national unity of our population, avoiding the formation of national minorities that could put this unity in danger.

World War I and League membership   No national objective impelled us to enter the First World War, although Brazil would have had reason to fear that a German victory could activate German imperialism among the immigrants of this nationality, concentrated in pockets in the south of our country, in the States of Santa Catarina and Rio Grande do Sul. We were, nevertheless, prepared to enter the conflict due to idealistic motives and pro-allied sympathies, from a time prior to the entry of the United States into the war. The sinking of Brazilian ships by German submarines brought us, finally, to a declaration of war on October 26, 1917. Our participation was limited, however, to the patrolling of the Atlantic by naval units, the sending of a medical mission to France, and the collaboration of Brazilian aviators and other military officers.

After the war Brazil participated in the League of Nations and served as a temporary member of the Council, being successively re-elected until 1926. Frustrated in its desire to be a permanent member of the Council, Brazil withdrew from the League of Nations in 1926. An important aspect of Brazilian activities in the League was a strong position against extending to all countries the program of protection of national minorities carried on by the League of Nations. Our delegate in the Council, Ambassador Afranio de Melo Franco, maintained that national minorities were European phenomena, resulting from historical vicissitudes of transfers of sovereignty and territorial annexations. It was, therefore, a concept that could not be extended to the Americas. His words amounted to a faithful translation of the Brazilian sentiment of self-protection and preoccupation with national homogeneity.

Restrictions on immigration   With the Revolution of 1930, nationalistic tendencies, stimulated by the First World War, took form. Constitutional and legal measures were taken to protect the Brazilian worker from the competition of immigrants as well as to reserve to nationals the exploitation of certain natural resources and the exercise of certain activities. So, in accordance with the provisions of the Constitution of 1934, reproduced along general lines by the Constitutions since then, only Brazilians by birth can be owners, outfitters or commanders of national merchant ships, or owners, shareholders, or directors of journalistic enterprises. Also required—in this and subsequent Constitutions—was that two thirds of the crews of merchant ships should be Brazilians by birth.[16] A concession from the federal government was necessary for exploitation of mines and waterfalls, but it could only be granted to Brazilians or to a firm organized in Brazil. The same Constitution ordered that there should be a progressive "nationalization"[17] of deposit banks, insurance companies, and mines and waterfalls. These objectives have not been fully realized up to the present time.[18]

The fear that national minorities might be created dictated restrictions on immigration which were adopted beginning in 1934. Alongside this ethnic motive, there was also an economic motive, because Brazil has a great excess of labor, especially unskilled, against which the foreign worker could easily compete. As the immigrant has in general a better level of education, he might advance more rapidly, thus provoking resentment of the

[16] A decree of 1931 requires that two thirds of the employees must be Brazilian—native born or naturalized—in all economic enterprises.

[17] "Nationalization" here is not a synonym of "socialization," but signifies only that the owners of the enterprises must be Brazilian.

[18] The Constitution of 1946 does not repeat the precept that would prescribe the "progressive nationalization" of these above-mentioned enterprises.

native-born Brazilian. For these reasons we followed the example of the United States and adopted a quota system for immigration.[19] The constitutional text declares that the "entrance of immigrants into national territory will suffer necessary restrictions to guarantee the ethnic integrity of the country" and adds shortly thereafter: "The concentration of immigrants in any part of the Union whatsoever is forbidden, and the law will determine the selection, locating and assimilation of the aliens."[20]

The rise of fascism   Although Brazil had returned to its old isolation, its doors could not be closed to the effect of events that happened in Europe in the decade of the thirties. The ideological and political offensives of the Communists and Fascists also unfolded on the Brazilian stage. In 1935 the Communists started a military uprising that was promptly smashed. The Fascist elements formed the *Partido Integralista* that advocated a corporate state. They adopted all the characteristics of their European models: paramilitary organization of the party, shock troops, shirt, salute, parades and mysticism of the leader.[21] They did not even overlook the preaching of anti-Semitism and a bitter anti-British and, in a smaller dose, anti-American nationalism. The epoch was one of the international rise of fascism and, with the aid of members of the *sigma* (symbol of *Integralismo*), Getulio Vargas accomplished the coup d'état that inaugurated his personal dictatorship. Afterwards he was

[19] The annual quota of immigrants of each nationality was fixed at 2 percent of the total of the respective immigration in the fifty years prior to 1934. This percentage is still maintained, but only for voluntary immigration; government controlled immigration is free of this limit. (Decree-Law Number 7,967 of September 18, 1945.)

[20] Constitution of 1934, Article 121, Sections 6 and 7.

[21] After the Second World War the majority of the integrationalists reunited in the Partido de Representação Popular (Popular Representation Party) and lowered the banner of anti-Americanism, which came to be wielded by the Communists and by extremely nationalistic factions.

to turn against the *integralistas,* who had ambitions to share in the power of the new state.

World War II   When the Second World War broke out, the Allies had the sympathy of the majority of Brazilians, especially the Democrats, who also tried in this manner to show domestic opposition to Vargas. Others were favorable to the Axis Powers. The Hitler-Stalin Pact silenced Communist criticism of Germany and gave occasion for criticizing British imperialism. This lasted until the German invasion of Russia reversed the Communist position. The *integralistas* were openly pro-German. Vargas himself, always so calculating with his words, expressed what amounted to applause for the victors when France went into collapse. Speaking to the Navy, on June 11, 1940, he took occasion to say: "We feel that the old systems and antiquated formulas are entering into decline." This phrase revealed his personal interest in the victory of the authoritarian system of government, but it could scarcely be interpreted as an expression of national interest. One cannot imagine what advantages there would be to Brazil, an underpopulated country of mixed races, if victory came to a racist Germany with a craving for "vital space."

In a short time there was a change of direction in the war, and Brazil repeated the history of 1917. The difference this time consisted in that the German aggressions against Brazilian shipping only occurred after Brazil had broken relations with Germany. The rupture came soon after the Japanese attack on Pearl Harbor, in December, 1941. During the same month, Brazil, faithful to commitments of continental solidarity, broke relations with the three nations of the Axis. But since March 1941, Brazil had permitted the United States to engage in construction of air-naval bases in Belém, Recife and Natal. In February of 1942 German submarines began sinking Brazilian ships. In August the government, in the face of popular excitement caused by successive sinkings, declared a state of war.

This time, Brazilian participation in the conflict represented a great aid. The air bases, especially that of "the trampoline of Natal," carried out a prominent role in the defense of the southern Atlantic and in the invasion of North Africa. Brazilian sailors and aviators collaborated actively in the defense of the Atlantic. Finally, an expeditionary force, composed of 25,-334 men, went to fight in Italy. They were the first and are so far the only Latin American troops that have fought on the soil of the Old World. In the final balance Brazil lost 37 ships, totaling 126,535 tons, and had, among its soldiers, 451 dead, 2,722 wounded and other casualties, not counting the victims of torpedoed ships, calculated in some hundreds. A Brazilian historian lamented that notwithstanding such heavy sacrifice the histories of the Second World War are silent, for the most part, about the participation of Brazil in this conflict.[22] No doubt, in face of the Dantesque hecatomb that was the Second World War, these figures are thin in the monstrous total of victims. But for Brazil, a weak and poor country, the price of this second extra-continental military experience was very high in terms of suffering and material losses.

The apprenticeship for World Power

After the Second World War the third and present stage of foreign policy of Brazil began. It is a period, to a certain extent, full of perplexities and in search of directions. The old objectives of our foreign policy, the defense of territorial integrity and preservation of national unity, as is obvious, have not lost their significance; indeed these are permanent objectives of all countries. But the most outstanding characteristic of the new phase is probably the *tendency to make foreign policy an instrument of our economic development.*

Balance between population and resources
Like all underdeveloped countries, Brazil is ex-

[22] Calmon, Pedro, *História do Brasil* (*History of Brazil*), José Olympio, Rio, 1959, vol. VI, p. 2267.

periencing several dislocating social changes. Among these, two are of tremendous importance, amounting to revolutions that create urgent problems. First, a demographic revolution — the "population explosion" referred to above. Second, a revolution of aspirations, that is to say the claims for better levels of living by the lower income groups that constitute the great majority of the nation. Expressing the situation in more concrete terms: each day Brazil has more persons to employ, to feed, to dress, to educate, and to house. For all of these, each day should bring higher standards as well. The claims of the masses, therefore, not only increase in number but also increase in quality. Inflation aggravates these factors of social unrest.

Since the Second World War the economic development of Brazil has been relatively rapid, especially in the industrial field. Industrialization has increased our import requirements. Besides wheat and fuels, we must import heavy equipment, some raw materials and semimanufactured products. Such demands, in addition to the payment of experts, royalties, and remittances of dividends (many of the new Brazilian industries were established with foreign capital), have since 1954 provoked constant deficits in our balance of international payments. This is in contrast to what occurred during the years of the war, when through the export of raw materials and strategic articles, we were able to accumulate a favorable trade balance. To maintain the rhythm of economic expansion, Brazil urgently needs to increase exports. We need new markets for our primary products and some articles of our flourishing industries, principally consumer items. Our new international policy is inspired for the most part by this search for new markets.

In a general manner, it may be said that this policy results from two opposite sentiments at the same time, our increasing power and our deficiencies. Hence contradictions may sometimes be noted in our attitudes on the international plane. Occasionally these contradictions are accentuated when foreign policy is transformed into a means for advancing certain objectives of internal policy. This is becoming more frequent because of the increasing interest in international affairs among the electorate.

Increasing nationalism   The consciousness of our growth as a nation as well as of our difficulties has intensified Brazilian nationalism, which had already been gaining strength since the Revolution of 1930. The nationalistic awakening that has agitated the sub-developed world since the Second World War has reinforced the phenomenon that was already on the march in Brazil. It is true that here, as in other countries, nationalism is a river of many tributaries, carrying waters of different colors. Tracing the motivations, we can make various distinctions. One may speak of a *tactical nationalism,* like that of the Communists, whose ideology is internationalist in nature. The nationalism of this species is, following the rules of the Cold War, principally anti-Americanism. It would be, nevertheless, an error to suppose that all anti-American sentiment comes from this source. With the United States as our largest customer, absorbing 42 percent of the Brazilian exports in 1959, any lowering of the price of our exportable products tends to arouse resentment against the United States. Besides this, there are complaints that Latin America has been neglected by Uncle Sam, whose attentions have moved, according to an order of priority dictated by events, to Europe, to Asia, and to Africa. Preoccupation with other parts of the World has been interpreted by many as evidence of the conviction in the United States that countries to the south of the Rio Grande are its natural tributaries. On account of this, the already sensitive Latin-American national pride becomes even more easily injured.

Since the launching of the Alliance for Progress we can see some improvement in Brazil-United States' relations. The first instalment of the allowances assigned to Brazil was promised during the visit of President João Goulart to Washington in April 1962, in an amount of 130 millions dollars destined for the poorest Brazilian region, the Northeast. Although the Alliance for Progress is just beginning, the Americans are no longer primarily on the defensive against the ideological offensive of the Communists. They have now some concrete proposals to offer, in addition to the attractive personality of John Kennedy whose policy is seen by many Brazilians as a resurrection of Franklin Roosevelt's good-neighbor policy.

Another variety of nationalism is the *electoral nationalism,* which would exploit popular emotions to obtain votes. Although the objectives of the Communists are principally revolutionary, they are not inimical to this form of nationalism when it becomes part of the electoral game. Since almost all of the politicians practice this type of nationalism, it is no longer a division of waters in the elections. Nationalism has thus lost its polemic character. No longer can some parties monopolize the exploitation of this sentiment and divide Brazilians into two well defined categories, *nacionalistas* and *entreguistas,* those who collaborate with foreign interests. If a party could obtain this monopoly, it would be armed with an invincible force of mass emotion, capable of transforming the political fight into a ferocious witch hunt. Although a Parliamentary Nationalist Front exists, its elements are affiliated with different parties. All claim to embody the authentic nationalism. When there is a fight, it is not against nationalism, but against a specific "nationalism."

Another species is *mercantile nationalism,* in which are gathered those industrialists anxious for tariff barriers and those exporters that clamor for price support for their products. Lastly, we have the *rational nationalism*[23] that would strive to find the most adequate ways to serve the economic emancipation and progress of the country.

Expectations for the future   For whatever the motives happen to be, nationalism is a dimension which one must take into account in the internal as well as foreign political life of Brazil. Brazilians are constantly acquiring a stronger awareness of the growth and the importance of their country, and they are anxious

---

[23] These categories are more or less arbitrary forms of classification which are not found in this pure state.

to see Brazil perform a greater role on the international stage. When they go abroad, Brazilians are easily piqued in observing how little Brazil is known, when not completely ignored. The average foreigner knows in general that he is talking about a country that produces much coffee. The somewhat better informed foreigner perhaps knows that Brazil has a well-developed architecture. After 1958, when the construction of Brasilia began, the new capital of the country increased curiosity about Brazil. The same effect was created during the seven months (February to August 1961) of the presidency of Jânio Quadros because of his audacious and enigmatic international policies.

On the other hand, nothing is more flattering to a Brazilian than the predictions of foreigners that Brazil is destined to be before very long the third World Power, as prophesied by Adolf Berle, Jr. in 1957. He justified his prediction with words to the effect that as a country that would have the same area as the United States if there were two Texases, with a present population of 60,000,000, an annual increment of 1,500,000, an organizational ability not to be despised, and natural resources that have been compared to those of the United States, Brazil ought to finish the twentieth century with a population of some 125,000,000, an economic capacity comparable to that of the United States of today, and a predominant position in the Latin, European and American world.[24] For some Brazilians this prognostication is already less than our potentialities. Consul Adolpho Justo Bezerra de Menezes, for example, begins his well circulated book *O Brasil e o Mundo Ásio-Africano* (*Brazil and the Asian-African World*) with this messianic tone: "That which is necessary from now is an answer from the leading classes, the Brazilian elite, to the question: Will Brazil be within a century the world power, or one of the world powers?"[25]

Without doubt there is divergence of opinion in response to this interrogation. We are forced to take a very long view, perhaps a century, even in this period of increasing "acceleration of history." But in the present, there already is a point of agreement between Brazilians: they will not permit Brazil to be a satellite to any nation in international politics. Brazilian policy, for various motives, including the pressure of public opinion, will take a route of increasing independence. Jânio Quadros proclaimed more than once that Brazil does not belong to any bloc, and alluded to an ambitious position of "fourth force." He wished to signify, undoubtedly, that Brazil would not be persistently pro-Western or persistently anti-Soviet, but neither would it be strictly neutralist. Behind this difficult definition appears an anxiety of Brazil to be no longer a second class actor but a "protagonist"[26] on the international scene. But Brazilians are still perplexed about exactly what the protagonist role involves that history is giving to them. There are many different views, but none of them has, as yet, become dominant.

[24] Berle, Adolf A., Jr., *O Mundo entre Ocidente e Oriente* (Tides of Crisis), Rio: Editora Fundo de Cultura, 1958, p. 42.

[25] The book, published in 1955, is now in its second edition (Rio: Edições GRD, 1960). The author frequently uses ethical arguments and a kind of theological interpretation of history. An example among many is his assertion: "The constants of Asiatic-African politics are unchangeable in the light of history, of morality, and of God's designs." (page 29.) It is nevertheless one of those interesting works on international relations where the Brazilian bibliography is very limited because of the secondary international importance of Brazil until the present time. Brazilian authors have dedicated themselves more to the juridical study of international relations than to their sociological aspects. Another interesting book published recently is General Antônio de Souza Junior's *O Brasil e a Terceira Guerra Mundial* (*Brazil and the Third World War*), Rio: Biblioteca do Exército, 1959. His study deals mainly with military problems of national security. An indicator of an increasing interest in these subjects is the existence of the *Revista Brasileira de Política Internacional* (*Brazilian Review of International Politics*) that has been edited quarterly in Rio since 1958 under the auspices of the *Instituto Brasileiro de Relações Internacionais* (Brazilian Institute of International Relations).

[26] The same expression was recently used by San Thiago Dantas in a speech on September 11, 1961, in taking office as Minister of Foreign Affairs: "Each time we are more conscious of our responsibilities as a protagonist in the international life."

DIRECTIONS IN CURRENT POLICIES

If we do not pretend to look very far into the future, if we restrict our vision to the nearby horizons, we believe we can point out the following directions in our foreign policy:

a) Latin American leadership in the sense of giving an economic basis to Pan-Americanism;

b) Maintenance of commercial, and perhaps diplomatic, relations with countries of the Soviet bloc;

c) Anti-colonialism and defense of the principle of self-determination of peoples;

d) Anti-racist policies;

e) Increasing relationships with African and Asiatic peoples.

These lines of direction have more or less wide support in public opinion, with the exception of the re-establishment of diplomatic relations with the nations of the Soviet bloc, which has been a rather controversial subject. Besides this, in many lines of foreign policy a certain continuity has been maintained by three successive governments, that of President Kubitschek, the ephemeral administration of Jânio Quadros, and the government of João Goulart, inaugurated in September 1961.

Latin-American leadership

The leadership of Latin America for Brazil is a natural result of territorial and demographic factors, as well as economic and cultural conditions. Brazil is unquestionably a key nation on the continent. Because of the circumstances of its historical formation, Brazil has not known clashes with the United States experienced by some Hispanic American countries. This puts Brazil in a good position as mediator of a policy of greater continental solidarity.

It was this position that caused President Juscelino Kubitschek to assume the initiative in what came to be called Operation Pan America, in a letter sent to President Eisenhower in May 1958, soon after Vice President Richard Nixon had encountered hostile demonstrations in some parts of his trip to South America. Operation Pan America visualized, according to its promoters, political, strategic, and economic objectives. The economic objectives, however, were predominant. The central idea urged that the frightful situation of underdevelopment in Latin America should be improved, giving an economic base to Pan Americanism without which the juridical-political framework of continental solidarity would always remain fragile. The proposal called for a kind of Marshall Plan for Latin America.

The first concrete result, although limited, was the creation of an Inter-American Development Bank. The bank, whose headquarters are in Washington, D.C., began its existence in December, 1959, with a capital of a billion dollars. The lessons of the Cuban revolution persuaded the Kennedy administration to amplify the Brazilian suggestion into a much larger one, the "Alliance for Progress." It formally came into being in the Conference of Treasury Ministers of the members of the Organization of American States, held at Punta del Este, Uruguay, in August 1961. The agreement then signed offered twenty billion dollars to the Latin American nations during a period of ten years, the United States promising to supply the larger share of this total.

With the same objective of fortifying the economic bonds between the countries of this hemisphere, Brazil, following the proposals of the United Nations Economic Commission for Latin America, signed the Treaty of Montevideo, in 1960, that created a zone of free commerce among Argentina, Brazil, Chile, Uruguay, Paraguay, Peru and Mexico. Colombia and Ecuador have joined recently. The treaty, which went into effect in 1961, follows the example of the European Common Market, whose creation caused the countries on this side of the Atlantic to fear that their exports to Europe would be partly replaced by similar products of African origin. The Zone of Free Commerce embraces a potential market of nearly 165,000,000 individuals. Although the commercial interchange between these nations is still a small percentage of their trade with the United States and Europe, it signifies a first phase toward making their economies complementary, expanding the consumer market and hastening the betterment of their standards of living. Following the model of the European Economic Community, the Treaty of Montevideo allows a span of time for the achievement of its objectives. This is a period not longer than twelve years from its effective date.

The political crisis in Argentina after the ousting of President Frondizi by the military in March, 1962, increased the importance of Brazil in the Latin-American world even more. The prominence of Brazil was emphasized a few days after Frondizi's fall by the visit of the Brazilian President, João Goulart, to the United States and Mexico. However, there is no relation between the two events. The trip of João Goulart to Washington strengthened the ties between Brazil and the United States. It helped to diminish the suspicions provoked in the latter country by the leftist fame of João Goulart and by the Brazilian position in the Meeting of Consultation of Foreign Affairs Ministers of the Organization of American States, held in January, 1962, at Punta del Este, Uruguay.

In that meeting, Brazil together with Argentina, Chile, Bolivia, Ecuador and Mexico, abstained from voting for the expulsion of Cuba from the Organization of American States. The behavior of the Brazilian delegation at Punta del Este is easily understandable if we take into account the internal situation of the new regime. Parliamentary government had just been inaugurated in Brazil, in September 1961, after the resignation of Jânio Quadros. Brazil could not deviate abruptly from Quadros' foreign policy without being accused by some vocal sections of the public of submission to the United States. Such an accusation would put the new government in an unfavorable position in comparison to the last presidential government. Thereafter, President João Goulart and the new cabinet government seemed to strive

for a more moderate foreign policy and for the betterment of continental solidarity.

Relations with the Soviet Bloc

A search for new outlets for its exports will open many new markets for Brazil, including those of the Soviet bloc. This policy, initiated rather timidly near the end of the Juscelino Kubitschek government (1956–1961), took an obvious step forward with the various commercial missions that President Jânio Quadros sent to the countries of Eastern Europe, to the U.S.S.R., and to Communist China. This policy does not encounter objections[27] in public opinion so long as it is maintained on a commercial level. The successor government to Jânio Quadros has already declared more than once that it will be pursued. Diplomatic relations are now limited to Poland, Yugoslavia, Czechoslovakia, Hungary, Rumania, and Albania. Relations with Soviet Russia were re-established on November 27, 1961, despite the fear of Communist infiltration. Symptomatic of this fear was the measure of the Prime Minister—prior to resumption of diplomatic relations—prohibiting the Post Office Department from handling Communist propaganda and the declaration to the press by the Cardinal of Rio de Janeiro that the Brazilian Episcopate was unanimously against the re-establishment of diplomatic relations with the Soviet Union.

Anti-colonialism and anti-racism

The anti-colonialist orientation of Brazil is based on our evident political and economic in-

[27] A pending commercial agreement with East Germany was frustrated due to protests by West Germany. West Germany is the second largest purchaser of Brazilian products.

terests. We are weak militarily, have large areas of as yet unexploited land, and stand to suffer economically from the maintenance of colonial regimes among other peoples, such as those of Africa, whose products compete with ours in the world market. In an article in the October, 1961 issue of *Foreign Affairs,* ex-President Jânio Quadros set forth in clear terms the realistic foundations of our anti-colonialism. Among other considerations, he pointed out that the exploitation of Africans by European capital is injurious to the Brazilian economy, permitting, as it does, the stimulation of commercial competition based on the poorly paid work of Negroes. Competition should be established at a civilized and humane level instead of quasi-slavery which exists because of inferior pay to a whole race. He continued that the present industrial growth of Brazil guarantees an important source of consumer goods to Africans which could serve as a base of agreement for co-ordinating the respective systems of production.[28]

The principles of self-determination and non-intervention in the internal affairs of other countries are closely connected to anti-colonialism, notwithstanding the obscure nature of these principles in this century of "international civil wars," the first of which was the Spanish Civil War. Brazil, as a weak nation which still remembers the unfriendly intervention of England in the past century, will surely continue to defend the principle of non-intervention. It was in this non-interventionist sentiment that Brazil always interpreted the Monroe Doctrine and supported it from the beginning.

[28] In his plan of government, presented to the House of Deputies on September 28, 1961, our Prime Minister expressed the same thought. Bezerra de Menezes, although he emphasized the moral arguments for our drawing nearer to Africa, also invoked this economic foundation. *O Brasil e o Mundo Ásio-Africano,* (*Brazil and the Asian-African World*), Second Edition, Rio: Edições GRD, 1960, p. 13. The same sentiment is found in Helio Jaguaribe, *O Nacionalismo na Atualidede Brasileira* (*Nationalism in Present-Day Brazil*), Rio: I.S.E.B., 1958, p. 286. In this book (pp. 225 and following) Jaguaribe divides our foreign politics into three phases that, excepting a few points, coincide generally with the divisions adopted in this study.

Anti-racism on the international plane is merely a corollary of the Brazilian "ideology" of being a racial democracy—a subject already explored in another part of this study.

Relations with African and Asian peoples

The two latter positions, anti-colonialism and anti-racism, undoubtedly favor the relationships between Brazil and the countries of Asia and Africa. In fact, the Brazilian government and certain educational institutions began recently to foster these relationships. In 1959 the University of Bahia founded the *Centro de Estudos Afro-Orientais* (Center of Eastern and African Studies) that has maintained cultural contacts with some peoples of western Africa. Following this precedent Jânio Quadros created the *Instituto de Estudos Afro-Asiáticos* (Institute of Asian and African Studies) directly under the control of the President of the Republic, and he hastened to establish diplomatic relations with the recently emancipated nations of Africa. The example of the University of Bahia was also imitated by the University of Rio Grande do Norte.

The most enthusiastic advocate of this policy, the already mentioned Consul Bezerra de Menezes, believes that in proportion as Europe loses ground among the peoples of the Asian and African continents, "Brazil is the country predestined to help, protect and lead them for its own benefit and even for that of the United States of America in those areas and matters in which its people are hindered by their racist practices."[29] However, there exist some economic obstacles to the attainment of these aims. As a subdeveloped country, Brazil cannot offer the capital and heavy equipment so badly needed by these peoples for their economic development, to say nothing of the circumstance that some Asian and African nations are our competitors in world trade.

[29] *O Brasil e o Mundo Ásio-Africano,* p. 29.

This fact causes contradictory situations in our relations with these countries. Thus, although Brazil was the author of the proposal for creation of the United Nations Economic Commission for Africa, the Brazilian ex-Minister of Foreign Affairs, Horácio Lafer, and our former Ambassador to Washington, Walter Moreira Sales, protested, on a certain occasion, against the sizable aids granted by the United States to our African competitors.[30] Obviously, Brazilian diplomacy will need to avoid such contradictions if we wish to collect the political and economic fruits that could stem from strengthened ties with the nations of Asia and Africa. These countries have fortified their position in the diplomatic game within the United Nations Organization and as a group have become the object of courtship from every side. Although the Asian and African peoples do not constitute a solid bloc, they have almost half of the votes of the United Nations General Assembly.[31]

THE AGENCIES THAT FORMULATE AND EXECUTE FOREIGN POLICY

The agencies that formulate and execute the external policy of Brazil become larger and more diversified with the increase of diplomatic duties. Representative government in Brazil goes back to the promulgation of the monarchical Constitution (1824), with the brief interruptions of the first and second Republics

(1889–1891 and 1930–1934) and of the period running from the *Estado Novo* (New State) to the promulgation of the Constitution of 1946 (1937–1946). There has always been parliamentary control over foreign policy, but during the Empire this control was at a minimum. The Emperor had to hear the State Council concerning a "declaration of war, peace settlements, negotiations with foreign nations" as well as to communicate these matters to the legislative branch (Articles 142 and 102, Numbers 8 and 9, of the Constitution). But only those matters were subject to the approval of Parliament which were "treaties concluded in times of peace" and which "involved cession or exchange of imperial territory, or of possessions to which the Empire has the right" (Article 102, Number 8). After the adoption of the first Republican Constitution (1891) all these matters became dependent on authorization from Congress. Congress also had to permit the movement or quartering of foreign troops on national territory, and had to approve international agreements. Besides this, since that date the Senate must approve nominations for diplomatic representation of a permanent character.

With the recent adoption of the parliamentary system of government, the President of the Republic retains the classic function of representative of the country in the international sphere, but the task of "maintaining relations with foreign states and directing foreign policy" has passed to the President of the Council of Ministers. This duty is executed through the Ministry of Foreign Relations, which has existed as a specialized department since the time of the United Kingdom of Brazil, Portugal, and Algarves. It was in 1821 that the post of "Minister of the Kingdom and Foreign Affairs" was created. Certain agencies outside the specific

[30] Delgado de Carvalho, *Atlas de Relações Internacionais (Atlas of International Relations)*, Rio: I.B.G.E., 1961, p. 156.

[31] Besides the directions of the Brazilian foreign policy above enumerated, the idea of a Lusitanian-Brazilian commonwealth, which would embody Brazil, Portugal, and the Portuguese possessions, is sometimes brought up. The ties between Brazil and Portugal are of a rather sentimental character. The Portuguese enjoy privileged treatment in Brazil, including easier naturalization procedures. The economic basis of the commonwealth scheme is, however, very fragile because of the small trade between the two countries. Besides this, closer relations to Portugal would probably damage our anti-colonial policy in Africa. But if the present difficulties were overcome, the suggestion of such a commonwealth could bring some gains in the future, through a stronger union of the Portuguese-speaking world, since language is until now the most important link between Brazil and Portugal.

portfolio lend aid in the formulation of external policy. In defense matters the most important is the National Security Council, created in 1927.[32]

The Ministry of Foreign Relations has been enlarged and implemented to cope with its increasing functions, especially in the economic field. The diplomatic posts are for the most part filled by career personnel, who secure them through direct competition or after a course at the Instituto Rio Branco. This institution was created in 1945 for the purpose of preparing specialized personnel in the diplomatic and consular fields. Our diplomats are losing that air of the refined aristocrat and man of leisure, which was proper to an epoch when Brazil had nothing to accomplish in the international orbit other than problems of territorial limits. Those denationalized, Europeanized, and especially Frenchified figures, imbued with a general and literary culture, exist no longer. In their place are emerging less decorative and more active diplomats to meet the new demands of our foreign policy.[33]

FORCES THAT INFLUENCE FOREIGN POLICY

The forces that mold foreign policy developed in Brazil in the same way as in all democratic countries. They became gradually enlarged and diversified. But only recently has the so-called "behind the scenes foreign policy" ended and the people evolved an interest in international problems. Prior to this "foreign policy was left to a small group of the initiated,

and the people were unconcerned with world events except on rare occasions when they reacted emotionally. . . . Only after World War II did Brazil awaken to international problems."[34]

Foreign policies as domestic issues

In general the themes of foreign policy are raised with the purpose of creating internal political effects. Writing in this respect, Deputy Afonso Arinos, who later became Foreign Minister, observed: "In my experience in the Brazilian Congress, international affairs assume increasingly greater interest, almost exclusively in relationship to internal politics."[35]

This does not occur only in the legislative branch. The same happens in the executive branch. In 1945, after being deposed by the armed forces, Vargas declared he had been a victim of foreign pressure. In 1954 his political "testament" renewed this accusation with dramatic emphasis. Jânio Quadros recently imitated the example, using equivalent expressions when he resigned the presidency. The fact, however, that foreign policy is continuing along almost the same lines as drawn by Jânio Quadros does not lend credence to his allegation, even though it is true that certain of his acts in foreign policy—primarily the decoration of Che Guevara with the Order of the Southern Cross—caused rebuke from various segments of public opinion, especially the military. But Jânio Quadros stated in his resignation letter that the military showed "exemplary behavior." Consequently, if any pressure existed for his resignation, it did not stem from the military.

The 1960 presidential election was the first

---

[32] It is regulated by Law-Decree Number 5,163 of December 31, 1942, and composed of the Ministers and the Chiefs of Staff of the Army, Navy, and Air Force, under the chairmanship of the President of the Republic.

[33] In August of 1961 Brazil had 66 embassies and six legations, not counting the delegations in the various international organizations.

[34] Bastian Pinto, Luis, "A Política Exterior do Brasil na América Latina" ("Brazilian Foreign Policy in Latin America"), *Revista Brasileira de Política Internacional,* Ano II, Number 8, pps. 52–53.

[35] *Estudos de Direito Constitucional* (*Studies in Constitutional Law*), Rio: Edição Revista Forense, 1957, pps. 272–273.

electoral campaign in which international problems assumed importance. Communists and "nationalists" presented their candidate, General Lott, as the standard bearer of nationalism, while accusing Jânio Quadros of being the incarnation of "entreguismo." Jânio's trip to Cuba during the campaign, while Lott characterized Fidel Castro as a "sanguinary," resulted in confusing the anti-Jânio propaganda, or at least in reducing the hostile tone of its most active spokesmen, the Communists. One suspects that Jânio's foreign policy, after assuming office, intended not only to silence the same vociferous Communist minority but also to solidify the popular support of the President, by satisfying national pride. Undoubtedly it resulted also in achieving the desired effects internationally, especially economic advantages.

Pressure groups

The degree of success with which government agencies obviate difficulties in formulating foreign policy depends on the conjunction of political forces and of pressure groups active in this sphere. Of these groups the more obvious are the armed forces, the Catholic Church, Communists and students.

The Armed Forces are, in certain aspects, instruments of foreign politics. Consequently, they cannot be fully characterized as a pressure group, since by definition a pressure group is an active organization outside the mechanism of government. Notwithstanding, in every country the military forces influence the course of foreign policy, the degree of influence being greater when there is less stability in the civil government. Hence, the important role of the military in areas like Latin America.

As in every nation, the main concern of the armed forces is defense of the country. They believe that Brazil's defense is better secured by alignment with the Western Powers. They advocate strengthening the United Nations and the Organization of American States, favoring also inter-American solidarity and compliance

with military agreements with the United States. The works of our military writers discuss primarily the geopolitical problems regarding defense of our boundaries, inadequate population of vast areas of our country, strategic importance of the northeastern bulge and the vulnerability of this region to modern long range weapons. The military, however, has begun to realize that this region is more vulnerable to psychological weapons of modern warfare than to mechanized weapons. As a rather underdeveloped country, most of Brazil belongs to what can be called the "external proletariat"— to use Toynbee's expression in a different connotation—whose support and sympathy are vied for by the two super-Powers of our time. Specifically, in the northeast there exists the largest and most abandoned part of this "proletariat," comprising a peasantry with one of the lowest standards of living in the world.

After the Cuban revolution and the recent success of Cheddi Jagan in British Guiana, the military are more alerted to the infiltration of anti-Western ideology, especially anti-Americanism. Even before these changes in Cuba and British Guiana, the northeast had provided an index of social fermentation with the formation of "Peasant Leagues," whose purpose is the creation of class consciousness among the peasants in order to regiment them for social and political action.[36]

The major ideological resistance to communism and the major opposition to diplomatic recognition of Russia come from the Catholic Church. The Church has only just awakened to the need of internal social action, but is already

[36] The first Peasant Leagues were set up in 1955 by Francisco Julião, a member of the Brazilian Socialist Party (P.S.B.) and a deputy to the State Legislature of Pernambuco. He claims to have peaceful purposes and speaks, at the same time, as a mystic and a shrewd politican: "If I could, I would put together the thought of Christ, Buddha, Saint Francis of Assisi (the greatest figure of the Catholic Church for his humility toward the poor), Lincoln, Lenin, Mao Tse-tung and Fidel Castro. I would make a synthesis of all of them and so I would find the solution to Brazil's problems." Interview with Carlos Leonam, Tribuna da Imprensa, Rio, issue of July 13, 1961.

revealing a tendency to increase activity as the ideological struggle is intensified.

The Communists, in their role as internationalists, are the only ones advocating a pro-Soviet position for Brazil. They never do it directly, however, but by preaching anti-Americanism, neutralism, or a rabid nationalism. That they are a minority with little electoral power was verified in the last presidential election. Although opposed by the Communists, Jânio Quadros received 5,600,000 votes, the most ever obtained by a presidential candidate in the history of Brazil. But the power of this minority in infiltration and propaganda is considerable.

The students participate actively in politics, although on a smaller scale than their colleagues in other Latin-American countries. They represent the young intelligentsia of a country which is more than half illiterate, and, as the adolescents they are, tend to react emotionally to problems of foreign policy, taking the positions most flattering to national feeling. There are ideological divisions in the midst of the student group, but the democratic majority is more or less passive, relinquishing leadership to the extremist minority. These latter tend to control the student organizations and to lead their colleagues to participate in political life, the while calling for group solidarity. Communists occupy some positions of student leader-

ship or are able to get student leaders to play the Communist game. Even among those who are not militant Communists, Marxism exerts a strong attraction. Student-worker pacts are popular, in which the university students join in support of worker strikes and the workers in turn support student strikes. The fact is that universities are the most sensitive focal point of social ebullition in Latin America, and Brazil is no exception.

As this summary of the forces active in Brazilian life verifies, there is no lack of discordant voices about what our foreign policy should be. There are sympathizers of the West and of the East, there are neutralists, and there are those who are in favor of an independent position. In taking the balance of these forces, we see that those which tend toward the Western side clearly predominate. Brazil is, then, an apprentice World Power without the unity in foreign policy which other nations struggling for international coming-of-age have known. These internal divisions may call the attention of the richer nations of the West to the necessity of accelerating the economic development of Brazil, but if these divisions are aggravated they bring the danger of transforming our country into one more stage of the "international civil war" that has torn apart so many peoples.

BIBLIOGRAPHY

Author's Suggestions

Bezerra de Menezes, Adolpho Justo. *O Brasil e o Mundo Ásio-Africano.* 2a. edição. Rio: Edições GRD, 1960.

Delgado de Carvalho. *História Diplomática do Brasil.* S. Paulo: Comp. Editora Nacional, 1959.

Jaguaribe, Hélio. *O Nacionalismo na Atualidade Brasileira.* Rio: ISEB, 1958.

Lambert, Jacques. *Os Dois Brasis.* Rio: Centro de Pesquisas Educacionais, 1959.

Honório Rodrigues, José. *Brasil e África: Outro Horizonte.* Rio: Civilização Brasileira, 1961.

Souza Jr., Antônio de. *O Brasil e a Terceira Guerra Mundial*. Rio: Biblioteca do Exército, 1959.

Vianna, Hélio. *História Diplomática do Brasil*. São Paulo: Edições Melhoramentos, n.d.

Supplementary Readings in English

Hill, Lawrence Francis, ed. *Brazil*. Berkeley, University of California Press, 1947.

Hunnicutt, Benjamin H. *Brazil: World Frontier*. Princeton, N.J.: Van Nostrand, 1949.

Johnson, John J. "Politics and Economics in Brazil," *Current History*, Feb. 1962 (Vol. 42, No. 246), pp. 89–95.

Quadros, Jânio. "Brazil's New Foreign Policy," *Foreign Affairs*, October, 1961 (Vol. 40, No. 1), pp. 19–28.

ABOUT THE AUTHOR

Francisco Cuevas Cancino received his LL.B. degree at the Free School of Law in Mexico City in 1943. He served as consultant to the Departments of Agriculture and Education of the Mexican Federal Government until he returned to his academic studies at McGill University in Montreal. He obtained his Master of Civil Laws in 1946 from McGill University. That same year he entered the Mexican Foreign Service and is presently Mexico's Alternate Delegate to the United Nations.

Mr. Cancino's diplomatic career was interrupted from 1950 to 1953 while he held a Guggenheim scholarship to study the Good Neighbor Policy. He then joined the Secretariat of the United Nations. During 1961 and part of 1962 he was the Director of the Center of International Studies of the College of Mexico.

He has added to the scope of his career by frequent publications; notable among these are: *Bolívar, el ideal panamericano del Libertador,* 1951, a work which received the Simon Bolivar Prize; *La doctrina de Suárez sobre el derecho natural,* 1952, which was awarded the "Suárez Prize"; and *Tratado sobre la Organización internacional,* 1962, which received a prize from the tenth Inter-American Conference.

ABOUT THE CHAPTER

Mexico's role in world affairs cannot be understood without paying careful heed to a number of factors which have given this nation a unique individuality. Her historical background, her location next to one of the Major World Powers, and the harsh realities of her economic problems must be taken into account.

From an early period when Mexican leaders clearly believed that a great empire was being born and that Mexico was destined to be a leading World Power, this nation slipped to the position where foreign intervention was rife and attempts were even made to make Mexico a dependent nation. The reliance of Mexico on international law as "the axis of foreign policy" was a direct result of the hostile international environment and the fact that "law was the only protecting shield she could use against ambitious nations."

Throughout this chapter one can clearly see the conflict between ideals and realities in international politics. Mexican leaders have always insisted on the "rule of law" and the rights of the small nations. But a world of international rivalry and the constant conflict of interests have provided the steady setting within which they have had to work in an attempt to achieve Mexico's aspirations.

This chapter was written while the author was on a leave of absence from the diplomatic service. It is not an official statement of the views and position of the Mexican government.

22

THE FOREIGN POLICY OF MEXICO

FRANCISCO CUEVAS CANCINO

Escuela Libre de Derecho, Mexico, D. F.

FOREIGN RELATIONS FRAMED BY HISTORY

Circumstances give each nation its own historical configuration and mark it with its own individuality. Although essentially changeable, they form the bases of all foreign policy. It is in conformity with them that a nation responds to the challenge of its own development or to the interests and ambitions of other nations. Each response leaves a residue which brings about the evolution of the foreign policy of the nation. And in that evolution we find the secret of many positions which otherwise might seem inopportune or unexpected. Our task here is to understand the course of conduct followed by Mexico in accordance with her national being and her historical personality in order that she might achieve those interests which she considers vital.

Great Power status, 1821–1836

On gaining her independence, Mexico thought, as did other nations, that a great empire was being born. She was called upon to exercise in the New World, if not hegemony, at least a markedly dominant position. The fame of her inexhaustible riches, the preference granted her by the motherland (Spain), her progress in the sciences and arts, her administration of the Oriental Spanish possessions and the practice of the *Situados* over other Caribbean colonies and even those of South America, her large population and her central geographical location, all led people to believe that Mexico was naturally and certainly destined to play a great international role.

This was the way the Mexican diplomats understood the situation. For fifteen years they worked in pursuit of that ideal; they thought that Mexico's external actions could be influential in all of America and beyond that, throughout the world. A series of statesmen—not as numerous nor constant and tightly-knit as the nation needed, but still a number of them—tried to mold a strong and vigorous Mexico that was not afraid to think about power—her own as well as alien power—about the use of force, about the balance of power, or about strategic obligations. In short, they attempted to shape a Mexico which went headlong into the great European currents of foreign affairs with the confidence that she could come out with clear advantages such as the consolidation and future well-being of the nation. Alamán, Gorostiza, Ramos Arizpe, Azcárate and Herrera managed Mexico's foreign policy on the assumption that they were guiding the interests of a Great Power.

Mexico acted as a Great Power from 1821 until 1836. There were errors and there were weaknesses. But the features of her foreign policy were those of a country which, convinced of her superiority in the international field, was clearly and decidedly disposed to exercise it. She quickly initiated towards the rest of Hispanic America a policy of leadership. This was evident in her lack of sympathy toward Bolivar's plans, in her victorious efforts to bring about the transfer of the headquarters of the Panama Congress to Tacubaya, and in the plan of the "family pact" proposed by Alamán which constituted the backbone of Mexican policy for years. Mexico sponsored the union of countries bound together by one history, one religion, one language, and common interests—a union under her leadership, to defend Latin America's destiny both on the continent and throughout the world.

There is no doubt that Mexico was seeking hegemony. This is clear from the instructions which Alamán gave to the Mexican diplomats. It is also reflected in the series of treaties of alliance and friendship through which Mexico outlined a system of commerce and shipping for the exclusive benefit of Latin America. These treaties enabled Mexico to act as representative of other Latin-American nations. South America—as opposed to the United States—was for the Mexican statesman a whole unit, bound together by nature and by reciprocal interests. They aimed at a union of states that would constitute "the most powerful rampart of liberty"[1] and in which, due to the greater weight of her power, Mexico would have the role of guide and mentor.

Some obvious consequences can be deduced from this attitude: one was Mexico's concern over the future of Cuba. It was noted that "politics demands of the government of Mexico that she dedicate herself to seize the said island," or at least not allow "any of her neighbors to become larger by the acquisition of such a rich possession." The Mexicans also looked towards what they called "the Mexican breast" (the Gulf of Mexico). Looking beyond, their statesmen affirmed that Cuba and Puerto Rico have "the same suitability in the sea of the North as the Marianas and the Philippines have in the sea of the South." With regard to Central America there was generosity. The decision of Guatemala to declare her independence was respected; but this was no obstacle in the way of Mexico's insistence on her dominant position in the central American region, which was of such vital strategic importance to her.[2]

Weaknesses and errors reduce power

Even during this early period of positive achievements, one can observe signs of weakness which were to prove fatal for the high and ambitious goals of Mexican foreign policy. To be successful Mexico needed an internal political center which would form its backbone, similar to the position served by the emperor in Brazil in the 19th century. In its absence, Mexican statesmen were "islands in the tempestuous sea . . . of demagogic din." An interminable succession of people filed through the Mexican chancellery; sixty-two persons headed it in the first twenty-five years of the

[1] *Archivo Histórico-Diplomático,* 1st series, vol. 33, p. 60.
[2] *Ibid.,* vol. 36; 2nd series, vols. 4 and 7.

political existence of the country.[3] All concept of continuity vanished; foreign policy was subject to the whims of an extremely agitated political life, and the real meaning of foreign affairs was lost. A significant and omnipresent penury began to plague foreign policy, a plague which will not disappear, and even continues to our time.

The first examples of non-intervention occurred: Mexico refused to uphold the legitimate government of Central America which sought military aid against insurrectionists (1827). She also abandoned all idea of dominance in the Gulf of Mexico, signing a treaty with Spain (Santa María-Calatrava, 1836) which included a secret article through which both Powers agreed to prevent any hostile act against the possessions of the co-signer.

Mexico also miscalculated gravely in her relations with Europe. Mexico had no reason either to beg or to show gratitude for being admitted to the family of nations. But she was weak enough to sign an unequal declaration with regard to France in 1827. In the same year she bowed before the conditional recognition granted her by Great Britain by signing a commercial treaty which was immensely prejudicial to Mexico's interests. Mexico appeared as a beggar of loans—onerous and one-sided—an image which for almost a half-century would leave Mexico in the role of a pauper-beggar before the proud Western Powers.

Genaro Estrada has argued that improvisation in international affairs was unavoidable in a country which "was testing its form of government."[4] Unfortunately, in international matters these errors could not simply be forgotten; they put into motion forces which the country later could not control. Mexico lacked the internal stability and the external continuity which her foreign policy required; she became the victim of the same qualities which compelled her to rise towards hegemony. Her situa-

tion, though privileged, brought with it grave dangers. Foreign relations were not for Mexico, a newly independent country, simply a schoolboy's exercise. They constituted a great challenge which, if not met, would leave her in a tottering position before the inevitable onslaught of ambitious Powers. Mexico was the great northern corner-stone of a civilization. Her "reason for being" called her to international greatness. Once this greatness failed, her situation necessarily became worse than that of the other Latin American Powers which stood protected by the very bulk of the geographical group.

Considering her links with Catholicism, Mexico should have entered international life as a great Catholic nation. The policy of the Roman Curia was largely responsible for her inability to do so. Rome refused to negotiate a concordat based on the rights of the Mexican state to exercise the same rights of patronage, presentation, and tithes which the Spanish crown had enjoyed. From the beginning it was understood that Mexico should count on two cardinalships and that the nuncio should be a Mexican citizen.[5] Rome refused to recognize these requests. As a consequence, Mexico was prevented from consolidating her position as a Catholic Power in international affairs and was obliged to follow a path which weakened her identity as a Power. An indication of the short-sightedness of Rome could still be seen as late as 1824 in an unfortunate encyclical of Leo XII which reiterated Spain's colonial interest.

Mexico, at the end of the second decade of her political existence, found herself torn by deep internal convulsions. From then on there appeared elements which have caused national crises over the years. Outstanding among them are the complexity of her being, the depth and diversity of her roots, the diverse, independent currents which were unable to fuse, and the absence of a clear-cut conviction of her destiny as a sovereign nation.

Mexico was overwhelmed by many problems which had to be solved under extremely un-

---

[3] *Ibid.*, vol. 7, p. 18. By "person" I mean the titular head or the person in charge of the Office of Foreign Affairs who is named by the Chief of State, although sometimes it may be the very same person.

[4] *Ibid.*, 1st series, vol. 25, prologue.

[5] *Ibid.*, vol. 33, p. 43 ff.

favorable conditions. The country needed external tranquillity so she could isolate herself from other nations and complete her metamorphosis. This was a vain wish. The new nation was surrounded by enemies, great or growing Powers which looked with greedy eyes at her territories and wealth. A series of external crises were added to the grave internal problems; they left permanent scars on the body of the nation and fixed her course in foreign policy for years ahead.

Disputes and war with the United States

Opposition to the United States was natural, as consequence of long centuries during which the rivalries of the Old World had been transplanted to the New. This opposition was recognized by statesmen of both countries who first directed the affairs of the two nations. The future of Cuba, the independence of Central America, the treaty of boundaries, Mexico's form of government, and, of course, the immediate claims of private debtors were matters of concern for the two nations from the outset. It is clear that Mexican statesmen were in a very disadvantageous position with regard to territorial matters. The Treaty of San Lorenzo (Pinckney-Godoy) and the Onis Treaty (1795 and 1819), by which Spain, for political reasons, made substantial concessions to American claims, set the stage for future developments.

The unending ambition of the United States soon came to the fore. Dissatisfied with the boundaries obtained from Onis, she was set on moving them to the Rio Grande and the Pacific. When Mexico was rising as a Great Power, use was made of the weapons of subversion and intrigue, to which a society such as that of Mexico of that day was particularly susceptible. Each error in our policy was taken advantage of by the ambitious neighbor. As soon as Mexico began to weaken, a multitude of adventurers proceeding from the Mississippi Valley "preyed upon the northern provinces of Mexico, just as the barbarians did on Rome."[6]

Mexico procrastinated and acted too late with regard to Texas. One could hardly expect a unified policy when in the first fifty years of independence no fewer than 128 persons were in charge of her foreign office. The opportunity to save the other western provinces at the time of Texas' secession was not taken. That opportunity would not return. Instead, the war with North America came about, a war which many Mexicans thought they could win. The peace treaty of Guadalupe-Hidalgo (1848) at least avoided "any stipulation of perpetual mortgage or ignominy," saved her nationality, and allowed the country to face the future as an independent nation.[7]

European Powers intervene in Mexico

At the end of this war Mexico was left truncated, nevermore able to consider herself a Great Power. The foreign policy of former years, the tool with which her destiny was to be carved, ceased to exist. Her statesmen now needed defensive weapons. North American ambitions had not yet been satisfied, nor was there a dearth of other Powers desirous of taking advantage of Mexico's weakness. As soon as it became apparent (through the defeat of San Jacinto and the virtual independence of Texas), that the Mexican Colossus had feet of clay, European pecuniary claims began to fall like rain on the troubled land. France was the chief interested party. Desirous of recouping the Napoleonic losses, she was the first of the European nations "to make use of her power rather than her rights in order to try to humiliate and vilify the new nation."[8] France's diplomacy was characterized by extreme harshness; she treated Mexico as a mendicant nation. And in the face of ultimata and threats of war, al-

[6] *Ibid.*, vols. 8 and 33, p. 9 ff.
[7] *Ibid.*, vol. 31, p. 139 ff.
[8] Message from President Bustamante to Congress, January 1, 1839.

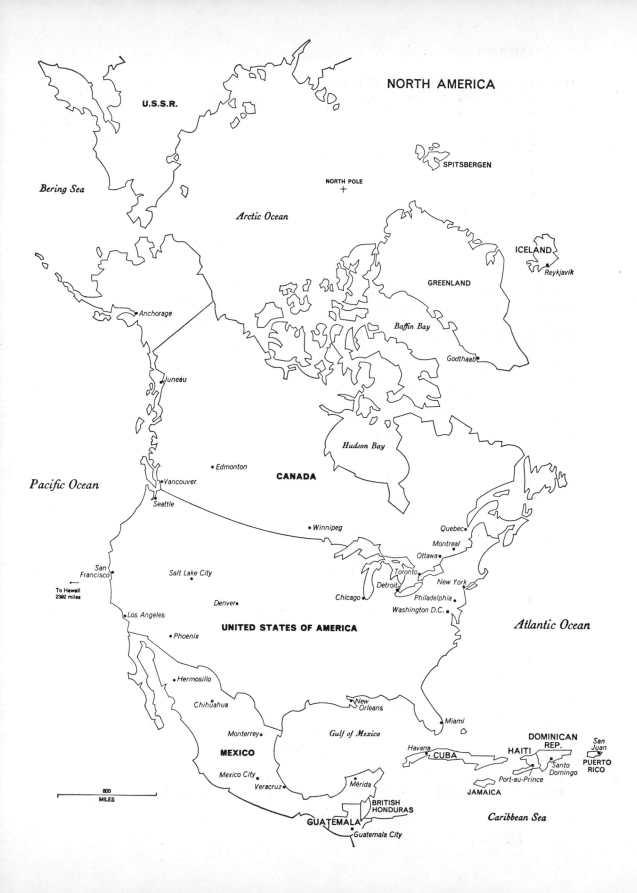

NORTH AMERICA

U.S.S.R.

SPITSBERGEN

Bering Sea

NORTH POLE
+

Arctic Ocean

ICELAND
Reykjavik

GREENLAND

Baffin Bay

Anchorage

Godthaab

Juneau

Hudson Bay

Pacific Ocean

Edmonton

CANADA

Vancouver

Seattle

Winnipeg

Quebec

Montreal

Ottawa

Toronto

San Francisco

Salt Lake City

Detroit

New York

To Hawaii
2392 miles

Chicago

Philadelphia

Denver

Washington D.C.

Los Angeles

UNITED STATES OF AMERICA

Atlantic Ocean

Phoenix

Hermosillo

Chihuahua

New Orleans

Miami

Monterrey

Gulf of Mexico

DOMINICAN
REP.

MEXICO

Havana

CUBA

HAITI

San
Juan

PUERTO
RICO

Mexico City

*Santo
Domingo*

Veracruz

Mérida

Port-au-Prince

JAMAICA

800
MILES

BRITISH
HONDURAS

GUATEMALA

Caribbean Sea

Guatemala City

ways accompanied by the most unfair and exaggerated pretensions,[9] Mexico was submerged in the quagmire of a total lack of political direction.

The battling of parties at home and the lack of directives in external affairs came to their end with the War of Intervention (1861–1867) during which the most aggressive of the European Powers attempted to subjugate Mexico. Several events during this period, however, helped to set the guide-lines for the foreign policy of Mexico. Firstly, the Civil War in the United States put a rein on that nation's territorial greed—for her economy ceased being agricultural and became industrial. Secondly, unstable conditions in Europe led the war machinery of European Powers in other directions. And thirdly, and even more important, the Mexican people came to realize their unity, and, now sure of themselves, they were willing to face the thrust of others. After a period of suffering and uncertainty, with the Republic restored, a new leadership came to the fore.

Through all of these dark periods, the idea grew that Mexico was receiving insults which were unfair. They were unfair because the claimant states relied more on their power than on the justice of their claims. Mexico, who had tried to establish with other nations of America a "magnanimous" international law, was forced to turn to the law then in force—European-Occidental law—to protect herself from exorbitant claims.[10] Juárez insisted that every obligation which Mexico accepted had to be "in conformity with the rights of the people and that the consideration of their weakness or their power, of their good or bad political organization, must not have any influence on the settlement of their differences."[11]

When the French intervention began, Juárez protested against the implied violation of the rights of the people on the part of the intervening Powers in not dealing with a legitimate government. His Minister of Foreign Relations

exposed the systematic aggressiveness of Napoleonic diplomacy which sought to outrage and exploit Mexico with no more right than that of the strong in taking advantage of the weak. Behind false shields, claims were presented which had no foundation in law, and these claims were couched in the most insolent terms.[12]

International law as the basis of policy

The new Mexico which surged up from these internal and external conflicts established her policy around international law. Positive law was placed at the service of the nation and served to promote her conservation and interests. The whole of Mexico's policy was aimed at attaining that ideal law to which she aspired through conviction and self-interest. This conviction was based on the reality that she found in law the only protecting shield she could use against ambitious nations. She was also convinced that a better world would exist only if all nations acted in consonance with such ideals.

Law became the axis of Mexican foreign policy. With it came a series of fundamental assumptions which were the cornerstones of a foreign policy which was clearly juridical. This policy assumed, in effect, that there existed among states a community which could be expressed juridically; that among states which accept the same juridical ideal there grows a true community of forces and interests, and also, that the partisans of law were sufficiently strong to oblige the enemies of law to recognize the indispensable rule of these juridical standards.[13]

This general policy reveals the juridical formalism inherited from Spain. Also, it reveals the spark of the age of enlightenment which had justified our independence. Some of its potentially most dangerous assumptions are: a belief

---

[9] *Archivo Histórico-Diplomático*, 1st series, vol. 26, Matías Romero a Seeward, October 2, 1862.

[10] *Ibid.*, vol. 23, p. 161 ff.

[11] *Ibid.*, vol. 13, pp. 156–57.

[12] *Ibid.*, vol. 10.

[13] *Ibid.*, 2nd series, vol. 10.

in an automatic harmony among nations, and a lessening of the natural rapacity of states and a full trust in the peaceful character of all democratic governments. The natural enmity which exists between neighboring states or opposing systems was belittled, and the idea that good faith does not demand as a counterpart a sacrifice of national interests was advanced.

The suffering which Mexico underwent to arrive at a political-juridical synthesis was very intense. Ever since that time—almost a century ago—her foreign policy has been based on such a synthesis. It would be just as mistaken as it would be unavailing to try to understand Mexican foreign policy today without basing a judgment on these great juridical underpinnings or to ignore the fact that Mexico places its hope for a better world on the role of law. The implicit assumptions inherent in the juridical basis of her foreign policy should be our point of departure in evaluating Mexico's foreign policy, even in a world which is significantly different from that which existed in 1866.

When the ephemeral attempt to impose a Franco-Austrian empire on Mexico failed, she looked at the outside world through very different eyes. Mexico had proved to the world that she was capable of defending her sovereign rights against an extremely powerful enemy and she was convinced that she did not need any foreign government to recognize her existence as an independent nation.[14] All of these struggles, at home and abroad, had not been fruitless. Mexico was now conscious of her identity. Freed from the nightmare of foreign debts—since the European governments had foregone their rights by recognizing the fallen empire—the republic could now raise her head without the weight of those onerous commitments. An element of legitimate pride appeared, and it consolidated an isolationist policy: friendship and trade were offered to all peoples of the earth but diplomatic relations were easy with none.[15]

The Republic of Mexico adopted a policy based on full international autonomy. She respects herself and, as a consequence, she respects others. Starting from the idea of her national integrity, she goes on to apply with strict impartiality the principle of self-determination. With unique idealism she goes no further than what is permissible under those same standards of justice to which she appealed during her days of trouble. The guiding light is the conviction that a Great Power, no matter how great it may be, is incapable of imposing itself on a nation desirous of being free. Out of these several ideas and principles, which are intimately interwoven, the ideal of non-intervention, a keystone of Mexican foreign policy, was born.

The era of Porfirio Díaz

There is not space here to trace the development of Mexico's foreign policy through all of the years that followed. But some major points should be noted. Mexico, no longer aspiring to be a Great Power, had the task of internal development, establishing a sound financial basis for the state,[16] and developing a reputation which the capitalistic Powers would class as "honorable." From the 1870's until his regime was toppled by the revolution of 1910, Mexico was ruled by the strong hand of Porfirio Díaz. It has been said that Díaz "was much more a governor than a statesman because he had no vision of the future, which in the statesman is a spontaneous obsession and cannot be held without a recognition of the past."[17] Under Díaz the policy was to sacrifice the long-term interests of the nation in exchange for immediate investments. Great problems were ignored and the government sought protection behind the prompt and immediate solution of any incident which grew out of foreign investments. A sys-

[14] Reply by Ezequiel Montes to the message of President Juárez to Congress, 1867.
[15] Reply by Palacio to the message of President Juárez to Congress, 1869.

[16] Emilio Rabasa, *La evolución política de México*, p. 127.
[17] *Ibid.*, p. 154.

tem in which foreigners enjoyed privileged positions over Mexicans, both within and outside the law, was in vogue at that time in the nation.[18]

While the long administration of Díaz was materially productive for Mexico, it was a period without an imaginative foreign policy. His many reports to Congress were totally lacking in those great external goals that were essential for the country. Insipid reading, his messages were those of a politician mainly concerned with administration, and not those of a statesman. For example, in 1910 he noted in one of those messages that "Mexico sees her efforts over many years compensated for, since she has definitely achieved in the family of nations the position which she had always hoped for."[19] Díaz's mistake was believing that he had personified Mexico's ultimate goals. As a matter of fact, he had weakened them.

During the Díaz period, the direction of internal affairs and foreign policy was personalized to the greatest possible extent. Mexican diplomacy was the fruit of the whims of the perpetual President; there was no chance for preparing for progress and for new generations. If we add to this the strong and inevitable break which occurred with the coming of the revolution, we can understand the serious breakdown of the nation. She could not count on that diplomatic tradition, that persistence of external objectives, that continuity in purpose which other nations have enjoyed.

In the twentieth century, Mexico found herself lacking in foreign policy machinery adequate for the implementation of her policies. Because of the lengthy struggle of the parties, and the equally lengthy personal dictatorship during the first and second halves of her first century of independent life, Mexico had no real diplomatic tradition. In periods of trial she appeared uncertain; in periods of positive policy she appeared lacking in the ability to follow a new course.

[18] Luis Cabrera, *La herencia de Carranza*, and Isidro Fabela, *Historia Diplomática de la Revolución Mexicana*, vol. I.
[19] Message of President Díaz to Congress, 1910.

The Revolution did not succeed in overcoming this fault which has become part and parcel of Mexican diplomacy. One of the immense difficulties of the revolutionary period was to implement a new policy without being able to count on adequate diplomatic means of articulating that policy. This flaw was particularly noticeable when the Revolution was finally established. It became apparent that frequently Mexico found herself operating in a vacuum, lacking the proper experience, and devoid of foreign traditions and clear-cut diplomatic directives.

The fixed goal of independent Mexico has been to develop as a Western country. Bold steps were taken in this direction by those who were connected with the colony, and were later implemented by the imbibers of 19th century liberalism, along with a brusque pruning that all true reform requires. Both types of reformers retained as a goal the progress of the nation, protecting and not destroying her. As Díaz's regime lost this goal, a debasement and depersonalization of the essence of true Mexican values followed. The golden calf of material progress was adored and all else was subjected to enormous wretchedness. The gates were opened to a real and fictitious imitation of foreign values. The aboriginal institutions which even the Colony had respected were ignored. Consequently, when the reaction came, it was a total one. The movement which began in 1910 constitutes a vast and vocal protest against institutions alien to Mexico.

The Revolution of 1910

The Mexican Revolution of 1910 was not based on universal ideologies and it did not lean on foreign values. It was the national conscience requesting a hearing and a return to its hard-won basic rights and privileges. The Revolution clearly stood against the continuation in power of a man who no longer had the support of public opinion and who had ceased to be high-minded towards the foreigner. It stood against an order imposed by force to maintain a status quo which was not supported by the majority. It stood against *latifundios* which were prejudicial to the great indigenous communities. It was against rapid and uncontrolled industrialization which preyed upon urban masses incapable of defending their own rights. It was against exploitation of new mineral resources which were abandoned to those great international enterprises which mushroomed everywhere at the time. Let us add to all this the general protest leveled against the extraterritorial privileges enjoyed by foreigners in Mexico, with its implicit assertion of racial equality, and we shall have the essence of the Revolution.

In the world of the nineteenth century, Mexico passed through a process of revaluating what was really Mexican and of consolidating her own identity. The Mexican Revolution did not seek to be the panacea of the world, but rather it sought what was just and proper for Mexico. The consolidation of the revolutionary government did not bring that universalization of its principles which was present in similar movements elsewhere. French foreign policy after 1789 became aggressive; under the Consulate and the Empire she constituted a great challenge for all of Europe. Soviet foreign policy, insofar as it seeks to change general assumptions, has similar characteristics. Mexican foreign policy, on the other hand, merely sought to implement ideals which were those of the nation: the ideals she had acquired when she was undergoing the trial by fire of her internal and external struggles. Non-intervention and self-determination again took the field as absolute values in Mexican foreign policy.

Huerta's criminal attempt to push things back is a good example of that attitude in foreign affairs against which the Revolution fought. In his report to the Congress in 1913 he spoke of Mexico's obligations to give "solid guarantees of her good will to those peoples with whom she is tied emotionally and by interest."[20] This system of guarantees was false

and contrary to Mexico's traditions and true interests. This accounts for the successful rise of Carranza against Huerta.

As a country which achieved her independence through her own sacrifices, Mexico had no reason to humiliate herself and render obeisance to nations which were materially more powerful. When the usurper's regime ended, Mexico ceased to be one of those nations which danced to the "tune of good will" of the Great Powers. She reaffirmed a Western personality in part, but also an aboriginal personality which was essentially her own. The vigorous protest which Carranza's government made against the validity of the Monroe Doctrine (as included in Article XXI of the League's Covenant) was an indication of Mexico's new independence.[21]

Tradition has unusual strength in Mexican foreign policy. Her revolutionary foreign policy flourishes in its continuity and bequeathes to its successors a line of conduct which presupposes the permanence of a number of elements. It recognizes that Mexico's great problems are internal and not international; that in the community of nations the only thing which small nations require, for their full development, is respect for their sovereignty, the general acceptance of their own laws as being the only ones in force in their own territory, and complete recognition of their equality.[22]

Gradually the Revolution became institutionalized. In external affairs, there were inevitable clashes with those countries which had gained great privileges for themselves in Diaz's Mexico. Of course they refused to give them up. The battle to maintain national integrity by frustrating their attempts to retain their privileges continued up to the opening of the Second World War. The agrarian policy—expropriation of great land holdings, including foreign-held ones—and the policy of giving the nation effective control over her mineral and oil resources, which were almost all in foreign hands, raised serious difficulties with the United King-

[20] Message of General Huerta to Congress, 1913.

[21] Message of President Carranza to Congress, 1918
[22] Message of President Calles to Congress, 1927.

dom and the United States. Again, claims for damages suffered by aliens during the Revolution appeared; again pleas were made for respect of those international norms which are supposedly above the rights of any one government. Political pressure on a weak neighbor was felt over and over again at the moment when a chink was discovered in her armor. But the revolutionary aims triumphed and must be taken into account by all those who would understand Mexican foreign policy and the goals of her diplomacy. For those goals are consistent with Mexico's permanent aims of helping the establishment of an enlightened and peaceful world community, based on the rule of law and always respectful of the right of self-determination of all nations.

FOREIGN POLICY FRAMED BY NATURE [23]

Idealism obscures realities of politics

While the natural endowments upon which a nation builds are important, it is obvious that the most important factor is the use man makes of these endowments. More than one Power, badly situated in terms of resources, has exercised hegemony over her neighbors through wise utilization of men and materials. It is through the work and mental efforts of the inhabitants that the natural endowments are shaped; through them a country achieves her international position and is able to mold her true interests.

Through her long, uncharted and defensive

foreign history, Mexico has come to depend more and more on a spiritual interpretation of history. We observe a conscious and voluntary contempt for those material things which shape international politics. Her statesmen, all through the middle decades of the twentieth century, have insisted on principles, not on interests. The assumption of being able to separate the nation's convictions from the requirements of her development underlie the whole concept. The same separation is observed with regard to certain principles whose force is reiterated with disregard to the realities of the world in which the nation lives. There is an insistence on the necessity of speaking about peace in a world which denies coexistence; about disarmament when we find ourselves in the midst of a gigantic arms race, and when, in our own sphere, the majority of the Hispanic-American countries are armed to the teeth. The needs of a population which is growing at an accelerated rate are never squared with the high goals which the nation as a whole is seeking. Time and time again, throughout almost a century, principles have been affirmed which present obstacles in the development of foreign policy plans which might benefit Mexico. Current international problems are not handled like an instrument which can be used by the Mexican government to further the immediate well-being of her citizens.

From among the several elements which shape her policy in the international community, Mexico has discarded the material ones. She relies almost exclusively on that element which shows "Mexicanism" to be a spiritual value. She either ignores the rest, or interprets them through the prism of her personality. Ours is a people made up of diverse racial groups which have not varied in the course of history, although there has been a lengthy process of unification and also of purification. Neither the character of the population nor its social habits have been substantially altered over the years.[24] The goal has always been to

[23] This title, and those which follow, have been taken from the report which the members of the Provisional Junta of the Empire—Ascaràte, Heras, and Sanchez Enciso—gave on Mexican foreign policy in the year 1821. Changes in contents, dictated by the changing needs of the times, have been made. *Archivo Histórico-Diplomático*, 1st series, vol. 33.

[24] A. von Humboldt, *Essai sur la Nouvelle Espagne*, Paris: 1811, vol. 1, p. 428 ff.; Victor L. Urquidi, *Pro-*

build a national being which is wholly upright and unified.

Geographical factors

Geography has helped considerably. To the great Pre-Columbian Indian population was added the Spanish population. Outside of these two groups, no other group had a substantial share in the formation of contemporary Mexico. A lengthy hybridization, now largely completed, has taken place during the period since the Revolution. There finally emerged an intermixed race, part European, part Indian, with one foot in the Old World, the other in the New. It offers its own interpretation of values, and while it belongs to the West, it is also profoundly linked to its Indian antecedents. The fact is, that this people developed in the face of a dual challenge imposed on it by the geography of the high plateau and by the lack of natural protection against its neighbors, both to the North and to the South.

Mexico has been called a geographic region of transition. From North America come her great mountain chains and great plains which make up the northern steppes of her territory. The ranges are joined together on the Isthmus of Tehuantepec where Meso-America begins. Clear geographical barriers do not exist either to the North or to the South. Once the Mississippi was crossed, nothing separated Mexico from the United States; in the North, then, she inherited a geo-political situation which was weak and indefensible. This is the reason for the existence today of an immense frontier of about 1,864 miles in length, which in part follows the Rio Grande and the Colorado, but which is exposed and unarmed. Even less precise is the border with Guatemala and Belize. The arbitrary character of the line explains the

---

blemas fundamentales de la economía mexicana, Cuadernos Americanos, 1961. Ifigenia M. de Navarrete, *La distribución del ingreso y el desarrollo económico de México.*

lengthy dispute with the former over Chiapas and Soconuzco. As for Belize, there exists the eventual possibility of extending the 17° 49′ line to divide a territory which never should have abandoned its Hispanic-American sovereignty.

As a region of transition, Mexico was subject to invasions. Her mountains served as an outer fort for a civilization which arose as an answer to the challenge that the high plateau provides. At a brief distance from the coasts—which until a short time ago were inhospitable and unhealthy—the two great ranges rise up and form between them an immense basin. It is there that the modern Mexico has developed, which today is beginning to extend herself to the most remote confines of her territory. The coasts, with their outer barriers, have served to isolate her.

On the high plateau there has developed a people which is manly, noble, and strong, but a people which does not like to look beyond the horizon of its mountains. The mountains are congenital for Mexicans; they know them and love them. From beyond them according to an experience already embodied in the Quetzalcoatl legend, come whites and bearded invaders. Mexicans have thus interpreted their future according to the development of their inner values. And instead of serving her as a barrier against the world, as a point of departure for external adventures, the Mexican mountain ranges form the natural seat of the nation, a place where her desires freely take flight and her hopes are firmly grounded.

This strong and noble attitude is appropriate to a people imprisoned by isolation. However, it offers a scant foundation for a foreign policy. It is an attitude based upon feelings rather than rational thought. There is an idea of what the country feels, but no analysis of what she requires. A position of principle, one wholly upright if seen from the immense heights of the Mexican high plateau, seems a little unreal when it descends to the details of implementation.

Since details do not form a part of Mexico's personality, they receive little attention. The spokesmen of Mexico reiterate, with laudatory consistency, the great ideals on which the conduct of the nation is based. On the other hand, they do not worry about counterposing the real situation of the globe with the policy of principles which they follow; nor do they ask themselves about the need for altering the former to fit the new currents which, like strong winds, sweep today's world.

Natural resources

The utilization of the country's resources to satisfy the needs of her growing population offers us a living example of the kind of foreign policy pursued by Mexico. The country was considered rich, immensely rich. Unbridled romanticism refused to come to terms with reality. Following this epoch of unwholesome optimism, successive governments concerned themselves with the proper development of Mexico. Since the partitioning of 1848, Mexico has neither had the territory nor the resources to become a Great Power. But she does contain large reserves, which are in part unexplored: there are regions where scarcely any exploration has taken place.

For the future, Mexico places her hopes on her own resources. A constant, uninterrupted development is offered as the legitimate call to glory for the revolutionary administrations. This move forward is, to a great extent, provoked and followed by a growth in population. This growth is so gigantic that it seems to repeat the myth of the cask of Danaides. The more efforts are made to raise the standard of living of the Mexicans, the more difficult it becomes because of the rapidly increasing number of mouths, which seem to multiply at a geometric rate.

In spite of this dilemma, Mexico has never departed from her principles. She persists in separating what her real position should be in the eyes of the world, from the benefits which a policy linked more closely to today's world might give the Mexicans. Other, less isolated countries, work to receive all kinds of help from the great opposing Powers. They play the game of political compromise with their votes in international organizations, and they collect from both the Right and the Left in the delicate game of international equilibrium.

In pursuing norms which are now a century old, Mexico insists on not mixing the direction of her international conduct with the needs of her people. This duality of purposes, which is pregnant with consequences, appears ominous. Meanwhile the dizzy race of industrial development, which is one of the great revolutions of our time, continues. And there is always the danger of getting to the table too late, where there are many guests and little food.

The national interests of Mexico, then, are interpreted in keeping with tradition. Traditionally, she tries to apply the principles of equity and justice to all nations, which she supposes to be free to determine their own role independently. Mexico subordinates the development of the country to an ideal world which is scarcely visible, and she believes that her interests should be planned not in immediacy, nor even in the statesman's life-time, but rather for a better world in the future. In such a world disputes will be reduced to finding out which of the contenders can be more useful to humanity, with scorn for nations which are only pursuing narrow selfish interests.

Mexico considers herself as the pioneer of the world of the future, as a nation able to dodge the dangers which enemies pose for her and able to consolidate herself in spite of ambitious thrusts. She believes that in today's international society it is enough to rely on her dignity and firmness. To attain the well-being of her children and the industrialization which the nation requires, it is not necessary to veer from her great framework. Offense is a vain ostentation. For her defense, all that Mexico needs, as of old, is the determination of Mexicans to be free.

In a world where violence and ambition reign, where even neutrality is made into a positive weapon, Mexico is proud of being a quiet pool of concord and peace. She does not believe that she is tied to the great struggles which are moving the world today; she still believes that her greatest contribution to the world resides in the worth of her example. This scorning of her interests constitutes one of the distinctive characteristics of her foreign policy. But in its implementation we find some alterations which are an indispensable concession to reality. With this dual doctrine—composed of the highest principles and of a minimum of concessions to those real pressures which are always present in the world of international politics—Mexico faces those nations to which she is perpetually tied by her geographical position: the contiguous states and the Caribbean world.

The United States—powerful northern neighbor

To her north, Mexico finds one of the Great World Powers. The leaders of this country watch the entire globe with attentive eyes. They are concerned over the great struggle between very different social systems, a struggle which characterizes our time. Mexico's own purposes are in no way contrary to those of her powerful neighbor. The Revolution has set forth the general lines of her conduct; she is above all concerned with increasing the well-being of her citizens and she attempts to maintain herself apart from the main stream formed by the great international currents of today.

Adjustment of earlier grievances　When the interests of the United States were less extensive, and when her investments in Mexican territory were much larger, there were great difficulties. These have been resolved. Mexico has made payments for expropriations and debts of other kinds. New and more precise norms fix and check North American investments. An equilibrium between the two expansive forces both within and without their respective borders, seems to have been found. At the end of more than a century of coexistence, under the aegis of the Good-Neighbor Policy, understanding was brought about through both

countries working within the law. They have agreed to ignore their great differences in power and have acted in accordance with a common interest. Since 1933—perhaps since 1928—there have existed between Mexico and the United States understanding, good-will, and very close relations which were maintained both during and since World War II.

Relations between the two nations are excellent, barely upset by small ripples which break the calm surface. One would assume then, that a definitive solution had been found for good neighborly conduct. However, upon close examination it is obvious that the present policy is merely postponing real problems and that relations between these two states are headed for rough seas.

Recent economic grievances　The strategic necessities in the struggle against communism clearly determine the policy of the United States. All other considerations are inexorably postponed. This explains her armament policy, the extension of her military bases, the enormous need for allies and finally even the policy of giving aid to countries like Yugoslavia which are attempting to follow a somewhat independent policy towards the Kremlin. The defense policy of the United States is joined to another which is derived from her internal conditions: that of maintaining an extremely high standard of living for her citizens, even though this means following policies which are harmful to the weaker nations. Virtually self-sufficient, the United States is not content to export manufactured goods. She is among the great exporters of raw materials, agricultural products among others, and this is done under conditions which are unfavorable to the less developed countries. The United States is following a dual policy: political-military consolidation and economic expansion in several lines of production.

Mexico's economy suffers from the whims of these policies. The losses which she has suffered because of the large sales of United States cotton are typical. Mexico's development depends on large and steady sales of raw materials. The natural market for these materials is the United States. But these exports from Mexico run into serious difficulties: tariffs are altered frequently, and prices are subject to great fluctuations. It becomes prohibitive to continue mineral production or the raising of certain crops which have been developed solely because of the American market.

Because of her consciousness of world interests, the United States refuses to concede to Mexico the same favored position politically that she has geographically. Mexico is simply thrown in with all other nations who petition the United States. And among the petitioners she receives consideration which is prejudicial to her. She has less to offer than others in the first line of defense against communism because of her geographical location. Moreover, Mexican foreign policy, founded on principles, seeks respect, rather than privileges. Reciprocity is a fundamental element which cannot be ignored in international politics; it can be ignored even less today when interests of a universal order unbalance the equilibrium among the Great Powers. Mexico, then, is disturbed to find herself placed way down the list of priorities which the United States has established in granting foreign aid.

Because of her historical development and because of vocal and inflexible public opinion at home, Mexico cannot tie onto the war-like wagon of the United States. Her long tradition as being the northernmost post of a different civilization prevents her from doing it. She cannot, then, grant to the United States the counterparts to technical and economic aid which the latter demands either directly or indirectly.

If Mexico were self-sufficient she could overlook these considerations. But her dependence on the United States is great with regard to her role as supplier, her need for foreign aid to keep up with the accelerated rate of her population growth, and with the rate of development of other countries. Mexico, then, is clearly in a position of inferiority. If this situation, in the long run, is not corrected—and perhaps the fund started by The Alliance for Progress does remedy the situation—it might bring the policies of the two nations into serious conflict sooner or later.

Other points of friction   There are a variety of other problems. Some problems have grown out of the limitations placed upon investments in Mexico. There is also the persistent problem created by the migrant workers. Even more delicate is the problem of the people of Mexican origin who live in the states of the Union which were formerly a part of Mexico. They continue bound to Mexico's traditions, to her language, and her customs. Their constant and pathetic petitions made to Mexican consular officials make it clear that the problems of this minority could raise serious differences between the two nations. There also remain certain territorial problems: that of Chamizal and the Pacific Islands. All of these problems are aggravated by the general stance of the United States which is inclined to be impatient towards those problems which seem small and which affect a country whose policy is of secondary importance in the fight against communism.

Mexico's policies towards the United States are extremely apt. She has tried to deal with the United States by completely ignoring the role which the strength of each plays between them. The history of the last fifteen years shows the correctness of Mexico's policy. But such a policy is based on the existence of conditions which, in the context of the Cold War and the preponderant interests of the United States in the world, seem to be transitory. Opposing interests will come into play; they already exist and they are basic.

Central America—exacting southern neighbor

A policy of strict non-intervention is operative in the relations between Mexico, Guatemala and Central America. From the moment in which these countries became independent, Mexico has applied this policy with great strictness.[25] If a distant region were involved, with

[25] *Archivo Histórico—Diplomático,* 1st series, vol. 33, p. 28.

other interests at play, then this policy of strict respect for the self-determination of peoples could be beneficent. But it involves a geographical unit to which Mexico belongs. She had ample and close bonds with those republics during the colonial period; her greater development, and the fact of having served as a reference point and as a cultural center, make it impossible for her to ignore what happens south of her border.

The traditional policy, moreover, could be justified if she had obtained from those peoples the good-will and affection which such abstentionism seeks. However, persistent signs point to just the opposite. Central America is divided into five diverse, and at times, antagonistic entities, and the region has found itself caught in a sea of problems and a never-ending stream of outmoded interests. Foreign aid is indispensable to Central America. Mexico, because of her position and tradition, is the one who should provide it.

Causes of friction There exists among these republics the traditional opposition held by small countries against a stronger one. Historical wounds (like Guatemala's over Mexican annexation of Chiapas and Soconuzco, or Nicaragua's over the intervention of 1928) have not yet healed over. In the face of the apparent indifference of Mexico, a whole series of ominous events occur intermittently. Such an event was the help received by Guatemala in 1958 from other Central American states in connection with the incident when several Mexican fishermen were machine-gunned and some were killed. Another such event is the verdict against Mexico which these countries have pronounced with regard to the future of Belize.

For Central America, Mexico is the Great Power of the North. Talleyrand's statement comes to the point: intervention and non-intervention hide the same concept in seemingly contradictory terms. It is inevitable that the smaller states of this region should attribute to the Mexican policy of non-intervention the perverse intention of leaving them in the bad situation in which they find themselves. It does not seem like a policy dictated by a respect for other peoples, but rather by an extremely serene selfishness.

Mexican ties to the Caribbean Mexico has geographical and historical obligations towards these countries which she cannot shrug off. So long as she does not implement a positive policy in which the Central American countries feel the warmth of friendship and an interest which is alert to their future, there will prevail in these nations currents of thought which may be contrary to Mexico's interests.

The Caribbean is, as Humboldt said, the Mediterranean of America. And as a mediterranean sea, it undoubtedly affects the continent and the riparian countries. The Caribbean has been the least tranquil region of America and the one that shows greatest backwardness. In the past this was a "pirate's nest," the weak spot which was exploited by Spain's enemies. This region was omitted from the great emancipation movement of 1810. It became a melting pot of races foreign to America and taken there by imperial interests.

Tied to this melting pot by geography, Mexico should have participated actively, and from the beginning, in its evolution. Such was the meaning of the initial policy of dominating Cuba, directly or indirectly, given the fact that Havana, during the entire colonial period, was the great military port of New Spain. This policy was also revealed by not ceding Belize to England and holding on to this territory until the late nineteenth century.

Non-intervention These initial policies were soon abandoned, in part, for political reasons. One reason was the profound isolation of a nation which was concerned above all with seeking solutions to urgent internal problems. Another factor which influenced policy were the conditions which prevail along the Mexican Caribbean coast: to the unhealthy climate is added the inhospitable Atlantic coast. There is also added the obstacle presented by the Mayan people until very recently. The cohesion of this group and their lack of unity with the nation, made of the Yucatan Peninsula more of a barrier than a route to the Caribbean.

As a result of these varied factors, Mexico turned her back on the Caribbean. Her Central-American policy of strict non-intervention is coupled with one of strictly ignoring this region. The great problems which have developed on her own doorstep have not elicited any positive action on her part. She has done little to put an end to colonialism aside from declarations, which are more theoretical than real, usually put forward at Inter-American meetings.

Towards Belize she has followed a strictly territorial and juridical policy. Later, policy is to be based on the idea of self-determination of the people who inhabit that colony. The Caribbean dictators, at times ferocious, have brought no reactions whatsoever from Mexico. Until the seventh meeting of American foreign ministers decided to break relations with the Dominican government, Mexico had not taken part in a movement which is concerned with guiding the political future of the Caribbean.

Trends of future policy As a result of this lengthy inaction, Mexico finds herself facing situations which profoundly affect her, but which she is no longer able to direct. The future development of the islands of the West Indies, and the status of Belize, will alter the equilibrium of this region. And the Cuban Revolution, in itself a consequence of many, many years of political corruption and colonial exploitation, also creates a situation of primary importance for Mexico.

Intimate geographical and strategic ties make it impossible for Mexico to maintain a position of onlooker with regard to what happens in Cuba. Towards the revolutionary government, she seeks refuge in her traditional policy of non-intervention. She believes that this government constitutes one more stage in the self-determination of the Cuban people. With this policy, she is trying to face the situation which changes assumptions which have existed since the Clayton-Bulwer Treaty (1850) which established Anglo-Saxon supremacy in the "American Mediterranean." Leaning on her conscience of law and on the free determination of peoples, Mexico acts on the assumption that the Cuban Revolution will unfold without affecting her own development. Her development, she thinks, is already mapped out by the axioms of her own revolution and has already borne fruit in the patent progress which can be observed in the Mexican nation.

FOREIGN RELATIONS FRAMED BY DEPENDENCE

Traditional ties to the West

The hegemony exercised by the Western World permitted it to carry its flags to the ends of the earth. Mexico was one of the first victims of that expansion. Since that time she has formed a part of the Western World, first as a colony, then as a country impregnated by Western religion and values.

Towards the end of the last century, Mexico established an equilibrium between her membership in the Western World and her own unique identity. Armed collection of debts and military intervention ceased; Mexico offered herself as a fertile field for capital investments and she became Europeanized through imitation. She appeared satisfied with the fact that the nations of the Old World considered her civilized.

The Revolution brought with it a return to what was genuinely her own; imitation disappeared and things Mexican again predominate. It was necessary to achieve this new equilibrium. New situations had to be faced. Europe had undergone fundamental changes. Her hegemony ceased; her internal battles precipitated her decline and she no longer claimed to be the cultural and political center of the earth. Mexico offered to this "New West" contributions which were exceptional, coming from a country which is Western because of a fortunate and unique hybridization.

There are limitations in the participation of Mexico as a part of the new Western World.

Mexico cannot offer full support in economic matters. Her people have a very low per capita income. Her methods for developing her resources are not attractive to Europe's interests. Mexico does find some enlightened groups in Europe—in the Low Countries, for instance—who believe that future advantages can be gained through understanding and co-operation. But other nations are more determined to keep what they have than to work towards general progress. Co-operation with nations whose eyes are riveted on their own interests and welfare only, is far from easy.

In political affairs, the differences are even greater. Mexico, now sure of herself and conscious of her own personality, claims the role of the representative of principles which have not been able to flourish in Europe. Respect for the effectiveness of international law has become a dogma for her. The ideal of peaceful co-existence is basic to all of her international doctrines, as is the idea that evolutionary progress of peoples is possible without armed battles. These are, doubtlessly, European principles; but in the West the Great Power complex has been operative and the principles of law have been largely ignored.

It was opportune and natural that these unorthodox voices should exist in times when the Western group enjoyed hegemony. They rounded out the European ideals; they made evident the value of Western hybridization in foreign civilizations, and they opened new horizons for the reaffirmation of values by countries which brought many of their own values with them.

Disagreements with Western policies

Such conditions no longer exist. Heterodoxy is no longer welcome and the need for loyal allies is great. The following example is symptomatic of this condition: in the United Nations certain issues, such as colonial problems, which affect vital Western interests are frequently discussed. Resolutions are presented which come from the Western and anti-Western countries. The policy of Mexico is to vote on the resolutions in an impartial manner: her representatives try to find the truth which opposing viewpoints hide. This position is not appreciated by the Western leaders who want a vote in their favor; they will accept abstention; but they do not take kindly to an independent compromise which tries to mediate differences which they believe cannot be arbitrated.

In the debates over many great issues which have come before the United Nations, Mexico finds herself separated from the Western bloc. In colonial matters, she cannot forget that she was a colony and obtained her independence with her children's blood. In the "Cold War" she does not lend "understanding ears" to the continuous and tenacious struggle against communism, and she looks skeptically upon the reiterated affirmation by the Europeans of their belief in strength only to keep peace. In the continuous arms race she counts herself among the critics of the West; she keeps insisting that it is necessary to postpone the suicidal race, that it is indispensable that armament monies be utilized for the development and betterment of those peoples who are still impoverished. The heterodox then becomes a heretic.

For her part, Mexico cannot expect from the West either new moral doctrines or advantageous political alignments. Present economic realities are of greater importance than cultural or historical bonds. The current revolts of peoples against Western states are a strong reminder of the past. Mexico finds herself, then, seriously separated from the West. Her policies do not coincide with those of the West and her aspirations are different.

A progressive Westernization of Mexico's foreign policy seems impossible; the historical being of Mexico revolts against it. In its zealous struggle to get Allies, the West scorns every aid which may be sensible but which is conditioned by non-Western interests. The Western Powers even go to the extreme of aiding, above all, those governments whose only reason for existence is anti-communism; or else, those whose geographical position singles them out as being on the boundary lines of the "common enemy" of the West.

The coincidence of interests is scanty; great, on the other hand, is the weight of tradition. Not far behind is the fact of Mexico's geographic proximity to a country, which, though not a European nation, is the country which today is the leader of the West. On the one hand, Mexico persists in preaching international European principles; she insists on believing that the future of humanity depends on the defense of the values achieved by this civilization. But within these principles, she maintains a firm position in her heterodoxy. As such, one can understand her persistent aid, now the only source left, to the Spanish Republican government. This deviation from her policy of non-intervention is firmly founded on Western values. Mexico considers herself as the warden of Western principles; she refuses, with characteristic firmness, to bend in the face of new political situations.

On the other hand, the proximity of the United States makes absolute freedom in the choice of alternative roads impossible. Mexico cannot consider, without incurring the gravest possible consequences, a break with the Western world. Such a break would harass the vital interests of the United States. Both Mexico and the United States need a minimum of good relations if they are to have "peaceful co-existence." That minimum would not exist if Mexico were to break with the Western tradition. It can be said, with regard to the West, that Mexican policy leans towards an "inverted neutralism."

Ties to the Latin American community

A second kind of dependence in which Mexico finds herself is that of belonging to the Latin American community. Such as it arose during the 19th century, the ideal of Latin American unity has always been one of the guide posts of Mexican policy. In 1927 Calles affirmed that "the pure and noble and traditional family ties which unite us with the Latin American nations have not been relaxed even for a moment." A similar concept was confirmed by Ruiz Cortines when he reported to Congress on the meeting of American presidents which took place in Panama in 1956. He reiterated the fact that Mexico is participating in the embodiment of Bolivar's ideal of making America a continent of friendship and international collaboration.[26] This was an excellent statement of a general objective. But it is necessary to get to the kernel of the problems which confront Latin America in her political, economic, and cultural development if we are to become aware of how significant Latin American unity is as a policy.

It is not enough to talk about the family union which should exist among nations which speak the same language, have similar customs, and venerate the same God with the same rites. What is necessary is to point out in what form that idea of Latin American unity contributes to the achievement of the national goals of Mexico; how it obstructs those aims, and how Mexico contributes to the Bolivarian ideal of unity.

In her larger aims, such as peace, international co-operation for economic development and co-existence within the context of self-determination among peoples, Mexico finds herself completely identified with the policy followed by the other Latin American republics. But this identification disappears if we try to give content to these general directives.

Disagreements with Latin American neighbors

In a world which notes the disappearance of Caucasian predominance, racial problems have acquired bold relief. And in this area, Latin American attitude is far from uniform. Coun-

[26] Message of President Calles to Congress, September 1, 1927; Message of President Ruiz Cortines to Congress, September 1, 1956.

tries with a large percentage of *mestizos* indicate their inclination towards favoring colored peoples; those of Creole origin—or those dominated by a Creole minority which dates from colonial times—appear much more closely linked to Europe. As a defender of racial equality and the elimination of colonialism in all its forms, Mexico is far from able to find support from all of her sister republics. Coexistence and racial equality, to which Mexico aspires, do not find a general Latin American echo.

No great political differences should exist if a group of nations is to act together, and thus buttress the foreign policy aims of each nation of the group. But Latin American history is replete with wars which gave clear-cut rights to the victors. Such contests have left resentments which spark anew at the slightest provocation. Neighbors wait for the moment when they can overthrow a status quo which they believe unjust; the victors fear such an eventuality. This results in an arms-building policy which is followed by almost all Latin American nations. Of course, this does not lessen tension. Mexico finds almost no echo for her policy of frank and loyal international co-operation coupled with a policy of complete disarmament, starting at home. In matters of armaments and territorial disputes Mexico does not deviate from her consistent foreign policy. But the great majority of the republics continue to support large armies and navies as the best arguments in favor of their rights thus endangering the whole gamut of their development.

Latin Americans should have a profound understanding of what Mexico is, of her aspirations, and the degree to which she is ready to make sacrifices for her ideals. But there exists among Latin American republics an immense and reciprocal ignorance of present policies, of their development, and even of their past history. It is not unusual for news stories originating in one of the republics to reach another by means of the "interested filter" of American or European news agencies. These filters—and the large background of ignorance and indifference—remove the content of the role to which Mexico aspires: to serve as an accurate barometer of continental social evolution. Consequently a "spiritual communion" is not achieved by either Mexico which has assumed that responsibility, or by those who should benefit from her experiences.

Common interests in Latin America

The help which Latin America gives to Mexico in the prosecution of her universal ideals is negative. Mexican–Latin American relations take on another aspect when they involve the continent itself. We find that increasing and immediate attention is being given to economic matters. These nations worry above all about the well-being of their peoples and find that "unity does constitute strength." Disagreements which arise from differences in the degree of their development do exist; but superimposed on this factor is the conviction that they are all in a similar position.

Hence, one can understand the importance of joint programs like CEPAL, the Economic and Social Inter-American Council, and the Latin American "common market." A great framework for joint economic development, as an alternative to inaction which only perpetuates low standards of living, has appeared. It offers a real guarantee for industrialized countries of the outside world. In the field of economic co-operation Mexico finds herself in complete agreement with her sister republics. The persistent struggle which Mexico has made to raise the Inter-American system to full-fledged economic co-operation counts on the substantial support, and reveals the unity of purpose, of twenty nations.[27]

There is another matter which should not be overlooked. The Inter-American system has tried to make a reality of representative democracy, not only as an internal goal, but also in the belief that it is required as a prerequisite

[27] Victor L. Urquidi, *Trayectoria del Mercado Común Latinoamericano*.

for international peace and tranquility. Let us leave aside the basis for this belief which comes directly from Rousseau. Let us note instead the failure of Mexican efforts to bring the continent closer to this ideal. The Mexican belief in democracy as the basic foundation of international peace is genuine and firm. But not many regimes have traversed the immense distance which separates them from that ideal, even if it is reduced to its most modest proportions. The principle of non-intervention appears in this context contrary to the democratic ideal; consequently the duality of purposes and policies continues.

The Bolivarian ideal of democracy tied to the goal of union could provide the foundation on which the Hispanic America of the future could be built. United, and at the same time, democratic, the republics which once formed a part of the Spanish Empire could play a leading role in the conduct of international affairs.

Mexico reiterates the existence of family ties with these republics, and we can conclude that she is still thinking in terms of unity. But it is not a question of unity which is political in its essence and Bolivarian in its manifestations. It rests on the ideal of non-intervention, on the primacy of juridical forms which postpone problems in order to permit their eventual solution, and on the autonomy and equality of all the peoples of America.

Conditions are much different today from what they were when Mexico achieved nationhood. Today's Mexico's Latin-American policy takes for granted that all of the Republics will not act together to obtain benefits which embrace the whole continent. Instead her policy is embodied in the application, somewhat theoretical, of juridical processes which are in keeping with Latin American thought (at least up until the time of the Cuban Revolution). Mexico understands her dependence on Latin America and has helped to shape the bilateral and multilateral paths that have developed. She understands this relationship in its widest possible context. She also believes that in helping to guide this multifaceted and even anarchistic evolution of the New World lies her true destiny and her greatest strength.

FOREIGN RELATIONS FRAMED BY NECESSITY

The twentieth century has witnessed the rise of multilateral relations carried on through permanent universal organizations. In these organizations is embodied the hope of finding new pathways which might assure peace and progress. Mexico participated in the first Hague Conference in 1899, and has been active in new organizations as they have developed. This generalization is true in spite of her long absence from the League of Nations.

Great and Small Powers participate in international organizations. The former have as a norm the present or future protection of their interests. The latter act, frequently, under the influence of parochialism, dwarfed by cowardice and indifferent to what does not affect them directly. Mexico cannot be counted among the former; but she is freed from the defects of the latter group by her firm and noble position in world affairs, by her well-founded idealism. With almost uninterrupted frequency her spokesmen are found among those who defend the applicability of principles of equity and of justice.

The proper scope of United Nations activities

Mexico participated in the San Francisco Conference which formally adopted the Charter of the United Nations. Her activities in that Conference were aimed at the achievement of universal peace and at the establishment of an organization which would benefit the whole world. The amendments she suggested to the Dumbarton Oaks proposals were very extensive; they sought to establish the principle of equality within the new organization and the principle of assuring the representation of the interests of all peoples. She did not seek the consolidation of rights which she thought should be protected by the new organization. She believed herself to be outside of the zones of tension of the postwar period. Consequently she attempted to synthesize the views which were to the advantage of all countries which were not Great Powers.

Some of Mexico's proposals were included in the Charter. Since then, Mexico has maintained the same position she took in 1945. She still believes that her own development permits her to avoid all international problems. She is proud of the fact that the organization has not had to concern itself with any Mexican problem and she continues acting as if her contribution embodies the conscience of mankind. "I have nothing to win," she seems to be saying, "by co-operating with other states in the solution of problems which are of no special interest to me. I do it out of a spirit of brotherhood, inspired by justice."

Mexico participates in the United Nations convinced that she has no specific international objectives. Her traditional non-intervention is transformed, within the United Nations, into a generic intervention which is beneficial to all. She tries to temper the inflexibility of a bilateral principle with the dictates of the general interest. Thus we witness that over and over again Mexico has insisted on the jurisdiction of the organization in cases which the interested states have considered to be matters of internal jurisdiction. She has established a tenuous but clear dividing line: she considers those acts through which one or several Powers try to implement their own purposes as being intervention; but no intervention takes place when it is a matter of applying the principles of the Charter in such cases as those involving the self-determination of all peoples, racial equality, or the establishment of representative democracy.

To these general positions can be added— as an inevitable concession to political realities —a certain flexibility concerning concrete problems. In these problems, Mexico does not act with the same vigor and clarity. Mexico's position usually rests on a restrictive interpretation of the domain of the United Nations when there is a conflict regarding the jurisdiction reserved to the nation. As a Small Power which has endured long decades of intervention, as a country which could not count on the internal tranquility necessary for implementing her own reforms, Mexico is not inclined to support completely and without restrictions the role of international organizations.

Disagreements with United Nations policies

It is in the field of collective security where we find the best example of her position. Mexico has not been able to rise to the point of understanding that collective security implies individual responsibilities, that it carries with it heavy fiscal charges, and that it can even require the shedding of blood of her own citizens. She has abstained from contributing, in personnel or financially, to the various collective operations which have been carried out by the United Nations. Likewise, she has opposed the creation of machinery which would make collective action somewhat automatic. But in spite of this attitude, she expresses faith in the United Nations. She believes that its very existence constitutes the best safeguard for the preservation of peace; she believes that as far as the existence of an international secular arm is concerned, it is not necessary to go beyond the bounds of principles.

Evolving modifications in the recognition of human rights as the basis of international law have not been accepted by Mexico. She remembers the constant interventions involving those rights in the past, how they were interpreted in favor of foreigners, and how they served to impose an extra-territorial regime on the country. Hence she looks with grave misgivings on any development which implies a reduction of her sovereignty, and on any new development that might be used as a pretext for foreign intervention. This explains the failure of Mexico—until very recently—to grant diplomatic immunity to representatives of international organizations, a status she believes should be reserved for diplomatic envoys.

A policy based on principle gives force and cohesion to Mexican policy in the United Nations; but as a counterpart, it becomes somewhat immune to the changes which occur within the organization. The opportunities for exercising greater influence, when the center of power within the organization moved from the Security Council to the General Assembly, passed without Mexico taking advantage of the change. The very substantial weight of the Afro-Asian bloc within the organization does not seem to be sufficiently appreciated. These former colonial countries loom as a majority which can impose itself on the Assembly, or, at the very least, halt all action which it opposes. These new nations, moreover, are the recipients of great amounts of international technical and financial aid. They are also adamant anti-colonialists who might not easily be satisfied with Mexico's view of the requirements of equilibrium and good sense.

The present situation in the United Nations is different from that of the immediate postwar period. The danger lies, consequently, in the possibility that Mexico may overlook her interests in favor of time-worn principles which cannot be immediately implemented. On some occasions she has acted in clear-cut defense of her interests; the weight of her influence has then been decisive. Such was the case during the two conferences concerned with limits of the territorial sea. Mexico's interests rested on safeguarding her rights to a strip of the sea which was wider than the present recognized limits. In pursuit of her goal she could count on the necessary strength to prevent the acceptance of new rules which were against her best interests.

Regional security—
The Organization of American States

The Organization of American States is shaped by its continental roots: it answers regional needs and it has its own goals. This organization presents an essentially different field for the development of Mexican foreign policy.

The union of two elements which are so dissimilar, albeit opposite (as are the Latin American countries and the United States), took place at an especially auspicious time. The United States had abandoned her policy of territorial expansion in America and wanted to be able to count on large new markets for her industrial production. The Latin American countries, who had tried in vain to form some unified organization of their own, agreed to accept an organization which had wider geographical boundaries and which encompassed more than the members of the Latin civilization. The Pan-American Union was established; regularly scheduled Inter-American Conferences were held; little by little juridical principles which were generally acceptable were agreed upon; United States' Good Neighbor Policy flourished; and an excellent constitution for a regional organization emerged in the form of a Charter, a pact for the settlement of disputes in the Western Hemisphere (the Charter of the O.A.S. and the Pact of Bogotá, 1948), and a pact of mutual defense (Treaty of Rio, 1947).

It would thus seem that union among these twenty-one republics has been realized to a degree without precedent in history. Once the differences which had divided them had been solved, their statesmen discovered that conception of continental unity which geography itself had determined. The New World presented itself as a united entity, under a law common to all, able to defend itself collectively and to seek jointly a solution to its diverse needs and problems. But the postwar era brought with it contrary elements which pointed to some cracks in an edifice which seemed to be so solid. As recent events have shown, this organization was built upon certain political assumptions; these assumptions were not stable, not susceptible of being crystallized, but essentially changeable. In fact, it is difficult to understand why the framers of the organization did not prepare for accommodation to political changes which were bound to come.

The need for reforming the O.A.S.

Divergent U.S. interests   The O.A.S. as a juridical edifice comes close to reaching perfection. But it has done nothing to bridge the gap that exists between the perfection of norms and patent political realities. This organization was based on conditions which existed before the Second World War. The same conditions are not operative today. For one thing, the United States is no longer a continental nation. Her interests no longer rest on her desire to maintain the New World as a refuge for the cast-offs of the Old World. Buried in her "grand strategy" of containing communism, the United States is not able to place the O.A.S. in the pre-eminent position which it presupposes as essential for the interests of the New World.

Latin America does not want to participate in the struggle against communism, nor can she do so in the way that the United States does. A Mexican statesman has affirmed that Mexico "cannot be a disinterested spectator to the downfall of civilization,"[28] but when the struggle is underground and obscure, people cannot be asked to make sacrifices which only the crisis of war can justify. Nor can it be believed that the defense of the interests of the great neo-continental Power are to the best advantage of the small neo-continental Powers. The identity of interests and the unity of viewpoints which existed before the war between the United States and Latin America has ended. This is the conclusion to which international developments give rise, as far as Mexico is concerned. It is a conclusion shared by many countries in the hemisphere.

Perpetuation of the status quo   One of the great objectives of the O.A.S. is the mainte-

nance of the status quo as it existed on the new continent prior to World War II. It tries to impose peaceful settlements for all controversies, with the protection that this implies for the countries which held significant advantages in the past. It does not recognize the validity of territorial conquests; but it respects as valid those which have already occurred. It also reiterates principles—such as representative democracy, non-intervention, equality of the foreigner in the eyes of the domestic law of any nation—as ideals to be followed today, when the evolution of the world has brought vast changes.

The O.A.S. represents the political past; once it has been crystallized, it impedes all peaceful solutions compatible with the organization itself. It is in this light that the achievements of the organization must be judged. One cannot help noting, at the outset, the great failure of an organization which has not satisfied a single one of the noble aspirations for which it was created. It has made no contribution towards eliminating the remains of colonial rule in America; it has done very little to better the economic situation of the Latin American countries. It has contributed nothing toward strengthening trust and thus obliterating the arms build-up which flourishes in almost all American republics; nor, finally, has it created among the Small Powers the feeling that they can count on the O.A.S. if they have some dispute with the United States. As an instrument of progress, peace, and equality among the member states, the O.A.S. has fallen far short of its ideals.

The regional form which it adopted in 1948 (Bogotá Charter), has been fatal. At that time it was hoped that it would be a positive force in shaping the postwar world. In this it has failed. The O.A.S. understands its function to be one of lessening regional disputes, eliminating possible areas of friction and the correction of continental ills through the application of judicial measures.

Mexico's contribution   Facing up to the great problems which confront the American regional organization is a necessity which can-

[28] Message of President Alemán to Congress, September 1, 1951.

not be postponed. Because of her geographical position, her cultural heritage, and her brilliant history, Mexico is the one which should take the initiative. She has been one of the tireless champions of the principles embodied in the O.A.S.; it is her role to carry out a reconsideration of what a regional organization can be, what its relations with the United Nations should be, and what ends Mexico and the other countries can bring to fruition through such an organization.

But Mexico finds herself caught by her own tradition. She has refused to recognize ever since 1867 that she holds in Latin America a privileged position, that that privilege implies that she should exercise her leadership, that her leadership today is indispensable. As a principle, respect for the self-determination of peoples is above reproach; so is the principle of non-intervention. It is necessary, nonetheless, to adapt them to the majority needs of all international organizations. Mexico will not be able to exercise leadership unless she deviates from her position of strict non-intervention; unless she agrees that the O.A.S. cannot be considered as entirely separate from the rest of the world.

Mexico continues to rely on the application of juridical principles; she believes they are the most adequate method for overcoming the ills which today plague the O.A.S. Her policy reaffirms that there is nothing wrong with the ideals embodied in the articles of the Charter of Bogotá. And over and over again, in the immediate application of principles, in the postponing of problems which seem urgent but which cannot be framed in juridical terminology, she reaffirms her faith in the goodness of justice and her confidence in the application of law.

Mexico is one of the most solid supporters of the O.A.S. And the O.A.S is one of the pillars of Mexican foreign policy. The very existence of the regional organization; the permanent effectiveness which it represents with regard to the juridical principles which are so dear; the negation of the notion that political realities weaken ideals; all these reasons make Mexican policy rest on the O.A.S.

FOREIGN RELATIONS FRAMED BY POLICY

The essence of revolutions

The study of great revolutions leads us to believe that they do not affect the essence of the nation where they occur.[29] They are commotions which confirm and consolidate the character of peoples, who, tired of slow or inefficient evolutionary developments, violently speed up the turning of the wheel of fortune, not to turn it off its course, but simply to speed it up. Those immense movements which apparently upset everything, pass by like great storms. After they have passed, the nation goes back to traditions and external patterns which have been persistent in the past.

The Mexican Revolution has not changed the character or the external traditions of Mexico. It first spread like a prairie-fire. A decade of struggle and commotion followed. But when the fire burned out, it revealed a foreign policy which was identical to the one which existed at the end of the War of Intervention. In Mexico, the revolutionary governments did not constitute a danger for any other countries; they did not aspire to offer any universal solutions; they did not appear under the form of an "old—yet new" kind of imperialism.

It is on this subjective evaluation of its own revolution that Mexico bases its political judgments of other and similar upheavals. She is inclined to judge all revolutions as if they were similar to the Mexican Revolution. The evaluation rotates around the concomitant process of hybridization that any evolution presupposes,

[29] The thesis which Sorel began with his *L'Europe et la Revolution Française* is repeated, among others, by Carr in *A History of Soviet Russia, Socialism in One Country*.

and thus the very characteristics of the hybridizing plant are ignored.

Great social movements, alongside of great struggles which destroy the primacy of the West, have occurred in our century. Mexico's judgment seems, towards them and despite adverse data, arbitrary and immutable. It is based on the conviction that all of these social movements are either similar to, or identical with, the Mexican Revolution. This conviction cannot conceive that any one of them can be the result of imperialistic desires and none of them appear to Mexico as an element that disturbs the peace. She consequently believes that coexistence with the new and revolutionary countries is necessary, possible, and even easy, since they all represent the efforts of peoples to achieve self-determination. It seems incomprehensible to Mexico that peoples who are struggling for self-determination for themselves would be willing to subordinate other peoples, equally desirous of being free.

For the sake of giving absolute supremacy to the revolutionary phenomenon in itself, Mexico ignores the very essence of the nations which have experienced revolutions. She forgets that the Mexican Revolution made peace with the traditions of the country and that these traditions were peaceful and isolationist. She consequently does not attempt to find out what traditions have guided those other countries which have undergone revolutions. The tradition to which these countries return, in many cases, is one of imperialism.

The revolution did not upset the union of Mexico with the West, even though she insisted on following an independent albeit heterodox course. Mexico consequently believes that the other revolutions (Russia's, China's, Islamic Renaissance, independence movements in Africa and the Orient), fall under a similar pattern. As a true mountaineer she is unable to see the main significance of the great movements in the plains. And her policy reveals itself to be incapable of keeping step with the new movements because they are tied to old traditions which stand in judgment on the Western world, the world on whose survival Mexico depends.

The Russian Revolution as seen through Mexican eyes

Mexico judges the Russian Revolution as if Marxism-Leninism had been adopted by a colorless and history-less people. She forgets that Mexico at one time had common boundaries with Czarist Russia, and she ignores the profound distrust her statesmen had towards this country. For the concepts embodied in the report which Azcárate submitted in 1821 seem to have application today: "This great power" he said about Russia "which is stretching her arms around Europe and Asia and seems intent on becoming lord and master of the Old World, also seems to have her eyes set on the New World." Bearing in mind her continuous maritime ventures in Upper California, and her desires to control Lower California, Azcárate continued, "her neighborliness is very dangerous." He concluded that "it is necessary to contain those adventurers; the spark that is not put out at its beginning becomes a spreading fire." As measures to carry out such a policy, he suggested the establishment of naval forces in the Pacific, with stations in Acapulco and Manila, and the signing of a boundary treaty.[30]

With our northern territories lost, Alaska sold, and Russia concerned with Euro-Asiatic expansion, it seemed that there would be no direct contact, or conflicting interests to mar the future. Mexico was able to suppose, for almost a century, that the two nations would develop without even coming into contact. But today one must ask if the old assumptions are still operative and if the October Revolution can cease having an effect upon the achievement of Mexico's interests.

Mexico's isolated place, in the benign shadow of the West, has disappeared. Two successive

[30] *Archivo Histórico-Diplomático,* 1st series, vol. 33, p. 22 ff.

supremacies have occupied the center of the international stage: British naval supremacy, and later, the economic-military supremacy of the United States. But these two supremacies are now in the same position as the *Infantes de Aragón.*" Neither Columbus' world nor Mexico's can follow a road which is immune, thanks to its great surrounding seas, to the great revolutions of our time. The insights of Azcárate are still valid today. The U.S.S.R. is extending her sovereignty over Europe and Asia. In forty years she has satisfied ambitions and desires which the Romanoffs were unable to reach in three hundred years.

Relations between Mexico and the U.S.S.R.

Mexico recognized the U.S.S.R. in 1924. The first diplomatic contact was not a happy one. The U.S.S.R. scorned the Mexican attempt to intercede in the Sino-Soviet dispute. Relations were broken off in 1927, to be renewed within the spirit of optimism of the Great Alliance. Mexico believes that her relations with the U.S.S.R. should be dictated by equality and mutual respect. She voluntarily ignores the political assumptions on which the Soviet government is based: that is, a revolution with universal goals, an unrestricted ideology, traditional expansionism which she has continued to follow since the war; and industrialization which—at the cost of sacrificing two generations—has placed the U.S.S.R. at the head of the economically advanced nations. And above all, she forgets the constant Messianic aspirations of a people which identifies its destiny with that of a Third Rome.

Dealing with the United States as an equal has been a wise policy for Mexico. There is room to doubt that such is the case with the U.S.S.R. The gravitational weight of the Soviet Revolution makes it impossible to restrict it to one country. The Soviet solution for a quick and today indispensable industrialization makes her example increasingly attractive to many nations.

Mexico attempts to preserve her traditional position of friendship and good will towards the U.S.S.R. She does not believe that the U.S.S.R. can endanger Mexico. Her foreign policy is clearly not anti-Soviet. Nevertheless, on a few questions, Mexico is obliged to follow the Western position. Events occur which occasionally require orthodoxy and Mexico then tempers her friendship with the U.S.S.R. by aligning herself with the Western position.

Mexico's ties with the West, combined with her independent position, prevent her from taking the same economic freedoms in the international field which are enjoyed by some countries. We are witnessing an immense battle between the two Great Powers in their attempts to extend their influence over countries which do not form part of the nucleus of either bloc. Some nations receive technical and economic aid from both of the Great Powers. Mexican policy, which is based on ideals and not on her interest, has not been manipulated to reach such a position. She is not one of the principal recipients from the Western bloc because she mistrusts aid which has prejudicial strings attached. And she is totally removed from aid which she could receive from the U.S.S.R.

This is the dignity which Mexico maintains in the face of this great struggle. She is a part of the West, but she does not manifest herself against the East except on few and exceptional occasions. She places her ideals for peaceful co-existence among peoples above her economic betterment, and she believes that her policy of friendship and trust will prevail in the long run. Perhaps Mexican policy is opposed to the political realities of our time; but she brings a breath of fresh air and hope, which are a major international contribution.

Relations with Far Eastern countries

The empire which Japan carved for herself in the Far East awakened nations from lethargy and brought resurgence to the civilizations of that fertile region. If to this awakening we add that of the immense Chinese Empire, we have two of the most important events of our century. The land area which they occupy and the population they contain, the vigor with which they enter the international world, their desire to regain the time lost under the aegis of the West are all vital factors which should not be ignored. However, it seems that Mexico overlooks them.

At one time Spain administered her possessions in the Far East through the Vice Royalty of Mexico. Early Mexican statesmen looked upon Cathay and the Philippines as part of their sphere of influence. But soon—too soon —a Western turn appeared and those former interests were reduced to naught. Even Passion Island, just a short distance away from Mexican coasts, was lost. As an independent nation Mexico has had no real or effective contact with the nations of the Orient. The political alignments which followed the Second World War have intrenched this isolationism rather than changed it. Mexico seems hardly aware of the meaning and birth of an organic and centralized China and of its implications for the world balance and the decline of Western interests in the Pacific. Mexico does not even try to establish relations with this new China and continues tied to that past phase now located at Taiwan.

Japan, Indonesia, and India   With Japan she should maintain a friendship based on a virtual international identity. For with the defeat of the Empire of the Rising Sun, this country—notwithstanding its great traditions and outstanding personality—can now be counted within the sphere of United States influence. A common heterodoxy towards the West could join intimately two countries whose commercial and diplomatic relations began in 1612. But this policy of generic friendship bears fruit only occasionally. It is thus worthy of note that Mexico did not take a very independent attitude with regard to the peace treaty imposed on Japan. For victory in World War II did give clear-cut rights to the victors. Even if Mexico did not share in these rights,

she did contribute to their imposition in San Francisco in 1951.

Commercial relations with Indonesia, Japan and India seem to be about the limits of Mexican policy in the Orient. Mexico was even slow to recognize the independence of India, even though these two nations have characteristics which should tie them together. Both of these nations rise above their geopolitical situations, both have pre-Christian civilizations which have borne fruit through a fortunate Western hybridization. A close political relationship would seem advisable. This has not occurred. The Mexican Embassy in New Delhi, with the exception of the brief enlightened ambassadorship of former President Portes Gil, has up to 1962, always been in the hands of a chargé d'affaires. The same has been true with regard to the Indian embassy in Mexico.

Mexico has also failed to develop close relations with the Philippines. In light of their past history, it would seem natural for Mexico to look to Manila for a sure ally and friend. But instead, separated by the Pacific Ocean, these two nations follow parallel and separate courses.

This pattern of ignorance shows us that Mexico still has not shed the colonial complex. She does not look upon the countries of the Far East as inhabitants of the coasts of the same sea; nor does she see their proximity within the Pacific area. It is an error to let oneself be controlled by European geographical conceptions; it is much worse to continue holding political concepts which are European and do not favor the international autonomy of Mexico. This ignorance of the problems of the Orient and their central position today shuts the door on many possible avenues of Mexican diplomacy. It makes her adopt, at the same time, positions which undermine the independent course of action she should follow.

The People's Republic of China   The recognition of the People's Republic of China is especially important. There is no room to doubt the popularity and strength of this government. Nor can it be doubted that this is the legitimate government of a great country which is making tremendous efforts to obliterate the past when China was considered as a fair prize for the West. Because of principle and of tradition, Mexico should have recognized this government a long time ago. She has no interest to be served by not doing so, nor does she augment her prestige in abstaining. Many Western countries have already recognized her.

In not following this lead, in reiterating her negative vote towards the People's Republic of China in the United Nations, Mexico has been accused—and rightly so in this case—of weakness and of being subjected to the will of the United States, because the latter is the only one who can benefit by Mexico's negative vote. She continues to judge the Orient through a Western filter—a United States filter in this case. She excludes herself thereby from one of the most important international avenues of today and allows herself to be drawn in the wake of an American warship towards waters which are stormy.

Relations with African states

Bonds with the Islamic peoples   Two other revolutions also characterize this epoch. They are the awakening of Islam and the gradual decline of colonialism in Africa. After considering the ideals of the Islamic people, it appears that a very close relationship should develop between these nations and Mexico, which also partakes of a portion of the great civilization established by the Caliphates in Spain. In practice, however, such bonds have not existed, with the exception of Lebanon. A good number of persons emigrated from Lebanon to Mexico at the beginning of this century. Another exception might develop from the recent relations which have been initiated with the United Arab Republic and the countries of the Mahgreb.

Islam is a world apart, which must be understood as a whole, rising above particular nationalisms. It constitutes a great movement of spiritual renovation. If it achieves its international objectives, Mexico will see her own objectives strengthened. With this current, Mexico should join and should co-operate towards building that better spiritual world to which she aspires. Unfortunately, in the international field, there is no direct way to get to understand what Islam is, to become aware of its problems, to understand its evolution. The natural bridge to the Islamic peoples was Spain where the traditions of Moorish studies and bonds with the Arab states have deep roots. But, deprived of this possible contact, because Mexico does not maintain diplomatic relations with the Spanish government, we find ourselves separated from Islam by a cultural and spiritual abyss. In the future, it must be bridged.

The newly independent nations   Africa at present finds herself in a situation similar to that of the Latin American Republics in 1810. The march of her peoples towards independence is inevitable. And independence for many countries will mean the tremendous leap from tribal to national organization.

As a partisan of self-determination for all peoples and as an enemy of colonialism, Mexico fully supports the independence movement in Africa. But condemning colonialism is one thing; it is quite another to face up to the great problems that the future holds for these new nations. It is one thing to receive them as sister nations in the community of nations, and quite another to become aware that their existence will alter political and economic situations which constitute pillars of Mexican foreign policy.

Most of these new nations show a profound distrust of everything which is Western. They have suffered under the worst kind of colonialism, and it would be super-human if they could understand values which have been so glaringly absent from their colonial lives. The new nations of Africa are clearly in the struggle being waged by the two Great Power blocs. They are the object of attention and pampering and the industrial Powers of both sides are preoccupied with trying to aid their development and improve the standard of living of their inhabitants. They find themselves in the center of the stage. Everybody wants to have the opportunity of helping them; no one wants to put a stop to their development.

This brings us to the economic consequences of their independence. When colonialism disappears, Africans will become competitors in the world markets for raw materials, competitors who have no reason to respect past agreements, no reason to worry about good relations with far-off countries with which they have nothing in common. African coffee, for example, is making a dent on what was, until very recently, a Latin American monopoly. There is no reason to suppose, given the political atmosphere of the present time, that there will be any countries who are desirous of pleasing Latin America at the expense of Africa by making any preferential market concessions.

Because of their number and characteristics, because of their doctrines of reform and their unity on major points of present-day politics, the African nations bring with them a new element of internal and international instability which will preoccupy the community of nations for a long time and which will vitally affect Mexico. Let it suffice as an example, to point out the time and resources which the Congo Republic has absorbed from the United Nations since gaining independence. Because of the character of her economy and because of the future of her production, Mexico will have to compete in international markets which, by their very nature, are limited. Looking beyond her sincere friendship for the new nations, Mexico is facing serious international problems brought on by the emergence of the new African republics. These problems need the most careful consideration.

BIBLIOGRAPHY

Author's suggestions

Castañeda, Jorge. *Mexico and the United Nations.* New York: Manhattan Publishing Company, 1958.

Ceniceros, José Angel. *Mexico's Attitude in its International Relations.* Mexico City: Ministry of Foreign Relations, 1935.

Cline, Howard Francis. *The United States and Mexico.* Cambridge: Harvard University Press, 1953.

Dulles, John W. F. *Yesterday in Mexico. A Chronicle of the Revolution, 1919–1936.* Austin: University of Texas Press, 1961.

Ministerio de relaciones exteriores. *La Diplomaciá Mexicana.* Mexico City: Federal Government Printing Office, n.d.

Scott, R. E. *Mexican Government in Transition.* Urbana: University of Illinois Press, 1959.

Tannenbaum, Frank. *Mexico: The Struggle for Peace and Bread.* New York: Alfred A. Knopf, 1950.

Villegas, Daniel Cosio. *Historia Moderna de México.* Mexico City: Hermes, 1959, 1960. This monumental work includes some chapters directly related to Mexico's foreign policy. Special attention might be given to *La República Restaurada—Vida Política Exterior;* and to *Los E. U. contra Porfirio Díaz.*

ABOUT THE AUTHOR

JAMES EAYRS was born in London in 1926 but has lived in Canada most of his life. He was educated at the University of Toronto, Columbia University and the London School of Economics. Since 1952 he has been a member of the Department of Political Economy, University of Toronto, where he is now an Associate Professor. He is co-editor of the *International Journal,* the quarterly periodical of the Canadian Institute of International Affairs. He has travelled and lectured widely outside Canada, most recently as Visiting Professor at Makerere College, Uganda, and Dartmouth College, Hanover, N.H.

His published writings include: *Canada in World Affairs,* 1955–1957, 1959; *Northern Approaches: Canada and the Search for Peace,* 1961; and *The Art of the Possible: Government and Foreign Policy in Canada,* 1961.

ABOUT THE CHAPTER

Even when Canadian leaders attempt to define a bolder, more aggressive, role for the nation in the foreign policy field, it is clear that "geography, tradition and an unyielding external environment, set a hard if not an iron hand upon the most daring of their ambitions." Within this context one can understand why Mr. Eayrs describes the Canadian style in external affairs as one which deals "with the world in a workaday way, eschewing doctrine and the long view, taking one thing at a time." He notes, however, that during the last few years, because of the changing setting of Canadian foreign policy which includes both domestic pressures and new circumstances abroad, national leaders "are readier than their predecessors were to look upon foreign policy as providing opportunities for creative initiatives."

Mr. Eayrs gives a penetrating account of the influence of geography, trade patterns, population distribution, political make-up, and other factors on Canada's role in international affairs. The author also adds valuable insights into the role of public opinion and the press as factors influencing national attitudes and the course of foreign policy developments.

Mr. Eayrs concludes his presentation with an analysis of the formulation of foreign policy in Canada and a brief survey of some current foreign policy problems and how they are viewed by Canadians.

23

THE FOREIGN POLICY OF CANADA

JAMES EAYRS

University of Toronto

A Middle Power at mid-century

On February 10, 1960, in his first major parliamentary address as Secretary of State for External Affairs, Mr. Howard Green undertook to define a brave new role for Canada in world affairs. Traditionally, he noted, Canada had played the part of interpreter in foreign policy. The highest achievement to which Canadian statesmen might aspire was thought to be reconciling differences among the Great Powers, particularly differences between the United States and the United Kingdom. The time had come, he now suggested,

to drop the idea that Canada's role in world affairs is to be an "honest broker" between the nations. We must decide instead that our role is to be to determine the right stand to take on problems, keeping in mind the Canadian background and, above all, using Canadian common sense. In effect, the time has come to take an independent approach.[1]

During the months to follow, Mr. Green discovered soon enough what all foreign ministers find out in time: that geography, tradition and an unyielding external environment set a hard if not an iron law upon the most daring of their ambitions. After little more than a year of effort, spent mainly in the inhospitable jungle of disarmament negotiations, the Secretary of State for External Affairs returned to Parliament with a less grandiose conception. "It is a fact which we must face," he told the House of Commons Standing Committee on External Affairs on May 1, 1961,

"that there are many of the middle and smaller powers which simply will not take a stand where the two key nuclear powers are at odds. It would be very nice if Canada or some other

---

[1] Canada, *H. of C. Debates*, 1960, vol. 1, p. 930.

nation, or Canada with other nations, could lead the middle and smaller powers into action which might be unpopular with the nuclear powers; but in the cold, hard facts of United Nations politics, it is just about impossible to do that.[2]

With these words—and with the deeds to which they led—Mr. Howard Green re-entered, after a brief period outside it, the tradition of his predecessors. It is a tradition marked by circumspection and by diffidence. It is sceptical of the bold stroke and of the grand design. The Canadian style in external policy has been to deal with the world in a workaday way, eschewing doctrine and the long view, taking one thing at a time and prepared to take much time over that one thing. "Cautious," "patient," "compromising," "flexible"—these are the adjectives by which Canada's foreign ministers are wont to describe their own endeavors; it is needless to add that they have no pejorative intent. Theirs is the way of gardeners, not of engineers; they are content to till and hoe the field of politics, leaving dams and dredging to others. Being mortal, they share with the rest of us the human trait of making necessities into virtues.

But, one should perhaps ask, is their modest role, in which they cast themselves, really the product of necessity? Is it imposed by objective limitations of power and influence? Or do they set their sights too low? Policy is the art of the possible. But what is possible? How much may legitimately be expected of a Middle Power in a nuclear age? Can it move forward boldly on its own path at its own pace? Or can it do no more than huddle helplessly in the shadow of its atomic allies?

During the years before the Second World War, Canada's Prime Minister sought with singular success to limit commitments for the coming conflict by stressing the restraints and pressures to which a Canadian government was inevitably prone. He spoke, on one occasion, of

> the real difficulties inherent in our preoccupation with the tremendous, absorbing and paramount tasks of achieving economic development and national unity . . . , and the unparalleled complexity of our position as a member of the British Commonwealth of Nations and one of the nations of the American continent;[3]

and, on another, of "the strain upon the unity of a country already strained by economic depression and other consequences of the last war and its aftermath."[4] Never, indeed, was Mackenzie King more satisfied than when ringing the changes on the theme that his country was difficult to govern. It was, and is, difficult to govern, but only in the sense that government is at all times and in all places an exacting and complicated craft. Compared to the ordeals undergone by nearly every modern nation—destruction and occupation in war, civil strife, malevolent and scouring tyrannies, the indignities of colonial rule—Canada's situation appears inordinately fortunate. In the perspective of a quarter-century, it is hard to escape the conclusion, harsh as it may be, that members of Canadian governments during the 1930's, reciting their litanies of grievances, exaggerated both to themselves and to their publics the obstacles to more effective, and more courageous, policies.[5]

Members of Canadian governments during the 1950's and early 1960's are readier than their predecessors were to look upon foreign policy as providing opportunities for creative initiatives. The world appears less as a congeries of perplexities than as a series of challenges. Theirs is a more attractive outlook than

---

[2] Canada, H. of C. Standing Committee on External Affairs, *Minutes of Proceedings and Evidence,* 1961, no. 1, p. 10.

[3] Canada, *H. of C. Debates,* 1936, vol. 4, p. 3862.
[4] *Ibid.,* 1938, vol. 3, p. 3184.
[5] See James Eayrs, " 'A Low Dishonest Decade': Aspects of Canadian External Policy, 1931–1939," in *The Growth of Canadian Policies in External Affairs* (Durham, N.C.: 1960), pp. 59–80.

that of the nay-sayers of the past. It would be pleasant to be able to ascribe it to the ascendancy in each of the statesman over the politician. That would be misleading. If there is a more constructive view than formerly, it is due more than anything to the changing setting of Canadian foreign policy, both in the domestic scene and in the external environment.

Let us begin with geography; for it is often asserted that the geographic factor in foreign affairs is as permanent as things can be in a world where, all things flowing, even the Pre-Cambrian shield must yield in time to the ravages of wind, rain, snow and ice.

GEOGRAPHY AND FOREIGN POLICY

The end of isolationism

Geography, during the 1920's and 1930's, could be, and was, summoned in aid of the prevailing policy of isolationism. The Great War had brought half a million Canadians to Europe; but it had brought the New World no closer to the Old. It had remade the map; but the scale and projection of that map remained untouched by a struggle wherein major gains were measured by hundreds of yards, and a generation exchanged for a few desolated acres of mud. The world still seemed wide. To the oceans and the fleet might now be added the great and friendly guardian to the South as purveyors of security. Canada was "a fire-proof house, far from inflammable materials," whose inhabitants peered indistinctly at distant continents from which invasion seemed so improbable. "At present, the danger of attack upon Canada is minor in degree and second-hand in origin."[6] So declared Mackenzie King as late as 1938, and nothing that happened during the next six years of war upset the accuracy of his

prediction. German U-boats torpedoed shipping in and about the Gulf of St. Lawrence; Japanese balloons of mulberry bark paper, armed with smallish charges of incendiary and high explosive, fell upon the Canadian West Coast and as far inland as Manitoba.[7] But this was hardly what the embattled residents of East London had understood by *blitzkrieg*.

Within a decade of Canada's declaration of war on Germany, the U.S.S.R., a nation heretofore hardly considered as a neighbor or an enemy, had detonated a nuclear device; within two decades, it had developed a thermonuclear arsenal and delivery systems of increasingly more terrifying range and accuracy. Geography, which so recently conferred invulnerability upon Canada, now placed it in the forefront of atomic attack. It had placed it, as well, in a unique, if not particularly enviable, situation. Western European allies of the United States, succumbing to the temptation of being "rather Red than dead," could opt for a status akin to satellites. This option is not open to Canadians. Pacts may be broken, treaties unilaterally denounced; but geography holds its victims fast. If the United States were to be brought under nuclear attack, Canada's territory and people, neutral or not, would be fearsomely punished. While 9,000 mile missiles, undersea delivery systems, satellites in space, and the possibility of Soviet bases in Latin America, make a nuclear attack upon the United States which would not be directed across Canadian territory theoretically possible, in practice such an attack would surely be accompanied by a trans-Polar strike, if only as a second wave of bombers and missiles. Probably the assault would be mounted mainly across the North Pole. Fall-out respects no frontiers. Moreover, most of what interception there might be of marauding missiles and bombers would occur over Canadian territory. "Dead-man fuses," causing detonation if stopped short of primary targets, could work as much devastation upon

---

[6] Canada, *H. of C. Debates*, 1938, vol. 3, p. 3179.

[7] Colonel C. P. Stacey, *Six Years of War: The Army in Canada, Britain and the Pacific* (Ottawa: 1955), pp. 177–8.

the innocent by-stander as upon the intended victim, possibly more.

The vocabulary of politics is still not so extensive that to introduce new terms is always a disservice. "Geopsychology" (geographers may fancy "psychogeography") usefully emphasizes that how people think they are situated is at least as important as their situation; and that these may not be the same. Canadians have been slow to grasp how the weapons revolution of the last ten years has transformed their geography from a defensive asset into a nerve-wracking liability. Looking at their place on the map, they more than likely encountered Mercator's distorting but re-assuring depiction of a Dominion sprawling hugely from sea to sea, protected to the North by a *glacis* of infinite duration. Its supremacy for a generation in the atlases of their children can scarcely excuse, however, mistaking the identity of the external enemy. This mistake Canadians have been prone to make. As late as the 1920's, perhaps later, a strategic plan for use in the event of invasion by the United States circulated among the Military Districts of the Dominion. No one any longer prepares for that eventuality. But the tocsins sounding raucously in the reports of Royal Commissions and in politicians' speeches are intended to arouse awareness of alleged dangers, in the form of economic penetration and cultural Fenianism, from south of the border, as often as of the far more threatening danger from the north. The resumption in September 1961 of nuclear weapons testing by the Soviet Union usefully reminded Canadians both of the proximity and of the ruthlessness of their not-so-friendly neighbor across the Pole.

Natural resources and trade policies

There is more to geography than a place on the map. The configuration of the land, and what it can produce, also help to shape a nation's foreign policy. Throughout its modern history Canada's has been a staple economy. Recent development, in the lee of sheltering tariffs, of some secondary industry is of less significance than the addition of new staples to traditional produce, with nickel, oil and uranium, joining fish, furs, wheat and wood. Canada remains a trading nation, for which autarky is unthinkable. Boycotts and embargoes are far from favored instruments of national policy. Used unilaterally against the United States, such devices are likely to visit greater misfortune upon the user than any hardships they might be designed to remedy. In 1923, for the first and possibly the last time, a Canadian government considered imposing an embargo upon newsprint to compel more favorable access for produce in United States' markets. On receiving this intelligence from the British chargé d'affaires—it was not until 1927 that the Canadian Government, by opening its first legation in Washington, could communicate with a United States administration through its own diplomatic representatives—the Secretary of State, Charles Evans Hughes, remarked

> that the Canadian Government must realize that in this matter if they proceeded along the lines suggested that they would be taking the American newspapers and our publishers by the throat, and that one could hardly imagine a case in which there would be a more serious and immediate reaction . . . Mr. Chilton said that he supposed what the Secretary meant was that this would lead to retaliation. The Secretary said that he did not care to indulge in any threat of retaliation; he wished the matter to be discussed in the most friendly way. It was perfectly apparent that if Canada started an economic war of this serious character, it would be continued, and the American Government would have abundant means of protecting itself against such injuries . . .[8]

[8] *Foreign Relations of the United States, 1923*, vol. 1, pp. 497–8.

The limitations imposed upon foreign policy by trading policy became painfully apparent during the later 1930's and early 1940's, when Canadian lead, nickel, aluminum, copper, zinc and scrap-iron, sent in large quantities to Japan, were quickly fed into the war-machine of the Tokyo militarists. Considerable protest throughout the Dominion did not cause the Government to curtail these exports. On February 11, 1938, the leader of the Co-operative Commonwealth Federation, Canada's party of democratic socialism, spoke out strongly against this policy. "If airplanes or warships come to the coast of British Columbia and attack this country with bombs and shells," declared J. S. Woodsworth,

we know that those bombs and shells will have been made from materials supplied by this country . . . Even though we have no sense of responsibility for the women and children of China, for our own sakes we should prevent one more ounce of war material going to Japan—and this whether or not any other nation takes similar action.

The Prime Minister replied:

May I say to my hon. friend that the Government is just as concerned as he is about the well-being and welfare of the women and children in the Orient . . . But what this government is particularly concerned about is the well-being and welfare of the Canadian people.[9]

No mine, no mill, could accordingly be closed. Two years later, when the flow of war matériel to Japan continued despite Canada's declaration of war upon Germany, Mackenzie King justified the policy in these words:

There are commodities, often quite . . . useful in themselves for war pur-

poses, of which the supply under Allied control is considerably in excess of all present and prospective Allied requirements. In such cases the refusal of an export permit for shipment to a neutral country may mean the complete closing down of a Canadian mine or factory and the loss of employment to people whose labour is presently bringing into the country considerable quantities of foreign exchange which we are able to use in financing our greatly expanding programme of armament purchases from the United States.[10]

It was about this time, after the conclusion of the Tripartite Pact, that the Japanese Government recalled its overseas ministers and ambassadors, and the Minister at Ottawa stopped by at the Department of External Affairs to pay his farewell visit. During his interview with the Under Secretary of State for External Affairs, O. D. Skelton, Baron Tomii raised the question of Canadian policy concerning exports to Japan. He said, Skelton noted,

that in so far as restrictions of exports were due to our own vital war necessity, no complaint could of course be made. He wondered, however, if it was not due to some extent to the hostile attitude of certain groups in Canada in connection with the present conflict in China. In the United Kingdom similar groups had been quite vociferous, but they had not dominated the policy of the Government of the United Kingdom . . . I told Baron Tomii that . . . I would readily agree that there was a vigorous demand for restricting shipments of munitions to Japan from a good many quarters on the ground (1) of sympa-

[9] *Canada, H. of C. Debates*, 1938, vol. 1, p. 381.

[10] Mackenzie King to Alex. Walker, September 4, 1940, King Papers. (Quotations from the King Papers are reproduced with the permission of Mackenzie King's Literary Executors.)

thy with China as the victim of aggression, and (2) because of the extraordinary open and unrestrained anti-British attitude of the leaders of the Japanese army and political opinion in recent months . . . We had not lifted a finger to help China, partly, it is true, because China did not have the money or the ships to buy and carry munitions. However that might be, as a matter of plain fact we had allowed the shipment to Japan of indispensable supplies for their war effort . . .[11]

The diversification of the economy, and some taming of its business cycle, made postwar Canada less dependent than formerly upon access to foreign markets, and so broadened the area of choice open to its governments. It became possible, for example, to comply without much restiveness with recommendations of the North Atlantic Treaty Organization that none of its members sell strategic commodities, such as nickel, aluminum and copper, to the Soviet Union. But Canadians still could not easily afford, nor had they much taste for, economic warfare on the grand scale. Their attitude was best revealed in their Government's refusal to join the United States in its total embargo of Communist China. The sale early in 1961 of 40 million bushels of wheat for $60 million cash was announced by an understandably jubilant Mr. Alvin Hamilton on "a great day for the Minister of Agriculture"; it was not such a bad day for the Secretary of State for External Affairs, either. A further illustration of the nonideological approach to dealings with People's Democracies may be seen in the fact that Canada was the first and only Western nation to take part in the Trade Exhibition at

---

[11] Memorandum for the Prime Minister by O. D. Skelton, August 28, 1940. King Papers. A social critic of the time commented in verse:

. . . Many a brave Canadian youth
  Will shed his blood on foreign shores,
And die for Democracy, Freedom, Truth,
  With his body full of Canadian ores . . .

Brno, Czechoslovakia, in 1959; two years later, it had been joined by fifteen others. And a third illustration is provided by Canada's policy towards Castro's Cuba, discussed below.

POPULATIONS AND POWER

The foreign policy of a country reflects, and ought to reflect, the character of its people. This is not to say that a government should wait for an explicit mandate before acting upon its own instinct and intelligence; it might as well be waiting for Godot. Ordinary men and women are preoccupied, in societies of affluence, with second cars and second mortgages; and these are their legitimate preoccupations. Governments, then, must govern. But no government can lead, not even a dictatorship can lead, oblivious to those who follow. A nation in which those behind cry "forward!" and those before cry "back!" can hardly do other than pursue an erratic and therefore an unsuccessful course in world affairs.

Relations between French and English elements

The population of Canada in 1935 was barely 11 millions; a quarter-century later, barely 18 millions. So large a country so thinly populated will never be a Great Power. No less significant than this increase—small enough in absolutes but displaying in relative terms an impressive vitality—has been the changing relationship of its principal peoples. Lord Durham had found French and English "warring within the bosom of a single state"; in 1939, a century later, they were still at it. The two cultures were out of kilter. By the early 1960's their co-existence had become more peaceable, though not wisely to be taken for granted. On March 18, 1961, the Montreal newspaper *La Presse* published the results of a poll in which 11,409 French-speaking Canadians of various occupations throughout the Province of Quebec had responded to interrogation such as the following:

Votre sentiment a l'égard des Canadiens anglais:	%
Supériorité?	4
Admiration?	2
Fraternité nationale?	24
Tolérance?	14
Mécontentement soutenu?	23
Antagonisme?	7
Indifférence?	11
Infériorité?	4

Comment les Canadiens français sont-ils traités par les gouvernants du pays?	
Favorisés?	1
Traités sur un pied d'égalité?	7
Défavorisés?	91

Les Canadiens anglais font-ils preuve de compréhension et de justice à l'endroit des Canadiens français?	
Oui	11
Non	85

Favorisez-vous, pour le Québec,	
La séparation de la province du reste de la Confédération?	45
L'annexion aux E.-U.?	3
La suppression de toutes les autres provinces et la formation d'un Etat centralisé?	4
Le maintien du régime actuel?	39

A separatist ideology, reminiscent of the movement for "Laurentie" which found some support during the embattled 1930's, and drawing inspiration from the Afro-Asian revolution, irresistibly attracted the younger French-speaking intellectual of the early 1960's whether or not he accepted the platform of the Rassemblement Pour L'Indépendance Nationale.

For the conduct of foreign policy, the significant development was the alteration of the external environment in ways permitting, for the first time in many years, French-speaking Canadians to respond to international crisis in much the manner of their compatriots. With the diffusion of power and responsibility for Commonwealth affairs—once lodged at Downing Street—among the far-flung capitals of multi-racial groupings of independent nations, the anti-imperialists of the 1930's became the Commonwealth's-men of the 1960's.

No less significant was the substitution of Communist for Fascist totalitarianism. There remained little chance of a repetition of the kind of division in the Dominion over the Spanish Civil War—when the sympathies of French Canada lay largely with "that army of heroes, justly called Christ's militia" who fought for General Franco—or, during the Second World War, over Vichy France. While Canada was the only NATO power with a military establishment maintained wholly without conscription, this doubtful distinction was due less to the unwillingness of Canadians to fight for freedom than to the unwillingness of their governments to risk opening wounds caused by conscription crises in two previous wars. But during the Korean conflict, the French-speaking Canadian demonstrated as much capacity for sacrifice as his English-speaking countryman from Toronto or Vancouver: of 10,587 men enlisting in the special volunteer force for Korean service, 3,134 were from the Province of Quebec, a proportion slightly higher than that of the population of Quebec to the population of the whole country. Moreover, the proportion of French-speaking Canadians in the special force was almost exactly the same as that of French-speaking Canadians to the total population.[12]

Ethnic minorities

In 1931, Canadians whose countries of origin were other than the United Kingdom or France numbered about 1,809,000 and ac-

---

[12] Canada, *H. of C. Debates*, 1951, 2nd. sess., vol. 2, p. 1532.

counted for about 19 per cent of the total population; by 1961 their number had reached 4,700,000, accounting for about 25 per cent of the total population. About a group so large, so scattered and so varied, which includes Canadians of Asian as well as of Western and Eastern European descent, generalization is difficult and perhaps misleading. But one general impression may be recorded. The Canadian ethnic minority has greater difficulty than its American counterpart in making an impact upon foreign policy. This is partly because its members are likely to be scattered and therefore less able to bring pressure to bear; partly because, Canada's voice in the chorus of nations being small, it has not been worthwhile to bring pressure to bear; partly because the parliamentary system is less responsive than the congressional to such pressure as may be brought to bear. All the same, Canada's foreign policy has not been unaffected by the presence within the country of sizeable minorities not of British or French descent, particularly those whose ancestors or who themselves had made their way from the nations of Eastern Europe fallen to Communist rule—from the so-called People's Democracies, from the Baltic States, from the Soviet Union itself. Canadians of Ukrainian origin alone numbered nearly half-a-million in 1961, and more than any other European-Canadian community had come to participate actively in the politics of their land of choice. Their influence may be detected in the government's continued refusal to recognize the People's Republic of China, and in its decision in 1951 to inaugurate broadcasting in the Ukrainian language to the Soviet Union, a policy which, on the face of it, appeared to conflict with the non-provocative approach favored by the Department of External Affairs. After 1957 the influence of European immigrant groups upon external policy may be presumed to have been greater than under the preceding administration, for the election of that year brought to power a Prime Minister who was himself a Canadian of neither British nor French descent, and into the Cabinet, as Minister of Labour, a Canadian of Ukrainian descent.

THE PUBLICS AND THEIR PRESS

Fear of nuclear war

Turn now from populations to publics, both attentive and inattentive. The latter, in Canada as elsewhere, greatly outnumbered the former. In 1961 2,000,000 adult Canadians—11 per cent of the total population—could neither read nor write. It must be presumed that this hard core of illiterates, together with a penumbra of the politically unaware comprising perhaps a majority of the population, had no real interest in, much less understanding of, the intractable problems of external policy with which their government attempted to grapple. But in times of crisis, even the most inattentive of publics may be roused from its accustomed private preoccupations. The early 1960's are such a time, and the crisis by which it has been aroused is the crisis of the nuclear age. In the fall of 1961, 140,000 Canadians affixed their signatures to a petition to the Government of Canada:

> Nuclear war could end civilization and most of the human race. The nuclear powers already have enough bombs to kill all the people in the world. The spread of nuclear weapons to more nations would increase the danger of nuclear war breaking out and would make disarmament harder to negotiate. The Canadian government is considering the acquisition of nuclear weapons. Such weapons offer Canada no defence whatever against the major threat, the intercontinental missile, and little if any defence against manned H-bombers. Their acquisition would also handicap or destroy the leadership Canada is giving toward disarmament.

For these reasons, we, the undersigned, oppose the spread of nuclear weapons to any country or military alliance not now possessing them. We petition the Canadian government to reject nuclear weapons for the armed forces of Canada and to prohibit their installation on Canadian soil.

The sponsors of this petition are highly attentive citizens, but it seems unlikely that most of those who signed it did so after careful examination of policy alternatives. Democratic governments, however, do not weigh votes, they count them. There is no doubt that so large a body of opinion wholly hostile to nuclear defense has caused prolonged postponement of such crucially important defense decisions as the nuclear arming of anti-aircraft missiles and fighter interceptors, and an offer of base facilities for the United States Strategic Force.

The interest generated by the hazards of the nuclear age among people ordinarily paying little or no attention to international affairs may carry over into other aspects of external policy, so contracting those "dark areas of ignorance" which in pre-atomic times were so characteristic a feature of the mass mind. "I was not prepared," confessed a former Secretary of State for External Affairs in February 1958, five months after taking up his new portfolio, "for the size of a Foreign Minister's mailbag, for the variety of its contents, and, above all, for the depth of concern for the state of the world which is revealed so clearly, often poignantly, in this correspondence."[13] Much will depend upon some tangible result of public concern. If petitioning proves unproductive, a relapse into apathy is not unlikely. "Wearied out by overwhelming novelties," noted Coleridge a century ago, "stunned by a series of strange explosions, sick of hope long delayed, and uncertain as to the real object and motive of the struggle . . . the public mind . . . lost

its tone and elasticity." Such could easily become the mood of a mass public too long exposed to the risks and frustrations of doomsday diplomacy.

Foreign policy leaders

The "attentive public" is defined by the originator of that phrase as the section of the population "which is informed and interested in foreign policy problems, and which constitutes the audience for the foreign policy discussions among the elites."[14] In Canada, elites and audience tend to coalesce. The nation's intellectuals are too few, too scattered and perhaps too ineffectual to provide a continuous performance at which other interested but less specialized citizens are merely onlookers. At the forums, seminars and conferences which now in Canada, as for long in the United States, play so large a part in the process by which elite opinions are formed, the speakers at one meeting are in the audience of the next, engaging in a kind of interior dialogue too infrequently leavened by infusions of expertise from outside. Many of the brains of the country are sucked, sometimes at a tender age, into the maw of the federal bureaucracy. There they engage in an interior dialogue of their own having little exchange of ideas with intellectuals beyond their bureaucratic universe. Expert knowledge of defense and foreign policy is largely a monopoly of the public service. The lack of any independent countervailing expertise at the service of the Canadian clerisy impairs to an extent not generally realized the quality of national debate and, in turn, the quality of national policy.

So it is that the Canadian policy-maker is far less often than the American tempted to turn to outsiders for advice. This no doubt helps the morale of the Foreign Service, whose mem-

---

[13] Address by the Secretary of State for External Affairs, Sidney E. Smith, to the Hamilton, Ont. Chamber of Commerce, February 4, 1958 (Information Division, Department of External Affairs).

[14] Gabriel A. Almond, *The American People and Foreign Policy* (New York: 1950), p. 138.

bers are not exposed to the indignity (for so it appears to a foreigner) of being by-passed in favor of some private research organization on such a problem as, say, whether to recognize Communist China. On the other hand, it is not so good for the bureaucratic imagination, more especially since the bureaucracy, in particular the Department of External Affairs, is hostile to the device of lateral entry. Those who rise, rise through the ranks, and so have ample opportunity to imbibe the departmental ethos—an ethos well described by words of Mr. George Kennan and intended as describing the diplomatic profession at large: "The task of diplomacy [is seen] as essentially a menial one, consisting of hovering around the fringes of a process one is powerless to control, tidying up the messes other people have made, attempting to keep small disasters from turning into big ones, moderating the passions of governments and of opinionated individuals."[15] These are necessary, even worthy, objectives, but not the kind ordinarily producing inspiring statesmen and inspired statecraft. New ideas are only with difficulty translated into policy. A case in point is the Canadian equivalent of President Kennedy's Peace Corps launched with such élan and enthusiasm in the United States. Although a Canadian version of the scheme was placed before the Ottawa bureaucracy while the Peace Corps was as yet only an idea, placed indeed before the Prime Minister, the authorities were unreceptive, in the sense of not doing anything about it.[16] To this day, no fed-

eral assistance has been given to the dozen or so young men and women presently working as volunteers in Ceylon, Sarawak and other faraway places. Is it too harsh to suggest that the Government's response was typically Canadian? A not unsympathetic visitor commented some years ago: "There is in Canada today somewhere seated on the throne of power a man who continually says 'No' to Life."[17]

The influence of the press

So much for publics. What of their press? Nothing any longer approaches either in quality or in distribution a "prestige paper" in the sense understood by Ithiel di Sola Pool,[18] although, during the 1920's and 1930's, the *Winnipeg Free Press* under J. W. Dafoe could be so described. "Reading its editorials day by day," one of its early admirers has recalled, "with their emphasis on broader national issues and on world affairs, you got the feeling that here was no provincial small town but a metropolitan centre in touch with intellectual currents throughout the world."[19] The excellence of this once great journal did not long survive

---

[15] George F. Kennan, "History and Diplomacy as Viewed by a Diplomatist," in Stephen D. Kertesz and M. A. Fitzsimons, eds., *Diplomacy in a Changing World* (Notre Dame: 1959), pp. 107–8.

[16] Access to the bureaucracy and to Cabinet ministers is relatively easy, for Canada is a small country and Ottawa a small, even provincial, capital. On this point it is worth recording the observation of the individual who attempted without success to obtain federal backing for the Canadian Overseas Volunteers: *"My personal impression of our experience in Ottawa is that the channels of approach to both administrative and policy-making levels of government are surprisingly free of obstacles to even the most uninfluential private citizen, provided that he comes armed with a plausible idea purporting to improve a particular aspect of for-*

eign policy, and with reasonable evidence of some preparation and conviction." (Letter to the author, December 20, 1959.)

[17] Quoted in F. H. Underhill, "A Country in Search of an Image," *Saturday Review of Literature*, October 24, 1959, p. 16.

[18] *"In each major power one newspaper stands out as an organ of elite opinion. Usually semi-official, always intimate with the Government, these 'prestige papers' are read by public officials, journalists, scholars and business leaders. They seldom have large circulations, yet they have enormous influence. They are read not only in their own countries, but also abroad by those whose business it is to keep track of world affairs . . . It is generally possible to name with fair confidence one paper in any given country which plays the role of prestige paper at any given time."* Ithiel di Sola Pool, The *"Prestige Papers,"* Hoover Institute Studies, Series C, Symbols, No. 2, January 1952, p. 1.

[19] F. H. Underhill, "Academic Freedom in Canada," *The C.A.U.T. Bulletin*, vol. 8, no. 2, December 1959, pp. 11–12.

the passing of its great editor, and nothing has taken its place. The *Globe and Mail* of Toronto is one of the few English-language newspapers offering sustained editorial comment at once informed and opinionated on world affairs. Its publisher's conviction of the importance of editorials in forming opinion has taken the form of reprinting them as paid advertisements in leading American newspapers. "Democracy and Disneyland," advertised in the *New York Times* for September 25, 1959, criticized the arrangements for Mr. Khrushchev's tour of the United States which did not allow him to visit the Los Angeles amusement park; others highly critical of American policy towards Communist China aroused much comment in the United States, both for and against, and were discreetly investigated by the State Department.

If there is no French-language equivalent of the *Globe and Mail,* there is, unfortunately, no English-language equivalent of *Le Devoir,* unique in the journalistic life of the nation in its freedom from the pressure of advertisers— the newspaper is held in trust by its directors and the annual deficit is usually made up by voluntary contributions from enthusiastic subscribers—its readiness to take a stand on controversial issues of social policy, and its high level of appeal—it is written by intellectuals for intellectuals. Its circulation is only about 30,000, but its influence inside French-speaking Canada—though not much beyond—is incalculable. In foreign affairs it has taken the line, at variance with the surrounding Catholic consensus, that the revolution in China is more nationalist than Communist; it is faithful to the traditions of "La Province" in its distaste for American influences both cultural and economic.

A newspaper's publisher understandably exaggerates its importance. A less biased, and more telling, index of editorial influence is the importance attached to it by members of governments. While this is not easily ascertained, particularly in recent years, it seems unlikely that Prime Ministers of Canada would any longer display Mackenzie King's tenacity in 1929 in attempting to win over the support of

an important newspaper.[20] If they have not done so, it is not because they are less sensitive than he to the need for securing public backing for public policy, but rather because they hold the editorial page as a means of influencing popular opinion in lesser regard.[21] The newspaper as such still exerts its influence, but through the largely subliminal effect of its headlines upon passers-by.

There are also its news columns. These are often condemned for their reliance on other than Canadian correspondents and Canadian news services for coverage of international events. "This is an unhealthy state of affairs," a recent critic insists.

The foreign agencies exist primarily to serve their own domestic clients; they

[20] On July 25, Mackenzie King wrote to W. G. Jaffray, the editor of the Toronto *Globe*: "*. . . It seems to me that The Globe might greatly aid the Government in its effort toward a goal which we have very much in common. Between now and the time discussion is to take place in Parliament, perhaps it could make clear that Liberal sentiment and opinion will never be satisfied merely by increase of tariffs against the United States . . . Some public discussion on these lines in the press would, I believe, be very helpful . . . in informing public opinion. . . .*" And on August 12: "*. . . I should be the last to wish The Globe or any paper to sacrifice the slightest degree of independence, but I think I have seen enough of public affairs to know that a Government's influence can be much greater in the causes it has at heart where it has a press that is sympathetic and in whose co-operation in furthering its ends and policies it is possible to count. . . .*"

[21] Representatives of other governments in Canada may value the press more highly. A former High Commissioner in Canada of the United Kingdom has recalled: "*. . . When I was in Canada and when the Cyprus story started to be of importance, we had a rather bad press in Canada, and I think it is broadly speaking true to say that public opinion in Canada, if they [sic] did not actually condemn the attitude our Government had taken, were extremely doubtful whether they had been right or not, and we asked for material with which to deal with that. We got an excellent response, and I think it is no exaggeration to say that within the course of a few months one began to see a change in the attitude of the press and to some extent in public opinion as a result. . . .*" Third Report from the Select Committee on Estimates, H.C., Session 1958–59, p. 117.

may even be quasi-official instruments of the government. The principles upon which they select and interpret the news may be very different from those which would govern an organization serving the Canadian public. Obvious examples of situations where distortion might be feared are American reports on Formosa or British despatches from Nyasaland or Cyprus. If Canada is to play a creative and independent role in world affairs, the public which ultimately determines foreign policy must surely cease to be dependent upon news sources which tend to assume, consciously or unconsciously, that American (or British, or French) interests are paramount when it comes to assessing significance. There is a clear case for greatly extending the international coverage of the Canadian Press . . .[22]

This argument assumes more than it examines. What is surely relevant is not the country of origin of agency or correspondent, but the quality of the dispatches to which the reader is exposed, and the hospitality shown to them by the newspaper he reads. A Canadian who daily reads the views of *The Observer, The Times* (of London), and the *New York Times* is not too badly treated. The legitimate grievance of those Canadians wishing to improve the quality of their information on international affairs is that the number of newspapers in the nation providing such a selection may be numbered on the fingers of a severely mutilated hand.

The Canadian Broadcasting Corporation

The absence of a "prestige press" is partly compensated for by the publicly owned and con-

trolled Canadian Broadcasting Corporation, providing in its news and public affairs programming "the most objective and unbiased source of information and opinion in Canada."[23] The Corporation operates both television and radio networks. Television is more popular, but radio is left freer to cater to the needs and expectations of a discriminating audience. The quality of discussion and debate does not yet approach the standards of the B.B.C's Third Program: Gresham's Law is as inexorable in the communications media as elsewhere, and bad programs drive out good programs in an effort, however misguided, to compete with the private broadcasters and their execrable output. Talks on national and international affairs may not be too recondite; nor may they last too long, the operating assumption of the program organizers being that the attention span of the intelligent Canadian adult is about five minutes on a week-day evening, nine on a Sunday night. But for what they thus receive, the favored few are truly thankful —or ought to be.

PARTIES AND POLICIES

The major parties

Sectional loyalties, deeply rooted in and coinciding with geographic regions of political importance, make for a Canadian party system in which doctrine is conspicuously absent. Two major political parties contend for the voters' favor like two great downtown department stores. The Liberal Party historically favors freer trade, lower tariffs, intimacy with the United States, something less than intimacy with the United Kingdom; the Conservative Party has been more ready to use the tariff as an instrument of external policy, to profess

[22] Neil Compton, "The Mass Media," in Michael Oliver, ed., *Social Purpose for Canada* (Toronto: 1961), pp. 73–4.

[23] *Ibid.*, p. 81.

loyalty to the Mother Country (Britain, not France), and to fend off American influences. But these generalizations, on close examination, become so riddled by exceptions as to be almost worthless as a reliable guide to how parties, once in power, actually behave. The striking thing, indeed, is how little, when either comes to form a government, each modifies the policies of its predecessor, how quickly the process of role reversal gets under way. In 1956, during the Suez crisis, the Conservative Party, then in opposition, chastised the Liberal Government of Mr. L. S. St. Laurent for its alleged disloyalty to the United Kingdom. Five years later a Conservative Government found itself obliged to defend its policies against charges from the Liberal opposition that, over the proposed entry of Britain into the Common Market, the Government had taken a "consistently anti-British line." The present Secretary of State for External Affairs, Mr. Howard Green, had in opposition persistently argued that Canada should apply for membership in the South East Asia Treaty Organization; once in office he showed no sign of moving in this direction and, reminded in the House of Commons of his previous preoccupation, remarked: "I have learned a lot since then."

The minor parties

The only parties venturing far from the conventional wisdom in foreign affairs are those yet to form a government. The Social Credit party, deprived of parliamentary representation in the General Election of 1958 (though it continued to flourish in British Columbia and Alberta where it formed the provincial governments) came back with astonishing force at the General Election of June 1962 to capture 30 of 265 seats in the House of Commons. 26 *Créditistes* came from the Province of Quebec, dispatched, one must suppose, by disaffected farmers, small shopkeepers and artisans of the countryside and the towns—the *Poujadistes* of North America. The imagination boggles in trying to foretell the probable impact upon the nation's foreign policy of such a ragged platoon, holding as it does the balance of power in Parliament, and having come there on the strength of its slogan, *"Rien à perdre."* Its influence can hardly be very salutary. The party in the past (to which the present group bears only a faint resemblance) derived its outlook upon the world from such right-wing political movements in the United States as those led by Joseph McCarthy and, more recently, by Senator Goldwater. The political theory of Social Credit, never convincingly repudiated by the party's leaders, relies heavily upon conspiracy theories of history, and a strident, negative anti-communism and an irrational regard for the Chiang Kai-shek regime are among the few distinctive themes of its spokesmen in foreign policy.

To the left of the Liberal and Conservative "department stores" there stood from 1933 to 1961 a structure unique in North America— the Commonwealth Co-operative Federation (C.C.F.), a party at once professing the precepts of democratic socialism and having considerable, if indirect, influence upon national policy despite its small parliamentary representation. During the 1930's, under the leadership of J. S. Woodsworth, the C.C.F. almost single-handedly compelled debate in the House of Commons upon international issues the Prime Minister preferred to leave in obscurity. During the war, the C.C.F., even more than the official Conservative opposition, made its mark upon government policy, and its leader, Mr. M. J. Coldwell, played a prominent part in the work of the delegation which went to San Francisco in 1945 to help finish drafting the Charter of the United Nations. During the postwar years, the C.C.F. continued to function as constructive critic of government policy. Its main concern has been to prod the Government along the course to which it was already committed: more foreign aid should be dispensed; Article II of the NATO Treaty ought to be taken more seriously; more should be done to make the ideals of an Afro-Asian Commonwealth a reality. At the time of the

Suez crisis, the C.C.F. in Parliament gave full support to the St. Laurent-Pearson policy of creating a United Nations Emergency Force and re-establishing the Anglo-American alliance, in marked contrast to the bitter and rancorous attack mounted by Conservative critics. However, it opposed the re-arming of Germany as a member of NATO in 1954, and advocated, in opposition to government policy, the immediate recognition of the People's Republic of China and its admission to the United Nations.

In 1961 the Co-operative Commonwealth Federation disbanded itself, re-emerging under the name of the New Democratic Party and enjoying, for the first time, the formal and financial support of the two largest trades union organizations, the Canadian Labour Congress and the Quebec Federation of Labour. A spirited attempt was made to take advantage of the metamorphosis to commit the New Party —as it was first and is still familiarly known— to a policy of neutralism in foreign affairs and national defense. The advocates of Canadian neutralism had for some years been a strongly vocal minority within the C.C.F. They argued that the Canadian role in world affairs could be fortified and made more useful by attempting to influence the behavior of the Afro-Asian nations growing year by year in numbers and importance. Such an endeavor, they held, required as its essential precondition a radical severance of existing alliances and defense arrangements with the United States. Canada should accordingly leave NATO, and contract out of the operation of radar early warning systems and the North American Air Defense Command.[24] The C.C.F. National Council and

parliamentary group resisted with increasing difficulty efforts to impose an official neutralist line upon the party. At the C.C.F. National Convention in 1960, a neutralist resolution, sponsored by younger delegates staying late at a session from which other delegates had departed, was carried by a vote of 85–72, despite the opposition of party leaders fearful of the resolution's effect upon the conservative trade union membership with which the C.C.F. was on the point of alliance. The New Democratic Party has so far been able to hold the more uncompromising neutralists at bay only by commitments to disband NORAD, and to leave NATO should the Alliance as such lose its non-nuclear innocence.

FOREIGN POLICY FORMATION

Government in Canada is parliamentary government. Foreign policy, like other policy, is made by ministers of the Crown, who are members of a Cabinet formed in the normal course of events from the members of the party obtaining in a general election a majority of seats in the House of Commons at Ottawa. So bare a statement obscures many of the realities of the foreign policy process, none so much, perhaps, as the extent to which in Canada the making of foreign policy is the Prime Minister's job.[25]

The Prime Minister's role

The Prime Minister bears inevitably a unique responsibility for his country's external rela-

---

[24] The most influential statement of the neutralist position is contained in a short book, *Peacemaker or Powdermonkey? Canada's Role in a Revolutionary World*, by James M. Minifie, well-known to Canadians as the Washington, D.C., correspondent of the C.B.C. A more rigorously analytical justification for Canadian neutralism, though less widely read, is the chapter on foreign policy by K. W. McNaught in *Social Purpose for Canada* (Toronto: 1961), pp. 445–72. It is characteristic of the neutralist approach in its romantic conception of the Commonwealth—"a triumph of political

education and experience"—and in its undisguised hostility towards the United States—"any socialist must be vaguely anti-American."

[25] Throughout this section, I have drawn freely upon my book *The Art of the Possible: Government and Foreign Policy in Canada* (Toronto: 1961).

tions, even if by taste or temperament he has little interest in them; circumstances make it likely that he will have too much interest rather than too little. Important officials concerned with the formulation and execution of foreign policy are appointed on his recommendation. To him are normally addressed communications from the political heads of foreign governments; with the technically non-foreign governments of the Commonwealth, consultation proceeds conventionally on a Prime Minister-to-Prime Minister basis. To him will be referred important foreign policy communications received not only in the Department of External Affairs but in other Departments having external contacts, such as Trade and Commerce, Finance, or National Defence. Visiting dignitaries wishing to exchange impressions of the international scene will want to confer with the Prime Minister rather than with some less prestigious figure. Good-will tours in foreign lands add to his range of influential contacts, providing sources of private information long after the journey's end. So do his excursions into the increasingly fashionable realm of summit diplomacy.

It is the Prime Minister's task to shape the recommendations of his foreign policy technicians—among whom his Foreign Secretary may or may not be numbered—to the requirements of domestic politics; by the same token of his omnipotence within his Cabinet—his, for he makes it and may break it—he may ride roughshod over pockets of domestic political discontent where the national interest, as he conceives it, may require. And in times of crisis, when the nation is roused from its private preoccupations to apprehensive awareness of external danger, it is the Prime Minister who through press and radio and television must play the father figure, providing reassurance and guidance and hope. Foreign policy is his prerogative; the range and intimacy of his concern are rarely matched by any of his colleagues, even by his Foreign Secretary.

The extent to which the Prime Minister allows members of his Cabinet to share in the mysteries of foreign policy is as much a matter of individual temperament and style as it is of constitutional law or political convention, perhaps a good deal more. One Prime Minister may in this resemble the Duke of Plaza Toro, leading his regiment from behind; another may prefer the vanguard. Some have been possessive, even secretive, in their conduct of external affairs; others take colleagues into their confidence and look to them for counsel. The increasing importance of Cabinet committees, of which the most influential in this context is the Cabinet Defence Committee, and of regular procedures for dealing with certain types of foreign policy problems—e.g., export control, the opening of new diplomatic missions—have made for a devolution of responsibility in external affairs. So has the convention by which the Secretary of State for External Affairs is ordinarily a separate member of the Government. This convention dates from 1946 when Mr. St. Laurent became the first member of the Cabinet other than the Prime Minister to hold the External Affairs portfolio.

Parliament's role

The role of Parliament in the foreign policy process is distinctly subordinate to that of the political executive. A foreign policy decision is a Cabinet decision. It is, or ought to be, a decision taken in the knowledge that too flagrant disregard of parliamentary opinion may disaffect its following in the House of Commons to the point of threatening its defeat. In practice this sanction is not severe. No Government M.P. wants to fight a General Election, and the weapon of dissolution is one of the instruments at the disposal of a Prime Minister anxious to keep his majority from becoming maverick. If Parliament, and in particular the House of Commons, is to set its mark upon external policy, it must do so by interrogation and discussion. What influence it has depends partly upon the quality of Opposition members, partly upon the readiness of the Government to allow them to perform their dialectical role as the parliamentary system requires.

Since 1945 a House of Commons Standing Committee on External Affairs has regularly and thoroughly scrutinized aspects of external relations. The Committee is not a policy-making body, but confines itself most usefully to eliciting information both on policy and administration. In the opinion of its own members, the success of the Committee is due to its direct questioning of officials of the Department of External Affairs and other public servants concerned with the foreign policy process, a privilege not allowed in the House of Commons. Conscious of the privilege, the members of the Committee are careful not to abuse it. Those civil servants appearing before them are given a respectful and considerate hearing, not pressed if they plead (as they often plead) that answers come better from responsible ministers than from themselves. There are other committees of Parliament in which matters of external policy are occasionally discussed; but the Standing Committee on External Affairs has unique standards of decorum and efficiency. The suggestion that a similar Standing Committee be created to deal with problems of defense policy has so far been resisted by the government of the day.

The quality of expertise on international affairs displayed in the House of Commons is not impressive. The ordinary Member has little incentive to develop detailed knowledge of the subject. What expertise he may possess is likely to lie fallow, for his opportunities to shape policy, in contrast with those of his colleagues in the Congress locked in their continuous struggle with the Executive, are slight. If he belongs to a large government majority, his modest aim in life will be to find enough to do to keep him busy and to keep his self-respect. A wise Prime Minister will find work for idle hands, sending back-benchers to the United Nations General Assembly, meetings of the Commonwealth Parliamentary Association or the Canada–United States Inter-Parliamentary group. But there are not enough of these consolatory missions to go round. While they enable those chosen to indulge in agreeable fashion an interest in foreign affairs, and flatter their sense of self-importance, they rarely bring them much closer to the actual centers of decision.

The problems of those in opposition are rather different. They have ordinarily too much to do, not too little. But whatever motives impel them to criticize foreign policy—conviction, an artisan's pride, or the thought that at the next General Election Hansards may be quoted on the hustings—they cannot realistically hope that their criticisms will cause the Government to change its mind or even modify its mind. A Government too often accepting the suggestions of the Opposition runs the risk of causing the electorate to draw the obvious inference that it has put the wrong people in power.

The Upper House in the Parliament of Canada, as in the United States Congress, is the Senate. But the Canadian Senator is not a power in the land. Of the American Senate, John Hay remarked that treaties enter it as bulls the arena, never to leave alive. In the Canadian Senate this is not true of treaties but it is of Senators. Senators are appointed by the government of the day for life. During the years to come—and for some there are many years to come—they rarely affect the course of external policy; the last significant deflection was in 1913, when the Liberal majority in the Senate was responsible for the defeat of Sir Robert Borden's Naval Bill.

The executive departments

The Canadian bureaucracy has enjoyed for many years the prestige and security attending a career public service whose members remain largely undisturbed by changes of administration. At its summit may be found a group of perhaps a dozen or twenty individuals to whom members of the Cabinet will turn, individually or collectively, for continuous advice and guidance on all matters of public policy. Within this group are usually to be found the deputy ministers and on occasion the associate and assistant deputy ministers of certain important departments—External Affairs, Finance, National Defense, Trade and Commerce, Transport—together with senior officials of the Bank of Canada, the Secretary of the Cabinet, perhaps the Prime Minister's principal private secretary. At this exalted level, divisions between domestic and foreign affairs, as indeed between departments, all but disappear, and the lofty gaze of the senior civil servant sweeps across the whole horizon of public policy. The members of the group are often moved from one key post to another. Since the Second World War, two or three very senior civil servants have rotated every three or four years among the Under Secretaryship of State for External Affairs, the Clerkship of the Privy Council, and the chairmanship of the Civil Service Commission.

The Department of External Affairs The Department most intimately associated with the foreign policy process is of course the Department of External Affairs. With over 400 foreign service officers on active strength in 1961, it is today a far cry from the three officials with which it began in 1909, a formidable bureaucracy in its own right. The Department operates as a career service, recruiting almost entirely among university students upon or shortly after graduation, training them on the job and, at least until recently, frowning upon lateral entry. Ambassadors are frequently appointed from outside, but the tendency is now to appoint most of the heads of the over sixty missions for which the Department is now responsible from the ranks of foreign service officers. The Department is still not large enough—perhaps the country is not large enough—to permit anything like the specialization found in the United Kingdom Foreign Office or the United States Department of State. It is still usual for a foreign service officer to be moved to another mission or another desk after two or three years on the previous job. Senior members of the Department have displayed what at times seems like an almost perverse attachment to the "generalist" ideal of public administration. Only very recently has serious attention been paid to building expertise in the affairs of Eastern Europe, the Far and Middle East, and Africa.

The Department of Trade and Commerce
Another Department whose officials help to shape external policy is the Department of Trade and Commerce. Commercial representation overseas preceded by several decades the first exercise of the right of legation in 1926, so that by comparison with the commercial attaché, the foreign service officer of the Department of External Affairs is something of an interloper. That relations between commercial and diplomatic representatives have been largely devoid of personal rivalries and jurisdictional disputes owes much to the tradition of inter-departmental co-operation and interchange of personnel. During the 1950's it was for a time uncertain which of the two departments should have primary responsibility for the control and administration of programs of capital and technical assistance coming to play an increasingly important part in external policy. The issue was not finally settled until 1961, when the formation of an External Aid Office, with a senior official of the Department of External Affairs firmly in charge, emphasized the Government's view that foreign aid was an integral aspect of foreign policy, and should be dealt with as such.

The military departments In Canada, as in every liberal democracy arming to deter Soviet aggression, the role of the military establishment in the formation of external policy has greatly expanded during the past decade. Civil-military relations in the Dominion have not been free from difficulty. Memories of the conscription crisis of 1944, when members of the High Command came close to resignation rather than accept the policy of the government, still persist, and one may detect in the attitudes of politicians and senior civil servants a thinly veiled distrust of the "military mind." The principle of civilian supremacy is firmly built into the institutions by which national security policy is made. In the Defence Committee of the Cabinet, normally attended by the Chiefs of Staff and the Chairman of the Chiefs of Staff Committee, personnel and tradition are such that the dominant voice is the voice of the civilian minister. The principal military advisers of the government are members of the Chiefs of Staff Committee, but even this is not entirely a military group for it includes the civilian chairman of the Defense Research Board. Additional civilian chaperonage is provided by regular attendance of the Under Secretary of State for External Affairs and the Deputy Minister of National Defence. An earnest attempt is made to infuse senior commanders with an awareness of the political aspects of military problems. Each year, at the National Defence College at Kingston, Ontario, a class of about 30 members, mainly though not exclusively serving officers, are instructed in "the principles of higher governmental administration and staff work, both in peace and war."

SOME CONTEMPORARY POLICIES AND ATTITUDES

Relations with the United States

Fence line disputes with the United States—disagreements over waterways and wheat, frontiers and fisheries—have always been the main concern of Canadian foreign policy. For as long as there continue to be two sovereign governments in North America, these traditional bilateral disputes will preoccupy Canadian governments and officials. In recent years a more perplexing issue has been added to the agenda —the terms on which Canada should cooperate with the United States in the defense of the continent which is their common home.

Difficult and intractable as some of these problems may be, they are becoming less of a threat to the harmonious relations of the two North American members of NATO than differences of opinion over the role Canada should play in response to the threat of militant Communist imperialism as it manifests itself in far-

away places—China, Laos, Latin America. "Perhaps we have come to take for granted disputes about trade, farm surpluses and drainage canals," a former senior member of the Department of External Affairs has recently written,

> recognizing that a state of litigation between neighbours is normal and perpetual. When a question of common policies towards the rest of the world is involved, however, the perspective is confused. On the one side there are complaints about "disloyalty" and on the other side grumblings about "arrogance."[26]

American complaints about Canadian "disloyalty" are as ill-founded as they may be imprecise. But while no Canadian government now or in the foreseeable future would willfully and unnecessarily betray United States interests to any of America's enemies, it will not be looking either for opportunities for slavishly following a Washington line. Precisely because Canadians and Americans are so much alike, or thought to be so much alike, Canadians and their governments want to be, or to be thought of being, different. It may be wondered why, if Canadians and Americans are so similar, anyone should go to such lengths to conceal their similarity. This is a natural way of looking at the matter—if one happens to be an American. For Americans will never be mistaken abroad as pale imitations of their Canadian cousins. Canadians are thought to be the palely imitating folk, and that is not quite so flattering.

Here, then, is the reason why the informed Canadian citizen, and his government, are preoccupied, sometimes to the neglect of common interests, with the area of distinctiveness between the two countries. They want to know what may be recognized as a distinctively Canadian ingredient in the North American re-

[26] John W. Holmes, "Canada and the United States in World Politics," *Foreign Affairs*, vol. 40, no. 1, October 1961, pp. 104–5.

sponse to the great issues agitating a suffering planet. If there is one thing Canadians as a people are agreed upon, it is that they do not want to be a carbon copy of the Americans, in foreign policy or in anything else. Canadians, then, are not looking for reasons to imitate the United States; they are looking, rather, for legitimate occasions on which to exercise a measure of individuality of style and independence of judgment.

Participation in United Nations affairs and NATO

Nowhere have greater opportunities for demonstrating a distinctively Canadian approach to international affairs appeared than at the United Nations. Therefore, every government since 1945, and every party, with the exception of the Social Credit group, has devoted energy as well as oratory in attempting to take as prominent a part in the work of the organization as its resources might allow. These could allow a good deal. The invasion of Egypt in 1956, when the breach between the United States and the United Kingdom over the propriety of using force against the Nasser regime threatened the break-up of the Western alliance, provided Mr. Lester Pearson with the opportunity of performing brilliantly the classical role of the Canadian statesman, bringing Britain and America together again.

The initiative leading to the creation of the United Nations Emergency Force, in which Canadian diplomacy and personnel played so large a part, encouraged the expectation that henceforth Canada's contribution to the defense of the West might most usefully be in the form of regular participation in para-military peacemaking. In this there resided much wishful thinking. The brilliance of Mr. Pearson's performance in the Suez crisis obscured the essential fact that it was a one-night stand, an exceptional turn in circumstances unlikely to recur. But, beyond that, the notion of Canada as a sort of saintly mediator, pursuing an an-

tiseptic course amidst the sordid maneuvers of greater Powers, sorely misconceived Canada's qualifications. Expectations much too great were reared upon the flimsy foundation of the claim to be free from what the Afro-Asian Powers meant by "colonialism." The soldier-policemen-diplomatists serving in the Middle East, the Congo and on the Truce Commissions in Indochina—these last not, of course, under United Nations auspices—have encountered humiliation and even assault by the inescapable fact of their white complexions. The national tradition, on balance, is a liability rather than an asset for this kind of work. Canada is unlikely to develop a taste for intervening in Latin American disputes (for reasons discussed below); in quarrels among Commonwealth nations there is a reluctance to express opinions, let alone to intrude troops; and Canada's membership in NATO will be, as it has been, exploited at the expense of whatever reputation it may have acquired as a disinterested mediator between East and West.

This last consideration leads directly to the neutralist contention, already noted, that Canada should abandon its alliances so as to be able to operate more effectively among the Afro-Asian nations both within the Commonwealth and at the United Nations. The Secretary of State for External Affairs, Mr. Howard Green, has on occasion seemed to show some sympathy for the objectives, though not for the methods, of non-alignment. But a sterner, and, one would judge, more influential voice in the Cabinet has ridiculed the suggestion that Canada is suited to such a role. "The responsible player in the international game," the Minister of National Defence, Mr. Douglas Harkness, declared in February 1961, "makes the most of the cards he has been dealt. We should invite jeers rather than cheers if we attempted to play India's game with Canada's hand."

The search for identity in foreign affairs helps to explain the reason why Canada, a full year before the United States—as the then United States Secretary of Defense noted with evident perplexity in his diary for April 9, 1948 —was working for a trans-Atlantic security pact linking the two nations of North America with the Western European states which had already signed the Brussels Treaty. It also helps to explain why successive Canadian governments, once in NATO, professed dissatisfaction with its emphasis on the military build-up, and strove, with something less than complete success, for the implementation of Article II, enjoining non-military co-operation upon the members.

The Commonwealth

The search for foreign policies demonstrably different from those of the United States has led Canadian governments, particularly the Government in power since 1957, to take a good deal of proprietary interest in the modern Commonwealth of Nations. Such interest marks a change from the era of Mackenzie King, fighting his good autonomist's fight against "Downing Street domination," determined that the Commonwealth should not collectively do anything detracting from the individual responsibility of member governments and therefore, to be on the safe side, should not do anything at all. So nay-saying an attitude has died hard. As recently as 1956, when the Prime Minister of Australia expressed concern at the lack of decisions taken at the Prime Ministers' Meeting of that year, Mr. Lester Pearson reacted with something of the suspicion of his old chief. "It was not a question of reaching decisions," he told the House of Commons, "it was a question of exchanging views." In reply to a member of the Opposition who observed that the Prime Ministers seemed to have been rather reticent even about exchanging views, he added:

> There are specific problems within the Commonwealth between Commonwealth Governments, and I admit that some of the most acute of them were not discussed. I can say that it was a very good thing that they were not discussed . . . If decision had been in-

sisted upon it might very well have broken up the meeting.[27]

That Mr. Pearson had not exaggerated the consequences of checking ministerial inhibitions at the door of Commonwealth gatherings became apparent five years later. At the March, 1961, Prime Ministers' Meeting, it was the Prime Minister of Canada who insisted, in defiance of all precedent, upon discussing and condemning South Africa's racial policy. This caused Dr. Verwoerd to withdraw his government's application to be allowed to remain in the Commonwealth as a Republic. "South Africa sought consent," Mr. John Diefenbaker later recalled,

> on the ground that continued membership was a virtual formality. I took the position that if we were to accept South Africa's request unconditionally our action would be taken as approval or at least condonation of racial policies which are repugnant to and unequivocally abhorred by Canadians as a whole.[28]

It is still too soon to assess the long-range significance of these momentous events, either for the Commonwealth as a whole or for Canadian attitudes toward it. But it is clear that Canada's new-found forthrightness at the 1961 Prime Ministers' Meeting reflected the rising influence of Afro-Asian states outside the Commonwealth as well as within it, and the Government's evident desire not to alienate this increasingly important grouping in world affairs.

It continued to be easier to profess faith in the Commonwealth as an example of co-operation among the nations than to adopt those policies which might give substance to the profession. But just because Canadians and their Government did not always practice what they preached does not mean that their interest in

[27] Canada, *H. of C. Debates*, 1956, vol. 7, p. 6830.
[28] *Ibid.*, 1961, vol. 4, pp. 3081–2.

the Commonwealth was either insincere or impelled merely by the negative motive of contriving a counter to the United States. Evidence of genuine interest in making the association work might be found in the allocation of capital assistance through the Colombo Plan to the principal members of the Commonwealth in Asia. The United Kingdom's decision in the fall of 1961 seriously to negotiate for membership in the European Economic Community afforded the Canadian Government a fresh opportunity to protest its fidelity to Commonwealth principles. These, it insisted, would be fatally compromised if the United Kingdom moved into Europe. Was this concern more than a cover for a less high-minded fear of what might happen to the Canadian economy in the event that imperial preferences were scrapped? The student may pose this question, but he cannot at present hope to do more than offer an opinion in reply. My opinion is that it was not more, or not much more.

Recognition of Communist China

Early in 1950, Canada was on the verge of extending recognition to the Peking regime as the de facto government of mainland China. Four other Commonwealth governments, including that of the United Kingdom, had already taken that step. Then the Korean War intervened. The entry of Chinese Communist troops transparently disguised as "volunteers" and the subsequent branding of the Chinese People's Republic as an aggressor by the General Assembly of the United Nations put the question of recognition aside for the next few years. By 1955 it was back in the limelight. A less irrational mood in the United States—signified by the Eisenhower Administration's allowing its ambassador to Czechoslovakia to sit down at a table with a representative of the Peking regime—and the patent failure of non-recognition either to weaken the Chinese Communists or to make them more sweetly reasonable, caused the Canadian Government

cautiously to circle the nettle. Neither Mr. Pearson nor any of his colleagues ever grasped it, partly because of their uncertainty about public reaction in their own country, partly—some felt mainly—because Mr. Eisenhower and Mr. Dulles had made no secret of how angry they would be if the Canadian Government moved unilaterally. It did not seem worthwhile, Mr. Pearson explained after the defeat of the Liberal Government in 1957, to have had "a first-class row with the United States over a matter on which public opinion in our country is strongly divided."[29]

Whereas the Liberal Government had tried to base its China policy neither on ideology nor on emotion, but on what Mr. Pearson had described as "a calculated weighing of advantages and disadvantages," the Conservative Government of Mr. John Diefenbaker proceeded to inject the vexed and troublesome factor of morality, speaking, as its predecessor had never done, in the baroque idiom of the Committee of One Million. "Until such time as the People's Government, the Communist Government, of China, expiates its wrong-doing under international law," Mr. Diefenbaker declared in the House of Commons in November 1957, "there will certainly be no justification for the granting of recognition."[30] The Prime Minister thus pitched his argument to principle so high-minded that either it would have to be abandoned at some later date, or recognition postponed forever. Nor was the cause of flexibility much helped by the introduction of an argument commonplace in American but heretofore conveniently neglected in Canadian discussion of the subject. "The main reason [for not recognizing Peking]," the new Secretary of State for External Affairs, Mr. Howard Green, told his constituents in January 1960, "is that in South East Asia there are countries standing up against Communism . . . If we recognize Red China we would be dealing a heavy blow to friends of ours in South East

[29] Lester B. Pearson, "Where Canada Stands in the World Crisis," *Maclean's Magazine*, July 6, 1957.
[30] Canada, *H. of C. Debates,* 1957, vol. 1, p. 654.

Asia."[31] In opposition, both Mr. Diefenbaker and Mr. Green had urged a sturdy independence from United States policy; in power, they echoed the arguments of the China Lobby. Such slavish imitation was as ignoble as it was unnecessary. Happily for the national self-respect, and for the national interest, it did not prevail in the Diefenbaker Government's response to events in the Western hemisphere.

Fidel Castro's Cuba

Like many Americans, Canadians had at first nothing but admiration for the gallant band of fighters under Fidel Castro, struggling against seemingly insuperable odds for the liberation of their country from a coarse, grab-bag Caribbean dictator. So far as they thought of the conflict at all—and Havana is a lot further away from, say, Saskatoon than from Miami— they thought of it as a struggle between the forces of light and the forces of darkness. They were elated, as much as surprised, when, for once, the forces of light—as they appeared— prevailed.

Fidel and his friends had thus built up in the Dominion a sizeable credit in goodwill which even an unusual amount of unpleasant post-revolutionary ruction did not immediately run down. Canadians were not particularly dismayed when the Castro regime began expropriating United States investment, particularly as theirs was left conspicuously alone. There was, some felt, a certain rough retributive justice in all that, the image of Cuban-American relations being mainly an image of a predatory imperialist relationship. There may even have been those not above reassurance at this demonstration that a final, if drastic, solution existed for the problem of American ownership of domestic resources. Much more unsettling was the rate at which the revolution

began to devour its children. The persistence long after the consolidation of power of drumhead trials, execution by firing squads, persecution of press and universities, the stream of harassed and evidently liberal refugees—all this seemed too reminiscent of the kind of totalitarian terror hitherto associated more with Eastern Europe than with Latin America. Even here, however, the Canadian reaction was less alarmist than reaction in the United States. Distance delayed disenchantment. Many Canadians were ready to give Castro the benefit of any doubt, and eager to draw a distinction between his freedom fighters, sea-green and incorruptible, and those of the rank and file who might be getting a bit out of hand. Reports of the extent to which the regime had gone over to the Communists excited in some quarters a mischievous pleasure that a People's Democracy had sprung up so close to the playground of People's Capitalism (and the proving ground of its missiles). Those not so amused tended to discount the reports of Communist influence as the exaggerations of a malevolently disposed communications system.

Reaction to the series of United States counter-measures which began with the sugar boycott of July 1960, continued with the more far-reaching embargo of October, and culminated in the severance of diplomatic relations at the end of the year, was remarkable for its unanimity. The consensus of Canadian opinion was that while the United States had been subjected to severe provocation, the imposition of the embargo had been a mistake. It was likely to lead to a tightening of totalitarian control, to add substance to Castro's propaganda, and, above all, to drive the regime more surely into the arms of the bear and the jaw of the dragon. There was almost universal dismay, even at first sheer disbelief, at word of the ill-fated operation of April 1961 ending in tragic and ignominious disaster in the swamps near Cochinos Bay. But while the Canadian Government refrained from policies of embargo or boycott in attempting to come to terms with the Castro revolution, it did nothing—contrary to widely held American opinion—to try to turn the disruption of Cuban–United States

[31] Quoted in "Mr. Green's Diplomacy," *The Globe and Mail* (Toronto), January 9, 1960.

trade to commercial advantage. Indeed, it used its export-control procedures to prevent what the Prime Minister described as "the bootlegging of goods of United States origin."

Membership in the Organization of American States

Joining the Organization of American States was one way, one of the very few ways, by which the new Diefenbaker Government, which had come to power talking grandly of new brooms and new departures only to discover how little room for maneuver there really was, could distinguish itself from its predecessor. Mr. Howard Green accordingly set out, soon after becoming Secretary of State for External Affairs, on a goodwill tour of the southern hemisphere, returning much enamored of Latin American *ambiente*. An announcement that Canada would seek membership in the O.A.S. was expected at any moment. It did not come; by December 1962 it had still not come. The Department's memorandists had done their work, and sober second thinking had, for the time being, won the day. There was, in fact, much to be said on the *con* side of position papers. The O.A.S. foreign ministers, convened as an "Organ of Consultation," might by a two-thirds majority vote make the imposition of diplomatic and economic sanctions binding upon all its members. To muster support for such a move against Cuba was a clear objective of United States policy. One of the first decisions Canada, as an O.A.S. member, might have to take was whether to abandon its own Cuban policy or risk charges that it was disrupting hemisphere solidarity.

Was there not more than one way, after all, of demonstrating a concern for the welfare of Latin America? The twenty-second chair might safely be left vacant for a few more months, at least. In the meantime, much might be done to strengthen the Dominion's diplomatic representation, both by increasing the number of missions and by getting rid of the notion that a Latin American embassy was primarily a pleasant place for a worn-out politician to put in time before retirement. The opening of new missions in Central America, and the appointment of a senior career officer of the Department of External Affairs as Ambassador to Cuba (both developments of 1961) showed that the Government was wisely not going to allow its hesitation over entering the O.A.S to appear as indifference to the growing importance of the hemisphere in its outlook upon world affairs.

The Berlin issue

In striking contrast to these preoccupations along what might be regarded as the periphery of the great conflict is the absence of Canadian initiatives at its center. If one goes straight to the heart of the matter—the frozen map of Central Europe and the problems of Germany—the remarkable thing is how little rather than how much successive Canadian governments have contributed over the years. There is no arena of conflict more dangerous for Canadians than Berlin: but no new idea about Berlin (apart from the suggestion that United Nations forces might somehow be usefully stationed along the access routes) has ever come out of Ottawa. Perhaps Canadian governments have experienced a certain diffidence in speaking out on this central issue of power politics; perhaps our failure to insist on an occupation role in Germany in 1945, or to take part in the relief of the Berlin blockade three years later, have induced an inferiority complex, a feeling that these are great problems best settled by Great Powers. If there are indeed such inhibitions, they should be quickly overcome: in the kingdom of the blind, the one-eyed man is king. But this is not in fact a very convincing explanation for Canadian reticence, since neither Mr. Diefenbaker nor Mr. Green have been particularly inhibited in their utterances on foreign policy (Mr. Green, in particular, has ruffled his colleagues in at least one NATO Council meeting by the bluntness of his views and the directness of his criticisms). It is more plausible to suppose that there is no distinct policy because there are no distinct ideas, and that this in turn is the result of the Government's preoccupation with other matters.

Disarmament

No such reticence has been displayed in the related area of disarmament. This has been well described as the "magnificent obsession" of the present Secretary of State for External Affairs. In his determination to keep the nuclear Powers negotiating, or to bring them back to the negotiation table, Mr. Howard Green has displayed a tireless energy and at times a touching faith. It must be said, however, that Mr. Green's ingenuity in suggesting procedural devices to get disarmament discussions going has not always been matched by originality in suggesting proposals likely to be useful if they ever did get going. Some of the Minister's answers to questions in the House of Commons reveal that he has not kept himself very well informed about the rapidly changing technological background of this baffling subject. Thus, in reply to a questioner who had asked him to explain the distinction between arms control and disarmament, Mr. Green implied that arms control is an inferior and somehow disreputable form of disarmament, whereas of course the beginning of wisdom is to understand clearly that disarmament is a form of arms control and that neither is prop-

erly an end in itself since the objective of both is (or ought to be) peace and tranquility among nations. The Minister's uncertain grasp of the subject is the more regrettable in view of the immense amount of time and effort he has devoted to it. One much needed reform is to bolster the numbers and quality of experts in the Departments of External Affairs and National Defence giving arms control their full-time attention. "I think the staff could be strengthened," Mr. Green conceded on May 2, 1961, and he added: "We are moving to do it."

While the Government's disarmament crusade has been handicapped by inexpertness and inexperience, its active role in the 16-nation discussions at Geneva concerning the terms of reference of the Truce Commission for Laos has obviously been fortified by direct participation since 1954 on the three Truce Observation Commissions in Indochina. No more authoritative statement of policy in recent years exists than that delivered by Mr. Green to the Geneva Conference on June 19, 1961, impressive no less for its forthrightness than for its knowledge of the subject. Together, firmness and expertise exert maximum influence; individually, one apart from the other, they are not much use.

If there is any basic criticism to be made of the Diefenbaker Government's conduct of foreign affairs since 1957, it is that the boldness of its statements has not always been matched by the diligence of its homework or by persistence in negotiation. If a Great Power makes its mark by following Theodore Roosevelt's prescription—"speak softly and carry a big stick"—the foreign minister of a Middle Power during the 1960's is well advised to speak firmly and carry a full briefcase.

BIBLIOGRAPHY

Author's Suggestions

Canada in World Affairs. Vols. I–IX, Biennial Survey, published by the Oxford University Press for the Canadian Institute of International Affairs.

Canadian Annual Review. 1960, 1961. University of Toronto Press. Chapters on "External Affairs and Defence," by Robert A. Spencer.

Eayrs, James. *Northern Approaches: Canada and the Search for Peace.* Toronto: Macmillan, 1961.

Eayrs, James. *The Art of the Possible: Government and Foreign Policy in Canada.* Toronto: University of Toronto Press, 1961.

Keenleyside, Hugh, *et al. The Growth of Canadian Policies in External Affairs.* Durham, N.C.: Duke University Press, 1960.

Pickersgill, J. W. *The Mackenzie King Record, I, 1939–1944.* Toronto: University of Toronto Press, 1961.

ABOUT THE AUTHORS

KENNETH W. THOMPSON is a well-known authority on international politics and American foreign policy. He received his A.B. degree from Augustana College and took his Ph.D. degree at the University of Chicago. He taught at Northwestern University and the University of Chicago before joining the staff of the Rockefeller Foundation in 1953. He is currently Vice-President of the Rockefeller Foundation. Mr. Thompson has written widely on international affairs. His major published works include: *Christian Ethics and the Dilemmas of Foreign Policy*, 1959; *Political Realism and the Crisis of World Politics*, 1960; *American Diplomacy and Emergent Patterns*, 1962. He is co-author of: *Principles and Problems of International Politics*, 1951; *Man and Society*, 1953; *Conflict and Cooperation among Nations*, 1960.

JOSEPH E. BLACK graduated from Utah State University in 1947 and took his M.A. and Ph.D. degrees at Northwestern University. In 1950 he joined the faculty at Miami University, Oxford, Ohio. He was made Professor and Chairman of the Department of Government at Miami in 1958. Starting in the summer of 1963, he will be on leave from Miami University for two years serving as Professor of Political Science at University College, Ibadan, Nigeria. He will also lecture at Makerere College in Kampala, Uganda, and at the Royal College at Nairobi, Kenya. He is the author of the study, *Charter Review and Revision*, 1955, and co-author with Reo Christenson, of *National and International Issues*, to be published by Harper & Row.

ABOUT THE CHAPTER

The United States, one of the giants on the international scene, is a relative newcomer to the stage of Great Power politics. This nation, which only a short time ago was espousing isolationism as a sound basis of her international behavior, now finds herself involved in attempting to shape events throughout the world.

This chapter examines the power position of the United States and the relationship between the power of a nation and the policies which she pursues. The difficulty of assessing the various elements of power is considered and special attention is given to particular areas which are in flux. For example, an adequate military posture and level of preparedness for one set of circumstances may not be at all adequate for another. It is made clear that even though it is practically impossible to correctly relate all of the elements of a nation's power to those of her competitors, evaluations must, nevertheless, be attempted.

The authors describe the foreign policy process in the United States with special attention to those features which distinguish the policy process within the presidential system. The chapter concludes with an examination of selected foreign policy problem areas.

24

THE FOREIGN POLICY OF
THE UNITED STATES OF AMERICA

KENNETH W. THOMPSON

The Rockefeller Foundation

JOSEPH E. BLACK

Miami University, Oxford, Ohio

ELEMENTS OF AMERICAN
FOREIGN POLICY

The relatively permanent material elements

Geographical factors   The United States is blessed with a favored geographical position, abundant natural resources and a capacity to feed and clothe itself and others. Its world location has placed it athwart developing lines of commerce and trade; its regional location has protected it from threats arising within the boundaries of strong neighboring states. Neither Canada nor Mexico endanger U.S. security either through rival ambitions or superior power. Thousands of miles of ocean separating it from Europe or Asia have frustrated any continuing alliance by a state in the Western Hemisphere with European or Asian Powers.

Napoleon's well-known phrase: *"La politique de toutes les puissances est dans leur geographie"* is borne out by the American experience. While geography is only one of the many factors that have conditioned external policies, it has been as relevant for John F. Kennedy as it was for George Washington that the Atlantic Ocean continues to separate Europe from the United States or that the ports of the St. Lawrence are largely blocked by winter ice. The basic policies of the United States grow out of its geographical position and the need and favorable conditions for defending the Western Hemisphere.

Further, the geography of the United States assured that expansionist drives for a century or more would be concentrated and largely exhausted within the American continent. Indeed, a particular theory of American foreign policy

699

called "continentalism" traces the history of our foreign relations primarily in these terms. The theory of "continentalism" seeks to account for the actions of American statesmen by instincts and aspirations to build a mighty nation with influence extending from the Atlantic to the Pacific.

Mountain ranges and river systems have not restricted the growth and unity of the nation. By contrast, in Switzerland and Scandinavia, towering mountain systems have divided these countries into separate ethnic communities, and rivers flowing parallel to one another without converging at some central communication point have intensified the division.

The United States, of course, to the present day, has suffered from localism and regionalism but only once to the point of political separatism (the American Civil War). With this exception, regionalism within the United States has stemmed more from economic specialization than from permanent geographical or ideological division. The topography and climate of the United States have for the most part enhanced rather than weakened the prospects of national unity.

In summarizing the geographical position of the United States, one authority has written: "The most favored state in the world from the point of view of location is the United States. It faces two oceans and has therefore direct access to the two most important trade areas of the world." Not until the construction of the Panama Canal were the full advantages of this position realized. With a simpler and easier route to the Pacific, the nation's economic development profited from access to the trade patterns of two great oceans. To the extent that foreign policy follows trade, expansion of international economic relations has led to worldwide foreign policies.

Natural resources　Natural resources are relatively stable and fixed, but not unchanging. New discoveries, or advances in technology essential to the exploitation of raw materials, may drastically alter resource-use patterns. Thus in 1913 the United States was the major producer of crude oil, followed by Russia,

Mexico, Rumania and the Netherlands East Indies. Today Venezuela, Iran, Iraq, Kuwait (and, perhaps in the future, the nation controlling Sahara production), have moved into prominent positions. In 1913, the United States produced seven times the amount of copper of that of Japan, which was second in output. Today, Chile, Canada, Northern Rhodesia and, until recently, the Belgian Congo, together are responsible for approximately half of the world's copper.

Self-sufficiency of a nation in basic resources, which by the laws of comparative advantage in international trade should be less vital than the best use of available resources, is nevertheless an index of a nation's capacity. Nations seek economic autonomy chiefly because they are thereby enabled to survive the rigors of economic warfare or all out war. The Soviet Union defended itself effectively in World War II partly because of its relative self-sufficiency in staple commodities like lumber, grains, coal, petroleum, iron, manganese and chromium. In these and other staples, the United States is, of course, in an even more enviable position, particularly if access to the resources of the Western Hemisphere continues. If economic autarky is an element of power, the United States can, if need be, protect itself against all threats; it stands in the forefront of present day nations. The practical uses of synthetic materials increase the favored position of the country even further.

In food production, its position is similarly advantageous. On the strength of almost every index, whether food consumption based on calories per capita or food exports exceeding consumption needs, the United States is singularly fortunate. Food production techniques and improved crop varieties have strengthened American agriculture. Through farm extension and progress in scientific agriculture, the gap between actual and optimum productivity has been narrowed.

Innovation in American agriculture has included use of hybrid corn, rust resistant wheats, commercial fertilizers, inoculation against hog cholera, improvements in livestock and poultry breeding, and effective sprays. Moreover, the know-how of scientific agriculture has proven exportable in the hands of experienced agriculturalists. Thus food production, which at one stage was viewed as a wholly domestic problem, has become an important facet of American international relations.

Defensive power

The effectiveness of American foreign policy is also linked with military power, which has not remained constant even within a given historical era. The military strength of a nation depends upon its material resources but is scarcely identical with them. The importance of forces in being is relative to the overall circumstances of international politics. When national security could be pursued behind the shield of British naval power, the urgency of American military preparedness was not self-evident. Today the United States, like other sovereign states, must depend for its security on forces more extensive than its own national defense system.

Yet when President Kennedy in the summer of 1961, facing the Berlin crisis, called for an acceleration of military training and speed-up of the draft, his action reflected the continuing importance of national military preparedness. He acted in the spirit of an American tradition going back to George Washington, who in his first annual address to Congress on January 8, 1790, declared: "To be prepared for war is one of the most effectual means of preserving peace."

Military power as deterrent to agression
For the United States historically and most obviously in the postwar years, the chief role of military power has been to deter adventuresome expansionist Powers. Democracies forever run the risk of tempting thieves, for they tend to be the last to arm and, following a war, the first to carry out full-scale demobilization. Yet since World War II, successive U.S. administrations have learned that favorable ne-

gotiations with other Great Powers also depend on the level of military preparedness. By a people schooled in civilian ways and staunchly dedicated to peace, military programs of large scale have been undertaken only with great reluctance. However, Republicans and Democrats alike, responding to the expansionist policies of the Communist Powers, have supported extensive programs of national defense.

Most informed observers in the early days of the Cold War were convinced that the Russian threat to Western civilization was identical to the Nazi menace. As such, the recipe for dealing with it was assumed to be the same. It was said that if our leaders had learned anything from over two centuries of national experience, it was that foreign policy divorced from strength was impotent. Had not the United States following two world wars dismantled its military establishment as an earnest of peaceful intentions and goodwill? And in both cases, had not aggressive forces bent on expansion pressed forward into areas defenseless against their power? Both Germany and the Soviet Union imposed their will on helpless nations that were situated within their zone of control.

The lesson this taught Western leaders was that weakness could be no substitute for security, that policies harnessed to power were more likely to succeed than those drawing strength from high ideals and noble expectations alone. We sadly observed that the Low Countries in World War I and the Baltic States in World War II succumbed not because they were lacking in morality, but because they found no means of securing their national frontiers.

The "balance of terror"   The West has carried this discovery into the atomic and thermonuclear age. It is possible to argue that such peace as we have known since 1945 is the outcome of a "balance of terror." There are signs that the Soviet Union more than once marched up to the brink, threatening to engulf Greece and Turkey, Iran and Berlin, only to march down again when it met resistance. Conversely, where resistance proved ambiguous, uncertain or divided, as in Egypt, Syria and the Far East, the Soviet or the Communist sphere of influence spread across boundaries that had long marked the limits of Russian power.

Seen in these terms, the immediate military threat is unquestionably the gravest danger and military power the most vital element of foreign policy. Those who hold to this view call for multiplication of more powerful weapons of destruction, for new strategic doctrines, and for missile bases and a nuclear weapons pool. The irreconcilable conflicts and tensions of the Cold War will come to an end, it is said, only when one side or the other forges decisively ahead.

Political and economic deterrents to the spread of communism At war with this approach to foreign policy is a second that places the element of military power in a less paramount role and urges us to display equal vision and energy in seeking political and economic solutions, as for example in launching expanded military programs. It points to the Soviet technical assistance program, pledging $1.5 billion to underdeveloped areas, and to the evidence of successful Soviet economic penetration into the Middle East.

The scene and tactics of Russian imperialism have shifted and new policies are being forged. Subversion, infiltration and indirect aggression (disguised as appeals to anti-colonialism, anti-interventionism, and anti-Westernism) have put the West on the defensive, not on the military front but, because of excessive preoccupation with the military problem, rather in the economic and political sectors.

Ultimate weapons in the vast emerging areas are bound to have ambiguous effects, since their use against great numbers of agrarian peoples spread across immense geographical areas seems doubtful at best. Crises that have passed without their deployment in Indochina, Korea and Egypt serve to reinforce such doubts. Because they neither possessed nor saw the relevance of these terrible weapons, the newer nations have led the movement for their outlawry.

But the reactions in the newer states to thermonuclear devices are contradictory, as is best seen in the effects of the sputniks. In the same countries that were most vocal in urging us to disarm, American prestige suffered a grievous blow when the Soviet Union launched the first satellite. Despite continuous criticism of the United States throughout Asia and Africa for its materialism and preoccupation with purely technological and military advances, confidence in American policy has been gauged by these very standards so deplored.

One is reminded once more of Europe's and Asia's response when the United States, through the United Nations, held the line in Korea. Then our sharpest critics (including some in India who had found us rigidly anti-Communist and obsessed with the military threat) applauded the successful deployment of American power, particularly until the fateful crossing of the 38th parallel.

The issue between the two approaches is not one that can be measured and appraised by a barometer of the rise and fall of Stalinism in the Soviet Union. If Stalinism means a brutal and heedless sacrifice of every goal to the goals of the Communist society, Stalinism lives as much today as ever. The fact is, however, that Stalin no less than his successors pursued Russian objectives along more than one front, even though the accent on economic-political warfare seems recently to have increased.

It is undeniable that the Russian military threat survives the death of Stalin. If anyone has any doubt, he need only look to the sputniks, to the stress on force, and to the hundreds of Russian divisions guarding Soviet frontiers. Or he can listen to the threats and counterthreats of the Russian tyrants brandishing the instruments of force at each emerging crisis— Suez, Hungary, Poland, the Turkish-Syrian and the Berlin disputes.

But the countless moves and counter-moves on the political and economic front are equally real. With Soviet tactics of advance and retreat, the contest shifts almost imperceptibly from one type of warfare to another, or sometimes is joined simultaneously on all sides. The greatest risk an observer can run is to exclude one or the other dimension of the crisis in his zeal to describe reality in shades of black and white.

Elements of military strength Assuming then that the present crisis is partly but not exclusively military in nature, there are other problems to be faced in considering military power. Three errors are commonly made in appraising the military component of foreign policy. First, military power is often confused with national power; a nation's capacity to impose its will is equated with its military establishments. By contrast, military power is like the fist whose force depends on the health and vitality of the body politic and the whole society. Troops in being are an important determinant of a successful foreign policy, but without other foundations they will not suffice. Second, the military element is often viewed in more static terms than is appropriate. The democracies in two world wars, while they were the last to arm, rallied their forces to gain victory in the end. Third, it is difficult to analyze and foresee the most effective distribution of the components of military force at any given period of time.

For example, what constitutes a strong military force today? Is it large ground forces, hydrogen bombs, or intensive research? Is a small, highly specialized army more desirable than a large number of ground forces, or are both essential for a nation that seeks to be strong? The answers to these questions will probably be decisive in determining future influence in the world of states, yet it is sobering that estimates must be made on the basis of contingencies that cannot be foreseen.

We know in a general way that an effective foreign policy must be supported by a military program that can safeguard national security. But this leaves those who make decisions with the painful task of distributing resources among alternative means of defense without any certainty of the kind of war they may have to fight.

Beyond this, the weapons of today may not be used in future wars, because technology may have rendered them obsolete. It is said that conventional weapons are fast being supplanted by new and more deadly weapons, and therefore traditional armaments fail to provide an adequate basis for foreign policy.

On the other hand, there are military experts who question whether atomic and hydrogen weapons will ever be used, given the prospect of mutual annihilation. The Kennedy administration has accelerated the buildup of conventional weapons. Is it not fair then to ask whether the stockpiling of an unlimited supply of weapons that no nation would dare to use furnishes a state with the requisite military support? A military establishment grounded in conventional weapons may fall short of providing a defensible military posture, but so may a policy aimed at superior atomic or hydrogen bomb capacities. These are the horns of the dilemma on which defense strategists might be impaled.

The same problems arise with other, less permanent, material elements. Industrial capacity, as we have seen, is subject to far-reaching changes as new technologies alter patterns of production and capacity. At the same time, the importance of a well-founded industrial base is vital, for progress in steel, electronics or nuclear physics depends upon it. Controversies over rates of growth or estimates suggesting that our growth of less than 3 percent compares unfavorably with the Soviet Union's 8–9 percent hardly obscure the strength and vitality of American industrialism. The industrial power of the United States has demonstrated in peace and war its remarkable capacity to serve the world and to assure national security.

Human resources

The material elements upon which national power is based remain latent until harnessed through human resources. Thus the vast resources of the region that was to become the United States had little impact until merged with human skills coming from Europe and elsewhere. Four hundred years ago the entire continental territory of the United States supported 200,000 or 300,000 Indians living on the margin of subsistence. Today the area supports 185,000,000 people of many racial origins.

Mere numbers of people are more likely to foreshadow than to assure the rise of an influential nation. To be effective, the force of numbers must be organized by human skills and cemented by social cohesion and unity of purpose. The huge populations of China and India are coming to be a factor with which others must contend only as these great Asian states modernize and industrialize.

Trends in population growth   The other important limitation relating to mere numbers arises from the uncertainty of forecasting trends and developments. Population statistics provide a rational and stable basis for projecting probabilities! The outstanding American demographer, Dudley Kirk, writes: "They [statistics] are one of the most certain elements in a most uncertain world." Yet recent history suggests that demography is subject to many of the same vicissitudes of scientific inquiries in other social spheres.

France and the United States are cases in point. France's casualties among its young men from 1914–19 totaled 1,400,000. By 1938, the birth rate no longer kept pace with the death rate. In World War II, French casualties were 650,000, or three times the losses in the United States—a country four times the size of France. Nevertheless, from 1946 to the present, population growth in France, despite its losses and an essentially static pattern for nearly a half century, has dramatically increased. Since World War II, births have exceeded deaths by 300,000 annually.

Similarly, the United States seemed destined to be numbered among countries facing probable future population decline—a roster which included most of the nations that led the world in material progress. However, following the cessation of World War II hostilities, the birth rate in the United States began to climb and we have already exceeded by a substantial degree past estimates and projections. Our advance to a population of 185,000,000 reflects a nationwide increase in the birthrate, even though the size of families continues to be in-

fluenced by factors such as religion, social class, and family income.

Significance of population growth spurts
From the standpoint of foreign policy, the shift in the curve of American population growth is significant only in relative terms. In the framework of the Cold War, it means we have not fallen behind the Soviet Union as expected. If by 1970 the Soviet Union achieves an estimated total population of 250,000,000, our own population may exceed 200,000,000.

More significant for the future of world politics, a globe which was inhabited by 875,-000,000 in 1750 had, by the 1960's, reached approximately 3 billion, and by the year 2000 may approach 6 billion people. The implications of this for a stable international world hardly require comment. Economic development and national self-determination both demand social and political systems so organized nationally and internationally that they satisfy basic human needs. If population outruns the capacity of social systems to sustain it, the prospects will not be bright.

American policy-makers, who for religious, political and humanitarian reasons would have preferred not raising the issue, have been obliged to face the problem of an expanding world population and its implications for international peace. They may sometime in the future be driven to more direct and interventionist policies, knowing full well the risks and hazards of such an approach.

Qualitative factors   However, the qualitative attributes of a nation's human resources are no less important. A people's technical know-how, diplomatic skills, perseverance in time of crisis and national unity and cohesion affect their nation's position in the world.

A few facts may illustrate the point. The per capita output of the average American worker is vastly superior to that of most non-Western workers, and this factor must be weighed in the balance alongside total number of workers. For more than three centuries British diplomats were widely recognized and generally respected throughout the international society.

Who could have predicted that the British and Russian people would withstand with such remarkable fortitude the awful rigors of World War II? Or who can say whether or not the American people would survive and recover from a thermonuclear attack if the casualties were 30–40,000,000—as most civil defense planners assume would be the case, even if minimum shelters were prepared?

Skill in the conduct of foreign affairs The folklore of popular thinking about America's human resources in these intangible areas may not provide a firm guide for analysis. For example, many Americans emphasize the inherent qualities of our people in the technological realm as distinct from the qualities relating to diplomacy and foreign policy. Considerable stress is placed upon the industrial superiority of the nation as a whole. Most writers assume that certain dominant national characteristics born of frontier experiences have fostered the abilities required for successful entrepreneurship.

The early success of Americans like Benjamin Franklin, Thomas Jefferson and John Quincy Adams in the field of diplomacy and statecraft is infrequently cited. The myth is widespread that in any confrontation with diplomats of foreign countries, American representatives are likely to come out second best. Partly for this reason foreign policy has suffered from the reluctance of an important sector of public opinion to entrust delicate negotiations to chosen representatives in foreign relations abroad.

The achievements of American diplomacy, from the time of French assistance to the Colonies struggling to attain their independence from Britain to the present concern with private negotiations over Berlin, reflect much the same viewpoint. For political and other reasons American diplomatic triumphs, such as the resolution of the Berlin blockade in 1948–9 or the political preparations leading up to the establishment of the Marshall Plan, tend to be downgraded.

Confidence in the American businessman as an instinctively skilful horse-trader is seldom transferred to pride and respect for the American negotiator, either at the United Nations or in direct bilateral discussions with representatives of individual foreign countries. The qualities of certain recent American negotiators such as Charles E. Bohlen, Philip C. Jessup, John Foster Dulles and Dean Rusk receive far less public attention and recognition than the facts would warrant.

Public misconceptions This widespread lack of public confidence in American negotiators may result from the curious combination of the public and private function of the diplomat. Harold Nicolson's distinction between negotiation and foreign policy has not been generally understood. Nicolson argues that negotiation, which is chiefly a process involving painstaking and extensive relationships with foreign diplomats, is quite distinct from the enunciation of goals and principles in foreign policy or the results of diplomatic exchanges. Where much of the work of the diplomat must forever remain outside the public domain and where too much stress on success in any given negotiation with representatives sensitive to their own national sovereignty comprise the essence of diplomacy, full public appreciation is destined to be restricted and limited.

Countries more experienced in the theory and practice of negotiation and foreign policy such as Great Britain have, over several centuries, evolved a viewpoint more in keeping with the realities. A national outlook of this kind probably awaits the passage of time and more prolonged responsibility for foreign policy leadership in the Western world. Meantime, it would be a mistake to over-emphasize the unique qualifications of Americans in technical fields, given the rapid advance of countries like the Soviet Union, while placing too low a value on the professional skills of American diplomats.

The common problem confronting any nation as observers seek to measure the intangible qualities of its foreign policy is the absence of any simple measure of national capacity. The observer can quantify national income or steel production or even military forces in being. He can seldom prejudge with comparable assurance the advance of diplomatic skills of a particular government or the capacity of a whole people to endure prolonged suffering and deprivation. Yet these qualities may, in the end, have as much to do with success or failure as the quantitative elements of national power.

The organization of the government for foreign policy

A further problem in evaluating American foreign policy is the essential complexity of the American machinery of government. Our friends abroad are continually mystified by the anatomy of a foreign policy decision in the United States. Where can they locate responsibility at any given time? Who has the authority for a particular course of action? The vitality and often the effectiveness of American foreign policy are frequently the result of the dispersion of responsibility within the system. The essential inertia of the bureaucracy of any Administration is offset by the flow of creative ideas from divergent sources.

The origination of policies   No one can say in advance where a policy will originate. It may have its roots in a memorandum by a visiting American Congressman returning from a trip abroad. It may stem from a position paper on an item on the United Nations agenda. It may result from the viewpoint of an outside consultant called in to assist as an adviser or engaged as a roving ambassador. It may also, of course, be an outgrowth of a policy paper originating in the White House or the Department of State.

Even when a policy directive has taken shape, it must run the gamut of competing departments and agencies of the government, each with some authority in the foreign relations field. The role of the President or Secretary of State often resembles that of a sheepdog rounding up spokesmen of contending viewpoints of agencies who are assigned or assign to themselves responsibility for an action. No party mechanism nor power within the executive branch can assure that an existing course of action may not be reversed.

The American government as a rule has functioned most successfully when some happy coincidence has placed leaders of both parties in alignment with the thought and action of the executive branch of government. The halcyon days of bipartisanship when Senator Arthur Vandenberg carried major responsibility for the support of policies within the legislative branch of government are an exception to the normal pattern of foreign policy-making. Frequently, the interests of the political opposition require that it avoid responsibility for policies which may grow sour with time. Indeed, when out of office, both Democrats and Republicans, throughout American history, have unquestionably been right politically in avoiding full responsibility for actions which, in the end, must rest with the government in power.

Consistencies and inconsistencies   For countries whose political system is unitary, the process of resolving problems and reaching decisions within the American system is inevitably confusing. They ask who speaks for the American government, and they expect the government to speak with a single voice. They are frustrated when commitments growing out of one set of relationships are reinterpreted in a new set of relationships. They point to the lack of consistency in American foreign policy.

Yet even a cursory review of recent American policies suggests that this weakness is more apparent than real. In any overall sense, the foreign policies of Dean Acheson, John Foster Dulles and Dean Rusk have much in common. In the postwar world, no American government which bears responsibility for the security of the American people and generations yet unborn could afford to ignore the Soviet threat. With greater experience in office, each successive President in turn has remarked upon a growing sense of the awesome responsibility for protecting American lives and national integrity from external threats of aggression and expansionism.

The burden of office of the American President has increased year by year as the United States has assumed ever wider responsibility for the security of Western civilization. The luxury of the private citizen who can experiment with alternative techniques of armament and disarmament is denied the American President. If this were not true, successive Administrations with quite divergent philosophies and ideologies as to the pursuit of American interests abroad, would have behaved far differently than they have.

The role of the President   In the end, the final source of authority for foreign policy inevitably must rest with the President. He may wish to delegate authority to implement and execute policies to various agencies of the government. It is the President, however, and he alone, who bears the responsibility for decisions—as President Kennedy was frank to assert in the Cuban debacle—and for the success or failure of American policies abroad. He is the Commander-in-Chief of the armed forces, the leader of his party, the principal administrator of government, the symbol of the nation abroad and, in former President Harry Truman's pungent phrase, he sits behind the desk at which the buck stops. Other legislative and political leaders are elected on a regional basis. The President along with his Vice President represents the nation as a whole.

Of course, the ultimate responsibility of the President in the foreign policy field should not obscure the fact that he can call upon a number of agencies for advice, he can counsel with confidential aides, and he can appoint special advisory groups to help explore the courses of action which are open in particular cases. Thus, one frequently hears of the "men close to the President," of consultations with Congressional leaders, and of special meetings of the National Security Council. Each President has to determine how major decisions will be made and no general rule can be set down on the actual process of policy formulation. Even within a single administration, a number of different methods are used to meet contingencies as they arise.

The National Security Council   Several special agencies are particularly important. First, the National Security Council was created in 1947 to advise the President "with respect to the integration of domestic, foreign, and military policies relating to the national security." The statutory members of this body are: the President, the Vice President, the Secretary of State, the Secretary of Defense, and the Director of the Office of Civil and Defense Mobilization. In addition, there are special assistants to the President and an Executive Secretary.

In actual practice, the National Security Council is larger than this. The Director of the Central Intelligence Agency and other high government officials are usually invited by the President to attend sessions of the Council. In fact, the regular meetings of this body have become so large that in special emergency cases, such as occurred during the Cuban crisis in October 1962, a special "Executive Committee" of the Council may be appointed to advise the President.

However, even when the National Security Council or an Executive Committee of the Council meets to assess and appraise the objectives, commitments, and risks of the United States in either particular or general cases, it does not make the decisions. It advises the President on courses of action which appear open. It is the task of the Council to explore options which are available; the President must make the final choice.

The Central Intelligence Agency   Second, the Central Intelligence Agency was established by the National Security Act of 1947 as a subsidiary body to the National Security Council. It was given the specific task of co-ordinating the intelligence activities of the various governmental departments and agencies which have special responsibilities in the national security field. In addition to its regular role of co-ordinating, gathering and evaluating intelligence, this agency has also, on occasion, been given certain operational assignments by the President and the National Security Council.

Other sources of advice   Third, there are a number of other agencies, many of them in the Executive Office of the President, which play advisory roles in matters related to both domestic and foreign policy. These agencies include the National Aeronautics and Space Council, headed by the Vice President, the Office of Civil and Defense Mobilization, the Council of Economic Advisers and the Bureau of the Budget.

The President also can appoint special "task forces" or study groups to deal with particular problems. Likewise, individuals whom the President especially respects and trusts can be called upon for advice. For example, the Attorney General, Robert Kennedy, has played an important advisory role in the field of foreign policy during the Kennedy Administration. But regardless of the various agencies which exist or the special advisory groups available, the fact remains that the President must ultimately take the responsibility for the policies which are adopted and for their execution.

The student of foreign policy must keep in mind that for long-run policy and for particular programs, especially those where appropriations are required, Congress plays an extremely important role. However, in the great matters of war and peace and the decisions which must be made as emergencies arise, the President is clearly in the "driver's seat."

The Department of State   The discussion above should not obscure the fact that the Department of State continues to be the major single source of foreign policy decisions in the government. The President obviously cannot make the myriads of decisions required each day for the conduct of United States foreign policy around the world. The Department of State has the specific responsibility of initiating and implementing foreign policies. The work of this, the oldest of the executive departments, and the Foreign Service is directed by the Secretary of State through the Under Secretary of State and the other officials of the Department.

The Department is organized both functionally and regionally. Thus, one finds within the Department such functional agencies as a Bureau of Intelligence and Research, a Bureau of Economic Affairs, and the Bureau of Public Affairs. On a geographical basis, there is a special bureau for each of the regions of the world. For example, there is a Bureau of African Affairs directed by an Assistant Secretary of State. Within this bureau there are offices for each of the major regions of Africa, and finally "desks" for various nations.

It is imperative that the President enjoy the most intimate and harmonious relationships with the Secretary of State. Each must perceive by reason or instinct the views of the other and understand the principles from which they are derived—often on the basis of limited exchange and discussion. No Secretary of State can be expected to bear the responsibility which the Constitution assigns to the President. The exact division of labor varies from Administration to Administration, but former Secretary of State Dean Acheson was undoubtedly right when he insisted that former President Truman must achieve the same mastery as the Secretary of the basic policy papers in order to fulfill his full constitutional responsibility in the conduct of foreign affairs.

The relationships between President and Secretary of State have run the gamut from the arrangements evolved by former President Franklin D. Roosevelt, under which he was in effect his own Secretary of State, to those worked out by former President Dwight D. Eisenhower and John Foster Dulles, under which Mr. Dulles carried many of the official as well as the non-official responsibilities of American foreign policy.

The cloth must be cut to fit individual circumstances and needs, and the personalities, interests and ambitions of the principals in any Administration must come into play. Yet in the end the President must recognize his duties as the major figure in the American government responsible for external relations.

The influence of military agencies The President is Commander-in-Chief of the armed forces of the United States and the Department of Defense is headed by a civilian secretary nominated by the President. Even though this is the Constitutional arrangement it is clear that the "military" has played an increasingly important role in the formulation of foreign policy during the past few years.

The Department of Defense and the three service departments under its direction share directly in the foreign policy process at all levels. In addition to being a member of the Cabinet, where important foreign policy issues are frequently discussed, the Secretary of Defense is also a member of the National Security Council.

It is a truism that military policy cannot be separated from the rest of the foreign policy of the nation. Military power is required both to secure particular interests of the nation abroad and for defensive purposes at home. It is also clear that a nation's military power, as an essential portion of its total power, greatly influences the full range of choices open to the nation at a particular time.

During the period since World War II the United States has assumed worldwide commitments. Is it any wonder then that the voice of the military has increased in the foreign policy field? And with ever more complex weapons systems one can assume that the "experts" in the military branch of the government will carry even greater weight.

This does not imply that the military speaks with a single voice and that there is a "military point of view." Indeed, Secretary of Defense McNamara and some of his subordinates, with their eye on foreign policy realities, insist that we must increase the number of "options" open to the United States at a particular moment. The "counterforce strategy" being developed aims not at war of mutual annihilation sometime in the future, but at finding alternatives to total destruction even if a major war should break out.

Other influential government agencies Other Departments such as Treasury, Agricul-

ture, and Commerce are also involved in the foreign policy field to some extent. And there are many sub-departments and other agencies, such as the Export-Import Bank, whose functions are directly related to foreign policy problems. The President as chief executive is in charge of these various departments and agencies. But again, because of the complexity of the modern world—the sheer magnitude of the problems, and man's limited span of control—it is almost an impossible task for the President to play a full part in their work.

The role of Congress The President must also work out a pattern of effective relations with the Congress. Not only does the Senate exercise its constitutional authority in areas such as the ratification of treaties on the basis of a two-thirds vote, but, as the cost of implementing our policies has grown geometrically, the importance of various committees and leaders within the Congress has increased apace.

A growing sense of public responsibility has evolved in the Congress, particularly in the Senate Foreign Relations Committee and the House Foreign Affairs Committee. Here the most searching discussions go on, often behind closed doors, and administrative officers who have spent long hours with Congressional committees have praise for the vision and objectivity of individual Congressmen. Initiatives in the field of diplomacy may come from individual Congressmen as in the case of Senator Walter F. George's proposal during the Eisenhower Administration for negotiations with Khrushchev at the summit.

The legislature also exercises checks upon proposals put forward by an Administration, and an overall educational function is performed by Congressmen who spend time abroad as part of their scrutiny of Congressional appropriations. The Congress is achieving a wider sense of national responsibility as the United States extends its interests in the postwar world, although there are more or less continual pressures at work on individual Congressmen to put parochial interests ahead of national interests. What is most surprising is not the existence of such pressures, but the number of cases in which they are transcended.

National goals and interests

Democratic constitutionalism The national goals and purposes of the United States in the early days of the Republic were relatively simple and clearcut. They centered around the establishment of an area of freedom for those who came in search of it from other lands. It should never be forgotten that their values were in part the largesse of history bequeathed to them by historic defenders of freedom in Europe and Great Britain. They stemmed from the fruits of a 2,000-year-old debate on the political consequences of the nature of man.

The new laboratory for the testing and implementing of these time-honored precepts was a vast and sprawling continent not marred by the ancient rivalries and feudal patterns of earlier days. The goals of the United States were freedom with equality. The more limited and specific constitutional and institutional aims of the new society were framed and ordered in a set of "Higher Law" principles of those ends of mankind that were conceived of as natural and objective. The competition for the spoils of public office and the struggle for political power went on within an accepted body of assumptions and principles that defined the rules of the political game.

The working principles of the "living constitution" were based on a wise and fruitful compromise between strong and limited government. If men were gods, wrote one of the Founding Fathers, democratic government would be unnecessary. If they were beasts, it would be impossible. Since each man combined within himself a touch of both the divine and the demoniac, democratic constitutionalism was essential. The goal of constitutionalism, therefore, has been to found political institutions strong enough to resolve national needs yet limited so as to prevent authoritarianism. Ours is a government based on separation

of powers and checks and balances, with delegation of responsibility to designated levels of legitimate authority. This underlying principle of division of responsibility is more fundamental than the specific institutional arrangements evolved within the federal system. The underlying principle, and not federalism or the precise distribution of powers among the executive, legislative and judicial branches of government, carries meaning and significance for other nations today.

Changing requisites of national security
If democratic constitutionalism embraces the political goals of American life, the nation's historic and strategic interests comprise our aims abroad. At minimum, the national interest as expressed by a long succession of changing governments has been protection of the security of a sovereign, independent state. For more than a century and a half no government of the United States could afford to jeopardize the safety of American soil.

At one stage and behind the protective shield of the British Navy, this called for a policy of non-alignment or, to be more precise, selective alignment in non-political fields. Later the Monroe Doctrine became the instrument for announcing firm opposition to intervention by European Powers in the affairs of any state in the Western Hemisphere. For more than a century, foreign policy leaders have insisted that any threat to vital interests would logically arise from a Power or combination of Powers within the New World. The threat could as well involve outside Powers acting in concert with one or more American states as it could collaboration exclusively among Western Hemispheric states.

With the revolutions in technology and communications lessening the importance of distances between world continents and regions, the international relations of states in Europe and Asia became matters of greater urgency for the United States. Our national interest in the twentieth century has decreed that we seek to prevent any single Power or combination of Powers from dominating all of Europe or Asia.

We entered the First and Second World Wars to turn back the threat of German expansionism which, had it gone unchecked, could have led to the control of all Europe. The objective of our Far Eastern policy was similarly to deny to Japan in Asia control and authority throughout that continent. American policymakers instinctively have sensed that sooner or later a major expansionist nation controlling the human and material resources of Europe or Asia would threaten American security.

The goal of Britain's foreign policy for nearly three centuries had been to maintain a balance of power in Western Europe. The goal of the United States has become the maintenance of freedom and self-determination for independent states whose sovereignty would be extinguished by the overwhelming power of a single ambitious and powerful state.

The United States in the first half of the twentieth century, as Britain in the nineteenth century, was able to withhold its power and force until the eleventh hour. It could act to reestablish a condition of equilibrium when it became clear that one or more nation-states within a world region threatened to overthrow the balance of power.

Today the principal weights in any balance of power lie outside Western Europe. Moscow and Washington have both committed their prestige and power, one for the transforming of the status quo and the other for its preservation. No longer can the United States hope to re-establish political stability by throwing its influence into the scales on the eve of a great military struggle. If a struggle is to be avoided, American prestige must be engaged around the world at points where Soviet expansionism is most threatening.

Reconciling conflicting principles   A coincidence of our national goals and interests is worth noting. The United States has embraced freedom within its borders and self-determination abroad. It has never taken the significance of either set of goals lightly. Democrats and Republicans are at one in espousing the cause of freedom. Moreover, the political and strategic interests of United States foreign policy dedicated to the maintenance of an equilibrium of power in the major world regions, coincide with and reinforce the American belief in national self-determination and freedom abroad. This coincidence of national goals and interests marks the broader outlines of a philosophy of American foreign policy. It provides a statement of what we stand for and where we seek to go. However, no one should imagine it gives the statesman a recipe for the steps he must take in the day-by-day conduct of foreign relations.

The complexity of decisions in American foreign policy stems from the fact that the United States today has commitments and treaties with more than forty nations and has representatives in more than one hundred. The pattern of freedom and the forms that it takes vary in different parts of the world. Our own loyalties and principles compete with one another. Thus we support self-determination of the newer nations and of those on the threshold of nationhood, while recognizing the identity of our mutual interests with France. We believe in the principle of non-intervention, particularly in Latin America, but our policies are also guided by the Monroe Doctrine.

In Cuba, these two principles collided head-on. According to the dictates of the Monroe Doctrine, we could not endanger American security by standing aside as Communist power expanded into the Western Hemisphere. The principle of non-intervention, however, prevented us from acting on any all-out full-scale basis within the jurisdiction of another sovereign state.

Therefore, the public official responsible for the fateful choices of the nation in its external policies is like a juggler who must keep not one but many balls in the air simultaneously. One distinguished American public servant, when asked what the best training might be for a prospective Foreign Service Officer, suggested he be placed in a room with a hundred white mice and be invited to deal with them all simultaneously.

Thus the principles of United States national interests and the goals that guide us are like a map of a vast region or continent. They mark out the broad lines of communication and the overall geographic features. But the traveler who must find his way must map out the hills and valleys as he goes along. Or to shift the analogy, he is like the platoon leader who must sketch out the details of the battlefield to locate the enemy and the local terrain, using the more general maps or orders of battle prepared at the divisional level for a broad picture of his position on a wide front.

Goals and values shared with other nations

Beyond this, the United States, no less than other countries with wide-ranging interests, must seek the points of concurrence between its goals and interests and those of other nations. Fortunately for the United States the principles of Articles 1 and 2 of the Charter of the United Nations state, on a worldwide scale, the dominant goals toward which America has worked for more than a century and a half. In theory at least there is a concurrence between America's interest in a free and peaceful world and those of other countries, not least the new nations.

If the goals and interests of the United States are to survive, they must to some limited extent be reflected in the goals of the international community. Thus the United States can hardly defend peace and order if the international community rejects it. American values depend on the form and content of worldwide values.

In the immediate postwar world, the United States found that its interest in a peaceful and stable Western Europe was identical with that of the states who set about reconstructing their economies and re-establishing their governments. Or, in more recent times, the interests of the North Atlantic community in achieving greater unity are seen by responsible officials in Washington as compatible with United States national interests.

Nature of the international community
The struggle over the future of the United

Nations is fundamentally a struggle over the nature of the international community. If other nations of the world recognize as a common interest the acceptance of the judgment of an international body like the United Nations, or an independent international civil service under the leadership of the Secretary General, this makes possible progress toward the American goal of justice and the rule of law throughout the world. If the international community rejects the principle of an independent "third party judgment" of disputes between sovereign states, this threatens the viability of American interpretations of the principles of international law and a legitimate international order.

The building of greater consensus among independent nation-states devoted to the rule of law in opposition to an international order of coercion has become a shared value of many of the members of the United Nations. When sovereign states are no longer capable of assuring their own national integrity through national security systems, they must, in the common interest, have recourse to some large-scale international security system. For states who are chiefly interested in preserving what they have and in maintaining international equilibrium, this goal is clear and unequivocal.

However, we have witnessed a succession of crises in which one or more parties to a dispute seek to overturn an existing state of affairs to advance their prestige and influence in the world. Under these circumstances, existing treaties and obligations which at best are a pale reflection of national systems of law are challenged by opponents of a given status quo.

The techniques of peaceful change Where law is insufficient for the maintenance of peace, nations historically have turned to other forms of justice for composing their differences. These forms include the many and varied techniques of peaceful change. They are embodied in the principles and the machinery of the Charter of the United Nations designed for the harmonizing of differences.

Mediation, conciliation and negotiation are the basis on which stability depends, where law yields to changing events.

Americans, in viewing their own constitutional system, run the risk of minimizing the many informal political methods that are used to achieve some tolerable stability and order. A political party in working out its platform proceeds not on the basis of law but compromise and adjustment. The genius of Anglo-Saxon politics has been the central role played by political give and take.

Thus at the same time the United States continues to defend law and order, it must also accept the inevitable role of political accommodation and peaceful change. Accommodation on the international scene is difficult to explain to an aroused and sensitive national public opinion. The Jay Treaty prompted so severe a reaction that its principal negotiator was hung in effigy. The painful compromises which the United States must inevitably accept on difficult and perplexing international problems call for political and moral courage of the highest order on the part of its leaders. If one considers the probable public reaction to a political agreement regarding Communist China or Cuba or Berlin, one sees immediately the difficulty of this approach.

Yet throughout history those nations who have contributed most to the advancement of justice and order have been flexible in the methods they employed and the compromises they accepted. This lesson above all and the anguish which must follow its application is one with which Americans must learn to live for generations to come.

GENERAL PRINCIPLES AND OBJECTIVES

The objectives of the United States, like those of other nations and empires, have always been a product of historical experience, geographical location and stubbornly rooted legend and belief. American isolationism, so-called, persisted until World War I because it seemed to account for and justify a century or more of national conduct. It enabled Americans to settle and populate a continent, master its natural resources, and become a Great Power.

Isolationism and its meaning in U.S. policy

But ours was always "isolationism with a difference," as exemplified by the thrust of America's dynamic westward expansion. It represented withdrawal—but also "Manifest Destiny." Early in American history, isolationism was belied by such events as the ratification of the Jay Treaty initiated in 1794 by President Washington's government shortly before he proclaimed his much-quoted dictum against entangling alliances in his celebrated Farewell Address. The assumptions of isolationism were even more dramatically challenged by the invasion of Washington, and the burning of the Capitol and the White House by a British army less than a quarter of a century before Abraham Lincoln declared in 1838: "All the armies of Europe, Asia and Africa combined . . . with a Bonaparte for a commander, could not by force take a drink from the Ohio or make a track on the Blue Ridge in a trial of a thousand years."

Nevertheless, in a larger sense the new American republic, for more than a century, was freed from international responsibility by the fortuitous coincidence of geographic isolation and a European equilibrium of power over which British policy and naval strength stood guard. In such a world, it was natural to assume that Americans were a chosen people, that domestic policies were more important than foreign policies, and that alliances, so prevalent in the history of Europe, were no more than an expensive and pernicious nuisance. The good fortune of our historical experience made for that peculiarly American version of self-righteousness about which Alexis de Tocqueville wrote:

If I say to an American that the country he lives in is a fine one, "Aye," he replies, "and there is not its equal in the world." If I applaud the freedom its inhabitants enjoy, he answers: "Freedom is a fine thing, but few nations are worthy of it." If I remark on the purity of morals . . . "I can imagine," says he, "that a stranger who has witnessed the corruption which prevails in other nations, would be astonished at the difference." At length I leave him to a contemplation of himself; but he returns to the charge and does not desist till he has got me to repeat all I had just been saying. It is impossible to conceive a more troublesome or more garrulous patriotism. . . .[1]

The political and intellectual change the United States has undergone since the early nineteenth century is profoundly significant. American foreign policy has cut loose from the moorings of "splendid isolation" and has consciously accepted firm ties of partnership with the peoples of Europe, Asia, Africa and the Middle East. We have bilateral and multilateral security arrangements with more than forty nations, and our loyalty to the UN, at least in principle, is beyond dispute. We can point to the Marshall Plan as an act of almost unrivaled generosity.

Chauvinistic tendencies

Yet the tendency to see ourselves as morally and spiritually, if not geographically, apart from the other nations of the world, although hidden beneath the surface, is always present, ready to erupt and engulf popular thinking. As a successful people we easily grow impatient

[1] *Democracy in America,* Galaxy edition, New York: Oxford University Press, 1947, p. 413.

with the failings both of nations whose greatness is presumed to lie in the past and of newly emerging states which painfully grope toward a better life. From our privileged world position we look at Europe as a civilization whose past greatness is beclouded by imperialism, colonialism and power politics, sins from which we assume we are free. Europe is like the aging father who has had his chance, while the United States, as the aspiring and buoyant youth, seeks to implant its newfound authority.

In much the same spirit we expect that the poverty of the under-developed countries will be removed by our material aid if only they will embrace the same economic and political institutions which account for our greatness. We forget that the ways by which a people move toward more enlightened political, economic and social structures constitute the most profound of the processes of national life. If one nation seeks overtly to influence the course of events within the borders of another, it does well to remember George F. Kennan's sage advice: "We must be gardeners and not mechanics in our approach to world affairs."

Within these limits, and recognizing that a nation's goals can never be universal, the United States cannot leave to others or to mere chance the formulation of its interests and objectives. This task is far more varied and exacting than it was in the less complicated days of our past history.

Safeguarding national security

The first objective of American foreign policy remains today, as in the past, the safeguarding of the territorial integrity and security of the United States. Experience makes clear, however, that the requirements of national security are not limited by the provision of an adequate zone of defense for Fortress America. A "great debate" has occurred with each successive geographical extension of the concept of national security, but at each stage the personal preferences of the country's leaders have yielded to the prevailing forces of history.

Territorial limits The conditions of a changing international environment have pushed the security principle ever more outward, from the national domain to the Caribbean littoral, then to the whole of the Western Hemisphere, and finally to the preservation of an equilibrium of power in Europe and Asia. Americans have come to recognize slowly and painfully that massive concentration of power in unfriendly hands is a threat to this nation's security.

Two world wars were needed to demonstrate that our advance line of defense requires the maintenance of a balance of power in Europe and Asia, although our final stand is in the Western Hemisphere. Postwar policies of creating collective strength and building deterrent power through NATO and, less successfully, SEATO, are designed to serve this end. Economic policies aimed at creating or reestablishing more stable and viable independent societies are properly conceived as programs of mutual security.

Moral values National security as a cardinal objective in United States foreign policy also has a moral and political content. Through it, enduring moral values inherent in the American national interest are protected and defended. The nation-state is both the problem child of international relations and the highest existing expression of genuine moral consensus on the part of a given people in a given geographic area. More progress has been made in creating freedom and equal opportunity within the United States than within the emergent but largely inchoate international community. Nations can, in practice, more readily give moral content, however modest, to the national interest than to international interests which tend to be vague and ill-defined. National values and the general welfare are an antidote to crass materialism or to subnational interests which are parochial and self-seeking.

A citizenry which takes its own history and traditions seriously is a guarantee that a nation's reputation shall not perish nor its will to stay alive be destroyed. A citizenry's sense of partnership in a common enterprise with ancestors who have gone before and heirs who are to follow gives moral stamina and political vitality. In this respect, national attachments remain the soundest basis for transcending narrow partisan political loyalties.

In general, a more tolerable relationship is achieved by nations which speak in the national interest than by those which claim to speak for the whole world. Hence, states, while asserting the moral integrity of their interests, ought never to see them too exclusively as universal ends. World patterns are so complex and variegated that perfect virtue cannot be claimed for a single state or a particular course of action. The periods of greatest decline in international morality have come when the purposes of one nation or another have been presented as pure and unsullied goals put forth for acceptance or rejection by the rest of the world.

Political considerations For the United States, as for all World or Regional Powers, the one thing which saves the national interest from itself is its essential reciprocity. Edmund Burke expressed this in the following words: "Nothing is so fatal to a nation as an extreme of self-partiality, and the total want of consideration of what others will naturally hope or fear." After a nation's leaders have determined its objective interests, they have an obligation to look at the world in perspective, and appraise coolly and realistically the interests of its neighbors.

There is no more hazardous a temptation than to treat other peoples as pawns in the struggle for one's own nation's basic interests. Yet, in the West's relations with the rest of the world, particularly with newly emergent societies in Asia, the Middle East and Africa, this temptation often seems irresistible.

The foreign policy objectives of the United States, then, are best conceived of as a series of concentric circles. At the heart or center is the requirement of assuring the security of existing territorial boundaries. This objective has been served since the days of the Monroe Doctrine by policies aimed at denying control over the Western Hemisphere to any unfriendly European or Asian Power.

Beyond this, the national interest has dictated that any American government would resist—it is hoped by means short of war—the spread of influence by nations or empires over all of Europe or Asia. It has been an implicit, if not articulated, premise that in both continents a balance of power should be fostered and preserved. In effect, the United States fought in two world wars to preserve such an equilibrium in Europe and Asia.

Our support today of West Germany in Europe, and of Japan and India in Asia, is based on the need for countervailing power against the U.S.S.R. and Communist China, respectively. Finally, within and outside the League of Nations and the UN, the United States has pursued the objective of creating and maintaining the type of international order in which democratic values have a fair chance of survival. We have worked for the kind of world in which the principles of freedom and individualism would be respected.

CONTEMPORARY FOREIGN POLICY PROBLEMS

The clash between East and West which dominates current U.S. foreign policy can best be illustrated by examples. The four case studies which follow will give concreteness to the Cold War and point up its manifold dimensions.

Cuba and the balance of power

The most dramatic and serious confrontation between the East and the West, at least since the Korean War, occurred during the last week of October, 1962. After several days of top-level meetings and a growing tenseness in the nation's capital, President Kennedy solemnly announced to the American people that "unmistakable evidence" had established the fact that Soviet Russia was preparing offensive missile sites in Cuba. The President pointed out that two different types of missile sites were under construction. The medium range missiles, some of them already in place, would be capable of carrying warheads for a distance of more than 1,000 miles. With the completion of installations designed for intermediate range missiles, most of the cities in the Western Hemisphere would be within the target range.

Cuba's turn to communism   The solid information of the offensive build-up came after a most frustrating period of attempting to deal with the "Cuban problem."[2] Historians will long debate the handling of relations with Castro in the months immediately following the fall of the Batista regime and the installation of the revolutionary government in January of 1959. The debate centers on the alternatives open to the United States at that time, and whether a different Cuba could have emerged if different policies had been followed.

After an extremely short "honeymoon period" with the United States, it became apparent that the foreign policy of Castro's Cuba was clearly oriented towards the Communist world. By May of 1960 Khrushchev announced that the Soviet Union would "defend" Cuba against any attempted American aggression. Cuban leaders paid visits to the Iron Curtain countries to receive the plaudits of the "comrades" and to arrange for technical assistance, technicians, and arms. Attempts were also made to "export the revolution" to other Latin American countries. Castro made clear the future he saw for the Western Hemisphere and Khrushchev announced that the Monroe Doc-

[2] See D. A. Graber, "United States Intervention in Latin America," *The Yearbook of World Affairs,* London: Stevens & Sons, Ltd., vol. 10, 1962.

trine had died "a natural death" and pointed with pride to the new arrangement in the Caribbean.

U.S. support for anti-Castro rebels American policy-makers gave the most careful attention to the "betrayal of the revolution" and the establishment of a Soviet base in the Western Hemisphere. The alternatives open to the United States were considered by President Eisenhower and his closest advisers. A plan emerged for supporting certain Cuban refugees who wished to overthrow the Castro regime. The Central Intelligence Agency was given extraordinary responsibilities for participating in the training of Cuban refugees as well as evaluating the stability of the Castro government and the support an invasion would have from different groups within Cuba.

Preparations for the Cuban operation continued under the Kennedy Administration, with a number of Security Council meetings devoted to the problem. It was decided that the invasion would have limited support but U.S. troops would not become directly involved in the venture.

The invasion, which occurred at the Bay of Pigs in April of 1961, ended in disaster. In its wake, the President, after taking full responsibility for the debacle, took a firmer grasp on policy-making machinery and the policy-making processes of the government were carefully reviewed, especially the role which had been assigned to the Central Intelligence Agency.

Demands for withdrawal of Soviet arms
The Soviet military build-up in Cuba, including the deployment of a large number of Communist technicians and military advisers, followed. Even with the placement of defensive anti-aircraft and anti-shipping missiles, the United States at first took the position that the status quo had not been altered. But the introduction of bombers, medium range missiles, and the preparation of intermediate-range missile sites altered the situation. It was this "upsetting of the precarious status quo" that could not be tolerated. The President de-

clared that the "deliberately provocative and unjustified change in the status quo cannot be accepted by this country if our courage and our commitments are ever to be trusted again, by either friend or foe."

After tracing the steps by which the United States had weighed the risks involved and with the knowledge that "even the fruits of victory in nuclear war would be ashes in our mouth" the President demanded that the offensive weapons be withdrawn from Cuba. The steps to be taken by the United States, including the quarantine on "all offensive military equipment" ended with the call to Chairman Khrushchev to "halt and eliminate this clandestine and provocative threat to world peace and to stable relations between our two nations."

The withdrawal of Soviet weapons and the victory for the forthright action by the United States are history. But one feels compelled to raise some questions about the grave Soviet miscalculations of the venture and also to draw some conclusions regarding United States foreign policy.

Khrushchev's miscalculations Students of Soviet behavior will long ponder both the willingness of Russia to pull back, and the fantastic miscalculations which led to the rash action of placing the offensive weapons in Cuba. It appears that Khrushchev, like Stalin before him, has shown a curious blind spot in assessing American capacities and intentions.

At an earlier period, Soviet leaders assumed that a speech by an American Secretary of State placing Korea outside of the sphere of interest of the United States meant that Communist forces could invade South Korea with impunity. Mr. Khrushchev apparently interpreted American policy at the Bay of Pigs to mean that the United States would not undertake overt action in defense of her vital interests. Or the Russian leaders may have assumed that the United States did not understand her own interests or did not have an appropriate framework for determining them.

Mr. Khrushchev may have reasoned that a young President, bent on social reform at home and abroad, was too preoccupied to nip aggression in the bud. As a Marxist, he may have assumed that a liberal regime was both too decadent and too peace-loving to confront power with power.

Or the Cuban action might have appeared to the Russians as a gamble. If the United States proved to be unwilling or incapable of preventing the establishment of missile bases in Cuba, then where would the United States draw the line? There is the possibility that the risk was taken with the hope that it would lead to a victory for Russia in Berlin and elsewhere. Another conclusion that may well be drawn is that Russia had less offensive power than had previously been conceded and that she was trying to "redress the balance" with medium and intermediate range missiles close to the United States.

Kennedy's role   It is also possible that President Kennedy and his advisers knew of the build-up in Cuba and had decided "to acquiesce by denying their existence."[3] One might argue that the Administration "invited the Soviet action" by its failure to talk to the American people in candor about changes in the world situation caused by the loss of America's nuclear monopoly. Indeed, even the President's earlier statements warning the Communists against an offensive build-up were usually contained within the context of denials that offensive weapons had been placed in Cuba.

As one views the Cuban crisis in perspective certain facets stand out:

This was a clear-cut case where no President could have ignored the threat to the security of the United States. One is impressed again with the central role of the President in determining the course of action in matters of the highest priority and with his ability to rally support for specific clear-cut policies. One also realizes that greater care must be taken in the future to prevent miscalculations by America's enemies about her willingness to defend her vital interests.

The crisis gave renewed proof that American leaders can take action which involves the greatest risks and still have the moderation and responsibility to know precisely where to stop. The United States gained as much prestige from the moderation of her action as from her show of strength and her willingness to take risks.

However, the action that the United States is prepared to take in one sector of the world does not give a clue to the response that would be required in another sector. Certainly the action taken in the Cuban crisis does not offer a ready-made recipe for future action in Southeast Asia or some other area of less strategic significance to the United States.

The aftermath   Finally, even with this successful pull-back it is clear that the fundamental relationship between the United States and the Soviet Union has not changed. As *The Economist* noted:

> The two sides have had a horrid shock at finding themselves on the brink of war, and have learned something about the techniques for scrambling back from the brink. But neither side has had any reason to change its estimate of the other's aims in life. Right or wrong, their deep-seated suspicions remain; and as long as they remain, there will be no meeting of their minds on the really major points at issue.[4]

In the long-run, the "Cuban problem" cannot be separated from the basic problems confronting all of Latin America. The United States is now well aware of the social and economic conditions in the Americas which give rise to revolutions and which offer a fertile field for communism. But even with the Alliance for Progress and a number of technical assistance programs it is not clear that reforms and economic growth can proceed at the required pace.

[3] Henry A. Kissinger, "Reflections on Cuba," *The Reporter,* November 22, 1962, p. 22.

[4] December 1, 1962, p. 886.

Europe and the German problem

The re-emergence of Europe and the problem of Germany are intimately associated in American policy. West Germany is politically, economically and militarily an integral part of renascent Europe, and this fact sets limits to negotiations over Germany's future. The rapprochement of France and West Germany, exemplified in the return of the Saar politically to Bonn on January 1, 1957, is the central condition of a strong Europe. Any discussion of the future status of Germany has to take this point into account and provide somehow for continued economic ties between Europe and West Germany.

This central fact sets the terms and underscores the problem of talks about reducing tensions in the heart of Europe or so-called policies of disengagement. It also explains why Europe and West Germany can never be viewed in isolation one from the other. Both are part of a single problem.

Europe was the first and perhaps the most crucial "battlefield" where Soviet and Western objectives clashed in the Cold War. After 1945 Soviet policy-makers expected the gradual alienation from the West of countries like France and Italy, which have substantial Communist parties numbering up to 40 percent of the electorate. Marxist doctrine assumed that Communist uprisings would take place in industrialized centers where overinvestment and underconsumption led to frustration and despair. Indeed, the present-day observer can only with the greatest difficulty reconstruct the precarious image Europe presented in 1945–46, ravaged by half a decade of total war and threatened by conventional Russian troops, who, competent observers predicted, could march to the English Channel in sixty days.

Europe as a "Third Force" Yet by 1956 the problem of Western Europe had been so radically transformed that one speaker on the BBC Third Programme predicted: "It is no longer so foolish . . . to think of Western Europe as a potential Third Force." Economic recovery has brought a new awareness of national independence. Nations like France and Britain whose postwar policies have often been subordinated to the policies of the United States are visibly astir, and are re-asserting their sovereign rights. They are boldly reconsidering their existing commitments such as the fulfillment of re-armament pledges.

Prime Minister Harold Macmillan of Britain feels secure enough to go to Moscow on an independent mission to explore Soviet intentions. France's withdrawal of its Mediterranean fleet from the NATO command structure and its unwillingness to accept nuclear weapons and intercontinental missile bases on its soil without full authority over their use are among the more dramatic examples of this recent trend. Even Chancellor Konrad Adenauer of West Germany calls for a united Europe capable of standing once again on its own feet in a world he fears is passing Europe by. Most dramatic of all, Britain has applied for membership in the European Common Market.

The re-emergence of Europe and its re-assertion of freedom of action are traceable, paradoxically, to the success of American policies for Europe. For nearly a decade the postwar "grand alliance" between Europe and America rested on two foundation stones of mutually identical interests. Europe's recovery and its military security were underwritten and guaranteed by American power. Its recovery was due to the immense vitality and vigor of the Europeans, stimulated by the most creative single act of Western statesmanship, the Marshall Plan. Its security rested ultimately on our atomic monopoly.

In this context, it mattered little that certain concrete European interests in Asia and the Middle East were sometimes at odds with those of the United States. Economic, political and military necessity required that Europe stand with the United States or invite catastrophe and possibly national suicide.

Ironically, Europe's economic recovery and the withdrawal of Marshall Plan aid undermined the first foundation stone of this concert of power. The Russian explosion of an atomic bomb shattered the other. Today Europe, far from being reassured by our stockpile of bombs, trembles at the thought of being pulverized by total weapons launched from either East or West.

Notwithstanding these changes, the bonds of community and mutual interest might have sustained the coalition had statesmen like Churchill or Roosevelt remained in power. Wounded feelings might have been assuaged, differences could have been healed, and the alliance patched up or kept intact if diplomatic communications had not broken down, as they did during the Suez crisis of 1956.

As Churchill said on the occasion of his visit to Washington in May 1959, what was needed was greater sympathy in understanding the legitimate hopes and fears, interests and aspirations of all the partners. Instead of making the best of a changing situation, adapting to it and reinterpreting it, the allies from 1956 to 1959 allowed mutual understanding to be frittered away until, in the phrase of James Reston of *The New York Times,* they "lost control of events" and their initiative in the world struggle.

Unrest in Eastern Europe   The most heartbreaking aspect of the decline of the Western alliance in the Suez crisis is that it coincided almost to the day with an eruption within the Soviet empire. The events which took place in the autumn of 1956 in Poland and Hungary continue to have a far-reaching effect within Europe even though Russian authority has been temporarily re-established.

Those ill-fated revolts proved that unity of purpose in the Soviet sphere could no longer be taken for granted, even under the shadow of the Red army. On November 3, 1956, *The Economist* of London wrote: "By swift changes, the consequences of which are still incalculable, the peoples of Eastern Europe have ceased to be mere pawns on the political chessboard." Poland revolted for "bread and freedom," gained a new leader—Wladyslaw Gomulka— who symbolically had earlier been imprisoned

for his "nationalist" tendencies, dismissed the Russian Marshal Konstantin K. Rokossovsky as minister of defense and installed a national Communist regime, which still continues its precarious existence.

Similarly, nationalist sentiment fanned the flames of revolt in Hungary, but Hungarians were unwilling or unable to accept anything approaching a Titoist solution. These contrasts illustrate the immense variety that can be found among human beings—including Communists—and the fallacy of generalizing about Eastern Europe any more than about Asia or Africa. Moreover, while demands for greater economic abundance were a factor in Poland, the physical condition of most Hungarian refugees would suggest that economic grievances were probably not a central feature of their revolt. Hence, the Marxist assumption that a solution of economic problems will satisfy all basic human needs is seen once more for what it is—a fantastic illusion at odds with human nature.

Some years after the event it is still too early to calculate the long-run historic effects of Poland's changeover and Hungary's revolt. No one can say, despite the seeming success of renewed Soviet oppression, whether they foreshadow an eventual upheaval in Eastern Europe.

Will East Germany, Czechoslovakia or other satellites follow the Polish lead? Or will Hungary's aspirations for liberty and free elections prove contagious outside its borders? Will the Russians succeed by naked force in preserving and completing domination within their sphere of influence? Or has the liberalization movement inherent in Khrushchev's departure from certain tenets of Stalinism attained such momentum that there can be no turning back? Will the Russians eventually be forced to accept a limited or total withdrawal from Eastern Europe as part of a more general political settlement? Or will their eternal fear of a band of even partly independent states, opening their borders to invasions from the West, drive them to repeated and ever more ruthless acts of military and economic oppression?

Who would be bold enough to make predictions amid fast-moving events? All one can say today is that these tragic yet reassuring recent episodes in the long history of the struggle for national independence present both an opportunity and a challenge to the West.

America's relations with her Western European allies   It would be comforting if we could prove that the stirrings of freedom in Eastern Europe had redounded to the credit of the United States. Unhappily, no one can make such a claim. Instead, many Europeans privately lament the fact that our protests and actions at the time of the Hungarian crisis were not more prompt and decisive. They contrast them with the timing of the American declaration against France and Britain during the Suez crisis.

The tragic irony of the doctrine of liberation expressed during an American election campaign may be that whereas it kept flagging hopes alive for a better day among Eastern Europeans, it also may have unwittingly inspired illusions that the United States was willing to do more than it actually could within the Soviet orbit. It is possible that economic and cultural programs by public and private agencies and well-timed diplomatic initiatives are better calculated to keep hope alive than are flamboyant governmental pronouncements about policies for which the resources and will to act are often lacking.

Moreover, the effect on other countries of an emergent Europe which is recovering its freedom of action should not be underestimated. The task of American policy-makers in dealing with strong and scrupulous leaders of states which are no longer economically dependent on the United States is at the same time more difficult and more promising. This change in relationship opens the way to creative acts of partnership never completely fulfilled before.

It would be tragic if the short-run irritations between the United States and Europe produced by the continent's resurgent nationalism and by growing European unity should cause American policy-makers to undertake a reappraisal of relations with our natural allies. We are easily piqued by manifestations of neu-

tralism in the Cold War, and much of present-day European nationalism has neutralist undertones. We are also often ready to resent the temporary inconveniences of the new trade patterns on the continent created by the Common Market. The reality we must recognize is a new Europe in which the various nations, on issues of national policy, will make their respective claims.

The European Community   This new entity is the so-called European Community—the Coal and Steel Community, based on the Schuman Plan, and the associated "supranational agencies" which, although not federal in nature, have consequences which are sometimes federal in quality. The Assembly of the Coal and Steel Community has evolved a more active role in the trend toward integration in Europe than its founders anticipated. Organized labor in six important European countries has actively supported the community, recognizing the concrete advantages that it provides.

The community, it should be recalled, came into being not because of the identity but because of the convergence of widely different views among labor and industrialist, public and trade association, groups. It has brought neither great dislocations of key national industries nor unemployment, and critics one by one have had to re-assess their positions. The Schuman Plan, however, is only one step toward a united Europe, and spill-over into the political realm has not taken place on any significant scale.

Europe is different today because in fragmented sectors of its economy like the Coal and Steel Community, Euratom and the European Economic Community (Common Market), partial integration has been achieved. The new European Parliamentary Assembly has members drawn from national parliaments and parties who, however, are more effective abroad as advocates of European integration than they have been in their own countries. Nevertheless, it is important to recognize both the particularism and the supranationalism at work in Europe today, since both contribute to the shape and character of the

Cold War and to the role Europe can play in the future.

The position of West Germany   If Western Europe has achieved a measure of the security and independence it lacked in 1945, the position of West Germany, and particularly West Berlin, is more precarious and uncertain. Germany remains the ultimate stake in the Cold War which neither side can afford to yield to the other. Walter Lippmann has said that Khrushchev, in the interview he granted Lippmann in October 1958, discussed the German question "with more passion than he showed on any other subject."

The Soviet attitude toward German power has been a blend of fear and aggressiveness, anxiety and threats. The Germans, in the twentieth century, have twice marched across Russia's boundaries, and it is in this perspective that Soviet fears of German nuclear re-armament carry the appearance of reality.

At the same time, Khrushchev has warned again and again that should a thermonuclear war be unleashed, Germany, as in 1939, would turn to the East and make arrangements with the Russians.

Soviet confidence rests on his boast that "if West Germany engaged in a war against the East, the U.S.S.R.—with its missiles—could quickly destroy West Germany." The Russians contend that since the Germans have more to fear from the East than the West and more to gain through re-adjustments in territorial frontiers, they will ultimately follow their interests and make a deal with Soviet leaders.

West Berlin   The rivalry over Germany comes to a focus in the current conflict over West Berlin. The Soviet Union has challenged the political and legal authority of this beleaguered island of freedom 100 miles inside Communist territory in East Germany. The Russians threaten to turn over to the East Germans control of the flow of traffic into West Berlin. Most observers agree that Soviet policy has the ultimate purpose of driving the Western Powers out of West Berlin and the tactical purpose of splitting the Western alliance. The East Germans have thrown up a wall demarcating the boundary between East and West Berlin and between slavery and freedom.

Their efforts thus far have had the effect of stiffening the resolve of the West to protect the lives of 2.25 million West Berliners. However, differences of emphasis have emerged on the issue of seeking an interim agreement for West Berlin. According to one point of view, espoused particularly by the West Germans and the French, any agreement negotiated with the Russians in response to their threats and ultimatums could only lead to a weakening of the position of West Berlin.

The other view is represented by the Kennedy administration in Washington and by British spokesmen like Churchill and Macmillan, who urge a protracted effort to obtain a commitment by Russia on a less equivocal status for West Berlin, particularly before the East Germans are given authority to monitor the movement of persons and goods into West Berlin.

Bases for settling East-West differences   The British go further to suggest that the West seek answers to broader hypothetical questions like the following: What price are the Soviet leaders prepared to pay for a Central Europe in which neither West Germany, East Germany, Czechoslovakia nor Poland would be given thermonuclear weapons? What, beyond this, are the prospects for a thinning out of conventional forces to achieve some form of genuine disengagement?

Are there ways in which outstanding issues can be joined together or packaged in some fashion to achieve a result disagreeable to both sides in certain respects but sufficiently palatable in broadest outlines to furnish a basis for a working settlement? Do Soviet fears of German nuclear re-armament coupled with Khrushchev's reported need for a political victory and his continued difficulties in the satellite states offer a basis for accommodation?

Does the current situation present an opportunity for devising the type of European security system based on mutual guarantees by

East and West or by the NATO and Warsaw Pact organizations which Churchill seriously considered in the early postwar years? The Kennedy administration has attached greater importance to the prospects for establishing an international authority for safeguarding free access to West Berlin and at one point considered an international authority representative of thirteen nations.

New issues in the Middle East and North Africa

In the Middle East and North Africa three conditions of international politics direct the course of the Cold War along lines which diverge fundamentally from the conflict we face in Europe.

Changes in power relationships   The first is the dramatic increase in the relative power and freedom of action of the native peoples. Their successful social and political revolutions introduce a new dimension in foreign policy. It is a truism, but one worth restating, that the Arabs and Africans are now subjects, no longer objects, in world politics. While Europe exemplifies a recovery of national autonomy, the Middle East symbolizes its discovery. Decisions vitally affecting the future of Algeria, the Suez Canal or the Gaza Strip are more often made in Tunis, Cairo and Tel Aviv than in London, Paris or Moscow. Egypt, Iraq and the Maghreb countries in North Africa are competing for the leadership of Arab nationalism.

Second, postwar Middle Eastern affairs have been marked by the introduction of Soviet power into the region. In the past, Russian policy had pursued a negative program aimed at undermining and destroying Western influence in the region. Russians allied themselves with whatever forces were struggling against the West: Syrian and Lebanese nationalism in 1945, Zionism in 1947–49, and Egypt and Syria in 1955–56.

The Suez defeat of Britain and France in the autumn of 1956 allowed the Soviet Union to break through the barrier which for centuries had held back the expansion of Russian influence into the Middle East. Now Russia, like the West before it, has positive stakes to defend in countries like Egypt and Iraq, and its position in the area has become simultaneously more formidable and complex.

Third, Western influence, in less than fifteen years, has fallen off sharply as positions held by the West in Cairo and Baghdad, Tunis and Nicosia, Rabat and Damascus, have been eliminated. A measure of this decline is the fact that France has lost her North African possessions. Britain retains larger stakes in the Middle East, but in Jordan, southern and eastern Arabia and Libya, British influence is unstable and precarious.

The United States has contributed, indirectly to be sure, to the weakening of the West's position in the region. In the Middle East, in contrast to Europe, we have been slow in establishing a solidarity of interests with Western colonial Powers, whose policies have offended our anticolonial sentiments. At the same time, the United States has inherited much of the onus of Western colonialism and has thus failed to build up a harmony of interests with indigenous forces.

Egypt and her political rivals   Until the summer of 1958, the central facts of Middle Eastern politics were the new character of Egyptian leadership and the upsurge of Arab nationalism. Egypt fell heir to the mantle of leadership partly because of its long cultural and political hegemony in the region—it had for decades exported its teachers and doctors to neighboring countries, just as the Swiss had once exported their mercenaries in Europe—and partly because of the dynamism of the popular revolt led by Gamal Abdel Nasser.

The Iraq revolt of July 14, 1958 brought to power the regime of General Abdul Karim Kassim, which made no concessions to the West and, like Nasser, symbolized victory over the old colonial order. Moreover, Iraq, potentially at least, enjoyed freedom from the economic harassment which led social revolutionaries in Egypt to seek external victories when internal reforms proved difficult to achieve. Iraq has wealth derived from its rich oil resources, and has reaped the fruits of limited reforms initiated by the efficient, if unpopular, regime of Nuri-al-Said. Under that regime, dams were erected, roads and factories were built, and the school population was increased from 204,000 in 1950 to 439,000 in 1956.

Thus a rival center of power had sprung up in the region, freed of the burdens a pro-Western government carries when neighboring nations are asserting their leadership in the struggle against European imperialism. The key to Middle-Eastern politics seemed to lie in the contest between Iraq and Egypt for Arab leadership. Then, in typical Mid-East fashion, alignments changed almost over night. A revolution brought a new government to power, headed by Nasser's friend, Colonel Abdul Salam Aref. How far rapprochement with Egypt will go, and how long it will last, remains uncertain.

Problems for U.S. policy   Beyond this contest the continuing Middle Eastern crisis raises three perennial issues which have troubled American policy-makers over the past four decades. These are the problems of deterring overt aggression, of meeting indirect aggression, and of diplomatic accommodation. American experience and imagination brought to bear on the first of these problems has been largely successful; it is with respect to the other two that we have suffered failures in concept and policy.

As has been suggested earlier, most Americans learned from events leading up to World War II that potential aggressors, left in doubt by international society as to its intention to resist, embarked on bold military expansionism which ultimately could be checked only by total war. After World War II, Western policy-makers agreed that nations, both in declarations and deeds, had to be ready to halt aggression before it spread.

Korea was the test of this doctrine, in a double sense. The initial failure to make our intentions clear may have led the Communists to miscalculate and invade South Korea, even

as subsequently the resoluteness shown by the UN and the United States helped to discourage them from reckless adventures elsewhere in Asia. The warning of the late Secretary of State John Foster Dulles to the Russians over Turkey in 1957 must be seen as a reasonable effort to anticipate another such miscalculation. The concerted action of the United States and Britain in Lebanon and Jordan during the summer of 1958 and more recently in Thailand and Vietnam are other examples, based on the assumption that force would be available to bolster official statements.

Though indirect aggression has been with us since the Bolshevik Revolution of 1917, responses now, as then, are uncertain, hesitant and often confused. However, signs point to a more realistic approach by the Kennedy Administration. American policy-makers have seemed alternately to assume that threats of internal disruption and subversion will be defeated as a kind of extra dividend of military security guarantees, or that generous infusions of economic aid will wipe out the problem altogether.

The Middle Eastern crisis, the conflict in Southeast Asia and the failures of Western policy raise doubts about the adequacy of both these assumptions. For much of the region the security problem is linked with economic problems which, in turn, rest on political foundations. Only a policy which interlocks all the issues at stake can deal effectively with internal disruption.

The context of the refugee problem   For example, the refugee problem has never been insoluble in purely economic terms. Both the Arabs and the Jews have preferred to keep it alive for political purposes. Israel has insisted that the admission into its territory of large numbers of Arab refugees would constitute a "Trojan Horse" and a threat to its internal security. Yet many Arabs already admitted have increasingly been integrated into Israel's national life. The Arabs, in turn, have talked less about possible opportunities for refugees in Iraq, Libya and the Jordan Valley than about Israeli intransigence.

It is at least conceivable that an arrangement might some day be possible whereby Israel would announce its willingness to accept Arab refugees in return for security guarantees from both within and outside the region. Similarly, the Middle Eastern countries, with problems of economic development and unstable regimes, may in time be prepared to accept, tacitly at least, the existence of the rugged little state of Israel.

The linking of economic development with the relaxation of Arab-Israeli tension was implicit in Mr. Dulles' proposal of August 1955, which may be in process of being revived in one form or another. In an often neglected speech to the Council on Foreign Relations, Mr. Dulles pledged American assistance for economic development and the resettlement of refugees if the Arab states and Israel settled their dispute over territorial boundaries.

Possibly the time has come when these views should be restated, not by simply dropping them as bread upon the waters, but by active intervention at appropriate diplomatic levels, and by linking them with a re-appraisal of the UN's refugee program. Short of this, the festering sore of Arab-Israeli conflict promises to poison every attempt at social and economic growth, no matter how generous the economic aid we may offer.

Left to themselves, neither the Arabs nor the Jews seem likely to take the first step, but with continuous prompting and subtle pressures both may welcome a way out of their present dilemmas. If a first step inspired by the United States were the announcement of Israeli willingness to accept some refugees, the way might be opened for a series of regional economic measures, such as the Jordan Valley Development, which have thus far remained in abeyance pending progress on political problems. There are signs that the Kennedy Administration is not indifferent to this situation.

The Middle East as Cold War battleground
The third issue we face in the Middle East is that of political accommodation—not only among the states within the area but also between Moscow and Washington. How are the Great Powers to look upon this theater of the Cold War? Is it an area where the temperature must remain forever near the boiling point, where armaments must be supplied in increasing amounts by both sides and where unremitting civil war must be regarded as a natural state of affairs? Or is there a prospect, however remote, of political settlement based on self-enforcing agreements? Would both Great Power blocs, faced by the peril of thermonuclear conflict, have an interest in drawing a ring around the Middle East or Southeast Asia and recognizing its special status in the Cold War?

It is easier to raise these questions than to answer them. Would it be fair to say that in the Middle East neither the dictates of communism nor of anti-communism can compete with the claims of nationalism and social revolution and that both Powers must ultimately recognize this fact? In the long run, do freedom and democracy depend on slow but gradual steps toward self-limitation of constant intervention by both sides, and especially the spread of disruption and disorder by the U.S.S.R.? Should we treat repeated Soviet proposals for neutralization and an arms moratorium as objects of negotiation, or signs of further deception? No one outside the United States government can realistically answer these questions, but they doubtless appear on someone's agenda in Washington—or will in the future.

The complicated rivalry among various Arab nations increases the need for settlement. Moscow would like to profit from inter-Arab feuds by helping Communist leaders to rise to power. But it cannot do so without alienating one or more states in the region whose friendship it desires. Western policy faces much the same predicament. The joint embarrassment of East and West may provide a basis for some form of *détente*. It may be that Egypt and Iraq will continue to contend for influence, and that new regional centers of authority may spring up—for example, some form of North African Federation. In the long run, a Middle East region with a multipower system of states might prove more stable than the alternative arrangements proposed or tried in the past.

Foreign aid: ideals and realities

No issue of foreign policy shows as clearly the link between ideals and realities as that of foreign aid. Even if there were no Russian threat, this country by virtue of its traditions and its interest in achieving a stable world where civilized values can survive would have an obligation to help the hungry and the underprivileged. No people can live any longer as "islands unto themselves," and the Judaeo-Christian tradition in particular teaches that because men have a touch of God within them, they cannot rest, so long as suffering, injustice and exploitation prevail.

Americans particularly have never, even in periods of isolationism, been willing to restrict themselves to narrowly parochial interests. De Tocqueville, with unrivaled penetration, observed, "If an American were condemned to confine his activities to his own affairs he would be robbed of one half of his existence."

Self-interest blended with altruism   Yet if we are honest with ourselves we must confess that acts of national generosity are prompted by a subtle blending of altruism and self-interest. Support in Congress for foreign aid, particularly the Marshall Plan, came from those who saw it as a means of holding back Russia's expansion. Our aid to the newly developing countries is justified in part by large-scale efforts of the U.S.S.R. to offer communism as key to the solution of the world's economic development problems. We do our cause more harm than good if, in our discussion of foreign aid, we impute sinister and selfish motives to the Communists and unqualified generosity to ourselves.

Moreover, technical assistance has now passed beyond the stage where noble intentions were an adequate expression of our responsibility. Moral impulses must, of course, remain the indispensable human ingredient of foreign aid If we need any reminder of this, a best-selling novel, *The Ugly American,* by William J. Lederer and Eugene Burdick, provides it. There are, however, two interconnected levels for thinking about foreign aid.

First, there is the level of man's relation to man, and, second, the level of public policy. Today a growing respect for human dignity is everywhere apparent even when it is only partly fulfilled. Most people in the world would rather be healthy than sick, fed than hungry, housed than destitute, and would want to give their children a fair chance in life. Obviously, vast differences persist both in desire and ability to attain these goals, but whether we like it or not, the universal desire of human beings for a better life places heavy burdens on us all.

In this common task, our man-to-man relations in the new nations confront us with a severe moral test. When you are the grand benefactor and your friend is the humble supplicant, the temptation to be less than moral tests a living ethic to its roots. A loving parent who sacrifices nobly for the good of his children runs a not inconsiderable risk of becoming obsessed with his own goodness. This risk is no less acute among nations and their officials, aggravated as it is by national obsessions about superior achievements and wealth. Our goal overseas is essentially that of translating the best in the missionary, dedicated enterprise into secular terms—but this calls for great understanding, patience and discrimination between what should and should not be done.

Problems of foreign aid allocation   In foreign policy, however, the harsh imperatives of national interest come into play at the second level, that of technical aid. American resources are not unlimited, and their allocation will be based on considerations of strategy and potentialities for economic and political development of those we aid. The initiative of enlightened senators like Mike Mansfield of Montana and J. William Fulbright of Arkansas to enlarge the scope of foreign aid should be hailed, because failure to combine wisdom with generosity will sooner or later spell the doom of this essential public undertaking.

Moreover, if informed Americans in an era of unparalleled prosperity leave the hard questions to a handful of public figures without consulting citizens at large, a national reaction will set in when financial demands appear to exceed our capacities. Among these questions are the following: Is effective technical assistance possible through short-run planning and annual appropriations? Is the real issue more aid or a streamlining of present programs? Is the purpose of aid to bolster unpopular regimes with greater instruments of oppression, or to co-operate in the transition toward a more tolerable political order?

What about the heavy preponderance of military aid in countries whose first need is for economic development? Have we achieved a proper balance between public and private investment abroad? Is the machinery of government in the United States geared to make wise decisions on foreign aid? Do we have a hard core of trained officials capable of carrying on tasks of utmost urgency?

Have we thought of economic development in other countries in terms of a model eminently suited to the American scene but alien to other people's problems? Is the model we present to others a fair representation of the "American Dream" with its emphasis on economic opportunity, profit-sharing, social welfare programs and concern for consumers and the "common good?"

Have we the language specialists, political and economic advisers, engineers and technicians needed for the task, or are we doing enough to supply these needs? Is there a role for international civil servants in countries whose memories of a colonial past color their attitudes today? Do we know the answer to the perennial question of whether multilateral or bilateral aid is the most promising in countries "x," "y" and "z?" Have we thought of an agency for reverse foreign aid, or receiving as well as giving to nations who are self-respecting and proud of their cultural, scientific and intellectual advancement?

Precise answers are not readily available for all the complicated and troubling questions. But future generations will never forgive the citizen and his chosen representatives if they consider only the broader issue and leave the details of fulfillment to chance. Success or failure in all great public endeavors hinges on the diligence with which the hard problems are tackled.

Today military policy and foreign aid have become everybody's business, for false answers can always be defended by the words, "This is what the people want." Unless an informed electorate becomes as concerned with complex difficult means as with noble ends, the United States will go the way of Greece and Rome. For the many challenges facing American foreign policy in fact form a single challenge facing us all.

The ultimate problem

Even if the American approach to these problems should yield unqualified success, the grim cloud of mutual annihilation would hang over all that we do. No matter how assiduously states prepare for military and non-military defense, the ever-increasing menace of nuclear disaster remains. The weight and expansion of armament capacities add to the general tension.

The Soviet Union has proposed a single formula of general and complete disarmament in four years. On March 21, 1961, a new American delegation led by Mr. Arthur Dean along with British and Soviet representatives resumed negotiations at Geneva on a treaty to ban the testing of nuclear weapons. A new approach was called for and a task force under John J. McCloy undertook a comprehensive study. In Secretary of State Dean Rusk's words: "The matter needs a fresh and imaginative review by all concerned."

The administration had no illusions about "the dismal history of man's attempts to lay down his arms" but it sought to chart a course enabling men "to move from endless discussion to practical steps—small steps if necessary, large steps if possible." One practical step that assuredly would not end the arms race but might lead to more significant measures was a test ban. The administration's approach was a pragmatic one, testing out Soviet intentions in areas of most probable immediate common interest.

Viewpoints on disarmament This approach falls midway between the two prevailing viewpoints on disarmament in modern society. On the one extreme, many of the most sensitive and noble spirits believe that disarmament and peace are synonymous. History is the melancholy record of states locked in deadly rivalry, driven by the haunting fear that a stronger neighbor threatens them and striving for security through ever-increasing armaments. War is the result of an arms race spiralling upwards until weapons which can no longer be hoarded are used. "The one thing you cannot do with bayonets is sit on them."

The evidence is clear that the new administration categorically rejects this interpretation of history. The President's disarmament adviser declared on February 25, 1961: "History shows that some wars can arguably be traced to a preceding arms race, and it shows that others can be as clearly related to disarmament and bad faith rather than armament." Democracies have a penchant for tempting thieves. They are often the last to arm and, like the shopkeeper who leaves his goods on the street exposed to all the natural and human elements, may invite crime and aggression. As Secretary of State Rusk observed:

> The American people bear arms, through necessity, not by choice. Emerging from World War II in a uniquely powerful military position, the United States demobilized its armed strength, and made persistent efforts to place under international control the use of atomic energy, then an American monopoly. The fact that the story of the postwar period has forced increased defense efforts upon us is a most grievous disappointment. This disappointment

teaches us that reduction of tensions must go hand in hand with real progress in disarmament.[5]

At the opposite extreme of the spectrum, opponents of continued disarmament talks urge that the free nations at most make one final effort to negotiate an arms agreement. They point to the endless round of discussions, the volumes of reports and studies, and the many fruitless months and years of futile negotiations. Why not bring matters to a head, force a showdown and, failing agreement, shore up every support of the garrison state and prepare for the worst?

The responsible leader must ask himself "is this fulfilling my trust?" He must brood over Robert Oppenheimer's warning that in all-out thermonuclear conflict the only issue will be whether there are sufficient survivors to bury the dead. He must ask whether diplomacy by ultimatum holds out hope for the future. He must measure his actions by our commitment through the United Nations Charter to disarmament as a solemn purpose. Finally, he must consider whether the example we wish to set for others at a time when some are proposing regional arms limitations is of a Great Power withdrawing from the field. If we abandon the search for limitation of armaments, will those who are considering limiting military preparations to arms essential to internal security purposes resume pursuit of the arms race on every front?

East-West negotiations at Geneva The progress of the Geneva talks has hardly been encouraging. On April 18, 1961, the West which since October 31, 1958, through 292 meetings, had endeavored to negotiate an agreement on a piecemeal basis, introduced a complete test ban proposal. A draft treaty would provide for banning all nuclear testing in the atmosphere, under water and in space. Underground tests of weapons smaller than the Hiroshima

---

[5] Dean Rusk, *The Winds of Freedom*. Boston: Beacon Press, 1963, p. 269.

bomb were to be dealt with by a separate moratorium pending research on a foolproof detection system.

Inspection teams would not include nationals of the country to be inspected, although there are signs this point might be negotiable. Inspections numbering twenty annually would be conducted in the Soviet Union, the United States and Britain and her dependencies.

The Soviets have consistently maintained that inspection was merely a cover for espionage activities by the West within Russian boundaries. The Soviet proposal, therefore, has been for three inspections annually. While the West has shown itself prepared to reduce its present requirement of 20 inspections to 12, it would be unlikely to accept the Soviet plan. The basic issue over inspection has been, of course, the reluctance of a closed society to accept incursions into its society when it had little to gain from inspections within the open territory of a free adversary.

A more serious and unexpected issue arises from Soviet demands for a veto over all inspection. Walter Lippmann in reporting an interview with Premier Khrushchev in the spring of 1961 noted:

He would never accept a single neutral administration. Why? Because, he said, while there are neutral countries, there are no neutral men . . . I will never entrust the security of the Soviet Union to a foreigner.[6]

In place of a single neutral administrator to administer the treaty, the Soviets propose a three-man council.

It had been agreed in talks at Geneva in 1960 that a commission would be established made up of two Russians, two Westerners and three officials from neutral countries. At the same time, the Russians had agreed there should be a single neutral administrator for this control commission. Then the Soviets, in the same way

[6] The Coming Test with Russia, Boston: Little, Brown & Co., 1961, p. 11.

they rejected the authority of the UN Secretary-General, overturned an earlier agreement and demanded in effect a veto-at-will over any inspection procedure.

Speculation over the shift in Soviet policy is probably pointless. The observer is tempted to ask whether continued successes in outer space and growing influence in the Western Hemisphere and the non-Western world have led to a less conciliatory stand. Whatever the forces to which Soviet leaders are responding, hopes and expectations of a test ban have been appreciably dampened.

Other approaches to disarmament issues

But the new position may be merely the latest Soviet tactic in the Cold War. Beyond that, the West may not have exhausted the alternatives open to it by discussions at Geneva. What are the prospects for reductions of armaments within countries other than the Great Powers? Is there a chance that East and West might thin out their forces in areas such as Central and Eastern Europe? What hopes can we reasonably entertain that Western Europe might increasingly provide for its own security within Europe except for protection through the ultimate threat of nuclear deterrence and retaliation from this side of the Atlantic? Could negotiations on armament reduction of this order be linked more closely with efforts to ameliorate political tensions? What of the relations between arms talks and the problem of Germany? When and how can or should the United Nations be drawn into the sphere of arms reduction?

The resumption of nuclear tests by the Soviet Union on the eve of the Belgrade Conference of non-committed states shattered the illusions of moralists and neutrals alike. Many of us in the past, in lecturing American policymakers on concessions that the United States should make, have failed to grasp the nature of the Soviet threat. When the Soviet Union sees that its relative power position can be strengthened through steps such as the resumption of tests, it will act irrespective of the judgment of world public opinion.

An ethic of protest that admonishes Western leaders alone without recognizing this fact is in the end an ethic of irresponsibility. An ethic of responsibility, by contrast, must accept the fact that the contest with Soviet Russia will not end through a single dramatic act. It seems destined to continue throughout the present generation with the ebb and flow of successive intensifications and reductions of tensions.

The struggle can perhaps be limited and contained, the means of violence restricted or reduced, the scale and temper of conflict checked and circumscribed, and deterrents be made more credible. We are doomed not to extinction but to living with dangers more terrifying than man has ever known, at least for the foreseeable future.

The moralist must help prepare men to live under these circumstances, not merely beckon him to a happier if imaginary land. We need moral resources not alone to be firm or flexible but to be both in dealings with Soviet leaders. There will be times, as in the autumn of 1961, when firmness must precede flexibility if the adversary is to resume serious negotiations. But there may also be moments in history when, from a position of strength, the West must be ready to initiate new and more flexible proposals for peace. To sense these moments and seize them at their tide is the ultimate challenge of statesmanship.

No one calling from the sidelines can solve the problem of timing: when to act and when to wait, when to be firm and when to be flexible, or when to resist and when to negotiate. Yet success or failure in this endlessly complicated and uncertain process, far more than exhortations or blueprints of utopia, will bring world wide peace or war to the tormented human race.

It may be that we shall flounder and make little progress on armaments until we ask the proper question. Foreign policy to a considerable degree lies in posing the right question. Once the right question is posed, the answer comes more nearly within reach. It may be that this question is "Can we negotiate a viable test ban safeguarded by essential provisions for inspection?" But even if success should elude our negotiators for the present here, there may be other "small steps" that will yield more readily to discussion. The phrase "one final attempt to reach agreement" is seldom helpful in diplomacy.

The challenge of the future   Arms agreements may require innovations or controls yet to be thrown up by the shifting waves of history. In this field, we may be awaiting new concepts, procedures or institutions. The need to adapt swiftly to new environmental factors invites us to reflect on the words of Alfred North Whitehead in his *Adventures of Ideas:*

> Tradition is warped by the vicious assumption that each generation will substantially live amid the conditions governing the lives of its fathers, and will transmit those conditions to mold with equal force the lives of its children. We are living in the first period of human history for which this assumption is false.
>
> In the past the time span of important changes was considerably longer than that of a single human life—today this time span is considerably shorter than that of human life, and accordingly our training must prepare individuals to face a novelty of conditions.[7]

The novelty of conditions in a thermonuclear age is the ultimate challenge to the wit of man. The urgency of the crisis with which all men are confronted by the utter destructiveness of the new instruments of warfare calls for imagination, prudence and vision. Those who hope for prompt and simple answers in approaches to disarmament will not be comforted by a recitation of these truths, nor will the cynics or the utopians. Yet for those who strive gallantly and continually to meet the problems of each new day, this almost unbearable crisis could bring their finest hour.

[7] New York, The Macmillan Company, 1956, pp. 117–18.

BIBLIOGRAPHY

Authors' Suggestions

Almond, Gabriel A. *The American People and Foreign Policy*. New York: Praeger, 1960.

Halle, Lewis J. *Civilization and Foreign Policy*. New York: Harper, 1955.

Jacobson, Harold, ed. *American Foreign Policy*. New York: Random House, 1960.

Kennan, George F. *Realities of American Foreign Policy*. Princeton: Princeton University Press, 1954.

Kennan, George F. *American Diplomacy, 1900–1950*. Chicago: University of Chicago Press, 1951.

Marshall, Charles B. *The Limits of Foreign Policy*. New York: Holt, Rinehart & Winston, 1955.

Kissinger, Henry A. *The Necessity for Choice*. New York: Harper, 1960.

Macridis, Roy C., ed. *Foreign Policy in World Politics*. 2nd ed. Englewood Cliffs, N.J.: Prentice Hall, 1962.

Morgenthau, Hans J. *The Purpose of American Politics*. New York: Alfred A. Knopf, 1960.

Rostow, Walt W. *The United States in the World Arena*. New York: Harper, 1960.

Rusk, Dean. *The Winds of Freedom*. Boston: Beacon, 1963.

Thompson, Kenneth W. *Political Realism and the Crisis of World Politics*. Princeton: Princeton University Press, 1960.

Thompson, Kenneth W. *Foreign Policy and Emergent Patterns*. New York: New York University Press, 1962.

Wolfers, Arnold, ed. *Alliance Policy in the Cold War*. Baltimore: Johns Hopkins Press, 1959.

List of Authors

Aguirre de Cárcer, Nuño *Spain*
Appadorai, A. *India*
Black, Joseph E. *United States of America*
Bourguiba, Habib, Jr. *Tunisia*
Boutros-Ghali, Boutros *Egypt*
Bracher, Karl Dietrich *Germany (Federal Republic)*
Coleman, James S. *Nigeria*
Cuevas Cancino, Francisco *Mexico*
De Sousa Sampaio, Nelson *Brazil*
Duroselle, J. B. *France*
Eayrs, James *Canada*
Eren, Nuri *Turkey*
Fernández de la Mora, Gonzalo *Spain*
Freymond, Jacques *Switzerland*
Henningsen, Sven *Denmark*
Khvostov, V. M. *Union of Soviet Socialist Republics*
Kiano, J. G. *East African Countries*
Kutakov, L. N. *Union of Soviet Socialist Republics*
Nincic, Dyura *Yugoslavia*
Qureshi, Ishtiaq Husain *Pakistan*
Rose, Saul *Britain*
Santa Pinter, José Julio *Argentina*
Scalapino, Robert A. *China (People's Republic)*
Seki, Yoshihiko *Japan*
Thompson, Kenneth W. *United States of America*
Toscano, Mario *Italy*
Webb, Colin de B. *Union of South Africa*

INDEX

Index

Herter, Christian, 608
Hertzog, General James Barry Munnik, 101
Hinduism, 487
Hispano-Arab Culture, Institute of, 212
Historical approach to study of foreign policy, 9, 15
History: *See* names of individual countries
Hitler, Adolf:
  and German policy, 118-19, 137
  and Mussolini, 176-77
  and Poland, 39
  and Rhineland remilitarization, 38
  on Turkey in World War II, 300
Hoare-Laval Plan, 37-38
Ho Chi-minh, President, 577
Hoffmann, Stanley, 74
Holmes, John W., 690
Home, Lord, 211
Huerta, Victoriano, 651
Hughes, Charles Evans, 476
Hull, Cordell, 231
Hussein, Ahmed, 344
Hussein, Tala, 332

I

Ibrahim Pasha, 324
Ideology:
  of China, 552
  and co-existence, 225, 228, 269-70
  of colonialism, 11, 140
  and foreign policy, 10, 11
  and imperialism, 26, 56
  and isolationism, 26
  and Marxism-Leninism, 11
  and neutrality, 80
  and Soviet foreign policy, 10, 11
Ikeda, Hayato, 580-81
Imperialism:
  British, 29
  Disraeli on, 32
  Indian, 442
  Italian, 175-76
  trends, new, 442-44
India:
  and China, border disputes with, 504-05
  and Communist bloc, 510
  Communist Party in, 470
  decision-making, 493
  dependent peoples, progress of, 496
  External Affairs Ministry, 492-93
  foreign policy
    characteristics, 484-91
    disputes, settlement of, 490-91
    effectiveness of, 513-14

    elements, 481-84
    formulation, 491-93
    means and ends, 488-89
    objectives, 483-84
    philosophy of, 489-90
  Goa seizure, 49
  Kashmir problem, 502-03
  National Congress, 483
  national interest, 482-83
  Nehru, Jawaharlal: *See* separate entry
  neutrality versus non-alignment, 486
  non-alignment, 484-87, 509-10
  nuclear tests, 509
  and Pakistan, 500-04
  Panch Sheel, 484, 489, 512
  peaceful settlement of disputes, 494-95
  racial problems, 497
  security problems, 511
  and Soviet Union, 507-08
  SUNFED proposal, 498
  underdeveloped countries, problems of, 497-98
  and United Nations, 493-500
  and United States, relations with, 506
  Uniting for Peace resolution, 495
  Trusteeship system, 496-97
  and Vietnam, 504
India Act of 1947, 502
Indian Council for Africa, 470
Indo-Soviet Agreement, 1960, 508
Indus Commission, 469-70
Industrial development, 16-17, 179-80
Indus Water Treaty, 1960, 469
Inonü, Ismet, 291, 301, 306
Inter-American Development Bank, 634
Inter-American System, 661-62
Inter-American Treaty of Reciprocal Assistance, 608
International Court of Justice, 437
International Statute of Tangier, 1923, 213
Iran, 459
Iraq, 309-10, 338-39
Ismail, Khedive, 324, 332
Ismail Sidky Pasha, 324-25, 344
Isolationism:
  in Britain, 29
  in Canada, 675-76
  in Egypt, 322
  in U.S.A., 713
Israel, 9, 340
Issawi, C., 320
Italia irredenta, 56
Italy:
  and Africa, relations with, 193
  and Albania, relations with, 191
  and Austria, relations with, 191

D
843
.653
1963

D
843
.B53

1963